CH2M Hill - Janet Snyder

MASTERING
ORACLE8i

MASTERING ORACLE8i™

Robert G. Freeman
Mark D. Blomberg

SYBEX®

San Francisco • London

Associate Publisher: Richard Mills

Acquisitions and Developmental Editor: Christine McGeever

Editors: Carol Henry, Marilyn Smith

Production Editor: Leslie E. H. Light

Technical Editor: Ashok Hanumanth

Book Designer: Patrick Dintino, Catalin Dulfu, Franz Baumhackl

Graphic Illustrator: Tony Jonick

Electronic Publishing Specialist: Adrian Woolhouse

Proofreaders: Nanette Duffy, Emily Hsuan, David Nash, Laurie O'Connell, Yariv Rabinovich, Nancy Riddiough

Indexer: Nancy Guenther

CD Coordinator: Christine Detlefs

CD Technician: Kevin Ly

Cover Designer: Design Site

Cover Illustrator: Sergie Loobkoff, Design Site

Copyright © 2002 SYBEX Inc., 1151 Marina Village Parkway, Alameda, CA 94501. World rights reserved. No part of this publication may be stored in a retrieval system, transmitted, or reproduced in any way, including but not limited to photocopy, photograph, magnetic, or other record, without the prior agreement and written permission of the publisher.

Library of Congress Card Number: 2001091742

ISBN: 0-7821-2929-3

SYBEX and the SYBEX logo are either registered trademarks or trademarks of SYBEX Inc. in the United States and/or other countries.

Mastering is a trademark of SYBEX Inc.

Screen reproductions produced with SnagIt. SnagIt is a registered trademark of TechSmith Corporation.

Screen reproductions produced with FullShot 99. FullShot 99 © 1991-1999 Inbit Incorporated. All rights reserved.

FullShot is a trademark of Inbit Incorporated.

TRADEMARKS: SYBEX has attempted throughout this book to distinguish proprietary trademarks from descriptive terms by following the capitalization style used by the manufacturer.

The author and publisher have made their best efforts to prepare this book, and the content is based upon final release software whenever possible. Portions of the manuscript may be based upon pre-release versions supplied by software manufacturer(s). The author and the publisher make no representation or warranties of any kind with regard to the completeness or accuracy of the contents herein and accept no liability of any kind including but not limited to performance, merchantability, fitness for any particular purpose, or any losses or damages of any kind caused or alleged to be caused directly or indirectly from this book.

Manufactured in the United States of America

10 9 8 7 6 5 4 3 2 1

Software License Agreement: Terms and Conditions

The media and/or any online materials accompanying this book that are available now or in the future contain programs and/or text files (the "Software") to be used in connection with the book. SYBEX hereby grants to you a license to use the Software, subject to the terms that follow. Your purchase, acceptance, or use of the Software will constitute your acceptance of such terms.

The Software compilation is the property of SYBEX unless otherwise indicated and is protected by copyright to SYBEX or other copyright owner(s) as indicated in the media files (the "Owner(s)"). You are hereby granted a single-user license to use the Software for your personal, noncommercial use only. You may not reproduce, sell, distribute, publish, circulate, or commercially exploit the Software, or any portion thereof, without the written consent of SYBEX and the specific copyright owner(s) of any component software included on this media.

In the event that the Software or components include specific license requirements or end-user agreements, statements of condition, disclaimers, limitations or warranties ("End-User License"), those End-User Licenses supersede the terms and conditions herein as to that particular Software component. Your purchase, acceptance, or use of the Software will constitute your acceptance of such End-User Licenses.

By purchase, use or acceptance of the Software you further agree to comply with all export laws and regulations of the United States as such laws and regulations may exist from time to time.

Software Support

Components of the supplemental Software and any offers associated with them may be supported by the specific Owner(s) of that material, but they are not supported by SYBEX. Information regarding any available support may be obtained from the Owner(s) using the information provided in the appropriate read.me files or listed elsewhere on the media.

Should the manufacturer(s) or other Owner(s) cease to offer support or decline to honor any offer, SYBEX bears no responsibility. This notice concerning support for the Software is provided for your information only. SYBEX is not the agent or principal of the Owner(s), and SYBEX is in no way responsible for providing any support for the Software, nor is it liable or responsible for any support provided, or not provided, by the Owner(s).

Warranty

SYBEX warrants the enclosed media to be free of physical defects for a period of ninety (90) days after purchase. The Software is not available from SYBEX in any other form or media than that enclosed herein or posted to www.sybex.com. If you discover a defect in the media during this warranty period, you may obtain a replacement of identical format at no charge by sending the defective media, postage prepaid, with proof of purchase to:

SYBEX Inc.
Product Support Department
1151 Marina Village Parkway
Alameda, CA 94501
Web: http://www.sybex.com

After the 90-day period, you can obtain replacement media of identical format by sending us the defective disk, proof of purchase, and a check or money order for $10, payable to SYBEX.

Disclaimer

SYBEX makes no warranty or representation, either expressed or implied, with respect to the Software or its contents, quality, performance, merchantability, or fitness for a particular purpose. In no event will SYBEX, its distributors, or dealers be liable to you or any other party for direct, indirect, special, incidental, consequential, or other damages arising out of the use of or inability to use the Software or its contents even if advised of the possibility of such damage. In the event that the Software includes an online update feature, SYBEX further disclaims any obligation to provide this feature for any specific duration other than the initial posting.

The exclusion of implied warranties is not permitted by some states. Therefore, the above exclusion may not apply to you. This warranty provides you with specific legal rights; there may be other rights that you may have that vary from state to state. The pricing of the book with the Software by SYBEX reflects the allocation of risk and limitations on liability contained in this agreement of Terms and Conditions.

Shareware Distribution

This Software may contain various programs that are distributed as shareware. Copyright laws apply to both shareware and ordinary commercial software, and the copyright Owner(s) retains all rights. If you try a shareware program and continue using it, you are expected to register it. Individual programs differ on details of trial periods, registration, and payment. Please observe the requirements stated in appropriate files.

Copy Protection

The Software in whole or in part may or may not be copy-protected or encrypted. However, in all cases, reselling or redistributing these files without authorization is expressly forbidden except as specifically provided for by the Owner(s) therein.

While this book was being written, the cowardly attacks on the World Trade Center, the Pentagon, and in Pennsylvania took place. Thus, this book is dedicated to all those who died there and in other terrorist tragedies throughout the world. This is dedicated to all the children who lost parents, the wives who lost husbands, and the husbands who lost wives. It is dedicated to the grieving families and friends and to the hope of peace, but also to the hope of justice for those who feel that terror and destruction are reasonable alternatives to peace and dialogue.

As always, this work is dedicated to my family—my father and my mother, my brother and sisters, and most of all, my wife and children, who sacrifice their time with me in the writing endeavors that I take on.
—Robert G. Freeman

ACKNOWLEDGMENTS

There are numerous individuals who deserve recognition, and if we could put them all on the front cover, we would. Thanks to Richard Basile and Shagun Tyagi, whose names do not appear on the front cover but who contributed to the original content of this book.

Thanks to my co-author Mark Blomberg, who really worked hard to make this happen.

Thanks, of course, to those who helped make this book what it is. To my friend Jeff Kellum, who put me in contact with everyone else—including Richard Mills, our supportive associate publisher. To the wonderful editing staff of this book, Leslie Light, Marilyn Smith, and Carol Henry. Many thanks, as well, to technical editor Ashok Hanumanth. In addition, thanks to Christine McGeever, acquisitions and development editor, who helped get the book off the ground. The CD team and Dan Mummert did a fine job of assembling the CD material. To the production staff, including talented compositor Adrian Woolhouse, thanks for making the book look great.

Of course, there are countless people who helped and didn't even know it. Special thanks to Steve Adams, Tim Stippler, Charles Pack, Mike Ault, Pete Sharman, John B., KG, and numerous other awesome people in the Oracle community!

Special thanks to the folks I work with: Nancy Von Dolteren, Yang Jiang, Don Mongeon, Bob Just, Bill Barker, Wendy Hausler, John King, Bill Sullivan, Gunjan Nath, Richard McClain, Nirupam Majumdar, and Maritza Gonzalez. You are all great! Thanks to those who provided moral support (and allowed me to not hold boards for board breaking while I was writing this!): Mrs. Skutnik, Mr. Alfaro, and all those at Master Clark's Karate America in Jacksonville. Thanks to our many friends, who always support us.

Finally, thanks to my wife and my five kids, who came into my work area about once a week just to refresh their memories of what I look like.

Robert Freeman

I would like to take this opportunity to thank the staff at Sybex for all their hard work through the long months of this project. The staff at Sybex were helpful, resourceful, and most of all, knowledgeable.

I would also like to thank my wife and family for being tolerant of my absence and not making the appropriate time to spend with them. So thank you to my wife Ann, and daughters Rebecca and Dana.

Finally, I would like to thank Robert Freeman for bringing me into this venture and giving me the opportunity to realize one of my personal goals.

To all involved, a truly grateful THANK YOU.

Mark D. Blomberg

CONTENTS AT A GLANCE

	Introduction	xxvii
PART I	**ORACLE ESSENTIALS**	**1**
1	Elements of Oracle Database Management	3
2	Installing, Upgrading, and Migrating Oracle	45
3	Creating Oracle Databases	87
4	The Data Dictionary	141
PART II	**ORACLE DATABASE ADMINISTRATION**	**173**
5	Understanding Oracle8i Architecture	175
6	Oracle Schema Object Management	215
7	Oracle Database Maintenance	291
8	Oracle Object-Oriented Features	335
9	Oracle Networking	389
10	Physical Backup and Recovery	423
11	Oracle Logical Backup and Recovery	491
12	Using Transportable Tablespaces	519
13	Oracle8i Recovery Manager	537
14	Oracle8i LogMiner	613
PART III	**BEYOND SIMPLE DATABASE MANAGMENT**	**627**
15	Oracle8i Performance Monitoring and Database-Level Tuning	629
16	Oracle8i SQL Performance Monitoring and Tuning	699
17	Monitoring and Tuning Latches, Locks, and Waits	795
18	Oracle8i Parallel Processing	843
19	Oracle8i Data Warehousing Features	863
20	Oracle8i Supplied Packages	907
21	Oracle8i Database Security	927
22	SQL*Loader	973

PART IV ORACLE8i DISTRIBUTED DATABASE   1009

23	Oracle Database Links	1011
24	Database Partitioning	1023
25	Simple and Advanced Replication	1049
26	High Availability	1075
27	Oracle8i and the Internet	1109

Index *1125*

CONTENTS

Introduction xxvii

PART I • ORACLE ESSENTIALS

1   Elements of Oracle Database Management   3
What Is a DBA? 4
Introducing Oracle8i 5
   Relational Theory—Briefly 6
   A Brief History of Oracle 12
Oracle Internals 13
   Instances vs. Databases 14
   The Physilogical Oracle 17
Fundamental Oracle Principles 19
   Database Consistency 19
   Transactions 19
   Constraints 20
   NULL Values 21
   Environment Settings 21
The Oracle SQL Interface Tools 22
   Server Manager 22
   SQL*Plus 24
   TNSPING 29
Using Oracle SQL 29
   Datatypes in Oracle8i 30
   The DML and DDL Languages 31
   Set Processing 32
   The SQL Query 33
   SQL Operations 34
Oracle PL/SQL 39
   Basic PL/SQL Structure 39
   PL/SQL Program Units 40
Moving On 43

2   Installing, Upgrading, and Migrating Oracle   45
Introducing the Universal Installer 47
   The Oracle Universal Installer 47
Preinstall Steps 48
   General Preinstallation Steps for All Platforms 48
   Preinstallation Steps on Unix 49

| Preinstallation Steps on NT 50
Installing the Database Software 50
    Starting the UI for Installation 51
    Running the Installation 53
    Postinstallation Steps 63
Patching the Oracle Software 64
Removing the Oracle Software 66
    Starting the UI 66
    Uninstalling Oracle with the UI 67
    Removing All Oracle Software from NT 68
Migrating/Updating to Oracle8i 70
    Migration vs. Upgrade 71
    Migrating a Pre-7.1 Database to Oracle8i 71
    Migrating an Existing 7.1+ Database to Oracle8i 73
    Some Advice for Your Migrations 80
    Migrating Using the Data Migration Assistant 84
    Upgrading within Major Versions 84
In Sum 86

3   Creating Oracle Databases   87

Oracle's Optimal Flexible Architecture (OFA) 89
    The Benefits of Using OFA 89
    OFA Structure 90
Determining Physical Requirements 97
    Disk Space Requirements 97
    Disk Configuration 101
    Sizing Database Files 108
    Determining Memory Requirements 111
Determining the Database Block Size 113
    Factors to Consider 113
Naming Conventions 115
    Deciding the Database Name 116
    Naming Database Objects 116
Creating the Parameter File (*init.ora*) 117
    Location of *init.ora* 118
    Setting the Parameters 120
    Configuring the SGA 120
    Setting Up File Paths 124
    Other init.ora Configuration Issues 126
Creating the Database 128
    Preparing to Create the Database 128
    Creating the Database Manually 133
    Using the Database Configuration Assistant 135
    After Creating the Database 136
Summary of Database Creation Steps 138
Moving On 139

4 The Data Dictionary — 141

- Data Dictionary Architecture 142
  - Dictionary Structure at Creation 142
  - Data Dictionary Views 144
  - Dynamic Performance Views 145
  - Protecting Your Data Dictionary 146
- Using the Oracle Data Dictionary 151
  - Using the X$ Tables 151
  - Using the DBA_, ALL_, and USER_ Views 155
  - Using the V$ Dynamic Performance Views 159
- Documenting the Database 160

PART II • ORACLE DATABASE ADMINISTRATION

5 Understanding Oracle8i Architecture — 175

- Oracle Storage Architecture 176
  - The Block 176
  - The Extent 178
  - The Segment 179
- Oracle Memory Structures 181
  - The System Global Area (SGA) 181
  - The Process Global Area (PGA) 187
  - Other Oracle Memory Structures 187
- Oracle Processes 188
  - Server Processes 188
  - Required Processes 189
  - Optional Processes 191
- Oracle Database Control Structures 192
  - Transaction Commits and Rollbacks 192
  - Checkpoints 192
  - The System Change Number (SCN) 195
  - Rollback Segments and Undo 197
  - The Database Datafiles 201
  - Control Files 202
  - Redo Logs 202
- Oracle Scalar Datatypes 205
  - NUMBER 205
  - Character Types 207
  - LONG, LONG RAW, and RAW 209
  - LOBs 209
  - ROWID and UROWID 213

6 Oracle Schema Object Management — 215

- An Overview of Object Management 216
  - Configuring an Object's Physical Attributes 217
  - The INITRANS and MAXTRANS Parameters 219
  - Specifying Storage Parameters 220

Managing Tablespaces 224
   Common Oracle Tablespaces 224
   Creating Tablespaces 226
   Altering Tablespaces 228
   Dropping Tablespaces 229
Managing Heap Tables 229
   Heap Table Fundamentals 229
   Creating Heap Tables 231
   Altering Tables 240
   De-allocating Unused Table Space 241
   Dropping Tables 241
   Viewing Table Information 242
Managing Indexes 247
   Index Fundamentals 248
   Creating Indexes 251
   Altering Indexes 256
   Dealing with Index Browning 258
   Dropping Indexes 259
   Viewing Index Information 259
Managing Index-Organized Tables 262
   Logical ROWIDs in IOTs 263
   Creating IOTs 263
   Compressing IOTs 266
   Altering, Moving, and Dropping IOTs 266
   Viewing IOTs 268
Managing Clusters 269
   Cluster Fundamentals 269
   Creating Clusters 271
   Altering Clusters 275
   Dropping Clusters 275
   Viewing Cluster Information 276
Managing Rollback Segments 277
   Planning Rollback Segments 277
   Creating Rollback Segments 279
   Altering Rollback Segments 279
   Dropping Rollback Segments 280
   Viewing Rollback Segment Information 280
Managing Views 282
   Creating Views 283
   Using Your Views 284
   Using Inline Views 287
   Viewing View Information 288

7 Oracle Database Maintenance   291

Managing Database Objects that Support Tables and Indexes 292
   Setting Up Synonyms 292
   Setting Up Database Links 294

Using Sequences 297
Setting Up Constraints 300
Managing LOBs 307
Understanding Database Startup and Shutdown 312
Starting Up the Database 312
Shutting Down the Database 315
Changing the Database Name 318
Managing Database Files 320
Managing Datafiles 320
Adding Control Files 322
Moving Online Redo Logs 322
Analyzing Database Objects 323
Gathering Statistics 324
Validating the Structure of an Object 328
Diagnosing Database Problems 329
Using Trace Files and the Alert Log 329
Using DBV 331
Using DBMS_REPAIR 332

8   Oracle Object-Oriented Features   335

Using Oracle Objects 336
Using User-Defined Object Types 339
Creating Types 340
Modifying and Dropping Types 341
Using Types as Attributes 342
Determining Dependencies 343
Managing Oracle Types 344
Introducing Row and Column Objects, OIDs, and REFs 346
Forward Declaring Types 347
Using Types in Relational Tables 350
Using Types in PL/SQL 350
Using Object Tables 351
Creating Object Tables 351
Altering Object Tables 355
Dropping Object Tables 356
Getting Information about Object Tables 356
Using Collection Types 357
Working with VARRAYs 357
Working with Nested Tables 361
Getting Information about Collection Types 364
Using Methods 365
Using Constructor Methods 366
Working with Member Methods 366
Creating Map and Order Methods 370
Getting Information about Methods 372
Querying Object Types 372
Using INSERT Statements 372

Using UPDATE Statements 374
Using SELECT Statements 376
Creating Object Views 380
Creating Joined Object Views 383
Creating Object Views on Relational Tables 383
Creating Relational Views on Object Tables 386

9 Oracle Networking   389

Introducing Net8 390
Net8 Client/Server Connections 390
Protocols Supported by Net8 391
Service Names 392
Naming Methods 393
Configuring Net8 394
Configuring and Managing the Listener 395
Configuring the Net8 Client 401
Using the Net8 Configuration Assistant 406
Using Oracle's Multithreaded Server (MTS) Option 407
Configuring MTS 408
Viewing MTS Information 410
Managing MTS on the Client 410
Using Oracle Names 411
How Oracle Names Works 411
Configuring Names Servers 415
Managing Names Servers 416
Introducing Oracle Connection Manager 419
Introducing the Advanced Security Option 420

10 Physical Backup and Recovery   423

Backup and Recovery Planning 424
Planning Your Backup Strategy 424
Planning for Disasters 425
Putting the Database in ARCHIVELOG Mode 429
Modifying the *init.ora* File 430
Completing the ARCHIVEMODE Process 433
Considering Online Redo Log Groups 434
Backup and Recovery in NOARCHIVELOG Mode 435
Performing Cold Backups in NOARCHIVELOG Mode 436
Recovering Cold Backups in NOARCHIVELOG Mode 439
Backups in ARCHIVELOG Mode 441
Performing Cold Backups in ARCHIVELOG Mode 441
Backing Up Archived Redo Logs 442
Performing Hot Backups in ARCHIVELOG Mode .443
Recoveries in ARCHIVELOG Mode 450
Preparing for Recovery 450
Using the Recover Command 452
Performing Complete Recovery 454
Incomplete Recovery 466

Control File Backups	480
Using the Backup Control File for Database Recovery	480
Using a Trace File	483
RESETLOGS and Recovery	486
Why and When to Use RESETLOGS	486
Recovering through RESETLOGS	487
When All Else Fails—Forcing Open the Database	489

11 Oracle Logical Backup and Recovery — 491

The Oracle Export Utility	492
What Can You Export?	493
Using the Export Utility	494
The Oracle Import Utility	504
What Can You Import?	504
Using the Import Utility	505

12 Using Transportable Tablespaces — 519

Introducing Transportable Tablespaces	520
Transportable Tablespace Requirements	520
What Can Be Transported?	521
Transporting a Tablespace Set	522
Generating a Tablespace Set	522
Plugging in the Transportable Tablespace Set	526
Moving Tablespaces	528
Sharing a Read-Only Tablespace	528
Transporting Partitioned Tables	529
Managing Transportable Tablespaces	531
Using Transportable Tablespaces for Point-in-Time Recovery	532
Determining Which Objects Could Be Lost	533
Resolving Dependencies	533
Preparing the Primary Database	534
Creating the Clone Parameter File	534
Preparing the Clone Database	534
Exporting and Importing the Tablespaces	535

13 Oracle8i Recovery Manager — 537

Introducing Recovery Manager	538
RMAN Features	538
RMAN Limitations	540
RMAN Architecture	540
Running RMAN	545
Connecting to Databases	547
Using RMAN Commands	548
Reviewing RMAN Output	559
Performing RMAN Backups	562
Backup Types	562
Cold Backups in NOARCHIVELOG Mode	564

Backups in ARCHIVELOG Mode 566
Archived Redo Log Backups 573
Datafile Copies 573
Duplexing Backups 575
Performing RMAN Recovery Operations 575
NOARCHIVELOG Mode Backup Recovery 575
ARCHIVELOG Mode Complete Recovery 579
Incomplete Recovery in ARCHIVELOG Mode 582
Recovering from Complete Loss of the Database without a Recovery Catalog 584
Recovering Archived Redo Logs 585
Recovering the Control File without a Recovery Catalog 587
Recovering a Datafile to Another Location 590
Using the Recovery Catalog 590
Creating the Recovery Catalog 591
Resynchronizing the Database to be Backed Up 594
Recovering a Control File 594
Resetting a Database 595
Storing RMAN Scripts 596
Maintaining the Recovery Catalog 598
Generating Reports and Lists 603
Producing Backup Reports 604
Producing Lists 607

14   Oracle8i LogMiner   613

Introducing LogMiner 614
LogMiner Features 614
LogMiner Limitations 615
Setting Up LogMiner 615
Establishing a UTL_FILE_DIR Entry 615
Creating the Dictionary File 616
Selecting Redo Logs to Mine 618
Staging Redo Logs 618
Viewing the Redo Log List 620
Using LogMiner 620
Mining Redo Logs 620
Viewing the Log Mining Results 623
Using the Placeholder Column Option 624
Retrieving the LogMiner Results 624

PART III • BEYOND SIMPLE DATABASE MANAGEMENT

15   Oracle8i Performance Monitoring and Database-Level Tuning   629

Tuning Problem Oracle Databases 630
Setting Oracle Events 632
Enabling Events 632
Using Events to Monitor Your Database 635

Using Oracle8i Dynamic Performance Views 638
    How Are V$ Views Created? 638
    Which V$ Views Are for Performance Monitoring? 639
    How Do You Get More Information from V$ Views? 643
Checking the SGA 645
    Monitoring and Tuning the Database Buffer Cache 646
    Monitoring and Tuning the Data Dictionary Cache 653
    Monitoring and Tuning the Library Cache 654
Checking for I/O Contention 658
    Monitoring System File I/O 658
    Monitoring Session File I/O 660
    Monitoring Rollback Segment Usage 662
Lurking Database Threats 664
    Monitoring User Setup 665
    Monitoring Fragmentation of Tablespace Free Space 666
    Monitoring Fragmentation of Segments 667
    Monitoring Inefficient Block Usage in an Object 669
    Monitoring Browned-Out Indexes 670
    Monitoring Resource Usage 672
Using Oracle Database Performance Monitoring Tools 673
    Gathering System Statistics 674
    Using the Oracle Statspack 676
Introducing a Monitoring Methodology 688
    Establishing Baselines, Benchmarks, and Trends 689
    What Should You Monitor? 690

16 Oracle8i SQL Performance Monitoring and Tuning   699

Overview of SQL Statement Processing 700
    The Cursor 700
    Parse Phase 701
    Bind Variables 703
    Execution, Fetch, and Close 704
The Oracle Optimizer 705
    Rule-Based Optimization (RBO) 705
    Cost-Based Mode Optimization (CBO) 707
    Setting Up the Optimizer 709
    Managing Migrated and Chained Rows 712
    Histograms: Analyzing Data Distribution 717
    Analyzing with Oracle Supplied Packages 719
Oracle Execution Plans 720
    Generating SQL Execution Plans 720
    Reading and Interpreting Execution Plans 734
    Oracle Data Access Methods 741
    Non–Data Execution Plan Operations 744
Tuning SQL Statements 749
    Before You Do Anything: Quantify Your Goals 749
    Improving Throughput and Response Time 750
    Making the Most of Indexes 753

Tuning Rule-Based Statements 758
Tuning Cost-Based Statements 761
Monitoring and Managing Excessive Hard Parsing 770
Other Tuning Suggestions 774
DBMS_STATS 778
DBMS_STATS vs. ANALYZE 778
Using DBMS_STATS 780
Oracle8i's Plan Stability 783
Creating Stored Outlines 784
Using and Modifying stored outlines 785
Data Dictionary Views of Stored Outlines 786
Managing Stored Outlines with OUTLN_PKG 786
An Addendum on Database Monitoring 787
Finding Problematic Code: Using V$SQL 788
Calling all SQL without Bind Variables! 793
SQL Monitoring and Notification 794

17 Monitoring and Tuning Latches, Locks, and Waits   795

Latches and Locks 796
What's a Latch? 796
What's a Lock? 802
Wait Management 813
Working with V$SYSTEM_EVENT 814
Working with V$SESSION_EVENT 815
Working with V$WAITSTAT 817
Common Wait Events 818
Working with V$SESSION_WAIT 824
Monitoring Scripts and Suggestions 826
Monitoring Events 826
Monitoring Locks 827
How Do We Monitor Latching? 832
Tuning Locks, Latches, and Waits 834
General Tuning Advice 834
General Tuning for Latch Contention 837
Last Word: Stay on Top of I/O Throughput! 841

18 Oracle8i Parallel Processing   843

Parallelizing Oracle Operations 844
Using Parallel DML and DDL 845
Enabling and Disabling Parallel DML 845
Creating a Table with Parallel DML 846
Using Parallel DDL 848
Parallel Loading with SQL*Loader 849
Executing Parallel Queries 849
Using One PX Slave 850
Using Two PX Slaves 852
Using Query Hints to Force Parallelism 853
Performing Parallel Recovery Operations 854

CONTENTS | **xxiii**

Tuning and Monitoring Parallel Operations 855
    Setting the Message Buffer Size 858
    Setting the Message Buffer Location 859
    Setting the Minimum and Maximum Parallel Servers 859
    Viewing Parallel Query Information 860
    Tuning Parallel Query Processes 860

19 Oracle8i Data Warehousing Features   863

Understanding Data Warehousing 864
    The Fact/Dimension Schema 865
Query Rewrite 866
    Using Query Rewrite 867
    How Does It Work? 868
    Enabling Query Rewrite 870
    Setting the Rewrite Integrity Level 871
Materialized Views 872
    Creating a Materialized View 873
    Data Dictionary Views for Mviews 879
    Refreshing Mviews 880
    Mview Logs 889
Dimensions 891
    Creating a Dimension 892
    Altering and Dropping Dimensions 899
    Displaying Dimensions 899
Other Data Warehousing Features 902
    Features Covered Elsewhere 902
    SQL Features for Data Warehouse Queries 902

20 Oracle8i Supplied Packages   907

Using the Oracle8i Supplied Packages 908
    Running the Supplied Packages 911
    Getting Information about Supplied Packages 912
Scheduling Jobs with the Job Scheduler 914
    Enabling the Job Scheduler 914
    Adding a Job to the Job Scheduler 915
    Modifying Jobs 918
    Suspending or Removing a Job 919
    Monitoring the Job Scheduler 919
Communicating through Pipes 921
    Using Public Pipes 921
    Using Private Pipes 921
    Sending and Receiving Messages 922

21 Oracle8i Database Security   927

Managing Oracle User Accounts 928
    Setting Up Password File Authentication 928
    Creating User Accounts 931

  Privileged Users 933
  Maintaining User Accounts 936
  Setting Up User Profiles 937
  Defining Grants 943
  Setting Up Roles 945
 Enforcing Row-Level Security 950
  Using Views for Row-Level Security 950
  Using FGAC 951
 Enforcing Column-Level Security 968
  Encrypting Data 969
  Decrypting Data 971

22 SQL*Loader 973

 Introduction to SQL*Loader 974
  SQL*Loader's Capabilities 975
  Conventional and Direct Path Loads 975
  Reserved Words 978
 The Input Files 979
  The Control File 979
  The Input Datafiles (Flat Files) 989
 The "Output": Discards and Rejects 991
  Bad File 992
  Discard File 993
 SQL*Loader Log Files 994
 Loading Objects, Collections, and LOBs 996
  Objects 996
  Collections 998
  LOBs 999
  Loading Partitioned Objects 1001
 Running SQL*Loader 1001
  SQL*Loader from the Command Line 1001
  SQL*Loader Script File Execution 1003
  SQL*Loader DDL Syntax 1004

PART IV • ORACLE8i DISTRIBUTED DATABASE

23 Oracle Database Links 1011

 Database Link Architecture 1012
  Advantages Offered by Database Links 1013
  Database Link Types 1014
  Connection Methods 1015
  Schema Object Names on a Distributed System 1018
 Administering Database Links 1018
  Creating Database Links 1019
  Schema Object Name Resolution 1020
  Data Dictionary Objects Relevant to Database Links 1021
 Using Database Links 1022

24 Database Partitioning — 1023
- Partitioning in Oracle8i — 1024
- Partitioning Basics — 1025
  - Partition Naming — 1026
  - Range Partitioning — 1026
  - Hash Partitioning — 1031
  - Composite Partitioning — 1033
  - Partitioning on LOB Columns — 1035
- Partitioning Indexes — 1036
  - Range Partitioning of an Index — 1036
  - Hash Partitioning of an Index — 1037
  - Composite Partitioning of an Index — 1037
  - Global Indexes — 1038
- The Importance of Partition Pruning — 1039
- Partition-Wise Joins — 1040
  - Example of a Partition-Wise Join — 1040
- Partition Management — 1043
  - Merging — 1043
  - Splitting — 1044
  - Exchanging — 1044
  - Dropping Partitions — 1044
  - Attributes and Partitioning — 1045
  - Data Dictionary Views Useful in Partitioning — 1046

25 Simple and Advanced Replication — 1049
- Simple Replication with Materialized Views — 1050
  - Choosing an Mview Build Option — 1052
  - Choosing an Mview Refresh Option — 1052
- Refresh Groups — 1055
  - Creating a Refresh Group — 1056
  - Adding Members to a Refresh Group — 1057
  - Removing Members from a Refresh Group — 1058
  - Changing a Refresh Group's Schedule — 1058
  - Deleting a Refresh Group — 1059
- Advanced Replication — 1059
  - Advanced Replication Requirements — 1060
  - Remote Procedure Calls for Replication — 1062
  - Replication Views — 1064
  - Setting Up Advanced Replication — 1065
  - Checking for Replication Errors — 1071
  - Detecting Replication Conflicts — 1071
  - Resuming Master Activity — 1073

26 High Availability — 1075
- Using a Standby Database — 1076
  - Standby Database Modes — 1077

Creating the Standby Database 1078
Maintaining a Standby Database 1089
Using Oracle Parallel Server 1093
The OPS Architecture 1094
Oracle8i OPS Enhancements 1097
OPS Limitations 1098
Creating the OPS Database 1098
Using Oracle Fail Safe 1105

27 Oracle8i and the Internet   1109
Using Java in Oracle8i 1111
Basic Methods 1111
The Java Virtual Machine (JVM) 1113
JServer Accelerator 1114
Java Configuration 1115
MTS vs. Dedicated Server 1116
Java Scripts 1117
Java Installation 1118
Verifying Java Installation 1119
Common Errors While Installing or Using JVM 1119
Creating Java Stored Procedures 1120
Java Utilities 1121
Using the LOADJAVA Utility 1121
Using the DROPJAVA Utility 1122
Java Security 1123
Additional Internet Features 1124
Oracle Internet File System (iFS) 1124
XML SQL Utility (XSU) 1124

Index *1125*

INTRODUCTION

"We want information... information..." Possibly you recognize these words as the primary interest of a somewhat clandestine group, and as told by a character called Number 2 to Patrick McGoohan's character Number 6 (in the old TV show *The Prisoner*). Indeed, in this day, information is king, and the speedy, accurate, and reliable retrieval of this information is paramount.

And if you wish to store and retrieve information quickly, Oracle's flagship database product is the way to go. Oracle Corporation currently "owns" the major share of the large database market, which is one sign of the superiority of Oracle's product. The Oracle product is robust in features and very fast—but it can also be complicated and expensive to run. As much as Oracle wishes to market its database product as being easy to manage and install, the truth is that an experienced DBA is generally needed for anything other than the most elemental installation and operation.

We hear often from aspiring or beginning DBAs wondering how they can join the ranks of Oracle DBAs. Experience is undeniably one of the primary requirements for DBA excellence. Yet, the need to acquire that experience also stands in the way of the junior DBA's advancement. This experience requirement has made senior DBAs somewhat scarce, and it's also a principal reason for the good salaries offered to truly good DBAs. In other words, you can't just pick up a book, go through the motions, and become a great DBA.

The bottom line for employers is that it's best to start out with the best and brightest. ("You can pay me now, or you can pay me later.") If you're investing millions in equipment and software, then you want to invest in talent, as well, at the beginning. Once you have a stable, well-designed system up and running, then you can bring on the juniors to maintain it.

Getting one's foot in the DBA door is difficult. What you can do, however, is learn from each book you study. Realize that just knowing the commands and how the processes work is not enough to become a good DBA. In addition, you need to know about backup and recovery. You need to know about tuning the database and tuning the SQL running in the database. You need to know how to ferret statistics out of the database and how to interpret them. That's what mastering Oracle database administration, and this book, are about.

This text goes beyond basic administration tasks, though it covers those as well. Within these pages you will find nuggets of our experience that might help you. We hope that you will also take away from this book the fact that administration of an Oracle database is a multifaceted job. Finally, remember that the best approach to management of Oracle is a proactive one. Don't sit and wait for problems to occur.

Is This Book for You?

We assume that the reader has fundamental knowledge of an Oracle database. If you are a beginning DBA with little or no understanding of Oracle, you should carefully read Chapter 1 before going further. In addition, we strongly suggest that you read a selection of the following books; these are in order from basic to advanced skills coverage:

- *Oracle DBA 101* by Marlene L. Theriault, et al
- The Sybex Oracle Certified Professional (OCP) series of certification study guides, including
  - *OCP: Oracle8i DBA SQL and PL/SQL Study Guide*, 0-7821-2682-0 (Sybex, 2000)
  - *OCP: Oracle8i DBA Architecture & Administration and Backup & Recovery Study Guide*, 0-7821-2683-9 (Sybex, 2001)
  - *OCP: Oracle8i DBA Performance Tuning and Network Administration Study Guide*, 0-7821-2684-7 (Sybex, 2000)

  Though this set of books is designed primarily for those working toward the Oracle OCP exams, the study guides really are a good introduction to the Oracle product.
- *Oracle8i Networking 101* by Marlene L. Theriault
- *Oracle8i Administration and Management* by Michael R. Ault

If you are a beginning DBA and do not have direct access to the Oracle product, you can download a copy of Oracle from Technet (www.technet.com), the Oracle website that contains demonstration copies of Oracle software. Technet also contains code samples and Oracle documentation.

Following are some other beneficial websites that you might use in your quest to master the Oracle database product:

www.revealnet.com This website provides information on the product offerings of RevealNet Labs (Quest Software), which develops state-of-the-art technical knowledge bases and development/administration tools for Oracle, DB2, and SQL Server. The site also includes the Oracle DBA Pipelines, a forum for Oracle database administrators to meet and share ideas and ask for help. The syntax diagrams throughout this book and in Appendix E (on the CD) were produced using the RevealNet Knowledge Base for Oracle Administration.

www.oracle.com   This is the main page of Oracle Corporation's website. Here you can find information on Oracle and download certain products.

education.oracle.com   This is Oracle Corporation's education site, which offers information on Oracle training courses and becoming an Oracle Certified Professional.

metalink.oracle.com   Metalink is the online website for Oracle users. If you are an Oracle support customer, you will have access to this site. Use it to search out help with existing Oracle bugs, to find Oracle documents, and to access Oracle forums on various subjects.

www.ixora.com.au   The Ixora site provides a great wealth of Unix-related Oracle internal knowledge, as well as scripts that you can use to monitor the health of your database.

What You Need to Know

As you pick up this book, understand that we have not devoted a great number of its pages to examining every fundamental detail of the Oracle database environment. You should already be comfortable with putting together SQL statements, and you should know what SQL*Plus is.

Although the book as a whole is not designed for beginners, beginning DBAs will find Chapter 1 to be a quick primer that may well be enough to help them on the way to mastering Oracle8i database administration.

If you are a junior DBA, this book is right up your alley. You'll be comfortable already with what's involved in starting and stopping the database and working with simple queries. You'll have some understanding of what the data dictionary is, and perhaps even be familiar with parts of it. It's our hope that you'll eat this book up and that it will give you the knowledge you need to become a truly great DBA.

If you're already a master DBA, we hope this text will be a trusted reference, and perhaps provide insight into some aspects of database administration that you want to improve.

Conventions Used in This Book

One of the themes you'll find in this book is *consistency*. Within these pages we follow a set of terminology standards that are in fairly common use in the Oracle community. We suggest that you adopt these standards in your daily operations, as well.

Within the text, Oracle keywords are in uppercase (SELECT, INSERT, FROM, V$PARAMETER, PARTITION BY HASH). Table and column names are in uppercase, as well, to distinguish them from the surrounding text (the EMP table; the EMP NO column).

In addition, the following elements appear in this book:

NOTE Notes like this will appear from time to time. Generally when we want add a comment that pertains to a particular section, we will do so in a note.

TIP Tips like this are used to highlight particularly important procedures or processes.

WARNING Warnings are used in the text to keep you from destroying something inadvertently. When a warning appears, make sure you read it carefully. We also use warnings to point out bugs in the Oracle8i product that we know about.

How to Use This Book

You may find it easiest to read the chapters in order, but it's not essential. One of our goals was to make it possible for you to pick the text up and read any individual chapter without having to study several other chapters first. We have grouped similar chapters logically, but otherwise (with a few exceptions) the chapters do not particularly "build" upon one another. To make it easier for you to move among the chapters, we have included plenty of cross-references throughout the book.

Of course, you'll get the most benefit from this book by putting the material to real use. Take the examples and the generic routines we've provided and expand on them. Add and subtract from them and incorporate them into your own database management activities. Experiment and enjoy!

What's On the CD

The CD is chock full of goodies!

First, you'll find a complete electronic edition of the book.

All nine appendices, which are not in the printed book, are on the CD. You'll find the Quick Reference appendices especially helpful. They're all in easy-to-search .PDF format.

We've also provided some trial versions of products that can help you better manage your database. Note that these demos require that you purchase a license for continued use; please read the provided supporting documentation and respect the rights of the vendors who were kind enough to provide these files. All of the following are from RevealNet Labs (Quest Software), www.revealnet.com:

- The Formatter Plus tool, which will do a quick syntax check of your SQL. It works on code that has no Oracle syntax errors and is compilable or executable on Oracle, but it is more permissive than the PL/SQL compiler or SQL*Plus environment.

- The RevealNet Knowledge Base for Oracle Administration, to help you find solutions for your questions about Oracle database administration.

- The Active PL/SQL Knowledge Base combines a comprehensive PL/SQL reference with an extensive PL/SQL Code Library. It offers a valuable source of technical expertise and a substantial library of procedures and functions.

Also included on the CD is the Oracle8i table, index, and SGA sizing spreadsheet discussed in Chapter 3 of the book, compliments of Mike Ault and TUSC.

 NOTE For late-breaking information about the CD, including additional files and utilities, see README.TXT in the root directory of the CD.

Come Visit Us

We hope that you will share with us your feelings about this book. Let us know what has helped you, and what you might like to see in the next incarnation of this work. You might well disagree with some things stated here—being a DBA is somewhat like being an artist, and not everyone agrees on what makes a work of art. We hope that you will communicate with us and let us know what you liked and what you didn't.

We have set up a website, www.masteringoracle.com, where you'll find a link to e-mail Robert. There are also some links to the book's errata and other nifty things!

PART I

Oracle Essentials

LEARN TO:

- *Install Oracle*
- *Migrate to Oracle*
- *Create an Oracle database*
- *Use the Oracle data dictionary*

CHAPTER 1

Elements of Oracle Database Management

FEATURING:

What is a DBA?	4
Introducing Oracle8i	5
Oracle internals	13
The physilogical Oracle	17
Fundamental Oracle principles	19
Environment settings	21
The Oracle SQL interface tools	22
Using Oracle SQL	29
Oracle PL/SQL	39

Welcome to *Mastering Oracle8i*. We hope you find this book useful in your DBA endeavors. We've made every effort to fit as much priceless information into this book as we could find, and hope you refer to it daily.

This book was written as a reference for the working Oracle DBA. We assume most of you already know Oracle well and want to explore Oracle8i in particular. And if you're new to Oracle, start right here. The pace might seem fast and furious, but you'll manage quite well.

Here in Chapter 1, we offer a broad view of Oracle and SQL fundamentals. We'll begin with a refresher on the DBA's role. Then we'll review some database theory and Oracle history. Following that is a discussion of Oracle internals, the building blocks you must master for successful database administration. Next up is a discussion of SQL*Plus and other elements of the Oracle database interface. In addition, we will briefly discuss the tools used to access the database, fundamental concepts of the SQL language, and how to use SQL in the database. All of these introductory subjects are, of course, covered in depth in later chapters.

What Is a DBA?

There seems to be an air of mystery surrounding database administrators and database management. But really, being a DBA boils down to just a few basic qualities:

- Willingness to work long, sometimes hard hours
- Ability to ferret out the answers
- Determination to be the best
- The drive to succeed
- Knowledge of database administration
- Experience in database administration

New DBAs can make up for a lack of the last two qualities by concentrating on the first four. As you gain knowledge and experience, you'll find that you don't need to work so many long, hard hours quite as often as when you first started. You'll make fewer mistakes, and you'll know where to look first for the answers—no ferrets required!

We aren't trying to snowball you, though. There will always be users who call you at midnight, needing your help to recover a database. But you'll be up to the task. With knowledge and experience comes a better DBA who can truly become a "lazy DBA." (In Chapter 15, which covers performance monitoring, you'll find a definition of a "lazy DBA"—and it's *not* someone who just sits around.)

Robert's Rants: Stick to Your Guns

As DBA, you're very much the heart of the database. If you fail, your database fails. Do not be complacent with your database just because it's performing well. Do not ease up on vigilance against risks to your systems, including policies and procedures that are not in the best interest of your database. Granted, there is a time to fight and a time to lay low, but this is your job. The life of your database is your job.

Yes, I'm on a soapbox; this is my chance to rant. I've met many a DBA who rolled over and gave up because a project manager ordered them to do this or do that. But don't forget that *you are the DBA*. Go on out and look at the top job-hunting web sites, and count the number of DBA jobs out there. If you're a DBA, you're in high demand, so you have the freedom to say no and stand by it. I've had more than a few encounters with a manager trying to bully me into doing something I just wasn't going to do. I've simply told them to go fly a kite. I might even have mentioned something about my black belt in karate, if they were particularly unpleasant.

Of course, please do make sure you can back up your point of view with some good solid facts. In the end, when you're proven right, you and your database will be better for it, and so will the community using that database. The point is, if you know you're correct, don't back down for a second. Compromise is fine, if it doesn't compromise the integrity of the database in your charge (or your own integrity). Someone may demand your head, but it's a sure bet that most of your company's management knows the value of your position—and if they don't, they will soon find out.

Of course, if you end up getting fired, I didn't say this and I'm not here.

Introducing Oracle8i

In this section we will briefly discuss some relational database theory and some Oracle history. We will take an overview of Oracle8i, the latest and greatest version of Oracle, and see how the Oracle database is both relational and object oriented.

 TIP Already an expert on relational theory? Already know that ACID means something else besides what you used to melt things in chemistry class? You can skip this section altogether; go ahead and move on to "Internals."

Oracle is a relational database geared to meet the information processing requirements of business. Its features include support for all of the following:

- A large number of users and high-concurrency activity.
- Read consistency among transactions, ensuring that other users will not see your changes until your changes are committed. Neither will your changes affect other users' queries that started before your changes were committed.
- A high degree of scalability.
- Multiple recovery methods, including recovery to point of failure and recovery to a specific point in time.
- High availability using several methodologies, including standby database and replication methodologies.

Relational Theory—Briefly

In a paper presented in June 1970, "A Relational Model of Data for Large Shared Data Banks," Dr. E. F. Codd introduced the relational database model we still use today. Of course, Codd and others have added to this theory. In particular, Dr. Peter Chen, professor of computer science at Louisiana State University, originated the Entity Relationship (ER) model. He described it in a 1976 paper entitled "The Entity Relationship Model - Toward a Unified View of Data."

Within the relational database, data is generally stored in two-dimensional tables. Contained within the tables are sets of rows and columns. A row represents a record in the table, and one or more columns represent the details of that record. When discussing relational theory, the acronym *ACID* is used to represent the four fundamentals of effective relational databases. Oracle8i provides robust support for all these relational fundamentals.

A   *Atomicity.* Each transaction is a separate and distinct entity. It happens in whole or not at all.

C   *Consistency.* Each database change is partitioned from other transactions. Results from another transaction won't mysteriously pop up in the middle of another transaction. One transaction moves the database from one consistent state to the next.

I   *Isolation.* A transaction is not available to other users until it has been committed. If you add a department and then add an employee to that department in the same transaction, someone else cannot see the new department added until you have committed the transaction, which takes place after you have added the employee record.

D   *Durability.* This fundamental implies that when a transaction is complete, its presence in the database will be preserved and will not be lost. Changes, once committed, can be recovered.

A relational database also demonstrates the principles of structures, operations, and integrity that Codd defined. *Structures* are tables, indexes, and views (for example). They are manipulated with *operations.* Operations are defined methods of allowing the user access to the database and of manipulating that database. Database operations adhere to *integrity* rules that govern the database. Integrity rules define what operations can be executed and when; all operations must follow these rules.

Normalization

When you're creating a database for an online transaction processing system (OLTP), there are generally two concerns: the speed and efficiency of transactions, and the overall storage space required by the database. One means of achieving the best results is *normalization*—the process of organizing and refining database tables to provide accurate, unambiguous results when the tables are accessed. For larger, data warehousing systems, the goals are generally the same, but the means to meet these goals tend to differ.

As a database is normalized, overall storage requirements are often reduced because there is less data redundancy. Normalization can also, however, have a negative impact on performance (a statement that causes an argument in many camps). That said, the benefits of normalization usually outweigh any potential loss of performance. In fact, normalization can improve performance because, overall, less data is processed.

Typically, we start with a normalized database. Often, however, the cost of performing the joins to retrieve data is higher than the additional disk space required to store the data in a denormalized state. Based on this and other performance factors, we may choose to denormalize the database—tables and materialized views are created to store data from various tables in denormalized format. Although denormalization should not be the first line of response to query performance problems, it can yield good results. In one case, we denormalized eight tables used in a recurring eight-table join and got runtimes down from several hours to just seconds. Indeed, just about any large data warehousing design comprises denormalized data stores.

Databases are typically described as being in *third normal form.* (You can actually normalize your database up to sixth normal form, but this is rarely done.) Here are the steps of normalizing an object in a database:

First Normal	Remove all repeating groups.
Second Normal	Link all entities to a primary key.
Third Normal	Link nonkey entities by keys, supported with foreign keys.

First Normal Form

When we normalize a database we begin with a given entity (for example, a table called PATIENT). This entity has attributes that uniquely identify each occurrence within the entity. Each attribute is in its own cell, and each cell has a single value. Entities in a given column must be the same kind of information (addresses and phone numbers cannot be mixed, for example).

When the PATIENT table is put in first normal form, all of the attributes of the table are atomic. Thus a patient's name will be in one column, the address in a separate column, and the zip code in a third column; no attributes will share a given column. Another rule is that an attribute cannot contain repeating groups. Thus, in the PATIENT table, all of the patient's doctors cannot be listed in an attribute called DOCTORS (unless there is truly only one doctor per patient—not very likely!) Once all this work has been done, the PATIENT table would be in first normal form as seen here:

```
PATIENT
-----------
Patient_id
last_name
first_name
address_1
city
state
zip
doctor_name
procedure
procedure_cost
```

Second Normal Form

In second normal form, we remove any item that is not directly dependent on the primary key (PK). For example, we have identified the PATIENT_ID as the primary key of the PATIENT table. The DOCTOR_NAME columns are not dependent on the PATIENT_ID column and thus should be removed from the PATIENT table. All these columns are moved to their own entity (table). We end up with the following entities, with the PATIENT table in second normal form:

```
PATIENT
-----------
Patient_id   -  PK
last_name
first_name
address
```

```
city
state
zip
procedure
procedure_cost

DOCTOR
_____

doctor_number   - PK
doctor_name

DOCTOR_ASSIGNMENT
_____

patient_id      - PK / FK
doctor_number   - PK / FK
Comments
```

Note that the PATIENT table attributes now all relate directly to the PATIENT_ID primary key. We have added DOCTOR table, which now contains the DOCTOR_NAME column, since the DOCTOR_NAME column is not related to the primary key. We also have a third table, DOCTOR_ASSIGNMENT, which relates the two tables (PATIENT and DOCTOR) that we have just created. Also note that we created the PATIENT_ID and DOCTOR_NUMBER columns in the DOCTOR_ASSIGNEMNT table as primary keys, and assigned them a foreign key relationship to the related columns in the DOCTOR and PATIENT tables. Finally, we added a COMMENTS column to the DOCTOR_ASSIGNMENT table so the doctor assigned to the patient could record some comment about the assignment.

Third Normal Form

In third normal form (often abbreviated to 3NF), all attributes in a given table are dependent on every key attribute. Any nonprimary attributes that are dependent on nonkey attributes are moved to their own table. We also ensure that no attribute is dependent on any set of nonprimary key attributes. Then we define key relationships between the various related tables. In our example, the PROCEDURE_COST attribute is dependent on a nonkey attribute, PROCEDURE. We create another table called PROCEDURE that links to the PATIENT table through a column called PROCEDURE_ID.

Foreign key relationships, which represent a relationship between two entities, are established in third normal form. The first entity (called the child) consists of one or more columns that are always related to all primary key attributes of the parent.

In this example the PROCEDURE column in the PATIENT table (the child table in this example) violates third normal form. We need to remove the PROCEDURE column from the PATIENT table and move it to a new table, which we will call PROCEDURE_NAME. Still, we want to relate the two tables (PROCEDURE and PATIENT), so we create the PROCEDURE_ID column in the PATIENT table, and relate it to the column of the same name in the PROCEDURE table. Finally, we make the PROCEDURE_ID column in the PROCEDURE table the primary key. Now, for each patient, we can track the procedure being performed, but there is still a problem that we need to deal with.

The PROCEDURE_ID doesn't really belong in the PATIENT table. This is because a given patient may need to have one or more procedures performed on them. If this occurred, we would violate 3NF because we would end up with repeating primary keys (multiple records for the same PATIENT_ID). Thus, we will move PROCEDURE_ID from the PATIENT table down to the DOCTOR_ASSIGNMENT table. Finally, we will add a PROCEDURE_DATE column in the DOCTOR_ASSIGNMENT table to make sure that each row in that table is unique, and thus fulfilling the requirements of normalization. Note in this case that the PROCEDURE_ID column in the PROCEDURE table is not a primary key column of that table, but it does have a foreign key relationship created between it and the PROCEDURE_ID column of the PROCEDURE table.

```
PATIENT
--------------------
Patient_id     -  PK
last_name
first_name
address
city
state
zip


DOCTOR
--------------------
doctor_number  -  PK
doctor_name


DOCTOR_ASSIGNMENT
--------------------
patient_id     -  PK / FK
doctor_number  -  PK / FK
procedure_date
procedure_id   -  FK
```

```
Comments

PROCEDURE
--------------------
procedure_id   - PK
procedure
procedure_cost
```

Joins

Often you will want to query two tables and produce a result from both, combined. You show the related rows of both tables together, with each row representing the merged rows from the two tables. This is known as a *join*. For example, assume you have an employee table containing employees' names and IDs, as well as the number of each employee's department. A second table, called DEPT, contains each department number and the name assigned to that specific department (Heating and Cooling, Lawn Equipment, and so on). With a join, you can query these tables to get an employee's name, and the name and number of the department in which they work. An example appears in Figure 1.1.

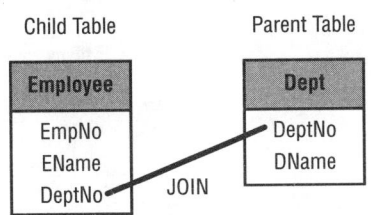

FIGURE 1.1
An example of a join between two tables

In the process of executing a join, the tables have various relationships to one another. If one table of the join will always have just one record, and the other table may have many records, this is known as a *one-to-many join*. If both tables of the join will have only one record as a result of the join, this is a *one-to-one join*. Sometimes both tables have many related records; this is a *many-to-many join*. Often these relationships are optional, or they may be required. When they are required, you end up with a *foreign key relationship*.

In a foreign key relationship, columns in one table relate to the primary key columns in another table. For instance, one or more columns in Table A (the child table) might have a relationship to one or more primary key columns in Table B (the parent table). The presence of parent/child relationships makes it a *foreign key relationship*, which creates another integrity rule. Oracle enforces the foreign key relationships via a *foreign key constraint* in which you define the parent/child relationship of the tables, and Oracle then ensures that the foreign key relationship between the two tables is enforced. Through enforcement of the foreign key relationship, logical data consistency is enforced.

Figure 1.2 shows the one-to-one, one-to-many, and many-to-many relationships possible in a relational design.

FIGURE 1.2
Relationships of tables

One-To-One Table Relationship

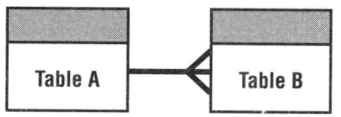

A row in Table A is related to a row in Table B

One-To-Many Table Relationship

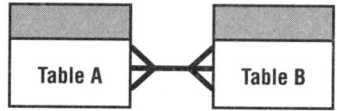

One row in Table A is related to
one or many rows in Table B

Table A — Table B

Many rows in Table A can be
related to many rows in Table B

A Brief History of Oracle

Oracle was founded by Larry Ellison in 1977 as Relational Software Inc. (RSI). The first version of RSI's database product was called Oracle. Oracle version 2 was introduced in 1979. It has quickly become the relational database of choice in most Fortune 500 businesses and a great number of Internet businesses. In late 1999, Oracle released its newest version, Oracle8i. At the time of this writing, release 8.1.7 of Oracle8i was the latest and greatest version of the Oracle database. Also, the beta for Oracle9i (release 9.0) has been announced. With Oracle8i, Oracle has introduced significant features that indicate a long, bright future for this product. Overall performance has been enhanced, and there have been improvements in Java support within the database, data warehousing, and a number of other aspects of Oracle8i.

Oracle as a Relational Database

Oracle supports the basic constructs of relational databases. It allows for the creation of tables and the definition of primary keys on those tables. It supports the ACID fundamentals as well as the principles of structures, operations, and integrity. In addition, Oracle supports multiple users and multiple transactions, all the while making sure that you can recover your data if disaster occurs. Oracle allows you to define foreign keys and enforce those relationships, yet Oracle offers you the flexibility to break those rules (or bend them a bit) when necessary.

Oracle as an Object-Oriented Database

Oracle8 introduced object-oriented functionality, which continues to evolve in Oracle8i. You can create user-defined datatypes that can be used in Oracle object tables, nested tables, VARARRAY types, and methods.

Though not yet fully object oriented, Oracle8i is a step in the right direction. As the company continues to improve the nature of object features in Oracle, more—and more truly object-oriented—features will be available. Chapter 6 explores the object-oriented architecture of Oracle8i.

Oracle Internals

This section covers the basics of Oracle internals: instances and how to create them, the SGA, Oracle processes, the physical and logical structures of an Oracle database, and some miscellaneous but important principles such as foreign keys and NULL values. If you're a beginning DBA, this section is critical. You need to really understand this stuff in order to master Oracle database administration. Until the internals are under your belt, you can go through the motions, but you won't really understand *why* you're doing what you're doing. So pay attention, and read on.

 NOTE For the most part, this book isn't directed toward beginners in database programming. If you're a beginner DBA, you will need supplemental information along your journey through this text. You might want to look at the Sybex Study Guides for Oracle Certified Professional (OCP) certification; several of them focus on certification for the DBA. Appendix I contains details about the Oracle Certified Professional Program.

So let's get started. First up: What is an Oracle instance, when is it created, and why?

Instances vs. Databases

An Oracle database and an Oracle instance are sometimes, incorrectly, lumped together. But the two are very different, and it's important to understand their distinctions.

The Oracle *instance* consists of the following:

- An area of allocated shared memory called the *System Global Area (SGA)*
- All the required Oracle processes

When you issue the STARTUP NOMOUNT command from one of the Oracle database interfaces (Server Manager or SQL*Plus, discussed shortly), you are actually starting an Oracle instance. As the instance starts, it reads the database parameter file. The parameter file contains a list of parameter settings that directs Oracle in configuring the various settings that apply to that instance.

An Oracle instance, then, is the collection of Oracle processes and shared memory. An *active* instance is a prerequisite to the successful mounting and opening of an Oracle database. Note that only one database can be mounted to a given instance at one time, unless you are running Oracle's Oracle Parallel Server (OPS) product, which we discuss in Chapter 26. With OPS, many instances can open the same database, which allows for higher availability. You can start the instance without the database being open (with the STARTUP NOMOUNT command); in fact, several administrative actions can be performed with only the instance started, including certain types of recovery, backup, and database creation. After Oracle has started the instance successfully, the database can then be mounted and opened.

Figure 1.3 diagrams the relationship between the instance and the database.

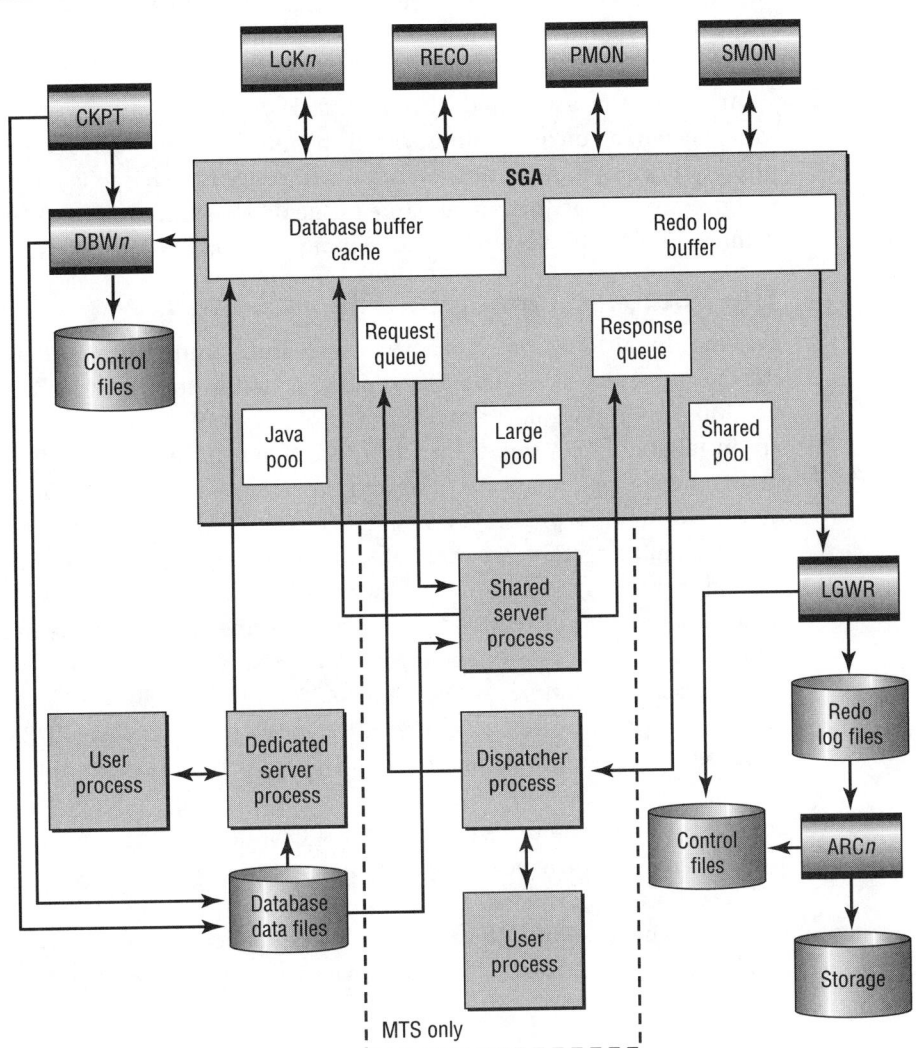

FIGURE 1.3
An instance and a database

Instance/Database Names

All Oracle databases have a *site identifier (SID)*. A system can have multiple databases, but you cannot have multiple databases within the same SID. You define the SID of a database when you create it, as a part of the CREATE DATABASE command (covered in Chapter 3 .

An Oracle database might also be referred to by its *service name,* which is a Net8 feature. This is really incorrect usage in Oracle8i, however, because service names in

Oracle networking can actually refer to more than one SID. Therefore, using a service name is not guaranteed to refer to one and only one database. See Chapter 8 for more information on service names.

Another name associated with the Oracle database is the *global name,* which comes into play when you are dealing with distributed Oracle databases (Part IV). The important thing to remember is that if you're going to rename your Oracle database, you need to change the global name of the database after the renaming operation is completed. We will discuss how to rename your Oracle database in Chapter 7.

The Database Parameter File, *init.ora*

Commonly called the `init.ora`, the Oracle initialization file contains parameters for the Oracle system. It is a text file, kept by default in the directory $ORACLE_HOME/dbs on Unix, or %ORACLE_HOME%\database on Windows NT. Often, with an OFA-compliant installation (OFA stands for Oracle Flexible Arthitecture), you'll find that the main database parameter file is kept in the database `admin` directory named %ORACLE_HOME%/admin/mydb/pfile/initpfile.ora. Then a one-line parameter file is created in the default directory; this file contains an IFILE pointer to the real parameter file in the `pfile` directory. Also, you can use the `pfile` parameter to cause Oracle to load the parameter file from the `admin` directory; or, in some operating systems (NT for example), you can change the system environment to point to a different parameter file location.

An Oracle install starts at ORACLE_BASE, and the database software is generally created in a product directory under the version number of the RDBMS being installed. This is an implementation of OFA, which is explored in Chapter 3.

Parameters are used to define Oracle database settings, directory locations, and to control the operation of certain processes. Comments can be included in the file, as well, via the use of the pound (#) symbol.

The full name of the database parameter file is generally init<*sid*>.ora. So if your database name is ROBERT, your `init.ora` will typically be called initROBERT.ora.

Here is an example of a partial database parameter file for a database called ora816:

```
db_name = "ora816"
instance_name = ora816
service_names = ora816
control_files = ("D:\Oracle\oradata\ora816\control01.ctl",
   "D:\Oracle\oradata\ora816\control02.ctl")
open_cursors = 100
max_enabled_roles = 30
db_file_multiblock_read_count = 8
db_block_buffers = 2048
shared_pool_size = 55428800
```

```
processes = 50
log_buffer = 32768
max_dump_file_size = 10240   # limit trace file size to 5M each
log_archive_start = true
log_archive_dest_1 = "location=D:\Oracle\oradata\ora816\archive"
log_archive_format = %%ORACLE_SID%%T%TS%S.ARC
rollback_segments = ( RBS0, RBS1, RBS2, RBS3, RBS4, RBS5, RBS6 )
# define directories to store trace and alert files
background_dump_dest = D:\Oracle\admin\ora816\bdump
user_dump_dest = D:\Oracle\admin\ora816\udump
db_block_size = 2048
compatible = 8.1.0
sort_area_size = 65536
sort_area_retained_size = 65536
```

NOTE Database SIDs are case sensitive on some platforms (namely Unix). On most others (namely Windows NT), they are not.

As you prepare the scripts required to create the database (Chapter 3), you'll create an init.ora parameter file for that database. If you use Oracle's Database Configuration Assistant (DCA), it will create the parameter file for you as the database is created.

The Physilogical Oracle

Oracle is truly *physilogical*—both physical and logical at the same time. Indeed, some Oracle internal educational manuals refer to the database as such. In this section we review both the physical and logical aspects of the Oracle database.

NOTE Thorough examination of Oracle physical and logical elements continues in subsequent chapters, and you'll find a discussion of Oracle architecture in general in Chapter 5.

Physical Oracle

At the physical level, Oracle exists in various files that have specific purposes.

Datafiles These physical files store Oracle data. One or more of these files is associated with an Oracle tablespace. Datafiles are examined throughout the book, and particularly in Chapters 3, 7, and 9.

Temporary Files Temporary files are associated with temporary tablespaces. Temporary files aren't really temporary, however. They are a bit different from normal database datafiles. First, they are used only for temporary segment creation, such as when your SQL statement results in a sort operation. Second, since these datafiles are only used for temporary sort work, you do not back them up during a database backup and thus they cannot be recovered. Third, redo is not generated on any operation involving a temporary file (except for global temporary tables). Temporary files and temporary tablespaces are discussed in Chapter 5.

Control Files Control files contain database information such as the location of datafiles, certain database status flags, and RMAN backup information. You can (and should) have more than one copy of the control files. We will discuss these files in more detail throughout the book, but particularly in Chapters 4 and 9.

Redo Logs The redo logs are like tape recorders, recording almost all activity that occurs in the database. Oracle requires that you have at least two redo logs for any database. You can multiplex redo logs, keeping multiple copies of the redo logs spread across various disks. See Chapters 3 and 9 for more on redo logs.

Configuration and Parameter files These various files include the `init<sid>.ora`, which controls instance and the database functionality; and the LISTENER, `sqlnet.ora`, and `tnsnames.ora` parameter files, which configure Net8 networking. Other configuration and parameter files may exist for various Oracle options, and we will discuss these files throughout the book.

Logical Oracle

The Oracle logical database is represented in several structures. Let's look at these structures in brief, and they'll be examined in more detail in later chapters.

Tablespaces Where the rubber meets the road. A *tablespace* is a logical storage entity that is assigned to one or more physical datafiles. We will discuss tablespaces in Chapters 3 and 7.

Segments A *segment* is made up of one or more extents that are allocated for one specific type of storage. The four types of segments, discussed in Chapter 5, are data segments, index segments, temporary segments, and rollback segments.

Extents An *extent* is a combination of Oracle data blocks that together make up a logical unit of storage. We will discuss extents in more detail in Chapter 5.

Blocks This is the most atomic unit of storage in Oracle. All Oracle objects are stored in units of blocks. The full discussion of blocks is in Chapter 5.

Fundamental Oracle Principles

We will now review a few fundamental principals of Oracle. First we will look at the issue of database consistency. Then we'll briefly define Oracle transactions and constraints; NULLs and related issues; and Oracle's environment parameters.

Database Consistency

Oracle supports and enforces database consistency. Such consistency implies several things. First, it means users will see a consistent view of their data, including their own changes. Second, it means the user will not see other users' uncommitted changes. Finally, consistency promises that the committed state of the database is the same for all objects in that database. Thus, two objects in the database will always be synchronized to the same point in time. For example, an EMPLOYEE table with all committed changes as of 3:10 P.M. cannot exist in the database simultaneously with a DEPT table having committed changes as they looked at 3:30 P.M.

Consistency is facilitated through several database mechanisms. Oracle locking mechanisms and rollback segments are the major structures that are used to support database consistency. These features can also cause problems; for instance, other sessions may be locked out, causing them to stall while waiting for a lock to be released. We will address such issues in the chapters about monitoring (15 through 17). When performing certain types of recoveries, you will need to pay close attention to the notion of consistency, and we will return to the subject in Chapter 9.

Transactions

A *transaction* defines the life of a unit of work in an Oracle database. The transaction starts when the user signs on to the database and continues until the user issues a COMMIT command in SQL, or causes an implied commit through some action, or rolls back the transaction.

All database actions within the transaction are committed as a group at the end of the transaction. If one transaction statement fails, this generally does not cause the entire transaction to fail (unless the error is so severe that it causes the database to crash or some other extreme event). Once the COMMIT is complete, the transaction is guaranteed to be accessible by all users in the database, and (if the DBA has established adequate backup and recovery procedures) guaranteed to be recoverable.

Constraints

Oracle supports various constraints to enforce data integrity. These constraints are described briefly here and in further detail in Chapter 7. Other constraints associated with Oracle features, such as partitioning, are discussed with related topics throughout this book.

Primary Key Constraints

A *primary key* represents an attribute or combination of attributes (columns) that uniquely identify a row in a table. Generally, primary key constraints are enforced through the use of a unique key. (This is not required in Oracle8i, however, because of the inclusion of the deferred constraint. We will discuss deferred constraints in Chapter 19.) Each table can have only one assigned primary key constraint.

Unique Key Constraints

Unique keys are similar to primary key constraints in that they are built on a table and require that the combination of columns in the key be unique within the table. A unique key requires an index, but the index need not be unique. The primary difference between a primary key and a unique key is that the columns of a primary key cannot be NULL, whereas in a unique key they can.

Foreign Key Constraints

Foreign keys (FKs) define a parent/child relationship (a relationship between a row in a child table and a row in a parent table). The foreign key ensures that if specific columns exist in the child table, then like columns exist in the parent table. Also, the columns in the parent table must be part of the primary key or a unique key. Foreign key constraints, as we will discuss in Chapter 7, can be enabled or disabled as required. By default, when a foreign key is re-enabled, it will validate that the foreign key column in each row of the child table actually exists in the parent table, thus verifying that the constraint between the two tables is still valid before it is enabled.

A few notes on foreign keys. First, we strongly suggest that all columns used in your unique keys and foreign keys be NOT NULL unless they truly must be able to handle NULL values. Also, foreign keys can have many options associated with them. For example, when you create a foreign key constraint, you can indicate that it should CASCADE any delete operation that might occur in the parent table. The CASCADE operation will cause all associated child rows to be removed when the parent row is removed. Other options that can be associated with constraints include deferring the enforcement of the constraint until the end of a transaction, or enabling the constraint without checking the existing records.

Full coverage of foreign keys is in Chapter 7.

Check Constraints

Check constraints cause a data validity check to occur on a single column of a single row. Check constraints enforce data-integrity rules and validate data to be stored in columns of a table. Examples of check constraints are that a value in a column cannot exceed a certain amount, or that it must be in all caps.

NULL Values

NULL values try really hard to mess everything up. A NULL is just that, null—not 0, not a blank, not even the absence of something. It's just a NULL.

NULLs tend to allow odd things to occur. SQL statements have special searching syntax associated with NULL values. NULLs are not stored in indexes and so can be a performance problem. Be aware that check constraints evaluating to NULL will pass. This is because a NULL is not TRUE and not a FALSE, and it is handled in various ways, some that will surprise you. We will discuss NULLs and their dangers in several places in this book.

Environment Settings

Oracle environment parameter settings must be established before you can install, create, or interact with an Oracle database. Sometimes, as in a Unix environment, these parameters are set in the environment itself. Sometimes the settings appear in the Registry and/or are set in the environment you are working in. In Windows NT, for example, you use a special program to set these in the Registry. Table 1.1 lists the most common Oracle environmental settings.

TABLE 1.1: TYPICAL ENVIRONMENT VARIABLES USED BY ORACLE

Parameter	Description
LD_LIBRARY_PATH	Should be set in most Unix versions (though it is falling out of use by Oracle).

Continued

TABLE 1.1: TYPICAL ENVIRONMENT VARIABLES USED BY ORACLE (CONTINUED)

Parameter	Description
ORACLE_BASE	The base installation location. When installing the Oracle database software, ORACLE_BASE defines the place to begin creating the OFA-compliant directory structures. See Chapter 3.
ORACLE_HOME	Base location of all the Oracle database software.
ORACLE_SID	The name of the local database to which you are connecting.
PATH	Should include the $ORACLE_HOME/bin.
TWO_TASK	Used in Unix to set up a TWO_TASK environment. Allows such things as linking certain Oracle tools with an environment other than that in ORACLE_HOME.

The Oracle SQL Interface Tools

A database would be pretty worthless without a means of using it. Oracle's tools for database access are SQL*Plus and Server Manager. This section explains these tools and how to use them to both manage and query the database. We will also look at the TNSPING utility, which helps you determine if your Oracle networking is set up properly. You'll see how to connect to remote databases, as well.

Server Manager

Server Manager is Oracle's character-based administrative tool. With Oracle8i, Server Manager allows you to connect to a database and perform several administrative functions including startup, shutdown, and backup and recovery.

Before you start Server Manager, you must set up your Oracle environment as explained in "Environment Settings" just above. Then you start Server Manager with the command svrmgrl. (This command varies based on the platform in use; for example, it is svrmgrl23 in early versions of Oracle for NT.)

Connecting to the database is done using one of two methods:

- Enter the CONNECT INTERNAL command, and then proceed to issue commands from Server Manager.

- Server Manager also supports Oracle's new DBA CONNECT method using the SYS AS SYSDBA verbiage. This new method replaces the CONNECT INTERNAL command, which will not be supported from Oracle9i.

NOTE Support for Server Manager and the CONNECT INTERNAL command are not included in Oracle9i. However, Server Manager's functionality is available in SQL*Plus (though some messages do not appear in SQL*Plus as of Oracle 8.1.6). If you have any existing Server Manager scripts, now is the time to alter them to using SQL*Plus.

Following is an example of using Server Manager with both CONNECT INTERNAL and CONNECT SYS AS SYSDBA:

```
C:\>svrmgrl
Oracle Server Manager Release 3.1.6.0.0 - Production
Copyright (c) 1997, 1999, Oracle Corporation.  All Rights Reserved.
Oracle8i Enterprise Edition Release 8.1.6.0.0 - Production
With the Partitioning option
JServer Release 8.1.6.0.0 - Production

SVRMGR> connect internal
Connected.
SVRMGR> shutdown immediate
Database closed.
Database dismounted.
ORACLE instance shut down.

SVRMGR> connect sys as sysdba
Password:
Connected.
SVRMGR> startup
ORACLE instance started.
Total System Global Area            61932812 bytes
Fixed Size                             70924 bytes
Variable Size                       57589760 bytes
Database Buffers                     4194304 bytes
Redo Buffers                           77824 bytes
Database mounted.
Database opened.
```

SQL*Plus

SQL*Plus is the primary administrative interface into Oracle, used to execute SQL statements. Current versions of SQL*Plus allow the DBA to manage the database, including starting it and stopping it.

SQL*Plus can be either character-based or windows-based, depending on the environment you're using. For example, the Solaris Unix SQL*Plus is a character-based version of SQL*Plus. Oracle for Windows NT, on the other hand, contains both a character-based version and a windows-based version of SQL*Plus.

Starting SQL*Plus

Typically, when you start SQL*Plus, you pass a username, password, and the service name of the database you wish to connect to at the command line. (Service names are defined earlier in this chapter. In-depth coverage of service naming is in Chapter 9.) Figure 1.4 shows you the Logon window displayed in SQL*Plus.

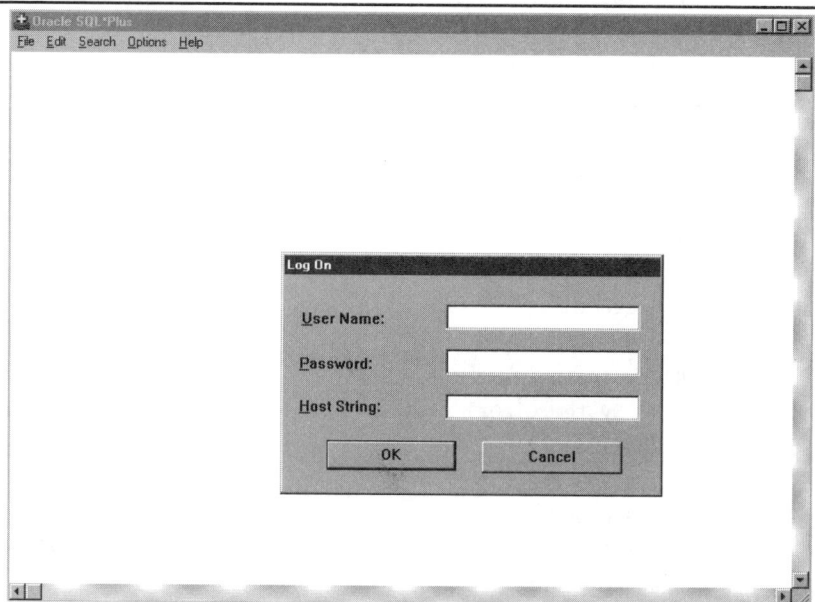

FIGURE 1.4
The SQL*Plus window

SQL*Plus, when started from the command line, has several parameters. Here is the general syntax of the SQLPLUS command, and Table 1.2 defines its parameters:

SQLPLUS {options} {"} username/password{@network_service_name}{"}
   {@sql} [/NOLOG]

TABLE 1.2: SQLPLUS COMMAND PARAMETERS

Parameter Name	Description
options	-MARKUP: Allows for HTML marked-up output to the screen and optionally to a spool file.
	-RESTRICT 1: Disables use of the EDIT and HOST commands in SQL*Plus.
	-RESTRICT 2: Same as Restrict 1, but also restricts the use of SAVE, SPOOL, and STORE commands.
	-RESTRICT 3: Same as RESTRICT 1 and 2, but also restricts the use of GET and START commands. SQL*Plus will not execute the login.sql file, and the glogin.sql file will be read but restricted commands will fail.
	-SILENT: Restricts all output to the screen.
""(quotes)	Note that the *username*, *password*, and *network_service_name* can all be included in quotes. This helps with special login cases such as the following: sqlplus "/ as sysdba"
username	Username of the database you are connecting to. Oracle will prompt you for this if you do not enter it.
password	Password of the database you are connecting to. Oracle will prompt you for this if you do not enter it.
@network_service_name	Optional Net8 database name. If this is not used, the default database name (as defined by the setting of ORACLE_SID) will be used. The @ sign must appear immediately after *password*.
@sql	Optional parameter that allows you to execute a SQL script from the command line.
/NOLOG	Eliminates the need for the *username/password* combination to enter SQL*Plus.

When connecting to an Oracle database, there are generally two ways to do it. You can connect to a local database using whatever method the operating system uses for interprocess communications, or you can connect to any properly configured database through Oracle's networking services, Net8. For a local connection, you need to set up the database environmental parameters.

Here are some examples of starting SQL*Plus using the command-line interface:

```
Sqlplus scott
Sqlplus system/manager@hrdata
Set ORACLE_SID=ora816
Sqlplus "sys/manager as sysdba"
```

NOTE Note the use of quotes on the second login shown—these are important!

In this example, the first SQLPLUS command connects to the SCOTT schema. SQL*Plus will prompt you for a password. The second SQLPLUS command causes SQL*Plus to connect to the database network service name HRDATA, as the user system using the password manager. Finally, the last SQLPLUS command allows you to connect to the ORACLE_SID that was set just above. It will connect to the ora816 database using the SYSDBA account.

Optionally, you can omit the password and SQL*Plus will prompt you for it, as shown in the following example output. (You would enter your password at the Enter password prompt.)

```
sqlplus scott
SQL*Plus: Release 8.1.6.0.0 - Production on Sun Jan 7 20:20:47 2001
(c) Copyright 1999 Oracle Corporation.  All rights reserved.
Enter password:
Connected to:
Oracle8i Enterprise Edition Release 8.1.6.0.0 - Production
```

To connect to a networked database using Net8, you use a connect string just as you do when connecting to a local database, except that you add the service name. In addition to an alias for a single database, a network service name can also represent multiple databases in a failover or load-balancing configuration. After the SQLPLUS command and the username/password, type an @ sign followed by the service name, as shown in this example:

```
sqlplus scott/tiger@scott_db
```

NOTE Full coverage of Oracle networking is in Chapter 9.

Profile Scripts

SQL*Plus provides for both a site profile script and user profile script to be run automatically when SQL*Plus is started. The site profile script is called glogin.sql. The user profile script is called login.sql. Setup and use of these scripts with SQL*Plus varies by operating system, so check the details for your specific version of Oracle.

Using SQL*Plus

Once you are logged onto the database, you can use SQL*Plus to execute queries (SQL statements) against the database.

 NOTE A *SQL*Plus command* is different from a *SQL statement*. A SQL*Plus command is one of the commands that controls the SQL*Plus interface. It does not interface with the database in any way, although it might control the output of the SQL statement (causing it to wrap, for instance, or controlling the look of column headers). A SQL statement, in contrast, is a structured command that follows the rules of the SQL language, causing specific information to be retrieved from the database and returned to the client.

One of the most important elements of SQL*Plus for the DBA is the interface's editable buffer, which contains the last executed SQL command or anonymous block. You access this buffer by using the SQL*Plus editing facilities, including the SQL line commands LIST (L), APPEND (A), INSERT (I), CHANGE (C), and EDIT (ED). Let's look at some instances of using these editing facilities

To list the last SQL statement run, use the L command. Each line of the SQL statement is assigned a number (or pointer), and you can list the specific numbered line as parameters for the L (or l, it's not case sensitive) command, as in L 5. You can also list a range of lines by separating two line numbers by a space as in L 5 10. Here are some examples:

```
SQL> l
  1  select empno, ename
  2  from emp
  3* where hiredate < sysdate - 10
SQL> l 1 2
  1  select empno, ename
  2* from emp
SQL> l 1 3
  1  select empno, ename
  2  from emp
  3* where hiredate < sysdate - 10
```

In the following example, we want to change the word *form* to *from* in line 2. To do this, you'd use the C command in this format: c/form/from.

```
SQL> l
  1  select empno, ename
  2  form emp
```

```
    3  where hiredate < sysdate
    4*
SQL> 2
  2* form emp
SQL> c/form/from
  2* from emp
```

To add additional text to the SQL statement, use the A command and then specify the additional text. For example: A from dba_data_files, as shown here:

```
SQL> select empno, ename
  2  from emp
  3  where hiredate < sysdate
  4
SQL> 1
  1* select empno, ename
SQL> a , hiredate
  1* select empno, ename, hiredate
```

To insert a line, use the I command. SQL*Plus will prompt you to insert additional test at the location of the current pointer.

A SQL*Plus command must be on one line only (this is not true for a SQL statement). If you explicitly want to use two or more lines to express the command, you must end each line with a space and then a dash (-). Then you can continue the command on the next line (which starts with a > symbol). Here's an example:

```
Column bytes -
> format 999,999,999
```

SQL*Plus also provides other features for the DBA. You can

- Format the output, including page breaks and totals summation on columns.
- Control the format of specific columns, including length of the output displayed in the column, and whether the output wraps or not.
- Supply title, header, and footer output for your SQL statements.
- Clear the screen.
- Calculate and print summary totals of columns.

All SQL*Plus commands are documented in Appendix C.

NOTE Several database management commands have been added to SQL*Plus since Oracle7, to facilitate the removal of Server Manager at some point in the future. These commands include starting up, shutting down, and recovering the database. Starting and stopping the database is discussed in Chapter 7. Setting up the database (including starting it without using CONNECT INTERNAL) is covered in Chapter 3. Database security relating to CONNECT INTERNAL is discussed in Chapter 21.

TNSPING

The Oracle utility called TNSPING helps you determine if your Oracle networking is set up properly. Here is the syntax for the command to run TNSPING:

TNSPING (*network_service_name*) [count]

The *network_service_name* is the name of the database you wish to check on. The COUNT parameter is the number of "pings" you wish to send to the database.

 NOTE The TNSPING command does not help you determine if your database is up and running. It only tells you whether the listener for that database is up and running.

If the TNSPING command is successful, Oracle responds with a display showing how long it took the ping to be returned by the Oracle listener. Following is an example:

```
C:\>tnsping ora816
TNS Ping Utility for 32-bit Windows: Version 8.1.6.0.0 -
   Production on 07-JAN-20  01 13:10:43
(c) Copyright 1997 Oracle Corporation.  All rights reserved.
Attempting to contact (ADDRESS=(PROTOCOL=TCP)
(HOST=ws-jax-w2820)(PORT=1521))
OK (650 msec)
```

Using Oracle SQL

SQL is the language of Oracle databases and the DBA's path into the database. You use SQL to store, remove, and retrieve information at will. This section provides a basic introduction to SQL, the fundamental precepts of SQL that you will see used throughout the rest of the book.

NOTE Don't forget to check the reading list at the end of this chapter if you need additional help working with SQL. You will have the opportunity to study the many SQL commands used throughout this book, and when you need more information about a command, you can look in Oracle's SQL Reference Guide. Also, there's a SQL quick reference guide in Appendix E of this book.

Datatypes in Oracle8i

When you query a table with a SQL statement, you access one or more columns in that table. The types of data stored in these columns are defined when the table is created. Each column is defined to be a particular datatype. This might be a *scalar* (native) datatype such as VARCHAR2, which stores characters. Or it might be a user-defined datatype. We will explore the Oracle datatypes throughout this book; Table 1.3 is a summarized list.

TABLE 1.3: NATIVE ORACLE DATATYPES

Datatype	Description
CHAR	Stores up to 2000 characters of data in a fixed-length format.
VARCHAR2	Stores up to 4000 variable characters of data. (Though it's not often used, Oracle still offers the VARCHAR datatype, which is the same as a VARCHAR2.)
NCHAR and NVARCHAR2	These datatypes store National Language Support (NLS) character data. They store data similarly to the CHAR and VARCHAR2 datatypes.
LOB and NCLOB	Can store up to 4GB of character data. These are part of the family of LOB data types.
BLOB	Stores up to 4GB of binary, unformatted data.
BFILE	Pointer to an outside operating system file.
LONG and LONGRAW	Stores up to 2GB of raw, unformatted data. Support for these data types will be dropped at some point in favor of LOBs.
DATE	Stores dates in Oracle. Stores both the date and time, up to hundredths of seconds.
NUMBER	Number datatype.
ROWID and UROWID	Stores Oracle ROWIDs. UROWID supports a wider variety of ROWIDs.

The DML and DDL Languages

In this section we'll look at Oracle's Data Manipulation Language (DML) and Data Definition Language (DDL), starting with the common syntax conventions.

First, all commands begin with a keyword. These are words that imply the action to be performed—for example, INSERT, UPDATE, and DELETE.

In SQL, certain characters have a special meaning, as follows:

;	End of SQL statement
/	End of SQL statement
--	Comment
/* */	Comment

So, for example, when you complete a DML or DDL statement, you end it with a semicolon to indicate that the statement is completed.

DML

DML statements are designed to display or modify database data. Following is a list of DML statements that you will be using in Oracle:

Statement	Purpose	Example
SELECT	The most common SQL statement; used to query the data in the database	SELECT * FROM emp WHERE empno < 2000;
INSERT	Adds new rows into a database table	INSERT INTO emp (empno, name) VALUES (1,'Robert');
UPDATE	Updates rows in the database table	UPDATE emp SET ename='Davis' WHERE empno=12345;
DELETE	Removes one or more rows from a database table	DELETE FROM emp WHERE empno=12345;

NOTE SELECT queries are sometimes considered a distinct type of statement, but in this book we will consider them DML.

DDL

Oracle's Data Definition Language (DDL) comprises every remaining SQL command that is *not* DML. In general, these are the statements that manipulate the database itself. DDL statements include CREATE TABLE, CREATE INDEX, and CREATE DATABASE.

Set Processing

Oracle SQL statements work with one group of records at a time. Unlike most standard programming languages that require you to loop through a set of records and process them one record at a time, Oracle facilitates what is called *set processing*. Many new developers who come from a background of COBOL or C have difficulty grasping this paradigm change, and at first tend to write inefficient code. For example, consider the following pseudocode:

```
For loop until EOF
Do
     Get record
     If column_to_change='2'
     then
          Change record so column_to_change='1'
     End if
     Write changed record
End of loop
```

This code works fine, of course, but in Oracle a simple SQL statement will generally work much faster:

```
UPDATE my_table
SET column_to_change=1
WHERE column_to_change=2;
```

Not only will it work much faster, but it's more compact as well. Set processing allows Oracle to perform one or more operations collectively. The result from one operation can interact with previous operations, and all of this is done via one SQL statement.

Let's look at a specific example. You need to collect a set of employee records for all employees of Department 7, sort them by hire date, and then remove from the result set all employees who happen to be retired. This type of logic would take several lines of other code but is done quickly in SQL by issuing a statement such as this:

```
SELECT employee_name, address, hire_date
FROM employee_data
WHERE status != 'Retired' AND dept_no=7
SORT BY hire_date;
```

WARNING SQL statements and set processing are more direct but can get complicated fast. The Oracle database engine is designed around set operations. As DBA, when reviewing programmers' code, be on the lookout for code that interacts with the database in a way that does not fully take advantage of set processing.

The SQL Query

A SQL query has several parts to it, some required and some optional. Its basic components are described in the following paragraphs. The SQL Quick Reference in Appendix F can be of assistance to you in crafting the perfect SQL statement.

The SELECT Clause

This clause starts with the SELECT keyword, followed by a comma-separated list of columns to display as a part of the query results. If you wish to bring back all columns of the table, use an asterisk (*). You can also include functions (your own or one of the many supplied by Oracle) to manipulate the columns appearing in the SELECT clause. For example, to display only a part of a character column, you might use the SUBSTR function in the SELECT query to limit the number of characters returned.

Throughout this book we will look at and use many of the native Oracle functions. In addition, a quick reference to functions can be found in Appendix F.

The FROM Clause

The FROM clause contains one or more of the following:

- A list of tables to be accessed as a part of the query
- An inline view that is to be accessed as part of the query

The WHERE Clause

This clause consists of several *predicates*, separated by AND keywords, that control the results of the SQL statement. The WHERE clause serves several purposes, including

- Making the query selective. Instead of bringing back all rows from the tables queried, the criteria in the WHERE clause's predicates serve to restrict the numbers of rows.
- Joining rows together. If several tables appear in the FROM clause, it is the WHERE clause that defines the related columns of the tables.

In the following example of a basic SQL statement:
```
SELECT empno, ename FROM emp WHERE empno=1;
```
the following is true:

- The SELECT clause will cause Oracle to return two columns, EMPNO and ENAME.
- The FROM clause identifies what table (EMP) we wish to bring back from the EMPNO and ENAME columns.

- The WHERE clause, with one predicate (`empno=1`), restricts the rows returned to just the row(s) where empno=1.

These are just the basic parts of a SQL statement, of course. There are other clauses, such as GROUP BY and HAVING, that format grouped results—for instance, a summation of values in the columns of a table. The ORDER BY clause sorts the result set. All of these commands and others are documented in the SQL Quick Reference in Appendix E, and you will find plenty of examples in this book.

SQL Operations

Several different kinds of operations are possible when issuing SQL statements.

Subqueries

A *subquery* is a SQL statement within a SQL statement. This allows nesting of queries in your SQL statement. The following example of a subquery returns a count of all employees who are paid less than the average salary:

```
SELECT count(*)
FROM employee
WHERE salary<(select AVG(salary)
            FROM employee);
```

Correlated Subqueries

These are subqueries that depend on the values of the parent query. Correlated subqueries return the same values as a join, but you use a subquery where you cannot use a join—in UPDATE and DELETE statements, for example. Consider the following correlated subquery that updates zip codes in the employee records, based on zip code changes in a ZIP_CHANGE table. What makes this a correlated subquery is that the subquery issuing the SELECT against the ZIP_CHANGE table is referencing the EMPLOYEE table, which we are updating.

```
UPDATE employee
SET zip_code=(SELECT new_zip
            FROM zip_change
            WHERE employee.zip_code=old_zip)
WHERE zip_code IN (SELECT old_zip FROM zip_change);
```

Joins

Joins allow two or more tables to be included in the same query, based on common key columns that relate the tables. There are several different kinds of joins.

Equijoin and Inner Join

An *equijoin* is a join involving a direct equivalence between the key columns of the tables involved in the join. In this example:

```
SELECT a.ename, a.deptno, b.dname
FROM emp a, dept b
WHERE a.deptno=b.deptno
```

the equijoin is between the EMP table and the DEPT table. The join is on the like or equivalent (hence the word equijoin) DEPTNO keys in both tables. From this join, we get the department number from the EMP table, and the name of the department is derived from the DEPT table.

An *inner join* is probably the most common join operation. It is the join of the rows from one table to those of others based on common key values. If a row in one table has a key that does not have a match in another table, then that row will not be displayed. For example, if an employee is assigned to a department that does not exist in the department table, then that employee will not appear in the results displayed by the following (a good example of referential integrity's importance in a database):

```
SELECT a.ename, a.deptno, b.dname
FROM employee a, dept b
WHERE a.deptno=b.deptno
```

Theta Joins

A *theta join* (also called a non-equijoin) is a join using an operator that involves equivalence along a range of values. SQL statement operators include < and >, BETWEEN, and others. Here is an example of a theta join:

```
SELECT a.ename, b. grade
FROM employee a, salgrade b
WHERE a.sal BETWEEN b.losal AND b.hisal
```

Outer Joins

An *outer join* causes rows in one table to be included in the resulting join, even if there is no matching row in the other joined table. Oracle uses a non-ANSI standard (+) operator to designate an outer join. The (+) operator goes in the WHERE clause, by the column/table combination that might not have the associated rows in it.

Let's say you are looking for employees and what they were paid last week, but you also want to see employees who were not paid anything last week. The PAY_TABLE table (which contains pay records) might not have rows for all the employees, since they might not all have been paid. To list all employees, then, including those not paid, we put the (+) in the WHERE clause next to the EMPNO column for the

PAY_TABLE table. So the query would look something like this (the outer join is in the last line):

```
SELECT a.empno, a.ename, b.pay_day, b.pay_total
FROM employee a, pay_table b
WHERE a.empno = b.empno (+)
```

Anti-Joins

An *anti-join* makes possible the selection of all rows in one table that do not have rows that match in another table. Specifically, you might want to find all the rows in one table that do not have the selected column values of those rows in another table. Anti-joins are typically performed using the NOT IN and NOT EXIST clauses.

Let's say you want a list of employees who have not been assigned a department. You can do that using an anti-join with a query such as this one:

```
SELECT a.empno, a.ename, a.deptno
FROM emp a
WHERE
a.deptno NOT IN (SELECT deptno FROM dept);
```

Self Joins

When you join a table to itself, it's called a self join. In a self join, the same table will appear twice (or more) in the FROM clause. Here's an example:

```
SELECT a.empno, a.ename, a.mgr, b.ename "Manager Name"
FROM employee a, employee b
WHERE b.empno=a.mgr;
```

Cartesian Joins

Cartesian joins are the result of a join between two tables when no join condition is defined the query's WHERE clause. Oracle will occasionally decide to do a Cartesian join when executing a SQL statement if it thinks that the join will provide the required row sources faster than other access methods.

The Effects of NULL Columns on Joins

The presence of NULLs in relational databases means we have a third logical value to deal with. Instead of just TRUE and FALSE, for instance, you now also have to consider NULL, which simply means that the data is missing or undefined. This causes some additional complications.

The impact of NULL values on queries is fairly easy to demonstrate. Here is an example:

```
SQL> SELECT COUNT(*) FROM emp WHERE job='CLERK'
  2  union
```

```
  3  SELECT COUNT(*) FROM emp WHERE job!='CLERK';

  COUNT(*)
----------
         4
        11

SQL> SELECT COUNT(*) FROM emp;

  COUNT(*)
----------
        16
```

This example perfectly demonstrates three-valued logic. In the first query, we have 15 total rows reported; yet when we issue a statement to count all rows, we get a total of 16 rows. What's up? The issue is that in one row the job column is set to NULL. The NULL is essentially a third value and will not evaluate to TRUE or FALSE. Thus, it fails both the test of being equal to 'CLERK' and the test of being unequal to 'CLERK'. The NULL is an unknown, and a special test must be done to check for that logical condition. In other words, neither the = nor the != test will find NULL values!

The presence of NULL values in data can have some interesting impact on join results, and you'll need to consider this when developing your queries. For example, take another look at our anti-join query:

```
SELECT a.empno, a.ename, a.deptno
FROM emp a
WHERE
a.deptno NOT IN (SELECT deptno FROM dept);
```

This gives the following output:

```
EMPNO ENAME           DEPTNO
----- --------------- -------------
    1 Freeman             99
```

What we want here is a listing of all employees who are assigned a department number that is not in the DEPT department. Only problem is, if an employee has NULL assigned to the DEPTNO column of the EMP table, that employee record will not appear—because the NULL is not considered a value at all. Thus, when a NULL column appears, it doesn't satisfy the NOT IN check and does not appear as part of the result set.

In this case, we might wish to rewrite the SQL slightly to take NULLs into consideration. To do this, we would use the NVL statement:

```
SELECT a.empno, a.ename, a.deptno
FROM emp a
WHERE
nvl(a.deptno,-1) NOT IN (SELECT deptno FROM dept);
```

This time the results are as follows:

```
EMPNO ENAME           DEPTNO
----- -------------- -------------
    1 Freeman             99
    2 Freeman
```

We can also use the IS NULL and IS NOT NULL to check for this condition and thus use NULLs to our advantage. For instance:

```
SELECT COUNT(*) from emp WHERE job='CLERK'
UNION
SELECT COUNT(*) from emp WHERE job!='CLERK'
OR job IS NULL;
```

In this case, we have added the `OR job IS NULL` clause to check for the additional logical possibility of a NULL, so we get the correct result when we run this query. The NOT NULL makes sure that columns that are NULL are not included in a given result set, such as in this example:

```
SELECT COUNT(*) FROM emp WHERE job IS NOT NULL;
```

Here we have indicated that we want to count all rows unless the job column is set to NULL, in which case we will not count it.

Aggregation

Oracle provides *aggregation operations* (returning a single result based on an operation performed on a group of rows) on columnar values. This is facilitated by various aggregation functions used in the SELECT clause. Aggregation options include functions such as SUM(), AVG(), and COUNT(). Aggregation often requires use of the GROUP BY clause to define the columns that are being aggregated. Also, you can include the HAVING clause to restrict the aggregate results being reported. See Appendix F for a list of Oracle's aggregation functions.

In the following example of aggregation, we determine the total size of the SYSTEM tablespace in bytes:

```
SELECT SUM(bytes)
FROM dba_data_files
```

```
    WHERE tablespace_name = 'SYSTEM'
    GROUP BY tablespace_name;
```

Oracle PL/SQL

SQL has little procedural structure. You execute a statement and bang, you get the results. Some functions do some logical processing (such as the DECODE and CASE expressions), but they still run in just one statement. SQL has no procedural processing to handle, for example, the result set of a given SQL statement. Oracle solves this problem with the *Procedural Structured Query Language (PL/SQL)* engine in the Oracle database. PL/SQL supplies procedural constructs for use by the DBA and developer in creating complex database interface logic.

 NOTE This is a brief introduction to PL/SQL. In Appendix F you'll find in-depth coverage.

Basic PL/SQL Structure

A *stored procedure* is PL/SQL that is stored in the database. This may be a function, procedure, package, or trigger. A PL/SQL *anonymous block,* on the other hand, is not stored in the database and therefore must always be loaded from the operating system (unless it has just run and you want to run it again).

PL/SQL programs generally have these parts:

- The DECLARE section, which stores the variables to be used in the PL/SQL code and is only present for anonymous blocks
- The BEGIN keyword
- The PL/SQL code in the body of the anonymous block
- The END keyword

PL/SQL code also contains several procedural constructs, including these:

- Looping constructs
- IF/THEN/ELSE structures
- Handling of statement results a row at a time, rather than relying on set processing

- Error checking
- Variable assignment
- Calling of other functions and procedures

PL/SQL Program Units

This section contains simple examples of PL/SQL anonymous blocks, procedures, functions, packages, and triggers, leaving more comprehensive discussion to Chapter 20.

Anonymous Blocks

An *anonymous block* is a block of PL/SQL that is loaded into the Oracle instance and executed. Unlike other types of PL/SQL (procedures, functions, and so forth) anonymous blocks are not stored in the database for easy recall. They do not return any kind of value. To execute an anonymous block, you must load it from an operating system file; if it's the last operation to execute, however, it gets stored in the SQL buffer and is available for recall and editing. Listing 1.1 is an example of an anonymous block.

Listing 1.1: An Anonymous PL/SQL Block

```
-- Two dashes indicate a remark in PL/SQL
-- The SET SERVEROUTPUT ON command is a SQL*Plus command;
-- not a part of PL/SQL anonymous block
SET SERVEROUTPUT ON


-- This is the start of the DECLARE section (or Declaration
-- section, if you prefer). Note this section is ONLY required
-- for anonymous blocks!
DECLARE

    -- This next line defines V_Num_rows as a variable of type number
    V_Num_rows     number;

-- The BEGIN section is next. The body of the PL/SQL code begins
-- after the BEGIN keyword.
BEGIN
   SELECT count(*)
   INTO v_num_rows
   FROM dba_tables;
```

```
        -- The Dbms_output.put_line package will output a message to the
        -- screen.
        Dbms_output.put_line('The number of rows is '||v_num_rows);
END;
-- The END declaration ends the body of the PL/SQL program.
```

This example introduces several concepts. First of all, you know this is an anonymous block because it includes a DECLARE section, which doesn't appear in any other type of PL/SQL (or SQL for that matter). Note the commands that come before the DECLARE section. They are both used to set up the SQL*Plus environment so that the DBMS_OUPUT.PUT_LINE package will work later in the anonymous block. You will find the SET SERVEROUTPUT command in the SQL*Plus command reference in Appendix C. The DBMS_OUTPUT package is an Oracle-supplied package that displays output to your screen from a PL/SQL block. (Oracle packages are discussed in Chapter 20.)

Note that we declared a variable called V_NUM_ROWS as a number type. Then comes the BEGIN keyword, followed by the PL/SQL block. In the PL/SQL block we do a simple SELECT INTO operation which causes the results of the SELECT to be loaded into the V_NUM_ROWS variable created in the DECLARE section. Finally, we output the line with the DBMS_OUTPUT package and end the PL/SQL block with the END keyword.

Procedures

Procedures are stored in the database but otherwise are much like anonymous blocks. Procedures do not contain a DECLARE statement, but rather are started with the keywords CREATE PROCEDURE or CREATE OR REPLACE PROCEDURE. Procedures can take parameters, as well. They do not return any values. Listing 1.2 is the anonymous block from Listing 1.1, after it was turned into a procedure.

Listing 1.2: A PL/SQL Stored Procedure

```
-- This is a SQL*Plus command
CONNECT sys/change_on_install
CREATE OR REPLACE PROCEDURE my_procedure
AS
     -- This next line defines V_Num_rows as a variable of type number
     V_Num_rows      number;

-- The BEGIN section starts next. The body of the PL/SQL code begins
-- after the BEGIN keyword.
BEGIN
   SELECT count(*)
```

```
      INTO v_num_rows
      FROM dba_tables;

      -- The dbms_output.put_line package will output a message to the
      -- screen.
      Dbms_output.put_line('The number of rows is '||v_num_rows);
END;
-- The END declaration ends the body of the PL/SQL program.
```

You would run this procedure using the EXEC command as shown here:

```
SET SERVEROUTPUT ON
EXEC my_procedure
The number of rows is 199
```

Java Stored Procedures

Oracle8i introduced the capability of storing Java code in a logical unit called a *Java stored procedure*. Running a Java stored procedure requires that Java be installed in the database. You can use the CREATE FUNCTION or CREATE PROCEDURE command with the AS LANGUAGE JAVA keywords to create a Java stored procedure. See Chapter 27 for details.

Functions

A *function* differs from a procedure in that the function returns a value. A function is run slightly differently, as part of a SELECT statement. To create a function, you use the CREATE FUNCTION or CREATE OR REPLACE FUNCTION command. Listing 1.3 contains our anonymous block, now written as a function.

Listing 1.3: A PL/SQL Stored Function

```
CREATE OR REPLACE FUNCTION my_function
Return NUMBER
IS
     -- This next line defines V_Num_rows as a variable of type number
     V_Num_rows    number;

-- The BEGIN section starts next. The body of the PL/SQL code begins
-- after the BEGIN keyword.
BEGIN
   SELECT count(*)
   INTO v_num_rows
   FROM dba_tables;
```

```
        -- The dbms_output.put_line package will output a message to the
        -- screen.
        Dbms_output.put_line('The number of rows is '||v_num_rows);
END;
-- The END declaration ends the body of the PL/SQL program.
```
You would run this procedure using the EXEC command as shown here:
```
SET SERVEROUTPUT ON
SELECT my_function from dual;
MY_FUNCTION
-----------
        199
```
Notice that we execute this function as part of a SELECT statement.

Packages

Packages are a combination of several procedures and functions that are contained in a *package body.* These procedures and functions are all predefined along with any global variables in a separate package header. You'll find plenty of examples of packages in Chapter 20.

Triggers

Triggers are PL/SQL programs that are executed after certain actions take place on a table. For example, when a new employee record is inserted in an EMPLOYEE table, the MEDICAL table must be updated accordingly, because the business makes medical insurance coverage effective on the day of hire. To support this MEDICAL table update, an INSERT trigger is written on the EMPLOYEE table to create the row in the insurance table when the employee record is added.

Moving On

Well, that's a brief overview of this database we call Oracle. In the chapters to come we will review in much more detail nearly all of the topics outlined in this first chapter. We trust this book will provide you with lots of help in managing your database. Now, let's move on to the topic of installing the Oracle software.

CHAPTER 2

Installing, Upgrading, and Migrating Oracle

FEATURING:

Introducing the Universal Installer	47
Preinstall steps	48
Installing the database software	50
Patching the Oracle software	64
Removing the Oracle software	66
Migrating/updating to Oracle8i	70

If you are installing Oracle for the first time, congratulations! You are implementing one of the finest relational database systems in the world. Whether you're new to Oracle, a veteran DBA with numerous installs under your belt, or preparing to migrate or upgrade an existing Oracle database to Oracle8i, don't worry. This chapter is your complete guide to Oracle software installs and upgrades. We will show you what to do and—just as important—what not to do.

There are three primary steps in the process of installing the Oracle software. The first step is preparing for the installation of the Oracle software. The second phase is the actual installation. Following that, the postinstallation stage includes such things as the actual creation of the database, setup of Oracle networking, and other tasks.

This chapter goes hand in hand with Chapter 3, which discusses creation of an Oracle database.

NOTE This chapter covers installation of the basic Oracle8i RDBMS software package from the Oracle CD-ROM. For installation information on a specific Oracle feature (such as Java in the database), refer to the chapter dedicated to that feature.

Oracle Platforms Covered in This Chapter

Oracle provides its database software for a vast number of different platforms. It runs on everything from HP-MP to Windows NT, on various flavors of Unix, and even on mainframes such as VAX and VMS (cough, cough, hack). Some ports of Oracle run on platforms so unique that only 200 or so licenses have ever been sold.

We have made this chapter as platform independent as possible, but that becomes difficult when you are discussing installation issues in particular. Therefore, when platform issues are of concern, we'll limit our discussions to the NT and Unix platforms. Generally, you'll get the details you need in your Oracle platform-specific documentation, so you can refer to that if something doesn't work or doesn't translate into the vernacular of your particular operating system.

Introducing the Universal Installer

The Oracle Universal Installer (UI) was introduced in Oracle8i to simplify the installation process. Unfortunately, with simplification sometimes come complications, and the UI is no exception to this rule. In this section we will briefly look at the UI.

The Oracle Universal Installer

Earlier versions of Oracle used one of two kinds of installation programs: a character-based installer or a platform-specific installation GUI. For Oracle8i, the installer has been "centralized" by switching to a Java-based program called the Universal Installer (UI). On a few platforms that don't support Java, Oracle still provides a character-based installer.

Switching to a Java-based installer doesn't come without a price to the user of the system. The first requirement is, of course, a system that includes the Java Runtime Environment (JRE). For a Unix system, running the UI may require incorporating an X Windows client that supports Java. Windows (NT/2000) gets the JRE on the Oracle install CD.

In addition, the absence of a simple character-based installer sometimes creates additional configuration problems. Depending on the type of system that's getting the Oracle software, you may need the assistance of your system or network administrator to get the installation utility running.

In addition, there are much greater memory, CPU, and disk requirements for the UI than for the previous installers. This larger resource requirement becomes even more significant when you are also running the memory-hungry Database Configuration Assistant (DCA, discussed shortly).

 WARNING Do not try to install a newer version of Oracle using an older version of the Universal Installer. Also, make sure you use an *unmodified* (except for Oracle-approved patches) *Oracle-supplied* JRE when running the Installer.

The Universal Installer, initially slightly buggy, is much improved in Oracle 8.1.6 and is excellent in 8.1.7. (One drawback, on some platforms such as Solaris, is that two CDs are required to install Oracle 8.1.7.) In spite of its shortcomings, the Universal Installer does provide a number of benefits. These include

- An easy-to-use common install/upgrade interface to Oracle products
- Support for Oracle patch-set installs

- Support for National Language Support (NLS), which provides for multiple languages
- Support for dependency resolution between products (Thus, if successful installation of one product depends on the existence of another, the UI will notify you of this dependency.)
- Support for multiple ORACLE_HOME locations
- A silent-mode installation process that does not need user interaction

The UI is started differently on various platforms. See "Starting the UI for Installation" later in this chapter.

Preinstall Steps

This section describes the steps necessary to prepare your system and environment for an Oracle installation. The general preparation items we cover first apply to installations on all platforms. Other than these general steps, NT installations require little else—but in a Unix system you'll need to meet several preinstall requirements. Of course, if you are using Oracle on some other platform, everything you need to do may not be included here. Each platform has its own installation and administration guides to which you should refer.

General Preinstallation Steps for All Platforms

Complete the following checks for any operating system before you install Oracle.

NOTE Many of the following items will be OS specific. Oracle includes both generic and OS-specific documentation with all installs. Depending on your operating system, you may find it on the documentation CD, in $ORACLE_HOME/doc, $ORACLE_HOME/rdbms/doc, $ORACLE_HOME\relnotes, or even in accompanying hard documentation.

- Read all the Oracle documentation that is specific to your system.
- Make sure the system hardware will support the Oracle database server and the expected user process loads.
- Make sure the operating system level, with all required patch sets, is supported by the Oracle version you are going to install.

- For any optional Oracle software that you are installing, find out about any specific preinstall requirements and make sure you have followed those instructions.

- Decide where your ORACLE_HOME will be located. Oracle will offer default, OFA-compliant value for this, but you may wish to choose a different location. If you want to install over a preexisting ORACLE_HOME, you must first remove the present software. See Chapters 1 and 3 for detailed information on OFA (Oracle Flexible Architecture) and ORACLE_HOME.

- Determine what Oracle software you want to install, and what Oracle software you are licensed to install. Just because the software is on the CD, that doesn't mean you own a license to use it. Items such as partitioning require a separate license (and thus cost you more) to use.

- Make sure you have enough disk space available. It's a good idea to set aside 2GB for an Oracle installation, just to be safe—the install image is getting bigger all the time. On some platforms, version 8.1.7 takes up two disks for the base Oracle RDBMS.

- Find out about any patches that will be needed after your initial RDBMS software install. In particular, check for patches for the Oracle Universal Installer.

NOTE Some platform-specific patches exist for the Oracle UI, particularly in early versions of Oracle8i. If you are having problems with the UI, check with Oracle support to see if there is a patch available for you to use.

Preinstallation Steps on Unix

For installation of Oracle on a Unix system, complete all the general preparations listed in the preceding section, and perform the following additional steps:

- Create the operating system account in the Unix environment that will own the Oracle software. Follow the OS-specific instructions for the privileges this account must have.

- Create a group called DBA. This group should include members whom you want to be able to administer databases through the Oracle software.

- Set the Unix shared memory and semaphore parameters as stated in the specific Oracle UNIX OS Install Guide. Generally these settings include changes to various settings in the /etc/system file.
- *Carefully* set your Oracle account's ULIMIT setting so that the Oracle account will be able to create files of the correct size.

Preinstallation Steps on NT

Oracle installations on Windows NT require very little preinstall activity. Of course, you need to make sure that you have enough disk space. There are a couple of gotcha's in this category to be aware of.

The first concerns temporary files. Oracle requires substantial temporary space on C: (somewhere around 100MB, depending on what you are installing). During the installation, Oracle creates a number of temporary files. Once these are used, most are not needed again, yet Oracle does not remove them until after the install. As a result, the installation seems to require more temporary space than it really needs. If you are pressed for space on your temporary drive, try removing some of the older temporary files created during the install. (They'll all have a number starting with 1.) In our experience, we've found that you can safely remove almost all temporary files except the very first one and the last few (since Oracle is probably still using them). Just be careful not to remove one that the installer will need, or you'll have to start the install process all over again.

Another issue is a quirk of the Oracle UI: It doesn't correctly calculate space requirements for the installation, either temporary space or actual space. Make sure you allow a comfortable margin for error when determining your space allocation.

Finally, make sure your NT box is running on a service pack that is supported by the version of Oracle you are installing. This has been critical especially with later versions of Oracle8i.

Installing the Database Software

It's time to install the database software. Indeed, some would say this is why you get paid the big bucks. This section tells you how to start the Universal Installer and describes each UI prompt during the installation. You'll see what you need to do at each stage. But now that you've read the early sections of this chapter, you're well prepared for the install, and this process should be a cinch!

Starting the UI for Installation

The Oracle installation process itself, by virtue of the Universal Installer, looks the same on all platforms. You'll see some slight variations here and there, depending on your particular system. For example, with AIX you will need to run a script called `rootpre.sh` after starting the UI and before installing the main Oracle code. The UI for AIX has a customized additional dialog box that instructs you to run this script. Beyond this additional prompt, however, the install on AIX has the same look and feel as it does for NT.

Following are the procedures for starting the UI for NT and Unix. These procedures are current as of Oracle8i, Release 8.1.7.

On NT

There are several methods of running the installer on NT. You do not need to set any environment variables (the UI prompts you for what's needed as it runs).

To run the UI from the installation CD-ROM, just insert the disk in the CD drive. Then, to start the installation:

- If you have Autorun enabled, when you insert the CD a front-end application will appear. Select the Install/Deinstall Products option.
- If you have Autorun disabled, go to Windows Explorer and click on the `setup.exe` folder on the CD drive.

If you already have Oracle installed, you can run the UI from the command line. Change directories to `files\oracle\oui\install`. Run the `setup.exe` program in that directory, and the UI will start up. You can also start the UI from this directory in Explorer.

On Unix

There are a couple of methods for running the UI on a Unix system. But first, you need to make sure your environment is set up appropriately.

Setting the Unix Environment to Run the UI

In Chapter 1 we discussed several Unix environment variables for running Oracle on the Unix system. Although the UI itself requires only one environmental variable to be set (DISPLAY), it's not a bad idea to set up an optimal environment for the UI. Consider designating the variables listed in the table just below, in addition to DISPLAY.

DISPLAY	The address of the client session. Example: `DISPLAY=mycomputer.mydomain.domain.com:0.0`
ORACLE_BASE	The base Oracle install directory. Example: `/ora01/oracle`

ORACLE_HOME   Location of the Oracle software. Example:
                   /ora01/oracle/product/8.1.7.0
ORACLE_SID   Name of the Oracle database you wish to create.
PATH   Make sure $ORACLE_HOME/bin is in the PATH.

NOTE The DISPLAY variable must be set if you use the UI to install Oracle from a remote client. In addition, you must run client software that will accept Unix X Windows connections.

As in any installation, refer to your specific operating system documentation. Talk to your Unix system administrator, as well, for guidance in setting these on your system. Many are defined as a part of the OFA discussion in Chapter 3, by the way.

Running the UI from the CD

Once your Unix environment is appropriately set, you can start the UI on Unix either from the CD-ROM or from the command line. For initial installations, of course, you'll start it from the CD, by executing the program runInstaller, stored on the root directory of the CD-ROM. Before you start runInstaller, you will be required to set the DISPLAY attribute for your Xclient in order for the installer to operate correctly.

If Oracle is already running on your system and the UI is already installed, you'll find the runInstaller program located in the ORACLE_HOME/bin directory. You can use this image of the UI to load additional Oracle features (for example, partitioning) or to install Oracle patches. Do *not* use this version of the program to install a new version of Oracle, however. It's important to run the UI with the same Oracle version it came with, and that version only!

Running the UI from the Command Line

When you install the Oracle software, the UI does not install by default. If you choose to install it, you must run the custom installation discussed later in this chapter. The UI is then stored under ORACLE_BASE in the oui directory. Typically, the Unix path (not to be confused with the variable PATH) is something like /ora01/oracle/oui.

To run the UI from the command line, look in the oui directory for the runInstaller program, and execute this program to start the UI. The oui directory is usually not in the Unix PATH environmental variable, so you'll need to prefix the program execution line with ./ or prefix the command line with the entire path. This causes the OS to start the program from the present working directory rather than traverse the path in an attempt to find it. For example, if ORACLE_BASE were

/ora01/ oracle, then we would issue the following command from the Oracle account to start the UI:

/ora01/oracle/oui/runInstaller

Or, if you're in the /ora01/oracle/oui directory:

./runInstaller

Generally when you install a newer version of the Oracle software, it will overwrite the previous version of the UI. This way, you never have to worry about mistakenly using an old copy of the UI when you are installing a patch or loading additional Oracle products.

Running the Installation

Once you've started the UI, you'll see the welcome screen. From here you can decide to continue or exit the installation. You can click the Installed Products button to get a display of any Oracle8i products that may already be installed on this system. There's a Help button, too, as there is on most of the UI screens.

The welcome screen also contains a Deinstall Products button, for use when you're running the UI to remove Oracle8i products. This process is discussed later in "Uninstalling Oracle with the UI."

To proceed with the installation, press the Next button and proceed to the File Locations window.

File Locations

The File Locations window, shown in Figure 2.1, allows you to designate the location of your Oracle software's source (the path to the software) and destination (the ORACLE_HOME).

FIGURE 2.1

The UI's File Locations window

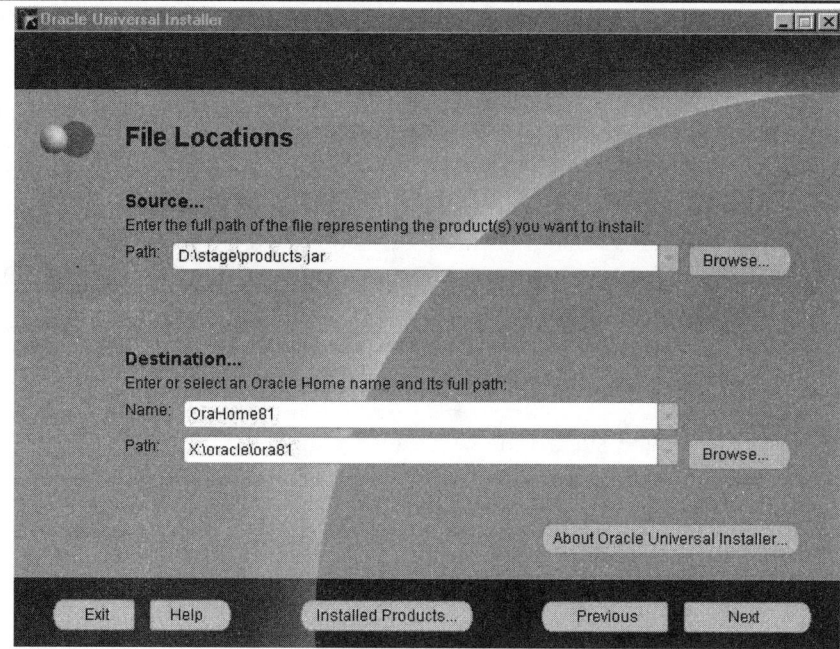

Oracle Software Source Path This is the location of the Oracle products .jar file, which lists all the software that is available to load through the UI. When doing a default installation, you can just accept the default value for the source path, typically d:\stage\products.jar for NT and /cdrom/oracle/stage/products.jar on Unix (where /cdrom/oracle is the name of the path).

If you are installing an Oracle patch, change this path to the path of the products .jar file associated with the Oracle patch.

Oracle Home Name The Oracle Home name is the name associated with this installation. In both NT and Unix, you can have multiple Oracle homes with their own names, as entered in the File Locations screen for each installation.

Oracle Home Path This is the path into which the software will be loaded, also known as ORACLE_HOME. After filling in the appropriate information for File Locations (or accepting the defaults), press Next to proceed with the installation.

Available Products

The Available Products window, an example of which is shown in Figure 2.2, provides a list and brief descriptions of Oracle product groups that you can install. Depending on your operating system, this screen may include options such as Oracle8i Enterprise

Edition, Oracle8i Client, and other product groups (such as Oracle8i Management and Integration shown in Figure 2.2).

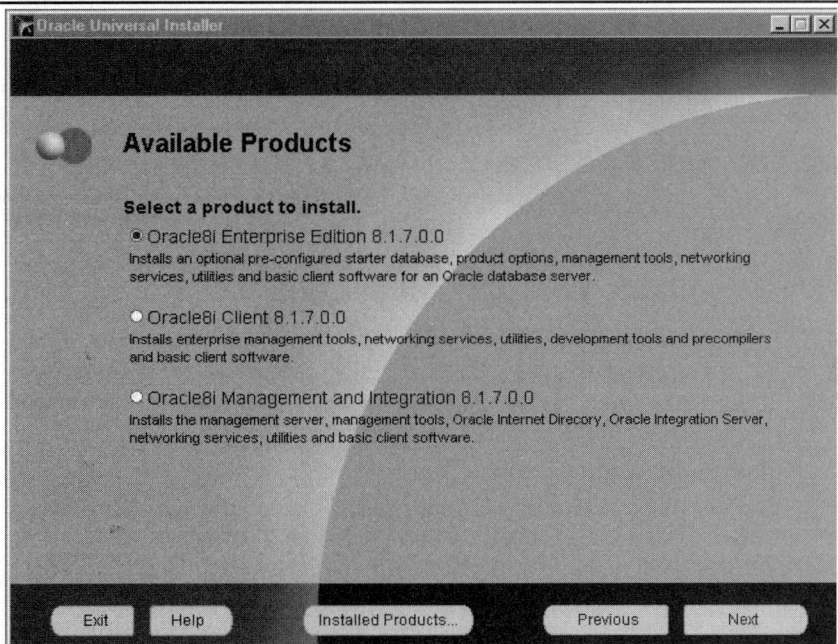

FIGURE 2.2

The UI's Available Products window

In Figure 2.2, we are loading the Oracle8i Enterprise Edition product grouping (this is the default). To install the Oracle client software (Net8 and SQL*Plus), we'd select the Oracle8i Client product grouping.

Note that products in the Oracle inventory have *dependencies*—they depend on the existence of other products and vice versa. During the product selection process, you might wish to deselect a product that Oracle has selected for install (for example, the Security Server Option). If this product has a dependency, you'll be informed that you cannot deselect it because it is needed by another product slated for the installation. After selecting the products you want to install, click the Next button to continue.

Installation Types

Use the next window, the Installation Types window, to select the type of install you want to do: typical, minimal, or custom.

Typical Install This installs the most common components of the Oracle database software. It also gives you the opportunity to install a preconfigured "starter" database through the Database Configuration Assistant (Chapter 3).

Minimal Install This option installs the minimal Oracle footprint. It, too, allows you to install a preconfigured starter database.

Custom Install This option is the one we are describing in this chapter. It is the most complex of the three because it lets you pick and choose most specifically what you want to install. In addition, for a new installation, it lets you find out what's new about the version you're installing. (We always choose this option because we just don't trust the default installation to be everything we want it to be.) The custom installation presents an additional window in the installation process: the Available Product Components window, where you browse and select the software you want to install.

Available Product Components

Figure 2.3 shows the Available Product Components window that you complete when you choose the Custom Install option. Each Oracle product is listed, and products scheduled to be installed have check marks next to them. For example, in Figure 2.3 the Oracle HTTP Server is checked. To designate that you don't want this product installed, simply click on the check mark to remove it. Then click Next to continue.

You'll want to review each product listed and make sure you understand what elements you are installing.

NOTE Don't forget that the Universal Installer is not installed by default. As stated earlier in this chapter, we recommend including the UI in your Oracle installation, if for no other reason than to make it easier to apply patches in the future.

INSTALLING THE DATABASE SOFTWARE

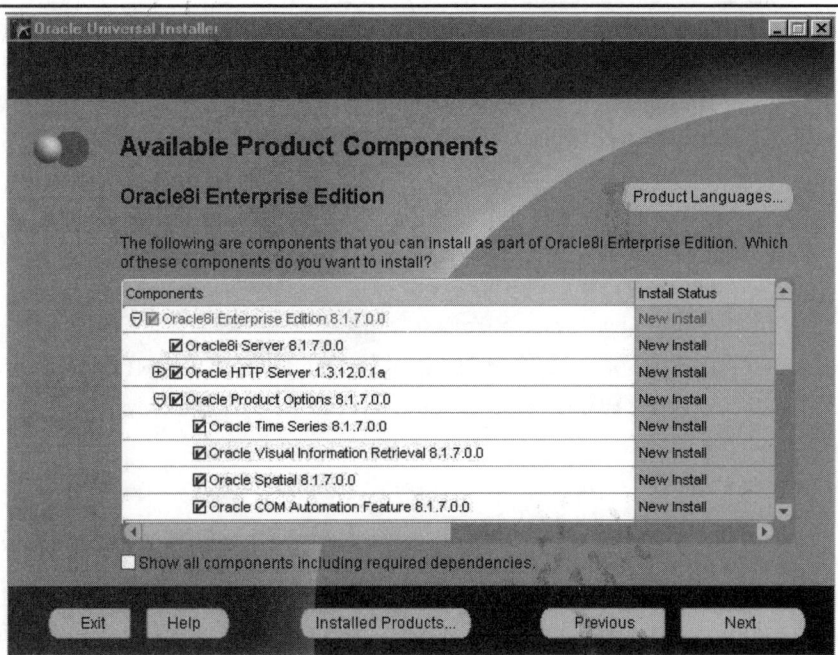

FIGURE 2.3
Choosing the products for a custom install

Loading Oracle Products Not Installed by Default

The following items are *not* installed by default. We recommend that you include the boldfaced items in your Oracle installation, by checkmarking them in the Available Product Components window.

Unix/NT Oracle Documentation

Universal Installer

Oracle SNMP Agent

Oracle Protocol Support

Oracle Performance Monitor for Windows NT (on NT systems only)

Oracle SQLJ (Note that there are substantial additional database requirements for SQLJ, which specifies integration of SQL statements in Java. You may or may not want to install SQLJ as a result. See Chapter 29 for more information.)

Continued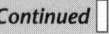

> **CONTINUED**
>
> Oracle OEM Management Server
>
> **Oracle DBA Management Pack** (helpful for beginning DBAs) This is a separately licensed product (as of this writing) that includes Schema Manager, Storage Manager, Security Manager, and Instance Manager.
>
> Various OEM Events options
>
> Oracle Migration Workbench
>
> Oracle Services for Microsoft Transaction Server
>
> Oracle Administration Assistant for Windows NT (on NT systems only)
>
> Oracle8i Windows documentation (on NT systems only)

Various Product Dialog Boxes

Depending on the products you have decided to install, various dialog boxes will appear, requesting setup information for those products. Usually there is nothing more to do but simply click Next and move on. Refer to the specific product documentation if you are not sure how to respond.

Component Locations

The Component Locations window (Figure 2.4) allows you to store Oracle products in specific ORACLE_HOME directories if those products support such an arrangement.

TIP We rarely install Oracle products in ORACLE_HOME directories other than the default locations, and we suggest you don't either—unless the product's installation instructions indicate that there is a particular benefit to choosing an alternate location.

FIGURE 2.4

The Component Locations window

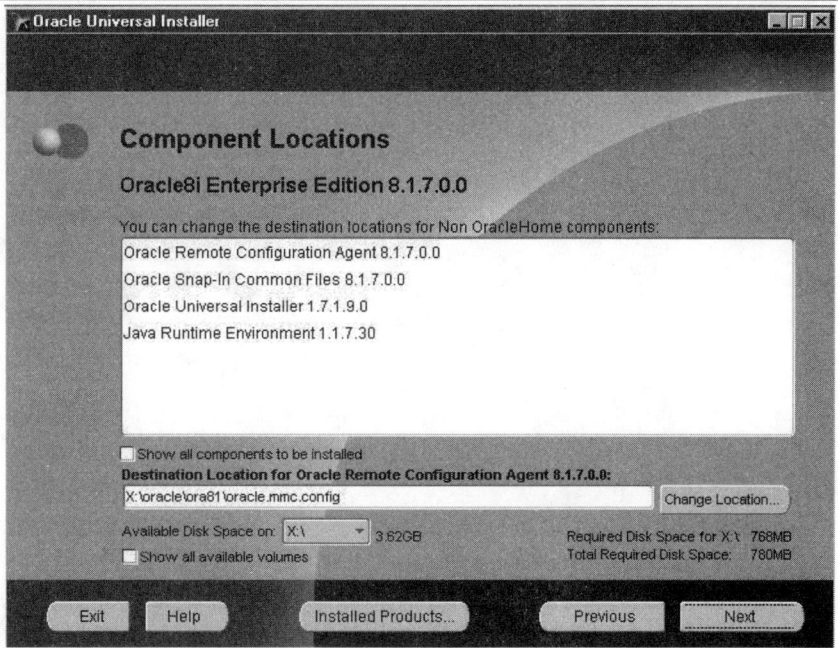

If you do want to designate a particular ORACLE_HOME directory for one or more components, simply select the component from the list and enter the directory in the Destination Location box at the bottom of the window (or click Change Location for a drop-down list of directories). Note that you can choose the location for only one component at a time.

Defining Oracle Protocol Support

In the Oracle Protocol Support window, shown in Figure 2.5, you define the communications protocols to be supported by your database software. Supported protocols include Named Pipes, TCP/IP, LU6.2, and SPX. See Chapter 9 for more on these protocols.

FIGURE 2.5
Specifying Oracle-supported protocols

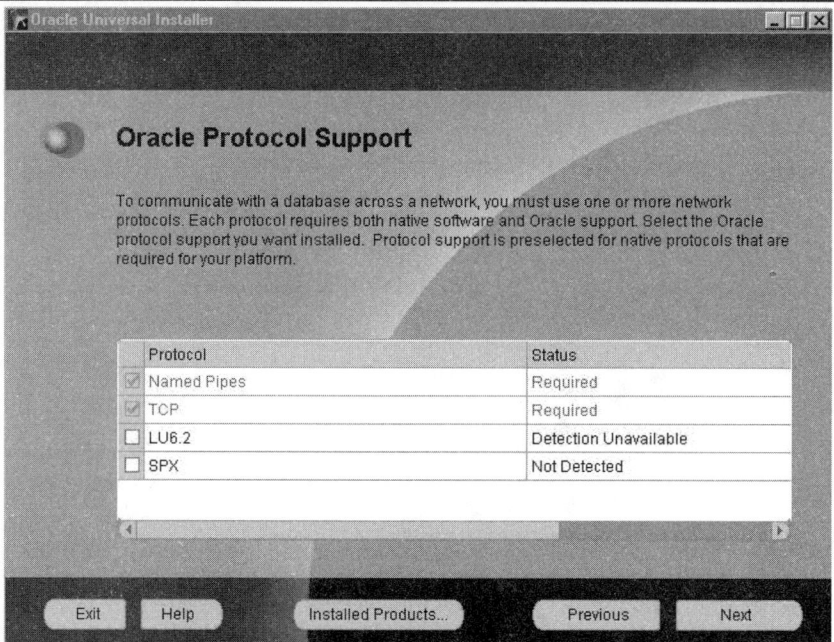

When You're Migrating Existing Databases

When it's preparing for an installation of the Oracle8i RDBMS software, the UI will detect any Oracle databases that are already installed. If it does find a database, the UI asks if you want to migrate these databases during the installation. If you select a database to upgrade or migrate, the UI starts the Database Migration Assistant (DMA) after completion of the RDBMS installation, and leads you through the migration process. (Note that the DMA is different from the DCA, Database Configuration Assistant, whose job is to create new databases.)

NOTE We prefer to do software loads and database migrations or creations separately. This is because of the additional memory constraints imposed by running the UI and the DMA or DCA at the same time. Also, we like to test the new Oracle software before we migrate or upgrade any existing databases.

The Create Database Screen

Before the Oracle software installation begins, you'll see one other inquiry. It's the option to have the UI start the Database Configuration Assistant after the RDBMS software has been installed and the UI has been shut down. The DCA aids you in database creation. The default answer is Yes, but we usually answer No because we prefer to create databases after the installation has finished.

The Summary Screen

The Summary window (Figure 2.6) is the last to appear before the actual product installation process begins. Each product to be installed is listed and you can view summary information about the installation, such as the amount of disk space required and the product's eventual location. Carefully check the contents of this window to confirm that the settings are the ones you chose. If all looks well, click Next and the installation will begin.

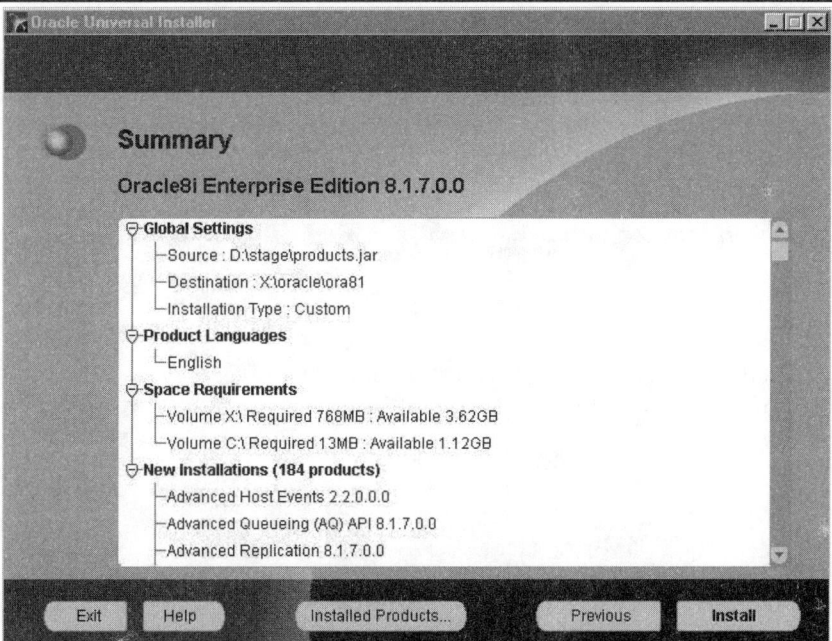

FIGURE 2.6

The Summary window

WARNING Just because Oracle thinks it has enough space to do the install doesn't make it so. You cannot depend on the UI to estimate the amount of space required for the installation process. We've sometimes had to free up space in a rush because the installation process hung. A good rule of thumb is to take the figure listed in the Summary window's Space Requirements section and add about 30%. If the result is more than what you have available, then you need to make some room on the destination drive.

Watching the Install Process

The Install window, shown in Figure 2.7, is displayed as the installation progresses. There isn't much to do here except sit and watch the progress bar, and the marketing billboard on the right bragging about how great Oracle8i is. Also, the component being installed appears beside the eclipsed star with the little moon running around it, or whatever that thing is. Note that you can cancel the install at this point by clicking the Cancel button just below the progress bar.

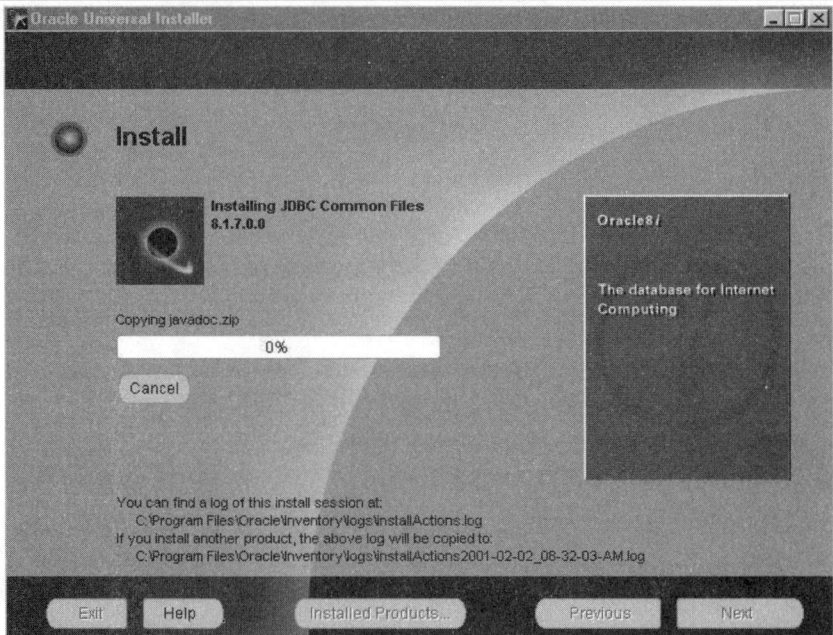

FIGURE 2.7
The Install window shows the progress of the installation

You will see the components you've selected as they are being installed or uninstalled. Also, Oracle will send appropriate messages as it links the different products.

Oracle8i keeps a log of the entire installation process. The log's filename and location are noted at the bottom of the Install screen. If you run another installation, the old log will be backed up with a new filename, as shown at the bottom of the window.

An Oracle8i installation is not a speedy thing. Of course, the time it takes depends on a number of factors, including CPU availability and clock speed, disk speeds and feeds, and CD-ROM speeds. Figure somewhere between 20 minutes and an hour to install the software.

If an error occurs during the installation, the first thing to check is available disk space. As stated earlier, the UI doesn't make very good estimates about disk space. Often this shortage will manifest in the middle of the installation, signaled by an error message. Typically this message will only complain that it cannot copy a file to the disk and may not explain that the problem is insufficient disk space. Check the disk to which you're installing, and the C: drive on NT (or the temporary file system for whatever operating system you are using), and make sure space is available on that file system. If there isn't any, you'll have to acquire some in order to continue. Another possibility is to reduce the number of products you are installing, as this might reduce the overall install footprint required. Once you've made some room on the disks, you can continue the installation by clicking Retry in the error window. If you have freed up enough space, the installation will continue.

Postinstallation Steps

The Configuration Tools window, shown in Figure 2.8, appears after the RDBMS software load has completed. This window allows you to run the NET8 Configuration Assistant (Chapter 8), the Database Creation Assistant (Chapter 3), and other utilities as required.

The configuration utilities will start automatically. The selection of utilities started will depend on which products you choose to install. If you choose not to run the configuration utilities at install time, they can be run later.

Review the product documentation for each of the Oracle products you are installing to determine what you need to do in order to complete their installation.

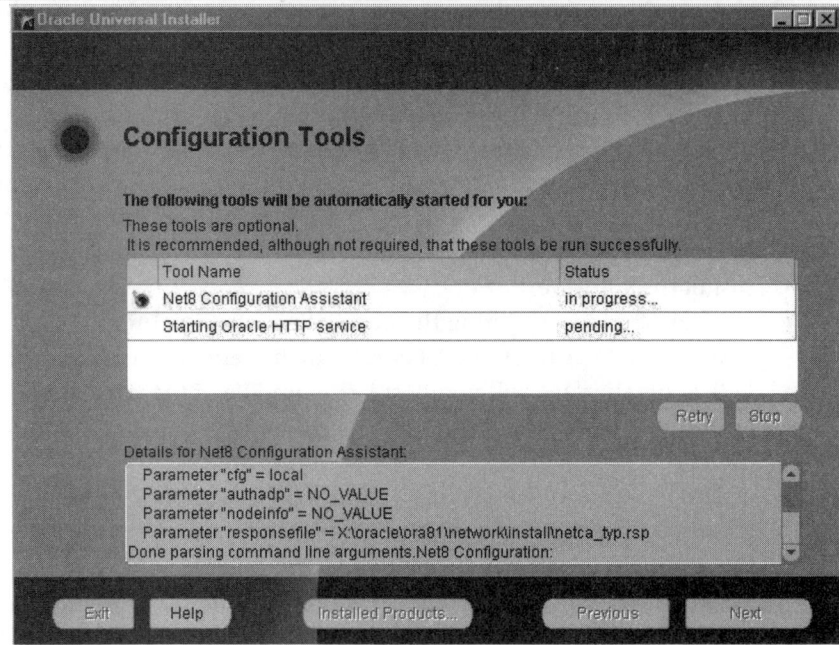

FIGURE 2.8
The Configuration Tools window

Patching the Oracle Software

When software is moving out the door as fast as it does at Oracle (not a condemnation; just a fact), programs are bound to end up with a bug or two. Oracle faithfully provides patches to its database management products. Although the patches come in two varieties, cumulative and "one-off," we usually refer to both as patch sets.

Cumulative patches are labeled for a given Oracle release. For example, if you are running Oracle 8.1.7, you might well apply a patch at some point that brings you up to release 8.1.7.1. But let's say you installed 8.1.7.0 without having applied patch set 8.1.7.1. If you were to then apply patch set 8.1.7.2, it would be cumulative and thus include all the patches included in the 8.1.7.1 patch set. Patch sets are available only from Oracle support, so you will need a support contract to get them.

What we call one-off patches are issued to fix specific bugs that have been discovered and reported. These individual patches usually apply specifically to the version of the database software you are currently working on. It's possible that you'll apply a one-off patch that will be overwritten by a subsequent patch set, so test your system after the patch. Also, if you install a new major Oracle software release and you plan on converting your databases to that release, you may find that your bug is not fixed in that new release.

WARNING After running a new installation, always check the release documentation and test the new software before depending on it. Bugs fixed by a one-off patch sometimes don't make it to the next major release (or patch). In fact, several bugs found and fixed in version 8.0 showed up again in 8i. This problem is characteristic of the development process and is to be expected. That being the case, just be sure to test everything, and then test it again.

Usually Oracle makes patches available on its support Web site or at an associated FTP address. They come compressed (a self-extracting .zip file or a tar file, depending on the operating system). Typically, you will use FTP to transfer the file and extract its contents into a directory according to the instructions associated with the file.

Patch sets are installed one of two ways.

The first is by using the Universal Installer. After extracting the patch files to a directory, say d:\patch, a *stage directory* will be created called d:\patch\stage. This directory is where the products.jar file for the patch set is located. Start the UI, and when the File Locations window comes up, change the Source box to point to the d:\patch\stage\products.jar file. (You can click on the Browse button and navigate to this directory.) Then click Next to continue the patch load process. The Oracle UI will pretty much take care of it from there. Respond to any prompts as required.

TIP Before installing a patch set, always browse its Readme files first.

Another way to install a patch set is to manually link the patch with an existing library. If Oracle instructs you to use this method, you'll be given very specific instructions. Contact Oracle customer support if you have any questions about how to install a patch set by linking to a library. (See the list of support sites at the end of this chapter.)

Removing the Oracle Software

This section includes instructions on removing Oracle software with the Universal Installer. Anytime you need to remove any piece of Oracle8i software from a system, it's best to use the UI to make sure the job is done completely. This is especially important if you intend to install other Oracle software later. Oracle8i tracks a software inventory across all the ORACLE_HOMEs you've created. In certain cases, if you try to install software that already appears in software inventory, you might get some odd results. You might be forced to remove the existing software. Also, as you might suspect, you may need to shut down the Oracle databases running on your system (depending on what you plan to uninstall).

Also included in this section are some special procedures for NT-based Oracle systems. Occasionally, the UI doesn't quite clean everything out when it's removing the software from an NT installation. We'll show you how to make sure that doesn't happen.

Starting the UI

On an NT System: If the UI is already installed, you can launch it from the Start menu (Start ➢ Oracle Installation Products ➢ Universal Installer). Or, to run the UI from the command line, change directories to `program files\oracle\oui\install`. Run the `setup.exe` program in that directory, and the UI will start up. You can also start the UI from this directory in Explorer.

 TIP Most DBAs eventually discover the wisdom of installing the UI when they install Oracle on an NT system. If you did not install the UI when you installed Oracle, you'll need to run it from the installation CD-ROM. Just insert the disk in the CD drive and let Autorun bring up the interface. If you have Autorun disabled, click on the UI's `setup.exe` program from Explorer.

On a Unix System: See "Starting the UI for Installation" and follow the instructions there for running the UI either from the command line or the Oracle installation CD.

Uninstalling Oracle with the UI

The UI makes removing software a snap. When the Installer's welcome screen appears, just select the Deinstall Products button. Oracle presents an inventory of the installed products on your system. Each ORACLE_HOME will be listed (see Figure 2.9).

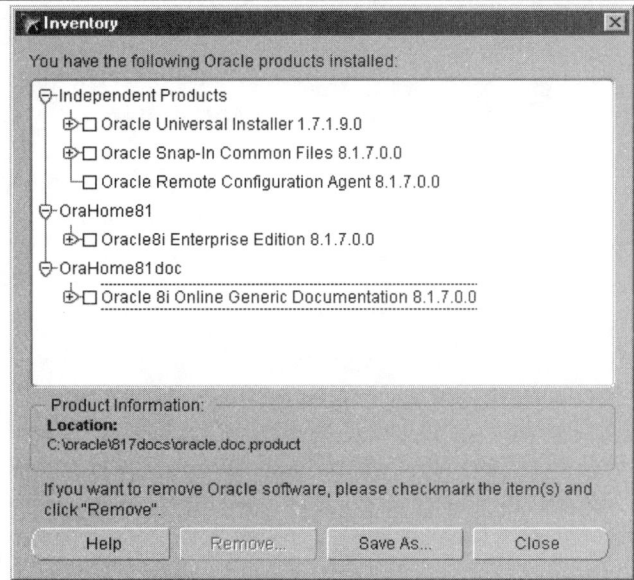

FIGURE 2.9

Getting ready to uninstall

You use the Inventory window to select the products you want removed. At first, the Remove button at the bottom is unavailable, but once you've selected one or more products to deinstall, the Remove button will become available.

The Oracle deinstall process includes a check for product dependencies. After you select products to be deleted and click Remove, Oracle displays a window asking you to confirm your action. You may see that other products, as well, are marked to be removed. If you're removing a product on which another product depends, Oracle will mark all dependent products for deletion, too. For example, remove the Oracle Remote Configuration Agent, and the UI will also try to remove the Oracle Server software along with a host of other products. Obviously, you need to be careful when removing products, or you may zap something else that you didn't want to remove. So check carefully in the list of products to be deleted, and go ahead and click the Yes button if you're certain of your action. The UI will do its thing, and then you can exit the Installer.

Removing All Oracle Software from NT

Windows NT can be a real pain when you're removing software. Sometimes, regardless of how hard you try, you just can't seem to get everything off of that box. Sometimes an Oracle service hangs around; sometimes a particular program just refuses to deinstall no matter what you do. Following is the foolproof, 100% tried-and-tested method of wiping out your Oracle install from an NT system—at least, your Oracle 8.1.7.0 install. Oracle sometimes throws you a curve when you're not watching. So we won't be surprised if, just as soon as this book is published, the company releases Oracle 8.1.7.2 and this foolproof technique won't work. We do promise that it works for version 8.1.7.0.

The process for removing Oracle software from an NT system has several steps, listed here and discussed in the sections that follow:

1. Stop all Oracle services.
2. Remove all Oracle services.
3. Remove all Oracle entries in the Registry.
4. Remove all Oracle software.

WARNING Please only use this technique as a *last resort* to clean Oracle from your Windows NT system. Before you take these steps, try and use the UI to remove the Oracle software from your system. Either way, make sure you back up everything, including the Registry, before you start.

Step 1: Stop All Oracle Services

To stop all Oracle services, open the NT Control Panel. From there, click on the Services icon. Figure 2.10 is an example of a Services window with many Oracle services. Select all Oracle services that are running and click the Stop button.

FIGURE 2.10

The Control Panel ➢ Services window showing Oracle services

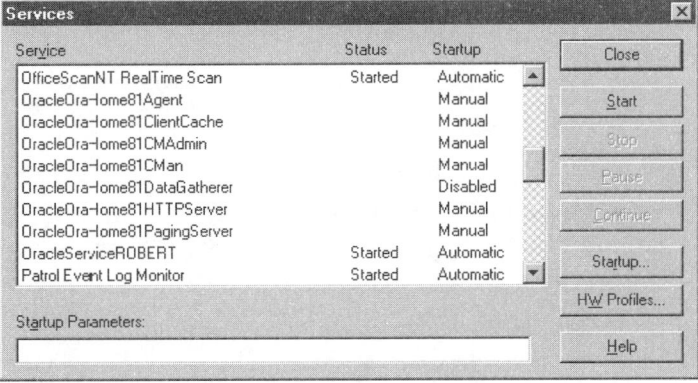

Most (if not all) Oracle services are prefixed with the word *Oracle* followed by the ORACLE_HOME name for that service. Thus, if the ORACLE_HOME name is ora817, then all your Oracle service names will end with ora817. It may be, of course, that you will have more than one ORACLE_HOME name and therefore will have duplicate instances of a service that start with different names (for example, OracleOra816TNSListener and OracleOra817TNSListener).

Following are some common services that you will stop:

- All Instance/Database Services (These services start with the word OracleService, followed by the name of the database. Thus for an instance called Robert, the name of the associated service would be OracleServiceRobert.)
- The Oracle TNS Listener

Other services that may be running include

- The Oracle Agent
- The client cache
- Oracle Connection Manager services (CMADMIN and CMAN)
- The Data Gatherer

Step 2: Remove All Oracle Services

 WARNING Do not do *anything* to your Registry until you have backed it up! Failure to follow this advice will cause this book to self-destruct. You have been warned... tick...tick...tick... tick....

Sometimes removing services manually is the only way to get it done right. To remove the services from the NT Registry:

1. Make sure you've stopped all Oracle services.

2. Now, before you do anything, back up your Registry.

3. Click Start ➢ Run and start REGEDIT.

4. Navigate to My Computer and then to the HKEY_LOCAL_MACHINE folder. Expand that folder and then expand SYSTEM, then ControlSet001, then SERVICES.

5. The SERVICES folder contains a subfolder for each service listed in the Control Panel Services window. Carefully remove each Oracle-related service from the Registry by highlighting its folder and pressing Delete.

Step 3: Remove All Oracle Entries in the Registry

The next step is to remove the software entries for Oracle from the Registry. Still in REGEDIT, find the HKEY_LOCAL_MACHINE folder and open the SOFTWARE subfolder. Find the ORACLE folder and remove it. Then exit REGEDIT.

Step 4: Remove All Oracle Software

You are now almost home free (free of Oracle files, that is). Your final step is to remove all the Oracle software. Using Explorer, simply click on the uppermost Oracle software folder and delete away. Once this is complete, you have completely wiped Oracle off your NT system.

Migrating/Updating to Oracle8i

This section is for those of you very intelligent DBAs who have decided that you need to get your Oracle database running on Oracle8i. First we'll make sure we know the difference between a migration and an upgrade. Then we'll explore the various options available for migrating to Oracle 8i, including the MIG utility, the Data Migration Assistant (DMA), the EXP/IMP utilities, and the SQL*Plus COPY operation. Some of you are moving databases that are not supported by the Oracle8i direct migration process, and here you'll find help with those sometimes more-complicated migrations. There's also an extensive, comprehensive checklist for the migration process, step by step.

> **NOTE** After doing literally hundreds of 7.x-to-8i migrations and several more hundred upgrades, we've included in this section some hints and suggestions from our experiences with these processes. We hope our advice about migrations in particular will help save you from a failed migration effort.

Migration vs. Upgrade

DBAs tend to use the terms *migration* and *upgrade* interchangeably when referring to transition from one version of the Oracle database to another. In fact, however, these terms have two very different meanings.

Version numbers of Oracle software start with a major version number (6, 7, or 8) followed by a dot, then the release number (giving you 7.2, 7.3, 8.0, 8.1), and then a patch number (giving you 7.3.3 or 8.1.6). This numbering scheme may extend even further into four and five digits for various "one-off" patch sets from Oracle. *Upgrading* means advancing to later release numbers within the same major version number. *Migrating* means advancing to subsequent major version numbers. Migrations often require a great deal more work, because significant changes usually occur when major version numbers change. Oracle generally supplies a migration utility to facilitate migrations. The process of upgrading is typically much easier; generally, you'll run a single upgrade script and then a couple of other standard Oracle scripts. Upgrades between the one-off patch sets are usually easier yet, requiring only the running of some standard Oracle scripts, depending on the options your database system uses.

Migrating a Pre-7.1 Database to Oracle8i

If you are running your current database on an Oracle version prior to 7.1 and you have decided to migrate to Oracle8i, you've made a wise decision. Unfortunately, your migration path will be somewhat more limited and potentially complex than for those who have already migrated to Oracle7 or Oracle8. With pre-7.1 databases, you have only a few migration options. You can use the Oracle Export and Import utilities to move the data to Oracle8i. You can also use the SQL*Plus COPY command to move the data. Or you can opt to first migrate your database to a version of Oracle7 that will support more robust migration options to Oracle8i.

Let's take a look at the various migration paths available to Oracle6 DBAs.

WARNING Migrations and upgrades are subject to many opportunities for massive failure. Don't put a production database at risk by failing to plan and test your migration strategy. Then test it again to make sure you are comfortable with it. Finally, take the additional precaution of having one of your DBA peers review it and test it again.

Using the Export and Import Utilities

The Import (IMP) and Export (EXP) programs are covered in much more detail in Chapter 11, but for now we'll examine their use for doing migration. First you use EXP to create a logical backup of your database. This logical backup is dumped out to an operating system file. The dump file can then be used by IMP, which loads the data back into the same or another database. Here are the basic steps for this process:

1. Create an Oracle8i database.
2. Do a full export of the pre-7.1 database.
3. Do a full import of the dump file created in step 2 into the new Oracle8i database.
4. Check for any invalid objects, failures to import specific objects, and so on, as required.

The Export/Import method isn't a bad choice as long as the database is relatively small. Typically, if the amount of data to be exported is greater than 2GB, this solution may become impractical. In this case, you'd consider the option to migrate first to a database under Oracle 7.0 or later, and then to Oracle8i (as explained shortly).

 TIP If your SYSTEM tablespace is badly fragmented, and your data dictionary tables are fragmented into many extents (SYS.SOURCE$), the Import/Export migration might be an advantage. That's because it will allow you to rebuild your data dictionary and the SYSTEM tablespace, and performance may improve.

Using the SQL*Plus COPY Command

In our opinion, using the SQL*Plus COPY command is, at best, a kludgy answer to migration. You have to create the Oracle8i database first, and then use the SQL*Plus COPY command to create the tables and copy the data into those tables. You then have to create any indexes, primary keys, foreign key constraints, load triggers, functions, procedures, and so on, as required. This is a great deal more work than what's needed for the migration utility, which we will discuss shortly.

Note that you can use a combination of these first two options, Import/Export and the SQL*Plus COPY command, to make the job easier. Here's how:

1. Create the Oracle8i instance and the basic database shell (SYSTEM tablespace, rollback segments, temporary tablespace, and so on), including all tablespaces that will be needed.

2. Do a full export of the Oracle database you are migrating. Use the ROWS=N parameter in the export so that only the logical structure of the database is exported and not the data. (See Appendix C for syntax of the SQL*Plus COPY command.)

3. Into the new Oracle8i database, import the exported dump file created in step 2. This creates all structures, indexes, tables, stored code, and so on.

4. You may wish to disable all primary keys and wait to build indexes until after the load has completed. This will speed up the load process significantly because index updates will not occur during the load processes.

Migrating to Oracle7 and Then to Oracle8i

If you are migrating a pre-Oracle 7.1 database, you won't be able to migrate directly to Oracle8i with the Oracle migration utility (MIG, discussed shortly) or the Database Migration Assistant (both of which we will discuss shortly). If your pre-Oracle 7.1 database is smaller than 2GB or so, it may be more expedient to migrate using just the Oracle Export and Import utilities. For larger databases, however, MIG is usually your best choice for upgrading.

In any of these cases, you'll need to determine how to migrate the pre-Oracle 7.1 database first to Oracle version 7.1 or later. This is because the Oracle8i migration process doesn't support migrating from a version of the Oracle database that is earlier than Oracle 7.1. Refer to the Oracle 7.1 migration instructions for the version from which you are migrating. Once you have migrated to Oracle 7.1, you can move forward to Oracle8i.

Migrating an Existing 7.1+ Database to Oracle8i

You've waited for Oracle8 to mature and you figure it's time to get on the Oracle8i bandwagon (not to mention that Oracle is pulling support for Oracle7). There are several options available for migrating your database to Oracle8i. These include the Oracle MIG utility, the Data Migration Assistant (DMA), the EXP/IMP utilities, and the SQL*Plus COPY operation. The last two options work just as described above for pre-7.1 databases. Here, let's look at the MIG utility and then the DMA.

The Oracle Migration Utility

The Migration utility (MIG) facilitates migrations from supported Oracle7 databases (usually 7.1 and above) to Oracle8i. This utility modifies the Oracle7 data dictionary, making it compatible with the new Oracle8i data dictionary structures. In the process, it re-creates the entire Oracle7 data dictionary as an Oracle8i data dictionary, adding and removing columns, tables, and indexes as required. The MIG utility does not change the fundamental database structures at all, and the original data dictionary tables are left intact (although the views on those tables are removed).

Because the Oracle7 data dictionary tables are left intact by MIG, you can recover the Oracle7 database easily should the MIG utility fail. You simply rerun the various database conversion scripts, such as `catalog`, `catproc`, and `catrep`, and you're in business. Once you determine why MIG failed, you can rerun it without any problem.

The MIG utility creates a schema in the database called MIGRATE. Before you start the migration process, make sure you don't already have a MIGRATE schema. After MIG is done working, it will have created a conversion file called `conv<sid>.dbf` file in the Oracle7 ORACLE_HOME. This file must be moved to the Oracle8i ORACLE_HOME, as shown in step 20 of the migration instructions later in this section.

Note that the MIG utility runs with the ORACLE_HOME of the database pointing to the Oracle7 software, not the Oracle8i software. This is because MIG precedes the actual conversion process that takes place when you issue the ALTER DATABASE CONVERT command. It's this fact that makes it easy to recover the database should MIG fail. Once the ALTER DATABASE CONVERT command has been issued, though, it's a whole different story.

Running MIGPREP

If you have already done some 7.3-to-8 migrations in UNIX, you'll be happy to know that the method of installing the MIG utility has changed. Previously, you had to load MIG into the 7.3 ORACLE_HOME from the Oracle8 CD-ROM. Now, MIG loads into the Oracle8i ORACLE_HOME directory when you install the 8i software, and you need only run a new utility called MIGPREP to move the migration software, including MIG, to the Oracle7 ORACLE_HOME.

The syntax for the MIGPREP utility is

```
Migprep <Oracle8i ORACLE_HOME> <Oracle7 ORACLE_HOME>
```

Thus, if you are installing the MIG utility from 8.1.6 to 7.3.4, your MIGPREP command would look something like this:

```
Migprep /ora01/oracle/product/8.1.6 /ora01/oracle/product/7.3.4
```

Note that this does not apply to migrations on NT. The MIG utility can be run from the Oracle8i install on NT without a problem.

A Checklist for Using MIG

The sidebar "Checklist for Migrating Oracle7 to Oracle8i" presents a step-by-step process for supported Oracle 7.*x* migrations to Oracle8i. This checklist has been through the test of time, updated and improved by Robert Freeman over the course of running many migrations and working through their problems. We recommend you print it out from the book's CD-ROM and use it during your migrations to Oracle8i. This checklist is current as of Oracle version 8.1.7. And hey, if Robert has left anything out, feel free to write him at the e-mail address in the Introduction!

Checklist for Migrating Oracle7 to Oracle8i

1. Verify successful backup of your database.
2. Install Oracle8i software on the server.
3. If you are running on NT, set the ORACLE_SID environment variable.

   If you are running on Unix, set up these environment variables for the Oracle7 environment: ORACLE_HOME, ORACLE_SID, PATH, LD_LIBRARY_PATH, ORA_NLS, ORACLE_BASE, and ORACLE_PATH (if set).

4. **Unix only:** If this is the first 7-to-8 migration for your Unix Oracle system, run the MIGPREP script to copy migration files to the Oracle7 environment.

   ```
   migprep
   /ora01/oracle/product/8.1.6.0
   /ora01/oracle/product/7.3.4.4
   ```

5. In /tmp, create a directory and subdirectory called mig and mig/<sid> (if they don't already exist).
6. Remove all rows (via TRUNCATE) from the aud$ table.
7. Modify the following parameters in the init*sid*.ora (don't forget to save a copy of the original file!):

   ```
   job_queue_processes=0
   audit_trail=None
   ```

Continued

CONTINUED

8. Confirm the version of the MIG utility. It should be the Oracle8i version to which you are migrating. To do this, print the MIG help screen, which will include the version of the utility. You'll run MIG from the Oracle 7.3 ORACLE_HOME on Unix, and from the newly installed Oracle8i ORACLE_HOME on NT. Run MIG with this command:

    ```
    Mig help=y
    ```

    which produces this output:

    ```
    ORACLE7 to ORACLE8 Migration Utility Release 8.1.6.0.0 - Production
    ```

9. Shut down the database with **SHUTDOWN IMMEDIATE**.
10. Run the MIG utility with the CHECK_ONLY option to ensure that enough space is available in the database for the migration process.

    Unix example:

    From the Oracle 7.3 ORACLE_HOME, enter this command (note that the slashes before the quotes are required):

    ```
    mig  CHECK_ONLY=TRUE SPOOL=\"/tmp/mig/<dbname>_check_only.out\"
    ```

    NT example:

    From the newly installed Oracle8i ORACLE_HOME, enter

    ```
    mig  CHECK_ONLY=TRUE SPOOL="c:\mig\<dbname>_check_only.out"
      pfile=<ORACLE7 parameter file>
    ```

11. Check the data dictionary tables for fragmentation and/or excessive numbers of extents. Modify the `migrate.bsq` as required. The following script will look for fragmented data dictionary objects. If an excessive number of these exist, consider modifying these objects in the `migrate.bsq` so they will fit in fewer extents.

    ```
    SELECT a.owner, a.segment_name, a.segment_type, a.extents,
       b.initial_extent, b.next_extent
    FROM dba_segments a, dba_tables b
    WHERE a.owner=b.owner and
    a.segment_name=b.table_name and
    a.owner='SYS' and
    a.extents > 5
    UNION
    SELECT a.owner, a.segment_name, a.segment_type, a.extents,
       b.initial_extent, b.next_extent
    ```

Continued

CONTINUED

```
FROM dba_segments a, dba_indexes b
WHERE a.owner=b.owner and
a.segment_name=b.index_name and
a.owner='SYS' and
a.extents > 5;
```

12. Make sure the SYSTEM rollback segment does not have an optimal setting. Use the following query to check the OPTIMAL setting for the SYSTEM rollback segment. If the SYSTEM rollback segment is set to OPTIMAL, you will need to use the ALTER ROLLBACK SEGMENT command to reconfigure it so that OPTIMAL is NULL.

    ```
    SELECT a.usn, a.name, b.optsize FROM v$rollname a, v$rollstat b
    WHERE a.usn = b.usn AND name = 'SYSTEM';
    ALTER ROLLBACK SEGMENT SYSTEM STORAGE (OPTIMAL NULL);
    ```

13. Check the SYSTEM tablespace of the database to ensure that it has sufficient contiguous space. The SYSTEM tablespace should have a few chunks of space that are moderate to large. If it does not, consider adding to the size of the existing system tablespace database datafiles, or adding a new datafile as required.

    ```
    SELECT tablespace_name, bytes FROM dba_free_space
    WHERE tablespace_name = 'SYSTEM';
    ```

14. Check the DBA_2PC_PENDING table for any unresolved distributed transactions. If there are any unresolved transactions, see Chapter 22.

    ```
    SELECT * FROM dba_2pc_pending;
    ```

15. Shut down the Oracle database with a normal or immediate shutdown. Do *not* do a shutdown abort.

16. Run the Oracle8i Migration utility:

    Unix example (still set up for the ORACLE7 environment):

    ```
    mig SPOOL=\"/tmp/mig/<sid>_migration.out\"
    ```

    NT example:

    ```
    mig SPOOL="c:\mig\<dbname>_check_only.out" pfile=<ORACLE7 parameter
        file>
    ```

17. Check the output file after running the Migration utility. If the utility ran correctly, you may wish to do another backup of the database at this point. (We rarely do this in practice, however, since we use a special backup/recovery method described later in this section, and it doesn't take as long to rerun the MIG process as it does to recover the database.)

Continued

CONTINUED

18. If you are running on Unix, set up the following environment variables for the Oracle8i environment: ORACLE_HOME, ORACLE_SID, PATH, LD_LIBRARY_PATH, ORA_NLS, ORACLE_BASE, and ORACLE_PATH (if set).

    If you are running on NT, take these steps:

    - Stop the Oracle service for your database:

    ```
    NET STOP OracleServiceORCL
    ```

    - Delete the Oracle7 service on NT using the ORADIM7x commands:

    ```
    ORADIM71 -delete -sid ORCL
    ORADIM72 -delete -sid ORCL
    ORADIM73 -delete -sid ORCL
    ```

    - Restart the system.

    - Create the Oracle8i service for the newly migrated Oracle8i database, using the ORADIM command. (See the NT-specific documentation for instructions on using ORADIM.) Here is an example:

    ```
    ORADIM -NEW -SID ORCL -INTPWD MYPASSWORD -MAXUSERS 200
    -STARTMODE AUTO
    -PFILE ORACLE_HOME\DATABASE\INITSID.ORA
    ```

19. Remove or rename the database control files. Alternatively, you can change the CONTROL_FILES initialization parameter to specify new location and/or names for the control files. The CONTROL_FILES initialization parameter typically is set in the init*sid*.ora file.

20. Move or copy the convert file from the Oracle7 ORACLE_HOME to the Oracle8i ORACLE_HOME. On most Unix systems, in both the Oracle7 and the Oracle8i environments, the convert file (conv*sid*.dbf, where *sid* is the Oracle8i database name), should reside in $ORACLE_HOME/dbs; in an NT system, it's in ORACLE_HOME\database.

Unix example:

```
cp  /ora01/oracle/product/7.3.4.4/dbs/convsid.dbf
   /ora01/oracle/product/8.1.6.0/dbs/convsid.dbf
```

NT example:

```
copy c:\oracle\product\7.3.4.4\database\convsid.dbf
   c:\ora01\oracle\product\8.1.6.0\database\convsid.dbf
```

Continued

CONTINUED

21. Copy the `init.ora` parameter file from the 7.3 ORACLE_HOME to the new 8i ORACLE_HOME.

22. Modify the copied `init.ora` parameter file to reflect any new Oracle8i parameters you wish to use. Be aware that, by default, the JAVA_POOL_SIZE will be allocated to 20MB! If you won't be doing Java within the database, you'll want to add the JAVA_POOL_SIZE parameter, setting the size of the pool to 0. Remove any obsolete parameters from the parameter file as well. Examples:

    ```
    JAVA_POOL_SIZE=0
    COMPATIBLE=8.1.5  (or 8.1.6 or 8.1.7)
    INSTANCE_NAME (see Chapter 8)
    SERVICE_NAME (see Chapter 8)
    LOCAL_LISTENER (see Chapter 8)
    ```

23. Change to the new Oracle8i `ORACLE_HOME/rdbms/admin` directory. From Server Manager or SQL*Plus, issue the commands to convert and open the database under Oracle8i.

    ```
    CONNECT INTERNAL
    STARTUP NOMOUNT
    ALTER DATABASE CONVERT;
    ALTER DATABASE OPEN RESETLOGS;
    ```

    CAUTIONS:

    You must use the STARTUP NOMOUNT option when first opening the database. MOUNT may crash the database, forcing a restore.

    Once you have issued the ALTER DATABASE CONVERT, you will need to recover the database before you can run the MIG utility again!

    If an error occurs during the ALTER DATABASE CONVERT process, carefully determine the nature of the error. It may or may not require you to recover the database.

24. Finish the conversion process by running the following conversion script from Server Manager or SQL*Plus. This script executes several other SQL scripts. You may need to include others not listed here if you are using optional Oracle products. To find out, refer to the Migration Guide, the OS-specific documentation, and the product-specific documentation.

Continued

> **CONTINUED**
>
> **Note:** If this script fails, correct the reason for the failure (lack of tablespace space, for example) and then rerun the script. After a script is completed, you don't have to rerun it if a subsequent script fails, but you do have to rerun the failed script and the subsequent scripts. Also, check the log file for any invalid constraints that might arise out of the execution of utlconst.sql.
>
> ```
> SPOOL /tmp/mig/<sid>_catoutm.log
> SET ECHO ON
> @u0703040.sql
> @catrep.sql
> @r0703040.sql
> @utlrp.sql
> @utlconst.sql
> SHUTDOWN IMMEDIATE
> STARTUP
> ```
>
> 25. Review the log from the migration process.
> 26. Change user OUTLN's password using the ALTER USER command as follows. Alter any additional new Oracle8i accounts that might be created:
>
>     ```
>     ALTER USER OUTLN
>     IDENTIFIED BY new_password;
>     ```
>
> 27. Modify the `listener.ora` file of the listener that was listening for the Oracle7 database. You will no longer need the SID description in the `listener.ora` for that database.
> 28. Verify client connectivity to the new Oracle8i database.
> 29. Perform a backup of the newly migrated Oracle8i database.

Some Advice for Your Migrations

The checklist in the sidebar is a good start when it comes to migrating your databases to Oracle8i. It does not, however, supplant your reading the Oracle Migration Guide, which is supplied with the Oracle8i documentation. Please—read the documentation, and then read it again. Then, if you feel comfortable with the migration process in general, test the process several times before trying it out on a real database. Following are our additional comments and suggestions for making your database migration experience a little easier.

Suggestions for Backup

Always, without fail, back up your system before you do any migration. In fact, we usually do two separate backups. The first one is a full backup of all tablespaces; hot backups are fine (see Chapters 10 through 13 for a full treatment on backups). Second, we back up only the SYSTEM tablespace and any tablespace with rollback segments. After doing these two backups, we put all the other tablespaces except SYSTEM and rollback segment tablespaces into READ-ONLY mode before continuing the migration process.

Making these tablespaces READ-ONLY is permissible because Oracle does not need to access them during the migration process. The benefit is that if you need to recover your database after a failed migration, you only have to recover the SYSTEM tablespace and rollback segment tablespaces; none of the other tablespaces will have changed and will thus be consistent. You can make the tablespaces READ-WRITE again after the migration is successful and you have run the migration scripts. These scripts include @u0703040.sql, @catrep.sql, @r0703040.sql, @utlrp.sql, @utlconst.sql, and possibly others demanded by your database software installation.

Finally, make sure you back up your new Oracle8i database after the migration is complete. Here again, a hot backup is sufficient.

Other Important Migration Tasks

Don't neglect these important issues.

Checking database parameters

Take care of the database parameter files. The migration checklist suggests several changes to these files, so always make a copy of the parameter file first. If you are using the Oracle job scheduler replication and such, it is very important that you turn the scheduler off before starting the migration, as shown in step 7 of the checklist. Just set JOB_QUEUE_PROCESSES=0 in the database init.ora parameter file, and that will take care of it.

Also, make sure you check the compatible parameter. Once the migration is complete, make sure you change it to the correct value (generally the version of the database you are migrating to). Also, keep an eye out for parameters that have become obsolete. Because these specific parameters are no longer supported, they will prevent your new database from coming up. There are also depreciated parameters. These are parameters that are no longer used by Oracle but their use will not keep your database from coming up, but will generate errors every time the database is started. It's a good idea to remove these parameters from the database because future versions of Oracle will likely not support them at all. Finally, there are some parameters that have become hidden parameters. There are not to many of these, but your database will complain about their use and refuse to start until they are either removed or changed to the correct hidden parameter. You can find lists of all obsolete and depreciated parameters in the Oracle8i documentation for the version of Oracle8i that you are running (they differ for each version).

Set Auditing OFF

If auditing is running, it can cause the migration to fail, so if you're using database auditing, turn it OFF (see step 7 of the checklist). Also, note that the checklist suggests truncation of the audit_trail in step 6 (SYS.AUD$ is the audit trail table). This is because Oracle will try to make a copy of the SYS.AUD$ table during the migration process. If the audit table is particularly large, the migration will take substantially longer to complete.

Check the System Items Before Migration

Before you start the migration process, consider checking the data dictionary tables for fragmentation and/or excessive numbers of extents (see step 12 of the checklist). This is your chance to rebuild the data dictionary if some of the tables (such as SOURCE$) are in bad shape. With any segment that appears in the .sql script provided with step 11, you should consider increasing the INITIAL and NEXT parameters for that object, in the file `mig.bsq` which is contained in the 8i $ORACLE_HOME directory. We strongly recommend assigning the same values to INITIAL and NEXT for that object, and setting PCTINCREASE to 0 for that object. Of course, you should always make a copy of the `mig.bsq` before changing it, and ensure that another user isn't making changes or doing a conversion with that copy of the `mig.bsq`.

Before migrating the database, ensure that the SYSTEM rollback segment does not have an OPTIMAL setting. Having OPTIMAL set will seldom cause a problem, but it may happen that you'll get a "snapshot too old" error and the migration process will die. It's better to reset OPTIMAL to NULL. Also, you must have the database shut down before you run the Migration utility. One of MIG's actions is to start up the database, and the utility will stall if the database is already up. The other thing to note is that when the migration utility starts, it will take off line all rollback segments except the SYSTEM rollback segment. So, when you check the SYSTEM rollback segment after running MIG with the CHECK_ONLY=TRUE flag, you may notice that the SYSTEM rollback segment is the only one. This is normal.

Migration Utility Notes

When you migrate a database with the MIG utility, a conversion file (conv<sid>.dbf) is created in the Oracle 7.3 ORACLE_HOME/dbs directory (ORACLE_HOME\database in NT). This file is critical to the conversion process. You will copy it to Oracle8i's ORACLE_HOME\dbs (or ORACLE_HOME\database) before you convert the database. The conversion file contains information that Oracle needs during the execution of the ALTER DATABASE CONVERT command, to check for changes in datafiles since the migration process was last run.

Watch out: If you're running multiple versions of Oracle8 and/or Oracle8i on your system, it's possible that the wrong version of MIG will be present in your 7.3 ORACLE_HOME directory in Unix. In NT, you might be in the wrong ORACLE_HOME directory or the PATH could be set such that an incorrect version of MIG will be executed. This problem arises from the fact that there is a version of MIG for each edition of the Oracle8 and Oracle8i database software that is installed on a given system. When running the migration utility, you need to make sure you are running the version of the utility that is associated with the Oracle software version to which you are migrating (see step 8). You will not immediately be made aware that you have used the wrong version of the migration utility. Oracle will happily migrate your database using the 8.0.5 version of the migration utility, even though you really mean to be using 8.1.7. In this case, you will not discover that you used the wrong migration utility until you try to actually convert the database, which may be sometime later in the migration process.

During MIG execution, you may find that a SYS.* table can't be extended due to an "out of extents" error. The MULTIPLIER parameter of the MIG command described earlier in this chapter may be the answer. This parameter causes certain system data dictionary tables to be created with a larger extent size than the Oracle 7.x data dictionary tables. MULTIPLIER's default setting is 15. If you encounter such errors, we recommended increasing this to 30; if errors persist, increase it again to 50. Note that this will increase the size of the objects in the data dictionary.

ALTER DATABASE CONVERT Problems

When you issue the ALTER DATABASE CONVERT command to convert the database, if you have used the wrong MIG utility, Oracle will produce an error message that the conv<sid>.dbf conversion file is incompatible with the database version you're trying to convert. You've accidentally run the wrong version of the migration utility, and fixing this is pretty simple (although it may take some time).

Shut Oracle down and run the correct version of the MIG utility. (In Unix, run MIGPREP to make sure that you have the right version in place. In NT, make sure you are in the correct ORACLE_HOME location.) Note, also, that in step 8 of the checklist you run the MIG process using the HELP=Y flag. This is so you can verify that the help banner displays the same Oracle version number as the database version to which you are moving.

> **WARNING** If the ALTER DATABASE CONVERT command fails, be very careful about what you do next. Just because the command fails does not mean you'll get automatic recovery. It might be that you forgot to remove the control files, or you didn't move the conversion file into its proper place. It might be that the new control files are too big for their disks. (The Oracle control files are significantly larger in Oracle8i than Oracle7.) Just don't panic if things don't work right the first time.

Again, as with all things, practice makes perfect. Please practice your migration efforts in a development environment before trying it in production.

Migrating Using the Data Migration Assistant

If the dark forces have hooked you into graphical interface addiction, the Data Migration Assistant (DMA) is for you. There are various platform-specific requirements for using this interface to migrate an Oracle database, so read the Oracle8i Migration Guide for details. It tells you how to prepare the database before using the DMA, as well as procedures to follow after the migration.

For the most part, the DMA automates the entire migration process. This is the primary benefit of the DMA and makes it easier for a novice DBA to migrate a database. On the downside, you cannot use some of MIG's command-line parameters (such as MULTIPLIER), which might be required. Another problem with the DMA is that if it fails, you are more likely to have to restore your database in order to try the migration again than if you had migrated the database manually. This is because you have more control over a manual migration and can more easily deal with failures.

To start the DMA from Windows, click Start ➤ Migration Utilities ➤ Migration Assistant. From Unix, start it from the ORACLE8i ORACLE_HOME, with the ORACLE7 path for your database set up. The DMA will take it from there.

Another benefit of the DMA is that it will handle upgrades of your database in addition to migrations. Should you need to upgrade from Oracle8 to Oracle8i, or even within versions of Oracle8i itself, the DMA can assist you in this process. We like to use the DMA for these types of upgrades, as opposed to migrations, because we don't have to worry about making typing errors in the upgrade script names during the upgrade. And, since the upgrade process is fairly simple, we can generally just point, click, and forget. All that's needed is to check that everything worked once the process is complete.

Upgrading within Major Versions

We have discussed migrations, which are movements to other major versions of the Oracle software. Now, let's look at the topic of upgrades. We'll discuss two types of upgrades: One is the upgrade to a different release level within the same major version (such as from 8.1.5 to 8.1.6). The second type of upgrade is the application of patches to a minor version of the Oracle software. In this case the minor version number stays the same; thus you will remain at the 8.1.6 release level.

Upgrading

Minor-version upgrades to Oracle can occur fairly frequently. A new minor version of the software gets released as often as every 9 to 12 months or so. With each upgrade, new functions (and often new bugs, as well!) are introduced. Upgrades within major versions of the Oracle software (8.0 to 8.1, or 8.1.x to 8.1.x, for example) are generally fairly simple processes. Of course, you should always get specific instruction from the Oracle documentation for the version to which you're upgrading.

More often than not, you'll find that the process consists of these steps:

1. Back up the database.
2. Shut down the database.
3. Restart the database using the new version of the Oracle software.
4. Run an upgrade script. You'll do this from $ORACLE_HOME/rdbms/admin on Unix, or ORACLE_HOME\rdbms\admin on NT. This script usually takes on the naming convention Uversion#.sql, with version# generally a seven-digit number representing the database version you are upgrading. Each part of the version number is proceeded with a zero (thus 8 is 08) except for the last digit, which normally is 0. Thus, if you are upgrading from an 8.1.5 to an 8.1.6 database, you'd run the upgrade script named u0805010.sql.

NOTE Looking through upgrade scripts and the scripts they call can reveal many interesting things about the version to which you are upgrading—including new features and maybe even an occasional undocumented command!

5. Run catalog.sql, catproc.sql, catrep.sql and other conversion scripts required to re-create the data dictionary views and to reload other database options such as advanced replication.
6. Back up the upgraded database.

Patching

The main difference between patch sets and upgrades is that patch sets are fixes and don't include any new features. When you apply one-off patches to the RDBMS software, as described earlier in this chapter, additional work is often required on any database using that ORACLE_HOME software. Sometimes, however, a one-off patch might be released for a nondatabase product such as SQL*Plus. Always study the patch set's Readme document to make sure you know what's necessary for applying the upgrade to each of your databases. Typically the procedure involves running the `catalog.sql` and `catproc.sql` scripts (discussed in more detail in Chapter 4), and other scripts necessary to the optional Oracle products you have loaded.

In Sum

It's true that migrating or upgrading your Oracle database can be an intimidating job. There is a good deal of preparation that needs to be done, and we hope you're ready for that after reading this chapter. You now know about the different types of software upgrades that you may encounter, and you've been cautioned about some of the pitfalls of the process. The bottom line is, and this is true with all DBA work, you must protect the database. Understand what you are doing, test it, and test it again before you do it for real. Back up the database before making any changes at all to it. Do these things and you're on your way to mastering Oracle installations.

And when you need help, there are a few things you can do. Hopefully, you're an Oracle customer, so you have access to support services. Oracle Metalink at `metalink.oracle.com` is Oracle's web-based support site, which you can sign up for as an Oracle support customer. There are other sites you might want to look at as well. Here are a few:

> `technet.oracle.com`—You need not be an Oracle support customer to join up. In addition to help, this site has a good deal of Oracle software available for download for trial use.
>
> `www.revealnet.com`—Home of the RevealNet products you will find on the CD that comes with this book. This site also has the DBA Pipeline and the PL/SQL Pipeline, where Robert participates as a sysop. This site is a true community of Oracle DBAs and developers, so come join us!
>
> `www.ixora.com.au`—This site belongs to Steve Adams and his company, Ixora. It is dedicated to information about Oracle internals.

CHAPTER 3

Creating Oracle Databases

FEATURING:

Oracle's Optimal Flexible Architecture (OFA)	**89**
Determining physical requirements	**97**
Determining the database block size	**113**
Naming conventions	**115**
Creating the parameter file (init.ora)	**117**
Creating the database	**128**
Summary of database creation steps	**138**

Creation of an Oracle database can seem an ominous task the first few times you try it. But like learning anything new, practice helps. This chapter gets you started on the right track, and you'll gain experience every time you create a new or change an existing database.

This chapter begins with a short discussion of the Oracle's Optimal Flexible Architecture (OFA), the standard on which Oracle databases are built. You'll learn about the important preparatory work that goes into the process of database creation: planning the foundation of physical space and the memory you'll need, configuring that foundation, and setting fundamental parameters. The important init<sid>.ora database parameter file contains most of the settings representing your decisions for these elements. We will then look at the steps of actually creating the Oracle database—either manually or via the Database Configuration Agent—and some of the important tasks to be done immediately afterward. At the end of the chapter is a summarized list of steps to help you remember to do everything necessary to create your Oracle database from start to finish.

NOTE This chapter is about creating the database proper. It is not about creating segments, tables, indexes, and the other objects in an Oracle database. These topics are covered in Chapter 6.

Robert's Rant: Read That Documentation!!

Many Oracle DBAs are not familiar or even comfortable with the Oracle documentation. While the documentation Oracle provides is not always complete or absolutely correct, it *is* (along with this book of course) a good first resource to use. Particularly important is documentation for your specific hardware. Because Oracle is available for so many hardware platforms, there is no way a book like this one can provide you with every bit of information you need to know about installing Oracle on your system.

So if you *are* one of these DBAs, we urge you to *stop right now.* Get out the documentation CD, start it up, and spend at least a good hour with it. Learn how to use the documentation search functions, awkward though they may be. Know what documents

Continued

> **CONTINUED**
>
> come with Oracle. Read your platform-specific documentation, read it again, then print it out and read it again—and then have your co-DBAs read it.
>
> We've lost track of how many times we've been asked by even senior DBAs about how to do or fix something. And the answer was right there in the OS-specific docs. Here's an example: Oracle on AIX requires that a specific driver called the post-wait driver be installed. If it isn't, and you don't know about it, you'll be looking at some fairly cryptic error messages when you try to even boot. To make things worse, getting help from Oracle Support can take some time because they're trying to support about a thousand different platforms! But it's all there in the documentation.
>
> By the way—Oracle used to ship paper copies of hardware-specific documentation. Unfortunately this is no longer the case. Nor is the documentation included on the server install disk—at least, not since 8.1.7. You now have to install the documentation from its own, separate CD.

Oracle's Optimal Flexible Architecture (OFA)

Oracle introduced the *Optimal Flexible Architecture (OFA)* back in Oracle7. OFA is designed to simplify the management and improve the performance of Oracle databases. The Oracle software and database are large and complex, and it is important to have a set of standards that define them. OFA provides naming standards for files and directories in Oracle databases, as well as standards for the placement of those files on your system. Generally when you install Oracle software, the installer tool installs that software in an OFA-compliant manner.

This section discusses the benefits of using the OFA guidelines and describes the elements of the architecture itself.

The Benefits of Using OFA

Standards are generally good things to have. They eliminate a lot of design guesswork, and they allow others to quickly come up to speed in understanding and maintaining your production environment. In using the OFA standard when installing and using Oracle, you gain these advantages and others.

In terms of the Oracle software, OFA provides several features:

- Provisions for the existence of multiple versions of the Oracle software on the same system.
- A common architecture that optimizes problem resolution time. This is particularly true because Oracle Support doesn't need to determine where and how the software is loaded before helping you solve a problem.
- Aid to the DBA in transitioning from site to site. This is particularly helpful to consultants who move among sites, and for large sites with many different databases and Oracle versions.

In addition to defining database software installation, it provides guidelines for the physical structure of your Oracle database. These guidelines serve several purposes, including

- Providing for the presence of multiple databases on the same system and even on the same file systems.
- Allowing database physical structures to reside on multiple disks, supporting distributed I/O and helping to protect the database from loss of one or more disk systems.
- Accommodating future growth of the database.
- Separating Oracle software and Oracle data, making the Oracle upgrade process easier.
- Consistent naming of database files and their related directories. This allows database files to be easily found and moved. The naming conventions also ensure close association with Oracle datafiles and their associated tablespaces.

OFA Structure

OFA differs slightly on various platforms. In this chapter we describe the standard Unix-based approach to OFA, but it normally isn't very difficult to extend this to other operating systems such as NT.

The Basic OFA Rules

The OFA guidelines consist of three basic rules:

Establish orderly operating-system directory structures in which any database file can be stored on any disk resource.
You should be consistent in your naming of directories in Oracle. In addition,

make sure that if a datafile is in a directory assigned to the Mydb database, that file actually belongs to the Mydb database.

Separate data objects (segments) having specific characteristics and behaviors into distinct tablespaces. Indexes and tables belong in separate tablespaces. Rollback segments belong in their own tablespaces, as do temporary segments. This rule can be extended to collections of objects with the same kind of structures (partitioned objects and transient tables, for instance); these objects, too, should be stored in distinct tablespaces.

Separate database components onto distinct I/O resources, in order to maximize I/O throughput. Following this one rule can significantly improve performance of your database. Place redo logs on disks separate from those for tablespace datafiles. Place index tablespace datafiles on their own disks. With today's various striped RAID configurations, this may be a difficult challenge. In addition to having multiple disk systems, consider spreading the I/O among multiple controllers.

Database Components

In applying OFA rules to database creation, you'll need to create multiple file systems to separate various database components. These components, listed just below, are discussed in detail throughout this book:

Online Database Redo Logs Online redo logs (sometimes just called redo logs) hold a record of all changes made to the database. The term *online* means they are associated with an active database, and as such are constantly undergoing changes to their data. As changes occur within the Oracle database, the online redo logs record all those changes. This record can be used later to recover the database, if required.

Oracle requires that at least two different groups of redo logs be created for every database. Most databases typically have three to five redo log groups, each consisting of one or more members (files). Each member in a group is a mirror copy of the other mirrors in that same group, giving additional protection to these very important files. As changes are made to the database, Oracle records the changes in one redo log group. Each online redo log member is preallocated; thus the redo logs, once created, do not grow or shrink unless they are re-created.

Archived Redo Logs These are copies of individual online redo logs. An archived redo log is only created for a database in ARCHIVELOG mode. The archived logs are used for backup and recovery purposes.

Database Control Files   These files, thoroughly examined in Chapter 5, contain database-specific information such as the location of the database datafiles, and other database structure information.

Tablespace Datafiles   An Oracle tablespace consists of one or more physical datafiles and is a logical entity that stores data and other information within the database. An Oracle database contains one or more tablespaces, but at a minimum the SYSTEM tablespace (with a minimum of one datafile) is required. Oracle tablespaces are used to hold a variety of database objects, such as:

- Tables
- Indexes
- Rollback segments
- The SYSTEM tablespace
- TEMPORARY tablespace(s)

Oracle Executables   The Oracle executables are the "guts" of the Oracle RDBMS—the programs, libraries, and help files that run and manage the Oracle database.

User Files   These are user scripts, output files, and other files that the Oracle database users creates.

Export and Import Files   These files are the result of the Oracle export (EXP) process, or those staged for the Oracle import (IMP) process.

Backup images   These files are the backups of the Oracle database.

NOTE To separate all these database components onto their own disks would require something like 12+ disks, and maybe more for optimal I/O. Rarely will you have this many disks, or even as many disks as you want. Later in the chapter we'll provide some suggested datafile placement strategies to use when you have a limited number of fixed disks, or when you are using a RAID array that stripes among many disks. See the section "Oracle File Placement."

Oracle Base and Oracle Home

This section explains the genesis of the Oracle software installation directory structures. In addition to ORACLE_BASE and ORACLE_HOME, we'll talk about the OFA-suggested administration directory structures.

Oracle Base

The OFA standard location for the Oracle software begins with the Oracle Base directory. Typically, *Oracle Base* refers to an environment variable called ORACLE_BASE that represents the base file system or directory (such as `c:\oracle`). The ORACLE_BASE directory is part of the overall OFA design. It provides for the installation of one or more concurrently operable Oracle software versions within it. Oracle Base also provides for installation of other related Oracle software (for example, the Oracle documentation) and even database administrative files. You'll note that the directory name `oracle` includes no version information and follows no particular intelligent naming conventions. This is important because OFA supports multiple versions of the Oracle software product in the same Oracle Base.

Oracle Base structures rarely contain database datafiles (though OFA allows for this). Oracle Base may include other Oracle directory structures, such as the product directory that stores the various versions of the Oracle software. Other possible directories here are APPL_TOP, associated with Oracle financials, and the database admin structure discussed shortly.

Oracle Home

Oracle Home—an extension of Oracle Base—is the location of the Oracle database software and the location from which all Oracle software is installed. Like ORACLE_BASE, ORACLE_HOME is an environmental variable pointing to the location of Oracle Home. The Oracle Home directory name is specific to a given version of the database software. This allows multiple versions of the Oracle software to exist in the same Oracle Base structure but not in the same Oracle Home structure.

The OFA standard calls for Oracle Home to be created with a directory called *product*, followed by a directory with the version number of the Oracle software. Thus, assuming Oracle Base is `c:\oracle`, and you have two Oracle Homes for versions 8.1.6.0.0 and 8.1.6.3.0, the two Oracle Home names will be `c:\oracle\product\8.1.6.0.0` and `c:\oracle\product\8.1.6.3.0`. It is important to include the entire version number, including the trailing 0's, in the Oracle Home name. This is a *fully versioned path*.

Oracle does not automatically use a fully versioned path to create the Oracle Home directory, but you should do so when you install the software. Though not strictly required by OFA, it's best to use a fully versioned path. It makes it easier for DBAs to maintain multiple versions of the Oracle software on the same system.

TIP We like to add an additional .0 to the version segment of the Oracle Home name, to allow for one-off patch set additions. Say you discover a peculiar bug and they send you a patch fix for it. After testing this patch (you always test everything, don't you?), you may want to roll it out only to a specific database or perhaps just roll it out slowly. Use of fully versioned paths keeps everything straight for everyone.

You'll see some variation in how Oracle names the directories in the product installations on various platforms (and in different release versions!). Thus the contents of ORACLE_HOME on various platforms may look very different. The Oracle directory names are often specific to an operating system, and even platforms such as Unix and NT will have different directory paths. Specific Oracle program files, Oracle libraries, and files specific to various Oracle products such as SQL*Plus or Net8 may be found in widely different locations at times (and might even have different names). Oracle appears to be trying to reconcile some of these differences in later releases of its software, which is a good sign!

Also OFA provides for the presence of Oracle database datafiles within Oracle Home. However, we strongly discourage this for several reasons, including performance ramifications and protection of critical datafiles from single points of failure.

The Database Administration Subdirectory

Also created as an extension of the Oracle Base structure is the *database administration subdirectory*. This structure begins with a directory called Admin in the Oracle Base directory. Under Admin is a subdirectory for each database on the system. This allows you to have separate Admin directories for each database. Following are some of the subdirectories included in an Admin\database, many of which are part of the OFA specification:

- A directory named pfile, for the database configuration file (init.ora).
- The various database dump directories (adump, udump, bdump and cdump) discussed later in this chapter. These directories hold database trace files and logging information.
- A create directory that stores the DDL used to create your Oracle database.
- An exp directory that holds dump files created by the EXP logical extraction facility (discussed in Chapter 11).
- Other directories created by the DBA.

For Unix-based systems, we often include in Admin/database a subdirectory for symbolic links, called link, which is an extension to OFA.

ORACLE'S OPTIMAL FLEXIBLE ARCHITECTURE (OFA)

 TIP You will see that we occasionally add an extension to the OFA structure. Logical, sensible extensions to the OFA minimum standard are perfectly acceptable.

The Oradata Directories

The *Oradata directory structure* standard defines the storage of database datafiles. These datafiles can be stored under Oracle Base (not recommended) or other file systems.

We use neutral names at the Oradata level, to allow the most flexible use of the file system. Let's say your database is named PAYROLL; you would not name the Oradata file system PAYROLL_DATA, but rather choose a less explicit name such as ora01. This lets you store data for databases other than PAYROLL, for instance, within this structure at some later time.

The OFA standard for this structure is a directory called oradata followed by a directory named after the database. For our PAYROLL example, then, the Oradata name would be d:\ora01\oradata\payroll or perhaps d:\ora02\oradata\payroll.

 NOTE We like to add an additional name to the structure, after the name of the database, such as data, redo, or control. For example: \ora01\oradata\payroll\redo. This provides another degree of separation and a touch more security.

An OFA Roadmap

The following diagram provides a complete "road map" of the OFA setup for a typical Oracle8i database on Windows NT. Remember that OFA is not a requirement but rather a recommended set of standards. You may have specific needs that are not met by OFA, and for these you will need some derivative of OFA. For the most part, however, OFA is a proven model.

Continued

CONTINUED

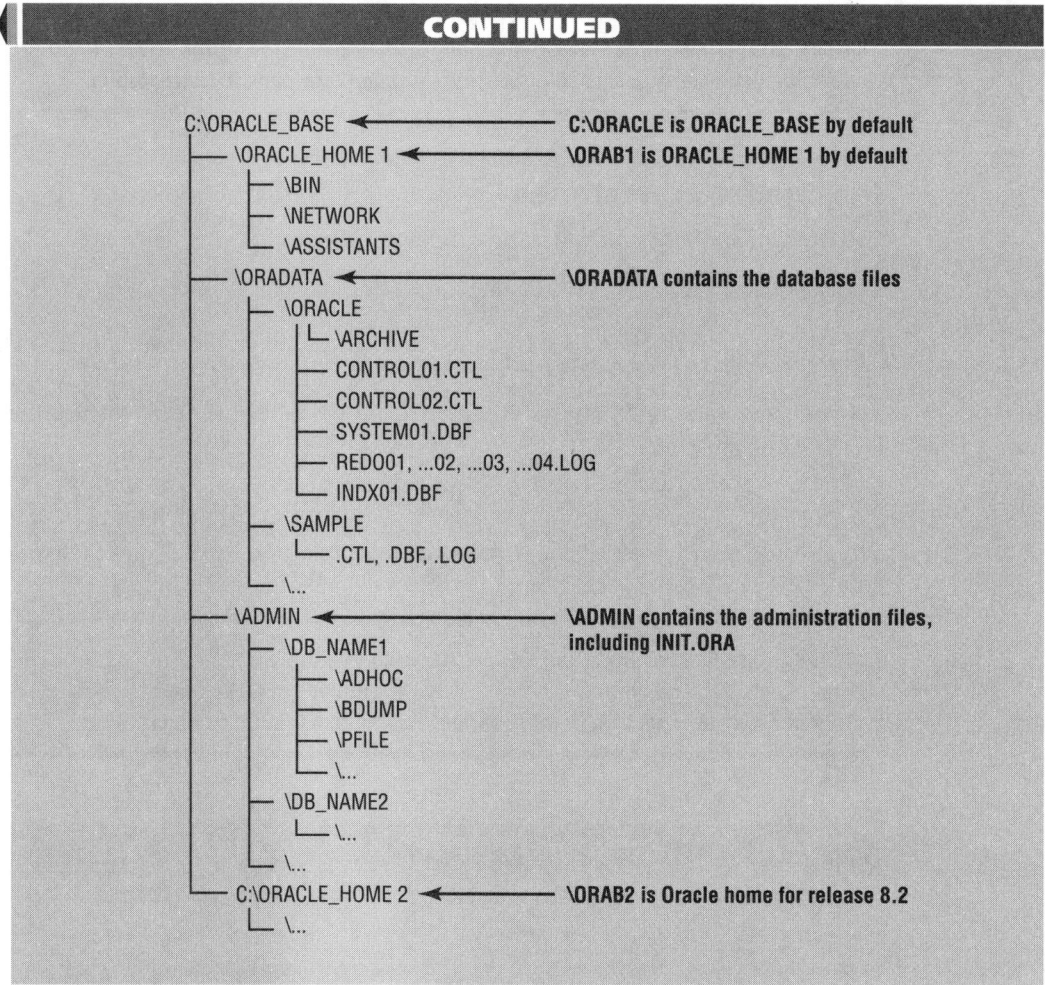

Preparing to Create the Database

The successful DBA spends far more time preparing for database creation than actually creating that database—and we're *not* referring to the fact that your hardware vendor

Continued

> **CONTINUED**
>
> probably can't deliver your hardware for six months. What we mean by preparation is the invaluable legwork done by the DBA, along with data administrators, developers, and management, before a database gets put into production. The majority of this chapter is devoted to that important work.
>
> Certainly it's true that many DBAs also act as developers and data architects, and in fact it's imperative that DBAs understand logical database design. But this chapter is meant to help you with the physical implementation of an existing database design, which is the heart of a DBA's job. We'll start with the physical requirements of your database, and then we will address the primary configuration issues that you need to consider before starting to create your Oracle database. Among the things to consider: choosing the database block size, designating naming conventions, creating the database parameter file, and other important organizational tasks. Finally, we will return to the topic of database creation.

Determining Physical Requirements

A lot of thinking and planning goes into the creation of an Oracle database—at least, it should. Typically, however, this doesn't happen, and this section will help you make sure it does. We will look at some of the physical requirements that the successful DBA will consider prior to creation of an Oracle database. Physical requirements include disk space, configuration choices, placement of Oracle files in the physical setup, memory needed for database files, and some general system requirements. Let's look in a bit more detail at some of the requirements that you will need to consider.

Disk Space Requirements

Databases use disk space the way humans use air, and skyrocketing requirements are the norm. There are several reasons for this.

Inadequate understanding of the database's actual usage of space Data volume needs are often poorly estimated. These errors can be the result of budgetary constraints or the velocity of the application design process or both.

Poor application or database design   Databases are often designed by people who don't really understand database design. Data may be missing, duplicated, or redundant, and any number of functional problems might have been created during the design.

Lack of defined data-retention standards   If data is kept forever, your database will grow and grow uncontrollably. It is critical that application development staff defines their data retention needs and the methods that will be used to purge that data. This affects both the size and performance of your database.

Normal and administrative database operations   Normal database operations can cause disk space requirements to increase. (Likewise, certain administrative controls can reduce this growth significantly.) Situations such as excessive index browning can boost disk usage, as can the effects of direct data loads on table high-water marks. Creation of indexes, and operations that require large sorts can require substantial disk space to be allocated. These may be perfectly normal operations, but oftentimes they are symptomatic of poor design.

So, How Much Space Do I Need?

Figuring out exactly how much disk space you'll need to allocate to your database is often an inexact science. Let's take it segment at a time.

The basic system will require a SYSTEM tablespace (see Chapter 6). Generally you can plan on 100GB for a base install, and upwards of 300GB for a complete install with all of the optional products such as Intermedia, Java, Spatial, and so on.

The data itself typically takes up the bulk of the space required in the database. We have seen a number of formulas that purport to calculate the correct space requirement for a given object in the database. The principal problem with these formulas is that many objects contain datatypes of different sizes, so space estimates can vary widely. Also, you'll be putting a diverse collection of objects in your database: tables, indexes, clusters, partitioned objects, object tables, and so on. Each of these has some overhead associated with its use, in addition to the space needed for storing its records.

Instead of complicated and inaccurate formulas, we suggest an alternative method for sizing your production database: Create a test database first, and guess at what's needed for the tablespaces. (If you guess wrong, you can always add space and redo the calculation.) Create the test database and each object in the database. The initial size of each table (INITIAL or NEXT) really doesn't matter. Next, from the data that will be loaded into the production database, select and load a representative sample into the test database. *Representative* is the key word here. In determining your sample, consider what your data will normally look like. If you anticipate a mix of long and short rows, make sure your sample includes this kind of data. When your tables are loaded with the representative data, create the indexes. Now you can determine the amount of space required to store the data you have just loaded. Then use this amount to calculate for a full-sized database.

NOTE If you do prefer to size your database using formulas, you'll find plenty of help in the *Oracle8i Administrators Guide*. There, Chapter 13 contains formulas for sizing tables, and Chapter 14 has them for index sizing. Also note that there is a sizing spreadsheet on the CD that comes with this book that you can use to size your database tables if you like. It's in the file Sizers.zip. Thanks to Mike Ault and TUSC for allowing me to include this spreadsheet in this book!

Let's look at an example. Say we've created a sample database with a tablespace called DATA, and INDEX for our indexes. We load the database with what we think is a 10 percent sample of representative data. Thus, we are creating a test database at 10 percent of the size of the real production database. We then calculate the sizes of the tables and indexes in this database by analyzing these objects and calculating the overall size of the data within them from the result of the ANALYZE operation. (See Chapter 7 for more on the ANALYZE command.)

So we analyze a table called MY_DATA. We then query the DBA_TABLES view. We find that MY_DATA contains 100 rows (from the NUM_ROWS column of DBA_TABLES), and the average row length (from the AVG_ROW_LEN column) is 120 bytes. We can then calculate the total size of the data in the object as 100 rows × 120 bytes, or a total of 12,000 bytes (12KB). From this number, we extrapolate that the overall table size will be about 120KB (the 12KB size of our 10 percent test table multiplied by 10). Finally, we like to include about 20 percent for growth, so we multiply the 120KB × 1.20 and get a final figure of about 144KB.

These same calculations can be applied to all the objects in the test database. Do the analysis on indexes, object tables, and so on, and add up all the numbers for each object in each tablespace. You will then find that you have a good guesstimate for the size of the tablespaces in which those objects will reside. And do consider throwing in the additional growth percentage of 20 percent, particularly for production systems. Nothing is worse than having to rescue a production system that's running out of space.

After you've figured out the space needed for user-type tablespaces, you'll need to plan for the space needed by the TEMPORARY and rollback segment tablespaces. The requirements for these tablespaces depend on a number of factors, including these:

- The number of concurrent users on the system
- The size and type of the average transactions on the system
- The numbers of sorts to disk vs. memory that will occur on the system

The subject of configuring rollback segments is thoroughly covered in Chapter 6. Moving on to the TEMPORARY tablespace, sizing that one is always a hit-or-miss proposition. Generally we begin by taking the size of our two largest tables and multiplying them by 20 percent of the expected number of concurrent transactions.

NOTE Once you have created the TEMPORARY tablespace, monitor its use constantly so that you're not wasting space that isn't being used. Conversely, if transactions are constantly failing because you've allocated too little space, then it's time to reanalyze the database and see if there's a spot where you need to create an index. Most sorts to disk (and thus most uses of the TEMPORARY tablespace) take place because Oracle can't find an index to use and so can't avoid the sort. You can often reduce reliance on the TEMPORARY tablespace by the simple addition of an index.

Armed with all your accurate tablespace estimates, you'll be ready to create tablespaces as described in Chapter 6. You need the sizing figures now because you may need to order disks, which can take time and money. Also, it's possible that your estimates and projected costs will lead to management's reassessment of the design or scope of the project. Furthermore, your DBA planning duties will require this sizing information, as well. Will your backup strategy accommodate a database of the size that you are planning? Will your hardware accommodate such a database?

Finally, one more important point to keep in mind is the fluidity of systems development. Often what developers think will be representative data falls short of what is eventually the real data. This can happen because business rules change during the development of the system, and perhaps these changes were not communicated to the DBA. It may be that the data itself changes in ways that made it inherently larger. It's important to stay in touch with the ongoing development process so that you don't get handed a nasty surprise.

Disk Configuration

Earlier in this chapter, we promised you some suggested disk placement configurations for achieving optimal I/O for your database. As you read this section, keep in mind that the goal here is to distribute I/O as evenly as possible among the available disks. Thus, you should consider the nature of your database. Will it be a read-intensive or write-intensive system? Are there some tables and indexes that are likely to be hot spots, getting large chunks of I/O requests?

Our configuration recommendations are just that: recommendations. After your database is actually in production, it's important to monitor its performance (Chapters 15, 16, and 17 will help you with this). You may find that you need to move a file here or there to get optimal I/O distribution. You may also, inevitably, have to add some additional disks to get the performance you need. Budget dollars will nearly always be available for adding disks when you can prove it's the solution to proper I/O distribution. Adding disks does decrease the MTBF (Mean Time Between Failure) of a database. However, the benefits of additional disks far outweigh the slight overall time between failures. Having more disks actually protects your database and reduces its MTTR (Mean Time To Recover) in most cases.

Physical Disk Configurations

When determining physical disk configurations you should consider the different disk technologies available to you. One of the most commonly used technologies is the use of a RAID (Redundant Array of Inexpensive Disks) technology. RAID comes with some negative and positive attributes. For example, when using one of the RAID technologies that includes disk striping, it is more difficult to know exactly where your datafiles are really being stored. Nevertheless, RAID setups offer substantial benefits, depending on the RAID level you decide to implement. Disk striping can be managed by the operating system. And several RAID levels allow data recovery without bringing the system down.

RAID configurations come in several flavors; here are descriptions of the most common:

RAID Level	Relative Cost	Description
RAID 0	Cheapest	This level of RAID is data striping across many (3–8) disks. In most cases, this provides very good read and write performance. Unlike other RAID solutions, RAID 0 provides no data redundancy. Thus, with RAID 0, if you lose a disk, you will need to recover that disk from backup.

RAID 1	Very Expensive	This is disk mirroring, which means changes to your physical disks are asynchronously being mirrored to other disks. Should one disk fail in the RAID 1 configuration, its mirror can be used to allow for uninterrupted operations. RAID 1 may be implemented through hardware or, less commonly, software.
RAID 0+1	Most Expensive	This is a combination of RAID 0 and RAID 1. It provides the performance benefits of striping across multiple drives plus recoverability of disks via disk mirroring. RAID 0+1 and RAID 5 are two of the most common disk configurations in use today. RAID 0+1 is the most secure RAID level you can use. Because it requires many disks (a minimum of twice the disk space you would otherwise need), it is also expensive.
RAID 5	Moderate Expense	This is disk striping as implemented in RAID 0, plus implementation of a parity bit that can be used to recover from the failure of a single disk in the RAID array. With most RAID 5 implementations, you can lose one drive and not experience any type of system outage because the data can be recovered by reading the striped parity bits on the undamaged disks. In most RAID 5 hardware, you can continue to use the disk array while the failed disk is being replaced and rebuilt using the parity bits present on the other disks in the array. During this time, you will probably experience some performance loss.

Typically for development and test systems, where data protection is not critical, RAID 5 is the recommended solution. It is a good compromise between the expensive RAID 0+1 and RAID nothing. For a production system, RAID 0 and RAID 0+1 are the best choices, depending on how much control you want over the placement of your datafiles. If the disk subsystem allowed, for critical systems where performance is paramount, we would probably opt for RAID 0+1. However, RAID 5 is less expensive, and in many cases may be preferable.

Often you have little control over the physical placement of data on a given disk system. In this case, the important thing is to stripe the data over as many disks and controllers as you can. If possible, always stripe horizontally rather than vertically. To stripe horizontally means that you take a set of disks (say 10) and you write your striped data across all 10 disks. With a vertical striping scheme, you will write to all 10 disks, but you might only be striping across 3–5 of them at any given time. Thus, you will fill up the first 3–5 disks first, before you ever start writing to the last 5 disks. Vertically striping data can make significant performance improvements to your database. You will find that it betters the performance of almost any operation because you have as many disk heads as possible working on the operation. See Figure 3.1.

FIGURE 3.1

Vertical vs. horizontal striping

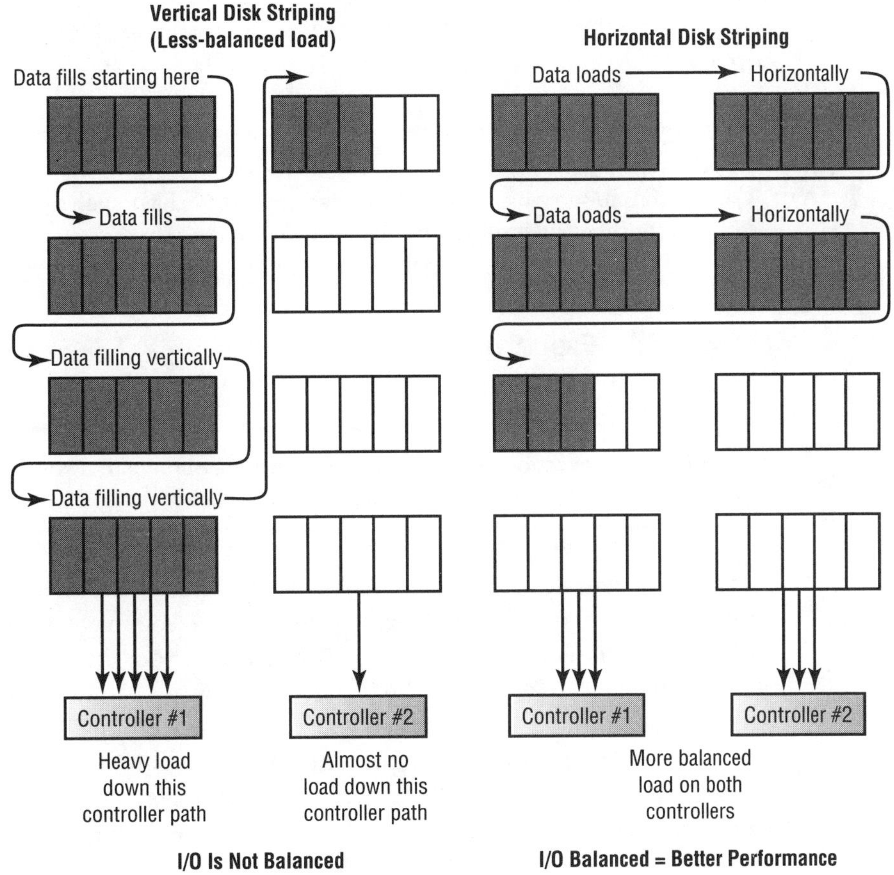

Vertical Disk Striping (Less-balanced load)

Data fills starting here

Data fills

Data filling vertically

Data filling vertically

Controller #1 — Heavy load down this controller path

Controller #2 — Almost no load down this controller path

I/O Is Not Balanced

Horizontal Disk Striping

Data loads → Horizontally

Data loads → Horizontally

Controller #1

Controller #2

More balanced load on both controllers

I/O Balanced = Better Performance

There are other solutions for your database physical configuration. For permanent storage (such as read-only tablespaces) you might consider rewritable CD-ROMs or even WORM drives. For critical-performance systems, consider some form of RAM disk (although RAM disks can add all sorts of administrative problems to system management, particularly in terms of lack of persistence of the memory!). Network appliances, too, are available. These solutions have the benefit of generally costing less than RAID arrays, but at the expense of the recoverability and uptime.

A word about speed: You want the fastest disks possible (or, as we like to say, the best of the feeds and the speeds). The faster the disk spins, the better your database will perform. Disks communicate at various speeds, too; generally, the faster the communications rate, the better the overall performance. Also, disks these days often have memory caches that buffer the disk writes, as well as buffering the most commonly used blocks on the disk. This further improves disk accesses for information. Therefore get as much memory on the disk as you can, and make sure it is configured correctly.

TIP When using RAID 0 or RAID 1 disk striping, make sure you test the various stripe size options to see which performs the best for you. We have seen significant performance gains from changing just this one element.

Oracle File Placement

NOTE In this section on file placement, we are assuming that you are not using some form of disk striping. File placement has less significance in configurations using disk striping.

As discussed in the section on OFA, proper placement of Oracle database datafiles is critical to the performance of any Oracle database. You may have occasion to work with several different combinations of disk configurations, but you will see that the common theme is to distribute the I/O as efficiently as possible. If you are working with a limited number of disks, then your task is to determine which will be the most active objects and separate them from the others. You might also need to consider when those objects will actually be active. For example, it is logical to assume that if you have a very active index tablespace, the temporary tablespace will be less active. This occurs because index usage leads to less of the sorting that occurs in the temporary tablespace. For a limited disk situation, then it would probably be acceptable to put index tablespaces and temporary tablespaces on the same disk.

Another example would be in the case of data tablespaces and index tablespaces. Since these tablespaces typically are accessed at the same time, it would be wise to separate these if at all possible onto separate disks. We do precisely that in the two-disk configuration below. Let's look at some example configurations for two-, five-, and seven-disk systems.

Two-Disk Configuration

Following is a two-disk configuration for Oracle—the bare bones, "I hope your users like long query response times" solution. Nevertheless, it can be adequate for a small development database or a very small budget. Even with just two disks, you can try to spread out I/O as evenly as possible.

Disk 1	Disk 2
The operating system	Datafiles for Oracle tablespaces that contain indexes
The Oracle RDBMS software and administrative files	Datafiles for Oracle tablespaces that contain rollback segments
Datafiles for the SYSTEM tablespace	Datafiles for Oracle temporary tablespaces
Datafiles for Oracle tablespaces that contain data	The second members of each of three online redo log groups
The first members of each of three online redo log groups	One copy of the current control files
One copy of the current control files	
Oracle database backup files	
Oracle database export files	
Archived redo logs	
The first members from each of three online redo log groups.	

NOTE If your database will be doing many full-table scans instead of index lookups, consider moving the index tablespaces to Disk 1. You might also isolate the tables on which you'll be doing the most full-table scans into their own tablespaces. Then you could stripe that tablespace's datafiles onto both Disk 1 and Disk 2, and gain some full-table scan performance benefits. This same idea applies if you will be doing mostly index lookups. You might well benefit from striping index tablespaces onto both disks.

Five-Disk Configuration

A five-disk configuration is getting better because you can spread out the I/O quite a bit more. But you'll need still more disk capability to make it optimal.

Disk 1	Disk 2	Disk 3	Disk 4	Disk 5
Operating system	Datafiles for Oracle tablespaces that contain data	Datafiles for Oracle tablespaces that contain indexes	Archived redo logs	Datafiles for the SYSTEM tablespace
Oracle RDBMS software and administrative files	The second members from each of three online redo log groups	The third members from each of three online redo log groups	Datafiles for Oracle tablespaces that contain rollback segments	Oracle database backup files
	One copy of the current control file	One copy of the current control file	Oracle temporary tablespaces	Oracle database export files
				The first members from each of three online redo log groups
				One copy of the current control files

Seven-Disk Configuration

A seven-disk setup is almost the ideal. You have nearly enough disks to separate all the Oracle file types onto their own disk.

Disk 1	Disk 2	Disk 3	Disk 4	Disk 5	Disk 6	Disk 7
The operating system	Datafiles for Oracle tablespaces that contain data	Datafiles for Oracle tablespaces that contain indexes	Datafiles for Oracle tablespaces that contain rollback segments	Datafiles for the SYSTEM tablespace	Archived redo logs	Oracle database backup files
The Oracle RDBMS software and administrative files				Datafiles for Oracle temporary tablespaces	The second members from each of three online redo log groups	Oracle database export files
				The first members from each of three online redo log groups	One copy of the current control files	The third members from each of three online redo log groups
				One copy of the current control files		One copy of the current control files

Protecting Against a Single Point of Failure

In deciding on placement of Oracle files, *single points of failure* are to be avoided at all costs. With Oracle (and assuming your backup and recovery process is working), the two most critical points of failure to be considered are the online redo logs and the Oracle control file.

There are many compelling reasons to ensure that the online redo logs are distributed onto separate disks and if at all possible, separate controllers. Probably the biggest reason is to protect your database from the loss of all members of a given online redo log group, which can cause an absolutely unrecoverable loss of data. Another reason to distribute your redo logs is for performance, as distributing the I/O to those log files can make a big difference in the time it takes Oracle to write to them.

Typically, you will have one member of every group on one disk, with the second members of those groups on a second disk. Even better is a third set of members on a third disk. Oracle writes to each member of the online redo logs synchronously. Because of this, performance is not significantly impacted by the addition of additional members. Because of potential problems it's best to avoid putting these redo log files on networked drives such as NFS drives. These problems can include loss of network connections and the fact that some network protocols (such as older NFS protocols) do not provide packet checking for corrupted packets. Newer networking protocols (NFS 3 for example) and better, more redundant hardware configurations may serve to reduce this concern.

Another critical single point of failure is the Oracle control file. As it does for the online redo logs, Oracle provides a facility to mirror the control file, and you should take advantage of this feature. Again, keep two copies at a minimum, and keeping three copies is best.

NOTE In Chapter 10 you'll see how to prepare for the loss of the control file and/or the online redo logs.

What about other single points of failure? Your best defense is to employ a sound backup and recovery strategy as discussed in Chapters 10 and 11. The bottom line is that planning your database must include plans for multiple copies of the control file and the online redo logs. That means allocating additional disk space when needed, as well as purchasing additional drives and/or controllers.

Sizing Database Files

One of the most common questions asked by DBAs is about how to decide on the size of various files associated with databases. Part of this task is covered here, where we look at the sizing of online redo logs (or just redo logs), the SYSTEM tablespace, and capacity planning for the control file. Additional matters of file-size planning include the rollback segments and rollback segment tablespaces, and Oracle database objects such as tables and indexes, which will directly affect the sizing of those tablespaces.

Sizing the Redo Logs

Oracle requires a minimum of two redo log groups for each database. We recommend you create a minimum of three, and preferably four. Oracle allows you to mirror each redo log file, creating multiple members for each group. Each member is a mirror of the other members of that redo log file group. Thus, if a redo log file group contains two members, they are mirrored copies of each other. Always create at least two mirrored copies of each redo log file, and put them on different disks and different controllers. This serves to protect the logs, which are critical to recovering your Oracle database in case of a failure.

Figure 3.2 illustrates an example of the placement of three redo log groups, each with two members, on two disks.

FIGURE 3.2

Mirroring and distribution of redo log groups

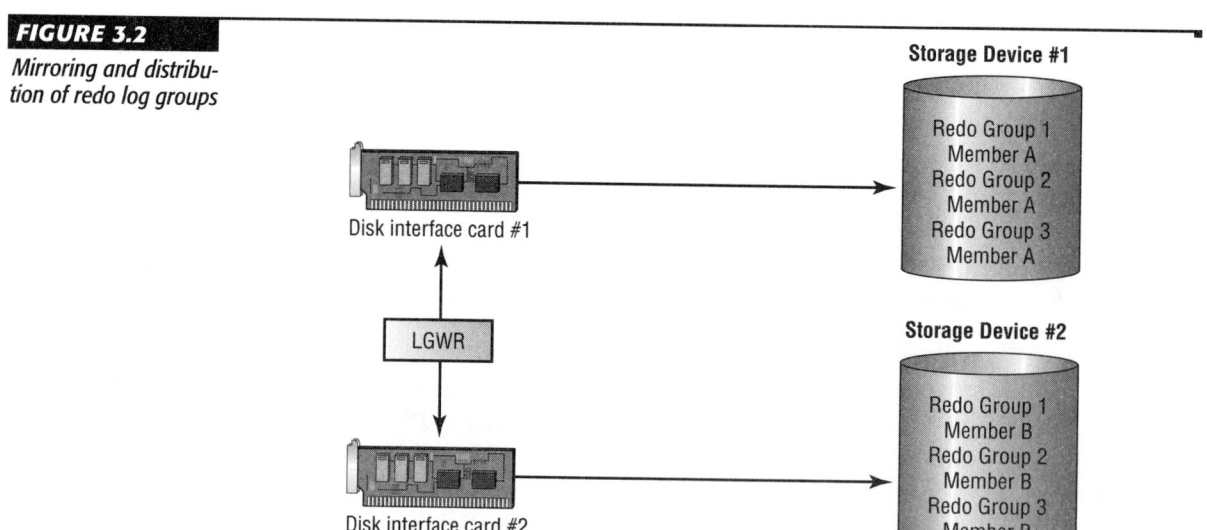

Initially, redo logs for a database are defined and sized when you execute the CREATE DATABASE command. Later in the life of a given database, you can also opt to create new redo logs of differing sizes and even remove old redo logs.

Typically, when sizing redo logs, you want log switches to occur every 10 to 20 minutes. Therefore, the best size for the redo logs is based on how often log switches are occurring on an active database. Table 3.1 provides suggested beginning sizes for redo logs, in several different databases.

TABLE 3.1: SUGGESTED SIZES OF ORACLE REDO LOGS

Database Size	Suggested Starting Redo Log Sizes for High / Medium / Low Database DML Activity
Small (up to 50mMB)	10MB/5MB/1MB
Medium (50m to 100 MB)	100MB/50MB/10MB
Large (100m to 250 MB)	1G/500MB/100MB
Huge (250MB to 1TB)	5G/1G/500MB
MegaDatabase (1TB+)	20G/5G/1G

Once your database is up and running, you'll monitor the alert log and determine how often the database is switching log files. If this is happening more often than once every 15 minutes, it's probably a good idea to re-create the online redo logs, making them larger. To figure out how much larger they need to be, extrapolate from the current size based on the number of log switches that occur. For example, if you have 500MB redo logs, and log switches occur every 5 minutes, then you should probably re-create them as 1.5GB files.

You can re-create the online redo log files while the database is still online. When you do, keep the following rules in mind:

- You must always have at least two redo log files available for the database to use.
- The current online redo log cannot be dropped.

The process is fairly simple:

1. Make sure that the redo logs you wish to re-create are not the current online redo logs, by looking at the STATUS column of the V$LOG data dictionary view.
2. Remove each redo log (each member of each group, one at a time) by using the ALTER DATABASE DROP LOGFILE command.

3. Once the redo log group is dropped, remove the physical redo log files on the database. Be very careful that you don't end up removing the wrong redo log files!

4. Re-create that group with the ALTER DATABASE ADD LOGFILE command, using the revised size parameter.

Listing 3.1 provides an example of replacing an existing redo log group with a new redo log group on an NT system.

Listing 3.1: Replacing a Redo Log Group

```
-- Make sure the redo log to be dropped is not the current log
SELECT group#, bytes, status FROM v$log;
    GROUP#      BYTES STATUS
---------- ---------- ----------------
         1    1048576 INACTIVE
         2    1048576 CURRENT
         3    1048576 INACTIVE
-- And where are the current logfile members?
SELECT * FROM v$logfile;
    GROUP# STATUS  MEMBER
---------- ------- ----------------------------------------
         1         D:\ORACLE\ORADATA\ORA816\REDO01.LOG
         2         D:\ORACLE\ORADATA\ORA816\REDO02.LOG
         3         D:\ORACLE\ORADATA\ORA816\REDO03.LOG
-- Let's re-create group 1 (since it's not active).
-- First, drop the existing group.
ALTER DATABASE DROP LOGFILE GROUP 1;
-- Note, since we are making the log file bigger, we will
-- need to drop the original.
Host del D:\ORACLE\ORADATA\ORA816\REDO01.LOG
-- Now, re-create logfile group 1 as 2MB logfile. Note that
-- group 1 originally only had one member, we will add
-- a second member to it as well.
ALTER DATABASE ADD LOGFILE GROUP 1 ('d:\oracle\oradata\ora816\redo01a.log',
    'e:\oracle\oradata\ora816\redo01b.log')
    SIZE 2M;
```

 NOTE When creating redo logs, you should consider configuration of the incremental checkpoint process. This is covered in detail in Chapter 5.

Sizing the SYSTEM Tablespace

The size of the SYSTEM tablespace includes a few variables that need to be taken into account:

- The primary consideration is the amount of PL/SQL that will be stored in the database.
- Account for the Oracle options that you will be implementing (for example, Oracle Spatial).
- To a lesser extent, consider the overall size of the database.

 TIP In calculating the SYSTEM tablespace, be sure to include a generous fudge factor. This is one tablespace you don't want filling up. See Chapter 6.

For the typical bare-bones Oracle database and a normal number of PL/SQL objects, we suggest you begin with the SYSTEM tablespace at 100MB. Each option that you add to Oracle (Spatial, Time Series, SQL J, Java, etc.) calls for an increase as recommended by Oracle in the documentation for that product. SYSTEM tablespaces sized at 250MB are not uncommon, and 500MB and larger is not unheard of.

Capacity Planning for Control Files

Although you do not size control files directly, you do need to plan for their placement. (And you *can* influence their size somewhat, as discussed in Chapter 13.) Expect to create at least two and preferably three control files, anywhere from 2 to 4MB in size and possibly larger. Make sure that you put each copy of the control file on a different disk, and on different controllers, if possible, for recovery purposes.

Determining Memory Requirements

Oracle requires memory, and a lot of it. In brief we will discuss configuring system memory for use by Oracle, and then we will tackle the topic of configuring Oracle memory structures. In this section, we will provide some suggested settings to start out with. Note that these are just suggestions and are in no way meant to be anything more than that. You should always monitor your databases to make sure you are getting the most out of your system.

System Memory

Before you start an Oracle database, you should ensure that you have enough memory on the system to support it. The Oracle Installation Guides include information on how much total memory you will need for all the products you wish to install.

Also, since the Oracle SGA requires shared memory, some systems (particularly Unix) will require that you configure that memory before it can be used. Again, the platform-specific Installation Guides are your source for operating system modifications that must be made before you can run Oracle.

Oracle Memory Structures

You need to consider the memory requirements of several Oracle structures, including

- The SGA
- Oracle processes
- User processes
- Other Oracle memory needs

Most of the memory requirements for the Oracle processes and user processes are platform specific. Refer to the Oracle platform-specific documentation for details about process memory requirements beyond those of the SGA. We will review configuration of the SGA later in this chapter.

A note to Unix folks: For Unix platforms you must configure shared memory for use at the OS level. This must be done before you can even start an Oracle instance, because Oracle depends on the use of shared memory with regard to SGA, which is allocated at instance startup. The requirements for each platform are different, so get further instructions from the OS-specific documentation for your version of Oracle.

TIP There is a good document that discusses Oracle best practices in a Sun environment (although a fair portion of this document can be expanded to include many different Unix flavors). It is called "Sun/Oracle Best Practices," authored by Bob Sneed of Sun's SMI Performance and Availability Engineering Group. You can find it at www.sun.com/blueprints. The part number is 806-6198-10.

Determining the Database Block Size

We're about to dive into what is sometimes called one of the Oracle Holy Wars: choosing the database block size. It is said that more paper wads have been lobbed over cubicle walls because of this argument than for any other in Oracle technology (with the exception, perhaps, of the Mountain Dew vs. coffee arguments, which we steer clear of). Juvenile behavior aside, it is critically important that you carefully choose the correct block size for your database, *before* you create it. Once the database is created, you can't change the block size without essentially rebuilding the database, which presents enormous difficulties especially for a mission-critical database.

Prior to Oracle 7.3, setting the block size also determined certain database restrictions, the primary one being a restriction on the number of extents a segment could consist of. These restrictions have been removed since Oracle 7.3. Oracle block sizes can range anywhere from 2K to upwards of 32K. When you are choosing a data block size, you need to consider both its benefits and detriments, as well as the operating system you are using.

Factors to Consider

For Online Transaction Processing (OLTP) systems, smaller block sizes are usually better. These systems typically are looking for random data, usually via indexed lookups. Smaller blocks translate into fewer rows per block, so you'll do fewer overall I/O operations to get the same row than you would with a larger block. For example, consider an index lookup of a single row. In any event, the number of logical I/Os will generally be the same (2–3 for the index, 1 for the block). The total bytes read to complete those I/Os, however, will be significantly less if you are using smaller block sizes. With a 2KB block database, Oracle needs to read only 6–8KB to get the data you need. With an 8KB-block database, Oracle would need to read 32KB to get the same information. Additionally, with smaller row sizes you won't be filling the SGA with nonessential rows, because fewer rows per block are read into the database.

If you are using systems that do sequential reads, such as data warehouses or Executive Information Systems (EIS), then you want to read in as much data in a single I/O as possible. This is because you typically want to read all the rows in the block. Thus larger block sizes are usually preferred in such environments. Warehouse databases with 16K and even 32K blocks are not unusual. Random, index-based queries, on the other hand, will suffer greatly with larger block sizes as Oracle moves data in and out of the database buffer cache more frequently and in higher volume. This can also lead to increased contention for data blocks, as well as to database writer (DBWR) performance problems.

As companies discover the power of the data in their systems, more and more databases these days are hybrids, a mix of OLTP and warehouse or EIS systems. Thus, it becomes more of a challenge to decide on a database block size.

It used to be that DBAs typically used smaller block sizes for their databases. The most commonly used block sizes were 2KB and 4KB. An 8KB block size was rare, and 16KB was very uncommon. For an OLTP database these days, an 8KB block size tends to perform best. For a data warehousing or EIS system, if you are expecting a mix of index lookups and full table scans, try 16KB blocks. If you are expecting mostly full table scans, consider 32KB blocks.

When setting the database block size, you also want to make sure that the block size times the DB_FILE_MULTIBLOCK_READ_COUNT is a multiple of the operating system I/O block read size. For example, on most Unix operating systems and NT, one I/O will consist of a 512KB block read from disk. Thus, if you have your Oracle block size set to 8KB, you should set this parameter to 64 (it defaults to 8), which will indicate to Oracle that a multiblock read of 64 Oracle blocks should be performed with each I/O. As a result, there is no I/O wastage.

Thus, the DB_FILE_MULTIBLOCK_READ_COUNT parameter has the effect of controlling how many blocks Oracle will read in a single I/O when doing a full table scan. The effects of setting this parameter are that full table scans will perform more efficiently. Higher values for this parameter can also cause the optimizer to consider full table scans (or index fast full scans, which use multiblock I/O as well) over other access paths.

As always, it's a good idea to set up a test and development environment before you create the production system. This is particularly true with the block size, because to reset the block size you must re-create the database—not a pleasant prospect if yours is terabyte-size!

There are other issues to consider. The default I/O block size of your operating system and your file system can have performance impacts. Also, other types of access control mechanisms, such as inodes in Unix, will have impact. In extreme situations, Unix inodes can cause access conflicts. These problems are less prevalent with the advanced technologies and disk caches in use today.

 TIP Beyond all the logical considerations, a test will give you the best input for choosing a block size. Create a database of a given block size and perform a test script on it that will simulate the expected load. Then re-create the database using a different block size and test it again. If you don't have time to test your system like this, we suggest 16K as a good place to start if you have enough memory to allocate sufficient blocks to the database buffer cache.

Table 3.2 summarizes all the things to consider in determining block size.

TABLE 3.2: BENEFITS AND DETRIMENTS OF VARIOUS BLOCK SIZES

Block Size	Benefits	Detriments	Comment
Small (2–4K)	Less contention for blocks, better random accesses.	High overhead for Oracle. Sequential access is generally slower.	Probably best for OLTP systems
Medium (8K)	Less block contention than with larger block sizes; good random access performance. Sequential access is moderately good. Overhead to the Oracle server is moderate.	Performance for OLTP may be better with small blocks. Performance in warehouses and EIS systems may be better with large blocks.	Probably best for hybrid systems
Large (16K)	Improved performance of sequential access. Less overall overhead cost.	Random access performance is degraded. Potential for block contention increases.	Good for data warehouse with some random access transactions
Humongo (32K)	Probably the best performance for sequential access. Least overhead costs.	Random access performance is seriously degraded. Block contention can be significant.	Probably best for pure data warehouse or EIS systems

Naming Conventions

At this point in the game, it's a good time to solidify some naming standards. In addition to database names, you'll want conventions for your physical database filenames. By enforcing solid standards as your database grows and as you add additional databases, you increase the quality and dependability of your system's information. Of course, OFA already provides some standards, but there are some other best practices to follow.

Deciding the Database Name

The name of a database is also known as the database System Identifier or SID. Each and every database name on a server must be unique.

Database names are best kept to eight characters or less (in fact, this is still a requirement on a few platforms). Database names can be in upper-, lower-, or mixed case. On some platforms, such as NT, Oracle does not make a case distinction. On other platforms, such as Unix, Oracle does distinguish between an instance called test and one called TEST. (We prefer all lowercase names for instances.)

It's usually smart to make the name of the database represent the database content. For an accounting database, you might start the name with acct, or perhaps fin. We suggest adding a tail to the name based on the type of database. A test system for accounting, for example, might be named accttest. For a production system, it might be acctprod, and a development system would be acctdevl. Database names like Thor, test, prod, or gonzo don't mean much of anything and can become really confusing in a large database environment.

Table 3.3 lists some suggested trailing identifiers for various kinds of databases, with examples for an HR database.

TABLE 3.3: DATABASE IDENTIFIERS

Database Type	Suggested Trailing Identifier	Example
Production	prod or p	hrprod or hrp
Test	test or t	hrtest or hrt
Development	devl or d	hrdevl or hrd
User Acceptance Testing	uact or u	hruact or hru
Unit Testing	utst or n	hrust or hrn
System Testing	stst or s	hrstst or hrs
Reporting	rpt or r	hrrpt or hrr

Naming Database Objects

Besides the name of the database itself, you'll need to identify naming standards for a variety of physical objects, including

- Database datafiles
- Control files

- Redo logs
- Directory naming standards

Table 3.4 provides some suggested naming standards along with examples.

TABLE 3.4: OBJECT NAMING STANDARDS

Object Type	Standard	Examples in Database Mydb
Database datafiles	Include the database name, the tablespace name, and a number to make the datafile unique for the tablespace. End with a .dbf extension.	For a tablespace named data: mydb_data_01.dbf
Control files	Include the database name, the word control, and a unique identifier for the file. End with a .ctl extension.	mydb_control_01.ctl
Redo logs	Include the name of the database, the word redo, a unique identifier for the redo log group, and a unique identifier for each member of that group. End with a .log extension.	For a redo log that is member 2 of group 3: mydb_redo_03b.log
Archived redo logs	Include the name of the database, the thread, and the sequence number of the archived redo log.	This would be set using the LOG_ARCHIVE_FORMAT parameter as %%ORACLE_SID%%%t%s.log

Creating the Parameter File (*init.ora*)

Your database parameter file contains many of the items discussed in this chapter—the database name, the SGA configuration, and much more.

 NOTE This section does not cover all database configuration issues. Matters such as MTS, parallelism, materialized views, and various recovery settings are discussed in other chapters.

The Oracle database parameter file is typically referred to as init.ora. The full naming standard is init<sid>.ora, where sid is the name of the database. Thus, for a database called brosep, the default name of the parameter file would be initbrosep.ora.

Location of *init.ora*

The default location for the parameter file is in the ORACLE_HOME\dbs directory (ORACLE_HOME\database in NT). Typically, however, you will create the parameter file in the ADMIN directory structure using the pfile directory.

- If your operating system supports file links, as Unix does, you will want to create a link in the ORACLE_HOME\dbs directory that points to the init.ora in pfile.
- If your operating system does not support links to files, then you will want to use the ifile parameter in a shell init.ora in the ORACLE_HOME\dbs directory (ORACLE_HOME\database in NT) directory and point the file to init.ora in the ADMIN directory structure. Thus, the init.ora in the default location only points to the true init.ora in the ADMIN directory.

TIP Rather than putting a link or a shell init.ora file in the ORACLE_HOME\dbs directory, you can just use the PFILE= option of the STARTUP command to point Oracle to the correct location of the parameter file.

TIP In Oracle8i for NT, you can actually modify a Registry entry and have it look for the parameter file in the ADMIN directory instead of the default location. To do this, change the key HKEY_LOCAL_MACHINE\SOFTWARE\Oracle\Home1 (or the appropriate Oracle Home). Then change the key ora_<sid>_pfile to point to the correct location of the init.ora file, and save the changes. Oracle will use the init.ora file at the new location the next time you start it.

You can, of course, call the init.ora file anything you want. You might want to start your database with an init.ora file other than the default one you have configured for that database. (For example, when creating or re-creating a database, you may want to comment out the ROLLBACK_SEGMENTS parameter.) In this case, when you use the STARTUP command to start the database, you will include the

PFILE parameter to define the location and name of the parameter file you want to use. Here's an example:

```
Startup pfile=c:\teststartup\initnorbs.ora
```

Following is an example of a database parameter file.

```
db_name = ora816
db_files = 1024
control_files = ("D:\Oracle\oradata\ora816\control01.ctl",
"D:\Oracle\oradata\ora816\control02.ctl",
"D:\Oracle\oradata\ora816\control03.ctl")
open_cursors = 100
max_enabled_roles = 30
db_file_multiblock_read_count = 8
db_block_buffers = 2048
shared_pool_size = 55428800
java_pool_size = 0
log_checkpoint_interval = 10000
log_checkpoint_timeout = 1800
processes = 50
parallel_max_servers = 5
log_buffer = 32768
#audit_trail = true   # if you want auditing
#timed_statistics = true   # if you want timed statistics
max_dump_file_size = 10240   # limit trace file size to 5M each
##### For archiving if archiving is enabled #####
log_archive_start = true
log_archive_dest_1 = "location=D:\Oracle\oradata\ora816\archive"
log_archive_format = %%ORACLE_SID%%T%TS%S.ARC
rollback_segments = ( RB01, RB02 )
# Global Naming -- enforce that a dblink has same name as the db it
                   connects to
global_names = true
# define directories to store trace and alert files
background_dump_dest = D:\Oracle\admin\ora816\bdump
user_dump_dest = D:\Oracle\admin\ora816\udump
db_block_size = 2048
compatible = 8.1.6
sort_area_size = 65536
sort_area_retained_size = 65536
```

Setting the Parameters

Setting `init.ora` parameters is kind of a hit-and-miss proposition. No matter what anyone tells you, there is no magic formula for doing it. Rules of thumb often apply, and certainly experience is a good guide. There are typically so many variables that fit into the mix, getting things to work just right becomes largely a matter of tuning. In the end, you need to monitor your database from its infancy, and make sure everything is set up to perform correctly.

When you find that you need to modify a parameter after the database is up and running, you may be able to do it dynamically for the entire system without needing to restart (or "bounce") the database. To find out whether a database parameter can be modified on-the-fly, with the database up, query the V$PARAMETER data dictionary view. This view includes two columns that indicate whether a listed parameter can be modified for a given session (ISSES_MODIFIABLE) or modified for the entire database (ISSYS_MODIFIABLE). Of course, many parameters cannot be modified dynamically at all.

If you find that the V$PARAMETER data dictionary view ISSES_MODIFIABLE column is set to TRUE, then you can modify the parameter for a given session with the ALTER SESSION command. If you find the ISSYS_MODIFIABLE column in V$PARAMETER is set to IMMEDIATE, then the setting can be changed for the entire database with an ALTER SYSTEM command and the change will take effect immediately. If the ISSYS_MODIFIABLE is reported as DEFERRED, then the setting can be changed, and will take effect, but only for new system logins; existing logins will not see the change. Finally, if either column is set to FALSE, then that parameter cannot be changed dynamically.

Chapter 5 contains a report for both normal parameters and hidden parameters. It also indicates the dynamic nature of these parameters.

To change parameters dynamically, use the ALTER SYSTEM and ALTER SESSION commands. An example is shown in Listing 3.2.

Listing 3.2: Changing Parameter Settings Dynamically

```
ALTER SYSTEM SET timed_statistics=TRUE;
System altered.
ALTER SESSION SET sort_area_size=100000;
Session altered.
```

Configuring the SGA

You learned in Chapter 1 that the System Global Area (SGA) contains the database buffer cache, the shared pool, and the redo log buffer. Here, we'll include two additional components in our discussion. They are not always directly associated with the SGA, but you need to know about them: the large pool and the Java pool.

In terms of preparing to create your database, your major concern is sizing—determining the optimum size for the buffers and pools in the SGA. That's what we are going to talk about next.

Sizing the Database Buffer Cache

The database buffer cache, as described in Chapter 1, is allocated in units of database blocks via the DB_BLOCK_BUFFERS parameter in the init.ora. You can calculate the total size of the database buffer cache by using the formula

DB_BLOCK_BUFFERS * DB_BLOCK_SIZE

Once you have determined the database block size, then you need to designate how many of those blocks you wish to allocate to the SGA's buffers and pools.

The sample database parameter file provided with Oracle8i contains suggested settings for the DB_BLOCK_BUFFERS parameter. These suggestions are probably not the best, however. Various Oracle experts have suggested benchmarks for setting the database buffer cache. We like to use from 3 percent to 10 percent of the total database size, depending on a number of factors including memory availability, type of database activity, and the expected volume of data changes. Of course, performance is always a concern when allocating memory to the buffer cache. A good figure to start out with is about 80MB for an average database (say, up to 1GB). After initially deciding on the size of your SGA, it's important to monitor closely the performance of your database. You may need less or more space, depending on the types of queries your database is performing.

Table 3.5 provides some suggestions based on the various database sizes.

TABLE 3.5: SUGGESTED SIZES FOR DATABASE BUFFER CACHE (DB_BLOCK_BUFFERS)

Database Size	Suggested Cache Size
500MB	50MB
1GB	80–100MB
10GB	200MB
20GB	400MB
100GB	600MB–1GB

Buffer pool caches larger than about 1.5GB seldom reap any real performance gains (though one of the themes of this book, we hope, is "never say never!"). So keep a close eye on your performance measurements if you allocate a particularly large database buffer cache. That memory may be better used elsewhere.

WARNING When you allocate memory to the SGA, be cautious that you don't induce disk paging or swapping on your system!

Setting Up the Buffer Pools

The database buffer cache, discussed just above, is the only one of Oracle's three data buffer cache pools for which memory must be allocated. Also out of that memory allocation can come memory for the optional recycle and keep buffer pools. These allocations are controlled with the init.ora parameters BUFFER_POOL_KEEP and BUFFER_POOL_RECYCLE.

Make sure you allocate enough default buffer pool memory to accommodate the two other buffer pools, if you choose to use them. Optionally, you can also assign a number of LRU latches to each buffer pool that's configured. Oracle requires a minimum of one LRU latch for every 50 buffers assigned to either the recycle or keep buffer pool, and will by default assign this ratio when allocating the two pools. Should latching become a problem, you can assign a larger number of LRU latches when configuring the buffer pool in the parameter file.

WARNING Be careful you don't allocate too many LRU latches to the buffer pools, or the database will not start. The total number of available LRU latches is controlled by the parameter DB_BLOCK_LRU_LATCHES, which defaults to 0.5 times the number of CPUs in your system (with a minimum of 1 LRU latch allocated). You may need to increase the DB_BLOCK_LRU_LATCHES parameter in order to use the multiple buffer pool feature of Oracle.

Following are examples of init.ora parameters for the buffer pools.
```
-- Assign a recycle buffer pool with default LRU list assignments
buffer_pool_recycle=100
-- Assign a keep buffer pool with 50 blocks and 2 LRU latches
buffer_pool_keep=("buffers:100", "lru_latches:5")
```

WARNING The documentation for some Oracle versions gives incorrect syntax for configuring multiple buffer pools. Note that in the BUFFER_POOL_KEEP setting just above, the single quotes are required.

Sizing the Shared Pool

The shared pool is sized with a single `init.ora` parameter, SHARED_POOL_SIZE. The value of this parameter is expressed in bytes, not blocks.

Specify the size of the shared pool in consideration of the following expectations:

- Overall size of the database
- Number of users in the database concurrently
- Number of concurrent transactions
- Amount of reusable SQL
- Number and size of PL/SQL objects and blocks
- Number of database objects
- Use of reusable SQL statements (see Chapters 15, 16, and 17 for more on this topic)
- Use of multithreaded servers (MTS) considering also allocation of the large pool, since some shared_pool structures can be created instead in the large pool.

The default size of the shared pool is 32MB, which is enough only for a database that does next to nothing. At a minimum, you should configure the shared pool at about 60MB. Shared pools bigger than a couple of hundred megabytes, in fact, are no longer unusual and may be upwards of 1GB and even larger with certain applications (though this can have performance implications).

WARNING Be careful of setting the shared pool too large (greater than about 300MB). This can have a detrimental effect on overall performance of your database (this is dependent on a number of factors). Likewise, a shared pool that is sized too small can have severe performance impacts as well. We generally recommend that a shared pool never be less than 60MB. Always monitor your database carefully after making any changes to memory. See Chapters 15 through 17 for more on this topic.

Sizing the Redo Log Buffer

The redo log buffer is sized via the LOG_BUFFER parameter and its default is platform specific. This buffer should be sized initially at about 512K.

Be very careful before you change the value of the redo log buffer. Some database performance problems may prompt you to try increasing the size. More often than not, this is a bad idea, because this can have an even more adverse impact on performance, as we will discuss in Chapter 17. Should performance-tuning issues dictate a change, you may want to increase the redo log buffer, but generally do not make the redo log buffer larger than 1MB at any time. In fact, frequently, the answer to performance tuning is decreasing the size of the redo log buffer.

Sizing the Large Pool

The large pool is an optional structure used for MTS session memory, I/O server processes, and RMAN. It is set by the parameter LARGE_POOL_SIZE, with a default size of 0. If we are using RMAN or MTS, we generally start by setting the large pool to about 20MB and then monitor its use afterward.

Sizing the Java Pool

The Java pool is an optional structure used by the Java memory manager (see Chapter 27). It is set by the parameter JAVA_POOL_SIZE and has a default size of 20MB. If you're going to use Java inside your Oracle database, you'll want to set this parameter accordingly. Otherwise, leave it at 0 to reduce memory overhead.

 WARNING A bug in Oracle 8.1.5.0 causes the database to not come up if you set JAVA_POOL_SIZE to 0. You'll need to set this parameter to about 1MB instead. The bug is fixed in later patch set fixes of Oracle 8.1.5, and in versions after 8.1.5, including 8.1.6 and 8.1.7.

Setting Up File Paths

Also in the database parameter file are directory locations for Oracle's use. You'll define the paths for such things as core dump files, user dump files, and other files generated by the database. Table 3.6 provides a complete list. Many of these parameters are discussed in more detail throughout this book.

TABLE 3.6: DIRECTORY PATH SETTINGS IN THE PARAMETER FILE

Parameter Name	Purpose	Default Value
AUDIT_FILE_DEST	Defines the location for database audit files.	Oracle_home\rdbms\audit
BACKGROUND_DUMP_DEST	Defines the location for the database alert log and for other background process trace files.	OS-specific
CORE_DUMP_DEST	Defines the location of database-related core files.	Oracle_home\dbs
LOG_ARCHIVE_DEST and LOG_ARCHIVE_DEST_N	Defines the location(s) to which Oracle will copy archived redo logs. The latter parameter is only supported by Oracle8i Enterprise Edition.	None
LOG_ARCHIVE_DUPLEX_DEST	This parameter, introduced in Oracle8, has been supplanted by LOG_ARCHIVE_DEST_N in Oracle8i Enterprise Edition. If you are not running Enterprise Edition, you must use this parameter instead.	None
ORACLE_TRACE_COLLECTION_PATH	Defines the directory path for the Oracle Trace collection definition, and data collection files associated with Oracle Trace.	OS-specific
ORACLE_TRACE_FACILITY_PATH	Defines directory path for Oracle Trace facility definition files	OS-specific
STANDBY_ARCHIVE_DEST	Only applies to stand-by databases. Defines the location of archived redo logs arriving from a primary database that will be processed by the stand-by database.	OS-specific
USER_DUMP_DEST	Directory location for user-generated trace files.	OS-specific
UTL_FILE_DIR	Directory location for operating system files generated by the Oracle package UTL_FILE. Repeat this parameter to add as many available paths as needed.	None

Other *init.ora* Configuration Issues

There are several other parameters you need to consider when setting up your database. These control everything from the number of datafiles you can have in your Oracle database to the location of control files, and a number of other database parameters.

Number of database files   Although the hard limit for the number of database datafiles is actually set by a parameter in the CREATE DATABASE statement, the DB_FILES parameter acts as a soft limit. If you try to add a datafile to the database and find you are unable to do so, you may find that this parameter is set artificially low.

Locations of control files   During database creation, the CONTROL_FILES parameter defines the number and location of control files. After the creation of the database, this parameter defines the location where the database will look for the control files.

Maximum number of open cursors   The Oracle database controls the total number of cursors that any given user session can open (see Chapter 16 for more on cursors). The parameter OPEN_CURSORS controls this limit. Often the default database value of 50 is not enough for even normal applications. We recommend that you set this value at 100 or 150 to begin with.

Maximum number of roles   The parameter MAX_ENABLED_ROLES controls the maximum number of roles that a user can enable. Often the default value of 20 is insufficient. We recommend setting this parameter initially to 50.

Maximum number of processes   PROCESSES defines the total number of operating system processes that can attach to the database. The default value is dependent on the value of the parameter PARALLEL_MAX_SERVERS, and may not be enough for larger databases. For most databases, we allow for at least three processes per expected concurrent user, plus 30 for system overhead. Thus, if you expect to have 10 concurrent users, you'd set processes to 60.

Maximum number of open cursors   Each SQL statement that is run on your database will require one or more cursors to operate. Since recursive SQL requires its own cursors, it's very possible that one query may require many cursors to be open simultaneously. Oracle controls the maximum number of open cursors in a given session, via the parameter OPEN_CURSORS. This parameter defaults to 50, which is rarely large enough. We suggest initially setting this parameter to 150 at first.

Size of dump files It may be that you will want to limit the size of trace files, core dumps, and so on. To allow you to control the size of these files, Oracle provides the MAX_DUMP_FILE_SIZE parameter. The default is to allow all dump files to be of unlimited length. Thus a single user could take up all the available disk space in your USER_DUMP_DEST directory if this parameter is not set. You can express this value in bytes, like this:

    USER_DUMP_DEST=1000

or in kilobytes or megabytes like this:

    USER_DUMP_DEST=1k
    USER_DUMP_DEST=1m

Initial setting of ROLLBACK_SEGMENTS parameter We will talk about setting up rollback segments later in this chapter. For now, during database creation, you should not set the ROLLBACK_SEGMENTS parameter at all. Until you have created your database rollback segments, there are no rollback segments to enable!

Other parameters The default values of most other database parameters should be sufficient to begin with. You'll be monitoring your new database closely at first, to make sure that you don't need to change such parameters as SORT_AREA_SIZE. Another example is the TIMED_STATISTICS parameter. This parameter allows you to derive timings on various database events including wait events and file I/O statistics. This parameter is disabled by default. Turning it on does entail additional overhead on the database, but this overhead seldom affects the overall performance of the database. Performance monitoring and tuning tips are covered in Chapters 15, 16, and 17.

ifiles The `ifile` parameter in a parameter file is like a "goto" command. It instructs the database to open and read the file contained in the command. Once that file has been executed, the original `init.ora` will be read. These ifiles are often employed in databases that use Oracle Parallel Server to define settings common to all instances. These ifiles can also be used to define specific types of database models (such as small, medium, and large database memory models).

TIP We are not crazy about using the `ifile` parameter. It sometimes makes things quite confusing. We recommend, instead, that each `init.ora` be unique to each database and that common parameters be grouped together. Thus, file definitions are grouped together, as are memory settings, network settings, and so on.

ARCHIVELOG mode parameters The database parameter file also contains LOG_ARCHIVE parameters that you'll set if your database will run in ARCHIVELOG mode. This mode allows you to do hot backups of your database. In general, however, you will probably want to go with NOARCHIVE log mode at first (which is the default setting when a database is first created with the CREATE DATABASE command). No archived redo logs will be created at this early stage, thus reducing the overall I/O load during database creation. If you created the database in ARCHIVELOG mode and then decide to disable it, follow these steps:

1. Mount but don't start the instance.
2. Issue the command `ALTER DATABASE NOARCHIVELOG;`.
3. Open the database in NOARCHIVELOG mode by issuing the SQL statement `ALTER DATABASE OPEN;`.
4. To put the database back into ARCHIVELOG mode, shut it down and mount it again. Issue the commands `ALTER DATABASE ARCHIVELOG;` and then `ALTER DATABASE OPEN;`.

Creating the Database

You've planned and calculated. You've sized and configured. It's time to really begin creating the database, and this section walks you through the process. We'll start with the work that must be done before you can issue the CREATE DATABASE statement (which actually creates the database). We'll study the CREATE DATABASE statement itself, including how we can change it to better suit individual purposes. Then we'll go through the steps of creating the database manually, followed by a discussion of the Database Configuration Assistant, Oracle's Wizard-like tool that helps you create databases. So, let's move on and get that database created!

Preparing to Create the Database

We are almost ready to actually create the database. This section gives you an overview of the CREATE DATABASE statement. We will also discuss modifications to SQL.BSQ, which is the file used by the CREATE DATABASE statement when creating the Oracle data dictionary. You can modify this file in order to reduce fragmentation of the SYSTEM tablespace. Finally, you'll see how to write a SQL script that contains all the required steps for database creation.

The CREATE DATABASE Statement

The CREATE DATABASE SQL statement is used to create the base database. Listing 3.3 is an example of the statement at work.

Listing 3.3: The CREATE DATABASE Statement

```
CREATE DATABASE ora816
LOGFILE 'D:\Oracle\oradata\ora816\redo01.log' SIZE 1024K,
        'D:\Oracle\oradata\ora816\redo02.log' SIZE 1024K,
        'D:\Oracle\oradata\ora816\redo03.log' SIZE 1024K
    MAXLOGFILES 32
    MAXLOGMEMBERS 4
    DATAFILE 'D:\Oracle\oradata\ora816\system01.dbf'
    SIZE 55M  REUSE AUTOEXTEND OFF
    MAXDATAFILES 128;
```

The CREATE DATABASE statement starts by defining the name of the database (ora816). Next, it defines the number, name, and size of the redo log groups. In Listing 3.3, we have defined three redo log groups. Following that are a couple of limits for the redo logs in the database: the maximum number of redo log groups that can be assigned to the database, and the number of members allowed per redo log group.

Next we define the datafile for the SYSTEM tablespace, including its size. Also, in this case we have disabled the Autoextend feature of the SYSTEM tablespace. The last line defines the maximum number of datafiles that can be added to the database. This is a hard limit; to change it requires rebuilding the control file.

 WARNING Carefully determine your MAXDATAFILES setting when creating your database. The only way to increase its value after the database has been created is to rebuild the control file.

You can see the CREATE DATABASE statement's complete syntax with all its parameters in Appendix F, or you can review the command in the Oracle SQL Reference Guide.

Modifying Data Dictionary Space Allocations

One of the primary actions of the CREATE DATABASE statement is to create the base Oracle data dictionary. This process is controlled through the execution of a script called `sql.bsq`, which is located in `oracle_home\rdbms\admin`.

You may wish to change the space allocations for the data dictionary objects in sql.bsq, and Oracle does support this action. The following storage attributes can be changed:

INITIAL	PCTINCREASE
NEXT	FREELISTS
MINEXTENTS	FREELIST GROUPS
MAXEXTENTS	OPTIMAL

Changing these settings can help to reduce unwanted fragmentation of the SYSTEM tablespace. Each database is different, of course, and various tables in a data dictionary are affected by what you do with your database, and what features you use the most. Table 3.7 lists the tables that often become very large and very fragmented, and whose storage settings you might need to change.

TIP If you would like your instance to run a script other than sql.bsq when you execute the CREATE DATABASE command, you can change the parameter _INIT_SQL_FILE in the init.ora to point to the location and name of the replacement file for sql.bsq. Note that this is a hidden and unsupported parameter, and thus you should use it with caution, as with all hidden and unsupported parameters.

TABLE 3.7: COMMON CHANGES TO TABLES IN SQL.BSQ

Object Name	Object Type	Suggested Change
ARGUMENT$	Table	Set INITIAL to about 10% of the value of INITIAL in the SOURCE$ table. Set NEXT to 20% of INITIAL.
AUD$	Table	It's wise to move this out of the SYSTEM tablespace altogether. Set INITIAL and NEXT based on the amount of auditing you expect to do.
C_OBJ$	Cluster	Set INITIAL to about 5MB. Set NEXT to about 1m.
DEPENDENCY$	Table	*Recommended*: Set INITIAL to 1MB, NEXT to 200KB.
EXT_TO_OBJ	Table	Set INITIAL to about 1MB, and NEXT to about 20% of INTIIAL.
I_ARGUMENT1	Index	Set INITIAL to about 20% of INITIAL of ARGUMENT. Set NEXT to about 20% of INITIAL.

Continued

CREATING THE DATABASE

TABLE 3.7: COMMON CHANGES TO TABLES IN SQL.BSQ (CONTINUED)

Object Name	Object Type	Suggested Change
I_AUD1	Index	Consider moving out of SYSTEM tablespace altogether. Set INITIAL to about 10% of AUD$ INITIAL value, and NEXT to about 20% of INTIIAL.
I_COL1	Index	*Recommended*: Set INITIAL to 1MB, NEXT to 200KB.
I_DEPENDENCY	Index	*Recommended*: Set INITIAL to 1MB, NEXT to 200KB.
I_DEPENDENCY2	Index	*Recommended*: Set INITIAL to 1MB, NEXT to 200KB.
I_SOURCE1	Index	Set INITIAL to about 50% of the INITIAL setting on SOURCE$. Set NEXT to about 50% of the INITIAL setting on SOURCE$.
IDL_CHAR$	Table	Set INITIAL to about 1MB, and NEXT to about 20% of INTIIAL.
IDL_SB4$	Table	Set INITIAL to about 2MB. Set NEXT to about 20% of INITIAL.
IDL_UB1$	Table	Set INITIAL to about 10MB. Set NEXT to 20% of INITIAL.
IDL_UB2$	Table	Set INITIAL to about 10MB. Set NEXT to 20% of INITIAL.
OBJ$	Table	*Recommended*: Set INITIAL to 1MB, and NEXT to 200KB.
SOURCE$	Table	If you will be using substantial PL/SQL, increase the NEXT and INITIAL sizes of this table. Also set PCTINCREASE to 0. *Suggested sizing*: 500KB to 5MB, depending on how much PL/SQL you will be using.
TRIGGER$	Table	Depends on the number and size of triggers in the system. *Recommended*: start with INITIAL set to about 1MB. Set NEXT to about 20% of INITIAL.
VIEW$	Table	Depends on the number of views in the database. *Recommended*: start with INITIAL set to about 1MB. Set NEXT to about 20%.

Using ORADIM in NT

Before you can create an Oracle database on an NT system, you must first use the ORADIM command to create an Oracle service. ORADIM is also used to modify an existing service or to remove a service. In the following example of using ORADIM to create an Oracle8i database service, the database is called MYDB:

```
ORADIM -NEW -SID MYDB -INTPWD PASSWORD -MAXUSERS 10 -STARTMODE AUTO
 -PFILE ORACLE_HOME\DATABASE\INITSID.ORA
```

In this example, the -NEW indicates we are creating a new service. The -SID parameter indicates the name of the new database SID. The -INTPWD and -MAXUSERS parameters provide settings for the password file that will be created for this database. The -STARTMODE command indicates whether the database should be started when the NT system boots (in this case, the AUTO says it should start up on system boot). Finally, the -PFILE command indicates the location of the parameter file for that database. You can type in ORADIM -HELP for a list of all valid commands for ORADIM, as seen here:

```
C:\>oradim -h
DIM-00002: Valid commands are: -DELETE, -EDIT, -NEW, -STARTUP, and
-SHUTDOWN
Please enter one of the following commands:
  Create an instance by specifying the following parameters:
-NEW -SID sid | -SRVC service [-INTPWD password] [-MAXUSERS number]
[-STARTMODE a|m] [-PFILE file] [-TIMEOUT secs]
  Edit an instance by specifying the following parameters:
-EDIT -SID sid [-NEWSID sid] [-INTPWD password] [-STARTMODE auto|manual]
[-PFILE filename] [SHUTMODE a|i|n] [-SHUTTYPE srvc|inst|srvc,inst]
[-TIMEOUT seconds]
  Delete instances by specifying the following:
 -DELETE -SID sid | -SRVC service name
  Startup services and instance by specifying the following parameters:
-STARTUP -SID sid [-USRPWD password] [-STARTTYPE srvc|inst|srvc,inst]
[-PFILE filename]
  Shutdown services and instance by specifying the following parameters:
-SHUTDOWN -SID sid [-USRPWD password] [-SHUTTYPE srvc|inst|srvc,inst]
[-SHUTMODE a | i | n]
  Query for help by specifying the following parameters: -? | -h | -help
```

Creating the Database Manually

Finally! After creating the init.ora parameter file, deciding where you want to put the redo logs and various other database files, and picking a spot for the control file and the SYSTEM tablespace, it is time to create the database. The database creation process takes place in several steps.

1. Consult your OS-specific Oracle documentation for any preliminary work that you need to do in order to start a given Oracle instance on your platform. For example, in Windows NT, you must first create a service for the Oracle database, using the ORADIM executable (see sidebar for more on ORADIM).

2. Set up the Oracle environmental parameters as required by your operating system. Typically, these will be ORACLE_HOME, PATH, and ORACLE_SID; see Chapter 1.

3. Start the database instance with the STARTUP NOMOUNT command from SQL*Plus or Server Manager. Here's an example:

```
D:\>set ORACLE_SID=ora816
D:\>svrmgrl
Oracle Server Manager Release 3.1.6.0.0 - Production
Copyright (c) 1997, 1999, Oracle Corporation.  All Rights Reserved.
Oracle8i Enterprise Edition Release 8.1.6.0.0 - Production
With the Partitioning option
JServer Release 8.1.6.0.0 - Production
SVRMGR> connect internal
Connected.
SVRMGR> STARTUP NOMOUNT
ORACLE instance started.
Total System Global Area                        61932812 bytes
Fixed Size                                         70924 bytes
Variable Size                                   57589760 bytes
Database Buffers                                 4194304 bytes
Redo Buffers                                       77824 bytes
SVRMGR>
```

2. Issue the CREATE DATABASE statement. For example:

```
CREATE DATABASE ora816
LOGFILE 'D:\Oracle\oradata\ora816\redo01.log' SIZE 1024K,
        'D:\Oracle\oradata\ora816\redo02.log' SIZE 1024K,
        'D:\Oracle\oradata\ora816\redo03.log' SIZE 1024K
    MAXLOGFILES 32
```

```
                    MAXLOGMEMBERS 4
                    DATAFILE 'D:\Oracle\oradata\ora816\system01.dbf'
                    SIZE 55M  REUSE AUTOEXTEND OFF
                    MAXDATAFILES 128;
```

3. Once the CREATE DATABASE statement has completed successfully, the database will be open. To continue the creation process, you'll need to run two scripts, `catalog` and `catproc` (at a minimum). These scripts build the data dictionary views and load various packages and procedures into the database for the DBA's use. In addition, there may be other scripts that you will need to run depending on any optional database components you will want to enable (such as Java).

Script/ Command	Command	Required/ Optional	Description
Catalog.sql	@catalog	Required	Creates the data dictionary views, such as the V$ views.
Catproc.sql	@catproc	Required	Creates the required packages and views for the Oracle procedural language, PL/SQL.
Catrep.sql	@catrep	Optional	Installs advanced replication.
Catblock.sql	@catblock	Optional	Creates various scripts to monitor blocking. See Chapters 15 through 17 for information about blocking of Oracle sessions by other sessions.
Catperf.sql	@catperf	Optional	Provides various performance-tuning views not created by default in Oracle. See Chapters 15 though 17.
Dbmspool.sql	@dbmspool	Optional	Creates the DBMS_SHARED_POOL utility package, covered in Chapter 20.
initjvm.sql	@initjvm	Optional	Creates the Oracle Java environment, which is required to use Java (i.e., Java Stored Procedures) within the Oracle database.

4. Consult the installation instructions for additional products that you are installing, to determine the scripts you need to run.

Using the Database Configuration Assistant

Oracle's Database Configuration Assistant (DCA) is a GUI wizard-style tool that guides you through the steps of creating a database and then actually creates it. This tool is helpful for beginning DBAs who need to get a database up and running quickly. In addition to adding a new database, you can use the DCA to change the configuration of or remove an existing database.

The DCA is pretty straightforward. If you wish to do something fancy such as modifying SQL.BSQ, you'll need to do that before you run the DCA. Also, be aware that using the DCA does not afford you all the options that are available when creating a database manually. However, for probably 90 percent of database creation options, the DCA works just fine.

When using the DCA to create a new database, you have two options. One is to create a "typical" database. This option requires little or no input from the user running the DCA (probably a DBA), and you end up with a small database. The second option creates a custom-designed database. In this case, the DCA presents a series of windows requesting your input to define the type of database you are configuring, such as OLTP or a data warehouse, as well as how many concurrent users you expect on the database. Oracle then asks if you wish to run the system in dedicated or shared-server mode. Generally, we prefer a dedicated server over shared server (MTS) mode.

As you continue, the DCA questions you about the database it is to create. It asks which database options you wish to install (such as time series, Oracle Spatial, JServer, and others). Remember that some of these options require separate licensing. Check with your Oracle representative to see what you are currently licensed for.

Next, you'll identify the global database name, which will also become the database SID. In this same screen you can choose the location for the parameter file, or use the default provided location. Also, you can choose the value for the compatible parameter, though generally the default is fine.

The next window allows you to define the location of the control files of the database, as well as values for the maximum number of database datafiles, log files, and log file members. The defaults are generally sufficient, except for the value of log file members. We like to set this to 3 because we like having three members in each log file group).

Additional questions regarding the configuration of individual tablespaces are presented in the next series of windows. You'll be able to define the tablespaces SYSTEM, USERS, TOOLS, RBS, TEMP, and INDEX, including their size, names, and locations. You can also configure the AUTOEXTEND settings for the datafiles of those tablespaces.

Next, Oracle prompts you for information about the redo logs, including the location and size of each log group. Three redo log groups are created. Then the DCA gives you the option of creating the database in ARCHIVELOG mode. It's best not to do that.

 WARNING We strongly suggest that you do *not* use ARCHIVELOG mode during database creation. If you do, there will be a large amount of redo generated and archived during the database creation process. By removing archiving, you reduce the I/O costs associated with archiving and free up system resources for the database creation process.

In the next screen you set parameters in the init.ora, such as the shared pool size and the number of database blocks allocated to the database buffer cache. This is also where you define the block size of the database (8KB is the default). After that comes a window to define the location for dump files for user and background processes. When you complete this screen, you will then have the option of creating a SQL script that will do the database creation for you, or you can have DCA create the database then and there.

- If you choose to have Oracle create a batch file for later database creation, Oracle will create a script file (an MS DOS batch file, or a shell script in Unix) as well as several SQL script files in a location you define. When you wish to create the database, simply run the shell or batch file and the database creation will begin.

- If you choose to have the DCA create the database, it proceeds to create the Oracle service (on NT) and issues the CREATE DATABASE command. Next, it runs the data dictionary scripts and creates the defined tablespaces. Finally, it starts the Net8 configuration assistant and any other configuration utilities that are needed. Once the DCA has completed its work, you will have a fully functional database.

After Creating the Database

There is still some work to do before you start adding segments to your newly created database.

Configuring Rollback Segments

Your first after-creation task is to create your rollback segment tablespace and the rollback segments it contains. Oracle will not allow you to create any objects in the database until you have completed this operation. Chapter 6 gives you all the details about configuration of rollback segments, and creation and management of other Oracle segments.

Configuring Oracle Networking

We discuss Oracle networking Chapter 9. Once a database is created, your networking services must be configured to support it. In Oracle8i, the database will automatically attach itself to the default listener service (port 1521), without any DBA involvement. If you want the database to listen on a different port, you will need to change one or more init.ora parameters. Also, you must configure your clients so they can connect to the database. This entire process, including the changes to init.ora, is outlined in Chapter 9.

Securing the New Database

Database security is discussed in Chapter 21. Immediately after database creation, you must change the passwords of several accounts, primarily SYS, SYSTEM, SCOTT, and OUTLN. Change the passwords on these accounts as quickly as you can. Use the ALTER USER command, as follows:

```
ALTER USER sys IDENTIFIED BY new_password;
```

Creating Tablespaces

The first tablespace you will want to create is for the rollback segments, as mentioned.

Following that, you'll create the TEMPORARY tablespace for temporary segments. The next step is to change the temporary tablespace assignments of all users to point to that tablespace. An example of this is shown here:

```
CREATE TABLESPACE temp DATAFILE
'c:\oracle\ora816\ora816_temp_01.dbf' SIZE 100m;
ALTER USER system TEMPORARY TABLESPACE temp;
```

 WARNING No user should ever use the SYSTEM tablespace to create temporary segments, not even user SYS.

Another tablespace created at this stage is often called USERS; you point the default tablespace setting for all users except SYS to this tablespace. This keeps authorized users from inadvertently creating objects in the SYSTEM tablespace. Here is an example of the CREATE TABLESPACE command for this purpose:

```
CREATE TABLESPACE users DATAFILE
'c:\oracle\ora816\ora816_users_01.dbf' SIZE 100m;
ALTER USER system DEFAULT TABLESPACE temp;
```

You will doubtless want to create other tablespaces soon after database creation, depending on your environment—for example, tablespaces for your database data, for indexes, and many different tablespaces for your database segments. We'll discuss tablespace creation in detail in Chapter 6.

Summary of Database Creation Steps

We have covered a lot of information in this chapter. Creation of a basic database is no small feat, but if you're prepared and properly organized, you'll have an easier time. The following is a summarized list of generic steps that will help you remember to do everything that you need to do. You can use this list in combination with the important specific information that comes from reading through your OS-specific documentation. Don't neglect to do this, because every Oracle platform has its own special characteristics in terms of database creation.

1. Determine the total disk space requirements for your database.
2. Create the database directory structures using OFA guidelines, including the database administration subdirectory structures and the database datafiles.
3. Create the `init.ora` parameter file in the `pfile` directory of the ADMIN directory structure. On a Unix system, create a line to init.ora in the ORACLE_HOME\dbs directory. On an NT system, create the parameter file in the ORACLE_HOME\database directory, with an `ifile` entry to the `init.ora` in the ADMIN directory structure.
4. Start the Oracle instance with the STARTUP NOMOUNT command.
5. Execute the CREATE DATABASE script.
6. Execute the `catalog.sql` and `catproc.sql` scripts.
7. Execute any other required setup scripts, based on the Oracle product options you will be using.
8. Create the rollback segment tablespace and rollback segments.
9. Create any other needed tablespaces.
10. Change the SYS, SYSTEM, and OUTLN passwords.
11. Change all default tablespaces from SYSTEM, for all users except for the SYS user.

12. Change all users' TEMPORARY tablespace assignments using the ALTER USER command. By default, these tablespaces are assigned to the SYSTEM tablespace; however, no user should ever be assigned a default temporary tablespace of SYSTEM.

Moving On

As a direct result of creating the database, we have created the data dictionary—a set of views that provides metadata about the database and the objects contained within it. In the next chapter we will look at the data dictionary in much more detail.

CHAPTER 4

The Data Dictionary

FEATURING:

Data dictionary architecture   *142*

Using the Oracle data dictionary   *151*

Documenting the database   *160*

The Oracle data dictionary is a collection of tables and views that contain information on the structure and composition of the database. DBAs must be familiar with the data dictionary and its function in the Oracle database. This chapter introduces you to the data dictionary, its components, and some of its internals. We will review the most commonly used views of the data dictionary, as well. At the end of the chapter, you'll find some suggestions for data dictionary reports that you can incorporate into the documentation of your database.

Data Dictionary Architecture

The Oracle data dictionary and its views are one of the most critical tools available to a DBA. These views are used for many administrative functions—from finding out which tables are in the database, to how much I/O is occurring on a particular datafile, to discovering where datafiles are actually located, and more. The architecture of the Oracle8i database data dictionary has changed within the releases of Oracle8i, but not dramatically so. This section explains the architecture of the data dictionary, in particular the base tables, the data dictionary views, and the dynamic performance views.

Dictionary Structure at Creation

When you run the CREATE DATABASE command, one of the things that occurs is execution of the script `sql.bsq`, and one of the first things accomplished by `sql.bsq` is creation of the *SYS account*. Once the SYS account is in place, database creation proceeds, beginning with the data dictionary *base tables, clusters,* and *indexes*. Thus the CREATE DATABASE process serves to initially create and seed the data dictionary tables contained within the SYS schema. (If you are migrating your database rather than creating a new one, the script `migrate.bsq` is used to create the data dictionary tables.)

NOTE In Oracle there is really very little distinction between an account and a schema, and in this book we use the terms interchangeably. Generally we will refer to a user account when discussing passwords or privileges, since these rightly belong to the *user account.* When discussing objects such as table and indexes, we will generally refer to the *user schema.* The bottom line is that objects reside in schemas, and accounts control access.

DATA DICTIONARY ARCHITECTURE

The data dictionary base tables, which contain few if any rows in the beginning, are designed to store *metadata* about your database. This metadata includes the datafiles that make up your database (SYS.FILE$), the objects taking up space in various tablespaces (SYS.UET$), and how much free space is available in a given tablespace (SYS.FET$). These and the other base tables grow as the database grows.

NOTE You may want to edit `sql.bsq` (or `migrate.bsq`) and modify settings for particular tables so that they are more efficiently using the space available to them in the SYSTEM tablespace. Chapter 3 gives a list of the storage attributes you can change, and a table of common modifications.

NOTE If you are migrating an Oracle7 database to Oracle8i, review your current data dictionary settings. Check the number of allocated extents and determine what you might need to alter in the `migrate.bsq`. See Chapter 2's "Checklist for Migrating Oracle7 to Oracle8i."

Apart from the base tables, the rest of the data dictionary comprises the user-accessible views, including those intended for DBAs, such as DBA_TABLES. These *data dictionary views* provide the actual database metadata. They tell the DBA about tables in the database, who owns them, what tablespace they are in, and so on. Information in the base tables typically only changes when DDL is executed against the database, causing some change to the database structure. These changes must be reflected in the data dictionary metadata. Thus the DDL will change the underlying base tables, and these changes are then reflected when views of those tables are queried.

Part of the base tables are the dynamically created internal tables often called the *X$ tables*. These tables are really representations of internal C structures that Oracle uses. Much as the base tables are the foundation for the dictionary data, the X$ tables are the foundation for the dictionary views that are used most commonly—the V$ views, or *dynamic performance views*. The X$ tables are rarely accessed by a DBA, although we'll be looking at some significant exceptions to that statement.

Dictionary Creation Scripts

After initial creation of the data dictionary, the DBA runs two required scripts: `catalog.sql` and `catproc.sql`. The primary job of `catalog.sql` is to create the data dictionary views that are built from the base tables. The `catproc.sql` script creates some data dictionary views as well, in addition to calling other scripts that install the PL/SQL functionality.

 NOTE If you are using the Database Creation Assistant (DCA), you won't need to run the CREATE DATABASE command, nor the `catalog.sql` or `catproc.sql` scripts. The DCA runs the scripts for you.

When you create your database, you might well run other scripts (see Chapter 3 for a list), depending on your operating system and the function of your database. These scripts are used to generate data dictionary objects (views, packages, and the like), and their names generally start with a prefix of `cat` to indicate that they are catalog creation scripts. For example, if you are installing advanced replication, you will run the `catrep.sql` script to create data dictionary views for use by the replication product and by the administrator of a database that uses advanced replication.

Typically, catalog creation scripts call many others during their execution. For example, `catalog.sql` in Oracle 8.1.6 calls some seven other scripts during its execution.

Data Dictionary Views

Data dictionary views typically start with one of three identifiers: DBA_, ALL_, or USER_.

- The DBA_ views, such as DBA_TABLES, DBA_USERS, and DBA_INDEXES, provide views of all objects in the entire database. Only users with DBA privileges can access the DBA-level accounts. These are among some of the most powerful views into the database, so take care before granting access to them. (Even greater caution should be used in granting DBA privileges, and we'll discuss that in Chapter 21.)

- The ALL_ views show information about all objects a given user has access to. Thus, if you are a user called TOM and you have access to tables in GUS's schema, you could query ALL_TABLES to see what those table names are.

- The USER_ views show you what objects you own, and nobody else.

These data dictionary views are generally built directly from the underlying base data dictionary tables, although joins to multiple data dictionary tables are frequent. You can find the SQL for the definition of these views in DBA_VIEWS.

Dynamic Performance Views

The dynamic performance (V$) views provide near-real-time statistical information on the database, as well as information on certain database structures. The statistics available in these views are critical to tuning your database and getting the most out of it, as discussed in Chapters 15 through 17. Also, performance view information about key database physical structures becomes especially important during database recovery situations. In particular, you'll use dynamic performance views to examine the online redo logs, control files, and various status and content information about these critical objects.

There is a kind of middle layer between the dynamic performance views and the underlying X$ tables: the GV$ views, from which the actual dynamic performance views are built. You can see the SQL used to create the V$ or the GV$ views (and as a result, the underlying X$ views and data dictionary tables) by querying the V$FIXED_VIEW_DEFINITION view.

NOTE If you are interested in understanding the base X$ tables, you can trace the dynamic performance views back through the GV$ views and learn a great deal about the internal workings of Oracle.

Listing 4.1 provides an example of the relationship between the V$ view V$PARAMETER, GV$ view GV$PARAMETER, and the underlying X$ tables.

Listing 4.1: The Relationship of V$ and GV$ Views and the X$ Tables

```
-- First, here is the SQL for the gv$parameter view that
-- v$parameter will be built on. Notice the X$ tables contained
-- in the FROM clause of this SQL statement.
select view_name, view_definition
from v$fixed_view_definition
where View_name like '%GV$PARAMETER'

VIEW_NAME
------------------------------
VIEW_DEFINITION
----------------------------------------------------------------
GV$PARAMETER
select x.inst_id,x.indx+1,ksppinm,ksppity,ksppstvl,ksppstdf,
decode(bitand(ksppiflg/256,1),1,'TRUE','FALSE'),
```

```
            decode(bitand(ksppiflg/65536,3),1,'IMMEDIATE',2,
            'DEFERRED', 3,'IMMEDIATE','FALSE'),
            decode(bitand(ksppstvf,7),1,'MODIFIED',4,'SYSTEM_MOD','FALSE'),
            decode(bitand(ksppstvf,2),2,'TRUE','FALSE'),   ksppdesc
            from x$ksppi x, x$ksppcv y
            where (x.indx = y.indx)
            and   (translate(ksppinm,'_','#') not like '#%' or
            (translate(ksppinm,'_','#')like '#%'and ksppstdf = 'FALSE'))

            -- And, here is the related SQL for the v$parameter view
            select view_name, view_definition
            from v$fixed_view_definition
            where View_name like 'V$PARAMETER'

            VIEW_NAME
            ------------------------------
            VIEW_DEFINITION
            ----------------------------------------------------------------------
            V$PARAMETER
            select  NUM , NAME , TYPE , VALUE , ISDEFAULT , ISSES_MODIFIABLE ,
            ISSYS_MODIFIABLE , ISMODIFIED , ISADJUSTED , DESCRIPTI/ON from
            GV$PARAMETER where inst_id = USERENV('Instance')
```

Protecting Your Data Dictionary

The SYS user owns the data dictionary. By default, this account is assigned to the SYSTEM tablespace, so that is where the data dictionary tables are created. DBAs should never allow any object that is not part of the data dictionary to be owned by the SYS schema. Likewise, the DBA should never allow objects to be created in the SYSTEM tablespace except those related to the data dictionary.

To this end, you'll need to be careful when you create new database user accounts. This is because the SYSTEM tablespace is, by default, the temporary and default tablespace assignment for all accounts. When creating user accounts, make sure to specify a default and temporary tablespace *other than* the SYSTEM tablespace. Also, change the SYSTEM account and any other Oracle system accounts that use the SYSTEM tablespace for default or temporary storage.

When creating a user account, use the DEFAULT TABLESPACE and TEMPORARY TABLESPACE clauses to correctly set these default tablespaces. An example of a CREATE USER command using these clauses would look something like this:

```
CREATE USER frankenstien IDENTIFIED BY madman
DEFAULT TABLESPACE alive_tbs
TEMPORARY TABLESPACE temp;
```

If a user is found to have these tablespaces incorrectly set, use the ALTER USER command to correct the problem. Here's an example of ALTER USER to reset a default tablespace and temporary tablespace:

```
ALTER USER frankenstien
DEFAULT TABLESPACE alive_tbs
TEMPORARY TABLESPACE temp;
```

The only account that is exempt from this imperative is the SYS account—and even so, we like to change the temporary tablespace specification for that account.

WARNING With virtually every Oracle release, there's a new account that is automatically created when the database is created. Make sure you change the default and temporary tablespace assignments for all these accounts. In Oracle8i, this includes SYS, SYSTEM, DBSNMP, and OUTLN. Also make sure you change the passwords to all of these accounts!

Accessing the Data Dictionary Views

All of the data dictionary views and dynamic performance views have a public synonym so that they can be queried from any account with the correct privileges. Often you will want to grant a user access only to a specific DBA-level view, and no others. This type of restriction can be facilitated by giving the user a direct grant to the view.

There may be some security issues with this arrangement, however, as when you must drop users who have granted privileges to other users. For example, if SYSTEM grants SELECT privileges to user ROBERT for DBA_TABLES with the grant option, and then ROBERT grants the same privileges to the TRACY user, you'll have a problem if you drop the ROBERT user. The direct grant from ROBERT to TRACY on DBA_TABLES will no longer be valid, and TRACY will wonder why her programs stop running all of a sudden. See Chapter 21 for more information on grants and related matters.

The following code demonstrates a situation where user SCOTT is granted access to the DBA_USERS view. Yet, he has no access to and cannot look at other views. Also, notice that we were unable to issue the same grant from SYSTEM until we gave SYSTEM a direct grant from SYS to DBA_TABLES. We gave this with the grant option to allow SYSTEM to pass the grant along.

```
-- Connecting as SYS will allow you to give a direct grant
-- to a DBA view...
```

```
CONNECT SYS
SQL> GRANT SELECT ON dba_tables TO scott;

-- Connect as system and it will not work
-- unless you have first given system a direct grant with admin.

CONNECT SYSTEM
SQL> GRANT SELECT ON dba_tables TO scott;
GRANT SELECT ON dba_tables TO scott
                *
ERROR at line 1:
ORA-01031: insufficient privileges
SQL> connect sys
Enter password:
Connected.
SQL> GRANT SELECT ON dba_tables TO system WITH GRANT OPTION
Grant succeeded.
SQL> connect system
Enter password:
Connected.
SQL> GRANT SELECT ON dba_tables TO scott;
Grant succeeded.
```

Security Alert: Accessing Data Dictionary Views from PL/SQL

A security issue occurs when PL/SQL programs need to access the data dictionary. Access to Oracle data dictionary views is granted through a role. Unfortunately, the default security model for PL/SQL requires that you have direct access to an object in order to use it in PL/SQL. (See Chapter 21 regarding roles and Oracle security in general.)

There are two workarounds to this problem. The first is to actually arrange for the user creating the PL/SQL object to be granted direct access to the DBA view that's needed. Of course, if the PL/SQL object is being created by user SYS, the conflict doesn't occur—but creating objects in the SYS schema is, in general, prohibited. Before you make adjustments to allow data dictionary access for PL/SQL programmers or other users, you should carefully consider the security implications of such activities.

Continued

CONTINUED

The second workaround is to create the procedure using the privileges of its owner (known as *definer's rights*) rather than the privileges of the invoker. This is a new option available in Oracle8i for all PL/SQL programs. In this case, you create the procedure in a schema that has access to the data dictionary view or tables in which you're interested. (This may be the SYS schema or another schema that you have set up.) Once the PL/SQL routine is created, you grant execute privileges to the users who will need to run the routine. When the routine is run, it will be the privileges of the user who owns the program, not the user running it.

When it's legitimately necessary, following is an example of granting access to a database view and creating PL/SQL that accesses that view. After that, you'll find an example of defining a procedure to use the security rights of the owner rather than of the user.

```
SQL> connect scott/tiger
Connected.
CREATE OR REPLACE PROCEDURE get_all_bytes
AS
total_bytes NUMBER;
BEGIN
SELECT SUM(bytes) INTO total_bytes FROM dba_data_files;
DBMS_OUTPUT.PUT_LINE('Total bytes: '||total_bytes);
END;
/
Warning: Procedure created with compilation errors.
SQL> show err
Errors for PROCEDURE GET_ALL_BYTES:
LINE/COL ERROR
-------- -----------------------------------
5/1      PL/SQL: SQL Statement ignored
5/41     PLS-00201: identifier 'SYS.DBA_DATA_FILES' must be declared


/* Note that dba_data_files is not recognized by the PL/SQL */
SQL> connect sys
Enter password:
Connected.
```

Continued

> **CONTINUED**
>
> ```
> -- Now, grant select on the dba_data_files view to scott.
> SQL> grant select on dba_data_files to scott;
> Grant succeeded.
> SQL> connect scott/tiger
> Connected.
> SQL> alter procedure get_all_bytes compile;
> Procedure altered.
> SQL> set serveroutput on
> SQL> exec get_all_bytes
> Total bytes: 141557760
> PL/SQL procedure successfully completed.
>
> -- Now, create a procedure that runs with the rights of the owner
> -- Create the procedure as SYS because it owns the tables.
> -- We could also create an account and grant each table to it directly.
> SQL> connect sys/change_on_install
> Connected.
> CREATE OR REPLACE PROCEDURE get_all_bytes
> AUTHID DEFINER
> AS
> total_bytes NUMBER;
> BEGIN
> SELECT SUM(bytes) INTO total_bytes FROM dba_data_files;
> DBMS_OUTPUT.PUT_LINE('Total bytes: '||total_bytes);
> END;
> /
> Procedure created.
> SQL> grant execute on get_all_bytes to scott;
> Grant succeeded.
> SQL> connect scott/tiger
> Connected.
> SQL> set serveroutput on
> SQL> exec sys.get_all_bytes
> Total bytes: 249561088
> ```

Using the Oracle Data Dictionary

Now that you know what the data dictionary is and how it came to be, we urge you not to stop here! Don't fall into the trap of being a DBA who doesn't know how to use your data dictionary to effectively manage your database. Unfortunately, many DBAs are not comfortable with the data dictionary's tables and views and don't use them regularly. This may be because they learned to administer the database itself through a GUI tool such as Oracle's Enterprise Manager, which reduces the need to refer to these tables. You'll be a better DBA, however, when you know how to navigate a productive course through the data dictionary and its contents.

Appendix H is a quick reference to all the data dictionary and dynamic performance views.

NOTE Beyond its maintenance as a result of Oracle's DDL operations, the data dictionary is also used during recursive SQL operations. When you execute a SQL statement, Oracle goes recursively through the data dictionary to make sure that your SQL statement is valid. Among the items checked are the presence of the object in the SQL statement (for example, do the tables being inserted into really exist?), and whether the columns in that object in fact exist. Often, when you see ORA-type errors, it's because something in the recursive table lookups didn't work out. You may have entered an invalid column or object name, and the recursive lookups failed to find it.

In this section, we introduce you to some of the common data dictionary views; you'll encounter these and others throughout this book. Then we end the chapter with some typical uses for data dictionary information; you can tailor these for use in your day-to-day administrative tasks.

Using the X$ Tables

You won't often need to look at the X$ tables. They are only minimally documented by Oracle, and they change from version to version of Oracle. The X$ tables may differ slightly across various Oracle releases. For a complete list of the X$ tables, you can traverse the V$FIXED_TABLE view (which also contains the V$, GV$ and other data dictionary items).

This section covers a few of the more commonly used X$ tables and a description of their purpose, in addition to occasions when you can find them useful. You'll see them used in other chapters of this book, as well.

- **X$BH** allows you to track the usage of the database buffer cache.
- **X$KCBFWAIT** allows you to track buffer busy waits to specific database datafiles.
- **X$KSMLRU** lists the ten largest allocations in the shared pool. You'll see an example shortly.
- **X$KSPPI**, together with X$KSPPCV, helps you find hidden Oracle parameters. Made for the pirate in all of us! Arrrrrghhhhh....
- **X$KSPPCV**, along with X$KSPPI, helps you to find hidden Oracle parameters. There's an example coming up.

X$BH

The X$BH table offers a great deal of potentially interesting information for the DBA. This view allows you to track the usage of the database buffer cache. For each buffer in the cache, you can see the file and block address that the buffer represents.

NOTE With the new touch-point algorithm in Oracle8i (which replaces the old LRU algorithm), we can tell how often a particular block has been "touched," or used, by the database. Thus, we now have a mechanism to determine which blocks in the database are truly hot.

Some of the more useful columns in the X$BH table include the following:

ADDR	Buffer address.
STATE	Current state of the buffer:
	0 - Free (never been used)
	1 - Either available or being used, depending on the status of the IRBA_SEQ column (if IRBA_SEQ=0, it is available; otherwise it is being used)
	3 - In use
IRBA_SEQ	If > 0, this is the type of operation being conducted on the block. If 0, the block is available for use.
TS#	Tablespace number to which the block is assigned. You can reference the TS$ data dictionary view (using columns TS# and NAME) to get the name of the associated tablespace.
FILE#	The absolute file number to which the block is assigned. You can reference the DBA_DATA_FILES column FILE_ID to get the name of the datafile or the tablespace name associated with the datafile.

DBABLK   Block's assigned number within the assigned datafile.
TCH   This is the "touch" counter, which is incremented each time the buffer is touched. Gives an indication of how "hot" (popular) the block is.

Listing 4.2 is the code for a report that tells us which database blocks are the hot blocks. It provides the name of the segment and the datafile in which it belongs. Be aware that this query can take some time to complete, depending on the size of your database buffer cache and the number of overall segments, as well as the number of datafiles in your database.

Listing 4.2: Listing the Hot Blocks in the Database Buffer Cache

```
COLUMN segment_name FORMAT a30
COLUMN file_name FORMAT a60
SET LINES 132
SELECT * FROM
(SELECT a.tch, a.file#, a.dbablk, b.segment_name, c.file_name
FROM x$bh a, dba_extents b, dba_data_files c
WHERE a.file#=b.file_id
AND a.dbablk >= b.block_id
AND a.dbablk < b.block_id+b.blocks
AND a.file#=c.file_id
ORDER BY 1 DESC)
WHERE rownum < 20;
```

X$KCBFWAIT

The X$KCBFWAIT table provides with a list of files that are experiencing a great number of buffer busy waits. Using the following query, you can determine which datafiles are experiencing the worst wait problems:

```
SELECT count, file#, name
FROM x$kcbfwait, v$datafile
WHERE indx + 1 = file#
ORDER BY count desc;
```

You'll find complete coverage of wait monitoring in Chapter 17.

X$KSMLRU

The X$KSMLRU table can be used to monitor the latest large object (LOB) allocations in the shared pool. In earlier versions of Oracle8i, the contents of this table were erased after a SELECT statement was issued against it. This is not the case with later versions—however, the table may change quickly, particularly in a dynamic environment.

X$KSMLRU returns the 10 latest allocations, so for use in ongoing analysis, it's a good idea to create a second table and dump the contents of X$KSMLRU into it from time to time.

Let's say you want to figure out which large PL/SQL objects you should pin in the shared pool. ("Pinning" an object means forcing Oracle to keep it. Pinning objects in the shared pool is discussed in later chapters.) You can use a query like that shown in Listing 4.3. This query returns the six largest users of the shared pool. You will probably want to change the number of rows returned as needed. In this example, we can see that a stored procedure gets loaded quite a bit, as well as some large SQL statements. We might well want to find those SQL statements and create them as PL/SQL statements instead.

Listing 4.3: Using X$KSMLRU to Determine Objects to Pin in the Shared Pool

```
SELECT * FROM
(SELECT ksmlrhon, ksmlrsiz
FROM x$ksmlru
ORDER BY ksmlrsiz)
WHERE rownum < 6;


KSMLRHON                              KSMLRSIZ
-----------------------------------   --------
SP_1438_SEL_S_INVOICE                     1060
SEG$                                      2232
PKG_3541_CALL_STATISTICS                  4120
BEGIN pkg_4488_sel_m_eqp_src...           4132
SELECT * FROM "CSTTDD"                    4292
select a.* from csttdd a, cs...           4324
```

X$KSPPI and X$KSPPCV

There is a class of parameters that is not available to you in V$PARAMETER or any V$ view: the *hidden* or *undocumented parameters*. But you can see them in the X$KSPPI and X$KSPPCV tables, which contain *all* the various parameters and their current and default settings in Oracle. These tables are made for the pirate in all of us!

Oracle has more hidden and undocumented parameters than it has documented ones. Many of these parameters are *dangerous* and should never be tinkered with unless you have guidance from Oracle Support, and not until they've been tested in a non-production environment first. Nevertheless, some of the hidden parameters can be very useful from time to time. Often when we install a new Oracle version, we produce a list of hidden parameters just to see what's out there. The SQL in Listing 4.4 gives you this list for Oracle8i.

Note that the SQL in this listing may change somewhat with new Oracle software versions (because Oracle never guarantees that database views won't change). Because the X$ tables might change in 9i, this code may well not work. As a result, you may have to do a little experimentation to see what might have changed (or you can buy the 9i version of this book when it comes out!).

Listing 4.4: Querying for Hidden Parameters

```
SELECT a.ksppinm "Name", b.ksppstvl "Current Value",
b.ksppstdf "Original Default?"
FROM x$ksppi a, x$ksppcv b
WHERE a.indx=b.indx
AND substr(ksppinm,1,1)='_'
ORDER BY 1;

-- and a partial result
Name                          Current Value              Origional Default?
---------------------------   ------------------------   ------------------
_trace_flushing               FALSE                      TRUE
_trace_multi_block_reads      FALSE                      TRUE
_trace_write_batch_size       32                         TRUE
_tts_allow_nchar_mismatch     FALSE                      TRUE
_unnest_subquery              FALSE                      TRUE
_use_ism                      TRUE                       TRUE
_use_nosegment_indexes        FALSE                      TRUE
_use_vector_post              TRUE                       TRUE
_wait_for_sync                TRUE                       TRUE
_walk_insert_threshold        0                          TRUE
_write_clones                 3                          TRUE
_yield_check_interval         100                        TRUE
```

Using the DBA_, ALL_, and USER_ Views

The DBA_, ALL_, and USER_ views are used primarily for database administration purposes. This is in contrast to the dynamic performance (V$) views that contribute primarily to database tuning (although they are handy for backup and recovery, as well).

As stated earlier in this chapter, a user's privileges determines which views he or she can query. In the ALL_ view, the grants to specific objects determine what objects the user can see. All users who have the ability to log in to the database can query the USER_ and ALL_ views, giving users a way to tell what objects they own and have access to.

Note that there are some DBA views that do not exist as ALL_ or USER_ views. This is generally for security purposes. Also, you will find that columns don't appear in all of these views. This is sometimes for security purposes, and sometimes because those columns are simply not needed for a particular view. For example, with the USER_ views, there is really no need for the username column NOW.

The DBA_ Views

These views are used by the DBA to get an overall look at the entire database. For example:

- Documenting the database. This involves locating all objects in the database, all datafiles, rollback segments and so on. We will cover this in more detail shortly.
- Performing security audits of the database.
- Finding out where and when certain problems, such as space problems, are likely to occur.
- Determining how much free space remains in the database.
- Determining what users are set up on the system, and what default and temporary tablespaces are assigned to those users.

WARNING There are no restrictions on the DBA_ views; their information is available to all DBAs—that's exactly why you need to be careful about giving DBA privileges. Access to DBA_ views is granted through use of the DBA role (see later in this section for instructions on granting users access to specific DBA_ views, if that is required). *Never* grant the DBA role just to accommodate temporary access to a DBA_ view. Substantial risk is associated with the DBA role, as discussed in Chapter 21.

Following is an example of using the DBA_USERS dictionary view to produce a report of all users. We want to make sure that no one is using the SYSTEM tablespace for the TEMPORARY tablespace (as is the default setting in Oracle).

```
SQL> SELECT username, temporary_tablespace FROM dba_users;

USERNAME    TEMPORARY_TABLESPACE
----------  --------------------
SYS         SYSTEM
SYSTEM      SYSTEM
OUTLN       SYSTEM
DBSNMP      SYSTEM
SID         SYSTEM
TEST        TEMP
SCOTT2      TEMP
SCOTT       TEMP
```

As you can see from the report above, we probably need to modify temporary tablespace settings for several users, in order to avoid the problems with sort segments in the SYSTEM tablespace (this problem is discussed in Chapter 6). The DBA_ reports offer all sorts of information like this. In the later section "Documenting the Database," you'll see many examples of queries and the resulting output that will help you document your database configuration.

NOTE A new role is available in 8i that allows you to give users access to the data dictionary views but not DBA privileges (as with the DBA role). The SELECT_CATALOG_ROLE role allows the user assigned to this role to select from all the data dictionary views.

The USER_ Views

Here is the output from a query to the USER_TABLES view for the SCOTT schema:

```
SQL> SELECT table_name, tablespace_name, pct_free,
pct_used, pct_increase
FROM user_tables;

TABLE_NAME                TABLESPACE_NAME   PCT_FREE   PCT_USED  PCT_INCREASE
------------------------  ----------------  ---------  --------  ------------
BONUS                     USERS                   10         40            50
CHILD                     USERS                   10         40            50
DEPT                      USERS                   10         40            50
DUMMY                     USERS                   10         40            50
EMPLOYEE                  USERS                   10         40            50
```

HOLD_EVENTS	USERS	10	40	50
NEWTABLE	USERS	10	40	50
PARENT	USERS	10	40	50
PAY_TABLE	USERS	10	40	50
SALGRADE	USERS	10	40	50
TEMP_EMP	USERS	10	40	50
TEMP_EMPLOYEE	USERS	10	40	50
TESTME	USERS	10	40	50
TEST_ME	USERS	10	40	50
TEST_RGF	USERS	10	40	50

In this query, we are looking for the list of tables owned by the user SCOTT, and SCOTT only. He may have access to other tables, but they will not be listed in this view. Because these objects are only objects that belong to the SCOTT schema, there is no need for an OWNER column. You will find that there is no OWNER column in most of the USER_ views.

Following is a second example of querying a USER_ view:

```
SQL> SELECT username, account_status, expiry_date, default_tablespace
FROM user_users;
```

```
USERNAME    ACCOUNT_STATUS    EXPIRY_DA  DEFAULT_TABLESPACE
----------  ----------------  ---------  ------------------------------
SCOTT       OPEN              31-MAR-01  USERS
```

Here we find only our own account information. We can see that our account password expires on March 31. We can also see in the ACCOUNT_STATUS column whether our password has expired and whether the system is allowing us to use grace logins.

You'll see many other examples of USER_ views throughout this book.

The ALL_ Views

Since users can access any Oracle object, provided the correct grants are given, you need a way to query the data dictionary metadata on those objects. Enter the ALL_ views, which provide a complete picture of objects you have access to, and other important database-level information. Because of security concerns, use of the ALL_ views is more restricted. For example, the ALL_USERS view only contains three columns, as opposed to ten columns for USER_USERS and twelve columns for DBA_USERS.

The next example is a query against the ALL_TABLES view. Contrast this against the earlier query on USER_TABLES. Note the inclusion of the OWNER column; this view can now report on multiple schemas if you have access to objects in multiple schemas. You can see some tables in the SCOTT2 schema in our example, which implies that we have some form of access to these tables. Of course, there are other views that will tell us what accesses we have, but we'll save that for Chapter 21.

```
SQL> SELECT owner, table_name, tablespace_name, pct_free, pct_used,
  pct_increase from all_tables WHERE OWNER NOT IN ('SYS','SYSTEM','OUTLN');
```

OWNER	TABLE_NAME	TABLESPACE_NAME	PCT_FREE	PCT_USED	PCT_INCREASE
SCOTT	DEPT	USERS	10	40	50
SCOTT	BONUS	USERS	10	40	50
SCOTT	SALGRADE	USERS	10	40	50
SCOTT	DUMMY	USERS	10	40	50
SCOTT	EMPLOYEE	USERS	10	40	50
SCOTT	TEST_RGF	USERS	10	40	50
SCOTT	TESTME	USERS	10	40	50
SCOTT	NEWTABLE	USERS	10	40	50
SCOTT	TEST_ME	USERS	10	40	50
SCOTT	PAY_TABLE	USERS	10	40	50
SCOTT2	EMP	LOCAL_UNIFORM	10	40	0
SCOTT2	DEPT	LOCAL_UNIFORM	10	40	0
SCOTT2	BONUS	LOCAL_UNIFORM	10	40	0
SCOTT2	SALGRADE	LOCAL_UNIFORM	10	40	0
SCOTT2	DUMMY	LOCAL_UNIFORM	10	40	0
SCOTT	TEMP_EMPLOYEE	USERS	10	40	50
SCOTT	TEMP_EMP	USERS	10	40	50
SCOTT	PARENT	USERS	10	40	50
SCOTT	CHILD	USERS	10	40	50
SCOTT	HOLD_EVENTS	USERS	10	40	50

Using the V$ Dynamic Performance Views

The V$ dynamic performance views are used primarily for the following purposes:

- For database performance monitoring and tuning, as discussed in Chapters 15 through 17.
- To facilitate recovery solutions for the database, as discussed in Chapters 10 through 13.

- For database documentation. In particular, the V$ views provide information on the redo logs and the control files. The rest of this chapter demonstrates this use in documenting particular database structures.

 NOTE Despite their name, the dynamic performance views are not truly "dynamic," in the sense that they are updated on a real-time basis. They should not be expected to provide real-time information.

Documenting the Database

This section presents a series of queries on data dictionary views that you can run to help you document your Oracle database. These reports will come in handy when you need to recover parts of your database, and when you run into odd problems with things such as user accesses. In addition, studying and understanding the reports will help you see how to better use the data dictionary.

We have included SQL*Plus formatting commands in the headers of these reports, so they should look as good on your screen as they do ours! Many of them utilize 132-character lines, so if you're going to print the output, you will want to do so in landscape mode. Also, notice that we've excluded the SYS and SYSTEM users in many of these reports. When you want to reinstate this data, simply remove the query lines that cause these users to be excluded.

All sorts of SQL code is used in these examples—outer joins, unions, and more. We hope the examples will get you started creating your own set of useful scripts for querying your data dictionary. The idea here is to get your feet wet, so that as you come across more detailed queries in other chapters of this book and in your everyday Oracle environment, you will develop a feeling of comfort with the data dictionary. When you can navigate it with ease, you will be a better DBA.

Database Tablespaces and Associated Datafiles

The query in Listing 4.5 will report on your database's tablespaces and the datafiles associated with those tablespaces. The output also includes the size of each datafile, and if you run this query in SQL*Plus, it will break on each tablespace, giving you the total size of each. In this listing we use several columns of the DBA_DATA_FILES data dictionary view, including TABLESPACE_NAME and FILE_NAME (to give us the name of the datafile associated with the tablespace, because each tablespace can have more than one datafile). Also, we include the BYTES column. The listing also shows the SQL*Plus report with sample output.

Listing 4.5: Report on Tablespaces and Datafiles

```
TTITLE CENTER "Database Tablespace and Datafile Report"
COLUMN no_prt NOPRINT
BREAK ON no_prt SKIP 2
COMPUTE SUM OF bytes ON no_prt
COMPUTE SUM OF bytes ON report
COLUMN bytes FORMAT 9,999,999,999
SELECT tablespace_name no_prt, tablespace_name, file_name, bytes
FROM dba_data_files
ORDER BY 1,2;
```

```
                     Database Tablespace and Datafile Report
TABLESPACE_NAME  FILE_NAME                                                           BYTES
---------------  ---------------------------------------------------------  --------------

LOCAL_UNIFORM    D:\ORACLE\ORADATA\ORA816\ORA816_LOCAL_UNIFORM_01.DBF            20,971,520
                                                                            --------------
                                                                                20,971,520


RBS              D:\ORACLE\ORADATA\ORA816\ORA816_RBS_01.DBF                      20,971,520
                                                                            --------------
                                                                                20,971,520


SYSTEM           D:\ORACLE\ORADATA\ORA816\SYSTEM01.DBF                           57,671,680
                                                                            --------------
                                                                                57,671,680


TEMP             D:\ORACLE\ORADATA\ORA816\ORA816_TEMP_01.DBF                     10,485,760
                                                                            --------------
                                                                                10,485,760


USERS            D:\ORACLE\ORADATA\ORA816\ORA816_USERS_01.DBF                    31,457,280
USERS            D:\ORACLE\ORADATA\ORA816\USERS02.DBF                             5,242,880
                                                                            --------------
                                                                                36,700,160
```

What can you deduce from this report? First of all, there is a problem with consistency in the naming convention for datafiles. This is always a serious management issue. (If you don't agree, you might want to reconsider your choice of career…or, at least, reread "Naming Conventions" in Chapter 3.). Whether you're naming file systems or datafiles or the objects within your database, be consistent!

Online Redo Logs

You can use the V$LOG and V$LOGFILE parameters to document the location and sizes of the online redo logs. Listing 4.6 shows a report that uses the data dictionary to document the location, number, and size of these logs on a Unix system. It is sorted by each redo log group, and then by the group member. Incidentally, this listing is a good example of spreading redo log group members among disks. The first members of the groups are sitting on disk /ora010, and the second member of each redo log group is sitting on disk /ora110.

Listing 4.6: Documenting Your Redo Logs

```
COLUMN member FORMAT a60
SET LINES 132
TTITLE CENTER "Redo Log Report"
BREAK ON REPORT
COMPUTE SUM OF bytes ON report
COLUMN bytes FORMAT 9,999,999,999

SELECT a.group#, b.member, a.bytes
FROM v$log a, v$logfile b
WHERE a.group#=b.group#
ORDER by 1,2;
```

GROUP#	MEMBER	BYTES
1	/ora101/oracle/DBDB/redo/dbdb_redo01a.log	104,857,600
1	/ora201/oracle/DBDB/redo/dbdb_redo01b.log	104,857,600
2	/ora101/oracle/DBDB/redo/dbdb_redo02a.log	104,857,600
2	/ora201/oracle/DBDB/redo/dbdb_redo02b.log	104,857,600
3	/ora101/oracle/DBDB/redo/dbdb_redo03a.log	104,857,600
3	/ora201/oracle/DBDB/redo/dbdb_redo03b.log	104,857,600
4	/ora101/oracle/DBDB/redo/dbdb_redo04a.log	104,857,600
4	/ora201/oracle/DBDB/redo/dbdb_redo04b.log	104,857,600
5	/ora101/oracle/DBDB/redo/dbdb_redo05a.log	104,857,600
5	/ora201/oracle/DBDB/redo/dbdb_redo05b.log	104,857,600
6	/ora101/oracle/DBDB/redo/dbdb_redo06a.log	104,857,600
6	/ora201/oracle/DBDB/redo/dbdb_redo06b.log	104,857,600

7	/ora101/oracle/DBDB/redo/dbdb_redo07a.log	104,857,600
7	/ora201/oracle/DBDB/redo/dbdb_redo07b.log	104,857,600
8	/or1a01/oracle/DBDB/redo/dbdb_redo08a.log	104,857,600
8	/or2a01/oracle/DBDB/redo/dbdb_redo08b.log	104,857,600
9	/or1a01/oracle/DBDB/redo/dbdb_redo09a.log	104,857,600
9	/or2a01/oracle/DBDB/redo/dbdb_redo09b.log	104,857,600
10	/or1a01/oracle/DBDB/redo/dbdb_redo10a.log	104,857,600
10	/or2a01/oracle/DBDB/redo/dbdb_redo10b.log	104,857,600
		--------------
sum		2,097,152,000

Control Files

You can use the V$PARAMETER and V$CONTROLFILE_RECORD_SECTION views to get the location and size of the control files. For example, should you need to re-create the `init.ora` parameter file, it helps to know where the control files used to be. Also, such a report helps you analyze the distribution of these files to ensure they are protected against accidental loss. Listing 4.7 is a nice little script that reports the location and size of each control file.

Listing 4.7: Documenting the Control Files

```
COLUMN NAME FORMAT a60
SET LINES 132
TTITLE CENTER "Control File Report"
BREAK ON REPORT
COMPUTE SUM OF bytes ON REPORT
COLUMN bytes FORMAT 9,999,999,999

SELECT c.name, b.db_block_value *
    (1 + 2 * sum(ceil(record_size * records_total
    / b.db_block_value))) bytes
    FROM sys.v_$controlfile_record_section a,
        (SELECT value db_block_value
            FROM v$parameter WHERE name='db_block_size') b,
            v$controlfile c
    GROUP by c.name, b.db_block_value;
```

```
Control File Report
NAME                                                          BYTES
-----------------------------------------------------   -----------
/ora101/oracle/DBDB/crtl/control01.ctl                    9,814,016
/ora201/oracle/DBDB/crtl/control02.ctl                    9,814,016
/ora301/oracle/DBDB/crtl/control03.ctl                    9,814,016
                                                        -----------
sum                                                      29,442,048
```

NOTE The number of bytes reported in this output is a close approximation. This script works fine on Solaris 2.6 with Oracle 8.1.6.3, but was about 8 blocks short on an NT system running 8.1.6. On other NT systems, however, it worked just fine (go figure!).

Current Parameters in Use

There are many times when the DBA needs to know the current setting of a database parameter. You'll also have frequent questions about the names and values of hidden parameters. In Chapter 3 we discussed the possibility of changing parameters dynamically. This report will provide the information you need in order to know if a parameter can be changed on-the-fly.

For session parameters, only two possibilities are reported: The parameter can either change (YES) or it cannot (NO). For system-level parameters, there are three possibilities: The parameter can change as soon as you issue the command (IMMEDIATE), or it will change as soon as your session exits (DEFERRED), or it cannot be changed at all (NO). The report also tells you whether the parameter is currently modified or is taking its default setting.

The report shown in Listing 4.8 has parameters sorted by name, with hidden parameters at the top. There's also a description of the parameter, which we have set up to display on a second line for each parameter in the report.

NOTE If you dig a little, you'll find that this report has many elements in common with the code for the V$PARAMETER view. This is one example of how you can study Oracle's handling of the data dictionary views and modify them to provide the data you really want. You might even consider turning this report into a view, named perhaps MYV$_ALL_PARAMETERS.

Listing 4.8: Report of Current Database Parameters

```
SET LINES 132
SET PAGES 66
TTITLE CENTER "Parameter Setting Report"
COLUMN "Parameter Name" FORMAT a25 WRAP
COLUMN "Value" FORMAT a20 WRAP
COLUMN "Default?" FORMAT a5
COLUMN "Session Modifiable" FORMAT a4
COLUMN "System Modifiable" FORMAT a12
COLUMN "Currently Modified" FORMAT a4
COLUMN "Oracle adjusted" FORMAT a4
COLUMN "Parameter Description" FORMAT a80
SELECT
ksppinm "Parameter Name",
ksppstvl "Value",
ksppstdf "Default?",
DECODE(BITAND(ksppiflg/256,1),1,'YES','NO') "Session Modifiable",
DECODE(BITAND(ksppiflg/65536,3),1,'IMMEDIATE',2,'DEFERRED',
   3,'IMMEDIATE','NO')
"System Modifiable ",
DECODE(BITAND(ksppstvf,7),1,'YES',4,'SYSTEM_MOD','NO')
   "Currently Modified",
DECODE(BITAND(ksppstvf,2),2,'YES','NO') "Oracle Adjusted",
SUBSTR(ksppdesc,1,80) "Parameter Description"
FROM x$ksppi x, x$ksppcv y
WHERE (x.indx = y.indx)
ORDER BY ksppinm;

Parameter Setting Report
Parameter Name            Value                 Defau Sess System    Mo  Curr Orac
------------------------- --------------------  ----- ---- --------- ---- ----
Parameter Description
------------------------------------------------------------
_use_vector_post          TRUE                  TRUE  NO   NO             NO   NO
use vector post
_wait_for_sync            TRUE                  TRUE  NO   NO             NO   NO
wait for sync on commit MUST BE ALWAYS TRUE
_walk_insert_threshold    0                     TRUE  NO   NO             NO   NO
maximum number of unusable blocks to walk across freelist
```

_write_clones	3	TRUE	NO	IMMEDIATE	NO	NO
write clones flag						
_yield_check_interval	100	TRUE	YES	IMMEDIATE	NO	NO
interval to check whether actses should yield						
active_instance_count		TRUE	NO	NO	NO	NO
number of active instances in the parallel server						
always_anti_join	NESTED_LOOPS	TRUE	NO	NO	NO	NO
always use this anti-join when possible						
always_semi_join	standard	TRUE	NO	NO	NO	NO
always use this semi-join when possible						
aq_tm_processes	0	TRUE	NO	IMMEDIATE	NO	NO
number of AQ Time Managers to start						
audit_trail	NONE	TRUE	NO	NO	NO	NO
enable system auditing						
background_dump_dest	D:\Oracle\admin\ora8 16\bdump	FALSE	NO	IMMEDIATE	NO	NO
Detached process dump directory						
backup_tape_io_slaves	FALSE	TRUE	NO	DEFERRED	NO	NO
BACKUP Tape I/O slaves						
bitmap_merge_area_size	1048576	TRUE	NO	NO	NO	NO
maximum memory allow for BITMAP MERGE						
blank_trimming	FALSE	TRUE	NO	NO	NO	NO
blank trimming semantics parameter						
buffer_pool_keep		TRUE	NO	NO	NO	NO
Number of database blocks/latches in keep buffer pool						
buffer_pool_recycle		TRUE	NO	NO	NO	NO
Number of database blocks/latches in recycle buffer pool						
commit_point_strength	1	TRUE	NO	NO	NO	NO
Bias this node has toward not preparing in a two-phase commit						
compatible	8.1.6	FALSE	NO	NO	NO	NO
Database will be completely compatible with this software versio						
control_file_record_keep_ time	7	TRUE	NO	IMMEDIATE	NO	NO
control file record keep time in days						

PL/SQL Objects in the Database

The report in Listing 4.9 documents the names and types of PL/SQL objects in the database, sorted by schema and object name. It can serve as a good cover page for the report described in the next section, which extracts the syntax of the PL/SQL code in the database.

Listing 4.9: PL/SQL Code in the Database

```
COLUMN object_name FORMAT a50
SET LINES 132
SET PAGES 66
TTITLE CENTER "Stored PL/SQL Object Listing"
SELECT owner, object_name, object_type
FROM dba_objects
WHERE object_type IN ('FUNCTI/ON','PROCEDURE','PACKAGE',
  'PACKAGE BODY','TRIGGER')
ORDER BY owner, object_type, object_name;
                       Stored PL/SQL Object Listing
OWNER                   OBJECT_NAME                                  OBJECT_TYPE
---------------------   ------------------------------------------   -----------
SCOTT                   GET_ALL_BYTES                                PROCEDURE
SCOTT                   MY_PROCEDURE                                 PROCEDURE
SCOTT                   EMPLOYEE_TRIGGER                             TRIGGER
```

PL/SQL Object Text

In the RevealNet Knowledge Base for Oracle Administration, you'll find a report on the text of all PL/SQL objects within the database, titled PL/SQL Source Report. With just a tiny bit of modification to the code, you could have it extract just a specific piece of PL/SQL, or just the PL/SQL for a specific user.

Users' Setups in the Database

The report produced by the code in Listing 4.10 documents the users in the database, sorted by username. (The output has been slightly modified to fit on this page.)

NOTE Don't forget about the importance of keeping your SYSTEM tablespace unfragmented and unfilled. Controlling the default tablespace settings for users is particularly important in preventing this. The report shown in Listing 4.10 can be used to alert you about users with incorrect temporary tablespace or default tablespace settings.

Listing 4.10: Database User Report
```
SET LINES 132
SET PAGES 66
SELECT a.username, a.default_tablespace, a.temporary_tablespace,
    NVL(b.num_objects,0) "Number of Objects"
FROM dba_users a,
    (SELECT owner, COUNT(*) num_objects
    FROM dba_objects GROUP BY owner) b
WHERE b.owner (+) = a.username
ORDER BY 1;


USERNAME    DEFAULT     TEMPORARY   Number of Objects
----------  ----------  ----------  -----------------
DBSNMP      SYSTEM      SYSTEM                      4
OUTLN       SYSTEM      SYSTEM                      5
PERFSTAT    PERFSTAT    TEMP                       59
REPO        REPOSITORY  TEMP                       99
REPOSITORY  REPOSITORY  TEMP                        0
SCOTT       USERS       TEMPTEMP                   15
SYS         SYSTEM      TEMP                     2160
SYSTEM      TOOLS       TEMP                       59
```

List of Current Roles

Listing 4.11 shows the SQL to produce a report that lists the current roles in your database, and the grants that those roles have. This report is specific to roles and excludes other types of grantees.

Listing 4.11: Role Grants Report
```
SET PAGES 66
SET LINES 80
BREAK ON role SKIP 1
TTITLE CENTER "Role Grants Report"
SELECT a.role, b.privilege
FROM dba_roles a, dba_tab_privs b
WHERE a.role=b.grantee
UNION
SELECT a.role, b.privilege
FROM dba_roles a, dba_sys_privs b
WHERE a.role=b.grantee
ORDER BY 1, 2;
```

List of Current Grants

The report produced from Listing 4.12 is a listing of all the grants that all users have, sorted by grantee, object, and type; it also includes direct grants to objects and system grants. In addition, you can see whether the users have the ability to grant the role they own to other users. This report uses a join and unions between several data dictionary tables, including DBA_ROLE_PRIVS, DBA_TAB_PRIVS, and DBA_SYS_PRIVS.

Listing 4.12: Current Grants to Users

```
SET PAGES 66
SET LINES 132
BREAK ON grantee SKIP 1
SELECT   a.grantee, 'Object Grant' AS grant_type, b.privilege,
     b.grantable AS "Grant Option"
FROM dba_role_privs a, dba_tab_privs b
WHERE a.grantee=b.grantee
UNION
SELECT   a.grantee, 'System Grant' AS grant_type, b.privilege,
     b.admin_option AS "Grant Option"
FROM dba_role_privs a, dba_sys_privs b
WHERE a.grantee=b.grantee
UNION
SELECT a.grantee, 'Role' AS grant_type, a.granted_role,
     a.admin_option AS "Grant Option"
FROM dba_role_privs a
ORDER BY 1, 2
```

Current Index Key Structures

Often, the DBA will want to produce a list of indexes and the columns they are built on. This is very handy when tuning SQL statements. Listing 4.13 is a SQL statement that will produce a report on indexes and their key structures. It presents the username, the table on which the index is built, the index type, and the key order of the columns. This report uses the DBA_IND_COLUMNS data dictionary view.

Listing 4.13: Index Key Report

```
SET LINES 132
COLUMN table_owner FORMAT a20
COLUMN index_name FORMAT a25
COLUMN column_name FORMAT a25
```

```
BREAK ON table_owner SKIP 1
BREAK ON index_name SKIP 3

SELECT table_owner, index_name,
    column_name, column_position
FROM dba_ind_columns
WHERE table_owner NOT IN ('SYSTEM','SYS','OUTLN')
ORDER BY table_owner, index_name, column_position;
```

Current Foreign Key Relationships Established

A list of foreign key relationships established between tables helps when you want to modify a table and you need to temporarily remove the foreign keys associated with that table. The report output from the query in Listing 4.14 shows the table that is the parent in the foreign key relationship. It then lists the child tables, and the columns in the relationship.

Listing 4.14: Foreign Key Relationships

```
SELECT b.owner, b.table_name "Parent Table",
    a.table_name "Child Table", a.constraint_name
FROM dba_constraints a, dba_constraints b
WHERE a.owner NOT IN ('SYS','SYSTEM','OUTLN')
AND a.constraint_type='R'
AND b.owner=a.r_owner
AND b.constraint_name=a.r_constraint_name;
```

OWNER	Parent Table	Child Table	CONSTRAINT_NAME
CSPS_OWN	SY_ERROR_SEVERITY	SY_ERROR_MESSAGE	FK_ERROR_SEVERITY_ERROR_MSG
CSPS_OWN	SY_SECURITY_POINT	SY_SECURITY_GROUP_ACCESS	FK_SCRTY_PNT_SCRTY_GRP_ACCESS
CSPS_OWN	SY_SECURITY_GROUP	SY_SECURITY_GROUP_ACCESS	FK_SECURITY_GRP_GRP_ACCESS
CSPS_OWN	SY_SECURITY_POINT	SY_SECURITY_POINT_OBJECT	FK_SCRTY_PT_SCRTY_PT_OBJCT
CSPS_OWN	AGENT_INFO	SY_SECURITY_USER_ACCESS	FK_AGNT_INFO_SCRTY_USR_ACCESS
CSPS_OWN	SY_SECURITY_GROUP	SY_SECURITY_USER_ACCESS	FK_SCRTY_GRP_USER_ACCESS
CSPS_OWN	CSIROUTE	CSILOCAL	FK_CALLGROUP_LOCALE
CSPS_OWN	CSIRSDIV	CSWUOWPM	FK_CSIRSDIV_CSWUOWPM
CSPS_OWN	CSILOCAL	CSILCCMT	FK_LOCALE_COMMENT
CSPS_OWN	CSIRSDIV	CSIGINFO	FK_CSIRSDIV_CSIGINFO
CSPS_OWN	CSIRSDIV	CSIDNISG	FK_RESPDIV_DNIS
CSPS_OWN	CSIROUTE	CSIDNISG	FK_ROUTE_DNIS

CSPS_OWN	CSWALERT	CSWALUOW	FK_ALERTLOG_ASSIGNMENT
CSPS_OWN	CSIROUTE	CSIRTCMT	FK_CALLGROUP_COMMENT
CSPS_OWN	CSWUOWS	CSWALUOW	FK_UOW_ASSIGNMENT
CSPS_OWN	CSICALLS	CSIXFERL	PK_CALL_TRANSFER
CSPS_OWN	CSWUOWS	CSWRASGN	FK_UOW_RESOURCE_ASGN
CSPS_OWN	CSWUOWGP	CSWGRPAS	FK_UOWGROUP_GROUPASGN
CSPS_OWN	CSHSYSCP	CSHSCRPT	FK_CSHSYSCP_CSHSCRPT
CSPS_OWN	CSBLSTTB	CSBRULTB	FK_CSBLSTTB_CSBRULTB
CSPS_OWN	CSBLSTTB	CSBSTHTB	FK_CSBLSTTB_CSBSTHTB

Dependencies

Knowing about dependencies for objects helps the DBA to predict the downstream impacts of changing a given object. Also, you'll often need to know all of the dependencies on a particular object type so you can alter it. Listing 4.15 provides a report that lists each object and all other objects that have a dependency on that object.

Listing 4.15: Object Dependencies

```
SET PAGES 66
SET LINES 132
COLUMN owner FORMAT a20 WRAP
COLUMN name FORMAT a20 WRAP
COLUMN referenced_owner FORMAT a20 WRAP
COLUMN referenced_name FORMAT a20 WRAP

SELECT owner, name, type,
    referenced_owner, referenced_name, referenced_type
FROM dba_dependencies
WHERE owner NOT IN ('SYS','SYSTEM','OUTLN')
ORDER BY owner, name, type;
```

OWNER	NAME	TYPE	REFERENCED	REFERENCED_NAME	REFERENCED_T
SCOTT	ADDRESS_TYPE	TYPE	SYS	STANDARD	PACKAGE
SCOTT	ADDRESS_TYPE_NT	TYPE	SYS	STANDARD	PACKAGE
SCOTT	ADDRESS_TYPE_NT	TYPE	SCOTT	ADDRESS_TYPE	TYPE
SCOTT	ADDRESS_VARRAY	TYPE	SYS	STANDARD	PACKAGE
SCOTT	ADDRESS_VARRAY	TYPE	SCOTT	ADDRESS_TYPE	TYPE
SCOTT	CHILD_TYPE	TYPE	SYS	STANDARD	PACKAGE
SCOTT	CHILD_TYPE	TYPE	SCOTT	NAME_TYPE	TYPE

SCOTT	CHILD_TYPE_NT	TYPE	SYS	STANDARD	PACKAGE
SCOTT	CHILD_TYPE_NT	TYPE	SCOTT	CHILD_TYPE	TYPE
SCOTT	GET_ALL_BYTES	PROCEDURE	SYS	STANDARD	PACKAGE
SCOTT	GET_ALL_BYTES	PROCEDURE	SYS	SYS_STUB_FOR_PURITY_ANALYSIS	PACKAGE
SCOTT	GET_ALL_BYTES	PROCEDURE	SYS	DBA_DATA_FILES	VIEW
SCOTT	GET_ALL_BYTES	PROCEDURE	PUBLIC	DBA_DATA_FILES	SYNONYM
SCOTT	GET_ALL_BYTES	PROCEDURE	SCOTT	DBA_DATA_FILES	NON-EXISTENT
SCOTT	GET_ALL_BYTES	PROCEDURE	SCOTT	DBMS_OUTPUT	NON-EXISTENT
SCOTT	GET_ALL_BYTES	PROCEDURE	PUBLIC	DBMS_OUTPUT	SYNONYM
SCOTT	GET_ALL_BYTES	PROCEDURE	SYS	DBMS_OUTPUT	PACKAGE
SCOTT	MY_PROCEDURE	PROCEDURE	SYS	STANDARD	PACKAGE
SCOTT	MY_PROCEDURE	PROCEDURE	SYS	DBMS_OUTPUT	PACKAGE
SCOTT	MY_PROCEDURE	PROCEDURE	SYS	DBA_TABLES	VIEW
SCOTT	MY_PROCEDURE	PROCEDURE	SCOTT	DBMS_OUTPUT	NON-EXISTENT
SCOTT	MY_PROCEDURE	PROCEDURE	PUBLIC	DBMS_OUTPUT	SYNONYM
SCOTT	NAME_TYPE	TYPE	SYS	STANDARD	PACKAGE
SCOTT	PARENT_TYPE	TYPE	SYS	STANDARD	PACKAGE
SCOTT	PARENT_TYPE	TYPE BODY	SYS	STANDARD	PACKAGE
SCOTT	PARENT_TYPE	TYPE BODY	SCOTT	PARENT_TYPE	TYPE
SCOTT	TEMP_TYPE	TYPE	SYS	STANDARD	PACKAGE
SCOTT	TEMP_TYPE	TYPE	SCOTT	ADDRESS_TYPE	TYPE

Certain operations, such as replacing PL/SQL code and upgrading or migrating the database, will cause dependent PL/SQL programs to go into an invalid state. You can discover these invalid objects by querying the DBA_OBJECTS table and looking for a status of INVALID. Usually the objects will recompile themselves the next time they are run, but not always. Also, database changes can sometimes invalidate an object because the change itself has invalidated the object. For example, say you've recreated a table and accidentally dropped a column that a PL/SQL function depends on. You'll want to know about this error as soon as possible, so it's always a good idea to recompile all invalid objects after performing database maintenance. To do this, log on as SYS or SYSTEM and run the Oracle script $ORACLE_HOME/rdbms/admin/utlrp.sql. It will recompile all database objects until it determines that the only objects left are those that will not compile. Then you can check DBA_OBJECTS for invalid objects, and anything leftover from utlrp.sqp should be investigated.

In closing, we want to emphasize that it's really important that you become comfortable with the data dictionary. If you are a DBA who is accustomed to using tools for managing your database, try to do your work manually next time. It might take you a little longer, but in the end you'll be a better, smarter DBA.

PART II

Oracle Database Administration

LEARN TO:

- *Manage tablespaces, indexes, and clusters*
- *Configure Net8*
- *Backup and recover databases*
- *Use LogMiner*

CHAPTER 5

Understanding Oracle8i Architecture

FEATURING:

Oracle storage architecture	176
Oracle memory structures	181
Oracle processes	188
Oracle database control structures	192
Oracle scalar datatypes	205

The key to managing Oracle databases is understanding the basic architecture of an Oracle database. Oracle presents a sophisticated orchestration of processes, volatile structures, and persistent structures that all play in harmony. Just as an orchestra has different types of instruments—the percussion, woodwinds, brass, and strings—Oracle has its own instruments that sing the song of a robust relational database.

Before you can successfully manage Oracle, you need to know how its mechanisms work and *why* they work. When you understand why a thing works the way it does, you will be prepared to deal with the times when it isn't working as it should.

In this chapter, we will try to peel back some of the architectural foundations of Oracle. We will begin with the basic storage units: blocks, extents, and segments. Next, we will cover the Oracle memory structures and processes. Then we will talk about the Oracle elements that provide the controls that ensure the integrity of a database, including transactions, SCNs, rollback segments, control files, redo logs, and the database datafiles themselves. Finally, we will cover the Oracle scalar datatypes.

Oracle Storage Architecture

Which came first—the segment or the block? The question of the ages, isn't it? In Chapter 1, you were introduced to the basic elements of Oracle: the block, the extent, and the segment. Here, we will go into the details of how each of these elements works.

The Block

The *block* in Oracle is the smallest allocation unit inside the Oracle database. All storage in an Oracle database boils down to units of blocks.

An Oracle block consists of a block header and whatever is stored in the block, such as row or index entries. Figure 5.1 illustrates the structure of the Oracle block. The block header grows from the top down, whereas the data in the block grows from the bottom up. This is to allow for expansion of the block header if required. Oracle manages free space fragmentation within the block itself, so the DBA does not need to be concerned with those fragmentation issues.

FIGURE 5.1
The Oracle block structure

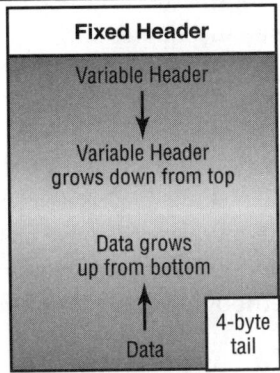

The block header is divided into four sections:

Fixed block header The fixed block header is about 57 bytes for a table and about 113 bytes for an index. This header holds various fixed information about the block, such as the block type (say, data or index), and also includes 4 bytes at the end of the block.

Variable transaction header This portion of the block header is 23 bytes times the setting of INITRANS and is present for both table and index blocks. This header can also grow dynamically as required, up to the size of 23 bytes times MAXTRANS. This structure holds information about transactions that will access the block. Space is reserved for only one transaction, but this can be overridden through the use of the INITRANS parameter. If additional transactions need to access the block, either free space in the block or an old transaction entry will be used. Once space for a transaction entry in a block has been allocated, it will never be de-allocated.

Table directory Table blocks include a table directory, which indicates the number of tables that the block is associated with. If the block is part of a non-clustered table, this section will be 4 bytes. If the block is part of a clustered set of tables, this section will grow by 4 bytes for each additional table in the cluster.

Row directory Table blocks also include a row directory. As each row is added to the block, 2 bytes are allocated for use in the row directory. As with the variable transaction header, this space is not reclaimed if a row is removed, but it is reserved for reuse.

The block size of a database is defined when the database is created, and the database block size cannot be changed unless the database is re-created. Oracle provides four parameters that allow you to control block usage: PCTFREE, PCTUSED, INITRANS, and MAXTRANS. We will discuss these parameters, as well as how to calculate block header size, in detail in Chapter 6.

The Extent

An *extent* is a collection of contiguous Oracle blocks used when allocating space to an object. In Oracle8i, blocks are allocated to extents using either dictionary-managed extent allocation (which was the only method available before Oracle8i) or bit-mapped extent allocations via locally managed tablespaces. Let's look at how these two allocation methods work in a bit more detail.

Dictionary-Managed Extent Allocation

When an extent is allocated using dictionary management, the blocks assigned to that extent are allocated from the data dictionary. When a dictionary-managed tablespace is created, the free space in that tablespace is recorded in the data dictionary table FET$. When an extent is to be allocated, Oracle will look in FET$ for a number of contiguous blocks to satisfy the extent allocation request. If the number of contiguous blocks is found, those blocks are removed from FET$ and registered with the data dictionary table UET$ as allocated blocks.

If Oracle cannot find a sufficient number of free blocks (either because not enough blocks exist or not enough contiguous free blocks exist), the extent allocation will fail. This extent allocation failure will cause a failure of the transaction that needed the segment to be extended, and that transaction will be rolled back. If a number of extents are de-allocated from a tablespace, the blocks are removed from the UET$ table and are reallocated to the FET$ table.

Because dictionary-managed extent allocation occurs in the data dictionary (such as tracking of free and used extents), all of the typical database activity revolving around dictionary operations also takes place during the operation. This includes redo generation and rollback segment usage, which can be I/O-intensive, causing performance problems.

Locally Managed Tablespace Extent Allocation

When dealing with locally managed tablespaces, the space management is handled by a bitmap in the datafile header of each datafile of the tablespace. Within the bitmap in each datafile, each bit is assigned to one extent within that datafile.

With locally managed tablespaces, the overhead associated with space management is reduced somewhat when compared to dictionary-managed tablespaces. However, there is still a great deal of dictionary activity related to locally managed tablespaces (that's why you need to do an export when you are moving a locally managed tablespace).

The Segment

Segments consist of one or more extents, and these extents must consist of contiguous blocks. Thus, the hierarchy of order from the most atomic to the least atomic object in an Oracle database is (smallest to largest) block to extent to segment. Figure 5.2 illustrates this hierarchy for the storage of an Oracle table, which is an Oracle segment.

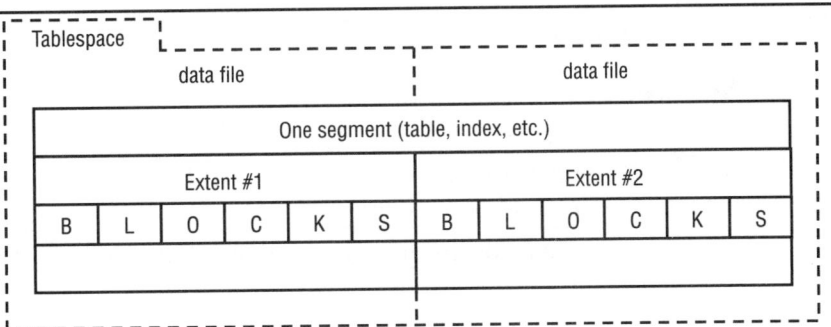

FIGURE 5.2

The Oracle storage hierarchy

The primary job of a segment is to act as a logical storage entity for a set of related physical information stored in the database. A given segment can exist in only one tablespace. Each segment is associated with a user object such as a table or an index. In fact, the terms *objects* and *segments* are synonyms, for the most part.

 NOTE We are limiting our discussion in this chapter to nonpartitioned objects/segments. Some of the rules about segments change a bit when you introduce partitioning into the mix (for example, a partitioned object can consist of multiple segments in multiple tablespaces). We will look at partitioning in Chapter 24.

There are four primary kinds of segments: data, index, rollback, and temporary. A segment may contain user data, perhaps in the form of a table. A segment may also contain sort information in the form of a sort segment, or it may contain certain parts of table data in sorted order in the form of an index. The following are examples of segments available in Oracle:

- Heap table (the default type of Oracle table)

- Hash cluster
- Index-organized table
- B*Tree index
- Function-based index
- Temporary segment
- Rollback segment
- Large Object (LOB) segment
- Object table
- Bitmap index

Segment Purposes

Segments have different purposes. Some are used to store data, some are used to help with the performance of retrieving that data, and others allow you to retrieve data in the format you want. Here is a summary of the four basic purposes of segments:

- Store user data (heap tables, object tables, index-organized tables, and LOB segments)
- Facilitate faster access to user data (indexes)
- Provide temporary segment space for sorting (temporary segments)
- Provide transactional read consistency and the ability to roll back transactions (rollback segments)

In some cases, a segment may actually take on a duality of roles, allowing the user to store data in it, but also storing it in a way that allows for fast lookups. This is the case, for example, with index-organized tables.

Segment Structure

Keep in mind that each segment really consists of a bunch of blocks. For each segment, one block is allocated as the header block. This block contains a great deal of information about the segment, including the following:

- A map of all extents allocated to the segment
- A set of free list entries (a process free list and a transaction free list)
- Control information about the segment

> **TIP** If you create a segment that has unlimited extents, other blocks in the segment can be allocated as needed to maintain the extent map.

The free lists control the number of concurrent INSERT operations that can occur to the segment that the header block belongs to. There are two kinds of free lists:

- *Process free lists* are for blocks that have been cleared by a process, but have not yet been committed (and thus, they are not available for other transactions to use). Process free lists are required to satisfy read-consistency requirements of the database and facilitate the rollback of Oracle transactions.
- *Transaction free lists* contain available blocks for a given transaction to use. When a transaction issues a COMMIT, the blocks on the process free list map are moved to the transaction free list map.

Oracle Memory Structures

In order to manage, monitor, and tune your databases, you'll need to understand what Oracle's memory structures are, how they are configured, and how they can impact database operations. In this section, we will talk about the System Global Area (SGA), private memory, and other memory areas that Oracle uses.

The System Global Area (SGA)

The SGA is a critical area of shared memory that is allocated as the database instance is started. Within the SGA, a *server process* is a database process that handles requests from connected user processes. Oracle *user processes* attach to the SGA to move data from the database to memory and then to the user. All database data is changed only within the SGA; data is never changed directly on the disk.

Think of the SGA as a "string" of database blocks, as illustrated in Figure 5.3. That string has a beginning and an end. The first blocks at the beginning of this string are the *most recently used (MRU)* part of the SGA. The last block of the SGA is the *least recently used (LRU)* part of the SGA. And, since Oracle8i, the middle (*midpoint*) of this string also must be considered.

FIGURE 5.3

The SGA MRU, midpoint, and LRU

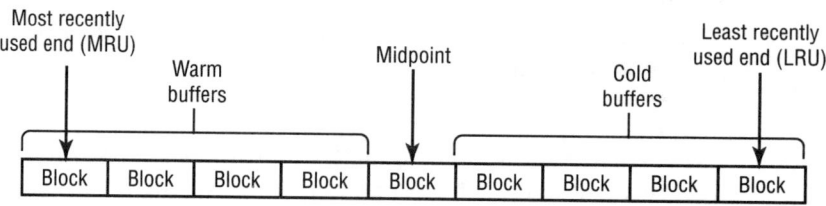

When a server process moves database blocks from the database datafiles into the SGA, Oracle processes those blocks based on what kind of access is occurring:

- If Oracle is reading blocks as the result of an index scan or a ROWID table lookup that occurs as the result of an index scan, Oracle will load the block containing that row into the midpoint of the LRU list. This is known as *midpoint insertion*.

- Each block in the SGA has a touch counter associated with it. As a block is used or reused, its touch counter is increased. Blocks with the highest touch counts are "hot" blocks. Those with the lowest touch counts are candidates for aging out and reuse by other operations that need SGA space. When a block is reused, its touch count will be reset.

 TIP If you want to see the touch count for a given block, you can look at the TCH column of the SYS.X$BH view. This view maintains a row for each block that is stored in the SGA.

- If Oracle is reading blocks as the result of a full table scan, it will read in a number of blocks (defined by the parameter DB_FILE_MULTIBLOCK_READ_COUNT) at one time, and load them into the SGA with a touch count of 1. Thus, during a full table scan, one I/O will result in several blocks being loaded into the SGA.

The SGA contains several substructures: the database buffer cache, the shared pool, and the redo log buffer. The SGA substructures are discussed in more detail in the following sections.

The Database Buffer Cache

The *database buffer cache* is an area of shared memory for storing database blocks. As the Oracle processes require access to blocks of data in the Oracle datafiles, the blocks are moved from the datafiles into the database buffer cache. Once a block has been moved into memory, the data within the block can be retrieved.

Note that at no time does the server process read rows directly from the datafiles or write to the datafiles. The server reads blocks only from the datafiles and places them into the database buffer cache. The process of writing out to the datafiles is the responsibility of the DBW*n* (Database Writer) process (described in the "Oracle Processes" section later in this chapter).

NOTE As with many things in Oracle, there are always exceptions. Sometimes, the server process does indeed write directly to the datafiles; these are known as *direct loads*. Direct loads circumvent the traditional Oracle architecture and are discussed in later chapters.

The database buffer cache is measured in database blocks. The database block size is established when the database is created, and it cannot be changed without dropping and rebuilding the database. Thus, the total overall size of the database buffer cache is the product of the DB_BLOCK_BUFFERS and DB_BLOCK_SIZE parameters in the `init.ora` file. Two databases can have the same number of DB_BLOCK_BUFFERS allocated but have significantly different amounts of overall memory allocated to the database buffer cache.

In Oracle8i, the database buffer cache structure may be made up of as many as three different kinds of buffer pools: the *default buffer pool*, *keep buffer pool*, and *recycle buffer pool*. The keep buffer pool and the recycle buffer pool are new structures in Oracle8i. The memory that is allocated to these buffer pools comes directly from the default buffer pool. The three caches serve the following purposes:

Default buffer pool The default buffer pool is the same as the database buffer cache in earlier versions of Oracle. The total size of the default buffer pool is based on the combination of settings for database initialization parameters DB_BLOCK_BUFFERS and BLOCK_SIZE.

Keep buffer pool The keep buffer pool stores data blocks that must be pinned in memory and not aged out. This might include key lookup tables or important partitions in a partitioned table.

Recycle buffer pool The recycle buffer pool stores database blocks that will be read infrequently. By assigning these blocks to the recycle buffer pool, you insulate the blocks in the default buffer pool from the effects of loading infrequently used data or index blocks. For example, you might assign to this pool tables that undergo frequent index lookups, but the same block is rarely read more than once over a long period.

NOTE Proper allocation of memory to the database buffer cache is critical to the database's overall performance. Undersize the cache, and you end up with more disk I/O, which is not a good thing for performance. Oversize the cache, and you may cause paging and swapping of memory in and out to disk—also not a good thing. See Chapter 15 for details on monitoring and tuning the database buffer cache.

The Shared Pool

The *shared pool* is a pool of memory allocated to several subpools. As a DBA, you allocate memory to the shared pool via the parameter SHARED_POOL_SIZE in the init.ora file. Unlike the database buffer cache, which is allocated in blocks, the shared pool is allocated in bytes. To allocate a small, 50MB shared pool, the init.ora setting would look like this:

shared_pool_size=50000000

The shared pool consists of the following structures:

Library cache This includes several structures, including the shared and private SQL areas, PL/SQL procedures and packages, and some control structures such as locks and library cache handles.

Data dictionary cache This is memory allocated for the storage of data dictionary views and tables. These objects contain information about the database, its objects, and its users.

Control structures These are the structures needed for basic database operation.

TIP Can you allocate too much space to the shared pool? Sure you can! In most cases, a large shared pool (generally starting at about 200MB) can begin to cause performance problems. The performance problems with large pool sizes include fragmentation (which is much less of an issue with later releases of 8i) and latch contention. Also, the hashing of SQL statements during the parse stages of SQL statement execution can be negatively impacted by large shared pools.

The Redo Log Buffer

The redo log buffer area in the SGA stores information about changes that have occurred in the database. This buffer holds the redo log records that are being buffered for writes to the Oracle redo logs by the Oracle LGWR (Log Writer) process (described in the "Oracle Processes" section later in this chapter. You can control the size of the redo log buffer by changing the init.ora parameter LOG_BUFFER.

 TIP There is a tendency to want to overallocate memory to the redo log buffer. Generally, setting LOG_BUFFER above 1MB will cause performance to suffer, rather than improve.

How Big Is the SGA?

You can determine the size of the SGA by looking at the V$SGASTAT dynamic performance view. Here is an example of a query against this view:

```
SQL> SELECT * FROM v$sgastat;

POOL         NAME                       BYTES
-----------  -------------------------  ----------
             fixed_sga                      75804
             db_block_buffers             1048576
             log_buffer                     66560
shared pool  free memory                  1108016
shared pool  miscellaneous                 414420
shared pool  trigger inform                   120
shared pool  table columns                  16916
shared pool  KQLS heap                     139176
shared pool  dlo fib struct                 40980
shared pool  java static objs               30560
shared pool  Checkpoint queue               73764

POOL         NAME                       BYTES
-----------  -------------------------  ----------
shared pool  latch nowait fails or sle      37632
shared pool  fixed allocation callback        320
shared pool  db_handles                     75000
shared pool  sessions                      366520
shared pool  enqueue_resources             129024
shared pool  State objects                 247360
shared pool  file # translation table       65572
shared pool  db_files                      370988
shared pool  SYSTEM PARAMETERS              63620
```

```
shared pool long op statistics array      74800
shared pool transactions                 166804

POOL        NAME                          BYTES
----------- ----------------------------- ----------
shared pool KGFF heap                      6552
shared pool PL/SQL DIANA                 311068
shared pool ktlbk state objects           80036
shared pool dictionary cache             164808
shared pool branches                      45120
shared pool DML locks                     89760
shared pool character set memory          32372
shared pool message pool freequeue       124552
shared pool library cache                357324
shared pool db_block_buffers              69632
shared pool sql area                     339448

POOL        NAME                          BYTES
----------- ----------------------------- ----------
shared pool PL/SQL MPCODE                 30664
shared pool processes                    121200
shared pool PLS non-lib hp                 2096
shared pool KGK heap                      17548
shared pool event statistics per sess   584800
large pool  free memory                 614400
java pool   free memory                  32768

40 rows selected.
```

This report shows the different memory allocations to the pools in the SGA. Notice that each pool actually consists of several different memory areas. It is also interesting to note that three of the memory areas have NULL pools, as indicated by the first three lines of the query output above:

- The FIXED_SGA line indicates the "overhead" that is required to maintain the SGA. This is not configurable, and it varies with different Oracle versions and even operating system versions and releases.
- The DB_BLOCK_BUFFERS line indicates the allocated size of the database buffer cache.
- The LOG_BUFFER line indicates the memory allocated to the redo log buffer.

NOTE The LOG_BUFFER allocation shown in the V$SGASTAT dynamic performance view may or may not be the same size as the LOG_BUFFER parameter that is set in the database parameter file. This is because there may be additional space added to the redo log buffer in the form of "guard" pages, which protect the pages of the redo log buffer. Also, there is a minimum size for the redo log buffer of four times the database block size.

The Process Global Area (PGA)

The PGA is stored in *private process memory*, which is just memory allocated to the process you are running. The PGA memory is a private structure, rather than a shared memory structure like the SGA. A PGA is established for each Oracle process when it is started and contains information for only that process. Along with data about various operating system resources and processes, the PGA also may store the User Global Area (UGA) and the Call Global Area (CGA).

The UGA contains session-specific information (your session state). It is allocated at the time the session is started and consists of a fixed area and a variable area of memory. The UGA contains the sort area (used for sorting primarily) and private SQL and PL/SQL areas. Storage of the UGA depends on the configuration of the database. For a normal database (one that is not configured with Oracle's multithreaded server option), the UGA is located in the PGA. In a multithreaded server-configured database, the UGA is contained within the large pool if allocated; otherwise, it is in the shared pool.

The CGA exists only for the duration of a single SQL statement call. The CGA is always stored within the PGA, unlike the UGA, which might find itself in the SGA or the large pool.

Other Oracle Memory Structures

In addition to the SGA, the Oracle database comprises some other significant memory structures:

Large pool This is an optional memory area configured by the DBA. It is used for multithreaded server (MTS) session memory (the UGA), I/O server process memory, and the Recovery Manager (RMAN).

Java pool This is an optional memory area used by the Java Memory Manager to allocate memory to Java processes. This memory area is contained in the SGA.

Sort areas Controlled by the parameter SORT_AREA_SIZE, sort area memory is taken from the SGA if MTS is being used. Otherwise, it's taken from outside the

SGA. Only one SORT_AREA_SIZE is allocated to a given process; then sorts will start to go to disk.

Request and response queues If MTS is enabled, request and response queues are created in the SGA. They serve as queuing areas for the shared server processes and for the client processes that connect to the queues through the dispatcher processes.

Oracle Processes

In order to make Oracle as efficient as possible, the way that the database processes are run depends on the operating system. For example, on Unix systems, individual processes are spawned for each of the Oracle processes that compose the instance. Each of these processes is called a *background process*. Each user session is also an individual Unix process (and thus has a Unix process ID associated with it). On a Windows NT system, when Oracle is started using one executable (`oracle.exe`), it spawns threads for all of the other needed processes. As users connect, additional threads are added for each connection. In this book, we use the term *processes* (or *background processes*) in a somewhat general manner.

There are three types of Oracle processes: server processes, required processes, and optional processes. The technical implementation of these processes may differ on various platforms, but they will operate on each platform.

Server Processes

The job of server processes is to provide a connection between a client application and the Oracle database. It is through this connection that SQL commands are processed and result sets are returned.

Server processes are responsible for many database operations, such as the following:

- Parsing the SQL query
- Managing any shared pool operations associated with that SQL
- Creating the query plan and its execution
- Finding the database in the database datafiles
- Moving that data to the database buffer cache, if that action is required (which we hope it will not be)

The Oracle server processes come in two flavors: dedicated and shared. Shared server processes (along with MTS Dispatcher processes) are associated with the Oracle

MTS option. One shared server process may represent a connection of several clients to the database. Dedicated server processes have a one-to-one relationship with each client attaching to the database.

Required Processes

The required processes are those that are necessary for the database to function normally. These include the Database Writer (DBW*n*), Log Writer (LGWR), System Monitor (SMON), Process Monitor (PMON), and Checkpoint (CKPT) processes. If one of these required processes fails, then the database fails.

Database Writer (DBW*n*)

The DBW*n* process is responsible for writing data to the database datafiles from the buffer caches. You can have multiple Database Writers (up to nine) if you are in an environment that does not support asynchronous I/O operations (hence the name DBW*n*, where *n* is the process ID of the Database Writer process).

DBW*n* is responsible for processing both incremental checkpoint operations and writing out to datafiles when checkpoint events are signaled. (Checkpoint operations are discussed in the "Checkpoints" section later in this chapter.) Basically, it's the job of DBW*n* to remove blocks from the dirty block queue in the SGA, write them out to the database datafiles, and then free that buffer for use by another process. Thus, DBW*n* ensures that free buffers are available in the SGA. When DBW*n* cannot do its job (because the SGA is configured too small), your database performance will suffer.

One rule to remember with regard to DBW*n* is that it is always behind the LGWR process. Thus, redo entries will always be written before the datafile changes associated with those redo entries will be written. (Redo entries are discussed in the "Redo Logs" section later in this chapter.) If DBW*n* is forced to write dirty buffers that have associated unwritten redo, DBW*n* will signal the LGWR to flush the redo log buffer so that the associated redo will be written. Once that occurs, DBW*n* may proceed to write out the batch.

Log Writer (LGWR)

The LGWR process moves redo records from the redo log buffer in the SGA to the online redo logs. Each database will have two or more redo log groups, and each group may have one or more members associated with it. Members are mirrored copies of the redo logs of that group. If multiple members of a given redo log exist, these are written to in parallel by LGWR. Thus, performance of LGWR can be impacted by placement of the redo logs. If you place them on separate disks, and even different controllers, not only will you improve the performance of LGWR, but you will also protect your online redo logs from failure or human error.

If one member of a redo log group becomes corrupted, that will not cause the rest of the database to fail. Rather, Oracle will simply close the log file, note an error in the LGWR trace file, and continue to write to the remaining log files. If all of the online redo logs become corrupted, LGWR will fail. Then you will need to shut down the database, investigate the cause of the problem, and probably recover the database. If Oracle cannot open an existing redo log file group, you will need to shut down the database, determine what the problem with the redo log file is, and then restart the database. Database recovery in the form of media recovery will likely not be required in this case.

System Monitor (SMON)

The SMON process is responsible for a variety of database operations, including the following:

- Cleaning up temporary segments
- Recovering from a database crash
- Coalescing database free space
- Running recovery transactions against unavailable datafiles
- Recovering an instance of a failed Oracle Parallel Server (OPS) node
- Registering instances with the listener
- Cleaning up the OBJ$ table
- Shrinking rollback segments back to their OPTIMAL size setting
- Managing offline rollback segments in PENDING OFFLINE mode
- Updating statistics if an object is set to monitoring

Process Monitor (PMON)

The PMON process is responsible for recovering failed user processes and cleaning up any resources that might have been allocated to that process. If you are running MTS, PMON is responsible for recovery of dispatcher and server processes. PMON also monitors background processes, restarting them if they fail or shutting down instances if required (though PMON shutdowns are not very gracious!). Also, PMON is responsible for registering the database with the Oracle listener.

Checkpoint (CKPT)

The CKPT process is responsible for updating certain structures in the database datafile headers, as well as in the control files of the database, so that these files are synchronized.

Every three seconds, CKPT will wake up and determine if there are checkpoint events to process. Also, CKPT is responsible for notifying DBW*n* to start checkpoint processing when a checkpoint event is raised. (Prior to Oracle8, if the CKPT process were not running, this job would fall to the DBW*n* process, which would further burden it.)

Optional Processes

The following processes are optional, and their use depends on the setup of your database:

- ARCH, the archiver process, is normally enabled when the database is in ARCHIVELOG mode. You can have it start automatically via the `init.ora` parameter LOG_ARCHIVE_START, or you can start it from SQL via the ALTER SYSTEM command.
- SNP*n*, the job queue (or Snapshot) processes, are associated with the Oracle Job Scheduler.
- RECO, the Distributed Database Recovery process, is associated with distributed transaction processing in Oracle. It is responsible for recovering transactions that are left in a prepared state after the loss of a connection to a remote database. This process can be disabled by setting the parameter DISTRIBUTED_TRANSACTIONS to 0.
- LCK*n* (Lock processes), LMON (Lock Manager), LMD (Lock Manager Daemon), and BSP (Block Server Process) are part of the Oracle Distributed Lock Manager (DLM) processes associated with OPS.
- D*nnn*, the MTS Dispatcher processes, are dispatcher processes that act as the liaison between the client sessions and the shared server processes in a Net8 configuration.
- S*nnn*, the MTS Shared Server processes, read requests from the request queue, process them, and then forward the result set to the response queue.
- Q*nnn*, the Queue Monitor processes, are associated with Oracle advanced queuing. This process is controlled with the `init.ora` parameter AQ_TM_PROCESS.
- LISTENER, the Oracle TNS listener process, facilitates Net8 connections between the database server and the client.

These processes are discussed in more detail in the chapters that describe the database functions with which they are associated.

Oracle Database Control Structures

In this section, we will review the concepts and internals of the Oracle database that contribute to maintaining the integrity of the database. First, we will discuss the nature of transactions in Oracle and the structures associated with transactions and data durability: commits, rollbacks, and checkpoints. Next, we will look at Oracle's internal numbering mechanism: the system change number (SCN). Then we will examine rollback segment generation in Oracle (also known as undo), database datafiles, control files, and Oracle redo logs.

Transaction Commits and Rollbacks

A transaction is at the heart of the Oracle database. Without transactions, the database data never changes—rows are never added, altered, or deleted—making the database pretty useless for the most part. A *transaction* is the life of a series of different Oracle DML statements. A transaction begins with an initial connection to the database by a user process or after a previous transaction has been completed.

Transactions end successfully (the changes are saved to the database) at the implementation of a commit. Commits can be forced through the use of the COMMIT command. Commits can also be implied through the use of certain DDL commands.

Transactions end unsuccessfully (database data changes are not saved) with the issuance of a ROLLBACK command or if the user process encounters some sort of fatal failure. Once a transaction has been committed, it cannot be rolled back. In many cases, such as with the default behavior of SQL*Plus, if you exit the process normally, an implied commit is issued, causing the transactional changes to be committed. Even terminations of certain user processes that might seem abnormal (such as hitting Ctrl+C in SQL*Plus and having SQL*Plus terminate, as it does in some cases) will cause an implied commit of the data.

Checkpoints

Because one of the goals of Oracle is speed, the changes to datafiles are not written out to the datafiles when a commit occurs. Changes are only written to the online redo logs (which we will discuss a bit later in this chapter). Of course, the data is written out at some point. This occurs when a checkpoint is signaled. A *checkpoint* is an event that causes the database to become synchronized to a single point in time (this may not be to the current point in time, however).

The DBWn process is responsible for processing checkpoint operations. During a checkpoint, the DBWn process fires up and starts writing data out to the database datafiles. In concert with the DBW*n* process, the CKPT process is responsible for updating certain structures in the database datafile headers, as well as updating the control files of the database so that they are also synchronized.

Checkpoints can be caused by a number of events, including the following:

- Taking a datafile or tablespace offline
- Issuing the ALTER TABLESPACE BEGIN BACKUP command
- Issuing the ALTER SYSTEM CHECKPOINT command
- Shutting down the database with a SHUTDOWN, SHUTDOWN NORMAL, or SHUTDOWN IMMEDIATE command

 TIP If you need to abort a shutdown, it's a good idea to force the system to perform a checkpoint by issuing an ALTER SYSTEM CHECKPOINT command. This will cause your shutdown to take a little longer, but it will allow your database to come back up much faster.

Checkpoint Processing

Oracle8i has changed how it handles checkpoints from previous versions of the database. In Oracle8i, you can have multiple checkpoints called and ready to be processed by DBW*n* at the same time (though checkpoints themselves occur in serial fashion). Oracle creates a checkpoint queue. All dirty buffers in the database buffer caches are linked to this list. The buffers in this queue are ordered according to when the changes occurred by using the low redo value in that block (an SCN value that indicates when the buffer was first changed).

When a checkpoint is signaled, the range of redo values that the specific checkpoint request is responsible for is sent. Once the last redo value has been processed, that checkpoint will be complete. Even though that particular checkpoint may be completed, DBW*n* may continue to process subsequently requested checkpoints. Each checkpoint is handled in the order requested, so the oldest dirty blocks are always written to disk first. Should a block change before it was written during the checkpoint, that dirty block will still be written by the original checkpoint.

There are five different kinds of checkpoints in Oracle:

Database All dirty blocks in memory that contain changes prior to the checkpoint SCN will be written to disk.

Datafile All dirty blocks in memory that contain changes that belong to a specific datafile will be written to that datafile.

Incremental These checkpoints do not update datafile headers and are used to reduce recovery time. Incremental checkpoints are discussed in more detail in the next section.

Mini-checkpoint These checkpoints are caused by certain types of DDL operations, such as dropping a table. This checkpoint impacts only the blocks of those objects.

Thread checkpoints These checkpoints are caused when an instance checkpoints in an OPS environment.

Incremental Checkpoints

In Oracle8i, the incremental checkpoint process limits the number of dirty buffers in the database buffer cache, in an effort to reduce the time required to restart the database in the event of a system failure. When an amount of redo equivalent to 90 percent of the size of the smallest log file is generated, an incremental checkpoint will be signaled.

During normal database operations, the DBWn process constantly writes out small batches of changes to the database datafiles. In doing so, an incremental checkpoint counter is maintained in each datafile, as well as in the database control file. This counter represents the progress of the incremental checkpoints. Because dirty blocks are written to disk in a more frequent fashion (to reduce I/O contention), Oracle will need to apply less redo from the online redo logs to recover the database. (This particular requirement has some restrictions associated with the size of the redo log buffer.)

You can set several parameters to control incremental checkpoints (each of these can be set in the `init.ora` database parameter file):

FAST_START_IO_TARGET This parameter is available only in the Oracle8i Enterprise Edition of the database. It defines the upper bounds on recovery reads, and it is measured by the maximum number of database buffer cache blocks that you want to recover after a database failure. In other words, you define the maximum number of I/Os that you want Oracle to process during recovery. Oracle will manage the incremental checkpoint process such that this target recovery figure will be maintained as best as possible. The smaller this number, the faster recovery will be (but there may be I/O and database performance impacts).

LOG_CHECKPOINT_INTERVAL This parameter is measured in redo log blocks (which is generally different from the database block size). It defines the maximum number of dirty redo log buffer blocks that can exist, unwritten, in the database. If this number of blocks is exceeded, an incremental checkpoint is signaled.

LOG_CHECKPOINT_TIMEOUT This parameter, which is measured in seconds, indicates that the tail of the incremental checkpoint should be where the last redo log record was *x* seconds ago. Thus, this parameter attempts to control the checkpoint process by causing incremental checkpoints no more than a set number of seconds behind in the redo stream.

LOG_CHECKPOINTS_TO_ALERT If you want to know how long it takes to complete a checkpoint (which can be a measure of overall database performance and a good trending tool), you can log the start and stop times of checkpoints to the alert log by using this parameter.

NOTE The logging time of checkpoints in Oracle8i version 8.1.6.3 does not appear to be working correctly. If you set the `init.ora` parameter LOG_CHECKPOINTS_TO_ALERT to report checkpoint completions, the times being reported do not seem to match when the checkpoints actually appear to have been completed. This may be due to changes in incremental checkpointing in Oracle8i.

You can see how the various parameters impact instance recovery by looking at the V$INSTANCE_RECOVERY view. If you want to know how many checkpoints have occurred on your system since it was started, you can query the V$SYSSTAT view and look for the statistic called DBWR Checkpoints. This value represents the number of checkpoint requests that have been completed.

The System Change Number (SCN)

The SCN is simply a counter that represents the state of the database at a given point in time. As an analogy, consider the counter on your VCR. As you record a movie on your videotape, the counter represents individual places on the tape. Thus, if you knew where the counter was when Neo says, "I know Kung-Fu" in *The Matrix*, you can always go back to that position and watch him strut his stuff. The SCN is somewhat like the VCR counter. It is a continuously flowing timeline that identifies when things happened.

The SCN is a 6-byte number that increases monotonically; that is, it goes from a small number (starting at 0) and moves up as transactions occur. Each database transaction is committed at a given SCN. The SCN consists of two parts: the base value and the wrap value. The base value of the SCN is increased first. If the base value rolls over, then the wrap value is increased. A new SCN is assigned every time a transaction is committed.

The SCN is central to several critical database operations, including providing read-consistent images, database consistency checks, and database recovery services. The role the SCN plays in these operations is described in the following sections.

Read-Consistent Images

Each committed change is associated with an SCN. That SCN is stored in the header of each block in the database, as well as in each rollback segment entry. As you know, if you start a report at 2 P.M., you will only see the data in the database as it looked at 2 P.M. This consistency is facilitated through the SCN. When you start your report at 2 P.M., the database will be at a given SCN.

NOTE The database does not care what time you started your report; it only cares what the SCN was when you started your report. This is why it doesn't matter if you change the system clock while the database is running.

For example, suppose you start your report at SCN 1000. Oracle will process the blocks from the database buffer cache if they are present there, or it will extract the correct blocks from the database datafiles. When it does so, it will read the header of the block, which contains, among other things, the SCN of the last time the block was updated. Now, what happens if that block happens to have been updated at SCN 1010? Can Oracle then use that block? No, since the report was started at SCN 1000, Oracle can use the data blocks only if the last update SCN is 1000 or less. So, you have a problem, don't you? The data block that contains the row(s) you need has been updated. What do you do?

The solution is to use the rollback segments to generate a *read-consistent image* of the block as it existed at SCN 1000. Having determined that the SCN of the actual data block is too high, Oracle will scan through the rollback segments (using some internal pointers that make the process rather fast), looking for the first image of that block that has an SCN less than or equal to 1000. Oracle will then create a read-consistent image of the rows that are needed by taking the original block and, using the rollback segments, constructing an image consistent to the time needed by the report.

Database Consistency Checks

The SCN provides methods of ensuring that the database is in a consistent state when it is started. Oracle will cross-check the SCNs stored in each database datafile header against those stored in the control file. If Oracle finds that the SCNs match, then the database is in a consistent state. If the SCNs do not match, then the database is not in a consistent state and some form of recovery will be required.

When a database is shut down normally, the shutdown process will cause a checkpoint to occur, and all datafiles will be updated. This will cause the SCNs in the datafile headers to be synchronized. The database will then update the SCNs in the control files, so that those SCNs will also be consistent. When the database crashes, or a SHUTDOWN ABORT is executed, these synchronization processes do not occur. Since the database datafiles will be out of synch with each other and the database, they will be considered inconsistent, and Oracle will apply recovery when the database is restarted.

Database Recovery Services

The SCN is used during database recovery to ensure that all database datafiles are recovered to a consistent point in time. If, during the recovery process, a database datafile is not consistent with the remaining datafiles of the database, Oracle will signal an error indicating that there is an inconsistent state in the database and that the database will not open. This means that all of your database datafiles must be recovered to the same point in time.

For example, if you want to recover one tablespace (and the objects in it) as they looked at 3 P.M., and the rest of the database as it looked at 4 P.M, you will need to consider some different options from a physical recovery of the data, such as performing a logical recovery or taking advantage of Oracle's transportable tablespace feature. We will discuss each of these options in more detail in Chapters 11 and 12.

Rollback Segments and Undo

We have already discussed the role of rollback segments in providing a read-consistent image of changes made to the database. These changes are in the form of *undo*. Undo is simply the representation of the data that was changed as it existed before the change took place. Undo is what is stored in rollback segments and allows a block change to be undone.

Different changes generate different levels of undo. Some changes, such as INSERT statements, generate minimal undo (since the undo for an INSERT operation is basically a deletion of the row). Other changes, such as the results of UPDATE or DELETE statements, can generate a lot of undo.

NOTE Don't confuse *undo* with *redo*. They are two very different things. *Redo* is associated with redo logs and represents atomic-level changes to the database, as explained in the "Redo Logs" section of this chapter. If you are interviewing for an Oracle DBA job, don't be surprised if you are asked to explain the difference between undo and redo!

More on Read Consistency

Read consistency is one of the fundamental principles of any truly relational database. Read-consistency implies that any query you execute at time *x* will use the data in the database as it looked at time *x*.

For example, suppose that you are going to query row number 1000, and the value in column B was 100. What happens if, before your query actually read column B, someone changed it to a value of 1010 and committed that change? Because you are using a read-consistent database, when your report gets to row number 1000, Oracle will know that the value 1010 is not consistent to the time you started the report. Oracle will then root around to find the rollback segment entries that were generated when the row value was changed from 1000 to 1010. Oracle will put this puzzle together and construct an image—a *snapshot*—of the row as it looked at time *x*, rather than as it currently looks. Thus, your report will get a row as it looked when the report started and not as it looked after the change.

In providing read consistency, Oracle has accepted that there will be some, shall we say, "wrinkles" in the process from time to time. The wrinkle I refer to is the Oracle error, ORA-1550, Snapshot Too Old message. This error has served to confuse more than a few DBAs, so let's discuss it in a bit more detail before continuing with the other architectural elements of Oracle.

The ORA-1555 Snapshot Too Old Error

As you just learned, when Oracle constructs a read-consistent image, it creates a consistent result set, or a snapshot; hence, the reference to "Snapshot" in the error ORA-1550 message.

The undo records (and the associated changed rows) for a given transaction are locked for as long as that transaction is active. So, there should be no problem finding the needed undo as long as the transaction is still churning away. However, a problem arises when a transaction commits its work. When this occurs, all the undo in the rollback segments associated with that transaction is unlocked, leaving those undo segment locations available to be reused by other transactions. Guess what happens if the undo segment location is reused and your report needs what was in that segment to generate the read-consistent image? You guessed it: Oracle returns the ORA-01555 error. So, of course, your report dies, and you want to go smacking some heads together.

There can be some other causes of the ORA-01555 besides missing rollback segment information. It is possible that the rollback segment information is present, but that the transaction slot information is missing from the rollback segment header. A *transaction slot* is kind of a directory in the rollback segment header that points to the location of the transaction within the rollback segment (it contains additional information on the transaction as well). The information in the transaction slot might be missing due to a feature of Oracle called *delayed block cleanout*, which is designed to assist with performance. When a transaction is complete, to save time, Oracle does not clean out the rollback segment entries. Rather, Oracle waits for the next user process that needs the entries to clean out those entries later on. Sometimes, the transaction slots in the rollback segment header may be overwritten, but the actual undo will not. In some cases, Oracle can reconstruct the transaction slot, as long as the undo image in the rollback segment is still present. Otherwise, an ORA-1555 is signaled.

PL/SQL programmers may run into ORA-1555 problems if they tend to perform large fetch-across-commit operations. This is because they end up overwriting their own session's before-image views or rollback segment transaction slots. This is more likely to happen if the program uses the SET TRANSACTION USE ROLLBACK SEGMENT command.

So, what can be done to eliminate the "Snapshot Too Old" problem? Here are a few pointers:

Make sure that your rollback segments are large enough. Just giving your rollback segments enough tablespace space to grow into is not sufficient. You need to allocate enough initial and growing space to make the extents of the segment big enough to handle the load you will be throwing at it. Remember that your rollback segments will not extend to avoid an ORA-1555 problem.

Watch EXTENDS and SHRINKS. The effects of the OPTIMAL clause in a rollback segment can be devastating to transactions needing read consistency. Guess what happens if Oracle shrinks a rollback segment back to its OPTIMAL size and you need a block that used to be allocated to the rollback segment but is no more? That's right, ORA-1555. This is one reason why Oracle tells you not to set OPTIMAL on the SYSTEM rollback segment during database migrations. Keep an eye on EXTENDS and SHRINKS. Rebuild rollback segments larger until EXTENDS are as near zero as possible.

Watch the size of the SGA. The size of the SGA can affect whether or not you run into ORA-1555. This is because Oracle will use an image in the database buffer cache if it is present. If the image of the rollback segment entry is in the SGA, Oracle will not need to go to disk to find it. Thus, this reduces the chance that when Oracle does go to disk, it will find that the entry is no longer there.

Add rollback segments. If you have many users and a lot of volume, adding rollback segments can help reduce contention for the transaction slots in the rollback segments.

Lock objects. When running large reports, you might consider locking the objects in SHARED or EXCLUSIVE mode by using the LOCK TABLE command. This will prevent other transactions from writing to these objects (thus requiring consistent reads by your session).

Try not to mix and match long-running and short-running transactions. If this is unavoidable, make sure that the rollback segments are sufficiently sized. This is probably the biggest cause of the ORA-1555 problem. If the problem is really large, consider creating a separate environment for reporting or ad-hoc users. For example, a standby database in read-only mode might be a good alternative.

Be careful of environments where there are large numbers of readers and writers. Readers are basically operations that cause reads to occur on the database. This would include things like reports and OLTP lookup operations. Writers are operations that cause a lot of database writing. This would include database load programs, OLTP operations, and certain analytic operations.

If you are writing PL/SQL, be aware of the impacts of fetching across commits. As you commit data, you risk losing the consistent image of that data that you may require. If you are using fetches across commits, write your code in such a way that you need to revisit blocks as little as possible. This can be done by forcing a full table scan or using an ORDER BY clause in the cursor.

Tune your queries to reduce total I/O as much as possible.
If your queries need to bring in fewer blocks, this will result in less I/O, fewer changes needing to occur in memory, fewer accesses to disk, and a reduction in ORA-1555 messages to boot. Also, consider breaking up long-running reports into smaller queries and combining the results.

Tune your applications. If an application issues five different UPDATE statements on the same row instead of just one, for example, you can make a significant difference by modifying the code so the UPDATE occurs only once.

The Database Datafiles

The database datafiles are the main part of the physical database. Each database datafile is associated with one tablespace, and multiple datafiles may be assigned to a given tablespace.

Datafile Headers

Database datafiles contain a header that is of a fixed length. This header includes various information about the datafile, including the following:

- Its current checkpoint SCN
- Its current incremental checkpoint SCN
- The datafile number
- The datafile name
- Its creation date, time, and SCN number

You can see the contents of a specific datafile header by setting the FILE_HDRS event, as follows:

```
ALTER SESSION SET EVENTS 'immediate trace name file_hdrs level 10';
```

See Chapter 15 for more information about setting events.

Datafile Fuzziness

We often talk about "fuzziness" in regard to database datafiles. Actually, fuzziness is a state that revolves around the setting of any of three different status flags in the datafile header.

One status flag is set when the database is opened. This is the online fuzzy bit. This bit will not be reset until the database is closed in a normal fashion (with a SHUTDOWN or SHUTDOWN IMMEDIATE command). In the case of a SHUTDOWN ABORT or any abnormal database termination, this bit will not be reset. When Oracle is restarted, this bit is checked. If it is set, the datafile is considered to be "fuzzy" and recovery will be required. This recovery may or may not require DBA intervention.

Other fuzzy flags are set when a hot backup is signaled for a given tablespace. It is this fuzzy flag that causes the database to signal you that a tablespace is in hot backup mode when you try to shut down the database. It is also this flag that prohibits you from opening the database if it was terminated abnormally during a hot backup. If this occurs, you will need to mount the database and use the ALTER DATABASE DATAFILE END BACKUP command for each datafile that is in hot backup mode. You will then be able to open the database backup. (See Chapter 10 for details on hot backups.)

The last fuzzy flag is the media recovery flag that is set when media recovery is executed. This flag will be reset once recovery of the datafile is complete.

Control Files

The control file is one of the central physical files of the Oracle database. Control files are used when starting up the database to ensure that it is in a consistent state. The control file is required to start any Oracle database.

A control file stores a vast amount of database information, including information on the datafiles that belong to the database, such as their size, status, and current SCN (which may not always be in synch with the actual SCN of the datafile). It also stores RMAN backup information, the name and location of the database redo logs, and other database control information.

Control files contain both a static section as well as a variable (or reuse) portion (also known as *circular reuse records*) in its structure. This variable area includes archived redo log history, backup history, and other historical information. This variable portion can grow so that the control file itself must expand, although there is a limit to the growth of the circular reuse area. If the control file is extended, you will see a message in the database alert log that looks something like this:

```
kccrsz: expanded controlfile section 9 from 56 to 112 records
requested to grow by 56 record(s); added 1 block(s) of records
```

This message simply means that one operating system block was added to the control file (on my NT 4 system, an operating system block is 512 bytes).

You can limit the number of records stored in the variable portion of the control file by setting the CONTROL_FILE_RECORD_KEEP_TIME parameter in the database `init.ora` file. This parameter, which is an integer, represents the number of days of records that Oracle should maintain in the variable portion. Oracle will then delete any records older than that number of days, should it require space in the variable portion of the control file and be unable to find it. Setting this parameter to 0 will effectively disable any growth of this variable portion of the control file.

You can dump the contents of the control file by setting an event, as in the following example:

```
ALTER SESSION SET EVENTS 'immediate trace name controlf  level 10'
```

Redo Logs

Redo logs are a critical set of files in the Oracle database. They provide for recovery of the database in the event of any type of failure.

Oracle redo logs record each and every change to the database. Redo logs (and stored redo logs called *archived redo logs*) are one of the most critical database structures. Here is an idea of how critical they can be: If your database is in ARCHIVELOG mode, you can essentially restore any datafile (with a few exceptions like the SYSTEM tablespace datafiles), even if you don't have a backup of that datafile. All you need to have is the archived redo logs generated since the datafile (or tablespace) was created. (See Chapter 10 for details on putting the database in ARCHIVELOG mode.)

Redo logs are identified uniquely by both a thread number (which is normally 1, unless you are running OPS) and a log sequence number. Each time the current online redo log changes, the sequence number of the next log will increase by one.

Each redo log has a header associated with it. The redo log header contains the low and high SCNs that are in that redo log. This is used by Oracle during media recovery to determine which redo logs it needs to apply. You can use the REDOHDR event to produce a trace file that contains event information, as in the following example:

```
ALTER SESSION SET EVENTS 'immediate trace name redohdr level 10';
```

What Is Redo?

To understand redo logs, you need to have a clear concept of what *redo* is. Every change to the database is recorded as redo. This includes changes to tables, indexes, and rollback segments. Redo is used to replay transactions during database recovery. Redo represents a single atomic change to the database. A single redo entry has three components: the redo byte address (RBA), change vectors, and redo records.

The RBA

We have already discussed the SCN, which is one of the atomic parts of all redo that is generated. Along with the SCN, there is another identifier called the *RBA*. The RBA is a 10-byte number that identifies and is stored with each redo record. The RBA stores three values: the log sequence number, the block number within the redo log, and the byte number within the block. Similar to the SCN the RBA is kind of like the counter on your VCR. In this case, Oracle uses it to locate specific records within a redo log quickly, thus speeding up various operations such as instance recovery. This is because the last RBA record that is associated with each datafile is stored in each datafile header. The RBA is also stored in the control file of the database. During recovery, Oracle can use the stored RBA to quickly locate the beginning of the redo that it needs to apply for that datafile.

Change Vectors

A change vector describes a single change to a single block in an Oracle database. The change vector begins with a header record that contains (among other things) the

SCN and the RBA of the change. There are different types of change vectors, such as insert, update, delete, and commit change vectors. The type is identified internally by a code associated with each change vector, called an *op code*.

For example, the commit vector guarantees that a change to the database will be recoverable. When you issue a COMMIT command from your user session (or you perform some action that causes a commit to occur automatically), a commit change vector will be written to the redo log. The COMMIT command issued by the session will not return as successful until the change vector has been written to the online redo log on disk.

NOTE When you issue a COMMIT command, Oracle does not write the changes to the database datafiles. Oracle relies completely on the commit vector and the other change vectors in the redo logs to provide database recoverability should the database fail. This should underscore the importance of protecting the online redo logs from failure. See Chapter 10 for details on backup and recovery.

Redo Records

Redo records consist of a series of change vectors that describe a single atomic change to the database. A given transaction can consist of multiple redo records. Redo records are written in ordered fashion based on the SCN and the RBA of the redo record.

Redo Log Switches

When Oracle writes to the online redo log, it eventually becomes full. When this occurs, an event known as a *redo log switch* occurs. During the log switch processing, Oracle will take a latch against the redo log buffer, which will prevent any processes from allocating space in the redo log buffer or writing to it. Next, Oracle will flush the contents of the redo log buffer to the online redo log file. Oracle will then release the switch to the next available online redo log. Once this is done, the latches against the redo log buffer will be released, and Oracle can again send redo to the redo log buffer.

As you might guess, the processing of a log switch can be an expensive operation, because it holds up any redo generation on the system, and it also causes additional I/O to occur because of the open and close actions occurring against the online redo logs. Additionally, if the database is in ARCHIVELOG mode, a log switch will cause additional I/O to begin to occur with the copying of the old online redo log to the archive log directory. Because of these costs (and also to reduce the costs of checkpointing in some cases), it is recommended that you size your redo log files so that your database executes log switches somewhere around every 15 minutes. You might end up with particularly large redo log files (online redo log files of several gigabytes are not unusual), but this is okay. As long as the online redo log files are properly protected and you have properly configured the incremental checkpointing process, larger online redo logs are not a problem.

Oracle Scalar Datatypes

Datatypes are associated with each column defined in a table, and are also used in SQL*Plus and PL/SQL programming. Datatypes are assigned to a column name or variable name and define a storage format, constraint, and valid range of values for that column or variable.

Oracle comes with a number of native, or *scalar*, datatypes, which we introduced in Chapter 1. A scalar type has no internal components. The following sections provide details on NUMBER, CHAR, and other Oracle8i scalar datatypes.

NUMBER

NUMBER types allow you to store numeric data (integers, real numbers, and floating-point numbers), represent quantities, and do calculations. You use the NUMBER datatype to store fixed-point or floating-point numbers of virtually any size. Its magnitude range is 1E–130 to 10E125. If the value of an expression falls outside this range, you get a numeric overflow or underflow error (and if it overflows with a positive number and the value represents your bank balance, give me a call—I'm sure you need some good full-time Oracle consulting!).

To define a column as a NUMBER type, you might issue the following CREATE TABLE statement:

```
CREATE TABLE test (id  NUMBER);
```

This creates a floating-point type of number with no precision or scale.

NUMBER Precision and Scale

With a NUMBER datatype, you can optionally define the precision and scale of the number. The syntax looks something like this:

```
NUMBER[(precision,scale)]
```

This precision is the total number of digits. If you do not specify precision, it defaults to 38 or the maximum supported by your system, whichever is less.

The scale is the number of digits to the right of the decimal point. The scale can range from –84 to 127. The scale also determines where rounding occurs. For instance, a scale of 2 rounds to the nearest hundredth (3.456 becomes 3.46). A negative scale rounds to the left of the decimal point. For example, a scale of –3 rounds to the nearest thousand (3456 becomes 3000). A scale of 0 rounds to the nearest whole number. If you do not specify scale, it defaults to 0.

An example of declaring a number with precision and scale in a table would look something like this:

```
CREATE TABLE test (id NUMBER(5,2));
```

This example creates a column that can hold a number of up to five digits. The last two digits are after the decimal point. Thus, the largest value you could put in this column would be 999.99. If you were to try to force a value larger than this into the column, Oracle would respond with the following error:

```
SQL> INSERT INTO test VALUES (9999.99);
INSERT INTO test VALUES (9999.99)
                         *
ERROR at line 1:
ORA-01438: value larger than specified precision allows for this column
```

You would get the same error if you tried to insert –9999.99. However, you could insert –999.99 without any problem, because the minus sign is not included in the precision of the number.

To declare an integer (which is a number with no fractional component), use this form:

NUMBER(*precision*)

This is essentially the same as specifying 0 as the scale.

NUMBER Subtypes

You can use the following NUMBER subtypes for compatibility with ANSI/ISO and IBM types or when you want a more descriptive name: DEC, DECIMAL, DOUBLE PRECISION, FLOAT, INTEGER, INT, NUMERIC, REAL, and SMALLINT. These subtypes are used as follows:

- Use the subtypes DEC, DECIMAL, and NUMERIC to declare fixed-point numbers with a maximum precision of 38 decimal digits.

- Use the subtypes DOUBLE PRECISION and FLOAT to declare floating-point numbers with a maximum precision of 126 binary digits, which is roughly equivalent to 38 decimal digits.

- Use the subtype REAL to declare floating-point numbers with a maximum precision of 63 binary digits, which is roughly equivalent to 18 decimal digits.
- Use the subtypes INTEGER, INT, and SMALLINT to declare integers with a maximum precision of 38 decimal digits.

Character Types

Character types allow you to store alphanumeric data, represent words and text, and manipulate character strings. There are two primary character datatypes in Oracle: CHAR and VARCHAR2. Oracle8i also provides National Language Support (NLS) character types.

All of the character datatypes take an optional parameter that lets you specify a maximum length:

```
CHAR[(maximum_length)]
VARCHAR2(maximum_length)
NCHAR[(maximum_length)]
NVARCHAR2(maximum_length)
```

You cannot use a constant or variable to specify the maximum length; you must use an integer literal.

You cannot insert values that are larger than the maximum size of the column datatype into a column, nor retrieve values that are larger than the maximum size of the character datatype into a character datatype variable. For example, a CHAR column's maximum size is 2000 bytes, so you cannot insert a CHAR value larger than that into a CHAR column. You can insert any CHAR(*n*) value into a LONG database column, because the maximum width of a LONG column is 2,147,483,647 bytes (or 2GB). However, you cannot retrieve a value longer than 2000 bytes from a LONG column into a CHAR(*n*) variable.

CHAR

The CHAR datatype stores fixed-length character data, specified in bytes. The maximum width of a CHAR database column is 2000 bytes. If you do not specify a maximum length, it defaults to 1.

 NOTE You specify the maximum length of the CHAR and VARCHAR2 datatype in bytes, not characters. So, if a CHAR(*n*) or VARCHAR2 variable stores multibyte characters, its maximum length is less than *n* characters.

The CHAR subtype CHARACTER has the same range of values as its base type. In other words, CHARACTER is just another name for CHAR. You can use this subtype for compatibility with ANSI/ISO and IBM types or when you want use an identifier that is more descriptive than CHAR.

VARCHAR2

You use the VARCHAR2 datatype to store variable-length character data, specified in bytes. The maximum width of a VARCHAR2 database column is 4000 bytes. The VARCHAR subtype has the same range of values as VARCHAR2. You can use this subtype for compatibility with ANSI/ISO and IBM types.

NOTE Currently, VARCHAR is synonymous with VARCHAR2. However, in future releases of PL/SQL, to accommodate emerging SQL standards, VARCHAR might become a separate datatype with different comparison semantics. So, it is a good idea to use VARCHAR2 rather than VARCHAR.

NLS Character Types

Although the widely used 7- or 8-bit ASCII and EBCDIC character sets are adequate to represent the Roman alphabet, some Asian languages, such as Japanese, contain thousands of characters. These languages require 16 bits (2 bytes) to represent each character. Oracle provides NLS types, which let you process single-byte and multibyte character data and convert between character sets. They also let your applications run in different language environments.

Oracle supports two character sets: the database character set, which is used for identifiers and source code, and the national character set, which is used for NLS data. The datatypes NCHAR and NVARCHAR2 store character strings from the national character set. How the data is represented internally depends on the national character set, which might use a fixed-width encoding, such as WE8EBCDIC37C, or a variable-width encoding, such as JA16DBCS. For fixed-width character sets, you specify the maximum length in characters. For variable-width character sets, you specify it in bytes.

NCHAR

The NCHAR datatype stores fixed-length (blank-padded if necessary) NLS character data. The maximum width of an NCHAR database column is 2000 bytes. If the NCHAR value is shorter than the defined width of the NCHAR column, Oracle blank-pads the value to the defined width. You cannot insert CHAR values into an NCHAR column. Likewise, you cannot insert NCHAR values into a CHAR column.

NVARCHAR2

The NVARCHAR2 datatype stores variable-length NLS character data. The maximum width of a NVARCHAR2 database column is 4000 bytes. You cannot insert VARCHAR2 values into an NVARCHAR2 column. Likewise, you cannot insert NVARCHAR2 values into a VARCHAR2 column.

LONG, LONG RAW, and RAW

The LONG datatype stores variable-length character strings. It is like the VARCHAR2 datatype, except that the maximum length of a LONG value is 2GB. LONG columns can store text, arrays of characters, or even short documents.

As with the other datatypes, you cannot insert values that are larger than the maximum size of the column datatype into a column, nor retrieve values that are larger than the maximum size of the character datatype into a character datatype variable.

You can reference LONG columns in UPDATE, INSERT, and (most) SELECT statements. You cannot reference LONG columns in expressions, SQL function calls, or certain SQL clauses, such as WHERE, GROUP BY, and CONNECT BY.

You use the LONG RAW datatype to store binary data or byte strings. LONG RAW data is like LONG data, except that LONG RAW data is not interpreted by Oracle. The maximum width of a LONG RAW column is 2GB.

TIP LONG and LONG RAW datatypes are not supported by many of the newer Oracle features and will be replaced by LOB datatypes. It is suggested that you use LOBs instead of LONG or LONG RAW datatypes whenever possible.

The RAW datatype stores binary data or byte strings. For example, a RAW variable might store a sequence of graphics characters or a digitized picture. RAW data is like VARCHAR2 data, except that Oracle does not interpret RAW data. Likewise, Net8 does not do character set conversion when you transmit RAW data from one system to another. The RAW datatype takes a required parameter that lets you specify a maximum length up to 2000 bytes.

LOBs

LOBs are an able replacement for the older and less flexible LONG datatype. Oracle has announced that it will eventually remove support for LONG datatypes (although it appears this will not be the case in at least the initial release of Oracle9i). What is it that makes LOBs better? Table 5.1 provides a summary of the features of LOBs and LONGs.

TABLE 5.1: LOB AND LONG FEATURES

Feature	LONG Support	LOB Support
Data copying	Requires writing of complex and generally inefficient code	Fully supported by the DBMS_LOB package
Distributed	Not supported transactions	Restricted distributed operations supported
Number allowed per Oracle table	One	Multiple
Update ability	Must update the entire LONG	More granular ability to update LOBs in pages (chunks)
Redo generation	Substantial—generally, the I/O generated will be 2 times the size of the data being inserted for any operation	Can be disabled for substantial performance improvement (but at the risk of prohibiting recovery)
Rollback generation	May be significant; read-consistency issues can be a problem	No rollback segment activity for any change to a LOB column in an object; Oracle handles read consistency differently in LOBs
General functionality	Generally, you can only read or replace a LONG; limited SQL functionality; only sequential access supported; not supported in index-organized tables	Additional features including search, append, strip, and other text-processing functions supported from within SQL; supported in index-organized tables
Indexing	Not supported	A LOB index is automatically created when a LOB is created
Size limitations	2GB	4GB
Data storage	Inline	Inline (if less than 4KB) or out-of-line
Triggers	Not supported	Restricted support within a trigger
Partitioning	Not supported	Supported
Object attribute	Not supported as an attribute in an Oracle object	Supported as attributes in an Oracle object (with the exception of NCLOBs)

There are two general types of LOBs: internal LOBs and external LOBs. Internal LOBs are stored inside the database itself. External LOBs, called BFILEs, are basically just pointers to external operating system files that can be accessed, read-only, from the database through the defined external LOB.

CLOBs, NCLOBs, and BLOBs

There are three different types of internal LOBs:

- The CLOB datatype is used to store large amounts of single-byte character data. The data stored in a CLOB must correspond to the character set that the database was created with. CLOBs store variable-length character data (like VARCHAR2s).

- The NCLOB datatype supports multibyte character sets that correspond to the national character set that is defined for your database. NCLOBs store fixed-length character data.

- The BLOB datatype is used to store binary data.

Any of the three internal LOB types can be either permanent or temporary in nature. Temporary LOBs are created through the use of the DBMS_LOB package. A temporary LOB, if created, will last only during the lifetime of the transaction that created it. Temporary LOBs are generally used as temporary storage for when you wish to manipulate an existing or new LOB entry. Temporary LOBs do not support read consistency, undo generation, backup and recovery, or transaction management. In many cases, if you encounter an error when using a temporary LOB, you will need to restart the operation.

LOB Storage

When you create a table that will contain internal LOB types, Oracle will create two additional objects as well: the LOB segment that will be associated with that column and the LOB index that will be associated with the LOB segment. The LOB segment and the LOB index will be stored in the same tablespace (this is new in Oracle8i). Because they will be stored together in the same tablespace, you need to be careful about I/O issues.

Oracle can actually choose to store LOB data in one of two ways (and you do have some influence over this when you create a table with LOBs).

Inline storage Oracle can choose to store the LOB data in the object to which the column is assigned. This is called *inline storage*. Basically, the LOB data will be handled like normal table data. You can disable inline storage with the use of the DISABLE STORAGE IN ROW clause when you are defining your LOB segments. If

the data to be stored is somewhere around 4KB, Oracle will opt to move the column data to out-of-line storage in the LOB segment.

Out-of-line storage   If the LOB data is to be stored out-of-line, a LOB locator is also stored in the row. The 20-byte LOB locator points to the LOB index entry for that LOB. (Even when the data is stored inline, the LOB locator is still created to reserve space should the LOB be updated and need to be stored out-of-line.) When using the DBMS_LOB package, several parameters reference the LOB locator.

LOBs and Read Consistency

LOBs provide their own form of read consistency. Using rollback segments to provide LOB read consistency would be a very expensive proposition. Besides the need for additional space, the constant I/O of moving LOB images to the rollback segment and the impacts that this would have on other transactions using rollback segments would be troublesome. LOBs could play havoc on reporting by causing Snapshot Too Old messages, because they would have overwritten read-consistent images in the rollback segments needed to reconstruct the data that a query is trying to access.

To solve this problem, Oracle does not use rollback segments for operations on out-of-line LOB data operations. If your LOB data is stored inline with the rest of the row data, it will be handled in the normal fashion.

Each out-of-line LOB row has an ID (or descriptor) stored in the table (the original table, not the LOB segment) associated with it that defines the version of that data. Oracle will retrieve the descriptor and use the LOB index entry to find the place in the LOB segment where that LOB data is stored.

Out-of-line LOBs stored in the LOB segment are stored in chunks. When you make a change to a LOB that is being stored out-of-line, Oracle makes a new copy of the chunk being changed and preserves the old chunk for read-consistency purposes. When the new chunk is created, the entry for the old chunk in the LOB index is replaced with the entry for the new chunk. Since the changes in the LOB index are recorded in rollback segments, if a transaction still needs access to the old data, it will simply look up the old chunk address rather than the new chunk address. Thus, when you change a LOB, the only thing that really changes is the chunk data in the LOB index for the chunk that was changed. Oracle can provide read consistency by referencing the appropriate chunk.

The benefit of this is that when using LOBs, you largely avoid the hassles of rollback segments. The downside is that you may lose your read-consistent image of the LOB anyway, just as you might with a rollback segment. Another problem is that you end up using more space to allow for consistent images than you might actually need.

LOB Restrictions

There are a few restrictions that are associated with the use of LOBs:

- You will not be able to perform parallel DDL or DML operations on any object that contains a LOB. Carefully consider this restriction when you are designing your database.
- You cannot write to a NULL LOB. The LOB must first be initialized by an Oracle function: EMPTY_BLOB() for a BLOB, EMPTY_CLOB() for a CLOB or NCLOB, or BFILENAME() for a BFILE.
- LOBs cannot be part of a cluster key in a set of clustered tables.
- LOBs cannot be part of a GROUP BY, ORDER BY, or SELECT DISTINCT operation.
- Aggregate operations and joins are not supported (although UNION ALL operations are allowed on tables with LOBs).

NOTE UNION, MINUS, and SELECT DISTINCT operations are allowed on LOB attributes of an object if the object type has a MAP or ORDER function.

- LOBs are not supported in partitioned index-organized tables or VARRAYs. However, they are supported in nonpartitioned index-organized tables.
- LOBs are not supported by the ANALYZE COMPUTE or ANALYZE ESTIMATE command.

ROWID and UROWID

Internally, every database table has a ROWID pseudocolumn, which stores binary values called ROWIDs. Each ROWID represents the storage address of a row. A physical ROWID identifies a row in an ordinary (heap) table. A logical ROWID identifies a row in an index-organized table.

The ROWID datatype can store only physical ROWIDs. However, the UROWID (universal ROWID) datatype can store physical, logical, or foreign (non-Oracle) ROWIDs.

TIP Use the ROWID datatype only for backward compatibility with old applications. For new applications, use the UROWID datatype.

When you select or fetch a ROWID into a UROWID variable, you can use the built-in function ROWIDTOCHAR, which converts the binary value into an 18-byte character string. Conversely, the function CHARTOROWID converts a UROWID character string into a ROWID. If the conversion fails because the character string does not represent a valid ROWID, PL/SQL raises the predefined exception SYS_INVALID_ROWID. This also applies to implicit conversions.

Physical ROWIDs provide fast access to particular rows. As long as the row exists, its physical ROWID does not change. Efficient and stable, physical ROWIDS are useful for selecting a set of rows, operating on the whole set, and then updating a subset. For example, you can compare a UROWID variable with the ROWID pseudocolumn in the WHERE clause of an UPDATE or a DELETE statement to identify the latest row fetched from a cursor. Physical ROWIDs are covered in more detail in Chapter 6, in the discussion of managing heap tables.

Logical ROWIDs provide the fastest access rows in an index-organized table. Oracle uses them when constructing secondary indexes on index-organized tables. Logical ROWIDs are also covered in more detail in Chapter 6, in the discussion of managing index-organized tables.

CHAPTER 6

Oracle Schema Object Management

FEATURING:

An overview of object management	**216**
Managing tablespaces	**224**
Managing heap tables	**229**
Managing indexes	**247**
Managing index-organized tables	**262**
Managing clusters	**269**
Managing rollback segments	**277**

Oracle object management is at the heart of every Oracle database. Objects are, after all, where your data is stored. As a DBA, there are many different types of objects that you will need to manage.

This chapter begins with an overview of Oracle object management. Next, we will cover how to create and manage tablespaces. We will then detail how to manage various Oracle objects, including tables, indexes, clusters, and rollback segments. You will learn the fundamentals of each type of object, as well as how to create, alter, drop, and view Oracle objects.

NOTE In this chapter, we use the terms *schema object* and *object* interchangeably to refer to schema objects. *Object* in this context does not have any reference to Oracle's object database technology, which is discussed in Chapter 8, unless specifically noted (such as when discussing VARCHARs or nested tables).

An Overview of Object Management

Typically, an Oracle object is created with a DDL statement such as CREATE TABLE, CREATE INDEX, and so on. The Oracle database engine creates temporary objects on an as-needed basis (for example, for sort operations). Some objects actually depend on the presence of other objects, such as indexes, which expect that the table they are being created on already exists. Some objects are created as the result of the creation of another object. Typically, these are dependent objects, such as LOBs that employ out-of-line storage segments.

NOTE For any interaction with an Oracle schema object, you must have the appropriate grant to perform that operation. For example to create a table, you must have the CREATE TABLE privilege. This is done via the GRANT command. An object grant gives the user the ability to interact with the object that the grant refers to in the way that the grant allows. See Chapter 21 for details on grants.

Objects (not the data in them) are generally manipulated through ALTER DDL statements. Often, you can alter storage parameters, or even re-create a segment on the fly if you need to. You can alter objects to modify their attributes and structures (as with the ALTER TABLE command). However, certain object attributes cannot be altered once the object has been created. For example, you cannot change the INITIAL parameter of tables or indexes.

To replace an object, you must first drop it (and its associated data) and then reallocate it. Objects are removed from the system with some form of a DROP DDL statement such as DROP TABLE or DROP INDEX. There are, as with everything else, exceptions to this rule. For example, the SMON process manages temporary segment cleanup (and if you are using a temporary tablespace, temporary segments are not cleaned up at all). Dependent objects, such as those associated with LOB storage, are removed when the dependent table associated with the LOB datatype is moved.

NOTE Temporary segments are used in Oracle for sorting of data during various operations. As a DBA, you do not create temporary segments, but rather you create one or more tablespaces that will contain temporary segments.

The removal of certain kinds of objects has a cascade effect on other segments. For example, if you remove a table, all associated indexes will be removed. This is also true with regard to removal of tables that contain LOB datatypes. If you remove a table that contains a LOB datatype, the associated LOB index and LOB segments will also be removed.

Before we delve into the details of the managing specific types of objects, we will examine two important settings associated with the creation and administration of many objects: physical attributes and storage.

Configuring an Object's Physical Attributes

When you create an object, you will often configure its physical attributes. The physical attributes clause allows you to instruct Oracle as to how it should manage the blocks of that segment (or object). The physical attributes clause can greatly impact disk space usage and I/O. If these parameters are set correctly, your blocks will be well packed, you will have few chained rows, and you will have good performance. Performance is improved because you have a larger average number of rows per block, so you end up with fewer blocks that need to be read. Also, with the elimination (or reduction) of chained rows, fewer I/O operations will be required.

NOTE A *chained row* is one that was inserted in the table and later expanded, so that it no longer fits its original block. See Chapter 16 for more on row chaining.

If the physical attributes clause parameters are set incorrectly, you may find that your chained row count will increase, and if so, you are likely to use more disk space than necessary. Also, you will find that your queries will take longer because the additional blocks assigned to the segment increase the I/O operations required to query the same data. This is a direct result of fewer rows existing in each data block, and also a result of chaining effects.

The parameters available in the physical attributes clause include PCTFREE, PCTUSED, INITRANS, and MAXTRANS. Let's look at how each of these works.

The PCTFREE and PCTUSED Parameters

The PCTFREE setting, when associated with a heap table, indicates what percentage of space in each block of the table to reserve for updates to existing rows. The object of the PCTFREE setting is to reduce row chaining. When free space in a block reaches the PCTFREE threshold, that block is removed from the free list. The block will first be removed from the process free list, and then after the transaction is committed, it will be removed from the transaction free list. Not only is block size affected by additional inserts and updates to existing rows in the table to which the block belongs, but the block's availability on the free list is affected by changes to the variable portion of the block.

By default, PCTFREE is set to 10 for tables that do not specify this clause. If you are creating a table that will have a great deal of update activity, consider reducing the setting of PCTFREE. The setting you should use depends on the nature of the expected activity on the table. For example, if you will have NUMBER columns changing the most often, you can set PCTFREE to a higher number than if you expect large VARCHAR2 columns to change frequently. Therefore, the smaller the overall size of the changes, the higher you can set PCTFREE.

Typically, for tables with no update activity, setting PCTFREE to 95 (or even higher) is acceptable. For tables with a moderate level of update activity, PCTFREE should be set somewhere around 80 to 90, depending on the nature of the activity.

Keep in mind that setting PCTFREE incorrectly can impact performance and cause a table to take up more disk space then it otherwise would need. If you set PCTFREE too low, such that a large portion of the block is being reserved for updates, then the average numbers of rows per block will decrease. This will require that more blocks be used to store the same amount of data. In other words, a table with a PCTFREE setting of 95 is going to store more rows, in fewer blocks, than a table with a PCTFREE setting of 80. For that table with PCTFREE set to 95, Oracle may need to read only 9 blocks to perform a full table scan of the table. If you set PCTFREE to 80, Oracle may need to read 12 blocks to get the same amount of data. Also, with the allocation of additional blocks comes additional disk space requirements, and even additional SGA

An Overview of Object Management

memory requirements to reduce the physical I/O impacts of reading more blocks. To avoid problems, make sure to monitor block usage after creating a table or changing its PCTFREE setting. (See Chapter 15 for details on monitoring block usage and I/O.)

When setting PCTFREE for an index, you are basically helping Oracle to initially balance the index, and nothing more. You cannot alter the PCTFREE setting for an index. Oracle uses the PCTFREE setting of an index only during the creation or re-creation of an index.

The PCTUSED setting defines a percentage of remaining space at which a given block can be returned to the free list after having been removed due to the PCTFREE setting. The PCTUSED parameter is based on how much of a given block is in use, unlike PCTFREE, which is based on how much space there is left in a given block. Once this threshold is reached, the block will be put on the process free list of the process that has caused the block to be freed. After the transaction commits, the block will be moved to the transaction free list of the table.

The default value of PCTUSED is 40, and the PCTUSED parameter is not valid when creating index or rollback segments. Figure 6.1 illustrates how the PCTFREE and PCTUSED parameters affect row storage in a block.

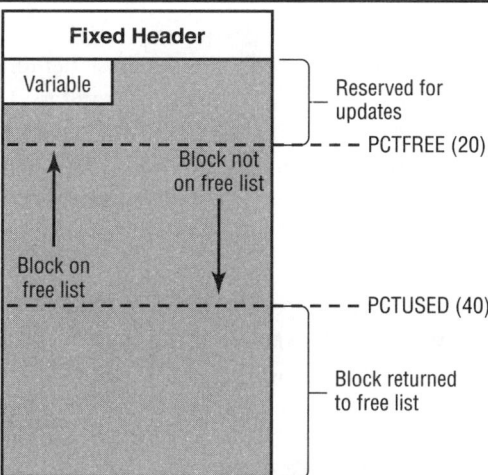

FIGURE 6.1
PCTFREE and PCTUSED block storage

The INITRANS and MAXTRANS Parameters

The INITRANS setting determines how many transaction entries will be reserved in the block header of the segment you are creating. It is only valid for tables. The INITRANS setting can have an impact if you have a table with many different concurrent transactions occurring. This parameter defaults to a value of 1 when you create a table and do not use the INITRANS setting.

The MAXTRANS parameter defines the maximum number of transactions that can concurrently access data in a data block. The purpose of MAXTRANS is to reduce the allocation of transaction entries beyond those defined in INITTRANS. This is because Oracle will create additional transaction entries on a space-available basis in other blocks in the segment. Once these entries are created, they are never removed. The default for MAXTRANS is a function of the block size of the database, and the default typically should be sufficient.

Specifying Storage Parameters

Through the STORAGE clause, you can specify storage parameters, such as how big to initially create the segment and how big to make the next and subsequent extents. The STORAGE clause also allows automatic adjustment of future extents by some percentage.

The database has defaults for each of the STORAGE clause parameters. When you create a tablespace, you can override these system defaults by defining tablespace-level defaults. When you create an object, it will use the tablespace-level defaults if you do not include a STORAGE clause in the DDL used to create the object. If tablespace defaults are not present, the database defaults will be used.

The effect of the STORAGE clause parameters depends on the type of tablespace of the object being created. The two different types of tablespaces are dictionary-managed and locally managed, which is the default tablespace type. When you create a locally managed tablespace, the default AUTOALLOCATE option allows Oracle to create the extents sized as it sees fit. Alternatively, you can define a uniform extent size when the tablespace is created.

The STORAGE clause parameters include INITIAL, NEXT, PCTINCREASE, MIN-EXTENTS, MAXEXTENTS, FREELISTS, FREELIST GROUPS, OPTIMAL, and BUFFER_POOL. The following sections describe how each of these parameters affect tablespaces.

The INITIAL Parameter

The INITIAL setting is the size of the initial extent of the segment being created. This value can be expressed in three ways:

- In bytes (such as 1024), which is the default allocation unit
- In kilobytes, by using the letter *k* at the end of the allocation value (such as 11k)
- In megabytes, by using the letter *m* (as in 11m)

The database default for this value is the size of five data blocks and can be no smaller than two database blocks for most segments. Bitmap segments require a minimum of three blocks. The maximum size of INITIAL is operating-system dependent, though any single extent is limited by the restriction that it must fit within a single database datafile. You cannot alter the INITIAL setting of a table once it has been created.

When dealing with locally managed tablespaces that are created using the uniform extent allocation option, the INITIAL clause works differently. This is because when you define the tablespace, you define the size of every extent in that tablespace. Thus, if you create a locally managed tablespace with a uniform extent size of 10MB, then all extents in that tablespace will be 10MB in size. If you create an object in that tablespace with an INITIAL setting of 20MB, you will end up with an object with two extents of 10MB each. If you create an object with an INITIAL setting of 5MB, the first extent will still be created at 10MB, the uniform extent size.

If the locally managed tablespace was created using the AUTOALLOCATE option, Oracle will define the size of the extents to be allocated. Generally, Oracle will start with 64KB extents and will manage the size of future extents as required. Oracle will create enough extents when an object is created to meet the requested INITIAL setting in the STORAGE clause. Thus, if you have an INITIAL setting of 100KB, Oracle will create two 64KB extents.

The NEXT Parameter

The NEXT parameter defines the size of the next extent allocation for a given segment. As with the INITIAL parameter, this value can be expressed in bytes, kilobytes, or megabytes. The default NEXT value is five blocks. The minimum size is one block. The maximum value of NEXT is operating-system dependent. The PCTINCREASE value, discussed next, can impact future settings of the NEXT parameter after Oracle allocates the first extent based on the NEXT parameter.

When dealing with locally managed tablespaces, regardless of the extent allocation option being used, the allocation of another extent will always result in the allocation of a single extent. Thus, the NEXT setting actually has little impact on the number or size of extents allocated.

The PCTINCREASE Parameter

The PCTINCREASE parameter is used to define the percentage to increase the NEXT parameter by after the next extent allocation occurs. Therefore, PCTINCREASE does not have an immediate impact on NEXT, but modifies it only after an extent is allocated using the NEXT parameter. Once that allocation has occurred, the NEXT parameter will be modified to a value of NEXT + (NEXT * PCTINCREASE). The new NEXT size will be rounded up to a multiple of the database block size during this calculation.

For example, suppose that you create a table with a PCTINCREASE of 50 in a database with a 2KB block size. You create this table with an INITIAL size of 100KB, and the NEXT value is 100KB. After the initial allocation, and after a subsequent allocation of a second extent of the size of NEXT, the next value will be modified to become 100 + (100 * 0.50) or 150KB (153,600 bytes—remember that 1KB is 1024 bytes). Each subsequent extent allocation will result in NEXT being further increased.

By default, the database setting for PCTINCREASE is 50 percent. However, setting PCTINCREASE can lead to all sorts of problems, including fragmentation issues, explosive growth of extent sizes, and the eventual inability to allocate an extent. I recommend that you set this parameter to 0 for each object that you create in your database.

As with the NEXT and INITIAL settings, you can also specify a tablespace default setting for the PCTINCREASE parameter. One thing to consider when setting the tablespace default for this parameter is that it will have an impact on SMON and its job of coalescing adjacent free blocks of space in tablespaces. It is recommended that you set PCTINCREASE to 1 as the default tablespace setting.

The MINEXTENTS and MAXEXTENTS Parameters

The MINEXTENTS parameter allows you to allocate multiple extents to a segment when you first create it. This parameter also prevents the object from having extents de-allocated (such as with rollback segments using the OPTIMAL setting, which we will discuss shortly) below the number defined by the MINEXTENTS parameter. The default setting for MINEXTENTS is 1. This parameter is typically used when creating rollback segments to add multiple extents for that segment. (See the "Managing Rollback Segments" section later in this chapter for details on rollback segment extents.)

The MAXEXTENTS parameter defines the maximum number of extents that the segment can grow to. This parameter basically limits the size of the object. Prior to Oracle 7.3, object growth was limited to a set number of extents. This limitation was a factor of the block size of the object. Starting with Oracle 7.3, a segment could consist of an unlimited number of extents by using the UNLIMITED keyword with the MAXEXTENTS parameter. The UNLIMITED keyword has the effect of removing any limitation on the number of extents in a segment.

It is common in databases that have been migrated from Oracle7 to find MAXEXTENTS set to some artificially low level because of the restriction in the number of extents in Oracle7. This can cause serious problems, and you should check any database to make sure that MAXEXTENTS is not artificially set low. In cases where you do find MAXEXTENTS set in an ill-advised way, you should consider setting the MAXEXTENTS parameter to UNLIMITED.

The database default value for this parameter depends on the block size for your database. The minimum value is 1 for all segment types except rollback segments, which have a minimum value of 2. The maximum value is UNLIMITED. As with the other STORAGE parameters discussed so far, the database defaults are overridden by tablespace defaults, which are overridden by object settings.

NOTE It is a common misconception (and sales bait used by more than one company selling defragmentation products) that performance suffers if an object consists of many extents. In fact, there is sufficient evidence to suggest otherwise. Several different test cases that I conducted showed that multiple extents did not cause any type of performance problems in regard to query execution times. I did find that an excessive number of extents (somewhere around 20,000, depending on a number of factors) caused some slowdowns in performance of certain DDL operations (DROP TABLE and TRUNCATE, for example). I also found that the impact of extent allocation during large operations (such as INSERT operations) was negligible.

The FREELISTS and FREELIST GROUPS Parameters

The FREELISTS parameter specifies how many free lists are to be established for each FREELIST GROUP. (There is normally one free list group for tables and indexes, unless you are using Oracle Parallel Server.) The default value for this parameter is 1. The maximum setting for this parameter depends on the database block size. Unlike the other storage parameters, this parameter cannot be set as a tablespace default. Therefore, if you wish to override the database default, you must do it when you create an object.

TIP In Oracle8i (release 8.1.6 and later), you can increase the number of free lists of an object by using an ALTER command. For example, to increase the free lists in a table called EMPLOYEE, issue the command ALTER TABLE employee STORAGE (FREELISTS 3). This is an important new feature that can help improve your system's performance.

The FREELIST GROUPS parameter defaults to 1. Normally, it is only changed when you are using Oracle Parallel Server (OPS).

The OPTIMAL Parameter

The OPTIMAL setting is valid only when you are creating rollback segments. When defined, the OPTIMAL setting will cause Oracle to de-allocate rollback segment extents allocated to a rollback segment. There is no database default for OPTIMAL.

When it is set, it cannot cause the rollback segment to shrink below the number of extents defined by the MINEXTENTS parameter of the rollback segment. If you attempt to create or alter a rollback segment in such a way that OPTIMAL will cause the number of extents to fall below that defined by MINEXTENTS, the statement will fail. We will discuss the OPTIMAL parameter in more detail in the "Managing Rollback Segments" section later in this chapter.

The BUFFER_POOL Parameter

The BUFFER_POOL setting defines the buffer pool that the object is assigned to. Valid values for this parameter are KEEP, RECYCLE, and DEFAULT. The default value is DEFAULT. This parameter cannot be set as a tablespace default.

Managing Tablespaces

Tablespaces are logical storage areas that contain schema objects. Tablespaces are the bridge between logical database storage and physical database storage in the form of database datafiles. A single tablespace is allocated space by virtue of the space allocated to one or more physical datafiles assigned to that tablespace. A tablespace may contain one or more datafiles. A datafile can belong to only one tablespace.

Common Oracle Tablespaces

Most Oracle databases contain certain tablespaces. Every database has a SYSTEM tablespace. Other tablespaces are created for temporary storage, tables, indexes, and rollback segments.

The SYSTEM Tablespace

The SYSTEM tablespace is the only tablespace that absolutely must exist in any Oracle database. This tablespace is created when you issue the CREATE DATABASE command. The SYSTEM tablespace is used to store all of the Oracle data dictionary objects. Also contained in the SYSTEM tablespace will be a SYSTEM rollback segment.

You should never create any objects in the SYSTEM tablespace. When you create a user account, that SYSTEM tablespace is assigned as its default tablespace and temporary tablespace. You should make sure that you change these settings to give the user account a different default tablespace and temporary tablespace. You can do this when creating the user or later, with the ALTER USER command. (See Chapter 21 for details on managing user accounts.)

The Temporary Tablespace

The temporary tablespace is used for storage of temporary database objects, such as those that are used during sorts to disk. Typically, this tablespace is called TEMP, but it can be called just about anything. As noted in the previous section, when you create a user account, it is assigned SYSTEM as its temporary tablespace by default. You should change this to the temporary tablespace you've created. Generally, you should never create any objects in a temporary tablespace.

Note in Oracle8i there are three different kinds of temporary tablespaces. The first is a normal tablespace, just like any other tablespace. The second type of tablespace is created through the use of the TEMPORARY clause of the CREATE TABLESPACE command. When a temporary tablespace is created in this manner, only temporary segments can be created in it (in other words, you can't accidentally create an index in it). Also, tablespaces created in this manner cannot be locally managed tablespaces.

 NOTE A temporary tablespace can be made permanent, and a permanent tablespace can be made temporary by using the ALTER TABLESPACE command. No activity can be present on the tablespace in order for the ALTER command to be successful.

Finally, the CREATE TEMPORARY TABLESPACE command creates a tablespace that allows objects to be created in it, but those objects will be removed once the session has disconnected. This type of tablespace can be created as a locally managed tablespace and can contain any type of object. This type of tablespace makes use of Oracle *tempfiles*.

Oracle tempfiles have the following features:

- No redo is generated for any operation in a tempfile.
- Tempfiles cannot be made read-only or renamed.
- Tempfiles cannot be created using the ALTER DATABASE command.
- Tempfiles cannot be recovered during media recovery. Control file backups display no information about tempfiles. When recovering your database, you simply add files to the existing tablespace definition.

To find the files associated with a temporary tablespace, use the V$TEMPFILE (not the V$DATAFILE view). For tempfile information, use the DBA_TEMP_FILES view, rather than DBA_DATA_FILES view.

The Data and Index Tablespaces

Typically, when creating a database, you will create one or more tablespaces for data and one or more separate tablespaces for the indexes. These tablespaces are created using the CREATE TABLESPACE command. Often, many objects are stored in the same tablespace. However, you may want to store a single object within its own tablespace to improve database performance or for ease of maintenance. If you are using large, partitioned objects, you may even create multiple tablespaces for a single object.

The Rollback Segment Tablespace

Normally, you will create a tablespace, using the CREATE TABLESPACE command, to store rollback segments. This tablespace must be large enough to accommodate the number of rollback segments you wish to create, including room for the likely growth of those rollback segments.

Creating Tablespaces

Creating tablespaces will likely be one of your first tasks after you create your database. The CREATE TABLESPACE command is used to create a tablespace. When creating a tablespace, you define the datafiles associated with that tablespace, along with the default STORAGE clause for that tablespace. The default storage settings will be used for the tablespace's schema objects that require storage allocations, but were created without a STORAGE clause. For example, if you issue a CREATE TABLE statement without a STORAGE clause, the default settings of that tablespace will be used for the table's INITIAL, NEXT, PCTINCREASE, and other parameters.

When creating a dictionary-managed tablespace, you can create it as a tablespace of type PERMANENT or TEMPORARY. If the tablespace is defined as type TEMPORARY, then only temporary segments can be stored in it. Permanent objects such as tables and indexes cannot be created in tablespaces of type TEMPORARY. Global temporary tables are not assigned to any specific tablespace at all.

You can define a tablespace to be LOGGING or NOLOGGING when it is created. This sets the default settings for tables, indexes, and other objects that support the NOLOGGING option.

Here are examples of creating tablespaces:
```
CREATE TABLESPACE my_tablespace
DATAFILE 'd:\oracle\oradata\recover\recover_my_tablespace_01.dbf'
SIZE 150m;

CREATE TABLESPACE my_tablespace
```

```
DATAFILE 'd:\oracle\oradata\recover\recover_my_tablespace_01.dbf'
SIZE 10m
DEFAULT STORAGE (INITIAL 100m NEXT 100m MAXEXTENTS UNLIMITED);
```

 TIP When creating a tablespace, give the tablespace a meaningful name. Make it something other than data or index, if possible. Descriptive tablespace names (for example, q4_99_partitioned_data) make maintenance operations easier.

The SIZE parameter defines the size of the datafile being created for the tablespace. All tablespace space is preallocated in Oracle. This can cause problems if an object attempts to grow outside the confines of the specified size of the tablespace. Oracle has provided a solution for this, by allowing tablespace datafiles to extend automatically when required. You tell Oracle that it can extend datafiles automatically by using the AUTOEXTEND clause of the CREATE TABLESPACE command.

With the AUTOEXTEND clause, you can define how large a datafile is allowed to grow and how large it can grow at any given time. Use of AUTOEXTEND is not a default setting, so if you wish to take advantage of this functionality, you will need to include it in the CREATE TABLESPACE command (or if you forget, you can use the ALTER DATABASE command to set it). This parameter is associated with a specific datafile, so you must define the datafile you are referencing with AUTOEXTEND.

In the AUTOEXTEND clause, you can use two keywords:

- NEXT represents the increment that the datafile will grow by each time it needs to be extended.

- MAXSIZE represents the maximum size to which the datafile can grow.

Here are examples of using AUTOEXTEND:

```
CREATE TABLESPACE my_extending_tbs
DATAFILE
'd:\oracle\oradata\recover\recover_my_extending_tablespace_01.dbf'
SIZE 10m
AUTOEXTEND ON NEXT 1m MAXSIZE 20m,
'd:\oracle\oradata\recover\recover_my_extending_tablespace_02.dbf'
SIZE 10m
AUTOEXTEND ON NEXT 1m MAXSIZE 20m,
'd:\oracle\oradata\recover\recover_my_extending_tablespace_03.dbf'
SIZE 10m
DEFAULT STORAGE (INITIAL 100m NEXT 100m MAXEXTENTS UNLIMITED);
```

This example creates a tablespace that consists of three datafiles. The first two datafiles have AUTOEXTEND clauses, and thus will be able to extend automatically as necessary. Both AUTOEXTEND clauses specify ON NEXT 1m MAXSIZE 20m. This means that the specific datafile associated with each clause will grow in 1MB increments, up to a total of 20MB. The third datafile created in this example does not have an AUTOEXTEND clause, so it will not extend automatically. Thus, this tablespace will be initially created as a 30MB tablespace. The maximum possible size that this tablespace can grow to is 50MB (20MB + 20MB + 10MB).

Altering Tablespaces

You can alter a tablespace with the ALTER TABLESPACE command. The following are some of the things you can do with the ALTER TABLESPACE command:

- Change the default storage characteristics of a tablespace.
- Bring a tablespace online or offline.
- Change the tablespace to type TEMPORARY or PERMANENT.
- Begin or end backups.
- Coalesce the free space in the tablespace.
- Change it from LOGGING to NOLOGGING.
- Add or rename a datafile.

The following are some examples of uses of the ALTER TABLESPACE command.

```
ALTER TABLESPACE my_tablespace
DEFAULT STORAGE (NEXT 10k);

ALTER TABLESPACE my_tablespace BEGIN BACKUP;

ALTER TABLESPACE my_tablespace COALESCE;
```

If you wish to disable or change the AUTOEXTEND setting of a tablespace's datafile, you will need to use the ALTER DATABASE command, as in the following examples.

```
ALTER DATABASE
DATAFILE
'd:\oracle\oradata\recover\recover_my_extending_tablespace_01.dbf'
AUTOEXTEND OFF;
```

```
ALTER DATABASE
DATAFILE
'd:\oracle\oradata\recover\recover_my_extending_tablespace_01.dbf'
AUTOEXTEND ON NEXT 2m;
```

Dropping Tablespaces

To drop a tablespace, you use the DROP TABLESPACE command. If the tablespace includes any objects, you will need to either drop those objects or use the INCLUDING CONTENTS clause of the DROP TABLESPACE command. Here are two examples:

```
DROP TABLESPACE my_tablespace;
DROP TABLESPACE my_extending_tablespace INCLUDING CONTENTS;
```

After you drop a tablespace, you will need to remove the database datafiles associated with that tablespace—Oracle does not do this for you.

Managing Heap Tables

Heap tables have been around since the beginning of Oracle; we just never called them "heap tables" until the advent of index-organized tables (discussed in the "Managing Index-Organized Tables" section later in this chapter). When you create a table with the CREATE TABLE statement, a heap table is the default type of table created. Heap tables are also known as *relational tables* or just *tables*.

Heap Table Fundamentals

Tables store data in rows and can consist of multiple columns, much like your favorite spreadsheet software. Each column in a table has a name assigned to it, as well as a datatype associated with it. That datatype may be NUMBER, DATE, CHAR, VARCHAR2, or any of the other valid Oracle datatypes.

Each row has an identifier, called a *ROWID*. The ROWID for each row in the table not only uniquely identifies the row within the table itself, but also identifies the row within the entire database. In Oracle, a ROWID is a pseudocolumn available for queries from each table. ROWIDs for tables are generated on the fly, and they are not stored in the database (with the exception of inside restricted ROWIDs, which are stored in indexes).

Oracle has two different types of ROWIDs: an extended ROWID and a restricted ROWID. Prior to Oracle8, the restricted ROWID was the native (and only) ROWID format used in Oracle. Because of changes to Oracle's architecture, including the addition of Oracle objects and partitioning, the format of the native database ROWID needed to be expanded, and the extended ROWID was born. Let's look at each of these ROWID types in a bit more detail.

Extended ROWIDs

The extended ROWID is the native form of a ROWID in Oracle8i and was first introduced with Oracle8. Extended ROWIDs are relative only to a given tablespace. This is different from the relative ROWID that was present in Oracle7, which made every row in the database unique throughout the entire database. The extended ROWID is an 18-character value that represents four different values:

Data object number This is a six-character representation of a 32-bit data object number. This number uniquely identifies the database segment. Each time an object changes, the data object number associated with this object changes as well. Thus, the data object number also serves as a version number for the object.

Relative datafile number This is a three-character representation of the relative datafile number. The relative datafile number is relative to the tablespace to which that tablespace belongs. Thus, objects in different tablespaces will likely have different relative datafile numbers.

Data block This is a six-character representation of the data block. This block number is relative to the tablespace to which it belongs.

Row number in the block This is a three-character representation of the row in the block.

An example of an extended ROWID is shown in the query below.

```
SQL> SELECT rowid FROM test;

ROWID
------------------
AAAAx/AABAAADhBAAA
AAAAx/AABAAADhBAAB
AAAAx/AABAAADhBAAC
AAAAx/AABAAADhBAAD
```

As you can see, the ROWID is a rather odd-looking thing. All of the different letters do not translate into anything usable by the DBA, except that they can be used directly in a SQL statement's WHERE clause in certain cases (for example, if you store ROWIDs in a table).

To effectively use an extended ROWID, you will probably need to employ the Oracle package DBMS_ROWID. This package has several functions that can be used to translate the extended ROWID into its component parts, which can then be used to determine such things as which datafile or block the row is in. The DBMS_ROWID package also provides procedures and functions that can convert extended ROWIDs into restricted ROWIDs, and vice versa.

Restricted ROWIDs

The restricted ROWID can be determined from the extended ROWID, and an extended ROWID can be created from a restricted ROWID. The restricted ROWID has three components:

- The first number in the restricted ROWID is an eight-digit number that represents the block number that the row belongs in. This number relates to the V$LOCK column in the DBA_EXTENTS dictionary view.
- The second number is a four-digit number that represents the row number in the block. The first row in each block is always a 0.
- The last number is a four-digit number that represents the absolute datafile to which the row belongs. This number relates to the FILE_ID column in the DBA_EXTENTS data dictionary view.

An example of a restricted ROWID looks something like this:
00000011.0000.0001

Each component of the restricted ROWID is separated by a dot, and unlike the extended ROWID, you do not need to use any package to determine the values being provided for each component.

NOTE It is a common misconception that the restricted ROWID has been totally done away with. In fact, Oracle indexes still store restricted ROWIDs for each table row that they point to. Also, there are those who mistakenly suppose that there is some sort of ROWID conversion that occurs during a migration from Oracle 7.3 to Oracle8i. This is not the case, since the ROWIDs for tables are not stored in the database, but are generated on the fly when the ROWID pseudocolumn is used in a query.

Creating Heap Tables

To create a table, use the CREATE TABLE DDL statement. In its typical form, the CREATE TABLE statement includes the following:

- The table name

- A list of column names, the datatype associated with the column, and certain constraints associated with that column (such as NOT NULL)
- The tablespace that the table is assigned to
- Table attributes such as PCTFREE and PCTUSED
- The STORAGE clause associated with the table
- Table attribute settings, such as CACHE or NOLOGGING

To create a table in your own schema, you must have the CREATE TABLE privilege. If you want to create a table in another user's schema, you need to have the CREATE ANY TABLE privilege. Also, you will need to have a sufficient QUOTA assigned to the tablespace(s) in which you will be creating tables (and any associated primary key indexes). If you create a primary key on the table, you also need to have the privileges to create an index, since the primary key is enforced through a unique index.

NOTE A QUOTA is a limitation on how much space a user can use in a given tablespace. For example, if your quota is 0 (the default for new users), you will not be able to add anything to the tablespace. Users are assigned a QUOTA as a part of their configuration and setup. See Chapter 21 for more details on setting up user accounts.

If you are using an Oracle TYPE in the table (we will discuss TYPEs in Chapter 8), you will need EXECUTE privileges on the TYPE you will be using, if your schema doesn't own the TYPE. If you wish to grant access to the table to other users, you will need to have EXECUTE privileges on the TYPE with the ADMIN option.

There are several miscellaneous types of settings that you may wish to consider when creating a table in Oracle. Table 6.1 lists these settings.

TABLE 6.1: MISCELLANEOUS TABLE OPTIONS

Option	Default	Purpose
CACHE	No	Causes full table scans to be put on the head of the LRU list. This clause has been deprecated in favor of the use of the new KEEP BUFFER_POOL option.
NOCACHE	Yes	Causes Oracle to follow the default full table scan behavior, by putting the blocks read for a full table scan on the tail of the LRU list.

Continued

MANAGING HEAP TABLES

TABLE 6.1: MISCELLANEOUS TABLE OPTIONS (CONTINUED)

Option	Default	Purpose
NOLOGGING	No	Reduces redo generated by DML activity on the table. Table data inserted after backup will not be recoverable. This can reduce the time required to create the table.
LOGGING	Yes	Sets the table in normal mode.
MONITORING	No	Causes Oracle to record DML activity on the table. You can then use the DBMS_STATS.GATHER STALE procedure to update the statistics of just the tables that have changed.
NOMONITORING	Yes	Sets the default for this parameter.

 NOTE CACHE remains in Oracle only for backward compatibility. You should configure and use a keep buffer pool (described in Chapter 5) and assign an object to that buffer pool rather than use the CACHE option.

Creating a Table

Listing 6.1 shows a simple example of using the CREATE TABLE statement.

Listing 6.1: Creating a Heap Table

```
CREATE TABLE PARENT
(parent_id    NUMBER PRIMARY KEY,
 last_name    VARCHAR2(30) NOT NULL,
 first_name   VARCHAR2(30) NOT NULL,
 middle_int   CHAR(1),
 sex          CHAR(1),
 married_status   CHAR(1)
)
TABLESPACE users
PCTFREE 10
PCTUSED 60
STORAGE(INITIAL 10m NEXT 10m PCTINCREASE 0);
```

This creates a table named PARENT with six columns. The first column, PARENT_ID, is defined as a NUMBER datatype and the primary key of this table.

Because the keyword PRIMARY KEY is included in the definition of the PARENT_ID column, an index will be created on this primary key column. Since we didn't give the index a name in this CREATE TABLE statement, Oracle will assign a name to it by default. The system-generated name will always start with a SYS and then be followed by a series of numbers. Also, the primary key index will be created in the default tablespace of the user creating the table, and the index associated with the primary key will also have a system-generated name. The query and results below show the primary key created as a result of the creation of this table.

```
SQL> SELECT table_name, index_name, tablespace_name
  2  FROM user_indexes
  3  WHERE table_name like 'PARENT';
```

TABLE_NAME	INDEX_NAME	TABLESPACE_NAME
PARENT	SYS_C00780	USERS

This shows that the system-generated index name is SYS_C00780. Also note that the primary key index has been assigned to the USERS tablespace, which is the default tablespace of the user who created the index. In the next section, you will see an example of how to give the primary key index a meaningful name and control where the primary key index is created.

The LAST_NAME and FIRST_NAME columns in the table are VARCHAR2 datatypes that are sized to hold up to 30 characters each. The MIDDLE_INT, SEX, and MARRIED_STATUS columns are fixed-length CHAR datatypes, each holding 1 byte.

Notice the NOT NULL keyword in the LAST_NAME and FIRST_NAME column definitions. The NOT NULL keyword establishes a constraint on the table. A *constraint* is a rule. In this case, the NOT NULL constraint prohibits this column from having a NULL value in it at any time. Thus, you will need to provide a value for the column in each INSERT statement, by including it in the INSERT statement, through the use of a trigger (see Chapter 1 and Appendix F for more on triggers) or by defining a default value for the column. When you create a primary key, the columns of the primary key will be set to the NOT NULL status automatically.

The other types of constraints you can create in Oracle are check, foreign key, NOT NULL, primary, and unique. When creating a table, you may define the various constraints in the CREATE TABLE statement either for individual rows (check constraints) or a group of rows (primary keys). (See Chapter 7 for a detailed discussion of constraints.)

Viewing the Table

After you've created the table, you can query the DBA_TABLES view to see your table:

```
SELECT owner, table_name,
tablespace_name, initial_extent, next_extent
FROM dba_tables
WHERE owner = 'SCOTT' AND table_name LIKE 'PARENT';
```

OWNER	TABLE_NAME	TABLESPACE_NAME	INITIAL_EXTENT	NEXT_EXTENT
SCOTT	PARENT	USERS	10485760	10485760

Also, you can query the DBA_TAB_COLS data dictionary view and discover that you have rows in it for each of the columns in your table:

```
  SELECT owner, table_name, column_name, data_type, nullable
2 FROM dba_tab_columns
3 WHERE owner='SCOTT'
4 AND table_name='PARENT'
```

OWNER	TABLE_NAME	COLUMN_NAME	DATA_TYPE	N
SCOTT	PARENT	PARENT_ID	NUMBER	N
SCOTT	PARENT	LAST_NAME	VARCHAR2	N
SCOTT	PARENT	FIRST_NAME	VARCHAR2	N
SCOTT	PARENT	MIDDLE_INT	CHAR	Y
SCOTT	PARENT	SEX	CHAR	Y
SCOTT	PARENT	MARRIED_STATUS	CHAR	y

The DBA_TABLES and DBA_TAB_COLS views are discussed in more detail in the "Viewing Table Information" section a bit later in this chapter.

Specifying the Primary Key and Index Location

Listing 6.2 shows another example of a CREATE TABLE statement.

Listing 6.2: Creating a Table with Primary Key and Index Location Specifications

```
CREATE TABLE children
(child_id   NUMBER CONSTRAINT pk_children PRIMARY KEY
  USING INDEX TABLESPACE indexes
  STORAGE (INITIAL 200k NEXT 200k),
parent_id   NUMBER,
```

```
        last_name    VARCHAR2(30),
        first_name   VARCHAR2(30),
        middle_int   CHAR(1),
        medical_code VARCHAR2(30) CONSTRAINT children_check_upper
                 CHECK (medical_code = UPPER(medical_code) )
)
TABLESPACE users
PCTFREE 10
PCTUSED 60
STORAGE(INITIAL 10m NEXT 10m PCTINCREASE 0);
```

This one looks a bit different from the CREATE TABLE statement in Listing 6.1. First, the second line, where the CHILD_ID column is being defined, includes a CONSTRAINT clause that names the primary key constraint. In this example, the primary key constraint is named PK_CHILDREN. The associated index enforcing that primary key will also be called PK_CHILDREN.

Next, the USING INDEX clause is associated with the first column. It is through this clause that you can control in which tablespace the primary key index is created, as well as define storage characteristics for that index with a separate STORAGE clause.

Finally, note the check constraint in the definition of the MEDICAL_CODE column. The definition of the constraint begins with the word CONSTRAINT, followed by the name of the constraint, then the keyword CHECK. Following the CHECK keyword is the actual constraint. This example uses the UPPER function to ensure that any values for MEDICAL_CODE are entered in uppercase. If someone tried to enter a lowercase medical code in this column, the transaction would fail and the following error would be returned:

```
ORA-02290: check constraint (SCOTT.CHECK_UPPER) violated
```

Creating a Two-Column Primary Key and Foreign Key Constraint

Let's look at another example of a CREATE TABLE statement. The example shown in Listing 6.3 re-creates the CHILD table with a two-column primary key and a foreign key constraint to the PARENT key.

Listing 6.3: Creating a Table with a Two-Column Primary Key and Foreign Key Constraint

```
CREATE TABLE children
(child_id     NUMBER,
 parent_id    NUMBER,
 last_name    VARCHAR2(30),
```

```
   first_name VARCHAR2(30),
   middle_int CHAR(1),
   medical_code VARCHAR2(30) CONSTRAINT children_check_upper
            CHECK (medical_code = UPPER(medical_code) ),
   CONSTRAINT pk_children PRIMARY KEY (child_id, parent_id)
   USING INDEX TABLESPACE indexes
   STORAGE (INITIAL 10k NEXT 10k),
   CONSTRAINT fk_child_parent FOREIGN KEY (parent_id)
   REFERENCES parent (parent_id)
   )
   TABLESPACE users
   PCTFREE 10
   PCTUSED 60
   STORAGE(INITIAL 10m NEXT 10m PCTINCREASE 0)
```

Both the primary key constraint and the foreign key constraint are created in the same clause where the table columns are created. Since the example creates a two-column primary key, it adds a separate CONSTRAINT clause, rather than just the PRIMARY KEY clause at the end of each column. In other words, you cannot create a two-column primary key like this:

```
CREATE TABLE children
(child_id    NUMBER PRIMARY KEY,
 parent_id   NUMBER PRIMARY KEY,
 last_name   VARCHAR2(30),
 first_name VARCHAR2(30),
 middle_int CHAR(1) );
```

This code would result in an error because you are incorrectly trying to define a two-column primary key.

Creating a Table from an Existing Table Definition

The CREATE TABLE AS SELECT (CTAS) command allows you to create a table from the definition of an existing table, or create a new table based on a join of one or more tables. This is handy to have for a variety of reasons. First, this is one method you can use to defragment a table. Also, you can use CTAS to create a separate table with a sample set of data. Listing 6.4 shows an example of using CTAS to create a table from two existing tables.

Listing 6.4: Using the CREATE TABLE AS SELECT (CTAS) Command

```
-- Using CTAS from an existing table (or tables in this case).
-- We are also limiting the number of rows returned to 9.
```

```
CREATE TABLE create_view_table_one
TABLESPACE users
STORAGE (INITIAL 100k NEXT 100k BUFFER_POOL RECYCLE)
AS
SELECT a.parent_id AS parent_id,
a.last_name AS parent_last_name,
a.first_name AS paremt_first_name,
b.last_name AS child_last_name,
b.first_name AS child_first_name
FROM parent a, children b
WHERE a.parent_id=b.parent_id
AND rownum < 10;
```

You can also use CTAS to create a table using a view, as shown in Listing 6.5. This example executes this statement using a view as the source for the new table.

Listing 6.5: Creating a Table Using a View with CTAS

```
-- Create the view first
CREATE VIEW v_parent_child AS
SELECT a.parent_id AS parent_id,
a.last_name AS parent_last_name,
a.first_name AS parent_first_name,
b.last_name AS child_last_name,
b.first_name AS child_first_name
FROM parent a, children b
WHERE a.parent_id=b.parent_id;

-- Now, create a table via CTAS using the view
CREATE TABLE ctas_from_view_pc
TABLESPACE data
STORAGE (INITIAL 100k NEXT 100k )
AS SELECT * FROM v_parent_child;
```

NOTE CTAS is particularly handy for use with LogMiner, which is discussed in Chapter 14. This is because some of the critical views that LogMiner populates with information are persistent only for the duration of the user session that created those views. Using CTAS to create a table allows you to retain the LogMiner results.

Creating a Temporary Table

A *temporary table* is like a regular table in many ways. It is created by the use of the GLOBAL TEMPORARY keywords in the CREATE TABLE command. The data in a temporary table is visible to only the session that created that data, yet the temporary table is available for use by all transactions.

The temporary table will persist until it is dropped; however, the data in the temporary table is not persistent. Using the ON COMMIT keywords, you can choose from two different options that control when the data in the temporary table is removed. If you create the temporary table using the ON COMMIT DELETE clause (the default), the session data in the table is removed as soon as the transaction completes. Using the ON COMMIT PRESERVE clause will cause that session's data to be removed only after the session is disconnected.

A temporary table uses temporary segments to store session data, and along with the data in the segments, the segments themselves are de-allocated. Since temporary tables use temporary segments, they use the temporary tablespace defined for the user who is using the temporary table. Therefore, no TABLESPACE clause, STORAGE clause, or physical attributes clauses are allowed in the CREATE TABLE statement. When an index is created on a temporary table, its data segments are temporary as well. Therefore, a USING INDEX clause is not permitted when creating a temporary table. The CONSTRAINT clause is allowed, but some constraints are not permitted.

Here is a summary of the restrictions on temporary tables:

- They can be only hash tables (so index-organized tables and clusters are not allowed as temporary tables).
- You cannot partition a temporary table.
- Most constraints are not supported, but you can specify check constraints and NOT NULL constraints. You can create temporary tables with primary keys, but foreign key relationships are not supported.
- Temporary tables do not support nested tables or VARRAYs, which are part of Oracle's object-oriented features.
- Parallel DML and parallel queries are not supported on temporary tables.
- You cannot use a temporary table as a part of a distributed transaction.

Listing 6.6 shows an example of creating a temporary table.

Listing 6.6: Creating a Temporary Table

```
CREATE GLOBAL TEMPORARY TABLE temp_children
(child_id    NUMBER CONSTRAINT pk_temp_children PRIMARY KEY,
 parent_id   NUMBER,
```

```
    last_name   VARCHAR2(30),
    first_name  VARCHAR2(30),
    middle_int  CHAR(1)
    );
```

Altering Tables

You can alter many of the settings of a table through the ALTER TABLE DDL command. The following are some of the things you can do with the ALTER TABLE command:

- Alter or drop column definitions, sizes, and constraints
- Alter table storage parameters, including NEXT and FREELISTS
- Enable constraints (without validating them) and disable constraints
- Move or rename a table
- Manually allocate an extent to a table
- Modify table parameters
- Add, drop, move, or alter partitions
- Modify several table attributes, such as CACHE and NOLOGGING

There are certain parameters that cannot be changed once an object is created. In particular, you cannot change the INITIAL parameter in the STORAGE clause.

The following are several examples of using the ALTER TABLE command:

- To alter the storage clause of a table:
  ```
  ALTER TABLE dodo STORAGE (NEXT 100k);
  ```
- To enable a constraint on the table:
  ```
  ALTER TABLE my_table ENABLE CONSTRAINT fk_my_table_01;
  ```
- To add a unique constraint to a table:
  ```
  ALTER TABLE phone_list ADD user_code
  CONSTRAINT line_code UNIQUE;
  ```
- To add a primary key to the table:
  ```
  ALTER TABLE student
  ADD CONSTRAINT pk_student_id
  PRIMARY KEY (student_id)
  USING INDEX
  TABLESPACE pk_index
  STORAGE (INITIAL 100k NEXT 100k);
  ```

- To add a column:
  ```
  ALTER TABLE student ADD COLUMN (maiden_name VARCHAR2(20));
  ```
- To drop a column:
  ```
  ALTER TABLE student DROP COLUMN maiden_name;
  ```

De-allocating Unused Table Space

You may discover that a table has had excessive space allocated to its structure. It might be that the unused space would be better used in another object. When this is the case, you can de-allocate space from the table using the DEALLOCATE UNUSED clause in an ALTER TABLE statement. When this command is issued, Oracle will de-allocate space from the table. Two settings influence how much space you can de-allocate with this command:

The high-water mark You can only de-allocate space in the table from the high-water mark up. Recall that the high-water mark is the highest position in the table that has ever been used to store data. Oracle will de-allocate space from the end of the table being de-allocated (this same command can be used for indexes, table partitions, and clusters as well) to the high-water mark. The optional KEEP clause allows you to reserve some space in the table, rather than de-allocate all of the space above the high-water mark.

The MAXEXTENTS clause Oracle will not allow you to de-allocate space such that the number of extents allocated to the object will fall below the MAX-EXTENTS clause of the object from which you are de-allocating space. The de-allocation process can actually cause Oracle to modify the INITIAL STORAGE clause value as well as the MINEXTENTS value, if the DEALLOCATE command will cause space to be de-allocated below these points.

Here are examples of using the DEALLOCATE UNUSED clause.
```
ALTER TABLE student DEALLOCATE UNUSED;
ALTER TABLE parent DEALLOCATE UNUSED KEEP 200m;
```

Dropping Tables

Removing a table (hash, temporary, or index-organized) is done via the DROP TABLE statement. In most cases, this is a straightforward process. The DROP TABLE command includes an optional CASCADE CONSTRAINTS clause. The CASCADE CONSTRAINTS clause will cause all associated referential integrity constraints to be removed when you drop the table. If there is a foreign key associated with the table to be dropped, you will need to use the CASCADE CONSTRAINTS clause in order to drop the table.

Here are examples of using the DROP TABLE statement:
```
DROP TABLE dodo;
DROP TABLE my_table CASCADE CONSTRAINTS;
```

Viewing Table Information

Several data dictionary views can be used to manage tables in Oracle. These views are used to locate the table and identify its columns and the other information in the table. Each of the views discussed here comes not only in the DBA_ variety, but also in USER_ and ALL_ versions.

The DBA_TABLES View

The DBA_TABLES view provides basic table information, including the owner of the table, the name of the table, the tablespace the table resides in, and many of the statistics collected by the Oracle statistics collection process. If you need to find out who owns a table or what its storage characteristics are, this is the place to go.

The following is a listing of the description of the view.

```
SQL> DESC dba_tables
 Name                                      Null?    Type
 ----------------------------------------- -------- ------------
 OWNER                                     NOT NULL VARCHAR2(30)
 TABLE_NAME                                NOT NULL VARCHAR2(30)
 TABLESPACE_NAME                                    VARCHAR2(30)
 CLUSTER_NAME                                       VARCHAR2(30)
 IOT_NAME                                           VARCHAR2(30)
 PCT_FREE                                           NUMBER
 PCT_USED                                           NUMBER
 INI_TRANS                                          NUMBER
 MAX_TRANS                                          NUMBER
 INITIAL_EXTENT                                     NUMBER
 NEXT_EXTENT                                        NUMBER
 MIN_EXTENTS                                        NUMBER
 MAX_EXTENTS                                        NUMBER
 PCT_INCREASE                                       NUMBER
 FREELISTS                                          NUMBER
 FREELIST_GROUPS                                    NUMBER
 LOGGING                                            VARCHAR2(3)
```

BACKED_UP	VARCHAR2(1)
NUM_ROWS	NUMBER
BLOCKS	NUMBER
EMPTY_BLOCKS	NUMBER
AVG_SPACE	NUMBER
CHAIN_CNT	NUMBER
AVG_ROW_LEN	NUMBER
AVG_SPACE_FREELIST_BLOCKS	NUMBER
NUM_FREELIST_BLOCKS	NUMBER
DEGREE	VARCHAR2(10)
INSTANCES	VARCHAR2(10)
CACHE	VARCHAR2(5)
TABLE_LOCK	VARCHAR2(8)
SAMPLE_SIZE	NUMBER
LAST_ANALYZED	DATE
PARTITIONED	VARCHAR2(3)
IOT_TYPE	VARCHAR2(12)
TEMPORARY	VARCHAR2(1)
SECONDARY	VARCHAR2(1)
NESTED	VARCHAR2(3)
BUFFER_POOL	VARCHAR2(7)
ROW_MOVEMENT	VARCHAR2(8)
GLOBAL_STATS	VARCHAR2(3)
USER_STATS	VARCHAR2(3)
DURATION	VARCHAR2(15)
SKIP_CORRUPT	VARCHAR2(8)
MONITORING	VARCHAR2(3)

Here is an example of a query against the view and its results:

```
SELECT owner, table_name, initial_extent, next_extent,
pct_free, pct_used
FROM dba_tables
WHERE owner='SCOTT';
```

OWNER	TABLE_NAME	INITIAL_EXTENT	NEXT_EXTENT	PCT_FREE	PCT_USED
SCOTT	BONUS	10240	10240	10	40
SCOTT	CHILD	10240	10240	10	40
SCOTT	DEPT	10240	10240	10	40
SCOTT	EMPLOYEE	102400	102400	10	40

SCOTT	GIJOE	10240	10240	10	40
SCOTT	PARENT	10240	10240	10	40
SCOTT	PLAN_TABLE	10240	10240	10	40
SCOTT	RANK	10240	10240	10	40
SCOTT	SALGRADE	10240	10240	10	40
SCOTT	STUDENTS	10240	10240	10	40
SCOTT	ZOCALO	10240	10240	10	40

The DBA_TAB_COLUMNS View

The DBA_TAB_COLUMNS view is used to locate specific information about columns in a table, including the name of the column, the datatype of the column, the precision of the column, and statistical information gathered by the Oracle statistics collection process. The following is a listing of the description of this view.

```
SQL> DESC dba_tab_columns
 Name                                      Null?    Type
 ----------------------------------------- -------- ------------
 OWNER                                     NOT NULL VARCHAR2(30)
 TABLE_NAME                                NOT NULL VARCHAR2(30)
 COLUMN_NAME                               NOT NULL VARCHAR2(30)
 DATA_TYPE                                          VARCHAR2(106)
 DATA_TYPE_MOD                                      VARCHAR2(3)
 DATA_TYPE_OWNER                                    VARCHAR2(30)
 DATA_LENGTH                               NOT NULL NUMBER
 DATA_PRECISION                                     NUMBER
 DATA_SCALE                                         NUMBER
 NULLABLE                                           VARCHAR2(1)
 COLUMN_ID                                 NOT NULL NUMBER
 DEFAULT_LENGTH                                     NUMBER
 DATA_DEFAULT                                       LONG
 NUM_DISTINCT                                       NUMBER
 LOW_VALUE                                          RAW(32)
 HIGH_VALUE                                         RAW(32)
 DENSITY                                            NUMBER
 NUM_NULLS                                          NUMBER
 NUM_BUCKETS                                        NUMBER
 LAST_ANALYZED                                      DATE
 SAMPLE_SIZE                                        NUMBER
 CHARACTER_SET_NAME                                 VARCHAR2(44)
 CHAR_COL_DECL_LENGTH                               NUMBER
```

```
GLOBAL_STATS                              VARCHAR2(3)
USER_STATS                                VARCHAR2(3)
AVG_COL_LEN                               NUMBER
```

Here is an example of a query against the view and its results:

```
SELECT owner, table_name, column_name, data_type,
data_length, column_id
FROM dba_tab_columns
WHERE owner='SCOTT'
AND table_name='GIJOE'
ORDER BY column_id;
```

OWNER	TABLE_NAME	COLUMN_NAM	DATA_TYPE	DATA_LENGTH	COLUMN_ID
SCOTT	GIJOE	PART_ID	NUMBER	22	1
SCOTT	GIJOE	TOY_NAME	VARCHAR2	30	2
SCOTT	GIJOE	TOY_RANK	NUMBER	22	3

The DBA_EXTENTS View

The DBA_EXTENTS view provides information about extent allocations for a given object in Oracle, including tables and indexes. Here is a description of the view:

```
SQL> DESC dba_extents
Name                                      Null?    Type
----------------------------------------- -------- -----------
OWNER                                              VARCHAR2(30)
SEGMENT_NAME                                       VARCHAR2(81)
PARTITION_NAME                                     VARCHAR2(30)
SEGMENT_TYPE                                       VARCHAR2(18)
TABLESPACE_NAME                                    VARCHAR2(30)
EXTENT_ID                                          NUMBER
FILE_ID                                            NUMBER
BLOCK_ID                                           NUMBER
BYTES                                              NUMBER
BLOCKS                                             NUMBER
RELATIVE_FNO                                       NUMBER
```

The following is an example of using this view to determine how many extents an object has been allocated.

```
SELECT owner, segment_name, segment_type, count(*) "Total_extents"
FROM dba_extents
```

```
WHERE owner='SCOTT'
GROUP BY owner, segment_name, segment_type
ORDER BY 1,3,2;

OWNER   SEGMENT_NAME    SEGMENT_TYPE       Total_extents
------  --------------  -----------------  -------------
SCOTT   TEST            CLUSTER                        2
SCOTT   TEST2           CLUSTER                        1
SCOTT   IX_TEST_RGF     INDEX                          1
SCOTT   IX_TEST_RGF_01  INDEX                          1
SCOTT   PK_CHILD        INDEX                          1
SCOTT   PK_CHILDREN     INDEX                          1
SCOTT   PK_PARENT       INDEX                          1
SCOTT   AUDIT_TABLE     TABLE                          1
SCOTT   BONUS           TABLE                          1
SCOTT   CHILD           TABLE                          1
SCOTT   DEPT            TABLE                          1
SCOTT   DUMMY           TABLE                          1
SCOTT   EMPLOYEE        TABLE                          1
SCOTT   GIJOE           TABLE                          1
SCOTT   HOLD_EVENTS     TABLE                          4
```

The DBA_SEGMENTS View

The DBA_SEGMENTS view provides a look at the individual segments in the database, including tables, indexes, and clusters. The following is a description of the view.

```
SQL> DESC dba_segments
Name                                      Null?    Type
----------------------------------------- -------- ------------
OWNER                                              VARCHAR2(30)
SEGMENT_NAME                                       VARCHAR2(81)
PARTITION_NAME                                     VARCHAR2(30)
SEGMENT_TYPE                                       VARCHAR2(18)
TABLESPACE_NAME                                    VARCHAR2(30)
HEADER_FILE                                        NUMBER
HEADER_BLOCK                                       NUMBER
BYTES                                              NUMBER
BLOCKS                                             NUMBER
EXTENTS                                            NUMBER
INITIAL_EXTENT                                     NUMBER
```

```
NEXT_EXTENT                              NUMBER
MIN_EXTENTS                              NUMBER
MAX_EXTENTS                              NUMBER
PCT_INCREASE                             NUMBER
FREELISTS                                NUMBER
FREELIST_GROUPS                          NUMBER
RELATIVE_FNO                             NUMBER
BUFFER_POOL                              VARCHAR2(7)
```

Here is an example of using this view to get information about segments:

```
SELECT owner, segment_name, segment_type,
tablespace_name, sum(bytes) bytes
FROM dba_segments
WHERE owner='SCOTT'
GROUP BY owner, segment_name, segment_type,
tablespace_name
ORDER BY 5;


OWNER  SEGMENT_NAME    SEGMENT_TY TABLESPACE_NAME     BYTES
------ --------------- ---------- ---------------    ----------
SCOTT  AUDIT_TABLE     TABLE      USERS                 10,240
SCOTT  BONUS           TABLE      USERS                 10,240
SCOTT  CHILD           TABLE      USERS                 10,240
SCOTT  DUMMY           TABLE      USERS                 10,240
SCOTT  GIJOE           TABLE      USERS                 10,240
SCOTT  IX_TEST_RGF     INDEX      INDEXES               10,240
SCOTT  HOLD_EVENTS     TABLE      USERS                 71,680
SCOTT  EMPLOYEE        TABLE      USERS                102,400
SCOTT  TEST2           CLUSTER    SYSTEM               102,400
SCOTT  NEWTABLE        TABLE      USERS              4,382,720
```

Managing Indexes

Indexes are important structures in Oracle. They can be an incredible boon to performance, and I don't think there is any database that should not have at least one index on just about every table in the tablespace. Indexes give the Optimizer many more access paths to consider when choosing how to execute a given SQL statement. Even small lookup tables that have indexes associated with them will perform better when they are being joined to other tables.

Index Fundamentals

Oracle uses different kinds of indexes. The primary index types are B*Tree indexes and bitmap indexes. Oracle8i introduces function-based indexes. Let's look at how these indexes are handled internally and when using an index is helpful.

 NOTE Indexes do not store columns with values that are NULL. Thus, if you have a query with a limiting condition that is NULL, Oracle will not be able to use any index to satisfy that particular condition. However, queries with NOT NULL limitation criteria can use indexes.

B*Tree Indexes

The standard type of index that Oracle uses is called a B*Tree index.

Think of a B*Tree index as something like a tree (hence the name). At the top of the tree is a single node called the *root*. Extending up (or down if you are in the southern hemisphere) from this node is a series of leaf blocks. There may be one or more leaf blocks associated with the root node. In the root, there are pointers to the different data stored in each leaf node.

For example, in a phone book, in the head node, all last names from A to L might have a pointer to the first leaf block, and all last names from M to Z might have a pointer to the second leaf block as shown in Figure 6.2. This progression will continue through a third (and perhaps more) level of nodes. Now suppose that you are looking for the name Adams. You would go from the root node to the first node below it, because the first node below the head node contains all last names beginning with A through L. In the second-level node, you find pointers for the values A through L again. This time, they are pointing to another level of leaf blocks below this level. Say, for example, that there are 13 leaf nodes below the middle leaf node. The middle leaf node, for the name beginning with A, would point to the node below it that contains the A records. Finally, in the bottom leaf node, you would search for Adams, which you would find quickly.

B*Tree indexes can be associated with one or more columns in a given table. Along with the values of the specific index columns, the B*Tree index also contains the ROWID of each row associated with an index entry. Oracle will return the ROWID to another process during the execution of the statement. Typically, that process will then access the table via ROWID, which is the fastest method of getting to distinct data in a table.

FIGURE 6.2
The structure of a B*Tree index

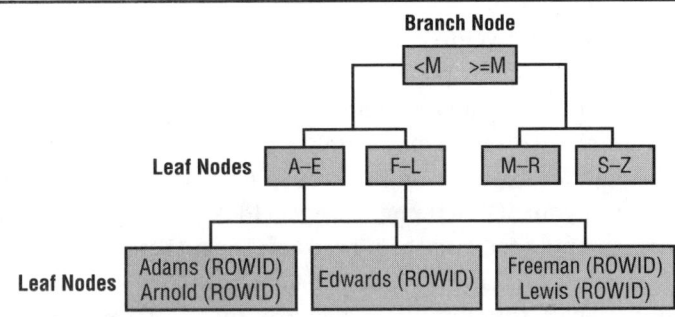

In most cases, an index search is fast. Because the indexed data is distributed among several nodes, Oracle can eliminate which leaf nodes do not need to be scanned, thus reducing the I/O needed to find the desired record. Also, the data in these nodes is stored in ordered fashion. However, there are times when indexes can be inefficient. You should build B*Tree indexes on columns with high cardinality, or a high degree of distinct values. If your column were populated with only Ys and Ns, it would not make a good candidate for a B*Tree index in most cases. This is because there are about two to four times the I/O operations required to get one row from a table using an index than are required to do a full table scan.

For example, suppose that you have a table with 10,000 rows. It has a column called YES_NO, which is populated with 6000 values of Y and 4000 values of N. If you want to count all records with a Y, how many I/O operations would that take? For a full table scan, you are looking at 10,000 logical I/O operations (one for each row). With an indexed lookup, there will be 6000 logical I/O operations to the index, plus 6000 lookups in the table, plus 1 or 2 I/O operations for the root and leaf block lookups needed to get to the proper leaf nodes. That makes 12,002 logical I/O operations for an indexed lookup, compared with 10,000 for a full table scan. In this case, the index is not the best way to get the information.

Now suppose that the YES_NO column in the sample table has 9999 Ys in it and just 1 N. In this case, a full table scan requires a 10,000-row lookup. With the index lookup, only three or four I/O operations are involved (two to three for the index lookup, and one for the table lookup). So, in this case, the index is the best choice.

Bitmap Indexes

Bitmap indexes were introduced in Oracle 7.3, and they can be very powerful if used properly. Bitmap indexes are used to provide performance improvements for queries against nonselective columns in a table, if these nonselective columns are part of the selectivity criteria (the WHERE clause). For example, performance might improve with a bitmap index where columns contain information such as sex (M or F), logic (T or F), or an answer to a question (Y or N). As you add more nonselective columns in the WHERE clause, performance gets even better.

When you create a bitmap index, a bitmap is created for each row in the column(s). This bitmap is simply a bunch of ones or zeros, depending on the value of the column. Each row in the bitmap represents the value of the column. So, when you run your SQL statement, Oracle looks through the bitmap, finds the value you are searching for, and then, based on the bit settings, determines which rows have that value in them. The Oracle database engine is written to be able to compare bitmap patterns of multiple columns quickly. Bitmaps become more helpful as more low-cardinality columns are added to the bitmap index.

There are a couple of negative aspects to using bitmap indexes. The first is that locking issues can arise with bitmap indexes, so if you have a database with a high transaction rate, using bitmap indexes may not be appropriate. Also, you should be aware that Oracle cannot perform range queries on bitmap indexes. Thus, if you have a SQL statement that would benefit from performing a range query on an index, a B*Tree index may be a better solution.

As with everything else DBA-oriented, there is no single right answer as to when to use a bitmap index. Try it, measure it, and determine if it is helpful. Even queries against columns with higher levels of distinctness can benefit from bitmap indexes. A full table scan will probably be faster than a bitmap index lookup of a single column.

Index Column Considerations

When creating an index, you need to carefully consider which columns you want to add to the index and in what order. If an index consists of multiple columns, the first column of the index is called the *leftmost column*. When looking up information in an index, Oracle starts looking from the leftmost column. This is important to understand because, if you want to use columns in an index, you can use only the unbroken string of columns starting at the leftmost column. Once the string is broken, columns after that string cannot be used to help satisfy the query.

For example, say an index is built on three columns: column A, column B, and column C. Depending on the WHERE clause of the SQL query, you may be able to use one, two, or all three of the columns in the index to quickly look up the data you need. If your query uses column A and column B, it can use the index, since column A is the leftmost column of the index, and column B is next to it. If your query uses column B and column C in the WHERE clause, it cannot use the index, since neither column is the leftmost column. If your query uses column A and column C, it would be able to use column A of the index, but not column C, since column C is not next to the leftmost column.

Bounded and Unbounded Range Scans

There are several different functions that Oracle can choose to perform on indexes in order to satisfy the requirements of a SQL query. One of these functions is a range scan, which is where Oracle traverses the index from one point in the index to another point in the index, thus eliminating the need to read the entire index (or its associated table). Range scans can be either bounded or unbounded.

Bounded range scans occur when Oracle knows a starting and stopping point in the index. For example, a bounded range scan may be used in cases where your WHERE clause has a greater-than range and a less-than range applied to the same column.

An *unbounded range scan* occurs when Oracle knows where to start the range scan, but does not know where it will end. Unbounded range scans are often caused by the use of greater-than or less-than operations. A full index scan (fast full scan) is a scan of the entire index. This type of scan replaces a full table scan. This is typically because the column(s) of the index are the only ones required to satisfy the query, making any reference to the underlying table unnecessary. Fast full scans can save overall I/O, which can boost performance.

Function-Based Indexes

Function-based indexes are a new feature in Oracle8i, designed to help improve performance of SQL statements. Prior to function-based indexes, any function used on a table column in a SQL statement WHERE clause would negate the use of an index on that column. Function-based indexes solve this problem by allowing you to create an index in which you include the function itself in the definition of the index. Function-based indexes are available only when using cost-based optimization (CBO).

Creating Indexes

To create an index, you use the CREATE INDEX command. When you create an index, you can use a STORAGE clause to define the size of its INITIAL extent and NEXT extent.

If you wish to create an index in your own schema, the table you want to create that index on must also be in your schema. If you created the table, you will need no other permissions in order to create an index on that table. If you are creating an index on a table created by another user, you need the INDEX privilege. In either case, you will need the appropriate QUOTA set for the tablespace in which you wish to create the index.

Creating a B*Tree Index

The CREATE INDEX statement is fairly straightforward, as you can see in Listing 6.7.

Listing 6.7: Creating a B*Tree Index
```
CREATE INDEX ix_parent_index
ON parent (last_name, first_name)
PCTFREE 20
TABLESPACE data
STORAGE (INITIAL 100k NEXT 100k PCTINCREASE 0);
```

This example creates a B*Tree index on two columns in the parent table: the LAST_NAME column and the FIRST_NAME column. The PCTFREE 20 clause helps balance the index when it is first created. (Remember that Oracle does not use the PCTFREE value with an index after the index has been created.) Finally, the STORAGE clause establishes the size of the INIITAL and NEXT extents at 100KB each. Notice that PCTINCREASE is set to 0, so that the next column will not be increased in size after the next extend operation.

The example in Listing 6.7 includes a TABLESPACE clause that defines the tablespace in which this index will be created. If the TABLESPACE clause were not included, the index would be put in the default tablespace of the user who is creating it. This is generally considered bad practice.

Creating a Reverse-Key Index

Reverse-key indexes store the keys in reverse order. A reverse-key index helps keep the index balanced, particularly when the key is a number that is growing in standard increments, such as with an increasing sequence number. Reverse-key indexes are created using the REVERSE keyword, as shown in Listing 6.8.

Listing 6.8: Creating a Reverse-Key Index
```
CREATE INDEX ix_reverse_parent_index
ON parent (parent_id)
TABLESPACE index
PCTFREE 20
REVERSE
STORAGE (INITIAL 100k NEXT 100k PCTINCREASE 0);
```

Creating a Unique Index

If you want to be sure that the combination of the columns in each record is unique in each index, you need to create a unique index. Oracle creates this type of index when you create a primary key. Unique indexes are created using the UNIQUE keyword, as shown in Listing 6.9.

Listing 6.9: Creating a Unique Index

```
CREATE UNIQUE INDEX ix_parent_index
ON parent (last_name, first_name)
TABLESPACE index
PCTFREE 20
COMPRESS 1
NOLOGGING
STORAGE (INITIAL 100k NEXT 100k PCTINCREASE 0);
```

With a unique index, you can have NULLs in one of more columns of the index. With a primary key in a table, you cannot have any NULLs. This is one of the primary differences between unique indexes and primary keys in Oracle.

Compressing an Index

Using the COMPRESS parameter when you create an index, as in Listing 6.9, can significantly reduce the size of an index if properly applied. Compression of the index also results in more rows being stored in each leaf block, so scans of the index will require fewer I/O operations.

When is the best time to use compression? You should use compression if you have a multiple-key index, where the leading columns do not often change. For example, if you have an index that has columns for an automobile manufacturer, model, and owner, you might consider compressing it. This is because there probably will be only a few manufacturers in your database.

The COMPRESS parameter breaks the key of the index into a prefix and a suffix entry. The repeating prefix entries are then removed from the leaf blocks of the index, leaving just the one common prefix entry. (If you do not include the COMPRESS keyword, no compression will take place.)

The COMPRESS parameter can optionally include an integer that represents the number of key columns (from the leading edge) that are likely to be repeating. The default value for this integer depends on the type of index:

- For a unique index, the default number of keys to compress is the number of key columns in the index minus one. The range of valid values for this parameter is between one and the number of key columns minus one.

- For nonunique indexes, the default is to compress all the keys of the index, and the range is from one to the number of key columns.

Bitmap, single-column unique, and partitioned indexes cannot be compressed.

Specifying NOLOGGING during Index Creation

Another parameter you can use when creating an index, also shown in Listing 6.9, is NOLOGGING. The benefit of using this parameter is that the time required to build the index will be reduced, because there will be fewer archived redo logs generated.

The downside of using NOLOGGING is that, if the database fails after you have created the index, you may not have a backup of the index to recover. If you have not backed up the database after the creation of the index, and the database fails, you will need to re-create the index. Note that it is often quicker to re-create the index than to restore its related tablespace (or datafile) from a backup.

The NOLOGGING parameter affects the index only during database creation. NOLOGGING has no impact on future changes to the index.

Creating a Bitmap Index

Listing 6.10 shows an example of a CREATE INDEX statement that creates a bitmap index. It is similar to a regular CREATE INDEX statement, except for the presence of the BITMAP command.

Listing 6.10: Creating a Bitmap Index

```
CREATE BITMAP INDEX bp_parent_index
ON parent (sex, married_status)
TABLESPACE index
PCTFREE 20
PARALLEL 5
STORAGE (INITIAL 10k NEXT 10k PCTINCREASE 0);
```

This example creates a bitmap index on the SEX and MARRIED_STATUS columns, which are low-cardinality columns. Also notice that the STORAGE clause establishes the size of the INIITAL and NEXT extents at 10KB each—quite a bit less than the extents specified in the examples in Listings 6.7, 6.8, and 6.9. This is because bitmap indexes tend to be much smaller than B*Tree indexes.

Creating Indexes Using Parallel Processing

You can create indexes in parallel by using the PARALLEL clause, as in Listing 6.10. In this case, the setting PARALLEL5 instructs Oracle to use five parallel processing slaves to create the index.

To create an index using parallel processing, you will need to have a significant amount of additional space available. You will need an equivalent of the initial extent size times the degree of parallelism used to create the index. For example, if you are creating a 1MB initial extent with ten parallel processes, you will need 10MB to create the index (assuming that you will not need more than one extent for the index). See Chapter 18 for more information about parallel processing.

Creating a Function-Based Index

There are several requirements for creating a function-based index:

- The function, when defined in the CREATE INDEX statement, cannot contain aggregate functions as parameters.
- The function must include parentheses, even if the function does not take any parameters.
- A function-based index cannot be built on LOBs, REFs, nested tables, or VARRAY columns.
- In order to use a user-defined function in the index, the function must have been created with the DETERMINISTIC keyword. This keyword basically tells Oracle that, for a given input to this function, the output from the function will always be the same.
- The Oracle COMPATIBILITY parameter must be set to 8.1.5 or higher.

To create a function-based index in your own schema and in your own table, you must have the QUERY REWRITE privilege. If you wish to create a function-based index in another schema or for a table that doesn't belong to you, you need GLOBAL QUERY REWRITE privileges. In either case, the owner of the table that the index is being created on must have EXECUTE privileges to the function contained within the function-based index.

As with the other types of indexes, you use the CREATE INDEX statement to create a function-based index. Listing 6.11 shows an example of creating a function-based index.

Listing 6.11: Creating a Function-based Index

```
CREATE INDEX fu_ix_parent_01
ON PARENT (UPPER(last_name) )
TABLESPACE indexes
STORAGE (INITIAL 10k NEXT 10k);
```

This example creates an index on the LAST_NAME column using the UPPER function.

Here is an example of a query that allows Oracle to use the function-based index to satisfy this query, its result, and its execution plan.

```
ALTER SESSION SET query_rewrite_enabled=TRUE;
SET AUTOTRACE on
SQL> SELECT count(*) FROM parent WHERE upper(last_name)='FREEMAN';
```

```
     COUNT(*)
   ----------
            2
Execution Plan
----------------------------------------------------------------
     0      SELECT STATEMENT Optimizer=CHOOSE (Cost=1 Card=1 Bytes=6)
     1    0   SORT (AGGREGATE)
     2    1     INDEX (RANGE SCAN) OF 'FU_IX_PARENT_01' (NON-UNIQUE)
                  (Cost=1 Card=2 Bytes=12)
```

Notice that you must set the QUERY_REWRITE_ENABLED parameter to TRUE for the session, using the ALTER SESSION SET command, so that Oracle will use the function-based index. Alternatively, you can set QUERY_REWRITE_ENABLED to TRUE in the `init.ora` file to set it for the whole system. There may also be times when you will need to add a hint to the SQL statement to get Oracle to use the function-based indexes.

The second line before the query enables the Oracle Autotrace facility. This displays the execution plan for this query after its execution. This execution plan shows that the index FU_IX_PARENT_01 was used and a range scan was performed. This simply means that the function-based index was used to satisfy the query.

 WARNING If you are using CBO, make sure that your tables and indexes are analyzed (see Chapter 7). Otherwise, the optimizer may not choose to use the best access path to get the data you request!

Altering Indexes

Oracle provides the ALTER INDEX statement to allow you to modify the settings of existing indexes, as well as to perform administrative tasks. You can change an index as follows:

- Modify its STORAGE parameters
- Rebuild the index online
- Enable or disable the index
- Set the index to the UNUSABLE state
- Coalesce the index

To alter an index, the index must exist in your schema. If the index is not in your schema, you must have the ALTER ANY INDEX privilege.

Disabling and Enabling Indexes

You can use the ENABLE and DISABLE commands with the ALTER INDEX statement to turn on and off the use of function-based indexes. This can be handy if you need to modify a function that is associated with a function-based index. You can use the DISABLE command to disable the function-based index. After you have modified the function, use the ENABLE clause to enable the index. Here is an example of the use of this clause:

```
ALTER INDEX fu_table_ix_01 DISABLE;
ALTER INDEX fu_table_ix_01 ENABLE;
```

Rebuilding Indexes

Rebuilding an index online is a new feature in Oracle8i that allows you to move and rebuild indexes while the database is still up and running. This makes index administration much easier.

WARNING There was a bug in Oracle8i with the online rebuild feature. In certain cases, this bug could cause you to need to rebuild your index again, and your index would be unusable during the rebuilding period. The bottom line is that you should use this feature with caution.

Online rebuilding of indexes is an alternative to dropping an index and moving it into another tablespace. This is because you can use the TABLESPACE parameter when rebuilding the index, effectively moving it to a new tablespace. Rebuilding an index is also an alternative to coalescing an index to deal with index browning issues, as discussed in the "Dealing with Index Browning" section, coming up shortly. When rebuilding an index, you can decide to make it a reverse-key index through the use of the REVERSE keyword. Likewise, a reverse-key index can be made into a regular index by using the NOREVERSE keyword.

Listing 6.12 provides an example of using the ALTER INDEX command with the REBUILD option to rebuild an index online.

Listing 6.12: Rebuilding an Index

```
ALTER INDEX ix_parent_index
REBUILD
TABLESPACE new_index
```

```
ONLINE
COMPUTE STATISTICS
STORAGE (INITIAL 100k NEXT 100k);

ALTER INDEX ix_parent_index
STORAGE (NEXT 200k);
```

This example uses the COMPUTE STATISTICS clause, which causes statistics on the index to be generated automatically after its creation. It also includes a STORAGE clause to redefine the storage characteristics of the index. Note that you cannot alter the value of PCTFREE when rebuilding an index. Also, you cannot rebuild an index on a temporary table.

Coalescing Indexes

The coalesce function is a new feature in Oracle8i that allows you to coalesce leaf blocks in a B*Tree index for future entries. The coalesce option also consolidates browned-out leaf nodes so that they are more densely packed, leading to better I/O performance. Coalescing the index is a possible solution to index browning issues, as described in the next section. Here is an example of using the ALTER INDEX command with the COALESCE keyword to coalesce an existing index:

```
ALTER INDEX ix_index_01 COALESCE;
```

Dealing with Index Browning

The leaf node of a B*Tree index will never be used unless the entire block has been cleared. This fact can lead to a condition called *index browning*, which is where the existing blocks are sparsely populated because they are not being reused, yet a great deal of data has been deleted. Browning occurs because Oracle will not reallocate a leaf block in an index until that leaf block is completely empty. This is because a leaf block is assigned to a range of values in the index, and until that range of values is completely removed, the leaf block cannot be reassigned to a new range of values.

Index browning can be resolved by using a couple of different methods. One solution is to create a reverse-key index, which is a B*Tree index that simply reverses the order of the key in the index when it is stored in the index. Other options are to re-create the index with the ALTER INDEX REBUILD command or to coalesce the index with the ALTER INDEX COALESCE command.

Coalescing an index has two main advantages over rebuilding an index: It is generally faster and takes less space. On the other hand, rebuilding an index may decrease the height of the index, whereas coalescing the index will not. The height of an index can be a performance issue. This is because Oracle will need to look through more blocks to get to the leaf nodes and the actual data. Thus, if your indexes are showing a height of more than about 4 in the DBA_INDEXES view BLEVEL column, you may wish to rebuild them rather than coalesce them. Another advantage of a rebuild operation is that you can also alter an index's storage characteristics. When coalescing an index, you cannot change any storage parameters.

Dropping Indexes

To drop an index, the index must exist in your schema or you must have the DROP ANY INDEX privilege. To drop a B*Tree, bitmap, or function-based index, use the DROP INDEX command:

```
DROP INDEX ix_parent_child_01;
```

Viewing Index Information

Three views provide index information: DBA_INDEXES, DBA_IND_COLUMNS, and INDEX_STATS. The DBA_INDEXES and DBA_IND_COLUMNS views also come in the USER_ and ALL_ flavors to suit your needs (and privileges).

The DBA_INDEXES View

The DBA_INDEXES view contains a listing of all indexes in the database. Also contained in this view is statistical information gathered by the Oracle statistics collection process. This view shows the tablespace that the index is created in, the owner of the index, the name of the table the index is built on, and other information about the index. This view does not provide information about the columns of the associated table contained within that index; that is the job of the DBA_IND_COLUMNS view, described in the next section.

The following is a listing of the description of the DBA_INDEXES view.

```
SQL> DESC dba_indexes
 Name                                      Null?    Type
 ----------------------------------------- -------- --------------
 OWNER                                     NOT NULL VARCHAR2(30)
 INDEX_NAME                                NOT NULL VARCHAR2(30)
 INDEX_TYPE                                         VARCHAR2(27)
 TABLE_OWNER                               NOT NULL VARCHAR2(30)
 TABLE_NAME                                NOT NULL VARCHAR2(30)
 TABLE_TYPE                                         VARCHAR2(11)
 UNIQUENESS                                         VARCHAR2(9)
 COMPRESSION                                        VARCHAR2(8)
```

PREFIX_LENGTH	NUMBER
TABLESPACE_NAME	VARCHAR2(30)
INI_TRANS	NUMBER
MAX_TRANS	NUMBER
INITIAL_EXTENT	NUMBER
NEXT_EXTENT	NUMBER
MIN_EXTENTS	NUMBER
MAX_EXTENTS	NUMBER
PCT_INCREASE	NUMBER
PCT_THRESHOLD	NUMBER
INCLUDE_COLUMN	NUMBER
FREELISTS	NUMBER
FREELIST_GROUPS	NUMBER
PCT_FREE	NUMBER
LOGGING	VARCHAR2(3)
BLEVEL	NUMBER
LEAF_BLOCKS	NUMBER
DISTINCT_KEYS	NUMBER
AVG_LEAF_BLOCKS_PER_KEY	NUMBER
AVG_DATA_BLOCKS_PER_KEY	NUMBER
CLUSTERING_FACTOR	NUMBER
STATUS	VARCHAR2(8)
NUM_ROWS	NUMBER
SAMPLE_SIZE	NUMBER
LAST_ANALYZED	DATE
DEGREE	VARCHAR2(40)
INSTANCES	VARCHAR2(40)
PARTITIONED	VARCHAR2(3)
TEMPORARY	VARCHAR2(1)
GENERATED	VARCHAR2(1)
SECONDARY	VARCHAR2(1)
BUFFER_POOL	VARCHAR2(7)
USER_STATS	VARCHAR2(3)
DURATION	VARCHAR2(15)
PCT_DIRECT_ACCESS	NUMBER
ITYP_OWNER	VARCHAR2(30)
ITYP_NAME	VARCHAR2(30)
PARAMETERS	VARCHAR2(1000)
GLOBAL_STATS	VARCHAR2(3)

```
DOMIDX_STATUS                                    VARCHAR2(12)
DOMIDX_OPSTATUS                                  VARCHAR2(6)
FUNCIDX_STATUS                                   VARCHAR2(8)
```

Here is an example of a query against the view and its results:

```
SELECT owner, index_name, tablespace_name, initial_extent,
Next_extent
FROM dba_indexes
WHERE owner='SCOTT';
```

```
OWNER   INDEX_NAME           TABLESPACE INITIAL_EXTENT NEXT_EXTENT
------  -------------------- ---------- -------------- -----------
SCOTT   IX_TEST_RGF          INDEXES             10240       10240
SCOTT   IX_TEST_RGF_01       USERS               10240       10240
SCOTT   PK_CHILD             USERS               10240       10240
SCOTT   PK_CHILDREN          MOVE_TBS            10240       10240
SCOTT   PK_PARENT            USERS               10240       10240
SCOTT   PK_PHONE_NUMBER      MOVE_TBS           102400      102400
SCOTT   PK_STUDENT_ID        INDEXES             10240       10240
SCOTT   SYS_C00895           USERS               10240       10240
SCOTT   SYS_C00896           USERS               10240       10240
SCOTT   UN_ZOCALO_ID         USERS               10240       10240
```

The DBA_IND_COLUMNS View

The DBA_IND_COLUMNS view provides a listing of the key columns contained in each index. The following is a description of this view.

```
SQL> DESC dba_ind_columns
 Name                                      Null?    Type
 ----------------------------------------- -------- -------------------
 INDEX_OWNER                               NOT NULL VARCHAR2(30)
 INDEX_NAME                                NOT NULL VARCHAR2(30)
 TABLE_OWNER                               NOT NULL VARCHAR2(30)
 TABLE_NAME                                NOT NULL VARCHAR2(30)
 COLUMN_NAME                                        VARCHAR2(4000)
 COLUMN_POSITION                           NOT NULL NUMBER
 COLUMN_LENGTH                             NOT NULL NUMBER
 DESCEND                                            VARCHAR2(4)
```

Here is an example of a query against the view and its results:

```
SELECT index_owner, table_name, index_name, column_name
```

```
FROM dba_ind_columns
WHERE table_owner='SCOTT'
ORDER BY 1,2,3,4;
INDEX_OWNER  TABLE_NAME  INDEX_NAME            COLUMN_NAME
-----------  ----------  --------------------  -----------

SCOTT        CHILD       PK_CHILD              CHILD_ID
SCOTT        CHILD       PK_CHILD              PARENT_ID
SCOTT        CHILDREN    PK_CHILDREN           CHILD_ID
SCOTT        CHILDREN    PK_CHILDREN           PARENT_ID
SCOTT        GIJOE       SYS_C00895            PART_ID
SCOTT        PARENT      PK_PARENT             PARENT_ID
SCOTT        RANK        SYS_C00896            TOY_RANK
SCOTT        STUDENTS    PK_STUDENT_ID         STUDENT_ID
SCOTT        TEST_RGF    IX_TEST_RGF           ID
SCOTT        TEST_RGF    IX_TEST_RGF_01        NAME
SCOTT        ZOCALO      UN_ZOCALO_ID          ID
```

The INDEXES_STATS View

The INDEX_STATS view is used during a statistics collection effort. The statistics collected in this view are only for the last object analyzed; therefore, the view is of limited use. However, it can be used to calculate index browning, as discussed in Chapter 16.

Managing Index-Organized Tables

Earlier in this chapter, we introduced the default type of table, a heap table, created by the CREATE TABLE statement. Until Oracle8, that was the only kind of table that you could create. Now, in Oracle8 and Oracle8i, you can also create index-organized tables (IOTs) with the CREATE TABLE statement.

When you create an IOT, you are really creating an index that masquerades as a table. With an IOT, the records are grouped together according to the primary key of the table. You should use IOTs in cases where you will be referring to the primary key of the table frequently in your queries. An IOT eliminates the need to read from a table after an index lookup, speeding up the overall process.

You can create secondary indexes on IOTs. This is a handy feature, but it also negates some of the performance benefits of the IOT.

Logical ROWIDs in IOTs

IOTs do not use normal ROWID types. Rather, they use *logical ROWIDs*, which are based on the primary key of the row in the table. Oracle uses the logical ROWIDs when accessing secondary indexes on IOTs.

Unlike physical ROWIDs, logical ROWIDs cannot be used to determine the organization of a table (you cannot relate a logical ROWID to a specific datafile). Rows in an IOT have no permanent physical address. This is because the physical location of row in an index may be changed if, for example, a primary key column is updated. In this case, a row may be assigned to a different leaf in the IOT.

A logical ROWID can optionally include a guess, which identifies the specific block location of a row at the time the guess is made. During a query, Oracle will bypass a full key search of the IOT, using a scan of the secondary index and the associated guess contained within that index to search the block directly. However, as new rows are inserted or existing rows are updated so that the row is moved to a different block, performance on an IOT will slow as the guesses become stale. This is because Oracle will first check to see if the guess is correct. If it is not correct, Oracle will then scan the IOT by the primary key to find the correct row. Thus, stale guesses can cause significant performance impacts. Therefore, guesses should be used only when a table will have little change activity.

You can use the ROWID pseudocolumn to select logical ROWIDs from an IOT. The ROWIDs are a bit different in format than the physical extended or restricted ROWIDs, in that they contain both the primary key and the guess information.

NOTE You can insert logical ROWIDs into a column of type UROWID, which has a maximum size of 4000 bytes.

Creating IOTs

You use the CREATE TABLE statement to create an IOT. The CREATE TABLE statement is similar to the statement used to create a heap table, but it includes the ORGANIZATION INDEX clause to indicate that it is an IOT rather than a heap table. As you might expect, since records are grouped by primary key, you must define a primary key for all IOTs. Listing 6.13 shows an example of a CREATE TABLE statement that creates a table named PARENT as an IOT.

Listing 6.13: Creating an IOT

```
CREATE TABLE parent
(parent_id    NUMBER CONSTRAINT pk_parent PRIMARY KEY,
 last_name    VARCHAR2(30) NOT NULL,
 first_name   VARCHAR2(30) NOT NULL,
 middle_int   CHAR(1),
 sex          CHAR(1),
 married_status    CHAR(1),
 comments     VARCHAR2(2000)
)
ORGANIZATION INDEX
STORAGE(INITIAL 10m NEXT 10m PCTINCREASE 0)
PCTFREE 10
TABLESPACE users
PCTTHRESHOLD 20
INCLUDING married_status
OVERFLOW TABLESPACE overflow
PCTFREE 20
PCTUSED 50
STORAGE(INITIAL 10m NEXT 10m PCTINCREASE 0);
```

First, the example defines PARENT_ID as the primary key, so this is the key on which the IOT will be built. After defining the other columns, the ORGANIZATION INDEX clause indicates this is an IOT. The next several parameters involve the optional overflow segment that can be created in a separate overflow tablespace. The OVERFLOW keyword creates the optional overflow segment. The overflow segment is used to help keep the structure of the IOT's B*Tree structure packed. The overflow tablespace is used to store nonkey rows that exceed the value of PCTTHRESHOLD, which defaults to 50 percent (valid values range from 1 to 50).

NOTE The overflow tablespace is optional. In some cases, Oracle will determine that your table requires an overflow tablespace (by evaluating each column) and generate an error to this effect. The requirement for an overflow tablespace depends on the overall maximum possible size of a single row in the IOT, including additional overhead.

In Listing 6.13, you see two STORAGE clauses, along with two different PCTFREE values. The first STORAGE clause indicates the storage attributes of the IOT itself. The second STORAGE clause, which appears after the OVERFLOW clause, defines the storage attributes for the overflow segment of the overflow tablespace. PCTUSED cannot be defined for an IOT, much like it cannot be defined for an index. However, PCTUSED can and should be defined for an overflow segment. Also note that since an IOT is really an index, the PCTFREE clause is only meaningful when creating or re-creating the IOT.

The next clause that you might notice that is different from a regular CREATE TABLE statement is the optional PCTTHRESHOLD clause. This clause defines the percentage of the index block that will be allocated to the head of the row.

When you insert a row into an IOT, the row may be split into two different parts: a head and a tail. The head portion of the row will be stored in the B*Tree of the IOT, along with the key column values. The tail portion of the row will be stored in an overflow segment in the overflow tablespace. A pointer to the overflow segment is then stored in the B*Tree row. The PCTTHRESHOLD value represents a percentage of the block size. Any part of the row below that percentage will become the head of the row and will be stored in the IOT. Any part of the row that exceeds this size (if that occurs) will be stored in the overflow segment. For example, if you have a block size of 8KB (or 8096 bytes) and PCTTHRESHOLD is set to 20, then each row head piece will be no more than 1620 bytes. Any part of the row larger than that will be stored in the overflow segment.

The optional INCLUDING clause can be used to also control the split of the head and the tail. Oracle will always store key columns in the IOT. The INCLUDING clause indicates to Oracle that all columns up to and including the column listed in the INCLUDING clause should be stored in the table, not in the overflow tablespace. However, any portion of any column that exceeds PCTTHRESHOLD will still be stored in the overflow tablespace. In the sample table created in Listing 6.13, the COMMENTS column would likely end up in the overflow tablespace.

 TIP The INCLUDING clause is not required, but it is good practice to use it if you will have large, less commonly used columns in your IOT. Typically, you would include all small and frequently used columns in the B*Tree structure, and larger, less-used columns in the overflow segment.

The OVERFLOW clause allows you to define the tablespace that the overflow segment will be assigned to. As rows are modified, Oracle will determine if columns need to be moved back and forth between the head and tail pieces of the IOT, based on the size of the columns. Again, the PCTTHRESHOLD determines which part becomes the head and which part is the tail.

Compressing IOTs

One of the benefits of an IOT is that you can use key compression with the table, just as you can with an index. To enable key compression, include the COMPRESS keyword in the ORGANIZATION INDEX clause, as shown in the example in Listing 6.14. Note that you can use compression only when you have a multiple-key primary key associated with your IOT.

Listing 6.14: Using Key Compression with an IOT

```
CREATE TABLE children
(child_id   NUMBER,
 parent_id  NUMBER,
 last_name  VARCHAR2(30),
 first_name VARCHAR2(30),
 middle_int CHAR(1),
 medical_code VARCHAR2(30) CONSTRAINT children_check_upper
        CHECK (medical_code = UPPER(medical_code) ),
 medical_history VARCHAR2(2000),
 CONSTRAINT pk_children PRIMARY KEY (child_id, parent_id),
 CONSTRAINT fk_child_parent FOREIGN KEY (parent_id)
 REFERENCES parent (parent_id)
)
ORGANIZATION INDEX COMPRESS
TABLESPACE users
PCTFREE 10
STORAGE(INITIAL 10m NEXT 10m PCTINCREASE 0)
PCTTHRESHOLD 20
INCLUDING medical_code
OVERFLOW TABLESPACE overflow
PCTFREE 10
PCTUSED 60
STORAGE(INITIAL 10m NEXT 10m PCTINCREASE 0);
```

Notice that there is no storage specification for the primary key in this example. No storage is allocated because the primary key is stored with the rows in the IOT. Also notice that multiple overflow segments can share the same tablespace.

Altering, Moving, and Dropping IOTs

Using the ALTER TABLE statement, you can modify the storage attributes of both the IOT and the overflow segment. Just remember that anything that occurs in an ALTER

TABLE statement after the use of the OVERFLOW clause will occur on the overflow segment and not on the IOT itself. Let's look at an example in Listing 6.15.

Listing 6.15: Altering an IOT

```
ALTER TABLE children
STORAGE (NEXT 100k FREELISTS 2)
OVERFLOW
PCTFREE 20;
```

This example changes the NEXT storage value to 100KB for the IOT, adds another free list to the segment, and changes the PCTFREE setting of the overflow tablespace to 20. You know that this modification applies to the overflow tablespace because the parameter appears after the OVERFLOW clause (and there is also the fact that you cannot alter PCTFREE for an IOT).

You can move an IOT to another tablespace by using the ALTER TABLE MOVE command, as shown in the example in Listing 6.16.

Listing 6.16: Moving an IOT

```
ALTER TABLE children MOVE TABLESPACE move_tbs;

CREATE TABLE phone_numbers
(country_code    VARCHAR2(10),
 area_code       VARCHAR2(10),
 phone_number    VARCHAR2(20),
CONSTRAINT pk_phone_number
PRIMARY KEY (country_code, area_code, phone_number)
) ORGANIZATION INDEX
TABLESPACE users PCTFREE 10
STORAGE(INITIAL 100k NEXT 100k PCTINCREASE 0);
```

In fact, if the IOT does not have an overflow segment and it is not compressed, you can perform an online move of the IOT, just as you can with an index, as follows:

```
ALTER TABLE phone_numbers MOVE ONLINE TABLESPACE move_tbs;
```

 WARNING There are several bugs in Oracle8i (particularly in early versions of 8i) with relation to online moves of IOTs. These bugs particularly revolve around movement of IOTs that contain LOBs. Carefully test all IOT moves in a test environment before moving them in your production system.

You can drop an IOT with the DROP TABLE command, just as you would any other table. See the "Dropping Tables" section earlier in this chapter for more information.

Viewing IOTs

In the DBA_TABLES view, IOTs are listed with a value of IOT in the IOT_TYPE column. (This column will be NULL for a non-IOT type.) Overflow segments associated with IOTs also appear in this view, because they are actually hash tables that store the remaining data. Overflow segments are denoted by the entry IOT_OVERFLOW in the IOT_TYPE column. Here is an example of a query against the DBA_TABLES view:

```
SELECT owner, table_name, iot_type, tablespace_name
FROM dba_tables
WHERE iot_type IS NOT NULL;
```

```
OWNER  TABLE_NAME                       IOT_TYPE      TABLESPACE_NAME
-----  -------------------------------  ------------  ---------------
SCOTT  PARENT                           IOT
SCOTT  SYS_IOT_OVER_4252                IOT_OVERFLOW  USERS
```

Notice that the tablespace for the IOT does not appear.

If you look in DBA_INDEXES, you will find an interesting entry associated with your IOT: a new index. If you named the primary key, then the index will have the name of the primary key you defined. Here is an example of a query against DBA_INDEXES:

```
SELECT table_name, table_owner, index_name,
tablespace_name, index_type
FROM dba_indexes
WHERE table_owner='SCOTT'
AND table_name='PARENT';
```

```
TABLE_NAME  TABLE_OWNE  INDEX_NAME       TABLESPACE  INDEX_TYPE
----------  ----------  ---------------  ----------  ----------
PARENT      SCOTT       PK_PARENT        USERS       IOT - TOP
```

Notice the output shows a table called PARENT, which really doesn't exist. This entry is similar to a synonym for the PK_PARENT index that contains the data. The INDEX_TYPE column shows IOT - TOP, which indicates that it is an IOT. Finally, you see the name of the tablespace name, USERS, that this IOT is assigned to.

The *_SEGMENTS and *_EXTENTS views also provide information on both the IOT (using the primary index name rather than the IOT name) and the overflow segment. Here is an example of a query against the DBA_SEGMENTS view:

```
SELECT owner, segment_name, segment_type
FROM dba_segments
WHERE owner LIKE '%SCOTT%'
AND segment_name LIKE '%IOT%' OR
segment_name = 'PK_PARENT'

OWNER  SEGMENT_NAME          SEGMENT_TYPE
-----  --------------------  ------------
SCOTT  SYS_IOT_OVER_4259     TABLE
SCOTT  PK_PARENT             INDEX
```

Here, you see the IOT in the form of PK_PARENT. Also, you see the system-assigned name of the overflow tablespace, SYS_IOT_OVER_4259.

Managing Clusters

Clustering is an option that allows you to combine related data into a single logical object. Clusters have gotten a bad reputation because of their poor performance during DML activities, but in some cases, clusters can significantly improve performance.

NOTE I found that clusters were helpful when I was working with tables of temporary results. These temporary tables were indexed, and were used by several related processes (thus, temporary tables in Oracle could not be used). Because of the volume of changes in these tables, the associated indexes browned-out very quickly. Performance collapsed in a nonlinear fashion. I moved these related temporary tables into a cluster and saw significant performance improvements.

Cluster Fundamentals

Clusters come in three varieties: table, indexed, and hash. In this section, we will review the different clustering options in Oracle and some of the performance issues that you might consider when using clusters.

Indexed Clusters

An *indexed cluster* (or just *cluster*) contains two or more tables. The *cluster key* is a column or multiple columns that can be used to join the data in these tables. When the tables of the cluster are populated with data, the data in the tables is stored in the same block, and the rows for both tables are related based on the cluster key columns. This has the basic effect of denormalizing the table. Thus, if you are going to cluster tables, they should be tightly related based on the keys.

The cluster key of the cluster is defined when you create the cluster. It can consist of up to 16 columns, and the cluster key size is limited to something like half the database block size. Also, the cluster key cannot consist of a LONG, LONG RAW, or LOB datatype (CLOB, BLOB, and so on).

One benefit of clustering tables is that the cluster key is stored only once. This results in a slight improvement in performance, because the overall size of the clustered tables is smaller than the size of two individual tables storing the same data, so less I/O is required. Another benefit of clusters is that, unlike indexes, they do not brown-out. Thus, performance of SELECT statements should not be negatively impacted by ongoing DML activity, as can happen with indexes.

Clusters can improve join performance, but this can be at the cost of slower performance on scans of the individual tables in the cluster and any DML activity on the cluster. To avoid problems, you should cluster only tables that are commonly joined together and that have little DML activity.

Hash Clusters

A *hash cluster* is an alternative to storing data in a table and then creating an index on that table. A hash cluster is the default type of cluster that will be created by the CREATE CLUSTER command.

In a hash cluster, the cluster key values are converted into a hash value. This hash value is then stored along with the data associated with that key. The hash value is calculated by using a hashing algorithm, which is simply a mathematical way of generating a unique identifier. (The same keys would generate the same hash value, of course.) You control the number of hash keys through the HASHKEYS parameter of the CREATE CLUSTER command. Thus, the total number of possible cluster key values is defined when the cluster is created. Be careful to correctly choose this number, or you will find that keys may end up being stored together.

There are two different kinds of hash clusters:

- With a *normal hash cluster*, Oracle will convert the values of the WHERE clause, if they contain the cluster key, to a hash value. It will then use the hash value as an offset value in the hash cluster, allowing Oracle to quickly go to the row being requested.

- With a *single-row hash cluster*, the hash keys relate directly to the key in the table stored in hash cluster. This eliminates the scan that would be required on a normal hash cluster, since Oracle would scan the entire cluster for a single table lookup by default.

When choosing the cluster key, you should consider only columns with a high degree of cardinality. You should also be careful about using hash clusters when a table will be subject to a great deal of range searches, such as searches on date ranges. Hash clusters generally are used when there is a constant need to look up specific and unique values, such as those you might find in a primary key or a unique index.

For the hashing algorithm, you have three options. The first is to use Oracle's internal algorithm to convert the cluster key values into the correct hash value. This works well in most cases. You can also choose to use the cluster key if your cluster key is some uniform value, such as a series of numbers generated by a sequence. The other option is a user-defined algorithm in the form of a PL/SQL function.

Creating Clusters

You use the CREATE CLUSTER command to create both indexed clusters and hash clusters. In order to create a cluster in your schema, you need the CREATE CLUSTER privilege. To create a cluster in another schema, you must have the CREATE ANY CLUSTER privilege. You also need the appropriate QUOTA set for the tablespace in which you wish to create the clusters.

Creating an Indexed Cluster

You use the CREATE CLUSTER command to create indexed clusters in your database. Listing 6.17 shows an example of creating an indexed cluster.

Listing 6.17: Creating an Indexed Cluster
```
CREATE CLUSTER parent_child
(parent_id NUMBER)
INDEX
SIZE 512
STORAGE (INITIAL 100k NEXT 100k);
```

It is the keyword INDEX in the CREATE CLUSTER command that makes this an indexed cluster. Omit this keyword, and Oracle will default to creating a hash cluster.

When you create the cluster, you define how many rows will be identified with each cluster key by using the SIZE parameter. The value associated with the SIZE keyword tells Oracle how much space to reserve for all rows with the same hash value, and this value should be a multiple of the database block size. If SIZE is not a multiple of the database block size, it will be rounded up to the next multiple of the database block size. For example, if you have 1600 bytes left in the block, and SIZE is set at 512, then you will be able to store three cluster key sets within that block.

 WARNING It is important to set the SIZE parameter correctly for both indexed clusters and hash clusters. If you set SIZE too small, you can cause rows to be chained, which can cause additional I/O.

After you have created the cluster, you can add tables to the cluster. Then you need to create a cluster index before you can use the cluster or the tables in the cluster.

Adding Tables to an Indexed Cluster

Listing 6.18 shows an example of creating two tables and adding them to the cluster created in Listing 6.17.

Listing 6.18: Adding Tables to a Cluster

```
CREATE TABLE parent
(parent_id    NUMBER PRIMARY KEY,
 last_name    VARCHAR2(30) NOT NULL,
 first_name   VARCHAR2(30) NOT NULL,
 middle_int   CHAR(1),
 sex          CHAR(1),
 married_status    CHAR(1)
)
CLUSTER parent_child (parent_id);

CREATE TABLE children
(child_id    NUMBER CONSTRAINT pk_children PRIMARY KEY
 USING INDEX TABLESPACE indexes
 STORAGE (INITIAL 200k NEXT 200k),
 parent_id   NUMBER,
 last_name   VARCHAR2(30),
 first_name  VARCHAR2(30),
 middle_int  CHAR(1),
 medical_code VARCHAR2(30) CONSTRAINT children_check_upper
         CHECK (medical_code = UPPER(medical_code) )
)
CLUSTER parent_child(parent_id);
```

Notice that you can still define primary keys on the tables, use the USING INDEX command to define where the primary key index is to be stored, and include the STORAGE clause. You can create indexes on tables in clusters, just as you would for any other table.

Creating a Cluster Index

Once you have set up the cluster, you need to create a cluster index so that you can add rows to our cluster. Until this step is done, no data can be added to any of the tables that exist in the cluster. To create the cluster index, you use the CREATE INDEX command using the ON CLUSTER keyword, as shown in the following example:

```
CREATE INDEX ic_parent_children
ON CLUSTER parent_child;
```

After creating the cluster index, you can work with the tables in the cluster.

NOTE If you accidentally drop the cluster index, you will not lose the data in the cluster. However, you will not be able to use the tables in the cluster until the cluster index is re-created.

Creating a Hash Cluster

Creating a hash cluster is similar to creating an indexed cluster. The differences are that you omit the INDEX keyword and add the HASHKEYS keyword. Listing 6.19 shows an example of using a CREATE CLUSTER statement to create a hash cluster.

Listing 6.19: Creating a Hash Cluster

```
CREATE CLUSTER parent_child
(parent_id NUMBER)
SIZE 512 HASHKEYS 1000
STORAGE (INITIAL 100k NEXT 100k);
```

The SIZE and HASHKEYS keywords are used to calculate how much space to allocate to the cluster. The SIZE keyword defines how much of each block will be used to store a single set of cluster key rows. This value determines the number of cluster key values that will be stored in each block of the cluster. SIZE is defined in bytes, and you can also append a *k* or *m* to indicate that the number is in kilobytes or megabytes.

The HASHKEYS clause (which is not used when creating an indexed cluster) defines the number of cluster key values that are expected in the cluster. Oracle will round up the number chosen to the next nearest prime number.

It is important to try to calculate the HASHKEYS and SIZE values as exactly as possible, but it is also sometimes a difficult task. If you already have the data stored in another database, or perhaps in a table that you were thinking of moving to a hash cluster, it might be easier to determine the settings for these values. You could simply set HASHKEYS to the number of unique rows in the table, based on a select set of columns that make up either a primary or unique key, or on a pseudo unique key if one does not exist.

The SIZE value is a bit more complicated. SIZE could be calculated by first taking the overall size of the data in the object that you are thinking about moving to a hash cluster, and dividing that size by the number of unique key values. This will give you some idea of where to start making the SIZE parameter. (I would add on a bit for overhead and a fudge factor.) By default, Oracle will allocate one block for every cluster key value (which is potentially very expensive). Also, the value given by SIZE cannot be greater than the block size of the database. If it is, Oracle will use the database block size instead.

TIP Like many other things in the database world, there is no exact science to calculating cluster sizes. It's important to get as close as you can to an accurate figure, but this may not be possible until you have seen how the data is actually going to come in and load. In practice, sizing may require one or two reorganizations of the object. So, sizing typically involves doing your best to calculate the right numbers, and then adjusting those numbers based on ongoing operations.

Both SIZE and HASHKEYS can have a significant impact on performance. If you allocate too much space (by making either SIZE or HASHKEYS too large), you will be wasting space. Since fewer data rows will exist per block, full scans (not using the hash key) or range scans of the hash cluster will be degraded. Also, Oracle uses the values of SIZE and HASHKEYS, along with the values of INITIAL and NEXT, to determine the initial extent allocations for the hash cluster.

The total amount of space that will be allocated to a hash cluster when it is created is the greater of SIZE * HASHKEYS or INITIAL. Thus, when the hash cluster is created, all of the initial space for the expected number of hash keys is mapped out in a structure called a *hash table*. Subsequent extents are created as overflow space and will be generated based on the NEXT parameter of the STORAGE clause. Any rows added to the cluster will first be added to the initial block in the hash table, based on the hash value of the cluster key column(s) in the row. If the block that is assigned to that cluster key is full, then the row will be stored in an overflow block, and a pointer will be stored in the block where the row should have gone. This can cause additional I/O operations, and it is why it is important to size your clusters correctly.

 WARNING Incorrectly setting the SIZE value can cause chaining to occur. This is because Oracle does not guarantee that any hashed data will remain in a given block (and often, this may not even be possible). Carefully set the SIZE parameter to avoid chaining.

Once you have created the hash cluster, you add tables to the cluster, just as you would with an index cluster (see Listing 6.18). You do not need to create a cluster index, as you do for an indexed cluster. After you add the tables to the hash cluster, the cluster is ready for use.

Altering Clusters

You can use the ALTER CLUSTER command to allocate an additional extent to the cluster in an index cluster (you cannot allocate an additional extent to a hash cluster) or to de-allocate an unused extent. You can also modify the STORAGE clause or the PCTFREE and PCTUSED settings for the cluster, as well as the other settings of the physical attributes clause. Here is an example of allocating an additional extent and modifying the STORAGE parameters of a cluster:

```
ALTER CLUSTER parent_child
STORAGE (NEXT 200k);
```

Dropping Clusters

To drop an indexed cluster, you must first drop the underlying cluster index, and then you must drop the underlying tables of the cluster. There is no way to decluster a table. Thus, you may need to use the CREATE TABLE AS SELECT command to move the data from tables in the cluster to tables outside the cluster.

After you remove the cluster index and the tables of the index, you can use the DROP CLUSTER command. If you don't care about the data in the tables of the cluster, you may use the optional parameter INCLUDING TABLES in the DROP CLUSTER command, and Oracle will remove the underlying tables for you. You may also need to include the CASCADE CONSTRAINTS clause if the tables have referential integrity constraints that will need to be dropped. Here is an example of dropping the PARENT_CHILD cluster created in Listing 6.19, including the tables:

```
DROP CLUSTER parent_child
INCLUDING TABLES
CASCADE CONSTRAINTS;
```

Viewing Cluster Information

The DBA_CLUSTERS view provides information about the clusters in your database. The following is a description of the view.

```
SQL> DESC dba_clusters
Name                                      Null?    Type
----------------------------------------- -------- ------------
OWNER                                     NOT NULL VARCHAR2(30)
CLUSTER_NAME                              NOT NULL VARCHAR2(30)
TABLESPACE_NAME                           NOT NULL VARCHAR2(30)
PCT_FREE                                           NUMBER
PCT_USED                                  NOT NULL NUMBER
KEY_SIZE                                           NUMBER
INI_TRANS                                 NOT NULL NUMBER
MAX_TRANS                                 NOT NULL NUMBER
INITIAL_EXTENT                                     NUMBER
NEXT_EXTENT                                        NUMBER
MIN_EXTENTS                               NOT NULL NUMBER
MAX_EXTENTS                               NOT NULL NUMBER
PCT_INCREASE                                       NUMBER
FREELISTS                                          NUMBER
FREELIST_GROUPS                                    NUMBER
AVG_BLOCKS_PER_KEY                                 NUMBER
CLUSTER_TYPE                                       VARCHAR2(5)
FUNCTION                                           VARCHAR2(15)
HASHKEYS                                           NUMBER
DEGREE                                             VARCHAR2(10)
INSTANCES                                          VARCHAR2(10)
CACHE                                              VARCHAR2(5)
BUFFER_POOL                                        VARCHAR2(7)
SINGLE_TABLE                                       VARCHAR2(5)
```

Here is an example of a query against the DBA_CLUSTERS view and its results:

```
SELECT owner, cluster_name, tablespace_name
FROM dba_clusters
WHERE owner NOT LIKE 'SYS';

OWNER   CLUSTER_NAME                       TABLESPACE
------  ---------------------------------  ----------
SCOTT   TEST                               USERS
SCOTT   TEST2                              SYSTEM
```

Managing Rollback Segments

When creating a database, the DBA needs to carefully consider the number, size, and extents to be allocated to rollback segments in the database. Rollback segments are used to provide rollback of incomplete transactions, read consistency, and database recovery.

Planning Rollback Segments

There are as many differing opinions about how to initially size a rollback segment as there are models of cars on the road. The answer to the question of how many rollback segments and what size to make them is the same as the answer to many such DBA questions: It depends.

There are a few considerations for planning rollback segments:

- The average size of a transaction
- The total number of concurrent transactions
- The type and frequency of transactions

The main concerns with rollback segments in terms of performance and operational success are the appropriate sizing of the rollback segment and contention for a given rollback segment. If you do not have enough rollback segments allocated, contention for rollback segments can occur.

You also need to have the appropriate sizing of the rollback segment tablespace. A single large job may cause a rollback segment to extend and take up the entire tablespace. If the rollback segment has OPTIMAL set (which should always be the case!), it will eventually shrink after the transaction using that rollback segment has completed or failed. In the meantime, however, any attempt to extend other rollback segments will lead to transaction failure.

Some DBAs create a separate large rollback segment in its own tablespace for large transactions. I personally don't like this approach, because these large rollback segments are rarely used, so they are a waste of space. I prefer to lump that extra space into one rollback segment tablespace that will allow the rollback segments to grow with the large transaction. Then I set the OPTIMAL parameter so the rollback segment will shrink back to its correct size later on.

 NOTE Keep in mind the concept of I/O distribution with regard to rollback segments. I've seen more than one DBA just plug the rollback segment tablespace datafiles on one disk, and then wonder why the system had such poor response time.

I generally will create rollback segments according to the following formula:

total extents = 2 × (expected number of concurrent transactions / number of overall rollback segments)

For example, if I expect 20 concurrent transactions and create 5 rollback segments, this formula leads to 8 extents each. I generally round this up to 10 extents, for a total of 5 rollback segments of 10 extents each. You should probably not have any rollback segment with more than about 30 extents initially. If you do, you need to either resize the extents or add another rollback segment.

I normally will make sure that the total size of each rollback segment (depending on how much space is available) is about 1.3 times the size of the largest table in the database. This allows me to modify all of the rows of any table without any problems. (Of course, if you have some particularly large tables, this might not be possible.) Finally, I always throw as much space as I can to the rollback segment tablespace (particularly in a production database). I am not fond of transaction failures due to lack of rollback segment space. For test or development systems where less disk space is available, I use smaller rollback segments. Again, it all depends on the environment.

TIP If you find that you have users that are constantly blowing your tablespaces up with ad-hoc queries that are poorly written, you should look into metering your users' resource use with Oracle's resource control facilities, rather then just allowing them to extend a tablespace to eternity.

The truth is that most DBAs guess at what they think is the right number and size of rollback segments, and then monitor the system for contention. Usually, when you first create a database, you have little idea of how many users will really be on it or how big the average transaction or largest table will be.

After you create your initial set of rollback segments, you need to monitor their usage. Chapter 15 provides details on monitoring rollback segment use. If you find that rollback segments have a significant number of extends, shrinks, or wraps, as determined from the V$ROLLSTAT performance view, you will need to rework the extent size and perhaps the number of extents in the rollback segment. You may also want to review the V$WAITSTAT performance view for classes that include the word UNDO in them. If you see waits for these segment types, you probably need to add rollback segments to your database.

Finally, you should use a uniform extent management policy with rollback segments. This implies that the INITIAL and NEXT storage parameters for a rollback segment will always be the same size. Also, INITIAL and NEXT should be the same for all rollback segments in any given tablespace. This helps eliminate any fragmentation issues in the rollback segment tablespaces.

Creating Rollback Segments

To create a rollback segment, use the CREATE ROLLBACK SEGMENT command. Creating a rollback segment is like creating any other segment in most respects. You define a STORAGE clause for the object, and you can define to which tablespace the rollback segment is assigned. Listing 6.20 shows an example.

Listing 6.20: Creating a Rollback Segment
```
CREATE ROLLBACK SEGMENT rbs01
TABLESPACE rbs
STORAGE (INITIAL 1m NEXT 1m OPTIMAL 10m MINEXTENTS 10);
```

The OPTIMAL option within the STORAGE clause allows you to define a size that you want Oracle to shrink the rollback segment back to. Thus, the rollback segment will expand as required, but Oracle will shrink it back down to the correct size later. As noted earlier, you should always use the OPTIMAL cause to prevent problems with a rollback segment taking too much tablespace.

The OPTIMAL and MINEXTENTS clauses cross-check each other. Thus, you cannot have an OPTIMAL parameter that will cause the rollback segment to drop below the value defined by MINEXTENTS.

As noted in the previous section, it is strongly encouraged that you make all of your extents uniform in size (thus, make sure that INITIAL and NEXT are set to the same value). If you choose to make INITIAL or NEXT larger, make sure it is a multiple of the smaller value.

When you create a rollback segment it is not initially available for use. You will need to use the ALTER ROLLBACK SEGMENT command (discussed next) to bring the rollback segment online. Also, you will want to add the rollback segment to the database parameter file so that it will be brought online immediately when the database is started. You use the ROLLBACK_SEGMENT parameter in the `init.ora` file to accomplish this.

Altering Rollback Segments

You can use the ALTER ROLLBACK SEGMENT command to alter the storage characteristics of a rollback segment, bring it online after creation, or take it offline before dropping it. You can also use the ALTER ROLLBACK segment command to force the rollback segment to shrink back to the size defined by OPTIMAL or, optionally, to a size you define in the ALTER ROLLBACK SEGMENT SHRINK command. Here are some examples of using the ALTER ROLLBACK SEGMENT command:

```
ALTER ROLLBACK SEGMENT rbs01 ONLINE;
ALTER ROLLBACK SEGMENT rbs01 OFFLINE;
ALTER ROLLBACK SEGMENT rbs01 SHRINK;
ALTER ROLLBACK SEGMENT rbs01 STORAGE (OPTIMAL 9m MINEXTENTS 9);
```

If you attempt to take a rollback segment offline while it is in use, it will go into an OFFLINE PENDING state (as you can see in the STATUS column of V$ROLLSTAT). The rollback segment will be taken offline immediately after the user transaction has completed. Since the ALTER ROLLBACK SEGMENT command is DDL, it will do an implied commit. Thus, if the user whose transaction was holding up the rollback segment before it was taken offline performed some sort of DML operation and did not commit it, the ALTER ROLLBACK SEGMENT command would commit it for that user.

Dropping Rollback Segments

Dropping a rollback segment is done with the DROP ROLLBACK SEGMENT command:

```
DROP ROLLBACK SEGMENT rbs01;
```

Oracle will generate an error message (ORA-1545) if you attempt to drop a rollback segment if it is in an ONLINE or OFFLINE PENDING state.

Viewing Rollback Segment Information

Three data dictionary views provide the primary information about rollback segments: DBA_ROLLBACK_SEGS, V$ROLLSTAT, and V$ROLLNAME.

The DBA_ROLLBACK_SEGS View

The DBA_ROLLBACK_SEGS view provides a list of all rollback segments that exist on the system, both online and offline. This view also includes information such as storage information (INITIAL, NEXT, and OPTIMAL) and the tablespace the rollback segment is occupying. Here is a description of the view:

```
SQL> DESC dba_rollback_segs
 Name                                      Null?    Type
 ----------------------------------------- -------- ------------
 SEGMENT_NAME                              NOT NULL VARCHAR2(30)
 OWNER                                              VARCHAR2(6)
 TABLESPACE_NAME                           NOT NULL VARCHAR2(30)
 SEGMENT_ID                                NOT NULL NUMBER
 FILE_ID                                   NOT NULL NUMBER
```

```
BLOCK_ID                                 NOT NULL NUMBER
INITIAL_EXTENT                                    NUMBER
NEXT_EXTENT                                       NUMBER
MIN_EXTENTS                              NOT NULL NUMBER
MAX_EXTENTS                              NOT NULL NUMBER
PCT_INCREASE                                      NUMBER
STATUS                                            VARCHAR2(16)
INSTANCE_NUM                                      VARCHAR2(40)
RELATIVE_FNO                             NOT NULL NUMBER
```

Here is an example of a query against the DBA_ROLLBACK_SEGS view and its results:

```
SELECT segment_name, owner, tablespace_name
FROM dba_rollback_segs
ORDER BY segment_name;

SEGMENT_NAME                    OWNER  TABLESPACE_NAME
------------------------------  -----  ---------------
RB01                            SYS    RBS
RB02                            SYS    RBS
RB03                            SYS    RBS
RBS01                           SYS    RBS
SYSTEM                          SYS    SYSTEM
TEST_ME                         SYS    LOCAL_UNIFORM
```

The V$ROLLSTAT and V$ROLLNAME Views

The V$ROLLSTAT and V$ROLLNAME views are typically used together. V$ROLLSTAT provides performance information about the individual rollback segments, as shown here.

```
SQL> DESC v$rollstat
 Name                                     Null?    Type
 ---------------------------------------- -------- ------------
 USN                                               NUMBER
 EXTENTS                                           NUMBER
 RSSIZE                                            NUMBER
 WRITES                                            NUMBER
 XACTS                                             NUMBER
 GETS                                              NUMBER
 WAITS                                             NUMBER
 OPTSIZE                                           NUMBER
```

```
HWMSIZE                                      NUMBER
SHRINKS                                      NUMBER
WRAPS                                        NUMBER
EXTENDS                                      NUMBER
AVESHRINK                                    NUMBER
AVEACTIVE                                    NUMBER
STATUS                                       VARCHAR2(15)
CUREXT                                       NUMBER
CURBLK                                       NUMBER
```

Unfortunately, as you can see, this view does not contain the name of the rollback segment, but rather the Undo Segment Number (USN) of the segment.

The V$ROLLNAME view resolves the USN to the rollback segment name, as you can see in its description:

```
SQL> DESC v$rollname
 Name                                     Null?    Type
 ---------------------------------------- -------- ------------
 USN                                               NUMBER
 NAME                                     NOT NULL VARCHAR2(30)
```

Here is a sample query that uses both these views and its results:

```
SELECT a.name, b.extents, b.rssize,
b.waits, b.extends, b.shrinks
FROM v$rollname a, v$rollstat b
WHERE a.usn=b.usn;
```

NAME	EXTENTS	RSSIZE	WAITS	EXTENDS	SHRINKS
SYSTEM	8	407552	0	0	0
RB02	16	1636352	0	0	0

Notice that not all of the rollback segments appear. Only those rollback segments that are online or have an OFFLINE PENDING status will appear in the V$ROLLSTAT and V$ROLLNAME views.

Managing Views

A *view* is a logical representation of a SQL statement that is stored in the database. Views are useful when certain SQL statements are commonly used on a given database.

View definitions are stored in the data dictionary, and they do not physically store data. As a result, views do not require any storage.

Prior to Oracle8i and the virtual private database (or fine-grained access control), views were frequently used to provide secured access to data within Oracle. Even now, fine-grained access control tends to be complicated to implement (and it makes performance tuning more difficult), so views are still sometimes uses to provide security.

Also, views can be used to tune otherwise untunable code. You can rename the table that the code is attempting to access, and then create a view with the name of the table. In this view, you can include hints that make accessing the table much more efficient. This solution doesn't always work, but it does in some cases.

You can use views to INSERT, UPDATE, and DELETE records from the database, with a few provisions in regards to key-preserved tables. You can even create triggers on views.

Another use of views is to provide access to certain features in Oracle8i SQL that are not yet available in Oracle8i PL/SQL, such as the CUBE and ROLLUP functions. You simply create the view providing the appropriate query, and then have your PL/SQL code call that view. Sometimes, a view is the only way around such limitations.

NOTE Sometimes, certain third-party tools are not "up to snuff" with Oracle8i. They have problems dealing with some of Oracle8i's more advanced features, such as partitions. You may need to create views to allow your tool to perform some of these operations.

Creating Views

You use the CREATE VIEW statement to create a view. You might also want to use the CREATE OR REPLACE VIEW command, should the view already exist. Here is an example of creating a view:

```
CREATE OR REPLACE VIEW v_emp
AS SELECT empno, ename FROM emp
WHERE ename BETWEEN 'A%' AND 'D%';
```

This example creates a simple view over the EMP table that displays only the employee number and name for all employees whose names begin with the letters between *A* and *D*.

The CREATE VIEW command also has a FORCE option that will cause Oracle to create the view even if the underlying tables of the view are not yet created, as in this example:

```
CREATE OR REPLACE FORCE VIEW v_emp
```

```
AS SELECT empno, ename FROM emp
WHERE ename BETWEEN 'A%' AND 'D%';
```

From time to time, views may become invalid. You can recompile a view with the ALTER VIEW command using the COMPILE keyword:

```
ALTER VIEW v_emp COMPILE;
```

Finally, when you are just sick and tired of your view, you can drop it with the DROP VIEW command:

```
DROP VIEW v_emp;
```

Using Your Views

The way you create views can have an impact on performance, just as the way you create SQL statements can have an impact on performance on those SQL statements. If you have two tables (or more) in the view joined together, the keys involved in the join cannot be updated. Basically, if your UPDATE operation will cause changes to rows in both tables, it will fail. Also, if in the SELECT portion of the view, you choose to include a column from a table that cannot be updated, you will find that your ability to remove records from that view will be compromised. To understand what can happen, let's look at some examples:

```
DROP VIEW giview;
DROP TABLE gijoe;
DROP TABLE rank;
CREATE TABLE gijoe
( part_id     NUMBER PRIMARY KEY,
  Toy_name    VARCHAR2(30),
  Toy_rank    NUMBER);

CREATE TABLE rank
(toy_rank    NUMBER PRIMARY KEY,
 rank_name VARCHAR2(30) );

INSERT INTO rank VALUES (1, 'Private');
INSERT INTO rank VALUES (2, 'Sgt');
INSERT INTO rank VALUES (3, 'Captain');

INSERT INTO gijoe VALUES (10, 'Joe',1);
INSERT INTO gijoe VALUES (20, 'Sarge',2);
INSERT INTO gijoe VALUES (30, 'Cappie',3);
```

```
-- Now, create a view.
CREATE VIEW giview AS SELECT a.part_id, a.toy_name, b. rank_name
FROM gijoe a, rank b
WHERE a.toy_rank=b.toy_rank;

-- Update a record… this works.
UPDATE giview SET toy_name='Joseph' WHERE part_id=10;

-- Insert a new record… this will fail!
INSERT INTO giview VALUES (4,'Barbie','Sarge');
```

Note that the INSERT fails. This is because one of the columns that the example is trying to INSERT INTO is not *key preserved*. To be key preserved, each column being updated must relate to the primary key in the base table that the column is in. In this example, we are trying to update a column in the RANK table (RANK_NAME). However, the primary key of the RANK table (TOY_RANK) is not part of the UPDATE statement (or the view). Since we are not able to reference the primary key columns of the RANK table in the INSERT statement (again, because these columns are not part of the view we are updating), the TOY_NAME column cannot be updated. The bottom line is that with the way this view is constructed, we cannot insert records into the underlying base tables through this view.

We might rebuild the view in a slightly different way to try to get the UPDATE operation to succeed:

```
DROP VIEW giview;
-- Now, create a view.
CREATE VIEW giview AS SELECT a.part_id, a.toy_name, b.toy_rank,
   b. rank_name
FROM gijoe a, rank b
WHERE a.toy_rank=b.toy_rank;

-- Insert a new record… this will fail!
INSERT INTO giview
(part_id, toy_name, toy_rank)
VALUES (4,'Barbie',2);
Still, it fails with this error:
ERROR at line 2:
ORA-01776: cannot modify more than one base table through a join view
```

Why is this? Another rule with views is that only one base table can be modified at a time. Look closely at the view definition. You will see that the example uses the

RANK.TOY_RANK column instead of the GIJOE.TOY_RANK column. Thus, it is trying to update two tables instead of one. Let's rewrite the view again:

```
DROP VIEW giview;
-- Now, create a view.
CREATE VIEW giview AS SELECT a.part_id, a.toy_name, a.toy_rank,
  b. rank_name
FROM gijoe a, rank b
WHERE a.toy_rank=b.toy_rank;

-- Insert a new record… this will fail!
INSERT INTO giview
(part_id, toy_name, toy_rank)
VALUES (4,'Barbie',2);
```

Once we use the GIJOE.TOY_RANK column rather than the RANK.TOY_RANK column, we have met the requirement that only one table can be updated at a time. Unfortunately, since this view accesses A.TOY_RANK, we will have a problem if we want to use the view to insert a record into the RANK table, as shown in this example:

```
INSERT INTO giview
(toy_rank, rank_name)
VALUES (10, 'General');
```

Same old song—we get an ORA-1776 error (the patriotic Oracle message!) again. So, how do we work around this problem? We might try to include both columns in the view:

```
DROP VIEW giview;
-- Now, create a view.
CREATE OR REPLACE VIEW giview AS
SELECT a.part_id, a.toy_name, a.toy_rank as girank,
  b.toy_rank as update_rank,  b. rank_name
FROM gijoe a, rank b
WHERE a.toy_rank=b.toy_rank;

INSERT INTO giview
(update_rank, rank_name)
VALUES (10, 'General');
```

But this doesn't work either. Basically, given this view, you will not be able to do INSERT operations on columns that are in the RANK table. This is because Oracle will not allow you to change (or add) a column that is part of the join criteria of the view. For example, if you try to update the RANK_NAME column in GIVIEW, this impacts the join of the view, because the TOY_RANK column is the join column in the view. Because of this, you cannot update the RANK_NAME in the GIVIEW table. However, if you want to change a TOY_NAME column value, this is acceptable because it is not part of the join between the two tables, and thus will not impact the change.

 TIP INSTEAD OF triggers can be used as an effective solution to the problem of non-key preserved DML. These triggers can be written to override DML actions against a view and implement those changes in the base tables of the view instead. Refer to the Oracle documentation for more information about INSTEAD OF triggers.

Views as Performance Problems

Views can be performance problems, as well as performance god-sends. Be cautious when you create views that they only bring back the rows you really need. Also be careful of situations where you have views, stacked on views, stacked on views. The performance of such designs can be terrible.

I knew a developer who wrote code to use such a stacked-view design. All the developer really needed was 2 columns of information, yet he was going through a view that was returning some 25 columns of information, via a stack of about four different levels of views. Each level contained joins that you would not believe (including outer joins, which views seem to have particularly hard times with).

The developer came to me asking why his code performed so poorly. Once I had him rewrite his query to not use the view, but directly query the two-table join that he needed, his code's performance was increased dramatically. This just serves to demonstrate that one of the follies of views is that they can make developers lazy in designing efficient code.

Using Inline Views

Oracle also offers an inline view that is very handy. An inline view is part of a SQL statement. It allows you, in the body of the SQL statement, to define the SQL for a view that the SQL statement will use to resolve its query. Here is an example of using an inline view:

```
SELECT *
FROM   /* This starts the inline view */
       (SELECT owner, table_name, num_rows
       FROM dba_tables
       WHERE num_rows IS NOT NULL
       ORDER BY num_rows desc)
       /* This is the end of the inline view */
WHERE ROWNUM < 10;
```

This example gives the top-ten largest tables in the database, in terms of row count. Note that this particular bit of code will work only with Oracle8i. This is because the ORDER BY operation that occurs in the body of the inline view was not supported before Oracle8i. The ORDER BY clause sorts the result set of the data, before it is passed to the main query.

Viewing View Information

The DBA_VIEWS view is used to assist in the management of views in the database. It provides information about the view, such as its owner, its name, and the SQL used to create the view. Here is a description of DBA_VIEW:

```
SQL> DESC dba_views
 Name                                      Null?    Type
 ----------------------------------------- -------- --------------
 OWNER                                     NOT NULL VARCHAR2(30)
 VIEW_NAME                                 NOT NULL VARCHAR2(30)
 TEXT_LENGTH                                        NUMBER
 TEXT                                               LONG
 TYPE_TEXT_LENGTH                                   NUMBER
 TYPE_TEXT                                          VARCHAR2(4000)
 OID_TEXT_LENGTH                                    NUMBER
 OID_TEXT                                           VARCHAR2(4000)
 VIEW_TYPE_OWNER                                    VARCHAR2(30)
 VIEW_TYPE                                          VARCHAR2(30)
```

The following is an example of a query that uses the DBA_VIEW and its result:

```
SELECT owner, view_name
FROM dba_views
WHERE owner != 'SYS';
```

```
OWNER   VIEW_NAME
------  --------------------
SYSTEM  AQ$DEF$_AQCALL
SYSTEM  AQ$DEF$_AQERROR
SCOTT   GIVIEW
```

In this example, you see that the SCOTT user owns a view called GIVIEW. If you wanted to see the SQL statement that as associated with that view, you could query the TEXT column of the DBA_VIEWS view. Note that TEXT is a LONG, therefore you will probably need to use the SET LONG and SET ARRAY commands in SQL*Plus.

CHAPTER 7

Oracle Database Maintenance

FEATURING:

Managing database objects that support tables and indexes	**292**
Understanding database startup and shutdown	**312**
Changing the database name	**318**
Managing database files	**320**
Analyzing database objects	**323**
Diagnosing database problems	**329**

In Chapter 6, we discussed management of different Oracle schema objects. Primarily, we dealt with schema objects that stored information, such as tables and indexes. In this chapter, we will describe the procedures for managing other database schema objects, such as constraints and synonyms.

Also under the DBA's jurisdiction are database startup and shutdown. An understanding of how these processes work is critical to maintaining and protecting your database. This chapter explains the startup and shutdown modes and when you might use them.

Routine database maintenance generally involves managing the database's physical files and may include gathering statistics (analyzing) database objects. Finally, if something goes wrong with your database, you will need to diagnose the problem so that you can fix it. The final parts of this chapter cover the procedures and tools for these database tasks.

Managing Database Objects that Support Tables and Indexes

To make your database operations run smoothly, you will need to set up and manage various supporting elements, including synonyms, links, sequences, constraints, and LOBs. In this section, you will learn how to create and use these database objects.

Setting Up Synonyms

If you want to access an object in another user's schema, you need to use dot notation to correctly point to that object. For example, if you want to look at the EMP table in my schema (called ROBERT, of course), you need to issue a SQL statement like this:

```
SELECT * FROM robert.emp;
```

Using dot notation every time you want to access a table or some other object in another schema can become rather tedious. As an alternative, you can set up an alias, or *synonym,* for the object. Then you can use that synonym instead of dot notation.

Using a synonym has several advantages:

- It makes access to the object easier (and less error prone) by requiring less typing.

- It makes maintenance easier. If you change the schema object name, all you need to do is modify the synonym, and the application will still work.

- It provides the ability to keep the source of the data (such as a table that might be queried through a database link) transparent to the user. The user does not even need to know which database provided the data.

Creating Synonyms

Synonyms can come in two flavors: public and private. A *public synonym* can be seen by the world and accessed by everyone (although everyone might not be able to access the alias's object). To create a public synonym, you must have the CREATE PUBLIC SYNONYM privilege. Then you can use the CREATE PUBLIC SYNONYM command, as in this example:

```
CREATE PUBLIC SYNONYM emp FOR robert.emp;
```

A *private synonym* is one that is visible to only a single user schema. When you create a synonym with the CREATE SYNONYM command in a specific user's account, only that user can access the object through the synonym. In order to create a private SYNONYM, you must have the CREATE SYNONYM privilege. If you want to create a private synonym within another schema, the CREATE ANY SYNONYM grant is required. For example, if you wanted to allow just the user named Charles to see the EMP table in the ROBERT schema, you would issue the following command in Charles' account:

```
CREATE SYNONYM emp FOR robert.emp;
```

A private synonym can also be useful when developers are using copies of tables in their own schemas, and they want to reference those copies rather than the copy pointed to by a public schema.

Using Synonyms

After you've created a synonym, you can use it instead of dot notation. For example, if you created a public synonym for the EMP table, the following query would now use that synonym:

```
SELECT * FROM emp;
```

There is an order of precedence with regard to referencing objects in schemas:

1. Using direct naming (dot notation) to refer to the object
2. Using a synonym to refer to any local table
3. Using a private synonym
4. Using a public synonym

It is possible (and in a development database, very likely) to have a public synonym and a private synonym with the same name in the same database. It is also possible for these synonyms to point to different objects, so there is a possibility of confusion. This is one reason why it is very important to control the production environment of a database. On more than one occasion, a developer has created a synonym that pointed somewhere other than the production tables and nobody noticed... for a couple of days, at least.

Dropping Synonyms

If a user no longer needs access to an object for which you have defined a synonym or if you are dropping that object, you will want to remove the synonym associated with that object. Use the DROP PUBLIC SYNONYM command to drop any public synonym or the DROP SYNONYM command to drop any private synonym.

If you own a synonym in your own schema, no privilege is required to remove it. If you want to drop a private synonym in another user's schema, you will need the DROP ANY SYNONYM privilege. You will need the DROP ANY PUBLIC SYNONYM privilege to remove a public synonym.

Viewing Synonyms

Of course, you need to be able to find out what synonyms are pointing to where, for whom, and so on. The DBA_SYNONYMS, USER_SYNONYMS, and ALL_SYNONYMS views show the owner of the synonym (except for the USER_SYNONYMS view), the synonym name, the table owner, the name that the synonym points to, and the name of the database link involved, if applicable. The following is an example of a query using the ALL_SYNONYMS view and its results. Notice the presence of two synonyms for the EMP table: one owned by PUBLIC and one owned by Charles.

```
SQL> SELECT * FROM all_synonyms
  2 WHERE table_owner NOT LIKE 'SYS%';
```

OWNER	SYNONYM_NAME	TABLE_OWNER	TABLE_NAME	DB_LINK
PUBLIC	EMP	SCOTT	EMP	
PUBLIC	BONUS	SCOTT	BONUS	
PUBLIC	DEPT	SCOTT	DEPT	
PUBLIC	SALGRADE	SCOTT	SALGRADE	
CHARLES	EMP	CHARLES	CP_EMP	

Setting Up Database Links

Database links allow you to establish a connection between one database and another simply by referencing an assigned alias to that database. Each database link is assigned to attach to a specific user account on the remote database. When defining the database link, you specify which user account you wish the link to point to, as well as giving the password for that account.

Creating Database Links

Database links, like synonyms, can be public or private. As you might guess, public database links are accessible to everyone (which is why we disdain them), whereas private database links are accessible to only the user schema in which the link was created.

To create a public database link (which requires the CREATE PUBLIC DATABASE LINK privilege), use the CREATE PUBLIC DATABASE LINK command. You refer to the name and password of the user you wish the link to connect to, as well as the Net8 service name of the database you wish to connect to. The following example creates a database link called to_production, connecting to the magma account with the account password volcano, and connects to the database through the Net8 connection called prod_db.

```
CREATE PUBLIC DATABASE LINK to_production
CONNECT TO magma IDENTIFIED BY volcano
USING prod_db;
```

 TIP When naming database links, it's a good idea to include the name of the database and the connecting schema in the link name, if possible.

If you wish to create a private database link (which requires the CREATE DATABASE LINK privilege), use the CREATE DATABASE LINK command. For example, suppose that user Charles needs to get to the SALARY table from your financial database called FINPD to the human resources (HR) database called PAYROLL. You could create a private database link named to_hr in the Charles account of FINPD to point to the HR database, and call this link payroll. Here is how you would create this link:

```
CREATE DATABASE LINK to_hr
CONNECT TO pay_owner IDENTIFIED BY payback
USING payroll;
```

Using Database Links

To use a database link, refer to the object that you want to query on the remote machine, and use the @ sign followed by the name of the database link to indicate that you should access the object via the database link. Here is an example of a SELECT statement using the to_hr database link created in the previous section:

```
SELECT SUM(net_pay) FROM salary@to_hr
WHERE pay_date=TRUNC(SYSDATE);
```

Note that all activity that occurs through the link is subject to the grants owned by the user account that the link attaches to. For example, if the SQL statement above were executed, the pay_owner account would need to either own the SALARY table or have SELECT privileges to that table. (See Chapter 21 for details on grants.)

Dropping Database Links

Dropping a local database link is as simple as using the DROP DATABASE LINK command, like this:

```
DROP DATABASE LINK to_production;
```

If the database link is a public database link, use the DROP PUBLIC DATABASE LINK command, as in the following example:

```
DROP PUBLIC DATABASE LINK to_production;
```

Be careful about invalidating other objects when you execute this command.

NOTE There is no ALTER DATABASE LINK command. Rather, you will need to drop and re-create database links. This happens most commonly when a password or user account name associated with a database link changes. Unfortunately, dropping and re-creating the database link has the potential to invalidate many schema objects. It is generally a good idea to check to determine if you need to recompile any invalid objects after dropping and replacing a database link.

Viewing Database Links

The DBA_DB_LINKS (or USER_ or ALL_ versions of this view) shows the owner, database link name, and host for database links. Here is an example of querying this view and the results:

```
SQL> SELECT owner, db_link, host FROM dba_db_links;

OWNER            DB_LINK              HOST
---------------  -------------------  ------------
PUBLIC           SLUM.WORLD           SLUM.WORLD
PUBLIC           TEST08.WORLD         TEST08.WORLD
REP_ADM          TEST08.WORLD         TEST08.WORLD
```

If you have access to the SYS schema, you can use the LINK$ data dictionary table to view link information.

 WARNING There is a major security concern relating to links: When a link is created, the data relating to that link is stored in the SYS schema in a data dictionary table called LINK$. That link contains the unencoded password to the account that the link is associated with. This is just one of many reasons that you need to make sure that you secure your database properly!

Using Sequences

A sequence is similar to a machine that just generates numbers. Sequences can be useful for many purposes, such as to populate a primary key column in a table to ensure that third normal form is not violated (by virtue of repeating columns). Sequences are also commonly used to assign identifiers to items. For example, a manufacturing company might use a sequence number to create a unique part number for new parts.

For the most part, sequence numbers are generated in ascending order, but do not assume that sequences are generated in exact numerical sequence for any transaction. There can be skipped numbers in assigned sequence numbers for a variety of reasons. Oracle does not guarantee that a sequence number will not be lost. Oracle does guarantee that a sequence number allocated to a transaction will be unique to that transaction. Thus, once allocated, a sequence number is never reused, even if the transaction is rolled back.

Sequences are preallocated for use in a database cache. This makes it much faster for a transaction to grab a sequence for use. However, in the case of an instance failure, all sequences allocated to memory will be lost.

Creating Sequences

To create a sequence, use the CREATE SEQUENCE command. You must have the CREATE SEQUENCE system grant to create a sequence in your own schema. You must have the CREATE ANY SEQUENCE grant to create a sequence in another user's schema.

Several options are available for use when creating a sequence. For example, if you want to start a sequence with a specific number, use the START WITH keywords. If you want to increment the sequence numbers by a particular value, use the INCREMENT BY keywords. The most common options are listed in Table 7.1.

TABLE 7.1: COMMONLY USE CREATE SEQUENCE COMMAND OPTIONS

Option	Description
CACHE *n* or NOCACHE	CACHE *n* (e.g., CACHE 5) indicates how many sequence numbers should be allocated and stored in memory for future use. Oracle caches 20 sequences by default. NOCACHE prevents Oracle from caching sequence numbers. This reduces the risk of losing sequence numbers (though it does not eliminate this risk).
INCREMENT BY *n*	Indicates how much to increment the sequence by each time a sequence is allocated. Oracle increments sequences by 1 by default. This number can be a negative number if you wish to allocate sequence numbers in reverse order.
START WITH *n*	Indicates which number the sequence should first allocate.
MAXVALUE *n* or NOMAXVALUE	MAXVALUE indicates the highest sequence number that should be allocated. If the sequence is a CYCLE sequence, the next sequence allocated will be the START WITH value. NOMAXVALUE is the default.
MINVALUE *n* or NOMINVALUE	MINVALUE indicates the lowest sequence number that should be allocated. If the sequence is a CYCLE sequence, the next sequence allocated will be the START WITH value. NOMINVALUE is the default.
CYCLE or NOCYCLE	CYCLE indicates the sequence is a cycling sequence, which is the default. If NOCYCLE is selected, an Oracle error will be generated if the MAXVALUE or MINVALUE is exceeded.

Here is an example of creating a sequence that starts with 1, has a maximum value of 1,000,000, and does not cycle or use a cache:

```
CREATE SEQUENCE seq_my_seq
START WITH 1
MAXVALUE 1000000
NOCYCLE NOCACHE;
```

Altering and Dropping Sequences

You may want to change how the sequence functions, such as the next number it will assign when called. To modify a sequence, use the ALTER SEQUENCE command. Before you can use this command to alter a sequence that is not in your own schema, you must have the ALTER ANY SEQUENCE system grant.

The ALTER SEQUENCE command offers the same options as the CREATE SEQUENCE command, with the exception of START WITH. Here is an example of changing the increment value of a sequence and also have it cycle and use a cache:

```
ALTER SEQUENCE seq_my_seq
INCREMENT BY 1
CYCLE CACHE 5;
```

Dropping sequences requires the DROP ANY SEQUENCE system grant if the sequence is not in your own schema. If you have the appropriate grants, simply issue the DROP SEQUENCE command to drop the sequence:

```
DROP SEQUENCE seq_my_seq;
```

If you want to reset a sequence, you can drop and re-create the sequence. Alternatively, you can change the increment to a value that represents the difference between the current value of the sequence and the value you wish to reset the sequence number to, as in this example:

```
ALTER SEQUENCE seq_my_seq
INCREMENT BY -10000;
```

Once this is done, you will need to use one of the sequence numbers. Then you can alter the sequence again to set the INCREMENT BY value to the appropriate value for the sequence increments.

Accessing a Sequence Number

To access a sequence number in SQL (or in PL/SQL), you reference the name of the sequence and then use one of two pseudocolumns to indicate what you want to do with that sequence:

- The CURRVAL pseudocolumn provides the current value of the sequence for that transaction.
- The NEXTVAL pseudocolumn provides the next sequence number to be assigned to that session. The sequence number allocated is not guaranteed to be the next sequence number in order.

Listing 7.1 provides an example of accessing a sequence number through a SQL statement, and then through a PL/SQL block.

Listing 7.1: Using a Sequence in SQL and PL/SQL

```
SQL> SELECT seq_my_seq.nextval FROM dual;
   NEXTVAL
   ----------
        1
```

```
SQL> SELECT seq_my_seq.currval FROM dual;
CURRVAL
----------
         1
SET SERVEROUTPUT ON
DECLARE
    my_var     number;
BEGIN
    SELECT seq_my_seq.currval
    INTO my_var
    FROM dual;
    DBMS_OUTPUT.PUT_LINE('Sequence is '||my_var);
END;
/
Sequence is 1
PL/SQL procedure successfully completed.
```

Setting Up Constraints

Constraints are defined limitations and restrictions on one table or between two tables in an Oracle database. Put simply, constraints constrain a table in some way. Here, we will review the types of constraints, look at the options for enabling constraints, and describe the views that provide information about constraints.

Types of Constraints

Oracle offers several types of constraints: NOT NULL, primary key, unique, foreign key, and check. You have already seen examples of using these constraints in previous chapters. Let's review them here, with a few more details about their use.

NOT NULL Constraints

The NOT NULL constraint prohibits the column from containing any NULL value. When a new row is to be inserted into the associated table, a column with a NOT NULL constraint must have a value defined for it in the INSERT clause or through a column default value.

NOT NULL constraints are created on columns of tables with the keywords NOT NULL, as shown in this example:

```
CREATE TABLE one_column (id    NUMBER NOT NULL);
```

Primary Key Constraints

A primary key constraint defines a set of columns in a table that make each row in that table unique. A primary key ensures that no duplicate values for the columns of the constraint are in the table. Primary keys in Oracle are enforced through the combination of a unique index and the NOT NULL constraint on the columns in the table. Each column that is part of the primary key takes on a NOT NULL characteristic.

There are a few rules regarding primary keys:

- A table can have only a single primary key.
- The following datatypes cannot be in a column that is part of a primary key: LONG, LONG RAW, VARRAY, nested table, user-defined datatype, LOB, BFILE, or REF.
- A composite primary key cannot contain more than 32 columns.
- If a column is in a primary key, it cannot be part of a unique key.
- The columns of a primary key must be unique and nonrepeating. No column may contain a NULL value.

When defining a primary key, you can define the name of the constraint, control in which tablespace the primary key is created using the USING INDEX clause, as well as define storage characteristics for that index with a separate STORAGE clause. Chapter 6 contains many examples of creating tables with primary keys (specifically, see Listings 6.1, 6.2, and 6.3 for heap tables with primary keys, and Listings 6.13 and 6.14 for IOTs with primary keys).

Unique Constraints

Unique constraints are much like primary key constraints, except that unique constraints allow for the existence of NULLs in the rows of the table. Unique constraints are enforced through the use of a unique index, which is created when the constraint is defined. Just as with a primary key, you can use the USING INDEX syntax to define which tablespace the unique index should be created in, as well as the STORAGE clause to define storage characteristics for that index. In Oracle8i, if an index on the key set that you wish to use for the unique index already exists, that index will be used (that index will become a unique index).

Here is an example of creating a unique constraint on a table:

```
CREATE TABLE zocalo
(id       NUMBER    CONSTRAINT un_zocalo_id UNIQUE,
 name     VARCHAR2(200) );
```

In this example, the first column in the table (ID) will be created with a unique constraint called un_zocalo_id.

You can also alter a table to add a unique constraint, as in this example:

```
ALTER TABLE babylon
ADD CONSTRAINT un_babylon_1 UNIQUE (language_id)
USING INDEX TABLESPACE the_one
STORAGE (INITIAL 1m NEXT 1m PCTINCREASE 0);
```

Here, we are adding a unique constraint to the BABYLON table called un_babylon_1 on the column LANGUAGE_ID. We also have identified the tablespace and storage characteristics for the unique index that will be created as a result.

Foreign Key Constraints

A foreign key (FK) constraint enforces relationships between two different tables. A foreign key constraint consists of one or more columns in a child table that references the primary key of a parent table. A table may have many foreign key constraints either pointing to it (such that the table is the parent table in the relationship) or pointing from it to other tables (indicating that the table is a child table in that relationship).

When creating the foreign key, you define the columns in the child table that are part of the foreign key to be created. Then you define the table that is being referenced (the parent table) and the column names in that table that the columns in your table reference.

There are a few rules regarding foreign keys:

- The columns in the referenced table (the parent table in the relationship) must already be assigned as the primary key in that table.
- Composite foreign keys cannot have more than 32 columns.
- Foreign keys are not supported across database links.

Here is an example of defining a foreign key:

```
ALTER TABLE child ADD CONSTRAINT fk_child_parent
FOREIGN KEY (parent_id)
REFERENCES parent (parent_id);
```

In this example, the CHILD table, which contains a column called PARENT_ID, references that column to the PARENT_ID column in the PARENT table. This means that all entries in the CHILD table must reference a valid record (as defined by the value of the PARENT_ID column) in the PARENT table.

Two options available with foreign keys have to do with what happens to related rows in the child table when you drop a row in the parent table:

- The ON DELETE CASCADE option causes the related rows in the child table to be dropped when the related rows in the parent table are removed.

- The ON DELETE SET NULL option causes the foreign key columns in the child table to be NULL set to.

For example, suppose that you issue the following statement:

```
DELETE FROM parent WHERE parent_id=1;
```

You will remove a single row from the PARENT table. If you created the constraint using ON DELETE CASCADE, all related records in the CHILD table will be removed. If you created the constraint using the ON DELETE SET NULL option, the related records in the child table will not be removed but will have the PARENT_ID column set to NULL (effectively orphaning those records).

If you don't use either ON DELETE CASCADE or ON DELETE SET NULL, you will need to remove data from the child table first, and then proceed to remove the data from the parent table.

Check Constraints

A check constraint allows you to define a constraint on a table that is specific to a column. A check constraint is generally used to enforce that data in a column takes on a specific format or letter case, or to validate new columnar data.

For example, if a column should have only a Y or N value, you can create a check constraint to make sure that the INSERT or UPDATE operation will fail if someone tries to put a Z in that column. As another example, you could construct a check constraint that prevents a specific entry in a column, like this one:

```
ALTER TABLE emp
ADD CONSTRAINT ck_emp CHECK
(empno != 0);
```

This example creates a check constraint that disallows a 0 in the EMPNO column.

Naming Constraints

Oracle will automatically name your constraints, but you should not just accept the system-generated names. Give your constraints meaningful names, so that you and others can recognize what they are and their purpose.

For example, I prefix primary key constraints with *pk_*, unique constraints with *uk_*, check constraints with *ck_*, and foreign key constraints with *fk_*. This makes it much easier to identify the type of constraint. When naming foreign key constraints, include the name of the two tables (or abbreviations if the names are too long) involved in the relationship. You can see examples of this naming convention in this chapter and throughout this book.

Enabling Constraints

There are several options that you can employ when enabling constraints in Oracle. You can defer the checking of constraints, enable constraints without checking the validity of those constraints, and tell Oracle not to enforce constraints. These options are generally useful for large tables with foreign key constraints. Let's look at how and when you might use each of these options.

Deferring Constraint Checking

Typically, a constraint on an object is checked each time the column in the object that the constraint refers to is changed in some way. However, in some cases, you might want to defer constraint checking until a transaction is committed.

For example, suppose that you need to change the primary key of a parent table and change all of the related columns in a child table that have a foreign key relationship to the parent key. With a regular constraint, you would run into a problem no matter which table you tried to update first. If you tried to update the child table, the update would fail during the constraint check because you had not yet changed the parent table. If you changed the parent table, the update would fail because there were related child records. The solution is to make the constraint deferrable. When a constraint is deferred, the constraint will be checked when the COMMIT command is issued. If the constraint is violated, the transaction will be rolled back and an error will be generated.

You can define a constraint as deferrable by using the DEFERRABLE clause of the ALTER TABLE ADD CONSTRAINT or MODIFY CONSTRAINT clause. If you wish to indicate that a constraint is not deferrable, use the NOT DEFERRABLE clause instead (this is the default).

If you define a constraint as DEFERRABLE, you can indicate that the constraint should be initially set as deferred by using the INITIALLY DEFERRED keyword. The default is to make the constraint initially immediate. If you like, you can optionally use the INITIALLY IMMEDIATE keyword to document this in the DDL.

Enabling Constraints without Validation

The process of constraint validation can be expensive. As large data warehouse load operations execute, each row added to the object must have any related constraints validated. This can significantly slow down the load process (particularly with foreign key constraints). In some cases, the data is sourced from another database, and you know that the data being loaded is valid.

Prior to Oracle8i, DBAs sometimes disabled constraints on the tables to be loaded before loading the data. They would then enable the constraints after the load was complete. This had the benefit of delaying the checking of the constraints until the table was loaded, speeding up the load process. The downside was that the constraints had to be validated when they were enabled, and this validation could take a great deal of time. During the validation process, users could not make any changes to the data within the tables that held the constraints being enabled.

With the use of the ENABLE NOVALIDATE clause, the DBA can create or enable an existing constraint in such a way that it does not validate the existing data within tables. Once the constraint is enabled with the ENABLE NOVALIDATE clause, any new activity on the table will be validated through the constraint. The default action is the ENABLE VALIDATE clause, which will cause the constraint to be validated as it is enabled.

Using the RELY Setting with a Constraint

The RELY setting for a constraint basically tells Oracle not to enforce the constraint, yet it will appear to be enabled. In a sense, when you use RELY, you are creating a constraint only for the purposes of documentation, since it will never be used as a constraint. The default action is NORELY.

In some cases, constraints set to RELY can be used in combination with query rewrite and materialized views. This is because QUERY_REWRITE_INTEGRITY parameter (set in the init.ora file or by using the ALTER SYSTEM or ALTER SESSION command) requires that constraints be established. When QUERY_REWRITE_INTEGRITY is set to TRUSTED (or STALE_TOLERATED), Oracle will use constraints that are in VALIDATE mode or that are in NOVALIDATE mode with the RELY parameter set to determine join information. (If QUERY_REWRITE_INTEGRITY is set to ENFORCED, Oracle will not be able to use constraints set with the RELY setting.) See Chapter 19 for details on query rewrite and materialized views.

Viewing Constraint Information

The first time you try to delve into the data dictionary and extract constraint information, you may find it a bit overwhelming. There are so many different kinds of constraints. Let's try to clarify how the Oracle data dictionary documents constraints.

The primary view for constraint information is DBA_CONSTRAINTS, which has related USER_ and ALL_ views as well. The DBA_CONS_COLUMNS view, and its related USER_ and ALL_ views, can be used to generate an ordered list of the columns associated with a constraint.

The DBA_CONSTRAINTS view lists all of the currently defined constraints in the system. This includes the name, type, and owner of the constraint. Also listed is the table that the constraint is assigned to, as well as the table that the constraint references (if it is a foreign key constraint).

The following is an example of a query against the DBA_CONSTRAINTS view and its results.

```
SQL> SELECT owner, table_name, constraint_type, constraint_name
  2  FROM dba_constraints
  3  WHERE owner = 'SCOTT'
  4  ORDER BY 1, 2,3;

OWNER       TABLE_NAME        C CONSTRAINT_NAME
----------  ----------------  - ----------------
SCOTT       DEPT              P SYS_C00818
SCOTT       EMP               C CK_EMP
SCOTT       EMP               C SYS_C00819
SCOTT       EMP               R FK_DEPT
```

In the DBA_CONSTRAINTS view, the CONSTRAINT_TYPE (C) column indicates the type of constraint being listed in the view. Each type of constraint is defined by a single letter code, as follows:

- C stands for check constraint.
- O stands for read-only view.
- P stands for primary key.
- R stands for referential.
- U stands for unique key.
- V stands for view with check option

One of the more difficult tasks when trying to document constraints is to document both sides of a foreign key relationship. This is because the objects involved in such a relationship actually sit in two separate rows in the DBA_CONSTRAINTS view. The first row is the row that defines the foreign key itself. This row represents the foreign key on the child table, listing the name of the constraint and the table on which the constraint is built. It does not list the table that the foreign key is pointing to. Rather, the R_CONSTRAINT_NAME column shows the name of the constraint that this foreign key constraint is referencing. Remember that all foreign key constraints must reference a table's primary key, which has a constraint name attached to it.

The second row of this foreign key relationship is the one that contains the constraint name in the CONSTRAINT_NAME column of the DBA_CONSTRAINTS view. This will lead you to your second table, which is the parent table in the foreign key relationship. You will want to join on not only the R_CONSTRAINT_NAME column, but also the R_OWNER column, since a given constraint name is only unique to each schema owner. Here is an example of a query against the DBA_CONSTRAINTS view that will produce a report of the foreign key relationships between two tables (with the output format modified slightly to fit on the page):

```
SQL> SELECT a.owner, a.table_name, a.constraint_name, a.constraint_type,
  2  b.owner||'.'||b.table_name "REFERENCES TABLE", a.r_constraint_name,
  3  b.constraint_type "REFERENCED CONSTRAINT", c.column_name
  4  FROM dba_constraints a, dba_constraints b, dba_cons_columns c
  5  WHERE a.owner='SCOTT'
  6  AND a.constraint_type='R'
  7  AND a.r_owner=b.owner
  8  AND a.r_constraint_name=b.constraint_name
  9  AND a.r_owner=c.owner
 10  AND a.r_constraint_name=c.constraint_name
 11  ORDER BY 1,2, position;
```

OWNER	TABLE_NAME	CONSTRAINT_NAME	C	REFERENCES TABLE	R_CONSTRAINT_NAME	R	COLUMN_NAME
-----	------	--------	-	-----------	------------	-	------
SCOTT	EMP	FK_DEPT	R	SCOTT.DEPT	SYS_C00818	P	DEPTNO

In this example, the EMP table has a foreign key relationship to the primary key of the SCOTT.DEPT table. Notice that we also joined to the DBA_CONS_COLUMNS table, so we could list the columns in the EMP and DEPT tables that are involved in the relationship.

Managing LOBs

The LOB datatype replaces the older LONG datatype for storing large amounts of data. The "LOBs" section in Chapter 5 describes the features of LOBs. Here, we will focus on how to create LOBs when creating a table or adding a LOB column to a table. Listing 7.2 provides an example of the creation of a table that contains two LOBs.

Listing 7.2: Creating a Table with LOBs

```
DROP TABLE gimmie_lobs;
CREATE TABLE gimmie_lobs (
lob_id      NUMBER,
raw_blob    BLOB,
text_clob   CLOB
)
STORAGE (INITIAL 100k NEXT 100k)
```

```
LOB (raw_blob) STORE AS raw_lob(
TABLESPACE users
STORAGE (INITIAL 100k NEXT 100k)
INDEX raw_lob_i
DISABLE STORAGE IN ROW
CHUNK 32k
PCTVERSION 25)
LOB (text_clob) STORE AS clob_lob(
TABLESPACE users
STORAGE (INITIAL 100k NEXT 100k)
INDEX clob_lob_i
ENABLE STORAGE IN ROW
CHUNK 32k
PCTVERSION 25);
```

You'll notice that the beginning of the CREATE TABLE command looks the same as it does for a regular table. It defines the table name, creates three columns (LOB_ID, RAW_BLOB, and TEXT_CLOB), and uses a STORAGE clause. At this point, a new twist is added to the CREATE TABLE statement in the form of the LOB STORAGE clause, which is used to define elements of the LOB segment and the LOB index.

Listing 7.2 first defines the LOB storage for the RAW_BLOB column, beginning with the name of the LOB storage segment (raw_lob), followed by the storage specification for that segment as well as the tablespace assignment. The definition for the TEXT_CLOB column is similar. The STORAGE clause contains the following items:

INDEX The INDEX clause assigns the name for the LOB index for this LOB segment as raw_lob_i. Unfortunately, this is about all you can control about this index. It will take its storage and tablespace assignments from what you've assigned for the LOB segment (not very efficient in terms of I/O distribution, is it?). If you do not assign the index a name, Oracle will assign it a system-generated name, which we personally hate.

NOTE It best practice to always assign the LOB index a name (as in Listing 7.2) rather than accepting a system-generated name. Defining the LOB index name is not documented in Oracle8i.

DISABLE/ENABLE STORAGE IN ROW   Next, the DISABLE STORAGE IN ROW clause forces all rows to be stored out-of-line for the LOB column.

Unfortunately, you cannot force in-line storage of a LOB column (as explained in Chapter 5, if it's greater than about 4KB, it will be stored out-of-line). The ENABLE STORAGE IN ROW clause used for the TEXT_CLOB column enables in-line storage of that LOB column.

CHUNK The CHUNK clause allows you to define the size of each individual chunk (or page). Oracle will round the chunk size up to the nearest multiple of the database block size. You should make the chunk size a multiple of the size of the NEXT and INITIAL settings of the LOB segment. The chunk size cannot be bigger than 32KB, and chunks cannot span extent boundaries (therefore, you can end up wasting space if you set the chunk size incorrectly). The chunk size cannot be changed without rebuilding the entire LOB segment and its associated index.

WARNING Be careful using the ALTER TABLE MOVE command when rebuilding tables with LOBs. There may be some bugs with the ALTER TABLE MOVE command with relation to LOBs, so test carefully before trying this on a production database.

PCTVERSION The PCTVERSION keyword indicates just how much of the total allocated space of the LOB segment, below the high-water mark, can be occupied by old versions of chunks that are not really needed anymore. When the number of old images exceeds the space allowed by PCTVERSION (in practice, PCTVERSION seems more like a guideline to Oracle than a hard-and-fast rule), Oracle will begin to remove the oldest images, thus managing the growth in the LOB segment. Unfortunately, as with rollback segments, you can still end up with the ORA-01555 Snapshot Too Old Error nemesis (covered in Chapter 5). Possible solutions to this problem are to increase the PCTVERSION value and check your storage settings to make sure that you are not wasting space somehow.

Several other settings are available for LOBs that allow you to disable logging and control LOB caching. The NOLOGGING clause allows you to disable redo generation for a given LOB segment. This reduces I/O overhead associated with LOB operations (which can be significant). The downside of this is that you won't be able to recover the data being manipulated in the LOB until you have performed another backup. LOGGING, the default setting, is the exact opposite of NOLOGGING. LOGGING causes all changes to a LOB to be recorded in the redo logs, which makes full recovery possible.

The CACHE parameter will cause Oracle to use the database buffer cache when moving data in and out of LOB segments. If you are going to use the CACHE parameter, you should assign the LOB to the recycle buffer pool. When NOCACHE (the default) is used, Oracle will use direct reads/writes to the LOB segment rather than the database buffer cache. This reduces the overhead associated with the Oracle kernel, as well as reduces the likelihood of causing some warm blocks to be aged out of the database buffer cache. Also, NOCACHE reads and writes to LOBs can use multiblock I/O calls, which can reduce the overall cost of the I/O operations. Finally, Oracle8i introduced the CACHE READS keyword, which will cause only reads of the LOB (not writes to the LOB) to be cached.

Using BFILES and Directories

BFILES are external LOBs that allow read-only access to specific external operating system files from the database. Before you can use a BFILE, you must use the CREATE DIRECTORY command to create a directory object. The directory you define will be an operating system directory that stores the physical files that will be accessed by BFILES. When you issue the CREATE DIRECTORY command, you will define an alias associated with that operating system directory, like this:

```
CREATE OR REPLACE DIRECTORY bfile_directory AS 'd:\oracle\bfile';
```

To be able to use the CREATE DIRECTORY command, you must have the CREATE ANY DIRECTORY privilege. Of course, you must also have the correct privileges on the operating system file system to be able to open the files you will want to access.

NOTE BFILES are handled much differently from internal LOBs. You do not define a LOB segment for a BFILE, and thus chunk sizes, caching, and all of the other attributes of the LOB segment are not defined.

Accessing LOBs through SQL

In most cases, you can insert, update, or delete Oracle LOB column values through SQL*Plus, although BLOBs and BFILEs are nearly impossible to deal with through SQL. Listing 7.3 shows an example of INSERT, UPDATE, and DELETE operations on a CLOB LOB type.

Listing 7.3: Inserting into a CLOB Datatype

```
CREATE TABLE clob_test_table
(id        NUMBER,
 clob_column CLOB )
 LOB (clob_column) STORE AS clob_column (
```

```
        TABLESPACE data
        DISABLE STORAGE IN ROW
        INDEX clob_index);

Table created.

INSERT INTO clob_test_table
VALUES
(1, 'This is another test');

1 row created.

SELECT * FROM clob_test_table;
        ID CLOB_COLUMN
---------- ------------------------------
         1 This is another test

UPDATE clob_test_table set clob_column='This is a changed column'
WHERE id=1;

1 row updated.

SELECT * FROM clob_test_table;
        ID CLOB_COLUMN
---------- ------------------------------
         1 This is a changed column

DELETE FROM clob_test_table where clob_column='This is a changed column';
DELETE FROM clob_test_table where clob_column='This is a changed column'
                                   *
ERROR at line 1:
ORA-00932: inconsistent datatypes

SQL> SELECT * FROM clob_test_table WHERE clob_column LIKE '%This%';
SELECT * FROM clob_test_table WHERE clob_column LIKE '%This%'
                                    *
ERROR at line 1:
ORA-00932: inconsistent datatypes
```

Notice that some SQL operations work just fine, but others don't work correctly. It's those problematic operations that the DBMS_LOB package is made for! The Oracle-supplied package provides various routines that can be used to manage and manipulate Oracle internal and external LOBs.

Viewing LOB Information

Several data dictionary views provide information about LOBs, such as the column name of the LOB, the LOB segment name, and the chunk size. Table 7.2 describes these data dictionary views.

TABLE 7.2: DATA DICTIONARY VIEWS FOR LOBS

View	Description
DBA_LOBS	Contains various information on LOBs, such as the name of the table that contains the LOB, the name of the LOB column, and so on
DBA_LOB_PARTITIONS	Contains partition-specific Information on LOBs in table partitions
DBA_LOB_SUBPARTITIONS	Contains partition-specific Information on LOBs in table subpartitions
DBA_PART_LOBS	Contains default partition settings for LOBs in table partitions
V$TEMPORARY_LOBS	Contains Information on temporary LOBs

Understanding Database Startup and Shutdown

It is important to understand the process of starting up and shutting down the database. This is because you will want the database to be in different modes for different types of recoveries (which are discussed in Chapter 10). In this section, we will discuss the various stages of database startup and shutdown.

Starting Up the Database

When you issue the STARTUP command on an Oracle database, it goes through three distinct stages: NOMOUNT, MOUNT, and OPEN. Several events occur during these stages as the database prepares to open. Database checks, datafile checks, consistency checks, and certain types of recoveries occur during the startup process. Another startup mode that is available to the DBA is restricted mode. In executing various tasks, it may (and will likely) be necessary for you to start the database in a mode other than OPEN mode.

NOMOUNT Mode

NOMOUNT mode, and the NOMOUNT stage of regular startup, is essentially only the startup of the Oracle instance. As Oracle proceeds through the NOMOUNT stage, it performs the following steps:

1. It locates the database parameter file. By default, it will look for the init.ora file in the $ORACLE_HOME/dbs directory on Unix systems or the $ORACLE_HOME\database directory on Windows NT.

TIP You can use the PFILE parameter in the STARTUP command to designate an alternate location for the parameter file. An example of using the STARTUP command with the PFILE parameter might look something like this: STARTUP NOMOUNT PFILE=d:\oracle\admin\database\pfile\init(*sid*).ora.

2. Oracle will open and read the parameter file, and then process and validate the parameters.
3. Oracle will allocate the SGA it will require to crank up the instance.
4. Oracle will proceed to start the processes of the instance, such as DBWR, LGWR, CKPT, SMON, and PMON.

Once the instance is started, the NOMOUNT phase of opening the database will have concluded.

You will start the database in NOMOUNT mode in just a few cases. First, you will start the instance in this manner when you wish to create a new database (or re-create an old one). Second, you will start the instance in this mode when you need to create a control file using the CREATE CONTROL FILE command (discussed in Chapter 10). To cause the database startup process to proceed only through the NOMOUNT stage and halt, issue the STARTUP NOMOUNT command from the Server Manager or SQL*Plus prompt.

You will note that when you start up the instance, the amount of memory allocated to the SGA is reported. Generally, the memory reported looks something like this (obviously the sizes of memory allocated will differ):

```
Total System Global Area    92280076 bytes
Fixed Size                     70924 bytes
Variable Size               87937024 bytes
Database Buffers             4194304 bytes
Redo Buffers                   77824 bytes
```

The Fixed Size entry shows the memory allocated to a small portion of the SGA that contains database and instance status information required by background processes. The Variable Size entry shows the overall size of the shared pool area. It is also influenced by the use of the large pool and Java pool sizes. The other entries are self-explanatory. This output can also be retrieved by using the SHOW SGA command or viewed in the V$SGA data dictionary view (which is the source of the output).

NOTE The Redo Buffers entry in this output may not match the setting in the `init.ora` file for your database. This is because there is a minimum setting for the redo log buffer of four times the maximum database block size for the system.

MOUNT Mode

Once the instance has been started, the next step in opening the database associated with that instance is to mount the database. In MOUNT mode (and during the MOUNT stage), Oracle locates and opens the control file of the database. It is also at the MOUNT stage that database media recovery occurs (if the database needs to be recovered while it is down).

To start the database in MOUNT mode, use the STARTUP MOUNT command. You might do this for several reasons: to put the database in ARCHIVELOG mode, to perform certain recovery operations, or to rename database datafiles. If you wish to open the database in this mode, issue the command ALTER DATABASE OPEN.

OPEN Mode

During the OPEN stage, Oracle takes the final steps to open the database. The datafiles are opened, and an error will be signaled if a datafile is missing or if Oracle is unable to open it for some other reason. Once the database datafiles are opened, Oracle will check them with the control file to make sure that the database was closed in a consistent fashion. If it was, Oracle will open the database for use. If the database was not closed in a normal fashion, Oracle will decide if instance or media recovery is required.

If instance recovery is required, Oracle will perform it automatically without any user interaction. During instance recovery, Oracle will apply the redo in the online redo logs to the database, open the database, and roll back any uncommitted transactions after the database is open. The process of rolling back transactions while the database is open is known as *fast start recovery*. Fast start recovery allows the database to be used while instance recovery is ongoing. During fast start recovery, the SMON process will roll back the uncommitted transactions, allowing users access to the database at the same time. In Oracle8i, SMON can actually take advantage of parallel processing while performing these operations.

NOTE During fast start recovery, a new feature in Oracle8i allows Oracle user processes to prioritize the recovery of specific, in demand blocks. Thus, user processes will not need to wait for SMON to recover a block, which can take some time during particularly large recovery operations. A user process will determine that the block needs recovery and will take care of that block's recovery itself.

If Oracle needs to apply media recovery, it will inform the user that media recovery is required. Oracle will not open the database in this case, and will return to the SQL prompt to allow the DBA to begin media recovery. See Chapter 10 for information about media recovery.

Restricted Mode

You (as the DBA) can put the database in restricted mode if the database needs to be open for some maintenance operation but you do not want users to be able to connect to the database. To start the database in restricted mode, issue the STARTUP RESTRICT command. If the database is already open and you wish to put it in restricted mode, you can issue the command ALTER SYSTEM ENABLE RESTRICTED SESSION. Restricted mode impacts only new logins to the database, so existing users will need to be disconnected to ensure that no one can make changes to the database.

Once you have completed your maintenance operations, you can take the database out of restricted mode by issuing the ALTER SYSTEM DISABLE RESTRICTED SESSION command. Also, if you shut down the database and restart it normally, it will no longer be in restricted mode.

Shutting Down the Database

The normal Oracle database shutdown sequence is much like the startup sequence, just in reverse order. First the database is dismounted.

During a normal shutdown, the database waits for all sessions to disconnect (while preventing new sessions from connecting to the database). Once all sessions disconnect (which has the result of determining the state of all transactions at shutdown time), the database datafiles are checkpointed and then closed. The checkpoint process is very important because it leaves the database datafiles in a consistent state, allowing the database to start up the next time without the database (or the DBA) needing to perform any type of recovery. (See Chapter 5 for more on checkpoints and the consistent state of the database.)

The database then proceeds through the dismount phase, in which the control file is closed. Finally, the instance is terminated with the normal shutdown of the Oracle processes and de-allocation of the SGA.

Along with the normal SHUTDOWN command, several other commands may be used to shut down the database, as explained in the following sections.

SHUTDOWN ABORT

A SHUTDOWN ABORT is essentially a crash of the database. At a minimum, this type of shutdown will result in an instance recovery when the database is restarted. The main difference between a SHUTDOWN ABORT and just pulling the plug on the database is that the database datafiles are closed normally (although they are not checkpointed in any way) and memory is de-allocated from the system in a somewhat controlled fashion. The normal closing of the database datafiles is perhaps a bit safer than just pulling the plug on a database.

SHUTDOWN IMMEDIATE

The SHUTDOWN IMMEDIATE command will cause all existing user processes to be terminated, following which a normal shutdown will ensue. All existing uncommitted transactions will be rolled back before the database is shut down, which can take some time to complete. Another thing that can slow down a SHUTDOWN IMMEDIATE is an ongoing instance recovery process.

You can get an idea of how long a SHUTDOWN IMMEDIATE will take by looking at the V$TRANSACTION table's USED_UBLK or USED_UREC column, which represents the total amount of undo that will need to be reapplied to the database datafiles before the database can shut down. Ongoing instance recovery processes will not show up in V$TRANSACTION. To see those, you can try looking at the V$SESSION_LONGOPS or V$RECOVERY_PROGRESS view, although neither of these may provide any information, depending on how much recovery Oracle is expecting to do.

SHUTDOWN TRANSACTIONAL

The SHUTDOWN TRANSACTIONAL command allows the user transaction to complete before signing off the user. Thus, if a user application is in the middle of making some change, the database will wait for a commit to occur before disconnecting the session. This can pose a problem if a transaction is being manually executed and the user doesn't commit that transaction for a long period of time.

When You Have the Choice—SHUTDOWN ABORT or SHUTDOWN IMMEDIATE?

When you need to shut down the database for normal maintenance operations, should you use SHUTDOWN ABORT or SHUTDOWN IMMEDIATE? This is another of those questions that everyone has an opinion about. There are those that take the position that a SHUTDOWN ABORT is just fine. It shortens the time for the outage, even though you know that the database will need to perform instance recovery when starting back up, However, there are problems with using SHUTDOWN ABORT to shut down the database for normal maintenance operations. What happens if you use SHUTDOWN ABORT, and then you accidentally remove all the copies of the current online redo log (or perhaps the system administrator accidentally wipes out the volumes or disks with these critical files on them)? Since the database was not shut down cleanly, it's going to need to perform instance recovery, which will not be possible without the current online redo log. Since the log file was the current log file, it will not yet have been archived, so there is no copy of it anywhere. Your database is now beyond recovery, unless you have some way to recover those online redo log files that were just removed.

Another issue with SHUTDOWN ABORT has to do with some nasty behavior in Oracle (I think it's a bug) involving the TRUNCATE command. Suppose that you create a table and add a large number of records to it. Now, say that after you have entered all these records (but with no commit), the database is shut down with a SHUTDOWN ABORT command. Now, the database starts up and instance recovery begins. Let's say that you decide (or perhaps another user does) to truncate the table. Of course, records in this table are being rolled back by the instance recovery process. If you try to truncate the table that is being rolled back during instance recovery, you will crash the database. And we don't just mean the one user session—the entire database will crash.

My point with all of this is that SHUTDOWN ABORT introduces too many variables into the equation. Probably 99.9 percent of the time, everything will be okay, but that one time in a thousand always seems to hit me. We try not to perform SHUTDOWN ABORTs for normal maintenance unless there is some emergency that requires an immediate database termination. If we do decide to do a SHUTDOWN ABORT, we generally try to force a log switch (ALTER SYSTEM SWITCH LOGFILE) on the database and then force a

Continued

> **CONTINUED**
>
> checkpoint (ALTER SYSTEM CHECKPOINT) as well, before issuing the SHUTDOWN ABORT command.
>
> My personal preference is the SHUTDOWN IMMEDIATE command. This has the impact of killing all user sessions, rolling back all uncommitted transactions, and then closing the database datafiles normally (with a checkpoint to boot!). When this mode is selected, the database will be shut down cleanly. You can lose the online redo log files and still be in good shape. Before performing a SHUTDOWN IMMEDIATE, we do a log switch. After the shutdown, if major system work is about to be performed (particularly if that system work involves disks), we back up all archived redo logs before we allow the work to begin. The downside of this is that the SHUTDOWN IMMEDIATE command (along with my suggestion of a log switch) generally will take longer to complete than the SHUTDOWN ABORT command will. The solution is to allow sufficient time to shut down the system, and coordinate the shutdown with the user community, so that a minimum number of transactions are occurring on the database when the shutdown occurs.

Changing the Database Name

If you need to, you can change the name of your database. You probably should not make a habit of this, but there may be times that you really don't have a choice. Changing the name of your database is a fairly straightforward process:

1. Issue the ALTER DATABASE BACKUP CONTROLFILE TO TRACE command. This will create a trace file in the UDUMP directory that will allow you to re-create the control file, which is required to rename the database.

2. Issue the SHUTDOWN IMMEDIATE or SHUTDOWN command for a consistent database shutdown.

3. Modify the trace file created in step 1. It should just contain the text of the CREATE CONTROL FILE statement. You will need to replace the REUSE statement with SET on the first line of the statement. Also, change the NORESETLOGS command to RESETLOGS. When you are finished, it should look something like this:
```
CREATE CONTROLFILE SET DATABASE "ORA817" RESETLOGS ARCHIVELOG
     MAXLOGFILES 32
     MAXLOGMEMBERS 3
     MAXDATAFILES 254
```

```
      MAXINSTANCES 1
      MAXLOGHISTORY 899
LOGFILE
  GROUP 1 'D:\ORACLE\ORADATA\ORA817\REDO01.LOG'    SIZE 1M,
  GROUP 2 'D:\ORACLE\ORADATA\ORA817\REDO02.LOG'    SIZE 1M,
  GROUP 3 'D:\ORACLE\ORADATA\ORA817\REDO03.LOG'    SIZE 1M
DATAFILE
  'D:\ORACLE\ORADATA\ORA817\SYSTEM01.DBF',
  'D:\ORACLE\ORADATA\ORA817\RBS01.DBF',
  'D:\ORACLE\ORADATA\ORA817\USERS01.DBF',
  'D:\ORACLE\ORADATA\ORA817\TEMP01.DBF',
  'D:\ORACLE\ORADATA\ORA817\TOOLS01.DBF',
  'D:\ORACLE\ORADATA\ORA817\INDX01.DBF',
  'D:\ORACLE\ORADATA\ORA817\TEMPTEMP01.DBF'
CHARACTER SET WE8ISO8859P1;
```

4. Back up the physical database control file. (It's always a good idea to make sure that you have a current backup of the database as well!) Remove the control file after backing it up.

5. If you are using Windows NT, you will need to stop the database service and then edit it to rename the service. Then restart the service. Perform these actions with ORADIM. (See Chapter 3 for more on ORADIM.)

6. You will need to rename the database parameter file and change any database name references inside that file, such as the database name, instance name, and service names.

7. If you are using a password file, you will need to rename the old password file.

8. Change your ORACLE_SID so that it is pointing to the new database name.

9. Issue a STARTUP NOMOUNT command to start the database in NOMOUNT mode. Execute the script you created in step 3.

10. After running the script, issue the RECOVER DATABASE command (if your are in ARCHIVELOG mode and did not shut down the database cleanly). Then issue the ALTER DATABASE OPEN RESETLOGS command. Your database should open normally.

11. Change the global name of your database with the ALTER DATABASE RENAME GLOBAL_NAME command, like this.
    ```
    ALTER DATABASE RENAME GLOBAL_NAME TO newname;
    ```

12. Make another backup of your database.

Managing Database Files

After you have your database up and running, you will need to manage various database files. Your datafiles may need some attention, and you might want to add a control file. Also, there may be cases where you need to move online redo logs. These topics are covered here.

Managing Datafiles

Your datafiles are defined with the tablespace that contains them. However, if necessary, you can move and resize them. Also, Oracle provides some data dictionary views that provide information about database datafiles.

Moving Datafiles

To move a datafile with the database up and running, you must first be in ARCHIVELOG mode. To move a datafile that is assigned to a tablespace, follow these steps:

1. Take the datafile offline.
2. Physically move it to the new file system.
3. Alter the datafile location internal to Oracle with the ALTER DATABASE RENAME FILE command.
4. Bring the datafile back online.

Listing 7.4 provides an example of moving an existing datafile.

Listing 7.4: Moving a Database Datafile

```
-- First, take the datafile offline.
ALTER DATABASE DATAFILE
'd:\oracle\oradata\recover\recover_my_extending_tablespace_01.dbf'
OFFLINE;

-- Now, copy the datafile.
Host copy
d:\oracle\oradata\recover\recover_my_extending_tablespace_01.dbf
e:\oracle\oradata\recover\recover_my_extending_tablespace_01.dbf

-- Now, rename it in the database.
ALTER DATABASE RENAME FILE
'd:\oracle\oradata\recover\recover_my_extending_tablespace_01.dbf'
```

```
                TO
                'e:\oracle\oradata\recover\recover_my_extending_tablespace_01.dbf';

                -- Bring the datafile online.
                ALTER DATABASE DATAFILE
                'd:\oracle\oradata\recover\recover_my_extending_tablespace_01.dbf'
                ONLINE;
```

If you are not running your database in ARCHIVELOG mode, you will need to shut down the database, physically move the datafile again, mount the database, and issue the ALTER DATABASE RENAME command to rename the datafile's location on the disk.

Resizing Datafiles

As explained in Chapter 5 (in the discussion of creating tablespaces), the AUTO-EXTEND clause lets you define how large a datafile is allowed to grow and how large it can grow at any given time. You can also use the ALTER DATABASE DATAFILE command with the RESIZE clause to resize database datafiles, as in this example:

```
                ALTER DATABASE DATAFILE
                'd:\oracle\oradata\recover\recover_my_extending_tablespace_01.dbf'
                RESIZE 10000k;
```

If you are making a datafile smaller, you can only remove free blocks from the end of the datafile. If the datafile has any used blocks, or any free space contained between used blocks, you will not be able to free that space.

Viewing Datafile Information

Oracle provides many different views for managing database datafiles. Table 7.3 lists the most commonly used views for managing datafiles.

TABLE 7.3: COMMON VIEWS FOR DATABASE DATAFILES

View	Description
DBA_DATA_FILES	Lists datafiles information, such as the datafile number and associated tablespace names.
DBA_FREE_SPACE	Provides free space information for datafiles. Can be used to determine how much free space can be de-allocated from a database datafile.
V$BACKUP	Indicates the backup status of a datafile.

Continued

TABLE 7.3: COMMON VIEWS FOR DATABASE DATAFILES (CONTINUED)	
View	Description
V$DATAFILE	Provides a large amount of information on database datafiles from the control file. This view is available after the database is mounted.
V$RECOVER_FILE	Provides information on database datafiles that require media recovery. This view is available after the database is mounted.
FET$	Lists datafiles and free blocks (or extents) within the datafiles.
UET$	Lists all used extents in a database datafile.
DBA_EXTENTS	Allows you to locate the datafile in which a specific extent is located.

Adding Control Files

You should have at least two control file copies at a minimum. If necessary, you can add a control file to your database. Simply follow these steps:

1. Shut down the system.
2. Copy an existing control file for the system to the new name and location of the control file you wish to add.
3. Modify the database parameter file to reflect the addition of the control file.
4. Restart the database.

Moving Online Redo Logs

Even as a seasoned DBA, it always makes me a bit queasy to even think about touching the online redo logs. This is because the redo logs are critical for database recovery operations, so if something should happen to them, you could end up with an unrecoverable database.

To move an online redo log (you might want to do this for I/O distribution purposes), you can choose one of two paths. One method is to just delete and re-create the online redo log group, using the ALTER DATABASE DROP LOGFILE and ALTER DATABASE ADD LOGFILE commands (see the "Sizing the Redo Logs" section in Chapter 3 for examples of using these commands). Alternatively, you can manually move the online redo logs and then rename them in the database using the ALTER DATABASE FILE RENAME command.

WARNING Remember how important the online redo logs are to Oracle. Act carefully when manipulating them.

To move a database redo log file, follow these steps:

1. Shut down the database and then mount it.
2. Rename the old log file.
3. Physically move the log file to its new location (for example, using the cp or copy command). Create it at the new location with its proper name.
4. To rename the redo log within the database itself, use the ALTER DATABASE RENAME FILE command.
5. Open the database.

Review Listing 7.4 for an example of moving a file in Oracle (redo logs are moved in the same manner as datafiles).

Analyzing Database Objects

The ANALYZE command collects a great deal of useful information about tables, indexes, and clusters. The ANALYZE command has the following main purposes:

- To collect or delete statistics about tables, indexes, clusters, and scalar object attributes
- To validate the structure of tables, indexes, clusters, and REFs
- To identify migrated and chained rows of a table or cluster
- To create histograms to analyze data distribution

Here, we will discuss the basics of gathering statistics and validating objects using the ANALYZE command. The topics of analyzing objects in conjunction with using cost-based optimization (CBO), identifying chained rows, and creating histograms are covered in Chapter 16. Also, analyzing database objects is a prerequisite for some Oracle maintenance and tuning activities, which are discussed in Chapters 15 through 17.

Gathering Statistics

The ANALYZE command provides statistics on tables, such as the number of rows in the table, the number of blocks above the high-water mark of the table, average free space in each block, and a great deal of additional information. When analyzing indexes, you gather statistics on the depth of the index from its root block to its leaf blocks, the number of leaf blocks in the index, the number of distinct index values, and other information.

You can either compute the statistics of the object, by using the COMPUTE STATISTICS clause of the ANALYZE command, or estimate the statistics of the object, by using the ESTIMATE STATISTICS clause. You can analyze a table, index, or cluster. If you analyze the table, all associated indexes are analyzed by default. However, you can specify that you do not want to analyze the indexes along with the table. You can also choose to analyze only specific columns in a table (all columns is the default), only specific partitions or subpartitions of a partitioned object (Chapter 24 discusses partitioned objects), or only local indexes.

 WARNING Never analyze an object owned by SYS. These are data dictionary objects and should not be analyzed.

Computing Statistics

The COMPUTE STATISTICS clause gives you the most accurate statistics possible on the object you are analyzing (short of building histograms, which we'll discuss in Chapter 16). Here are examples of computing statistics for a table and an index:

```
ANALYZE TABLE employee COMPUTE STATISTICS;
ANALYZE INDEX ix_employee COMPUTE STATISTICS;
```

The downside to computing statistics is that you need a significant amount of temporary space—enough to hold and sort the entire table. As a benchmark, figure that you need about three times the size of the table as workspace for an analysis using the COMPUTE STATISTICS method. (Note that if indexes are being analyzed, no additional space is required.) Also, a complete analysis of a table takes significantly more processing time than for an analysis using the ESTIMATE STATISTICS clause. This can be particularly noticeable in a warehousing or Decision Support System (DSS) environment, where you are dealing with very large objects.

Estimating Statistics

Computing statistics may not be a realistic option because of the demand on resources. As an alternative, you can use ANALYZE with the ESTIMATE STATISTICS clause. When you estimate a given object's statistics, Oracle reads through a sample set of rows or blocks, and based on that sample set, generates estimated object statistics. You can estimate based on either a specific number of rows or on a percentage of the total number of rows in the object.

NOTE If you choose to have the CBO estimate more than 50 percent of the table, it will actually compute the statistics instead. (Of course, Oracle doesn't bother to tell you that it's doing so.)

Let's look at a few examples of the ANALYZE command using the ESTIMATE STATISTICS clause:

- To estimate statistics for a table based on the first 2000 rows:
  ```
  ANALYZE TABLE employee ESTIMATE STATISTICS SAMPLE 2000 ROWS;
  ```
- To estimate statistics for a table based on a sample of 20 percent of the rows:
  ```
  ANALYZE TABLE employee ESTIMATE STATISTICS SAMPLE 20 PERCENT;
  ```
- To estimate statistics for an index using a sample size of 2000 rows:
  ```
  ANALYZE INDEX ix_employee ESTIMATE STATISTICS SAMPLE 2000 ROWS;
  ```

If you issue the ANALYZE TABLE ESTIMATE STATISTICS command without defining how many or what percentage of rows to sample, Oracle will, by default, use a 1064-row sample to estimate the statistics.

Is there any difference between doing an ANALYZE ESTIMATE using ROWS or an ANALYZE ESTIMATE using PERCENT? Some DBAs have found that using PERCENT generates statistics that more closely align with the actual statistics of the object. We have seen consistently better performance of queries against objects where PERCENT was used, as opposed to ROWS. Thus, we strongly suggest that you use PERCENT when analyzing an Oracle object.

NOTE If you attempt to analyze an index that has been marked UNUSABLE (such as a partitioned table and a partition of a global index), the ANALYZE operation will fail. You will need to rebuild the UNUSABLE index before you can analyze it.

Viewing Statistics

The ANALYZE command populates many columns in the DBA_INDEXES, DBA_TABLES, _TAB_COL_STATISTICS, and DBA_TAB_COLUMNS tables. This also applies to the USER and ALL versions of these data dictionary tables. Table 7.4 lists all of the columns populated by the ANALYZE command, and Table 7.5 describes the commonly referenced columns.

TABLE 7.4: TABLES POPULATED BY THE ANALYZE COMMAND

Table (DBA, USER, and ALL)	Columns with Analyze Results
_INDEXES	BLEVEL, LEAF_BLOCKS, DISTINCT_KEYS, AVG_LEAF_BLOCKS_ PER_KEY, AVG_DATA_BLOCKS_PER_KEY, CLUSTERING_FACTOR, NUM_ROWS, SAMPLE_SIZE, LAST_ANALYZED
_TABLES	NUM_ROWS, BLOCKS, EMPTY_BLOCKS, AVG_SPACE, CHAIN_ CNT, AVG_ROW_LEN, AVG_SPACE_FREELIST_BLOCKS, NUM_FREELIST_BLOCKS, SAMPLE_SIZE, LAST_ANALYZED
_TAB_COL_STATISTICS	NUM_DISTINCT, LOW_VALUE, HIGH_VALUE, DENSITY, NUM_NULLS, NUM_BUCKETS, LAST_ANALYZED, SAMPLE_SIZE, GLOBAL_STATS, USER_STATS, AVG_COL_LEN
_TAB_COLUMNS	NUM_DISTINCT, LOW_VALUE, HIGH_VALUE, DENSITY, NUM_NULLS, NUM_BUCKETS, LAST_ANALYZED, SAMPLE_SIZE

TABLE 7.5: COMMONLY REFERENCED ANALYZE STATISTICS

Column	Table, Index, or Column	Description
LAST_ANALYZED	All	Date the object was last analyzed.
SAMPLE_SIZE	All	Size of the last analyze sample.
AVG_COL_LENGTH	Column	Average length of data in the table column.
LOW_VALUE/HIGH_VALUE	Column	High value and low value for the data points contained in the column.
NUM_NULLS	Column	Number of NULL values currently in the column.

Continued

TABLE 7.5: COMMONLY REFERENCED ANALYZE STATISTICS (CONTINUED)

Column	Table, Index, or Column	Description
AVG_DATA_BLOCKS_PER_KEY	Index	Average of how many index blocks a single key resides in.
AVG_LEAF_BLOCKS_PER_KEY	Index	Average of how many index leaf blocks a single key resides in.
BLEVEL	Index	Height of an index—indicates the number of levels from the root block to the node blocks.
DISTINCT_KEYS	Index	Number of distinct keys present in the index. The closer this number is to NUM_ROWS, the more selective the index.
LEAF_BLOCKS	Index	Number of leaf blocks contained in the index.
AVG_ROW_LEN	Table	Average length of a row in a table. You can multiply this by NUM_ROWS to discover the total amount of data you are actually storing in a table.
AVG_SPACE	Table	Average amount of free space, in bytes, in a block in the table.
BLOCKS	Table	Number of blocks in the table.
CHAIN_CNT	Table	Number of chained rows in the table.
CLUSTERING_FACTOR	Table	Clustering factor—indicates the ordering of the rows in the table as compared to the order in the index. A lower number is generally better. (See Chapter 16 for details.)
EMPTY_BLOCKS	Table	Number of unused blocks allocated to the table above the high-water mark.
NUM_ROWS	Table/Index	Number of rows in the table. Use this number to keep track of table growth.

Removing Statistics from an Object

Using the DELETE STATISTICS clause of the ANALYZE command, you can remove statistics that have been generated with the ANALYZE command. You can remove statistics on a table, cluster, or index. You can also delete statistics for a specific partition of a partitioned table. If you remove statistics from a table, the statistics of any associated index are also removed. Here's an example of using the ANALYZE DELETE command:

```
ANALYZE TABLE employee DELETE STATISTICS;
```

So, why would you want to use the DELETE STATISTICS command? Perhaps you have decided not to keep existing statistics on a given object because you wish the queries using that table to use rules-based optimization (RBO), rather than CBO. Or, you might have objects that you don't keep statistics on because you wish them to use RBO, yet you want to have the statistics available for management purposes. In this case, you would analyze the object, copy the statistics somewhere else, and then delete the statistics. For example, Chapter 15 describes how to generate average block usage reports for a table. If you are using Oracle in an RBO environment and you want to actually run these reports, you can analyze the table, run the report, and remove the statistics using the ANALYZE TABLE DELETE STATISTICS command.

Validating the Structure of an Object

The ANALYZE VALIDATE command allows you to validate the structure of tables, table partitions, indexes, and clusters. You might validate an object if you suspect all or part of it has become corrupted. Also, validating an index is a way to collect statistics that are not otherwise collected. Here is a summary of the effects of validating each type of object:

Table validation   Each row and each data block in the table is validated. If you wish to validate that all of the table's rows are properly stored in all associated indexes, use the CASCADE clause of the ANALYZE VALIDATE command. When you validate a partitioned table, in addition to the validation routines executed for normal tables, each row is checked to ensure that it is in the correct partition. If an invalid row is discovered, an entry is made in a table called INVALID_ROWS.

Index validation   Each data block in an index is validated and checked for corruption. However, no cross-checking is done against the table on which the index is built to make sure that all entries in the index are valid. Oracle also collects useful statistics that are loaded in tables called INDEX_STATS and INDEX_HISTOGRAM, which store statistics from only one index at a time. For example, the INDEX_STATS table includes information about the number of distinct keys in the index, number and total length of deleted leaf rows in the index, how often the most repeated key is repeated, total space allocated and used in the B*Tree, and the height of the B*Tree.

Cluster validation The structure of the cluster's tables is validated. You can use the CASCADE keyword with the ANALYZE VALIDATE command to force validation of the cluster table's associated indexes.

WARNING Use caution when validating an object. During the period of the validation, you will not be able to make any changes to the object, and all DML activity on that object will wait for the validation to be completed.

Diagnosing Database Problems

As a DBA, you know that databases occasionally have problems. Perhaps a process keeps failing, or maybe the database keeps shutting down for what appears to be no good reason. Of course, you need to identify the cause of a problem before you can fix it. Oracle provides several tools that you can use for diagnosing and troubleshooting database problems. These include trace files, the alert log, the DBV utility, and the DBMS_REPAIR packages.

Using Trace Files and the Alert Log

Oracle trace files provides varying levels of information about the database. In particular, they can provide some insightful information about why the database or an associated process has failed. The alert log is created by the database and can be used to monitor the database for ongoing events.

Reviewing Process Trace Files

Database processes generally create process trace files when they encounter some situation that causes process failure or could indicate some problem condition (for example, encountering a bad block that could be repaired). Sometimes, processes will create informational messages in their trace files. The location of process trace files is controlled by the `init.ora` parameter BACKGROUND_DUMP_DEST. The file-naming convention differs on different operating systems, but it generally includes the process name in the name of the file. An example of a process trace filename on a Windows NT system is `ora816ARC0.log`, containing the trace file for the ARC0 archive logging process.

Networking processes also create trace files. For example, the listener process creates a listener trace file and stores it in `$ORACLE_HOME/network/trace` by default.

If you have a database crash, be sure to look for trace files written about the time of the crash. Oracle will probably be interested in these as a part of the diagnosis process.

NOTE Each ARCH process will create a trace file by default. The parameter LOG_ARCHIVE_TRACE is supposed to prohibit this action. There is a bug (1307166) that causes a trace file to be created, regardless of the setting of LOG_ARCHIVE_TRACE. This bug is corrected in Oracle8i version 8.1.7.0.

Reviewing User Trace Files

User trace files are generally created at the request of a user session. The trace files generated are created in the directory location specified by the `init.ora` parameter USER_DUMP_DEST. These trace files generally contain run information from specific sessions that can be analyzed for performance-tuning purposes.

User trace files are also used by the system when the DBA issues the ALTER DATABASE BACKUP CONTROLFILE TO TRACE command at the SQL prompt. When issued, this command will create a trace file that contains the required SQL commands to re-create the control file of the database. We will discuss this command in more detail in Chapter 10.

Finally, the system processes themselves will create trace files as they operate. These trace files can be helpful in cases where the database processes have crashed.

Using the Alert Log

You can use the alert log to monitor database events such as log switches, startup and shutdown, tablespace coalesce operations, and certain database error conditions. Like the process trace file location, the alert log location is controlled by the `init.ora` parameter BACKGROUND_DUMP_DEST.

In terms of monitoring a production database, you should keep an eye on the alert log. Database problems that will be reported in the alert log include segments that could not extend and certain Oracle database errors. You will also find other important day-to-day operating messages in the alert log.

Purging Trace and Log Files and Directories

Although the trace and log files are useful, over time, they can grow to an unwieldy size. You should watch the growth of the alert log and truncate it as required. Also, you may wish to control the growth of the process and user trace files (in the directories specified by the USER_DUMP_DEST and BACKGROUND_DUMP_DEST parameters), as well as the trace files created by the listener and client processes.

TIP Also watch the size of the core dump files, in the directory defined by the CORE_DUMP_DEST `init.ora` parameter. You can control the growth and size of dump files by using the MAX_DUMP_FILE_SIZE `init.ora` parameter.

Using DBV

Oracle provides the DBV (also called DBVerify) utility to check database datafiles, online or offline, for any type of corruption. The name of the utility may differ, based on your operating system.

When you execute DBV, you must specify the name of the datafile you wish to check, using the FILE parameter. If the database block size is greater than 2KB, you must also pass the block size of the database datafile you are checking. Here is an example of using DBV:

```
D:\ORACLE\oradata\ora816>dbv file=ora816_overflow_01.dbf
DBVERIFY: Release 8.1.6.0.0 - Production on Sun Apr 22 23:28:53 2001
(c) Copyright 1999 Oracle Corporation.  All rights reserved.
DBVERIFY - Verification starting : FILE = ora816_overflow_01.dbf
DBVERIFY - Verification complete
Total Pages Examined         : 51200
Total Pages Processed (Data) : 0
Total Pages Failing   (Data) : 0
Total Pages Processed (Index): 0
Total Pages Failing   (Index): 0
Total Pages Processed (Other): 3
Total Pages Empty            : 51197
Total Pages Marked Corrupt   : 0
Total Pages Influx           : 0
```

You can also use other DBV parameters to control what is checked and specify other options. Table 7.6 describes the valid parameters for the DBV utility.

TABLE 7.6: DBV PARAMETERS

Parameter	Default Value	Description
BLOCKSIZE	2048	Defines the block size of the datafile being checked
END	None	Defines the last block to check during the verification process
FEEDBACK	0	Provides constant feedback in the form of a period per block checked (0 disables feedback; 1 enables it)
FILE	None (but required)	Specifies the name of the datafile to be verified
HELP	None	Displays the help screen
LOGFILE	None	Specifies the name of the log file to dump results generated by the verify process
PARAFILE	None	Allows you to define a parameter file for DBV
START	None	Allows you to define the block where you wish DBV to start the verification process

Using DBMS_REPAIR

The DBMS_REPAIR package allows you to check Oracle database objects for logical corruption, such as corruption that has resulted from software bugs, hardware failure, or memory problems. DBMS_REPAIR does not check for or fix physical corruption. Table 7.7 describes the DBMS_REPAIR functions.

TABLE 7.7: DBMS_REPAIR FUNCTIONS

Function	Description
ADMIN_TABLES	Creates database objects required to use the DBMS_REPAIR package
CHECK_OBJECT	Checks an object and reports on any corruption in that object
DUMP_ORPHAN_KEYS	Reports on keys in indexes that point to corrupted rows in data blocks
FIX_CORRUPT_BLOCKS	Marks software-corrupted data blocks discovered by the CHECK_OBJECT procedure as unusable

Continued

TABLE 7.7: DBMS_REPAIR FUNCTIONS (CONTINUED)

Function	Description
REBUILD_FREELISTS	Rebuilds an object's free lists (not used to add free lists)
SKIP_CORRUPTED_BLOCKS	Causes Oracle to ignore corrupted blocks during index scans (helpful in the event you are getting ORA-01578 errors, but be aware that the results may be unreliable)

Actual use of DBMS_REPAIR is limited to soft corruption of Oracle database objects. Soft corruption occurs much less frequently than other types of corruption, such as physical datafile corruption.

CHAPTER 8

Oracle Object-Oriented Features

FEATURING:

Using Oracle objects	336
Using user-defined object types	339
Using object tables	351
Using collection types	357
Using methods	365
Querying object types	372
Creating object views	380

The Oracle database has traditionally been a relational database; that is, it is designed to provide the structures to support the rules of relational database design. This includes tables, foreign keys, constraints, and so on. Purely relational databases have rules, such as a table cannot have repeating rows and a row must contain only one record. In a relational database, there is (theoretically) some performance loss because of the additional work needed to join related data in different tables together to resolve a given query.

A relational database is not the only kind of database that exists, of course. There are hierarchical databases, proprietary format database formats using a combination of flat files and indexing, and a number of other database schemes. One of these database-management schemes is the object-oriented database.

Oracle8 began to introduce object-oriented features in the Oracle database. While Oracle8i does not offer many new object-oriented features, it does improve the performance of the existing features and offers a few new twists. In Oracle8, you needed to install the Object option before you could use Oracle's object-oriented features. In Oracle8i, this is no longer required, because these features are installed in the database by default. Objects in Oracle8i are also part of the standard licensing, so no additional licensing costs are required to use Oracle's object-oriented features.

Using Oracle's object-oriented features, you now can store multiple records in a single row. For example, you can store all of an employee's dependent records in one column of the employee table, rather than create a separate table for dependents. (Yes, we hear you relational hard-cases screaming bloody murder.) In this chapter, we will look at Oracle's object-oriented database features. We will first review some basic object-oriented principles and terms. Then we will cover each of the different types of Oracle objects, including user-defined types, object tables, and collection types. Finally, you will learn about creating methods and using views with object-oriented database objects.

Using Oracle Objects

In this section, we are going to cover, at 10,000 feet, how a database designer might use Oracle objects. First, if you are going to deal with object-oriented features in Oracle, you will need to become familiar with several new terms. Following are definitions of the main object-oriented terms. We will review most of these terms in greater detail later in this chapter. If you are familiar with object-oriented methodologies, you may notice that, in some cases, the definition is slightly different from the traditional definition. This is because the terms are defined as Oracle uses them. When in Rome....

Attributes   The various data elements associated with an object. Similar to columns in a table.

Class   A blueprint of an object. With one class, you can create as many objects as you want. In Oracle, this is an object type.

Collection objects   Objects that allow you to store multiple rows of data within a single row. The two collection objects in Oracle are VARRAYs and nested tables.

Encapsulation   Implies that the attributes of an object can be modified only through the use of the methods associated with the object, and basically protects the data within that object and keeps that data compartmentalized within that object. Thus, if an object were truly encapsulated, you could not directly modify it. Oracle does not currently support true encapsulation.

Instance   An object of a class. One class can instantiate any number of similar type of objects with different data in them. The instantiated object will contain its own methods and attributes in its own memory instance.

Method   One or more programs that are directly associated with a type. In a truly object-oriented environment, methods are the only way to alter data in an object. Oracle supports four types of methods: constructor, member (including the method subtypes normal member and static member), map, and order.

Object   A collection of related data elements (attributes) and programs (methods). An object can physically store data. There can be only one object of a given name in any database.

Object table   A database table based on defined object types.

Persistent object   An object that remains in place until removed by the DBA. This includes user-defined datatypes and object tables.

Polymorphism   In traditional C programming concepts, this is called overloading. Polymorphism is making use of same method name to perform different tasks. Even though, the method names are the same, the type and number of parameters passed to the method are different. Therefore, calling the same method with different parameters will invoke different methods of the code, which would be transparent to the user.

Scalar datatypes   The native datatypes provided in Oracle. The features present in the Oracle object database allow you to define new datatypes beyond the scalar datatypes.

Transient object An object that disappears after use. PL/SQL tables and data in temporary tables are examples of transient objects.

Type (user-defined datatype) Logical definition of attributes that an object will be made up of. A type cannot physically store data, and thus requires no storage. Objects are a definition, or a template, of the structures that will become an object. The object will then store data using an instance of the type.

As an example, suppose that a database designer has decided to create an object table for an employee database. The object table will contain both the employee records and all of the dependent records for the employee. The designer will also create some methods to provide standard reports and sorting for the object table.

To begin his work, the designer will create one or more types using the CREATE TYPE command. This *type* is the framework for a logical object structure. It does not consume any storage space and is not allocated any memory. These types will consist of one or more attributes. *Attributes* are much like a column in a regular relational table, and they can contain other types. Each attribute in the type will have a name and an associated datatype, but there are no constraints defined for an attribute, since the type does not store any data itself. The type is basically just a template of the one or more structures that the developer will put together to make up the object table.

When designing the type, the designer might then create some PL/SQL code called methods. *Methods* are various PL/SQL procedures and functions associated with a given type (and instances of that type) that allow for interaction with the attributes of an instance of an object. For example, the designer might create a PL/SQL function that will retrieve the employee number of every employee who has no dependents, and return that value in an object table of the type of that object.

After developing the types and methods, the designer is ready to create the actual object table out of the type. An *object table* is an Oracle table that is wholly derived from a single type in the database (though that single type may itself include multiple types within it). The designer will create the object table using an instance of the type he created. An *instance* of a type is created when a type is used to create an actual object; thus, only instances of objects require storage. When creating the object table, the developer defines storage characteristics of the object table, as would be done for a normal relational table.

On the application side, several object-oriented programming languages can take advantage of Oracle's object-oriented features. C++, Java, and a host of other object-oriented languages allow you to define data structures as objects, just as you can in the database. Thus, similar structures can be created in the programs and databases, making the movement of data between these two entities easier and faster.

Given this overview, you can begin to get an idea of how Oracle's object-oriented features can be used. In the rest of this chapter, you'll learn the details about each of Oracle's object-oriented features.

 NOTE This chapter is not about designing an object-oriented database, and it does not take a stand on whether using object-oriented technologies is better or worse than relational technology. Whether or not you choose to use Oracle objects depends on your needs and your experience. In some cases, the object-oriented features may make your life and your data design a little easier. Then again, you may choose never to use them.

Using User-Defined Object Types

When you want to use Oracle objects, you usually start by creating of one or more types. In its most elemental form, an *object type,* or just *type,* defines an Oracle object and its associated attributes and methods. The type itself requires no storage (except for some very minimal dictionary storage), and you do not store anything in a type.

For example, you could create a type called employee that will contain several attributes that describe a given employee, as shown in Figure 8.1. The employee type may also contain one or more methods, although none are required. (We will discuss methods later in this chapter, in the "Using Methods" section.)

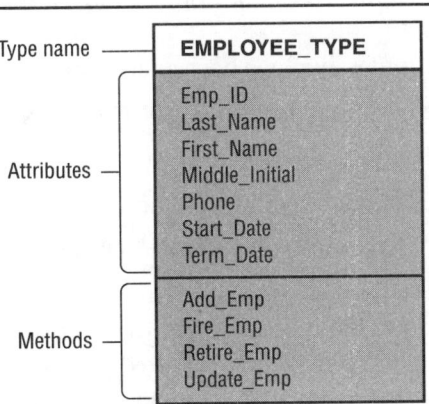

FIGURE 8.1

An object type with attributes and methods

After creating the type, you would then create instances of that type (such as defining that type as a column in a relational table) when creating other objects. When an instance of a type is defined as a part of a database segment, the instance of that type is allocated storage.

Once created, a type may find itself being used in several places, including object tables, relational tables, PL/SQL constructs, or even as an attribute of another type. For example, you may create a type called ADDRESS_TYPE, which you will then use in a type called EMPLOYEE_TYPE (ADDRESS_TYPE would store the employee's address in this case). A type may be persistent or volatile, depending on where it is declared. Typically, an object type instance used in an application (such as PL/SQL) will be volatile, whereas a type used in a database (such as in object tables) will be persistent.

 WARNING Once you create a type, and you build other types and objects using that type, it becomes harder and harder to modify that type. Carefully consider this limitation, and make sure that your object-oriented database designs are complete and well thought out before you start building them.

Creating Types

To create an object type, you use the CREATE TYPE command. CREATE TYPE is a DDL statement, so it cannot be used inside PL/SQL. However, use of the CREATE TYPE in dynamic SQL is allowed. To create the object, the CREATE TYPE privilege must have been granted, which can be done through a role (the resource role has this grant as a part of it).

The attributes of a type have a few restrictions:

- They cannot consist of a LONG or LONG RAW value.
- NLS types such as NCHAR and NCLOB are not supported.
- The column types ROWID and UROWID are not supported.
- PL/SQL constructs such as %TYPE and %ROWTYPE are not supported.

Listing 8.1 provides the basic structure of a type called EMPLOYEE. Everything you want to know about a given employee will be contained in this type: the name, phone number, and so on. (Admittedly, in real life, this would probably infer that you don't know nearly enough about your employee!)

USING USER-DEFINED OBJECT TYPES

Listing 8.1: Creating a Type

```
CREATE OR REPLACE TYPE employee_type AS OBJECT (
Emp_id       NUMBER,
Last_name    VARCHAR2(30),
First_name   VARCHAR2(30),
Middle_init  CHAR(1),
Phone        VARCHAR2(30),
Start_date   DATE,
Term_date    DATE )
/
```

You might have noticed that the CREATE TYPE statement is a bit different from most SQL statements. Instead of ending the statement with a semicolon, you always end the statement with a forward slash, as you would PL/SQL. If you use a semicolon, the statement will not execute.

Notice that we used a _type suffix for the type name, EMPLOYEE_TYPE. We use this suffix for all of the types that we create. It's important to use a naming convention for the different objects you create in the Oracle database, so that you can recognize their purpose.

Modifying and Dropping Types

As you define types, you will find that you are developing a hierarchy of types—one type becomes part of another type, which becomes part of another type, and so on. This is typical when dealing with object-oriented programming. Unfortunately, these dependencies can make it hard to modify your types. As you build types upon types, you cannot alter a given type unless you first remove the types that are dependent on it. For example, suppose that you create a type called ADDRESS_TYPE, as shown in Listing 8.2.

Listing 8.2: Creating an Address Type

```
CREATE OR REPLACE TYPE address_type AS OBJECT (
Street_address_one    VARCHAR2(50),
Street_address_two    VARCHAR2(50),
City                  VARCHAR2(30),
State                 VARCHAR2(2),
Zip_code              NUMBER )
/
```

If you wish to re-create the employee type to use this new type, you will first need to drop the old employee type. This is because you cannot add, remove, or update attribute definitions in Oracle8i types. To drop the type, you use the DROP TYPE command:

```
DROP TYPE address_type;
```

You can then re-create the employee type with the CREATE TYPE command, including the ADDRESS_TYPE in it.

 NOTE The ALTER TYPE command is used for managing methods associated with types. We will discuss methods later in this chapter, in the "Using Methods" section.

Using Types as Attributes

Listing 8.3 demonstrates using the ADDRESS_TYPE type (created in Listing 8.2) as an attribute of another type called EMPLOYEE_TYPE. Notice that you treat the ADDRESS_TYPE attribute as you would any other scalar datatype when you define it as an attribute in another type. In this case, the example gives the attribute a name, EMP_ADDRESS, which is of type ADDRESS_TYPE.

Listing 8.3: Re-creating the Employee Type

```
CREATE OR REPLACE TYPE employee_type AS OBJECT (
    Emp_id        NUMBER,
    Last_name     VARCHAR2(30),
    First_name    VARCHAR2(30),
    Middle_init   CHAR(1),
    Emp_address   address_type,
    Phone         VARCHAR2(30),
    Start_date    DATE,
    Term_date     DATE )
/
```

Now suppose that you have discovered that you need to modify the address type because it doesn't support Canadian zip codes. Unfortunately you cannot just issue a CREATE OR REPLACE TYPE command. If you attempt to do that, you will get the following error:

```
CREATE OR REPLACE TYPE address_type AS OBJECT (
            *
```

```
ERROR at line 1:
ORA-02303: cannot drop or replace a type with type or table dependents
```

This is one of the difficult and unfortunate characteristics of objects in Oracle. When a given type is a dependency of another type, it cannot be altered (or dropped) until the types that are dependent on the type you wish to change are dropped first. Because of the hierarchical nature of using objects in Oracle, you need to plan your database carefully before you begin to create it.

NOTE The ability to modify type attributes may be added in Oracle9i. If this feature is implemented, it will make objects in Oracle much easier to use.

Determining Dependencies

To determine which types are dependent on your type, you can use the DBA_DEPENDENCIES view. Here is an example of using this view to determine which types are dependent on the type ADDRESS_TYPE.

```
SELECT owner, name FROM dba_dependencies
WHERE referenced_name='ADDRESS_TYPE';

OWNER                              NAME
------------------------------     -------------
SCOTT                              EMPLOYEE_TYPE
```

This tells you that you will need to drop this type before you can replace the address type. Listing 8.4 shows the gyrations you need to go through just to replace the ADDRESS_TYPE type.

Listing 8.4: Replacing a Type

```
DROP TYPE employee_type;

CREATE OR REPLACE TYPE address_type AS OBJECT (
Street_address_one      VARCHAR2(50),
Street_address_two      VARCHAR2(50),
City                    VARCHAR2(30),
State                   VARCHAR2(2),
Zip_code                VARCHAR2(10) )
/
```

```
CREATE OR REPLACE TYPE employee_type AS OBJECT (
Emp_id         NUMBER,
Last_name      VARCHAR2(30),
First_name     VARCHAR2(30),
Middle_init    CHAR(1),
Emp_address    address_type,
Phone          VARCHAR2(30),
Start_date     DATE,
Term_date      DATE )
/
```

NOTE The DROP TYPE command does include a FORCE clause that will allow you to drop the type even if there are dependencies on that type (this is particularly helpful if the type you are trying to drop is involved in a circular relationship with another type). Unfortunately, there is no recovering from this command, and any information that may be stored using a type would be permanently lost. Therefore, when modifying types, it's a good idea to remove and re-create all dependent types first, rather than using the FORCE option. This way, you will be sure that you have backed up any pertinent data.

Managing Oracle Types

There are several data dictionary tables you can use in Oracle to manage types:

- DBA_DEPENDENCIES
- DBA_TYPES
- DBA_TYPE_ATTRS
- DBA_OBJECTS
- DBA_COLL_TYPES
- DBA_NESTED_TABLES
- DBA_OBJECT_TABLES
- DBA_REFS
- DBA_TYPE_ATTRS

We have already discussed the DBA_DEPENDENCIES view, which is used to determine the various objects that a type is dependent on. Here, we will look at the DBA_TYPES, DBA_TYPE_ATTRS, and DBA_OBJECTS views. We will look at the other views throughout this chapter, as we cover the different layers of the Oracle object model.

The DBA_TYPES View

The DBA_TYPES view shows information about the various types in the database. It also includes the number of attributes and methods associated with each type. Here is an example of using the DBA_TYPES view:

```
SELECT owner, type_name, attributes, methods
FROM dba_types
WHERE owner NOT LIKE ('%SYS%');
```

OWNER	TYPE_NAME	ATTRIBUTES	METHODS
SCOTT	NAME_TYPE	3	0
SCOTT	ADDRESS_TYPE	6	0
SCOTT	PARENT_TYPE	5	1
SCOTT	CHILD_TYPE	2	0

The DBA_TYPE_ATTRS View

The DBA_TYPE_ATTRS view is used to look up information on the various attributes of a type in the database. This includes the name of the attribute, the variable type, precision, scale, and other pertinent information. The following is an example of using the DBA_TYPE_ATTRS view.

```
SELECT owner, type_name, attr_name, attr_type_name, length
FROM dba_type_attrs
WHERE owner NOT LIKE '%SYS%';
```

OWNER	TYPE_NAME	ATTR_NAME	ATTR_TYPE_NAME	LENGTH
SCOTT	ADDRESS_TYPE	ADDRESS_NUMBER	NUMBER	
SCOTT	ADDRESS_TYPE	STREET_ADDRESS_ONE	VARCHAR2	50
SCOTT	ADDRESS_TYPE	STREET_ADDRESS_TWO	VARCHAR2	50
SCOTT	ADDRESS_TYPE	CITY	VARCHAR2	30
SCOTT	ADDRESS_TYPE	STATE	VARCHAR2	2
SCOTT	ADDRESS_TYPE	ZIP_CODE	VARCHAR2	10
SCOTT	CHILD_TYPE	CHILD_ID	NUMBER	
SCOTT	NAME_TYPE	FIRST_NAME	VARCHAR2	30
SCOTT	NAME_TYPE	LAST_NAME	VARCHAR2	30
SCOTT	NAME_TYPE	MIDDLE_INIT	CHAR	1
SCOTT	PARENT_TYPE	FIRST_NAME	VARCHAR2	30
SCOTT	PARENT_TYPE	LAST_NAME	VARCHAR2	30

SCOTT	PARENT_TYPE	MIDDLE_INITIAL	CHAR		1
SCOTT	PARENT_TYPE	PHONE_NUMBER	VARCHAR2		20
SCOTT	PARENT_TYPE	LAST_CONTACT	DATE		

The DBA_OBJECTS View

The DBA_OBJECTS view provides information on objects in the database, including types. You can use this view to determine the status of a type, the last time the type was manipulated (via the LAST_DDL_TIME column), and when the type was originally generated (via the CREATED column). Here is an example of a query against DBA_OBJECTS for all types owned by SCOTT:

```
SELECT owner, object_name,
TO_CHAR(created, 'mm/dd/yyyy hh24:mi:ss') CREATED_DATE
FROM dba_objects
WHERE owner='SCOTT' AND
object_type='TYPE';
```

```
OWNER       OBJECT_NAME      CREATED_DATE
----------  ---------------  -------------------
SCOTT       ADDRESS_TYPE     03/20/2001 22:20:39
SCOTT       EMPLOYEE_TYPE    03/20/2001 22:25:32
```

Introducing Row and Column Objects, OIDs, and REFs

In an Oracle database, there are two types of persistent objects: a column object and a row object. The *column object* is an object that is included in the creation of a relational table, as shown in this example:

```
CREATE TABLE employee
( empl_id    NUMBER,
  empl_info  my_employee,
);
```

Here, EMPL_INFO is a column object of type MY_EMPLOYEE. It contains information about the employee. Thus, a column object is an object that is stored in a table as a part of the table definition.

A *row object* is the type of object that is created when an object table is created. The type that the row object will contain is defined by the CREATE TYPE command. Then the CREATE TABLE command will be executed to create the object type. An object table can contain many row objects within it (each row being one row object).

As you've learned in previous chapters, each row in an Oracle relational table has a ROWID. Each row in an object table—each row object—has an OID, or an object ID.

In an object table, the OID is a pointer to that row object, much like a ROWID is a pointer to the location of a unique row, rather than the data in the row itself. The OID for a row in an object table is unique and will never be reused (unlike a ROWID).

A column object does not have an OID associated with it. Only persistent objects have OIDs. Thus, objects used inside PL/SQL do not have OIDs associated with them. Oracle also has a second type of OID associated with object views, which we will discuss later in this chapter, in the "Creating Object Views" section.

Because OIDs are unique to each row object, it is handy to be able to reference those OIDs in other objects in the Oracle database, which is exactly what a REF allows you to do. Here is an example of the creation of an object with a REF:

```
CREATE TYPE child_type (
Child_name        name_type,
Child_address     REF address_type,
Teacher           parent_type)
/
```

In this case, the CHILD_ADDRESS contains a reference to the type ADDRESS_TYPE. Thus, when an object table is created using this type, the CHILD_ADDRESS attribute will store an OID as a reference to a row object in some other object table. To make even better use of OID REFs, Oracle provides several different SQL functions, including VALUE, REF, DREF, and DANGLING operators.

Using REFs can be, in some ways, like defining a foreign key relationship between the two objects. Unfortunately, the relationship is not enforced, as it would be with a foreign key. As a result, you can end up with dangling REFs, where there are references to OIDs in an object, yet those OIDs do not exist in the referenced object. This is much like a situation where a child table contains records that do not have related records in the parent table.

In Oracle8, it was a pain to deal with dangling REFs. Oracle8i makes it much easier by allowing you to use the ANALYZE command and set all dangling REFs to NULL. Here is an example:

```
ANALYZE TABLE my_table VALIDATE REF UPDATE SET DANGLING TO NULL;
```

Forward Declaring Types

On occasion, you may end up having types that have recursive relationships within an object. For example, suppose that you have a parent table that holds information about parents and a child table that contains information about children. For each child, you will list the teacher of the child, which happens to be in the parent table (because teachers are parents, too!). Further, since some parents might have exchange students in their households, you want to list the exchange student. How would you create such a relationship? The CREATE TYPE commands might look something like this:

```
CREATE OR REPLACE TYPE address_type AS OBJECT (
Street_address_one    VARCHAR2(50),
Street_address_two    VARCHAR2(50),
City                  VARCHAR2(30),
State                 VARCHAR2(2),
Zip_code              VARCHAR2(10) )
/

CREATE TYPE name_type (
First_name     VARCHAR2(30),
Last_name      VARCHAR2(30),
Middle_init    CHAR(1) )
/

CREATE TYPE child_type (
Child_name       REF name_type,
Child_address    address_type,
Teacher          REF parent_type)

CREATE TYPE parent_type (
Parent_id        NUMBER,
Parent_name      REF name_type,
Parent_address   REF address_type,
Child_name       REF child_type,
Exch_student     REF child_type)
/
```

However, this code will not work because of the curricular references between the CHILD_TYPE type and the PARENT_TYPE type. To avoid this, Oracle allows you to *forward declare* a type that may be also declared in another type. When you forward declare a type, you create just a shell of a type. This shell does not include any attributes or methods, but acts as a placeholder of sorts for the ultimate creation of the type. Listing 8.5 provides the solution by forward declaring the PARENT_TYPE type.

Listing 8.5: Creating Parent and Child Tables with a Recursive Relationship

```
CREATE OR REPLACE TYPE address_type AS OBJECT (
Street_address_one    VARCHAR2(50),
```

```
    Street_address_two      VARCHAR2(50),
    City                    VARCHAR2(30),
    State                   VARCHAR2(2),
    Zip_code                VARCHAR2(10) )
/

CREATE OR REPLACE TYPE name_type AS OBJECT(
    First_name      VARCHAR2(30),
    Last_name       VARCHAR2(30),
    Middle_init     CHAR(1) )
/

-- Forward declaring the type parent_type.
CREATE OR REPLACE TYPE parent_type
/

CREATE OR REPLACE TYPE child_type AS OBJECT (
    Child_name      name_type,
    Child_address   address_type,
    Teacher         parent_type)
/

CREATE OR REPLACE TYPE parent_type AS OBJECT (
    Parent_name     name_type,
    Parent_address  address_type,
    Child_name      REF child_type,
    Exch_student    REF child_type)
/
```

Notice that you forward reference the PARENT_TYPE type with a CREATE OR REPLACE TYPE command. In this command, you just define the type and do not use the AS OBJECT syntax or define any attributes for the type. If you input the code in Listing 8.5, you will get an error when you create the CHILD_TYPE type. This is okay, because the error is only indicating that the type PARENT_TYPE is malformed, which it is at this point. This problem is corrected with the replacement of the PARENT_TYPE type in the last CREATE TYPE statement in the listing.

Listing 8.5 also uses the REF clause, which will allow you to later query this relationship through SQL statements. Another reason for using the REFs here is that they help establish the relationship between object tables, as you will see shortly.

Using Types in Relational Tables

You can create relational tables that include user-defined datatypes. For example, you could create an employee table with the ADDRESS_TYPE type (created in Listing 8.2), as shown in Listing 8.6. Later in this chapter, in the "Querying Object Types" section, we will look at how to access these user-defined datatypes with SQL.

Listing 8.6: Creating a Relational Table with a User-Defined Datatype

```
CREATE TABLE employee
( Emp_id      NUMBER,
Last_name     VARCHAR2(30),
First_name    VARCHAR2(30),
Middle_init   CHAR(1),
Emp_address   address_type,
Phone         VARCHAR2(30),
Start_date    DATE,
Term_date     DATE )
TABLESPACE users
STORAGE (INITIAL 100k NEXT 100k);
/
```

Using Types in PL/SQL

Instances of object types can be defined in PL/SQL code. Of course, the persistence of the data in these objects is only as long as the PL/SQL program continues to run. Listing 8.7 provides an example of a PL/SQL program that creates an instance of the address type and populates it using the type constructor (which we will discuss later in this chapter, in the "Using Methods" and "Querying Object Types" sections).

Listing 8.7: Creating an Instance of an Object in PL/SQL

```
DECLARE
    v_address    address_type :=
                 Address_type('222 Somewhere Lane',
                 NULL, 'Somewhereville','FL','44030');
BEGIN
    Dbms_output.put_line('Your address is : ');
    Dbms_output.put_line(v_address.street_address_one);
END;
```

Using Object Tables

Another Oracle object-oriented feature is an object table—a table made solely from a single user-defined type (which can be made up of multiple types). In this section, we will look at how to create and manage object tables. We will also look at some additional details about Oracle objects, including more on OIDs and REFs.

 TIP If you used objects in Oracle8 and have migrated to Oracle8i, you should know that object table storage has changed in 8i. The new storage methods are more efficient in terms of overall storage and performance. Unfortunately, when you upgrade from Oracle8 to Oracle8i, your objects are not modified to take advantage of this new format. If you want to use the new format, you will need to re-create your objects using either CREATE TABLE SELECT statements or Oracle's Export and Import utilities.

Creating Object Tables

To create an object table, use the CREATE TABLE command, just as you would to create a relational table. When you create an object table, you use the OF keyword to define the object type for which you want to create the table. Listing 8.8 shows an example of creating an object table using the CHILD_TYPE and PARENT_TYPE types that were created earlier in this chapter, in Listing 8.5.

Listing 8.8: Creating Object Tables

```
CREATE TABLE child
OF child_type
TABLESPACE users
STORAGE (INITIAL 10k NEXT 100k PCTINCREASE 0);
```

Notice how tablespaces and storage for object tables are defined just as they are for regular tables. The only real difference is that the example uses the type definition CHILD_TYPE to define the attributes of the object table (using the OF CHILD_TYPE clause), rather than listing column attributes as you would for a relational table.

As you might suspect, you have all sorts of options that you can use when creating an object table. One option is to define an object table as a GLOBAL TEMPORARY table. In doing so, you can define the persistence of the rows in that table with the ON COMMIT clause. You can also create a primary key for an object table, just as you would for a relational table.

Another option for an object table is to define the primary key of the table to be the OID, using the OID clause of the CREATE TABLE statement. If you use the primary key as the OID for the table, it will only be unique to the table itself. This is an alternative to using the default system-generated OID (a 128 byte, base 64 number), which is globally unique throughout the database. If you specify that the table should use the system-generated OID, then you will want to specify the STORAGE clauses for the related OID index that will be created. Thus, using the system-generated OID will require more storage space than using the primary key.

Listing 8.9 provides an example of the creation of both the child and the parent object tables, using a few of the options just described.

Listing 8.9: Creating Object Tables

```
-- Drop all types and tables to make this easier.
DROP TABLE child;
DROP TABLE parent;
DROP TYPE parent_type FORCE;
DROP TYPE child_type FORCE;

CREATE OR REPLACE TYPE name_type AS OBJECT(
    First_name      VARCHAR2(30),
    Last_name       VARCHAR2(30),
    Middle_init     CHAR(1) )
/

-- Create our forward type declaration for the child_type type so we
-- can create the parent_type type.
CREATE OR REPLACE TYPE child_type
/

-- Create the parent_type type.
-- Note the two REFs to the child_type.
CREATE OR REPLACE TYPE parent_type AS OBJECT (
    Parent_id       NUMBER,
    Parent_name     name_type,
    Parent_address  address_type,
    Child_name      REF child_type,
    Exch_student    REF child_type)
/
```

```sql
-- Now, create the child_type. Again, note the REFs to the
-- parent_type type.
CREATE OR REPLACE TYPE child_type AS OBJECT (
    Parent_id       REF parent_type,
    Child_id        NUMBER,
    Child_name      name_type,
    Child_address   address_type,
    Teacher         REF parent_type)
/

-- Now, create the parent table. We will use an OID index for this
-- table. This is generally required for the main table in a
-- parent/child relationship. The OIDINDEX clause will help speed up
-- REF lookups between this and the child table.
CREATE TABLE parent
OF parent_type
OIDINDEX idx_parent (TABLESPACE indexes)
TABLESPACE users
PCTFREE 10
PCTUSED 70
STORAGE (INITIAL 100k NEXT 100k PCTINCREASE 0);

-- Now, we are going to add a primary key constraint to the parent
-- table.
ALTER TABLE parent ADD
CONSTRAINT pk_parent
    PRIMARY KEY (parent_id)
USING INDEX
PCTFREE 10
TABLESPACE indexes
STORAGE (INITIAL 10k NEXT 10k);

CREATE TABLE child
OF child_type
(parent_id WITH ROWID SCOPE IS parent,
teacher WITH ROWID SCOPE IS parent)
OIDINDEX oid_child (TABLESPACE indexes)
TABLESPACE users
STORAGE (INITIAL 100k NEXT 100k PCTINCREASE 0);
```

There is a lot going on in Listing 8.9, but much of it is building on what you have already learned (and we will build even more on this example shortly). Let's dissect what this code is doing.

First, we drop the types and tables that we will be creating. This just makes the overall re-creation process much easier. Next, we create a forward type declaration for the CHILD_TYPE type, since we will need it to create the PARENT_TYPE type. Next, we create the parent type and then the child type. As before, each type has REFs (references) to each other (yes, we know, true evil nastiness).

Then we begin to create the object tables. The first thing you may be wondering about is the OIDINDEX clause that you see in both CREATE TABLE statements. The OIDINDEX clause will create an index on the OID of the tables. This is not unlike a regular index on a primary key. The OID index can significantly speed up REF queries between object tables. Since both tables will be referencing each other, both indexes will be helpful. If you had only one table with REFs, then you definitely would want an OID index on the table being referenced. In this case, an OID index on the other table—the one that has no references to it—would not be needed.

The parent table creation is a fairly straightforward operation that you have already seen in earlier examples. The child table creation is a bit different. Here, you see some new syntax in the form of:

```
(parent_id WITH ROWID SCOPE IS parent,
teacher WITH ROWID SCOPE IS parent)
```

What we are doing here is completing what we started. When we defined the PARENT_ID and TEACHER_ID attributes of the PARENT_TYPE type (in the CREATE TYPE statement), we used the REF clause to indicate that the PARENT_ID and TEACHER_ID attributes would reference row objects in some other object table. I'm sure that you were wondering just what that REF was going to be used for. Well, here is your answer. When we first created the REF, we didn't have an actual object to reference it to. Remember that types are just templates, and beyond that, they do not store anything. Thus, when you create a type, you don't need anything to reference an attribute to. Now that we have created the object tables (and thus allocated some storage to an instance of the PARENT_TYPE), we can define what object these REFs are referring to. In Listing 8.9, we have two different operations going on. This is known as *scoping* the REF.

Also notice in Listing 8.9 that we are storing the ROWID pseudocolumn with the OID of each row. Like scoping the REF to a specific table, this can speed up certain query activities. Neither of these actions is required, but taking them will reduce space requirements and can speed up access to the table being referenced.

Have you noticed that something is still missing? Think about it for a moment and see if you can figure out what it is. There is something we still have not done yet, and that leads us to the topic of altering object tables.

Altering Object Tables

After you create an object table, you may need to later alter the nature of that table. As you might guess, the ALTER TABLE statement is what you are looking for.

So, going back to the previous section, did you figure out what it was we still needed to do? What we have not done yet is to scope out the REFs for the parent table. This is because when we created the parent object table, we had not yet created the child table. After creating the child table, we can scope the circular references that are in the parent table, as well as set up the ROWID storage. We execute these operations in the last two ALTER TABLE statements, shown in Listing 8.10.

Listing 8.10: Altering Object Tables

```
-- This enables our circular reference from parent to child for
-- the parent table. This is the same as the "parent_id WITH
-- ROWID SCOPE IS parent" line in the CREATE TABLE statement
-- for the child table. Since the child table was not present
-- when we created the parent table, we could not do this yet.
-- Now that the child table has been created, we can create the
-- scoped REF.
ALTER TABLE parent ADD
(REF(child_name) WITH ROWID, REF(exch_student) WITH ROWID)
/

ALTER TABLE parent ADD
(SCOPE FOR (child_name) IS CHILD,
SCOPE FOR (exch_student) IS CHILD)
/
```

As you would expect, you can also use the ALTER TABLE statement to change a number of characteristics of an object table, just as you would a relational table. This includes STORAGE clauses, partitioning, and so on.

 NOTE One big difference between object tables and relational tables is that it is not possible to add a column to an object table. This is because an object table is wholly defined by a user-defined type.

Dropping Object Tables

Well, it doesn't get much simpler than this. You use the DROP TABLE clause to drop an object table:

```
DROP TABLE parent;
```

As you might expect, there are a couple of nasty potential results from dropping an object table. If you drop a parent table and leave a child table (or even vice-versa, as in our example), you can end up with dangling REFs—the orphaned table will have references to rows in a table that no longer exists. This can also occur if you drop parent rows but do not clean up the child records. This is bad news, but Oracle has provided a way to deal with this problem through the use of the ANALYZE command, using the VALIDATE REF UPDATE SET DANGLING TO NULL option. As explained in the "Introducing Row and Column Objects, OIDs, and REFs" section earlier in this chapter, this option will update all ROWIDs for REFs, and set dangling REFs to NULL.

Getting Information about Object Tables

There are a couple of data dictionary views that are useful for managing object tables. These include the DBA_OBJECT_TABLES view and the DBA_REFS data dictionary views.

The DBA_OBJECT_TABLES View

Do you want to see a listing of object tables? You won't find them in the DBA_TABLES view. You'll need to use the DBA_OBJECT_TABLES view, which provides information about the object table, such as the owner name, object table name, the tablespace name that the object table is assigned to, as well as the results of the ANALYZE process executed against that object table. Here is an example of a query against the DBA_OBJECT_TABLES view and its results:

```
SELECT owner, table_name, tablespace_name, initial_extent,
next_extent
FROM dba_object_tables
WHERE owner='SCOTT';
```

OWNER	TABLE_NAME	TABLESPACE_NAME	INITIAL_EXTENT	NEXT_EXTENT
SCOTT	CHILD	USERS	102400	102400
SCOTT	PARENT	USERS	102400	102400

NOTE Even though you won't find object tables in the DBA_TABLES view, you will find the columns of an object table in the DBA_TAB_COLUMNS view.

The DBA_REFS View

The DBA_REFS data dictionary view describes the REFs present in an attribute of an object type. This view describes the owner and object that contains the REF, as well as other information about the REF. Here is an example of a query against this data dictionary view and its results:

```
SELECT owner, table_name, column_name,is_scoped, scope_table_owner,
scope_table_name
FROM dba_refs
WHERE owner NOT LIKE '%SYS%';


OWNER      TABLE_NAME COLUMN_NAME      IS_ SCOPE_TABL SCOPE_TABLE_NA
---------- ---------- ---------------- --- ---------- --------------
SCOTT      CHILD      PARENT_ID        YES SCOTT      PARENT
SCOTT      CHILD      TEACHER          YES SCOTT      PARENT
SCOTT      PARENT     CHILD_NAME       NO
SCOTT      PARENT     EXCH_STUDENT     NO
```

Using Collection Types

If you have had any programming experience, you know what an *array* is. A collection is not unlike an array. A *collection* allows you to store one or more object types in a given row. In other words, with a collection type, you can denormalize a table, storing multiple related objects of information in a given row that is related to that information. The two collection types in Oracle are VARRAYs and nested tables. Each has its own distinguishing characteristics, but they are similar in nature.

Working with VARRAYs

A VARRAY (or varying array) is much like an array in a programming language such as C or BASIC. A VARRAY column allows you to store multiple values in the same allocated datatype. You can define a VARRAY as an attribute of a table or as a volatile element in a PL/SQL routine.

A VARRAY is an ordered set of data elements of the same type. Each element of a VARRAY contains an index. An index is a number that points to the order of the data element in the array. Because you need to define the boundaries of the array (or how many records it can store), the VARRAY is somewhat more limiting than its cousin, the nested table. Once created, the boundaries of the array cannot be redefined without dropping and re-creating the VARRAY object. A VARRAY cannot contain another collection type in its definition. Also, VARRAY types cannot store LOBs, while nested tables can. Finally, a VARRAY has a storage limit of 2GB. These restrictions obviously limit the effectiveness of the VARRAY collection type.

Just as you can store LOBs out of line in a given object to improve performance, you can also store VARRAYs out of line with the rest of the data in the object table. The associated LOB storage segment must be contained in the same tablespace as the object table. When you define the object that contains the VARRAY, you can force Oracle to store the data out of line with the DISABLE STORAGE IN ROW clause of the CREATE TABLE command.

The elements of a VARRAY must be packed, meaning that you need to start with index 0 for the first record, store the second in index 1, and so on. You cannot store record one in position two and record three in position four. This also implies that you cannot remove records from a VARRAY except from the uppermost used index.

Creating VARRAYs

To create a VARRAY, use the CREATE TYPE command, just as you would to create a user type. When creating a VARRAY, you must provide a type name for that array. The type name can be a built-in datatype (such as NUMBER or VARCHAR2), a REF, or an object type (such as ADDRESS_TYPE). Listing 8.11 provides an example of creating a VARRAY.

Listing 8.11: Creating a VARRAY

```
DROP TABLE parent;
DROP TYPE address_type FORCE;
DROP TYPE name_type FORCE;
DROP TYPE parent_type FORCE;

-- First, create the address_type type.
CREATE OR REPLACE TYPE address_type AS OBJECT (
Address_number         NUMBER,
Street_address_one     VARCHAR2(50),
Street_address_two     VARCHAR2(50),
City                   VARCHAR2(30),
```

```
    State               VARCHAR2(2),
    Zip_code            VARCHAR2(10) )
/

CREATE OR REPLACE TYPE address_varray AS VARRAY(5) OF address_type
/
-- Create the name_type type.
CREATE TYPE name_type AS OBJECT(
    First_name    VARCHAR2(30),
    Last_name     VARCHAR2(30),
    Middle_init   CHAR(1) )
/

-- Create the parent_type type.
CREATE TYPE parent_type AS OBJECT (
    Parent_id          NUMBER,
    Parent_name        name_type,
    Parent_address     address_varray
    )
/

-- Create the object table with the VARRAY.
CREATE TABLE parent OF parent_type (
PRIMARY KEY (parent_id)
USING INDEX TABLESPACE indexes
STORAGE (INITIAL 10k NEXT 10k PCTINCREASE 0) )
OBJECT ID PRIMARY KEY
VARRAY parent_address STORE AS LOB parent_address_varray
(DISABLE STORAGE IN ROW )
PCTFREE 10
PCTUSED 70
STORAGE (INITIAL 100k NEXT 100k PCTINCREASE 0);
```

In this example, we begin by dropping the table and types that we will be creating. This is so we get a fresh start with each creation. Next, we create the ADDRESS_TYPE type. Following that is the creation of the VARRAY type. Notice that when we create the VARRAY type, we are, again, just creating a type. There is still no storage associated with this type; it is just another type defined in the data dictionary. We proceed to create the other types (NAME_TYPE and PARENT_TYPE) that we will need in the object table to be created in this example.

Now comes the fun part—the actual creation of the object table that we call PARENT. The creation syntax is straightforward. First, we indicate that the parent object table will be of the type PARENT_TYPE. Next, we define the primary key for the object table to be the PARENT_ID column, and we use the USING INDEX clause to define the tablespace and storage characteristics of the primary key index, just as we would with a normal relational table. Next, we define the OID to be the primary key of the table. (Recall that the OID is a unique identifier for each row in the table.)

Following the definition of the primary key as the OID, we define the VARRAY that will be contained in this table, starting with this command:

```
VARRAY parent_address STORE AS LOB parent_address_varray;
```

The VARRAY is the attribute PARENT_ADDRESS in the type PARENT_TYPE. We are storing the VARRAY data as a LOB datatype, and the LOB segment that will be created is PARENT_ADDRESS_VARRAY. Note the use of the DISABLE STORAGE IN ROW clause, which is optional. This forces Oracle to store all of the data associated with the VARRAY out of line, in the LOB segment. If the DISABLE STORAGE IN ROW clause is not used, or the default ENABLE STORAGE IN ROW clause is used, then the first 4000 bytes of the data (more or less, depending on how finicky Oracle is feeling on a given day) will be stored in line. The remaining data will be stored out of line in the LOB segment.

Note that you can also create a VARRAY as a PL/SQL variable, as shown in this example:

```
CREATE OR REPLACE TYPE number_varray AS VARRAY(10) OF NUMBER;
```

Altering and Dropping VARRAYs

There isn't really anything to alter with regard to a VARRAY. If you need to make changes to the definition of a VARRAY, you will need to drop the type and re-create it. This implies that you will need to preserve your data before you make the change. If you created a VARRAY and then decide that it just isn't working out, you can drop the thing (in Nevada, there is no waiting period required). To drop a VARRAY, simply use the DROP TYPE command.

You can use the ALTER TABLE statement to modify some of the attributes of the actual VARRAY assigned to the table. This would include the LOB STORAGE clause (you can change the PCTVERSION and CHUNK parameters, for example). Here is an example of changing the PCTVERSION:

```
ALTER TABLE parent
MODIFY VARRAY parent_address
(PCTVERSION 20);
```

Note that once you have created or added a VARRAY, you cannot change the setting for storing rows in line.

Working with Nested Tables

The second cousin (once removed) to the VARRAY is the nested table. The nested table type has the same job as the VARRAY, which is to store repeating data for a single row. The primary differences between a nested table and a VARRAY are that a nested table is not bounded and that the elements of a nested table can be sparsely populated. If you have a nested table with three elements, you can remove the middle element without affecting the other elements.

The data in a nested table is stored out of line in an object that you define when you create the table with the nested table. The table created to store the nested table data is stored in the same tablespace as the table that the data is associated with, and this default cannot be changed.

Creating Nested Tables

When you create a nested table, you define a primary key index for the nested object, just as you would for any other table. You can also define the storage of the nested table as a hash table, which is the default, or as an index-organized table. As with VARRAYs, nested tables cannot contain other collection types; thus, a nested table type cannot contain a reference to another nested table.

Listing 8.12 shows an example of creating a nested table. This example makes the ADDRESS_TYPE type a nested table in the PARENT table (assume our parents have multiple homes).

Listing 8.12: Creating a Nested Table

```
DROP TYPE address_type FORCE;
DROP TYPE address_type_nt FORCE;
DROP TYPE name_type FORCE;
DROP TYPE parent_type FORCE;
DROP TABLE parent;

-- First, create the address_type type.
CREATE OR REPLACE TYPE address_type AS OBJECT (
Address_number          NUMBER,
Street_address_one      VARCHAR2(50),
Street_address_two      VARCHAR2(50),
City                    VARCHAR2(30),
```

```
   State                VARCHAR2(2),
   Zip_code             VARCHAR2(10) )
/

-- Now, create a nested table type.
CREATE TYPE address_type_nt AS TABLE OF address_type
/

-- Create the name_type type.

CREATE TYPE name_type AS OBJECT(
   First_name     VARCHAR2(30),
   Last_name      VARCHAR2(30),
   Middle_init    CHAR(1) )
/

-- Create the parent_type type.

CREATE TYPE parent_type AS OBJECT (
   Parent_id           NUMBER,
   Parent_name         name_type,
   Parent_address      address_type_nt
   )
/

-- Create the object table with the nested table.
CREATE TABLE parent OF parent_type (
PRIMARY KEY (parent_id)
USING INDEX TABLESPACE indexes
STORAGE (INITIAL 10k NEXT 10k PCTINCREASE 0) )
OBJECT ID PRIMARY KEY
NESTED TABLE parent_address STORE AS parent_address_nestab (
(PRIMARY KEY ( nested_table_id, address_number ) ) )
TABLESPACE users
PCTFREE 10
PCTUSED 70
STORAGE (INITIAL 100k NEXT 100k PCTINCREASE 0);
```

Altering and Dropping Nested Tables

Like VARRAYs, nested tables don't really have anything to alter, but you might consider using some ALTER TABLE options for active tables containing nested tables. You can use the ALTER TABLE statement to add a nested table to an existing table. You can also change the nested table so that it returns the locator value of the data in the nested table rather than the data contained in it. This is handy for situations where you might get a great deal of information from a query that includes a nested table. Since, by default, you would get all of the data in the nested table that met the criteria of the query, this could end up being a significant amount of data. By using the RETURN AS LOCATOR clause (and you can create the nested table to do this as well), Oracle will simply return a locator value that is a pointer to the rows that match the criteria of the query. You can use the Oracle Call Interface (OCI) interfaces or the package UTL_COLL_IS_LOCATOR to return the row detail using this value.

Listing 8.13 provides an example of an ALTER TABLE command that you might run against a relational table with a nested table in it. In this case, the example adds a nested table of type CHILD_TYPE to the parent table. This particular nested table will return a locator to any rows that are retrieved by a query, rather than the data itself.

Listing 8.13: Altering a Relational Table That Contains a Nested Table

```
-- Drop the type first.
DROP TYPE name_type FORCE;
DROP TYPE name_type_nt FORCE;
DROP TYPE child_type_nt FORCE;
DROP TYPE child_type FORCE;
DROP TABLE parent;

-- Create the name_type type.
CREATE TYPE name_type AS OBJECT(
    First_name      VARCHAR2(30),
    Last_name       VARCHAR2(30),
    Middle_init     CHAR(1) )
/

-- Make this a nested table.
CREATE TYPE name_type_nt AS TABLE OF name_type
/

-- Now, create the child_type.
CREATE OR REPLACE TYPE child_type AS OBJECT (
```

```
        Child_id        NUMBER,
        Child_name      name_type
    )
/
-- Now, create a nested table type.
CREATE TYPE child_type_nt AS TABLE OF child_type
/

CREATE TABLE parent (
    Parent_id           NUMBER PRIMARY KEY,
    Parent_name         name_type_nt
    )
NESTED TABLE parent_name STORE AS parent_name_nestab (
(PRIMARY KEY ( nested_table_id ) ) )
TABLESPACE users
PCTFREE 10
PCTUSED 70
STORAGE (INITIAL 100k NEXT 100k PCTINCREASE 0);

ALTER TABLE parent ADD (child_name child_type_nt)
NESTED TABLE child_name STORE AS parent_child_name_nestab
RETURN AS LOCATOR;
```

As noted earlier, this example only works on a relational table. Unfortunately, you cannot add columns to an object table.

Getting Information about Collection Types

If you want to know something about the collection types present in your database, the DBA_COLL_TYPES view is the place to go. This view will show you the name and owner of the collection type, what type of collection it is, and other useful information. The following is an example of a query against this DBA view and its results.

```
SELECT owner, type_name, coll_type,
elem_type_owner "EOwner",
elem_type_name "Ename"
FROM dba_coll_types
WHERE owner NOT LIKE '%SYS%';
```

OWNER	TYPE_NAME	COLL_TYP	EOwner	Ename
SCOTT	ADDRESS_TYPE_NT	TABLE	SCOTT	ADDRESS_TYPE
SCOTT	CHILD_TYPE_NT	TABLE	SCOTT	CHILD_TYPE
SCOTT	ADDRESS_VARRAY	VARYING ARRAY	SCOTT	ADDRESS_TYPE_2

Notice that it indicates the type of collection (nested tables are identified by the word TABLE and VARRAYs by the words VARYING ARRAY).

To generate a report on all the nested tables defined in your database, use the DBA_NESTED_TABLES view. Here is an example of a query against this view and its results:

```
SELECT owner, table_name, table_type_name, parent_table_column
FROM dba_nested_tables;
```

OWNER	TABLE_NAME	TABLE_TYPE_NAME	PARENT_TABLE_COLUMN
SCOTT	PARENT_NAME_NESTAB	NAME_TYPE_NT	PARENT_NAME
SCOTT	PARENT_CHILD_NAME_NESTAB	CHILD_TYPE_NT	CHILD_NAME

Notice that the name and owner of the nested table appear in the OWNER and TABLE_NAME columns (this is the name of the actual segment that is storing the table data). You also see the type name of the nested table, as shown in the CREATE TYPE OF TABLE statement, in the TABLE_TYPE_NAME column. In the PARENT_TABLE_COLUMN column, you find the name of the column that the nested table is assigned to.

Using Methods

Methods are PL/SQL or Java programs that are associated with user-defined types. In this chapter, we will stick to PL/SQL methods.

 NOTE This chapter includes some examples of using PL/SQL. For more information about PL/SQL, such as overloading PL/SQL methods, using the AUTHID clause to indicate if the user or creator's privileges should be used when executing a method, and other PL/SQL details, see Appendix F on the CD.

There are four types of methods that you can associate with any type that you create:

- Constructor methods
- Member methods (including static member methods)
- Map methods
- Order methods

To call a method, you use named decimal notation. In some cases, you can send parameters to a method; in other cases, you may create methods without any parameters. Constructor methods are created automatically. If you want to use the other types, you will need to create them.

Using Constructor Methods

A *constructor* is a PL/SQL function that is created automatically with the creation of any type or collection object. Constructors are used to insert data into user-defined datatypes and collection objects, as you will learn in the "Querying Object Types" section later in the chapter.

A constructor is named the same as the type that it is based on. Therefore, if a VARRAY or nested table is based on a type called ADDRESS_TYPE, the constructor is also called ADDRESS_TYPE. The constructor contains several parameters, one for each of the attributes of the type it is associated with, in the order that they were created. Thus, if the type the collection type was based on has three attributes, then the constructor will have three parameters.

Working with Member Methods

When creating a member method, you define the method when you issue the CREATE TYPE statement to create the user-defined type. Just as with other PL/SQL program units, you can define a member method to run with the rights of either the invoker or the creator. Use the AUTHID clause to indicate if the user or creator's privileges should be used when executing a method. As with a package, you define the method in the initial definition of the type. You then proceed to create the actual code for the method by using the CREATE TYPE BODY statement.

When you call an instance of a member method, the first parameter of that method is always called SELF. This parameter identifies the instance of the object within that object. SELF is bound automatically when you refer to an object in a method that was created (instantiated) in that method. If you want to pass the instance of an object to another method, or reference it in an argument to a function or procedure, you need to preface the instance of that object with the SELF keyword.

When using the CREATE TYPE statement to create a method, you can define two types of member methods: functions or procedures. The methods created can be defined as either static or member methods. A member method can have any number of parameters associated with it, and it can also be overloaded.

Static member methods were introduced in Oracle8i. This type of method is a derivative of the member method. It is associated and invoked with the object type, rather than an instance of that object. A static method, since it is associated with the type rather than any instance of that type, cannot refer to the attributes of the current object. If you create a static method, the PL/SQL procedures will not have a SELF parameter.

Creating Member Methods

To create a member method, use the CREATE OR REPLACE TYPE BODY command. In this command, you define the type and name of the member. If it is a function, you declare the value type to be returned. Following this is the body of a PL/SQL block of code. Listing 8.14 provides an example of the creation of a type that contains one method—a function that returns the name and phone number of the record selected—followed by the command to create the associated PL/SQL block.

Listing 8.14: Creating a Member Method

```
-- First, create the type.
CREATE OR REPLACE TYPE parent_type AS OBJECT
(
     first_name          VARCHAR2(30),
     last_name           VARCHAR2(30),
     middle_initial      CHAR(1),
     phone_number        VARCHAR2(20),
     last_contact        DATE,
     MEMBER FUNCTION name_and_phone RETURN VARCHAR2
)
/

-- Now, create the members.
CREATE OR REPLACE TYPE BODY parent_type AS
MEMBER FUNCTION name_and_phone RETURN VARCHAR2 IS
BEGIN
     RETURN(SELF.first_name||' '||SELF.last_name||' Phone:
     '||SELF.phone_number);
END name_and_phone;
END;
/
```

Listing 8.14 just creates a template of the user-defined object. What you need to do next is create an instance of it. Here is an example of creating the table and then inserting some records into it:

```
CREATE TABLE parent OF parent_type;

-- Insert a couple of records.
INSERT INTO parent VALUES
('Robert','Freeman','G','904.200.2020',to_date('01-JAN-01'));
INSERT INTO parent VALUES
('Deborah','Freeman','L','014.200.2020',to_date('01-MAY-01'));
```

Now you can use the NAME_AND_PHONE function, like this:

```
SELECT p.name_and_phone() FROM parent p;


P.NAME_AND_PHONE()
-----------------------------------------
Robert Freeman Phone: 904.200.2020
Deborah Freeman Phone: 904.200.2020
```

Notice that the method is called using the name of the object (or its alias, as in the case of the listing above) and then the name of the method.

You can also create and use a member method in PL/SQL, as demonstrated in the example in Listing 8.15.

Listing 8.15: Creating and Using a Method Instance in PL/SQL

```
DECLARE
V_output    VARCHAR2(60);
V_parent    parent_type := parent_type
('Robert','Freeman','G','904.200.2020',to_date('01-JAN-01'));
BEGIN
     V_output=v_parent.name_and_phone();
END;
/
```

Creating Static Member Methods

To define a static member method, use the keyword STATIC in both the header and the body of the code you are using to create the method. The method can refer to an object passed to it and to the attributes of a new object.

A static method can be used as an alternative to the default constructor method for a given type. Using a static method, you can create the constructor with a name other than the name of the object. Listing 8.16 provides an example of using a static method associated with an object type.

Listing 8.16: Creating a Static Member Method

```
DROP TYPE parent_type FORCE;

-- First, create the type.
CREATE OR REPLACE TYPE parent_type AS OBJECT
(
    first_name          VARCHAR2(30),
    last_name           VARCHAR2(30),
    middle_initial      CHAR(1),
    phone_number        VARCHAR2(20),
    last_contact        DATE,
    STATIC PROCEDURE my_static_procedure (p_var1 IN VARCHAR2)
)
/

-- Now, create the members.
CREATE OR REPLACE TYPE BODY parent_type AS
STATIC PROCEDURE my_static_procedure
(p_var1      IN      VARCHAR2)
IS
BEGIN
    Dbms_output.enable(1000);
    Dbms_output.put_line(p_var1||' Passed into the static Procedure');
END my_static_procedure;
END;
/
```

Here is an example of using the static procedure:

```
SQL> SET SERVEROUTPUT ON
SQL> EXEC parent_type.my_static_procedure('This is a test of the
     procedure!');

This is a test of the procedure! Passed into the static Procedure!
```

Creating Map and Order Methods

Map and order methods are used to facilitate ordering and grouping of attributes in an object. By default, Oracle supports comparisons of values within an instance of an object (not the comparison within an instance of an object) only if those comparisons are equality or inequality based. A type can have only one order or map method, so they are mutually exclusive.

Both map and order methods use the SELF parameter. A map method returns a VARCHAR2 value and requires no other parameters. An order method takes one other parameter, which represents the value being compared to the current record. The order method will then return one of three values:

- –1 when the value of SELF is less than the input parameter
- 0 when the value of SELF is equal to that of the input parameter
- 1 when the value of SELF is more than that of the input parameter

Listing 8.17 provides examples of creating map and order methods for a type.

NOTE In Oracle8i, you will find that ordering within an instance of a type works just fine, without a map or order method.

Listing 8.17: Creating a Map and Order Method

```
-- First, create the type.
CREATE OR REPLACE TYPE parent_type AS OBJECT
(
        first_name         VARCHAR2(30),
        last_name          VARCHAR2(30),
        middle_initial     CHAR(1),
        phone_number       VARCHAR2(20),
        last_contact       DATE,
        MAP MEMBER FUNCTION parent_map RETURN VARCHAR2
)
/

-- Now, create the map method.
CREATE OR REPLACE TYPE BODY parent_type AS
MAP MEMBER FUNCTION parent_map RETURN VARCHAR2 IS
BEGIN
```

```
            Return(SELF.first_name||' '||SELF.last_name);
END;
END;
/

DROP TYPE parent_type FORCE;

-- First, re-create the type for the order method.
CREATE OR REPLACE TYPE parent_type AS OBJECT
(
      first_name          VARCHAR2(30),
      last_name           VARCHAR2(30),
      middle_initial      CHAR(1),
      phone_number        VARCHAR2(20),
      last_contact        DATE,
      ORDER MEMBER FUNCTION parent_order (OTHER parent_type)
          RETURN NUMBER
)
/

-- Now, create the order method.
CREATE OR REPLACE TYPE BODY parent_type AS
ORDER MEMBER FUNCTION parent_order (other parent_type)
RETURN NUMBER IS
   My_name    VARCHAR2(2000):=
   self.last_name||self.first_name||self.middle_initial;
   compare_name    VARCHAR2(2000):=
   other.last_name||other.first_name||other.middle_initial;
BEGIN
     IF my_name < compare_name
     THEN
         RETURN -1;
     ELSIF my_name < compare_name
     THEN
         RETURN 1;
     ELSE
         RETURN 0;
     END IF;
END;
```

```
END;
/
```

Getting Information about Methods

There are a few data dictionary tables that you can use to gather information about methods (each of these views has a related ALL_ and USER_ version):

- The DBA_METHOD_PARAMS view provides the parameters required for all methods in the database.
- The DBA_METHOD_RESULTS view describes the method results from all methods in the database.
- The DBA_TYPE_METHODS view describes all methods associated with all types in the database.

Querying Object Types

Now that you have created all sorts of objects with types, collections, methods, and so on, you will want to know how to use DML to add data to these structures. This section is all about how to do that.

Using INSERT Statements

The INSERT SQL required for dealing with types and collection objects is somewhat different than that for dealing with tables that just contain columns. To insert values into a collection type, you need to use the constructor of the type on which the collection type is based. (Constructors were described earlier in the chapter, in the "Using Constructor Methods" section.)

For example, here is the code to create a row in a table that contains a collection type, using the VARRAY in the object table created in Listing 8.11.

```
INSERT INTO parent (parent_id, parent_name, parent_address) VALUES
(1,
name_type('Robert','Freeman','G'),
(address_varray(
address_type(1,'550 Water St.',NULL,'Jax','Fl','32202'),
address_type(2,'500 Water St.',NULL,'Jax','Fl','32202') ) ) );
```

The INSERT statement starts like any other INSERT statement. It lists the table that you are inserting into, and then uses the VALUES clause. (You can list each column in parentheses, if you prefer that style.) Next, start listing the values to insert, all enclosed in parentheses, just as with a normal INSERT statement. First, insert the value for the PARENT_ID table, which is a NUMBER type. That value is 1.

Next comes the INSERT INTO statement for the PARENT_NAME attribute, which is of type NAME_TYPE. The NAME_TYPE type consists of three attributes. When you created the NAME_TYPE type, a constructor was automatically created, just as when you created ADDRESS_VARRAY. Use the constructor NAME_TYPE() to insert the new values into the instance of that type, contained in the PARENT table. The instance of NAME_TYPE in the PARENT table is PARENT_NAME. Since the type NAME_TYPE has three attributes, the constructor takes three parameters, one for each attribute. For quick reference, here is the definition of NAME_TYPE:

```
First_name    VARCHAR2(30)
Last_name     VARCHAR2(30)
Middle_init   CHAR(1)
```

And here is the part of the INSERT statement that is using the constructor to insert values into the PARENT_NAME attribute, which is of type NAME_TYPE:

```
name_type('Robert','Freeman','G'),
```

Can you see how it works then? The 'Robert' will be stored in the FIRST_NAME attribute, the 'Freeman' will be stored in the LAST_NAME attribute, and the middle initial 'G' will be stored in the MIDDLE_INIT attribute.

Adding the multidimensional VARRAY or the nested table to the mix makes this slightly more complicated, because you now need to provide for multiple rows of data for one column in one INSERT operation. If you have ever tried to insert more data than columns, no doubt you have noticed that Oracle traditionally frowns on such an action. This is not the case with collection types such as VARRAYs. Here are the lines that create the rows in the VARRAY (recall that the attribute that is the VARRAY is called PARENT_ADDRESS on the object table):

```
address_varray(
address_type(1,'550 Water St.',NULL,'Jax','Fl','32202'),
address_type(2,'500 Water St.',NULL,'Jax','Fl','32202') ) )
```

Notice that there are references to two collection types here. First, the ADDRESS_VARRAY constructor is what allows you to do multiple inserts into the VARRAY using one INSERT statement. When the VARRAY type is created, this constructor is created for just that purpose. Next, the ADDRESS_TYPE constructor, which was created when you created the ADDRESS_TYPE type, is referenced twice. This constructor allows you to insert actual values into the instance of the type that you created when you created the PARENT table.

The INSERT INTO statement for the nested table is just like the INSERT INTO statement for the VARRAY, except that the type names change (this next INSERT is based on the objects created in Listing 8.12):

```
INSERT INTO parent (parent_id, parent_name, parent_address) VALUES
(2,
name_type('Debbie','Freeman','L'),
(address_type_nt(
address_type(1,'0293 Gonzo Way',NULL,'Jax','Fl','32202'),
address_type(2,'500 Water St.',NULL,'Jax','Fl','32202') ) ) );
```

These examples illustrate that there is a hierarchy of sorts when you are inserting into objects that contain types. Consider this when you are constructing DML statements to interact with objects that contain various types. The hierarchy starts from the base type on which the attribute that you want to modify depends. You then move up through the hierarchical stages using each collector of that type, until you reach the attribute into which you want to insert.

Using UPDATE Statements

Now that you know how to insert into collection types, you'll want to know how to update these same structures. In this section, we will look at updating type columns in object tables, which will include a review of the PL/SQL built-in functions to access VARRAYs (which cannot be accessed from SQL directly) and nested tables.

Updating Types

Updating types in object tables is fairly easy. Again, just use named decimal notation, and you have it. Here is an example of updating a type in an object table:

```
UPDATE parent p SET p.parent_name.last_name='Freeman'
WHERE p.parent_name.last_name='FREEMAN';
```

Updating VARRAYs

One of the disadvantages of using VARRAYs is that SQL does not allow piece updates for them. You can UPDATE an entire table row, however, as in this example:

```
UPDATE parent
SET parent_address=
Address_varray(
    address_type(1,'550 Water St.',NULL,'Jax','Fl','32202')
    )
WHERE parent_id=2;
```

Note some odd behavior here though. If PARENT_ID is not truly unique when you execute this statement, and you had two rows with PARENT_ID=2 before you executed the statement, you will end up with only one row after the UPDATE. Thus, when you are updating a VARRAY type, you are really replacing the entire row rather than updating the VARRAY.

If you want to update individual elements of a VARRAY, you will need to use PL/SQL to do this. In PL/SQL, Oracle provides several methods (known as static methods) that allow you to traverse each index element of the VARRAY. Table 8.1 provides a list of the methods supported for VARRAYs in Oracle8i.

TABLE 8.1: VARRAY ACCESS METHODS SUPPORTED IN PL/SQL

Method	Description
COUNT	Returns the number of elements in the collection
DELETE	Causes the removal of one, all, or a given range of elements in a VARRAY
EXISTS	Returns TRUE if the element exists
EXTEND	Adds a given number of elements to the VARRAY
FIRST	Returns the first index in the VARRAY
LAST	Returns the last index in the VARRAY
LIMIT	Returns the maximum number of elements in the VARRAY
NEXT	Returns the next index number in the VARRAY
PRIOR	Returns the previous index number
TRIM	Removes one or more elements from a collection

Listing 8.18 provides a sample piece of PL/SQL that adds an element to a VARRAY and updates an existing record.

Listing 8.18: Maintaining a VARRAY with PL/SQL

```
DECLARE
     V_address_varray        address_varray;
BEGIN
     SELECT parent_address
     INTO v_address_varray
     FROM parent
     WHERE parent_id=1;
     -- Add to the VARRAY.
     v_address_varray.EXTEND;
```

```
                v_address_varray(v_address_varray.LAST):=
                    address_type(2,
                    '2145 W. Oak', NULL,
                    'Seattle','Wa','98042');
                -- Now, we are going to update the first element.
                v_address_varray(1).street_address_one:='Somewhere';
                v_address_varray(1).zip_code:='00000';
                -- Now, update the object itself
                UPDATE parent SET parent_address=v_address_varray
                WHERE parent_id=1;
            END;
            /
            COMMIT;
```

Notice that the code in Listing 8.18 reads the VARRAY into a PL/SQL variable. You can then manipulate the VARRAY element in memory with the various access methods supplied by Oracle. Finally, once you have made the necessary changes, you can update the entire VARRAY, since this is the only way that SQL supports changing VARRAYs in Oracle.

Updating Nested Tables

Updating nested tables is much easier than updating VARRAYs. This is because Oracle supports direct updates of each element of a nested table. By using the TABLE expression to locate the specific record (or records) in the object table you want to manipulate, you can change individual columns in the nested table, as in this example:

```
UPDATE table
(SELECT parent_address FROM parent WHERE parent_id=2)
SET street_address_one='500 Water St.'
WHERE address_number=1;
```

Using SELECT Statements

Selecting objects and collections from SQL is, as you might expect, a bit different. This section describes these differences and how to properly issue SELECT statements against these different object types.

Selecting from Types

As with updating a type, selecting a type is fairly straightforward. You simply use named decimal notation to indicate the attribute to update, as in this example:

```
SELECT parent_id, s.parent_name.last_name,
```

```
s.parent_name.first_name
FROM parent s
WHERE parent_id=1;


 PARENT_ID PARENT_NAME.LAST_NAME            PARENT_NAME.FIRST_NAME
 ---------- -------------------------------- ------------------------
         1 ROBERT                           FREEMAN
```

This SELECT statement prints the value of the LAST_NAME column of the PARENT_NAME type that is associated with PARENT_ID column value 1. In the SELECT statement, the column is referenced as S.PARENT_NAME.LAST_NAME, using named decimal notation. You are saying that you want the LAST_NAME attribute in the PARENT_NAME type. The S in the notation is an interesting (and odd, we think) requirement of SQL. The S is an alias for the parent table. You must alias the table and use that alias in the reference to the type attributes you wish to display. If you do not, you will get an Oracle error. For example, the following statements will fail in Oracle8i:

```
SELECT parent_id, parent_name.last_name,
parent_name.first_name
FROM parent
WHERE parent_id=1;

SELECT parent_id, parent.parent_name.last_name,
parent.parent_name.first_name
FROM parent
WHERE parent_id=1;
```

Selecting from Collection Objects

To extract values from nested tables and VARRAYs, you can use what is called the *unnesting syntax* in SELECT statements. This is also known as *declustering tables*. This syntax allows you to derive specific values from a collection object when issuing a SELECT statement, because it causes the table to appear as a flattened, relational form.

Unnesting Queries

The TABLE clause is central to the unnesting syntax. This clause is used to define which collection object you are unnesting and allows you to use the attributes of that object directly in the SELECT statement.

NOTE The TABLE syntax was introduced in Oracle8i, and it supersedes the THE keyword that was available in Oracle8 (although THE is still available for backward compatibility).

The following is an example of an unnesting query and the resulting rows from that query.

```sql
SELECT a.parent_id "Parent_ID",
a.parent_name.first_name "First_Name",
a.parent_name.last_name "Last_Name",
b.street_address_one "Address",
b.city "City",
b.state "State",
b.zip_code "Zip"
FROM parent a, TABLE(a.parent_address) (+) b;
```

```
Parent_ID First_Nam Last_Name Address          City  St Zip
--------- --------- --------- ---------------- ----- -- -----
        1 FREEMAN   ROBERT    550 Water St.    Jax   Fl 32202
        1 FREEMAN   ROBERT    500 Water St.    Jax   Fl 32202
        2 FREEMAN   ROBERT    550 Water St.    Jax   Fl 32202
        2 FREEMAN   ROBERT    500 Water St.    Jax   Fl 32202
        3
```

Notice how the two rows in the parent table have now been exploded into four rows. This is because there were two records in each row in the PARENT_ADDRESS VARRAY. Also, did you notice the outer join syntax (+)? This allows you to also get the row for PARENT_ID 3, which has no record in the PARENT_ADDRESS collection type. If you do not include the outer join syntax, the query result will not include the row with PARENT_ID 3.

The following example shows a larger query in the TABLE clause. (Note that the output from this query has been modified slightly to fit the page.)

```sql
SELECT a.parent_id, b.* FROM
parent a,
TABLE(SELECT t.parent_address
      FROM parent t
      WHERE t.parent_id=1) b
WHERE a.parent_id=1;
```

```
PARENT_ID  ADDRESS_NUMBER STREET_ADD_ONE   STREET_ADD CITY ST ZIP_CODE
---------  -------------- ---------------- ---------- ---- -- --------
        1               1 550 Water St.               Jax  Fl 32202
        1               2 500 Water St.               Jax  Fl 32202
```

This query essentially moves the listing of the attributes of the collection into the TABLE clause.

Nested Cursors

Another option for SELECT statements for collection objects is to use the CURSOR function. This is known as a *nested cursor*. A nested cursor is opened as you begin the fetch in the SELECT statement. Thus, the nested cursor is always directly related to the row that holds the parent cursor. Here is an example:

```
SELECT a.parent_id,
CURSOR(SELECT * FROM table(a.parent_address) )
FROM parent a
WHERE parent_id=1;


PARENT_ID  CURSOR(SELECT*FROMTA
---------- --------------------
         1 CURSOR STATEMENT : 2

CURSOR STATEMENT : 2

ADDRESS_NUMBER STREET_ADDRESS_ONE   STREET_ADD CITY ST ZIP_CODE
-------------- -------------------- ---------- ---- -- --------
             1 550 Water St.                   Jax  Fl 32202
             2 500 Water St.                   Jax  Fl 32202
```

Simple SELECT Queries

You can also just issue SELECT * queries from tables with collection types, or you can use the VALUE function in the SELECT statement to return the object instances that are stored in the object you are querying. Here is an example of a SELECT VALUE query and its result:

```
SELECT VALUE(p) FROM parent p;

VALUE(P)(PARENT_ID, PARENT_NAME(FIRST_NAME, LAST_NAME, MIDDLE_INI
-----------------------------------------------------------------
PARENT_TYPE(1, NAME_TYPE('FREEMAN', 'ROBERT', 'G'), ADDRESS_VARRAY
(ADDRESS_TYPE(1, '550 Water St.', NULL, 'Jax', 'Fl', '32202'),
ADDRESS_TYPE(2, '500 Water St.', NULL, 'Jax', 'Fl', '32202')))

PARENT_TYPE(2, NAME_TYPE('FREEMAN', 'ROBERT', 'G'), ADDRESS_VARRAY
(ADDRESS_TYPE(3, '550 Water St.', NULL, 'Jax', 'Fl', '32202'),
ADDRESS_TYPE(4, '500 Water St.', NULL, 'Jax', 'Fl', '32202')))
```

Creating Object Views

After you've created an object table or two, you might want to create views for them, just as you do with relational tables. To do this, you simply use the CREATE VIEW command and other normal SQL statements, just as you would to create a view for a relational table. Listing 8.19 provides an example of the creation and use of such a view (and some of the groundwork for later examples of views).

Listing 8.19: Creating an Object View

```
DROP TABLE child;
DROP TABLE parent;
DROP TYPE parent_type FORCE;
DROP TYPE child_type FORCE;
DROP TYPE address_type FORCE;
DROP TYPE name_type FORCE;

CREATE TYPE name_type AS OBJECT (
    First_name      VARCHAR2(30),
    Last_name       VARCHAR2(30),
    Middle_init     CHAR(1) )
/

CREATE OR REPLACE TYPE address_type AS OBJECT (
    Street_address_one      VARCHAR2(50),
    Street_address_two      VARCHAR2(50),
    City                    VARCHAR2(30),
    State                   VARCHAR2(2),
    Zip_code                VARCHAR2(10) )
/

-- Create our forward type declaration for the child_type type
-- so we can create the parent_type type.
CREATE OR REPLACE TYPE child_type AS OBJECT (
    Parent_id       NUMBER,
    Child_id        NUMBER,
    Child_name      name_type,
    Child_address   address_type)
/
```

```
-- Create the parent_type type.
-- Note the two REFs to the child_type.
CREATE OR REPLACE TYPE parent_type AS OBJECT (
   Parent_id        NUMBER,
   Parent_name      name_type,
   Parent_address   address_type)
/

-- Now, create the parent table. We will use an OID index for this
-- table. This is generally required for the main table in a
-- parent/child relationship. The OIDINDEX clause will help speed up
-- REF lookups between this and the child table.
CREATE TABLE parent
OF parent_type
OIDINDEX idx_parent (tablespace indexes)
TABLESPACE users
PCTFREE 10
PCTUSED 70
STORAGE (INITIAL 100k NEXT 100k PCTINCREASE 0);

-- Now, we are going to add a primary key constraint to the
-- parent table.
ALTER TABLE parent ADD
CONSTRAINT pk_parent
     PRIMARY KEY (parent_id)
USING INDEX
PCTFREE 10
TABLESPACE indexes
STORAGE (INITIAL 10k NEXT 10k);

CREATE TABLE child
OF child_type
OIDINDEX oid_child (tablespace indexes)
TABLESPACE users
STORAGE (INITIAL 100k NEXT 100k PCTINCREASE 0);

ALTER TABLE child ADD
CONSTRAINT pk_child
     PRIMARY KEY (parent_id, child_id)
```

```sql
USING INDEX
PCTFREE 10
TABLESPACE indexes
STORAGE (INITIAL 10k NEXT 10k);

-- Insert some records.
INSERT INTO parent (parent_id, parent_name, parent_address) VALUES
(1,
name_type('Debbie','Freeman','L'),
address_type('0293 Gonzo Way',NULL,'Jax','Fl','32202') );

INSERT INTO parent (parent_id, parent_name, parent_address) VALUES
(2,
name_type('Pack','Charles',NULL),
address_type('2340 Somewhere Place',NULL,'Jax','Fl','22222') );

COMMIT;

INSERT INTO child(parent_id, child_id, child_name) VALUES
(1,1,name_type('J', 'Freeman','R') );

INSERT INTO child(parent_id, child_id, child_name) VALUES
(1,2,name_type('S', 'Freeman','K') );

INSERT INTO child(parent_id, child_id, child_name) VALUES
(1,3,name_type('F', 'Freeman','R') );

INSERT INTO child(parent_id, child_id, child_name) VALUES
(1,4,name_type('J', 'Freeman','R') );

INSERT INTO child(parent_id, child_id, child_name) VALUES
(1,5,name_type('E', 'Freeman','R') );

INSERT INTO child(parent_id, child_id, child_name) VALUES
(2,1,name_type('Peanut', 'Pack','R') );

-- Create the object view.
CREATE VIEW v_obj_parent
OF parent_type AS
SELECT * FROM parent;
```

Creating Joined Object Views

If you wish to create a complex object view that contains a join of one or more object tables (or even relational tables), you need to use the special clause WITH OBJECT IDENTIFIER in the CREATE VIEW command. Listing 8.20 provides an example of such a case.

NOTE If you used objects in Oracle8, you may be used to the term WITH OBJECT OID. This has been deprecated in favor of the WITH OBJECT IDENTIFIER clause.

Listing 8.20: Creating a Joined Object View
```
DROP TYPE t_parent_child FORCE;

-- Create the type that represents the view.
CREATE OR REPLACE TYPE t_parent_child  AS OBJECT
(
      parent_id               NUMBER,
      parent_name             name_type,
      address_info            address_type,
      child_id                NUMBER,
      child_name              name_type )
/

-- Now, create the view.
CREATE OR REPLACE VIEW v_parent_child
OF t_parent_child
WITH OBJECT IDENTIFIER (parent_id) AS
SELECT a.parent_id, a.parent_name, a.parent_address,
b.child_id, b.child_name
FROM parent a, child b
WHERE a.parent_id=b.parent_id
ORDER BY a.parent_id, b.child_id;
```

Creating Object Views on Relational Tables

As you begin to make the transition to an object-based design philosophy from a relational one, or if you are working with languages such as C++ that use object-oriented concepts, you may want some of the existing relational tables in your database to look like object tables. Oracle has read your mind and provided an *object view* for you to use in these cases. An object view will allow you to query a relational table as if it were an object table.

Object views are created with the CREATE OR REPLACE VIEW command. To create the view, you define a type that has attributes that are the same as the columns of the table that you wish to appear like an object type. Then you can use the CREATE OR REPLACE VIEW command to create the object view, as shown in Listing 8.21.

Listing 8.21: Creating an Object View on a Relational Table

```
-- Create a type that will represent the view.
DROP TYPE t_parent_1 FORCE;

CREATE OR REPLACE TYPE t_parent_1 AS OBJECT
(
    parent_id            NUMBER,
    parent_last_name     VARCHAR2(30),
    parent_first_name    VARCHAR2(30),
    street_address       VARCHAR2(50),
    city                 VARCHAR2(30),
    state                VARCHAR2(2),
    zip                  VARCHAR2(10) )
/

-- Now, create the view syntax.
CREATE OR REPLACE VIEW v_parent_1
OF t_parent_1 AS
SELECT a.parent_id, a.parent_name.last_name, a.parent_name.first_name,
a.parent_address.street_address_one,
a.parent_address.city, a.parent_address.state,
a.parent_address.zip_code
FROM parent a
ORDER BY a.parent_id;
```

You may also want to join object tables to create a join view. Heck, you may even want to add in a relational table. Listing 8.22 provides an example of this type of view. Note the use of the WITH OBJECT IDENTIFIER again.

NOTE We assume for this example that the structures created in Listing 8.11 are still around. If not, re-create the parent and child tables from that exercise before using the code in Listing 8.22.

Listing 8.22: Creating a View with Both a Relational and Object Table

```
-- Create a type that will represent the view.
CREATE TABLE placement_date
(
     parent_id         NUMBER,
     child_id          NUMBER,
     placement_date    DATE
);

INSERT INTO placement_date VALUES (1,1,SYSDATE);
INSERT INTO placement_date VALUES (1,2,SYSDATE);
INSERT INTO placement_date VALUES (1,3,SYSDATE);
INSERT INTO placement_date VALUES (1,4,SYSDATE);
INSERT INTO placement_date VALUES (1,5,SYSDATE);
INSERT INTO placement_date VALUES (2,1,SYSDATE);

CREATE OR REPLACE TYPE t_parent_child_2   AS OBJECT
(
     parent_id              NUMBER,
     parent_last_name       VARCHAR2(30),
     parent_first_name      VARCHAR2(30),
     street_address         VARCHAR2(50),
     city                   VARCHAR2(30),
     state                  VARCHAR2(2),
     zip                    VARCHAR2(10),
     child_id               NUMBER,
     child_last_name        VARCHAR2(30),
     child_first_name       VARCHAR2(30),
     placement_date         DATE )
/

-- Now, create the view syntax.
CREATE VIEW v_parent_child_2
```

```
     OF t_parent_child_2
     WITH OBJECT IDENTIFIER (parent_id) AS
     SELECT a.parent_id, a.parent_name.last_name, a.parent_name.first_name,
     a.parent_address.street_address_one,
     a.parent_address.city, a.parent_address.state,
     a.parent_address.zip_code, b.child_id,
     b.child_name.last_name, b.child_name.first_name, c.placement_date
     FROM parent a, child b, placement_date c
     WHERE a.parent_id=b.parent_id
     AND a.parent_id=c.parent_id
     AND b.child_id=c.child_id
     ORDER BY a.parent_id, b.child_id;
```

Creating Relational Views on Object Tables

Just as you may want to create object views to look at relational tables as object tables, you might want to create relational views to deconstruct object tables to make them look like relational tables. Again, you use the CREATE OR REPLACE VIEW command to do this. But first, use the CREATE TYPE command to create the type to represent the object structure that you want the relational data displayed in. When you create the view, you almost cast the columns in the table to the columns of the type they will be associated with. What you are doing is using the constructor of the type to put the values into the proper format. When the view executes, these columns are then represented in the same format that they would have if they had been in an actual object. Listing 8.23 provides an example of this type of operation.

Listing 8.23: Creating an Object View on a Relational Table

```
DROP TYPE my_name_type FORCE;
DROP TABLE my_name;

-- Create the relational table.
CREATE TABLE my_name
  (Name_id          NUMBER,
   first_name       VARCHAR2(30),
   last_name        VARCHAR2(30),
   middle_initial   VARCHAR2(1)
);

INSERT INTO my_name VALUES (1, 'Robert','FREEMAN','G');
```

```sql
-- Now, create the type to display the name value in.
CREATE TYPE my_name_type AS OBJECT
( first_name       VARCHAR2(30),
  last_name        VARCHAR2(30),
  middle_initial   VARCHAR2(1)
)
/

-- Now, create the object view.
-- Note how we "cast" the first_name, last_name and middle_initial
-- columns to the my_name_type in the view definition. We are using
-- the my_name_type constructor to present the columns in object
-- format.
CREATE OR REPLACE VIEW obj_v_my_name
( name_id, my_name_type)
AS
SELECT name_id, my_name_type(first_name, last_name, middle_initial)
FROM my_name;
```

When you query the view, it looks like an object view:

```
SQL> SELECT * FROM obj_v_my_name;

   NAME_ID
----------
MY_NAME_TYPE(FIRST_NAME, LAST_NAME, MIDDLE_INITIAL)
---------------------------------------------------
         1
MY_NAME_TYPE('Robert', 'FREEMAN', 'G')
```

As you can see from this chapter, Oracle's implementation of objects is a robust and powerful option in Oracle8i. Objects are being used more often in new database designs, and DBAs must become familiar with the benefits, use, and management of object-oriented features in an Oracle database.

CHAPTER 9

Oracle Networking

Introducing Net8	390
Configuring Net8	394
Using Oracle's multithreaded server (MTS) option	407
Using Oracle Names	411
Introducing Oracle Connection Manager	419
Introducing the Advanced Security Option	420

Oracle's networking services are provided through Net8. With Net8 installed and properly configured, clients and servers can connect to remote databases. This chapter begins with an introduction to Net8, and then explains how to configure Net8 on servers and clients. You'll also learn how to configure Oracle 8i's multithreaded server (MTS) feature, as well as the Oracle Names directory service. Finally, you'll get an overview of two other Oracle network-related tools: Oracle Connection Manager and the Advanced Security Option.

Introducing Net8

In a *distributed computing environment,* client processes are separated from shared services across a network of logically and physically separated hosts. Net8 enables client/server and server/server database communication in a distributed computing environment. Net8 was introduced with Oracle 8 as the next generation of SQL*Net and is backward compatible with SQL*Net version 2.

Before you configure Net8, you should understand how it makes connections, which protocols it supports, how it uses service names, and how it resolves those names. These topics are covered in the following sections.

Net8 Client/Server Connections

A connection to an Oracle service from a client application is made using a connect string that includes the username, password, and connect identifier. The following example illustrates a connect string with the username robin, the password princess, and the connect identifier toffee.

```
connect robin/princess@toffee
```

The connect identifier maps to a network (net) service name through a known naming method. The net service name resolves to a connect descriptor that tells Net8 how to establish the connection to the Oracle service. The connect descriptor includes information about the network route to the service, including the location of the listener through a protocol address, and the service name, usually the global database name (composed of the database and database domain names). Once the Net8 client knows how to handle the connection request, it will forward the request to the listener address identified by the connect descriptor.

The Net8 listener receives the connection request on the server and processes the connection request, first by verifying the requested service, and then by spawning a server process or using a pre-spawned server process to enable communication between the client application and the Oracle instance. After passing a client connection request to a server process, the listener continues to monitor for new connection requests.

Protocols Supported by Net8

The Transparent Network Substrate (TNS) is the foundation of Net8 that provides transparent database communication across several industry-standard protocols. Net8 supports six client/server protocols, as well as a native process protocol:

TCP/IP (Transmission Control Protocol/Internet Protocol)
This is the most common protocol used for client/server communication over a network. Net8's support of TCP/IP enables an Oracle client to communicate with an Oracle service over a TCP/IP network.

TCP/IP with SSL SSL (Secure Sockets Layer) is the industry-standard protocol designed by Netscape Communications Corporation for securing network connections. SSL provides authentication, encryption, and data integrity by using public key infrastructure (PKI).

SPX (Sequenced Packet Exchange) This protocol is predominantly used in Novell NetWare environments.

Named pipes This is a high-level interface protocol that provides interprocess communication between distributed applications. Net8 support of the named pipes protocol allows an Oracle client to communicate with an Oracle service over a named pipes network.

LU6.2 (Logical Unit Type 6.2) This protocol is part of the IBM Advanced Program-to-Program Communication (APPC) architecture. APPC is the IBM peer-to-peer protocol for an SNA (System Network Architecture) network. Net8 support of LU6.2 allows an Oracle client on a PC to communicate over an SNA network with an Oracle service residing on a host that supports APPC.

Bequeath This protocol works if the client and instance reside on the same host. The listener will spawn a dedicated server process that allows the client to communicate directly with the instance without going through the listener.

IPC (Inter-Process Communication) This protocol does not support client/server communications. It supports communication between processes native to the Oracle server.

Service Names

Prior to Net8, communication was established referencing the Oracle system identifier (SID). With Net8, the connection is established using a service name. A *service name* is a logical representation of one or more Oracle instances.

Service names are always defined at the instance level. A single instance can be identified by one or more service names, and a service name can represent one or more Oracle instances.

You can identify the service names for an Oracle instance by querying the value of the SERVICE_NAMES parameter from the V$PARAMETER view, as in this example:

```
SQL> SELECT name, value
  2  FROM v$parameter
  3  WHERE name = 'service_names';

NAME                  VALUE
--------------------  --------------------
service_names         toffee.cafecandy.com
```

The default service name for any instance is the global database name, which is the fully qualified name that uniquely identifies a single instance from any other instance on your network. The default global database name is represented in the form of *database_name.database_domain*, such as toffee.world, where toffee is the database name and world is the domain name.

Any user can identify the global database name with the following query:

```
SQL> SELECT * FROM global_name;

GLOBAL_NAME
-----------
TOFFEE.WORLD
```

The global database name is specified at the time of database creation by the values of DB_NAME and DB_DOMAIN in the database parameter file (`init.ora`). If DB_DOMAIN is not specified, the default domain name for an Oracle instance is world, as in toffee.world.

NOTE Changing the values of DB_NAME or DB_DOMAIN after database creation will not change the global database name. To change the global database name after database creation, issue the DDL statement SQL> ALTER DATABASE RENAME GLOBAL_NAME TO *newname*.

You may optionally specify the service name of an Oracle instance by setting the SERVICE_NAMES parameter in the `init.ora` file. I recommend setting the service name in this manner as good practice, to eliminate guesswork. The following example illustrates setting the service name of an Oracle instance. In this example, two service names are specified for a single instance.

```
service_names = toffee.cafecandy.com, orange.cafecandy.com
```

Naming Methods

The Net8 client resolves net service names through one of five known naming methods:

Local naming   Local naming is specific to each Oracle client and requires extensive administration. With local naming, net service names are stored in the `tnsnames.ora` file residing in `$ORACLE_HOME/network/admin` on a Unix system or in `%ORACLE_HOME%\network\admin` on a Windows NT system. Local naming is most appropriate for small networks with a limited number of services and clients.

Oracle Names   Oracle Names is an Oracle directory service comprised of a system of Oracle Names servers, which can be centrally managed by the DBA. Oracle Names is a good solution for a high-volume, dynamic, and complex environment.

NOTE Oracle Names will be deprecated in Oracle9i. Because of this, if you need a centralized naming resolution solution, it is recommended that you use Oracle Directory Naming rather than Oracle Names.

Oracle Directory Naming   Oracle Directory Naming uses an LDAP (Lightweight Directory Access Protocol)–compliant directory server to store net service names and connect descriptors. The network directory becomes the central repository for all data on databases, network components, and user and corporate policies and preferences, replacing client-side and server-side localized files. Administrators can centrally manage these objects, and all systems on the heterogeneous network can refer to the directory for information. Net8 supports Oracle Internet Directory, Microsoft Active Directory, and Novell Directory Services (NDS).

Host naming   Host naming uses a known name resolution service in a TCP/IP environment, such as Domain Name System (DNS) or Network Information Services (NIS).

External naming External naming support allows sites to resolve Oracle service names using industry-standard name services, including Sun NIS+, NDS, and the Open Software Foundation/Distributed Computing Environment (OSF/DCE) Cell Directory Service (CDS).

Local naming and host naming fall under the localized management network configuration model. Localized management involves configuring name resolution on each Oracle client in a tnsnames.ora file. Oracle Names, Oracle Directory Naming, and external naming fall under the centralized management network configuration model. Centralized management eases management of Oracle clients, because you do not need to reconfigure each client every time a new Oracle service is added to the network.

Configuring Net8

Net8 is typically installed along with other Oracle8i products. For example, when you install the database server or SQL*Plus, Net8 will be installed at the same time. You can choose to install Net8 without any other client software (though some dependent libraries will still be installed). If you need to install Net8, simply insert your server installation CD (or SQL*Plus installation CD), start the Universal Installer, and choose to do a Custom Install. From the Available Product Components window, choose Net8. (See Chapter 2 for details on the Oracle Universal Installer and installing Oracle8i components.)

NOTE In addition to installing Net8 you will need to install one or more protocol adapters, to allow Net8 to communicate using the protocol you wish to use. By default, Oracle will try to install the correct protocol adapter, but it's always a good idea to make sure that the correct one is being installed.

Net8 is configured using configuration files located on the client and network server hosts. The following configuration files contain information about where services are located and how to establish connections between the application client and an Oracle service:

- listener.ora, located on the server, contains configuration information about listeners on a server.

- `tnsnames.ora`, located on the client, contains information about net service names and connection data.
- `sqlnet.ora`, located on the client and/or server, contains information about the net service name resolution method and Net8 configuration options.
- `names.ora`, located on the client, contains information about an Oracle Names server.

These configuration files are typically found in $ORACLE_HOME/network/admin on a Unix system, in %ORACLE_HOME%\network\admin on Windows NT system, or in the location specified by the TNS_ADMIN environment variable or registry entry.

The `listener.ora` and `tnsnames.ora` files are covered in the following discussions of configuring the listener and client. The `sqlnet.ora` and `names.ora` files are discussed later in this chapter, in the "Using Oracle Names" section.

Configuring and Managing the Listener

You must employ a listener on each host where an Oracle service resides. The Net8 listener process monitors for and processes incoming database connection requests from client applications. The listener process runs independently of any Oracle instances running on the host. In fact, one listener process can service connections for any instance running on the host. The Net8 listener verifies the connection data passed to it by matching this information to the services that have been registered with the listener.

The listener has a default name of LISTENER and will be automatically configured to listen on the TCP/IP protocol on port 1521, or on the IPC protocol for external procedures.

Just as you can run multiple Oracle instances on a single node, you can also configure multiple listeners for that node. If you configure multiple listeners, each listener will have the name you specify in the `listener.ora` configuration file. A single listener can service multiple service names, and multiple listeners can service a single service name.

Registering Service Names

A service name can be registered with the listener either through configuration information saved in the `listener.ora` file or through automatic registration at instance startup. Beginning with Oracle8i, the PMON process will register the service names for that instance with the listener through a feature known as *service registration*. Service registration is automatic at instance startup if the listener is already running. If the listener is not already running at instance startup, Oracle will periodically check to see if the listener has started. When the listener is started, the Oracle instance will register its service names with the listener.

 NOTE If you are running an Oracle instance under a version of Oracle prior to Oracle8i, you must manually configure the listener for those services. Listener configuration is also required when using certain products such as Oracle Enterprise Manager (OEM).

You can control service name registration by specifying the name of the listener in the `init.ora` file using the LOCAL_LISTENER parameter. Set this parameter to a listener name alias that is resolved either through `tnsnames.ora` or an Oracle Names server. In the following example, the Oracle instance is configured to register its service names with the listener brewlist.

```
local_listener=brewlist
```

The listener alias is then resolved through a known naming method. In this example, the resolution is through local naming in the `tnsnames.ora` file:

```
brewlist=
    (address=(protocol=tcp)(host=oregano)(port=1521))
```

Following instance startup, the PMON process will then register the service names for that instance with the brewlist listener running on host oregano and listening on port 1521.

Configuring the *listener.ora* File

Listing 9.1 shows a sample `listener.ora` file with a Net8 listener configuration.

Listing 9.1: A listener.ora File with a Net8 Listener Configuration

```
# Listener Address Section
listener=
  (description=
    (address_list=
      (address=(protocol=tcp)(host=oregano)(port=1521))
      (address=(protocol=ipc)(key=toffee.cafecandy.com))
    )
  )

# Static Service Section
sid_list_listener=
  (sid_list=
```

```
      (sid_desc=
        (global_dbname=toffee.cafecandy.com)
        (oracle_home=/u01/app/oracle/product/8.1.7)
        (sid_name=toffee)
      )
    )

    # Listener Control Options
    connect_timeout_listener=5
    logging_listener=off
```

 NOTE You can use the formatting style you prefer for the `listener.ora` file, but you should try to be consistent. Note that some versions of the Net8 software will generate an error if parentheses are written in the first column.

There are three sections within the `listener.ora` file for each listener configured: the listener address section, the static service section, and the control parameters section. Let's look at these sections in a bit more detail.

The Listener Address Section

The listener address section defines the protocol addresses for the listener. In other words, this section tells the listener where to listen for incoming connection requests. This section starts with the name of the listener, such as LISTENER, followed by a description that is a list of protocol addresses.

```
    # Listener Addresses
    listener=
      (description=
        (address_list=
          (address=(protocol=tcp)(host=oregano)(port=1521))
          (address=(protocol=ipc)(key=toffee.cafecandy.com))
        )
      )
```

The address in this example is a TCP/IP protocol address that specifies the name of the destination host and the port that the listener is monitoring. The host can be the current host or another host to which the listener will forward the connection request. The second protocol address in this listing is an IPC address. In this address definition, the key parameter specifies the name of the service that receives the IPC protocol communications.

For systems that handle many connection requests, you may want to configure a queue for the listener process. This feature enables the listener to dynamically handle a larger volume of connection requests. Check your platform-specific documentation for availability of listener queues and default queue sizes. To configure a queue for a protocol address, specify the QUEUESIZE parameter at the end of the address definition. The following example demonstrates how to configure a queue size of 20 for the first listener address only.

```
# Listener Addresses
listener=
  (description=
    (address_list=
      (address=(protocol=tcp)(host=oregano)(port=1521)
        (queuesize=20)
      )
      (address=(protocol=ipc)(key=toffee.cafecandy.com))
    )
  )
```

The Static Service Section

The static service section includes the static service name configurations for the listener. This section also supports backward compatibility for instances running versions prior to Oracle8i, as well as for certain add-ons such as OEM. This section starts with the parameter SID_LIST_*<listener name>*, such as SID_LIST_LISTENER, followed by a list of SIDs.

```
# Static Service Section
sid_list_listener=
  (sid_list=
    (sid_desc=
      (global_dbname=toffee.cafecandy.com)
      (oracle_home=/u1/app/oracle/product/8.1.7)
      (sid_name=toffee)
    )
  )
```

In this example, the GLOBAL_DBNAME parameter specifies the service name for which the listener is receiving requests. The ORACLE_HOME parameter should match the definition of the ORACLE_HOME parameter for the instance. SID_NAME is the SID of the instance.

Listener Control Parameters

The control parameters are optional and control the operation of certain features of the listener, such as listener tracing and connection time-outs. Each parameter in this section is suffixed with the name of the listener, such as CONNECT_TIMEOUT_LISTENER. Table 9.1 describes the available control parameters.

TABLE 9.1: LISTENER CONTROL PARAMETERS IN THE *LISTENER.ORA* FILE

Parameter	Default	Description
connect_timeout	10	Specifies the time (in seconds) that the listener will wait for a valid connection to be made
log_directory	$ORACLE_HOME/network/log	Specifies the destination directory for the listener log file
log_file	<listener_name>.log	Specifies the name of the listener log file
logging	ON	Turns listener logging on or off
passwords	oracle	Sets an unencrypted password for the listener control (lsnrctl) utility and allows one or more passwords; an encrypted password can be set using lsnrctl change_password
save_config_on_stop	FALSE	If set to TRUE, saves to the `listener.ora` file any configuration changes set using lsnrctl
startup_wait_time	0	Specifies the time (in seconds) that the listener will sleep before responding to the lsnrctl status command
trace_directory	$ORACLE_HOME/network/trace	Specifies the destination directory for the listener trace files
trace_file	<listener_name>.trc	Specifies the name of the listener trace file
trace_filelen	Unlimited	Specifies the maximum size of the listener trace file, in kilobytes
trace_fileno	1	When trace_filelen is also specified, specifies the maximum number of listener trace files; when this setting is exceeded, the listener will recycle the listener trace files
trace_level	OFF	Turns listener tracing on or off and specifies incremental tracing levels: OFF (no trace output), USER (user trace information), ADMIN (administrative trace information), or SUPPORT (Oracle worldwide customer support trace information)

Continued

TABLE 9.1: LISTENER CONTROL PARAMETERS IN THE *LISTENER.ORA* FILE

Parameter	Default	Description
trace_timestamp	OFF	Specifies whether to add a timestamp in the format of *dd-month-yyyy hh:mm:ss* to a trace event; set using ON|TRUE|OFF|FALSE
use_plug_and_play	OFF	Tells the listener to register services with an Oracle Names server

The following example sets the CONNECT_TIMEOUT parameter to 5 seconds and turns listener logging off.

```
# Listener Control Options
connect_timeout_listener=5
logging_listener=off
```

Managing the Listener

You can manage the listener with the Listener Control utility, lsnrctl. You can issue a single command from the operating system prompt by passing arguments to lsnrctl, as follows:

```
$ lsnrctl command [listener_name]
```

In this syntax, *listener_name* is the name of the listener defined in the listener.ora file. It is not necessary to identify the listener if you are using the default listener, named LISTENER. Table 9.2 describes the basic lsnrctl commands.

TABLE 9.2: COMMONLY USED LISTENER CONTROL (LSNRCTL) COMMANDS

Command	Description
START	Starts the listener
STOP	Stops the listener
RELOAD	Reloads the listener configuration
STATUS	Shows the current status of the listener, including the version of the listener, start time, up time, tracing level, logging and tracing options, the name and location of the listener configuration file, a list of services registered with the listener, and the addresses the listener is monitoring
HELP	Lists all available lsnrctl commands, or if a command is specified, shows help information about that command

Continued

CONFIGURING NET8

TABLE 9.2: COMMONLY USED LISTENER CONTROL (LSNRCTL) COMMANDS

Command	Description
SET	Lists the available parameters that can be passed to the SET command, or if passed a parameter, modifies the setting of the parameter
SHOW	Lists the available parameters that can be passed to the SHOW command, or if passed a parameter, shows the setting of the parameter
CHANGE_PASSWORD	Sets an encrypted password for the listener
SERVICES	Provides detailed information about the services registered with the listener
TRACE	Turns on tracing for the listener
VERSION	Shows the current lsnrctl version

Configuring the Net8 Client

The Net8 client might be an application running on a PC or a database that requests information from another database through a database link. The Net8 client resolves connect identifiers to connect descriptors through a net service name identified by a known name resolution method, as discussed in the "Naming Methods" section, earlier in this chapter. Here, we will discuss the local naming method and basic Net8 client configuration.

Local naming resolves service names to network addresses by using information configured in the tnsnames.ora file that is stored locally on each client node. Before a database server can receive connections from clients, the clients must have a tnsnames.ora file with service names that map to the service addresses listed in the database server's listener.ora file. You configure the client by creating a list of service names (which are aliases for database network addresses) and addresses of network destinations (database server names or IP addresses) in the tnsnames.ora file.

In the tnsnames.ora file, the net service names are mapped to database network addresses contained in a connect descriptor. A connect descriptor contains the location of the listener through a protocol address and the service name of the database to which to connect. Clients and servers that are clients of other servers use this net service name when making a connection to an application.

Here is the basic syntax for a net service name entry in the tnsnames.ora file:

```
<net service name>=
  (description=
```

```
(address=(protocol=<protocol>)(host=<host>)(port=<port>))
(connect_data=
  (service_name=<service name>)
)
)
```

For each connect identifier referenced by a Net8 client, a matching net service name entry should be listed in the tnsnames.ora file to allow the client to make the proper connection. Listing 9.2 illustrates how a connect identifier is mapped to a connect descriptor through the net service name toffee.

Listing 9.2: Mapping a Connect Identifer to a Connect Descriptor in the tnsnames.ora File

```
toffee=
  (description=
    (address=(protocol=tcp)(host=oregano)(port=1521))
    (connect_data=
      (service_name=toffee.cafecandy.com)
    )
  )
```

In the event that a service name represents more than one instance, you may identify a specific instance in the connect descriptor. This is particularly useful if you are using Oracle Parallel Server (OPS). Listing 9.3 shows an example that specifies the instance name, which matches the INSTANCE_NAME parameter in the init.ora file of that instance.

Listing 9.3: Identifiying an Instance in a Connect Descriptor in the tnsnames.ora File

```
toffee=
  (description=
    (address=(protocol=tcp)(host=oregano)(port=1521))
    (connect_data=
      (instance_name=toffee)
      (service_name=toffee.cafecandy.com)
    )
  )
```

Client Load Balancing

If you have configured multiple listeners for a service, you can configure the Net8 client to randomize connection requests to the listeners through a feature called *client load balancing*. This feature causes the Net8 client to randomly select which listener it will attempt to connect with. To enable client load balancing, you define two protocol addresses and set the LOAD_BALANCE parameter in the net service name description, as shown in Listing 9.4.

Listing 9.4: Using Client Load Balancing

```
toffee=
  (description=
    (load_balance=on)
    (address=(protocol=tcp)(host=oregano)(port=1521))
    (address=(protocol=tcp)(host=thyme)(port=1521))
    (connect_data=
      (service_name=toffee.cafecandy.com)
    )
  )
```

Enabling Connect Time Failover

If you have configured multiple listeners for a service, you can configure the Net8 client to fail over from one listener to the other if a connection request to the first listener fails. You may use this option with or without client load balancing. To enable connect time failover, you define two protocol addresses and set the FAILOVER parameter in the net service name description. Listing 9.5 shows an example of enabling load balancing and connect time failover.

Listing 9.5: Enabling Connect Time Failover

```
toffee=
  (description=
    (load_balance=on)
    (failover=on)
    (address=(protocol=tcp)(host=oregano)(port=1521))
    (address=(protocol=tcp)(host=thyme)(port=1521))
    (connect_data=
      (service_name=toffee.cafecandy.com)
    )
  )
```

Using Transparent Application Failover

Transparent Application Failover (TAF) is a runtime failover method that enables a Net8 client to reestablish connection to a service through the same listener, or through an alternate listener if the first connection fails. Optionally, you can have TAF resume a

SELECT statement. The failover works transparently to the user. TAF is especially useful for high-availability architectures such as OPS and Oracle Fail Safe (discussed in Chapter 25).

TAF is different from connect time failover. Connect time failover handles redirecting initial connections. TAF is concerned with established connections. You may use TAF along with the connect time failover and client load balancing features described in the previous sections.

 NOTE TAF works only with services registered with the listener through service name registration. Static configuration of a service name with a listener will disable TAF.

TAF is implemented by adding the FAILOVER_MODE parameter to the CONNECT_DATA portion of the connect descriptor. The general syntax of the FAILOVER_MODE parameter is:

```
failover_mode=
  (backup=<backup connection ID>)
  (type=<failover type>)
  (method=<failover method>)
  (retries=<number of retries> )
  (delay=<wait time between retries> )
```

FAILOVER_MODE takes the following parameters:

- The BACKUP parameter specifies a connect identifier for the backup connection.

- The TYPE parameter specifies the type of failover. Three types are possible:
    - SESSION, so a failed session will reconnect
    - SELECT, so a failed session will reconnect and resume SELECT statements in progress at the time of session failure
    - NONE, which is the default and explicitly disables TAF

- The METHOD parameter specifies the method of failover. Two methods are possible:
    - BASIC will establish failover connection at the time of failover.
    - PRECONNECT will preestablish idle failover connection to the backup server.

- The RETRIES parameter specifies the number of times to retry a failed connection. If the DELAY parameter is set, RETRIES defaults to 5.
- The DELAY parameter specifies the time, in seconds, to wait between retry attempts. If the RETRIES parameter is set, DELAY defaults to 1.

Basic Failover

Listing 9.6 shows an example of using the SELECT type and BASIC method of TAF. In this configuration, Net8 will reestablish a session with the second listener when the original connection fails. The session will resume processing of any SELECT statements that were in progress at the time of session failure.

Listing 9.6: Enabling Basic Failover

```
toffee=
  (description=
    (address=(protocol=tcp)(host=oregano)(port=1521))
    (address=(protocol=tcp)(host=thyme)(port=1521))
    (connect_data=
      (service_name=toffee.cafecandy.com)
      (failover_mode=
        (type=select)
        (method=basic)
      )
    )
  )
```

Preconnect Failover

When you use the PRECONNECT method of TAF, Net8 establishes both the initial connection and an idle failover connection to a backup instance. This configuration is faster than basic failover, at the cost of additional overhead. In the example shown in Listing 9.7, TAF is configured to preestablish a backup connection to the net service name orange and will fail over to that connection should the primary session opened with the net service name toffee fail.

Listing 9.7: Enabling Preconnect Failover

```
toffee=
  (description=
    (address=(protocol=tcp)(host=oregano)(port=1521))
    (connect_data=
      (service_name=toffee.cafecandy.com)
      (failover_mode=
```

```
            (backup=orange)
            (type=select)
            (method=preconnect)
          )
        )
     )
   orange=
     (description=
       (address=(protocol=tcp)(host=oregano)(port=1521))
       (connect data=
         (service_name=orange.cafecandy.com)
       )
     )
```

Connection Retry

When you use the RETRIES parameter, Net8 will attempt to reconnect to a service until a connection is reestablished or the retry limit is reached. In the example shown in Listing 9.8, TAF will retry the connection 20 times before failure.

Listing 9.8: Enabling Connection Retries

```
toffee=
  (description=
    (address=(protocol=tcp)(host=oregano)(port=1521))
    (connect_data=
      (service_name=toffee.cafecandy.com)
      (failover_mode=
        (type=select)
        (method=basic)
        (retries=20)
      )
    )
  )
```

Using the Net8 Configuration Assistant

You might have noticed that there is a lot of manual work to the configuration of Net8. One slip of the finger, one misplaced parenthesis, and you are in a world of hurt. Oracle provides a somewhat simpler method of maintaining your Net8 configurations through the use of the Net8 Configuration Assistant. This graphical utility offers the following options for configuring Net8:

- The Listener Configuration allows you to create, update, remove, or rename an Oracle listener. This option is valid only for a system on which the database server is running; it is not used on clients.

- The Naming Methods (Oracle Names) Configuration option allows you to configure Net8 naming methods. You can choose from the naming methods described in the "Naming Methods" section earlier in this chapter.

- The Local Net Service Name Configuration option allows you to maintain a local copy of the `tnsnames.ora` file.

- The Directory Service Access Configuration option is used to configure access to an LDAP directory server. Choose this option if you are using Oracle Directory Naming or Oracle Advanced Security.

Once you have selected the type of Net8 configuration you wish to complete, just follow the prompts, and the Net8 Configuration Assistant will complete the Net8 configuration for you.

Using Oracle's Multithreaded Server (MTS) Option

Net8 connections are established using two different models: the dedicated server model or the multithreaded server (MTS) model. With the dedicated server model, the listener starts a server process dedicated to the client session and passes the connection to that server process.

With MTS, the listener passes the connection to a dispatcher, which supports multiple client sessions concurrently. Each session is bound to a virtual circuit, which is a unit of memory used by the dispatcher to manage that session. The dispatcher places the virtual circuit in a queue when communication from the client arrives. An idle shared server process picks up the virtual circuit from the queue and services the request. Because any individual client session is relatively idle, this architecture allows a small pool of server processes to handle a larger number of client sessions and also consumes less memory on the host.

NOTE When an Oracle instance configured for MTS is started and a listener to support the service is running, each dispatcher is registered with the listener. Registration can take up to a minute. If a client session request is received before the dispatchers are registered with the listener, the listener may assign a dedicated server process.

You should use MTS only if your application is using technology that mandates it (like Enterprise JavaBeans) or if you have reached your scalability limits in terms of process counts or possibly virtual memory. With MTS, you need fewer processes, thus context switching is cheaper and the total virtual memory size is a little lower (but the SGA is much larger). This means that MTS can let you support more users on a system that is already running at capacity, but increasing that capacity is normally a better solution.

Configuring MTS

MTS is configured for an Oracle instance using the MTS_DISPATCHERS parameter in the `init.ora` file for the instance. This is the only required parameter for configuring MTS; all of the other MTS parameters are optional.

The following is the basic syntax for MTS_DISPATCHERS:

```
mts_dispatchers="(<attribute>=<value>)[(<attribute>=<value>)... ]"
```

At a minimum, the MTS_DISPATCHERS parameter must set one attribute: the address, description, or protocol attribute. These and the other, optional, attributes available for MTS_DISPATCHERS are described in Table 9.3.

TABLE 9.3: MTS_DISPATCHERS ATTRIBUTES

Attribute	Description
address	Specifies the network protocol address of the endpoint on which the dispatchers listen. This attribute must be set if the description or protocol attribute is not specified.
description	Specifies the network description of the endpoint on which the dispatchers listen, including the network protocol address. This attribute must be set if the address or protocol attribute is not specified.
protocol	Specifies the network protocol for which the dispatcher generates a listening endpoint. This attribute must be set if the address or description attribute is not specified.
connections	Specifies the maximum number of network connections to allow for each dispatcher.
dispatchers	Specifies the initial number of dispatchers to start. The number of dispatchers does not change dynamically but must be incremented with the ALTER SYSTEM command, so be sure to configure enough dispatchers for your system.

Continued

USING ORACLE'S MULTITHREADED SERVER (MTS) OPTION

TABLE 9.3: MTS_DISPATCHERS ATTRIBUTES (CONTINUED)

Attribute	Description
listener	Specifies a listener alias with which the PMON process will register dispatcher information. Refer to the "Registering Services" section earlier in this chapter for information about registering with a nondefault listener.
multiplex	Enables connection concentration.
pool	Enables connection pooling.
service	Specifies the service name to register with the listener. By default, MTS will use the service_names setting.
session	Specifies the maximum number of sessions to allow for each dispatcher.
ticks	Specifies the size of a network tick in seconds. The value set is multiplied by the pool time-out value to get the total connection pool time-out. The default is 15 seconds. Oracle recommends a tick size of about 1 second for a fast network and about 3 to 4 seconds for a slow network.

For example, to set up MTS on the TCP/IP protocol with 20 initial dispatchers, you would add the following line to your `init.ora` file:

`mts_dispatchers="(protocol=tcp)(dispatchers=20)"`

Other MTS parameters can be used to tune the performance of MTS. The following parameters are optional:

- MTS_MAX_DISPATCHERS specifies the maximum number of MTS dispatchers.
- MTS_SERVER specifies the number of MTS shared server processes to be started at instance startup.
- MTS_MAX_SERVERS specifies the maximum number of MTS shared servers.
- MTS_CIRCUITS specifies the maximum number of MTS virtual circuits.
- MTS_SESSIONS specifies the maximum number of MTS sessions to allow.

 TIP When configuring MTS, you may also need to adjust the LARGE_POOL_SIZE and SESSIONS parameters. The LARGE_POOL_SIZE parameter specifies the size of the large pool, in bytes. The SESSIONS parameter specifies the maximum number of sessions available to the Oracle instance.

Viewing MTS Information

Oracle provides some V$ views that offer useful information about MTS. For example, the V$DISPATCHER view shows information about dispatcher processes. The VMTS, VSGA, and V$SGASTAT views provide information that may be useful for tuning MTS. Table 9.4 describes the MTS views.

TABLE 9.4: MTS VIEWS

View	Description
V$DISPATCHER	Provides information on the dispatcher processes, including name, network address, status, various usage statistics, and index number
V$DISPATCHER_RATE	Provides rate statistics for the dispatcher processes
V$QUEUE	Contains information on the multithread message queues
V$SHARED_SERVER	Contains information on the shared server processes
V$CIRCUIT	Contains information about virtual circuits, which are user connections to the database through dispatchers and servers
V$MTS	Contains information for tuning MTS
V$SGA	Contains size information about various system global area (SGA) groups
V$SGASTAT	Shows detailed statistical information about the SGA
V$SHARED_POOL_RESERVED	Lists statistics to help tune the reserved pool and space within the shared pool

Managing MTS on the Client

You may optionally configure a client to use only dedicated or shared servers using the server parameter in the CONNECT_DATA portion of the connect descriptor in the tnsnames.ora file. If a shared server is requested but not available, the connection request fails. In the example shown in Listing 9.9, the connect descriptor for toffee is set up to use only dedicated servers, while orange is configured to use only shared servers.

Listing 9.9: Configuring Clients to Use Only a Dedicated Server or Only a Shared Server

```
toffee=
  (description=
    (address=(protocol=tcp)(host=oregano)(port=1521))
    (connect_data=
      (service_name=toffee.cafecandy.com)
      (server=dedicated)
    )
  )
orange=
  (description=
    (address=(protocol=tcp)(host=thyme)(port=1521))
    (connect_data=
      (service_name=orange.cafecandy.com)
      (server=shared)
    )
  )
```

Using Oracle Names

Oracle Names is a distributed directory service made up of a system of integrated Oracle Names servers that provide name-to-address resolution for each Net8 service on the network. Oracle Names simplifies Net8 setup and administration in complex, distributed computing environments.

How Oracle Names Works

Clients configured to use Oracle Names refer connection requests to an Oracle Names server. The Oracle Names server resolves the service name provided by the client to a network address and returns that information to the client. The client can then use that address to connect to the service.

Oracle Names employs administrative regions. An *administrative region* is a logical entity for organizing Net8 services. Each administrative region consists of a collection of one or more Oracle Names servers that administer services for that region. Administrative regions are transparent to clients in that Oracle Names servers forward name resolution requests from clients in foreign administrative regions to the proper Oracle Names server. An administrative region can span multiple domains. Domain names in Oracle exist independently of network domains, although you may follow the same domain naming conventions to ease administration.

Oracle Names includes three features to improve network performance and ease of administration:

- Dynamic service registration
- Client discovery of Names servers
- Name resolution optimization

Let's look at each of these features in a bit more detail.

Service Registration

Net8 services can register themselves with a Names server, and their addresses are made available to all the other Names servers in the region. Upon startup, a Net8 service looks for a Names server with which to register. This process is as follows:

- If a service has a `sqlnet.ora` file, it looks for the NAMES.PREFERRED_SERVER parameter. If the parameter exists, it registers with the first Names server listed.
- If there is no `sqlnet.ora` file, it looks for a Names server with a well-known address. The well-known Names server address on a TCP/IP network is a host aliased to oranamesrvr0, oranamesrvr1, and so on, using port 1575.
- If it can't find a well-known address, the Oracle Installer prompts the user to provide a Names server address.

NOTE Administrators can also register services manually using namesctl. Using this utility is discussed a bit later in this chapter.

Once the service is registered, its address is made available to all other Names servers in the region. The address information is shared in one of two ways: through service replication or through an Oracle Names database. In service replication, service information is stored in a Names server's cache and is instantly replicated to the caches of all other Names servers in the region. If an Oracle database is used as the registration repository, the registration information is stored in the database, and from there is accessible to all the Oracle Names version 8 servers in the region.

Client Discovery of Names Servers

By referring to a list of Oracle Names servers, a client or another Oracle Names server can contact an Oracle Names server. This process of creating the list is called *discovery*.

When a client tries to discover an Oracle Names server (with the namesctl utility or Net8 Assistant), one Oracle Names server is found first. Once the client finds an Oracle Names server, it pings all other Oracle Names servers in the region. A list of Oracle Names servers is then created on the client and saved to a file named `.sdns.ora` on Unix systems and `sdns.ora` on Windows platforms. This list is sorted in order of response time.

The discovery process allows the client to retrieve a list of all the existing Names server addresses and to find out about new Names servers as they appear in the network. This allows for dynamic changes in the network topology with minimal involvement on the user's part and with little or no impact on the performance of a normal query.

Clients discover Names servers in much the same way that services find them for registration:

- A client first looks in its own client-side cache. If it has contacted a Names server within the past 24 hours, the address of a Names server may be in the cache.
- If a client has a `sqlnet.ora` file, it looks for the NAMES.PREFERRED_SERVER parameter. If one exists, it queries the first Names server listed.
- If there is no `sqlnet.ora` file, a client looks for a Names server with a well-known address. The well-known Names server address on a TCP/IP network is a host aliased to oranamesrvr0, oranamesrvr1, and so on, using port 1575.
- If Net8 is being installed on the client and the client cannot find a Names server address, the Oracle Installer prompts the user to provide a Names server address. The user must provide a Names server address in order to continue.

Once a Names server is found, the addresses of all the other Names servers in the region are made available to the client.

Name Resolution Optimization

There are two features of Oracle Names that optimize the speed with which client name queries can be resolved:

- A client-side daemon process to find the fastest responding Names server
- A client-side cache

The following sections describe how each of these features optimizes client name queries.

The Client-Side Daemon Process

When a client is installed with Net8 and Oracle Names, it finds a Names server and retrieves a list of all the Names servers in the region. A client-side daemon process contacts each of the Names servers in turn, and orders the list on the basis of the

speed of each Names server's response. The result of this process is stored in an `sdns.ora` file. Subsequently, when a client makes a query to a Names server, the Names server at the top of the list in the `sdns.ora` file is contacted first. Whenever the client queries a Names server, the time of the round-trip is used to modify the order of entries in the list.

A Names server list reordering consists of asking one live Names server for all of its Names server addresses within the region. If fewer than two are found, or if fewer than two are live when asked by the initial Names server, a list of Name servers in the parent region is requested (if one exists). Each Names server that responds is then added to the list that is being constructed. The resorted list is then written to `sdns.ora`. By featuring periodic reorders, Oracle Names version 8 ensures that the client receives the best response time to a query. The reordering algorithm takes no longer than a few seconds.

A full Name server reorder is performed at the following times:

- At installation of the Net8 client
- When requested by the user using namesctl (discussed shortly)
- At shutdown of the Net8 client

The Client-Side Cache

On most platforms, a local client cache is created when a client is started. Once a current list of Names servers is retrieved, that list is stored in the local client cache. Similarly, when a Names server resolves a name query, the result of that query is stored in the client-side cache. Clients attempt to find the result of a query by first looking in their cache, so that subsequent requests for name resolution can be answered, in most cases, more quickly than a network round-trip between the client and a Names server. Forwarding the query on to the Names server retrieves any names that are not in the local client-side cache or have timed-out.

The local client-side cache is particularly advantageous if at some time no Names server is available. In this case, the local client-side cache has the current list of recently accessed services.

 NOTE All the information in the client cache has a time to live (TTL). At the end of that TTL, the information is flushed from the cache. The purpose of this feature is to avoid having stale information in the client cache. The default TTL is 86,400 seconds (24 hours). It cannot be changed.

Not all platforms support the client-side cache. See your Oracle platform-specific documentation for further information. If the client platform does not have a cache, the result of the initial discovery process is stored in .sdns.ora in the client's $ORACLE_HOME/network/names directory.

Configuring Names Servers

An Oracle Names server stores the following information:

- Global database names and addresses
- Other Oracle Names server names and addresses
- Net service names
- Global database links
- Aliases
- Oracle Connection Managers

There should be at least two Names servers in a region, for fault-tolerance. Each Names server in the network requires an individual configuration file called names.ora. This file contains control parameters for the Names server and points the Names server to the database where the network definition is stored. Listing 9.10 shows an example of a names.ora file.

Listing 9.9: A names.ora File

```
names.server_name = NameServer.world
names.admin_region =
  (REGION=
  (NAME = LOCAL_REGION.world)
  (TYPE = ROSDB)
  (USERID = names)
  (PASSWORD = names)
  (DESCRIPTION =
    (ADDRESS_LIST =
      (ADDRESS = (PROTOCOL=tcp)(Host=nineva)(Port=1387)
    )
  )
  (CONNECT_DATA=(SID=EM))
)
(DOCNAME=sbox)
(REFRESH=14400) #4 hours#
```

```
(RETRY=600) #10 minutes#
(EXPIRE=259200) #3 days#
(VERSION=34619392) #2.1.4#
names.addresses = (address=(protocol=tcp)(host=george.world)(port=1522))
names.domains =
  (DOMAIN_LIST =
    (DOMAIN=(NAME=dname1)(MIN_TTL=20864))
    (DOMAIN=(NAME=world)(MIN_TTL=20864))
)
names.config_checkpoint_file = cache.ckp
names.trace_level = OFF
names.trace_unique = FALSE
```

Managing Names Servers

The Names control (namesctl) program is a basic utility for controlling Oracle Names servers. The namesctl utility can be run in three modes: INTERPRETER, COMMAND LINE, and BATCH COMMAND.

With INTERPRETER mode, namesctl is loaded and all operations are executed within it. When loaded, the program displays the following prompt:

```
namesctl>
```

You can also execute most commands from the operating system in COMMAND LINE mode by running the namesctl program with a complete command as a parameter to the program, as in this example:

```
namesctl START
```

In this case, namesctl will load and execute the command, then return to the operating system prompt.

In BATCH COMMAND mode, you can combine commands in a standard text file, then run them as a sequence of commands. To execute in batch mode, use this format:

```
namesctl @file_name
```

You can use either REM or a hash mark (#) to identify comments in the batch script; all other lines are considered commands. Any commands that would typically require confirmation do not require confirmation during batch execution.

Requiring Passwords

You have the option of configuring a Names server to require a password for any namesctl command that alters how it operates. If you do not enter anything in the Password field on the Nameserver property sheet in the Oracle Network Manager, no password is required to control any Names server function. If you do supply a password on the Nameserver property sheet in the Network Manager, you must also set the password property in the namesctl program. If this is not done, the Names server will not respond to some namesctl commands.

If you are concerned with the security implications of explicitly putting a Names server password in the administrator's client sqlnet.ora file, you can omit the parameter and always use the command:

SET PASSWORD

After you issue this command, you will be prompted for the password.

NOTE When passed over the network, the namesctl password is *always* encrypted, regardless of how it is set in namesctl.

Issuing Names Control Commands

Some of the namesctl commands require your confirmation before they are executed. When you issue the command, you are prompted:

confirm:[yes or no]

Type yes to execute the command, or type no to cancel the command. You can turn confirmation mode off by setting this parameter in the sqlnet.ora file:

namesctl.NOCONFIRM = TRUE

When this parameter is set to TRUE, all commands execute without asking for confirmation.

Table 9.5 lists the namesctl commands.

TABLE 9.5: COMMONLY USES NAMES CONTROL (NAMESCTL) COMMANDS

Command	Description
EXIT	Exits namesctl
FLUSH	Flushes all foreign names from the cache
FLUSH_NAME	Flushes an individual name from the foreign data cache
HELP	Gets brief general or specific help on commands
LOG_STATS	Logs the current statistics to the log file

Continued

TABLE 9.5: COMMONLY USES NAMES CONTROL (NAMESCTL) COMMANDS (CONTINUED)

Command	Description
PING	Tests for the existence of a Names server and gets the time it took for the Names server to respond
QUERY	Queries for the existence or contents of a network object name
QUIT	Quits namesctl
REGISTER	Registers a network object to a Names server
RELOAD	Reloads the local region data into the cache
REPEAT	Performs a query repeatedly for *n* iterations
RESET_STATS	Resets the current Names server statistics to the same state as they were in at startup
RESTART	Restarts the Names server
SET DEFAULT_DOMAIN	Sets or changes the default domain for the namesctl client
SET FORWARDING_AVAILABLE	Turns on or off name request forwarding for a Names server
SET LOG_STATS_INTERVAL	Changes the frequency with which statistics are logged to the log file
SET NAMESCTL_TRACE_LEVEL	Sets the level at which namesctl can be traced
SET PASSWORD	Registers a password for privileged Names server operations such as RELOAD and STOP
SET REQUESTS_ENABLED	Determines whether the current Names server will respond to requests
SET RESET_STATS_INTERVAL	Changes the time between statistics being reset to zero or initial values in the current Names server
SET SERVER	Changes the current Names server
SET TRACE_LEVEL	Changes the trace level for tracing the current Names server
SHOW CACHE_CHECKPOINT_INTERVAL	Shows the frequency with which the Names server cache is written to the checkpoint file
SHOW FORWARDING_AVAILABLE	Shows whether the Names server is forwarding requests or redirecting them
SHOW DEFAULT_DOMAIN	Displays the default domain of the current Names server
SHOW LOG_FILE_NAME	Shows the name of the Names server log file

Continued

TABLE 9.5: COMMONLY USES NAMES CONTROL (NAMESCTL) COMMANDS (CONTINUED)	
Command	Description
SHOW LOG_STATS_INTERVAL	Displays the frequency with which statistics are logged to the log file
SHOW NAMESCTL_TRACE_LEVEL	Displays the current trace level of namesctl
SHOW REQUESTS_ENABLED	Shows whether or not the Names server is responding to requests
SHOW RESET_STATS_INTERVAL	Displays the frequency with which internal statistics are reset
SHOW SERVER	Displays the name and version of the current Names server
SHOW STATUS or STATUS	Displays general status information about the Names server
SHOW SYSTEM_QUERIES	Displays information about system queries from the Names server
SHOW TRACE_FILE_NAME	Shows the name of the Names server trace file
SHOW TRACE_LEVEL	Displays the trace level of the current Names server
SHOW VERSION or VERSION	Displays the Names server version
SHUTDOWN or STOP	Stops the Names server
START or STARTUP	Starts the Names server
TIMED_QUERY	Shows all registered data in the Names server cache
UNREGISTER	Removes a network object from a Names server

Introducing Oracle Connection Manager

Oracle Connection Manager (OCM) is a tool that adds to the manageability of Net8. OCM is a router through which a client connection request may be sent either to its next hop or directly to the database server. Clients who route their connection requests through a Connection Manager can then take advantage of the connection concentration, Net8 access control, and multiprotocol support features configured on that Connection Manager. OCM is separately available for installation with Oracle8i Enterprise Edition via the Oracle Universal Installer (described in Chapter 2).

The following are the basic features of OCM:

Connection concentration   This feature enables you to multiplex or funnel multiple client network sessions through a single transport protocol connection to a multithreaded server destination.

Net8 access control   You can use this feature to control client access to designated servers in a TCP/IP environment. By specifying certain filtering rules, you may allow or restrict specific clients access to a server based on the source host name or IP address for clients, the destination host name or IP address for servers, or the destination database service name.

Multiprotocol support   Because OCM supports multiple protocols, clients and servers can communicate between and across separate protocols. For example, OCM can allow clients running SPX to communicate with a database server across a network running TCP/IP. Multiprotocol support is limited only by the protocols supported by the hardware and operating systems on your network.

OCM performs its tasks with the help of two processes: the OCM Gateway Process (CMGW) and the OCM Administrative Process (CMADMIN). CMGW acts as a hub for OCM. CMADMIN is a multithreaded process that handles administrative requests for OCM. OCM is managed via the OCM Control (cmctl) utility.

Introducing the Advanced Security Option

Oracle introduced the Advanced Networking Option (ANO) in Oracle8 as a package of security products. With Oracle8i, Oracle has renamed this the Oracle Advanced Security Option (ASO). ASO is an additional layer that sits on top of Net8, delivering industry-standard encryption, authentication, and remote access. ASO is a separately licensable option available with Oracle8i Enterprise Edition and Oracle8i Personal Edition. It is not available with the Standard Edition. ASO includes three components: network security, single sign-on, and Distributed Computing Environment (DCE) Integration.

This Oracle network data encryption and checksumming service ensures secure transmission of data over networks. ASO uses encryption and checksumming engines from RSA Data Security, Incorporated. For encryption, the DES_40 (domestic and export versions), RC4_40 (domestic and export versions), RC4_56 (domestic and export versions), and RC4_128 (domestic version) algorithms are supported. For checksumming, ASO uses the MD5 algorithm.

Single sign-on enables users to access multiple accounts and applications with a single password. This feature eliminates the need for multiple passwords for users and simplifies management of user accounts and passwords for system administrators. Centralized, secure authentication services verify the identity of users, clients, and servers in distributed environments. Network authentication services can also provide the benefit of single sign-on for users. The CyberSAFE, Identix (Biometric), Kerberos, RADIUS, SecurID, and SSL authentication methods are supported.

DCE Integration enables users to transparently use Oracle tools and applications to access Oracle8i databases in a DCE environment. The Oracle DCE Integration product consists of two major components: the DCE Communications/Security method and DCE Cell Directory Service (CDS) Naming method.

CHAPTER 10

Physical Backup and Recovery

FEATURING:

Backup and recovery planning	424
Putting the database in ARCHIVELOG mode	429
Backup and recovery in NOARCHIVELOG mode	435
Backups in ARCHIVELOG mode	441
Recoveries in ARCHIVELOG mode	450
Control file backups	480
RESETLOGS and recovery	486
Forcing open the database	489

With Oracle, there are actually two different types of backups (and recoveries): physical and logical backups. A *physical backup* takes place when you back up the physical structures of the Oracle database, including database datafiles, the control files, and in some cases the online redo logs or the archived redo logs. This chapter is devoted to physical backup and recovery. *Logical backups* are backups of the logical structures within the database itself. These backups are typically facilitated though the use of an outside utility such as Oracle's Export and Import programs. Logical backups are covered in Chapter 11.

When the database is configured correctly, physical backups also support point-in-time recovery. In other words, you can use a physical backup to recover the database to the point of failure (say, the loss of a physical disk drive). Physical backups even allow you to recover the database to a point in time before some action occurred. Therefore, if a user accidentally dropped every table in the database, you could recover the database to the point in time before the DROP action occurred.

This chapter begins with the important topic of backup and recovery planning. Then it discusses the two Oracle modes that affect how you do backups (and recoveries): NOARCHIVE and ARCHIVE mode. The remainder of the chapter is devoted to the various backup and recovery procedures you can use.

Backup and Recovery Planning

DBAs have many responsibilities, but one of the most critical is backup and recovery. As the DBA, you need to make sure that the database is recoverable at all times. This requires carefully planning and documenting your backup and recovery strategy. Here, we will look at the issues a DBA needs to consider when planning for backup and recovery, including how to develop a general backup strategy and a disaster recovery plan.

Planning Your Backup Strategy

There are several issues that you need to consider when planning your backup and recovery strategy. You need to meet with your users and decide on the answers to some fundamental questions:

- How critical is the data in the database? Is this a mission-critical database? Is this a test or development database?
- How often does the database need to be backed up?
- Does the data need to be recovered from a specific point in time, or can it be recovered at the point that the backup took place?

- Do you need to back up archived redo logs?
- How long does a given backup need to be retained?
- What is the allowable outage time for recoveries?
- Where will you store backups?
- How will you report on the status of backups?
- What happens in the event of a disaster?

Once you have answered these questions, you need to proceed to put together a backup and recovery plan. This plan should outline what types of database backups you will make, the frequency, and so on. Present this plan to management personnel, and anyone else who is involved, for their review and approval.

Make sure that you monitor your backups once they are in place. You'll need to test your backups on a regular basis. Nothing is more useless than a backup that failed, and nothing gets a DBA fired faster than being unable to recover a critical database.

Planning for Disasters

Disasters—floods, fire, tornadoes, stupid operators who spill soda on the keyboard, and so on—are a fact of life. Because life and nature tend to conspire against us at times, we need to make sure our critical databases are prepared for disaster. Planning is the key to successful disaster recovery. Of course, any good disaster recovery plan will apply to your entire business, not just your Oracle databases.

Considering the Worst

You should plan for the disasters that are most likely to occur in your location. If you are in Florida, plan for a hurricane or perhaps fire. If you live in Oklahoma, plan for a tornado or a huge lightning strike. In Seattle, you might prepare for Mt. Rainier to blow its top. In California, be ready for a major earthquake. Assume that your disasters will not allow you back into the building for some time (if ever). For example, after the Oklahoma City bombing, several businesses could not be accessed for some time.

You also should consider that major disasters (such as earthquakes, or even nuclear, chemical, or biological warfare) might affect communications and the ability to travel. For example, if your plan includes a group of recovery personnel taking a commercial flight out of town to your recovery site, you should think again. During major disasters, the airlines tend to fill up quickly! A better idea might be to identify off-site personnel to act as disaster backups, if possible. Perhaps you have offices in New York and Seattle. Maybe there are no DBAs in the Seattle office, but you could train someone to at least learn the basics of recovering your mission-critical databases.

This way, you distribute the risk. If your personnel can't get out of town (or perhaps they are all dead), your business has a fallback plan. Nobody wants to think of the worst happening, but that is what disaster planning is about.

Consider the nature of your business when you are disaster planning. In the event of a major disaster, who will be counting on you to stay in operation? Perhaps your business is a critical asset to the national defense structure (say, for example, your company is an airline, railroad, or military supplier). You need to consider these responsibilities in your disaster planning.

Also, in your disaster planning you need to consider the safety of your employees. In the event of a major event, such as a bombing, you need to decide where you will evacuate your people to, and you should execute such plans immediately upon occurrence of any situation. Often, when disaster strikes, people are not sure what to do or where to go. Keep in mind that during a disaster, people may be panicking and concerned about their families. Try to consider these facts when creating your plan.

An Eye Witness Account: The Oklahoma City Bombing

I was at ground zero during the Oklahoma City bombing, working at a downtown office with about 300 people. When the bomb exploded, it broke windows for a couple of miles around. Shrapnel from the blast impacted an area several blocks wide. We found rebar from the building literally impaled in the driver's seat of a car. Pieces of the building littered the ground.

After the bomb went off, the 300 employees sat in the front parking lot. Many of them were shocked at what they had seen and experienced. A few of us suggested that personnel should be removed from the area because of the possible dangers. What if a gas main had been compromised? What if there were another bomb? Still, the shock factor was a powerful thing, and it took some time for people to be convinced that they should go home. The point of this is that you need a plan for extreme disaster, and you need to stick to it. Safety of your people should always be your primary concern.

Creating a Disaster Recovery Plan

To complete your disaster preparation, you need to create and execute a disaster recovery plan. A disaster recovery plan includes the following critical elements:

- A timeline for recovering your databases
- A disaster recovery document

- Off-site storage of backups and procedures to recover those backups
- Disaster recovery plan testing (at least once a year)

Let's look at each of these elements in a bit more detail.

Developing Disaster Recovery Timelines

Disaster recovery timelines define when certain recovery tasks will begin and when they are expected to end. You may have several different timelines, depending on the various disaster situations that you might encounter. These timelines will also determine the critical personnel who are required and where they need to be at given times during the disaster process. Typically, you will mark the timeline from the point of the disaster. You would include details such as the following:

- One hour after a disaster, all critical personnel notified.
- Three hours after a disaster, DBAs and the disaster coordinator head for the off-site recovery center.
- Twelve hours after a disaster, the operating systems at the recovery center are ready for use.

You want to give people a clear idea of where they need to be during an emergency, when they need to be there, and what they need to be doing. You want to allow people to focus on the process of recovering the systems, removing all other concerns as much as possible.

Creating a Disaster Recovery Document

Before the disaster, you need to document your disaster recovery timeline and define who is responsible for various assignments in the disaster recovery plan. You should also list the duties of each person. At a minimum, you need to assign the following responsibilities:

Disaster recovery coordinator and alternate The disaster recovery coordinator is directly responsible for managing the disaster recovery plan. In the event that there is a disaster, the coordinator will be responsible for managing the disaster recovery process, making sure everything goes smoothly. An alternate coordinator needs to be named in case the primary one is unavailable.

Lead technical representatives from each technical group Any disaster plan needs to look beyond just the database. Since the database depends on an operating system, networks, and various other media, you need to have primary disaster contacts for each of these areas.

Outside vendor emergency contacts This list should include contact information for all vendors, as well as information for product ordering (should you need to order software or hardware during a disaster) and support lines. Make sure that you include support identification numbers, such as the Oracle CSI number.

Include contact information for all personnel assigned to these various disaster recovery duties in the disaster recovery document. Each person who is a member of the recovery team should have a copy of this document at his or her home.

Off-Site Backup Storage and Recovery

You need to store your backups of critical systems off-site for disaster recovery purposes. Here are a few criteria for off-site recovery:

- Find a site that is a reasonable distance from your primary site. This is because many types of disasters—fires, earthquakes, floods, and so on—can impact a locality. Imagine a biological disaster that affected an entire city.
- Establish a good system of managing your off-site backup rotation.
- Ensure that the backups will be accessible when needed.
- Security is an important concern. You don't want just anyone to be able to go in and pick up your backups, do you?

There are several companies that provide off-site recovery services. Many of these will even help you with your disaster recovery planning and allow you to use their sites for tests of your disaster recovery plan. It is important that your disaster recovery site be committed to the process. It is also important that the site maintains hardware that is as much like the hardware you have at your site as possible.

Off-site recovery locations can be expensive. If you find it's a bit pricey to sign a contract with such a site, consider a mutual off-site recovery agreement with another company. You could provide a location at your site for the other company to install a basic system that would be available for their personnel to use for disaster recovery purposes. In return, you could install a system at their site for the same purposes.

During disaster recovery, you probably won't need to install all of your systems, but only your primary ones. This implies that you might be able to purchase recovery hardware at an affordable cost. Of course, a careful analysis needs to be done before embarking on any path.

Testing Your Disaster Recovery Plan

Testing your disaster recovery plan is critical to success. On more than one occasion, I have seen clients turn ashen when I told them, in no uncertain terms, that they would never be able to recover their backups. A DBA never assumes anything. Generate your disaster recovery plan and test it—not just once, but as often as possible. At one client's site, I saw three disaster recovery tests fail in a row for different reasons. Disaster recovery is like anything else worthwhile—it takes practice.

Putting the Database in ARCHIVELOG Mode

Oracle backup and recovery solutions start with the database being in one of two different modes: ARCHIVELOG mode or NOARCHIVELOG mode. You can tell which mode your database is in by querying the V$DATABASE table, as follows:

```
SELECT log_mode FROM v$database;
```

NOARCHIVELOG mode is the default mode that the database will be created in. Therefore, if you haven't put the database in ARCHIVELOG mode, the query's result will be:

```
LOG_MODE
------------
NOARCHIVELOG
```

When the database is in NOARCHIVELOG mode, the archived redo logs are not backed up. This limits your physical backup and recovery options. You can perform only *cold backups*, which require the database to be down. *Hot backups*—backups performed while the database is operating—and point-in-time recovery of your database will not be possible. However, you do gain some disk space and a slight reduction in the CPU and I/O requirements.

Putting the database in ARCHIVELOG mode causes Oracle to create archived redo logs, which are backups of each online redo log, stored in one or more archive log directories. Until the archived redo log copies are complete, the online redo logs associated with these archived redo logs will not be reused by the system. When the database is in ARCHIVELOG mode, you can perform hot backups and recover the database to point of failure, or some point prior to that failure.

If you want to expand your physical database recovery options, you should put the database in ARCHIVELOG mode. There are actually several steps that you need to complete to put the database in ARCHIVELOG mode:

1. Modify the `init.ora` file.
2. Create the archive log directory.
3. Shut down the database.
4. Mount the database.
5. Put the database in ARCHIVELOG mode.
6. Open the database.

Let's look at the process of putting the database in ARCHIVELOG mode in a bit more detail.

Modifying the *init.ora* File

In preparation for setting up the database in ARCHIVELOG mode, you need to make some changes to the database's `init.ora` file. For the most part, what you are configuring in this file is the optional ARCH process. The parameters are listed in Table 10.1.

 NOTE There is a difference between the database being in ARCHIVELOG mode and enabling the ARCH process. Both steps need to be completed before the database is ready for hot backup and recovery.

TABLE 10.1: *INIT.ORA* PARAMETERS ASSOCIATED WITH ARCHIVELOG MODE

Parameter	Default Setting	Description
log_archive_dest	None	Establishes the location to copy archived redo logs to. This parameter is deprecated with Oracle8i.
log_archive_dest_n	None	In Oracle8i Enterprise Edition, establishes up to 5 archive log destinations. You can use the LOCATION keyword to denote a local file system to copy archived redo logs to. You can use the SERVICE keyword to denote a destination, such as to allow Oracle to transmit archived redo logs for standby database use. Each given path can be designated as MANDATORY or OPTIONAL.
log_archive_dest_state_n	Enable	Indicates the status of the associated archive log destination and can be set to enable or deferred. If set to deferred, then archive logs will not be sent to that destination.
log_archive_duplex_dest	None	In Oracle8i Enterprise Edition, designates an archive log destination, but its use is deprecated in favor of the log_archive_dest_*n* parameter.

Continued

PUTTING THE DATABASE IN ARCHIVELOG MODE

TABLE 10.1: *INIT.ORA* PARAMETERS ASSOCIATED WITH ARCHIVELOG MODE (CONTINUED)

Parameter	Default Setting	Description
log_archive_format	Operating system dependent	Defines the format of archived redo logs generated by the instance. See the example following the table for variables that you can use when defining the log filename.
log_archive_max_processes	1	Specifies the number of ARCH processes that Oracle will initially invoke.
log_archive_min_succeed_dest	1	Defines how many archive log destinations must be successfully copied to in order for an online redo log to be made available for reuse. This number can be up to 5 if you are using Oracle8i Enterprise Edition, or up to 2 with other versions.
log_archive_start	FALSE	This parameter, if set to TRUE, will cause the ARCH process(es) to start when the Oracle database starts.
log_archive_trace	0	Enables tracing of the ARCH process.
standby_archive_dest	None	Used by standby databases to define the location of the archived redo logs sent from the primary database.

 WARNING Failure to properly set up these parameters can cause the database to not start, or can cause the database to fail after a period of usage.

Here are examples of several of the settings listed in Table 10.1 in an init.ora file for a Windows NT system:

```
log_archive_start = true
log_archive_dest_1 = "location=D:\Oracle\oradata\ora816\archive"
log_archive_dest_2 = "service=standby_db reopen=10"
log_archive_format = %%ORACLE_SID%%T%TS%S.ARC
```

The LOG_ARCHIVE_FORMAT setting sets the archived redo log filename, as follows:

- The %%ORACLE_SID%% parameter includes the Oracle database name in the filename. ORACLE_SID is an environment variable, which NT encloses in % symbols. By enclosing the environment variable in double % symbols, this variable will be used in the name of the archived redo log file.
- Following %%ORACLE_SID%% is a hard-coded T, which will cause a *T* to appear in the archived redo log name.
- The hard-coded T is followed by a %T, which will cause a zero-filled thread number to be included in the archived redo log name. If a %t were used instead, the thread number would not be zero-filled.
- Next is another hard-coded value, S, which puts an *S* in this position of the log filename.
- The next parameter is %S, which sets a zero-filled thread number. You can also use the %s variable to set a log sequence number.
- Finally, the .ARC appends an .ARC extension to the filename.

With this specification, an archived redo log filename will end up looking like this:
ORA817T001S00090.ARC

In this case, this archived redo log is from the ORA817 database, its thread number is 001, and the log sequence number is 90.

To specify the same filename format in a Unix system, you need to hard-code the database name (rather than using an environment variable):
LOG_ARCHIVE_FORMAT=ORA817T%TS%S.ARC

Many of these parameters can be changed dynamically through the use of the ALTER SYSTEM command. Also, you can use the ARCHIVELOG clause of the ALTER SYSTEM command as another way to start archiving, force log switches (discussed in the next section), switch archive log destinations, and other operations. Table 10.2 provides a summary of the different ALTER SYSTEM ARCHIVELOG clause operations.

TABLE 10.2: ALTER SYSTEM ARCHIVELOG COMMANDS

Command	Description
ARCHIVE LOG	Defines the start of the ARCHIVELOG clause.
SEQUENCE #	Causes the listed log sequence number to be archived.

Continued

PUTTING THE DATABASE IN ARCHIVELOG MODE

TABLE 10.2: ALTER SYSTEM ARCHIVELOG COMMANDS (CONTINUED)

Command	Description
ARCHIVE LOG	Defines the start of the ARCHIVELOG clause.
SEQUENCE #	Causes the listed log sequence number to be archived.
CHANGE #	Causes Oracle to archive the online redo log file that contains the given SCN. If the affected log is the current log file, a log switch occurs.
CURRENT	Causes Oracle to archive the current online redo log. This command essentially forces a log switch.
GROUP #	Causes a given log group number to be archived. All previous log file groups must already have been archived, or an error will occur.
LOGFILE *'filename'*	Causes the given online redo log file to be archived. All previous log file sequence numbers must already have been archived, or an error will occur.
NEXT	Causes Oracle to archive the next unarchived online redo log group.
ALL	Causes Oracle to archive all full, unarchived redo logs. This command does not cause a log switch.
START	Causes Oracle to start the ARCH process.
STOP	Causes Oracle to stop the ARCH process.

Here are a few examples of using the ALTER SYSTEM command:

```
ALTER SYSTEM SET log_archive_dest_1="location=d:\oracle\archive"
ALTER SYSTEM SWITCH LOGFILE;
ALTER SYSTEM ARCHIVELOG ALL;
```

Completing the ARCHIVEMODE Process

After you've configured the ARCH process, you can complete the process of putting the database into ARCHIVELOG mode, as follows:

Create the directories that the ARCH process will copy the archived redo logs to.
It's a good idea to put this directory on its own set of disks if possible. This way, the I/O associated with the process of writing the archived redo logs will not interfere with your database. Also, your archived redo logs will be protected from disk failure.

Shut down and remount the database. This is required to put the database in ARCHIVELOG mode. Once the database is shut down, proceed to mount it again. After you remount it, the ARCH process should be running.

Put the database in ARCHIVELOG mode and open it. At this point, you can put the database in ARCHIVELOG mode by using the ALTER DATABASE ARCHIVELOG command. Then open the database by issuing the ALTER DATABASE OPEN command.

Next, you will want to test the configuration of the ARCH process. Why? Well, if you incorrectly set up ARCH so that it is writing to a directory that doesn't exist, guess what will happen soon: The database will come to a screeching halt. This happens because Oracle will not allow you to overwrite the online redo log file until ARCH can write out the archived redo logs successfully. If you are trying to archive to a destination that doesn't exist, these attempts to create the archived redo logs will fail. To test your configuration, issue an ALTER DATABASE SWITCH LOGFILE command. Then check the archived log destinations a few moments later. You should see an archived redo log file created in those directories. If these files are created, you are in good shape.

After you put the database in ARCHIVELOG mode and test your configuration, you should proceed to perform a hot backup as quickly as possible. Then you will be able to recover your database using the archived redo logs, if necessary.

Considering Online Redo Log Groups

In NOARCHIVELOG mode, there is only one basic rule that Oracle follows in relation to redo log switches: Before an online redo log can be used, the changes represented within the redo it contains from its last use must have been written to the database datafiles. Thus, Oracle will not reuse a redo log if its previous contents have not been written to the database datafiles. This rule is in place to facilitate crash and instance recovery of the database.

In ARCHIVELOG mode, things get a bit more complicated. When a log switch occurs, Oracle will first update the control file, indicating that the redo log needs to be archived. It will then signal the ARCH process, indicating that it has a redo log to process. The ARCH process will wake up (assuming it's not processing another online redo log file already) and begin to copy that online redo log to the archived redo log directory defined in the init.ora file (by the ARCHIVE_LOG_DEST_n parameter). During the ARCH copy process, Oracle will proceed to the next available online redo log and continue database activity as normal.

If Oracle proceeds through the remaining redo log groups and returns to the redo log group you are archiving, it will not reuse that online redo log until the archiving process has completed successfully for that online redo log file. If Oracle cannot use that online redo log, it will look for another available online redo log. If no online redo log is available, then the Oracle database will be suspended until the ARCH process has completed its moves. Once ARCH completes the move of the online redo log, it will update the control file, indicating that the online redo log has been archived. At that point, LGWR will be able to open and use the online redo log.

The log switch process in ARCHIVELOG can pose a problem if you don't have enough online redo log files (and/or if they are too small), because Oracle may not be able to write out the archived redo logs fast enough to keep up with the redo creation within the online redo logs. Thus, you may find that your database activity becomes suspended quite often—not a condition that users or managers desire.

Something else to consider is the number of archive log destinations you will have. Adding a destination will increase the time it takes to archive your online redo logs. If you add a network destination, that will further erode the performance of the archiving process. There are several possible solutions to this problem:

- Add enough log file groups of sufficient size to reduce contention with the archiving process.
- Reduce the number of archiving destinations.
- Carefully tune the I/O. Try to separate the archived logs onto their own disks to reduce the I/O contention that ARCH might incur.

Backup and Recovery in NOARCHIVELOG Mode

With the database in NOARCHIVELOG mode, the online redo logs are overwritten without regard to recoverability of the database. Thus, the only backup option is a cold backup. A *cold backup* of a database is a backup that takes place while the database is shut down. Thus, during the period that the cold backup takes place, users will have no access to the database or the data within it.

When you perform a cold backup in NOARCHIVELOG mode, you simply back up the entire physical structure of the database. A cold backup in NOARCHIVELOG mode includes backups of the following:

- All database datafiles
- All database control files

- All online database redo logs
- Other required database files such as `init.ora`

The following sections describe the procedures for backing up and recovering a database in NOARCHIVE mode.

Performing Cold Backups in NOARCHIVELOG Mode

To perform a cold backup, you simply identify the database files to be backed up, shut down the database, and back up the physical files to the backup medium. Then you can start the database again.

You might wonder why you need to shut down the database for a cold backup if you can ensure that nobody will make any changes to the database while it is up. As explained in Chapter 5, one method that Oracle uses to determine that the database is in a consistent state is by virtue of a fuzzy file flag maintained in each database datafile. If the fuzzy datafile flag is set when the database starts, the database will consider the datafile to be fuzzy. Thus, if you recover a datafile that was backed up while the database was running, even if the database had no activity, that backup is not usable for recovery purposes. This is because the fuzzy flag will have been set in the open position. There are some ways to force the database open in these cases (as you will learn later in this chapter), but these methods are not recommended.

Identifying the Files to Back Up

To locate the database datafiles, control files, and online redo logs to back up, you can use some data dictionary queries. Use the DBA_DATA_FILES data dictionary view to find the database datafiles, as in this example:

```
SELECT tablespace_name, file_name, file_id
FROM dba_data_files
ORDER BY tablespace_name, file_name;
```

TABLESPACE_NAME	FILE_NAME	FILE_ID
IDX	D:\ORACLE\ORADATA\RECOVER\RECOVER_IDX_01.DBF	4
RBS	D:\ORACLE\ORADATA\RECOVER\RECOVER_RBS_01.DBF	2
SYSTEM	D:\ORACLE\ORADATA\RECOVER\SYSTEM01.DBF	1
TEMP	D:\ORACLE\ORADATA\RECOVER\RECOVER_TEMP_01.DBF	5
USERS	D:\ORACLE\ORADATA\RECOVER\RECOVER_USERS_01.DBF	3

To find the database control files, query the V$CONTROL_FILE data dictionary view:
```
SQL> SELECT * FROM v$controlfile;
```

```
STATUS   NAME
-------  ----------------------------------------
         D:\ORACLE\ORADATA\RECOVER\CONTROL01.CTL
         D:\ORACLE\ORADATA\RECOVER\CONTROL02.CTL
         D:\ORACLE\ORADATA\RECOVER\CONTROL03.CTL
```

Finally, use a query to the V$LOGFILE data dictionary view to locate the database online redo log files:

```
SQL> SELECT * FROM v$logfile;

GROUP#  STATUS   MEMBER
------  -------  ----------------------------------------
     1           D:\ORACLE\ORADATA\RECOVER\REDO01.LOG
     2  STALE    D:\ORACLE\ORADATA\RECOVER\REDO02.LOG
     3           D:\ORACLE\ORADATA\RECOVER\REDO03.LOG
```

Running the Backup

After you've identified the database files, you're ready to perform a cold backup. To do so, you must first shut down the database. When shutting down the database for a cold backup, it is strongly recommended that you use either the normal SHUTDOWN command or the SHUTDOWN IMMEDIATE command. This will cause DBWn to flush all dirty buffers to the database datafiles. As long as you have issued either a SHUTDOWN or SHUTDOWN IMMEDIATE command, you will not need to recover (or back up) the online redo log files for the database.

Now, you can proceed to back up the physical database files that you identified. To shorten the time of the overall outage required to back up the database, you may wish to back up the datafiles to disk, open the database, and then back up the other files to slower backup medium, such as tape. It is often advisable to include in your final backup image a copy of a backup control file (aside from the backup of the current control file). A *backup control file* is a backup of the control file that can be used to recover the control file in the event that it is lost. We will discuss the creation of a backup control file later in this chapter, in the "Control File Backups" section. When you're finished backing up the database, you can open the database again. Listing 10.1 shows an example or running a cold backup in NOARCHIVELOG mode.

NOTE All of the examples in this chapter were done on Windows NT. The principles are the same, regardless of the operating system. Only the operating system commands (such as copy, cp, tar, or tape backup) are different.

Listing 10.1: Performing a Cold Backup in NOARCHIVELOG Mode

```
D:\ORACLE\ORA816\DATABASE>sqlplus "sys/robert as sysdba"
SQL> SHUTDOWN IMMEDIATE
Database closed.
Database dismounted.
ORACLE instance shut down.
-- Now we are going to back up the database. Note that we have a
-- pretty poorly set up database here, because everything is on one
-- drive. We did that mostly just to keep the example easy and
-- to save page space.
SQL> HOST MKDIR d:\backup_oracle
SQL> HOST COPY d:\oracle\oradata\recover\*.* d:\backup_oracle\*.*
d:\oracle\oradata\recover\CONTROL01.CTL
d:\oracle\oradata\recover\CONTROL02.CTL
d:\oracle\oradata\recover\CONTROL03.CTL
d:\oracle\oradata\recover\REDO01.LOG
d:\oracle\oradata\recover\REDO02.LOG
d:\oracle\oradata\recover\REDO03.LOG
d:\oracle\oradata\recover\SYSTEM01.DBF
d:\oracle\oradata\recover\RECOVER_RBS_01.DBF
d:\oracle\oradata\recover\RECOVER_USERS_01.DBF
d:\oracle\oradata\recover\RECOVER_TEMP_01.DBF
d:\oracle\oradata\recover\afiedt.buf
d:\oracle\oradata\recover\recover_idx_01.dbf.backup
d:\oracle\oradata\recover\RECOVER_IDX_01.DBF
        13 file(s) copied.

-- Backup is complete, restart the database.
SQL> STARTUP
ORACLE instance started.
Total System Global Area    92280076 bytes
Fixed Size                     70924 bytes
Variable Size               87937024 bytes
Database Buffers             4194304 bytes
Redo Buffers                   77824 bytes
Database mounted.
Database opened.
```

NOTE Listing 10.1 and many other examples start SQL*Plus or connect to the database using the "/ as sysdba" or "sys/robert as sysdba" string. This is done for two reasons. First, Oracle will be dropping support for CONNECT INTERNAL in Oracle9i, so we are trying to prepare for that eventuality. Second, with Oracle release 8.1.6, we are forced to put the username and password on the command line. This is due to a bug in 8.1.6 that was fixed in 8.1.7. If you are running 8.1.7, you can use "system as sysdba" with SQL*Plus, and then respond to the password prompt that follows.

Recovering Cold Backups in NOARCHIVELOG Mode

Recovering a database from a cold backup taken in NOARCHIVELOG mode is fairly simple. Issue a SHUTDOWN ABORT command on the database instance to make sure that all the database processes are stopped and all operating system locks on files that might remain are released. Then recover all of the database files to their original locations, if possible. If this is not possible, record the new location of the database files for later use. If any of the files were recovered to a different location, you will need to reset the location as follows:

- If the control files were recovered to a different location, edit the database parameter file to reflect the new location for the control files. Change any other directory paths that might have changed as a result of the recovery process.

- If the database datafiles or the redo logs were recovered to another location, you will need to mount the database by issuing a STARTUP MOUNT command. Issue the ALTER DATABASE RENAME FILE command for each datafile that was recovered to another location.

- If the online redo logs were recovered to another location, issue the ALTER DATABASE RENAME FILE command to reset the location of the database online redo logs.

When all of the database files have been recovered, issue the STARTUP command, and the database should open normally. Listing 10.2 provides an example of recovering a database that was backed up in NOARCHIVELOG mode. (Note that due to book page line-length restrictions, some code is broken into multiple lines.)

Listing 10.2: Performing a Cold Backup Recovery in NOARCHIVELOG Mode

```
D:\ORACLE\oradata\RECOVER>sqlplus "sys/robert as sysdba"
SQL> STARTUP
```

```
ORACLE instance started.
Total System Global Area    92280076 bytes
Fixed Size                     70924 bytes
Variable Size               87937024 bytes
Database Buffers             4194304 bytes
Redo Buffers                   77824 bytes
Database mounted.
ORA-01157: cannot identify/lock datafile 4 - see DBWR trace file
ORA-01110: datafile 4: 'D:\ORACLE\ORADATA\RECOVER\RECOVER_IDX_01.DBF'
SQL> SHUTDOWN ABORT
ORACLE instance shut down.
-- Recover the database from the backup we made earlier.
SQL> HOST COPY d:\backup_oracle\*.*
d:\oracle\oradata\recover\recover_idx_01.dbf
d:\backup_oracle\CONTROL01.CTL
d:\backup_oracle\CONTROL02.CTL
d:\backup_oracle\CONTROL03.CTL
d:\backup_oracle\REDO01.LOG
d:\backup_oracle\REDO02.LOG
d:\backup_oracle\REDO03.LOG
d:\backup_oracle\SYSTEM01.DBF
d:\backup_oracle\RECOVER_RBS_01.DBF
d:\backup_oracle\RECOVER_USERS_01.DBF
d:\backup_oracle\RECOVER_TEMP_01.DBF
d:\backup_oracle\afiedt.buf
d:\backup_oracle\recover_idx_01.dbf.backup
d:\backup_oracle\RECOVER_IDX_01.DBF
        1 file(s) copied.
SQL> STARTUP
ORACLE instance started.
Total System Global Area    92280076 bytes
Fixed Size                     70924 bytes
Variable Size               87937024 bytes
Database Buffers             4194304 bytes
Redo Buffers                   77824 bytes
Database mounted.
Database opened.
```

If you were not able to recover the online redo logs from the backup medium, you can still recover the database in many cases. First, if you were able to recover at least one member of each redo log group, you can create a copy of that online redo log, naming it with the name of the missing online redo log. If none of the online redo logs are available, as long as you shut down your database normally (or with the IMMEDIATE option), all you need to do is open the database with the following command:

```
ALTER DATABASE OPEN RESETLOGS;
```

We will discuss the RESETLOGS command in more detail later in this chapter, in the "RESETLOGS and Recovery" section. For now, suffice it to say that issuing this command will cause the database to create new redo logs. Also, if the control file is missing, you can recover using the backup control file, as described in the "Control File Backups" section later in this chapter.

Backups in ARCHIVELOG Mode

The principle difference between NOARCHIVELOG mode and ARCHIVELOG mode is the creation of archived redo logs, and associated with that, the ability to back up the database while it is still running and recover the database to point of failure, or some point prior to that failure. It is this functionality and reliability that make Oracle the most popular database in the world.

Performing Cold Backups in ARCHIVELOG Mode

Cold backups in ARCHIVELOG mode are much the same as those in NOARCHIVELOG mode, except that you don't need to back up the online redo logs or the control files. It is best not to back up online redo logs during backups in ARCHIVELOG mode (unless you are not saving the archived redo logs), because you do not want to accidentally recover them over existing online redo logs during a recovery. Also, overwriting the existing control file will hamper your ability to recover the database to the point of failure. Instead, create a backup control file, as discussed later in this chapter in the "Control File Backups" section.

The steps for performing a cold backup in ARCHIVELOG mode are as follows:

1. Identify the database datafiles to be backed up.
2. Shut down the database.
3. Back up the physical datafiles to the backup medium.
4. Start the database.

5. Back up the existing archived redo log. (This is not really a requirement at this point if you shut down the database normally, but it's good practice.)

6. Back up the archived redo logs on a regular basis.

All of these steps, except the last two, are the same as those for a cold backup in NOARCHIVE mode. Steps 5 and 6 pertain to backing up archived redo logs, which is covered in the next section.

Backing Up Archived Redo Logs

When you are doing any backup in ARCHIVELOG mode, it is assumed (and in the case of hot backups, required) that the archived redo logs created during the time of the backup are themselves backed up. It is the backup of these logs (and subsequent backups of newly created archived redo logs) that allows an Oracle database in ARCHIVELOG mode to be recovered.

When recovering from hot backups, all of the archived redo logs generated during the hot backup are required during the recovery process. In addition, if you wish to recover the database to a point beyond the point of recovery, you will need all of the generated archived redo logs as well. As explained earlier in this chapter, the location of the archived redo logs is defined in the init.ora file using the LOG_ARCHIVE_DEST_*n* parameter. You can query the V$ARCHIVE_DEST data dictionary view to determine the current location of the archived log directories, as follows:

```
SELECT destination FROM v$archive_dest;

DESTINATION
----------------------------------------
D:\Oracle\oradata\Recover\archive
```

NOTE The V$ARCHIVE_DEST data dictionary view contains a row for each destination, even if the destination is not defined.

How often should archived redo logs be backed up? The answer to the question is really another question: How much data loss can you tolerate? Since the archived redo logs are typically stored on the same system as the database that generated them, there is some risk of loss of these files. When configuring your database, you should give careful consideration to using alternative storage locations, such as network appliances or other options, to reduce the risk of datafile loss.

Also keep in mind the performance implications of your archived redo log configurations. The more archived redo log destinations you configure, the longer the ARCH process will take to copy each archived redo log. If you are copying these over the network (to a standby database in Net8), this may even further impact the overall performance of the ARCH process. Remember that Oracle will not be able to reuse an online redo log until all required copies to archive locations are complete.

 NOTE Besides being useful for recovery, archived redo logs can also be run through the Oracle8i utility called LogMiner, which we will cover in Chapter 14. LogMiner allows you to review the archived redo logs for security audits and other purposes. Archived redo logs are also used to keep standby databases current, as explained in Chapter 26, which discusses high-availability options.

Performing Hot Backups in ARCHIVELOG Mode

Now we reach the big time—hot backups in ARCHIVELOG mode. When you implement hot backups in your database, you enter a whole new world of recovery options. When doing hot backups, you simply do not back up control files and online redo logs. What you do is put tablespaces in hot backup mode. These tablespaces are associated with the datafiles that you have chosen to back up.

When you put tablespaces in hot backup mode, Oracle generates block-level redo to the online redo logs, as opposed to the normal atomic redo records that are created when the tablespaces are not in hot backup mode. This means that all redo generated for the tablespace is generated as an image of the entire block, rather than as just redo records. Thus, redo generation is substantially increased during hot backup operations (however, this is not true with RMAN hot backups, which are discussed in Chapter 13).

Block images are recorded in the redo logs to avoid problems with operating system block splitting. Since Oracle continues to write to database datafiles during hot backups, there is a possibility that the backed up image of the datafile will contain fractured blocks. This is because the operating system write batch size may be smaller than the block size of the database, so the backup image of a given datafile may contain a block that is of two different versions. The generation of block images in the online redo logs solves this problem by allowing the block to be restored during the backup process.

> **TIP** Because of the increased level of redo generation during hot backups, as well as the general performance impacts associated with moving large amounts of data (such as copying database datafiles to tape), you should try to schedule database backups during low-usage hours.

Performing hot backups is not a complicated task. Here are the basic steps:

1. Identify the database datafiles to be backed up. You also need to identify the associated tablespace names.
2. Determine the current log sequence number.
3. For each tablespace that is associated with the datafiles to be backed up, put that tablespace in hot backup mode.
4. Back up the physical database datafiles that are associated with the tablespace put in hot backup mode.
5. As each tablespace backup is complete (or you have completed backups for all the datafiles of a given tablespace), take that tablespace out of hot backup mode.
6. Once the backups are complete and all tablespaces are out of hot backup mode, force a log switch.
7. Back up all of the archived redo logs.
8. Create backup control files.
9. Back up the archived redo logs on a regular basis.

Let's look at these steps in a bit more detail.

Identifying the Database Files and Associated Tablespaces

Since you need to put the tablespaces of the database datafiles in hot backup mode, you need to know not only the location of the database datafiles, but also the tablespaces they are associated with. You can find this information via a query to the DBA_DATA_FILES data dictionary view (as shown in Listing 10.3, a bit later in this chapter).

Hot backups allow you to selectively back up different tablespaces at different times. Therefore, if you wanted to back up the DATA tablespace tonight, and the INDEX tablespace tomorrow night, you could—although good arguments could be made not to do this. In fact, you don't even need to back up every datafile of a given tablespace. Again, this isn't good practice, because it becomes a lot more difficult to manage backups created this way and can lead to situations where the database may be unrecoverable.

For example, suppose that you backed up one datafile belonging to the DATA tablespace two weeks ago and the other two datafiles a week ago. Now suppose that your database crashes, and you lose all three datafiles. You would need to recover the one datafile from two weeks ago and the two other datafiles from a week ago. Also, you would need to recover the archived redo logs to apply recovery. If you couldn't get the one datafile off the tape from two weeks ago, you would be in bad shape and would probably be unable to recover the database. Thus, it is normally good practice to back up all associated datafiles with a given tablespace during a backup.

Determining the Current Log Sequence Number

Before starting the backup, you should determine the current log sequence number. You will need to make sure that you back up this log sequence number, along with all logs generated during the backup, after the backup has completed. Use the ARCHIVE LOG LIST command to get this information (see Listing 10.3).

Putting Tablespaces in Hot Backup Mode

The hot backup bit is set in the database datafiles when you issue the ALTER TABLESPACE BEGIN BACKUP command:

```
ALTER TABLESPACE idx BEGIN BACKUP;
```

This command places the tablespace in hot backup mode, flipping the fuzzy backup bit.

If you want to determine if a database datafile is in hot backup mode, you can query the V$BACKUP view. The STATUS column in this view will indicate the value ACTIVE if the tablespace is in hot backup mode (see Listing 10.3).

If the database should crash or you issue a SHUTDOWN ABORT command while a tablespace is in hot backup mode, you will need to reset the datafiles associated with the tablespace so that they are no longer in hot backup mode. To do this, you use the ALTER DATABASE DATAFILE *filename* END BACKUP command. Here is an example:

```
SQL> ALTER TABLESPACE idx BEGIN BACKUP;
Tablespace altered.
SQL> SHUTDOWN ABORT
ORACLE instance shut down.
SQL> STARTUP
ORACLE instance started.
Total System Global Area    92280076 bytes
Fixed Size                     70924 bytes
Variable Size               87937024 bytes
Database Buffers             4194304 bytes
Redo Buffers                   77824 bytes
```

```
Database mounted.
ORA-01113: file 4 needs media recovery
ORA-01110: datafile 4: 'D:\ORACLE\ORADATA\RECOVER\RECOVER_IDX_01.DBF'
SQL> ALTER DATABASE DATAFILE 4 END BACKUP;
Database altered.
SQL> ALTER DATABASE OPEN;
Database altered.
```

This example uses the file identifier (4) rather than the file path and name in the END BACKUP command. Alternatively, you could use the filename, like this:

```
ALTER DATABASE DATAFILE 'D:\ORACLE\ORADATA\RECOVER\RECOVER_IDX_01.DBF' END
BACKUP
```

Backing Up the Datafiles

You can use any standard copy facility (cp, copy, tar, gzip, and so on) to copy the database files to the backup media that you wish to use. As mentioned earlier, it's probably a good idea to back up all of the associated datafiles, but this is not required. All that is required for recovery is the presence of all the associated datafiles (backed up with the database in hot backup mode or the current database datafiles) and the archived redo logs to make those files consistent.

Completing the Backup

Once you have completed backing up the datafiles for a given tablespace, take that tablespace out of hot backup mode, using the ALTER TABLESPACE END BACKUP command (see Listing 10.3).

Your next step is to force a redo log switch. This is because you will need all of the redo generated during the hot backup (and since the database is open to users during a hot backup, you will be generating redo) to recover the database datafiles you have backed up. After forcing a log switch, back up all archived redo logs generated during the backup, as well as the archived redo log generated by the log switch.

To force the redo log switch after you have taken each tablespace out of hot backup mode, issue the ALTER SYSTEM SWITCH LOGFILE command. You can determine which log sequence numbers you need to make sure are backed up by issuing the ARCHIVE LOG LIST command from either Server Manager or SQL*Plus when connected as INTERNAL. Run this command both before the hot backups (finding the current log sequence number) and before issuing the ALTER SYSTEM SWITCH LOGFILE command (again finding the current log sequence number). This will tell you the low and high log sequence numbers that you must back up in order to recover the hot backup you just made.

Listing 10.3 provides an example of a complete hot backup. In this example, the database files reside in d:\oracle\oradata\recover. These datafiles are backed up to d:\oracle_backup\hot, and the archived redo logs are backed up to d:\oracle_backup\hot\archive.

Listing 10.3: Running a Hot Backup

```
-- First, get the tablespace names and filenames and locations.
SQL> SELECT tablespace_name, file_name, file_id
FROM dba_data_files
ORDER BY tablespace_name, file_name;

TABLESPACE_NAME    FILE_NAME                                              FILE_ID
-----------------  -----------------------------------------------------  -------
IDX                D:\ORACLE\ORADATA\RECOVER\RECOVER_IDX_01.DBF                 4
RBS                D:\ORACLE\ORADATA\RECOVER\RECOVER_RBS_01.DBF                 2
SYSTEM             D:\ORACLE\ORADATA\RECOVER\SYSTEM01.DBF                       1
TEMP               D:\ORACLE\ORADATA\RECOVER\RECOVER_TEMP_01.DBF                5
USERS              D:\ORACLE\ORADATA\RECOVER\RECOVER_USERS_01.DBF               3

-- Get the current log sequence number
SQL> ARCHIVE LOG LIST
Database log mode              Archive Mode
Automatic archival             Enabled
Archive destination            D:\Oracle\oradata\Recover\archive
Oldest online log sequence     216
Next log sequence to archive   218
Current log sequence           218

-- Now, put the tablespaces in hot backup mode.
-- Note that if we wanted to just back up a specific
-- tablespace, we would execute this statement only
-- for that tablespace.
SQL> ALTER TABLESPACE idx BEGIN BACKUP;
Tablespace altered.
SQL> ALTER TABLESPACE rbs BEGIN BACKUP;
Tablespace altered.
SQL> ALTER TABLESPACE system BEGIN BACKUP;
Tablespace altered.
SQL> ALTER TABLESPACE temp BEGIN BACKUP;
Tablespace altered.
```

```
SQL> ALTER TABLESPACE users BEGIN BACKUP;
Tablespace altered.

-- Check the status of all the database datafiles.
SQL> SELECT * FROM v$backup;

     FILE# STATUS              CHANGE# TIME
---------- ------------------ ---------- ---------
         1 ACTIVE              176503 28-APR-01
         2 ACTIVE              176502 28-APR-01
         3 ACTIVE              176505 28-APR-01
         4 ACTIVE              176501 28-APR-01
         5 ACTIVE              176504 28-APR-01

-- Now, back up the database datafiles. Notice that we do not back up
-- the online redo logs or the control file.
SQL> HOST COPY d:\oracle\oradata\recover\*.dbf d:\oracle_backup\hot\*.*
d:\oracle\oradata\recover\SYSTEM01.DBF
d:\oracle\oradata\recover\RECOVER_RBS_01.DBF
d:\oracle\oradata\recover\RECOVER_USERS_01.DBF
d:\oracle\oradata\recover\RECOVER_TEMP_01.DBF
d:\oracle\oradata\recover\RECOVER_IDX_01.DBF
        5 file(s) copied.

-- Now, end the backup status of the tablespaces.
SQL> ALTER TABLESPACE idx END BACKUP;
Tablespace altered.
SQL> ALTER TABLESPACE rbs END BACKUP;
Tablespace altered.
SQL> ALTER TABLESPACE system END BACKUP;
Tablespace altered.
SQL> ALTER TABLESPACE temp END BACKUP;
Tablespace altered.
SQL> ALTER TABLESPACE users END BACKUP;
Tablespace altered.

-- Check the status of all the database datafiles.
-- They should all now show not active.
SQL> SELECT * FROM v$backup;
```

```
     FILE# STATUS              CHANGE# TIME
---------- ------------------ ---------- ---------
         1 NOT ACTIVE           176503 28-APR-01
         2 NOT ACTIVE           176502 28-APR-01
         3 NOT ACTIVE           176505 28-APR-01
         4 NOT ACTIVE           176501 28-APR-01
         5 NOT ACTIVE           176504 28-APR-01

-- Find out what the active online redo log sequence number
-- is. We need to make sure this one gets backed up. We want
-- to make sure we back up from log sequence number 218 to 219.
SQL> ARCHIVE LOG LIST;
Database log mode              Archive Mode
Automatic archival             Enabled
Archive destination            D:\Oracle\oradata\Recover\archive
Oldest online log sequence     217
Next log sequence to archive   219
Current log sequence           219

-- Now, force a log switch.
SQL> ALTER SYSTEM SWITCH LOGFILE;
System altered.

-- Now, back up the archived redo logs generated during the backup.
-- Optionally, you can delete the archived redo logs once they are
-- backed up to save space.
SQL> HOST COPY d:\oracle\oradata\recover\archive\*.*
d:\oracle_backup\hot\archive\*.*
d:\oracle\oradata\recover\archive\RECOVERT001S00215.ARC
d:\oracle\oradata\recover\archive\RECOVERT001S00216.ARC
d:\oracle\oradata\recover\archive\RECOVERT001S00217.ARC
d:\oracle\oradata\recover\archive\RECOVERT001S00218.ARC
d:\oracle\oradata\recover\archive\RECOVERT001S00219.ARC
        3 file(s) copied.

-- The backup is complete. The database is recoverable.
```

Ongoing Backups of Archived Redo Logs

The Achilles heel of hot backups is their dependence on archived redo logs for recovery. You simply must have all of the logs in order to recover the database completely. If you have a gap in the redo log sequence numbers, recovery to the point of the crash will not be possible (although you should be able to do an incomplete recovery, unless you don't have all the archived redo log files generated during a backup).

Because the archived redo logs are so important, you need to have a good backup strategy to make sure that they are protected. In some environments, disk space to store archived redo logs is limited as well. Again, a good backup strategy in such a situation is critical. A full archive log directory will eventually cause the database to stall, because ARCH will not be able to process archived redo logs, and therefore it will not be able to release online redo logs for the database to use.

Recoveries in ARCHIVELOG Mode

One of the huge advantages of using ARCHIVELOG mode is that it offers a wealth of recovery options. You can perform complete or incomplete recoveries. Complete recoveries include recovery of datafiles, tablespaces, or the entire database. The three kinds of incomplete recoveries that Oracle provides are time-based, change-based, and cancel-based.

Preparing for Recovery

You generally know when you have a problem—the users start calling and your monitoring system starts sending out panic e-mail messages. It's time for you to don your cape and earn your keep. When presented with a recovery situation, you first need to figure out what the problem is. This is where understanding the internals of the Oracle database comes in handy. Sometimes that experience and understanding can make the difference between a 30-second outage and having the system down for days.

When presented with a problem, you need to proceed through a mental checklist. Start your checklist with the easiest things to fix and the most likely things to go wrong, and work your way down to the unlikely. Has the whole database crashed? Are the users getting any error messages? Has the database really crashed or is it just stalled? Check the alert log for any messages that might be helpful. Have the users send you any messages they may be getting (though applications frequently trap these messages, so the users never send them).

TIP When presented with a database that will not come up (say, after a power outage or an aborted shutdown) and says it needs media recovery, your first response should always be to issue a RECOVER DATABASE command. Just because the database says it needs media recovery doesn't mean you need to recover database datafiles.

When your database is troubled, the V$ views are frequently of great help. Table 10.3 lists the V$ views that can be handy to use during backup and recovery operations. Generally, many of these views become available as the database startup process proceeds. For example, when the database is mounted, you have access to the V$DATAFILE view. This view provides you with a wealth of information on the status of the database datafiles. This same view will let you know if a database datafile has gone AWOL, by indicating a status of OFFLINE for that datafile. Also, mismatches between the control file and the FILE$ data dictionary table will be reported in this view. If you see a file named MISSING*xxx* in this view, that's the problem. We will talk more about this later in this chapter in our discussion on control file recovery issues.

TABLE 10.3: V$ VIEWS FOR BACKUP AND RECOVERY

View Name	Description
V$DATAFILE	Provides datafile information from the control file.
V$ARCHIVE_DEST	Provides various information on the archive log destinations.
V$ARCHIVED_LOG	Provides information on archived redo logs.
V$ARCHIVE_PROCESSES	Provides information on the ARCH processes currently running on the database.
V$BACKUP	Provides status information on database datafiles in hot backup mode.
V$DATABASE	Provides various database information, such as if it is in ARCHIVELOG mode or NOARCHIVELOG mode.
V$INSTANCE_RECOVERY	Provides various information on the different systems used by Oracle to speed up recovery. These different recovery processes are influenced by parameters such as fast_start_io, log_checkpoint_timeout, and log_checkpoint_interval.
V$LOG	Contains various information on the current redo logs that comes from the control file.

Continued

TABLE 10.3: V$ VIEWS FOR BACKUP AND RECOVERY (CONTINUED)

View Name	Description
V$LOGFILE	Contains information on the current redo logs.
V$LOG_HISTORY	Contains information on the archived redo logs generated by the database.
V$RECOVER_FILE	Contains information on the recovery status of a datafile.

After you've identified the problem, you need to determine what it will take to correct the problem. Sometimes, you just need to get a system administrator to remount a file system that went away for some odd reason. Other times, it's a hardware issue that needs to be resolved. If it turns out to be a problem with lost database datafiles, recover only those datafiles that have problems. There is no need to recover the entire database, unless the whole database has problems.

In general, determining what you need to recover requires the following steps:

1. Make sure that all hardware problems are corrected.
2. If the database is still running, recover only the datafiles or tablespaces that were lost. Check to ensure that you did not lose a redo log member or a control file copy.
3. If the database has crashed, try to start the database. If it says it needs media recovery, issue the RECOVER DATABASE command. Often, this will work.
4. If the database instance will not start, check again for hardware problems, particularly memory and memory configuration issues.
5. If the instance will start but the database complains that it cannot find the control file, you will need to use a backup control file to recover the database.
6. Once the instance will mount, use the V$ views (see Table 10.3) to determine which database datafiles need recovery.
7. Proceed with the most expedient type of database recovery (datafile, tablespace, or entire database) for your situation.

Using the Recover Command

The RECOVER command is used to recover entire databases, specific tablespaces, or specific datafiles, as well as for the three types of incomplete recoveries. Table 10.4 shows the most common parameters used with the RECOVER command. The

RECOVER command should be issued from a database account that has DBA privileges such as SYS or SYSTEM, or when connected to the database as INTERNAL.

TABLE 10.4: COMMONLY USED RECOVER COMMAND PARAMETERS

Optional Command	Description
USING BACKUP CONTROLFILE	Indicates that a backup control file is being used during the recovery process
UNTIL CANCEL	Indicates a cancel-based recovery
UNTIL TIME <time string>	Indicates a time-based recovery
UNTIL CHANGE <scn>	Indicates a change-based recovery
FROM <location>	Provides an alternate archived redo log location to use during the recovery.
AUTOMATIC	Causes the RECOVER command to generate its own list of suggested redo logs to apply, and will apply those logs without stopping for user interaction
FROM	Defines an alternate location for the archived redo logs that are to be applied
PARALLEL [degree] NOPARALLEL	Allows for parallel recovery processing or disabling of parallel processing (this parameter overrides the setting of the RECOVERY_PARALLELISM parameter)

When the database starts its recovery exercise, it will start applying the archived redo logs to the database datafiles to make them consistent. As the recovery process cycles through each log file, it will prompt you for an action with a message that looks like this:

```
SQL> RECOVER DATAFILE 4
ORA-00279: change 76361 generated at 04/25/2001 19:15:30
needed for thread 1
ORA-00289: suggestion :
D:\ORACLE\ORADATA\RECOVER\ARCHIVE\RECOVERT001S00206.ARC
ORA-00280: change 76361 for thread 1 is in sequence #206
Specify log: {<RET>=suggested | filename | AUTO | CANCEL}
```

So, what is the meaning of this? Oracle says that it needs a particular log sequence number to start the recovery process. Oracle will sit and wait for you to respond with some form of input.

In the example here, it needs log sequence number 206, which contains change number 76361. Oracle also makes some assumptions about the location of this particular log file. In this case, it thinks the log file is in the d:\oracle\oradata\RECOVER\ARCHIVE directory, which just happens to be the directory pointed to by the databases LOG_ARCHIVE_DEST_1 parameter. Thus, by default, Oracle will look for redo log files in this directory. However, Oracle gives you several options for specifying the log. If you press Enter, you accept the suggested directory and filename. However, you may have restored these log files to another directory. In this case, you would respond with a new directory and filename for the archived redo logs, as shown in the last line here:

```
SQL> RECOVER DATABASE
ORA-00279: change 76375 generated at 04/25/2001 19:18:13
needed for thread 1
ORA-00289: suggestion :
D:\ORACLE\ORADATA\RECOVER\ARCHIVE\RECOVERT001S00207.ARC
ORA-00280: change 76375 for thread 1 is in sequence #207
Specify log: {<RET>=suggested | filename | AUTO | CANCEL}
e:\oracle\recover\archive\recovert001s00207.arc
```

You can also choose to cancel the recovery by issuing the CANCEL command, or you can instruct Oracle to apply the archived redo logs without any input by using the AUTO command.

Performing Complete Recovery

Complete recovery is just what it sounds like—the complete recovery of a datafile, tablespace, or the whole database to the point of the last transaction recorded in the redo logs. When complete recovery is applied successfully, there will be no loss of data in the database.

When performing a complete recovery, you generally will recover only the affected datafiles. You will have the online redo logs, as well as the control file, available. Lack of either the online redo logs or the current control file may require incomplete recovery methods to be used, but this is not always the case.

One of the principle benefits of running in ARCHIVELOG mode is the ability to recover a datafile or even a tablespace while the rest of the database is up and running. Generally, the process you will follow is to take the datafile or tablespace you are going to recover offline, recover it, and then bring it online again. If users attempt to access an object that is contained within that tablespace, they will receive an error. Users who do not use any objects in that tablespace will not notice any problems (except possible slowdowns during the recovery process).

Certain types of recoveries cannot be done with the database up and running. These include recovering from the loss of the entire database (no surprise there) and recovering from the loss of a datafile in the SYSTEM tablespace. Recoveries from loss of a tablespace with an active rollback segment will likely begin with the database down as well. These special cases are discussed in the sections following the descriptions of how to recover datafiles, tablespaces, and the entire database.

Determining Which Archive Log Files to Recover

Once you have recovered the database datafiles, you will want to know which archived redo logs you need to recover. Recall that archived redo logs are primarily tracked by their unique log sequence number. Oracle keeps track of each archived redo log in the control file, including that log's sequence number. Also in the control file, with each archived redo log record, Oracle keeps track of the first and last SCN (or change number) that is contained in that redo log. This information is available to the DBA when the database is mounted or opened via the V$ARCHIVED_LOG data dictionary view.

Once you have identified which datafiles need to be recovered, and once you have recovered those datafiles, you will use the V$RECOVER_FILE view to determine the last change number present in that datafile. Using this information, you then look up the sequence number that is required for the next change number, and that will be the sequence number of the archived redo log that you will need to start your recovery with. Here is an example of the type of queries you might run to determine the log sequence numbers of the archived redo logs you will need to recover:

```
SELECT a.name, b.change# FROM v$datafile a, v$recover_file b
WHERE a.file#=b.file#;

NAME                                                CHANGE#
-------------------------------------------------  ----------
D:\ORACLE\ORADATA\RECOVER\RECOVER_IDX_01.DBF         76361

SELECT sequence#, name
FROM v$archived_log
WHERE first_change# >= 76361;

SEQUENCE# NAME
---------- ----------------------------------------------------------
       207 D:\ORACLE\ORADATA\RECOVER\ARCHIVE\RECOVERT001S00207.ARC
       208 D:\ORACLE\ORADATA\RECOVER\ARCHIVE\RECOVERT001S00208.ARC
       209 D:\ORACLE\ORADATA\RECOVER\ARCHIVE\RECOVERT001S00209.ARC
```

```
210  D:\ORACLE\ORADATA\RECOVER\ARCHIVE\RECOVERT001S00210.ARC
211  D:\ORACLE\ORADATA\RECOVER\ARCHIVE\RECOVERT001S00211.ARC
```

In this case, you see that you need to recover five archived redo logs in order to restore the given datafile. After running this query, you should recover the archived redo logs from your backup medium in preparation for recovering the database, tablespace, or datafile.

Datafile Recovery

Datafile recoveries generally have the least impact on your system. For the most part, recovery of a datafile can be completed while the rest of the database is up and running. Datafile recovery does not need to be a synchronous operation. You can recover multiple datafiles using multiple sessions to the database, although only one datafile can be recovered per session at any one time. Typically, datafile recovery will occur in cases such as the following:

- Some hardware failure occurred that caused the loss of a few database datafiles.
- An administrator accidentally removed the datafile or the directory.
- Database corruption has occurred due to a bug or perhaps faulty memory.

To perform a datafile recovery, follow these steps:

1. If the database is already open, take any affected datafiles offline. (You may find that Oracle has already taken them offline.) To take a datafile offline, use the ALTER DATABASE DATAFILE OFFLINE command. If the database was shut down and is refusing to open because of a missing datafile, take the datafile offline, and then issue an ALTER DATABASE OPEN command.

2. Recover only the affected datafile(s) from the last backup taken in ARCHIVE-LOG mode.

3. Recover all archived redo logs created since the start of the last hot backup. (See the previous section for details on determining which archived redo logs to recover.)

4. Recover each datafile individually with the RECOVER DATAFILE *<datafilename or datafile number>* command.

5. Once the datafiles are recovered, bring the datafiles back online with the ALTER DATABASE ONLINE command. Make sure you don't need to also bring the associated tablespace online. Once this step is complete, your database has been recovered.

Listing 10.4 provides an example of a datafile recovery. In this example, we lost a datafile called `recover_idx_01.dbf`, which belongs to our IDX tablespace. When we tried to start the database, we were alerted to the missing file. In order to get the database up quickly, we first take the file offline, and then open the database. Finally, we proceed to restore the missing datafile from disk and recover it.

Listing 10.4: Recovering a Datafile

```
-- First, we try to start the database. We have a hot backup.
SQL> STARTUP
ORACLE instance started.
Total System Global Area    92280076 bytes
Fixed Size                     70924 bytes
Variable Size               87937024 bytes
Database Buffers             4194304 bytes
Redo Buffers                   77824 bytes
Database mounted.
ORA-01113: file 4 needs media recovery
ORA-01110: datafile 4: 'D:\ORACLE\ORADATA\RECOVER\RECOVER_IDX_01.DBF'
-- Oracle has signaled us here that a datafile is in need of recovery.
-- Normally, we would first issue a recover database command to see if
-- that will fix the problem. In this case, let's assume it's corrupt
-- and correct the problem.
-- Find out what archived redo logs we need.
SQL> SELECT a.name, b.change# FROM v$datafile a, v$recover_file b
  2  WHERE a.file#=b.file#;

NAME                                                            CHANGE#
--------------------------------------------------------------- ----------
D:\ORACLE\ORADATA\RECOVER\RECOVER_IDX_01.DBF                      76361

SQL> SELECT sequence#, name
  2  FROM v$archived_log
  3  WHERE first_change# >= 76361;

SEQUENCE# NAME
---------- -----------------------------------------------------------
       207 D:\ORACLE\ORADATA\RECOVER\ARCHIVE\RECOVERT001S00207.ARC
       208 D:\ORACLE\ORADATA\RECOVER\ARCHIVE\RECOVERT001S00208.ARC
       209 D:\ORACLE\ORADATA\RECOVER\ARCHIVE\RECOVERT001S00209.ARC
       210 D:\ORACLE\ORADATA\RECOVER\ARCHIVE\RECOVERT001S00210.ARC
       211 D:\ORACLE\ORADATA\RECOVER\ARCHIVE\RECOVERT001S00211.ARC
```

```
-- Now, take the datafile offline and open the database so users can
-- use it.
SQL> ALTER DATABASE DATAFILE 4 OFFLINE;
Database altered.
SQL> ALTER DATABASE OPEN;
Database altered.

-- Now, copy the last backup of the datafile into its proper place.
-- This was done on NT.
SQL> HOST COPY recover_idx_01.dbf.backup RECOVER_IDX_01.DBF
     1 file(s) copied.
-- Note the status of the datafile is offline right now.
SELECT file#, name, status FROM v$datafile;
SQL> /
     FILE# NAME                                                STATUS
---------- --------------------------------------------------- -------
         1 D:\ORACLE\ORADATA\RECOVER\SYSTEM01.DBF              SYSTEM
         2 D:\ORACLE\ORADATA\RECOVER\RECOVER_RBS_01.DBF        ONLINE
         3 D:\ORACLE\ORADATA\RECOVER\RECOVER_USERS_01.DBF      ONLINE
         4 D:\ORACLE\ORADATA\RECOVER\RECOVER_IDX_01.DBF        OFFLINE
         5 D:\ORACLE\ORADATA\RECOVER\RECOVER_TEMP_01.DBF       ONLINE

-- Now that the backup datafile is in place, issue the recover command.
-- We will apply the redo logs as required.
SQL> RECOVER DATAFILE 4;
ORA-00279: change 76361 generated at 04/25/2001 19:15:30
needed for thread 1
ORA-00289: suggestion :
D:\ORACLE\ORADATA\RECOVER\ARCHIVE\RECOVERT001S00206.ARC
ORA-00280: change 76361 for thread 1 is in sequence #206
Specify log: {<RET>=suggested | filename | AUTO | CANCEL}

ORA-00279: change 76375 generated at 04/25/2001 19:18:13
needed for thread 1
ORA-00289: suggestion :
D:\ORACLE\ORADATA\RECOVER\ARCHIVE\RECOVERT001S00207.ARC
ORA-00280: change 76375 for thread 1 is in sequence #207
ORA-00278: log file
```

```
'D:\ORACLE\ORADATA\RECOVER\ARCHIVE\RECOVERT001S00206.ARC'
no longer needed for this recovery
Specify log: {<RET>=suggested | filename | AUTO | CANCEL}

ORA-00279: change 76378 generated at 04/25/2001 19:18:30
needed for thread 1
ORA-00289: suggestion :
D:\ORACLE\ORADATA\RECOVER\ARCHIVE\RECOVERT001S00208.ARC
ORA-00280: change 76378 for thread 1 is in sequence #208
ORA-00278: log file
'D:\ORACLE\ORADATA\RECOVER\ARCHIVE\RECOVERT001S00207.ARC'
no longer needed for this recovery

Specify log: {<RET>=suggested | filename | AUTO | CANCEL}
ORA-00279: change 76383 generated at 04/25/2001 19:18:48
needed for thread 1
ORA-00289: suggestion :
D:\ORACLE\ORADATA\RECOVER\ARCHIVE\RECOVERT001S00209.ARC
ORA-00280: change 76383 for thread 1 is in sequence #209
ORA-00278: log file
'D:\ORACLE\ORADATA\RECOVER\ARCHIVE\RECOVERT001S00208.ARC'
no longer needed for this recovery

Specify log: {<RET>=suggested | filename | AUTO | CANCEL}
Log applied.
Media recovery complete.

-- Now that recovery is complete, online the datafile.
SQL> ALTER DATABASE DATAFILE 4 ONLINE;
Database altered.
-- Now, check the status of the datafile again.
SQL> SELECT file#, name, status FROM v$datafile;

     FILE# NAME                                                 STATUS
    ------ ---------------------------------------------------- -------
         1 D:\ORACLE\ORADATA\RECOVER\SYSTEM01.DBF               SYSTEM
         2 D:\ORACLE\ORADATA\RECOVER\RECOVER_RBS_01.DBF         ONLINE
         3 D:\ORACLE\ORADATA\RECOVER\RECOVER_USERS_01.DBF       ONLINE
         4 D:\ORACLE\ORADATA\RECOVER\RECOVER_IDX_01.DBF         ONLINE
```

```
     5 D:\ORACLE\ORADATA\RECOVER\RECOVER_TEMP_01.DBF        ONLINE
```
```
-- The datafile has been recovered.
```

Note that we could have allowed the archived redo logs to be applied automatically (and we will in all the other examples in this chapter where this is possible).

Tablespace Recovery

As with datafile recoveries, for the most part, tablespace recoveries can be completed while the rest of the database is up and running. You can perform multiple tablespace recoveries using multiple sessions to the database, although only one tablespace can be recovered per session at any one time. Typically, tablespace recovery will be required for the same reasons as datafile recovery.

To perform a tablespace recovery, follow these steps:

1. If the database is still up, take the tablespace offline (if it is not already offline) by using the ALTER TABLESPACE OFFLINE command. You can check the status of a tablespace by looking at the DBA_TABLESPACES data dictionary view. Of course, if the database is down, this view will not be available.

2. Recover only the affected tablespace datafile(s) from the last backup taken in ARCHIVELOG mode. You can recover all of the tablespace datafiles, if that is easier, but this is not required.

3. Recover all archived redo logs created since the start of the last hot backup. See the "Determining Which Archive Log Files to Recover" section earlier in this chapter for details.

4. Recover the tablespaces individually with the RECOVER TABLESPACE <tablespace_name> command.

5. Once the tablespace is recovered, if the database was up, you may bring it back online with the ALTER TABLESPACE ONLINE command.

Listing 10.5 provides an example of a tablespace recovery. In this example, we lost all the datafiles to the tablespace called TEST_TBS. We will restore those datafiles and then recover the tablespace.

Listing 10.5: Recovering a Tablespace

```
-- Create a table in the tablespace we are going to recover and
-- add records to it.
SQL> CREATE TABLESPACE test_tbs
  2  DATAFILE 'd:\oracle\oradata\recover\recover_test_tbs_01.dbf'
  3  SIZE 100k;
Tablespace created.
```

```
SQL> ALTER TABLESPACE test_tbs
  2  ADD DATAFILE 'd:\oracle\oradata\recover\recover_test_tbs_02.dbf'
  3  SIZE 100k;

Tablespace altered.
SQL> CREATE TABLE example_table (id number) TABLESPACE test_tbs;
Table created.
SQL> INSERT INTO example_table VALUES (1);
1 row created.
SQL> INSERT INTO example_table VALUES (2);
1 row created.
SQL> COMMIT;
Commit complete.

-- Perform a hot backup of the database or just the tablespace.
-- Now, something has happened to our datafile; it is gone. Try to
-- insert a new record into it.
SQL> INSERT INTO example_table SELECT * FROM example_table
INSERT INTO example_table SELECT * FROM example_table
            *
ERROR at line 1:
ORA-00376: file 7 cannot be read at this time
ORA-01110: datafile 7: 'D:\ORACLE\ORADATA\RECOVER\RECOVER_TEST_TBS_01.DBF'

-- We have determined that we have lost the datafiles due to
-- a disk crash.
-- Take the tablespace offline. Use offline immediate in this case,
-- because one of the datafiles is already offline.
SQL> ALTER TABLESPACE test_tbs OFFLINE IMMEDIATE;
Tablespace altered.

-- Copy the backed up datafiles back over.
SQL> HOST COPY d:\oracle_backup\hot\recover_test_tbs*.dbf
d:\oracle_backup\hot\RECOVER_TEST_TBS_01.DBF
d:\oracle_backup\hot\RECOVER_TEST_TBS_02.DBF

-- Recover the needed redo logs.
SQL> HOST COPY d:\oracle_backup\hot\archive
d:\oracle\oradata\recover\archive
```

```
d:\oracle_backup\hot\archive\RECOVERT001S00215.ARC
d:\oracle_backup\hot\archive\RECOVERT001S00216.ARC
d:\oracle_backup\hot\archive\RECOVERT001S00217.ARC
d:\oracle_backup\hot\archive\RECOVERT001S00218.ARC
d:\oracle_backup\hot\archive\RECOVERT001S00219.ARC
        5 file(s) copied.

-- Now, recover the tablespace.
SQL> RECOVER TABLESPACE test_tbs;
Media recovery complete.

-- Now, online the tablespace.
SQL> ALTER TABLESPACE test_tbs ONLINE;
Tablespace altered.

-- Check to make sure our table is recovered.
SQL> SELECT * FROM example_table;

        ID
----------
         1
         2
```

Complete Recovery of the Entire Database

Well, if you have the last two recovery types down, you'll find that recovering a database is a piece of cake! By now, I hope you have noticed a pattern of operations: You restore the datafiles, you restore the archived redo logs, and then you recover the datafile, tablespace, or database. In the case of a full database recovery, you have likely lost most (if not all) of your database files. It is also possible that you have lost your control files and your online redo logs. Later in this chapter, we will address cases of control file loss and/or redo log loss. For now, let's assume that you have lost many of your database datafiles, but that all of your online redo logs and control files are present.

The basic steps for performing a database recovery are as follows:

1. If you need to perform a full database recovery, the database is likely to be down already. If not, shut down the database.

2. Restore all of the database datafiles from your last database backup. You can, of course, selectively recover just the missing database datafiles if you prefer. It

may be faster to restore just the lost datafiles, depending on the size of the overall backup image and the size of the surviving datafiles.

3. Recover all archived redo logs required to recover the database.
4. Issue the RECOVER DATABASE command and proceed to recover the database.
5. Once recovery is complete, open the database for use.

Seems pretty easy doesn't it? Listing 10.6 provides an example of such an operation.

Listing 10.6: Recovering the Entire Database

```
-- Create a table in the tablespace we are going to recover and
-- add records to it. Use the previous example_table again in this
-- example, so we will drop it first.
-- In this example, the control file and online redo logs will survive
-- the failures.
SQL> DROP TABLE example_table;
Table dropped.
SQL> CREATE TABLE example_table (id number) TABLESPACE test_tbs;
Table created.
SQL> INSERT INTO example_table VALUES (1);
1 row created.
SQL> INSERT INTO example_table VALUES (2);
1 row created.
SQL> COMMIT;
Commit complete.

-- Perform a hot backup of the database or just the tablespace.
-- After performing the backup, the database crashes. When we try to
-- start the database, we get the following error.
SQL> STARTUP
ORACLE instance started.

Total System Global Area    92280076 bytes
Fixed Size                     70924 bytes
Variable Size               87937024 bytes
Database Buffers             4194304 bytes
Redo Buffers                   77824 bytes
Database mounted.
ORA-01157: cannot identify/lock datafile 1 - see DBWR trace file
ORA-01110: datafile 1: 'D:\ORACLE\ORADATA\RECOVER\SYSTEM01.DBF'
```

```
-- We copy all of the database files into place from the backup.
-- We also copy the archive logs into place from the backup.
SQL> HOST COPY d:\oracle_backup\hot\*.dbf
d:\oracle_backup\hot\SYSTEM01.DBF
d:\oracle_backup\hot\RECOVER_RBS_01.DBF
d:\oracle_backup\hot\RECOVER_USERS_01.DBF
d:\oracle_backup\hot\RECOVER_TEMP_01.DBF
d:\oracle_backup\hot\RECOVER_IDX_01.DBF
d:\oracle_backup\hot\RECOVER_USERS_02.DBF
d:\oracle_backup\hot\RECOVER_TEST_TBS_02.DBF
d:\oracle_backup\hot\RECOVER_TEST_TBS_01.DBF
        8 file(s) copied.

-- Recover the needed redo logs.
SQL> HOST COPY d:\oracle_backup\hot\archive
d:\oracle\oradata\recover\archive
d:\oracle_backup\hot\archive\RECOVERT001S00219.ARC
d:\oracle_backup\hot\archive\RECOVERT001S00220.ARC
d:\oracle_backup\hot\archive\RECOVERT001S00221.ARC
        3 file(s) copied.

-- Now we try to start up the database with the datafiles back in place.
SQL> SHUTDOWN ABORT
ORACLE instance shut down.
SQL> STARTUP
ORACLE instance started.

Total System Global Area    92280076 bytes
Fixed Size                     70924 bytes
Variable Size               87937024 bytes
Database Buffers             4194304 bytes
Redo Buffers                   77824 bytes
Database mounted.
ORA-01113: file 1 needs media recovery
ORA-01110: datafile 1: 'D:\ORACLE\ORADATA\RECOVER\SYSTEM01.DBF'

-- Note that now the database is giving us an ORA-01113. We need to
-- apply media recovery. So we recover the database.
SQL> RECOVER DATABASE
```

```
Media recovery complete.

-- And we open it.
SQL> ALTER DATABASE OPEN;
Database altered.

-- Check to make sure our table is recovered.
SQL> SELECT * FROM example_table;

        ID
----------
         1
         2
```

Recovering the SYSTEM Tablespace

In the event that the SYSTEM tablespace is lost, the database will have come crashing down. Recovering in this situation is fairly simple:

1. Identify the datafile(s) that are corrupted.
2. Issue a SHUTDOWN ABORT command on the system if it failed abnormally. This is to make sure everything is shut down properly.
3. Issue a STARTUP MOUNT command.
4. Once the database is up, proceed to issue a RECOVER DATABASE command. You can, if you prefer, issue a RECOVER DATAFILE or RECOVER TABLESPACE command. In this situation, it will not make much of a difference.
5. Once the recovery is complete, open the database for user access.

Recovering Tablespaces with Rollback Segments

If a tablespace with active rollback segments is lost, your database will likely crash. First, you need to get the database up and running. Then you can deal with the tablespace that needs to be recovered. The solution is to mount the database and take offline the datafiles associated with the tablespace that the rollback segment is in. Next, open the database. Then you can restore and recover the database datafiles for the tablespace in question. The steps in such a recovery are as follows:

1. The database will likely be shut down from a crash. Use the STARTUP MOUNT command to mount the database.
2. Determine which datafiles are bad and take those offline with the ALTER DATABASE DATAFILE OFFLINE command.

3. Proceed to open the database. You may need to create new rollback segments for users to use if all of the rollback segments are in the tablespace you are recovering.

4. Restore and recover the tablespace (or datafiles of the tablespace) with the rollback segment.

5. Put the datafiles and the rollback segment tablespace online. You will also need to put the rollback segments in that tablespace online.

6. You can now take offline and drop any new rollback segments you created in step 3.

NOTE Recovering the SYSTEM tablespace and recovering a tablespace with active rollback segments as described here apply only to databases in ARCHIVELOG mode. If either of these situations occurs and your database is in NOARCHIVELOG mode, you will need to perform a full recovery using your cold backup.

Incomplete Recovery

Most of the time, when your database needs recovery, you want to recover it to the point of the failure—you don't want to lose any changes that occurred just before the crash. However, sometimes something goes very wrong, and you want to recover the database to a point in time before that thing went wrong. It's like a time machine in a way. You can wipe out an accidental TRUNCATE operation or an accidental DELETE operation, for example. Maybe that script the developer was sure he tested gave everyone a 100 percent raise instead of the 1 percent raise (and perhaps that was by design, but management tends to notice those types of things). This is when you will want to use the incomplete recovery features of Oracle.

Incomplete recovery comes in three flavors:

- Time-based recovery allows you to recover the database to a specific point in time.

- Change-based recovery allows you to recover the database to a specific change number. (This is handy if recovering through a RESETLOGS operation.)

- Cancel-based recovery allows you to recover through archived redo logs one by one, canceling recovery at any prompt along the way.

Another issue to be aware of with regard to incomplete recovery is that you will need to issue a RESETLOGS command when opening the database. This serves to clear out the database's redo logs, reset the redo log sequence number, and define a new incarnation for the database. We will discuss the RESETLOGS command later in this chapter, in the "RESETLOGS and Recovery" section. For now, let's look at steps for preparing for an incomplete recovery, and then examine each type of incomplete recovery.

Preparing for Incomplete Recovery

When preparing for incomplete recovery, you should consider several factors:

- Determine the specific backup to recover.
- Determine which type of incomplete recovery you wish to perform. Based on the type of recovery you are going to perform, determine where to stop recovery.
- Make sure your user population will not be negatively impacted by the proposed recovery. Performing incomplete recovery on a database can have unexpected consequences, depending on the nature and sensitivity of the system.

Time-Based Recovery

Because of database consistency issues, time-based recovery is not an easy task. For example, if you have a large database, and a user accidentally truncates the employee table, it's a big deal to recover that table back to the point before the TRUNCATE operation using time-based recovery. This is because you need to roll back the entire database for consistency purposes. Keep in mind that Oracle demands that each datafile be consistent with the other datafiles in the database. If your database is at SCN 10000 and you try to recover the employee tablespace to SCN 9000 to roll back that TRUNCATE operation, your database will be inconsistent and will not open.

If you want to roll back a database using incomplete recovery, you must restore each datafile in the database from a backup that took place before the time that you want to restore the database to, and apply archived redo to all the database datafiles. Using incomplete recovery, you cannot restore an individual tablespace to a different point in time from the other tablespaces in the database.

TIP There are some ways around the time-based recovery constraint of needing to restore all tablespaces to the same point in time. Logical exports, stub databases, and transportable tablespaces are among the most common. If you have a logical export that you can use to recover the object, that is usually the easiest approach. We will talk about logical database backup and recovery in the next chapter. See Chapter 12 for details on how to use transportable tablespaces.

Time-based recovery will allow you to define what time you wish to recover your database to. Using the RECOVER DATABASE UNTIL TIME <time_string> command, you can instruct the database to stop the recovery process at a specific time. The *time_string* part of this command takes the format of '*YYYY-MM-DD:HH24:MI:SS*'. For example, to recover to 12:01 A.M. on December 1, 2002, you would issue the following command:

```
RECOVER DATABASE UNTIL TIME '2002-12-01:00:01:00';
```

Once the recovery process has reached the time defined, it will stop recovering the database. At that point, you may choose to recover the database further, or you may choose to open the database.

WARNING Be careful of the impacts of changing the system time with regard to time-based recovery. Changing the system clock can make time-based recovery over a given period of time impossible. This is particularly true when you set the system clock back.

Listing 10.7 provides an example of time-based recovery. In this example, we first back up the database, then create a table and add some rows to it. We note the time, and then wait a few minutes, note the time again, and then add two more records to the database. We then perform a time-based recovery to the time between the addition of the first two records and the later records.

Listing 10.7: Time-Based Recovery

```
-- We create a table again, populate it with data, and wait
-- for about 5 minutes. We then add another row.
-- We will then assume some situation has occurred that requires
-- us to roll back the table to the point before the time that
-- the last record was added.

-- First, we do a complete hot backup. Then we create the table.
SQL> CREATE TABLE time_table (the_time   date) TABLESPACE test_tbs;
Table created.


-- Insert a new record into the table. This record will record the
-- time that the insert took place.
SQL> INSERT INTO time_table VALUES (sysdate);
1 row created.


-- We wait 1 minute and insert another record.
```

```
SQL> INSERT INTO time_table VALUES (sysdate);
1 row created.

-- Commit these changes.
SQL> COMMIT;

-- Get the rough time of the commit.
SQL> SELECT to_char(sysdate, 'mm/dd/yyyy hh24:mi:ss') FROM dual;

TO_CHAR(SYSDATE,'MM
-------------------
04/28/2001 21:35:07

-- Now, we wait 5 minutes and do another insert.
SQL> INSERT INTO time_table VALUES (sysdate);
1 row created.

-- Now, let's look at the table.
SQL> SELECT TO_CHAR(the_time, 'mm/dd/yyyy hh24:mi:ss') FROM time_table;

TO_CHAR(THE_TIME,'M
-------------------
04/28/2001 21:33:24
04/28/2001 21:35:02
04/28/2001 21:48:03

-- Next, we determine the archived redo logs that will be required to
-- recover to the point in time we need (which is 21:35:02).
SQL> SELECT sequence#,
  2    TO_CHAR(first_time,'mm/dd/yyyy hh24:mi:ss'),
  3    TO_CHAR(next_time,'mm/dd/yyyy hh24:mi:ss')
  4  FROM v$archived_log
  5  UNION
  6  SELECT sequence#,
  7    TO_CHAR(first_time,'mm/dd/yyyy hh24:mi:ss'),
  8    NULL
  9  FROM v$log
 10  WHERE sequence# NOT IN (SELECT sequence# FROM v$archived_log)
 11  ORDER BY sequence#;
```

```
SEQUENCE# TO_CHAR(FIRST_TIME, TO_CHAR(NEXT_TIME,'
---------- ------------------- -------------------
       220 04/28/2001 16:39:05 04/28/2001 19:35:31
       221 04/28/2001 19:35:31 04/28/2001 21:20:54
       222 04/28/2001 21:20:54 04/28/2001 21:25:10
       223 04/28/2001 21:25:10 04/28/2001 21:31:20
       224 04/28/2001 21:31:20 04/28/2001 21:56:51
       225 04/28/2001 21:56:51
-- Commit the whole shooting match.
SQL> COMMIT;
-- Shut down the database.
SQL> SHUTDOWN IMMEDIATE
Database closed.
Database dismounted.
ORACLE instance shut down.

-- Recover the last backup.
SQL> HOST COPY d:\oracle_backup\hot\*.* d:\oracle\oradata\recover
d:\oracle_backup\hot\SYSTEM01.DBF
d:\oracle_backup\hot\RECOVER_RBS_01.DBF
d:\oracle_backup\hot\RECOVER_USERS_01.DBF
d:\oracle_backup\hot\RECOVER_TEMP_01.DBF
d:\oracle_backup\hot\RECOVER_IDX_01.DBF
d:\oracle_backup\hot\RECOVER_USERS_02.DBF
d:\oracle_backup\hot\RECOVER_TEST_TBS_02.DBF
d:\oracle_backup\hot\RECOVER_TEST_TBS_01.DBF

-- We recover the required archived redo logs. It appears that
-- we will need to recover until archived redo log sequence 224.
-- Recover the needed redo logs from the archived redo log directory.
SQL> HOST COPY d:\oracle_backup\hot\archive\*.*
d:\oracle\oradata\recover\archive
d:\oracle_backup\hot\archive\RECOVERT001S00220.ARC
d:\oracle_backup\hot\archive\RECOVERT001S00221.ARC
d:\oracle_backup\hot\archive\RECOVERT001S00222.ARC
d:\oracle_backup\hot\archive\RECOVERT001S00223.ARC
d:\oracle_backup\hot\archive\RECOVERT001S00224.ARC
        5 file(s) copied.
```

```
-- Mount the database.
SQL> STARTUP MOUNT
ORACLE instance started.
Total System Global Area    92280076 bytes
Fixed Size                     70924 bytes
Variable Size               87937024 bytes
Database Buffers             4194304 bytes
Redo Buffers                   77824 bytes
Database mounted.

-- We begin the point-in-time recovery.
-- Notice we use automatic application of archived redo logs
-- in response to the recovery prompt.
SQL> RECOVER DATABASE UNTIL TIME '2001-04-28:21:35:07';
ORA-00279: change 196739 generated at 04/28/2001 21:26:44
needed for thread 1
ORA-00289: suggestion :
D:\ORACLE\ORADATA\RECOVER\ARCHIVE\RECOVERT001S00223.ARC
ORA-00280: change 196739 for thread 1 is in sequence #223
Specify log: {<RET>=suggested | filename | AUTO | CANCEL}
auto
Log applied.
Media recovery complete.

-- We open the database. Note the use of RESETLOGS.
SQL> ALTER DATABASE OPEN RESETLOGS;
Database altered.

-- We query the table, and now we have only two records!
SQL> SELECT TO_CHAR(the_time, 'mm/dd/yyyy hh24:mi:ss') FROM time_table;

TO_CHAR(THE_TIME,'M
-------------------
04/28/2001 21:33:24
04/28/2001 21:35:02
```

WARNING When dealing with time-based recovery, keep in mind that it is based on the time that the transaction was committed, not the time that the change was first made to an object. For example, suppose that you inserted an object at 1530, but you waited to commit until 1600. If you try to recover until 1540, you will not see the insert made at 1530.

Change-Based Recovery

Change-based recovery allows you to apply incomplete recovery up to a given SCN number. This type of recovery is not used often, but it does come in handy in certain cases (such as recovery past RESETLOGS, which we will discuss later in this chapter). To execute a change-based recovery, you use the RECOVER DATABASE UNTIL CHANGE <change_number> command. The change number is the decimal representation of the SCN following the last change you wish to recover. Thus, if you know the change number you wish to recover to, add one to it and use that as the SCN. Listing 10.8 provides an example of a change-based recovery.

Listing 10.8: Change-Based Recovery

```
-- This is to test change-based recovery.
-- We create a table again, populate it with data, and wait
-- for about 5 minutes. We then add another row.
-- We will then assume some situation has occurred that requires
-- us to roll back the table to the point before the time that
-- the last record was added.

-- First, we do a complete hot backup. Then we create the table.
SQL> DROP TABLE time_table;
Table dropped.
SQL> CREATE TABLE time_table (the_time   date) TABLESPACE test_tbs;
Table created.

-- Add two rows to the table.
SQL> INSERT INTO time_table VALUES (sysdate);
1 row created.

SQL> INSERT INTO time_table VALUES (sysdate);
1 row created.
```

```
-- Commit these changes.
SQL> COMMIT;

-- It's hard to find out the exact SCN. To get a close approximation,
-- let's force a log switch. Then we can look at v$log and find out the
-- SCN we probably want to recover to.
SQL> ARCHIVE LOG LIST
ORA-01031: insufficient privileges
-- Connect as the privileged sysdba user.
SQL> connect / as sysdba
Connected.
SQL> ARCHIVE LOG LIST
Database log mode              Archive Mode
Automatic archival             Enabled
Archive destination            D:\Oracle\oradata\Recover\archive
Oldest online log sequence     1
Next log sequence to archive   2
Current log sequence           2

-- Force a log switch. Log sequence 3 will become the current redo log.
-- We will recover to the first change for log sequence 3.
SQL> ALTER SYSTEM SWITCH LOGFILE;
SQL> SELECT sequence#, first_change# FROM v$log;

SEQUENCE# FIRST_CHANGE#
---------- -------------
        1         35869
        2         35899
        3         35936

-- Now add two more rows and commit.

-- Add two rows to the table.
SQL> INSERT INTO time_table VALUES (sysdate);
1 row created.
SQL> INSERT INTO time_table VALUES (sysdate);
1 row created.
-- Commit these changes.
SQL> COMMIT;
```

```
-- Now, let's look at the table.
SQL> SELECT TO_CHAR(the_time, 'mm/dd/yyyy hh24:mi:ss') FROM time_table;

TO_CHAR(THE_TIME,'M
-------------------
04/29/2001 00:24:52
04/29/2001 00:24:54
04/29/2001 00:27:26
04/29/2001 00:27:26

-- Shut down the database.
SQL> SHUTDOWN IMMEDIATE
Database closed.
Database dismounted.
ORACLE instance shut down.

-- Recover the last backup.
SQL> HOST COPY d:\oracle_backup\hot\*.* d:\oracle\oradata\recover
d:\oracle_backup\hot\RECOVER_RBS_01.DBF
d:\oracle_backup\hot\RECOVER_USERS_01.DBF
d:\oracle_backup\hot\RECOVER_DATA_01.DBF
d:\oracle_backup\hot\RECOVER_INDEX_TBS_01.DBF
d:\oracle_backup\hot\RECOVER_TEMP_01.DBF
d:\oracle_backup\hot\RECOVER_TEST_TBS_01.DBF
d:\oracle_backup\hot\SYSTEM01.DBF

-- Mount the database.
SQL> STARTUP MOUNT
ORACLE instance started.
Total System Global Area    92280076 bytes
Fixed Size                     70924 bytes
Variable Size               87937024 bytes
Database Buffers             4194304 bytes
Redo Buffers                   77824 bytes
Database mounted.

-- We begin the change-based recovery.
-- Notice we use automatic application of archived redo logs
-- in response to the recovery prompt.
```

```
-- Change 35936 is the first change in the online redo log after
-- we forced the log switch, thus we will recover up to but not
-- including that point.
SQL> RECOVER DATABASE UNTIL CHANGE 35936;

-- We open the database. Note the use of RESETLOGS.
SQL> ALTER DATABASE OPEN RESETLOGS;

-- We query the table, and see only two records!
SQL> SELECT TO_CHAR(the_time, 'mm/dd/yyyy hh24:mi:ss') FROM time_table;

TO_CHAR(THE_TIME,'M
-------------------
04/29/2001 00:24:52
04/29/2001 00:24:54
```

Cancel-Based Recovery

Cancel-based recovery allows you to manually apply archived redo logs to the database during a recovery, but be able to stop the recovery after the application of each archived redo log and open the database. This is handy in cases where you have lost a control file or the online redo log, and you need to recover the database as much as possible.

To use cancel-based recovery, use the command RECOVER DATABASE UNTIL CANCEL. Then, as you are prompted for archived redo logs to apply, enter CANCEL to stop the recovery process. We will demonstrate the use of cancel-based recovery in the next section.

Recovery from Loss of Online Redo Logs

A special case is recovery from the loss of the online redo log. This is a particular problem if the online redo log that is lost is the current online redo log and no other members exist. In this case, if your database crashes along with the loss of the redo log, you will likely lose some data.

NOTE As noted earlier, the online redo log is the Achilles heel of Oracle. This is why you must protect it by creating at a minimum two different members of each redo log group (and I prefer three). Each of these should be on a separate disk and use a separate controller, if possible.

Should you lose the online log file and the database doesn't crash, you may find that it hangs. In this case, you can try to issue the ALTER DATABASE CLEAR LOGFILE command, and this may solve the problem.

Suppose that you accidentally deleted the online redo log during maintenance, after shutting down the database with the SHUTDOWN NORMAL or SHUTDOWN IMMEDIATE command. In this case, you can perform an easy bit of magic to solve the problem, as shown in Listing 10.9.

Listing 10.9: Recovering from the Loss of the Online Redo Logs after a Normal Database Shutdown

```
-- In this first case, we shut down our database to do some maintenance.
-- Unfortunately, we didn't test our script and we accidentally deleted our
-- online redo logs. We shut down the database normally with a SHUTDOWN
-- IMMEDIATE command, so recovery in this case is a snap.
-- All we need to do is issue a recover database until cancel command,
-- and then open the database with RESETLOGS. (RESETLOGS will re-create
-- the redo logs!)
SQL> STARTUP
ORACLE instance started.

Total System Global Area    92280076 bytes
Fixed Size                     70924 bytes
Variable Size               87937024 bytes
Database Buffers             4194304 bytes
Redo Buffers                   77824 bytes
Database mounted.
ORA-00313: open failed for members of log group 1 of thread 1
ORA-00312: online log 1 thread 1: 'D:\ORACLE\ORADATA\RECOVER\REDO01.LOG'
SQL> RECOVER DATABASE UNTIL CANCEL;
Media recovery complete.
SQL> ALTER DATABASE OPEN RESETLOGS;
Database altered.
```

If you issued SHUTDOWN ABORT, or some other problem caused a database crash (such as a power failure), then you have a bigger problem. Assuming that you have lost one or more of the online redo logs required to get the database up and going again, you will need to restore all database datafiles from the last good backup and recover the database. In this kind of recovery situation, complete database recovery will not be possible. After you have completed the recovery, you will need to issue the ALTER DATABASE OPEN RESETLOGS command. The use of the RESETLOGS command will cause new online redo logs to be created. Listing 10.10 provides an example of such a situation.

Listing 10.10: Recovering from Loss of the Online Redo Logs after an Abnormal Database Shutdown

```
-- A slightly different problem. This time we crashed the database (via
-- a SHUTDOWN ABORT perhaps), so recovery is more complicated. In this
-- situation, there is a likelihood of data loss. We performed another
-- hot backup before this exercise.
SQL> SELECT count(*) FROM time_table;
  COUNT(*)
----------
      4096

SQL> ALTER SYSTEM SWITCH LOGFILE;
System altered.
SQL> INSERT INTO time_table SELECT * FROM time_table;
4096 rows created.

SQL> SELECT COUNT(*) FROM time_table;
  COUNT(*)
----------
      8192


SQL> COMMIT;
Commit complete.
SQL> connect / as sysdba
Connected.

-- Oh no!! System crash big time!
SQL> SHUTDOWN ABORT
ORACLE instance shut down.

-- Restart the database.
SQL> STARTUP
ORACLE instance started.
Total System Global Area    92280076 bytes
Fixed Size                     70924 bytes
```

```
Variable Size              87937024 bytes
Database Buffers            4194304 bytes
Redo Buffers                  77824 bytes
Database mounted.
ORA-00313: open failed for members of log group 3 of thread 1
ORA-00312: online log 3 thread 1: 'D:\ORACLE\ORADATA\RECOVER\REDO03.LOG'
ORA-27041: unable to open file
OSD-04002: unable to open file
O/S-Error: (OS 2) The system cannot find the file specified.

-- We lost our online redo log file. It is nowhere to be found.
-- So, we need to recover the database. Can we do a regular recovery?
SQL> RECOVER DATABASE;
ORA-00283: recovery session canceled due to errors
ORA-00313: open failed for members of log group 3 of thread 1
ORA-00312: online log 3 thread 1: 'D:\ORACLE\ORADATA\RECOVER\REDO03.LOG'
ORA-27041: unable to open file
OSD-04002: unable to open file
O/S-Error: (OS 2) The system cannot find the file specified.

-- No way … that missing redo log is murder. We need to do cancel-
-- based recovery or change-based recovery. Let's do cancel-based.
-- What log sequences do we have available?

SQL> ARCHIVE LOG LIST
Database log mode              Archive Mode
Automatic archival             Enabled
Archive destination            D:\Oracle\oradata\Recover\archive
Oldest online log sequence     2
Next log sequence to archive   4
Current log sequence           4

-- So, the lost log sequence number is 4 (this shows as the current
-- log file). We need to recover to log sequence number 3, which
-- we should have available. Let's do that with cancel-based recovery.

-- Apply log sequence 1.
SQL> RECOVER DATABASE UNTIL CANCEL;
ORA-00279: change 56033 generated at 04/29/2001 00:52:37 needed
```

```
ORA-00289: suggestion :
D:\ORACLE\ORADATA\RECOVER\ARCHIVE\RECOVERT001S00001.ARC
ORA-00280: change 56033 for thread 1 is in sequence #1

Specify log: {<RET>=suggested | filename | AUTO | CANCEL}
ORA-00279: change 56047 generated at 04/29/2001 00:53:53 needed
ORA-00289: suggestion :
D:\ORACLE\ORADATA\RECOVER\ARCHIVE\RECOVERT001S00002.ARC
ORA-00280: change 56047 for thread 1 is in sequence #2
ORA-00278: log file
'D:\ORACLE\ORADATA\RECOVER\ARCHIVE\RECOVERT001S00001.ARC'
no longer needed for this recovery

Specify log: {<RET>=suggested | filename | AUTO | CANCEL}
ORA-00279: change 56056 generated at 04/29/2001 00:55:02 needed
ORA-00289: suggestion :
D:\ORACLE\ORADATA\RECOVER\ARCHIVE\RECOVERT001S00003.ARC
ORA-00280: change 56056 for thread 1 is in sequence #3
ORA-00278: log file
'D:\ORACLE\ORADATA\RECOVER\ARCHIVE\RECOVERT001S00002.ARC'
no longer needed for this recovery

Specify log: {<RET>=suggested | filename | AUTO | CANCEL}
ORA-00279: change 56065 generated at 04/29/2001 00:56:44 needed
ORA-00289: suggestion :
\D:\ORACLE\ORADATA\RECOVER\ARCHIVE\RECOVERT001S00004.ARC
ORA-00280: change 56065 for thread 1 is in sequence #4
ORA-00278: log file
'D:\ORACLE\ORADATA\RECOVER\ARCHIVE\RECOVERT001S00003.ARC'
no longer needed for this recovery
Specify log: {<RET>=suggested | filename | AUTO | CANCEL}
cancel
Media recovery canceled.
SQL> ALTER DATABASE OPEN RESETLOGS;
Database altered.

-- Note the data loss. We have only half the number of rows in
-- time_table that we should have!!
SQL> SELECT COUNT(*) FROM time_table;
```

```
  COUNT(*)
----------
      4096
```

WARNING While using SHUTDOWN ABORT may work 99.99 percent of the time, you should realize that there is some risk to your database in doing this. If you do a SHUTDOWN ABORT, and you lose your online redo log file, you will likely suffer some data loss. To reduce this risk, issue an ALTER SYSTEM SWITCH LOGFILE command and then an ALTER SYSTEM CHECKPOINT command before forcing a SHUTDOWN ABORT. It will make the shutdown take a bit longer, but it reduces your risk somewhat (but not completely).

Control File Backups

Control file backups come in two flavors:

- *Backup control files* are generated through the use of the ALTER SYSTEM BACKUP CONTROL FILE TO *'filename'* command, as in this example:
  ```
  ALTER DATABASE BACKUP CONTROL FILE TO
  'd:\oracle_backup\control\backup_control_01.ctl';
  ```
- Trace files can be created that contain the DDL required to re-create the current control file. This is facilitated through the use of the ALTER SYSTEM BACKUP CONTROL FILE TO TRACE command.

Both methods are useful when you need to recover the database. The trace file generated by the ALTER SYSTEM BACKUP CONTROL FILE TO TRACE command also serves as a good piece of documentation for your database, because it lists various database configuration information.

NOTE The backup control file itself is not readable. It is in the same format as the Oracle control file.

Using the Backup Control File for Database Recovery

If you use the backup control file to recover a database, you must use the USING BACKUP CONTROL FILE syntax of the RECOVER command. Listing 10.11 provides an example of using a backup control file to recover a database. Note that when recovering with a backup control file, you will need to use RESETLOGS to open the database.

NOTE In many cases, when you use the CREATE CONTROL FILE command to recover from a lost control file, you will not need to issue a RESETLOGS command. You always need to use RESETLOGS when recovering with a backup control file.

Listing 10.11: Using a Backup Control File when Recovering a Database

```
-- First, create a backup control file.
SQL> ALTER DATABASE BACKUP CONTROLFILE TO
  2 'd:\oracle_backup\control\backup_control_01.ctl';
Database altered.

-- Shut down the database.
SQL> SHUTDOWN IMMEDIATE
Database closed.
Database dismounted.
ORACLE instance shut down.

-- Now, remove the existing control files.
SQL> HOST DEL d:\oracle\oradata\recover\*.ctl

-- Try to start up the database.
SQL> STARTUP
ORACLE instance started.

Total System Global Area    92280076 bytes
Fixed Size                     70924 bytes
Variable Size               87937024 bytes
Database Buffers             4194304 bytes
Redo Buffers                   77824 bytes
ORA-00205: error in identifying controlfile, check alert log for more
info

-- A snippet from the alert log looks like this:
-- ORA-00202: controlfile: 'D:\Oracle\oradata\Recover\control01.ctl'
```

```
-- ORA-27041: unable to open file
-- OSD-04002: unable to open file
-- O/S-Error: (OS 2) The system cannot find the file specified.

-- The database won't start due to missing control files.
-- Shut it down again.
SQL> SHUTDOWN
ORA-01507: database not mounted
ORACLE instance shut down.

-- Copy backup control file into place.
SQL> HOST COPY d:\oracle_backup\control\backup_control_01.ctl
d:\oracle\oradata\recover\control01.ctl
SQL> HOST COPY d:\oracle_backup\control\backup_control_01.ctl
d:\oracle\oradata\recover\control02.ctl
SQL> HOST COPY d:\oracle_backup\control\backup_control_01.ctl
d:\oracle\oradata\recover\control03.ctl

-- Now, startup mount the database.
SQL> STARTUP MOUNT
ORACLE instance started.

Total System Global Area    92280076 bytes
Fixed Size                     70924 bytes
Variable Size               87937024 bytes
Database Buffers             4194304 bytes
Redo Buffers                   77824 bytes
Database mounted.

-- Now, determine the current online log file sequence numbers.
-- We may have to recover using an online sequence number.
SELECT a.group#, a.member, b.sequence#
FROM v$logfile a, v$log b
WHERE a.group#=b.group#;

    GROUP# MEMBER                                           SEQUENCE#
---------- ---------------------------------------- ----------
         1 D:\ORACLE\ORADATA\RECOVER\REDO01.LOG             10
```

```
            2 E:\TESTRECOVER\REDO02.LOG                     11
            3 D:\ORACLE\ORADATA\RECOVER\REDO03.LOG           9

-- Now, recover the database.
SQL> RECOVER DATABASE USING BACKUP CONTROLFILE;
ORA-00279: change 136287 generated at 04/29/2001 22:48:45
needed for thread 1
ORA-00289: suggestion :
D:\ORACLE\ORADATA\RECOVER\ARCHIVE\RECOVERT001S00011.ARC
ORA-00280: change 136287 for thread 1 is in sequence #11

Specify log: {<RET>=suggested | filename | AUTO | CANCEL}
e:\testrecover\redo02.log
Log applied.
Media recovery complete.

-- Note that we had to apply the current online redo log (redo02.log)
-- instead of taking the prompted archive log sequence number.
-- This isn't always going to be required, but it does happen.
-- Now, we open the database with RESETLOGS.
SQL> ALTER DATABASE OPEN RESETLOGS;
Database altered.
```

Using a Trace File

If you are going to use a trace file resulting from the BACKUP CONTROL FILE TO TRACE command, you will need to edit it first, because Oracle adds a trace file header on the trace file before generating the RECOVERY command. The trace file will contain a CREATE CONTROL file command. Review the command and make sure it is suitable. Once you are satisfied that the command is correct, connect to the database and start the instance with STARTUP NOMOUNT command. Following that, run the script with the CREATE CONTROL FILE inside of it to re-create the control file. Depending on the condition of your online redo logs, RESETLOGS may or may not be required. If the online redo logs are intact, you should not need to issue a RESETLOGS command. In fact, if the database was shut down cleanly, you won't even need to recover the database.

Listing 10.12 provides an example of using the results of the ALTER DATABASE BACKUP CONTROL FILE TO TRACE command to recover a database.

Listing 10.12: Using the Trace File Results to Recover a Database

```
-- First, create the trace file with the ALTER DATABASE COMMAND.
SQL> ALTER DATABASE BACKUP CONTROLFILE TO TRACE;
Database altered.

-- We will need to edit the trace file to remove the file header.

-- Now, shut down the database.
SQL> SHUTDOWN IMMEDIATE
Database closed.
Database dismounted.
ORACLE instance shut down.

-- Now, delete the control files.
SQL> HOST DEL d:\oracle\oradata\recover\*.ctl
-- Execute the edited trace file.
-- This is the code in the trace file that is executed.
SQL> STARTUP NOMOUNT
ORACLE instance started.

Total System Global Area    92280076 bytes
Fixed Size                     70924 bytes
Variable Size               87937024 bytes
Database Buffers             4194304 bytes
Redo Buffers                   77824 bytes

-- Create the control file.

SQL> CREATE CONTROLFILE REUSE DATABASE "RECOVER" NORESETLOGS ARCHIVELOG
  2      MAXLOGFILES 12
  3      MAXLOGMEMBERS 3
  4      MAXDATAFILES 120
  5      MAXINSTANCES 1
  6      MAXLOGHISTORY 224
  7  LOGFILE
  8      GROUP 1 'D:\ORACLE\ORADATA\RECOVER\REDO01.LOG'  SIZE 1M,
  9      GROUP 2 'D:\ORACLE\ORADATA\RECOVER\REDO02.LOG'  SIZE 1M,
 10      GROUP 3 'D:\ORACLE\ORADATA\RECOVER\REDO03.LOG'  SIZE 1M
 11  DATAFILE
```

```
    12    'D:\ORACLE\ORADATA\RECOVER\SYSTEM01.DBF',
    13    'D:\ORACLE\ORADATA\RECOVER\RECOVER_RBS_01.DBF',
    14    'D:\ORACLE\ORADATA\RECOVER\RECOVER_USERS_01.DBF',
    15    'D:\ORACLE\ORADATA\RECOVER\RECOVER_DATA_01.DBF',
    16    'D:\ORACLE\ORADATA\RECOVER\RECOVER_INDEX_TBS_01.DBF',
    17    'D:\ORACLE\ORADATA\RECOVER\RECOVER_TEMP_01.DBF',
    18    'D:\ORACLE\ORADATA\RECOVER\RECOVER_TEST_TBS_01.DBF',
    19    'A:\NEW_RBS.DBF'
    20   CHARACTER SET WE8ISO8859P1;
Control file created.

-- Does the database need recovery?
SQL> RECOVER DATABASE;
ORA-00283: recovery session canceled due to errors
ORA-00264: no recovery required
-- No recovery needed (this is because we had a clean shutdown).
-- Open the database.
SQL> ALTER DATABASE OPEN;
Database altered.
```

Other Oracle Backups

There are some other files that you might need to consider backing up from time to time. These include the following:

- The parameter (init.ora) file should be backed up after any changes.
- Any other database configuration files (ifiles, and the oratab file, for example) should be backed up after any changes.
- Any listener or Net8 configuration files such as the listener.ora, tnsnames.ora, and sqlnet.ora files should be backed up after any changes.
- All database creation scripts should be backed up after the creation of the database. Any scripts that change the design of the database (DDL) should be backed up as they are implemented.
- Keep a current backup of your Oracle software for easy recovery. Back up the software directory any time a change (such as a patch application) is made.

RESETLOGS and Recovery

The use of the RESETLOGS command seems to be an area of confusion for beginning and even some intermediate-level DBAs. In this section, we will try to remove some of the mystery.

When you use RESETLOGS, you are creating another *incarnation*, or version, of the database. Recovery between incarnations is generally not supported by Oracle (though we will discuss a way to recover between incarnations shortly). Thus, it is very important that you back up the database immediately after issuing the RESETLOGS command. Consider that the logical lifetime of a given database is between its creation, or the execution of the last RESETLOGS command, and the execution of the RESETLOGS command. Thus, you cannot recover different logical versions of the database.

TIP As you will see shortly, it is always a really good idea to back up your online redo logs before issuing the RESETLOGS command.

Before Oracle will open the database with the RESETLOGS command, several consistency checks are performed:

- Datafile compatibility set in the datafile headers must not be greater than the compatible setting for the database. The current compatible setting for the database is set by the COMPATIBLE parameter in the `init.ora` file.
- Offline immediate files must be brought online or dropped.
- Datafiles cannot have any of the fuzzy bits set, and all datafiles must be at the same SCN level, except read-only tablespace datafiles.

These checks can be a bit tough at times and can cause you to need to force open the database (which we will discuss shortly).

Why and When to Use RESETLOGS

Once you have applied incomplete recovery, the remaining unapplied redo generated by the database after the point you have recovered to becomes useless. Therefore, there needs to be a way to clear the unusable redo and reset various other internal settings. This is the purpose of the RESETLOGS command.

You use RESETLOGS when doing a point-in-time recovery of the database. This command is also used when you are recovering the database using a backup control file and recovering a database with a control file created using the CREATE CONTROL FILE command that includes the RESETLOGS option. The RESETLOGS option in the CREATE CONTROL FILE command must be used if you are recovering a database when both the control file and the current online redo logs are missing. If you are recovering a database with a backup control file, the RESETLOGS option will need to be used if the online redo logs have been lost.

When the RESETLOGS command is issued, the following actions take place:

- Oracle will reset the log sequence number for the next online redo log to 1. This also has the effect of rendering unusable any archived redo log (and any online redo) generated in the online redo logs after the creation of the new incarnation.
- A log file group is chosen to be the current online redo log group.
- The control file and all the datafiles are resynchronized. Datafile headers for online datafiles are updated. Offline datafiles are marked as needing recovery.
- The control file and the FILE$ table are cross-checked. Oracle will consider the FILE$ table to be correct. Therefore, if a file is in the FILE$ table and it is not in the control file, it will be marked in the control file with a MISSING*xxx* placeholder. If the file is in the control file but not in FILE$, it will be dropped from the control file.
- All redo in the online redo logs will be cleared.
- Any missing online redo logs will be created.

Recovering through RESETLOGS

You should always make a backup of your database after using the RESETLOGS command. This is one of those rare cases where I like to do a cold backup, because it makes sure that the database remains consistent until after I have completed my backup.

However, performing a cold backup may not possible. It does, after all, increase your time to recover. You may opt for a hot backup, or you might decide to wait for the normal nightly backup so the backup process does not impact the user community. While these decisions are somewhat related to business needs, you should make sure that management clearly understands the risks of such decisions.

What happens if you perform an incomplete recovery, issue the RESETLOGS command, and before you can back up the database, it comes crashing down again? In this case, you are not only faced with a recovery, but you also need to recover through the use of the RESETLOGS command. Fortunately, there is a way to perform such a recovery (obviously, the database must be in ARCHIVELOG mode for this to work). The bad news is that the requirements to be able to perform this recovery are rather exacting. To do this kind of recovery you must have the following:

- The datafile backup from before the issuing of the RESETLOGS command
- A copy of the control file from the database backed up before the RESETLOGS command
- All archived redo logs from before and after the issuing of the RESETLOGS command
- A copy of the online redo logs as they looked just before you issued the RESET-LOGS command (in other words, right before you issue the RESETLOGS command, back up the online redo logs)

 WARNING It is strongly suggested that you discuss your plans to roll forward through RESETLOGS with Oracle support before you do it.

Here are the steps you take to roll forward through the last RESETLOGS:

1. Create a backup control file for the current database. (Use the ALTER SYSTEM BACKUP CONTROLFILE TO TRACE command.)
2. Restore the datafiles using the last backup of the database made before you issued the RESETLOGS command. Make sure you have copies of the online redo logs from before issuing the RESETLOGS command.
3. Restore the backup control file from the last control file backup that you took before the RESETLOGS command. Restore it to a location other than the location of the current control file. Modify the `init.ora` file of the database to point to the new control file location.
4. Mount the database by issuing a STARTUP MOUNT command.
5. From the alert log, find the change number for the open RESETLOGS command.
6. Recover the database using the backup control file until the change number found in the previous step.
7. When recovery completes, shut down the database with a normal shutdown.
8. Change `init.ora` to point back to the original location of the control files.
9. Mount the database by issuing a STARTUP MOUNT command.

10. Recover the database using the current control file. Open the database without RESETLOGS.

When All Else Fails—Forcing Open the Database

We saved this section for last, and this is because forcing open the database is an absolute last resort. Table 10.5 provides a list of the parameters that can be used to force open a database. Often, if you are trying to force open a database, you will need to use more than one parameter.

 WARNING Talk to Oracle before using these parameters. They may change between versions, and their uses may even change.

TABLE 10.5: PARAMETERS TO FORCE OPEN AN ORACLE DATABASE

Parameter	Description	Example
_offline_rollback_segments	Allows a rollback segment to be dropped, even though it has active transactions. It allows read access to the rollback segment while preventing write access. This parameter needs to be left in place until all the database blocks with changes in the rollback segments have been recovered.	_offline_rollback_segments=rb01
_corrupted_rollback_segments	If a rollback segment is unavailable or corrupted, can be used to force the database open. Any transaction that is in the affected rollback segment will be considered committed, thus leading to a very serious possibility of database consistency problems, including the data dictionary.	_corrupted_rollback_segments=rb01

Continued

TABLE 10.5: PARAMETERS TO FORCE OPEN AN ORACLE DATABASE (CONTINUED)

Parameter	Description	Example
_allow_resetlogs_corruption	Causes all consistency checks during the execution of RESETLOGS to be skipped. It allows database files to have different SCNs or even have the fuzzy bits set. This can be used, for example, if you lose a datafile and it cannot be recovered completely because of missing archived redo logs.	_allow_resetlogs_corruption=TRUE
_allow_read_only_corruption	New in 8i, allows you to open the database in read-only mode, even if it is corrupted.	_allow_read_only_corruption=TRUE

WARNING Using many of the parameters listed in Table 10.5 is not supported by Oracle. You should talk to Oracle support before using them. Use of some of these parameters will almost guarantee that your database will be in an inconsistent state. They can cause your database to be destroyed (and you to ask yourself why you ever did what you did!).

You should use these parameters only if your database is hopelessly dead in the water, Oracle support personnel have thrown up their hands in failure, and your system administrator has said you do not have a good backup available. Oracle will probably not suggest some of these to you—ever. I am not suggesting that you use these for anything other than fun and frolic. (I love to play with stuff I'm not supposed to!) So, again, you are warned to use them at your own risk.

CHAPTER 11

Oracle Logical Backup and Recovery

FEATURING:

The Oracle Export utility	*492*
The Oracle Import utility	*504*

Logical backups are backups of the logical structures within the database itself. A logical backup does not back up the physical database; therefore, you must restore some part of the physical database before you can use a logical backup to recover it. Logical backups do not provide point-in-time recovery, as do physical backups.

Logical backups do provide several useful features. They facilitate Oracle8i features such as transportable tablespaces, and they also provide the ability to recover specific objects that were backed up at a specific point in time. For example, you might want to use logical backups with databases that are part of a development system, where a lot of destructive testing occurs. With logical backups, you can restore certain tables to how they looked before a test. Also, logical exports are one method that can be used to move an Oracle database between different operating systems.

Logical backups are supported by Oracle through the use of two tools: the Import utility and the Export utility. In this chapter, we will address the use of these two utilities.

The Oracle Export Utility

The Oracle Export utility (EXP) has been around since the early days of Oracle. It provides a means of producing a logical extract of the data from an Oracle database into a operating system file, often called the *export dump file*, or just the *dump file*. This file is created in a format that allows it to be used by the Oracle Import utility (IMP) to re-create the data (and database structures) in the same database or another database, at a later date. The following are some common uses of logical exports:

- Extracting specific objects for recovery and re-creation purposes
- Defragmenting a database
- Rebuilding a database in order to defragment the SYSTEM tablespace
- Protecting the database from user errors, such as a user accidentally truncating a table
- Saving the structure of the database, including table definitions, indexes, constraints, and stored program units (such as PL/SQL functions and procedures)
- Creating a historical archive of a given state of the database

Basically, once the export file is created, it can be copied to any other system running Oracle (for example, via NFS or FTP transfer) and used to re-create that database (or some part of it) on that other system. Together, the Export and Import utilities allow you to move an Oracle database between operating systems, on the same operating system, or even the same database.

Logical backups provide the ability to extract the database in a consistent manner; that is, the data in the export will be consistent to the time that the export was taken. Another interesting benefit you get with the Export utility is that as each block is read, the export process will detect logically corrupt blocks. When corrupt blocks are detected, the export will fail. You can then correct the problem and restart the export. Most physical backup software will not detect corrupt blocks, making it possible to back up (and recover) corrupted data without ever knowing about it.

NOTE RMAN provides block checking when performing physical backups. See Chapter 13 for details on using RMAN.

What Can You Export?

The Export utility works with more than data. When configured properly, it can be used to export the following database objects:

- Tablespaces
- Schema objects (tables and indexes)
- Constraints, grants, and synonyms
- Users
- Data
- Stored PL/SQL code (procedures, functions, triggers, and so on)

The Export utility cannot be used to re-create the database itself. The base database must be created (via the CREATE DATABASE command) before an export file can be used to load data into that database. However, once the base database is created, the Export utility can create all of the tablespaces, including the datafiles and the other associated objects.

The Export utility does not back up all of the objects in the database. Specifically, objects owned by SYS (such as the data dictionary tables) will not be exported. Other schemas that will not be exported include ORDSYS, MDSYS, CTXSYS, and ORDPLUGINS. If you create objects using these schemas, those objects will not be exported.

NOTE Use of the Export utility (or its complementary program, Import) is not a substitute for physical backup and recovery. Use of logical backups does not provide for point-in-time recovery, as do physical backups. Also, typically, recovering an entire database from a logical backup takes longer and can be somewhat messier from an administrative perspective than recovering from a physical backup.

Using the Export Utility

The Export utility allows you to perform three different types of logical extractions:

- Full export extracts the entire database.
- User export extracts objects owned by a specific user or users.
- Table export extracts specific tables in the database.

To use the Export utility, you must have the EXP_FULL_DATABASE privilege to export tables in other schemas than your own. To export from your own schema, you need the CREATE SESSION privilege.

Table 11.1 lists the most commonly used EXP parameters, their default values, and a brief description of each.

TABLE 11.1: COMMONLY USED EXP COMMAND-LINE PARAMETERS

Parameter	Default Value	Description
BUFFER	Operating system-specific	Sets the size of the data buffer to be used while exporting. Increasing the size of this buffer can help the performance of the export.
COMPRESS	Y	Causes Oracle to use the current size of the object as the setting for the NEXT parameter when re-creating the object.
CONSISTENT	N	When set to Y, bases the export on a consistent image of the database as of the time the export started. (This cannot be used if you are doing an export connected as SYSDBA.)
DIRECT	N	Uses direct mode when performing the export.
FILE	expdat.dmp	Defines the export filename. Oracle8i supports multiple export files to avoid file size limitations. Each filename is separated by a comma.

Continued

TABLE 11.1: COMMONLY USED EXP COMMAND-LINE PARAMETERS (CONTINUED)

Parameter	Default Value	Description
FILESIZE	None	Defines the maximum size of each of the dump files to be created (used to facilitate creation of multiple export dump files).
FULL	N	When set to Y, indicates that the entire database should be exported.
LOG	None	Defines a log file to send screen output to.
OWNER	None	During a user-level export, indicates the owner(s) to be exported. A comma separates each owner in the list of owners.
PARAFILE	None	Causes EXP to read in a parameter file to derive any other command-line parameters.
QUERY	None	Allows you to define a query that will further restrict the rowset being exported.
ROWS	Y	Allows you to restrict the export of row-level data. This results in an export that contains logical structure creation information (such as creation of tables and indexes) without related data.
STATISTICS	ESTIMATE	Defines the type of statistics gathering that should be done when the export file is imported. Options include ESTIMATE, COMPUTE, and NONE.
TABLES	None	During a table-level export, indicates the specific tables to export. A comma separates each table in the list of tables.
USERID	None	Identifies the username and password of the user that EXP should use to perform the extraction. Should be the first parameter in the command line, and does not need to have the USERID parameter name included.

The Export utility can be run in one of three different modes: interactive, command-line, or parameter-file-driven. The following sections describe each of these modes and the different types of extractions.

Interactive Mode Export

With an interactive mode export, you call EXP without any parameters. In this case, EXP will prompt you for certain required information, such as a username and password, the name of the dump file, the type of export, and other related information. Listing 11.1 provides an example of an interactive mode export. It also shows a full export, which extracts the entire database.

Listing 11.1: Performing an Interactive Mode Export

```
D:\ORACLE\admin\RECOVER\exp>exp
Export: Release 8.1.6.0.0 - Production on Mon Apr 30 22:39:26 2001
(c) Copyright 1999 Oracle Corporation.  All rights reserved.
Username: system
Password:
Connected to: Oracle8i Enterprise Edition Release 8.1.6.0.0 - Production
With the Partitioning option
JServer Release 8.1.6.0.0 - Production
Enter array fetch buffer size: 4096 >
Export file: EXPDAT.DMP >
(1)E(ntire database), (2)U(sers), or (3)T(ables): (2)U > 1
Export grants (yes/no): yes >
Export table data (yes/no): yes >
Compress extents (yes/no): yes >
Export done in WE8ISO8859P1 character set and WE8ISO8859P1
NCHAR character set
About to export the entire database ...
.
. Various informational messages appear during the export.
. These have been removed in this listing.
.
Export terminated successfully without warnings.
```

Command-Line Mode Export

The command-line export method involves including various command-line parameters. The ability to use command-line parameters (or a parameter file, which we will discuss shortly) makes automating the export process much easier. The Export utility has many parameters associated with it that make it a robust program. You can see these parameters by issuing the HELP=Y parameter at the command line, as shown here:

```
D:\ORACLE\oradata\RECOVER>exp HELP=Y
Export: Release 8.1.6.0.0 - Production on Mon Apr 30 00:52:29 2001
(c) Copyright 1999 Oracle Corporation.  All rights reserved.
You can let Export prompt you for parameters by entering the EXP
command followed by your username/password:
      Example: EXP SCOTT/TIGER
Or, you can control how Export runs by entering the EXP command
Followed by various arguments. To specify parameters, you use keywords:

      Format:  EXP KEYWORD=value or KEYWORD=(value1,value2,...,valueN)
      Example: EXP SCOTT/TIGER GRANTS=Y TABLES=(EMP,DEPT,MGR)
               or TABLES=(T1:P1,T1:P2), if T1 is partitioned table

USERID must be the first parameter on the command line.

Keyword    Description (Default)         Keyword       Description (Default)
--------------------------------------------------------------------------
USERID     username/password             FULL          export entire file (N)
BUFFER     size of data buffer           OWNER         list of owner usernames
FILE       output files (EXPDAT.DMP)     TABLES        list of table names
COMPRESS   import into one extent (Y)    RECORDLENGTH  length of IO record
GRANTS     export grants (Y)             INCTYPE       incremental export type
INDEXES    export indexes (Y)            RECORD        track incr. export (Y)
ROWS       export data rows (Y)          PARFILE       parameter filename
CONSTRAINTS export constraints (Y)       CONSISTENT    cross-table consistency
LOG        log file of screen output     STATISTICS    analyze objects (ESTIMATE)
DIRECT     direct path (N)               TRIGGERS      export triggers (Y)
FEEDBACK   display progress every x rows (0)
FILESIZE   maximum size of each dump file
QUERY      select clause used to export a subset of a table

The following keywords only apply to transportable tablespaces
TRANSPORT_TABLESPACE export transportable tablespace metadata (N)
TABLESPACES list of tablespaces to transport
```

Listing 11.2 provides an example of a command-line driven export. This export is, for all practical purposes, the same type of export performed in Listing 11.1, except that the parameters are included on the command line rather than set interactively. Again, this is a full export of the whole database.

Listing 11.2: Performing a Command-Line Mode Export

```
D:\ORACLE\admin\RECOVER\exp>exp system/robert
file=expdat.dmp full=y buffer=4096

Export: Release 8.1.6.0.0 - Production on Mon Apr 30 22:47:24 2001
(c) Copyright 1999 Oracle Corporation.  All rights reserved.
Connected to: Oracle8i Enterprise Edition Release 8.1.6.0.0 - Production
With the Partitioning option
JServer Release 8.1.6.0.0 - Production
Export done in WE8ISO8859P1 character set and
WE8ISO8859P1 NCHAR character set

About to export the entire database ...
.
. Various informational messages appear during the export.
. These have been removed in this listing.
.
Export terminated successfully without warnings.
```

Parameter-File-Driven Export

The parameter-file-driven method of executing an export is facilitated through the creation of a text parameter file and the use of the PARFILE parameter in the command line. The parameter file is simple a text-based file that contains each parameter and its setting, delimited by carriage returns and linefeeds. You can use a combination of command-line parameters and parameter file settings if you like.

WARNING Be careful when using parameter files and command-line parameters together. The parameter file setting will always override the command-line parameters.

Listing 11.3 provides an example of a parameter file and its use in an export operation.

Listing 11.3: Performing a Parameter-File-Driven Export

```
D:\ORACLE\admin\RECOVER\exp>type parm.fil
file=expdat.dmp
full=y
buffer=4096
consistent=y
```

```
D:\ORACLE\admin\RECOVER\exp>exp system/robert parfile=parm.fil
Export: Release 8.1.6.0.0 - Production on Mon Apr 30 22:53:06 2001
(c) Copyright 1999 Oracle Corporation.  All rights reserved.
Connected to: Oracle8i Enterprise Edition Release 8.1.6.0.0 - Production
With the Partitioning option
JServer Release 8.1.6.0.0 - Production
Export done in WE8ISO8859P1 character set and
WE8ISO8859P1 NCHAR character set
About to export the entire database ...
.
. Various informational messages appear during the export.
. These have been removed in this listing.
.
Export terminated successfully without warnings.
```

User-Level Export

A user-level export allows you to export the schema objects of a specific user. Only specific objects are exported when doing a user-level export. This includes the object-creation DDL (creation DDL for tables, indexes, views, grants, and so on), stored PL/SQL code for that user, any private database links, and data row information for the exported tables. Listing 11.4 shows an example of exporting the SCOTT schema.

Listing 11.4: Performing a User-Level Export

```
D:\ORACLE\admin\RECOVER\exp>exp scott/tiger file=userlevel.dmp
Export: Release 8.1.6.0.0 - Production on Mon Apr 30 23:49:30 2001
(c) Copyright 1999 Oracle Corporation.  All rights reserved.
Connected to: Oracle8i Enterprise Edition Release 8.1.6.0.0 - Production
With the Partitioning option
JServer Release 8.1.6.0.0 - Production
Export done in WE8ISO8859P1 character set and
WE8ISO8859P1 NCHAR character set
About to export specified users ...
. exporting pre-schema procedural objects and actions
. exporting foreign function library names for user SCOTT
. exporting object type definitions for user SCOTT
About to export SCOTT's objects ...
.
. Various informational messages appear during the export.
```

. These have been removed in this listing.

Export terminated successfully without warnings.

Notice that this export was done logging in as the SCOTT user. You can also perform a user-level export of a user who you are not logged in as. This is done through the use of the OWNER parameter, as shown in Listing 11.5.

Listing 11.5: Performing a User-Level Export as Another User

```
D:\ORACLE\admin\RECOVER\exp>exp system/robert owner=scott file=userlevel.dmp
Export: Release 8.1.6.0.0 - Production on Mon Apr 30 23:52:50 2001
(c) Copyright 1999 Oracle Corporation.  All rights reserved.
Connected to: Oracle8i Enterprise Edition Release 8.1.6.0.0 - Production
With the Partitioning option
JServer Release 8.1.6.0.0 - Production
Export done in WE8ISO8859P1 character set and
WE8ISO8859P1 NCHAR character set
About to export specified users ...
. exporting pre-schema procedural objects and actions
. exporting foreign function library names for user SCOTT
. exporting object type definitions for user SCOTT
About to export SCOTT's objects ...
.
. Various informational messages appear during the export.
. These have been removed in this listing.
.
Export terminated successfully without warnings.
```

Table-Level Export

A table-level export allows you to export specific tables. Different schemas or the same schema can own the tables to be exported. With a table-level export, only table definitions, associated rows, grants, indexes, and constraints are exported.

To specify a table, prefix it with the schema owner using dot notation:

`my_schema.my_table`

If you are exporting a specific partition of a table, use a colon to denote the partition, along with dot notation for the object:

`my_schema.my_table:partition_2`

Listing 11.6 provides an example of a table-level export of two tables in different schemas. This example exports one table from the SCOTT schema and a second table from the SCOTT2 schema.

Listing 11.6: Performing a Table-Level Export

```
D:\ORACLE\admin\RECOVER\exp>exp system/robert tables=scott2.emp,scott.dept
file=userlevel.dmp
Export: Release 8.1.6.0.0 - Production on Tue May 1 00:10:00 2001
(c) Copyright 1999 Oracle Corporation.  All rights reserved.
Connected to: Oracle8i Enterprise Edition Release 8.1.6.0.0 - Production
With the Partitioning option
JServer Release 8.1.6.0.0 - Production
Export done in WE8ISO8859P1 character set and
WE8ISO8859P1 NCHAR character set
About to export specified tables via Conventional Path ...
Current user changed to SCOTT2
. . exporting table                  EMP         14 rows exported
Current user changed to SCOTT
. . exporting table                  DEPT         4 rows exported
Export terminated successfully without warnings.
```

Compression of Extents

Using the COMPRESS parameter of the Export utility can be particularly useful if you have a database that is severely fragmented or if you have many tables that are suffering from poor space allocations or chained rows. The COMPRESS parameter will cause Oracle to re-create the object within a single extent when it is imported back into the database. (It does not cause the export file itself to be compressed.) Realize that although COMPRESS eliminates fragmentation, it does not eliminate the cause of the fragmentation, which is typically poor object management policies.

The default action for Oracle is to re-create the object in the same number and size of extents that it currently resides in. LOB data objects will not be compressed; they will maintain their original configuration settings.

 WARNING If the tablespace that the object is to be created in is not large enough or does not have enough contiguous free space to create the single extent, setting COMPRESS=Y can cause the import process to fail.

> **Tips on Defragmenting with the Export and Import Utilities**
>
> If you are going to use the Export and Import utilities to defragment most objects in your database, consider the following:
>
> - When re-creating the database, modify the `sql.bsq` file to avoid fragmenting the SYSTEM tablespace.
> - Review the objects' physical attributes (PCTFREE and PCTUSED) to make sure that they are set correctly. You should do this before the export is completed.
> - When creating an export file in order to defragment a database, create a second export file that does not contain rows. Set COMPRESS=Y on the export file that contains the data, but set COMPRESS=N on the second export file, just in case you need it to re-create the object using its existing storage attributes.

Direct-Mode Export

Using the DIRECT parameter causes Oracle to use the optional direct method of exporting data from the database. Essentially, this causes the Export utility to circumvent the standard Oracle kernel and extract the requested data directly from the database datafiles. Generally, using a direct-mode export can positively impact the performance of an export operation.

NOTE The Import utility does not support direct-mode operations. However, you can import a file created by the Export utility, regardless of whether the export was done in the default or direct mode.

There are some restrictions to using direct-mode exports:

- Interactive exports are not allowed.
- The character sets on the client and server must be the same.
- The BUFFER parameter has no effect on the export process.
- Certain datatypes cannot be exported using a direct-mode path. These include LOBs, BFILEs, REFs, or any object type. These objects will be exported using the

conventional export path. The rest of the export will be able to use the direct-mode path, however.

- The QUERY parameter cannot be used with a direct-mode export.

Support for Multiple Export Files

Many operating systems have limitations on the size of a given datafile, which can be a problem if the export file from a database exceeds those limitations. Additionally, you may find that you do not have enough space on a particular file system to support the entire export file. A solution might be to distribute the export files among two or three file systems. Oracle8i introduces the ability to split export files into multiple datafiles though the use of the FILE and FILESIZE parameters. The FILESIZE parameter is new to Oracle8i.

To export to multiple files, separate each datafile by a comma in the FILE parameter. Then, in the FILESIZE parameter, specify the file size that each datafile should be. This file size can be specified in bytes (in which case, there is no size identifier), kilobytes (using a *k* identifier), or megabytes (using an *m* identifier). Listing 11.7 provides an example of an export that exports the database into two different datafiles. The size of each of those datafiles will not be bigger than 100KB.

Listing 11.7: Creating Multiple Dump Files with EXP

```
D:\ORACLE\admin\RECOVER\exp>exp sys/robert file=exp001.dmp, exp002.dmp
filesize=100k full=y buffer=4096 consistent=y
Export: Release 8.1.6.0.0 - Production on Mon Apr 30 23:11:04 2001
(c) Copyright 1999 Oracle Corporation.  All rights reserved.
Connected to: Oracle8i Enterprise Edition Release 8.1.6.0.0 - Production
With the Partitioning option
JServer Release 8.1.6.0.0 - Production
Export done in WE8ISO8859P1 character set and
WE8ISO8859P1 NCHAR character set
About to export the entire database ...
.
. Various informational messages appear during the import.
. These have been removed in this listing. Note though that
. EXP reports when it's changing dump files.
.
. exporting synonyms
continuing export into file exp002.dmp
. exporting views
.
```

. Various informational messages appear during the export.
. These have been removed in this listing.
.

Export terminated successfully without warnings.

Let's look at the resulting physical export dump files.

```
D:\ORACLE\admin\RECOVER\exp>DIR EXP*.dmp
 Volume in drive D has no label.
 Volume Serial Number is 3C0E-D639
 Directory of D:\ORACLE\admin\RECOVER\exp
04/30/01  11:11p              102,400 exp001.dmp
04/30/01  11:11p               49,152 exp002.dmp
```

The Oracle Import Utility

The Import (IMP) utility, the companion to the Export utility, can be used to process an Oracle export file and import the contents of that file into another database. The Import utility can recover the logical structures, data, constraints, and stored program units contained inside export files.

The Import utility can be used to accomplish several tasks, including the following:

- Re-creating the entire database (tablespaces, users, and schema objects) with or without populating it with data
- Re-creating and populating selected tables in an export file
- Recovering from statement or user error that may cause an object to be accidentally changed, truncated, or dropped
- Resetting schema objects to a static state after the objects have been changed due to testing
- Defragmenting an existing database
- Recovering objects in cases where point-in-time recovery is not possible
- Moving transportable tablespaces (discussed in Chapter 12) and performing tablespace point-in-time recovery

What Can You Import?

The Import utility, depending on the import mode selected, will import all of the database schema objects contained in the export file. You can choose to import only specific types of objects by choosing a different import mode than the mode in which the export file was created.

Before you can use the Import utility, you must have a database that it can interact with. If a database does not already exist, you will need to create it (via the CREATE DATABASE command) before an export file can be used. Once the database is created and you start the import process, Oracle imports objects in a specific order, as follows:

- Type definitions
- Table definitions
- Table data
- Related table index
- Constraints
- Views
- Procedures
- Triggers
- Bitmap and function-based indexes

Using the Import Utility

Like the Export utility, the Import utility allows you to use one of three import modes:

- With a full import, the Import facility will import all objects in the export file into the database.
- With the user-level import, all objects belonging to a specific user will be imported into the database.
- With a table-level import, you can specify the tables to be recovered from the export file.

To be able to perform an import, the user who will be executing the import must have the CREATE SESSION privilege. If a specific user wishes to import an export dump file that was not created by that user, the IMP_FULL_DATABASE role must be assigned to that user.

Each schema that is to have an object imported into it must have the appropriate rights to create that type of object. For example, if the object is a table, the schema must have the CREATE TABLE privilege, as well as the appropriate QUOTA on the tablespace in which the table is to be created.

If you wish to import grants, the user who initiates the import must either own the object or have a grant to it using the WITH ADMIN option or the WITH GRANT option, depending on if the grant to be imported is a system or object grant.

NOTE From time to time, you may issue special grants on system objects to other users—direct grants of a system-level object to a user. For example, suppose that you gave a direct grant to user Charlie on SYS.DBA_USERS. If you were to export the database that contained this grant, and then re-create the database with that export file, user Charlie would lose the special system-level grant. This is because Oracle will not export grants on data dictionary objects (objects owned by SYS).

The Import utility has many different parameters, a few of which are required. The parameters are listed in Table 11.2.

TABLE 11.2: COMMONLY USED IMP PARAMETERS

Parameter	Default Value	Description
ANALYZE	Y	Determines if objects are analyzed after they are imported.
BUFFER	Operating-system dependent	Determines the size of the data buffer used when importing into the database. Increasing the size of this buffer can improve performance of the import, since more data will be written per I/O.
COMMIT	N	Causes IMP to commit rows after each array insert. The default is to commit after each table is loaded.
CONSTRAINTS	Y	Sets import object constraints.
DATAFILES	None	Used with transportable tablespaces.
DESTROY	N	Causes existing datafiles to be overwritten when IMP attempts to create a tablespace.
FEEDBACK	0 (disabled)	Causes a dot to be displayed each time the number of rows defined by this parameter is imported.
FILE	expdat.dmp	Identifies the export file to import. If multiple export files are to be used, the filenames are separated by commas.

Continued

TABLE 11.2: COMMONLY USED IMP PARAMETERS (CONTINUED)

Parameter	Default Value	Description
FILESIZE	None	If, when creating the export file, you opted to create multiple export files, you defined a file size for each of those files. This parameter must be used when importing multiple files and must be set to the same size as it was during the export.
FROMUSER	None	Allows you to select a subset of schemas in an export file for import. This parameter is generally used with the TOUSER parameter.
FULL	N	Defines the import as a full import.
GRANTS	Y	Allows you to control the creation of grants that are contained in the export file. Set this parameter to N if you do not wish grants contained in the export file to be imported during this import session.
HELP	N	Displays the help screen.
IGNORE	N	Ignores errors generated during the export that might otherwise cause the export to fail. This generally applies to object-creation errors, such as attempts to create a tablespace or table that already exists. The default action of IMP is to fail if these errors occur. Import-generated errors for row data, such as primary key violations, are always reported to the screen but always ignored.
INDEXES	Y	Allows you to control the creation of indexes that are contained in the export file. By default, IMP will attempt to create indexes during the import process. This can be disabled by setting this parameter to N.
INDEXFILE	None	Creates a file that contains various database DDL. If this parameter is used, the export file is not imported into the database.
LOG	None	Creates a log file that contains all messages generated during the import process.
PARFILE	None	Points to a user-defined parameter file that contains parameters to be used during the import process.
RECALCULATE_STATISTICS	N	Provides the option to recalculate Optimizer statistics after an object is imported.

Continued

TABLE 11.2: COMMONLY USED IMP PARAMETERS (CONTINUED)

Parameter	Default Value	Description
ROWS	Y	If set to N, restricts the import of data rows into the database.
SHOW	N	Causes the contents of the export file to be displayed to the screen rather than imported.
SKIP_UNUSABLE_INDEXES	N	Causes IMP to skip building indexes that are unusable. You can later re-create the indexes using the INDEXFILE parameter.
TABLES	None	Indicates a table-level import.
TABLESPACES	None	Used for transportable tablespaces.
TOUSER	None	Indicates a list of users to import specific objects into. This parameter is generally used with the FROMUSER parameter.
TRANSPORT_TABLESPACE	N	Used with transportable tablespaces.
TTS_OWNERS	None	Used with transportable tablespaces.
USERID	None	Specifies the username and password of the user performing the import operation. It must be the first parameter (can be included without using the USERID parameter name).
VOLSIZE	None	Defines the maximum number of bytes that can be exported to a given tape volume.

Like the Export facility, the Import facility can be run in one of three different modes: interactive, command-line, or parameter-file-driven. To see a listing of all of the valid IMP parameters, use the HELP=Y parameter, as follows:

```
C:\>imp HELP=Y
Import: Release 8.1.6.0.0 - Production on Tue May 1 22:45:26 2001
(c) Copyright 1999 Oracle Corporation.  All rights reserved.
You can let Import prompt you for parameters by entering the IMP
command followed by your username/password:
     Example: IMP SCOTT/TIGER
Or, you can control how Import runs by entering the IMP command followed
by various arguments. To specify parameters, you use keywords:

     Format:  IMP KEYWORD=value or KEYWORD=(value1,value2,...,valueN)
```

```
Example: IMP SCOTT/TIGER IGNORE=Y TABLES=(EMP,DEPT) FULL=N
         or TABLES=(T1:P1,T1:P2), if T1 is partitioned table
```

USERID must be the first parameter on the command line.

```
Keyword    Description (Default)           Keyword      Description (Default)
-------------------------------------------------------------------------------
USERID     username/password               FULL         import entire file (N)
BUFFER     size of data buffer             FROMUSER     list of owner usernames
FILE       input files (EXPDAT.DMP)        TOUSER       list of usernames
SHOW       just list file contents (N)     TABLES       list of table names
IGNORE     ignore create errors (N)        RECORDLENGTH length of IO record
GRANTS     import grants (Y)               INCTYPE      incremental import type
INDEXES    import indexes (Y)              COMMIT       commit array insert (N)
ROWS       import data rows (Y)            PARFILE      parameter filename
LOG        log file of screen output       CONSTRAINTS  import constraints (Y)
DESTROY    overwrite tablespace data file (N)
INDEXFILE write table/index info to specified file
SKIP_UNUSABLE_INDEXES   skip maintenance of unusable indexes (N)
ANALYZE    execute ANALYZE statements in dump file (Y)
FEEDBACK display progress every x rows(0)
TOID_NOVALIDATE   skip validation of specified type ids
FILESIZE maximum size of each dump file
RECALCULATE_STATISTICS recalculate statistics (N)

The following keywords only apply to transportable tablespaces
TRANSPORT_TABLESPACE import transportable tablespace metadata (N)
TABLESPACES tablespaces to be transported into database
DATAFILES datafiles to be transported into database
TTS_OWNERS users that own data in the transportable tablespace set
```

Full Import Mode

Full import mode causes the entire export dump file to be imported into the database. When performing a full import, system objects such as grants, public database links, profiles, public synonyms, roles, rollback segment definitions, system privileges, tablespace definitions and quotas, and other system-level objects are imported. Also imported are schema-level objects, such as tables, indexes, private database links, and synonyms.

Full import mode can be used to logically restore a complete database. A full mode import is specified with the FULL=Y parameter. Note that a full import will try to create all database objects, including tablespaces, rollback segments, and so on. The import will fail with an error the first time it attempts to create an object that already exists. To avoid this, use the IGNORE=Y parameter to indicate that you wish to ignore errors.

TIP If you are performing a full import into a new database, it is a good idea to pre-create the rollback segments for that database before running the import (or import the dump file twice, using the ROW=*n* flag during the first import). This is because Oracle will create the rollback segments and the rollback segment tablespace(s), but the rollback segments created will be offline. You will need to bring the rollback segments online before you attempt to import rows into the table, or the import will fail.

Listing 11.8 shows an example of a full import of a database. (In this example, the base database has already been created, by starting an instance and using the CREATE DATABASE command to create the SYSTEM tablespace.)

Listing 11.8: Performing a Full Import

```
D:\ORACLE\admin\RECOVER\exp>imp system/robert
file=fullexp.dmp full=y ignore=y log=output.log

Import: Release 8.1.6.0.0 - Production on Thu May 3 19:49:54 2001
(c) Copyright 1999 Oracle Corporation.  All rights reserved.
Connected to: Oracle8i Enterprise Edition Release 8.1.6.0.0 - Production
With the Partitioning option
JServer Release 8.1.6.0.0 - Production

Export file created by EXPORT:V08.01.06 via conventional path
import done in WE8ISO8859P1 character set and
WE8ISO8859P1 NCHAR character set
. importing SYS's objects into SYS
. importing SYSTEM's objects into SYSTEM
. importing SYS's objects into SYS
  .
. Various informational messages appear during the import.
. These have been removed in this listing.
  .
```

```
. importing SCOTT's objects into SCOTT
. . importing table          "BONUS"          0 rows imported
. . importing table          "DEPT"           4 rows imported
. . importing table          "DUMMY"          1 rows imported
. . importing table          "EMP"           14 rows imported
. . importing table          "SALGRADE"       5 rows imported
. . importing table          "TIME_TABLE"  4096 rows imported
. importing SCOTT2's objects into SCOTT2
. . importing table          "BONUS"          0 rows imported
. . importing table          "DEPT"           4 rows imported
. . importing table          "DUMMY"          1 rows imported
. . importing table          "EMP"           14 rows imported
. . importing table          "SALGRADE"       5 rows imported
. importing SYSTEM's objects into SYSTEM
. importing DBSNMP's objects into DBSNMP
. importing SYSTEM's objects into SYSTEM
. importing OUTLN's objects into OUTLN
. importing SYSTEM's objects into SYSTEM
About to enable constraints...
Import terminated successfully without warnings.
```

User-Level Import Mode

User-level import mode allows you to import specific users only. User-level imports also allow you to import data partitions. The import process does not create the user account itself, nor does it create the tablespaces in which the objects need to be created. Therefore, before you perform a user-level import, you will need to set up the user account, assign any grants to that account, and make sure that the tablespaces are created as well.

Listing 11.9 shows an example of a user-level import, using the FROMUSER parameter. This example imports objects from a schema called TEST to a schema called PRODUCTION.

Listing 11.9: Performing a User- Level Import to the Same User

```
D:\ORACLE\admin\RECOVER\exp>imp system/robert
fromuser=scott file=scott.dmp
Import: Release 8.1.6.0.0 - Production on Thu May 3 20:00:08 2001
(c) Copyright 1999 Oracle Corporation.  All rights reserved.
Connected to: Oracle8i Enterprise Edition Release 8.1.6.0.0 - Production
With the Partitioning option
```

```
JServer Release 8.1.6.0.0 - Production
Export file created by EXPORT:V08.01.06 via conventional path
import done in WE8ISO8859P1 character set and
WE8ISO8859P1 NCHAR character set
. importing SYSTEM's objects into SYSTEM
. importing SCOTT's objects into SCOTT
 . . importing table         "BONUS"           0 rows imported
 . . importing table         "DEPT"            4 rows imported
 . . importing table         "DUMMY"           1 rows imported
 . . importing table         "EMP"            14 rows imported
 . . importing table         "SALGRADE"        5 rows imported
 . . importing table         "TIME_TABLE"   4096 rows imported
Import terminated successfully without warnings.
```

Another option when you are importing is to import the objects from one user's schema into a different user's schema. To perform this operation, you use the FROMUSER and TOUSER parameters. The FROMUSER parameter is the name of the schema that the objects were exported from. This parameter can take multiple schema names, each separated by a comma. The TOUSER parameter contains a comma-delimited list of schemas that represent the schemas in which to import objects.

The lists of schemas in the FROMUSER and TOUSER parameters are aligned such that the first schema in the FROMUSER list is imported into the first schema listed in the TOUSER list, the second schema in the FROMUSER list is imported into the second user listed in the TOUSER list, and so on. If the number of users in the FROMUSER list exceeds the number in the TOUSER list, the last schema in the TOUSER list will be used. Listing 11.10 shows an example of moving SCOTT's objects into a schema named TED.

Listing 11.10: Performing a User-Level Import to a Different User

```
D:\ORACLE\admin\RECOVER\exp>imp system/robert
fromuser=scott touser=ted file=scott.dmp
Import: Release 8.1.6.0.0 - Production on Thu May 3 20:02:51 2001
(c) Copyright 1999 Oracle Corporation.  All rights reserved.
Connected to: Oracle8i Enterprise Edition Release 8.1.6.0.0 - Production
With the Partitioning option
JServer Release 8.1.6.0.0 - Production

Export file created by EXPORT:V08.01.06 via conventional path
import done in WE8ISO8859P1 character set and
WE8ISO8859P1 NCHAR character set
```

```
. importing SCOTT's objects into TED
. . importing table         "BONUS"          0 rows imported
. . importing table         "DEPT"           4 rows imported
. . importing table         "DUMMY"          1 rows imported
. . importing table         "EMP"           14 rows imported
. . importing table         "SALGRADE"       5 rows imported
. . importing table         "TIME_TABLE"  4096 rows imported
Import terminated successfully without warnings.
```

Table-Level Import Mode

A table-level import allows you to specify the tables to be imported into the database. Unlike with the Export facility, the schema owner of the table cannot be prefixed to the table name in this list. Instead, you need to use the TABLES clause with the FROM-USER and TOUSER parameters to effectively complete a table mode import. The FROMUSER clause indicates the owner of the table within the export file. If you did not use this clause, Oracle will not be able to locate the table. Also, when you import an object, the data is updated and various related schema objects, such as associated indexes, are built as well.

In the TABLES clause, include a list of tables within the import file to be imported into the database. (An * indicates all tables.) Listing 11.11 provides a couple of examples of table-level imports.

Listing 11.11: Performing Table-Level Imports

```
-- Here is an example of importing a specific table into the
-- same schema it was exported from.
-- Note that we have to use the fromuser and tables parameters
-- so that we can get the specific table that we are interested
-- in out of the export.
D:\ORACLE\admin\RECOVER\exp>imp system/robert tables=emp
file=emptable.dmp fromuser=scott
Import: Release 8.1.6.0.0 - Production on Thu May 3 20:06:49 2001
(c) Copyright 1999 Oracle Corporation.  All rights reserved.
Connected to: Oracle8i Enterprise Edition Release 8.1.6.0.0 -
Production
With the Partitioning option
JServer Release 8.1.6.0.0 - Production
Export file created by EXPORT:V08.01.06 via conventional path
import done in WE8ISO8859P1 character set and WE8ISO8859P1
NCHAR character set
```

```
. importing SYSTEM's objects into SYSTEM
. importing SCOTT's objects into SCOTT
. . importing table         "EMP"          14 rows
imported
Import terminated successfully without warnings.


-- Here, we want to take a table that was exported from the scott
-- schema and import it into the new_scott schema.

D:\ORACLE\admin\ORA817\exp>imp system/robert tables=emp
fromuser=scott touser=new_scott file=expdmp.dmp ignore=y
Import: Release 8.1.7.0.0 - Production on Sun Aug 26 18:11:50 2001
(c) Copyright 2000 Oracle Corporation.  All rights reserved.
Connected to: Oracle8i Enterprise Edition Release
8.1.7.0.0 - Production With the Partitioning option
JServer Release 8.1.7.0.0 - Production
Export file created by EXPORT:V08.01.07 via conventional path
import done in WE8ISO8859P1 character set and WE8ISO8859P1
NCHAR character set
. importing SCOTT's objects into NEW_SCOTT
. . importing table         "EMP"          43 rows
imported
Import terminated successfully without warnings.
```

Row Array Type Commits when Importing

By default, Oracle will commit INSERT operations after each table insert. If a large table is being inserted into, a tremendous amount of undo (rollback) will be generated during such operations. In a very large operation, you may generate more undo than there is rollback segment space available, which will cause the import to fail, and the rows imported into the object will be rolled back. To avoid such a problem, Oracle provides the COMMIT parameter with the Import utility.

When the COMMIT parameter is set to Y, Oracle will commit the rows as they are being inserted. Oracle writes rows during the import process using an array-type insertion process, importing many rows in one array operation. When COMMIT is set to Y, these rows are committed during every array insert. This way, several rows will be inserted at a time and then will be committed.

Support for Multiple Export Files

When you've split export files into multiple datafiles, as described in the "Support for Multiple Export Files" section earlier in the chapter, you will need to use the FILESIZE and FILE parameters when importing them. Using the FILESIZE parameter, you define the assigned file size for each import file. (FILESIZE must be set to the same size as it was during the export.) With the FILE parameter, you list each export dump file in a comma-delimited format. An example of an import using multiple export files is shown in Listing 11.12.

Listing 11.12: Performing a Multiple Export File Import

```
D:\ORACLE\admin\RECOVER\exp>imp system/robert full=y
filesize=100k file=expfull1.dmp, expfull2.dmp ignore=y
Import: Release 8.1.6.0.0 - Production on Thu May 3 20:51:50 2001
(c) Copyright 1999 Oracle Corporation.  All rights reserved.
Connected to: Oracle8i Enterprise Edition Release 8.1.6.0.0 - Production
With the Partitioning option
JServer Release 8.1.6.0.0 - Production
Export file created by EXPORT:V08.01.06 via conventional path
import done in WE8ISO8859P1 character set and
WE8ISO8859P1 NCHAR character set
. importing SYS's objects into SYS
. importing SYSTEM's objects into SYSTEM
. importing SYS's objects into SYS
. importing SYSTEM's objects into SYSTEM
.
. Various informational messages appear during the import.
. These have been removed in this listing.
.
. importing SCOTT's objects into SCOTT
. . importing table        "BONUS"           0 rows imported
. . importing table        "DEPT"            4 rows imported
. . importing table        "DUMMY"           1 rows imported
. . importing table        "EMP"            14 rows imported
. . importing table        "SALGRADE"        5 rows imported
.
. Various informational messages appear during the import.
. These have been removed in this listing.
.
. importing SYSTEM's objects into SYSTEM
```

. importing DBSNMP's objects into DBSNMP
. importing SYSTEM's objects into SYSTEM
. importing OUTLN's objects into OUTLN
. importing SYSTEM's objects into SYSTEM
About to enable constraints...
Import terminated successfully without warnings.

DDL Production with INDEXFILE

Using the INDEXFILE parameter of the Import utility produces the DDL required to create the objects contained within the export file. This parameter takes the name of the output file that should be created. This output file will contain the DDL associated with the creation of indexes for the selected schemas. This allows the indexes to be created manually, if that is required. This is handy if you used the SKIP_UNUSABLE_INDEXES parameter and you wish to create those indexes after the import. When you use the INDEXFILE parameter, no objects will be imported into the database. Listing 11.13 demonstrates the use of this parameter.

Listing 11.13: Generating DDL with INDEXFILE

```
D:\ORACLE\admin\RECOVER\exp>imp system/robert full=y
filesize=100k file=expfull1.dmp expfull2.dmp indexfile=indexfile.sql
Import: Release 8.1.6.0.0 - Production on Thu May 3 21:00:54 2001
(c) Copyright 1999 Oracle Corporation.  All rights reserved.
Connected to: Oracle8i Enterprise Edition Release 8.1.6.0.0 - Production
With the Partitioning option
JServer Release 8.1.6.0.0 - Production
Export file created by EXPORT:V08.01.06 via conventional path
import done in WE8ISO8859P1 character set and
WE8ISO8859P1 NCHAR character set
 .
. Various informational messages appear during the import.
. These have been removed in this listing.
 .
. . skipping table "BONUS"
. . skipping table "DEPT"
. . skipping table "DUMMY"
. . skipping table "EMP"
. . skipping table "SALGRADE"
 .
. Various informational messages appear during the import.
```

. These have been removed in this listing.
.

Import terminated successfully without warnings.

The following is example of the output generated by the INDEXFILE parameter:

```
REM   CREATE TABLE "SCOTT"."EMP" ("EMPNO" NUMBER(4, 0) NOT NULL ENABLE,
REM   "ENAME" VARCHAR2(10), "JOB" VARCHAR2(9), "MGR" NUMBER(4, 0),
REM   "HIREDATE" DATE, "SAL" NUMBER(7, 2), "COMM" NUMBER(7, 2), "DEPTNO"
REM   NUMBER(2, 0)) PCTFREE 10 PCTUSED 40 INITRANS 1 MAXTRANS 255 LOGGING
REM   STORAGE(INITIAL 10240 NEXT 10240 MINEXTENTS 1 MAXEXTENTS 121
REM   PCTINCREASE 50 FREELISTS 1 FREELIST GROUPS 1 BUFFER_POOL DEFAULT)
REM   TABLESPACE "USERS" ;
REM   ... 14 rows
CONNECT SCOTT;
CREATE INDEX "SCOTT"."IX_EMP_EMPNO" ON "EMP" ("EMPNO" ) PCTFREE 10
INITRANS 2 MAXTRANS 255 STORAGE(INITIAL 10240 NEXT 10240 MINEXTENTS 1
MAXEXTENTS 121 PCTINCREASE 50 FREELISTS 1 FREELIST GROUPS 1 BUFFER_POOL
DEFAULT) TABLESPACE "SYSTEM" LOGGING ;
```

Notice that table-creation DDL, including constraints, is created as well, although these statements are remarked out. You will need to remove the remarks from the output file in order to create these objects.

CHAPTER 12

Using Transportable Tablespaces

FEATURING:

Introducing transportable tablespaces	**520**
Transporting a tablespace set	**522**
Sharing a read-only tablespace	**528**
Transporting partitioned tables	**529**
Managing transportable tablespaces	**531**
Using transportable tablespaces for point-in-time recovery	**532**

Oracle8i introduced transportable tablespaces as a new feature for improving the performance of data-movement operations. This feature joins the other features that Oracle has introduced over the years to help DBAs manage large amounts of data: the TRUNCATE command for bulk deletions, the APPEND hint and SQL*Loader direct-path loads for insertions, partitions for dividing tables and indexes into smaller sets of data, and parallel processing.

This chapter begins with an introduction to the transportable tablespace feature. Then you will learn how to generate a transportable tablespace and copy or move it to a new database. Next, we will discuss using the transportable tablespace feature to share read-only tablespaces and to transport partitioned tables. Finally, we will cover a flexible recovery option that uses temporary tablespaces to allow you to recover tablespaces to a different point in time than that of the rest of the database.

Introducing Transportable Tablespaces

As you know, an Oracle tablespace is a locally managed division of data within a database. The *transportable tablespace* is like any other tablespace, except that it can be moved or copied from one database to another.

When configured and used properly, transportable tablespaces can be an efficient means of moving large amounts of data between databases. For example, you might use transportable tablespaces to copy or move a set of tablespaces, share a read-only tablespace between multiple databases, or quickly rearrange database contents. In previous versions of Oracle, you would need to use SQL*Loader or another tool to accomplish what you can now do with transportable tablespaces. This feature handles most of the necessary verification automatically. Another use of transportable tablespaces is for point-in-time recovery, allowing you to restore a particular tablespace to a point in time that is different from that of the rest of the database.

A transportable tablespace contains all the datafiles for the tablespaces being moved, including the metadata. For a tablespace to be transportable, it must meet certain requirements. Also, you need to know what can and cannot be transported. These transportable table requirements and capabilities are described in the following sections.

Transportable Tablespace Requirements

You must have the Oracle8i Enterprise Edition to generate a transportable tablespace set. In order for a tablespace to be transportable, the tablespace and your system must meet the following requirements:

- It must be a locally managed tablespace.

- It must be self-contained. This means that the objects should depend on objects only from this tablespace, not from other tablespaces.
- The source and target database must be on the same operating system. For example, you can transport a tablespace from one NT cluster to another, but not from an NT cluster to database running under a Unix system.
- The source and target databases must have the same database block size and must use the same character set. (Although this requirement may change with Oracle9i or a later release.)
- The name of tablespace being transported must be unique to the target database; that is, the name of the tablespace must not be in use on the destination database.
- You must always export primary key constraints.
- Both the source and destination database must have a COMPATIBLE parameter of 8.1.0 at a minimum.

Several Oracle scripts create the views and packages required for the transportable tablespace feature to work properly. These scripts should have been run during the installation of your database. However, if you have problems using the transportable tablespace feature, you can run the scripts manually. For NT and Sun Solaris systems, you will need to run `catplug.sql`, which can be found in `ORACLE_HOME\rdbms\admin` on NT or in `$ORACLE_HOME/rdbms/admin` on Unix. Refer to your Oracle documentation for the scripts to run to enable transportable tablespaces on other operating systems.

What Can Be Transported?

With a transportable tablespace, you can transport data, indexes, LOBs, and nested tables. However, if you are transporting LOBs, you must move the BFILE separately, because these are not moved with the LOBs.

You cannot transport the following items:

- Bitmap indexes
- Function-based indexes
- Domain indexes
- Data containing collectors
- Snapshots
- Replication
- Rollback segments

- Scoped REFs
- Oracle 8.0-compatible advanced queues with multiple recipients

Transporting a Tablespace Set

The steps for creating a transportable tablespace set are to check that the tablespaces are self-contained, make the tablespaces read-only, and then export them. Once you have generated the transportable tablespaces, copying or moving them is a simple matter of importing them and making their data accessible. This section describes the procedures for generating and plugging in transportable tablespaces.

Generating a Tablespace Set

The key to generating a transportable tablespace set is to produce a self-contained set of tablespaces. The better you organize and distribute your data and index objects among different tablespaces, the easier it is to generate a self-contained set of tablespaces.

A self-contained set of tablespaces does not contain any references that point outside the set. Any of the following situations would violate this rule:

- A table not included in the tablespace being transported has an index associated with that table.

- A partitioned table is not fully contained in the set of tablespaces. (However, you can transport a subset of a partitioned table by first moving the data you want to transport into a new table, as described in the "Transporting Partitioned Tables" section later in this chapter.)

- A table inside the set of tablespaces contains a LOB column that points to a LOB outside the set of tablespaces.

- A referential integrity constraint on a table refers to a parent table that is not in the set of tablespaces. (However, if you do not need to maintain the relationship, you can choose not to include referential integrity constraints when you export the tablespaces.)

For example, suppose that you want to move your PRODUCT table from your production database to your development database. If you want to transport the PRODUCT table, you will also need to transport all of the tables that are in the same tablespace as the PRODUCT table. First, consider the indexes associated with the tables. You might transport all tablespaces that contain indexes that are attached to these tables, or you may transport only the tables and re-create the indexes when the data is plugged into the development instance.

Other items to keep in mind are the referential integrity constraints and other supporting objects of the PRODUCT table and other tables in this tablespace. If all of the supporting objects of the tables are already in existence on the target database, you do not need to transport the supporting objects. As with indexes, you can transport all of the referential integrity constraints, or you can rebuild them after you plug in the tablespace.

If you choose to include the referential integrity constraints, keep in mind that the objects needed to keep the constraints intact will increase the size of the transportable tablespace set. This is because it will contain the tables necessary to maintain and check the constraints, as well at the metadata for loading on the receiving end. Excluding the referential integrity constraints will simplify and speed up the movement of the tablespace to its destination database.

If you design your database with these operations in mind, objects will be distributed among tablespaces in anticipation of their later movement among databases. The design decisions you make up front (which tablespaces you create and what tables are in those tablespaces) can significantly impact your ability to use transportable tablespaces effectively.

Checking the Transportable Tablespace

Oracle8i provides a tool that makes it easy to determine if a tablespace is self-contained: the TRANSPORT_SET_CHECK procedure of the DBMS_TTS package. Here is the syntax of this procedure:

```
DBMS_TTS.TRANSPORT_SET_CHECK (
    ts_list          IN VARCHAR2,
    incl_constraints IN BOOLEAN);
```

As you can see, this procedure takes two input parameters:

- The TS_LIST parameter is a list of the tablespaces being moved, separated by commas.

- The INCL_CONSTRAINTS parameter is a Boolean flag. Set this parameter to TRUE to move the referential integrity constraints with the tablespaces, or set it to FALSE if you do not want to include the referential integrity constraints.

The following is an example of using the DBMS_TTS.TRANSPORT_SET_CHECK procedure to check the MDB_DATA and MDB_INDEXES tablespaces for movement, without including referential integrity constraints:

```
SQL> EXECUTE DBMS_TTS.TRANSPORT_SET_CHECK ('mdb_data,mdb_indexes','false');
```

If Oracle finds any violations in the specified set, it will populate the TRANSPORT_SET_VIOLATIONS data dictionary view. If there are no violations, the view will be empty. Use this query to check for violations:

```
SQL> SELECT * FROM transport_set_violations;
```

The TRANSPORT_SET_VIOLATIONS view will not be created until you run the TRANSPORT_SET_CHECK procedure for the first time. This view will be accessible only to the schema in which it is created, since no synonyms are created. This view will also be cleared when the user who created it logs out. So, if you want to keep the results, you will need to save them somewhere.

NOTE Unfortunately, object references, such as REFs, are not checked for validity by the TRANSPORT_SET_CHECK routine. You will need to check the REFs manually (where they are stored) to see if they are self-contained in the tablespace.

You should also note the names of the accounts that own objects in the transportable tablespace set. Each object's owner will come across with the tablespace, and these owners will need to exist in the destination database before you plug in the transportable tablespace.

Remember that the transportable tablespace cannot have the same name as a tablespace that exists on the destination database. Use the DBA_TABLESPACES view to check if the tablespace already exists on the destination database.

Also, the source and target databases must use the same character set for the tablespace transport operation to be successful. You can query the PROPS$ table to check the database's character set. The NLS_CHARACTERSET column shows the database character set, and the NLS_NCHAR_CHARACTERSET column shows the NCHAR character set.

Making the Tablespaces Read-Only

After you have checked the tablespaces and resolved any violations, you need to make the tablespaces read-only, as shown here:

```
SQL> ALTER TABLESPACE mdb_data READ ONLY;
SQL> ALTER TABLESPACE mdb_indexes READ ONLY;
```

Exporting the Metadata

Your next step is to export the metadata for the tablespace, using the Export utility's TRANSPORT_TABLESPACE and TABLESPACES commands. Oracle's EXP command with a tablespace exports only the data dictionary for the tablespace contents, not the physical data. The following example exports the MDB_DATA and MDB_INDEXES tablespaces, and uses the FILE parameter to place the export contents in the mdb_database.dmp and mdb_indexes.dmp files:

```
SQL> EXP transport_tablespace=y tablespaces=mdb_data, mdb_indexes
  file=mdb_database.dmp, mdb_indexes.dmp
```

By default, constraints, grants, and triggers are included in the export. If you want to exclude any of these, you will need to specify the CONSTRAINTS, GRANTS, and TRIGGERS parameters appropriately. Here is an example of exporting the metadata without constraints or triggers:

```
SQL> EXP transport_tablespace=y tablespaces=mdb_data, mdb_indexes
  constraints=n grants=y triggers=n
```

Notice that this example does not specify the FILE parameter. In this case, the export contents will go into a file named expdat.dmp, by default.

When prompted for a username, you must enter SYS AS SYSDBA (using the appropriate syntax for your operating system). Only the SYS user can transport a tablespace, because the stored procedures required to transport a tablespace are owned by SYS.

WARNING If you export triggers, they will be exported without a validity check. Any invalid triggers will cause compilation errors during the import.

If you want to be prompted for the various parameters, just enter the EXP command followed by your username and password. Then the Export utility will display a series of questions on how you want the export to proceed, like this:

```
SQL> EXP username/password
FULL=y
FILE=mdb_test.dmp
GRANTS=y
INDEXES=y
CONSISTENT=y
```

See Chapter 11 for details on using the Export utility, including its various parameters and modes.

Copying the Tablespace Datafiles

Now you can copy the tablespace datafiles to a separate area for movement. All you need to do is copy the datafiles to a location that the destination database will be able to access. You can use any command available to the operating system, such as copy, cp, or FTP.

If the source and destination databases can access the file system on which the datafiles reside, this step is not required. This is because both databases can access the location where the export file resides.

 TIP You can also copy tablespace datafiles to CD-Rs. Then they can be added to the target database without actually moving them to the hard disk.

Plugging in the Transportable Tablespace Set

Your transportable tablespace files are now moved to an area that is accessible to the target location. To "plug in" the transportable tablespace set, you simply need to import it and then put the tablespaces back into read/write mode.

Importing the Tablespace

To move the transportable tablespace set into the target database, you use Oracle's Import utility to bring in the exported metadata. You can simply specify the datafiles that were part of the EXP command used to export the desired tablespaces. Here is an example of using the IMP command to import the data exported in the previous section:

```
SQL> IMP transport_tablespace=y datafiles=(mdb_data, mdb_indexes)
```

As with the EXP command, you can also simply issue the IMP command followed by your username and password. Then the Import utility will prompt you for the parameters, as follows:

```
SQL> IMP username/password
FILE=mdb_test.dmp
GRANTS=y
FROMUSER=scott
TABLES=(project,task)
```

Another way to import the data is to create a parameter file containing each parameter and its setting, and save it under an appropriate name (`mdb_database.txt` in this example), like this:

```
TRANSPORT_TABLESPACE=Y
DATAFILES=(mdb_data,mdb_indexes)
FILE=mdb_test.dmp
LOG=mdb_test.log
```

Then run the Import utility using the PARFILE parameter (which imports the data using the settings in the specified parameter file):

```
IMP parfile=mdb_database.txt
```

When prompted for a username, enter SYS AS SYSDBA.

 WARNING There must be a corresponding user ID in the target database for all the owners of objects in the transported tablespace; otherwise, the import will fail.

TRANSPORT_TABLESPACE and DATAFILES are required parameters when you import transportable tablespaces. Table 12.1 describes several optional Import utility parameters that you can use with transportable tablespaces. See Chapter 11 for details on the general use of Oracle's Import utility.

TABLE 12.1: OPTIONAL IMPORT PARAMETERS FOR TRANSPORTABLE TABLESPACES

Parameter	Description
TABLESPACES	A list of tablespaces to be imported. The list is surrounded with quotation marks, and each tablespace is separated with a comma.
TTS_OWNERS	A list of users who own the data in the transportable tablespace set.
FROMUSER	The owner of the objects in the source database. This parameter can be used with TOUSER to change ownership of objects when they are imported into the target database.
TOUSER	The owner of the objects in the target database. This parameter can be used with FROMUSER to change ownership of objects when they are imported into the target database.

Making the Data Accessible

Upon completion of the import, check the log file to ensure that no errors have occurred. If the import was successful, you will now want to place the tablespaces back in read/write mode in their current database, so they will be accessible. Use the ALTER TABLESPACE command to switch modes, as follows:

```
SQL> ALTER TABLESPACE mdb_data READ WRITE;
SQL> ALTER TABLESPACE mdb_indexes READ WRITE;
```

Backing Up the Control Files

After you have successfully transported the tablespace set to a new location, it's a good idea to back up the control files, for documentation purposes. Back up the control files for both the target and source databases using the following command:

```
SQL> ALTER DATABASE BACKUP CONTROLFILE TO TRACE;
```

Moving Tablespaces

If you want to move the tablespace, rather than just copy it, you simply remove it from its original location after completing the transport process. Drop the tablespace you moved from the source database, as shown here:

```
SQL> ALTER TABLESPACE mdb_data OFFLINE;
SQL> DROP TABLESPACE mdb_data INCLUDING CONTENTS;
```

Sharing a Read-Only Tablespace

Sharing a read-only tablespace among multiple databases is useful when you have a series of tables that never or hardly ever change, such as tables that hold information on states and cities. By taking this approach, you can save space on multiple databases, because you will have only one set of these tables in existence. You will also be able to save time and effort in backup and recovery operations and other maintenance tasks.

To set up a read-only tablespace to share, take the following steps:

- Select a source database that owns the tablespace.

- Generate a transportable tablespace set from the source database (as described in the "Generating a Tablespace Set" section earlier in the chapter).

- Plug the tablespace set into each of the target databases, using the procedures described in the preceding "Plugging in the Transportable Tablespace Set" section, except do *not* put the tablespace into read/write mode; leave the tablespace in read-only mode.

 WARNING Do not take the tablespace out of read-only mode in any of the databases, because doing so could corrupt the tablespace. If at a later time you drop the transported tablespace from all but one of the databases, you can put it in read/write mode.

Transporting Partitioned Tables

Partitioned tables are as easy to transport as nonpartitioned tables. The only difference in the procedures for transporting tablespaces described earlier in this chapter is that you will need to remember to identify each and every partition for the tablespace you want to transport.

WARNING   If you forget to move a partition that you wanted, you will no longer have access to that data when the transport is complete.

If you don't want to transport all of the partitions, there is a way to transport only some of them. For example, suppose that you have a large table with multiple partitions, and you want to use the transportable tablespace feature to move only one partition's worth of data. To move just selected data, in the source tablespace, create a table for the data you want to move (thus creating a table with no partitions). For example, you can use a CREATE TABLE AS SELECT command with a WHERE clause that selects only the data you want from one or more of the partitions and puts it into the new table. Optionally, you can create indexes for the new table, in either the new tablespace or in a separate, isolated one.

TIP   Parallel processing will speed up the process of querying the partitioned table to extract the data and putting it into a new table. See Chapter 18 for details on parallel processing in Oracle.

Remember that the tablespace being moved needs to be in read-only mode. Place the tablespace in read-only mode as follows:

```
SQL> ALTER TABLESPACE trans_tablespace READ ONLY;
```

Next, insert the data into the target tables on the new database. You can do this with INSERT AS SELECT command or, if the target table is partitioned, by using the EXCHANGE PARTITION option to make the newly plugged-in table a partition within the target table. Commit the inserted data, and verify that everything worked. Finally, back up the control files for the source and the target database.

Be aware that the transportable tablespace exists only until you have completed the move and stored the data in the source database, and it may possibly exist only temporarily in the target database as well. Each time you move a partitioned table, you will need to decide if you wish to move all of the partitions or only some of the partitions. You will need to identify the data that is going to be moved and decide if you will be using the EXCHANGE PARTITION option or the CREATE TABLE and INSERT commands to fulfill your needs. Unless you use the EXCHANGE PARTITION option, the tables you use to store the data during the data transfer are not considered part of the permanent database until you issue a COMMIT command after the INSERT command is complete.

NOTE Following the procedures outlined here ensures that the files and database objects you use to support data movement are separate and independent from the rest of the database. Each of the procedures requires the preceding process to be successful. You may want to have error checking in place to ensure the success of each process.

The result of these operations is a database that can support the storage of large data volumes (via partitions), as well as the movement of large data volumes (via transportable tablespaces).

Transportable Tablespaces and the Data Warehouse

The transportable tablespace feature can help DBAs meet the ever-growing need for accurate and up-to-date data on a 24/7 basis. Along with need for 24/7 availability is the challenge of managing the great amount of data that is required to keep everybody happy and functional. The data warehouse environment is probably one of the most demanding in terms of data updates and volume. Currently, we use the old standby of the Export and Import utilities and REFRESH command to meet these demands. Moving many gigabytes from an OLTP database to the data warehouse through the traditional staging tables is time-consuming. By combining the present methods with the new transportable tablespace feature, you can bring the OLTP database up faster.

The combination of partitioning with transportable tablespaces makes it much faster and easier to populate a data warehouse or data mart. You can now design the proper tablespace and transport the tablespaces required to update the destination, regaining much of the time spent using the existing methods of exporting and importing or unloading and loading. Transporting a tablespace involves only copying datafiles and

Continued

> **CONTINUED**
>
> plugging in the tablespace metadata. You also can move the indexes required, rather than needing to rebuild the indexes on the destination database.
>
> For example, suppose that you have a warehouse with years of historical data that is partitioned by range, with one partition for each quarter. Now assume that your data warehouse is on a quarterly cycle for refreshing from your OLTP system. You could create a table in the OLTP database (or a staging database) that would contain summarized data from the OLTP system's transaction table for the quarter in question. Then you could transport the tablespace containing the summary to the warehouse. By using the transportable tablespace feature, you can update the warehouse in a fraction of the time it would have taken using older methods. Next, you could create a new partition in the source table to hold the next quarter's data.
>
> Of course, using the transportable tablespace feature requires some design on your part. However, you will likely see the benefit of moving datafiles and metadata in this manner, instead of using SQL scripts.

Managing Transportable Tablespaces

As with most database features, transportable tablespaces require some management. Following are some of the tasks:

- Monitor the size of the datafiles to ensure adequate free space for the new tablespace.
- You may need to restrict AUTOEXTEND to control the datafiles' sizes.
- Because the source and target databases must have the same database block size, you may want to implement a standard database block size for all the databases you set up. Remember that you can establish block size only when the database is created.
- Plan your backups carefully. Backups may require more time and space to complete, since you will be adding new tablespaces.
- All hard-coded scripts must be updated to reflect the new tablespace and/or datafile names.
- If you do not transport referential integrity constraints, maintain a common set of these constraints.

Using Transportable Tablespaces for Point-in-Time Recovery

Tablespace point-in-time recovery (TSPITR) is a convenient way to quickly recover any non-SYSTEM tablespaces to a particular point in time that is different from the point in time of the rest of the database. When you use this option, you are recovering a whole tablespace, rather than an object in the tablespace.

Simply put, you use the transportable tablespace feature to move the needed tablespaces from the clone database to the recovery database, known as the *primary database*. All of the requirements that apply to transportable tablespaces (outlined in the "Transportable Tablespace Requirements" section earlier in this chapter) apply to TSPITR as well.

For the TSPITR process, you need two sets of items:

- The *recovery set,* which includes the tablespace or tablespaces that are in need of recovery

- The *auxiliary set,* which includes the other items that assist in the recovery, such as the backup control file, SYSTEM tablespaces, datafiles containing rollback segments, and temporary tablespace

Recovering a tablespace when the primary and clone databases are on different computers requires the following steps:

1. Determine which objects could be lost.
2. Resolve any dependencies.
3. Prepare the primary database.
4. Create the clone parameter file.
5. Prepare the clone database.
6. Export the tablespaces.
7. Import the tablespaces.

The following sections provide more details on accomplishing these steps.

Determining Which Objects Could Be Lost

You will need to query the TS_PITR_OBJECTS_TO_BE_DROPPED view to see if any objects have been created on the primary database after the point in time of the objects on the clone database. This can be accomplished with the following query:

```
SELECT
    Owner
    , name
    , tablespace_name
    , to_char(creation_time, 'YYYY-MM-DD:HH24:MI:SS')
FROM ts_pitr_objects_to_be_dropped
WHERE tablespace_name IN ('list of tablespace to recover')
AND creation_time > to_date(date and time for recovery)
ORDER BY
    tablespace_name
    , creation_time;
```

Resolving Dependencies

On the primary database, use the TS_PITR_CHECK view to check for objects that are related and overlap the boundaries of the recovery set. (If the view is empty, you can proceed to the next step.) The following is a query you can use to assist with this process.

```
SELECT *
FROM sys.ts_pitr_check
WHERE (tablespace_name IN ('list of tablespaces')
AND    tablespace_name2 NOT IN ('list of tablespaces'))
   OR (tablespace_name NOT IN ('list of tablespaces')
   AND tablespace_name2 IN ('list of tablespaces'));
```

TIP Given the size of some of the columns in the TS_PITR_CHECK view, you may want to format the columns for readability.

Remember that you will need to have a tablespace that is self-contained. Also, if you are transporting only one partition of a partitioned table, you will need to create a stand-alone table of that partition and use it as the recovery table. You will want to keep track of all of the steps you take to resolve dependencies, so you will be able to re-create the relationships on the primary database if required.

Preparing the Primary Database

To prepare the primary database for receipt of the data, follow these steps:

1. Execute the ALTER SYSTEM ARCHIVE LOG CURRENT command to archive the current redo logs.
2. Execute the ALTER ROLLBACK SEGMENT *segment_name* OFFLINE command to take any rollback segments in the recovery set offline.
3. If you need to recover a lot of datafiles, execute the ALTER TABLESPACE *tablespace_name_to_recover* OFFLINE FOR RECOVER command to improve the recovery performance.

Creating the Clone Parameter File

You can create the clone parameter file by copying the primary file or by creating a new `init.ora` file. You will need to set the following parameters:

- CONTROL_FILES
- LOCK_NAME_SPACE
- DB_FILE_NAME_CONVERT
- LOG_FILE_NAME_CONVERT

If you use the production `init.ora` file as the basis of the clone parameter file, you can reduce the values of the DB_BLOCK_BUFFERS, SHARED_POOL_SIZE, and/or LARGE_POOL_SIZE parameters to help save memory. However, be aware that setting these parameters too low may prevent the clone database from starting when other parameters are set too high.

Preparing the Clone Database

To prepare the clone database for startup, follow these steps:

1. Put the recovery set and the auxiliary set in a location that is different from that of the primary database.
2. Execute the ALTER DATABASE MOUNT CLONE DATABASE command to mount the clone database.
3. Execute the ALTER DATABASE DATAFILE '*datafile_name*' ONLINE command to bring the recovery and auxiliary set files online.

Exporting and Importing the Tablespaces

To create the transportable table set, run the EXP command on all tablespaces in the recovery set. Then drop the tablespaces in the recovery set on the primary database with the DROP TABLESPACE command.

Next, run the IMP command to plug in the transportable tablespace set on the primary database. Finally, if desired, place the recovered tablespaces in read/write mode by using the ALTER TABLESPACE READ WRITE command.

Since you can recover dropped tablespaces, you can test this process by recovering to a database other than the primary database. For a complete discussion of Oracle recovery options, see Chapter 10.

CHAPTER 13

Oracle8i Recovery Manager

FEATURING:

Introducing Recovery Manager	***538***
Running RMAN	***545***
Performing RMAN backups	***562***
Performing RMAN recovery operations	***575***
Using the recovery catalog	***590***
Generating reports and lists	***603***

The preceding chapters have covered various aspects of Oracle backup and recovery. In this chapter, we will complete our coverage of this topic by discussing Oracle's own backup and recovery solution, Recovery Manager (RMAN). RMAN provides an easy-to-use interface that allows you to back up and recover Oracle databases.

This chapter begins with an introduction to RMAN's features and architecture. Then you will learn how to use RMAN commands to perform backups and recoveries. Finally, we will look at the optional recovery catalog that you can set up and use with RMAN.

Introducing Recovery Manager

Prior to Oracle8, Oracle provided a backup product called EBU, which wasn't very popular. In Oracle8, Oracle introduced the replacement to EBU, called Recovery Manager, or RMAN for short. It was a good first step, but there were many in the Oracle community that felt that it still wasn't the best solution, and they largely ignored it. Oracle8i's version of RMAN is a significant improvement over the original product. Oracle has addressed many of the shortcomings of RMAN in Oracle8 (though not all) and has produced a backup and recovery product that appears to be competitive.

NOTE There are many non-Oracle backup and recovery solutions available. RMAN's competition ranges from homegrown backup and recovery scripts to product offerings from companies such as BMC, Quest, and others.

RMAN Features

RMAN offers a great number of benefits to the DBA and includes some unique features that set it apart from its competition. A big plus is that RMAN is free. It is licensed with the Oracle8i Enterprise Edition of the Oracle database. Most other backup tools have some cost associated with them. This also eliminates another vendor to deal with and those annoying, finger-pointing episodes.

RMAN backups, in ARCHIVELOG mode, typically will have a smaller impact on ongoing operations. This is because tablespaces being backed up during a hot backup are never put in hot backup mode. This significantly reduces redo generation, which is typically high during hot backups. Other backup and recovery tools will put one or more tablespaces in hot backup mode during backups. This increases the redo generated because Oracle will start recording entire block images in the online (and archived) redo log files.

Also, RMAN is smart about which tablespaces it backs up. Because of the architecture of RMAN backups, it is possible for RMAN to stop the backup of a given tablespace before it's completed if that tablespace becomes "hot" (or the subject of a great deal of I/O). Oracle can proceed to back up other tablespaces and return to the hot tablespace at a later time, when it may no longer be hot. This is especially handy for backups of data warehouses, for example, where large loads might occur during the backup window. Other tools just back up the tablespaces, without consideration for the activity occurring in those tablespaces.

RMAN also offers true block compression. This means that RMAN backs up only a database's used blocks, and blocks that are not in use are not backed up. This makes incremental backup strategies possible and, in some cases, reduces the size of backup images. Other database backup utilities that offer incremental backups will back up the entire object, not just the changed blocks. Unfortunately, Oracle has not seen fit to introduce true compression to its backup output files, which can result in some large backup images if your database is nearly full.

RMAN uses server sessions to facilitate backup and recovery tasks. This allows RMAN to automate such things as locating the backup files that are needed to recover your database, removing the burden on the DBA during recovery time. Since RMAN knows when backups occurred and when archived redo logs were backed up, it's an easy process for it to determine what needs to be restored and applied to recover a database.

The following are some other features of RMAN that are worthy of mention:

- You can use an optional recovery catalog that will allow you to easily restore control file backups, store your backup and recovery scripts, and store backup and recovery history over a longer period of time than supported by use of database control files alone.
- RMAN backs up the database and archived redo logs in both ARCHIVELOG mode and NOARCHIVELOG mode.
- RMAN supports cold and hot backups, and full and incremental backups.
- RMAN supports making and recovering backup sets that include backups of the entire database, a set of tablespaces, or a set of datafiles.
- RMAN supports making and recovering from exact copies of datafiles (known as image copies).
- You can make copies of your database elsewhere with RMAN backups.
- You can create standby databases and duplicate databases.

- RMAN interfaces with many third-party media-management software products.
- RMAN supports parallelism of backup and recovery processes.
- RMAN backups can be tested in a nondestructive fashion.
- RMAN checks database blocks during backups to ensure they are not corrupt.
- RMAN provides reporting so that you can determine the status of backup sets and the backup status of a given database.

RMAN Limitations

Although RMAN offers many benefits, there are a few things that it does not do:

- RMAN does not support databases earlier than Oracle8.
- RMAN does not offer true compression of backup files, as do some other backup tools. If you are backing up large and relatively full databases, consider this when deciding on a tool to use to back up your database. RMAN will generally require as much, if not more, storage space as other tools that offer true compression of backup images (such as BMC Software's SQL BackTrack).
- RMAN does not back up operating system files or certain important database files, including the parameter file, the listener file, or any log files (such as the alert log). You'll need separate backup solutions for these types of files.
- RMAN does not include a scheduling facility. However, Oracle does provide such a facility in the form of the Oracle Job Scheduler (discussed in Chapter 20).

RMAN Architecture

RMAN consists of several components that work together to make backup and recovery operations manageable. The RMAN architecture consists of the following components:

- The database control files
- The target database
- The media management layer
- RMAN channels
- The RMAN recovery catalog
- RMAN backup sets and backup pieces
- RMAN image copies

- The snapshot control file
- The RMAN executable

The RMAN executable provides the user interface to the RMAN program, and it is discussed in the "Running RMAN" section later in this chapter. The other components are described in the following sections.

NOTE Oracle Enterprise Manager also provides a graphical interface for RMAN. See the Oracle documentation for more information about using Enterprise Manager.

Database Control Files

The database control file is at the core of Oracle's RMAN backup and recovery strategy. You can use RMAN just by using the database control file, which will store the backup and recovery information. If you choose to do this, you will not be able to use RMAN stored scripts, and you will not be able to recover the control file from RMAN if it becomes corrupted (though a manual procedure is available). If you are not using a recovery catalog, it is probably a good idea to manually back up your control files.

NOTE Several dynamic V$ views are provided by Oracle to allow you to view the control file's information pertaining to RMAN backup and recovery operations. These views are described in Chapter 10.

Backup control files do retain backup history when they are created. Therefore, a backup strategy using backup control files created with the ALTER DATABASE BACKUP CONTROLFILE TO command is preferable to using those created with the ALTER DATABASE BACKUP CONTROLFILE TO TRACE command. Also, if you re-create the control file with the CREATE CONTROL FILE SQL command, you will lose all backup history that was contained in the old control file! Thus, be cautious if you are using this command.

The Target Database

The *target database* is the database on which you are going to perform a RMAN backup or recovery operation. When starting RMAN, you will direct it to connect to the target database that you wish to back up. If you are running Oracle Parallel Server (OPS), you can connect to multiple instances of the OPS database, which can improve the performance of the backup process.

Each instance of a database has a unique 32-bit identifier called a DBID, which is used to identify the target database. This identifier is assigned when the CREATE DATABASE command is issued and never changes for a given database, even after using RESETLOGS. You can find the DBID of your database in the V$DATABASE data dictionary view.

NOTE When you use one database to create another, the new database will have the same DBID as the old database. This can cause problems if you are using the recovery catalog, since you will have two databases with different names but the same DBID. Currently, there is no documented way of changing the DBID of a database. Thus, if you have two databases with the same DBID, you will need two recovery catalogs (or you will not be able to use one of the databases if you choose to use a single recovery catalog).

The Media Management Layer

The *media management layer* is a layer of software that allows RMAN to interface with third-party storage devices. It is the responsibility of this layer to load (or prompt the operator to load) tapes, label them, sequence them as required, control writes to tapes, and then unload tapes (or prompt the operator to unload tapes), as required during RMAN backup and recovery operations.

NOTE The Oracle installation media, on some platforms, provides a media management layer that allows you to interface with the Legato Storage Manager. Refer to your operating system-specific documentation to see if this is supported on your system.

Sometimes the media management layer will take over the operation of backing up and restoring the data. If this is the case, it is known as a *proxy copy,* which RMAN supports. Refer to your media management operating instructions to see how this might affect your use of RMAN.

RMAN Channels

An *RMAN channel* provides the means for RMAN to communicate with the database. When you perform an RMAN backup or recovery operation, you must open one or more channels. For each channel allocated, a separate Oracle server session will be started. Using multiple channels serves to parallelize the operations for which the channels were established. Channels are automatically closed after the RMAN operations are completed, or they can be manually closed. Channels are established with the ALLOCATE CHANNEL and ALLOCATE CHANNEL FOR MAINTENANCE commands. When you allocate a channel, you also define what type of device the channel will be assigned to write from or to. This device may be a disk, or it may be the media management layer.

When allocating channels, you are controlling the amount of operating system overhead that is associated with a given RMAN operation. The more channels that are allocated, the more system resources that will be required.

NOTE When determining how many parallel sessions you wish to run, keep in mind that there is a point of diminishing returns. Our experience shows that on a box with a normal load, this point of diminishing returns is typically around the number of CPUs minus 1. This assumes that only one backup is occurring, there isn't a great deal of other database activity, and you are writing to a disk device. Test varying degrees of parallelism when implementing your backup strategies. Too much parallelism can actually be worse than too little. Depending on the media management software layer installed, you may need to allocate only a single channel (or a channel per tape device). Refer to the vendor's documentation for suggestions.

When you establish channels, you can set I/O limits, size limits of individual backup files (called *pieces*), and the upper limit of files that you can have open at one time. You can also send vendor-defined commands through the media management layer. If you are using OPS, you can use different connect strings to connect to different OPS instances.

The RMAN Recovery Catalog

The RMAN *recovery catalog* is an optional feature that provides several capabilities, such as storage of RMAN scripts and long-term storage of backup and recovery information. Although the recovery catalog is optional, there are some RMAN features, such as certain lists and reports, that require the recovery catalog to be in place. When starting the RMAN executable, if you have a recovery catalog, you will indicate its location.

RMAN Backup Sets

Every completed RMAN backup of a database or of the database's archived redo logs (and each of these must be a different operation) is considered a *backup set*. A backup

set is a logical entity rather than a physical one. A backup set is created for every channel that is allocated, and Oracle will try to divide the load of the backup as evenly as possible among the backup sets. This is known as *multiplexing*. You can also choose to duplex a backup set, which simply creates up to four duplicate images of the entire backup set in different locations.

A backup set is associated with a given database incarnation. When the database is first created, this will be its first incarnation. Each time the database is opened using the RESETLOGS command, a new incarnation of that database will be created. Backup sets for one incarnation cannot be used to recover a database that is a member of a different incarnation. Thus, once a new database incarnation has been created, old backup sets are of limited usefulness unless you wish to return to a point in time before the RESETLOGS command was issued. This also implies that performing a full backup of the database is a very good idea after you issue a RESETLOGS command.

A *tag* is simply a name you assign to a given backup (backup set or image copy). You can use the same tag name over and over again for backup operations. When you perform a recovery operation and refer to that tag, the latest item to be assigned to that tag will be what is recovered.

RMAN Backup Pieces

A full backup of a database may consist of more than one backup set. A backup set contains one or more physical files that are called *backup pieces*. Backup pieces can store database backups, control file backups, or archived redo logs. Unfortunately, because of the nature of database datafiles and archived redo logs, the two cannot be stored in the same backup piece or the same backup set (this has to do with the different block sizes used for the two types of objects). A single RMAN backup or restore command will write only through a single allocated channel. However, a single backup or restore command can generate or read from multiple backup sets through that single channel, in parallel. This is controlled through settings in the BACKUP command, which we will cover in the "Backup Commands" section later in this chapter.

When RMAN creates the files for the backup pieces, default naming and location conventions can be used, or you can define the file location and naming convention if you prefer. If you choose the latter, take care that the convention you use will make the backup piece filenames unique. Oracle provides substitution variables that can be used with the backup commands to craft unique, user-defined filenames.

You can control the size of individual backup pieces. This allows you to stay within the confines of operating-system file size restrictions. You can also control the number of backup pieces.

Image Copies (Datafile Copies)

An *image copy* is simply a copy of a single database datafile, archived redo log, or database control file. RMAN provides the ability to make image copies via the COPY command. RMAN supports writing image copies to disk. If you make image copies at the operating-system level, you can store these in the database control file or the RMAN recovery catalog through the RMAN interface.

The Snapshot Control File

During a backup operation, RMAN makes a copy of the control file called a *snapshot control file* and backs up this copy with the backup set. This ensures that there is a consistent image of the control file available to RMAN during the backup process. By default, this snapshot control file is created in the $ORACLE_HOME\database (or $ORACLE_HOME/dbs) directory. You can change the location by using the SET command.

NOTE If you include the control file in a backup set, it will be written to the backup set first. This implies that if you recover the control file during a backup, the control file image will be the image of the control file before the backup took place (which means it will have no record of the backup you just restored from!). You should always back up the control file after a successful backup, either with RMAN or manually.

Running RMAN

To start RMAN, you simply enter RMAN from the operating system prompt, followed by any of the valid parameters you wish to include. If you do not include any parameters when starting RMAN, you will get the RMAN prompt. If you want to know what parameters are accepted on the RMAN command line, you can call up the RMAN help screen by typing in RMAN HELP, which results in the following output (we have reformatted the output slightly to fit in this book):

```
C:\>RMAN HELP

Argument     Value            Description
-----------------------------------------------------------
target       quoted-string    connect-string for target database
rcvcat       quoted-string    connect-string for recovery catalog
debug        none             if specified, activate debugging mode
```

```
cmdfile     quoted-string   name of input command file
msglog      quoted-string   name of output message log file
trace       quoted-string   name of output debugging message log file
append      none            if specified, msglog opened in append mode
nocatalog   none            if specified, then no recovery catalog
```

Both single and double quotes (' or ") are accepted for a quoted-string. Quotes are not required unless the string contains embedded white-space.

```
RMAN-00571: ===========================================================
RMAN-00569: =============== ERROR MESSAGE STACK FOLLOWS ===============
RMAN-00571: ===========================================================
RMAN-00552: syntax error in command line arguments
RMAN-01005: syntax error: found "identifier": expecting one of:
"append, at, auxiliary, catalog, cmdfile, clone, debug, log, msglog,
mask, msgno, nocatalog, pipe, rcvcat, slaxdebug, send, target,
timeout, trace"
RMAN-01008: the bad identifier was: help
RMAN-01007: at line 2 column 1 file: command line arguments
```

This output is somewhat helpful, but it is marred by the pesky error message accompanying it. Table 13.1 provides a brief description of each RMAN command-line parameter.

TABLE 13.1: RMAN COMMAND-LINE PARAMETERS

Parameter	Description
TARGET	The username and password for the target database. Use a Net8 network identifier if required (e.g., robert/password@ora817).
RCVCAT or CATALOG	The username and password for the recovery catalog database. Typically, you will connect to the catalog using a Net8 network identifier (e.g., recover/recover @recover).
DEBUG	Enables the RMAN debugger. This is rarely used unless Oracle support requests it.
CMDFILE	Denotes a script file that contains valid RMAN commands to execute. This command file may include commands to back up or recover the database, for example.

Continued

TABLE 13.1: RMAN COMMAND-LINE PARAMETERS (CONTINUED)	
Parameter	Description
MSGLOG	The location and name for a log file that will contain a copy of all output sent from RMAN.
TRACE	Defines an output file for debugging messages.
APPEND	Causes MSGLOG to be opened in append mode.
NOCATALOG	Indicates that no recovery catalog is being connected to. This is required if you are not going to use a recovery catalog.

Connecting to Databases

RMAN supports connecting to a database directly (through IPC, for example) or through Net8. You must use Oracle's password file facility if you are going to connect RMAN to the target database or the recovery catalog through Net8. See Chapter 21 for more on Oracle's password file security.

Connect to a database directly by setting the ORACLE_SID environment variable to point to the appropriate local database. An example of this type of connectivity is shown here:

    SET ORACLE_SID=ora817
    RMAN TARGET=sys/robert nocatalog

If you are using the recovery catalog, you will need to use Net8 to connect to it or to the target database being backed up. To use Net8, use the normal connect string syntax, including the @ symbol, as shown here:

    RMAN TARGET=sys/robert@ora817 nocatalog

An example of connecting to a recovery catalog would look something like this:

    SET ORACLE_SID=ora817
    RMAN TARGET=sys/robert catalog rman_own/rman_own@rmandb

Or, you could use Net8 to connect to both databases (though from a performance point of view, this may not be preferable), as in this example:

    RMAN TARGET=sys/robert@ora817 catalog rman_own/rman_own@rmandb

You can also choose to connect to the target database or the recovery catalog from the RMAN prompt. Simply use the CONNECT TARGET or CONNECT CATALOG command, along with the correct connect string, as in this example:

    RMAN> CONNECT TARGET sys/robert@ora817

Using RMAN Commands

You enter RMAN commands at the RMAN prompt. These commands can be entered from the command-line interface, or they can be put into a script in an operating system file. All RMAN commands, like Oracle SQL commands, end in a semicolon. Many RMAN commands have a great number of parameters and keywords associated with them. We will discuss many of these commands and their parameters as we progress through this chapter.

RMAN uses two basic types of commands: stand-alone commands and job commands. The job commands must appear within the confines of the RUN command, which combines multiple commands (or a block of commands) into a single job stream. The stand-alone commands don't require the RUN command (with a few exceptions). Table 13.2 lists the stand-alone commands, and Table 13.3 lists the job commands.

NOTE RMAN command syntax has varied in different versions of Oracle8i. For complete syntax information, refer to the *Oracle8i Recovery Manager User's Guide and Reference*.

TABLE 13.2: RMAN STAND-ALONE COMMANDS

Command	Description
ALTER DATABASE	Allows you to mount or open a database, and to issue a RESETLOGS command.
CATALOG	Allows you to add information to the recovery catalog about backups that were not taken by RMAN. This allows you to record datafile backups taken before RMAN was implemented and use RMAN to recover those backups.
CHANGE	Checks the status of physical backup files (backup sets, archived redo logs, and datafile copies). This command also facilitates updates of recovery catalog records.
CONNECT	Connects to the target database or the recovery catalog.
CREATE CATALOG	Creates the RMAN recovery catalog.
CREATE SCRIPT	Allows you to create a script that will be stored in the recovery catalog.
CROSSCHECK	Allows you to cross-check the physical backup set pieces against the recovery catalog. Any physical backup set piece that is missing will be marked as EXPIRED in the recovery catalog (or control file).

Continued

TABLE 13.2: RMAN STAND-ALONE COMMANDS (CONTINUED)

Command	Description
DELETE EXPIRED	Causes RMAN to remove all records of backup sets marked EXPIRED by the CROSSCHECK command.
DELETE EXPIRED BACKUPSET	Allows you to delete backup sets that have been expired via the CROSSCHECK command.
DELETE SCRIPT	Allows you to remove a script stored in the recovery catalog.
DROP CATALOG	Drops an existing RMAN recovery catalog.
LIST	Provides various reports for the DBA to use when managing RMAN.
REGISTER DATABASE	Registers the target database with the recovery catalog, if a recovery catalog is being used.
REPLACE SCRIPT	Allows you to replace an existing script in the recovery catalog.
REPORT	Provides various reports for the DBA to use when managing RMAN.
RESET DATABASE	Resets a database in the recovery catalog after it is opened using the RESETLOGS command. Essentially, this command causes a new incarnation of the database to be created in the recovery catalog.
SET	Allows you to define a different directory structure for RMAN to back up or recover archived redo logs. This is one of the few commands that has a different syntax for job commands and stand-alone commands.
SHUTDOWN	Causes RMAN to shut down the database.
STARTUP	Allows you to start up the database from RMAN, using the NOMOUNT, MOUNT, or OPEN parameter.
UNTIL	Allows you to define a window of time that a specific recovery operation should restore to. For example, you can use the UNTIL command to perform incomplete recovery based on time, SCN, or log sequence number.
UPGRADE CATALOG	Upgrades a RMAN recovery catalog after an upgrade of the recovery log database.

TABLE 13.3: RMAN JOB COMMANDS

Command	Purpose
ALLOCATE CHANNEL	Allows you to allocate a channel between RMAN and the database server to be used for backup or recovery operations.

Continued

TABLE 13.3: RMAN JOB COMMANDS (CONTINUED)

Command	Purpose
BACKUP	Allows you to perform backups of the database, control file, or archived redo logs. Supports whole, full, and incremental backups of the database, tablespaces, and datafiles.
COPY	Creates datafile image copies of database datafiles.
DUPLICATE	Allows you to create a duplicate database with a RMAN backup.
RECOVER	Allows you to recover an Oracle database after a RMAN restore operation has been completed. You can recover the entire database, a tablespace or specific datafiles. Also, the RECOVER command supports point-in-time recovery.
RELEASE CHANNEL	Causes a channel allocated with the ALLOCATE CHANNEL command to be released.
RESTORE	Causes RMAN to begin recovering backup images from previously created backup sets. This can include all of the datafiles of a database, only specific datafiles, the control file, or archived redo logs.
SWITCH	Instructs RMAN to alter the location that the database expects a datafile to exist in. The SWITCH command is used if you must restore datafiles to a directory other than the one that the datafile is associated with in the database control file.
EXECUTE SCRIPT {script_name}	Allows you to execute the named script that is stored in the recovery catalog.

Backup Commands

In this section, we will look at the most commonly used backup commands. First, let's look at an example of the structure of a typical set of backup commands in Listing 13.1.

Listing 13.1: RMAN Backup Code

```
RUN
{
     ALLOCATE CHANNEL d1 TYPE DISK;
     BACKUP FULL (DATABASE);
     RELEASE CHANNEL d1;
}
```

The first thing you see in Listing 13.1 is the RUN command. The RUN command starts with the RUN keyword, followed by an open bracket. Within that bracket and its matching closing bracket are a series of job commands that should be run as a unit. If a single command in the unit fails, all of the commands executed after that command will fail as well. The commands shown in Listing 13.1—ALLOCATE CHANNEL, BACKUP, and RELEASE CHANNEL—are job commands. All job commands must be run within the RUN command structure.

NOTE If a job command fails within a RUN block, the remaining commands will not be executed. When the RUN command completes (either failing or successfully), the resources allocated during that RUN command's execution will be released automatically.

The ALLOCATE CHANNEL Command

The ALLOCATE CHANNEL command is used to allocate channels as needed. Each channel that is allocated is assigned an identifier that is used within RMAN. If you are using multiple channels, you can use the channel ID to reference the specific channel to use.

When allocating a channel, you define which I/O device the channel is to write to. Typically, this will be either DISK, which writes directly to disk (as in Listing 13.1), or SBT_TAPE, which causes RMAN to interface with the media management layer. (If you allocate a channel to type DISK, RMAN does not call the media management layer.) Here is an example of allocating a channel to the media management layer:

```
ALLOCATE CHANNEL d1 TYPE 'SBT_TAPE';
```

NOTE In the future, you may also be able to use the NAME parameter in lieu of the TYPE parameter if you wish to specify a particular device to use (such as /dev/rmt0). At the time this book was written, this functionality had not yet been implemented.

The FORMAT parameter allows you to define a file naming convention that is fairly codified yet remains unique, as required by RMAN. These format string codes are listed in Table 13.4. The most commonly used code is %U, which you will see in the examples in this chapter. This code guarantees that the generated backup files will have unique names. If you do not specify a format, RMAN uses %U by default.

TABLE 13.4: FORMAT STRING CODES

Format String	Description
%c	Specifies the copy number of the backup piece within a set of duplexed backup pieces. If you did not issue the SET DUPLEX command, this variable will be 1 for regular backup sets and 0 for proxy copies. If you issued SET DUPLEX, the variable identifies the copy number: 1, 2, 3, or 4.
%p	Specifies the backup piece number within the backup set. This value starts at 1 for each backup set and is incremented by 1 as each backup piece is created.
%s	Specifies the backup set number. This number is a counter in the control file that is incremented for each backup set. The counter value starts at 1 and is unique for the lifetime of the control file. If you restore a backup control file, duplicate values can result. CREATE CONTROLFILE initializes the counter back to 1.
%d	Specifies the database name.
%n	Specifies the database name, padded on the right with *x* characters to a total length of 8 characters. For example, if PROD1 is the database name, then PROD1xxx is the padded database name.
%t	Specifies the backup set timestamp, which is a 4-byte value derived as the number of seconds elapsed since a fixed reference time. The combination of %s and %t can be used to form a unique name for the backup set.
%u	Specifies an 8-character name made up of compressed representations of the backup set number and the time the backup set was created.
%U	Shorthand for %u_%p_%c, which guarantees uniqueness in generated backup filenames. If you do not specify a format, RMAN uses %U by default.

The ALLOCATE CHANNEL FOR MAINTENANCE or DELETE Command

The ALLOCATE CHANNEL FOR MAINTENANCE or DELETE command is a close relative to the ALLOCATE CHANNEL command. It is used specifically for RMAN maintenance operations. Several RMAN operations require the use of the ALLOCATE CHANNEL FOR MAINTENANCE or DELETE command. These include CHANGE BACKUPSET ... DELETE and CROSSCHECK, CHANGE BACKUPPIECE ... DELETE and CROSSCHECK, and CROSSCHECK.

The RELEASE CHANNEL Command

The RELEASE CHANNEL command simply de-allocates a channel that was previously allocated by the ALLOCATE CHANNEL or ALLOCATE CHANNEL FOR MAINTENANCE or DELETE command. The channel ID is the only parameter for the RELEASE CHANNEL command. You will see plenty of examples of the use of the RELEASE CHANNEL command in the examples in this chapter.

The BACKUP Command

The BACKUP command defines what is to be backed up during the RMAN backup session. The BACKUP command supports several different kinds of backups, including database, tablespace, datafile, control file, and archived redo log. All backup types are supported if the database is in ARCHIVELOG mode. In NOARCHIVELOG mode, only database and control file backups are supported. The BACKUP command syntax includes a number of optional parameters. The most commonly used parameters are listed in Table 13.5.

TABLE 13.5: COMMONLY USED BACKUP COMMAND PARAMETERS

Parameter	Description
FULL	Performs a full backup. This backup will not be considered a part of an incremental backup.
INCREMENTAL = {n}	Part of an incremental backup. If $n = 0$, it is a base incremental backup. Any higher-level backup (from 1 to 4 is valid) is considered either a differential or incremental backup. Lower-level backups will back up all blocks previously backed up by higher-level backups.
PARMS = {channel_params}	Allows you to specify parameters for the device to allocate (up to 1000 characters).
NOCHECKSUM	Suppresses the default block checksumming that occurs during normal RMAN operations.
CHECK LOGICAL	Performs logical corruption tests on data and index blocks that pass physical corruption checks. RMAN records any logical corruption it discovers in the database alert log and the trace file for the session that discovered the corruption. If the sum of physical and logical corruptions detected for a file remain below its MAXCORRUPT setting (set with the SET command), the RMAN backup operation completes, and Oracle will populate V$BACKUP_CORRUPTION with corrupt block ranges. If MAXCORRUPT is exceeded, the backup terminates.

Continued

TABLE 13.5: COMMONLY USED BACKUP COMMAND PARAMETERS (CONTINUED)

Parameter	Description
FILESPERSET = {n}	Indicates the maximum number of input files allowed per backup set. RMAN will never cause more than n files to be included in a given backup set. The default for this parameter is the lesser of two values: 64 or the number of input files divided by the number of channels.
FORMAT = {format_string}	Used to format the names and locations of the backup pieces that will be associated with the backup set that will be created by this channel. See Table 13.4 for the format string codes.
CHANNEL {channel_id}	Specifies the name of a specific channel to use when creating the backup sets. The default is to dynamically assign backup sets to any available channels.
SKIP {READONLY | OFFLINE | INACCESSIBLE}	Indicates that read-only datafiles should not be included in the backup set.
INACCESSIBLE	Indicates that any datafile or archived redo log that cannot be read due to I/O errors should not be included in the backup.
TAG = {tag_name}	Defines a user-specified tag for the backup set.
SETSIZE = {n}	Defines the maximum size for a backup set, in 1KB units. For example, to limit a backup set to a maximum of 2GB, use SETSIZE = 2000.
POOL = {n}	Defines the media pool in which the backup should be stored. Your media management software may or may not support this parameter.
BACKUPSPEC {backup_spec_list}	Contains one or more of the backup specification clauses (see Table 13.6). Each BACKUPSPEC clause will generate one or more backup sets.

Associated with the backup command is the backup specification list. The rubber really meets the road as far as the backup is concerned when you enter the backup specification list as a part of the BACKUPSPEC parameter in the BACKUP command. This list defines what is going to get backed up and how it's going to get backed up. You will find a great number of examples of this clause throughout this chapter. Table 13.6 lists the valid values within this clause.

TABLE 13.6: THE BACKUPSPEC LIST SPECIFICATION CLAUSES

Clause and Parameters	Description
DATAFILE {*datafileSpec*}	Indicates a datafile backup. The parameter is a list of one or more datafiles to be backed up, separated by commas. You can use the datafile name (as stored in Oracle, fully pathed) or the datafile number to define the datafiles. If you back up the system tablespace (datafile 1), the control file will be included in the backup set you are creating.
DATAFILE COPY *'filename'* TAG {*tag_name*}	Indicates that you are making a datafile copy (or image copy) of the specified filename, rather than a backup set. Also included is an optional tag name that can be assigned to the datafile copy.
TABLESPACE {*tablespace_name*}	Indicates that you wish RMAN to back up all database datafiles associated with a specific tablespace (or tablespaces).
DATABASE	Causes RMAN to back up all datafiles of the given database, as well as the control file.
ARCHIVELOG {*archivelogrecord-specifier clause*}	Indicates a backup of archived redo logs. The archive log record specifier clause indicates which archived redo logs are to be backed up. You can choose to back up archived redo logs by various criteria, including a range of archive log sequence numbers, time, SCN number, or pattern matching.
CURRENT CONTROLFILE	Indicates that the backup is of current control file.
CONTROLFILE COPY *'filename'*	Indicates that the backup should be a copy of the control file to a backup control file of the name specified.
PARMS	Not currently supported in RMAN at the BACKUP command level.
FILESPERSET = {*n*}	Indicates the maximum number of input files allowed per backup set. RMAN will never cause more than *n* files to be included in a given backup set. The default for this parameter is the lesser of two values: 64 or the number of input files divided by the number of channels.
FORMAT = {*format_string*}	Formats the names and locations of the backup pieces that will be associated with the backup set that will be created by this channel. See Table 13.4 for the format string codes.

Continued

TABLE 13.6: THE BACKUPSPEC LIST SPECIFICATION CLAUSES

Clause and Parameters	Description
CHANNEL {channel_id}	Specifies the name of a specific channel to use when creating the backup sets.
SETSIZE = {n}	Defines the maximum size for a backup set in units of 1KB.
TAG = 'tag_name'	Associates a given tag with the backup set being created.
DELETE INPUT	Causes all source input files to be removed after being backed up. This clause is normally used with archived redo log backups to remove the source files after a successful backup operation.
SKIP	Causes the RMAN backup to skip any datafiles that are OFFLINE, READONLY, or INACCESSIBLE.
POOL = {n}	Defines the media pool in which the backup should be stored. Your media management software may or may not support this parameter.
INCLUDE CURRENT CONTROLFILE	Includes a snapshot of the current control file in the backup set being created by the backup.

Recovery Commands

There are two principal commands that are used in the recovery of a database from an RMAN database backup: RESTORE and RECOVER. Just as with backups, these commands are used in within the confines of a RUN block, along with ALLOCATE CHANNEL and other commands that help facilitate special types of recoveries, such as point-in-time recovery (which we will discuss later in this chapter). A typical recovery script, without any frills, looks something like the one shown in Listing 13.2.

Listing 13.2: RMAN Database Recovery Script

```
RUN
{
    ALLOCATE CHANNEL d1 TYPE DISK;
    RESTORE DATABASE;
    RECOVER DATABASE;
    RELEASE CHANNEL d1;
}
EXIT;
```

The RESTORE Command

The purpose of the RESTORE command is to restore database datafiles, archived redo logs, or control files from RMAN backups in preparation for recovering from some sort of database failure. RMAN can recover the entire set of database datafiles, datafiles associated with a given set of tablespaces, or individual datafiles, as required. With the RESTORE command, you can restore these files to their original locations, or if these locations are not available (due to disk failure, perhaps), to alternate locations. Table 13.7 summarizes the RESTORE command options.

TABLE 13.7: THE RESTORE COMMAND OPTIONS

Parameter	Description
restoreObject	Specifies the type of object to be restored. Valid values for this parameter are listed in Table 13.8.
restoreSpecOperand	Allows you to override the RESTORE command level parameter for each individually restored object. This operand takes three parameters: CHANNEL {channel_id} indicates that you wish to use a different channel for this restore (if not used, the restore will use any channel that is available), FROM TAG {tag_name} causes the backup or file copy with the associated name to be used (if more than one backup set has the same tag, the most recent is used), and PARMS {channel_parms} passes operating-system specific information during each restore.
VALIDATE	Causes RMAN to validate that the backup sets, datafile copies, and archived logs that would be restored by the RESTORE command are valid. No actual restore is performed.
CHECK LOGICAL	Checks the database and index blocks for any logical corruption. (RMAN automatically checks for physical corruption.) RMAN logs any logical corruption found to the V$BACKUP_CORRUPTION or V$COPY_CORRUPTION data dictionary views, unless the value for MAXCORRUPT is exceeded. The corrupt blocks are also logged in the alert log and a process trace file.
CHECK READONLY	Causes RMAN to check and restore any read-only database datafiles.

The *restoreObject* parameter of the RESTORE command can be any of the values listed in Table 13.8.

TABLE 13.8: RESTORE OBJECT SPECIFICATION OBJECTS

Parameter	Type of Object Restored
CONTROLFILE	Causes the control file to be restored and written to all current control file locations. Optionally, you can specify a different path name and RMAN will restore the control file to that location only.
DATABASE	Causes all datafiles associated with the database to be recovered. The control file backup is not restored by this command (use the controlfile command for that operation). Offline and read-only datafiles are not restored unless the CHECK READONLY option is selected with the RESTORE command.
DATAFILE {datafileSpec}	Restores the database datafiles included in the *datafileSpec* parameter. You can refer to the datafiles by filename (include the path name) or by datafile number.
TABLESPACE {tablespace_name}	Causes all database datafiles associated with the tablespaces listed in the *tablespace_name* parameter to be recovered.

The RECOVER Command

The RECOVER command is similar to the RECOVER command used in Oracle to recover a database. You can recover the entire database, one or more tablespaces, or datafiles. You can perform point-in-time recovery (which we will discuss later in this chapter) with the RECOVER command as well. Table 13.9 summarizes the parameters for this command.

TABLE 13.9: THE RECOVER COMMAND PARAMETERS

Parameter	Description
DATABASE	Indicates that the entire database should be recovered.
TABLESPACE {tablespace_name}	Indicates that the datafiles associated with the listed tablespaces should be recovered.
DATAFILE {datafileSpec}	Indicates that the datafiles listed should be recovered. The datafiles can be specified as fully pathed names, as listed in the control file or the recovery catalog, or absolute datafile numbers.
SKIP [FOREVER] TABLESPACE {tablespace_name}	Causes specific tablespace datafiles not to be recovered. Commonly used to postpone recovery of specific tablespaces. The datafiles for these tablespaces will be marked offline during the recovery operations.

Continued

TABLE 13.9: THE RECOVER COMMAND PARAMETERS (CONTINUED)

Parameter	Description
DELETE ARCHIVELOG	Causes RMAN to remove archived redo logs after they are applied and no longer needed.
CHECK READONLY	Ensures that read-only files do not require recovery. The default is to not recover read-only tablespaces and datafiles.
NOREDO	Stops the application of redo logs during the recovery process and is used during the recovery of NOARCHIVELOG databases using incremental backups.

The UNTIL Clause

Both the RESTORE and RECOVER commands offer the use of the UNTIL clause. This clause allows you to specify which backup sets are recovered, based on time, SCN, or log sequence number. This is particularly useful for point-in-time recovery. The values you use with the UNTIL clause are high-limit values. All values less than the value listed will be recovered; any value equal to or greater than the value listed will not be recovered. Table 13.10 lists the parameters for this clause.

TABLE 13.10: THE UNTIL CLAUSE PARAMETERS

Parameter	Description
UNTIL TIME {'NLS date string'}	Specifies the end date for a series of archived redo log files. Date must be in NLS format and can include SYSDATE.
UNTIL SCN {n}	Defines the ending SCN for a sequence of archived redo logs. The default is to use the lowest SCN available.
UNTIL LOGSEQ {n}	Causes all archived redo logs to be recovered until the log sequence number specified.

Reviewing RMAN Output

RMAN creates a great deal of output during its operation. Because it can be so voluminous, we do not include the output from the commands in this chapter's examples. It is worthwhile, however, to review some of the output that RMAN gives. Listing 13.3 provides an example of a successful RMAN backup operation.

Listing 13.3: Output from a Successful RMAN Operation

```
D:\ORACLE\admin\ORA817\archive>rman
target='sys/robert@ora817 as sysdba' nocatalog
Recovery Manager: Release 8.1.7.0.0 - Production
RMAN-06005: connected to target database: ORA817 (DBID=1598904557)
RMAN-06009: using target database controlfile instead of recovery catalog
RMAN> RUN
2> {
3>     ALLOCATE CHANNEL d1 TYPE DISK;
4>     BACKUP FULL (DATABASE
5>     FORMAT "d:\oracle\admin\ora817\backup\ora817.full.%u");
6>     BACKUP CURRENT CONTROLFILE;
7>     RELEASE CHANNEL d1;
8> }

RMAN-03022: compiling command: allocate
RMAN-03023: executing command: allocate
RMAN-08030: allocated channel: d1
RMAN-08500: channel d1: sid=8 devtype=DISK

RMAN-03022: compiling command: backup
RMAN-03023: executing command: backup
RMAN-08008: channel d1: starting full datafile backupset
RMAN-08502: set_count=5 set_stamp=433943941 creation_time=01-JUL-01
RMAN-08010: channel d1: specifying datafile(s) in backupset
RMAN-08522: input datafile fno=00001
name=D:\ORACLE\ORADATA\ORA817\SYSTEM01.DBF
RMAN-08011: including current controlfile in backupset
RMAN-08522: input datafile fno=00002
name=D:\ORACLE\ORADATA\ORA817\RBS01.DBF
RMAN-08522: input datafile fno=00003
name=D:\ORACLE\ORADATA\ORA817\USERS01.DBF
RMAN-08522: input datafile fno=00004
name=D:\ORACLE\ORADATA\ORA817\TEMP01.DBF
RMAN-08522: input datafile fno=00006
name=D:\ORACLE\ORADATA\ORA817\INDX01.DBF
RMAN-08522: input datafile fno=00005
name=D:\ORACLE\ORADATA\ORA817\TOOLS01.DBF
RMAN-08013: channel d1: piece 1 created
```

```
RMAN-08503: piece
handle=D:\ORACLE\ADMIN\ORA817\BACKUP\ORA817.FULL.05CTQTC5
comment=NONE
RMAN-08525: backup set complete, elapsed time: 00:01:18
RMAN-03022: compiling command: backup
RMAN-03023: executing command: backup
RMAN-08008: channel d1: starting full datafile backupset
RMAN-08502: set_count=6 set_stamp=433944019 creation_time=01-JUL-01
RMAN-08010: channel d1: specifying datafile(s) in backupset
RMAN-08011: including current controlfile in backupset
RMAN-08013: channel d1: piece 1 created
RMAN-08503: piece
handle=D:\ORACLE\ORA816\DATABASE\06CTQTEJ_1_1 comment=NONE
RMAN-08525: backup set complete, elapsed time: 00:00:10
RMAN-03022: compiling command: release
RMAN-03023: executing command: release
RMAN-08031: released channel: d1
RMAN> exit;
Recovery Manager complete.
```

Notice that RMAN goes through a compile phase before the backup ever begins. The compile phase is where the syntax of the commands that are sent to RMAN are checked to make sure that they follow the command syntax conventions. Once the compile phase is complete, RMAN proceeds to execute the backup or recovery operation.

In this output, the following line includes information about the backup operation:

```
RMAN-08502: set_count=5 set_stamp=433943941 creation_time=01-JUL-01
```

The SET_COUNT value indicates the backup set identifier number (your first RMAN backup will have a SET_COUNT of 1, then 2, and so on). The SET_STAMP value is the current SCN. The CREATION_TIME value shows the date of the backup creation. Also notice in Listing 13.3 that the name of each database datafile that is to be backed up is logged, as is its location.

The backup in Listing 13.3 actually consists of two different backup commands: a full backup and a backup of the current control file. Because there are two different backup operations, there will be two backup sets created: the actual full backup of the database and a separate backup set of the control file backup. The location and name of each piece of the backup sets are identified in the following lines:

```
RMAN-08503: piece
handle=D:\ORACLE\ADMIN\ORA817\BACKUP\ORA817.FULL.05CTQTC5
comment=NONE
```

```
RMAN-08503: piece
handle=D:\ORACLE\ORA816\DATABASE\06CTQTEJ_1_1
comment=NONE
```

The example defines a location other than the default for the first backup set piece (as well as the name of that piece). For the second piece, it takes the default name and directory location.

Also notice that the elapsed time of each backup set is reported. This information is helpful to have when you want to schedule many different backups and you need to know how long the backups are taking.

You can log the output from RMAN to a log file by using the MSGLOG parameter from the RMAN command line, as shown here:

```
D:\ORACLE\admin\ORA817\archive>RMAN TARGET='sys/robert@ora817 as
sysdba' nocatalog MSGLOG=d:\oracle\rman\output.log
```

When this command is used, no output from RMAN will be generated to the console.

Performing RMAN Backups

Now that we have reviewed the basic RMAN commands, let's look at the various methods that can be used to back up databases with RMAN. First, we will review the backup types. We will then look at performing the various types of backups. Next, we will cover backing up archived redo logs, making datafile copies, and creating duplex backups.

 TIP Through the media management layer, you can back up your databases on tape. However, disks tend to be much faster than tape when it comes to recovering your databases. For mission-critical databases, if you can afford the disk space, you might want to consider backing up to disk when building your backup and recovery strategies. Also, if you do not have a media management layer available, you can back up your databases to hard disks, and then have an operating system utility copy these backups to disk at a later time.

Backup Types

Associated with RMAN (and in some cases, backup and recovery in general) are some specific backup types: full backups, whole backups, incremental backups, hot (open) backups, and cold (closed) backups. Let's quickly review each of these types in a bit more detail.

Incremental Backups

Incremental backups allow you to back up just the changed blocks of a database. Incremental backups start with a level 0 backup, which is essentially a backup of the entire database. This is your *base incremental backup*. You then can proceed to perform a level 2 incremental backup, which will back up all changes since the last level 2 or lower backup. This is known as a *differential backup*. Once a week, you might opt to perform a level 1 incremental, which would back up all changes since the last level 0 backup. This is known as a *cumulative backup*. During the following week, you would continue with the level 2 differential backups, which would then back up only blocks changed since the level 1 cumulative backup. Thus, the level 1 cumulative backup serves to "wrap up" all of the changes reflected in the level 2 differential backups taken during the week into one backup image (allowing the weekly tapes to be reused). Here is an example of an incremental backup strategy for a four-week period:

	Mon.	Tue.	Wed.	Thurs.	Fri.	Sat.	Sun.
Week 1	Base	Diff.	Diff.	Diff.	Diff.	Diff.	Diff.
Week 2	Cum.*	Diff.	Diff.	Diff.	Diff.	Diff.	Diff.
Week 3	Base**	Diff.	Diff.	Diff.	Diff.	Diff.	Diff.
Week 4	Cum.*	Diff.	Diff.	Diff.	Diff.	Diff.	Diff.

*Previous differential backups no longer required.
**Previous base incremental and cumulative backups no longer required.

In this example, we take a base incremental backup on Monday. On Tuesday through Sunday, we perform differential backups. On the following Monday, we perform a cumulative backup. The cumulative backup saves all of the changes that were backed up by the differential backups taken over the week. As a result of the accumulation of the backups in one backup set, the differential backups are no longer needed for recovery, so we can reuse those tapes to perform this week's worth of differential backups. On the following Monday, we perform a base incremental backup again, restarting the cycle.

Incremental backups have the benefit of shortening the backup window and reducing the overall amount of backup storage requirements. If your network is already having bandwidth problems, incremental backups can help. Also, incremental backups enable the recovery of data in objects affected by UNRECOVERABLE operations. On the downside, incremental backups can cause the recovery window to grow, because more data needs to be read during the recovery operation.

Full and Whole Backups

A *full backup* of a database is a backup of the entire database. Oracle supports full backups of the Oracle database datafiles, image copies, tablespaces, control files, the entire database, and archived redo logs. Be aware that a full backup cannot be used as the base of an incremental backup. Any subsequent base incremental backup would still back up all of the blocks of the database, ignoring the full backup just taken.

A *whole backup* includes all of the files of a database (full or incremental) and the control file. Thus, a full backup does not include the control file, whereas a whole backup does back up the control file.

Hot (Open) and Cold (Closed) Backups

An RMAN *hot*, or *open*, *backup* of a database is taken with the database up and running. This type of backup is supported only if the database is in ARCHIVELOG mode. By its nature, a hot database backup is considered to be an inconsistent backup—that is, all the data in the database is not consistent to the same point in time. Therefore, recovery will require the application of archived and online redo logs to make the recovered objects consistent.

An RMAN *cold*, or *closed*, *backup* is taken with the database mounted but not open. RMAN requires the database be mounted before it can perform a backup because it requires access to several of the V$ views that provide control file information. This type of backup is supported if the database is in ARCHIVELOG or NOARCHIVELOG mode (although most backups of a database in ARCHIVELOG mode are hot backups). A cold database backup is said to be consistent—that is, all the data in the database is consistent to the same point in time—if the database was shut down cleanly (with a SHUTDOWN, SHUTDOWN IMMEDIATE, or SHUTDOWN TRANSACTIONAL command).

Cold Backups in NOARCHIVELOG Mode

As explained in Chapter 10, databases running in NOARCHIVELOG mode provide the DBA with a limited number of backup and recovery solutions. Quite limited in the case of physical backups—cold backups are the only option.

NOTE Of course, you can perform a cold backup of a database in ARCHIVELOG mode as well. Just be sure to back up the related archived redo logs so you can perform the various recoveries that are possible with a database in ARCHIVELOG mode.

Writing the Backup Script

Although the BACKUP command can be run from the RMAN command line, it is usually a much better idea to create the script in an operating system file that you can simply instruct RMAN to execute. The examples in this chapter take this approach. Fire up your favorite text editor, open a text file, and give it a name that conforms to your database naming conventions (d:\oracle\admin\ora817\recover_script\rman_cold_backup.rman, in this example). Create the RUN script that will perform a RMAN cold backup, shown in Listing 13.4, and save the file.

 NOTE The default location for backup pieces is operating-system dependent. On NT systems, the location is $ORACLE_HOME\database. On Unix systems, the default location is $ORACLE_HOME/dbs.

Listing 13.4: RMAN Cold Backup Script

```
RUN
{
      SHUTDOWN IMMEDIATE;
      STARTUP MOUNT;
      ALLOCATE CHANNEL d1 TYPE DISK;
      BACKUP FULL (DATABASE);
      RELEASE CHANNEL d1;
      ALTER DATABASE OPEN;
}
EXIT;
```

This script shuts down the database and then mounts the database, as necessary for performing a cold backup (allowing access to the database control file). Note that you can use the PFILE= parameter with the STARTUP command if the init.ora file isn't in the default location.

 WARNING If you wish to use RMAN to shut down and restart an Oracle database, you cannot use Oracle's auto listener registration feature. Instead, you must manually configure the instance in the listener.ora file. Failure to do this may cause RMAN to fail to connect to the database.

After mounting the database, the script allocates a channel called d1. This particular backup will be going to disk. It then executes the backup by using the BACKUP FULL command, for a full database backup using the default parameters. Next, the script releases the channel. This is not necessary, since the channel will be released automatically after the RUN command is complete, but it is good practice to do it explicitly. The final lines reopen the database for user access and then exit RMAN.

Performing the Backup

To perform the backup, start the RMAN interface. To run the script, you can use the CMDFILE parameter of the RMAN executable to define the script to execute, as shown here:

```
c:\>d:
d:\>CD \oracle\admin\ora817\recover_script
d:\oracle\admin\ora817\recover_script> rman TARGET='sys/robert@ora817
    as sysdba'
CMDFILE=rman_cold_backup.rman NOCATALOG
```

Or you can use the command-line parameter @ to indicate that you want to run a specific file, as shown here:

```
C:\> RMAN TARGET='sys/robert as sysdba@ora817' NOCATALOG

Recovery Manager: Release 8.1.7.0.0 - Production

RMAN-06005: connected to target database: ORA817 (DBID=1598904557)
RMAN-06009: using target database controlfile instead of recovery catalog

RMAN> @d:\oracle\admin\ora817\recover_script\rman_cold_backup.rman
```

 NOTE Some RMAN documentation and some error messages indicate that certain RMAN failures are restartable, and even suggest there is a restart command. This is not the case; however, this functionality may be made available in Oracle9i.

Backups in ARCHIVELOG Mode

Putting your database in ARCHIVELOG mode offers a much wider range of database backup possibilities. The commands for each backup type are slightly different, but the basic format stays the same. In this section, we will review the differences in the scripts that are used to perform full database backups, tablespace backups, datafile backups, and incremental backups. We will introduce some additional backup options as well, such as formatting the backup piece names and changing the default locations for the backup pieces.

Once you have the backup scripts written, you can run the scripts as described in the previous section.

 TIP The recovery catalog, which we will discuss later in this chapter, allows you to store RMAN scripts within an Oracle database for later use. Consider this as one reason to create a recovery catalog.

Full Database Backups

Listing 13.5 provides an example of a script that performs a full database backup of a database in ARCHIVELOG mode. You can create this script in your favorite editor and name and store it appropriately. In this example, we call it back_full_database.rman and save it in the \oracle\admin\ora817\recover_script directory.

Listing 13.5: Full Database Backup Script

```
RUN
{
    ALLOCATE CHANNEL d1 TYPE DISK;
    BACKUP FULL (DATABASE
    FORMAT "d:\oracle\admin\ora817\backup\ora817.full.%u");
    SQL "ALTER SYSTEM ARCHIVE LOG CURRENT";
    BACKUP CURRENT CONTROLFILE
    FORMAT "d:\oracle\admin\ora817\backup\ora817.crtl.%u";
    BACKUP ARCHIVELOG ALL
    DELETE INPUT
    FORMAT "d:\oracle\admin\ora817\backup\ora817.arch.%u";
    RELEASE CHANNEL d1;
}
EXIT;
```

 WARNING If you use the ALTER SYSTEM ARCHIVE LOG CURRENT command in the BACKUP command, and no archived redo logs are present, the backup will fail.

Notice that this script does not shut down the database and then mount it. Since the database is in ARCHIVELOG mode, you do not need to do this. We have again allocated a channel to disk for the purposes of this backup. We then issue the BACKUP FULL command, just as in the full backup in NOARCHIVELOG mode shown in Listing 13.4. The BACKUP FULL simply indicates the type of backup, not what is getting backed up. The keyword DATABASE indicates the scope of the backup and what is getting backed up.

The BACKUP command in this example also contains the FORMAT keyword. Earlier, we mentioned that the FORMAT command's purpose is to format the naming convention of the backup pieces, as well as to cause them to be created in a location other than the default location. In this example, all of the backup pieces will be put in the d:\oracle\admin\ora817\backup directory. The naming convention for these backup pieces is also established here. Each backup piece will start with the name ora817.full. The %u format string code represents an eight-character name made up of compressed representations of the backup set number and the time the backup set was created (Table 13.4 earlier in this chapter defines all the format codes).

Next, the script includes the BACKUP CURRENT CONTROLFILE command to back up the control file after the database backup has been completed. This is useful if you are using an RMAN recovery catalog. This control file backup will reflect the last backup of the database that was taken. When recovery time comes around, you will have the most current information on backups possible. If you were to restore the control file backup taken at the time of the backup, that control file would not contain any information about the backup that it was associated with. This is because the control file is backed up first during a full backup.

Next, the script forces a log switch with the ALTER SYSTEM ARCHIVE LOG CURRENT command, and then backs up the archived redo logs using the BACKUP ARCHIVELOG ALL command. This is a really important step, and when and how it is done can be critical to recovering your database in certain recovery situations (such as time-based recovery). Again, these backups use the FORMAT command to format the name of this backup set as well. (Recall that database datafiles and archived redo logs must be in separate backup sets.)

NOTE Oracle's documentation seems to suggest that you don't need to force a log switch (at least most of their examples don't include this). In reality, in some specific recovery situations (recovering changes that occurred during the backup, for example), you will not be able to recover your backup unless you switched the log file and backed it up.

Notice the DELETE INPUT keywords the script uses when backing up the archived redo logs. This causes RMAN to delete the archived redo logs after they are backed up. Finally, we release the channel and exit RMAN.

 NOTE If you prefer to manually remove archived redo logs rather than allow RMAN to do so, you will need to issue a CHANGE ARCHIVELOG ALL VALIDATE command. Failure to do so may lead to occurrences of RMAN 6089 errors, and the archived redo log backup will fail.

Tablespace Backups

When backing up databases in ARCHIVELOG mode, you can opt to back up only specific tablespaces rather than the whole database. When you back up a tablespace, you are really backing up all of the database datafiles associated with that tablespace. Oracle provides the tablespace backup option just to make the process a little easier for you. Listing 13.6 provides an example of a script that is used to back up multiple tablespaces of a database.

Listing 13.6: Tablespace Backup Script

```
RUN
{
     ALLOCATE CHANNEL d1 TYPE DISK;
     BACKUP FULL TABLESPACE rbs, users, tools
     FORMAT "d:\oracle\admin\ora817\backup\ora817.tbs.%u";
     RELEASE CHANNEL d1;
}
EXIT;
```

In this example, we have simply changed the BACKUP command. Instead of using the keyword DATABASE, we use the keyword TABLESPACE, followed by the names of the tablespaces we wish to back up. We also changed the format of the backup set piece naming conventions to indicate that this was a tablespace backup rather than a database backup, but this is an optional step.

Datafile Backups

The most granular backup possible in RMAN is the datafile backup, although in reality, all backups in RMAN are really just datafile backups. Even though RMAN provides you with the ability to do database or tablespace backups, RMAN is still resolving the objects to datafiles and backing up those datafiles. Listing 13.7 shows an example of a script to back up two datafiles in a database.

Listing 13.7: Datafile Backup Script

```
RUN
{
     ALLOCATE CHANNEL d1 TYPE DISK;
     BACKUP FULL (DATAFILE 1, 2, 4
     FORMAT "d:\oracle\admin\ora817\backup\ora817.dat.%u")
     (ARCHIVELOG ALL
     FORMAT "d:\oracle\admin\ora817\backup\ora817.arch.%u");
     BACKUP CURRENT CONTROLFILE
     FORMAT "d:\oracle\admin\ora817\backup\ora817.crtl.%u";
     RELEASE CHANNEL d1;
}
EXIT;
```

Notice that this example uses the datafile numbers, rather than the fully qualified names. This just makes the DBA's job a little easier. We could just have easily written the command like this:

```
BACKUP FULL (DATAFILE 'd:\oracle\oradata\ora817\system01.dbf',
                     'd:\oracle\oradata\ora817\rbs01.dbf',
                     'd:\oracle\oradata\ora817\temp01.dbf',
FORMAT "d:\oracle\admin\ora817\backup\ora817.dat.%u");
```

Incremental Backups

Incremental backups give you the option of backing up only that part of a database that has been changed since the last incremental backup. For this type of backup, prepare three scripts to perform each type of incremental backup: the full base incremental backup, the differential backup, and the cumulative backup.

Listing 13.8 shows the RMAN script to perform the base incremental backup.

Listing 13.8: Base Incremental Backup Script

```
RUN
{
     ALLOCATE CHANNEL d1 TYPE DISK;
     ALLOCATE CHANNEL d2 TYPE DISK;
     BACKUP INCREMENTAL LEVEL 0 FILESPERSET 2 SETSIZE 70000
         (DATABASE
           FORMAT "d:\oracle\admin\ora817\backup\ora817.inc.%u")
```

```
        ARCHIVELOG ALL
            FORMAT "d:\oracle\admin\ora817\backup\ora817.arch.%u";
    BACKUP CURRENT CONTROLFILE
    FORMAT "d:\oracle\admin\ora817\backup\ora817.crtl.%u";
    RELEASE CHANNEL d1;
    RELEASE CHANNEL d2;
}
```

First, notice that we have opened two different channels in this example. Each channel will establish a new session with the Oracle server and make it available for RMAN to use. RMAN will discover this is the case and try to take advantage of both channels during the backup process. The allocation of multiple channels allows you to parallelize the backup operation.

In the BACKUP command, we use the INCREMENTAL keyword to indicate that this is an incremental backup rather than a full backup. Next, we specify the level of the backup. Level 0 becomes the base incremental backup. This means that all the used blocks of the database will be backed up. We have also added a couple new parameters in this example. The FILESPERSET parameter defines the maximum number of backup pieces that will be allowed to be created for a given backup piece. The SETSIZE parameter allows you to set the maximum size of any backup piece. You might use this particular command if your operating system limits the size of an individual file, for example. In this example, the 70000 indicates that a single backup piece will be no larger than 70MB (since the values are in kilobytes). The FILESPERSET and SETSIZE parameters can be used for either incremental or full backups.

To perform the differential backup, you simply change the level of the backup from a 0 to a 2 (or 3 or 4, depending on our backup scheme). This is shown in the script in Listing 13.9.

Listing 13.9: Differential Incremental Backup Script

```
RUN
{
    ALLOCATE CHANNEL d1 TYPE DISK;
    ALLOCATE CHANNEL d2 TYPE DISK;
    BACKUP INCREMENTAL LEVEL 2 FILESPERSET 2 SETSIZE 70000
        (DATABASE
            FORMAT "d:\oracle\admin\ora817\backup\ora817.inc.%u")
        (ARCHIVELOG ALL
            FORMAT "d:\oracle\admin\ora817\backup\ora817.arch.%u");
    BACKUP CURRENT CONTROLFILE
    FORMAT "d:\oracle\admin\ora817\backup\ora817.crtl.%u";
```

```
    RELEASE CHANNEL d1;
    RELEASE CHANNEL d2;
}
```

The main point here is that the level for the differential backups (which are the backups you will make every day) needs to be higher than the once-every-two-weeks base incremental (which is level 0). In addition, the level for this backup needs to be higher than the once-a-week cumulative backup, which is a level 1 backup in our strategy, as shown in Listing 13.10.

Listing 13.10: Cumulative Incremental Backup Script

```
RUN
{
    SET COMMAND ID TO 'RMAN IS ALLOCATING CHANNELS';
    ALLOCATE CHANNEL d1 TYPE DISK;
    ALLOCATE CHANNEL d2 TYPE DISK;
    SET COMMAND ID TO 'RMAN IS BACKING UP';
    BACKUP INCREMENTAL LEVEL 1 FILESPERSET 2 SETSIZE 70000
        (DATABASE
          FORMAT "d:\oracle\admin\ora817\backup\ora817.inc.%u")
        (ARCHIVELOG ALL
          FORMAT "d:\oracle\admin\ora817\backup\ora817.arch.%u");
    SET COMMAND ID TO 'RMAN IS BACKING UP THE CONTROL FILE';
    BACKUP CURRENT CONTROLFILE;
    SET COMMAND ID TO 'RMAN IS DEALLOCATING CHANNELS';
    RELEASE CHANNEL d1;
    RELEASE CHANNEL d2;
}
EXIT;
```

Notice that besides changing the level of the backup, we have also added several SET COMMAND ID TO lines. This allows you to track the progress of the backup by querying the CLIENT_INFO column of the V$SESSION view, as in this example:

```
SQL> SELECT sid, serial#, username, client_info
  2  FROM v$session
  3  WHERE client_info IS NOT NULL;
```

SID	SERIAL#	USERNAME	CLIENT_INFO
9	83	SYS	id=RMAN is backing up,ch=d2
12	43	SYS	id=RMAN is backing up,ch=d1
13	16	SYS	id=RMAN is backing up

Archived Redo Log Backups

The previous listings include backing up archived redo logs, but we thought it would be nice to provide a simple RMAN script that does just that. Listing 13.11 provides such a script.

Listing 13.11: Archived Redo Log Backup Script

```
RUN
{
    ALLOCATE CHANNEL d1 TYPE DISK;
    SQL "ALTER SYSTEM ARCHIVE LOG CURRENT";
    BACKUP (ARCHIVELOG ALL
    DELETE INPUT
    FORMAT "d:\oracle\admin\ora817\backup\ora817.arch.%u");
    RELEASE CHANNEL d1;
}
EXIT;
```

NOTE The log file switch in this example is not required, but it does prevent RMAN from returning an error if no log files are available to back up.

Datafile Copies

Datafile copies, also called image copies, are exact copies of database datafiles that are just copied elsewhere and given an RMAN naming convention. Datafile copies can only be made to disk; copies to tape are not supported.

To make a datafile copy, use the COPY command. Datafile, archived redo logs, and control files can be backed up using the COPY command. Note that image copies are exact copies of the physical files, and they are not part of any RMAN backup set.

The optional parameters for the COPY command include the following:

- TAG {*tag name*} associates a tag name to the backup that can be used as an alias to the backup.
- LEVEL{*n*} includes the copy in the incremental backup strategy.
- NOCHECKSUM disables block checksum calculations.
- CHECK LOGICAL enables data and index logical block checking.

The input file parameter defines the type of input file. The following parameters are valid:

- DATAFILE {*datafileSpec*} lists the datafile names or absolute file numbers to back up.
- DATAFILECOPY lists one or more datafiles copies that should be used as the input. This datafile cannot be listed in the database as a current datafile.
- ARCHIVELOG '*filename*' defines the filename of an archived redo log to copy.
- CURRENT CONTROLFILE specifies that the copy should be of the current control file.
- CONTROLFILECOPY '*filename*' defines the filename of the control file(s) to copy. This control file copy will be marked as a backup control file, so its use will require database recovery, just as a backup control file would.

Finally, the TO '*filename*' parameter defines where the copy is to be made and what its name should be.

An example of this command is shown in Listing 13.12.

Listing 13.12: Datafile Copying

```
RUN
{
    ALLOCATE CHANNEL ch1 TYPE DISK;
    COPY datafile 1 TO
    'c:\oracle\mydb\backup\070101\system_backup_01.dbf';
    current controlfile TO 'c:\oracle\mydb\backup\070101\control.ctl';
}
```

The LIST COPY command can be used to inventory the datafile copies that RMAN has performed. To recover datafile copies, simply use the operating system copy command to move them back into place (there is no special RMAN command to perform this function). You can also use the RMAN SWITCH command and the SET {*newname*} command to cause the database to switch to using the datafile copy, if you do not wish to move the datafile copy first.

 NOTE Consistency rules apply to datafile copies. The database must not be open when you make a datafile copy or the tablespace must be in hot backup mode.

Duplexing Backups

When you duplex a backup, you make two copies of that backup at the same time to further protect the backups from some failure or disaster. You can duplex a backup by using the SET DUPLEX command, as shown in Listing 13.13.

Listing 13.13: Duplexing a Backup

```
RUN
{
    SET DUPLEX=2;
    ALLOCATE CHANNEL d1 TYPE 'SBT_TAPE';
    SQL "ALTER SYSTEM ARCHIVE LOG CURRENT";
    BACKUP (ARCHIVELOG ALL
    DELETE INPUT
    FORMAT "d:\oracle\admin\ora817\backup\ora817.arch.%u");
    RELEASE CHANNEL d1;
}
EXIT;
```

This example creates two separate backups to tape of the archived redo logs. Each backup will be to a different backup set name; thus, the backups remain unique.

Performing RMAN Recovery Operations

Your options for recovering your RMAN backups depend on whether your database is in NOARCHIVELOG mode or ARCHIVELOG mode. As you've learned, your options with a NOARCHIVELOG mode database recovery are limited. The following sections describe how to recover in both modes, including point-in-time or point-of-failure recovery in ARCHIVELOG mode. You will also learn how to recover archived redo logs, control files, and datafiles to another location.

NOARCHIVELOG Mode Backup Recovery

With a NOARCHIVELOG mode database recovery, you do not have the option of point-in-time recovery or recovery to the point of failure. All you can do is recover the datafiles from the last good backup and restart the database.

To recover a database in NOARCHIVELOG mode, the database must be mounted but not open. This assumes that you have the control file available. If the control file has been lost and you are not using a recovery catalog, then you should have implemented a plan to back up the control file. You will need to recover this control file before you can perform a recovery. The control file should be either a copy of the database control file that was taken after the backup of the database (with the database still down) or a backup control file (the result of an ALTER DATABASE BACKUP CONTROL FILE TO '*filename*' command).

What are the ramifications of not having a control file backup that is current? The biggest problem is that you will not be able to recover the database backups that RMAN has taken without a lot of grief. However, if you are using an RMAN recovery catalog, recovering after the loss of a control file is much easier. Using a recovery catalog is described later in this chapter, in the "Using the Recovery Catalog" section.

Preparing for the Recovery

Listing 13.14 shows a script with the commands to prepare for and start the NOARCHIVELOG mode recovery. You can create this script and save it in an appropriately named file (this example is named `recover_db.rman`). It assumes that there is a current backup of the database and that the control file has been recovered.

Listing 13.14: RMAN Database Recovery Script

```
RUN
{
    SHUTDOWN ABORT;
    STARTUP MOUNT;
    ALLOCATE CHANNEL d1 TYPE DISK;
    RESTORE DATABASE;
    RECOVER DATABASE;
    RELEASE CHANNEL d1;
    ALTER DATABASE OPEN;
}
EXIT;
```

This script shuts down the database (assuming it is still up) and then mounts it. It then allocates a channel to disk to facilitate the restore process, restores the database datafiles with the RESTORE command, and performs the database recovery with the RECOVER command. Finally, it releases the channel, opens the database for use, and exits RMAN.

Performing the Recovery

To perform the recovery in this example, we decided to just cut and paste the RUN command at the RMAN prompt and let it do its thing, as shown in Listing 13.15. We will break with the typical format of this chapter and show you the output from this recovery run.

Listing 13.15: RMAN Database Recovery Execution

```
C:\>SET ORACLE_SID=ora817
C:\>RMAN TARGET=sys/robert nocatalog

Recovery Manager: Release 8.1.7.0.0 - Production

RMAN-06005: connected to target database: ORA817 (DBID=1598904557)
RMAN-06009: using target database controlfile instead of recovery catalog

RMAN> RUN
2> {
3>      SHUTDOWN ABORT;
4>      STARTUP MOUNT;
5>      ALLOCATE CHANNEL d1 TYPE DISK;
6>      RESTORE DATABASE;
7>      RECOVER DATABASE;
8>      RELEASE CHANNEL d1;
9>      ALTER DATABASE OPEN;
10> }

RMAN-03022: compiling command: shutdown
RMAN-06402: Oracle instance shut down

RMAN-03022: compiling command: startup
RMAN-06193: connected to target database (not started)
RMAN-06196: Oracle instance started
RMAN-06199: database mounted

Total System Global Area      7665692 bytes
Fixed Size                      75804 bytes
Variable Size                 6463488 bytes
Database Buffers              1048576 bytes
Redo Buffers                    77824 bytes

RMAN-03022: compiling command: allocate
RMAN-03023: executing command: allocate
```

```
RMAN-08030: allocated channel: d1
RMAN-08500: channel d1: sid=10 devtype=DISK


RMAN-03022: compiling command: restore


RMAN-03022: compiling command: IRESTORE
RMAN-03023: executing command: IRESTORE
RMAN-08016: channel d1: starting datafile backupset restore
RMAN-08502: set_count=39 set_stamp=434068604 creation_time=02-JUL-01
RMAN-08089: channel d1: specifying datafile(s) to restore from backup set
RMAN-08523: restoring datafile 00001 to
D:\ORACLE\ORADATA\ORA817\SYSTEM01.DBF
RMAN-08523: restoring datafile 00002
to D:\ORACLE\ORADATA\ORA817\RBS01.DBF
RMAN-08523: restoring datafile 00003 to
D:\ORACLE\ORADATA\ORA817\USERS01.DBF
RMAN-08523: restoring datafile 00004 to
D:\ORACLE\ORADATA\ORA817\TEMP01.DBF
RMAN-08523: restoring datafile 00005 to
D:\ORACLE\ORADATA\ORA817\TOOLS01.DBF
RMAN-08523: restoring datafile 00006 to
D:\ORACLE\ORADATA\ORA817\INDX01.DBF
RMAN-08023: channel d1: restored backup piece 1
RMAN-08511: piece handle=D:\ORACLE\ORA816\DATABASE\17CTUN3S_1_1
tag=null params=NULL
RMAN-08024: channel d1: restore complete
RMAN-03022: compiling command: recover
RMAN-03022: compiling command: recover(1)
RMAN-03022: compiling command: recover(2)
RMAN-03022: compiling command: recover(3)
RMAN-03023: executing command: recover(3)
RMAN-08054: starting media recovery
RMAN-08055: media recovery complete
RMAN-03022: compiling command: recover(4)
RMAN-03022: compiling command: release
RMAN-03023: executing command: release
RMAN-08031: released channel: d1
RMAN-03022: compiling command: alter db
RMAN-06400: database opened
```

```
RMAN> EXIT;
Recovery Manager complete.
```

In this example, we accessed the database directly by setting the SID and using sys/robert as the connect string. In previous examples, we used a Net8 connect string (like sys/robert@ora817). Either way is valid, although you may find that there are times that connecting to a target database through Net8 doesn't work very well. Also, connecting to the target through Net8 adds overhead to the recovery process.

NOTE If you are using automated instance registration with your listener, you may find that Net8 connections don't always work if you shut down the database and then try to start it up again. Sometimes, the listener will release the service and not recognize it when RMAN tries to attach again. If you wish to perform RMAN startup and shutdown operations through Net8, you will need to manually register the database service in the `listener.ora` file.

Notice in the listing that RMAN automatically selected the most recent backup to recover from. We just told it to restore the most recent datafiles and recover the database. RMAN took care of the rest; heck, it even opened our database for us!

ARCHIVELOG Mode Complete Recovery

RMAN, by default, will recover the database to the point of failure during a restore operation for a database that is in ARCHIVELOG mode. You can also do point-in-time recoveries (which is probably why you put the database in ARCHIVELOG mode and bought that extra disk space for those archived redo logs anyway), which we will discuss in the "Incomplete Recovery in ARCHIVELOG Mode" section later in this chapter.

RMAN allows you to recover the entire database, a tablespace or a number of tablespaces, or a database datafile or a number of database datafiles. RMAN also allows you to take a tablespace or datafile offline and bring it back online again; both of these operations may be required or desired during a recovery.

The recovery methods do not change, regardless if you have performed full or incremental backups. RMAN is smart enough to determine which backups need to be recovered and which will cause the recovery to happen the fastest.

The following sections show recovery scripts for the entire database, for specific tablespace recoveries, and for individual database datafiles. You will find all three scripts are similar, with only a few changes to the RESTORE command and some additional statements to take tablespaces or datafiles offline. You can save these scripts in a RMAN command file and run them, or cut and paste them at the RMAN prompt. If you have a recovery catalog, a third alternative is to store the scripts there. We will discuss this possibility in more detail later in this chapter.

Full Database Recovery

The recovery process is pretty straightforward here—you simply issue the RESTORE and RECOVERY commands. RMAN will take care of the rest automatically. It will find the most current backups, apply them, and then recover the database applying the archived redo logs (including restoring them if required) to make the database current. The script for a full database recovery is shown in Listing 13.16.

Listing 13.16: RMAN Full Database Recovery Script

```
RUN
{
    SHUTDOWN IMMEDIATE
    STARTUP MOUNT
    ALLOCATE CHANNEL d1 TYPE DISK;
    RESTORE DATABASE;
    RECOVER DATABASE;
    RELEASE CHANNEL d1;
    ALTER DATABASE OPEN;
}
EXIT;
```

Note that you may not need the SHUTDOWN command if the database has already shut itself down (and indeed RMAN will generate an error if this is the case).

NOTE If you have lost your online redo logs, this procedure will not work. Refer to the section on incomplete recovery for information on how to deal with this situation.

Tablespace Recovery

The script for recovering a tablespace, shown in Listing 13.17, is only slightly different than one for recovering the entire database. In this script, we assume that the INDX tablespace has gone AWOL and we need to recover it. We also assume that the tablespace is offline.

Listing 13.17: RMAN Tablespace Recovery Script

```
RUN
{
    ALLOCATE CHANNEL d1 TYPE DISK;
    RESTORE TABLESPACE indx;
    RECOVER TABLESPACE indx;
    RELEASE CHANNEL d1;
    SQL "ALTER TABLESPACE indx ONLINE";
}
EXIT;
```

Notice that the RESTORE and RECOVER command syntax indicates that tablespace recovery is being performed. Finally, to bring the tablespace back online, we use the SQL command to send a SQL statement to the target database.

Datafile Recovery

Recovering datafiles is a piece of cake. The script, shown in Listing 13.18, is not much different from the ones you have seen thus far.

Listing 13.18: RMAN Database Datafile Recovery Script

```
RUN
{
    ALLOCATE CHANNEL d1 TYPE DISK;
    RESTORE DATAFILE 6 7;
    RECOVER DATAFILE 6 7;
    RELEASE CHANNEL d1;
    SQL "ALTER DATABASE DATAFILE 6 ONLINE";
    SQL "ALTER DATABASE DATAFILE 7 ONLINE";
}
EXIT;
```

Notice that this example uses the absolute datafile numbers to reference the datafiles to restore. We could have also used the datafile name (but that tends to be long, messy, and prone to "fat fingering"). In the RESTORE and RECOVER commands, we use the DATAFILE keyword. Finally, we again use the SQL command to send a SQL statement to the target database to bring the datafile online after its recovery.

Incomplete Recovery in ARCHIVELOG Mode

As we discussed in previous chapters, for an incomplete recovery, you must recover the entire database back to the point in time, so that all the datafiles will be consistent to the same point in time. Therefore, you will use only the RESTORE DATABASE and RECOVER DATABASE commands.

The real difference in the scripts is the inclusion of the SET UNTIL statement, which allows you to define at what point you wish recovery halted. The SET UNTIL command allows you to recover to a point in time, to a given database SCN number, or to a given log sequence number. The other requirement is to open the database with RESETLOGS. The following sections include scripts for time-based, log sequence number-based, and changed-based RMAN recovery. (See Chapter 10 for more on incomplete recovery principles.)

Time-Based Recovery

The script for a time-based recovery is shown in Listing 13.19. This script will restore the database to where it was three hours ago.

Listing 13.19: RMAN Time-Based Database Recovery Script

```
RUN
{
    SHUTDOWN IMMEDIATE;
    STARTUP MOUNT;
    SET UNTIL TIME 'SYSDATE - 3/24';
    ALLOCATE CHANNEL d1 TYPE DISK;
    RESTORE DATABASE;
    RECOVER DATABASE;
    RELEASE CHANNEL d1;
    SQL "ALTER DATABASE OPEN RESETLOGS";
}
EXIT;
```

The recovery script looks much like the other recovery scripts shown in this chapter, but with the addition of the SET UNTIL command. The 3/24 indicates to recover to SYSDATE, 3 hours (there are 24 hours in a day, and we want 3 of those hours). This is not the only format for time that you can use. Depending on your NLS_DATE_FORMAT, you might use a format like this:

```
SET UNTIL TIME '07/03/2001 22:36:32';
```

To change the NLS_DATE_FORMAT, you set the NLS_DATE_FORMAT environment variable, as in this example from NT:

```
C:\>SET NLS_DATE_FORMAT=mm/dd/yyyy hh24:mi:ss
```

This will change the NLS_DATE_FORMAT at the client level, where you will be running RMAN.

After performing the incomplete, time-based recovery, the script issues the ALTER DATABASE OPEN RESETLOGS command to the database through the RMAN SQL command. This will cause the database to be opened and a RESETLOGS command (which is required after incomplete recovery) to be performed.

 WARNING Do a backup anytime you have performed any operation that requires you to use the RESETLOGS command. Otherwise, the database will fail to open.

Log Sequence Number-Based Recovery

You will recall that each online redo log is assigned a unique sequence number, which increments by one for each log switch. As the online redo log is archived, this log sequence number continues to be associated with it as it is copied to the archived redo log directory. Usually, this log sequence number is part of the archived redo log physical filename to make it easy to distinguish which archived redo log represents which sequence number. Listing 13.20 provides an example of a recovery script that restores a database to a specific log sequence number.

Listing 13.20: RMAN Log Sequence Number-Based Database Recovery Script

```
RUN
{
    SHUTDOWN IMMEDIATE;
    STARTUP MOUNT;
    SET UNTIL LOGSEQ 6 THREAD 1;
    ALLOCATE CHANNEL d1 TYPE DISK;
    RESTORE DATABASE;
    RECOVER DATABASE;
    RELEASE CHANNEL d1;
    SQL "ALTER DATABASE OPEN RESETLOGS";
}
EXIT;
```

TIP You can look at V$LOG_HISTORY to get an idea of which log sequence number you want to recover. This view contains each archived redo log, along with its log sequence number, the first SCN within the log, the last SCN in the log, and the time that the log sequence number was first written to.

Change-Based Recovery

Change-based recovery is probably the most infrequently used method of incomplete database recovery, because few people know which SCN the transaction of interest occurred during. However, you might use change-based recovery for resetting through RESETLOGS. This is a complicated process, and RMAN makes it even more complicated because you will need to reset the database incarnation in order to do this. Listing 13.21 provides an example of change-based database recovery.

Listing 13.21: RMAN SCN (Change)-Based Database Recovery Script

```
RUN
{
    SHUTDOWN IMMEDIATE;
    STARTUP MOUNT;
    SET UNTIL SCN 123456;
    ALLOCATE CHANNEL d1 TYPE DISK;
    RESTORE DATABASE;
    RECOVER DATABASE;
    RELEASE CHANNEL d1;
    SQL "ALTER DATABASE OPEN RESETLOGS";
}
EXIT;
```

Recovering from Complete Loss of the Database without a Recovery Catalog

If you have lost your control files and your online redo logs as well, and you are not using a RMAN recovery catalog, you must use an incomplete recovery (log sequence number-based) to restore the database. (This procedure is slightly different if you are using a recovery catalog, since the control file is recoverable from the RMAN backup as long as you have access to the recovery catalog.) This recovery assumes that you have used the ALTER DATABASE BACKUP CONTROL FILE TO *'filename'* command to back up your control file, and that this was done after the last current backup of your database. The results of a CREATE CONTROL FILE command will not help you recover your database with RMAN without direct support from Oracle. Once you have copied your backup control file into place, you are ready to recover your database. Listing 13.22 shows the RMAN script for this procedure (we assume that the database is already down):

Listing 13.22: RMAN Database Loss Recovery Script

```
RUN
{
    STARTUP MOUNT
    SET UNTIL LOGSEQ 4 THREAD 1;
    ALLOCATE CHANNEL d1 TYPE DISK;
    RESTORE DATABASE;
    RECOVER DATABASE;
    RELEASE CHANNEL d1;
    SQL "ALTER DATABASE OPEN RESETLOGS";
}
EXIT;
```

In this example, log sequence 3 was the last log sequence we had available to apply. Thus, any transactions that occurred after the log switch from log sequence 3 will be lost.

NOTE If you lose only your control files (all of them) and you are not using an RMAN recovery catalog, all you need to do is recover the control files from the backup control file. You should not need RMAN to accomplish this operation.

Recovering Archived Redo Logs

In Chapter 14, we will discuss how LogMiner can be used to read the contents of an archived redo log and how you can generate reports on the results of LogMiner's operations. To be able to do that, you need to have the archived redo logs that you want to mine available. Since, in most cases, archived redo logs are removed after being backed up, you need some way to recover archived redo logs that are contained in RMAN backup sets.

The RESTORE command syntax calls for the use of the ARCHIVELOG record specifier clause. Table 13.11 lists its parameters.

TABLE 13.11: THE ARCHIVELOG RECORD SPECIFIER PARAMETERS

Parameter	Description
ALL	Recovers exactly one copy of each log sequence number.
LIKE {'string'}	Allows recovery of specific archived redo logs. Used for OPS recovery.
UNTIL TIME = {'NLS date string'}	Specifies the end date for a series of archived redo log files. The date must be in NLS format and can include SYSDATE.
FROM TIME {'NLS date string'}	Specifies the beginning date for a series of archived redo log files. The date must be in NLS format and can include SYSDATE.
UNTIL SCN = {n}	Defines the ending SCN for a sequence of archived redo logs. The default is to use the lowest SCN available.
FROM SCN {n}	Defines the beginning SCN for a sequence of archived redo logs. The default is to recover all archived redo logs from the earliest available.
UNTIL LOGSEQ = {n}	Causes all archived redo logs to be recovered until the log sequence number specified.
FROM LOGSEQ {n}	Causes all archived redo logs beginning at the defined sequence to be recovered.
THREAD {n}	Defines the thread that contains the archived redo logs that you wish to recover. This is for OPS configurations.

Listing 13.23 provides an example of a script that will perform a recovery of archived redo logs.

Listing 13.23: RMAN Archived Redo Log Recovery Script

```
RUN
{
    ALLOCATE CHANNEL d1 TYPE DISK;
    SET ARCHIVELOG DESTINATION TO 'c:\oracle\temarch\recover';
    RESTORE ARCHIVELOG FROM LOGSEQ 9 UNTIL LOGSEQ 12;
    RELEASE CHANNEL d1;
}
EXIT;
```

This example uses the RESTORE command with the ARCHIVELOG keyword. Using the FROM keyword, it restores the archived redo logs starting with sequence 9 and completing the restore operation with sequence 12. Also, notice the use of the SET keyword to modify the destination where the archived redo logs are recovered. By default, RMAN recovers the archived redo logs to the database archive log destination.

Recovering the Control File without a Recovery Catalog

The RMAN executable cannot recover a control file backup unless you are using a recovery catalog, but you can recover a control file from a backup set from the SQL prompt. To perform this feat, use the Oracle package DBMS_BACKUP_RESTORE, which RMAN uses to facilitate its own backup and recovery operations.

 NOTE Unfortunately, the DBMS_BACKUP_RESTORE package is not documented anywhere (at least in the Oracle 8.1.7 documentation). Still, you can use its functions and procedures to recover a control file, as described in this section.

The first thing you need to do is discover which is your latest control file backup set. To do this, start RMAN and use the LIST command (which we will discuss in detail later in this chapter, in the "Generating Reports and Lists" section) to list backup sets that contain control files. Here is the output from that command (the output format is slightly modified to fit this page):

```
RMAN> LIST BACKUP OF CONTROLFILE;

RMAN-03022: compiling command: list
RMAN-03025: performing implicit partial resync of recovery catalog
RMAN-03023: executing command: partial resync
RMAN-08003: starting partial resync of recovery catalog
RMAN-08005: partial resync complete
List of Backup Sets
Key     Recid       Stamp       LV Set Stamp  Set Count  Completion Time
------- ----------  ----------  -- ----------  ----------  ---------------
142     95          434215135   0  434215052   99          04-JUL-01

List of Backup Pieces
Key   Pc# Cp# Status     Completion Time  Piece Name
----- --- --- ---------- ---------------- --------------------------
143   1   1   AVAILABLE  04-JUL-01        D:\ORACLE\ADMIN\ORA817\
                                          BACKUP\ORA817.FULL.33CU364C

        Controlfile Included
```

```
         Ckp SCN    Ckp time
         ----------  ---------------
         444014     04-JUL-01

List of Backup Sets
Key     Recid       Stamp         LV Set Stamp   Set Count  Completion Time
-------  ----------  ----------    -- ----------  ----------  ---------------
155     96          434215167      0  434215161   100        04-JUL-01

List of Backup Pieces
Key     Pc# Cp# Status       Completion Time    Piece Name
---  --- --- ----------      ---------------    ---------------------------
156     1   1   AVAILABLE    04-JUL-01          D:\ORACLE\ADMIN\ORA817\
                                                BACKUP\ORA817.CRTL.34CU367P

         Controlfile Included
         Ckp SCN    Ckp time
         ----------  ---------------
         444019     04-JUL-01
```

Notice that this example shows two different backups of control files that are available. You can tell which is the latest by looking at the CKP SCN column, which shows the SCN of the time that the control file was checkpointed. In this case, the control file checkpoint SCN 444019 is the latest, so that is the control file we will want to recover. Write down the filenames of the backup pieces that are contained in this backup set. These backup pieces will be specifically referred to during the recovery and will be known as the handle when you do the recovery.

Now that we have the information we need, it's time to recover the control file. Listing 13.24 shows the SQL script to perform this operation.

Listing 13.24: SQL Control File Recovery Script

```
DECLARE
DEVTYPE VARCHAR2(256);
DONE BOOLEAN;
BEGIN
DEVTYPE:=DBMS_BACKUP_RESTORE.DEVICEALLOCATE(NULL);
DBMS_BACKUP_RESTORE.RESTORESETDATAFILE;
DBMS_BACKUP_RESTORE.RESTORECONTROLFILETO -
('c:\oracle\ctrlfile\controlfile.ctl');
DBMS_BACKUP_RESTORE.RESTOREBACKUPPIECE
```

```
('d:\oracle\admin\ora817\backup\ora817.crt1.34cu367p', DONE=>done);
END;
/
```

In the fifth line of the script, we allocate the channel to the device we will need. NULL indicates the default, which is disk (there is no DISK device to define here). The other option is SBT_TAPE, for when you are using the media management layer.

The control file restoration is handled in this line:

```
DBMS_BACKUP_RESTORE.RESTORECONTROLFILETO -
('c:\oracle\ctrlfile\controlfile.ctl');
```

It tells Oracle where to restore the control file to and what to call it.

Finally, the restore operation is started in this line:

```
DBMS_BACKUP_RESTORE.RESTOREBACKUPPIECE('d:\oracle\admin\ora817\backup\
ora817.crt1.34cu367p', DONE=>done);
```

We are telling Oracle to start the restore using the backup piece handle that contains the backup. If your backup has more than one backup piece, you will need to create a line for each backup piece.

Once you have restored the control file, copy it as required, mount the database, and recover it as required.

The RESTORE CONTROLFILE command can be used to restore a control file from a backup set to another location, even if there isn't a recovery catalog, as long as the database that the backup belongs to is still available. You can then replicate the control file to the different database locations if necessary by using the REPLICATE CONTROL FILE command. Here is an example of such an operation:

```
RUN
{
    ALLOCATE CHANNEL dsk1 TYPE DISK;
    RESTORE CONTROLFILE TO 'c:\oracle\ctrl_file.ctl';
    SHUTDOWN IMMEDIATE
    REPLICATE CONTROLFILE FROM 'c:\oracle\ctrl_file.ctl';
    STARTUP MOUNT;
}
```

In this example, we recover the control file to a different location, shut down the database, and then issue the REPLICATE CONTROLFILE command. The REPLICATE CONTROLFILE command will cause the control file to be distributed to the different control file locations. This method is useful if you are not using a recovery catalog and you wish to recover the database to a previous incarnation.

Recovering a Datafile to Another Location

A common recovery operation is to restore certain database datafiles to other locations. This might be required, for example, if a given disk system fails and you need to recover a database datafile to a different file system name. The SET command facilitates this process. Listing 13.25 provides an example of such an operation.

Listing 13.25: RMAN Database Recovery that Recovers a Datafile to a Different Location

```
RUN
{
    SQL "ALTER DATABASE DATAFILE 6 OFFLINE";
    ALLOCATE CHANNEL d1 TYPE DISK;
    SET NEWNAME FOR DATAFILE 'd:\oracle\oradata\users01.dbf' TO
         'c:\oracle\oradata\users01.dbf';
    RESTORE DATAFILE 6;
    SWITCH DATAFILE ALL;
    RECOVER DATAFILE 6;
    RELEASE CHANNEL d1;
    SQL "ALTER DATABASE DATAFILE 6 ONLINE";
}
EXIT;
```

Note that in addition to using the SET command, this example also uses the SWITCH command. The SWITCH command is used to cause the target Oracle database to alter the internal location where it looks for a physical file. In this example, it is used to update the database so that it will switch from the old database datafiles locations to the new database datafile locations, as defined in the RMAN SET NEWNAME command. The SWITCH command is also used for datafile copies (which we discussed earlier in this chapter) to indicate that the datafile copy should be used by the database.

Using the Recovery Catalog

The recovery catalog is a schema in an Oracle database that keeps track of the status of RMAN backup sets, much like the database control file does. The recovery catalog is optional. Consider using the recovery catalog if you wish to be able to do the following:

- Store RMAN scripts in the database for easy recall.

- Recover the database control file using RMAN, should the control files of the database be lost.
- Keep a longer history of backup and recovery operations than supported by the database control file (roughly 365 days).

Creating the Recovery Catalog

The creation of the recovery catalog takes place in several steps:

1. Create the recovery catalog database.
2. Create the recovery catalog schema.
3. Create the recovery catalog.
4. Register the database

Let's look at each of these steps in more detail.

NOTE Once created, the recovery catalog consumes about 1MB worth of space to begin with. The recovery catalog will grow as the number of databases you are backing up grows. Also, the recovery catalog will grow as the backup history contained within it grows.

Creating the Recovery Catalog Database

The recovery catalog sits in a normal Oracle database. There is nothing special to do during normal database creation in order for the database to contain a recovery catalog. In fact, if your resources (CPU, memory, or disk) are limited, you can use an existing database and just add a schema to it to contain the recovery catalog.

One thing to consider with the recovery catalog database is how you plan to back it up. You can use RMAN, but you must make provisions for back up of the control files of that database, since they will not be recoverable in the event of a database failure.

In our examples, we have created a database just for the recovery catalog. We have called this database rmanrdb.

TIP Insulate the recovery catalog database from other databases as much as possible. Eliminate as many common points of failure between the recovery catalog and other databases to preserve the ability of the recovery catalog to facilitate recovery in the event of the loss of another database.

Creating the Recovery Catalog Schema

Once the recovery catalog is created, it's time to create the schema and establish the appropriate grants for that schema. We also strongly suggest that you create a separate tablespace just for the recovery catalog objects. Here are the steps to follow when creating the schema:

1. Create the tablespace in which you will store the recovery catalog objects. (We will call ours REPO_TBS.)

2. Create the database user/schema that will own the recovery catalog objects. (We call ours REPO_OWN.) Set the default tablespace to the new tablespace created in step 1. Also make sure that you make the temporary tablespace something other than the default SYSTEM tablespace. Make sure that you grant the user an unlimited QUOTA on the recovery catalog tablespace.

3. Grant the schema the RECOVERY_CATALOG_OWNER role. You may also want to grant the CREATE SESSION privilege to the user.

Here is an example of the steps listed above:

```
D:\tempzip>sqlplus "/ as sysdba
SQL*Plus: Release 8.1.7.0.0 - Production on Wed Jul 4 13:29:41 2001
(c) Copyright 2000 Oracle Corporation.  All rights reserved.
Connected to:
Oracle8i Enterprise Edition Release 8.1.7.0.0 - Production
With the Partitioning option
JServer Release 8.1.7.0.0 - Production

SQL> CREATE TABLESPACE repo_tbs
  2  DATAFILE 'e:\oracle\oradata\rmandb\rmandb_repo_tbs_01.dbf'
  3  SIZE 20m;

Tablespace created.
SQL> CREATE USER repo_own IDENTIFIED BY repo_own
  2  TEMPORARY TABLESPACE temp
  3  DEFAULT TABLESPACE repo_tbs
  4  QUOTA UNLIMITED ON repo_tbs;
User created.

SQL> GRANT RECOVERY_CATALOG_OWNER TO repo_own;
Grant succeeded.
```

```
SQL> GRANT CREATE SESSION TO repo_own;
Grant succeeded.
```

Creating the Recovery Catalog

Your next step is to create the recovery catalog. In Oracle8i, this is done by starting the RMAN interface, connecting to the recovery catalog, and issuing the CREATE CATALOG command. To connect to the recovery catalog, use the CATALOG command-line parameter of RMAN, and then enter the username and password for the recovery catalog. Typically, you will connect to the recovery catalog using a Net8 service name rather than connecting directly through IPC. This is because you can connect to only one database directly with RMAN, and generally it's better if you connect to the database you are going to back up directly for backup performance reasons. Here is an example of connecting to the recovery catalog database and creating the recovery catalog:

```
E:\oracle\oradata>rman catalog repo_own/repo_own@rmandb
Recovery Manager: Release 8.1.7.0.0 - Production
RMAN-06008: connected to recovery catalog database
RMAN-06428: recovery catalog is not installed
RMAN> CREATE CATALOG;

RMAN-06431: recovery catalog created
```

 NOTE The CREATE CATALOG command has an optional TABLESPACE clause that allows you to define the tablespace to create the recovery catalog objects in.

Registering the Database with the Recovery Catalog

Before you can use the recovery catalog for RMAN database operations, you need to register the database. To do this, simply use the REGISTER DATABASE command, as shown in this example:

```
E:\oracle\oradata>rman target sys/robert catalog repo_own/repo_own@rmandb
Recovery Manager: Release 8.1.7.0.0 - Production
RMAN-06005: connected to target database: ORA817 (DBID=1598904557)
RMAN-06008: connected to recovery catalog database

RMAN> REGISTER DATABASE;
```

```
RMAN-03022: compiling command: register
RMAN-03023: executing command: register
RMAN-08006: database registered in recovery catalog
RMAN-03023: executing command: full resync
RMAN-08002: starting full resync of recovery catalog
RMAN-08004: full resync complete
```

Resynchronizing the Database to be Backed Up

From time to time, it may be a good idea to resynchronize the databases you are backing up with RMAN with the recovery catalog. Resynchronizing the database with the recovery catalog makes sure that all changes to the database since the last synch call have been propagated to the recovery catalog. This would include such things as newly generated archived redo logs and new tablespaces or datafiles. Anytime you perform a backup in RMAN, a resynch is automatically completed, but it might be a good idea to schedule resynch operations on a more frequent basis.

To resynchronize the database with the recovery catalog, issue the RESYNC CATALOG command from the RMAN prompt while connected to the recovery catalog database and the target database that you wish to resynch. This command also offers the FROM CONTROLFILECOPY *'filename'* parameter, which allows the specification of a control file copy as the source of the resynchronization. When this parameter is used, physical schema information will not be updated in the recovery catalog.

WARNING Make sure that you resynch the database (or make sure that you are backing up your database so the automatic resynch will occur) at intervals no less than that of the CONTROL_FILE_RECOVER_KEEP_TIME parameter in Oracle. Otherwise, you may find that the recovery catalog will fall hopelessly out of synch with the database.

Recovering a Control File

One of the benefits of using the recovery catalog is the ability to recover the control file should it get lost or corrupted. The process for recovering the control file is fairly easy if you have a recovery catalog—you simply use the RESTORE command with the CONTROLFILE keyword. Here is an example:

```
RUN
{
    ALLOCATE CHANNEL dsk1 TYPE DISK;
```

```
        RESTORE CONTROLFILE;
        ALTER DATABASE MOUNT;
}
```

You can incorporate this into a complete database recovery script, as shown in Listing 13.26.

Listing 13.26: RMAN Database and Control File Recovery with the Recovery Catalog

```
RUN
{
        STARTUP NOMOUNT
        ALLOCATE CHANNEL dsk1 TYPE DISK;
        RESTORE CONTROLFILE;
        ALTER DATABASE MOUNT;
        ALLOCATE CHANNEL d1 TYPE DISK;
        RESTORE DATABASE;
        RECOVER DATABASE;
        RELEASE CHANNEL d1;
        RELEASE CHANNEL dsk1;
        ALTER DATABASE OPEN;
}
EXIT;
```

Issuing the RESTORE CONTROLFILE command causes the control file to be restored and replicated to each location specified by the CONTROL_FILES database initialization parameter.

Resetting a Database

If you are using a recovery catalog, and you perform any type of recovery on the database that requires the use of the RESETLOGS command, you will need to issue a RESET DATABASE command to indicate to the recovery catalog that a new incarnation of the database has been created. This command is used only if you are using a recovery command, and it is not required if you are using just the database control file. An example of such a recovery is shown in Listing 13.27.

Listing 13.27: RMAN Database Reset

```
RUN
{
        SHUTDOWN IMMEDIATE;
```

```
        STARTUP MOUNT;
        SET UNTIL LOGSEQ 6 THREAD 1;
        ALLOCATE CHANNEL d1 TYPE DISK;
        RESTORE DATABASE;
        RECOVER DATABASE;
        RELEASE CHANNEL d1;
        SQL "ALTER DATABASE OPEN RESETLOGS";
}
RESET DATABASE;
EXIT;
```

The RESET DATABASE command can also be used to reset the incarnation of a database, so that a previous incarnation's backup can be recovered. Again, this is only possible if you are using a recovery catalog. An example is shown in Listing 13.28.

Listing 13.28: RMAN Database Incarnation Reset

```
SHUTDOWN IMMEDIATE
RESET DATABASE TO INCARNATION 1;
RUN
{
        ALLOCATE CHANNEL d1 TYPE DISK;
        RESTORE CONTROLFILE;
        STARTUP MOUNT;
        RESTORE DATABASE;
        RECOVER DATABASE;
        RELEASE CHANNEL d1;
        SQL "ALTER DATABASE OPEN RESETLOGS";
}
RESET DATABASE;
EXIT;
```

In this example, all of the available archived redo logs assigned to incarnation 1 will be recovered, and the database will be opened to the point at which incarnation 1 ceased to exist. By issuing the RESETLOGS command, you create a new incarnation.

Storing RMAN Scripts

Another feature of the recovery catalog is its ability to store RMAN scripts that can be called from RMAN. To store scripts in the recovery catalog, you use the CREATE SCRIPT command, assigning each script a unique name that identifies it. Typically, you will assign the script a name that identifies its purpose, such as backup_prod_db. Here is an example:

```
CREATE SCRIPT backup_prod_db
{
    ALLOCATE CHANNEL d1 TYPE DISK;
    BACKUP FULL (DATABASE
    FORMAT "d:\oracle\admin\ora817\backup\ora817.full.%u");
    SQL "ALTER SYSTEM ARCHIVE LOG CURRENT";
    BACKUP CURRENT CONTROLFILE
    FORMAT "d:\oracle\admin\ora817\backup\ora817.crtl.%u";
    BACKUP ARCHIVELOG ALL
    DELETE INPUT
    FORMAT "d:\oracle\admin\ora817\backup\ora817.arch.%u";
    RELEASE CHANNEL d1;
}
```

NOTE When you use a script, you do not need to include a RUN command in it. This is because when you EXECUTE a script, it is executed within the confines of a RUN command.

The EXECUTE SCRIPT command, which is a job command, allows you to execute the script. Here is an example:

```
RUN
{EXECUTE SCRIPT backup_prod_db;}
EXIT;
```

The REPLACE SCRIPT command replaces existing RMAN scripts with new scripts, as shown here:

```
REPLACE SCRIPT BACKUP_PROD_DB
{
    ALLOCATE CHANNEL disk1 TYPE DISK;
    BACKUP FULL (DATABASE
    FORMAT "d:\oracle\admin\ora817\backup\ora817.full.%u");
    SQL "ALTER SYSTEM ARCHIVE LOG CURRENT";
    BACKUP CURRENT CONTROLFILE
    FORMAT "d:\oracle\admin\ora817\backup\ora817.crtl.%u";
    BACKUP ARCHIVELOG ALL
    DELETE INPUT
```

```
            FORMAT "d:\oracle\admin\ora817\backup\ora817.arch.%u";
            RELEASE CHANNEL disk1;
}
```

The PRINT SCRIPT command will cause the contents of the script to be printed to the screen:

```
PRINT SCRIPT backup_prod_db;
```

The DELETE SCRIPT command removes the script:

```
DELETE SCRIPT backup_prod_db;
```

Maintaining the Recovery Catalog

Now that you have created the recovery catalog, you need to maintain the records in it. In this section, we will first discuss the recovery catalog views that you can use to check the records of the recovery catalog. Next, we explain how to perform cross-checking to make sure that physical datafile statuses are properly recorded in the recovery catalog. Finally, we will cover how to purge old recovery catalog records.

Recovery Catalog Data Dictionary Views

There are a number of views created when the recovery catalog is created that you can use to write reporting scripts and the like (though Oracle provides its own reporting through the LIST and REPORT commands). Most of these views derive their information from the recovery catalog. Many of them have corollary views that derive the same information from the database control file. These views have the same name except for their prefixes: RC_ for the recovery catalog views and V$ for the control file views. For example, if you want to find the view in the recovery catalog that is like V$ARCHIVED_LOG, you would look for RC_ARCHIVED_LOG. Table 13.12 lists the recovery catalog views, a brief description, and the corollary control file view (if one exists).

TABLE 13.12: RMAN RECOVERY CATALOG VIEWS

View	Description	Corollary Control File View
RC_ARCHIVED_LOG	Provides historical information on archived redo logs	V$ARCHIVED_LOG
RC_BACKUP_CONTROLFILE	Provides information on control files that are contained in backup sets	

Continued

TABLE 13.12: RMAN RECOVERY CATALOG VIEWS (CONTINUED)

View	Description	Corollary Control File View
RC_BACKUP_CORRUPTION	Provides block corruption information	V$BACKUP_CORRUPTION
RC_BACKUP_DATAFILE	Lists recovery catalog information on backup sets	V$BACKUP_DATAFILE
RC_BACKUP_PIECE	Lists recovery catalog information on backup set pieces	V$BACKUP_PIECE
RC_BACKUP_REDOLOG	Lists recovery catalog information on archived redo logs	V$BACKUP_REDOLOG
RC_BACKUP_SET	Lists recovery catalog information on backup sets for all incarnations of the database	V$BACKUP_SET
RC_CHECKPOINT	Provides recovery catalog resynch information, but Oracle recommends that you use the RC_RESYNC view instead	
RC_CONTROLFILE_COPY	Provides information on control file copies on disk	
RC_COPY_CORRUPTION	Lists recovery catalog information on corrupt blocks in datafile copies	V$COPY_CORRUPTION
RC_DATABASE	Lists recovery catalog information on databases registered with the recovery catalog	V$DATABASE
RC_DATABASE_INCARNATION	Provides information on all database incarnations registered in the recovery catalog	
RC_DATAFILE	Lists recovery catalog information on all datafiles registered in the recovery catalog	V$DATAFILE
RC_DATAFILE_COPY	Lists recovery catalog information on datafile copies on disk	V$DATAFILE_COPY
RC_LOG_HISTORY	Lists recovery catalog information on online redo log history	V$LOG_HISTORY
RC_OFFLINE_RANGE	Lists recovery catalog information on the offline ranges for datafiles	V$OFFLINE_RANGE

Continued

TABLE 13.12: RMAN RECOVERY CATALOG VIEWS (CONTINUED)

View	Description	Corollary Control File View
RC_PROXY_CONTROLFILE	Lists recovery catalog information on control file copies made using the proxy copy function	V$PROXY_CONTROLFILE
RC_PROXY_DATAFILE	Lists recovery catalog information on datafile backups made while using the proxy copy function	V$PROXY_ DATAFILE
RC_REDO_LOG	Provides information about online redo logs for all incarnations of the database stored in the recovery catalog	
RC_REDO_THREAD	Provides information about online redo log threads for all incarnations of the database stored in the recovery catalog	
RC_RESYNC	Provides information on resynch operations between a target database and the recovery catalog	
RC_STORED_SCRIPT	Provides information on scripts stored in the recovery catalog	
RC_STORED_SCRIPT_LINE	Provides detail on each line of each script stored in the recovery catalog	
RC_TABLESPACE	Lists recovery catalog information on all tablespaces, including dropped tablespaces and those from old incarnations	V$TABLESPACE

Cross-Checking Backup Sets

You might wonder what happens if a tape becomes unavailable or is overwritten for some reason. The RMAN CROSSCHECK command can be used to check all backups currently on tape and compare (cross-check) them with the cataloged backups. The status of the backups will be marked accordingly. Any backup not found will be marked with an EXPIRED status, for later removal. If, on the other hand, the backup set has an EXPIRED status, but it actually exists on the backup media, its status will be set to AVAILABLE. Table 13.13 describes the parameters for the CROSSCHECK command.

USING THE RECOVERY CATALOG

TABLE 13.13: CROSSCHECK COMMAND PARAMETERS

Parameter	description
of *listObjList*	Restricts the types of objects operated on by the command to those specified. (See Table 13.15 later in this chapter.)
TAG <*tag_name*>	Defines a tag for a backup set to be cross-checked.
completedTimeSpec	Defines a time range to run the CROSSCHECK command over. The options are AFTER = {*date string*} to define when the backup was completed, BETWEEN {*date string*} and {*date string*} to define a time range between backup completions, and BEFORE = {*date string*} to define a time range before the backup was complete.

NOTE Prior to Oracle 8.1.7, the CROSSCHECK command required the recovery catalog. In 8.1.7, this is no longer the case.

Listing 13.29 shows an example of using the CROSSCHECK command.

Listing 13.29: RMAN Backup Set Cross-check

```
E:\oracle\oradata>rman target sys/robert catalog repo_own/repo_own@rmandb

Recovery Manager: Release 8.1.7.0.0 - Production
RMAN-06005: connected to target database: ORA817 (DBID=1598904557)
RMAN-06008: connected to recovery catalog database
RMAN> ALLOCATE CHANNEL FOR MAINTENANCE TYPE DISK;

RMAN-03022: compiling command: allocate
RMAN-03023: executing command: allocate
RMAN-08030: allocated channel: delete
RMAN-08500: channel delete: sid=8 devtype=DISK

RMAN> CROSSCHECK BACKUP;

RMAN-03022: compiling command: XCHECK
RMAN-03023: executing command: XCHECK
RMAN-08074: crosschecked backup piece: found to be 'EXPIRED'
```

```
RMAN-08517: backup piece
handle=D:\ORACLE\ADMIN\ORA817\BACKUP\ORA817.ARCH.31CU1I
QB recid=93 stamp=434162508
RMAN-08074: crosschecked backup piece: found to be 'EXPIRED'
RMAN-08517: backup piece
handle=D:\ORACLE\ADMIN\ORA817\BACKUP\ORA817.ARCH.32CU1I
QJ recid=94 stamp=434162516
RMAN-08074: crosschecked backup piece: found to be 'AVAILABLE'
RMAN-08517: backup piece
handle=D:\ORACLE\ADMIN\ORA817\BACKUP\ORA817.FULL.33CU36
4C recid=95 stamp=434215057
RMAN-08074: crosschecked backup piece: found to be 'AVAILABLE'
RMAN-08517: backup piece
handle=D:\ORACLE\ADMIN\ORA817\BACKUP\ORA817.CRTL.34CU36
7P recid=96 stamp=434215164
RMAN-08074: crosschecked backup piece: found to be 'AVAILABLE'
RMAN-08517: backup piece
handle=D:\ORACLE\ADMIN\ORA817\BACKUP\ORA817.ARCH.35CU36
8A recid=97 stamp=434215180
RMAN-03023: executing command: partial resync
RMAN-08003: starting partial resync of recovery catalog
RMAN-08005: partial resync complete

RMAN> RELEASE CHANNEL;

RMAN-03022: compiling command: release
RMAN-03023: executing command: release
RMAN-08031: released channel: delete
```

As an alternative, you can issue the CROSSCHECK command using a date range, as in this example:

```
CROSSCHECK BACKUP COMPLETED AFTER 'SYSDATE - 30';
```

Purging Old Recovery Catalog Records

We all need to take out the trash from time to time, and this applies to maintaining the recovery catalog as well as your household. Without some reoccurring maintenance, the recovery catalog will grow and grow. The CROSSCHECK command marks backups that are no longer available with an EXPIRED status, but this command does not remove them from the recovery catalog. The DELETE EXPIRED BACKUP command is the one that handles this chore. This command will remove all records in the recovery catalog associated with expired backups.

 NOTE Prior to Oracle 8.1.7, the DELETE EXPIRED command required the recovery catalog. In 8.1.7, this is no longer the case.

Listing 13.30 shows an example of using the DELETE EXPIRED command.

Listing 13.30: RMAN Recovery Catalog Record Deletion

```
RUN
{
ALLOCATE CHANNEL FOR DELETE disk1 TYPE DISK;
CROSSCHECK BACKUP OF TABLESPACE user;
DELETE EXPIRED BACKUP OF TABLESPACE user;
RELEASE CHANNEL disk1;
}
```

In this example, we first allocate a channel, but this time we use the FOR DELETE syntax, which indicates to RMAN that we are likely going to be removing some physical backup pieces. The CROSSCHECK command will mark as expired all tablespace backups of the USER tablespace that no longer have physical backup sets. The DELETE EXPIRED BACKUP command will then physically remove those backups from RMAN. Housecleaning at its best!

Although the CHANGE command allows you to mark backup items with a DELETED status, currently, there is no RMAN command that allows you to remove these DELETED records from RMAN. Fortunately, Oracle has provided the prgrmanc.sql script, which will remove all records that have a DELETED status from the recovery catalog. This script can be found in the $ORACLE_HOME/rdbms/admin directory of your Oracle software installation.

Generating Reports and Lists

DBAs need information, and RMAN is poised to provide that information. RMAN facilitates reporting of backup sets, image copies, and many other facets of the backup and recovery landscape through the use of the REPORT and LIST commands. In this section, we will look at each of these types of RMAN information output.

Producing Backup Reports

The REPORT command provides information on the state of the database with regard to backups. With the REPORT command, for example, you can determine which datafiles have not been backed up in a certain number of days. You can also generate reports on database datafiles that need to be backed up because UNRECOVERABLE operations have been performed on them since the last backup.

Most output from the REPORT command can be run without a recovery catalog, but there are few exceptions (use of the AT clause parameters, described shortly).

The NEED BACKUP Option

The NEED BACKUP {*report criteria*} parameter lists all datafiles of the target database that require a backup. (If a file has not been backed up, it will not appear on the report.) The following report criteria are valid:

- INCREMENTAL {*n*} sets a maximum number of backups that should be required for full recovery. If this number is exceeded, a level 0 incremental backup is required.

- DAYS {*n*} defines the maximum number of days of redo log file application that any datafile should require. Thus, if this were set to 5, any datafile that was backed up more than 5 days ago would appear on the report.

- REDUNDANCY {*n*} defines a minimum number of backups or datafiles copies that must exist for a datafile. If this number of copies does not exist, the datafile will appear on the report.

Let's say that you want a list of all the datafiles in the database that have not been backed up in two days. Here is the REPORT command and the resulting output that shows the desired information:

```
RMAN> REPORT NEED BACKUP DAYS 2;
RMAN-03022: compiling command: report
Report of files whose recovery needs more than 2 days of archived logs
File Days  Name
---- ----- ----------------------------------------
1    6     D:\ORACLE\ORADATA\ORA817\SYSTEM01.DBF
2    6     D:\ORACLE\ORADATA\ORA817\RBS01.DBF
3    6     D:\ORACLE\ORADATA\ORA817\USERS01.DBF
4    6     D:\ORACLE\ORADATA\ORA817\TEMP01.DBF
5    6     D:\ORACLE\ORADATA\ORA817\TOOLS01.DBF
6    6     D:\ORACLE\ORADATA\ORA817\INDX01.DBF
```

The report shows the datafiles that are in need of backup because it would take more than two days of archived redo logs to recover them. This report provides the file number, the actual number of days' worth of archived redo logs that would be required to recover the datafile, and the names of the datafiles themselves.

As another example, suppose that you have decided that you need a minimum of three backups of every database datafile to feel that you have a sufficiently redundant backup strategy. These backups don't need to be at the same time—you just want three different backups (you can apply the archived redo logs, of course). So, you might produce this report:

```
RMAN> REPORT NEED BACKUP REDUNDANCY 3;

RMAN-03022: compiling command: report
Report of files with less than 3 redundant backups
File #bkps Name
---- ----- ----------------------------------------
1    1     D:\ORACLE\ORADATA\ORA817\SYSTEM01.DBF
3    2     D:\ORACLE\ORADATA\ORA817\USERS01.DBF
4    1     D:\ORACLE\ORADATA\ORA817\TEMP01.DBF
5    2     D:\ORACLE\ORADATA\ORA817\TOOLS01.DBF
6    1     D:\ORACLE\ORADATA\ORA817\INDX01.DBF
```

This report indicates that you do have some datafiles that do not meet your minimum redundancy requirement. Some of them, like SYSTEM01.DBF, require another backup to meet the requirement; others, like TOOLS01.DBF, require two backups. Any datafiles that have a sufficient number of backups to meet the criteria do not appear on the report.

The UNRECOVERABLE Option

Perhaps you want to know if any UNRECOVERABLE actions have occurred that might necessitate a backup of a datafile. You can get this information with the REPORT UNRECOVERABLE parameter:

```
RMAN> REPORT UNRECOVERABLE
RMAN-03022: compiling command: report
Report of files that need backup due to unrecoverable operations
File Type of Backup Required Name
---- ----------------------- ----------------------------------
3    full or incremental     D:\ORACLE\ORADATA\ORA817\USERS01.DBF
```

From this report, you see that the USERS01.DBF datafile is in need of either a full or incremental backup. This is because you have performed some UNRECOVERABLE operation on it. Since an UNRECOVERABLE operation does not generate redo, there is no way to recover that operation with archived redo logs. Thus, you need to make sure that you back up this tablespace, or you might lose the objects in it that you created as UNRECOVERABLE.

Report Object Definition

The *reportObject* clause allows you to define the datafiles that are included in the report. The following are valid parameters:

- DATAFILE {*datafileSpec*} causes RMAN to report on the datafiles listed. You can list the entire datafile name or use the absolute datafile number.
- TABLESPACE {*tablespace_name*} causes RMAN to report on the datafiles of the tablespaces listed in the *tablespace_name* parameter.
- DATABASE causes RMAN to report on all datafiles of the current target database.
- SKIP TABLESPACE {*tablespace_name*} causes RMAN to skip the datafiles of the specified tablespaces listed in the *tablespace_name* parameter.

The OBSOLETE Option

The OBSOLETE parameter lists backups and datafiles that are no longer required and can be removed. It takes the following optional parameters:

- REDUNDANCY {*n*} defines how many copies of backups must exist in order for a backup to be considered obsolete. For example, a REDUNDANCY of 3 indicates that three backups must exist before any backup set can be considered obsolete. REDUNDANCY defaults to a value of 1.
- The UNTIL clause defines time constraints for which a backup can be considered obsolete.
- ORPHAN defines backups as obsolete because they belong to a previous incarnation of the database.

The SCHEMA Option and AT Clause

The SCHEMA parameter reports on all datafiles of the target database, including the file number, name, and size of the tablespace that the datafiles belong to.

The AT clause allows you to specify a snapshot point in time that you wish the SCHEMA report to reflect. Thus, you can have RMAN provide you with a report of the database datafiles at some specific period of time. Use of this parameter requires the recovery catalog. The following are valid parameters for this clause:

- AT TIME {*date string*} reports on the database schema as it looked at a specific time.

- AT SCN {*n*} reports on the database schema as it looked at a specific SCN.
- AT LOGSEQ {*n*} reports on the database schema as it looked at a specific log sequence number.

The DEVICE TYPE Option

The DEVICE TYPE {*device*} parameter restricts the report to a specific device. For example, to see information about disk backups, use the command REPORT DEVICE TYPE DISK.

Producing Lists

Lists are another method of reporting RMAN information. Lists provide specific information on backups, rather than on database datafiles. Thus, if you want to know when a specific backup took place, use a LIST report.

The LIST command can be used, for the most part, without the recovery catalog (exceptions are noted in Table 13.14). Table 13.14 summarizes the parameters of the LIST command.

TABLE 13.14: LIST COMMAND PARAMETERS

Parameter	Description
INCARNATION	Provides information about the incarnations of the target database, including each incarnation primary key (which is the incarnation key used to reset the database incarnation if required.) Optionally, you can add the parameter OF DATABASE {*database name*}. This command requires the use of a recovery catalog.
COPY	Provides information about RMAN datafile image copies, archived redo logs, and image copies of archived redo logs.
BACKUP	Provides information about RMAN backups, backup sets, and their related backup pieces. Each backup set and backup piece has a unique key associated with it in the report. You can use this key with the CHANGE and DELETE EXPIRED BACKUPSET commands.
listObjList	Defines the object types to be reported on (see Table 13.15).
completedTimeSpec	Defines a range of time for which the reported backup or image copy should have completed its operation. The options are AFTER = {*date string*} to define when the backup was completed, BETWEEN {*date string*} and {*date string*} to define a time range between backup completions, and BEFORE = {*date string*} to define a time range before the backup was complete.

Continued

TABLE 13.14: LIST COMMAND PARAMETERS (CONTINUED)

Parameter	Description
TAG = {tag_name}	Restricts the report to those datafiles or datafile copies that contain the listed tag name.
RECOVERABLE	Causes the resulting output to be restricted to only those backups that are candidates for restore operations. Thus, backups taken before a RESETLOGS operation, for example, are not listed unless the files were read-only. Also, incremental backups without a base backup are not listed.
DEVICE TYPE {deviceSpecifier}	Causes the report to be restricted to backups made through specific devices (i.e., DISK).
LIKE {string pattern}	Allows you to restrict datafile copy reporting by using a filename matching pattern. The Oracle matching patterns '%' and '_' are accepted.

The *listObjList* parameter is used in the LIST command to define the object that is to be reported on and in some cases a range of time to report on the specific object. Table 13.15 describes the parameters of the *listObjList* parameter.

TABLE 13.15: LIST OBJECT LIST PARAMETERS

Parameter	Description
DATAFILE <datafile name list>	Defines the datafile, either by name or by absolute file number. One or more datafiles can be listed.
TABLESPACE <tablespace_name>	Defines one or more tablespaces this clause is to act on.
archivelogRecord	Specifies a range of archive logs for the command to act on.
database	Specifies to check backup sets or image copies of the current database. Optionally, the SKIP TABLESPACE argument causes the check to skip specific tablespaces.
controlfile	Specifies the current control file.

The LIST command can tell you a great deal about the backups on your system. Let's look at a few examples.

Listing Archive Log Backups

Suppose that you want to see all archive log backups in the last seven days. You would issue the following command from RMAN and get the resulting output (the output format is slightly modified to fit this page):

```
RMAN> LIST BACKUP OF ARCHIVELOG FROM TIME 'SYSDATE - 7';

RMAN-03022: compiling command: list

List of Backup Sets
Key     Recid       Stamp      LV Set Stamp  Set Count  Completion Time
------- ----------  ---------- -- ---------- ---------- ----------------
94      94          434162516  0  434162515  98         04-JUL-01

List of Backup Pieces
Key Pc# Cp# Status    Completion Time   Piece Name
--- --- --- --------- ----------------  -------------------------------
94  1   1   EXPIRED   04-JUL-01         D:\ORACLE\ADMIN\ORA817\BACKUP\
                                        ORA817.ARCH.32CU1IQJ

    List of Archived Logs Included
    Thrd Seq     Low SCN    Next SCN   Low Time         Next Time
    ---- ------- ---------- ---------- ---------------- -----------
    1    12      423987     423989     04-JUL-01        04-JUL-01

List of Backup Sets
Key     Recid       Stamp      LV Set Stamp  Set Count  Completion Time
------- ----------  ---------- -- ---------- ---------- ----------------
97      97          434215181  0  434215178  101        04-JUL-01

List of Backup Pieces
Key Pc# Cp# Status    Completion Time   Piece Name
--- --- --- --------- ----------------  -------------------------------
97  1   1   AVAILABLE 04-JUL-01         D:\ORACLE\ADMIN\ORA817\BACKUP\
                                        ORA817.ARCH.35CU368A
```

```
List of Archived Logs Included
Thrd  Seq     Low SCN     Next SCN    Low Time         Next Time
----  ------- ----------  ----------  ---------------  ---------------
 1     9      423981      423982      04-JUL-01        04-JUL-01
 1    10      423982      423985      04-JUL-01        04-JUL-01
 1    11      423985      423987      04-JUL-01        04-JUL-01
 1    12      423987      423989      04-JUL-01        04-JUL-01
 1    13      423989      443994      04-JUL-01        04-JUL-01
 1    14      443994      444018      04-JUL-01        04-JUL-01
```

This report indicates that there are two backup sets that contain archive log backups. One set (ID 94) has an EXPIRED status, so it is unusable. The second set (ID 97) is still marked AVAILABLE, and it appears to have six archived redo logs in it. We see that archived redo log sequences 9 through 14 are in this backup set.

Listing Recoverable Backups

Next, suppose that you want information on the backups in the database that are still recoverable. You would issue this command and get the following output (the output format is slightly modified to fit this page):

```
RMAN> LIST BACKUP OF DATABASE RECOVERABLE;
RMAN-03022: compiling command: list

List of Backup Sets
Key     Recid       Stamp       LV Set Stamp   Set Count   Completion Time
------  ----------  ----------  -- ----------  ----------  ---------------
 95      95         434215135    0  434215052   99          04-JUL-01

List of Backup Pieces
Key  Pc# Cp# Status     Completion Time   Piece Name
---  --- --- ---------  ---------------   ------------------------------
 95   1   1  AVAILABLE  04-JUL-01         D:\ORACLE\ADMIN\ORA817\BACKUP\
                                          ORA817.FULL.33CU364C

List of Datafiles Included
File Name                                       LV Type Ckp SCN   Ckp Time
---- ---------------------------------------    -- ---- ---------- --------
 1   D:\ORACLE\ORADATA\ORA817\SYSTEM01.DBF       0  Full  444015    04-JUL-01
 2   D:\ORACLE\ORADATA\ORA817\RBS01.DBF          0  Full  444015    04-JUL-01
 3   D:\ORACLE\ORADATA\ORA817\USERS01.DBF        0  Full  444015    04-JUL-01
 4   D:\ORACLE\ORADATA\ORA817\TEMP01.DBF         0  Full  444015    04-JUL-01
```

```
5     D:\ORACLE\ORADATA\ORA817\TOOLS01.DBF   0  Full  444015    04-JUL-01
6     D:\ORACLE\ORADATA\ORA817\INDX01.DBF    0  Full  444015    04-JUL-01

List of Backup Sets
Key       Recid       Stamp       LV Set Stamp   Set Count   Completion Time
-------   ---------   ---------   -- ---------   ---------   ---------------
98        98          434757821   0  434757805   102         10-JUL-01

List of Backup Pieces
Key  Pc# Cp# Status      Completion Time   Piece Name
---  --- --- ---------   ---------------   -------------------------------
98   1   1   AVAILABLE   10-JUL-01         D:\ORACLE\ADMIN\ORA817\BACKUP\
                                           ORA817.TBS.36CUJ05D

List of Datafiles Included
File  Name                                     LV Type Ckp SCN   Ckp Time
----  ---------------------------------------  -- ---- ---------  ---------
2     D:\ORACLE\ORADATA\ORA817\RBS01.DBF       0  Full 464073     10-JUL-01
3     D:\ORACLE\ORADATA\ORA817\USERS01.DBF     0  Full 464073     10-JUL-01
5     D:\ORACLE\ORADATA\ORA817\TOOLS01.DBF     0  Full 464073     10-JUL-01
```

Here, you see that you have two recoverable backup sets. The first backup set with key number 95 contains full backups of five database datafiles in one backup piece. The second backup, which is key 98, contains backups of three database datafiles, which are also full backups. This output also shows the physical filenames of the backup pieces involved in the backup, the date of the backup, and the level of the backup for incremental backups.

Getting Incarnation Information

You may need to see some basic database incarnation information, especially if you are faced with recovering a database with a backup taken before the RESETLOGS command was issued. In this case, you might issue this command:

```
RMAN> LIST INCARNATION OF DATABASE;

RMAN-03022: compiling command: list
RMAN-03025: performing implicit partial resync of recovery catalog
RMAN-03023: executing command: partial resync
RMAN-08003: starting partial resync of recovery catalog
RMAN-08005: partial resync complete
```

```
List of Database Incarnations
DB Key  Inc Key  DB Name   DB ID             CUR  Reset SCN   Reset Time
-------  -------  --------  ----------------  ---  ----------  ----------
1        138      UNKNOWN   1598904557        NO   423906      03-JUL-01
1        2        ORA817    1598904557        YES  423949      03-JUL-01
```

This report shows that the database has had two incarnations in its RMAN lifetime. Notice that the DBID remains the same. The DB key also stays the same. Only the incarnation key (INC KEY) changes. Thus, it is a combination of the DB key and the incarnation key that makes each line in this report unique. Also of interest is the reset SCN. If you ever want to try to recover past the RESETLOGS command, you will need the reset SCN. (See Chapter 10 for more on recovering past RESETLOGS.)

CHAPTER 14

Oracle8i LogMiner

FEATURING:

Introducing LogMiner	**614**
Setting up LogMiner	**615**
Selecting redo logs to mine	**618**
Using LogMiner	**620**
Retrieving the LogMiner results	**624**

There is a wealth of information that can be derived from redo logs. In earlier releases of Oracle, there was no easy way to extract this information. New to Oracle8i is LogMiner, which provides the tools to retrieve the information in redo logs.

This chapter begins with an introduction to LogMiner. We will then show you how to set up LogMiner and use it to mine redo logs.

Introducing LogMiner

LogMiner is a powerful add-on feature to the Oracle database that lets you "mine" the information in redo logs. LogMiner is embodied in two PL/SQL packages and some views.

As you've learned, redo logs contain a record of almost every transaction and change that occurs in the database. The information contained within the redo logs can be used for a number of database management tasks, including the following:

- Security review and auditing
- Data recovery
- Data removal
- Database change velocity measurement
- Database trending
- Problem resolution, such as detecting when logical data corruption occurred

Let's look at the features and the restrictions of using LogMiner.

LogMiner Features

LogMiner allows you to select the redo logs you wish to mine, and even define specific time periods within those redo logs from which to extract transactional records. Once LogMiner extracts the contents of selected redo logs, it translates them and provides them for review in a user-accessible view. LogMiner has some other interesting features to note:

- You can analyze redo logs that belong to one database in a completely separate database.
- The SQL to undo or redo the transaction is provided when the redo log is mined.

LogMiner Limitations

LogMiner does have a few limitations. The restrictions are not really that imposing for the most part, but some of them do reduce the effectiveness of LogMiner in certain situations. Restrictions of LogMiner include the following:

- LogMiner cannot be used with Oracle7 (or earlier) database redo logs. LogMiner can be used with redo logs from an Oracle8 database, but it runs only on Oracle8i databases.
- The database that you are mining and the database doing the ANALYZE process must have the same character set, database block size, and hardware platform.
- Operations on the following objects are currently not supported by LogMiner:
  - Index-organized tables
  - Clustered tables and indexes
  - Nonscalar datatypes (types created with the CREATE TYPE command)
  - Chained rows
  - Direct path operations
  - Extraction of DDL operations

Setting Up LogMiner

If you build it, they will come... well, something like that. Before you can use LogMiner, you need to do some setup. Fortunately, this process is fairly straightforward. First, you need to establish a UTL_FILE_DIR entry in the database parameter file. Then you can use the DBMS_LOGMNR_D.BUILD procedure to create the dictionary file. These steps are described in the following sections.

Establishing a UTL_FILE_DIR Entry

The UTL_FILE_DIR entry in the database parameter file defines a directory where Oracle can open, close, read, and write physical files using the UTL_FILE package. Here is an example of the UTL_FILE_DIR setting in the `init.ora` file:

```
UTL_FILE_DIR="e:\oracle\oracle_output"
```

LogMiner uses the UTL_FILE package to write out a dictionary file, described next.

Creating the Dictionary File

The dictionary file provides object-resolution information that LogMiner uses when mining redo logs. Within the redo log itself, the names of objects are not used. Instead, the redo log uses object IDs, or numbers that represent the objects. Of course, the output of LogMiner would be a bit harder to use if all it provided was the object number of the objects being modified. You would then need to resolve each object ID for each object—a painstaking process if your database has several thousand tables in it.

The dictionary file solves this problem by resolving each object ID to the name and owner of that object. The dictionary file is not required to run LogMiner, but it makes analyzing the output much easier. To create the dictionary file, you use the DBMS_LOGMNR_D.BUILD procedure. The package takes two parameters, as shown here:

```
SQL> DESC dbms_logmnr_d.build
PROCEDURE dbms_logmnr_d.build
 Argument Name                  Type                    In/Out Default?
 ------------------------------ ----------------------- ------ --------
 DICTIONARY_FILENAME            VARCHAR2                IN
 DICTIONARY_LOCATION            VARCHAR2                IN
```

The first parameter, DICTIONARY_FILENAME, represents the name of the dictionary file. The second parameter, DICTIONARY_LOCATION, represents the location where the dictionary file should be written to. The DICTIONARY_LOCATION should be the same location as defined in the UTL_FILE_DIR parameter.

Listing 14.1 shows an example of the creation of a dictionary with the DBMS_LOGMNR_D.BUILD procedure, along with a listing of the resulting output file (I removed some unneeded output for brevity).

NOTE The space and hyphen (-) at the end of the EXEC command lines throughout this chapter are SQL*Plus continuation indicators (rather than SQL indicators). As noted in Chapter 1, if you wish to use two or more lines to express a SQL*Plus command, you must end each line with the space and hyphen to indicate continuation of the lines.

Listing 14.1: Creating a Dictionary File

```
D:\ORACLE\ORA816\RDBMS\ADMIN>sqlplus "/ as sysdba"
SQL*Plus: Release 8.1.7.0.0 - Production on Sat Jul 14 21:16:10 2001
(c) Copyright 2000 Oracle Corporation.  All rights reserved.
Connected to:
Oracle8i Enterprise Edition Release 8.1.7.0.0 - Production
```

SETTING UP LOGMINER

```
With the Partitioning option
JServer Release 8.1.7.0.0 - Production
SQL> EXEC dbms_logmnr_d.build('ora817_dictionary', -
'e:\oracle\oracle_output');
PL/SQL procedure successfully completed.
SQL> QUIT
Disconnected from Oracle8i Enterprise Edition Release 8.1.7.0.0
D:\ORACLE\ORA816\RDBMS\ADMIN>DIR e:\oracle\oracle_output
 Directory of e:\oracle\oracle_output

07/14/01  09:18p            1,894,148 ora817_dictionary
             3 File(s)      1,894,148 bytes
                          241,795,072 bytes free
```

Now that you have created a dictionary file, you are ready to choose redo logs from the database that you can mine. We will cover that in the next section.

 TIP You can create a LogMiner database, where its sole job is to facilitate log-mining activities. Simply create dictionary files for all of your databases and move them into one single directory (obviously the filenames must be unique). You can then mine redo logs from any database by moving those log files over to a special directory set aside for that purpose. When you mine a database redo log file, you simply define the dictionary file to use to resolve all the references, and Oracle will do the rest.

Handling ORA-06532 Errors

When running the DBMS_LOGMND_D.BUILD routine, you may run into an ORA-06532 error. To correct this, you will need to copy the dbmslmd.sql script in the $ORACLE_HOME/rdbms/admin directory, as you see in this example:

```
cp dbmslmd.sql dbmslmd_new.sql
```

Then open the dbmslmd_new.sql script and search for the following line of code in it:

```
TYPE col_desc_array IS VARRAY(513) OF col_description;
```

Continued

> **CONTINUED**
>
> Replace this line with the following line of code:
>
> ```
> type col_desc_array IS VARRAY(1000) OF col_description;
> ```
>
> Then log in as SYS or INTERNAL (*only* SYS or INTERNAL—no other user!) and run the dbmslmd_new.sql script that you just modified:
>
> ```
> sqlplus sys/robert
> SQL> @d:\oracle\ora817\rdbms\admin\dbmslmd_new.sql
> ```
>
> If you still get the ORA-06532 error when you run LogMiner (and you will if any schema contains more than 1000 objects), simply increase the size of the VARRAY to the largest number of objects within the largest database schema.

Selecting Redo Logs to Mine

Before you can start using LogMiner to mine redo logs, you need to take a few preliminary steps:

- Determine what time period you wish to mine information from.
- Determine what redo logs were generated during that period.
- Stage the redo logs you wish to mine.

Use the V$LOGMNR_LOGS view to check the list of selected redo logs.

You can recover the redo logs that you wish to mine from backup, in the case of older archived redo logs, or identify those redo logs that may be still available on disk, including online redo logs if you so choose. The V$ARCHIVED_LOG view and the V$LOG views can be of great help to you when you need to figure out what redo logs you need to mine. The staging and viewing steps are discussed in more detail in the following sections.

Staging Redo Logs

After you have identified the redo logs that were created during the period in question, your next step is to stage these redo logs before they can be mined. This staging process is facilitated through the DBMS_LOGMNR.ADD_LOGFILE procedure. Here is the description of this procedure:

```
PROCEDURE ADD_LOGFILE
 Argument Name                  Type                    In/Out Default?
 ------------------------------ ----------------------- ------ --------
 LOGFILENAME                    VARCHAR2                IN
 OPTIONS                        BINARY_INTEGER          IN     DEFAULT
```

The LOGFILENAME procedure is the name of the redo log you wish to add (fully pathed). The OPTIONS column is one of three options that indicate the type of registration activity you wish to perform (these options are hard-coded values within the DBMS_LOGMNR package itself):

- The DBMS_LOGMNR.NEW option adds the redo log file, removing any existing log files from the list of redo logs available for mining.
- The DBMS_LOGMNR.ADDFILE option adds the listed redo log file, while leaving the other registered log files available for mining.
- The DBMS_LOGMNR.REMOVEFILE option removes the listed redo log file from mining consideration.

Listing 14.2 shows some examples of using the DBMS_LOGMNR.ADD_LOGFILE procedure.

Listing 14.2: Staging Redo Logs

```
EXEC DBMS_LOGMNR.ADD_LOGFILE( -
'd:\oracle\admin\ora817\archive\ora817T001S00019.ARC', -
options=>DBMS_LOGMNR.NEW);
EXEC DBMS_LOGMNR.ADD_LOGFILE( -
'd:\oracle\admin\ora817\archive\ora817T001S00020.ARC', -
options=>DBMS_LOGMNR.ADDFILE);
EXEC DBMS_LOGMNR.ADD_LOGFILE( -
'd:\oracle\admin\ora817\archive\ora817T001S00021.ARC', -
options=>DBMS_LOGMNR.ADDFILE);
EXEC DBMS_LOGMNR.ADD_LOGFILE( -
'd:\oracle\admin\ora817\archive\ora817T001S00019.ARC', -
options=>DBMS_LOGMNR.REMOVEFILE);
```

In this example, we add a redo log file using the NEW parameter, which clears all previously staged log files. Then we add two more log files with the ADDFILE parameter. Finally, we remove the first log file from the staging area using the REMOVEFILE option.

Viewing the Redo Log List

Now that you have added a few redo logs to the LogMiner staging list, it would be nice to be able to view that list and see what redo logs have been assigned. To do that, you can look at the V$LOGMNR_LOGS view, as in this example:

```
SQL> SELECT log_id, filename FROM v$logmnr_logs;

    LOG_ID FILENAME
---------- ------------------------------
        20 d:\oracle\admin\ora817\archive
           \ora817T001S00020.ARC

        21 d:\oracle\admin\ora817\archive
           \ora817T001S00021.ARC
```

As you can see, there are two log files staged for mining. This is the result of the DBMS_LOGMNR.ADD_LOGFILE procedures shown in Listing 14.2.

NOTE The V$LOGMNR_LOGS view (and the staging list) is cleared when you end your session. So, if you add a lot of logs to be mined and quit, or lose your network connection, you will need to start again (one of my least favorite features of LogMiner).

Using LogMiner

After you have some logs staged for mining, you're ready to use the DBMS_LOGMNR.START_LOGMNR procedure to actually mine the logs you have selected and populate the results of that operation in the V$LOGMNR_CONTENTS view. In this section, we will demonstrate mining the logs selected in Listing 14.2, and then we will look at the V$LOGMNR_CONTENTS view.

Mining Redo Logs

To mine the redo logs you have staged, use the DBMS_LOGMNR.START_LOGMNR procedure. This procedure has the following parameters:

```
SQL> DESC dbms_logmnr.start_logmnr
PROCEDURE dbms_logmnr.start_logmnr
```

Argument Name	Type	In/Out	Default?
STARTSCN	NUMBER	IN	DEFAULT
ENDSCN	NUMBER	IN	DEFAULT
STARTTIME	DATE	IN	DEFAULT
ENDTIME	DATE	IN	DEFAULT
DICTFILENAME	VARCHAR2	IN	DEFAULT
OPTIONS	BINARY_INTEGER	IN	DEFAULT

You can call the procedure without any parameters, since all of the parameters have default values. This will result in each selected redo log being mined and the results being populated in the V$LOGMNR_CONTENTS view. However, you may want to restrict your mining operations to a specific range of SCNs or a time period, or use the other parameters, as follows:

- The STARTSCN and ENDSCN parameters allow you to pick a beginning SCN and an end SCN (one or both). Thus, you can limit the log-mining activities to a range of SCNs, have it start at a specific SCN and mine from there, or start at the first SCN in the staged logs and mine to a specified end SCN.

- The STARTTIME and ENDTIME parameters allow you to define a time range that you wish to mine logs over. You can also start at a specific time and mine from there, or stop at a specific time and mine to there from the first log file. You can use the time and SCN parameters together, to define both time and SCN ranges.

- The DICTFILENAME parameter allows you to identify the dictionary file that you want to use to translate object IDs to object names (the dictionary file is described earlier in this chapter, in the "Creating the Dictionary File" section).

- The OPTIONS parameter offers the SKIP_CORRUPTION and DBMS_LOGMNR .USE_COLMAP options.

  - The SKIP_CORRUPTION flag causes LogMiner to skip any corruption that might be present in the redo logs being analyzed. This option works only if the corruption is in a redo block (not the header data) of the redo log.

  - The DBMS_LOGMNR.USE_COLMAP option allows you to map specific columns in objects to one of five special columns, known as the PH columns, in the V$LOGMNR_CONTENTS view. These columns are discussed in the "Using the Placeholder Column Option" section, a bit later in this chapter.

In order to mine a log file based on date, you must somehow *not* send in the parameters for the start and stop SCNs (which will allow you to mine the entire range of

SCNs in the log file). To do this, you need to either pass NULLs into the two parameters or use *named notation*, and send nothing to those parameters to use the default values instead. Here is an example of using positional notation, which simply means that the values listed in the procedure call are in the order that the procedure expects them to be:

```
EXEC dbms_logmnr.start_logmnr(null, null, sysdate - 10, sysdate, -
'd:\oracle\logs\redo01.log');
```

The following is an example of using named notation:

```
EXEC dbms_logmnr.start_logmnr( -
    starttime=>sysdate - 10,
    endtime=>sysdate,
    dictfilename=>'d:\oracle\logs\redo01.log');
```

As you can see, named notation uses the exact name of the parameter, then the characters => to indicate named notation, and finally the parameter value itself.

Listing 14.3 shows an example of mining a set of redo logs.

Listing 14.3: Mining Redo Logs

```
SQL> SELECT log_id, to_char(low_time, 'mm/dd/yyyy hh24:mi:ss'),
  2  to_char(high_time, 'mm/dd/yyyy hh24:mi:ss')
  3  ,low_scn, next_scn
  4  FROM v$logmnr_logs;

    LOG_ID TO_CHAR(LOW_TIME,'M TO_CHAR(HIGH_TIME,'    LOW_SCN   NEXT_SCN
---------- ------------------- -------------------  ---------- ----------
        20 07/14/2001 20:45:13 07/14/2001 21:50:58      484111     484199
        21 07/14/2001 21:50:58 07/14/2001 21:51:29      484199     484217

SQL> EXEC dbms_logmnr.start_logmnr(startscn=>484112, endscn=>484216, -
> starttime=>to_date('07/14/2001 21:51:00', 'mm/dd/yyyy hh24:mi:ss') -
> ,endtime=>to_date('07/14/2001 21:51:25', 'mm/dd/yyyy hh24:mi:ss'), -
> dictfilename=>'e:\oracle\oracle_output\ora817_dictionary');

PL/SQL procedure successfully completed.
```

In this example, we query the V$LOGMNR_LOGS view to determine which redo logs are staged for mining. Two logs appear in the output. Notice that we displayed the low and next SCN columns, as well as the beginning and ending dates of the transactions in the redo logs. We then proceeded to mine the logs, using STARTSCN and ENDSCN constraints, as well as the STARTTIME and ENDTIME constraints. We also provided the dictionary filename, so that we can get object name and owner resolutions from that file. We will look at the results of this operation in the next section.

 WARNING If you mine logs and then log out of the system, or lose your network connection, you will lose the results of the LogMiner session. I strongly suggest that you back up the view to a table using the CREATE TABLE AS SELECT command to prevent loss of the mined data.

Viewing the Log Mining Results

Seeing the results is the whole reason for using LogMiner. The results of the log mining appear in the V$LOGMNR_CONTENTS view. This view contains a number of columns. The most commonly used ones are described in Table 14.1.

TABLE 14.1: COMMONLY USED V$LOGMNR_CONTENTS COLUMNS

Column	Description
SCN	The SCN of when the change occurred
TIMESTAMP	The time the change occurred
THREAD#	The thread number of the instance (used for OPS)
LOG_ID	The redo log sequence number containing the change
ABS_FILE#	The absolute file number of the data block being affected
REL_FILE#	The relative file number of the data block being affected
DATA_BLK#	The data block number being affected
DATA_OBJ#	The data block object number being affected
DATA_OBJD#	The data block data object number being affected
SEG_OWNER	The owner of the segment
SEG_NAME	The name of the affected segment
SEG_TYPE	The segment type being affected
TABLE_SPACE	The tablespace the segment is assigned to
ROW_ID	The row ID of the row being changed
SESSION#	The session number making the change
SERIAL#	The serial number making the change
USERNAME	The username the change is being made under

Continued

TABLE 14.1: COMMONLY USED V$LOGMNR_CONTENTS COLUMNS (CONTINUED)

Column	Description
SESSION_INFO	Various session information, such as the machine name, the Oracle login username, and the operating system username (this information appears when it's available)
OPERATION	Text description of the operation type, such as DELETE, INSERT, or COMMIT
SQL_REDO	SQL redo to apply to reapply the change
SQL_UNDO	SQL undo (rollback) to remove the change

Using the Placeholder Column Option

There are also several PH columns in the V$LOGMNR_CONTENTS view. These are designed to facilitate the use of the placeholder column option. To use this option, you must first create a column map in a file called `logmnr.opt`. This file must be in the same directory as the dictionary file. Within the `logmnr.opt` file, you define the PH column the table columns are assigned to.

For example, suppose that you have a table called APPOINTMENTS in the DOCTORS schema. In that table, you have a column called LAST_NAME. You set up a `logmnr.opt` file with the following entry:

```
colmap = doctors appointments (1, last_name);
```

Then, when you mine the redo logs, any changes to the LAST_NAME column will appear in the PH1 column. For each PH assignment in the `logmnr.opt` file, there are three related columns in the V$LOGMNR_CONTENTS view:

- PH?_NAME shows the name of the column.
- PH?_REDO shows the redo value required to reapply the change to that column.
- PH?_UNDO shows the undo value required to remove the change to that column.

Retrieving the LogMiner Results

Now that you have reviewed the V$LOGMNR_CONTENTS view, let's see some output from it. In this first example, we create a table called LOG_TEST, which has a single column called ID. We then insert some records into it, commit the operation, and mine the resulting redo logs. Having done that, we query the V$LOGMNR_CONTENTS view and find these records (we have stripped away other changes):

```
SQL> SELECT sql_redo FROM v$logmnr_contents
  2  WHERE seg_owner='SYS' AND
  3  seg_name='LOG_TEST';

SQL_REDO
-----------------------------------------------
insert into "SYS"."LOG_TEST"("ID") values (1);
insert into "SYS"."LOG_TEST"("ID") values (2);
insert into "SYS"."LOG_TEST"("ID") values (2);
```

Here, you see the INSERT records that are associated with the redo records that were mined. You can use these INSERT statements to replay the transactions, if necessary. Furthermore, you know that an undo operation would be required to reverse these changes. You can retrieve these undo operations, as shown in this next example:

```
SQL> SELECT sql_undo FROM v$logmnr_contents
  2  WHERE seg_owner='SYS' AND
  3  seg_name='LOG_TEST';

SQL_UNDO
-----------------------------------------------------------------
delete from "SYS"."LOG_TEST" where "ID" = 1
and ROWID = 'AAAA7WAABAAAHGeAAA';
delete from "SYS"."LOG_TEST" where "ID" = 2
and ROWID = 'AAAA7WAABAAAHGeAAB';
delete from "SYS"."LOG_TEST" where "ID" = 2
and ROWID = 'AAAA7WAABAAAHGeAAC';
```

The DELETE statements that result from this query represent the work that must be done to undo each individual change.

Perhaps you are more interested in who made the changes. You can see what account the changes were made from by using this query:

```
SQL> SELECT username, to_char(timestamp, 'mm/dd/yyyy hh24:mi:ss')
  2  FROM v$logmnr_contents
  3  WHERE seg_owner='SYS' and
  4  seg_name='LOG_TEST';
```

```
USERNAME                          TO_CHAR(TIMESTAMP,'
-------------------------------   -------------------
SCOTT                             07/14/2001 21:51:19
SCOTT                             07/14/2001 21:51:22
SID                               07/14/2001 21:51:24
```

So, now you know who made the changes, what changes were made, and what time the changes were made. This should give you an idea of the power of LogMiner. Use it and see how many different applications you can think of for it.

PART III

Beyond Simple Database Management

LEARN TO:

- *Find lurking database threats*
- *Monitor database performance*
- *Secure databases*
- *Use SQL*LOADER*

CHAPTER 15

Oracle8i Performance Monitoring and Database-Level Tuning

FEATURING:

Tuning problem Oracle databases	630
Setting Oracle events	632
Using Oracle8i dynamic performance views	638
Checking the SGA	645
Checking for I/O contention	658
Lurking database threats	664
Using Oracle database performance monitoring tools	673
Introducing a monitoring methodology	688

One of the most important jobs of the DBA is to monitor the overall performance of the database and to tune the database instance. Monitoring is related to, but different from, tuning. Tuning generally takes place after a problem has been discovered. In other words, monitoring is a preemptive activity, while tuning is usually reactive, although it doesn't always need to be. Generally, monitoring is easier than tuning because it is nondestructive. Monitoring doesn't require changes to the database in order to be effective, whereas tuning can require significant changes to the database.

Problems are much easier to solve early on. A problem with a production database that is discovered in its first two or three days of life with few users on the system is much easier to solve than one detected weeks later when you finally manage to turn on monitoring. This is why it's important to set up and monitor your databases early in the database life cycle. Also, problems are much easier to solve if you know how the database normally acts before the problem occurs. In other words, performance monitoring allows you to develop a tuning baseline. Time is an important factor in successful monitoring. The faster a problem is detected, the cheaper the cost to correct the problem will be. The less it costs to fix a problem, the more likely it will be that you become the hero.

In this chapter, we'll begin with a summary of database tuning, and then you'll learn how to set events in Oracle. Next, we'll discuss the V$ performance views Oracle provides to assist you in performance monitoring. Then we'll move onto specific queries that you can use to monitor the database, what the data in those queries means, and how to use the information you learn from the queries to better tune your database. Next, we'll look at a few Oracle tools that you can use to monitor the database. Finally, we'll outline a methodology for monitoring to develop baselines, benchmarks, and trends.

This is the first of three chapters on monitoring and tuning. We'll address SQL tuning in Chapter 16. Chapter 17 describes how to tune waits, latches, and locks.

Tuning Problem Oracle Databases

Some people believe that there is some magic solution that DBAs can pull out of their hats to fix poor database performance problems. I've lost track of how many times people have suggested changing this or that setting, because they read in a book that the particular setting is the panacea of database problem resolution. The truth is that database tuning represents only about 10 percent of the overall performance gains you can achieve when dealing with a problem database.

Oracle suggests that you tune your database in this order:

- Business rules
- Data design
- Application design
- Logical structure of the database
- Database operations
- Access paths
- Memory allocation
- I/O and physical structure
- Resource contention
- Underlying platform(s)

Tuning is a recursive process. You may tune the application design, and then tune the logical structure of the database, which will require that you tune the application design again. Oracle's recommended tuning order indicates that a great deal of tuning can actually occur before the database is ever created. In tuning the business rules and the database design in particular, you can be truly proactive about performance issues.

This chapter is about the process of tuning database operations. This step is lower than others on Oracle's list of tuning priorities, but it seems to be the first thing people consider when they think about fixing a problem database. If you approach tuning in the order Oracle suggests, you will find you have fewer overall database problems.

I Want You to Be a Lazy DBA

Yes, you read the title correctly—I want you to be a lazy DBA. A lazy DBA is one who has done a great deal of work in the beginning of the creation and use of a given database. A lazy DBA is one who has created a framework to constantly monitor the databases in his or her charge, and to report about potential problems long before they occur. Once these tasks have been completed, the DBA is free to move onto other tasks (reading this book, say), safe in the knowledge that nothing terrible will happen to his or her database without advance warning.

Being a lazy DBA is about taking preemptive versus reactive measures in your approach to database administration. It's about not needing to update your résumé that often.

Setting Oracle Events

An *event* is some defined action in the database. Events can be used to trigger special database functionality or to enable additional troubleshooting functionality. Sometimes, events are set to enable specific database error processing. There are several events that can be useful to DBAs. The DBA can use events to start tracing others sessions, to trace the execution of the Optimizer, and to learn more about Oracle internals.

Events and event codes are poorly documented by Oracle. This is, in part, because many of them have the capacity to do damage to your system. Before you set an event on a production system, test it in a development system. In the development system, don't just enable the event and check that it doesn't crash the system. Run transactions through the system. Verify that the event is doing what it's supposed to be doing. Test your backup and recovery strategy, and make sure that the event does not have a negative impact on that strategy. Remember that backup and recovery are your primary duties as a DBA. Everything else is secondary, even the use of some really cool events.

WARNING Events in Oracle are not all that well documented (in fact, many are not documented at all), and they can change from version to version. Often, it takes some trial and error to get an event to work the way you really want it to, if it works at all. Always try a new event out on a test database first. Do not use events until you are confident that they will not adversely affect your database. Improper use of events can cause a database failure.

Enabling Events

You can enable an event code in one of the following ways:

- Set the event in the `init.ora` file
- Use the ALTER SYSTEM SET EVENTS command
- Use the ALTER SESSION SET EVENTS command
- Use the DBMS_SYSTEM.SET_EV procedure

When you enable an event, you use the following event command components to control how the event executes and for how long:

```
{event code} TRACE {trace type name},{trace parameter}
```

SETTING ORACLE EVENTS

When you set up events using the ALTER SYSTEM or ALTER SESSION commands, use the following syntax:

{immediate} {event number} trace {name {event name to trace}},
{level {level number}}

When setting an event in the init.ora parameter file of the database, use this syntax:

EVENT = "{immediate} {event number} trace {name {event name to trace}},
{level {level number}}"

The DBMS_SYSTEM package contains two procedures that can assist you with events: the READ_EV procedure to determine which events are set for your system and the SET_EV procedure to set events for your session. You'll see an example of using the SET_EV procedure a bit later in this chapter, in the "Using Events to Monitor Your Database" section.

The event codes, trace types, and trace parameters are described in the following sections.

Event Codes

An event code is a number such as 10262 or 10235. If you are using Oracle on a Unix system, you can find the event codes in the $ORACLE_HOME\rdbms\mesg\oraus.msg file. Unfortunately, Oracle has encrypted that file on NT systems, so it is unreadable.

NOTE The event code numbers are part of the larger set of Oracle error numbers. Oracle has reserved the set of error code numbers from 10000 to 10999 for event codes.

Each event code has a different meaning and instructs Oracle to do something specific. For example, the event code 10046 causes Oracle to start tracing your session. Associated with each event code are different levels that define the depth of information that is provided by that event. Many events have just one level; others have many levels. For example, the 10046 event code has four levels. One level provides regular trace information, and the other levels provide additional details, including bind variable information, wait information, and combinations of bind and wait information.

For the *event code* parameter in the event command, you can use a specific event code number. Alternatively, when you are enabling an event with the ALTER SYSTEM or ALTER SESSION command, you can use the IMMEDIATE keyword as the *event code* parameter to indicate that the event should be executed immediately and that its execution is unconditional.

Trace Types

For the *trace type name* parameter in the event command, you can optionally use the types listed in Table 15.1.

TABLE 15.1: EVENT TRACE TYPE NAME PARAMETERS

Trace Type Name	Description
BLOCKDUMP	A database block dump (the associated level is the block address in decimal)
BUFFERS	A buffer header dump
CONTEXT	Determines how detailed a dump should be
CONTEXTAREA	Dumps the cursor context area
CONTROLF	A control file header dump
ERRORSTACK	Error stack information, to store information related to a specific Oracle error
FILE_HDRS	Datafile header information
LATCHES	Dumps latches
ENQUEUES	Dumps enqueues
LOCK	Lock information
LOGHIST	Log history from the control file
PROCESSSTATE	Dumps the process state of a session
REDOHDR	Redoes the header block
SAVEPOINTS	Dumps the currently defined savepoints
SYSTEMSTATE	A system state dump (may be requested by Oracle in the event of hard-to-diagnose system problems)

Trace Parameters

The *trace parameter* parameters that can be used in event commands are listed in Table 15.2. As you might guess, not all combinations of parameters will work with all events.

TABLE 15.2: EVENT TRACE PARAMETERS

Trace Parameter	Description
FOREVER/OFF	Using FOREVER indicates that the event should remain active for the life of the session or as long as the instance is active. Using OFF turns off the event.
LEVEL {n}	Indicates the level of detail that should be processed by the event. Most events have multiple levels assigned to them, normally 1 through 10 (though some go higher). LEVEL can also have other meanings, depending on the event being executed.
AFTER {n} TIMES	Indicates that the trace should be started after the event happens n times.
LIFETIME {n}	Indicates that the trace should occur for only n times. It will be disabled after that.
TYPE INCREMENT	Sets the trace level to the highest possible.
TYPE DECREMENT	Sets the trace level to 0, effectively disabling it.

Using Events to Monitor Your Database

Now that you know something about events, let's look at some examples of setting them. Table 15.3 provides a list of commonly used events. Included in the table are the event code, a description of what it is used for, and an example of how to use it from the SQL command line.

TABLE 15.3: COMMONLY USED EVENTS

Event Code	Description	Example
10013	Used to determine rollback corruption problems that prevent the database from starting.	EVENT="10013 trace name context forever"
10015	Used to determine rollback corruption problems that prevent the database from starting.	EVENT="10015 trace name context forever"
10029	Provides information on session logons.	EVENT="10029 trace name context forever"
10030	Provides information on session logoffs.	EVENT="10030 trace name context forever"

Continued

TABLE 15.3: COMMONLY USED EVENTS (CONTINUED)

Event Code	Description	Example
10033	Provides details about sorts to disk.	ALTER SESSION SET EVENTS '10033 trace name context forever, level 4';
10046	Used to trace a session. Valid levels are 1 (regular trace), 4 (dump bind variables), 8 (dump wait information), and 12 (dump all).	ALTER SESSION SET EVENTS '10046 trace name context forever, level 4';
10053	Provides details on how the CBO decided which execution plan to use. Valid level is 1, which gives information on the CBO execution decisions.	ALTER SESSION SET EVENTS '10053 trace name context forever, level 1';
10128	Provides details on partition elimination decisions. Valid levels are 1, 2, and 4.	ALTER SESSION SET EVENTS '10128 trace name context forever, level 1';
10210	Provides table block checking.	EVENT="102100 trace name context forever, level 10"
10211	Provides index block checking.	EVENT="10211 trace name context forever, level 10"
10212	Provides index block checking.	EVENT="10212 trace name context forever, level 10"
10231	Skips corrupted blocks during table scans.	EVENT="10231 trace name context forever, level 10" To turn off block checking once the database is up and running, issue ALTER SYSTEM SET EVENTS '10231 trace name context off';
10232	Dumps corrupted blocks to a trace file.	EVENT="10232 trace name context forever, level 10"
10240	Dumps the DBA of blocks that incur waits.	EVENT="10240 trace name context forever, level 10"
10391	Traces parallel query execution.	EVENT="10391 trace name context forever, level 10"

As an example, suppose that you want to dump the control file header to see the last checkpoint SCN. You can use the following command to do a control file header dump:

```
ALTER SESSION SET EVENTS 'immediate trace name controlf level 10';
```

This creates a trace file in the location defined by the init.ora parameter USER_DUMP_DEST, which will contain the control file dump that you want to review.

As another example, suppose that you want to trace your user session, dumping the bind variables as well as the wait events. To enable this trace, you can use event 10046 set at level 4:

```
ALTER SESSION SET EVENTS '10046 trace name context forever, level 12';
```

This creates a session trace file, just as you would get with the ALTER SESSION SET SQL_TRACE=TRUE command.

If you want to set an event that always executes when the database starts, you can set it in the database init.ora file. For example, if you want to trace session logons and logoffs, you can set events 10029 and 10030:

```
EVENT="10029 trace name context forever, level 10"
EVENT="10030 trace name context forever, level 10"
```

In this case, the level 10 indicates tracing with additional detail. The CONTEXT FOREVER parameter means that this event will continue to be reported. If you want to turn this event off, use CONTEXT OFF instead.

You can also set an event for a specific session by using DBMS_SYSTEM.SET_EV. This procedure takes five parameters, as shown in its description below:

```
PROCEDURE SET_EV
 Argument Name                  Type                In/Out Default?
 ------------------------------ ------------------- ------ --------
 SI                             BINARY_INTEGER      IN
 SE                             BINARY_INTEGER      IN
 EV                             BINARY_INTEGER      IN
 LE                             BINARY_INTEGER      IN
 NM                             VARCHAR2            IN
```

The first parameter (SI) is the session identifier. The second parameter (SE) is the serial number of the session. The session identifier and the serial number of a session uniquely identify a given user session and can be discovered by querying the V$SESSION view. The third parameter (EV) is the event number (see Table 15.3). The next parameter (LE) is the level that you wish to set the event to (see Table 15.2). Finally, the last parameter (NM) is the event name (see Table 15.1). This last parameter cannot be NULL, but it may be blank. Depending on the event (again, sometimes it's a matter

of trial and error to get the right setting), you may need to enter the last parameter as empty quotation marks, as in this example:

    EXEC SYS.DBMS_SYSTEM.SET_EV(9,407,10046,4,' ');

This sets event 10046 for session 9 (serial number 407), to level 4, sending " as the name.

TIP You can set regular error events so that they will cause trace files to be generated when they occur. For example, when a user tries to perform an action that he or she does not have the rights to do, this will generally cause an ORA-1031 to occur. You can set the 1031 event to cause a trace file to be dumped each time that this event occurs: EVENT="1031 trace name errorstack forever, type increment". Although you can get more information from a custom event trigger, being able to set the event and trap it is a handy tool.

Using Oracle8i Dynamic Performance Views

Dynamic performance views generally start with a V$ prefix, and they are also referred to as *V$ views*. Dynamic performance views give a snapshot of the database's various performance statistics. For the most part, all the information you will need to tune and monitor your database will come from the V$ views. As with any endeavor, if you want to be an expert, you should know how the tools you use actually work. So, first we'll look at how the V$ views are constructed. Then you'll learn about the V$ views that are useful for performance monitoring.

NOTE One mistake DBAs commonly make is to expect dynamic performance views to be truly dynamic—updated immediately all of the time. Unfortunately, this isn't always true. In some cases, dynamic performance views may lag too far behind to provide the timely information you need.

How Are V$ Views Created?

The V$ views that you query, such as V$SYSSTAT, are actually synonyms that point to views. If you look up V$SYSSTAT in the SYNONYM_NAME column of DBA_SYNONYMS, you'll find that V$SYSSTAT is a synonym for a view called V_$SYSSTAT. The V_$ views are the underlying views that you look at when querying the V$ views.

You might think that you could find the SQL text that comprises the V_$ view in DBA_VIEWS. However, because V$ views are really internal data dictionary views, the method by which they are implemented differs slightly from regular views. Rather than going to the DBA_VIEWS view to find the creation text of the view, you go to V$FIXED_VIEW_DEFINITION to find the SQL statements used to create the V$ views.

If you look at the view definitions in V$FIXED_VIEW_DEFINITION, you'll find that the V_$ views are further based on a series of GV$ views. These views are, in turn, based on a series of tables called the X$ tables. The X$ tables are often called fixed views. These tables represent various structures that the Oracle database populates at system startup. The Oracle DBA does not normally need to access the X$ tables (although we do refer to these and other underlying base tables in this book). The V$ views (and the underlying X$ tables) get their information from various sources, including the database itself, the database control file, the data parameter files, and so on.

NOTE Be careful if you choose to use the X$ views. Oracle changes such structures from release to release, so a query that works in Oracle8i may not work in 8i release 2. The queries you see here (many of which were written using Oracle 8.1.6.3) may not work in later versions.

Which V$ Views Are for Performance Monitoring?

Table 15.4 lists the V$ views that pertain to performance monitoring, along with a brief description of each view.

NOTE V$ view statistics are cumulative in nature. They will be reset when the database starts and will accumulate values as the database continues to function. Some of them will even roll over if the database has been running long enough.

TABLE 15.4: ORACLE V$ VIEWS FOR DATABASE PERFORMANCE MONITORING

View Name	Description
V$DATABASE	Describes database information derived from the database control file. You can use this view to join with dynamic performance views to report on the database name.
V$DBFILE	Resolves datafile numbers to the name/location of the datafile. You can use this view to join with other dynamic performance views to report the names and locations of datafiles. This view is similar to the DBA_DATA_FILES data dictionary view.
V$DB_OBJECT_CACHE	Displays objects that are in the library cache, such as tables and indexes. You can use this view with others to look at object memory use, the number of times the object has been loaded, and other information that might indicate that the shared pool needs to be tuned.
V$DISPATCHER	Monitors dispatcher processes in a distributed environment.
V$DISPATCHER_RATE	Provides additional statistics on the dispatcher processes.
V$FILE_STAT	Provides information on database file I/O. You can use this view to monitor database datafiles to make sure that the database does not become I/O bound.
V$FIXED_TABLE	Lists all dynamic performance views. Note that some V$ tables are actually real tables and will not be listed in this view.
V$FIXED_VIEW_DEFINITION	Lists the SQL text that comprises a V$ view.
V$INSTANCE	Lists the instance name, the startup date and time, and if the instance is hung waiting for the ARCH process to clear archived redo logs.
V$LATCH	Displays latching statistics for parent latches and summary statistics for child latches.
V$LATCH_CHILDERN	Displays latching statistics for child latches.
V$LATCH_MISSES	Contains statistics on latch acquisition failures.
V$LIBRARY_CACHE	Contains various statistics on the performance of the library cache.
V$LOG_HISTORY	Contains information on redo log switches. You can use this view to determine if you are switching redo logs too often or not often enough.
V$OPEN_CURSOR	Lists cursors that each user session has opened and parsed. You can use this view to identify SQL statements that are being run by a specific session.

Continued

TABLE 15.4: ORACLE V$ VIEWS FOR DATABASE PERFORMANCE MONITORING (CONTINUED)

View Name	Description
V$PARAMETER	Lists database parameter settings.
V$PQ_SESSTAT	Shows session statistics for parallel queries.
V$PQ_SLAVE	Shows parallel query slave process statistics.
V$PQ_SYSSTAT	Shows system-level statistics for parallel query processing.
V$PX_PROCESS	Contains information about sessions using parallel query processing.
V$PX_PROCESS_SYSSTAT	Contains information about sessions using parallel query processing.
V$PX_SESSION	Contains information about sessions using parallel query processing.
V$RESOURCE_LIMIT	Displays information about resource use for certain system resources.
V$ROLLNAME	Displays rollback segment name information.
V$ROLLSTAT	Contains various rollback segment information.
V$ROWCACHE	Contains statistics for the data dictionary.
V$RSRC_CONSUMER_GROUP	Contains information on active resource consumer groups.
V$SESSION	Contains session-level database information.
V$SESSION_CURSOR_CACHE	Contains information on current cursor usage. You can use this view to determine if the OPEN_CURSORS setting parameter is set appropriately.
V$SESSION_LONGOPS	Displays information on certain long-running database operations. You can use this view to see if any long-running processes might have been started inadvertently.
V$SESS_IO	Lists I/O statistics for each user session.
V$SESSTAT	Contains specific session statistics.
V$SGA	Lists memory allocations of various SGA components.
V$SGASTAT	Contains memory allocation information for various SGA components.
V$SHARED_POOL_RESERVED	Contains information on the reserved part of the shared pool.
V$SQL	Lists statistics on SQL in the shared pool.
V$SQLAREA	Contains information on the shared SQL area of the shared pool. You can use this view to see if inefficient SQL is being executed.

Continued

TABLE 15.4: ORACLE V$ VIEWS FOR DATABASE PERFORMANCE MONITORING (CONTINUED)

View Name	Description
V$STATNAME	Displays statistic names to allow for resolution when only the statistic number is available from a V$ view.
V$SYSSTAT	Contains various system-level statistics. You can use this view to join with V$STATNAME to resolve the statistic names.
V$TEMPSTAT	Contains temporary datafile read/write statistics.
V$THREAD	Contains various instance information from the control file.
V$TRANSACTION	Contains transaction information. You can use this view to identify transactions that are using excessive resources.

NOTE This chapter will not address V$ views that don't pertain to performance monitoring. For a comprehensive list of dynamic performance views, refer to Appendix H or query the Oracle8i V$FIXED_VIEW_DEFINITION table.

We recommend monitoring the following database information using the V$ views:

- Various SGA hit ratios, including the database buffer cache and the various shared pool hit ratios (VSGA, VSYSSTAT, and V$SGASTAT)
- I/O contention, because too much I/O can impact system performance (V$FILE_STAT and V$SESS_IO)
- Memory contention, because allocating too little or too much memory to certain structures can impact system performance (VDB_OBJECT_CACHE, VSGA, and V$SGASTAT)
- Latching and waiting (V$LATCH, V$LATCH_CHILDERN, and V$LATCH_MISSES)
- Efficiency of SQL statements, because inefficient SQL can cause performance problems (V$SQLAREA and V$SQL)
- Potential internal database problems, such as a segment unable to extend or rollback segments that are not as efficient as they could be (V$ROLLSTAT)
- Long-running database operations, which can negatively impact overall database operations such as index rebuilds and some SQL operations (V$SESSION_LONGOPS)

In this chapter, we'll build scripts using several V$ performance views to monitor various aspects of database performance. Methods for monitoring latching, waiting, and long-running database operations are covered in Chapters 16 and 17.

How Do You Get More Information from V$ Views?

Some of the V$ views provide more performance information if you enable the TIMED_STATISTICS parameter in the database. The TIMED_STATISTICS parameter defaults to a FALSE setting. When it is set to TRUE, the database gathers time-related statistics on various operations. Be aware that this collection effort has some overhead associated with it, so you might want to measure the impact of enabling the parameter before forging ahead.

NOTE Oracle8i release 8.1.5 had trouble enabling the TIMED_STATISTICS parameter, and this caused serious performance problems. This was corrected in the 8.1.5.1 patch for that release. Later releases don't have the problem. If you are using release 8.1.5, make sure that you've installed the 8.1.5.1 patch.

You can use one of several different methods to set the TIMED_STATISTICS parameter:

- Set it in the `init.ora` database parameter file, where the setting will take effect on the next database reboot.
- Dynamically enable it for a given session by using this command:
  `ALTER SESSION SET timed_statistics=TRUE`
- Enable it for the entire system by using this command:
  `ALTER SYSTEM SET timed_statistics=TRUE`

To disable the parameter, either for the session or system, reset it to FALSE.
The following V$ views have columns that are affected by enabling the TIMED_STATISTICS parameter:

- V$FILE_STAT
- V$SESSION_EVENT
- V$SESSION_WAIT
- V$SYSTEM_EVENT
- V$TEMPSTAT
- V$WAITSTAT

Enabling TIMED_STATISTICS before looking at these views will cause Oracle to provide additional time-related information, such as how long the session waited and the total time that a particular event occurred. For example, suppose that you issued the following query to see the total number of wait events in V$WAITSTAT:

```
SQL> SELECT * FROM v$waitstat;
```

CLASS	COUNT	TIME
data block	22	0
sort block	0	0
save undo block	0	0
segment header	0	0
save undo header	0	0
free list	0	0
extent map	0	0
bitmap block	0	0
bitmap index block	0	0
unused	0	0
system undo header	0	0

CLASS	COUNT	TIME
system undo block	0	0
undo header	0	0
undo block	0	0

14 rows selected.

This query shows that you have 22 data block waits, but this number doesn't really mean anything by itself. What matters is how long the waits took. This is where TIMED_STATISTICS comes in. After enabling TIMED_STATISTICS and allowing the system to run for a while, you might come up with these numbers:

CLASS	COUNT	TIME
data block	42	205
sort block	0	0
save undo block	0	0
segment header	0	0
save undo header	0	0

```
free list                  0          0
extent map                 0          0
bitmap block               0          0
bitmap index block         0          0
unused                     0          0
system undo header         0          0


CLASS                    COUNT       TIME
------------------      --------   --------
system undo block          0          0
undo header                1          1
undo block                 0          0
```

Now the TIME column is populated. This column represents the time (in hundredths of a second) that these specific waits took, so the database has spent 2.05 seconds on data block waits. If this number was generated over a period of just a few minutes (rather than a few weeks), you might need to consider some tuning.

NOTE There seem to be three camps in regards to setting TIMED_STATISTICS. One says to never set it, because it has a huge performance impact. Another camp says to always have it on, because it really is of no performance impact. Finally, there is the group that says to enable it when you need it. I tend to be a member of the group that says have it on all the time. For your own system, I suggest turning it on and measuring its impact. If the impact is insignificant, leave it on.

Checking the SGA

One of the first things DBAs typically check in a database is the health of the SGA. As a critical database structure, it is rightly the subject of constant concern and scrutiny. You can monitor and tune the SGA from several vantage points. The following structures in the SGA should be monitored:

- The database buffer cache
- The library cache in the shared pool
- The data dictionary cache in the shared pool

In the following sections, we'll look at the various ways to monitor the database instance and improve the numbers you see, if necessary.

WARNING Monitoring a database is not without cost. Monitoring requires that you interact with the database, and that interaction takes database resources. Constant monitoring can have a negative effect on the database at times, particularly if the database is already struggling with performance. You must carefully balance the impact of the monitoring process against the benefits of that monitoring.

Monitoring and Tuning the Database Buffer Cache

One of the most commonly referred to numbers in the Oracle DBA world is the database buffer cache hit ratio. The database buffer cache is the area of the SGA that stores database data in memory blocks for access by user processes. Prior to Oracle8, the database buffer cache consisted of one buffer pool area. Starting with Oracle8, Oracle introduced multiple buffer pools. The primary buffer pool is referred to as the default buffer pool, and you can allocate optional keep and recycle buffer pools. The advent of multiple buffer pools also introduces the need to calculate the database buffer cache hit ratio for all three buffer pools, if you have allocated them.

The database buffer cache hit ratio represents the percentage of block-read requests that were satisfied by a logical read to the database buffer cache. A high ratio means that more reads from memory (logical reads) took place, and a low ratio means that more physical reads (from the disk) are required. Because logical reads involve reads to memory and physical reads involve reading from disks, it stands to reason that one would prefer that logical reads occur rather than physical ones.

NOTE The database buffer cache hit ratio, along with the many other ratios touted for monitoring and tuning purposes, is perhaps given a bit too much importance in the overall scheme of things. Granted, it is the classical method to use, but it is not the most effective. There are times when ratios can be incorrect. For example, certain database operations (such as recursive SQL and rollback segment operations) can artificially increase or reduce the database buffer cache hit ratio. Also, the nature of the database (data warehouse versus OLTP) can affect the hit ratio. In general, tuning and monitoring wait statistics (discussed in Chapter 17) is a more effective approach.

If you want to calculate the database buffer cache hit ratio of any of the buffer pools, you can use this fairly simple formula:

buffer cache hit ratio = 1 – (*physical reads*) / (*memory reads*)

To derive the numbers to use in this formula, you can use several methods:

- The V$SYSSTAT view to calculate the hit ratio of the default buffer pool only
- The X$KCBWS and X$KCBWBPD tables to calculate the hit ratio for any buffer pool
- The V$BUFFER_POOL_STATISTICS view to calculate the hit ratio for any buffer pool

The following sections describe how to use these views and tables, and then how to tune the hit ratio if necessary.

Calculating the Hit Ratio for the Default Buffer Pool

To calculate the hit ratio of the default buffer pool, you can use the V$SYSSTAT view. Use two of the V$SYSSTAT view's columns: the NAME column, which contains the name of the statistic, and the VALUE column, which contains the value of the statistic. You are interested in three different statistics:

- Physical reads, which is the total number of physical reads to the database datafiles
- Db block gets, which is the number of blocks in the buffer cache that were accessed for INSERT, UPDATE, and DELETE operations
- Consistent gets, which is the number of blocks accessed, using the consistent get mechanism, in the database buffer cache for I/O

Here are a query that uses the V$SYSSTAT view to calculate the hit ratio of the database and its results:

```
SELECT (1 - (sum(decode(name, 'physical reads', value, 0)) /
(SUM(DECODE (name, 'db block gets', value, 0)) +
SUM(DECODE (name, 'consistent gets', value, 0))))) buffer_hit_ratio
FROM v$sysstat;

BUFFER_HIT_RATIO
----------------
       .91295284
```

So, the hit ratio for this database is 91 percent—not bad, but it probably could be better. We'll look at some ways to tune the database buffer hit ratio after exploring the other methods for calculating it.

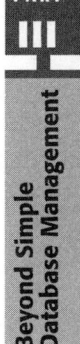

Calculating the Hit Ratio for Any Buffer Pool

An alternative to using the V$SYSSTAT view is to use two undocumented tables introduced in Oracle8i: X$KCBWS and X$KCBWBPD. As explained earlier in this chapter, V$ views are created from X$ tables. When an appropriate V$ view is not available, you can sometimes use X$ tables.

This method can be used to calculate the hit ratio of any of the buffer pools. Here is an example of a query that will provide the hit ratios for all the buffer pools (this particular query works in Oracle release 8.1.6.3 but not 8.1.7.0):

```
SELECT kcbwbpd.bp_name "Pool Name",
SUM(kcbwds.dbbget) "Block Gets",
SUM(kcbwds.conget) "Consistent Gets",
SUM(kcbwds.pread) "Physical Reads",
(1 - (SUM(kcbwds.pread)+1 ) / ( ( SUM(kcbwds.dbbget) + SUM(kcbwds.conget) +
   1) ) ) "Hit Ratio"
FROM x$kcbwds kcbwds, x$kcbwbpd kcbwbpd
 WHERE kcbwds.set_id >= kcbwbpd.bp_lo_sid
   AND kcbwds.set_id <= kcbwbpd.bp_hi_sid
   AND kcbwbpd.bp_size != 0
 GROUP BY kcbwbpd.bp_id, kcbwbpd.bp_name
 ORDER BY 1;
```

As another alternative, Oracle provides a script called `catperf.sql` that creates a view called V$BUFFER_POOL_STATISTICS, which will provide the same information as the preceding query. The V$BUFFER_POOL_STATISTICS table provides other buffer pool information in addition to hit ratio statistics, so it's worth running this script in your database if you are using multiple buffer pools. To calculate the hit ratio of your database using V$BUFFER_POOL_STATISTICS, use this query:

```
SELECT name, ( 1 - (physical_reads) /
( (db_block_gets + consistent_gets))) "Pool Hit Ratio"
FROM v$buffer_pool_statistics
WHERE db_block_gets + consistent_gets > 0;
```

Which will result in the following output:

```
NAME                 Pool Hit Ratio
-------------------- --------------
KEEP                              1
RECYCLE                           1
DEFAULT                    .8465218
```

CHECKING THE SGA   649

NOTE Due to bug 1491213, the X$KCBWDS table and V$BUFFER_POOL_STATISTICS view queries shown here will not work in Oracle release 8.1.7. This problem is supposed to be corrected in later releases. These queries do work in earlier versions.

Tuning the Database Buffer Cache Hit Ratio

The hit ratio can be skewed, either up or down, depending on your database. For example, if you are running a data warehouse environment, it would not be unusual to see hit ratios significantly less than 90 percent, especially if a great deal of ad hoc query activity is occurring. Still, the better you can tune the hit ratio, the better your database performance will be.

Also, keep in mind that the statistics used to calculate the hit ratio are cumulative, having been gathered since the database was last started. You might have an overall high hit ratio masking a very low hit ratio of a critical process. Fortunately, both the Oracle Statspack and the monitoring methodology we describe later in this chapter (in the "Using the Oracle Statspack" and "Introducing a Monitoring Methodology" sections, respectively) provide a method of seeing the statistics between a specific starting and ending time.

You can do several things to address a low hit ratio. The first is simply to add memory resources to the database buffer cache. To add memory to the database buffer cache, change the DB_BLOCK_BUFFERS parameter in the `init.ora` file.

WARNING Be careful not to increase memory to the point that the operating system starts paging memory in and out to disk. Paging has serious negative implications on database performance. To avoid paging, do not allocate more than 40 percent of overall available memory to the SGA. If you have multiple databases on the same system, this benchmark should be adjusted accordingly. For example, if you have ten databases and a large amount of memory installed on the system, it may be okay to use 50 percent of available memory.

If memory is a premium, what else can you do to improve the database buffer cache hit ratio? You can sometimes derive significant performance gains by tuning SQL statements, as explained in Chapter 16. By reducing I/O (which is the goal of SQL statement turning), you will reduce the need to access blocks in the SGA, thus reducing the need to go to disk to collect those blocks. Reducing I/O can also reduce latching issues and contention for blocks by different sessions.

While tuning SQL statements can help, a common misconception is that full table scans always seriously affect the hit ratio of a database. This is only partially true. In reality, full table scans do cause a great deal of physical I/O, but they do not age out that many blocks in the database buffer cache. Therefore, it is unlikely that a hot block (a block that is used often) in a properly allocated SGA will need to be reread from disk because of the effects of a full table scan. Full table scans are performance hogs for a lot of reasons, but knocking blocks out of the SGA isn't usually one of them.

NOTE You might be familiar with the DB_BLOCK_LRU_STATISTICS parameter and its associated X$KCBRBH table, which allowed the DBA to "simulate" adding or removing memory from the SGA. While this was available in versions as recent as Oracle release 8.0.6, it is not available in Oracle8i.

Analyzing the Database Buffer Cache

While you're considering hit ratios, you might want to analyze the database buffer cache itself. The X$BH view affords this opportunity. There is an associated view called V$BH, but there is more information in the X$BH view.

TIP To access the X$ tables, you should be logged in a SYS or INTERNAL. You can create synonyms and grant access to these tables to other schemas if you need to.

Using the X$BH view, you can determine how many of the allocated blocks are free, how many are currently in use, and how many have been modified. You might use this query to get the information:

```
SELECT decode(state, 0, 'Unused', 1, 'Modified', 2, 'Not Modified',
3,'Being Read','Other') dbbc_block_status, count(*)
FROM sys.x$bh
GROUP BY DECODE(state, 0, 'Unused', 1, 'Modified', 2, 'Not Modified',
3,'Being Read','Other')
```

Which will result in the following output:

```
DBBC_BLOCK_S    COUNT(*)
-----------   ----------
Modified          1451
Unused             597
```

This is just the tip of the iceberg in terms of the information you can derive from X$BH in Oracle8i. Let's look at a few other ways that you can use this table, which will give you some ideas for you own queries.

 WARNING *Never* change data in an X$ table (usually you can't anyway). In fact, a good rule of thumb is that you should never change *anything* in the SYS schema.

As explained in Chapter 5, midpoint insertion is Oracle's new method of controlling when a block is aged out of the SGA. Internally, the aging of a block depends on the touch count of each buffer. As the buffer is used, its touch count is increased. Oracle uses a formula to decide if the buffer should be aged out:

```
IF (touch count of buffer > _db_aging_hot_criteria) THEN
     Keep the buffer and increment the touch count.
     IF (_db_aging_stay_count >= _db_aging_hot_criteria)
     THEN
          half the touch count of the buffer
     ELSE
          set the buffer touch count to _db_aging_stay_count.
     END IF;
ELSE
     You may use this buffer
END IF
```

Notice that the criteria for the hidden parameters used in the formula are _DB_AGING_HOT_CRITERIA with a default value of 2 and _DB_AGING_STAY_COUNT with a default value of 0.

The advent of the touch count means that you can actually tell which object's buffers are in the SGA and how often they are used. Now you have a way of telling which blocks of an object are hot and which are not. Here is a query that will do just that:

```
COLUMN tch HEADING "Touch|Count"
SELECT a.owner, a.segment_name, c.file_name, b.dbablk "block", b.tch
FROM dba_extents a, x$bh b, dba_data_files c
WHERE b.file#=c.file_id and
b.dbablk >= a.block_id
AND b.dbablk <= a.block_id + a.blocks
AND b.tch > 0
AND a.owner != 'SYS'
ORDER BY 5 desc;
```

Here are the partial results of this query:

OWNER	SEGMENT_NA	FILE_NAME	block	Touch Count
SCOTT	NEWTABLE	D:\ORACLE\ORADATA\ORA816\SYSTEM01.DBF	2,240	18
SCOTT	NEWTABLE	D:\ORACLE\ORADATA\ORA816\SYSTEM01.DBF	2,350	18
SCOTT	NEWTABLE	D:\ORACLE\ORADATA\ORA816\SYSTEM01.DBF	2,356	18
SCOTT	EMPLOYEE	D:\ORACLE\ORADATA\ORA816\SYSTEM01.DBF	6,259	17
SCOTT	NEWTABLE	D:\ORACLE\ORADATA\ORA816\SYSTEM01.DBF	2,357	16
SCOTT	NEWTABLE	D:\ORACLE\ORADATA\ORA816\SYSTEM01.DBF	2,755	1
SCOTT	NEWTABLE	D:\ORACLE\ORADATA\ORA816\SYSTEM01.DBF	2,243	1
SCOTT	NEWTABLE	D:\ORACLE\ORADATA\ORA816\SYSTEM01.DBF	2,244	1

To find out how hot specific tables are, you might craft a query like this:

```
SELECT a.owner, a.segment_name, sum(b.tch) "Sum Touches"
FROM dba_extents a, x$bh b
WHERE b.dbablk >= a.block_id
AND b.dbablk <= a.block_id + a.blocks
AND a.owner != 'SYS'
GROUP BY a.owner, a.segment_name
ORDER BY 3 desc;
```

Which will result in the following output:

OWNER	SEGMENT_NA	Sum Touches
SCOTT	NEWTABLE	739
SCOTT2	BONUS	520
SCOTT2	SALGRADE	399
SCOTT	EMPLOYEE	237
SCOTT2	DUMMY	169
SCOTT2	EMP	46
SCOTT2	DEPT	45
SCOTT	DUMMY	13
SCOTT	SYS_C00767	5
SCOTT	PAY_TABLE	4
SCOTT	HOLD_EVENT	3

So, it appears that the NEWTABLE object in SCOTT is a hot table. This might imply that you should concentrate on making the queries that access this table more efficient.

Monitoring and Tuning the Data Dictionary Cache

In Chapter 5, we reviewed the structures that comprise the SGA. One such structure is the shared pool. A component of the shared pool is the data dictionary cache, which is used to store data dictionary rows in the SGA. Much like the database buffer cache, the shared pool has various hit ratios that can be calculated to determine its performance. Here, we will look at the data dictionary cache hit ratio and the dictionary cache miss ratio.

Calculating the Data Dictionary Cache Hit Ratio

The formula for calculating the data dictionary cache hit ratio is a bit different from that used for the database buffer cache hit ratio. Here, you are looking for the ratio of attempts to get an object from the cache to the number of times you were not able to get the object (and thus, needed to read it from disk). The formula to calculate the ratio is as follows:

dictionary cache hit ratio = 1 − ((# failed attempts to get object) / (# successful block gets + # failed attempts to get block))

You can get these numbers from the V$ROWCACHE view. Use two of this view's columns: the GETMISSES column, which represents the number of failed attempts to get the object, and the GETS column, which represents the number of successful gets. This leads to a query and results that look like this:

```
SELECT (( 1 - (sum(getmisses) /
(sum(gets) + sum(getmisses)))) * 100) "Hit Ratio"
FROM v$rowcache
WHERE gets + getmisses <> 0;

Hit Ratio
---------
90.341686
```

If the hit ratio is less than 95 percent, you probably need to add memory to the shared pool. To do so, increase the SHARED_POOL_SIZE parameter in the database parameter file (init.ora). Unfortunately, doing so will add memory to the entire shared pool, so it is difficult to the gauge the impact of adding a specific amount of memory. Note that this ratio will be 0 when the system has started, because there will be nothing in the data dictionary cache to get.

Calculating the Dictionary Cache Miss Ratios

The dictionary cache miss ratio tells you how often the system went into the dictionary cache and found what it was looking for. You can use the following formula to calculate the dictionary cache miss ratio:

dictionary cache miss ratio = dictionary cache get misses / dictionary cache gets

To get these numbers, use the GETMISSES and GETS columns in the V$ROWCACHE view. The query to monitor the dictionary cache miss ratio and its results look like this:

```
SELECT (SUM(getmisses)/SUM(gets))*100 "Dict Cache Miss Ratio"
FROM v$rowcache;


Dict Cache Miss Ratio
---------------------
            17.877095
```

What you want to see for the dictionary cache miss ratio here is a big, fat zero. If you are seeing a number more than 10 percent or so, as in the example here, consider increasing the shared pool. There isn't much more you can do to tune this performance.

Monitoring and Tuning the Library Cache

The library cache is where Oracle stores object definitions, SQL statements, and PL/SQL objects for use in areas called *namespaces*. For monitoring purposes, you're interested in the efficiency of the use of the library cache.

Library cache misses can occur in either the parse or execute phase of a SQL operation. If a parse call is made by an application, and the parsed statement is not already in the shared pool, Oracle will need to parse the statement, and a library cache miss will result. If an application makes an execute call for a SQL statement, it is possible that the parsed representation of that statement will have been aged out of the library cache by another operation. In this case, Oracle will reparse the statement before executing it. The first solution to both of these problems is to make sure that you have sufficient memory allocated to the shared pool. This is done using the SHARED_POOL_SIZE parameter in `init.ora`. If you are having problems with misses on the parse calls, review your SQL statements for reusability (see Chapter 16 for more on SQL statement tuning).

To monitor the library cache, you are interested in three statistics: the cache hit ratio, the cache reload ratio, and the library cache pin hit ratio. The queries to retrieve this information use the V$LIBRARYCACHE view. As with most dynamic performance views, this view provides statistics about the library cache since system startup. The view contains several rows, each of which contains statistics for a type of item kept in the library cache (SQL, triggers, procedures, and so on).

You also want to monitor the shared pool to determine if the shared pool reserved size is allocated properly. You can find shared pool information in the V$SHARED_POOL_RESERVED view.

Calculating the Library Cache Hit Ratio

The library cache hit ratio is a measure of how often the system finds the library cache objects already loaded in the cache and how many times the system needs to get them off the disk. The formula for calculating the library cache hit ratio is:

> library cache hit ratio = # times object found in cache / (# times object found in cache + # times object needed to be reloaded from disk)

To calculate the hit ratio, use the V$LIBRARYCACHE view. The RELOADS column represents the number of times Oracle went looking for a statement in the library cache, didn't find it (or a part of it), and therefore needed to reload it. The PINS column represents the number of times that Oracle tried to *pin* the object. An item must be pinned in order to be used, and an item can be pinned several times after being looked up. You want to see that library cache objects are pinned without needing to be reloaded.

The query to monitor the library cache hit ratio and its results look like this:

```
SELECT SUM(pins) / ( SUM(pins) + SUM(reloads) )
"Lib Cache Hit Ratio"
FROM v$librarycache;

Lib Cache Hit Ratio
-------------------
         .97988166
```

What you are looking for here is a number close to 100 percent. Anything greater than 94 percent is fine.

Calculating the Library Cache Reload Ratio

The library cache hit ratio measures the overall hit ratio of the library cache. The library cache reload ratio differs from the hit ratio in that it measures the reuse of SQL objects that have already been in the library cache, aged out, and then reloaded.

The library cache reload ratio should be as near to 0 as possible. A low cache reload ratio indicates that Oracle did not need to reload any previously loaded library cache items (say, for example, a piece of PL/SQL code). If the library cache reload ratio is high (say greater than 0.5 to 1 percent, depending on your database), you should check for SQL statement reusability (see Chapter 16). A high cache reload ratio indicates that the database needs to reload library cache items once they have already been loaded. Since this requires additional disk I/O, it becomes an expensive operation. A high library cache reload ratio is likely to be associated with a low library cache hit ratio.

The formula for calculating the library cache reload ratio is:

*library cache reload ratio = (reloads / pins) * 100*

You can use the RELOADS and SUM columns of the V$LIBRARYCACHE view to calculate this ratio, with this query:

```
SELECT ((SUM(reloads) / SUM(pins) ) * 100) "Library Cache Reload Ratio"
FROM v$librarycache;


Library Cache Reload Ratio
--------------------------
                 2.0347098
```

This example shows a reload ratio of 2 percent, which is too high. Adding memory to the shared pool would likely help. Also, you can pin certain packages in the shared pool with the Oracle-supplied package DBMS_SHARED_POOL.KEEP, preventing them from being aged out. It's a good idea to figure out what large packages are commonly used in your database and pin them in the SGA every time you start your database. Also, keep in mind that unlike the hit ratio, the library cache reload ratio is not affected by database startup and shutdown operations.

TIP In Chapter 16's discussion of tuning SQL statements, we emphasize tuning issues that relate to library cache reuse of SQL statements, such as bind variables. In a nutshell, it's important to make sure that a SQL statement that is going to be used often is reusable.

Calculating the Library Cache Pin Hit Ratio

The library cache pin hit ratio is a measure of how often Oracle executed an object that was already in the library cache and was valid. This ratio should be as close to 100 percent as possible. The formula for the library cache pin hit ratio is simple:

library cache pin hit ratio = pin hits / pins

Use the PINHITS and PINS columns from the V$LIBRARYCACHE view to calculate the pin hit ratio, with this query:

```
SELECT (sum(pinhits)/sum(pins))*100 "Lib Cache Pin Hit Ratio"
FROM v$librarycache;
```

```
Lib Cache Pin Hit Ratio
-----------------------
             85.919215
```

The result of 85 percent could mean that the database needs to be tuned. However, in this case, the database had just been started, so the ratio is low.

Monitoring the Reserved Area of the Shared Pool

The shared pool contains the reserved area of memory, which is dedicated to the loading of large objects. The reserved area is designed to reduce fragmentation of the shared pool. Oracle automatically sets the reserved area in the shared pool to 5 percent of the overall shared pool size. Generally, this setting works fine. However, if the reserved area is too small or too big, you need to know about it and do something about it. (If your system is not using all of the space allocated to the shared pool, you're wasting memory.)

To see how much memory is allocated to the shared pool reserved area, use this query:

```
SELECT name, value
FROM v$parameter
WHERE name = 'shared_pool_reserved_size';

NAME                      VALUE
------------------------- -------
shared_pool_reserved_size 150000
```

To monitor the shared pool, you want to look at the V$SHARED_POOL_RESERVED view. Here, you are interested in free space, requests, request misses, and request failures information. The query and result look like this:

```
SELECT free_space, requests, request_misses, request_failures
FROM v$shared_pool_reserved;

FREE_SPACE   REQUESTS  REQUEST_MISSES  REQUEST_FAILURES
----------   --------  --------------  ----------------
    150000         20               3                 1
```

The REQUEST_MISSES column indicates that there was insufficient memory in the shared pool reserved area, and Oracle needed to drop some objects from the shared pool reserved area to make room for the new object. In other words, Oracle employed the LRU algorithm to age out objects from the shared pool reserved area. By itself, this does not mean that anything is wrong.

The REQUEST_FAILURES column shows a count of the number of times that no memory could be found to load an object into the reserved area of the shared pool.

The value of this column is associated with ORA-4031 errors (indicating Oracle was unable to allocate memory in the shared pool).

You can use the following criteria to determine if the shared pool reserved size is allocated properly:

- If REQUEST_MISSES is 0 or very small and not increasing over time, this may indicate that there is excessive memory allocated to the structure.
- If FREE_SPACE is more than 50 percent of the space allocated to the shared pool reserved size, you may have too much memory allocated to the shared pool reserved area.
- If REQUEST_FAILURES is anything above 0 and it continues to increase, this indicates that insufficient memory has been allocated to the reserved pool area.

Checking for I/O Contention

I/O contention can cause serious database performance problems. To monitor the database's I/O performance, you can check for problems with system I/O, session I/O, and rollback segment usage.

Monitoring System File I/O

The number one cause of database-related problems (that is, problems where the database is to blame) is related to file I/O issues. The primary view for monitoring database datafile performance is V$FILESTAT. This view, like many others, is reset at database startup, so the figures you get from the raw view are those for the database during its entire life since startup. The following query will show you the file system names, the datafile names, the numbers of physical reads on the file systems, the number of physical writes on the file systems, the total read time, the total write time, and the average I/O time.

```
SELECT name, phyrds "PRD", phywrts "PWR", readtim "RTM",
writetim "WTM", avgiotim "ATM"
FROM v$filestat a, v$dbfile b
WHERE a.file#=b.file#
ORDER BY avgiotim;
```

NAME	PRD	PWR	RTM	WTM	ATM
D:\ORACLE\ORADATA\ROBT\SYSTEM01.DBF	1861	10	2904	4	0
D:\ORACLE\ORADATA\ROBT\RBS01.DBF	7	8	13	2	0
D:\ORACLE\ORADATA\ROBT\QUARTER_THREE_01.DBF	3	1	0	0	6
D:\ORACLE\ORADATA\ROBT\TEMP01.DBF	3	1	0	0	7
D:\ORACLE\ORADATA\ROBT\QUARTER_FOUR_01.DBF	3	1	0	0	8
D:\ORACLE\ORADATA\ROBT\RBS_TEST.DBF	3	1	0	0	8
D:\ORACLE\ORADATA\ROBT\LOCAL_AUTO_01.DBF	3	1	0	0	8
D:\ORACLE\ORADATA\ROBT\DR01A.DBF	3	1	0	0	12
D:\ORACLE\ORADATA\ROBT\QUARTER_TWO_01.DBF	3	1	0	0	12
D:\ORACLE\ORADATA\ROBT\QUARTER_ONE_01.DBF	3	1	0	0	12
D:\ORACLE\ORADATA\ROBT\USERS01.DBF	3	1	0	0	13
D:\ORACLE\ORADATA\ROBT\ROBT_OBJECTS_01.DBF	3	1	0	0	13
D:\ORACLE\ORADATA\ROBT\OEMREP01.DBF	3	1	0	0	13
D:\ORACLE\ORADATA\ROBT\INDX01.DBF	3	1	0	0	14

Note that the total read time (RTM), total write time (WTM), and average I/O time (ATM) columns will not be populated if the TIMED_STATISTICS parameter is not turned on, as discussed in the "How Do You Get More Information from V$ Views?" section earlier in this chapter.

You're looking for a few things in this report. The first is unbalanced I/O. In the sample report, notice that all of the database datafiles are in one file system. This may be bad news, depending on the hardware. On hardware where each physical disk is represented by a directory, or file system, you should spread these datafiles onto different disks for better performance.

TIP Try to stripe your data out evenly among as many disks as possible. Work with your disk manufacturer, your operating system manufacturer, and the manufacturer of the computer itself to determine how you can best spread out your data on multiple disks. Also, work with the different manufacturers to determine such things as the best stripe size for the combination of equipment, the best way to reduce single points of failures on disk systems, and any other issues that might be specific to your hardware.

The second thing to look at is the balance of I/O times among the different datafiles to confirm that no single tablespace is getting blasted by reads or writes—a condition that can affect performance. Don't underestimate the impact of distributing I/O. It can make a huge difference and it's worth the time, effort, and cost to do it right.

Finally, you want to check the average I/O time (ATM) column. This column, new in Oracle8i, represents the average time, in hundredths of a second, spent on I/O. Anything above a 40 warrants review. A high average I/O time may indicate several problems, including an I/O imbalance or excessive full table scans on the database. It could even be a prelude to a disk problem (often, before a disk will crash, I/O times will start increasing because of errors and error corrections that occur).

 TIP If you have a hot database datafile that contains just a single large table (or that large table represents a majority of the data in the tablespace), you might benefit from Oracle's partitioning option. Refer to Chapter 24 for more information about using this Oracle feature. If you determine you need to move datafiles and the like, refer to Chapter 7 for more information.

Monitoring Session File I/O

One rough session can spoil a DBA's lazy workday. This is particularly true if you have many users who don't have a clue about how to write efficient SQL (which, in my experience, is more often than not). Well, we've got the goods on them. We'll show you how to monitor specific session I/O use, and later in this chapter, we will put in place a monitoring program to wake us ... I mean alert us ... when a user is abusing the system.

The query for monitoring specific session I/O uses a join between the V$SESSION view, which contains session information, and the V$SQLAREA view, which contains the specific SQL being executed by users, as well as I/O information for those sessions. It uses the following columns in these views:

- **SID,** which identifies the session that is running. Each connection to the database is given an SID.

- **USERNAME,** which identifies the user who signed onto the system.

- **EXECUTIONS,** which is the number of times the SQL statement was executed. A low execution number indicates several things, including the possibility that the statement was not written to be reusable.

- **STATUS,** which is the status of the session. It might be active or inactive.

- **DISK_READS,** which is the total disk reads that this SQL statement has caused during its execution.

- LOADS, which is how many times this SQL statement been loaded. The higher this number, the more times that the SQL statement has been aged out and needed to be reloaded.
- SORTS, which is the number of sorts for this statement and any children.
- SQL_TEXT, which is the text of the associated SQL statement associated with this SQL area.
- PHYSICAL READS, which is the total physical reads that this session has performed. Note that this is the number of blocks read, *not* the number of I/O requests, which is an important distinction, since multiple blocks can be written in a single I/O.
- PHYSICAL WRITES, which is the total physical writes that this session has performed.
- SORTS (DISK), which is the total number of disk sorts that the session has performed.

This query contains information specific to the session and information specific to the SQL statement that the session is running. The query and result are shown below. Note that the results extend well beyond 80 characters, so we've divided them into two sections to fit here (repeating the SID column for reference).

```
SELECT a.sid, a.username, b.executions, a.status,
b.disk_reads "DskRds", b.loads, b.sorts, c.value "PReads",
d.value "PWrites", e.value "SortDsk" , b.sql_text
FROM v$session a, v$sqlarea b, v$sesstat c,
v$sesstat d, v$sesstat e,
v$statname f, v$statname g, v$statname h
WHERE a.sql_address=b.address
AND f.statistic#=c.statistic#
AND g.statistic#=d.statistic#
AND h.statistic#=e.statistic#
AND f.name = 'physical reads'
AND g.name = 'physical writes'
AND h.name = 'sorts (disk)'
AND a.sid=c.sid
AND a.sid=d.sid
AND a.sid=e.sid
ORDER BY 1 desc;
```

```
SID  USERNAME  EXECUTIONS  STATUS    DskRds  LOADS  SORTS  PReads  PWrites
---  --------  ----------  ------    ------  -----  -----  ------  -------
249  CICS01            29  CACHED         0      1      0    3359        0
248  CICS03          1064  INACTIVE      51      1      0       0        0
continued
SID  SortDsk   SQL_TEXT
---  -------   ----------------------------------------------------------
249        0   BEGIN pkg_3593_sel_m_state_waybill.close_cursor; END;
248        0   select value$ from props$ where name = 'GLOBAL_DB_NAME'
```

In this example, the report is ordered by the SID of the session. You can just as easily sort it by any of the other columns. For example, if you are concerned about sessions doing a lot of physical I/O, you might sort by physical reads. In fact, you might want to produce multiple versions of this report, sorting on different criteria.

 WARNING The previous query works in Oracle releases 7.3.4.4 and 8.1.6.3. However, on Oracle release 8.1.5.0, you'll run into a bug (#929577) that causes it to crash with an ORA-600 error (because of the descending order by clause in the query).

Monitoring Rollback Segment Usage

Rollback segments are sometimes overlooked as an area to monitor. We, being lazy DBAs, want to monitor rollback segment usage, to make sure that problems with the rollback segments don't sneak up on us.

If your rollback segments extents are too small, this can cause performance problems when Oracle is forced to add extents to the rollback segment during query operations. Comparing the total size of rollback segments to the amount of available space in the rollback segment tablespace can show you if there is a problem. If there is little free space in the tablespace, you may have rollback segments that are too large (perhaps the rollback segments do not have an OPTIMAL setting). If you find that the rollback segment tablespace is often full of free space, you may have allocated too much space to the rollback segment tablespace.

The primary view of interest here is V$ROLLSTAT, which provides information that helps to determine if the rollback segment is optimally set up, including a column that reports the high-water mark for each rollback segment. Here is a description of the columns used in the query to monitor rollback segment usage:

- NAME, which is the name of the rollback segment.

- RSSIZE, which is the current size of the rollback segment.
- EXTENTS, which is how many extents make up the current rollback segment. While running long transactions, you can watch the rollback segment grow by monitoring this column and the RSSIZE column.
- WRITES, which is how many bytes have been written to that rollback segment overall since instance startup.
- TRANS_TBS_WAITS, which shows whether the rollback segment headers had waits for them. Generally, this indicates that you need to add rollback segments.
- GETS, which is the number of header get requests for the rollback segment.
- WAITS, which is how many segment header waits have occurred.
- OPTSIZE, which is the OPTIMAL setting for the rollback segment.
- HWMSIZE, which is the high-water mark of the rollback segment. This is the largest that the rollback segment has grown to since the database last started up. The current size of the rollback segment may be smaller than this if OPTIMAL is set.
- SHRINKS, which is the number of extent de-allocations that have occurred in an effort to shrink a rollback segment back to its OPTIMAL setting. The operation to shrink the rollback segment to OPTIMAL takes place in several different extent de-allocation operations. The SHRINKS statistic is increased with each extent de-allocation operation. If this number is excessive, rollback segments may be sized improperly.
- WRAPS, which shows how many times a transaction moves from one extent to the next in a rollback segment. Wraps are generally not very expensive operations. Excessive wraps might indicate that the rollback segment extent sizes are too small.
- EXTENDS, which indicates if new extents were created. If the transaction needs to enter another extent, but an extent is not available, Oracle will create a new extent in the rollback segment for the transaction to use. Extends are very expensive operations. If you are seeing excessive extends, you should consider rebuilding your rollback segments so they are sized properly. Review Chapter 6 for information on the creation and sizing of rollback segments.
- STATUS, which is the status of the rollback segment. It may be ONLINE or OFFLINE PENDING. OFFLINE rollback segments will not appear in this view.

The query looks something like this:

```
SELECT a.name, b.rssize, b.extents, b.writes, b.gets,
b.waits, b.optsize, b.hwmsize, b.shrinks, b.wraps,
b.extends, b.status
FROM v$rollname a, v$rollstat b
WHERE a.usn=b.usn;
```

Here are the results of the query. This report extends well beyond 80 characters, so we've divided the results into two sections to fit here (repeating the NAME column for reference). I generally print it in landscape mode. You can set the line size to 132 in SQL*Plus when you generate this report, so it will be more readable.

NAME	RSSIZE	EXTENTS	WRITES	GETS	WAITS	OPTSIZE	HWMSIZE
SYSTEM	407552	8	1284	31	0		407552
RB0	7268352	29	214	27	0		7268352
RB1	12900352	51	0	17	0		12900352

continued

NAME	SHRINKS	WRAPS	EXTENDS	STATUS
SYSTEM	0	0	0	ONLINE
RB0	0	0	0	ONLINE
RB1	0	0	0	ONLINE

Lurking Database Threats

Part of monitoring database use is finding threats that, like a submarine, lie just beneath the surface. Sometimes, small problems can mount up, and suddenly, you have a major problem. An example of this might be a user whose temporary tablespace is not changed from the default of SYSTEM. At the beginning, this won't be a big problem. Down the road, it can cause a huge problem. Let's look at some ways to monitor for these types of threats.

NOTE Migrated and chained rows in a table are also a database threat. In cases where a row was inserted in the table and later expanded, that row may no longer fit its original block. Depending on the size of the row and the space available in the object, Oracle may choose to chain or migrate the row. See Chapter 16 for details on row chaining, spanning, and migration, and how to correct these problems when you discover them.

Monitoring User Setup

You need to monitor how users are set up. You want to make sure that no users are inadvertently set up to use the SYSTEM tablespace as their default tablespace or as their temporary tablespace (which, unfortunately, is the Oracle default). Also, you may want to keep an eye on users whose accounts are about to expire, and you may want to know when their accounts were created.

NOTE If you have users, even SYS, whose tablespaces default to SYSTEM, you need to change the default tablespaces of those users to something else. For temporary tablespace, I generally leave SYS's default tablespace set to SYSTEM.

The following query produces a report that provides all of the user setup monitoring and reporting you need:

```
SELECT username, account_status, lock_date,
    expiry_date, default_tablespace, temporary_tablespace, created
FROM dba_users
WHERE account_status != 'OPEN' OR
Lock_date IS NOT NULL OR
Expiry_date IS NOT NULL OR
Default_tablespace = 'SYSTEM' OR
Temporary_tablespace = 'SYSTEM';
```

USERNAME	ACCOUNT_STATUS	LOCK_DATE	EXPIRY_DA	DEFAULT_TA	TEMPORARY_	CREATED
SYS	OPEN			SYSTEM	TEMP	21-DEC-00
SYSTEM	OPEN			SYSTEM	SYSTEM	21-DEC-00
OUTLN	OPEN			SYSTEM	SYSTEM	21-DEC-00
DBSNMP	OPEN			SYSTEM	SYSTEM	21-DEC-00

Monitoring Fragmentation of Tablespace Free Space

Free space fragmentation can cause an object that normally would be able to extend in the tablespace to not be able to be created or allocated an additional extent because there appears to be insufficient contiguous space to Oracle. While it is true that SMON does coalesce adjacent tablespace free space chunks, it is also true that it doesn't do this all the time, and it can be disabled by setting the PCTINCREASE default for a tablespace to 0.

Generally, fragmented free space in a tablespace is not a performance issue, but rather an operational issue. This is because it can cause user processes to fail due to Oracle's inability to allocate space for an extent. Since it is an issue that can affect availability of the database for an application, free space fragmentation should be monitored on a regular basis.

You can use the DBA_FREE_SPACE view to monitor the free space fragmentation situation. This query looks at each tablespace and reports how many chunks of free space there are and the size of the largest chunk of free space:

```
SELECT tablespace_name, COUNT(*) "Chunks", MAX(bytes) "Largest Chunk"
FROM dba_free_space
GROUP BY tablespace_name;
```

TABLESPACE_NAME	Chunks	Largest Chunk
DRSYS	1	1536000
INDX	1	10483712
LOCAL_AUTO	1	2031616
OBJECTS	1	9388032
OEM_REPOSITORY	1	5240832
QUARTER_FOUR	2	5087232
QUARTER_ONE	2	4984832
QUARTER_THREE	1	5128192
QUARTER_TWO	2	5046272
RBS_TEST	1	387072
SYSTEM	7	34250752
TEMP	1	2095104
USERS	2	61440

If the number of chunks is high, and the largest chunk is very low, you have a problem. The first thing to do is to issue an ALTER TABLESPACE {*table_name*} COALESCE command. This will force Oracle to coalesce the adjacent free space chunks in the tablespace. If this does not solve the problem, you will need to either defragment the tablespace or add space to it. Which option you choose depends on a number of factors, such as how much contiguous space you can gain if you defragment the tablespace and the cost in time to defragment the tablespace versus the cost of adding additional space to the tablespace.

Monitoring Fragmentation of Segments

As the database adds extents to segments, Oracle doesn't promise to add them in contiguous form. It is beneficial for segments to be written contiguously, because then the disk head doesn't need to move from place to place to find all the data. The less contiguous the data, the more likely the system is prone to I/O issues, as the disks are being forced to move back and forth. Junior DBAs sometimes mistake the issue of contiguous extents with the notion that multiple extents are a bad thing. This is not altogether true. You can have an object of many extents that will perform just as well during a read as an object of one extent, as long as those extents are contiguous. If an object is made up of multiple extents (and this was not done on purpose), this might be a sign of a couple of things:

- The object may be sized incorrectly such that it is creating additional extents (which are expensive operations) with some frequency.

- Large numbers of extents can cause performance problems with certain DDL statements (such as the TRUNCATE *table* command).

- The object's extents could be noncontiguous, and therefore causing performance problems. This is more of a problem with sequential access to segments (for example full table scans) than with random access to segments (for example, index lookups).

To discover if there are any noncontiguous extents, you should monitor objects with multiple extents. Here is a query that will do just that:

```
SELECT DISTINCT a.owner, a.segment_name, b.extents
FROM dba_extents a, (select owner, segment_name, count(*) AS extents
FROM dba_extents
WHERE owner != 'SYS'
GROUP BY owner, segment_name) b
WHERE (SELECT COUNT(*) FROM dba_extents WHERE owner=a.owner AND
segment_name=a.segment_name) > 1
AND block_id+blocks NOT IN (SELECT block_id FROM dba_extents WHERE
   owner=a.owner AND
segment_name=a.segment_name)
AND extent_id != (SELECT MAX(extent_id) FROM dba_extents
```

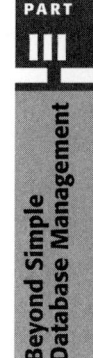

```
WHERE owner=a.owner AND segment_name=a.segment_name)
AND a.owner != 'SYS'
AND a.owner=b.owner
AND a.segment_name=b.segment_name;
```

NOTE Note that the SYS user is excluded here. You can choose to include SYS or not, as you wish. I typically do not include SYS, because it would include the data dictionary, which I am not likely to defragment since it means I need to re-create the database. See Chapter 4 for information about how to build your database so the data dictionary is less likely to become fragmented.

Here is the output of the query:

OWNER	SEGMENT_NAME	EXTENTS
BMC_SMGR	BMC_BTD	2
SYSTEM	DBA25$	5
SYSTEM	EPC_MULTI_VIEWS	2
SYSTEM	PLAN_TABLE	2
SYSTEM	RETURN_COUNT	7
SYSTEM	TEST_RGF	4
SYSTEM	XP_INSTANCE_PARAMS	2
SYSTEM	XP_OBJECT	2
SYSTEM	XP_SQL	2
SYSTEM	XP_USER_RULE	3
SYSTEM	XP_USER_RULE_IDX_01	3

WARNING This query is somewhat slow and can be disk-intensive. I suggest running it only on off hours and perhaps once a week.

This query will detect segments with noncontiguous extents. Keep in mind that noncontiguous extents (even a large number of them) are not in and of themselves a bad thing. They can cause problems with certain DDL operations, and they may impact sequential disk-access performance slightly. The first things to check if an object is adding extents at a rapid pace are the object's storage settings (for example, INITIAL and NEXT) and physical attribute settings (for example, PCTFREE).

Monitoring Inefficient Block Usage in an Object

In Chapter 6, we discussed the importance of the STORAGE clause when creating an object like a table or an index. In particular, the PCTFREE and PCTUSED keywords can be used to aid Oracle in efficiently storing data in the blocks assigned to the object. Unfortunately, incorrectly setting these parameters can lead to a situation where Oracle data blocks are not being used to their fullest capacity. Of course, you can't always know how much a table is going to be used—whether or not it will have a great deal of INSERT/UPDATE or DELETE activity. Because DBAs are not fortune-tellers, we need to have a way to monitor these objects and make sure that they are storing the data in such a way that space is not being wasted.

The following query is for tables. It will work only if you have analyzed the table.

```
SELECT /*+ ORDERED */  u.name owner, o.name   table_name,
   SUBSTR(TO_CHAR(100 * t.rowcnt / (
         FLOOR((p.value - 66 - t.initrans * 24) /
             GREATEST(t.avgrln + 2, 11))
         * t.blkcnt ),'999.00' ), 2) ||'%'   density
FROM
   sys.tab$  t,
   ( SELECT value FROM sys.v_$parameter
     WHERE name = 'db_file_multiblock_read_count' ) m,
   sys.obj$  o, sys.user$  u,
   (SELECT value FROM sys.v_$parameter WHERE name = 'db_block_size')  p
WHERE
   t.tab# IS NULL AND t.blkcnt > m.value AND
   t.chncnt = 0 AND   t.avgspc > t.avgrln AND
   CEIL(( t.blkcnt - t.rowcnt /
       FLOOR((p.value - 66 - t.initrans * 24) /
           GREATEST(t.avgrln + 2, 11))) / m.value ) > 0 AND
   o.obj# = t.obj# AND o.owner# != 0 AND
   u.user# = o.owner#
ORDER BY 2;
```

TIP If you are not analyzing tables because you want to run in rule mode, you can analyze the table, run this query, and then delete the statistics. Refer to Chapters 7 and 16 for more information about using the ANALYZE command and creating and deleting statistics on objects.

Here is the resulting output from the query:

```
OWNER        TABLE_NAME            DENSITY
----------   --------------------  -------
POR_OWN      SSEPDOCUMENT          74.56%
POR_OWN      SSEPMESSENGER         28.65%
POR_OWN      SSEPOBJECTREPOS       73.36%
POR_OWN      SSEPPROFILE           66.11%
POR_OWN      SSEPRELATIONSHIPS     72.05%
POR_OWN      SSEPTEMPLATELOOKUP    82.46%
POR_OWN      SSEPTRANSLOG          88.89%
POR_OWN      SSEPUSER              61.39%
```

You are interested in tables where the average block utilization is low, say 75 percent or less. Now, for some tables, there may be a reason for the low utilization. Small lookup tables typically seem to have low utilization, but this is of inconsequential impact since they are small tables. However, you might find tables where space is not being used to its potential. In that case, review your use of PCTFREE and PCTUSED.

NOTE The first time I ran the table block usage query at a client site, I found several tables that were very poorly used. It was quite evident that the DBAs didn't monitor their databases very well. I found tables that had many multiple extents where most of the blocks were sitting around 50 percent used. I found tables that they were doing direct loads into with SQL*Loader. The client was deleting the old data from the tables rather than truncating, which caused the tables to grow. The client kept adding space, thinking the loads were just getting bigger. As you can see, monitoring a database can save a lot of things, including the cost of buying additional disk storage.

Monitoring Browned-Out Indexes

We discussed the concept of browned-out indexes in Chapter 6. This query reports on browned-out indexes:

```
SELECT /*+ ordered */
  u.name Index_Owner , o.name   index_name,
  SUBSTR(TO_CHAR(100 * i.rowcnt * (SUM(h.avgcln) + 11) /
       (i.leafcnt * (p.value - 66 - i.initrans * 24)),
     '999.00'), 2) || '%'  density,
  FLOOR((1 - i.pctfree$/100) * i.leafcnt - i.rowcnt *
  (SUM(h.avgcln) + 11) /
```

```
      (p.value - 66 - i.initrans * 24)) extra_blocks
FROM
   sys.ind$   i, sys.icol$   ic, sys.hist_head$   h,
   ( SELECT kvisval   value from sys.x$kvis
      WHERE kvistag = 'kcbbkl' )   p,
   sys.obj$   o, sys.user$   u
WHERE
   i.leafcnt > 1 and i.type# IN (1,4,6) AND
   ic.obj# = i.obj# AND h.obj# = i.bo# AND
   h.intcol# = ic.intcol# AND o.obj# = i.obj# AND
   o.owner# != 0 AND u.user# = o.owner#
GROUP BY u.name, o.name, i.rowcnt, i.leafcnt,
   i.initrans, i.pctfree$, p.value
HAVING
   50 * i.rowcnt * (sum(h.avgcln) + 11)
   < (i.leafcnt * (p.value - 66 - i.initrans * 24)) *
         (50 - i.pctfree$) AND
         FLOOR((1 - i.pctfree$/100) * i.leafcnt -
      i.rowcnt * (SUM(h.avgcln) + 11) /
      (p.value - 66 - i.initrans * 24)
      ) > 0
ORDER BY 3 desc, 2;
```

INDEX_OWNER	INDEX_NAME	DENSITY	EXTRA_BLOCKS
POR_OWN	SSEP_REL_PARENT	59.44%	19
POR_OWN	SSEP_REL_CHILD	55.13%	24

The DENSITY column indicates how full an average block of an index is. In this example, the indexes are about half full. The EXTRA_BLOCKS column indicates how many blocks would likely be recovered if you rebuilt (or coalesced) the index. If an index shows up on this report, it's a good idea to rebuild it. Of course, with Oracle's online index rebuild feature, this is a piece of cake.

You can add even more block information to your analysis if you use the statistics in the INDEX_STATS table, generated by the ANALYZE VALIDATE command (discussed in Chapter 7). This lets you learn a great deal more about your indexes—not just whether they are browned out, but also whether you have properly set the PCTFREE value. Indeed, you should consider validating your indexes regularly (unless it seriously impacts system performance, and you do need to be careful about that). You can store the INDEX_STATS data in another table (say, INDEX_STAT_HISTORY) and perform later queries against that table (assuming its structure is the same as INDEX_STATS and that it also includes a date column and a schema owner column to make each row unique).

Monitoring Resource Usage

New in Oracle8i is the ability to monitor resource limitations. This means that you can measure resource usage, such as the maximum number of processes that have been attached to the database since the database was first up and how many processes are currently attached. This is facilitated through the new Oracle8i view V$RESOURCE_LIMIT. This view reports the resource name, current use, maximum use since the system was up, the initial limit that the resource was set to, and the absolute limiting value for the resource.

The limit shown as the initial limit is a soft limit of sorts; many of the SGA initial limits are expanded dynamically as required. Any resource's CURRENT_LIMIT column value that is approaching the LIMIT_VALUE column value should be viewed as a potential problem. The following query will report any resource within 10 percent of its hard, absolute limit:

```
SELECT resource_name, current_utilization, max_utilization, limit_value
FROM v$resource_limit
WHERE
current_utilization >
limit_value * .90
AND limit_value NOT LIKE '%UNLIMITED%';
```

RESOURCE_NAME	CURRENT_UTILIZATION	MAX_UTILIZATION	LIMIT_VALUE
processes	49	92	55
sessions	50	96	60

Most of the resource limit names correspond to an `init.ora` parameter for the database. Table 15.5 shows the resource limit name and the corresponding `init.ora` value that should be reviewed should the CURRENT_LIMIT column value come close to the LIMIT_VALUE column.

TABLE 15.5: V$RESOURCE_LIMIT VIEW RESOURCE LIMIT NAMES AND CORRESPONDING init.ora VALUES

RESOURCE Limit Name	init.ora parameter
_lm_procs	
distributed_transactions	distributed_transactions
dml_locks	dml_locks
enqueue_locks	enqueue_locks
enqueue_resources	enqueue_resources
lm_cache_ress	
lm_locks	lm_locks
lm_ress	lm_ress
max_rollback_segments	max_rollback_segments
mts_max_servers	mts_max_servers
parallel_max_servers	parallel_max_servers
processes	processes
sessions	sessions
sort_segment_locks	
temporary_table_locks	
transactions	transactions

Using Oracle Database Performance Monitoring Tools

Oracle supplies a few tools to assist you in monitoring database performance. In this section, we will look at the `utlbstat/utlestat` report and the newest Oracle8i feature, the Oracle Statspack.

These tools produce reports that are reactive ways of dealing with database problems (though Statspack can be used somewhat proactively, as you will see). They are ways of gathering information and dealing with database problems that may seem to just appear out of nowhere. However, if you are proactive about your administrative duties, as we've stressed in this chapter and throughout the book, your need for reactive response to problems will be limited.

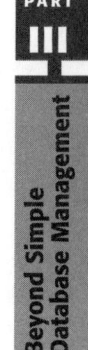

Gathering System Statistics

Oracle7 and Oracle8 provide a method for gathering system statistics over a given period of time. This method is provided through the use of two scripts: `utlbstat.sql` and `utlestat.sql`, which can be found in the $ORACLE_HOME/rdbms/admin directory.

The `utlbstat.sql` script creates some temporary tables and then stores a snapshot of the current system statistics in those tables. Typically, execution of the `utlbstat.sql` script will occur as the SYS or SYSTEM user or (even better) a special DBA-level user account created for statistics collection. You should run the `utlbstat.sql` and `utlestat.sql` scripts during periods of normal database activity to ensure that representative statistical database data is generated.

WARNING Before you run the `utlbstat` and `utlestat` scripts, you should change the temporary tablespace and the default tablespace for the user who creates these views. Doing so will prevent the SYSTEM tablespace from being fragmented or filled up.

DBAs tend to run `utlbstat.sql` on a reoccurring basis to generate various benchmarks. The DBA will wait a period of time between `utlbstat.sql` executions. Typically, this interval is after a normal operational period, after a run of a particularly heavy bit of processing, or perhaps during a peak operational hour when the database seems to be the slowest.

The `utlestat.sql` script populates temporary tables with additional statistical data, and then generates a report with the resulting statistical sample over that period of time. The `utlbstat.sql` script will produce a report in a file called `report.txt`, typically in the default directory your session is in. This report contains the output of the statistical sample for the DBA to review. Finally, the `utlestat.sql` script will remove all of the temporary tables it created.

NOTE If you run `utlbstat` and then shut down your database, you will need to run `utlbstat` again after restarting the database. If you do not rerun `utlbstat` after a restart, the `utlbstat` report will not be correct.

The output contained in `report.txt` is a snapshot of the database over a given period of time. The report can be broken down into sections, as summarized in Table 15.6.

TABLE 15.6: SECTIONS OF THE `utlbstat` REPORT

Section	Description
Library cache statistics	Statistics on the different library cache namespaces. This section shows the numbers of gets, pins, the get hit and pin hit ratios, and the number of reloads and invalidations that took place during the period of the report.
Database statistics	The multitude of statistics that Oracle collects. Most of them you will never need to refer to, but some can be important. These statistics include CPU information, the buffer cache hit ratio, full table scans, and sorts to disk.
Average write queue length	Not used in Oracle8i (well, it just shows up as a blank). For earlier versions of Oracle, this number can be a good determinant of how busy the database is.
System-wide wait events (for nonbackground processes)	Data on system-wide wait events (discussed in Chapter 17).
System-wide wait events (for background processes)	Data on system-wide wait events for background processes (discussed in Chapter 17).
Latch statistics	Information on various possible latch-contention situations (discussed in Chapter 17).
Buffer busy waits	Information on buffer waits (discussed in Chapter 17).
Transaction table waits	Information on transaction table waits (discussed in Chapter 17).
Nondefault `init.ora` parameters	A list of the nondefault `init.ora` parameter settings.
Dictionary cache performance statistics	Statistics on the data dictionary cache in the shared pool. Since the dictionary cache is self-managed in Oracle8i, this section generally can be ignored.
Tablespace I/O reports	Reports on read and writes operations. If you see imbalanced I/O operations occurring on a particular datafile, you may want to check the objects sitting on that datafile (the datafile that an object is sitting on can be found by querying the DBA_EXTENTS view).
Report date/time and banner	The date and time the report was executed, and the version of the database.

NOTE To save space, we do not provide a sample `utlestat` report here. These reports tend to be long, and to be honest, a great deal of the information supplied is not terribly important most of the time.

You should first look over the report and note if any negative figures appear in it. If so, this probably indicates that the database was shut down and restarted between the time you ran the `utlbstat` and `utlestat` scripts. In this case, your reports are worthless.

You will see that a lot of the report has to do with waits and latching. We will cover these topics in detail in Chapter 17. However, note that the following wait events listed in the report can be ignored:

- SQL*Net message from client
- SQL*Net more data from client
- RDBMS IPC message
- Pipe get
- Null event
- PMON timer
- SMON timer
- Parallel query dequeue

These are known as "idle" waits, which are generally representative of the database waiting to do some work, and therefore are of little or no consequence.

Many of the items on the report provide the same information as we have already discussed earlier in this chapter. For example, the file I/O report replicates the file I/O query that you saw in the "Monitoring System File I/O" section earlier in this chapter, but it's providing that information in a cumulative fashion.

The `utlbstat/utlestat` report is nice to have, and it augments any monitoring that you are doing, but the report is not a facility to replace ongoing monitoring and reporting. We will discuss the monitoring process in the "Introducing a Monitoring Methodology" section later in this chapter.

Using the Oracle Statspack

One of the problems with the `utlbstat/utlestat` report, and even the other reports we have presented throughout this chapter, is that it is difficult to generate a true baseline with them. Also, it is hard to gauge trends in these reports, because they are just snapshots at a point in time. In addition to these reports, DBAs often create repositories to store historical information about databases. These repositories usually contain performance data, table sizing, and table growth information. This information allows the DBA to determine trends and predict future space and processing requirements. To help collect this information, Oracle introduced Statspack in version 8.1.6 (Oracle8i release 2).

Statspack is different from the `utlbstat.sql` and `utlestat.sql` scripts in several ways:

- It collects additional information that is specific to Oracle8i.
- It stores this data permanently in Oracle tables that are owned by a user called PERFSTAT.
- Certain ratios (such as the buffer cache hit ratio) are calculated for you.
- Data collection and the generation of the Statspack report are separate functions.

Data collection can be scheduled through the Oracle Job Scheduler so that it occurs on a regular basis, allowing the DBA to generate a baseline of normal database performance over time. Thus, when there is a database performance problem, you can compare the baseline statistics against the current statistics, which should allow you to target your database tuning efforts.

Installing Statspack in the Database

To install Statspack, you run an installation script called `spcreate.sql`. You can find this script in the $ORACLE_HOME/rdbms/admin directory on Unix systems, or in the $ORACLE_HOME\rdbms\admin directory on NT systems. Note the following about the installation process:

- You need to run the installation script from SQL*Plus, not Server Manager. The `spcreate.sql` script uses SQL*Plus commands to prompt you for the user and default tablespaces. The creation of Statspack will fail if you use Server Manager.
- You can run this script for each node in a parallel server configuration. Each instance's data is stored, and the primary keys are created in such a way that the instance data is always unique, in case you later want to combine data from multiple instances.
- The Statspack tables take a minimum of about 35MB to create, because all of the tables have a 1MB initial extent. You may need to modify the creation scripts to create smaller tables, if this is a problem. If you find you need to modify the storage parameters for the tables, you will find those parameters in the `statsctab.sql` script, which is in $ORACLE_HOME\rdbms\admin.

- Make sure that you change the password of the PERFSTAT user once the spcreate.sql script has successfully completed.

Statspack is fairly easy to install. The spcreate.sql script will create the PERFSTAT user, and then it will prompt you for the default and temporary tablespaces that the PERFSTAT user should use. Once the script has completed, Statspack will have been installed. The following is an example of the installation of Statspack. Note that running spcreate.sql actually results in the execution of several other SQL programs, as shown in the example below. We removed some of the redundant output for space reasons.

```
D:\ORACLE\ORA816\RDBMS\ADMIN>sqlplus "/ as sysdba" /nolog

SQL> SPOOL d:\oracle\spcreate.log
SQL> @spcreate.sql
SQL> REM $Header: statscre.sql 06-dec-99.18:33:17 cdialeri Exp $
SQL> REM statscre.sql
SQL> REM   Copyright (c) Oracle Corporation 1999. All Rights Reserved.
SQL> REM     NAME
SQL> REM           statscre.sql - Statistics Create
... Installing Required Packages
Package created.
Grant succeeded.
View created.
… blah blah… more of the same output here truncated by author…
.. Creating PERFSTAT user
Below are the list of online tablespaces in this database.
Decide which tablespace you wish to create the Statspack tables
and indexes. It is not recommended to use the system tablespace
for storing statistics data.

TABLESPACE_NAME
------------------------------
RBS
USERS
TEMP
TOOLS
INDX

Specify PERFSTAT user's default tablespace: tools
```

```
User altered.
User altered.

Specify PERFSTAT user's temporary tablespace: temp
User altered.
... blah blah... more of the same output here truncated by author...
Below is the list of online tablespaces in this database.
Decide which tablespace you wish to create the Statspack tables
and indexes. It is not recommended to use the system tablespace
for storing statistics data.

Ensure the PERFSTAT user has sufficient quota in the tablespace
you specify.

TABLESPACE_NAME
------------------------------
RBS
USERS
TEMP
TOOLS
INDX
Enter tablespace where Statspack objects will be created: tools
... Creating STATS$SNAPSHOT_ID Sequence
Sequence created.
... blah blah... more of the same output here truncated by author...
Below are the list of online tablespaces in this database.
Decide which tablespace you wish to create the STATSPACK tables
and indexes. This will also be the PERFSTAT user's default tablespace.
Using the SYSTEM tablespace to store statistical data is
NOT recommended.
TABLESPACE_NAME
------------------------------
RBS
USERS
TEMP
TOOLS
INDX
TEMPTEMP
PERFSTAT
```

```
7 rows selected.
Specify PERFSTAT user's default   tablespace
Enter value for default_tablespace: perfstat
Using perfstat for the default tablespace
User altered.

Specify PERFSTAT user's temporary tablespace
Enter value for temporary_tablespace: temp
Using temp for the temporary tablespace
User altered.
... blah blah... more of the same output here truncated by author...
Creating Package STATSPACK...
Package created.
No errors.
Creating Package Body STATSPACK...
Package body created.
No errors.
NOTE:
SPCPKG complete. Please check spcpkg.lis for any errors.
```

NOTE No indexes, except primary key indexes, are created during the Statspack installation process. As you add historical data, you may find that you need to add more indexes to help performance.

In different versions of Oracle8i, the names of the SQL procedures used with Statspack have changed. The procedures you see listed in this chapter are associated with Oracle release 8.1.7. The following lists the old names (pre-8.1.7) and the new names in 8.1.7:

Pre-8.1.7 Name	8.1.7 Name
statspack.doc	spdoc.txt
statscre.sql	spcreate.sql
statsrep.sql	spreport.sql
statsauto.sql	spauto.sql
statsdrp.sql	spdrop.sql

TIP spdrop.sql can be used to remove the Statspack tables. It is contained in $ORACLE_HOME/rdbms/admin.

Taking Database Snapshots

Now that Statspack has been installed, you can start collecting database data. The principle package used with Statspack is the STATSPACK package. In particular, you will use the SNAP procedure within the STATSPACK package to create what is called a *snapshot*. A snapshot, in this case, should not be confused with a snapshot in reference to replication. This snapshot is the collection of database performance information at a given time.

The SNAP procedure takes a snapshot of your database and stores the information collected in that snapshot in the Statspack repository. Later, you can generate Statspack reports based on the differences in snapshots, which occurred over a given period of time.

The STATSPACK.SNAP package has the following definition:

```
PROCEDURE SNAP
Argument Name                  Type                    In/Out Default?
------------------------------ ----------------------- ------ --------
I_SNAP_LEVEL                   NUMBER                  IN     DEFAULT
I_SESSION_ID                   NUMBER                  IN     DEFAULT
I_UCOMMENT                     VARCHAR2                IN     DEFAULT
I_NUM_SQL                      NUMBER                  IN     DEFAULT
I_EXECUTIONS_TH                NUMBER                  IN     DEFAULT
I_PARSE_CALLS_TH               NUMBER                  IN     DEFAULT
I_DISK_READS_TH                NUMBER                  IN     DEFAULT
I_BUFFER_GETS_TH               NUMBER                  IN     DEFAULT
I_SHARABLE_MEM_TH              NUMBER                  IN     DEFAULT
I_VERSION_COUNT_TH             NUMBER                  IN     DEFAULT
I_ALL_INIT                     VARCHAR2                IN     DEFAULT
I_PIN_STATSPACK                VARCHAR2                IN     DEFAULT
I_MODIFY_PARAMETER             VARCHAR2                IN     DEFAULT
```

The parameters and their meanings are shown in Table 15.7.

TABLE 15.7: STATSPACK.SNAP PARAMETERS

Parameter	Default Value	Purpose
I_SNAP_LEVEL	5	Determines the level of detail collected by the Statspack snapshot
I_SESSION_ID	0 (report on all sessions)	Allows you to define a specific session ID to snapshot

Continued

TABLE 15.7: STATSPACK.SNAP PARAMETERS (CONTINUED)

Parameter	Default Value	Purpose
I_UCOMMENT	Blank	A comment that will be stored with the snapshot
I_NUM_SQL		Undocumented (Oracle internal use only)
I_EXECUTIONS_TH	100	Reports on only SQL statements that have been executed a minimum of the specified number of times
I_PARSE_CALLS_TH	1000	Reports on only SQL statements that have been parsed a minimum of the specified number of times
I_DISK_READS_TH	1000	Reports on only SQL statements that have caused a minimum of the specified number of disk reads
I_BUFFER_GETS_TH	10000	Reports on only SQL statements that have caused a minimum of the specified number of buffer gets
I_SHARABLE_MEM_TH	1048576	Reports on only SQL statements that have used a minimum of the specified amount of shared memory
I_VERSION_COUNT_TH	20	Reports on only SQL statements that have a minimum of the specified number of versions
I_ALL_INIT		Undocumented (Oracle internal use only)
I_PIN_STATSPACK		Undocumented (Oracle internal use only)
I_MODIFY_PARAMETER	FALSE	Allows you to save these parameters for future runs of the STATSPACK.SNAP procedure

Note that each of these parameters has a default value associated with it. This allows you to execute the SNAP procedure without any parameters, like this:

SQL> EXEC STATSPACK.SNAP

On the other hand, you may wish to provide parameters to customize the statistics that are gathered. You can collect data at various levels of detail and set thresholds. Of course, the more detail you collect, the more space required for that data, and the bigger the impact on your system of running the collection process.

There are three levels of detail you can collect: level 0, level 5, and level 10. At level 0, general performance statistics are collected. These include wait statistics, system event statistics, rollback segment information, row cache information, SGA statistics, background events, session events, lock status and statistics, buffer pool statistics, and parent latching information.

Level 5 includes all of the statistics included with level 0, plus information about SQL statements that have high-resource usage. This means that SQL statements will be stored by Statspack if they exceed four threshold parameters:

- The total number of times the SQL statement was executed (the default is 100)
- The total number of disk reads the SQL statement has caused (the default is 1000)
- The total number of parse calls the SQL statement has caused (the default is 1000)
- The total number of buffer gets the SQL statement has caused (the default is 10000)

Level 10 collection consists of all of the information collected in level 5 plus the parent and child latch information.

You can modify the threshold defaults by changing them in the STATS$STATSPACK_PARAMETER table. Alternatively, you can set the I_MODIFY_PARAMETER in the STATSPACK.SNAP package, and the defaults will be changed to reflect the defaults selected in the execution of STATSPACK.SNAP. Here is an example of setting some STATSPACK.SNAP parameters:

```
SQL> EXEC STATSPACK.SNAP(i_snap_level=>10, i_disk_reads_th=>10000);
```

This command sets data collection level 10 and limits the collection of SQL statements to just those that are causing 10,000 or more disk reads.

Automating Statistics Collection

To collect statistics on a regular, frequent basis, you will want to automate the process. One way to schedule statistics collection is to use Oracle's Job Scheduler in the Oracle DBMS_JOB package to set up a recurring job that executes the STATSPACK.SNAP SQL script.

NOTE You can also use your operating system's scheduling facility (such as cron in Unix) to schedule the execution of the statistics collection job using SQL*Plus. See your operating system documentation for information about how to use your operating system's job scheduling facility.

Before you can use the Job Scheduler, you need to make sure that it's enabled by checking the `init.ora` parameter JOB_QUEUE_PROCESSES. This parameter should be greater than 0. (The Job Scheduler is discussed in detail in Chapter 20.) Once you have enabled the Job Scheduler, issue the following command to have statistics collected on your system once every 6 hours:

```
DECLARE
jobno NUMBER;
BEGIN
DBMS_JOB.SUBMIT(:jobno,'STATSPACK.SNAP;', -
TRUNC(sysdate+1/6,'HH'),'TRUNC(SYSDATE+1/6,''HH'')' );
END;
/
```

 TIP Oracle provides a SQL script called `spauto.sql` that can help you automate the running of your statistics jobs (after you've set up the Job Scheduler). This script, which can be found in the `$ORACLE_HOME/rdbms/admin` directory, will set up a scheduled job that will run STATSPACK.SNAP every hour.

Viewing the Statspack Report

After you've collected several Statspack snapshots, you'll be ready to look at that data and see how your database is doing. Oracle provides a single report that contains the collected information. This report is run by using the script `spreport.sql`. When you run `spreport.sql`, it will provide you with a list of snapshots currently stored in the database. You will then be prompted to select the beginning and ending snapshot to report on and to specify the output report name. Here is an example of running `spreport.sql`:

```
SQL> @spreport

    DB Id    DB Name      Inst Num Instance
----------- ------------ --------- ------------
 1598904557 ORA817               1 ora817
```

USING ORACLE DATABASE PERFORMANCE MONITORING TOOLS

```
Completed Snapshots
                          Snap                        Snap
Instance      DB Name      Id   Snap Started        Level Comment
------------  ------------ ----- ----------------- ----- -------
ora817        ORA817         1 23 Jul 2001 16:00      5
                             2 23 Jul 2001 16:10      5


Specify the Begin and End Snapshot Ids
~~~~~~~~~~~~~~~~~~~~~~~~~~~~~~~~~~~~~
Enter value for begin_snap: 1
Begin Snapshot Id specified: 1

Enter value for end_snap: 2
End    Snapshot Id specified: 2


Specify the Report Name
~~~~~~~~~~~~~~~~~~~~~~~
The default report file name is sp_1_2.  To use this name,
press <return> to continue, otherwise enter an alternative.
Enter value for report_name: c:\sql\snap.rpt

Using the report name c:\sql\snap.rpt

STATSPACK report for

DB Name        DB Id       Instance  Inst Num    Release  OPS Host
--------    -----------   ---------  --------  ----------- --- ----
ORA817      1598904557     ora817        1      8.1.7.0.0  NO  WS-JAX

                Snap Id    Snap Time         Sessions
                -------  ------------------  --------
   Begin Snap:       1   23-Jul-01 16:00:53      9
     End Snap:       2   23-Jul-01 16:10:31      9
     Elapsed:              9.63 (mins)
```

Notice that the script also outputs the amount of time that has elapsed since the two snapshots (in this example, 9 minutes). The script will then proceed to produce the snapshot report (both to the screen and to the report name selected at the prompt). Table 15.8 summarizes the sections in the Statspack report.

TABLE 15.8: SECTIONS OF THE STATSPACK REPORT

Section	Description
Report header	Identifies the instance you are reporting on and the start and stop snapshot numbers that are being reported on.
Cache size information	Shows the defined sizes of the various SGA memory caches, such as the database buffer cache and the shared pool.
Load profile information	Shows the average load of the database per second during the period reported on. Also included are the per-transaction averages during the snapshot periods, how many rows, on average, were processed per sort, and other averaged information.
Instance efficiency percentages	Shows the various hit ratios (such as the database buffer cache hit ratio) that you needed to calculate manually when using the utlbstat/utlestat reports.
Wait event information	Shows the top five wait events, followed by a list of all wait events (discussed in Chapter 17).
Expensive SQL statements	Provides several lists of expensive SQL statements. Each is sorted by different criteria, including total gets, physical reads, and total rows processed.
Instance activity statistics	Shows instance statistics, such as the number of checkpoints that occurred during the reporting period, db_block_gets, and physical reads.
Tablespace and file I/O summary statistics	Lists each tablespace for the database, the total reads and writes to the tablespace, and the average read and wait times. The file I/O statistics include average read times, total writes and reads, and other information.
Rollback segment information	Shows wait, extend, and shrink information, as well as sizing information for the rollback segments.

Continued

TABLE 15.8: SECTIONS OF THE STATSPACK REPORT (CONTINUED)

Section	Description
Latching information	Shows information about latching (discussed in Chapter 17).
Buffer pool information	Shows information on the different buffer pools available in Oracle8i.
Dictionary cache and library cache information	Provides get and miss information. Information on all the library cache namespaces is also provided.
SGA memory allocation information	Includes a breakdown of the various memory areas and how much memory is allocated to them. It presents the differences in memory allocations to aid in troubleshooting. If your system has slowed down, this report will show you if another DBA has reduced memory on the system.
init.ora parameters	Lists the parameters in the init.ora file. If there is a difference in parameter settings between the start and stop snapshots, this will be displayed as well.

Beyond the Canned Report

You can access the Statspack tables directly to generate your own reports. As a step further, you can access the Statspack tables with another application, like Microsoft Excel, to generate graphs and reports.

When you run a snapshot of the instance, it is given a unique snapshot ID. Also, the instance has its own unique ID, called the DBID. This information, along with the time of the snapshot, is stored in the table STATS$SNAPSHOT. You can use this table to join to the other tables, such as STAT$.FILESTATXS, to create your own reports, charts, and/or graphs.

The following are the tables that are created when you install Statspack. All of these tables will be owned by the PERFSTAT user.

STATS$BG_EVENT_SUMMARY
STATS$BUFFER_POOL_STATISTICS
STATS$ENQUEUESTAT
STATS$IDLE_EVENT
STATS$LATCH_CHILDREN
STATS$LEVEL_DESCRIPTION
STATS$PARAMETER

STATS$BUFFER_POOL
STATS$DATABASE_INSTANCE
STATS$FILESTATXS
STATS$LATCH
STATS$LATCH_MISSES_SUMMARY
STATS$LIBRARYCACHE
STATS$ROLLSTAT

STATS$ROWCACHE_SUMMARY
STATS$SESSTAT
STATS$SGAXS
STATS$SQL_SUMMARY
STATS$SYSSTAT
STATS$WAITSTAT

STATS$SESSION_EVENT
STATS$SGASTAT_SUMMARY
STATS$SNAPSHOT
STATS$Statspack_PARAMETER
STATS$SYSTEM_EVENT

Looking through these tables, you'll find several interesting columns. Some of the primary metrics you will be interested in (and interested in looking at trending in) are shown in Table 15.9.

TABLE 15.9: SOME IMPORTANT STATISTICS AND METRICS IN THE STATSPACK TABLES

Statistic Name	Why It's Important
Database buffer hit ratio	It measures the effectiveness of the database buffer cache.
Sorts	You are primarily interested in sorts to disk, because they can cause performance problems.
Physical disk reads	The primary goal of database tuning is reducing disk I/O.
Physical disk writes	Disk writes can have an impact on Oracle performance. If disk writes are excessive, you may need to look at how often you are checkpointing, the size of your redo logs, and the frequency of log switches
I/O waits	Monitoring I/O contention is very important.
Buffer busy waits	Buffer busy waits indicate contention within an Oracle data block in the database buffer cache.
Redo log space requests	Excessive space requests may indicate that the redo logs are too small.
Table fetch continued row	This indicates that you may have problems with row chaining in tables (see Chapter 16).
Sorts (disk)	Sorts to disk can cause serious performance problems.

Introducing a Monitoring Methodology

Many of the scripts provided in this chapter (and in Chapters 16 and 17) should be run once a day and reviewed. However, there is another class of reporting that needs to be done more frequently. By watching critical items, such a database availability, you will be proactive, and well on your way to becoming a lazy DBA.

Establishing Baselines, Benchmarks, and Trends

Along with spotting potential problem areas, your database monitoring should be designed to help you establish baselines, benchmarks, and trends. Baselines tell you about the normal operations of our system. When you have baseline information, you can do a better analysis of the system when it is suffering for some reason.

Benchmarks are important because they give you something to quantify when there is a problem. You want to know what the average growth of a table is, the average runtime of SQL statements in the system, the average number of users on the system, and the normal I/O rates are for all the datafiles. If you know how long a given SQL statement or batch job ran during the normal course of the day, you are better prepared to deal with problems when they are reported. When the user claims that the SQL used to run in 20 minutes and now takes an hour, your benchmarks can prove or disprove that statement. Benchmarks also can help you quantify the results of your tuning efforts. If a given process used to run in 45 minutes, but after your database or SQL tuning effort, it now runs in 10 minutes, you can quantify that.

You also want to monitor trends. What is the average growth of a given table? How many new users start using the system at a given time? When are the peak loads? When are the low volume times?

As you pursue your career as a DBA, think beyond simple monitoring. Think about baselining and trending. In doing so, you will be a better and more valuable DBA.

Tools for Applying Your Monitoring Methodology

There are some good monitoring tools out there. Companies like BMC, Precise, and Quest sell monitoring tools, and Oracle provides some monitoring through Oracle Enterprise Manager (OEM). Most monitoring tools can be configured to send pages and e-mails to the DBA if some area that is being monitored violates some given criteria. But it is highly possible that you will not have access to these tools, and that your boss isn't likely to part with precious budget money anytime in the near future just because you want to buy some fancy tools. Indeed, I'm told that a certain pointy haired boss in a well-known cartoon was modeled after a database manager in a large Oracle database shop. Of course, that's only a rumor, and I'm not one to spread rumors.

Continued

> **CONTINUED**
>
> What is the cash-starved DBA to do? I suggest that you build scripts that monitor some basic database operations and implement them in your own monitoring methodology. You can design these scripts to use whatever method of communication is available (say, e-mail or pager) to notify you if there is a problem. Generally, I like to be paged with a quick description of the problem ("Freespace Problem <SID> <Tablespace>," for example) and also send an e-mail with the output of the report itself.

What Should You Monitor?

So what should you monitor? As a beginning, I suggest that you monitor the items shown in Table 15.10, on the schedule and frequency indicated. Also listed in the table is the warning threshold, which determines a condition that will cause your monitoring system to report a problem. We'll discuss each of these conditions and the scripts that monitor them in more detail in the following sections.

TABLE 15.10: BASIC DATABASE ITEMS TO MONITOR

Item to monitor	Frequency to monitor	Warning Threshold
Database availability (database is up)	Every 20 minutes	Alert if the database is down
Database objects that will not be able to extend in tablespace due to lack of tablespace space	Every hour	Alert if any object cannot extend
Database objects that will not be able to extend because of lack of contiguous free space	Every hour	Alert if any object cannot extend
Free space in tablespace	Every hour	Generally, if tablespace allocated free space is less than 20%.
Objects near maximum extents	Every hour	Report any object within 5 extents of its maximum extents setting.

> **TIP** Individual databases may have different monitoring requirements. For example, lower volume databases and test databases may require less overall monitoring than production databases will. Databases with higher transactional volume or those critical to the business may require a higher level of monitoring.

Monitoring Database Availability

Database availability is a basic monitoring issue that can be addressed by a number of methods. If you are running Oracle on a Unix system, simply issue a ps command:

```
ps -ef|grep <sid>|grep lgwr
```

The result will indicate if the instance is up, but the presence of lgwr does not provide 100 percent proof that the database is actually open. A more sophisticated method is required to be fully sure.

> **NOTE** In pre-Oracle8i versions, an undocumented feature called oiconnect allowed you to test actual database connectivity. Unfortunately, Oracle has omitted this feature in Oracle8i.

The method I recommend for checking database availability involves connecting to the database with SQL*Plus, and then querying the data dictionary (if you were able to connect) to determine the mode in which the database is open. The query is simple:

```
SELECT name, open_mode FROM v$database;
```

If, in the result, OPEN_MODE doesn't say OPEN (it might say MOUNTED), or if you cannot connect to the database, your script needs to send an alert to you. Listing 15.1 is a basic Unix script you can use as a framework for monitoring database availability on other operating systems. You can rewrite the script in Listing 15.1 to suit your specific needs.

Listing 15.1: Unix Script for Monitoring Database Availability

```
# checksend.sh
# Author : Robert Freeman
# Date   : 24 Dec 2000 (ho ho ho)
# Purpose : This script checks for database availability. If the
# database is down, we will send a mail message to the user
# identified in the mail_address variable. This is a sample
# script you can modify to suit your needs. This script was
```

```
# written and tested on Solaris 2.6 with Oracle 8.1.6.
# No warranty or guarantee is expressed or implied in any way
# about this script or its results.
#
# Change the mail_address to your email address.
MAIL_ADDRESS="my_address @somewhere.com"

# If a downdb.lst exists, then we failed sending a message.
# Resend the last failed message.
IF [ -f /tmp/downdb.lst ]
THEN
 cat /tmp/downdb.lst | /usr/lib/sendmail $MAIL_ADDRESS
 if [ $? -eq 0 ]
 then
      cat /tmp/downdb.lst >> /tmp/downdb.lst.history
      if [ $? -eq 0 ]
      then
           rm /tmp/downdb.lst
      fi
 fi
fi
# Now, parse the oratab file for all databases on the system.
for d in `cat /etc/oratab|grep -v "#"`
do
  # Get date and time
  DATE_RUN=`date +%m%d%y`
  TIME_RUN=`date +%H%M%S`
  # Get SID & ORACLE_HOME information from the oratab file entry.
  ORACLE_SID=`echo $d|cut -f 1 -d :`
  ORACLE_HOME=`echo $d| cut -f 2 -d :`

  # Set the Oracle environment for this SID.
  ORAENV_ASK="NO"
  . oraenv

  # Check that the Unix lgwr process for this SID is running
  proc_count=`ps -ef|grep $ORACLE_SID|grep lgwr|grep -v grep|wc -l`
  if [ proc_count -eq 0 ]
  then
```

INTRODUCING A MONITORING METHODOLOGY

```
              # If the Unix process is not running, send an error
              echo "$ORACLE_SID is down! $DATE_RUN   $TIME_RUN"  >> /tmp/downdb.lst
        else
        # The SID processes are up. Can we connect?
        $ORACLE_HOME/bin/sqlplus -s   system/wa1060<<-WEOF>>/dev/null 2>>/dev/null
              WHENEVER SQLERROR EXIT 1
              Set echo off
              Set feedback off
              select name||'should be $ORACLE_SID' from v\$database;
              DECLARE
                    V_Db_name varchar2(30);
                    V_Open_mode varchar2(20);
              BEGIN
                    SELECT name, open_mode
                    INTO v_db_name, v_open_mode
                    FROM v\$database;
                    -- We are going to make sure the database is open.
                    -- If not, we will send an error!
                    IF :v_db_name != '$ORACLE_SID' and
                          IF v_open_mode != 'OPEN'
                    THEN
                          SELECT 'Database $ORACLE_SID is down!'
                          FROM dual;
                    END IF;
              END;
              quit;
        WEOF
              if [ $? -ne 0 ]
              then
                    echo "$ORACLE_SID is down! ">> /tmp/downdb.lst
                    echo "$DATE_RUN    $TIME_RUN">> /tmp/downdb.lst
              fi
         fi
     done
     if [ -f /tmp/downdb.lst ]
     then
     cat /tmp/downdb.lst | /usr/lib/sendmail $MAIL_ADDRESS
     if [ $? -eq 0 ]
     then
```

```
                cat /tmp/downdb.lst >> /tmp/downdb.lst.history
                if [ $? -eq 0 ]
                then
                        rm /tmp/downdb.lst
                fi
        fi
fi
```

 TIP While the database may be up and running (fat and happy is the technical term), Net8 could be down. You can check for the Net8 process on your specific system (on Unix, for example, do a ps -ef and grep for tns, and then grep for your listener name). Alternatively, you can modify the script in Listing 15.1 so that you connect to the databases through Net8 instead of through a local connection. If the Net8 listener is down, the script will fail, and an error will be reported.

Using the Database to Send E-mail Notifications

In addition to having shell scripts operate to provide e-mail notifications, you can also take advantage of Oracle8i's new Java features and the UTL_STMP package to send e-mail messages. The UTL_STMP package is designed to send out e-mail, but it does not provide facilities to receive e-mail. In order to use the UTL_STMP package, you must first install the JServer option of the Oracle database. Once that is complete, you can take advantage of the UTL_STMP package to send e-mail. The following code provides the basic framework for sending e-mail:

```
PROCEDURE send_mail (sender      IN VARCHAR2,
                     recipient IN VARCHAR2,
                     message   IN VARCHAR2)
IS
    -- This is your mail server. Use IP address if possible.
    mailhost    VARCHAR2(30) := '10.0.0.0';
    mail_conn  UTL_SMTP.CONNECTION;
BEGIN
```

Continued

CONTINUED

```
      -- We are going to open the connection to the mail server.
      -- 25 is the port number of the smtp server to connect to.
      mail_conn := UTL_SMTP.OPEN_CONNECTION(mailhost, 25);
      -- This next statement provides the basic handshaking
      -- required to connect to the mail server.
      UTL_SMTP.HELO(mail_conn, mailhost);
      -- This next statement initiates the mail transaction.
      -- It defines who the sender of the message is.
      UTL_SMTP.MAIL(mail_conn, sender);
      -- The next statement defines who is supposed to get the
      -- message. If you want to send to multiple recipients,
      -- issue this statement multiple times.
      UTL_SMTP.RCPT(mail_conn, recipient);
      -- This next statement transmits the e-mail message.
      UTL_SMTP.DATA(mail_conn, message);
      -- The next statement indicates we have completed sending
      -- the message and disconnects us from the mail server.
      UTL_SMTP.QUIT(mail_conn);
      DBMS_OUTPUT.PUT_LINE('Email sent.');
EXCEPTION
   WHEN OTHERS THEN
       DBMS_OUTPUT.PUT_LINE('An error occurred trying to send the
       email'||sqlerrm);
END;
```

Note that there are some limitations when sending e-mail this way. First, the username for the recipient cannot be longer than 64 characters. This limitation is also true for the domain name. The individual e-mail text cannot be longer than 1000 characters, and you cannot buffer more than 100 recipients at any one time.

Also note that in some versions of Oracle8i, `initjvm.sql` does not work properly, so the UTL_SMTP package will not work. To correct this problem, go to the ORACLE_HOME of the version of Oracle8i that you are using. Change to the `plsql/jlib` directory, and then issue the following command:

```
loadjava -user sys/<password> plsql.jar
```

Once this code has been executed, you should be able to execute the UTL_SMTP package.

Monitoring Tablespace Space

Objects that will not extend because the tablespace lacks sufficient free space can cause problems, such as not being able to insert or update rows in the table. You want to monitor tables, indexes, and clusters to make sure that there is enough space in the tablespace they are assigned to for those objects to extend again. For this monitoring, use a query that looks something like this:

```
SELECT 'Table' "Object Type", owner, table_name,
tablespace_name, next_extent
FROM dba_tables a
WHERE next_extent > (select sum(bytes) FROM dba_free_space
WHERE tablespace_name = a.tablespace_name)
UNION
SELECT 'Index' "Object Type", owner, index_name,
tablespace_name, next_extent
FROM dba_indexes a
WHERE next_extent > (SELECT SUM(bytes) FROM dba_free_space
WHERE tablespace_name = a.tablespace_name)
UNION
SELECT 'Clusters' "Object Type", owner, Cluster_name,
tablespace_name, next_extent
FROM dba_clusters a
WHERE next_extent > (SELECT SUM(bytes) FROM dba_free_space
WHERE tablespace_name = a.tablespace_name);
```

Monitoring Contiguous Tablespace Space

Another condition that elevates the risk of not being able to insert or update table rows is when the tablespace lacks sufficient contiguous free space. You want to monitor tables, indexes, and clusters to confirm that there is enough contiguous space in the tablespace they are assigned to for those objects to extend again. You can monitor contiguous space with a query like this:

```
SELECT 'Table' "Type", owner "Owner", table_name "Name",
a.tablespace_name "Tblsp", next_extent "Next",
b.available_space "Available"
FROM dba_tables a,
(SELECT tablespace_name, MAX(bytes) Available_Space
FROM dba_free_space
GROUP BY tablespace_name) b
WHERE next_extent > (SELECT MAX(bytes) FROM dba_free_space
```

```
WHERE tablespace_name = a.tablespace_name)
AND b.tablespace_name=a.tablespace_name
UNION
SELECT 'Index' "Type", owner "Owner", index_name "Name",
a.tablespace_name "Tblsp", next_extent "Next",
b.available_space "Available"
FROM dba_indexes a,
(SELECT tablespace_name, MAX(bytes) Available_Space
FROM dba_free_space
GROUP BY tablespace_name) b
WHERE next_extent > (SELECT MAX(bytes) from dba_free_space
WHERE tablespace_name = a.tablespace_name)
AND b.tablespace_name=a.tablespace_name
UNION
SELECT 'Cluster' "Type", owner "Owner", cluster_name "Name",
a.tablespace_name "Tblsp", next_extent "Next",
b.available_space "Available"
FROM dba_clusters a,
(SELECT tablespace_name, MAX(bytes) Available_Space
FROM dba_free_space
GROUP BY tablespace_name) b
WHERE next_extent > (SELECT MAX(bytes) FROM dba_free_space
WHERE tablespace_name = a.tablespace_name)
AND b.tablespace_name=a.tablespace_name;
```

Here is an example of the results of this query:

Type	Owner	Name	Tblsp	Next	Available
Index	PERFSTAT	STATS$FILESTATXS_PK	TOOLS	1,048,576	227,328
Index	PERFSTAT	STATS$LATCH_PK	TOOLS	1,048,576	227,328
Index	PERFSTAT	STATS$ROLLSTAT_PK	TOOLS	1,048,576	227,328
Index	PERFSTAT	STATS$SESSTAT_PK	TOOLS	1,048,576	227,328

Note that objects that show up on this report may not show up on the report resulting from the script shown in the previous section for monitoring the lack of free space condition, which is why the contiguous space condition is monitored separately.

Monitoring Free Space in Tablespaces

If free space falls to less than 20 percent of a tablespace's allocated space, you need to add some space. The following script creates a report on the percentage of free space left in a given tablespace, displaying the result in a column labeled FREE BYTES. If the result is less than 20 percent, the query generates an alert.

```
SELECT a.tablespace_name, SUM(a.BYTES) "Free Bytes",
SUM(b.bytes) "Allocated Bytes",
( (SUM(a.bytes)/SUM(b.bytes) ) * 100) "Free Space %"
FROM dba_free_space a, dba_data_files b
WHERE a.bytes < (SELECT SUM(bytes) * .20
                 FROM dba_data_files b WHERE
                 b.tablespace_name=a.tablespace_name)
GROUP BY a.tablespace_name;
```

Monitoring Objects Near Maximum Extents

Oracle introduced the concept of unlimited extents in Oracle7, yet many DBAs do not take advantage of this feature in their databases. The following query keeps an eye on the objects that have MAX_EXTENTS set to something less than unlimited and reports on any object that is five extents or less from reaching its maximum:

```
SELECT a.owner, a.segment_name, b.max_extents, COUNT(*)
FROM dba_extents a, dba_tables b
WHERE a.owner=b.owner
AND a.segment_name=b.table_name
HAVING COUNT(*) > b.max_extents - 5
GROUP BY a.owner, a.segment_name, b.max_extents;
```

All of these scripts can be customized to correct problems as well as report on them. For example, you can change the above script so that it not only senses that an object is about to run out of extents, but also changes the MAX_EXTENTS parameter to fix the problem. The idea is to limit, particularly with production databases, any type of outage or failure. Uptime, availability, recoverability, and performance are the goals of the DBA. To achieve them, you need to be proactive in your approach to database administration.

The next two chapters continue with the tuning process, building on the monitoring strategy we've started here. Continue on and learn the keys to being a lazy DBA (it's the best type of DBA to be!).

CHAPTER 16

Oracle8i SQL Performance Monitoring and Tuning

FEATURING:

Overview of SQL statement processing	700
The Oracle optimizer	705
Oracle execution plans	720
Tuning SQL statements	749
DBMS_STATS	778
Oracle8i's plan stability	783
An addendum on database monitoring	787

In terms of database performance, perfecting your SQL statements will derive the biggest gains on average of any tuning process that occurs on an existing database. In this chapter, we'll look at how to make that happen.

In order to fix something, you have to know how it works, so our first task is to have a thorough understanding of how SQL statements are processed. Then we'll discuss how the optimizer, Oracle's program for tuning SQL, does its job. You contribute to this process by analyzing Oracle objects, and we'll look at the various methods for gathering these analyses. Next, the chapter explores the subject of Oracle execution plans, how to produce them, and how to interpret them.

You'll see plenty of SQL tuning examples in this chapter. You'll learn how to keep an eye out for problem SQL statements and the users who are operating them. We'll also examine Oracle8i's new plan stability feature, and discuss ways to integrate SQL statement performance monitoring into overall database monitoring methodology.

Overview of SQL Statement Processing

When you submit a SQL statement to the database, Oracle must process that statement and present the data in the format you specify. This section takes an overview of Oracle's six stages of preparation for and execution of a SQL statement.

1. Creation of the cursor or private SQL area
2. Parsing
3. Bind variables to the statement
4. Execution
5. Fetching the rows from the query
6. Closing the cursor

NOTE In the interest of simplification, this overview does not cover parallel processing, partitioning, and other optional Oracle features that can affect SQL statement processing. These features are addressed in subsequent chapters.

The Cursor

A *cursor* is created in expectation of a SQL statement, and is the first step in the overall process of executing a SQL statement. A cursor is a name for an allocated *private SQL area*, an area of memory allocated by Oracle to a given SQL statement and specific to the user session creating the cursor. In the cursor, Oracle stores the parsed and unparsed version of the SQL statement, the *execution plan* of the statement, and a pointer to the current row being processed by the statement.

The cursor information can be retained by the session after the session's SQL statement has completed, or the memory allocated to the cursor may be freed for use by other statements. Generally, Oracle cursor creation is automatic and not seen by the user.

A given Oracle session can open as many cursors as it needs, though the total number of cursors that can be opened by any one session is limited by the OPEN_CURSORS database parameter. This concept is particularly important with programming languages such as PL/SQL, C, and Cobol, with which you might open several cursors at the same time. Recursive SQL needed to complete a requested operation requires cursors in addition to those needed for a given SQL statement. (Recursive SQL is SQL issued by Oracle to satisfy internal needs. For example, Oracle issues recursive SQL against data dictionary views to validate that the columns used in a SELECT statement actually exist.)

Parse Phase

During the *parse phase*, a number of operations are performed on your SQL statement in order to digest it. First, Oracle determines if an identical statement exists in the shared pool. If so, the parse phase usually ends there. This is known as a *soft parse* and is the preferred situation.

To allow for the reuse of SQL statements and thus incur only the impact of a soft parse, Oracle maintains an area in the shared pool (in the Library cache) called the shared SQL area. This is where previously parsed SQL statements and their associated execution plans are stored. If Oracle determines that no identical statement has been cached, Oracle performs a *hard parse*, in which the following events occur:

- The syntax of the SQL statement is checked in order to determine that the SQL statement is valid. All keywords and operators are checked to ensure that they have been correctly used.

- A series of data dictionary lookups are done to validate the objects in the FROM clause, the columns listed in the SELECT statement, and so on. The impact of the hard parse may be lessened if these objects already exist in the data dictionary cache.

- A semantic check of the statement is performed, which verifies that objects referenced in the statement actually exist in the database.

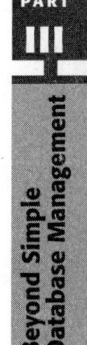

- Parse locks are acquired, so that definitions of objects do not change during the parse process.
- User access rights to the queried object are verified. If the user doesn't have access rights to an object, an error is returned.
- The optimizer is called, and an execution plan is generated.
- If required, the object is loaded into a shared SQL area.

Note how much work occurs in a hard parse. Since hard parsing takes time and affects the overall runtime of a SQL statement, soft parses are a much better option.

 TIP See the section "Monitoring and Managing Excessive Hard Parsing" later in this chapter.

Rules for Shared SQL Statements

Because Oracle uses a hashing algorithm to check the shared SQL area for matching SQL, the SQL statement being executed must be exactly like the one in the shared SQL area. If they are not identical in every way, the current statement will be reparsed, which increases its overall execution time, which is not desirable. Since SQL statements often contain constant values in the WHERE clause, and these values tend to change quite a bit (such as WHERE col1=1 in SQL statement 1, and col1=2 in SQL statement 2). This performance problem can be solved with the use of bind variables, and we'll take a look at those shortly.

Oracle uses the following rules to identify SQL statements that are considered similar:

The text of the shared statements must be identical. This extends to spaces, carriage returns, letter case, and even the position of semicolons. For example, Oracle will treat these two following statements as different, because the second statement contains a carriage return after the semicolon:

```
SELECT * FROM EMPLOYEE;
-- The next statement is different
SELECT * FROM EMPLOYEE;
```

All of the statements' references to schema objects must be to the same schema object. If we're querying the SCOTT.EMPLOYEE table with one SQL statement and the PROD.EMPLOYEE table with another statement, a separate shared SQL area will be created for the PROD.EMPLOYEE statement.

This is true regardless of whether the SQL statements differ. If the SQL statement schema object in the FROM clause is prefixed with the schema name (that is, SELECT * FROM SCOTT.EMPLOYEE; as opposed to SELECT * FROM PROD.EMPLOYEE;) then these two statements will not be considered alike and would be reparsed. Also, if the SQL statements are alike but the objects in those statements resolve to different schema objects by virtue of a synonym, the statements will have different shared SQL areas. Statements that prefix the same schema can be reused.

The statements' bind variables must match. Both the name and datatype of the bind variables must be the same.

The statements' optimization must match. Statements considered similar must by optimized using the same optimization approach (RULE or COST) and the same optimization goal (FIRST_ROWS or ALL_ROWS). These optimization concepts will be discussed shortly.

Invalidation of Shared SQL Areas

In addition to problems with improper SQL statement reuse, other database activities can cause shared SQL areas to become invalidated (and thus cause hard parsing to occur). Several typical DBA operations can cause this invalidation, including the following:

- Anytime you ANALYZE a table, all shared SQL areas that contain SQL for that table object will be removed. Thus any SQL statement that references an object that has been analyzed must be reparsed.
- If a schema object is modified in any way, any SQL statement in the shared SQL area that references that object will be invalidated.
- When the global name of the database is changed, the shared pool is flushed.
- The DBA can flush the shared pool manually using the ALTER SYSTEM FLUSH SHARED_POOL; command.

Bind Variables

A significant issue in making SQL reusable is that literal values in the WHERE clauses are likely to change, which negates the reuse of the SQL statement. For example, a SQL statement like this:

```
UPDATE employee
SET sal = sal * 1.10
WHERE emp_id=1234;
```

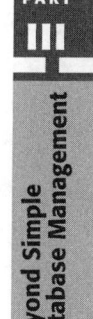

will likely not be reusable because the value of EMP_ID (1234) is going to change. For example, the next statement might be something like this:

```
UPDATE employee
SET sal = sal * 1.10
WHERE emp_id=2222;
```

Notice that the SQL statement is exactly like the earlier one except for the different EMP_ID; the literal for it is now 2222. Thus the representation of this statement in the shared SQL area will not be reusable. Fortunately, Oracle8i provides a solution for this situation in the form of *bind variables*.

Bind variables are fixed variable names. The values of these variables are defined before the SQL code is executed, and the values can be modified between SQL executions. Bind variables are stored in the user's private SQL area, typically stored in the PGA and not in the Library cache of the shared pool. Since the bind variable name itself does not change, the SQL statement will look the same—and hash the same—in the shared SQL area, so it will be reused. After Oracle has parsed the statement, or if the statement is found in the shared SQL area, Oracle will replace the bind variables in the statement with their proper values.

Here's an example of a SQL statement using a bind variable:

```
Variable v_employee_num   number
Begin
:v_employee_num:= 7369;
end;
/
SELECT ename, sal
FROM employee
WHERE empno=:v_employee_num;
```

Execution, Fetch, and Close

After the parse phase has completed, SQL statement gets executed in the execution phase of query operation. As this occurs, each row that is to be modified (with an INSERT, UPDATE, or DELETE statement) will be locked, ensuring database integrity.

The fetch phase tends to be the longest running part of the entire operation as rows are read and modified as required. During the fetch phase, the rows are selected and the results returned back to the application.

After all the rows have been fetched, the cursor is closed.

The Oracle Optimizer

The Oracle optimizer calculates the most efficient way to execute a SQL statement, using either a cost-based or rule-based approach. In the next few sections we'll study the optimizer's modes of operation and the parameters that control its functions.

There's an old saying about there being more than one way to skin a cat and this sentiment also applies to data access. Oracle's optimizer operates on the idea that there's more than one way to access requested data, some ways more efficient than others, and the most efficient means is the best one to use. How the optimizer makes this determination depends on a number of factors, but primary among them is the mode in which the optimizer is run: rule based and cost based. When the optimizer is in rule-based mode, its operation is fairly simple. It follows a set of specific rules that help it choose the proper access paths to your data. When the optimizer is in cost-based mode, the process is a bit more complex.

Rule-Based Optimization (RBO)

Rule-based optimization (RBO), the default setting for Oracle optimization, follows a hard-coded set of rules. The rules tell the optimizer it must do a particular operation if that operation is possible. For example, under RBO you will always do an index lookup if it's possible, rather than a full table scan. RBO is not built to accommodate data volumes and distribution of values, and it cannot take advantage of some newer optimization features that Oracle provides with cost-based optimization.

Choosing the Driving Table

Optimizer in RBO utilizes a ranking of 15 different data-access paths. If multiple paths are available, RBO will take the highest-ranking path for each table in the SQL statement (1 being the highest). Thus, the joins are being constructed as the optimizer proceeds to rank the access paths for the tables. For example, the RBO will always access a table by primary key (rank 4) if a key is available, even if it could also use a full table scan (rank 15). Table 16.1 defines the access paths and their rankings.

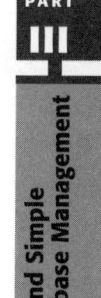

TABLE 16.1: RBO DATA-ACCESS PATH RANKINGS

Rank	Access Path
1	Access of single row by ROWID
2	Access of single row by cluster join
3	Access of single row by hash cluster key with unique or primary key
4	Access of single row by unique or primary key
5	Access via cluster join
6	Access via hash cluster key
7	Access via indexed cluster key
8	Access via composite key
9	Access via single-column indexes
10	Access via bounded range search on indexed columns
11	Access via unbounded range search on indexed columns
12	Access via sort-merge join
13	Access via MAX or MIN or indexed column
14	Access via ORDER BY on an indexed column
15	Access via full table scan

RBO generally chooses the table with the best access path as the one to be the *driving table* (see "Reading and Interpreting Execution Plans" later in this chapter).

With RBO, your SQL tuning options are more limited than they are with CBO. In fact, more than a handful of Oracle operations are not available at all in rule-based mode, including the following:

Partitioned tables	Index joins
Index-organized tables	Bitmap indexes
Reverse indexes	Function indexes
Parallel execution and parallel DML	SAMPLE clause in a SELECT statement
Star transformations	Use of the extensible optimizer.
Star joins	Query rewrite
Sample table scans	Hash joins
Fast, full index scans	

 NOTE Running any of the above operations will result in CBO use, even when the OPTIMIZER_MODE parameter is set to RULE.

Cost-Based Mode Optimization (CBO)

Cost-based optimization (CBO) in Oracle takes into account a variety of factors as it calculates the best execution plan for your query. When using CBO, you must first use the ANALYZE command (see Chapter 7) to analyze the tables and indexes of the database. This process provides CBO with the information it needs about data volumes, number of rows, data distribution, and a host of other factors.

There are downsides to CBO. It is very dependent on database statistics. If tables are volatile, statistics will not be very current and CBO may choose an inefficient execution plan. In Oracle8i, there's a way to manage this difficulty using automated statistics updates, which offer some additional benefits, too. We'll cover this new feature, enabled by setting a table to monitoring status, later in this section.

The CBO was introduced in early Oracle 7 and, in terms of performance, did not have an auspicious beginning. Even today, it is far from perfect. It is, however, more flexible than RBO. For any new or ongoing long-term project, we strongly suggest you use the CBO.

Let's start by examining the CBO's three primary elements: the query transformer, the estimator, and the plan generator.

The Query Transformer

The *query transformer's* job is to determine whether the parsed version of the query will benefit from any *transformations,* such as those described in the following paragraphs.

View Merging

View merging occurs if the query transformer determines that a query using a view will benefit from actually merging the SQL used to create the view into the query. This merging process can produce a more optimal query execution plan. If the exception plan for the view is not merged into the SQL statement, the exception plan is generated separately. When the view is merged into the statement, however, the optimizer generates a single plan that incorporates the view results and is therefore improved.

Certain view-merging operations are more complex than others, such as those containing GROUP BY and DISTINCT operations. Oracle does not automatically enable the merging of these types of views. You can enable merging by setting the optimizer_features_enable parameter, using a MERGE hint or using the hidden/undocumented Oracle8i parameter _COMPLEX_VIEW_MERGING. (Hints are discussed later in this chapter, in "Tuning Cost-Based Statements.")

Unnesting Subqueries

Often, a join will be more efficient than a subquery because the execution plan for the subquery is calculated separately from the execution plan for the rest of the query. Oracle may choose to transform a subquery into a join if possible, in an effort to optimize the execution plan of the statement by transforming the subquery into a join to improve accesses.

Materialized Views

The new materialized views feature in Oracle8i is discussed in more detail in Chapter 19. Essentially, it allows the optimizer to rewrite a query that would benefit from accessing a materialized view. Generally these queries involve aggregating values from tables.

The Estimator

The *estimator's* job is to estimate the cost of an overall plan. Using available statistics, the estimator determines the costs of the various plans under consideration. The plan with the lowest cost is then generally selected for use. In determining the overall cost, the estimator is interested in three types of measures:

Selectivity   This is the fraction of the total number of possible rows that will be returned. It is determined by the use of the WHERE clause in a SQL SELECT statement and the associated predicates in that WHERE clause. The estimator uses generated statistics on tables and indexes to determine the selectivity of each analyzed access path. If histograms are available, those are used as well.

Cardinality   There are several kinds of cardinality.

- *Base cardinality* represents the total number of rows in a given table.
- *Effective cardinality* is the total number of rows that will be selected from that table.
- *Join cardinality* is the total number of rows that will be returned from a join of two tables.
- *Distinct cardinality*, which is especially significant to DBAs, measures the total number of distinct rows in a given rowset. In a given rowset of 200 rows, If distinct column values are found in 50 of those rows, then the cardinality is said to be 50.
- *GROUP BY cardinality* occurs after the operation of a GROUP BY on a row source. Because a GROUP BY operation can reduce the total row source even further, it has the effect of increasing the overall cardinality of a given row source.

Cost   Cost is the overall amount of work that the database will have to perform for a given access plan. In determining the cost of each access plan, the estimator considers the impact of the operation on CPU, disk I/O, memory, and so on.

The Plan Generator

The *plan generator's* job is to select the plan with the lowest cost. The plan generator will continue to generate and try plans until it identifies the optimum; however, it does not check every possible permutation of plan. You can adjust the limit to the number of permutations the plan generator will check, by changing the hidden parameter _OPTIMIZER_SEARCH_LIMIT.

WARNING   The _OPTIMIZER_SEARCH_LIMIT hidden parameter (like other hidden parameters) is not documented or supported by Oracle. We've used it before with no problems, but you should test it in a nonproduction environment first.

Setting Up the Optimizer

Some DBAs don't realize that the Oracle database by default uses RBO (the actual default value is CHOOSE, which we will discuss shortly), or they don't bother to change the default setup. To make sure your SQL statement is using CBO, you can do one of the following:

- Set the OPTIMIZER_MODE parameter to CHOOSE (the default) FIRST_ROWS or ALL_ROWS. If set to CHOOSE, CBO will be used whenever any table in a given query has statistics built on it. If other tables are accessed in a join and just one table has statistics, CBO will be used and assumptions about the other tables will be made.
- Issue an ALTER SESSION SET OPTIMIZER_MODE statement to enable CBO use for your session.
- Use any hint other than RULE.

For optimal setup of optimization in your Oracle environment, you'll want to pay attention to several init.ora parameters that affect the optimizer's behavior (see Table 16.2). Several of these parameters refer to data access methods, such as hash joins and full table scans, which are described in more detail later in this chapter.

TABLE 16.2: *INIT.ORA* PARAMETERS AFFECTING OPTIMIZER OPERATIONS

Parameter Name	Valid Values	Default	Description
ALWAYS_ANTI_JOIN	NESTED_LOOPS, MERGE, HASH	NESTED_LOOPS	Used often in warehousing operations, this parameter defines what type of anti-join Oracle chooses to use.
BITMAP_MERGE_AREA_SIZE	OS-dependent	1MB	Size of the memory used to merge different bitmaps that match a range predicate.
DB_FILE_MULTIBLOCK_READ_COUNT	OS-dependent	8	Affects the number of blocks read in a single I/O during a full table scan. The higher this number, the more likely the CBO is to perform a full table scan. This parameter times the DB_BUFFER_BLOCKS should equal 64 on a 32-bit system and 128 on a 64-bit system.
HASH_AREA_SIZE	Range from 0 to an OS-dependent value	2 times the SORT_AREA_SIZE parameter	Amount of memory to be dedicated to hash joins. The higher this value, the more likely the CBO is to choose a hash join as an execution plan.
HASH_JOIN_ENABLED	TRUE and FALSE	TRUE	Enables or disables the hash join feature.
HASH_MULTIBLOCK_IO_COUNT	Query-dependent	OS-dependent	Can be increased to lower the cost of hash joins. It's best to keep the Oracle setting for this parameter.
OPTIMIZER_FEATURES_ENABLED	Any Oracle version from 8.0.0 to 8.1.7	8.1.6	Enables several optimizer features, including fast full scans.
OPTIMIZER_INDEX_COST_ADJUST	Range from 1 to 10000	100	Adjusts the cost of using indexes to make their use more favorable. As you increase the value of this parameter you increase the likelihood of using any index, not just those with the best selectivity.

Continued

THE ORACLE OPTIMIZER | 711

TABLE 16.2: *INIT.ORA* **PARAMETERS AFFECTING OPTIMIZER OPERATIONS (CONTINUED)**

Parameter Name	Valid Values	Default	Description
OPTIMIZER_INDEX_CACHING	Range from 0 to 100	0	Favors use of more selective indexes. The lower this value, the more likely the CBO will use an index that is very selective.
RULE, CHOOSE, FIRST_ROWS, ALL_ROWS	RULE, CHOOSE, FIRST_ROWS, ALL_ROWS	CHOOSE	Determines the optimizer mode in which the database will run.
OPTIMIZER_PERCENT_PARALLEL	Range from 0 to 100	0	Defines the amount of parallelism that the optimizer uses in its cost estimates.
OPTIMIZER_MAX_PERMUTATIONS (formerly OPTIMIZER_SEARCH_LIMIT)	Range from 4 to about 4.3 billion	80000	Defines the number of possible join permutations the CBO will consider before selecting an execution plan. Oracle's tuning guide suggests that this rarely needs to be changed, but it does make a difference on occasion.
SORT_AREA_SIZE	Range from 6 database blocks to an OS-dependent maximum	OS-dependent	Larger sort areas can lower the cost of sorting, which can increase the optimizer's use of sort merge joins.

 WARNING One of the dynamics affecting the execution plans of the CBO is the size of the tables being queried. If your test and development environments do not match your production environments, you might have to retune SQL statements after they're in production.

Making Allowances for RBO

Sometimes allowances have to be made for old applications that were designed under RBO, when you want the alternative of adding new objects to the database that you'll query using CBO. Doing so is fairly easy. In the database's default optimizer mode, CHOOSE, Oracle will use RBO if the tables do not have any statistics created for them. However, if you're doing a join and one of the affected tables has statistics, Oracle will use CBO—and use default values for tables and indexes without statistics! You can also choose to modify your existing queries to use a RULE hint (more on hints later in this chapter). Finally, if you want the database to always run under RBO, you can set the OPIMIZER_MODE = RULE, which will force all queries to run under RBO regardless of the presence of statistics.

WARNING Be careful in databases with both analyzed and unanalyzed tables. You might get some unexpected execution plans.

Managing Migrated and Chained Rows

Migrated and chained rows in a table can cause significant performance slowdowns on your database. Both these conditions occur as a result of a row insertion in a table that is later expanded such that the row can no longer fit in the block to which it was originally assigned.

In *row migration,* the row is moved to a new block, and a pointer to the new row is created in the old block. The existence of the pointer allows the row to maintain the same ROWID even though it's been moved. In *row chaining,* Oracle splits the row into multiple blocks. At the end of the row piece in each block, there's a pointer to the next block that contains a row piece. Again, the row maintains the same ROWID throughout the process.

Oracle always prefers to migrate a row rather than chain it. Chaining generally occurs only if the block size of the database is too small to contain the entire row.

NOTE In the remainder of this chapter, we will use *chaining* to refer to *both* chaining and migration (because Oracle tends to combine the two), unless there is a specific reason to differentiate.

In Chapter 6 you learned some object management tricks to avoid the occurrence of chained rows. Here in this chapter about SQL tuning, we'll take a closer look at why chained rows occur, how to find tables that have them, and how to repair those tables to be more efficient.

Chaining can happen for various reasons. Whoever designed the database may have misunderstood the real nature of the data, and/or misestimated the velocity of changes to that data. The tables may have been configured carelessly in the rush to complete the database creation. Often the nature of the data changes and becomes more fluid (that is, the pace of DML activity is more volatile, particularly UPDATE activity), requiring changes to the internal storage settings of the object. With migration specifically, the database block size may not be large enough, or the nature of the data in that object might simply require that it be chained.

Because of these issues, you may find that your tables are all of a sudden racked with migrated or chained rows. Ideally, no more than 0.5 percent of your rows should be chained (again, if this is a block size issue, you may not be able to do anything about it). Using information calculated by the ANALYZE command about a table's chained rows, you can actually locate those rows and move them without having to defragment the entire table.

Finding Tables with Chained Rows

The chained rows report (which also provides information on migrated rows) provides a list of tables in which the number of chained rows is so significant that it can impact performance. Here is the query to report on tables with chained rows:

```
SELECT owner, table_name, chain_cnt
FROM dba_tables
WHERE chain_cnt > 0;
```

Here are the results of this query:

OWNER	TABLE_NAME	CHAIN_CNT
COPS_OWN	CSFMISCN	4
COPS_OWN	CSTCOI	2677
COPS_OWN	CSTINS	915
COPS_OWN	CSTTDE	19490
COPS_OWN	CSTTDT	2006
COPS_OWN	CSTTIC	26045
COPS_OWN	CSTGCA	21488
COPS_OWN	CSTOTE	13528
PATROL	P$USER_EPOCH	1
ETI_OWN	RPT_AUDIT_TRAIL	26995
ETI_OWN	RPT_XFER_DETAIL	8311
ETI_OWN	CSICALLG	25923

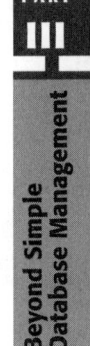

TIP This query looking for chained rows is a good one to add to your monitoring toolkit.

NOTE When reviewing statistics for rows in a given table, if you find that the average row length is larger than the database block size, you likely have chaining of rows occurring more often than you have migration. In this case, the real solution may be to increase the block size of the database (which requires rebuilding the database). You will have to carefully analyze the risks and rewards of such an action before you do it.

Fixing Tables with Chained and Migrated Rows

Once we have identified a table with migrated or chained row problems (and determined that chaining because of the database block size is not the real issue), we can fix the block allocation settings PCTUSED and PCTFREE, as described in Chapter 6. Specifically, we want to store fewer rows per block. Generally, when you analyze a table and find that the blocks are not well packed, you may end up decreasing the PCTFREE value—assuming you don't expect significant UPDATE activity to rows in that table. If you *do* expect significant UPDATE activity, make sure that it's not going to change the average row length before you go about decreasing PCTFREE. Also, based on the average block usage of an object, you may or may not want to increase the PCTUSED value. This upward adjustment would allow blocks in a given object to be reused with some more frequency.

Your next step, then, is to determine what rows are currently chained or migrated, in order to move those rows so that they are no longer chained. We gather this information by analyzing the table using the LIST CHAINED ROWS keyword (this will also get us migrated rows).

Create a table called CHAINED_ ROWS by using either the `utlchain.sql` or `utlchn1.sql` script. Both scripts are found in `$ORACLE_HOME/rdbms/admin` on a Unix box, and in `$ORACLE_HOME\rdbms\admin` on an NT system. The `utlchain.sql` script can be used for regular tables, and the `utlchn1.sql` script for regular tables or index-organized tables. Execute either script from the schema from which you'll run the ANALYZE command.

Now, to get the list of chained rows for a given table, issue an ANALYZE command like the following, which works on the EMPLOYEE table:

```
ANALYZE TABLE employee LIST CHAINED ROWS;
```

Oracle proceeds to populate the CHAINED_ROWS table with the ROWID for each chained row in the employee table. Here is an example of the output of a query to the CHAINED_ROWS table after the ANALYZE process has completed:

```
SELECT owner_name, table_name, head_rowid
FROM chained_rows
WHERE rownum< 5;
OWNER_NAME  TABLE_NAME  HEAD_ROWID
----------  ----------  ------------------
SCOTT       EMPLOYEE    AAAFEjAADAAAADDAAE
SCOTT       EMPLOYEE    AAAFEjAADAAAADDAAF
SCOTT       EMPLOYEE    AAAFEjAADAAAADDAAG
SCOTT       EMPLOYEE    AAAFEjAADAAAADDAAH
```

The output from this query tells us that there are some migrated or chained rows in the EMPLOYEE table (each row is a migrated or chained row in the object that was analyzed). An informed DBA knows that we fix this tiny, little problem quite easily by moving all of those uncooperative chained rows out of the table and into a temporary table. Then we simply delete them from the temporary table and reinsert them again. Here is how we do it:

1. Begin by making sure that after the deletion and reinsertion, you'll end up with the same number of rows you started with. So, let's find out the total number of rows in the table, as well as the total number of chained rows. Assuming you've analyzed the table, this query should work just fine:

    ```
    SELECT a.table_name, a.chain_cnt, b.emp_count, a.chain_cnt/b.emp_count
    FROM user_tables a, (select count(*) emp_count from employee) b
    WHERE a.table_name='EMPLOYEE';
    ```

    And here are the results:

    ```
    TABLE_NAME  CHAIN_CNT   EMP_COUNT  A.CHAIN_CNT/B.EMP_COUNT
    ----------  ----------  ---------  -----------------------
    EMPLOYEE         31380      32014                 .980196164
    ```

2. Fully 98 percent of our rows are chained! Let's resist the impulse to yell at the DBA who set up this database, and instead go forward to figure out the problem with the table. We have statistics from our analysis, and in step 1 we've generated a baseline against which to measure everything after we're done. We enter this query:

    ```
    SELECT table_name, pct_free, pct_used
    FROM user_tables WHERE table_name ='EMPLOYEE';
    ```

And here are the results:

```
TABLE_NAME   PCT_FREE   PCT_USED
----------   --------   --------
EMPLOYEE            1          1
```

It's pretty obvious that the problem is that the block storage settings have been very badly done indeed.

3. Let's fix the block storage parameters with an ALTER TABLE command:

   ```
   ALTER TABLE employee PCTFREE 20 PCTUSED 40;
   ```

   Of course, you will set your PCTFREE and PCTUSED values based on the velocity and nature of changes to the table.

4. Having fixed the table's block storage parameters, we now move the chained rows from the EMPLOYEE table to a temporary table called TEMP_EMP. (This temporary table is *not* a global temporary table, mind you, but one we'll create simply to populate this data. Afterward, we'll remove the table.) Here is the SQL statement for this operation:

   ```
   CREATE TABLE temp_emp AS
   SELECT * FROM employee
   WHERE rowid IN (select head_rowid from chained_rows);
   ```

NOTE Note that we don't use a "real" temporary table for this table because we don't want to accidentally lose this data should the database crash or the session fail. Core dumps always happen when they are the most inconvenient, don't you think?

TIP Of course, in creating your own TEMP_ table, you may want to add STORAGE clauses, TABLESPACE clauses, and the like, but for our purposes here we've not done so. The CREATE TABLE...AS SELECT... command (CTAS) is very useful for operations such as this. It allows us to create a table using another table as a template, and then will even populate the table for us. Notice the subquery that selects from the EMPLOYEE table all the rows based on the ROWIDs stored in the CHAINED_ROWS table.

5. Before we continue, please raise your right hand and repeat after me: *"I will back up my database, or at least the object I'm removing chained rows from, before I do the next step. I promise, so help me, Codd."*

6. Having done the necessary backup (you did keep your promise, didn't you?), you're ready to delete records. First clear the offending chained rows from the EMPLOYEE table:
```
DELETE FROM employee
WHERE rowid in (select head_rowid from chained_rows);
COMMIT;
```

7. Insert the rows from the TEMP_EMP table to repopulate the EMPLOYEE table with the chained rows that were deleted:
```
INSERT INTO employee
SELECT * FROM temp_emp;
```

8. All that remains is to make sure the number of rows in the table is correct, and that there are no chained rows remaining. To do this, ANALYZE the table again, and then run the same checksum query as before (step 1):
```
ANALYZE TABLE employee COMPUTE STATISTICS;
SELECT a.table_name, a.chain_cnt, b.emp_count, a.chain_cnt/b.emp_count
From user_tables a, (select count(*) emp_count from employee) b
Where a.table_name='EMPLOYEE';
```

The results of this query are:

```
TABLE_NAME   CHAIN_CNT   EMP_COUNT  A.CHAIN_CNT/B.EMP_COUNT
----------   ---------   ---------  -----------------------
EMPLOYEE             0       32014                        0
```

9. It appears we still have 32,014 rows in the table, and our chain count is now 0. All systems go. Complete the process by dropping the temporary table you created.

Histograms: Analyzing Data Distribution

Sometimes column data in a table is skewed so that one or two values make up a significant percentage of the values in the column of the table. This may cause fluctuating query performance on that table. When you access the table looking for a value (such as NO) that is present in a great percentage of the rows, using an index to do that lookup will not be very efficient. Likewise, if the value NO shows up only once in the column and the table is very large, an index lookup will certainly be preferable to a full table scan.

Unfortunately, the normal statistics Oracle generates don't provide a table data view that is wide enough that we can determine whether a specific query would benefit from an index or a full table scan. The normal statistics do track the number of distinct values in the table, but they do not track the distribution of those values. In

Oracle 7.3, *histograms* were introduced in an effort to correct this omission. Histograms are performance enhancers in cases where data values in a column are skewed and some imbalance exists. If the data is not skewed, histograms will likely not help performance.

You create histograms via the ANALYZE command, for both tables and indexes. An example of creating a histogram on the DEPT column in the EMPLOYEE table would look something like this:

```
ANALYZE TABLE EMPLOYEE COMPUTE STATISTICS FOR COLUMNS
Deptno SIZE 10;
```

A histogram has a fixed width, but variable height. The width of the histogram is measured in "buckets." The histogram we just created, then, will be 10 buckets long and will remain 10 buckets long forever unless we re-create it. The height of the histogram is balanced along the width of the bucket. Thus every bucket has an equal number of rows.

TIP If you are using bind variables in your SQL (which is good), Oracle will not be able to use histograms when generating the execution plan.

Now you can examine one of the data dictionary views and find information on the histograms you've created for the EMPLOYEE table. Table 16.3 lists the primary views that contain histogram information.

TABLE 16.3: DATA DICTIONARY VIEWS THAT PERTAIN TO HISTOGRAMS

View Name	Histogram Information Provided
*_PART_HISTOGRAMS	Partitions in a partitioned table
*_SUBPART_HISTOGRAMS	Table subpartitions
*_TAB_HISTOGRAMS	Nonpartitioned tables
INDEX_HISTOGRAM	Any index analyzed with ANALYZE INDEX...VALIDATE STRUCTURE

* These views will be prefixed with ALL, USER, or DBA.

Analyzing with Oracle Supplied Packages

In addition to the ANALYZE command, you can use one of the Oracle-supplied packages to analyze the database. Here we'll briefly look at these Oracle packages that perform the same actions as the ANALYZE command. For a complete listing of their parameters, see Appendix D. Using these packages in many cases can be easier than running the ANALYZE command. For example, you can analyze the entire database or an entire schema, a process that otherwise would require the issuance of a great number of ANALYZE commands.

DBMS_UTILITY.ANALYZE_DATABASE

The DBMS_UTILITY.ANALYZE_DATABASE procedure analyzes the entire database, with the exception of data dictionary objects. Following is an example of a statement to run the procedure:

```
Exec DBMS_UTILITY.ANALYZE_DATABASE('ESTIMATE', estimate_rows=>1000);
```

This example will analyze the entire database except for SYS objects. Each object in the database will be analyzed using 1000 as the number of rows to scan to generate estimated statistics. You can also compute database statistics when using this procedure.

DBMS_UTILITY.ANALYZE_SCHEMA

The DBMS_UTILITY.ANALYZE_SCHEMA procedure analyzes a specific schema in the database. In the following example:

```
Exec DBMS_UTILITY.ANALYZE_SCHEMA
     ('SCOTT','ESTIMATE', estimate_rows=>1000);
```

the SCOTT schema is analyzed. The procedure does an ESTIMATE scan, using 1000 as the number of rows to scan to generate the estimated statistics. You can also choose to compute statistics for all objects in the schema.

DBMS_DDL.ANALYZE_OBJECT

The DBMS_DDL.ANALYZE_OBJECT procedure analyzes a specific object in the database. Note that this procedure allows you to analyze a partition in an object, whether that object is a partitioned table or a partitioned index. Here's an example of running the DBMS_DDL.ANALYZE_OBJECT procedure:

```
Exec DBMS_UTILITY.ANALYZE_OBJECT
     ('TABLE', 'SCOTT', 'EMPLOYEE', 'ESTIMATE', estimate_rows=>1000);
```

This call will analyze the EMPLOYEE table in the SCOTT schema. It will use 1000 rows to estimate the table statistics.

DBMS_UTILITY.ANALYZE_PART_OBJECT

The DBMS_UTILITY.ANALYZE_PART_OBJECT procedure analyzes a partition of a specific partitioned object in the database. An example of running this procedure would be as follows:

```
Exec DBMS_UTILITY.ANALYZE_PART_OBJECT
     ('TABLE', 'PART_TAB', 'T', 'E',sample_clause=>'SAMPLE 10 PERCENT');
```

This will analyze the partitioned table SCOTT, using the ESTIMATE method of analyzing the partitioned table, and using a sample of 10 percent of the rows when analyzing the partition.

Oracle Execution Plans

The "bottom line" output of the optimizer is the *execution plan*—the heart of a SQL statement's operation. The execution plan is Oracle's plan of attack for getting the data you request with your SELECT statements.

In this section we show you how to get your hands on the execution plans of your SQL statements, and even those of other users' SQL running in your system. You'll learn how to read a SQL statement's execution, so you can know how you're getting your data. All of this is in preparation for tuning your SQL statement so it runs like a greased monkey on fire. (Apologies to PETA. No animals were injured in the making of this book.)

Generating SQL Execution Plans

Before you can read and interpret an execution plan, you must first generate the plan via any of the following methods:

- Use TKPROF to analyze the session's trace file and generate execution plans.
- Use the AUTOTRACE command in SQL*Plus.
- Use the EXPLAIN PLAN command to generate the execution path for a given SQL statement.

Tracing Oracle Sessions and TKPROF

One method of generating execution plans for SQL statements is to trace the user session in which the statement is running. Once you have traced the session, you use the Oracle utility TKPROF to format the trace file into a more readable format. You set a flag in TKPROF so that it will generate an execution plan for each SQL statement that's run. Let's first look at the process for tracing your Oracle session, and then we'll generate a report on the resulting trace file using TKPROF.

Tracing Your Session

To trace a session in which you'll execute a SQL statement (including execution of any PL/SQL program units), issue the command

```
ALTER SESSION SET SQL_TRACE=TRUE;
```

Oracle will create a trace file in the `user_dump_dest` directory that is defined in the `init.ora` parameter file.

Table 16.4 shows other database parameters that affect tracing.

TABLE 16.4: *INIT.ORA* **PARAMETERS THAT AFFECT TRACING**

Parameter Name	Description
USER_DUMP_DEST	This is the directory for user-directed dumps on a database. You can change this parameter dynamically with either the ALTER SYSTEM or ALTER SESSION command.
TIMED_STATISTICS	Allows timing statistics to be enabled (see Chapter 15).
MAX_DUMP_FILE_SIZE	Defines the maximum size of the trace file.
SQL_TRACE	Enables the Oracle trace facility. Can be turned on for a session with ALTER SESSION or database-wide with ALTER DATABASE.

 WARNING Although it is possible to do so, setting TRACE on for the entire database can have negative effects on system performance. You can usually do what you need to do by tracing a session rather than the database.

You can find the specific location of the `user_dump_dest` directory by querying V$PARAMETER:

```
SELECT name, value FROM v$parameter WHERE name = 'user_dump_dest';
```

The name of the trace file on a Unix system is typically in this form:

```
{db_name}_ora_{spid}.ora
```

where db_name is the name of the database, and spid is the operating system process identifier (SPID) value from V$PROCESS for the session being traced. Thus, a trace file's name might look like ora8i_ora_1102.trc on Unix for a database called ora8i and for a session with a SPID of 1102.

On NT the filename format is a bit different:

{db_name}{spid}.ora

where db_name is the name of the database, and spid is the SPID value from V$PROCESS for the session being traced. The SPID is zero filled to five digits. (Before Oracle8i you had to do some pretty wild conversions to get the right trace filename, but this is no longer true.)

NOTE As always with Oracle, anything can change. The naming convention of trace files is not documented all that well, and may change in subsequent releases.

Using TKPROF to Reformat the Trace File

Once the trace file has been generated and you have completed the execution of the SQL statements on which you want to see the executions plans, you'll run the TKPROF utility. TKPROF reads the trace file and formats and sorts it into a friendlier format.

For the entire session traced, TKPROF output provides

- Total counts for parse, execute, and fetch operations
- Total CPU and elapsed time for parse, execute, and fetch operations
- Cumulative disk I/O statistics for parse, execute, and fetch operations
- Total number of rows processed by the session

For each individual statement execution, TKPROF provides

- Total counts for parse, execute, and fetch operations for that statement
- Total CPU and elapsed time for parse, execute, and fetch operations for that statement
- Cumulative disk I/O statistics for parse, execute, and fetch operations for that statement
- Total number of rows processed for that session
- Optimizer goal used for the query
- Number of library cache misses encountered by the query

ORACLE EXECUTION PLANS

- An execution plan for each SQL statement executed (if the EXPLAIN parameter of TKPROF is used)

Following is the syntax for the TKPROF command, and Table 16.5 lists its command-line parameters:

```
TKPROF tracefile outputfile [explain= ] [table= ]
              [print= ] [insert= ] [sys= ] [sort= ]
```

TABLE 16.5: TKPROF COMMAND-LINE PARAMETERS

Parameter	Description
AGGREGATE={**YES**/NO}	The default YES causes identical SQL statements to be shown only once in the report, and the overall run statistics are combined. Setting aggregate to NO causes identical SQL statements to be shown individually.
EXPLAIN=USER/PASSWORD	Creates an execution plan for each SQL statement executed, using the schema selected for the plan. Selected schema must have the CREATE SESSION system grant and have access to the objects accessed during SQL statement execution.
FILENAME ONE	The trace to be formatted.
FILENAME TWO	The output file that will contain the formatted TKPROF results.
INSERT={*filename*}	Causes TKPROF to create a SQL script called *filename* that contains commands to create a database table. TKPROF then populates the script with INSERT statements that will cause the trace file statistics to be INSERTed into the created table.
PRINT={*n*}	Lists only the first *n* SQL statements. The default is to print all statements.
RECORD={*file_name*}	Creates a SQL script that contains all nonrecursive SQL executed by the session so it is available for replay if desired.
SORT {*options*}	Sorts the SQL statements on the *options* specified. Valid *options*: EXECNT = By number of execute calls made EXECPU = By CPU execution time spent EXECU = By number of buffers for current read during execute EXEDSK = By number of disk reads during execute EXEELA = By elapsed execution time EXEMIS = By number of library cache misses during execute EXEQRY = By number of buffers for consistent read during execute

Continued

TABLE 16.5: TKPROF COMMAND-LINE PARAMETERS (CONTINUED)

Parameter	Description
	EXEROW = By number of rows processed during execute
	FCHCNT = By number of times fetch was called
	FCHCPU = By CPU fetch time spent
	FCHCU = By number of buffers for current read during fetch
	FCHDSK = By number of disk reads during fetch
	FCHELA = By elapsed fetch time
	FCHQRY = By number of buffers for consistent read during fetch
	FCHROW = By number of rows fetched
	PRSCNT = By number of times parse was called
	PRSCPU = By CPU parse time spent
	PRSCU = By number of buffers for the current read during parsing
	PRSDSK = By number of disk reads during parsing
	PRSELA = By elapsed parsing time
	PRSMIS = By number of misses in library cache during parsing
	PRSQRY = By number of buffers for consistent read during parsing
	USERID = Sort by the USERID of user who parsed the cursor
SYS={**YES**/NO}	Enables (default) and disables the inclusion of SQL statements that are issued by SYS in the TKPROF output file, including recursive SQL or any statement executed by SYS. This parameter has no effect on the output to the SQL file created by use of the INSERT parameter.
TABLE={*schema.table_name*}	Directs TKPROF to load execution plans temporarily into an alternate table. (By default, TKPROF uses PROF$PLAN_TABLE.) TKPROF will create, use, and remove the alternate table if it does not exist. If the alternate table does exist, TKPROF will delete any existing rows in that table and then populate it.

About Setting TIMED_STATISTICS

You'll notice that some information reported in trace files and in the ultimate TKPROF output from those trace files (as well as in execution plans generated using SET AUTO-TRACE ON) is dependent on the TIMED_STATISTICS parameter being enabled in the database `init.ora` file. This is because TIMED_STATISTICS provides elapsed-time information for each operation that is being traced.

There is a great deal of contention over the advisability of leaving TIMED_STATISTICS enabled all the time. The truth is that there is not that much overhead associated with having it set this way. The benefits are significant, and leaving the parameter enabled provides the DBA with additional information for database tuning.

Finally, note that TIMED_STATISTICS is a dynamic parameter; it can be turned on or off using either the ALTER SYSTEM or ALTER SESSION commands.

Output Generated by TKPROF

Let's look at an example from the wealth of information provided by TKPROF. The trace file you use will be generated by a session that issued just one query:

```
SELECT COUNT(*) FROM employee;
```

Once you have the trace file, you process it with TKPROF. For this sample, we have used the following TKPROF command line:

```
TKPROF ora00104.trc traceout.txt explain=scott/tiger sys=no
```

This command causes TKPROF to process the trace file `ora00104.trc` and create an output file called `traceout.txt`. Using the EXPLAIN parameter, we instructed TKPROF to create execution plans (which is what we are after in this chapter). Finally, using SYS=NO, we instructed Oracle to remove all SYS queries, which includes any recursive SQL.

Listing 16.1 shows the output trace file, including the execution plan.

Listing 16.1: TKPROF Output File

```
TKPROF: Release 8.1.6.0.0 - Production on Fri Dec 29 23:51:07 2000
(c) Copyright 1999 Oracle Corporation. All rights reserved.
Trace file: ora00104.trc
Sort options: default
********************************************************************
```

```
select count(*)
from
  EMPLOYEE

call     count       cpu    elapsed       disk      query    current       rows
------- ------  --------- ---------- ---------- ---------- ---------- ----------
Parse        1       0.03       1.30          0          0          0          0
Execute      1       0.00       0.00          0          0          0          0
Fetch        2       0.06       0.46        281        280          4          1
------- ------  --------- ---------- ---------- ---------- ---------- ----------
total        4       0.09       1.76        281        280          4          1

Misses in library cache during parse: 1
Optimizer goal: CHOOSE
Parsing user id: 25  (SCOTT)

Rows     Row Source Operation
-------  ---------------------------------------------------
      1  SORT AGGREGATE
  32014  INDEX FAST FULL SCAN (object id 20774)

Rows     Execution Plan
-------  ---------------------------------------------------
      0  SELECT STATEMENT   GOAL: CHOOSE
      1   SORT (AGGREGATE)
  32014    INDEX   GOAL: ANALYZED (FAST FULL SCAN) OF 'ID_EMP'
               (NON-UNIQUE)

********************************************************************************

OVERALL TOTALS FOR ALL NON-RECURSIVE STATEMENTS
call     count       cpu    elapsed       disk      query    current       rows
------- ------  --------- ---------- ---------- ---------- ---------- ----------
Parse        1       0.03       1.30          0          0          0          0
Execute      2       0.01       0.01          0          0          0          0
Fetch        2       0.06       0.46        281        280          4          1
------- ------  --------- ---------- ---------- ---------- ---------- ----------
total        5       0.10       1.77        281        280          4          1

Misses in library cache during parse: 1
Misses in library cache during execute: 1

OVERALL TOTALS FOR ALL RECURSIVE STATEMENTS
call     count       cpu    elapsed       disk      query    current       rows
------- ------  --------- ---------- ---------- ---------- ---------- ----------
Parse       12       0.10       1.09          0          0          0          0
Execute     14       0.02       0.27          0          0          0          0
```

```
Fetch        29      0.02       0.41          3         52          0         23
-------    ------   --------  ----------  ----------  ----------  ----------  ----------
total        55      0.14       1.77          3         52          0         23
```
Misses in library cache during parse: 11
    2   user SQL statements in session.
   12   internal SQL statements in session.
   14   SQL statements in session.
    1   statement EXPLAINed in this session.
****
Trace file: ora00104.trc
Trace file compatibility: 8.00.04
Sort options: default
        1   session in tracefile.
        2   user SQL statements in trace file.
       12   internal SQL statements in trace file.
       14   SQL statements in trace file.
       13   unique SQL statements in trace file.
        1   SQL statements EXPLAINed using schema:
              SCOTT.prof$plan_table
                Default table was used.
                Table was created.
                Table was dropped.
      127   lines in trace file.

The output file starts out with a header that includes simply the banner with version information, the name of the trace file, and the sorting done on the output. Then comes the SQL statement, and then this section, which gives statistics for the SQL statement parse phase, execute phase, and fetch phase:

```
call       count        cpu     elapsed        disk      query     current      rows
-------   ------    --------  ----------  ----------  -------   ---------  --------
Parse        1        0.03       1.30           0          0          0         0
Execute      1        0.00       0.00           0          0          0         0
Fetch        2        0.06       0.46         281        280          4         1
-------   ------    --------  ----------  ----------  -------   ---------  --------
total        4        0.09       1.76         281        280          4         1
```

Table 16.6 defines the information provided for each phase.

TABLE 16.6 COLUMNS IN TKPROF'S SQL EXECUTION STATISTICS

Column Name	Description of Contents
CALL	A list of the SQL execution phase being reported, with totals at the bottom.
COUNT	Number of times the phase occurred. Statements that are parsed once but executed 10 times will have a 1 in the Parse line for this column, and a 10 in the Execute line for this column.
CPU	If TIMED_STATISTICS is enabled, this column shows the CPU time required for the phases.
ELAPSED	If TIMED_STATISTICS is enabled, this shows the total elapsed time required for the phases. Includes non-CPU time such as time required by networking connections and disk I/O waits.
DISK	Total number of disk reads required.
QUERY	One part of logical reads. Add this to values in CURRENT column to get the total number of logical reads.
CURRENT	Second part of logical reads. Add this to values in QUERY column to get the total number of logical reads.
ROWS	Total number of rows processed. Only the fetch stage will display non-0 numbers for this column.

Pertinent Ratios in TKPROF Output

In the SQL execution output of the TKPROF output, there are several ratios of particular interest to the DBA.

Disk Reads vs. Query + Current Because physical I/O is always much more expensive than logical I/O, look at the total values in the disk column compared to the total combined values of the query and current columns (DISK : QUERY + CURRENT). This ratio is a measure of the database buffer cache hit ratio, so use that formula to determine if you are getting good hits out of the buffer cache. Anything less than 90 percent is bad news.

Continued

> **CONTINUED**
>
> **Disk Reads vs. Total Rows Returned**   If you have a large number of physical reads as well as a large number of rows returned, some possible culprits could be significant full table scans, or even an undersized SGA.
>
> **Total Blocks Read vs. Total Rows Returned**   Review the number of blocks read (CURRENT + QUERY) and the number of rows returned to the user (ROWS). If you are reading a great many blocks and returning only a single row, there may be a better way to write your SQL statement. Or it may be that changing the database architecture (indexes particularly) could improve the query's performance. In the output shown in Listing 16.1, we combine the total QUERY and CURRENT columns (280 + 4 = 284) and take the total of the ROWS column (1), giving an astounding 284:1 ratio of blocks read for each row. Experts say that ratios greater than 20:1 beg to be tuned; the standard is somewhat lower for indexed lookups or partitioned table/index accesses. Shoot for about 5:1 to 10:1 maximum.
>
> **Parse Rate vs. Executions**   If the number of parses relative to the number of executions is high, review your SQL statements for reusability and check your applications to make sure they are reusing cursors.
>
> **Rows Fetched vs. Number of Fetches**   The ratio of rows fetched to the number of fetches is a measure of the effectiveness of the array fetch facility in certain Oracle tools and applications. If the ratio is low, you may be able to tune your application to take advantage of Oracle's array fetching feature. Review your application development manuals (PRO*C, Java) for more information on how to take advantage of array fetching.

After the numbers associated with the execution of the SQL statement come the following lines of the output:

```
Misses in library cache during parse: 1
Optimizer goal: CHOOSE
Parsing user id: 25  (SCOTT)
```

These statements tell you that you had a library cache miss during SQL statement execution; that the optimizer goal is set to CHOOSE; and that SCOTT is the user who executed this particular bit of SQL. If multiple users executed the statement, the user who last executed the statement is listed.

Next comes the execution plan for the statement: This plan actually contains two execution plans, as shown just below, and you'll find detailed discussions of how to read them in the upcoming section "Reading and Interpreting Execution Plans."

```
Rows     Row Source Operation
-------  ---------------------------------------------------
      1  SORT AGGREGATE
  32014    INDEX FAST FULL SCAN (object id 20774)
Rows     Execution Plan
-------  ---------------------------------------------------
      0  SELECT STATEMENT   GOAL: CHOOSE
      1   SORT (AGGREGATE)
  32014     INDEX   GOAL: ANALYZED (FAST FULL SCAN) OF 'ID_EMP'
                (NON-UNIQUE)
```

Next up in the TKPROF output are the total overall statistics for the entire session. These are in the same format as the earlier individual statement statistics, but here they're divided into statistics for recursive SQL and nonrecursive SQL.

Finally, you get some summary information for the session traced. This information includes the number of user and internal (recursive) SQL statements, the number of sessions and users, and so on. This summary section also tells you which schema was used to generate the execution plan for the SQL statements.

Examples of Running TKPROF

Let's study a few examples of running TKPROF. This first example shows TKPROF with no parameters other than the required input and output file names:

```
TKPROF ora00104.trc traceout.txt
```

If we wanted to execute a TKPROF, generating execution plans for all SQL statements, we would issue a command like this:

```
TKPROF ora00104.trc traceout.txt explain=scott/tiger
```

Say we wanted to sort this report by the total elapsed time spent fetching, and then by the total disk reads during the fetch stage. Here's the command for that report:

```
TKPROF ora00104.trc traceout.txt explain=scott/tiger
    sort= (fchela, fchdsk)
```

The following command eliminates system calls from the output and creates a script called `insert.sql` that will load the TKPROF results into an Oracle table:

```
TKPROF ora00104.trc traceout.txt explain=scott/tiger
    sort= (fchela, fchdsk) insert=insert.sql
```

What if you wanted to create a `.sql` script that contained all the SQL statements in the trace file? If you wanted to run this script from SQL*Plus to replay all SQL statements on a database, you would include the RECORD parameter as shown here:

```
TKPROF ora00104.trc traceout.txt explain=scott/tiger
    sort= (fchela, fchdsk) insert=insert.sql record=record.sql
```

As you can see, TKPROF is a powerful tool for overall performance tuning. It's generally not used as a proactive monitoring tool, however, because the cost of session and database tracing can be expensive. Oracle does offer some alternatives, which we'll discuss next.

Using SQL*Plus Autotrace

Because tracing is expensive in terms of system resources and a bit cumbersome to implement, Oracle offers some other choices for monitoring. One is the excellent SQL*Plus Autotrace facility, which was added in the Oracle 7.3 days. Autotrace allows you to generate execution plans after every SQL statement. It also provides you with additional information such as physical and logical read information.

Setting up Autotrace doesn't take a lot of effort. The user/schema you are signed in to must have a *plan table* (PLAN_TABLE) installed; without this table, you'll get an error message. The PLAN_TABLE is populated with the current SQL execution plan and then read. The execution plan is formatted and presented to the user automatically.

To create the PLAN_TABLE, use the Oracle script utlxplan.sql in the $ORACLE_HOME/rdbms/admin directory.

Because the signed-on user must have the plan table installed in order to run Autotrace, the DBA may need to create multiple plan tables. An even better arrangement is to create one plan table, grant everyone else access to it, and set up synonyms pointing to that table. (Grants and synonyms are covered in Chapter 21 on database security.) In Listing 16.2 you can see an example of creating PLAN_TABLE using the utlxplan.sql script. We log in as user PLAN, which has already been created for this purpose. We then grant the user SCOTT access to the plan table, facilitating access through a synonym.

Listing 16.2: Setting Up the Plan Table for Autotrace

```
C:\>sqlplus plan/plan
SQL*Plus: Release 8.1.6.0.0 - Production on Sat Dec 30 01:40:26 2000
(c) Copyright 1999 Oracle Corporation.  All rights reserved.
Connected to:
Oracle8i Enterprise Edition Release 8.1.6.0.0 - Production
With the Partitioning option
JServer Release 8.1.6.0.0 - Production
SQL> @d:\oracle\ora816\rdbms\admin\utlxplan.sql
Table created.
SQL> grant all on plan_table to scott;
Grant succeeded.
SQL> connect scott/tiger
```

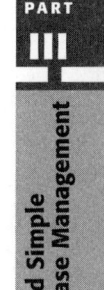

```
Connected.
SQL> create synonym plan_table for plan.plan_table;
Synonym created.
```

With the plan table established, you can enable Autotrace, with the command SET AUTOTRACE ON. Note that this command works only in SQL*Plus; it does not work with Server Manager.

When Autotrace is running, Oracle will return to you the execution plan of every SQL statement that executes. You'll also get various runtime information, such as physical and logical reads that occurred during the execution of the SQL statement, and the number of sorts and disk sorts that occurred.

NOTE About Sorting: When examining run statistics, watch the sorts that occur. If you see lots of sorts to disk, shown as sorts (disk), check the SORT_AREA_SIZE setting. Verify that it's allocating enough memory for sorting. Sorts to disk are going to be slower on the order of a magnitude than a sort in memory. When tuning SQL, make every attempt to get sort operations overall, whether to disk or memory, down to 0. Sort stats can tell you when an index needs to be built. Operations such as ORDER BY, DISTINCT, and GROUP BY can force Oracle to perform sort operations if indexes are not available on the objects being queried.

Listing 16.3 shows output from a SQL*Plus session with Autotrace enabled.

Listing 16.3: Output from SQL*Plus with Autotrace

```
SQL> set autotrace on
SQL> select count(*) from EMPLOYEE;
  COUNT(*)
----------
     32014
Execution Plan
----------------------------------------------------------
   0      SELECT STATEMENT Optimizer=CHOOSE (Cost=43 Card=1)
   1    0   SORT (AGGREGATE)
   2    1     INDEX (FAST FULL SCAN) OF 'ID_EMP' (NON-UNIQUE) (Cost=43
              Card=32014)
Statistics
----------------------------------------------------------
          0  recursive calls
          4  db block gets
```

```
    280  consistent gets
      0  physical reads
      1  sorts (memory)
      0  sorts (disk)
      1  rows processed
```

Using EXPLAIN PLAN

The old standby method of generating execution plans is to use the SQL command EXPLAIN PLAN (see Appendix F for the complete syntax of this command). As explained for Autotrace just above, EXPLAIN PLAN requires the presence of a plan table that is generated by executing the utlxplan.sql script. Execute this script in the schema in which you want to generate execution plans.

The EXPLAIN PLAN command requires that you feed it a SQL statement and an identifier for the statement. In return, the EXPLAIN PLAN command populates PLAN_TABLE with the execution plan for that SQL statement. A call to the EXPLAIN PLAN command looks like this:

```
EXPLAIN PLAN set statement_id='1' FOR
SELECT COUNT(*) FROM EMPLOYEE;
```

To get the execution plan out of the plan table, you query PLAN_TABLE. There are several versions of queries that do this, but Oracle provides a couple that work relatively well. Called utlxpls.sql and utlxplp.sql, they are both found in the $ORACLE_HOME/rdbms/admin directory. The primary difference between the two is that utlxplp.sql provides some parallel query statistics. An example of the utlxpls.sql output is shown just below (utlxplp.sql looks pretty much the same). In the upcoming section on reading execution plans, we'll actually dissect this particular plan.

```
Plan Table
--------------------------------------------------------------------------
| Operation              | Name    | Rows  | Bytes| Cost  | Pstart| Pstop |
--------------------------------------------------------------------------
| SELECT STATEMENT       |         |    1  |      |   43  |       |       |
|  SORT AGGREGATE        |         |    1  |      |       |       |       |
|   INDEX FAST FULL SCAN |ID_EMP   |   32K |      |   43  |       |       |
--------------------------------------------------------------------------
```

Tracing Other Users' Sessions

Sometimes a DBA or other user needs to trace another's session to which they do not have direct access. This may be the case when an application does not afford you the opportunity to turn on tracing before the application executes. Or it might be that a

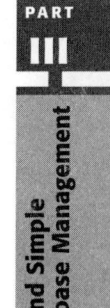

DBA notices odd behavior in a particular user's session (perhaps it's using substantial CPU resources or doing lots of disk sorts), and you want to trace the session unobtrusively. Oracle8i provides a procedure to do just that: It's a procedure called SET_SQL_TRACE_IN_SESSION, in the largely undocumented package DBMS_SYSTEM. (See Chapter 20 and Appendix D for a look at Oracle-supplied packages.)

Here's the definition of the procedure:

```
DBMS_SYSTEM.SET_SQL_TRACE_IN_SESSION
(SID        NUMBER     IN
 SERIAL#    NUMBER     IN
 SQL_TRACE  BOOLEAN    IN );
```

The procedure takes three parameters. The first two, the user SID and SERIAL#, are derived from V$SESSION; together they uniquely identify the user session. The final parameter is a Boolean, either TRUE (session trace turned on) or FALSE (session trace turned off).

Let's say we want to trace the session that Scott is currently running. First, we query the V$SESSION table to determine the SID and SERIAL# column values for his session:

```
SQL> select sid, serial#
  2  from v$session
  3  where username='SCOTT';
     SID    SERIAL#
---------- ----------
      13       5407
```

Now we execute the SET_SQL_TRACE_IN_SESSION procedure of DBMS_SESSION to start tracing this session, as follows:

```
SQL> exec dbms_system.set_sql_trace_in_session(13,5407,TRUE);
PL/SQL procedure successfully completed.
```

Once you've collected all the trace information you need, end the trace of the session with this command:

```
SQL> exec dbms_system.set_sql_trace_in_session(13,5407,FALSE);
PL/SQL procedure successfully completed.
```

Reading and Interpreting Execution Plans

In our opinion, reading and interpreting execution plans is a bit of an art. Now that you've learned how to get hold of one, let's examine its parts and see what it tells us.

The Execution Plan's Order of Operations

Each step in the execution plan has an output in the form of a *row source* that is passed on to the next step. Some steps, called *access paths,* produce the row sources from the database. Other steps, such as sort operations, just manipulate the rowsets passed to them. Some operations can return rowsets as they are being processed, and other operations wait until the entire rowset is processed before working on it. All of these approaches affect your tuning efforts. All of these operations put together ultimately produce the output that you requested in your SQL statement. So our first task is to determine the order in which the operations run.

The optimizer's job is to find the most efficient way to get to the required output. In doing so, it chooses from a variety of possible access paths and picks the ones that appear to be the most efficient. As the optimizer selects these paths, it assigns an efficiency cost to the various paths and execution plans.

Example 1

Here's the first example of an execution plan (generated using Autotrace in SQL*Plus) and its related query:

```
SET autotrace on
SELECT a.empno, a.ename, b.dname
FROM EMPLOYEE a, dept b
WHERE a.deptno=b.deptno;
Execution Plan
----------------------------------------------------------
0      SELECT STATEMENT Optimizer=CHOOSE (Cost=2590 Card=6723 Bytes=242028)
1    0   HASH JOIN (Cost=2590 Card=6723 Bytes=242028)
2    1     TABLE ACCESS (FULL) OF 'DEPT' (Cost=1 Card=21 Bytes=462)
3    1     TABLE ACCESS (FULL) OF 'EMPLOYEE' (Cost=2581 Card=32014 Bytes=448196)
```

When parsing an execution plan, Oracle uses a *reverse transversal* algorithm. Einstein might have loved this term, but for the rest of us it's a little abstract. It means that Oracle starts with the deepest operations first (those indented the farthest) and moves up from there. The preceding example shows three operations, each marked with an operation number at the far left. Operation 1 is a hash join. Operation 2 is a full table access of the DEPT table. Operation 3 is a full table access of the EMPLOYEE table. For now, don't worry about what these operations are. Just try to understand which one takes place first. (In case you were wondering, the second column of numbers in the execution plan identifies the parent step of the plan. In the foregoing example, step 1 is the parent step to steps 2 and 3.)

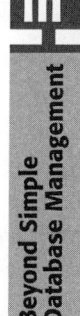

Here are some basic rules to keep in mind about execution plans:

1. The statement that is indented the most is the first step.

2. If two or more statements are indented at the same level, the topmost of these statements is executed first.

3. An index lookup associated with a table scan should be considered a single step. This is important because certain types of index scans are not coupled with table lookups.

4. If a parent step can process the row source returned from the child operation, Oracle will execute that step. This process can be cascaded up the entire execution plan chain until execution reaches an operation that requires all row sources to be executed. The operations that typically require all row sources are sorts and certain types of joins. (We'll discuss such operations later in this chapter.)

Based on these rules, the full table scan of DEPT (operation 2) is executed first. This is followed by the full table scan of EMPLOYEE (operation 3) and then the hash join (operation 1). Again, ignore the actual purpose of the operations for now.

Example 2

Let's look now at a slightly more complicated example. Here is the query:

```
SET autotrace on
SELECT a.empno, a.ename, b.dname
FROM EMPLOYEE a, dept b
WHERE a.deptno=b.deptno
and empno<7600;
```

and the resulting execution plan:

```
Execution Plan
----------------------------------------------------------
   0      SELECT STATEMENT Optimizer=CHOOSE (Cost=46 Card=30 Bytes=1080)
   1    0   HASH JOIN (Cost=46 Card=30 Bytes=1080)
   2    1     TABLE ACCESS (FULL) OF 'DEPT' (Cost=1 Card=21 Bytes=462)
   3    1     TABLE ACCESS (BY INDEX ROWID) OF 'EMPLOYEE' (Cost=44
                Card=144 Bytes=2016)
   4    3       INDEX (RANGE SCAN) OF 'ID_EMP' (NON-UNIQUE) (Cost=4 Card=144)
```

In this execution plan, the first column is the *step number* of the step in the plan. A *parent step* is the topmost statement, or any statement to which another statement is related. Here, statement 0 is the parent statement for the entire plan. Statement 1 is the parent statement for statements 2 and 3. The parent statement in an execution plan can be seen in the second column of the plan itself. A *child step* is any step that has a parent. All statements in this plan are children of another step, except step 0.

This execution plan has four operations. The first two are the same as in Example 1: a hash join (operation 1) and a full table scan of the DEPT table (operation 2). From this point, things begin to differ. This time, operation 3 is a table access by index ROWID; and there's another step, operation 4, which is an index range scan lookup.

So, in what order do these steps execute? You might be tempted to say 4, 2, 3, 1, but you'd be wrong. Operation 4 is an index scan that is associated with operation 3 (granted, we have not covered access paths yet, so you are excused if you missed this one). Therefore, operation 4 will not run until operation 3 runs. The correct order is really 2, 4, 3, and then 1. Here is what is really happening:

First we do the full table scan of the DEPT table. This is a hash join (see step 1). So, during the full table scan, the entire DEPT is loaded into memory.

Now, Oracle needs to make the join on DEPTNO between the DEPT table and the EMPLOYEE table. It finds there is an index, ID_EMP, which contains the column DEPTNO in it. That index is used in step 4 to speed up the query. Oracle will look for the DEPTNO value in all the rows in the EMPLOYEE table, in step 3. That rowset is returned to step 2, and processing continues, running steps 2-4-3 over and over until all rows are processed.

Step 2 is special in that there is no additional processing (like a sort) that has to be done to the rowsets being returned to it. Because of this, each time the step 2-4-3 iteration occurs, the rowset returned to step 1 is passed on to the user without delay. If an operation that required a sort of the entire rowset were present (for example, a GROUP BY operation), the user would have to wait for the results until all the rows were returned. In other words, some operations (such as nested loop operations) pass rowsets up the line of execution as they get them, somewhat like a river of data. Some operations (such as a sort merge join) must receive the entire rowset before passing it upstream, something like a dam in the middle of a river.

When tuning a query, you might find that a particular operation is preventing the initial results from being speedily returned. You may well want to tune that operation to return rowsets as soon as they are received. This is often the case with OLTP systems. Typically, inclusion of indexes and removal of SORT and GROUP BY operations will call for generating execution plans that return rowsets as they are processed. On the other hand, your choice will be different if you are running a data warehouse or EIS system. Since in this case you're probably looking for good overall throughput rather than a fast return of the first processed row, the best choice will be operations that wait until all rows are processed.

Oracle provides two hints to help you indicate your choice to the CBO:

- If you use the /*+ FIRST_ROWS */ hint, Oracle will try to optimize to return the first row as soon as possible.

- If you use the /*+ ALL_ROWS */ hint, Oracle will try to optimize using operations that process rows in bulk, rather than processing a row at a time.

Other hints, as well, can influence the CBO in this regard, and we'll discuss them as the chapter progresses.

An Easier Way to Follow the Execution Order

You might have had trouble understanding the two preceding examples of execution order. We have an alternate method of diagramming operations that just might help. The diagrams in this section walk you through the process of diagramming the execution order of a statement (we will use Example 2 for this discussion). The plan will look a little like a tree, so that's what we call it. Start from the top of the execution plan at statement 1. That's the top of your tree. On a piece of paper, draw a circle and put the number 1 in it (see Figure 16.1). That's step 1, which we also call a *node*.

FIGURE 16.1

Step 1 of diagramming the execution plan

Now draw a line starting from the bottom of circle 1 and moving southwest, as shown in Figure 16.1. Draw another circle and put in a 2; this represents statement 2 (see Figure 16.2). The line indicates that the two statements are connected, and we'll get to that in a moment. So now we have a *branch*, which is all the nodes so far, connected together from one common source.

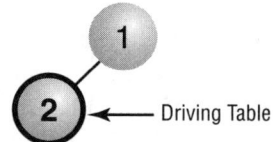

FIGURE 16.2

Step 2 of the execution plan diagram

At this point, because statement 2 is the first operation (and it is an access path to data), it is considered the *driving table* of the query. That means the entire query is driven off the resulting row sources returned by this one access.

NOTE In performance tuning, it's critical that you are using the correct driving table. The driving table of a query generally should be the row source returning the fewest numbers of rows (the smallest row source).

Now, move on to step 3 in the execution plan. Since step 3 is at the same level as step 2, it is a child of step 1 and returns a row source to step 1. Step 3 is also at the same level of indention as step 2, so you'll diagram step 3 as coming from step 1. Drop a line southeast from the step 1 circle, draw another circle, and enter a 3 (Figure 16.3).

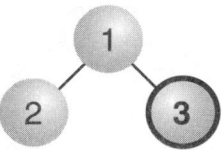

FIGURE 16.3
Step 3 of the execution plan diagram

You're now ready to deal with step 4. Since operation 4 is indented farther in than step three, that makes 4 a child of 3. So we draw a line down southeast from the step 3 circle and create another circle for step 4 (Figure 16.4).

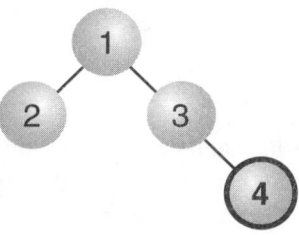

FIGURE 16.4
Step 4 of the execution plan diagram

Now that we have diagramed the statement, it's easy to diagram its execution. Start at step 1 and stay to the left. Continue downward to the left until you can go no farther (step 2). When you have gone as far downward as possible on the left side of the tree, the step you're on at that point is the first step that executes. In this case, then, you traverse the tree downward on the left from step 1 to step 2. Since there are no more steps below step 2 on this branch of the tree, step 2 is the first one that executes. Figure 16.5 demonstrates the steps of execution to this point.

FIGURE 16.5
Tracing the flow of execution

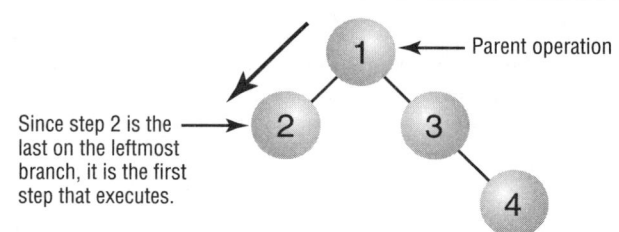

Now, move to the right side of the leftmost branch of the tree and move up that branch to the parent operation of that branch (step 1). Move to the next branch to the right, and then all the way to the bottom of the branch again; you're now at step 4. Move to the right side of the tree. The bottom-most node of the tree (step 4) is the next operation to execute. So the order of execution thus far is 2, 4. Move up the tree to the next node; that is the next operation (step 3). Finally, move up to the parent again (step 1). Since there are no more branches off to the right, the parent will now execute. Figure 16.6 is the last diagram in the tracing of this process.

FIGURE 16.6
Conclusion of tracing the flow of the execution plan

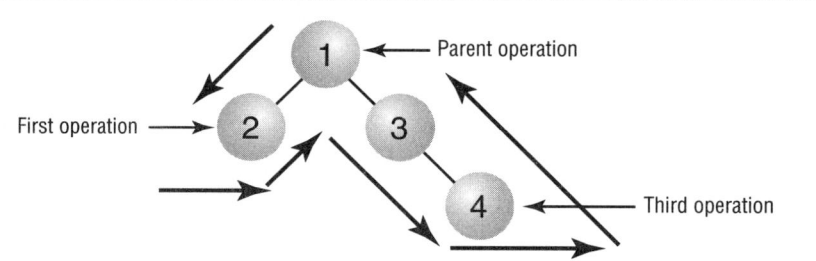

You can use this diagramming method to trace the path of any execution plan. Just remember that you list all like indented operations off their parent, with the first operation to the left and others off to the right of that first one. Then just trace it as you would trace your hand and fingers. Start from the left side, and follow all the fingers. Every time you reach the bottom of a finger, trace back up. As you trace up, those operations are firing.

> **TIP** In execution plan diagrams, along with the numbers of the operations, we like to show the number of rows being processed. (This data is not available when using Autotrace, but it is when using the EXPLAIN PLAN command.) We also like to note what operation is occurring (for example, we might show a SORT-MERGE-JOIN). This is very helpful when you are trying to tune a SQL statement.

Oracle Data Access Methods

Now let's talk about those access paths we've mentioned several times in the chapter so far. You already know that access paths are the methods Oracle uses to get to data. Oracle can use full table scans, index lookups, table lookups by ROWID, and several other types of access. Table 16.7 lists them all.

TABLE 16.7: TABLE AND INDEX DATA ACCESS PATHS

Operation	Execution Plan Designation	Description
FULL TABLE SCAN	TABLE ACCESS (FULL)	Scan of every row in the table; specifically, a scan of every block up to the high-water mark.
CLUSTER TABLE SCAN	TABLE ACCESS (CLUSTER)	Access to the data is via an index cluster key.
HASH SCAN	TABLE ACCESS (HASH)	Access to the rows in the table is through a hash key lookup.
ROWID TABLE LOOKUP	TABLE ACCESS (BY ROWID) or (BY INDEX ROWID)	Access to the table is facilitated through a lookup by the row's ROWID. Generally follows an index lookup of some sort.
SAMPLE TABLE LOOKUP	TABLE ACCESS (SAMPLE)	Access to the table as a result of the SAMPLE clause (available access paths are discussed later in this section).
COMBINATION INDEX SCANS	AND-EQUAL	Results from one or more index scans that are combined.
UNIQUE SCAN OF INDEX	INDEX (UNIQUE SCAN)	An index lookup that returns the ROWID of one and only one row.
INDEX RANGE SCAN	INDEX (RANGE SCAN)	An index lookup that returns multiple ROWIDs. Generally caused by a range lookup (for instance, a theta join) or because the index is not unique.
SAMPLE INDEX SCAN	INDEX (SAMPLE {fast_full_scan})	Taken by virtue of the SAMPLE clause (available SAMPLE access paths are discussed later in this section).

Continued

TABLE 16.7: TABLE AND INDEX DATA ACCESS PATHS (CONTINUED)

Operation	Execution Plan Designation	Description
INDEX FULL SCAN	INDEX (FULL)	A full scan of an index to scan for values that are not on the leading edge of the index. A FULL scan can be forced to eliminate sort operations.

Full Table Scans

During a full table scan, Oracle reads all rows of the table. Later operations remove rows from the returned row source that do not meet various SQL predicate requirements (the WHERE clause). Full table scans read the entire table, up to the high-water mark, which is one reason for the slowness of full table scan operations. Here's an execution plan for doing a fast full scan of a table:

```
Execution Plan
-----------------------------------------------------------
   0      SELECT STATEMENT Optimizer=CHOOSE (Cost=2581 Card=32014 Bytes=128056)
   1   0     TABLE ACCESS (FULL) OF 'EMPLOYEE' (Cost=2581 Card=32014 Bytes=128056)
```

Full table scans and indexed lookups are handled differently in the database buffer cache. Oracle loads full table scans into blocks at the end of the LRU list. Several blocks are loaded at one time (as designated by the init.ora parameter DB_MULTIBLOCK_READ_COUNT). See Chapter 5 for more information on the database buffer cache.

Table ROWID Lookups and Index Scans

Looking up a row by its ROWID is absolutely the fastest way to access that row. Unfortunately, ROWID lookups on tables generally follow index lookups, which results in additional I/O. Often the additional I/O associated with the index lookup is more than offset by the total reduction in I/O caused if you had to do a nonindex full table scan. However, there are cases when a full table scan will actually be faster. Generally, you should opt for index lookups over full table scans because they perform better and offer a larger variety of access path options.

In the execution plan studied in this section, we see a ROWID lookup on a table occurring after an *index range-scan lookup* of a nonunique index associated with the table. Because the index is not unique, the lookup of the index is a range scan. This means Oracle will start reading the index at some point, and will scan a range of index leaf nodes until it reaches a point at which it knows it can stop.

There are two types of index range scans: bounded and unbounded. The *bounded range scan* starts at one location in the index and traverses it until reaching a point where it can stop the lookup. An *unbounded range scan* begins at one point and continues through the entire index. Unbounded scans are often caused by predicates using a single > or < condition. This provides a starting point (say, WHERE empno > 500) for the index scan, but no ending point. In the bounded range scan, the predicate of the SQL statement might include both a > and < clause (say, WHERE empno > 500 AND empno < 1000). Bounded range scans are preferable to unbounded range scans in terms of performance.

In this next example, the index range scan will push ROWIDs to the table access operation. The table access operation will then pluck rows out of the EMPLOYEE table based on the ROWID returned in the preceding operation.

```
Execution Plan
----------------------------------------------------------
   0      SELECT STATEMENT Optimizer=CHOOSE (Cost=4 Card=2 Bytes=620)
   1    0   TABLE ACCESS (BY INDEX ROWID) OF 'EMPLOYEE' (Cost=4 Card=2 Bytes=620)
   2    1     INDEX (RANGE SCAN) OF 'ID_EMP' (NON-UNIQUE) (Cost=3 Card=2)
```

Sample Table Lookups

A new feature in Oracle8i—the ability to get a random sampling of data from a table—has added a new access path for both table and index lookups. You can do sample lookups based on the percentage of rows (the default) or by selecting a random number of blocks (using the BLOCK clause) that you want to read. The sample lookups are random in nature, so you won't get the same set of rows (or even the same number of rows) twice. See Appendix F for the syntax of the SAMPLE clause. Here's an example:

```
SELECT empno, ename
FROM emp sample (5)
order by ename;
SELECT empno, ename
FROM emp sample block (5)
order by ename;
```

Index Accesses

Index accesses are generally precursors to table accesses. Oracle selects the indexes to use based on the values in the SQL predicate (the WHERE clause). If a column in the WHERE clause is contained in an index, and it is the leading column of that index, Oracle generally will use that index. If two columns are contained in a given index, and they are the outer two columns of the index, that index may be used in addition to another index. Oracle can also do full index scans of indexes when the predicate is not on the leading edge. This approach requires a full scan of the index, which can be expensive in terms of system resources, but the advantage is that it can eliminate the need for a sort operation.

When an index is accessed in order to find rows in its associated table, Oracle finds the ROWID of the rows. The index is scanned starting with the header block, traversing the structure of the B*Tree through branch blocks, and finally to the leaf block where the desired values exist. In the leaf block, the values are associated with the ROWIDs of the referenced rows. Typically, after ROWIDs are retrieved from the index, they are passed to a subsequent table scan operation, which uses the ROWIDs to locate the rows quickly.

Sometimes the index contains all the columns that are requested in the query. In this case, Oracle only needs to scan the index and does not go to the table. Oracle8i can actually combine one or more indexes to resolve the query, again without needing to touch a table. Furthermore, if the query involves a join and the indexes on the tables of the join can resolve the query without needing to read those tables, they will do so.

Non–Data Execution Plan Operations

You'll encounter several other types of operations in the execution plans. These include join, set, miscellaneous, and aggregate operations. Table 16.8 lists and briefly describes them; you'll find more detail on their execution plans in the paragraphs that follow.

TABLE 16.8: NON–DATA EXECUTION PLAN OPERATIONS

Operation	Execution Plan Designation	Description of Operation
CONNECT BY (join operation)	CONNECT BY	Facilitates the execution of the SQL CONNECT BY command.
MERGE JOIN (join operation)	MERGE JOIN	Combines the row sources of two child operations. Note: Will also cause an additional SORT (JOIN). Typically, a MERGE JOIN occurs when two tables are accessed via full table scans.
MERGE JOIN (join operation)	MERGE JOIN (OUTER)	A merge join that does an outer join on the two row sources.

Continued

TABLE 16.8: NON–DATA EXECUTION PLAN OPERATIONS (CONTINUED)

Operation	Execution Plan Designation	Description of Operation
NESTED LOOP (join operation)	NESTED LOOP	Typically used when at least one table lookup involves an index.
NESTED LOOP (join operation)	NESTED LOOP (OUTER)	Performs an outer join on the two row sources. Typically used when at least one table lookup involves an index.
INDEX JOIN (join operation)	HASH JOIN	Joins the row sources of several index scans. If used, this operation indicates that no table was needed for the operation because all data was available in the indexes.
HASH JOIN (join operation)	HASH JOIN	Typically used when one of the joined tables is small. The smaller table is loaded into memory, a hash table is built from it, and the second table is joined to the hash table.
CONCATENATION (set operator)	CONCATENATION	Used to merge multiple rowsets passed into the operation.
INTERSECTION (set operator)	INTERSECTION	Causes two result sets to be compared; only rows common to both are returned.
MINUS (set operator)	MINUS	Given result set A and result set B, the MINUS operator removes rows in result set B from result set A. Occurs when the MINUS operator is used.
UNION-ALL (set operator)	UNION-ALL	Combines both row sources into one row source. Duplicates are returned in the resulting row source.
UNION (set operator)	UNION	Combines both row sources into one row source. Duplicates are not returned in the resulting row source.

Continued

TABLE 16.8: NON–DATA EXECUTION PLAN OPERATIONS (CONTINUED)

Operation	Execution Plan Designation	Description of Operation
VIEW (set operator)	VIEW	Indicates that a view has been accessed, or a temporary table.
FOR UPDATE (miscellaneous)	FOR UPDATE	Indicates that the row sources returned are locked as a result of the FOR UPDATE clause.
FILTER (miscellaneous)	FILTER	Removes rows from the result set that do not match the selection criteria.
REMOTE (miscellaneous)	REMOTE	Indicates use of a database link for that part of the operation.
SEQUENCE (miscellaneous)	SEQUENCE	Indicates that the sequence generator is being used to obtain a sequence number.
COUNT (aggregation)	COUNT	Counts the rows in the result set. Used in response to a COUNT function in the SQL statement.
COUNT (aggregation)	COUNT(STOPKEY)	Used when the ROWNUM pseudo-column is used to limit the number of rowsets returned to the user.
SORT (aggregation)	SORT(AGGREGATE)	Occurs when an aggregate function such as MAX is used on data that is already grouped. Can also occur when a SELECT contains a subquery using an aggregate.
SORT (aggregation)	SORT(JOIN)	Sorts the rows in preperation for a merge join. Generally happens after a full table scan.
SORT (aggregation)	SORT(UNIQUE)	Eliminates all duplicate rows from the row source passed into the sort.
SORT (aggregation)	SORT(GROUP BY)	Groups the row source in response to the presence of a GROUP BY clause.
SORT (aggregation)	SORT (ORDER BY)	Indicates that a row source is being sorted to satisfy an ORDER BY clause.

MERGE JOINS

When a merge join operation (also called a sort merge join) occurs, it takes the two row sources and merges them together into one row source output. A merge join cannot process the row sources until the child processes creating the row sources have completed their work. Therefore, a merge join typically does not return the first row quickly; generally, however, it will execute faster over time, particularly when full table scans are occurring. Merge joins typically occur when two full table scans are returning row sources. Typically a sort operation occurs after both full table scans. The row sources from these sorts are then passed on to the merge join operation.

A Cartesian join might occur if two tables are joined together and no join criterion is expressed between the two tables. Oracle uses Cartesian joins from time to time to reduce the overall runtime of a query. This is particularly true if one of the tables is small, such as a lookup table.

NESTED LOOPS

This type of join operation typically occurs when one of the tables involved in the join is accessed via an indexed lookup. With the nested loop operation, you start with a driving table. Oracle will fetch each valid row of that driving (or outer) table (possibly using indexed accesses) and then proceed to the inner table to find any corresponding values. Typically the lookup on the inner table is via an index, so it tends to be very fast and efficient.

One consideration when you have a SQL statement using nested loops is that the driving table should be the table with the smallest row source. If it is not, your query will not run optimally. Also, if the driving table returns a large number of rows that causes excessive scanning of the inner table, a nested loop access is probably not be the best access method.

HASH JOINS

Hash joins were introduced in Oracle 7.3 and are available only in cost-based optimization. Oracle uses hash joins when one of the row sources being joined is fairly small. This smaller table is scanned, and an in-memory hash table is built using the smaller table. Oracle then scans the larger table, using the values from the hash table to identify the matching rows. Hash joins are available only with equijoins.

The `init.ora` parameter HASH_AREA_SIZE is critical to the effective operation of hash joins. This parameter defines the maximum amount of private process memory that can be allocated to the hash join. The larger the HASH_AREA_SIZE, the more likely Oracle will select a hash join (and the more efficient the hash join process will be).

WARNING Oracle will use temporary segments when performing hash joins, which can negatively impact performance. Setting HASH_AREA_SIZE appropriately can negate the use of temporary segments.

Which Join Is Right for You?

Sort merge joins and hash joins provide good response in generally the same situations. In the following cases, they can be the better choice:

- In data warehousing and certain DSS systems, when creating reports that may take a long time to run
- When you're interested in overall throughput versus retrieval of the first row
- When you're joining to a large number of tables, and a large set of rows is being processed
- When you have sufficient memory and CPU available
- When you intend to parallel the operation

Nested loop operations are quite different from sort merge join operations and hash joins, and you'll use them in quite different situations. Consider nested loop operations when response time is critical, when you are supporting an OLTP system, or when indexes are available to support joins. Nested loops are rarely effective when indexes are not available to support the operation.

These are just general guidelines. Should you use nested loops or sort merge joins? As with many other answers to database administration questions, the answer really is, "it depends."

TIP If you're an expert at interpreting execution plans, or perhaps you just want to increase your understanding of Oracle's decision making on execution plan selection, then we have an event for you. If you use SET EVENT 10053 in your session, Oracle will generate a trace file that indicates the steps it took in deciding what execution plan to take. Try using this event if you're having problems understanding why an index you created isn't being used.

Tuning SQL Statements

You studied database tuning in general in Chapter 15, and SQL statement tuning is just one part of the overall tuning process. Nevertheless, SQL tuning generally gives you the biggest bang for your tuning buck—something on the order of 75 to 80 percent of your total return (as measured in throughput increases).

There are a great many books dedicated to the topic of tweaking SQL statements. We're going to hit the highlights here: the things you absolutely need to know, and the things that will produce the most noticeable results. Becoming a tuning expert is a never-ending process, and you'll want to keep working at it. As Oracle matures, new features are added and new access paths become available. Be sure to stay abreast of all these changes.

In this section we'll look at the primary goals of SQL tuning. We'll discuss fundamental SQL tuning mechanisms in both RBO and CBO environments. Finally, we'll look at a few examples of tweaking a SQL statement to make it the best it can be.

Before You Do Anything: Quantify Your Goals

Forrest Gump liked to take long walks without really knowing where he was going, but a DBA can't afford that luxury. We can't waste time on tuning efforts that have no real purpose or goal. A developer who asks you to tune some SQL to make it "run faster" isn't telling you want you need to know. To do it right, you need to ask some questions of the person needing the tuned statements.

How much faster do you want the application to run? How fast does it run now? Does it always run for the same amount of time or does the runtime vary? Have you tried to tune this statement yourself? The answers to these questions will help you quantify the goal of the tuning effort. The following list of questions is a good start for the DBA preparing to tune SQL code. You can always add your own environment-specific questions to the list.

- Is this a batch process or an online process?
- What do you consider is a reasonable time to allow for completion of this SQL statement?
- What is the minimum acceptable time for completion of this SQL statement?
- Have you tuned this statement to the best of your ability? What have you done to tune the statement? What helped, what didn't help, and why?
- What is the history of this SQL statement? Did it work well at first and then start to slow down? Did performance degrade gradually or all at once? Do you have

any baseline performance information about this query? (Objective data is more helpful here than user reports or subjective "gut feelings.")

- If this statement's performance has just recently slowed down, is there anything new happening with the application that might be the cause?

 TIP Remember that the developers may be unaware of the importance of the information they have. It's up to you to extract it with direct, probing questions.

Robert's Rant: Who Is Responsible for Tuning?

The DBA should be the *last* stop on the road to tuning assistance, in my opinion. This is particularly true in a large environment. Developers, not DBAs, should be responsible for principle tuning tasks. How come? Consider that working through the process of tuning SQL makes a better writer of SQL. And who writes the most SQL (and certainly the SQL with the most impact) in your business? The developer, of course. So if developers are charged with tuning the SQL they themselves write, you end up with much better developers. There's nothing like a 24-hour, up-all-night tuning exercise to encourage tidier, more efficient SQL code.

Improving Throughput and Response Time

Generally the goal of tuning SQL is to improve either the throughput or the response time of the statement. (Of course, you may be asked just to make the SQL statement return the correct values, but that is not a tuning issue.)

- Increasing throughput is most often the goal in a batch system. Typically, you'll be working on a SQL statement that worked fine for a while but suddenly doesn't. You'll see either a linear degradation in performance, or a sharp drop.

- Reducing response time is related to online processing. Attempts to reduce response time are usually related to data volume or growth, or a change in the nature of a business. SQL statements may stop working well because new processes or users are added to the system over time. As the database is taxed more and more, problems with waits, locking, and other issues will occur.

Solving throughput and response time problems requires reduction of both logical and physical I/Os to the database. That is what tuning is really all about.

The Importance of Having a Baseline

When the DBA analyzes a problem in preparation for tuning SQL, historical data is invaluable. We like to look at table row growth trends, user growth and use trends, trends of certain database statistics, and more. Unfortunately, Oracle does not provide these historical statistics.

Fortunately, however, as a lazy DBA, you have been proactive and have set up some monitoring yourself. You store historical row-growth statistics in a table for later use. You store statistics on user sessions that log in to the database at given points in the day. It's likely you've established plenty of other statistics-gathering mechanisms that occur regularly, to give you what you need in order to establish a baseline for the database's performance. Perhaps you're really on the ball and you even store past SQL activity statistics from the various V$VIEWS available. Of course, you have to weigh the need for statistics against the cost of collecting them, but as you do, remember that baselines are important.

TIP If you're still not clear on the concept of a lazy DBA, take another look at Chapter 15.

A baseline is critical to tuning because it gives you something against which to measure. If you see that, for some reason, the EMPLOYEE_HISTORY table grew from 100 rows to 10,000,000, perhaps that is the reason for the problem with the SQL statement. Maybe it's not the SQL statement at all, but it's a problem with the data. How did this table grow so fast? You can't afford to be myopic, so consider the whole picture. Be holistic in your approach to tuning and use those baseline stats. You'll be more successful.

Robert's Rant: Quantify the Problem!

It's hard to tune something if you have not first quantified what the problem is. A developer who just says "Well, the SQL statement runs slower" is not helping. How much slower is it running? Who is saying it's running slow? How fast did it used to run? The

Continued

> bottom line is that you need to probe to make sure there really is a problem. Sometimes you run into situations where you have a new employee who just thinks the report is too slow. Sometimes (and you'd be surprised how often this is the case) it turns out that the statement runs just fine but the developer heard that it was troubled from someone who heard it from someone who mentioned it in a meeting last Thursday.
>
> The issue is that you are a high-priced DBA; your time is money. If you only have one database to worry about, then it's not a big deal, but if you are managing tens of hundreds of databases, then it becomes a big deal. You have to manage your time, and if developers won't help you by quantifying the problem, and making sure there is a problem, then you need to do that. Nothing is worse than spending a great deal of time tuning a SQL statement just to find out that, hey, this thing runs just fine as it is.

Reducing I/Os

Having quantified the problem and reviewed your benchmarks, what is the bottom line for SQL statement tuning? It is reducing the number of I/Os, both physical and logical. The more I/Os that occur during the execution of a SQL statement, the longer that statement is going to take to run. Physical I/O is more expensive than logical I/O. Your first goal, then, is to eliminate or greatly reduce disk I/O. Logical I/O should be kept to a minimum, as well, even though it is less expensive. Logical I/O causes the database to work harder, and the more logical I/Os you have, the longer your query will take to run. Reducing a query from millions of logical I/Os to a few hundred can have a huge impact on the performance of the query.

Make Sure the Database Is Tuned

Maybe it goes without saying, but we'll say it anyway. Don't neglect the importance of tuning the database itself.

> **CONTINUED**
>
> If you're a lazy DBA, you do it on an ongoing basis. If you're not a lazy DBA or you're new to database analysis, then it should be among your first tasks. Make sure the memory structures (SGA) are optimal. Make sure you've arranged the most efficient placement of the database datafiles on the disks. Review Chapters 3 and 15 and ensure that all of the required elements are in place. A poorly tuned database will cause all sorts of problems and can wreak havoc on your SQL tuning efforts.

Making the Most of Indexes

Using indexes allows for more access options, including nested loop accesses. Even if you have small lookup tables, index them on the columns that are very selective. A SQL statement that has a WHERE clause may well benefit from an index. If the columns in the WHERE clause are selective, it's a good idea to create an index on those columns. Create a concatenated index if at all possible. The RBO will nearly always use an index if possible.

Using indexes provides the following benefits:

- Indexes make nested loops occur more often, which tends to improve response times.

- Indexes provide alternate methods of accessing the requested data, from single-value lookups to bounded and unbounded range scans. You gain additional flexibility and performance over using just an Oracle table alone.

- Indexes can significantly reduce the SQL statement's I/O, which is what tuning is all about.

Some DBAs use indexes sparingly because of their maintenance cost during DML operations. Certainly there is some cost, but it's outweighed in nearly every case by the benefits when querying the data. If index maintenance is a major issue in your environment, consider dropping the index, doing the maintenance required, and then rebuilding the index. You might also consider options such as partitioned tables and materialized views if you find your maintenance and load processes are suffering because of index maintenance overhead.

NOTE We can't overemphasize the importance of indexes, and DBAs with less experience may not realize this. Robert remembers one consulting assignment where he found not a single index in the database. The performance problems were solved fairly quickly with some strategic CREATE INDEX statements. (Robert says indexes are like oil wells—if you don't have one, get one! And if this pun brings back memories, be sure to e-mail him.)

When tuning a SQL statement, consider the following ways of maximizing index use:

Creating new indexes   This involves studying the query and the underlying table and determining if new indexes need to be created to improve query performance.

Tuning existing indexes   Will existing index structures (and the query) benefit from adding an additional column? Performance improves when you have more columns in the query's WHERE clause that are columns in the index. Always make sure that the first columns of the index are the most selective. For example, if you're indexing the EMPNO and NAME columns of the EMPLOYEE table, make sure the EMPNO column is listed first because it is more selective. There may be 500 Smiths but only one employee number 2200.

Alternative index types and table clustering   Oracle offers table clustering, hash clustering, bitmap indexing, and other indexing and performance-enhancement options. Consider the entire range of Oracle features when tuning your SQL statement.

Histograms   (Not available in RBO) Consider creating histograms on tables. Histograms help the CBO understand the distribution of data in the table. This helps it make better choices as to what indexes to use, or whether to use indexes at all).

Hints   (Not available in RBO) Hints are covered in detail in the section on tuning CBO-based statements.

The nature of the data   Consider or reexamine the database architecture. It may be that you are doing a vast number of joins and thus degrading performance to a level where tuning is basically hopeless. You may need to reconsider the architecture of the database and even denormalization of the data.

> **TIP** Also, if you are currently using RBO, consider a plan to migrate to CBO. Limiting yourself to RBO means you and your organization are missing out on the full range of tuning options. You can always force a statement to use RBO later if it isn't running quite right under CBO and you don't have the time to fine-tune it.

Disabling Indexes (on Purpose)

Now that we've sung the praises of indexes, we're going to tell you the other side of the story. Yes, it's true—in certain cases, indexes can be detrimental to the performance of your SQL statement. It's all about I/O; specifically, about the I/O required to read an index and then read the associated row in a table.

For each index read, you incur a minimum of two I/Os per row read, plus one additional I/O to read the header block of the index. You might incur additional I/Os to read leaf blocks, and if the index is inefficiently built, there might be even more I/Os to read through additional leaf blocks or index blocks that are empty. Say you have an EMPLOYEE table that indicates the gender of each employee. The gender column in the table will accept only two values, either M or F. An index created on this column would have some pretty poor selectivity. Let's assume there are 500 rows in the table and thus 500 index entries. Compare the number of I/Os (logical, in this case) required for (1) an index lookup for all values of M and (2) a full table scan for the same value.

For an index lookup, we would read through 499 entries of the index. That's 499 I/Os. Then we add one for the header block and one more for a leaf block, so we have 501 I/Os so far. Now we have to go to the table and do 499 more I/Os to look up the 499 rows that meet the index criteria. Total I/Os for this index lookup: 1000. Now compare this to a full table scan. We would scan through all the rows (that's 500 logical I/Os) and... That's all: 500 logical I/Os. There's no question in this case that we'd want to disable the costlier access to the index.

To disable use of an index, simply affix a blank to the end of the line of the WHERE clause that is causing the index lookup. For example, this statement results in an index lookup:

```
SELECT empno, dname
FROM    dept b, EMPLOYEE a
WHERE dname='RESEARCH'
and empno< 7950
and a.deptno=b.deptno;
```

which results in the following execution plan and statistics from Autotrace:

```
Elapsed: 00:00:00.41
Execution Plan
----------------------------------------------------------
   0      SELECT STATEMENT Optimizer=RULE
   1   0    NESTED LOOPS
   2   1      TABLE ACCESS (BY INDEX ROWID) OF 'EMPLOYEE'
   3   2        INDEX (RANGE SCAN) OF 'ID_EMP' (NON-UNIQUE)
   4   1      INDEX (RANGE SCAN) OF 'ID_DEPT' (NON-UNIQUE)
Statistics
----------------------------------------------------------
          0  recursive calls
          0  db block gets
         24  consistent gets
          0  physical reads
         14  rows processed
```

Notice the index lookup on the EMPLOYEE and DEPT tables. Every employee in EMPLOYEE is a member of the research department. Notice also that EMPLOYEE is the driving table. We know that DEPT is going to be a better driving table, however, because only one row is needed from it (as compared to reading every row from EMPLOYEE). So we're scanning the index on the EMPLOYEE table for every employee, and then we have to scan the DEPT index for every row in the EMPLOYEE table. This is costing us 24 consistent gets. What if we just did a full table scan of the EMPLOYEE table? We're reading every row anyway, so wouldn't it help? Let's see.

To force the optimizer to do a full table scan, append a +0 to the left side of the EMPNO < 7800 line in the WHERE clause:

```
SELECT empno, dname
FROM   dept b, EMPLOYEE a
WHERE dname='RESEARCH'
and empno+0< 7950
and a.deptno=b.deptno;
```

In the following output, you'll see there's not much improvement. In fact, we've managed to *increase* the number of logical I/Os by 12. Also, the runtime has about doubled.

```
Elapsed: 00:00:00.51
Execution Plan
----------------------------------------------------------
   0      SELECT STATEMENT Optimizer=RULE
```

```
    1    0    NESTED LOOPS
    2    1      TABLE ACCESS (FULL) OF 'EMPLOYEE'
    3    1      INDEX (RANGE SCAN) OF 'ID_DEPT' (NON-UNIQUE)
Statistics
----------------------------------------------------------
          0  recursive calls
         12  db block gets
         24  consistent gets
          0  physical reads
          0  sorts (memory)
          0  sorts (disk)
         14  rows processed
```

Tuning is an iterative thing, so you try and try again. Let's try again. We know we want DEPT to be the driving table. Let's disable the index on the DEPT table and see what happens:

```
SELECT empno, dname
FROM    dept b, EMPLOYEE a
WHERE dname='RESEARCH'
and empno< 7950
and a.deptno||' '=b.deptno||' ';
```

Now look at the runtime; it's slightly better—and the logical I/Os are very much improved!

```
Elapsed: 00:00:00.40
Execution Plan
----------------------------------------------------------
    0       SELECT STATEMENT Optimizer=RULE
    1    0    NESTED LOOPS
    2    1      TABLE ACCESS (FULL) OF 'DEPT'
    3    1      TABLE ACCESS (BY INDEX ROWID) OF 'EMPLOYEE'
    4    3        INDEX (RANGE SCAN) OF 'ID_EMP' (NON-UNIQUE)
Statistics
----------------------------------------------------------
          0  recursive calls
          4  db block gets
         11  consistent gets
          0  physical reads
          0  sorts (memory)
          0  sorts (disk)
         14  rows processed
```

So the big gain here appears to have come from disabling the DEPT index, which caused the RBO to make the DEPT table the driving table. Instead of 24 logical I/Os, we got 15—a 62 percent improvement in performance. Not bad. As you can see, disabling indexes can be a good thing or it can be a bad thing.

If you are using CBO, you can also disable the use of an index by using the NO_INDEX hint. You can use the hint without any parameters, or you can include parameters that cause certain indexes to be ignored by the optimizer. For example, if you didn't want to use the IX_EMPLOYEE index, you'd use

```
NO_INDEX(ix_employee)
```

Tuning Rule-Based Statements

One of the unfortunate facts of life about RBO is that the tuning options are somewhat limited. In this section we will discuss some issues that can make an impact on the overall performance of your RBO-based SQL statements.

Choosing the Driving Table Wisely

As discussed, the driving table is the table that provides the row sources to be resolved in the second table in the join. Often the driving table will be accessed through a full table scan, if the column is not indexed. In a rule-based statement, the driving table is generally the table with the lowest access path, but not always. When the access paths are alike between two tables, you can change the join order in RBO by reversing the table order in the FROM clause. This is because the last table in the FROM clause will be the driving table, if the access paths for both tables are the same. Because the driving table is the main row source, you always want it to be the table that will generate the smallest and thus most selective row source.

Let's examine an example in which you can see the impact of a well-chosen driving table. Assume you have an EMP table and a DEPT table, both of which are not indexed. Here is the first query:

```
SELECT a.empno, b.dname
FROM emp a, dept b
WHERE a.deptno=b.deptno;
```

And here are the execution plan and performance stats:

```
Elapsed: 00:00:39.87
Execution Plan
-----------------------------------------------------------
   0      SELECT STATEMENT Optimizer=RULE
   1   0    MERGE JOIN
   2   1      SORT (JOIN)
```

```
    3    2        TABLE ACCESS (FULL) OF 'DEPT'
    4    1      SORT (JOIN)
    5    4        TABLE ACCESS (FULL) OF 'EMP'
Statistics
----------------------------------------------------------
       2072  recursive calls
        325  db block gets
       2227  consistent gets
       3324  physical reads
      25536  redo size
    1391187  bytes sent via SQL*Net to client
     212546  bytes received via SQL*Net from client
       1913  SQL*Net roundtrips to/from client
          7  sorts (memory)
          1  sorts (disk)
      28672  rows processed
```

In this case, the DEPT table is the driving table. Notice that both tables are using full table scans, so they are ranked equally. To continue our example, let's reverse the order of the tables in the FROM clause and make the employee table the driving table, as follows:

```
SELECT a.empno, b.dname
FROM dept b, emp a
WHERE a.deptno=b.deptno;
```

Take a look at the execution plan and performance stats now, and notice the reversal of the join order of the DEPT and EMP tables:

```
Elapsed: 00:00:30.14
Execution Plan
----------------------------------------------------------
    0      SELECT STATEMENT Optimizer=RULE
    1    0   MERGE JOIN
    2    1      SORT (JOIN)
    3    2        TABLE ACCESS (FULL) OF 'EMP'
    4    1      SORT (JOIN)
    5    4        TABLE ACCESS (FULL) OF 'DEPT'
Statistics
----------------------------------------------------------
       2072  recursive calls
        297  db block gets
       2227  consistent gets
```

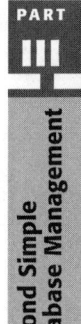

```
      3068  physical reads
     25736  redo size
   1391187  bytes sent via SQL*Net to client
    212546  bytes received via SQL*Net from client
      1913  SQL*Net roundtrips to/from client
         7  sorts (memory)
         1  sorts (disk)
     28672  rows processed
```

Notice that this plan executes almost 10 seconds faster than the first. A 10-second difference may not seem like much at first glance, but consider the significance if this same statement were executed several thousand times, perhaps as part of a month-end or payroll report. Those seconds add up quickly.

Accounting for Indexes

Of course, indexes can make for even more interesting tuning. Assume you have an index on the DEPT table that you are querying. You create the index on the join columns for DEPT, DEPTNO, and DNAME. What do you suppose will happen? Let's run the original query first. Then we'll reverse the order of the tables in the query and change the driving table.

```
Elapsed: 00:00:23.84
Execution Plan
----------------------------------------------------------
   0      SELECT STATEMENT Optimizer=RULE
   1    0   NESTED LOOPS
   2    1     TABLE ACCESS (FULL) OF 'EMP'
   3    1     INDEX (RANGE SCAN) OF 'IX_DEPT' (NON-UNIQUE)
Statistics
----------------------------------------------------------
       444  recursive calls
         6  db block gets
     36176  consistent gets
      1625  physical reads
        60  redo size
    908283  bytes sent via SQL*Net to client
    212546  bytes received via SQL*Net from client
      1913  SQL*Net roundtrips to/from client
         8  sorts (memory)
         0  sorts (disk)
     28672  rows processed
```

As you might expect, Oracle has picked up the index and used it. This has improved the overall performance of the query over the original by some 45 percent (which is a lesson unto itself). Now, let's see what happens when we reverse the FROM clause:

```
Elapsed: 00:00:24.65
Execution Plan
----------------------------------------------------------
   0      SELECT STATEMENT Optimizer=RULE
   1   0    NESTED LOOPS
   2   1      TABLE ACCESS (FULL) OF 'EMP'
   3   1      INDEX (RANGE SCAN) OF 'IX_DEPT' (NON-UNIQUE)
Statistics
----------------------------------------------------------
       444  recursive calls
         6  db block gets
     36175  consistent gets
      1625  physical reads
         0  redo size
    908283  bytes sent via SQL*Net to client
    212546  bytes received via SQL*Net from client
      1913  SQL*Net roundtrips to/from client
         8  sorts (memory)
         0  sorts (disk)
     28672  rows processed
```

In this case, Oracle did not change the execution plan. Regardless of the order of the objects in the FROM clause, Oracle is still going to follow the rules. So with the introduction of the index, Oracle in RBO will always choose to use the index and will choose to do a nested loop.

Tuning Cost-Based Statements

CBO tuning is a whole different animal than RBO tuning. In cost-based optimization, you have many more options available to you in terms of access paths. CBO is smarter than RBO because CBO takes advantage of generated statistics. And CBO queries are easier to tune because you can utilize hints to tell the optimizer which access paths are optimal.

Using Hints

Hints are part of CBO magic and probably your most important SQL tuning tool—they only work with CBO (except for the RULE hint). Hints let you direct the CBO on what access paths to take when generating the execution plan for your SQL statement. The CBO will not always follow your hints, for one reason or another, and you might find that it takes a combination of hints to get the response you want from SQL statement.

To use a hint in a SQL statement, you place it immediately after the SELECT statement in a comment (/* */) bracket, with a + immediately after the first /* symbol. For example:

```
/*+ RULE */
```

The format of the hint designation is important. You must put the + immediately after the /*. If you leave a space between the /* and the +, you invalidate the hint. You can also use the alternate --+ syntax for hint inclusion (as in --+ RULE).

A SQL statement can comprise multiple hints; each hint is separated by a space. Hints often have associated parameters, one of which is often the name of the table to which you want the hint applied. For example, when using the FULL hint to get full table scans, you give the hint a parameter specifying the name of the table you want to have the full table scan, as in

```
/*+ FULL(EMPLOYEE) */
```

You must use the table alias if it is defined. So if an alias, EMP, is used for the EMPLOYEE table, then the hint would be

```
--+ FULL(EMP)
```

 NOTE Oracle does not report an error when it encounters an invalid hint. It just ignores the hint and processes the SQL statement using whatever plan the optimizer would have generated apart from the hint. On the other hand, if you have a valid hint and an invalid hint in the same hint SQL statement, Oracle will accept the valid hint and throw out the invalid hint. So, when you do use hints, it's important to check the execution plans to make sure your hints are being incorporated.

When you use multiple hints, Oracle may ignore some of them depending on the access paths it decides to use. If a certain hint is very important but is not being implemented, you can try to force it by controlling the order of the join (using the ORDERED hint). Thus, if you force the table with the preferred hint to be the driving table of the join by using the ORDERED hint, Oracle is more likely to use the access path directed in the hint.

Tables 16.9 through 16.14 list and classify all hints available in Oracle8i and how to use them.

TABLE 16.9: OPTIMIZATION APPROACH HINTS

Hint Name	Parameters	Purpose/Example
ALL_ROWS	None	Causes Oracle to optimize the SQL statement for throughput rather than response. This mode tends to prefer full table scans and merge joins over index lookups. Example: /*+ ALL_ROWS */
FIRST_ROWS	None	Causes Oracle to optimize the SQL statement for response rather than throughput. This mode tends to prefer index lookups and nested loop lookups. Example: /*+ FIRST_ROWS */
CHOOSE	None	Causes the statement to run in RULE mode if no statistics are available. If statistics are available, then the statement will run in cost-based mode. Example: /*+ CHOOSE */
RULE	None	Causes the statement to run in rule-based mode regardless of the current system setting OPTIMIZER_MODE. Example: /*+ RULE */

TABLE 16.10: ACCESS METHOD HINTS

Hint Name	Parameters	Purpose/Example
FULL	Table name	Forces a full table scan of the listed table. If table has an alias, then the alias rather than the table name must be used in the hint. Example: /*+ FULL(e) */
ROWID	Table name	Suggests that the optimizer do a table scan by ROWID for the listed table. Example: /*+ ROWID(e) */
CLUSTER	Table name	Suggests that the optimizer do a cluster scan to access a specific table. Example: /*+ CLUSTER(e) */

Continued

TABLE 16.10: ACCESS METHOD HINTS (CONTINUED)

Hint Name	Parameters	Purpose/Example
HASH	Table name	Suggests that the optimizer do a hash scan to access the table specified. Applies only to tables stored in a cluster. Example: `/*+ HASH(e) */`
INDEX	Table name and index names	Specifies the index to be used to access the given table. Oracle will not consider a full table scan or a scan on another index on the table. Applies to both B*Tree and bitmap indexes. See also INDEX_COMBINE, which Oracle suggests when using bitmap indexes. When this hint specifies multiple indexes, Oracle selects the one that offers the best access. If no index name is specified, the optimizer chooses from all indexes available on the table. Full table scans are not considered. In multiple index listings or where no index is listed, Oracle may decide to scan multiple indexes and merge the results. Example: `/*+ INDEX (e ix_emp_01 ix_emp_02) */`
INDEX_ASC	Table name and index names	Designates an index scan for the table specified. Essentially the same as the INDEX hint. Example: `/*+ INDEX_ASC(e ix_bit_emp_01) */`
INDEX_COMBINE	Table name bitmap index names	Designates the specified bitmap index as the access path to the table specified. If no indexes are listed, the optimizer uses whatever combinations of bitmap indexes have the best-calculated cost. If multiple indexes are listed, Oracle will use the best combination of indexes that it finds. Example: `/*+ INDEX_COMBINE (e ix_bit_emp_01)*/`
INDEX_JOIN	Table name and index names	Designates an index join containing the specified indexes as the access path to the table specified. Example: `/*+ INDEX_JOIN */`

Continued

TABLE 16.10: ACCESS METHOD HINTS (CONTINUED)

Hint Name	Parameters	Purpose/Example
INDEX_DESC	Table name and index names	Causes the optimizer to choose a plan that instigates an index scan for the given table. If during the execution the query an index range scan is used, the index will be scanned in *descending* order (the reverse of the default Oracle setting for index scans). Example: /*+ INDEX_DESC */
INDEX_FFS	Table name and index name	Designates a fast full scan on the index specified, instead of a full scan of the associated table. Example: /*+ INDEX_FFS(emp ix_emp_01) */
NO_INDEX	Table name and index names	Causes the specified indexes associated with the listed table to be ignored by the optimizer. If no indexes are listed in this hint, then no indexes will be considered for the table. Example: /*+ NO_INDEX(emp ix_emp_01) */
AND_EQUAL	Table name and index names	Causes the optimizer to choose an execution plan for access to the listed table that includes a merge scan of the indexes listed. At least two indexes must be specified in the hint, and no more than five. Example: /*+ AND_EQUAL (emp ix_emp_02 ix_emp_03 ix_emp_04) */
USE_CONCAT	None	Forces a SQL statement using OR conditions in the WHERE clause to be transformed into a compound query (i.e., using a UNION ALL keyword). Example: /*+ USE_CONCAT */
NO_EXPAND	None	This hint removes OR expansions from consideration when the query is being optimized. It is the opposite of the USE_CONCAT query. Example: /*+ NO_EXPAND */
REWRITE	View name	Causes Oracle to search for eligible materialized views that could be used to rewrite the SQL query associated with the hint. You may specify one or more materialized view names to be considered. Example: /*+ REWRITE */

Continued

TABLE 16.10: ACCESS METHOD HINTS (CONTINUED)

Hint Name	Parameters	Purpose/Example
NOREWRITE	None	Disables query REWRITE for the given SQL statement, regardless of the QUERY_REWRITE_ENABLED setting. Example: /*+ NOREWRITE */

TABLE 16.11: JOIN ORDER HINTS

Hint Name	Parameters	Purpose/Example
ORDERED	None	Causes Oracle to join tables in the order shown in the statement's FROM clause. The join order is from left to right. Example:: /* ORDERED */
STAR	None	Suggests that the optimizer use a star query plan if possible, which causes the largest table (assumed to be the fact table) in the query to be joined last in the join order. This table must have a concatenated index with at least three columns that are part of the query in question. Applies only when there are three or more tables in the join. Do not include conflicting accesses or join hints with the STAR hint. See Chapter 19. Example: /*+ STAR */

TABLE 16.12: JOIN OPERATION HINTS

Hint Name	Parameters	Purpose/Example
USE_NL	Table names	Designates a nested loop join when joining the specified table to another row source. Specified table will be the inner table of the join. Example: /*+ USE_NL */

Continued

TABLE 16.12: JOIN OPERATION HINTS (CONTINUED)

Hint Name	Parameters	Purpose/Example
USE_MERGE	Table names	Designates a sort merge join when joining the specified table with another row source. Example: `/*+ USE_MERGE */`
USE_HASH	Table names	Causes Oracle to join the specified table with another row source by using a hash join. Example: `/*+ USE_HASH */`
DRIVING_SITE	Table name (remote)	Causes the row source from the local table being joined to the specified remote table to be sent to the remote system and processed on that system. Query result is then returned to the local site. Example: `/* DRIVING_SITE(emp) */`
LEADING	Table name	Causes the specified table to be used as the first table (or the driving table) of the join. Specifying multiple tables causes this hint to be ignored. The ORDERED hint overrides this hint. Example: `/*+ LEADING */`
HASH_AJ or MERGE_AJ	Table name	Used with a NOT IN subquery. Designates a sort merge anti-join or a hash anti-join, depending on the hint selected. Has the same effect as setting the always_anti_join parameter=MERGE or HASH. Example: `/*+ HASH_AJ (emp) */`
HASH_SJ	None	Used when doing EXISTS subqueries. Can cause an EXISTS subquery to be transformed into a hash semi-join or a sort merge semi-join to occur. Has the same effect as setting the parameter always_semi_join=HASH or MERGE. Example: `/*+ HASH_SJ */`

TABLE 16.13: PARALLEL EXECUTION HINTS

Hint Name	Parameters	Purpose/Example

PARALLEL	Table name; degree of parallelism; number of instances	Specifies desired number of concurrent parallel server processes to be used for the parallel table scan operations. Applies to SELECT, INSERT, UPDATE, and DELETE statements. Hint is ignored if parallel processing is disallowed. Oracle will decide these parameters based on `init.ora` settings if degree of parallelism isn't specified; if number of instances isn't specified; or if the keyword DEFAULT is used.
		Examples:
		`/*+ PARALLEL(emp 3,2) */`
		`/*+ PARALLEL(emp 4,1) PARALLEL(dept 4,1) */`
		`/*+ FULL(emp) PARALLEL(emp 5) */`
		`/*+ PARALLEL(emp DEFAULT,DEFAULT) */`

NOPARALLEL	Table name	Causes Oracle to override the specified table's PARALLEL setting, ensuring that access to the table will not be via parallel server processing. Example: `/*+ NOPARALLEL(dept) */`
APPEND	None	Used only with an INSERT clause, causing it to be a direct insert operation. No free space in currently allocated blocks is used. If an INSERT is parallelized, then APPEND mode will be used by default. Example: `/*+ APPEND */`
NOAPPEND	None	Causes APPEND operations to be overridden. Example: `/*+ NOAPPEND */`

PARALLEL_INDEX	Index name; degree of parallelism; number of instances	Specifies desired number of concurrent parallel server processes to be used for the parallel index operations. Applies only to partitioned indexes. Hint is ignored if parallel processing is disallowed. Oracle will decide these parameters based on `init.ora` settings if degree of parallelism isn't specified; if number of instances isn't specified; or if the keyword DEFAULT is used.
		Examples:
		`/*+ PARALLEL_INDEX(ix_emp 3,2) */`
		`/*+ PARALLEL(ix_emp DEFAULT,DEFAULT) */`

Continued

TABLE 16.13: PARALLEL EXECUTION HINTS

Hint Name	Parameters	Purpose/Example
NOPARALLEL_INDEX	Table name and index names	Disables parallel index scans on specified indexes. Example: `/*+ NOPARALLEL_INDEX(emp ix_emp_01) */`

TABLE 16.14: MISCELLANEOUS HINTS

Hint Name	Parameters	Purpose of hint
CACHE	Table name	Directs Oracle to place the blocks retrieved from the specified table during a full table scan at the MRU end of the database buffer cache rather than the LRU end. Example: `/*+ CACHE(emp) */`
NOCACHE	Table name	Overrides specified table's CACHE setting, and causes full scans to load rows into the LRU end of the database buffer cache (the default behavior). Example: `/*+ NOCACHE(emp) */`
MERGE	Table name	Applies to views that are part of a SQL statement (such as inline views). Enables complex merging behaviors such as merging the inline view into the SQL statement and using the inline view when the inline view contains GROUP BY or DISTINCT operators. Example: `/*+ MERGE (d) */` Note: Complex view merging is not the default CBO behavior. It must be enabled by setting the parameter optimizer_features_enable, or by using the MERGE hint, or by setting the parameter _complex_view_merging.
NO_MERGE	Table name	Causes Oracle not to merge mergeable views on the specified table. Example: `/*+ NO_MERGE */`

Continued

TABLE 16.14: MISCELLANEOUS HINTS (CONTINUED)

Hint Name	Parameters	Purpose of hint
UNNEST	None	Causes the optimizer to check validity of subquery block in a SQL statement, allowing unnesting to be enabled without Oracle checking the subquery's heuristics. Example: /*+ UNNEST */
NO_UNNEST	None	Disables query unnesting. Example: /*+ NO_UNNEST */
PUSH_SUBQ	None	Causes nonmerged subqueries to be evaluated as early as possible in statement's execution. Example: /*+ PUSH_SUBQ */
STAR_TRANSFORMATION	None	Forces the optimizer to use the best star transformation access plan. Does not guarantee that the transformation will take place. Example: /*+ STAR_TRANSFORMATION */
ORDERED_PREDICATES	None	Causes the optimizer to preserve the order of predicate evaluation. Does not apply to predicates used as index keys. Unlike other hints, this one goes in the WHERE clause. Example: /*+ ORDERED_PREDICATES */

Monitoring and Managing Excessive Hard Parsing

You can use several methods to analyze your SQL statements and determine if excessive parsing is happening in your Oracle system:

- You can trace the statement's execution in your session using Oracle's trace facility. This method is explained in a later section.

- Another option is to use the V$SQLAREA dynamic performance view. If the value in the PARSE_CALLS column is close to that in the EXECUTIONS column for the same statement (and the number of executions is significant), it's a signal that you should investigate why the statement is being reparsed.

- You can use V$SESSTAT view to get two other valuable statistics: PARSECOUNT (HARD) and EXECUTIONS. For example, this query will produce the values you need:

```
SELECT a.sid, a.statistic#, b.name, a.value
FROM v$sesstat a, v$statname b
WHERE a.statistic# IN (SELECT statistic# FROM v$statname
                       WHERE name IN
                       ('parse count (hard)','execute count') )
AND a.statistic#=b.statistic#
ORDER BY sid;
```

When you do see a great disparity in counts for hard parses and executions, one of the likely culprits is an application that is opening a cursor, closing it, and reopening it. Often this action will cause the statement to be parsed again. Such reparsing actually has to do with the private SQL area, which is stored in the PGA rather than the shared pool's library cache. If you didn't know this, you might try to add memory to the shared pool and would see no positive affect on parse/execute ratios. The solution that *will* work is to analyze the application and look for a way to reduce overall parse calls coming from it. In other words, this is a problem with the private memory allocated by the application, rather than shared database memory.

Further discussion of how to actually change applications in order to reduce parse calls is beyond the scope of this book.

NOTE If you are running MTS, the private SQL area is stored in the SGA. For more about MTS and configuration differences when running in that mode, see Chapter 9.

In terms of shared SQL areas, you can determine if you have reparsing issues by using this query from Chapter 15:

```
SELECT ((SUM(reloads) / SUM(pins) ) * 100) "Library Cache Reload Ratio"
FROM V$LIBRARYCACHE;
```

If the resulting number is low (less than 0.5 to 1 percent), few reloads are occurring and you're in good shape. If this number is high, however, consider adding memory to your SGA via the SHARED_POOL_SIZE parameter. (But take care not to allocate so much memory that you incur memory-to-disk swapping.)

If you find that the library cache reload ratio is bad, it may well mean that the size of the shared pool is insufficient for the database. In this event, Oracle will deallocate shared SQL area memory for new statements that need to be parsed. If you are not using reusable SQL, you'll find SQL statements with a small number of executions, and the number of parse calls will be almost the same as the number of execution calls.

Be careful when you're setting the size of the shared pool, however. It's quite possible to make it too large. Does that surprise you? Remember that for each SQL statement parsed, Oracle must verify that the statement is already in the shared pool. If you have a large shared pool, and it has also become particularly fragmented, you may find that parse times (hard and soft) will grow longer and longer. Eventually it takes longer to find like SQL statements than it would to just parse the statement in the first place.

The CURSOR_SHARING Parameter in Oracle8i

In Oracle 8.1.5 and later, an additional solution to parsing problems is the CURSOR_SHARING parameter. Setting CURSOR_SHARING=FORCE in the databases parameter file has the effect of replacing literal values in SQL statements with system-generated bind variables. The parameter has two values: EXACT (the default) and FORCE. Setting CURSOR_SHARING = FORCE can reduce the time required for reparse operations (but does not eliminate parse operations). It also reduces the amount of memory required for the SGA and may improve SQL query performance.

The CURSOR_SHARING parameter can be a great boon. Look at the results of using it on an Oracle system with the SCOTT/TIGER EMP table. Here is the first query executed against the table:

```
SELECT * FROM EMP WHERE empno=7369;
```

Now, here is an excerpt of what the V$SQLAREA looked like after this query:

```
SELECT substr(sql_text,1,40) sql_text, executions, loads, parse_calls
FROM v$sqlarea;
```

and here is the output:

```
SQL_TEXT                                 EXECUTIONS LOADS PARSE_CALLS
---------------------------------------- ---------- ----  -----------
SELECT * FROM EMP WHERE empno=:SYS_B_0        1       1         1
```

Notice the bind variable :SYS_B_0. Oracle replaced the literal value 7369 with the system-generated bind variable :SYS_B_0.

Let's run a similar query:

```
SELECT * FROM EMP WHERE empno=7900;
```

Oracle replaces the system bind variable :SYS_B_0 with the value 7900, and when you query V$SQLAREA you get this result:

```
SQL_TEXT                                 EXECUTIONS LOADS PARSE_CALLS
---------------------------------------- ---------- ----  -----------
SELECT * FROM EMP WHERE empno=:SYS_B_0        2       1         2
```

The EXECUTIONS parameter has increased, as has the PARSE_CALLS parameter (this is the same action you would see if you explicitly used a bind variable). The LOADS parameter has not increased, however, because this statement had to be loaded only once rather than twice. There is only one row in V$SQLAREA for this query, which indicates that Oracle replaced the literal with the bind value and used the existing SQL query in the shared SQL area.

You can see that if the shared SQL area contains lots of SQL statements that are similar except for certain literals in the WHERE clause, you might benefit from the use of CURSOR_SHARING set to FORCE. The default for this setting is CURSOR_SHARING=EXACT, which will require that SQL statements be exactly alike to be reused.

NOTE Oracle does not recommend setting CURSOR_SHARING to FORCE in a DSS environment.

TIP You shouldn't set CURSOR_SHARING to FORCE if you are using complex queries, query rewrite, or stored outlines. However, experience tells us never to rule out anything until it's proven unworkable. Try it: Set CURSOR_SHARING = FORCE and run some tests. If you see improvements, great. If not, reset CURSOR_SHARING and don't use it.

The CURSOR_SPACE_FOR_TIME Parameter

The `init.ora` parameter CURSOR_SPACE_FOR_TIME can also be of some help with parsing problems. This parameter has two values: TRUE and FALSE (the default). When set to TRUE, it allows the deallocation of a shared SQL area only when all cursors associated with the statement have been closed. Oracle's default behavior is that shared SQL areas may be released, even if there are current cursors (inactive) using that shared SQL area. This approach saves time because Oracle doesn't need to verify that the shared SQL area is in the cache. Also, setting this parameter to TRUE prevents the deallocation of private SQL areas until the associated cursors are closed.

By default, Oracle can (and will) remove the shared SQL area if it is aged out for another statement. Doing so can cause a small performance impact, but it is generally insignificant. If you set CURSOR_SPACE_FOR_TIME to TRUE, it is possible that Oracle will be unable to allocate memory in the shared SQL area, and it will unfortunately return an error to the user. So leave CURSOR_SPACE_FOR_TIME set to the default unless you can clearly demonstrate that it has a positive impact on performance.

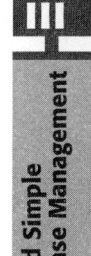

Other Tuning Suggestions

Some of the following miscellaneous tuning suggestions apply only to RBO, and some apply to both RBO and CBO.

Using Function-Based Indexes

The notion of function-based indexes is new as of Oracle8i. These indexes allow you to use a function in the predicate of a WHERE clause. (Prior to Oracle8i, use of a function in a WHERE clause's predicate forced an I/O-expensive full table scan.)

A function-based index is based on the function you use in the SQL statement. For example, the following SQL statement contains the UPPER function in the WHERE clause, to accommodate mixed-case names:

```
SELECT empno, ename, sal
FROM employee
WHERE upper(ename) = 'KING';
```

In this case, the execution plan tells the story, a full table scan of the EMPLOYEE table:

```
Execution Plan
----------------------------------------------------------
   0      SELECT STATEMENT Optimizer=CHOOSE
   1    0   TABLE ACCESS (FULL) OF 'EMPLOYEE'
```

If we create a function-based index, however, we end up with an index scan. Here is the statement to create the function-based index:

```
CREATE INDEX id_func_employee_ename_01 on employee (upper(ename));
```

We now query the EMPLOYEE table again, and voilà! Here is the new execution plan:

```
Execution Plan
----------------------------------------------------------
   0      SELECT STATEMENT Optimizer=CHOOSE (Cost=1 Card=1 Bytes=11)
   1    0   TABLE ACCESS (BY INDEX ROWID) OF 'EMPLOYEE' (Cost=1 Card=1 Bytes=11)
   2    1     INDEX (RANGE SCAN) OF 'ID_FUNC_EMPLOYEE_ENAME_01' (NON-UNIQUE)
                (Cost=1 Card=1)
```

There are several database configuration (init.ora) requirements associated with function-based indexes:

- The parameter QUERY_REWRITE_INTEGRITY must be set to TRUSTED.
- The parameter QUERY_REWRITE_ENABLED must be set to TRUE.
- The parameter COMPATIBLE must be 8.1.0.0.0 or greater.

Also, remember these rules:

- In order to use the function-based index after it is created, the table must be analyzed.
- Since NULL values are not stored in indexes, the query must not return any NULL values from the function.

 TIP Make sure you check your execution plans if you expect to use a function-based index. You'll often have to include a hint to get the SQL statement to use a function-based index, because the optimizer does not choose it as the access path of choice.

Accidentally Forcing Table Scans

Unfortunately, it's possible to code a SQL statement that inhibits index accesses, so watch out. Here are a few statements that will do it:

Using the != operator   (RBO only) Oracle will not use an index if you use the != operator. If you want to make sure an index is used, replace the != operator with an IN clause that contains the acceptable values. For example, replace this statement:

```
SELECT empno FROM EMPLOYEE
WHERE deptno != 30;
```

with this statement:

```
SELECT empno FROM EMPLOYEE
WHERE deptno in (10,20,40,50);
```

 NOTE When using CBO, != operators can take advantage of indexes by using full index scans. You may need to use hints to force this action.

Searching for NULL values in columns   (RBO, CBO) Because NULL values are not stored in indexes, query searching for NULL values in a column will force a full table scan. If you are going to create an index on a column, consider making that column NOT NULL so as to avoid this problem.

Searching for values using the NOT NULL clause   (RBO only) This search does not necessarily disable an index, but the optimizer tends to do full table scans when NOT NULL operations are performed. With CBO you can use hints to force index usage.

Disabling an index with a function   (RBO, and CBO if not using function-based indexes) If you use a function on either side of a line of the WHERE clause, it disables that column's ability to be part of an index scan. This restriction is negated in Oracle8i, however, with the function-based index capability. In the following example, Oracle would not be able to use an index on the ENAME column of the EMPLOYEE table because the UPPER function is employed to ensure that the name comparison is done in uppercase:

    SELECT empno from EMPLOYEE where upper(ename) = 'KING';

TIP   Function-based indexes in Oracle8i are available only with CBO.

Using the LIKE operator   (RBO, CBO) Use of the LIKE operator can inhibit some indexes. If you issue this query:

    SELECT * FROM EMPLOYEE WHERE ENAME LIKE 'TOAD%'

an index can be used. Flip the % around, however, and the query

    SELECT * FROM EMPLOYEE WHERE ENAME LIKE '%OAD'

will force a full table scan. With CBO you can use hints to force the optimizer to use an index, if that index contains the column.

NOTE   Wildcard searches can benefit significantly from the presence of an index. If you are using % searches (i.e., using the LIKE operator), review your indexing strategy.

Watch Out for the FOR UPDATE Clause

The FOR UPDATE clause can cause problems. Because it locks all the rows during the execute stage of the SQL operation rather than at the fetch stage, rows end up being locked a lot longer than normal. Also, because the whole rowset has to be read in before any fetch can occur, you can tune a FOR UPDATE statement only for throughput, not for response time.

TIP In the FOR UPDATE clause, an undocumented feature called SKIP LOCKED will cause the SELECT FOR UPDATE statement to skip any rows that are already locked. It works only in PL/SQL program units, though.

Watch for the High-Water Mark

The high-water mark of a table can cause serious performance degradation for your SQL query. The high-water mark is the highest point to which data has been loaded into the table. As more data is loaded (assuming all blocks are full), the high-water mark increases.

Don't confuse the high-water mark with the overall size of the table. The size of an Oracle table is allocated when the table is created (via the INITIAL parameter, and the NEXT parameter if the table is more than one extent at creation). The high-water mark, on the other hand, is set to 0 when the table is first created. If a 200-byte row is then inserted, the high-water mark will be 200 bytes.

To determine the high-water mark of a table, look at the DBA_TABLES view if the table is analyzed. The following query will show you the high-water mark and the amount of space allocated to the table. The column called BLOCKS indicates the high-water mark, and the EMPTY_SPACE column indicates the amount of space above the high-water mark.

```
SELECT owner, table_name, blocks, empty_blocks
FROM dba_tables
WHERE owner != 'SYS';
```

Reducing the Impact of Full Table Scans

The real impact of a full table scan is that it must read every block up to the high-water mark of the table. There are several ways to mitigate the impacts of full table scans.

Keep an eye on the table's high-water mark. If you find that the high-water mark is moving up constantly, yet the number of rows is not growing, you may have a problem with a load into the table. Keep an eye on things using the SQL query shown in the section just above. If you find a table with a high-water mark that is excessively high, try rebuilding the table with the ALTER TABLE REBUILD command.

Pack the blocks of the table. If the table in which you're doing the full table scan isn't set with the correct PCTFREE and PCTUSED parameters, block space will be inefficiently used. See "Monitoring Inefficient Block Usage in an

Object" in Chapter 15 for a query that will help you determine if tables are storing data inefficiently. If they are, you may want to increase PCTFREE and decrease PCTUSED.

Are full table scans really necessary? It may be that an index will help performance of the query.

Move large columns to another table. Good candidates are columns used infrequently (LONG or large VARCHAR2 columns, for example). Doing so will not affect BLOBs because they use out-of-line storage.

Use a parallel query to access the table. Doing so can significantly improve the runtime performance of queries against the table.

DBMS_STATS

In this section we discuss the DBMS_STATS package, new in Oracle8i. This package is used to generate statistics much as the ANALYZE command does, but DBMS_STATS does more. It allows you, for example, to store object statistics in a user-defined table rather than in the data dictionary. This package also allows you to swap statistics back and forth between the data dictionary and user-defined statistics tables. You might move object statistics between, say, a production database and a test database. This can be most helpful in confirming that execution plans for queries in the test environment will look the same in production.

DBMS_STATS vs. ANALYZE

Oracle8i's DBMS_STATS package offers the following benefits over the ANALYZE command for generating database statistics:

- In DBMS_STATS, statistics-gathering operations can be performed in parallel rather than in serial (as is the case with ANALYZE).
- Statistics gathered with DBMS_STATS are likely to be more accurate for partitioned tables than those generated by the COMPUTE command.
- You can collect statistics in the data dictionary (for optimizer use) or in a separate user-defined statistics table.
- DBMS_STATS includes functionality with which you can save and restore current system statistics, create user-generated statistics on objects, and export and import statistics from other databases.

In comparison to DBMS_STATS, the ANALYZE command has its own benefits:

- ANALYZE gathers certain statistics that are not gathered by the DBMS_STATS package, including such columns as the chained row count, average free space, and the number of unused blocks in the table. Also, column level statistics are not collected.
- ANALYZE has been in use longer and is likely more dependable.

Note that the ANALYZE command will not be able to overwrite statistics created by the DBMS_STATS package. Within the DBMS_STATS package there are several procedures that can be used to analyze objects in your database. The available procedures also allow you to maintain object statistics. These procedures are listed in Table 16.15.

TABLE 16.15: COMMON PROCEDURES IN DBMS_STATS

Procedure	Purpose
GATHER_INDEX_STATS, GATHER_TABLE_STATS, GATHER_SCHEMA_STATS, GATHER_DATABASE_STATS	Collects statistics on the index, table, or all objects in the schema or database.
SET_COLUMN_STATS, SET_INDEX_STATS, SET_TABLE_STATS	Sets column, index-, or table-related statistics.
GET_COLUMN_STATS, GET_TABLE_STATS, GET_INDEX_STATS	Gets all column-, table-, or index-related information.
DELETE_INDEX_STATS, DELETE_TABLE_STATS, DELETE_COLUMN_STATS, DELETE_SCHEMA_STATS, DELETE_DATABASE_STATS,	Deletes index-, table-, column-, schema-, or database-related statistics.
CREATE_STAT_TABLE	Creates table in schema to store statistics.
DROP_STAT_TABLE	Drops statistics storage table.
EXPORT_COLUMN_STATS, EXPORT_TABLE_STATS, EXPORT_INDEX_STATS, EXPORT_SCHEMA_STATS, EXPORT_DATABASE_STATS	Gets specific column, table, index, schema, or database dictionary statistics and stores in user-defined statistics table.
IMPORT_COLUMN_STATS, IMPORT_TABLE_STATS, IMPORT_INDEX_STATS, IMPORT_SCHEMA_STATS, IMPORT_DATABASE_STATS	Retrieves statistics for specified column, table, index, schema, or database from user-defined stat table and installs in data dictionary.
GENERATE_STATS	Generates statistics on object from previously collected statistics on similar objects.

Moving Statistics Among Databases

If you are doing development on databases that do not have the same production environment, you may see significant differences in the execution plans generated for your SQL. You may want to move your database statistics among various databases to try and stabilize the execution plans. The DBMS_STATS package makes this very easy to do. Here are the steps:

1. Build the user-created statistics table with the procedure DBMS_STATS.CREATE_STAT_TABLE.

2. Export statistics from the data dictionary to the user-created statistics table using the procedure DBMS_STATS.EXPORT_?_STATS. These statistics can be table, index, schema, or database statistics.

3. Using the Export and Import utilities, export the user statistics table and import it into the appropriate database.

4. Use the DBMS_STATS.IMPORT_?_STATS procedure to import the statistics from the statistics table into the data dictionary.

DBMS_STATS Common Parameters

The common parameters STATOWN, STATTAB, and STATID in DBMS_STATS allow you to store your own statistics somewhere other than the data dictionary. In this manner you can generate statistics in your own set of dictionary tables, thus avoiding the danger of affecting the optimizer's overall operation.

- STATOWN (defaults to the current schema) and STATTAB (defaults to the data dictionary) allow the user to define the names of the owner and table for storing the statistics.

- With STATID you can define a "version" of the statistics being loaded into the table. This lets you store more than one set of statistics in a table, eliminating the need to create multiple tables to store statistics.

Using DBMS_STATS

Listing 16.4 shows several examples of using the DBMS_STATS package.

Listing 16.4: Examples of using DBMS_STATS

```
-- Create the user-defined statistics table. It will be
-- called STATTABLE and will be put
-- in the SCOTT schema using the default tablespace for SCOTT.
exec dbms_stats.create_stat_table('SCOTT','STATTABLE');
```

```
-- Now let's generate some statistics! This next statement will
-- generate statistics, and put them in the data dictionary for the
-- optimizer to use.
exec dbms_stats.gather_table_stats('SCOTT','EMPLOYEE');
-- This next run will populate the stats for the EMPLOYEE table in
-- the statistics table we created called STATTABLE. It will
-- update the data dictionary also. This will also generate column-
-- level statistics.
exec dbms_stats.gather_table_stats('SCOTT','EMPLOYEE', -
stattab=>'STATTABLE', statid=>'RF');
-- Now, let's gather for the entire schema!
exec dbms_stats.gather_schema_stats('SCOTT',stattab=>'STATTABLE');
-- Let's drop statistics on the EMPLOYEE table
exec dbms_stats.delete_table_stats('SCOTT','EMPLOYEE',
  -stattab=>'STATTABLE');
-- let's export the statistics to the data dictionary!
exec dbms_stats.export_table_stats('SCOTT','EMPLOYEE', -
    stattab=>'STATTABLE');
-- let's import the statistics from the data dictionary!
exec dbms_stats.import_table_stats('SCOTT','EMPLOYEE', -
    stattab=>'STATTABLE');
-- Let's look at the statistics contained in the statistice table
set serveroutput on
exec dbms_output.enable(10000)
declare
v_numrow number;
v_numblks number;
v_avgrlen number;
begin
dbms_stats.get_table_stats('SCOTT','EMPLOYEE',numrows=>v_numrow,
    numblks=>v_numblks,avgrlen=>v_avgrlen, stattab=>'STATTABLE',
    statown=>'SCOTT');
dbms_output.put_line('Number of rows: '||v_numrow);
end;
/
Number of rows: 15
PL/SQL procedure successfully completed.
-- Finally, we will drop the stats table
exec dbms_stats.drop_stat_table('SCOTT','STATTABLE');
```

Maintaining Current Statistics

The CBO depends on the statistics collected on the various objects used during execution of a given query. Of course, because database data changes by virtue of DML operations (INSERT, UPDATE, DELETE), the statistics for particular objects may change. Part of the DBA's challenge is to keep these statistics as current as possible. Oracle8i offers some new features that can help you manage this issue much more effectively.

The COMPUTE Option on CREATE INDEX

When you rebuild an index in Oracle, the statistics associated with that index are by default lost, and you have to analyze the index again. Using the COMPUTE clause of the CREATE INDEX command, you can tell Oracle to generate index statistics during the index build process. This eliminates the need to analyze the index later.

The MONITORING Option

Once you have analyzed an object, there is no need to go back and do it again unless its contents change. But if the object is static, why waste time analyzing it again? Recognizing this fact, Oracle8i has added the MONITORING option. You use the MONITORING option with the CREATE TABLE or ALTER TABLE command, to monitor for INSERT, UPDATE, and DELETE activities, as well as TRUNCATE activities.

Here's an example of activating the MONITORING option when you alter your table:

```
ALTER TABLE employee MONITORING;
```

Now Oracle will keep track of all changes to the object. Every three hours, or when the system is shut down and restarted, SMON will review all the changes and incorporate them into a view called SYS.DBA_TAB_MODIFICATIONS. This view lists all operations (INSERT, UPDATE, DELETE, and TRUNCATE) that occur on a table.

NOTE In testing, we didn't notice that the MONITORING clause had much performance impact, but you'd be wise to test performance carefully after enabling the feature.

TIP MONITORING can be useful in determining whether the PCTUSED and PCTFREE settings are set up reasonably for a particular table. This clause will help you determine the velocity of changes, by reviewing the SYS.DBA_TAB_MODIFICATIONS table.

GATHER STALE

Having enabled monitoring, you can use the GATHER STALE option to update the data dictionary with the tables that have changed. This option is available to the two DBMS_STATS programs, GATHER_SCHEMA_STATS and GATHER_DATABASE_STATS.

NOTE The GATHER STALE option updates only the statistics listed in the SYS.DBA_TAB_MODIFICATIONS view. If this view has not been updated because SMON has not yet populated it, the table statistics will not be updated.

Here's an example of GATHER STALE with DBMS_STATS.GATHER_SCHEMA_STATS:

```
exec dbms_stats.gather_schema_stats('SCOTT',stattab=>'STATTABLE', -
   options=>'GATHER STALE');
```

TIP You might want to schedule the execution of the DBMS_STATS.GATHER_SCHEMA_STATS stored procedure with the GATHER STALE option with a database job so that it runs on a regular basis.

Oracle8i's Plan Stability

Oracle's plan stability features protect the database and the DBA from "overenthusiastic" optimization. The optimizer has this irritating habit of changing execution plans after a database change—even when we don't want that to happen.

Execution plans can change for a number of reasons, including addition of new objects to a database (such as an index) or addition of significant volumes of data. This is what is supposed to happen, and the optimizer is supposed to be "intelligent" enough to see the changes and find cheaper and smarter ways to get to the data you want. These adjustments can cause a quick-running, well-behaved query to become suddenly slow and undependable. It's sometimes a result of some change to the tables that is picked up by an ANALYZE operation (even though the old plan works just fine, thank you very much). For the most part we want these execution plan changes to occur, but sometimes we don't. There are often special cases where queries were tuned to get the best execution path. Perhaps we just don't want old execution plan changed. Many times, the addition of an index to speed up the performance of one query can have an unexpected negative impact on another query.

It is for all these situations that *plan stability* was introduced in Oracle8i. With plan stability, we can protect execution plans from being changed by the optimizer. We can save execution plans before we make database changes; we can make those changes and determine the impact on the queries in question. If a given execution plan is unsatisfactory after the changes are made, but we still want to keep the changes in place because of positive performance impact, then we can simply force a query to use the existing, saved execution plan.

NOTE For any stored execution plan to be used for any given SQL statement, the stored statement must match exactly. The rules outlined earlier in this chapter for reusing shared SQL statements apply here, as well.

When you create an Oracle8i database, a user called OUTLN is created as a part of SQL.bsq, as well as two tables called OL$ and OL$HINTS. The OL$ table stores the outlines, including their names, the associated SQL text, the category, and the timestamp of the outline's creation. The OL$HINTS table stores any hints associated with the SQL stored in each OL$ table. Two views, ?_OUTLINES and ?_OUTLINE_HINTS, allow you to see the stored plan information.

Creating Stored Outlines

To take advantage of plan stability, you must create stored outlines of the SQL for which you want to secure the execution plan. You can generate stored outlines at either the session level or the system level. When creating stored outlines, you can assign a group of outlines to a unique category name. Doing so allows you to store multiple plans for the same SQL statement.

Creating stored outlines is a simple, three-step process:

1. Enable the storage of stored outlines for the SQL you are preparing to execute, using the ALTER SYSTEM or ALTER SESSION commands:
   ALTER SYSTEM SET CREATE_STORED_OUTLINES={TRUE|*category*};
   ALTER SESSION SET CREATE_STORED_OUTLINES={TRUE|*category*};

   Note that setting CREATE_STORED_OUTLINES to TRUE uses a default category, but you can also name the category to which the statement belongs. This simplifies the management of stored outlines.

2. Execute the SQL statements for which you are generating outlines.
3. Disable the storage of stored outlines, using the ALTER SYSTEM or ALTER SESSION commands:
   ALTER SYSTEM SET CREATE_STORED_OUTLINES=FALSE;
   ALTER SESSION SET CREATE_STORED_OUTLINES=FALSE;

That's all there is to it!

You can manually create a stored outline, as well. Use the CREATE OR REPLACE OUTLINE statement, as shown here:

CREATE OR REPLACE OUTLINE scott_emp_outline
FOR CATEGORY scott
ON
SELECT COUNT (*) FROM emp
WHERE empno=790;

With this method, the system will validate the SQL just as it would if you were executing it from the command line. This is because the SQL goes through the entire parse stage including syntax checks, as well as execution plan generation.

Using and Modifying Stored Outlines

After the stored outlines are created, you must enable their use by executing the ALTER SYSTEM or ALTER SESSION commands:

ALTER SYSTEM SET USE_STORED_OUTLINES={TRUE | Named Category};
ALTER SESSION SET USE_STORED_OUTLINES={TRUE | Named Category};

Oracle will start using the named outlines of either the default or named category at this point. To stop using stored outlines, issue the same commands with a FALSE parameter.

NOTE USE_STORED_OUTLINES and CREATE_STORED_OUTLINES are not parameters that can be set in init.ora. They can only be set only at the system or session level by using the ALTER SYSTEM or ALTER SESSION commands.

To alter existing stored outlines, use the ALTER OUTLINE statement. This command allows you to rename outlines, rebuild a stored outline's execution plan, or rename a category. Examples:

ALTER OUTLINE Robert RENAME TO old_robert;

```
ALTER OUTLINE Robert Change category to Gonzo;
ALTER OUTLINE Robert REBUILD;
```

In addition, you can drop outlines with the DROP OUTLINE command.

Data Dictionary Views of Stored Outlines

Oracle provides several data dictionary views for getting information about stored outlines that reside in the database.

- V$SQL has the OUTLINE_CATEGORY column that tells you whether the SQL statement in the V$SQL view is using a stored outline.
- ?_OUTLINES provides information about each individual outline, including its name and the SQL text that is stored.
- ?_OUTLINE_HINTS provides information about all hints associated with a stored outline.

Managing Stored Outlines with OUTLN_PKG

Oracle provides the OUTLN_PKG package for managing stored outlines. It is created automatically when you create your Oracle database. OUTLN_PKG contains the following three procedures (among others):

- Use DROP_UNUSED, for dropping outlines that have never been used for SQL statement compilation.
- DROP_BY_CAT, for dropping all outlines that belong to a specific category.
- UPDATE_BY_CAT, to change all outlines in one category, merging them into another category. Any outline that already exists in the category will not be overwritten.

Dealing with Unchangeable SQL

Ever have problems with SQL that you can't change? Say it's an application for which you don't have access to the source code, or perhaps it's a wrapped PL/SQL package.

Continued

> **CONTINUED**
>
> In Oracle8i, you can create stored outlines for this code and modify the hints as required. Here are the steps to perform this little miracle (and you can read more about this process in Oracle note 92202.1):
>
> 1. Determine what hints you want to use. Create the SQL statement you want to tune, with the new hints. *Note:* You can only change the statement's hints, not the SQL statement itself.
> 2. Create the outline for the original SQL statement. (You might need to enable stored outlines for the entire system in order to do this.) Use the CREATE OR REPLACE OUTLINE command, calling the outline OUTLINE1.
>
>   **Important:** Make sure the names of the outlines created in steps 2 and 3 are unique.
>
> 3. Create an outline for the SQL statement with the changed hints. Again, use the CREATE OR REPLACE OUTLINE command, and name the outline OUTLINE2.
> 4. Now exchange the outline plan between the two SQL statements. Use the following SQL statement:
>
> ```
> UPDATE OUTLN.OL$HINTS
> SET ol_name = DECODE(ol_name, 'OUTLINE2', 'OUTLINE1', 'OUTLINE1',
>    'OUTLINE2') WHERE ol_name in ('OUTLINE2','OUTLINE1');
> ```
>
> 5. Drop the outline for OUTLINE2 using the DROP OUTLINE command.
>
> Now the outline plan for OUTLINE1 will be the same as the plan for OUTLINE2.

An Addendum on Database Monitoring

You've made it through a long and involved chapter on SQL tuning. Even so, we have addressed only the *reactive* side of tuning. Let's turn our attention to the *proactive* side. Being proactive is really the underlying theme of this chapter and the rest of the book. It's important to continue asking the question: What can you do to monitor the SQL executing on your system, and how can you detect problem areas?

This chapter builds substantially on the monitoring methodology we started discussing in Chapter 15. So let's end the chapter with some more material on that subject—specifically, about monitoring ongoing SQL statement execution and keeping track of other database statistics that can affect SQL statement performance.

The dynamic performance view you're most interested in is V$SQL. It contains several statistics that will help you discover problematic SQL in the system. Once you find the offending statements, hunt down the responsible users or procedures with a vengeance. Then get busy and find someone to rewrite the SQL code. (For more on the V$ views, see Chapter 15.)

Time for a Reports Repository?

Paper reports are great. They are generally easy to read, and they stack up in the corner really nicely. You can recycle the paper they're on and make a coupla bucks. The used reports are perfect for the kids' drawing and coloring projects. That said, paper reports are not the most effective way to distribute information, particularly not enterprise-wide information. That's why you should always put a database statistics repository in place whenever you can.

Once the repository is in place, you can automate the reports' execution so that you don't have to think about them—they just go where they're supposed to go. Set up a nice interface (typically using HTML), and you can get to your reports anytime, from any site. Probably the best bonus is that you can create reports for your pesky power users. That way, they can look up their stuff themselves rather than interrupting your nap...er, training session.

So. Lazy DBA requires repository.

Finding Problematic Code: Using V$SQL

The V$SQL view is invaluable for monitoring SQL and looking for statements that aren't working well. V$SQL gets cleared every time the database is shut down and restarted, so the queries represented in the view are only significant after the database has been up for a while.

Remember that tuning SQL statements is about decreasing logical and physical I/O. So it stands to reason that you'll be monitoring I/O and things related to it. You'll want to pay attention to the following V$SQL view columns. Sort on these, and you'll cause offensive SQL to float to the top just like oil on water.

- SQL_TEXT
- SORTS

- EXECUTIONS
- LOADS
- INVALIDATIONS
- PARSE_CALLS
- DISK_READS
- BUFFER_GETS
- ROWS_PROCESSED

Each of these columns contains critical information about the efficiency of recently executed SQL statements. Some common events and relationships to watch out for are as follows:

Ratio of buffer_gets to disk_reads If this proportion is high, you likely are getting a lot of full table scans. This is bad news.

SQL statements that are similar and that repeat These are possible candidates for rewriting and use of bind variables.

Ratio of SORTS to EXECUTIONS If the proportion is high, consider taking greater advantage of index scans.

Loads, invalidations, and parse calls If any of these counts is high, you might have a problem with memory or reusable SQL.

These numbers are going to vary from site to site, of course. Busier and faster databases will have larger numbers; warehousing applications will have higher ratios of BUFFER GETS to DISK READS. That said, no one benchmark can be applied to the monitoring process. As you will soon see, you can't even depend on finding the real difficulty by sorting the output so that SORTS, DISK READS or BUFFER GETS come out at the top. There are problem SQL statements that will lurk in the shadows unless you know how to get at them.

Some Helpful Queries on V$SQL

One helpful statistic you can obtain from V$SQL reports is on SQL that is causing the greatest number of sorts. This condition probably means the query is doing a great many full table scans and then must do sort merge joins. A high sort count may also indicate that ORDER BY or GROUP BY conditions are included in the SQL statement. Whatever the causes, lots of sorts typically indicates one thing clearly: the need to add indexes. Here is an example of the V$SQL report:

```
SELECT rows_processed, sorts, sorts/rows_processed "Ratio",
    executions, loads, invalidations, parse_calls, disk_reads,
    buffer_gets, sql_text
FROM v$sql
WHERE rows_processed > 10000
AND executions > 5
ORDER BY 3 desc;
```

Notice in this query that we limited the results to queries that returned more than 10,000 rows. Establishing reasonable reporting limits is an important consideration when you're analyzing performance. A query that processes 1000 rows total over the course of the database's uptime, and then sorts those 1000 rows, is probably not terribly significant.

TIP You might wonder why we use V$SQL instead of V$SQLAREA. Both views report the same information, except that V$SQLAREA also does a GROUP BY, which makes querying V$SQLAREA a more expensive operation. Thanks to Jonathan Lewis for pointing this out on his website.

You'd probably want to run this query once or twice a day, depending on how often statements are aged out of the shared pool. The point is to focus on exception processing. You want to look at as little data as possible, but the data you look at should be the data that stands out and challenges you to fix whatever is wrong.

The foregoing query gives us the results in Listing 16.5. Three SQL statements show up with a fairly large number of sorts per execution, so they would merit our review to see what the problem is.

Listing 16.5: V$SQL Report of High Sort Count

```
ROWS_PROCESSED  SORTS     Ratio EXECUTIONS  LOADS INVALIDATIONS PARSE_CALLS DISK_READS BUFFER_GETS
--------------  -----  -------- ----------  ----- ------------- ----------- ---------- -----------
SQL_TEXT
--------------------------------------------------------------------------------
         19297  19297         1      19297      1             0        7319          0       57586
SELECT MIN(CREATE_TS)    FROM CSWDTASK    WHERE TD_I = :b1
         16418  16418         1      16418      1             0        2483          0       32836
SELECT MAX(LAST_UPDT_TS)    FROM IMGAUD    WHERE ACTION_X = 'STDINIT'
         16418  16418         1      16418      1             0        2483          3      147762
SELECT COUNT(*)    FROM IMGOCR    WHERE OCR_STATUS_C = 'OCRPROC'    AND OCR_PROCESS_C
 = 'OCR'
```

AN ADDENDUM ON DATABASE MONITORING

```
      28603     22577   .7893228       22577       1            0        2244      13850       94354
SELECT RAL.ARTCL_DESC_X,RAL.RATE_QUAL_C,RAL.RATE_WT_M,RAL.ACCOUNT_C,RAL.RATE_WEI
GHT_C,RAL.NMBR_OF_PKGS_C,RAL.RATE_PRICE_UNIT_Q   FROM CSTRAL RAL    WHERE RAL.TD_I
= :b1   AND RAL.TD_SEQ_I = :b2 ORDER BY RAL.RATE_LINE_SEQ_I
      25139     19840   .78921198      19840       1            0         650      20116       77878
SELECT CSBADLTB.LINE_NMBR_I,CSBADLTB.ADRS_DTL_X    FROM CSBADLTB    WHERE CSBADLTB.
LE_AT_LCTN_I = :b1   AND CSBADLTB.LE_ADRS_I = :b2 ORDER BY CSBADLTB.LINE_NMBR_I
     789430      8870   .01123596       8870       1            0        2475        343       44354
SELECT DISTINCT A.FUNC_C,A.FUNC_OBJ_N,A.FUNC_X    FROM CSWUOWFN A    WHERE A.FUNC_X
  NOT LIKE   'ISS%' ORDER BY A.FUNC_X
     5518194    13137  .00238067     5518314       1            0      371198      83245     23167525
SELECT COUNT(*)    FROM CSTCRW    WHERE CSTCRW.TD_I = :b1
```

Let's look at another monitoring query. This time we are interested in substantial disk I/O caused by a SQL statement. This can occur when indexes on the tables being queried are missing, or when large sorts are occurring. This query is similar to the preceding one, except that the sort is different and some of the column positions have changed.

```
SELECT rows_processed, disk_reads, disk_reads/rows_processed "Ratio",
    buffer_gets, executions, sorts,  loads, invalidations,
    parse_calls, sql_text
FROM v$sql
WHERE rows_processed > 10000
AND executions > 5
ORDER BY 3 desc;
```

Listing 16.6 shows the results. Notice the high number of disk reads vs. the number of rows processed.

Listing 16.6: V$SQL Report on High Disk I/O

```
ROWS_PROCESSED DISK_READS      Ratio BUFFER_GETS EXECUTIONS    SORTS   LOADS INVALIDATIONS PARSE_CALLS
-------------- ----------  --------- ----------- ----------   ------  ------ ------------- -----------
SQL_TEXT
----------------------------------------------------------------------------
        12496      57938  4.6365237    1632826      194510    -2103        1             0       14245
DELETE FROM CSTDIV WHERE TD_I = :b1  AND TD_SEQ_I = :b2  AND RATE_LINE_SEQ_I IN
  (SELECT RATE_LINE_SEQ_I    FROM CSTRAL   WHERE TD_I = :b1  AND TD_SEQ_I = :b2   AND
  STOP_SEQ_I IS NULL )
        49981      54327  1.086953     2300115      174958        0        2             0         643
      UPDATE CSTTDE SET EQUIP_MOVE_I=:b1,EQUIP_MOVE_SEQ_I=:b2,LAST_UPDT_USER_I=:b3,LAS
```

```
T_UPDT_TS=SYSDATE WHERE EQUIP_I = :b4 AND TD_I = :b5
       62545    11127 .17790391    1103122      62576    0    1    0       738
INSERT INTO CSTRDE ( INVOICE_I,TD_I,SEQ_I,INTER_SEQ_I,BUSINESS_UNIT_I,EVENT_I,EV
ENT_EXCP_TYPE_C,ACTUAL_TS,SCHED_TS,REVISED_TS,EVENT_TS,PAY_REF_I,PAY_REF_QUAL_C
) VALUES ( :b1,:b2,:b3,:b4,:b5,:b6,:b7,:b8,:b9,:b10,SYSDATE,:b11,:b12  )
      117178     6626 .05654645     751722     274607    0    1    0     25935
SELECT 'Y'   FROM RPTDTASK  WHERE DETAIL_TASK_I = :b1
     5518527  83245 .01508464    23170050    5518647 13470    1    0    371213
SELECT COUNT(*)    FROM CSTCRW  WHERE CSTCRW.TD_I = :b1
       87766       88 .00100267     460783      87766    0    1    0      2290
SELECT CSTEXE_SEQ_01.NEXTVAL    FROM DUAL
       19297        0         0      57586      19297 19297    1    0      7319
SELECT MIN(CREATE_TS)   FROM CSWDTASK  WHERE TD_I = :b1
```

In the next query, we'll examine the ratio of buffer gets to rows processed. When this proportion is high, it means Oracle is working hard to get your rows. The results are shown in Listing 16.7.

```
SELECT rows_processed, buffer_gets,
buffer_gets /rows_processed "Ratio",
Disk_reads, executions, sorts,  loads, invalidations,
parse_calls, sql_text
FROM v$sql
WHERE rows_processed > 10000
AND executions > 5
ORDER BY 3 desc;
```

Listing 16.7: V$SQL Report on Ratio of Buffer Gets to Rows Processed

```
ROWS_PROCESSED BUFFER_GETS     Ratio DISK_READS EXECUTIONS   SORTS   LOADS INVALIDATIONS PARSE_CALLS
-------------- ----------- --------- ---------- ---------- ------- ------- ------------- -----------
SQL_TEXT
--------------------------------------------------------------------------------
         12496     1633448 130.71767      57963     194602    2011       1             0       14255
DELETE FROM CSTDIV WHERE TD_I = :b1  AND TD_SEQ_I = :b2  AND RATE_LINE_SEQ_I IN
(SELECT RATE_LINE_SEQ_I    FROM CSTRAL  WHERE TD_I = :b1  AND TD_SEQ_I = :b2  AND
 STOP_SEQ_I IS NULL )
         87830      461118 5.2501195         88      87830       0       1             0        2291
SELECT CSTEXE_SEQ_01.NEXTVAL    FROM DUAL
         19300       57592 2.9840415          0      19300   19300       1             0        7321
SELECT MIN(CREATE_TS)   FROM CSWDTASK  WHERE TD_I = :b1
        789608       44364 .05618484        343       8872    8872       1             0        2475
```

```
SELECT DISTINCT A.FUNC_C,A.FUNC_OBJ_N,A.FUNC_X   FROM CSWUOWFN A  WHERE A.FUNC_X
NOT LIKE  'ISS%' ORDER BY A.FUNC_X
```

Based on these results, you would likely try to improve some queries. Perhaps the table join order could be changed, or perhaps the wrong index is being used.

Calling All SQL without Bind Variables!

Another issue that needs to be checked proactively is similar SQL statements differing only in the use of literals instead of bind variables. You need a way to determine if this condition is problematic and a way to continue monitoring for the condition. We have a query that will do this, but at a probable cost in system performance. Still, the results are valuable, so consider using the query, running it at a time when the system has some CPU available.

NOTE This query checks only the first 40 characters of the SQL statements in V$SQL, so it might not work for you. Change the query as required to get the level of comparison you want.

```
SELECT substr(SQL_TEXT,1,40), count(*) "Count",sum(executions) "Exes",
sum(rows_processed) "Rows", sum(buffer_gets) "Gets",
sum(disk_reads) "DiskR"
FROM V$SQL
Group by substr(SQL_TEXT,1,40)
Order by 2 desc;
```

Listing 16.8 shows the results (reformatted slightly to allow for page width).

Listing 16.8: V$SQL Report on Similar SQL Statements

SUBSTR(SQL_TEXT,1,40)	Count	Exes	Rows	Gets	DiskR
SELECT BLOCK_ID, BLOCKS FROM SYS.DBA_FRE	4	4	7	222	0
SELECT TO_CHAR(FHBCP_SCN), FHBCP_TIM FRO	2	2	2	8	0
DELETE FROM CSTCNH WHERE TD_I = :b1	1	1	0	2	1
SELECT TO_CHAR(FHBSC), FHBTI FROM dto$kc	1	1	1	4	0
insert into p$autoext values('ORDERPROCO	1	456	44	88	0
SELECT TD_INTERRUPT_C FROM CSTTDD WHE	1	17933	5184	22550	2
SELECT GROUP# FROM V$LOG WHERE STATUS =	1	4051	4051	0	0
SELECT /*+ remote_mapped(REP_COPS_EISP_L	1	1	0	0	0
SELECT /*+ rule */B.IIDS_I,A.EQUIP_I	1	209	22458	55389	15213

The bottom line in this case is that if you see a significant number in the COUNT column (say, over 10), look at the entire SQL statement and see if it can be made more reusable. You should run these queries probably once a day, more often if you have a hybrid system with a mix of OLTP and reporting. Hang on to the results for a while; they are valuable baseline information.

In fact, you could keep them in that special statistics storage location described in the earlier sidebar "Time for a Reports Repository?" Then you could query the repository to chart the statistics. At the same time, you'll be charting the effectiveness of your tuning efforts right in readiness for your next performance review. It'll give you ammunition to pitch for a big raise!

SQL Monitoring and Notification

Finally, in terms of reporting, the thresholds you select for monitoring SQL usage will depend on the business needs of your database. It may be that your database will simply have to do lots of full table scans or sorting, and there won't be any way around that. When setting monitoring thresholds, consider the business requirements. If you'll be tasked with substantial large sorts in a data warehouse environment, for example, you probably won't want to set up your system to page you in the middle of the night when the sorts-to-disk number grows.

There are no Oracle reports that specifically identify bad-running SQL. Typically, if a SQL statement is causing problems, you'll know about it through Oracle's reporting on waits, locking, or something similar (see Chapter 17). That's not to say, however, that you shouldn't establish some thresholds, and for this task you can use the output of the V$SESSION_LONGOPS view. New in Oracle8i, this view provides a unique look at the history of long-running SQL, including how long it's been running, when it started, and an estimate of how much longer it has to run. You get a birds-eye view of any Oracle operation that has been running for longer than six seconds. Of course, this includes backup, long data loads, and other operations. You might want to monitor for queries that threaten to run longer than some predetermined amount of time at specific hours, such as during the workday. This way, if one user starts up an ad hoc killer report, you'll find out about it before other users start to complain.

The V$SESSIOIN_LONGOPS view requires the use of CBO, and you have to have TIMED_STATISTICS turned on for the database.

CHAPTER 17

Monitoring and Tuning Latches, Locks, and Waits

FEATURING:

Latches and locks	**796**
Wait management	**813**
Monitoring scripts and suggestions	**826**
Tuning locks, latches, and waits	**834**

This is the last piece of the tuning trilogy that began with Chapter 15. In this chapter we will look at latches, locks, and waits—mechanisms in Oracle database processing that can all cause significant execution delays. Users' sessions can start to "pile up," waiting for an available resource. If you can proactively monitor the database and know when and where a problem is occurring, you'll have an opportunity to tune these mechanisms before users even know anything is amiss.

We'll start with a discussion of locking, latching, and waiting and how they affect the database. When you understand the purpose and effects of these events, you can more easily identify the problems that are most closely associated with them. From there, we'll cover monitoring these mechanisms and tuning them based on the results.

Latches and Locks

Much of the memory that Oracle allocates to the database process is shared memory—shared among all of Oracle's processes for both reading and writing. In many cases, Oracle needs to limit access to a particular area of memory to just one process. Limiting access to blocks and other memory structures helps ensure that other processes do not interfere in the ongoing operations of other sessions. Also, because of the concurrency and consistency requirements of the database, Oracle must be able to restrict access to user objects such as tables, clusters, partitions, and the data in the rows in those objects.

Two Oracle mechanisms facilitate some form of restricted access to memory blocks: the *latch* and the *lock* (also known as an *enqueue*). Although very different in their implementation of access control, latches and locks have something else in common: They both can be symptoms of database performance problems. Much as fever and coughing are symptoms of the flu, the behavior of latches and locks can help you diagnose underlying problems in database operations. By monitoring various statistics related to locks and latches, you can improve the effectiveness of your tuning efforts on the database and on SQL statements.

What's a Latch?

A latch is an elemental locking mechanism used by Oracle to serialize access to various memory structures. Oracle uses latches on structures that are expected to remain unlocked for a long period of time. Latches protect memory structures and processes such as redo-log buffer copy operations, the structures that manage the buffers in the database buffer cache, and other operations that interact with the SGA.

Oracle uses many different kinds of latches, and a given process may use more than one latch. In fact, more than one latch may be used for a single operation of a process. For example, when an Oracle process needs to write to the redo log buffer, one or two latches are used to control that access, depending on the size of the redo to be written.

Latches are low-level locking mechanisms and are more restrictive than most of the locks used by Oracle. Latching is an atomic operation. In fact, locks use latches as part of the overall locking mechanism. With a few exceptions, latches restrict any kind of access (read or write) to the memory area to the process that is holding the latch.

Latch Contention

So, what happens during the life of a process waiting to acquire a latch? Getting a latch is like winning the Cannonball Run—the first one to the latch wins. More specifically, the first process to request the latch acquires the latch. Once a latch is acquired by a process, other processes wait based on the mode in which the latch was requested. These modes are willing-to-wait mode and no-wait mode.

Willing-to-Wait Latches

If a process acquires a latch in *willing-to-wait* mode, other processes requesting that latch with a willing-to-wait request will stack up waiting for the latch to become available to them. These waiting processes go through two distinct operations while waiting: a *spin* operation, which involves continual attempts to reacquire the latch over and over again. If the subsequent latch get attempts are not successful after a fixed period of spinning, the process enters a *sleep* operation.

The waiting process's spin operation is essentially a timed loop. The length of spin time is controlled by the hidden parameter _SPIN_COUNT. Through each iteration of the spin process Oracle checks again to see if the latch is available. Spin operations are CPU intensive because the process is active, looping and doing very little of worth. Still, spinning is much preferred to sleeping in most cases. Spinning represents intense use of CPU resources, but sleeping generally has more negative ramifications on overall process performance. The reasons for this are discussed throughout this chapter.

Sleeping occurs when the requesting process fails to get the latch after coming out of the spin operation (or, in some cases, after awakening from another sleep operation). The sleep operation is a suspension of the thread or process for a given amount of time or until the sleeping process is awakened. Putting a process in sleep mode works the CPU fairly hard because of context switching (or the cost of moving the process and its related structures in and out of memory). When Oracle puts the process to sleep, it also indicates how long the process should sleep. After this sleep operation expires, the process awakens and attempts to acquire the latch. If that fails, the process enters the sleep cycle again, and so on until the latch get is successful—or the power company runs out of coal! As a waiting process moves from one sleep operation to the next, the overall sleep time grows exponentially as Oracle increases the sleep cycle duration.

All this can have an adverse effect on the performance of the process because latches are not taken in any designated order. So when a process wakes, the latch it wants may have already been acquired by another process. The process sleeps yet again, unable to acquire the latch it wants. And with each sleep operation, the sleep duration increases, sometimes taking far longer than it should have to get the latch. One way to reduce the delay to a minimum is to raise the system's _SPIN_COUNT parameter so that processes spin for a longer time before sleeping. We'll get into this later in the sections on monitoring and tuning.

Latch Wait Posting

Another measure for controlling sleep operations is to use *latch wait posting*. When latch wait posting is used, the process holding the latch will wake the sleeping process that is waiting for the latch. This is a more expensive arrangement, but it can decrease the overall time waiting to acquire a latch.

By default, only requests for the library cache and the shared pool latches use latch wait posting. If you want to take advantage of latch wait posting for all latches, set the hidden parameter _LATCH_WAIT_POSTING to 2. You can also disable this feature completely by setting the parameter to 0.

TIP You can tell how many times a process has slept by looking for the Latch Free Wait statistics in the V$SESSION_EVENT view, explained in the later section about Oracle waits.

Monitor latching very carefully if you choose to change the _LATCH_WAIT_ POSTING or the _SPIN_COUNT parameters, to make sure that the changes have a positive impact. In particular, watch the V$LATCH and the V$SYSTEM_EVENT data dictionary views for excessive latch contention. Look for significant wait times in the latch free waits event in V$SYSTEM_EVENT. In both views, look for increased wait times for latches in general. (You can see why having TIMED_STATISTICS turned on is so important!)

When a willing-to-wait process uses latch wait posting, the process is still put to sleep because it cannot acquire the required latch. Beforehand, however, the process posts a request for the latch in the latch wait list, which notifies processes that currently own the latch that other processes are waiting. Based on the latch wait list, the process acquiring the latch wakes up the sleeping process when the latch is freed.

No-Wait Mode Latches

When a process takes a latch in *no-wait mode,* the process will not sleep or spin in order to wait for a given latch. The process immediately tries to obtain the latch again, without waiting, until it succeeds. Generally, no-wait latches are used in cases where latch acquisition deadlocks between two or more processes might occur, and other latches have already been acquired at the same or lower level. In this case, if Oracle cannot service the process's request, the latches already allocated are released and the entire operation must be repeated. Very few latches use no-wait mode.

Parent/Child Latches

Oracle allows *parent latches* and *child latches*. Structures that require multiple latches, such as the shared pool, will have a parent latch (shared pool latch) and one or more child latches. Some parent latches have only one child (for example, the cache buffers LRU chain, which has one child latch in the database we use) and some have many children (for example, cache buffer chains, which has 512 in the database we use). The use and number of parent/child latches vary among releases of Oracle.

Latch Levels

The V$LATCH view (discussed shortly) includes a LEVEL# column. Oracle assigns level numbers to latches in order to avoid deadlocks. Frequently, an operation requires acquisition of multiple latches, and multiple processes may attempt to acquire the same latch. Deadlock problems are prevented by Oracle's assignment of an order for the acquisition of latches. The level numbers range from 0 to 15, and Oracle acquires latches beginning at a lower level and proceeding to higher levels. When a process attempts to get a latch, Oracle checks to make sure that a latch at the same or higher level is not already being held.

Say that Processes 1 and 2 need Latches A and B. If Process 1 acquires Latch B first and then tries to allocate Latch A, and Process 2 grabs A first and then tries to acquire B, you'd have a deadlock condition. The two processes are each trying to acquire a latch already acquired by the other process. Oracle prevents this by means of its latch-level architecture. Processes 1 and 2 will always try to grab a latch first, because it's a lower-level latch. If Process 1 grabs Latch A, Process 2 will spin or sleep until Process 1 releases latch A. Process 2 never tries to grab Latch B until it has acquired Latch A, thus preventing a potential deadlock situation.

Important Latches for Monitoring

Oracle's V$LATCH view comprises 152 different latch types (in Oracle 8.1.7). Which ones are the significant latches that you should be keeping an eye on? The following list of important latches is organized based on the parts of the SGA that are protected by a particular latch group.

Database Buffer Cache Latches The *cache buffers LRU chain* is responsible for protecting the blocks of the database buffer cache. This important latch is used to allow the addition of a new block into the database buffer cache.

The *cache buffers chain* is requested when a process needs access to a block in the SGA.

Library Cache Latches The *library cache latch* must be obtained by a process in order to add a new statement to the library cache. The latch is not used if the SQL statement is already in the library cache.

The *library cache pin latch* must be obtained when a statement in the library cache is to be reexecuted.

The *row cache objects latch* must be acquired by a user process in order to access the data dictionary.

Redo Buffer Latches The well-known *redo allocation latch* is required so that space can be allocated in the redo log buffer for redo log entries.

The *redo copy latch* is uniquely handled by Oracle. First of all, it's not one latch but several. The number of redo copy latches is defined by the setting of the `init.ora` parameter _LOG_SIMULTANEOUS_COPIES, which is calculated by Oracle automatically, generally based on the CPU count of the system. If the request for a latch fails, Oracle goes down the list of redo copy latches until it reaches the last one. Oracle tries to acquire this last latch in willing-to-wait mode, incurring the spinning and sleeping operations described earlier.

Shared Pool Latch The *shared pool latch* is required when space in the shared pool needs to be allocated or deallocated.

Where to Find Latch Information

The primary views for information on latches are V$LATCH, V$LATCH_PARENT, and V$LATCH_CHILDREN.

V$LATCH This view contains statistics for every type of latch used in Oracle and is critical to latch monitoring. We will use the V$LATCH view later in this chapter as part of our proactive database monitoring and tuning strategy. Following are the important columns in this view:

- NAME and LEVEL#: These two columns identify the latch being monitored and its level.
- GETS: The number of times a willing-to-wait request for the latch was successful. This is *not* the number of requests, but the number of successes; the count in this column does not increase until the latch get is successful.

- **MISSES:** The number of times a willing-to-wait request for a latch failed. Each miss results in a spin operation. This is a cumulative total of all failed attempts to get a latch. So if a process fails four times before a successful latch get, this column will show a 4 for those misses.

- **SLEEPS:** The number of times a willing-to-wait request for this latch missed and the process ended up sleeping.

- **SPIN_GETS:** The number of times a latch was acquired after the requesting process went into spin mode.

- **IMMEDIATE_GETS:** The number of successful no-wait requests for the latch.

- **IMMEDIATE_MISSES:** This column displays the number of failed no-wait requests for the latch.

- **SLEEP1 through SLEEP4:** The number of times the latch went through sleep operations. The SLEEP1 column lists the number of times a latch slept once, the SLEEP2 column lists the number of times that the latch swept twice, and so on. Columns SLEEP5 through SLEEP11 in V$LATCH are not used in Oracle8i.

V$LATCH_PARENT and V$LATCH_CHILDREN These views provide a more detailed look at the statistics for parent and child latches. V$LATCH_PARENT includes parent latches as well as latches with no associated child latches. Its columns are the same as for V$LATCH. In V$LATCH_CHILDREN you get an additional column, CHILD#.

You can get a feel for the relationship of parent and child latches by using the following query (which only works in Oracle8i):

```
SELECT b.name, b.num_parent, c.num_child
FROM
(select name, count(*) num_parent from V$LATCH_parent group by name) b,
(select name, count(*) num_child from V$LATCH_CHILDREN group by name) c
WHERE b.name=c.name (+);
```

NOTE If you need details about the columns of V$LATCH, V$LOCK, and the other Oracle views mentioned in this chapter, refer to the Oracle8i Reference Manual.

What's a Lock?

Multiple statement processing means an object may be needed by multiple transactions at the same time. A *lock* (also known as an *enqueue*) is an automatic internal mechanism that protects access to Oracle data structures, similarly to the way latches protect access to memory. For example, when a process has issued a DML statement (INSERT, UPDATE, or DELETE) that changes a row in a table, Oracle locks that row in order to prevent other processes from changing it. The lock remains in place until the related process commits the transaction or issues a rollback that negates the DML action. Rollbacks can take a long time, which means the object remains locked for a long time.

NOTE An Oracle oddity: If you ROLLBACK to a SAVEPOINT, the locks taken after SAVEPOINT will be released—but they are not made available to any waiting transaction. New transactions will be able to access rows affected by the locks, however.

Fortunately, Oracle handles locks automatically, so application developers don't have to worry about them. Also, Oracle always uses the lowest level of locking possible, so you don't end up with locking that's more restrictive than required. Waiting sessions are held in a queue until the lock is released. Unlike latches, this queue is managed on a first-in, first-out (FIFO) basis. Therefore, the first process to request and wait for a lock is the first process serviced after the lock is released. Subsequent requesting processes will be handled in the order of the requests.

NOTE Though Oracle handles locking automatically, it also provides tools needed by application developers to preemptively lock objects when the application design calls for custom locking. Unless otherwise noted, in this section we address issues related to automatic locking.

Native Oracle locks do not prevent read access to the data in a table (but you can opt to use restrictive locks that do so). Keep in mind that when you query a table, the data you see is the value of the data *before* application of any uncommitted transactions from other sessions. Thus, if you UPDATE in a SQL*Plus session but do not COMMIT, you won't see that data in a different SQL*Plus session. Your UPDATE will be visible in your session, however, even before you COMMIT it. That's Oracle data concurrency and consistency in action!

Also, Oracle's enqueue locking system provides a queuing system for lock requests. Thus, if a process is blocked from acquiring a lock, that request for the lock is queued up and will be processed in the order received. Note that this differs from latching, where the fastest process gets the latch whether it was first or not. Locking, on the other hand, provides a first-in first-out (FIFO) queueing system, that provides access to resources to requesting processes in order.

Working with the V$LOCK View

At the risk of belaboring the point, locking can cause serious performance problems and is often the cause of very slow running queries. To get information about who is locking what objects in your database, a primary tool is the V$LOCK view. It tells you about locks on tables and rows, and who is taking those locks. If users performing INSERTS, UPDATES, and DELETES are complaining that their systems aren't moving smoothly, check V$LOCK—you'll probably find the session that is causing the problem.

Lock Types and Locking Modes

Locks come in different shapes and sizes. Oracle uses the following:

Data or DML Locks   Used to protect data, DML locks can lock an entire table or specific rows of a table. While it's locked, your data is protected from other users' actions; and if you are making a change, other users' actions will not conflict with that change.

Data Dictionary or DDL Locks   DDL locks are used for data dictionary protection (duh!). These locks generally are used to prevent the removal of objects from the database, and to prevent changes in the structure of objects in the database while those objects are being used. Dictionary locks are maintained during both the parse and execute stages of SQL statement processing and are held for the lifetime of the transaction.

Internal Locks   These locks protect the internal structure of the database datafiles. Internal locks are used in association with latches to protect various internal database structures.

For each lock listed in the V$LOCK view, you'll encounter codes representing the types of lock and graduated methods of locking objects. Together, the codes tell you what type of locking is occurring (a DML row lock, for instance) and the extent of the locking (exclusive or shared, for instance).

Lock Type Codes

The *lock type* indicates what type of lock is being acquired. This might be a row-level lock, a table lock, or a lock created by a user. In the TYPE column you'll see the associated codes for each lock type, as defined in Tables 17.1, 17.2, and 17.3.

NOTE You can find more information on DDL locks by looking at the V$LOCKED_OBJECT view.

TABLE 17.1: DML LOCK TYPES

DML Lock Type	Code	Description
Row lock	TX	This is a row-level lock, the most granular lock in Oracle. Row-level locks are always exclusive.
Table lock	TM	Acquired with various DML operations including INSERT, DELETE, UPDATE, SELECT FOR UPDATE, and when the LOCK TABLE clause is used.
User lock	UL	A lock created explicitly by the user via use of the DBMS_LOCK package.

TABLE 17.2: DDL LOCK TYPES

DDL Lock Type	Code	Description
Exclusive DDL lock	N/A	A lock on a resource being modified. Prevents simultaneous DDL operations on the same object. For example, you won't be able to drop a partition and move the same partition at the same time.
Share DDL lock	N/A	Prevents exclusive DDL locks from being taken against the object locked. Thus, this prevents a table from being dropped while you are updating a procedure that references the table.

Table 17.3 describes the internal lock codes that appear in the TYPE column of V$LOCK. In general, you don't need to worry about them, but you may need to handle them in your monitoring scripts.

TABLE 17.3: INTERNAL LOCK TYPES

Lock code	Description	Lock Code	Description
BL	Buffer hash table instance	NA to NZ	Library cache pin instance (A..Z = namespace)
CF	Control file schema global enqueue	PF	Password file
CI	Cross-instance function invocation instance	PI and PS	Parallel operation
CU	Cursor bind	PR	Process startup
DF	Data file instance	QA..QZ	Row cache instance (A..Z = cache)
DL	Direct loader parallel index create	RT	Redo thread global enqueue
DM	Mount/startup db primary/secondary instance	SC	System COMMIT number instance
DR	Distributed recovery process	SM	SMON
DX	Distributed transaction entry	SN	Sequence number instance
FS	File set	SQ	Sequence number enqueue
HW	Space management operations on a specific segment	SS	Sort segment
IN	Instance number	ST	Space transaction enqueue
IR	Instance recovery serialization global enqueue	SV	Sequence number value
IS	Instance state	TA	Generic enqueue
IV	Library cache invalidation instance	TS	Temporary segment enqueue (ID2=0)
JQ	Job queue	TS	New block allocation enqueue (ID2=1)
KK	Thread kick	TT	Temporary table enqueue
LA to LP	Library cache lock instance lock (A..P = namespace)	UN	User name
MM	Mount definition global enqueue	US	Undo segment DDL
MR	Media recovery	WL	Being-written redo log instance

NOTE It's not uncommon to see media recovery (MR) locks for each datafile in the database. In Oracle8i, MR locks appear for each online datafile associated with the Oracle database.

Locking Modes

A lock placed against an Oracle object is generally in one of two modes: *exclusive* or *shared*. An exclusive lock prevents sharing of the resource being locked. Only the transaction locking the object can access the object, and other transactions wait for the lock to be released. When a shared lock is placed, multiple transactions can use the locked resource.

Oracle also allows NULL lock holders, which is not the same as "no lock." If a session has cached information about an object, the NULL lock causes the cached information to become invalidated if the associated resource is invalidated. Table 17.4 describes the DML locking modes and their codes (which appear in the LMODE column of V$LOCK view).

TABLE 17.4: ORACLE LOCKING MODES

Lock Mode	Lock Mode Number in LMODE Column	Lock Type Represented	Description
None	0 or Blank	None	No lock at all.
NULL	1	NULL	Indicates that cached session information exists about an object. Used to invalidate the information should the resource become invalid. A NULL lock is different from no lock at all.
Row share	2	RS or SS	Occurs when a transaction has locked rows in a table with the intention of updating them. This is the least restrictive of the DML table locks. Does not prevent any type of DML activity from occurring on the table.
Row exclusive	3	RX or SX	Occurs when a transaction has made a change to a table row, via INSERT, UPDATE, or DELETE operations. Allows DML activity to continue on the table. Exclusive table access can be enforced via the LOCK TABLE command.

Continued

TABLE 17.4: ORACLE LOCKING MODES (CONTINUED)

Lock Mode	Lock Mode Number in LMODE Column	Lock Type Represented	Description
Share table	4	S	Occurs when the LOCK TABLE statement is used. Allows transactions only to query the table involved in the lock, but does not prevent the use of SELECT FOR UPDATE. Updates by other transactions are not allowed.
Share row exclusive	5	SRX or SSX	Can only be obtained by one transaction at a time per object, and is acquired only by use of the LOCK TABLE SHARE ROW EXCLUSIVE MODE command. Other transactions can query the table, but no updates are allowed.
Exclusive	6	X	Acquired only by use of the LOCK TABLE EXCLUSIVE MODE command. Prohibits any other access to a table by any other transaction.

Lock Conversions

Oracle converts locks rather than escalates them. What's the difference? Lock *escalation* occurs when a given database holds several lower-level locks (such as row level) and escalates them to a higher level (such as table level) as an operation executes, in order to reduce locking conflicts. Oracle accomplishes this by *conversion*. For example, if you perform a SELECT FOR UPDATE, Oracle takes out row share (RS) locks on the rows that are part of the SELECT FOR UPDATE statement. Oracle also takes out a row share (RS) table-level lock. As the transaction progresses and rows are changed, the RS locks are converted to row exclusive (RX) table-level lock.

Table 17.5 provides a summary of the various DML statements and the kinds of locks they acquire.

NOTE SELECT FOR UPDATE statements vis-à-vis locking are covered in more detail later in this chapter, so read on.

TABLE 17.5: DML STATEMENT LOCKING

Statement Type	Lock Mode Acquired	Causes Row Locks?
SELECT		No
INSERT	RX	Yes
UPDATE	RX	Yes
DELETE	RX	Yes
SELECT FOR UPDATE	RS	Yes
LOCK TABLE ROW SHARE	RS	No
LOCK TABLE ROW EXCLUSIVE	RX	No
LOCK TABLE SHARE MODE	S	No
LOCK TABLE SHARE EXCLUSIVE MODE	SRX	No
LOCK TABLE EXCLUSIVE MODE	X	No

The ID1 and ID2 columns in the V$LOCK view take on a different meaning depending on the value in the TYPE column. Table 17.6 explains the contents of ID1 and ID2 associated with the TYPE value.

TABLE 17.6: V$LOCK'S ID1 AND ID2 COLUMN CONTENTS

Lock Type	Column ID1 Meaning	Column ID2 Meaning
Transaction (TX)	Decimal value of the ROLLBACK segment number and slot number.	Decimal value of the wrap number, or the number of times the ROLLBACK slot has been reused.
Table lock (TM)	Object ID of table being modified.	Always 0.
Media recovery (MR)	File ID of file against which the lock is being held.	Always 0.

An Example of Lock Monitoring Using V$LOCK

Let's consider an example of using V$LOCK to handle a "blocking lock" state—that is, a situation where one session's locks are blocking another session from completing its work. A SQL*Plus session has updated a table record, but the transaction has not yet committed the record. A second SQL*Plus session is trying to update the same record, without success.

Having read this far, you know the problem is that the first session is blocking the second session. Once you've detected the blocking session, you can call the user and investigate. Listing 17.1 provides a SQL script that detects the blocking session, using information in the V$LOCK view.

Listing 17.1: Using V$LOCK to Find a Blocking Lock

```
Sqlplus scott/tiger
-- In Session 1, we update employee 7369's job description.
SQL> SELECT empno, ename, job, sal from employee where empno=7369;

    EMPNO ENAME      JOB              SAL
---------- ---------- ---------- ----------
      7369 Robert     CLERK            800
SQL> UPDATE employee set job='PooBah' where empno=7369;
1 row updated.
-- Now, in a second session, we try to update the salary of the employee.
Sqlplus scott/tiger
SQL> UPDATE employee set sal=20000 where empno=7369;
-- Note that there is no message "1 row updated." This session will
-- hang here forever until Session 1 issues a COMMIT. This is because
-- both sessions are trying to change the same row. If the user in the
-- second session calls us wondering who is holding them up, we can
-- query V$LOCK.
  1  SELECT sid, id1, id2, lmode, request, block
  2  FROM v$lock
  3* order by block desc, id1, id2
SQL> /

       SID        ID1        ID2      LMODE    REQUEST BLOCK
---------- ---------- ---------- ---------- ---------- ------
        17     131075        674          6          0      1
         2          1          0          4          0      0
         3          1          0          6          0      0
         2          2          0          4          0      0
         2          3          0          4          0      0
         2          4          0          4          0      0
         2          5          0          4          0      0
        15       2890          0          3          0      0
        17       2890          0          3          0      0
        15     131075        674          0          6      0
```

```
-- Here the blocking session is shifted to the top.
-- Where the BLOCK column=1, that SID is the bad guy. So in this
-- example it appears that Session 17 is causing the lock.
```

Now we know that Session 17 is a blocking session because the block column associated with that session is set to 1. If your V$LOCK query revealed several blocking sessions, how would you know the culprit is Session 17, and how would you find out what user is running Session 17?

Let's address the latter question first: Who is Session 17? Because we know the SID of the blocking session (from the SID column in V$LOCK), we need only a simple query against V$SESSION to find the offender. Listing 17.2 shows an example of this query.

Listing 17.2: Using V$SESSION to Find the User Assigned to a SID

```
SQL> 1
  1  select sid, serial#, username, osuser, machine, terminal, program
  2  from v$session
  3* where sid=17
SQL> /


SID SERIAL# USERNAME OSUSER            MACHINE                 PROGRAM
--- ------- -------- ----------------- ----------------------- -----------
 17   10289 SCOTT    MYNT_WORKSTN_MYID WORKGROUP\MYID          SQLPLUS.EXE
```

You learn a lot from this query. You see the user's Oracle sign-on (SCOTT), the machine Scott is working on (MYNT_WORKSTN_MYID), and the OSUSER logged in to the machine (MYID). You probably know enough now to go and ask the person about the lock.

Of course, as a DBA, you never have enough information, do you? Before you lop off this user's head, let's identify the object that is actually experiencing the locking problem. You can do a couple of things here. The V$LOCK view tells you which object is being blocked. Perhaps even more valuable is the fact that V$SESSION tells you exactly what is blocking that session.

Listing 17.2 executes a query against V$SESSION for the SID of the blocked session. Join it with DBA_OBJECTS, and voilà—you know what object is being blocked. More than that, you'll know the file number where the object is, the block number, and what row is being blocked. Listing 17.3 shows you how to find this information, and it has a query using the reported V$SESSION ROWID to find the row that is locked.

Listing 17.3: Finding the Blocked Table/Row

```
SELECT a.sid, a.serial#, b.object_name, b.object_type, c.file_name
FROM v$session a, dba_objects b, dba_data_files c
```

```
WHERE a.row_wait_obj#=b.object_id and
a.row_wait_file#=c.file_id
and a.sid=15;

SID SERIAL# OBJECT_NAM OBJECT_TYPE FILE_NAME
--- ------- ---------- ----------- ----------------------------------------
 15     422 EMPLOYEE   TABLE
D:\ORACLE\ORADATA\ORA816\ORA816_USERS_01.DBF

-- Get the restricted rowid information!
SQL> l
SELECT row_wait_file#, row_wait_block#, row_wait_row# from v$session
WHERE sid=15;

ROW_WAIT_FILE# ROW_WAIT_BLOCK# ROW_WAIT_ROW#
-------------- --------------- -------------
             3            4318             0

-- To look at the actual row, we need to convert
-- these values into Hex with our handy dandy scientific calculator
-- or one of the many available Decimal-to-Hex converter functions.
-- The number 4318 = 10DE in Hex. So, the final query to see
-- the actual locked row shows up next!
SELECT empno, ename, job, sal from employee
WHERE rowid=dbms_rowid.rowid_to_extended('000010DE.0000.0003',NULL,NULL,1);

    EMPNO ENAME      JOB            SAL
---------- ---------- --------- ----------
     7369 Robert     PooBah         800
```

Lock Issues of Concern to DBAs

There are some specific lock-related issues meaningful to the DBA's monitoring efforts, including lock interactions with foreign keys, and use of the SELECT FOR UPDATE statement. These issues have direct performance implications, so let's get to them.

Problems with Foreign Keys

If you take advantage of foreign key relationships in Oracle, it's a good idea to index the foreign key columns of the child table. If you don't, every time you delete a record in the parent table you'll get a full table scan of the child table to ensure that there are no related records. (Unless, of course, you have disabled the foreign key or set it to NORELY.) Full table scans can be a serious performance problem, so do yourself a favor and index the foreign key columns of the child table.

 TIP Previous versions of Oracle had problems with unindexed foreign keys. If you changed a row in the child table, Oracle would take a table-level shared lock on the parent table. This is no longer the case with Oracle8i, which takes row exclusive locks instead. If you work with a version earlier than Oracle8i, index your foreign key columns to ensure that you don't get adverse locking.

Problems with SELECT FOR UPDATE

By default, Oracle uses an *optimistic locking strategy,* which means that it assumes that it will be able to get a lock on a required row when that row is required. When you employ the SELECT FOR UPDATE clause, however, it uses what is known as a *pessimistic locking strategy.* This means a row-level lock is taken for all the rows that will be affected by the statement during the parse stage. Rather than applying row-level locks when the data is changed, Oracle applies row-level locks to each row to be impacted by the statement before the statement executes. As a result, the rows are likely to be locked longer than they would be otherwise.

So when, on occasion, you need to use the SELECT FOR UPDATE clause, be aware of the impacts of doing so. Review your application code and PL/SQL for all SELECT FOR UPDATE usage, and make sure that they're warranted.

Here's an example: In the course of locking the rows in the table, the SELECT FOR UPDATE statement reaches a record that is already locked, which causes the statement to fail. Typically, the response of the application code is to retry the cursor until it succeeds—an exceedingly inefficient approach. In this situation, you could try including the undocumented SKIP LOCKED keywords in the SELECT FOR UPDATE command. The one caveat to this solution is that it will work only when you're using dynamic SQL.

Another issue with SELECT FOR UPDATE statements involves the fact that locks are not cleared until the session is committed. If users are firing off some massive update to run over the weekend, watch out, because the locks that are acquired might affect users come Monday morning. Always make sure users are aware of the impacts that SELECT FOR UPDATE statements have on a system.

Wait Management

During database operations, various *events* occur, such as the database writer (DBWR) writing to a datafile, a server process acquiring a lock on a buffer, or a process taking a latch on a row in the library cache. Many of these events can experience performance delays because of waits that occur during the event's operation.

Why worry about waits? Because wait statistics are a key indicator for determining what's ailing your database. They tell you when your database is experiencing too much delay while waiting for log file switches, waiting for cached database blocks in the SGA (buffer busy waits), waiting to get at a row in a table, and waiting on data dictionary rows (row cache lock waits)—to name just a few. And when you know how to monitor, analyze, and manage wait events, you have mastered another tool for making your database perform at top proficiency.

You can examine events from the session level or at the level of the whole database, using several Oracle-supplied views that provide wait statistics for events. These views record a wide range and multiple classes of events, and you'll see them used throughout this chapter.

- V$SYSTEM_EVENT
- V$SESSION_EVENT
- V$SESSION_WAIT
- V$WAITSTAT
- V$LOCK

NOTE These views are primarily used for identifying events that cause significant waits. If a wait has not occurred for a particular event, it will not appear in any of these views.

To determine the cause of a wait problem, three of these views are good tools for a top-down approach. First, you look at the V$SYSTEM_EVENT view, which provides systemwide statistics. When you have evidence of a systemwide wait problem, you then look at the V$SESSION_EVENT view to get statistics for a specific session. Once you have narrowed the problem down to a session and a specific type of wait, you look at V$SESSION_WAIT for dynamic wait information. In addition, the V$WAITSTAT view gives you needed details when you're tackling waits in a particular buffer.

The V$LOCK view, described in the preceding section on locks, can be a significant aide in determining database locking problems. With this view you can locate the sessions causing the blocking situations, and even how long the blocking has been in effect. Later in this chapter we'll discuss some additional views Oracle provides that present locking information in a format that is easier to read.

The following sections examine each of these views and give suggestions for their use.

NOTE The wait statistics views can provide timing information on waits, such as total time spent waiting and the average wait, if you have set the TIMED_STATISTICS parameter to TRUE. See "How Do You Get More Information from V$ Views?" in Chapter 15.

Working with V$SYSTEM_EVENT

The V$SYSTEM_EVENT view provides a look at event waits in the database, system-wide. This is the view we'll use to monitor the database looking for wait problems that might be occurring. It includes the name of the wait event, the total number of waits and timeouts, the total time waited, and the average time per wait. (These last two statistics will not appear if TIMED_STATISTICS is not enabled.) The various wait events are discussed in a later section.

Here's a query against V$SYSTEM_EVENT:

SELECT * from v$system_event;

and the result:

EVENT	TOTAL_WAITS	TOTAL_TIMEOUTS	TIME_WAITED	AVERAGE_WAIT
latch free	54	54	0	0
pmon timer	634	628	0	0
checkpoint completed	1	0	0	0
buffer deadlock	1	1	0	0
buffer busy waits	45	1	0	0
log file sequential read	66	0	0	0
log file single write	13	0	0	0
log file parallel write	571	0	0	0
log file sync	657	1	0	0
db file sequential read	538	0	0	0
db file scattered read	145	0	0	0
db file single write	5	0	0	0
db file parallel write	53	0	0	0
db file parallel read	2	0	0	0

direct path read	30	0	0	0
direct path write	20	0	0	0
instance state change	2	0	0	0
smon timer	10	5	0	0
library cache pin	19	3	0	0
library cache load lock	1	0	0	0
file identify	37	0	0	0
file open	116	0	0	0

Following is another query of V$SYSTEM_EVENT with a slightly narrower focus:

```
SELECT event, total_waits, time_waited, average_wait
FROM v$system_event;
```

and the result:

EVENT	TOTAL_WAITS	TIME_WAITED	AVERAGE_WAIT
buffer busy waits	4	0	0
log file sequential read	23	0	0
log file single write	7	0	0
log file parallel write	133	0	0
LGWR wait for redo copy	2	0	0
log file sync	54	0	0
db file sequential read	603	0	0
db file scattered read	141	0	0
db file single write	5	0	0
db file parallel write	42	0	0
direct path read	20	0	0

Working with V$SESSION_EVENT

Here's an example of a query against V$SESSION_EVENT:

```
Column timeouts heading "TIMEOUTS"
SELECT * from v$session_event order by sid;
```

and the result:

SID	EVENT	TOTAL_WAITS	TIMEOUTS	TIME_WAITED	AVERAGE_WAIT	MAX_WAIT
1	pmon timer	768	762	0	0	0
2	latch free	4	4	0	0	0
2	rdbms ipc message	712	701	0	0	0
2	direct path read	10	0	0	0	0

2	file open	11	0	0	0	0
2	file identify	5	0	0	0	0
2	db file parallel write	68	0	0	0	0
3	latch free	10	10	0	0	0
3	log file sequential read	8	0	0	0	0
3	direct path write	5	0	0	0	0
3	file open	20	0	0	0	0
3	file identify	12	0	0	0	0
3	direct path read	5	0	0	0	0
3	log file parallel write	571	0	0	0	0
3	log file single write	12	0	0	0	0
3	rdbms ipc message	1182	664	0	0	0

You could use the V$SESSION_EVENT view if a user were reporting specific problems with their running session and you wanted to investigate. Or perhaps a query on V$SYSTEM_EVENT is showing something peculiar. For example, suppose the V$SYSTEM_ EVENT report reveals database file sequential reads at 603. Let's say that this is an excessive figure and you want to know if any of the current sessions have high numbers of waits for this event. (Keep in mind that the statistics are cumulative, so sessions running currently might well be doing okay.) Here's a query that will tell you specific session information for this event:

```
SELECT sid, event, total_waits, time_waited, average_wait
FROM v$session_event
WHERE event='db file sequential read'
Order by sid
```

and the result:

SID	EVENT	TOTAL_WAITS	TIME_WAITED	AVERAGE_WAIT
5	db file sequential read	29	0	0
6	db file sequential read	4	0	0
12	db file sequential read	204	0	0
16	db file sequential read	2	0	0
18	db file sequential read	17	0	0

Notice the substantial number of database file sequential reads for SID 12 is 204. Although 204 is probably not unusually high, the proportion of waits for this session compared with other sessions is compelling and worth troubleshooting.

Working with V$WAITSTAT

The V$SESSION_EVENT and V$SYSTEM_EVENT views provide summaries of all buffer busy waits. If you see a significant number of buffer busy waits in either view, you can obtain a more detailed breakdown of buffer block waits in the V$WAITSTAT view. Here's a sample query and its results:

```
SELECT * from v$waitstat;

CLASS                COUNT      TIME
------------------   --------   --------
data block           31         0
sort block           0          0
save undo block      0          0
segment header       1          0
save undo header     0          0
free list            0          0
extent map           0          0
bitmap block         0          0
bitmap index block   0          0
unused               0          0
system undo header   0          0
system undo block    0          0
undo header          1          0
undo block           0          0
```

The CLASS column lists buffer block classes associated with the wait COUNT number. Table 17.7 defines the classes reported in this query.

TABLE 17.7: WAIT CLASSES OF INTEREST IN V$WAITSTAT

Wait Class	Description
Data block	A wait on a data block in the buffer cache. Might indicate that you need to increase FREELISTS or INITTRANS settings on the table experiencing the wait.
System undo header	The number of waits for only the header blocks in the SYSTEM rollback segment.
System undo block	The number of waits for all buffers of the SYSTEM rollback segment *except* header blocks.

Continued

TABLE 17.7: WAIT CLASSES OF INTEREST IN V$WAITSTAT (CONTINUED)

Wait Class	Description
Undo header	The number of waits for only the header blocks in the non–SYSTEM rollback segments.
Undo block	The number of waits for all buffers in the no–SYSTEM rollback segment, *except* header block waits.

To locate a specific datafile where waits are occurring, use this query:

```
SELECT name, count
FROM x$kcbfwait, v$datafile
WHERE indx + 1 = file#
Order by count;
```

for these results:

```
NAME                                                         COUNT
------------------------------------------------------------ ----------
D:\ORACLE\ORADATA\ORA816\ORA816_TEMP_01.DBF                       0
D:\ORACLE\ORADATA\ORA816\ORA816_LOCAL_UNIFORM_01.DBF              0
D:\ORACLE\ORADATA\ORA816\ORA816_RBS_01.DBF                        1
D:\ORACLE\ORADATA\ORA816\SYSTEM01.DBF                             5
D:\ORACLE\ORADATA\ORA816\ORA816_USERS_01.DBF                     39
```

Common Wait Events

The V$SESSION_EVENT and V$SYSTEM_EVENT results reveal quite a few wait events that occur in Oracle. Actually, many of them are of no consequence in terms of performance monitoring. A good number of them are known as timeout events, for example (when a database process has timed out and is just looking for work). This section reviews the wait events that do have important implications to the DBA.

You can safely ignore the following events if they appear in V$SYSTEM_EVENT and V$SESSION_EVENT views:

- client message
- parallel query dequeue wait
- RDBMS IPC message
- SQL*Net more data from client
- dispatcher timer
- pipe get
- SMON timer
- virtual circuit status WMON goes to sleep
- NULL event
- PMON timer
- SQL*Net message from client

Buffer Waits

The following wait events represent waits for a buffer lock in the database buffer cache: buffer busy, *buffer busy due to global cache,* and *write complete.* They occur because a buffer needed by one session is being read into the buffer cache by another session. Another cause is that the requested buffer is being held by another process in an incompatible mode. This might be the case, for example, if an exclusive table lock were held on the table associated with the buffer.

These three buffer waits differ slightly. *Buffer busy* waits occur when a process wants a block in the database buffer cache. A *buffer busy due to global cache* wait is used with Oracle Parallel Server configurations and thus will not show any waits in a standard database configuration. *Write complete* waits occur if the database writer process has locked the requested block in the buffer cache because it is currently processing that block. These waits also have varying timeout periods that control the length of the waits.

When checking for the cause of these waits events, look at V$SESSION_WAIT to find out which session is experiencing the bulk of the waits. Often one or two sessions will be the primary obstacles. Once you have identified the problem sessions, the options for resolution are simple:

- Tune the SQL. Find the most troublesome sessions and examine the SQL statements associated with them. This SQL is very likely a good candidate for tuning.

- Investigate the cause of the waits by using V$SESSION_WAIT. You can also try to trace remote sessions, setting event 10046 to level 8 or 16, as described in Chapter 15.

- If you're doing indexed lookups on large tables and the lookups are random in nature, consider assigning those tables to the recycle buffer pool. This will reduce contention for the default buffer pool.

- This last one's no big surprise: *tune your disk I/O.* If you have read times of >40ms on datafiles, see what you can do to reduce that. The V$FILESTAT view will help you locate hot datafiles. Throughput issues are discussed at the end of the chapter.

Db File Scattered Read

The *db file scattered read* wait occurs as a result of a full table scan from the database buffer cache that requires the server process to get the block from the datafile first. If you are seeing a significant number of these waits, it means you have some I/O contention or perhaps some SQL that needs to be tuned. If you find that full table scans are unavoidable, consider tuning your database to accommodate full table scans.

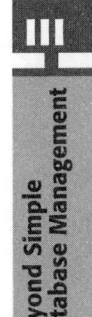

When searching for suspect sessions, look for sessions that are doing lots of physical reads. (Use V$SESSTAT to find the physical reads statistic for these sessions.)

Here are the options for dealing with db file scattered read waits. Many are the same as for buffer wait problems:

- Adjust DB_FILE_MULTIBLOCK_READ_COUNT. This parameter, multiplied by the DB_BLOCK_SIZE value, should equal 64 on a 32-bit system and 128 on a 64-bit system. So if you're using an 8KB database block size, this parameter should be 8; and for an 16KB database block size the parameter should be 4 on a 32-bit system.

NOTE Making the DB_BLOCK_SIZE*DB_FILE_MULTIBLOCK_READ_COUNT = 64 is a general rule, and may vary based on the method your OS uses for I/O at the OS level. On 64-bit systems, the rule of thumb is DB_BLOCK_SIZE*DB_FILE_MULTIBLOCK_READ_COUNT = 128.

- Tune the SQL on the sessions that are having the biggest problems.

- Use the keep buffer pool. Consider assigning any table that will generally experience full table scans to the keep buffer pool if you have enough memory available. This is particularly true for unindexed lookup tables.

- Index tables as much as you can—even smaller lookup tables. Often the presence of an index will allow the optimizer to choose more efficient execution plans. Full index scans and partitioned indexes can improve performance, as well. Usually, index scans are better than full table scans.

- Investigate the cause of the waits by using V$SESSION_WAIT. You can also try to trace remote sessions, setting event 10046 to level 8 or 16, as described in Chapter 15.

- As when dealing with buffer waits, *tune your disk I/O*. If you have read times of >40ms on datafiles, see what you can do to reduce that. The V$FILESTAT view will help you locate hot datafiles.

Db File Sequential Read

The *db file sequential read* wait occurs when an indexed block read from the database buffer cache requires the server process to get the block from the datafile first. In a majority of cases, the cause is faulty SQL. Other factors are a badly tuned database or inefficient I/O distribution. Your database buffer cache may be sized too small, so adding memory to this structure might help.

The index clustering factor may have an impact as well. Check the CLUSTERING_FACTOR column in DBA_INDEXES. If this number is large (1 is perfect), consider rebuilding your table, making sure you order the rows. Why? In a B*Tree index, the columns are in descending order. Because the columns are ordered, the values are all clustered together in the index. For example, in an index built on the department number, all employees in Department 1 are clustered, employees in Department 2 are clustered, and so on.

In contrast, consider that Oracle doesn't order data that is put in a table. So it can end up anywhere. The 15 employees in Department 1 can be scattered around 15 different blocks. To get all the employees in Department 1, you'd need to perform 18 logical I/Os to get the data: three I/Os minimum for the index, and 15 I/Os for the table. Here's the breakdown:

1 index header + 1 leaf + 1 index node + 15 blocks in table = 18 I/Os

Now suppose the table has been re-created and the data loaded in the correct order (by department number). In this case, assume that all 15 employees are now in just one block. The I/Os are reduced to four:

1 index header + 1 leaf + 1 index node + 1 block in table = 4 I/Os

Certainly this ordering approach won't work all the time, but in some cases it can significantly reduce I/O. This method also requires constant maintenance if new records are added, old ones deleted, and so on. This methodology probably has the most meaningful application in decision support systems (DSS) and data warehousing, where data is more static.

Enqueue

Enqueue waits occur as the result of a session waiting to obtain a lock on a resource. Normally this resource is a buffer in the database buffer cache. In most cases, the wait occurs because of an existing user-session lock or Oracle internal database lock on that resource.

Free Buffer

A *free buffer* wait occurs when an Oracle server process cannot find an available free buffer in the database buffer cache. This can be caused by several problems, with inefficient I/O among the top candidates. Often the database writer cannot keep up with the demand to write dirty buffers to disk, thus freeing those buffers for reuse. An inadequately sized database buffer cache can also cause free buffer wait problems, as can improperly tuned SQL statements. Even an oversized SGA can be at fault if excessive paging and swapping are occurring.

Note that some documentation indicates that excessive sorting to disk can cause free buffer waits, but this is incorrect. In Oracle8i, all sorts to disk bypass the database buffer cache and thus never cause free buffer waits.

Latch Activity

The *latch activity* wait occurs when a server or Process Monitor (PMON) process fails to acquire a latch and executes a latch activity test. If the process determines that latch cleanup is required, it will post PMON to wake and get busy performing cleanup of prematurely deceased sessions. When not posted, PMON wakes every three seconds to perform its normal latch cleanup duties. During the latch activity test of the Oracle session, and any resulting PMON latch activity cleanup, latch activity waits will accrue.

Latch Free

The *latch free* wait indicates that a session had to wait to acquire a latch. Each time a process attempts to acquire a latch, is unable to get it, and is forced to sleep, the latch free statistic is updated. (See the "Latch Contention" section earlier in this chapter.)

Library Cache Lock and Library Cache Pin

These waits occur when sessions are waiting for a lock or a pin on a library cache object. Sessions waiting to acquire a library cache lock will generate library cache lock waits. Sessions waiting to pin an library cache row object will generate library cache pin waits.

- Library cache locks are applied when library cache objects are used in SQL statements. Further, the locks can be recursively applied to other library cache objects as required. These locks are held in shared mode while parse operations are ongoing, and are then converted to NULL mode locks once the parse of the SQL statement has completed.

- When a library cache object is being compiled, parsed or executed, a pin is applied to that object. The pin protects the object from having the library cache lock removed (or broken), as might occur if a DDL statement tried to modify a table being queried. Thus, the act of executing a SQL statement causes that statement to be pinned in the shared pool. If there's an attempt to modify the table on which the SQL statement was operating, the statement will fail, in part because of the pinned status of the SQL statement in the shared pool.

Log Buffer Space

The *log buffer space* statistic indicates that the LGWR is not clearing the log buffer fast enough, causing sessions to wait. A session needs to write a redo log entry to the redo log buffer, but there is not enough space to accommodate the request. This wait can also be a result of contention for the redo copy latch or the redo allocation latches, when the waiting session cannot acquire the latch it needs.

A popular idea is that increasing the size of the log buffer will correct log buffer space wait problems, but it rarely works. It may help to a point, but we don't recommend going much over 300KB, and that's on the high side. It's more likely that these waits are occurring because Log Writer (LGWR) is having a hard time keeping up with the amount of redo being generated. You'll have better results if you improve I/O distribution and increase the size of redo logs to reduce excessive log switches (more than once every 10–15 minutes). Overhead associated with the switches can cause log buffer space waits. The redo log files, if not properly allocated for I/O distribution, can really bog down a high-transaction-rate system. Make sure all redo log files are on separate disks and that there is sufficient bandwidth.

Here are some other possibilities:

- Increase the number of redo log file groups.
- Consider *reducing* the size of the redo log buffer. Yes, that's right, reduce it. This might mean that LGWR has smaller redo batches to write and can improve performance as a result.
- If you're seeing contention for the redo allocation latch along with log buffer space waits, consider reducing the LOG_SMALL_ENTRY_MAX_SIZE parameter. This will force more frequent use of the multiple redo allocation copy rather than the one redo allocation latch.

Log File Parallel Write

This wait occurs as redo log files are being written to by LGWR. Oracle writes to the members of the same redo log group in parallel, in an effort to reduce the overall time for this wait.

Log File Sequential Read

This wait occurs as redo records within a redo log file are being read.

Log File Single Write

This wait occurs as log file headers are being written. This often occurs when members are being added to a redo log group, or when the headers of the group members are being updated. Updates might include adjusting the redo log file status, modifying the start SCN or the stop SCN of the redo log file, or assigning a new sequence number to the log file during a log switch.

Log File Switch

Log file switch waits occur when a process needs to write to the redo log buffer, but Oracle is in the middle of flushing the buffer and executing a log file switch. These waits are a result of one of the following listed conditions:

Archiving Needed   Sometimes the ARCH process is struggling to move the archived redo log files. Oracle, in ARCHIVELOG mode, had to wait to complete a log switch because a completely archived log was not available.

Checkpoint Incomplete   A log file switch cannot occur because an online redo log file's associated checkpoint has not yet completed and Oracle must wait for it. This generally indicates that your redo logs are too few or too small. You should look at ways of optimizing DBWR throughput to the database datafiles.

Clearing Log File   This happens when a log switch is waiting on a log file that is being cleared as a result of the CLEAR LOGFILE command.

Log File Switch Completion

This wait indicates that Oracle had to wait for a log file switch to complete.

Log File Sync

The *log file sync* wait statistic indicates the amount of time that was taken from the point of a COMMIT command by a session, and the time taken by LGWR to complete the writing of the contents of the redo log buffer, including the COMMIT vector, and to post the write complete signal to the user session.

Write Complete

Write complete waits occur as DBWR is writing out dirty buffers. While the buffer block is being written by DBWR, processes are prevented from changing it. The wait occurs as a user session attempts to lock a row in a buffer that DBWR is writing. The key to solving this wait problem is tuning DBWR so it will have the throughput required.

Working with V$SESSION_WAIT

At times, the V$SESSION_WAIT view can be the mother lode for the DBA trying to minimize the effects of waits on database processing. This view helps you to pinpoint the waits for a given session, and it provides various levels of detail on those waits.

For example, suppose a query of V$SESSION_EVENT indicates that SID 22 is showing significant buffer busy waits. These buffer busy wait events might suggest that the datafiles are not optimally placed for I/O purposes, or maybe there's some bad SQL in use. So we know that there's a problem, but we don't know where in the database the waits are occurring. That is where V$SESSION_WAIT comes in.

Here's a V$SESSION_WAIT query:

```
select sid, seq#, event, p1, p2, p3 from v$session_wait
where event='buffer busy waits';
```

and the result:

```
 SID  SEQ# EVENT                P1 P1TEXT    P2 P2TEXT   P3 P3TEXT
----- ----- -------------------- ----- ------ ----- ------ ----- ------
  22    67 buffer busy waits      3 file#   4320 block#  220 id
```

Let's analyze these statistics. We know that a buffer busy wait event indicates that this session waited for a buffer lock. In this case, we only have one session reporting such a wait, so it's probably not of much importance. Many of the V$SESSION_WAIT events populate columns P1 through P3. Sometimes this information is useful and sometimes it's not.

Look at the P1, P2, and P3 columns and their associated P?TEXT columns. For each type of wait, one or more of these columns may be populated with information that can assist in diagnosing the problem at hand. The P1 column gives the file number (3) of the file that contained the block Oracle was trying to access; this is designated by the FILE# that appears in the P1TEXT column. Column P2 tells us the block number (4320) of the block that Oracle was trying to access, designated by the BLOCK# shown in the P2TEXT column. In this situation, you can do a simple query against DBA_EXTENTS and discover the object causing problems. You could also query the DBA_DATA_FILES view to uncover the troublesome datafile. Armed with this knowledge, you can look deeper into recurring problems.

In the following example, the problem object is the employee table on datafile ORA816_USERS_01.DBF:

```
SELECT tablespace_name, file_name from dba_data_files where file_id=3;
```

Here's the result of our query:

```
TABLESPACE_NAME  FILE_NAME
---------------  ------------------------------------------------
USERS            D:\ORACLE\ORADATA\ORA816\ORA816_USERS_01.DBF
```

We can use the DBA_EXTENTS data dictionary view to figure out which object is causing us a problem.

```
SELECT owner, segment_name from dba_extents
WHERE (block_id<=4320 and block_id + blocks >4320)
And file_id=3;
```

```
OWNER                SEGMENT_NAME
-------------------- --------------------
SCOTT                EMP_TEST
```

One problem with V$SESSION_WAIT is its dynamic nature. Wait events can move very fast. Although a 0.5-second wait may not seem very important, when you multiply that half-second wait by several thousand you can see that even short waits can add up to something significant. Unfortunately, while looking at V$SESSION_WAIT, you might just miss a bunch of those half-second waits. Also, querying V$SESSION_WAIT incurs a cost in and of itself. So how do you generate wait information for a session that is complete? The answer is to do a trace on the session.

There are several ways to trace sessions, and they're covered pretty well in Chapter 16's section on tracing other users' sessions. In a nutshell, when you tracing a session, if you set the trace event to level 8 you get all the wait information for that session. (Level 16 gives you binding variable values, by the way.) This wait information is helpful in solving problems with that session.

Solutions to wait problems can be complex. Let's move on to the next section and see some tools for monitoring your database.

Monitoring Scripts and Suggestions

Now that we've discussed the internals of Oracle latches, locks, and wait events, you'll need some scripts to help you monitor these things. No doubt you have seen the beginnings of such scripts in some of the examples provided thus far. Here we'll examine specific scripts and other helps for detecting problems with these elements of Oracle processing.

Once you've found a problem, the question will be to figure out how bad a problem it is. Locking, for example, happens all the time. If you get a fleeting blocking lock, is that really a concern? We'll work on clarifying these and other issues in this section, so you can move forward and develop your own reliable decision-making process.

Monitoring Events

When monitoring system events, it's important to monitor for a meaningful period of time. This is where your baselines come into play.

During a normal operational period of time (and after properly tuning your database, of course), you determine the total wait times your database experiences. Having determined the baseline wait times, monitor your system over a fixed period (for example, every 15 minutes) to establish a benchmark.

Once the benchmark is established, you set two threshold criteria for monitoring. We recommend a yellow (warning) threshold and a red (danger) threshold. When monitoring determines that the warning threshold has been eclipsed, we might send an informational e-mail. When the threshold eclipses the red threshold, we start paging, and performing other notifications as required. Depending on the event, we might allow Oracle to bust the yellow or red criteria more than once before sending out warnings, if that is the normal behavior of the database. Again, benchmarking and really understanding the personality of your database goes a long way toward establishing an effective monitoring routine.

Monitoring Locks

When monitoring locks, what you are most interested in are blocking locks. Locking is a serious problem, and you need to stay on top of it.

Though you can write your own scripts to do this, Oracle provides some additional views that you can create (such as DBA_BLOCKERS) that will give you all the information you need. We will talk about creating those views first, and then we will discuss using those views and determining when to flag a locking problem in your monitoring processes.

Using V$LOCK

While we've already discussed the V$LOCK view, we should spend some more quality time with it, reviewing some of the finer details and getting comfortable with it. Then we'll use some Oracle scripts to create a few views that will eliminate your need to use V$LOCK most of the time anyway. Isn't that just the way of things?

V$LOCK can be used for ongoing monitoring. Unfortunately, it can be a very cryptic view to read. V$LOCK provides total locking and waiting times.

When it comes to resolving blockers and blocked sessions, querying V$LOCK can get complicated. Often it's much easier to use DBA_WAITERS (discussed shortly) when monitoring with TIMED_STATISTICS on. You can create a simple SQL statement that will trigger an alarm (e-mail or pager, perhaps) when a set number or length time of overall waiting for locks is exceeded. The SQL script in Listing 17.4 demonstrates this method of monitoring for blocking locks. Note that this script is for Unix, but you could do something similar in NT. We often wrap these into shell scripts, as the example demonstrates.

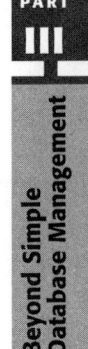

Listing 17.4: Generating an Alarm for a Blocking Lock Condition

```
#!/bin/ksh
# report blocking lock problem
# will report on any blocking locks that have
# blocked > 30 seconds.
# requires timed_statistics to be set on.
SET ORACLE_SID=oracle
SET ORAENV_ASK=NO
. oraenv
alarm=`sqlplus -s /nolog<<WEOF
connect scott/tiger
set heading off
set feedback off
select count(*) from V$LOCK
where block=1
and ctime > 30;
quit
WEOF`
If alarm -ge 1
Then
     # your action goes here
fi
```

TIP Set up whatever thresholds that are appropriate for your own environment. We generate a report on any wait over about 30 seconds, or when a set cumulative total of waits (say, 100) have occurred over a given period of time (say, 1 minute). Also, we like to dump the snapshot of waits to some historical repository, to help in establishing a baseline for system information.

Once your script has alerted you to a potential blocking problem, you can use V$LOCK to determine who is causing the blocking. Or you can use the DBA_LOCKS and DBA_WAITERS views that we will create in the next section. Let's look at the result of a query from V$LOCK:

SID	TY	ID1	ID2	LMODE	REQUEST	CTIME	BLOCK
2	MR	5	0	4	0	0	0
2	MR	1	0	4	0	0	0

2	MR	2	0	4	0	0	0
2	MR	3	0	4	0	0	0
2	MR	4	0	4	0	0	0
3	RT	1	0	6	0	0	0
13	TX	65541	1571	6	0	1251	1
13	TM	2890	0	3	0	1251	0
16	TM	2890	0	3	0	1236	0
16	TX	65541	1571	0	6	1236	0

Note the row that has "1" in the block column. This entry indicates that the session (SID 12) is blocking other sessions. Look at the values in column ID1 and ID2 for that TX lock in SID 12. To find the sessions that this session is blocking, look at the other TX lock types. As you look at the other TX lock types, look in the ID1 and ID2 rows. Any TX lock type that has ID1 and ID2 rows that are the same as the blocking session will be the sessions that are waiting for the blocking session. If you want to identify the objects causing the blocking, you can look at the TM locks associated with those sessions. There, in the ID1 column, you'll see the OBJECT_ID of the object that the locks are currently being taken against.

Using catblock.sql

The indispensable Oracle-provided SQL script called `catblock.sql` is located in the $ORACLE_HOME/rdbms/admin directory in Unix, and $ORACLE_HOME\rdbms\admin in NT. You run this script while connected as INTERNAL or using the SYS AS SYSDBA sign-on. Listing 17.5 shows an example.

Listing 17.5: Running *catblock.sql* to Create Views for Blocking Lock Resolution

```
D:\ORACLE\ORA816\RDBMS\ADMIN>sqlplus "sys as sysdba"
SQL*Plus: Release 8.1.6.0.0 - Production on Sat Jan 20 11:02:11 2001
SQL> @catblock
View created.
Synonym created.
Grant succeeded.
<etc…etc… this is about all you see>
```

Catblock.sql creates several views you can use to resolve locking problems. The views you'll use most often are as follows:

- DBA_BLOCKERS: Information on sessions that are being locked.
- DBA_DDL_LOCKS: Various locking information. Particularly helpful if you are trying to change an object that appears to be locked by another session.

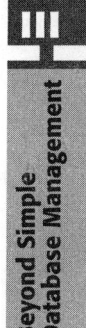

- **DBA_DML_LOCKS**: Information on DML locks in the database. Also provides the owner and name of the object being locked.
- **DBA_LOCKS**: A view of all database locks. Converts several of the locking codes into text, simplifying your diagnosis efforts.
- **DBA_LOCK_INTERNAL**: Information on internal database locks.
- **DBA_WAITERS**: Session ID of waiting sessions and of the session that is doing the blocking. Includes several elements of V$LOCK, including the lock ID and the lock mode requested.

Let's look at the most commonly used views, DBA_LOCKS and DBA_WAITERS.

The DBA_LOCKS View

The DBA_LOCKS view is the same as the more cryptic V$LOCK view, except it's easier to read. In DBA_LOCKS, Oracle includes decode statements for the V$LOCK coded columns, so you can see a description of the actual values in the column. Listing 17.6 gives an example of the output from a query against the DBA_LOCKS view.

Listing 17.6: Seeing Locks Using DBA_LOCKS

```
SELECT session_id sess_id, lock_type, mode_held,
mode_requested requested, lock_id1 lock1,
lock_id2 lock2, blocking_others
from dba_locks;
```

SESS_ID	LOCK_TYPE	MODE_HELD	REQUESTED	LOCK1	LOCK2	BLOCKING_OTHERS
2	Media Recovery	Share	None	5	0	Not Blocking
2	Media Recovery	Share	None	1	0	Not Blocking
2	Media Recovery	Share	None	2	0	Not Blocking
2	Media Recovery	Share	None	3	0	Not Blocking
2	Media Recovery	Share	None	4	0	Not Blocking
3	Redo Thread	Exclusive	None	1	0	Not Blocking
15	DML	Row-X (SX)	None	2890	0	Not Blocking
15	Transaction	None	Exclusive	65544	1670	Not Blocking
16	Transaction	Exclusive	None	65544	1670	Blocking
16	DML	Row-X (SX)	None	2890	0	Not Blocking

In this output, you can ignore the batch of media recovery locks, which appear for all online datafiles in Oracle8i. The same is true of the redo thread exclusive lock, which is set by the LGWR process and will pretty much always be there. The first thing of real interest is the DML lock by SESSION_ID 15. A DML lock is a row exclusive lock (as indicated by ROW-X in the MODE_HELP column). By looking at the BLOCKING_OTHERS column, we see that this particular lock is not blocking other sessions. You can determine which table is locked by looking at the LOCK1 column. There, the number 2890 is the OBJECT_ID of the object being locked. We can use this number in the following query to determine which object is being blocked:

```
SELECT owner, object_name, object_type from dba_objects
WHERE object_id=2890;
```

Here are the results:

```
OWNER    OBJECT_NAME      OBJECT_TYPE
-------  ---------------  ---------------
SCOTT    EMPLOYEE         TABLE
```

which tell us that the transaction is locking a row in the SCOTT.EMPLOYEE table.

The next line of the DBA_LOCKS report also focuses on Session 15. This time it's an exclusive transaction lock. The numbers in LOCK1 and LOCK2 columns in this case are of little use with transaction locks. The next line, however, is more helpful. It indicates that Session 16 is also causing a blocking situation with an exclusive transaction lock, and the BLOCKING OTHERS column tells us that we definitely have a problem. This session is blocking other sessions, causing them to wait.

Look at the next line; that DML lock looks suspicious. Note that it's on the same object that is being used by Session 15. Bingo! Session 16 is blocking Session 15. Knowing that, you can monitor the length of the locking action. If the blocking situation doesn't resolve itself soon, you should probably start calling users.

As you can see, one of the shortcomings of the DBA_LOCKS view is the lack of a column indicating how long the blocking situation has existed. For that information, you need to return to the V$LOCK view column CTIME.

The DBA_WAITERS View

DBA_WAITERS gives you a restricted report focused on locks that are waiting for blockers. Here is an example of a query:

```
SELECT waiting_session wait_ses, holding_session hold_ses, lock_type,
    mode_held mode_requested, lock_id1, lock_id2 from dba_waiters;
```

and the result:

```
WAIT_SES   HOLD_SES  LOCK_TYPE      MODE_REQUE  LOCK_ID1   LOCK_ID2
---------- --------- -------------- ----------  ---------- ----------
      15          16 Transaction    Exclusive       65544        1670
```

Notice that our old friend Session 16 is still blocking Session 15. Whoever's running that Session 16 is being really rude.

How Do We Monitor Latching?

For the most part, monitoring for latch contention issues requires the V$LATCH view. Listing 17.7 is a basic monitoring script using V$LATCH. It gives information about latches that are missed, and processes that are spinning and sleeping.

Listing 17.7: Using V$LATCH to Monitor Latching

```
Set lines 132
Column name format a25 heading "Name"
Column gets format 9,999,999 Heading "Gets"
Column misses format 999,999 Heading "Misses"
Column immediate_gets format 9,999,999 heading "Immed|Gets"
Column immediate_misses format 999,999 heading "Immed|Miss"
Column sleeps format 999,999 heading "Sleeps"
Column spin_gets format 999,999 heading "Spin|Gets"
Column miss_gets_r format 999,999 heading "Miss|Gets|Ratio"
Column sleep_gets_r format 999,999 heading "Sleep|Gets|Ratio"
Column spin_gets_r format 999,999 heading "Spin|Gets|Ratio"
Column nw_misses_r format 999,999 heading "No Wait|Misses|Ratio"
Column immediate_gets format 999,999 heading "Immed|Gets"

SELECT distinct a.name,
a.gets, a.immediate_gets, a.misses, a.immediate_misses,
a.sleeps, a.spin_gets,
round(a.misses/a.gets,3) miss_gets_r,
round(a.sleeps/a.gets,3) sleep_gets_r,
round(a.spin_gets/a.gets,3) spin_gets_r,
decode(immediate_gets,0,0,
round(a.immediate_misses/a.immediate_gets,3) ) nw_misses_r
FROM V$LATCH a
WHERE a.gets!=0 and
( (a.misses/a.gets > .01) or
  (a.sleeps/a.gets > .01) or
  (a.spin_gets/a.gets > .01) or
  (a.immediate_misses/a.gets > .01) or
  sleeps > 0
)
order by 4 desc
/
```

Because of the width of the report, the results are going to look much better if printed in landscape mode. Notice we've used the COLUMN command to create stacked headers for some of the columns (for instance, `column spin_gets...heading "Spin|Gets"` puts the Spin and Gets on two lines). And to accommodate the report's width on the printed page, we've divided it into two sections, repeating the NAME column for reference.

Name	Gets	Immed Gets	Misses	Immed Miss	Sleeps
library cache	655,492	0	74	0	78
cache buffers chains	831,514	16,826	39	0	52
session idle bit	199,904	0	8	0	8
enqueue hash chains	39,414	0	6	0	8
redo writing	51,704	0	5	0	5
shared pool	91,307	0	4	0	4
redo allocation	74,107	0	3	0	4
session allocation	37,598	0	2	0	2
Checkpoint queue latch	45,876	0	1	0	1
redo copy	12	59,900	0	28	0

Continued

Name	Spin Gets	Miss Gets Ratio	Sleep Gets Ratio	Spin Gets Ratio	No Wait Misses Ratio
library cache	0	0	0	0	0
cache buffers chains	0	0	0	0	0
session idle bit	0	0	0	0	0
enqueue hash chains	0	0	0	0	0
redo writing	0	0	0	0	0
shared pool	0	0	0	0	0
redo allocation	0	0	0	0	0
session allocation	0	0	0	0	0
Checkpoint queue latch	0	0	0	0	0
redo copy	0	0	0	0	0

This report sorts the various latches based on misses, assuming that the latches with the highest number of misses are the ones we want to look at first. The ratios listed (MISS GET, SPIN GET, and SLEEP GET) are the ratios of the misses, sleeps, and spins to the total number of gets. The higher these numbers, the more likely you have a problem with that latch. In particular, these numbers should never rise above 0.005 percent. If they do, consider tuning for latch contention.

Tuning Locks, Latches, and Waits

Tuning for latches, locking, and waits is all about reducing I/O to the disks and improving database usage. When you do latch tuning and lock tuning, you're really addressing the problem of waits. This section reviews some time-tested methods and strategies and gives you some tips and tricks on tuning in general—with a slant toward the elements discussed in this chapter.

General Tuning Advice

With so many options at your disposal, the advice we dispensed in Chapter 15 bears repeating here: Tune the database from the top down. Start with the system. Then tune database I/O distribution, the shared pool, and SQL statements, in that order. It may be true that you get the best overall performance improvement from SQL tuning, but such efforts will be less effective or even fruitless if the underlying database engine associated with those statements is struggling.

When Is Latch Contention a Problem?

Latch contention in the form of waits, sleeps, and no-wait misses happen all the time in normal database processing. If you were to chase down every latch sleep, you'd never get to sleep yourself. So how do you decide when contention is actually causing difficulties? In our experience, we've found we can gauge the severity by noting the average duration and frequency of contention for a specific latch. You can use the ever-helpful V$ views to gather this information, along with the sample queries provided in this chapter.

Identifying latch contention is another case for benchmarking your database. By setting a benchmark based on normal periods of activity (and by keeping that benchmark current), you'll never find yourself wondering about the extent of changes to your database's activity.

NOTE Do you need to tune the system? Right out of the gate, check your OS for basic soundness. You know the drill: Is the system performing at peak efficiency? Is it configured to do so? How hard are your CPUs working? Do you have sufficient CPU capability? Are you getting the disk-transfer times you expect? Is the network sending packets at the desired rate? Is the memory configured properly? And get your system administrator involved, too. Once you're certain that the system is purring along like a well-oiled machine, you can take the next tuning step.

Check Up on I/O Distribution

Latch contention issues and wait events are often symptomatic of an I/O problem. Chapter 4 tells you how to ensure that database datafiles are appropriately distributed for optimal I/O. Of course, in these days of big disks and volume managers, tuning I/O is tougher than it used to be. If you have a choice, choose a configuration with many smaller disks rather than one huge disk. Simply said, you can get better performance from distributing your database I/O to multiple disks (and, if possible, multiple disk channels) than by confining it to one huge disk.

TIP The subject of disk configuration and its effect on database I/O is hugely controversial, even within DBA ranks. Many think that, by virtue of the huge caches on these disks, you won't suffer performance hits if you configure a database using one big disk. That's fine and dandy, but if you're disk shopping, ask the sales rep to bring in a big-disk system so you can benchmark it and confirm that it's truly advantageous. We contend that several disks means more disk heads, which irrefutably results in more throughput.

Regardless of today's monolithic caches, I/O distribution is still everything. Quick writes to the redo logs from the redo log buffer are important, and being able to efficiently write to and read from the database datafiles is everything. If your I/O setup causes contention, your performance will suffer.

In Chapter 4 we covered Oracle Flexible Architecture (OFA) and tablespace placement in a given database. Of course, your database may not be the only database on the system, so the question is whether the other database is causing your database I/O problems. The subject gets murky when you factor in virtual disks. Virtual file systems create a middle layer between the operating system and the disk drives, called a *logical volume manager*. This middle layer comprises logical file systems that sit on top of one or more physical disks. With logical volume management, one file system can actually reside on the same physical disk, and you may not even know it.

If your system administrator manages these systems, you may not be privy to the mapping of physical disks. Perhaps, in part, the administrator doesn't understand the importance of such mapping or doesn't know how to create such a map. Either way, it's imperative that you make clear to your system administrator that you need to know where this data resides, and with what other systems it interacts.

Correcting I/O problems can make a huge difference in performance. This action alone can transform you into a hero. Trust me. I've been there.

How's the Shared Pool Doing?

After tuning I/O, you may still be seeing a good deal of latch contention. Now's the time to look at the shared pool and take advantage of the scripts provided in Chapter 15. A poorly tuned shared pool can cause all sorts of latch issues. Run the various scripts that monitor the hit ratios of the shared pool. Are your hit ratios low? If so, you must add memory.

WARNING Any time you add memory to any Oracle memory structure such as the shared pool, make sure you don't add so much that you cause the system to start thrashing memory pages between the swap disks and memory. This will inevitably result in performance problems. You'll only wind up worse off than before.

If the hit ratios are not low, and you see thrashing, make sure you have not overallocated memory to the point that you are paging or excessively swapping memory to and from the disk. If you are, you must correct this problem immediately. You'll need to enlist the help of your system administrator to determine if you're having system memory contention issues.

In keeping with the theme of reducing I/O is the idea that the fewer numbers of blocks you have to deal with, the less work the database will have to do, and latch contention will be minimized. Do everything you can to reduce I/Os during queries. Make sure your tables are allocating block storage correctly (look at PCTUSED/PCTFREE). Making sure tables load in order of the primary key (or most often used) index columns, and tuning your SQL to return the result set in the fewest number of block I/Os (logical or physical) will result in a reduction in latch contention—we guarantee it.

Finally, don't just throw CPUs, disks, and memory at the problem: that's the wrong kind of lazy solution and often doing so prolongs the problem. As your database system grows, even the faster hardware will not be able to handle the load. The only exception to this rule is if you simply do not have enough disk space to properly distribute the I/O of the database. If this is the case then you simply have to buy more disk pronto.

NOTE In some cases, lack of memory in the shared pool or the database buffer cache actually *is* the problem. This can be true if you see low hit ratios in any of the memory areas.

Fragmentation of the shared pool can also be a problem. Consider changing the
```
shared_pool_reserved_size
```
parameter, which is associated with the parameter
```
_shared_pool_reserved_min_alloc
```
These parameters affect the location in the shared pool for storing PL/SQL code. If the code is of a size greater than _SHARED_POOL_RESERVED_MIN_ALLOC, it will be stored in an area of the shared pool set aside by the parameter SHARED_POOL_RESERVED_SIZE. If there isn't enough memory available for that chunk to be stored in reserved memory, it will be stored in the normal memory area of the shared pool. You can positively affect shared pool fragmentation by increasing the SHARED_POOL_RESERVED_MIN_ALLOC parameter so that your largest PL/SQL programs are loaded there. This approach will eliminate fragmentation issues.

Another method that can be used to limit fragmentation of the shared pool is the use of the DBMS_SHARED_POOL.KEEP procedure to pin often used PL/SQL objects in the shared pool. (See Chapter 20 for more on DBMS_SHARED_POOL.) You might consider pinning commonly used objects in the SGA every time the database starts up. Doing so will help improve performance, and will go a long way toward reducing performance problems.

Tune Up Your SQL

If everything looks hunky-dory with the shared pool then make sure you are using reusable SQL statements with bind variables as much as possible. If you aren't, you can cause all sorts of problems, including latching contention. See Chapter 16 for more information on how to write reusable SQL and how to determine if SQL needs to be rewritten. You may also want to take advantage of cursor sharing in Oracle8i, which is also discussed in Chapter 16.

General Tuning for Latch Contention

Because there are various levels of latches, contention for one latch can cause contention against other, lower-level latches. A perfect example is the attempt to acquire a redo copy latch to quickly allocate memory in the redo log buffer. Depending on the size of the redo to be written, Oracle will often opt to use one of the several redo allocation latches rather than use the one redo copy latch. Having acquired the redo allocation latch, Oracle will then quickly try to acquire the level-six redo copy latch. Oracle needs this latch only long enough to allocate space in the redo log buffer for the entries it needs to write; then it releases the latch for other processes to use. Unfortunately, a delay in getting the redo copy latch can keep other processes from acquiring the available redo allocation latches. The bottom line is that you must always deal with latch contention level by level, tuning from the highest level (15) to the lowest (0).

Consider increasing the _SPIN_COUNT parameter if you are seeing excessive sleeps on a latch. On many systems it defaults to 2000, but yours might be different. If you're seeing problems with redo copy latches or other latch sleeps, see what you can do by playing with this parameter.

You can use the ALTER SYSTEM command to reset the spin count as well, which means you don't have to shut down the database. Here's the syntax for this:

ALTER SYSTEM SET "_SPIN_COUNT" = 4000;

After you have reset the spin count, let the system run normally for a few minutes and then check to see if the number of spins has dropped. Also, has there been any change in the number of sleeps? (Note that sleeps for the redo copy latch are not unusual.)

WARNING Remember that hidden or undocumented parameters are not supported by Oracle in most cases. That includes _SPIN_COUNT (though it was a documented parameter until Oracle8). With this in mind, test all hidden parameters before you decide to use them in production, and find out about any bugs by checking Oracle's registered information.

TIP In conjunction with your latch contention tuning, keep in mind that tuning bad SQL statements can have a huge impact on latching overall. So by all means tune the instance as best you can—but often your best results will come from SQL tuning.

Tuning Redo Copy Latch Problems

Oracle's multiple redo copy latches are designed to relieve the hard-pressed single redo allocation latch. When using the redo copy latch, Oracle acquires the redo allocation latch only long enough to get memory in the redo log buffer allocated. Once that operation is complete, it releases the redo allocation latch and writes the redo log entry through the redo copy latch. Note that sleeps for the redo copy latches are normal and unique to this latch.

The process will sleep if it fails to acquire one of the redo copy latches. When it wakes up, it tries to acquire the next redo copy latch in order, trying one at a time until it is successful. Oracle executes a sleep operation between each acquisition attempt, so you see the increases in the SLEEP columns of the V$LOCK data dictionary view. That being the case, if you get multiple processes fighting for this latch, you are going to get contention. You can do a couple of things to try to correct this problem.

Increase the number of redo copy latches by increasing the default value of the parameters LOG_SIMULTANEOUS_COPIES and LOG_ENTRY_PREBUILD_THRESHOLD. Check your operating system documentation for restrictions on increasing these values.

Tuning Redo Allocation Latch Problems

Oracle's lone redo allocation latch serializes access to the redo log buffer, allocating space to it for the server processes. Sometimes this latch is held for the entire period of the redo write, and sometimes just long enough for the allocation of memory in the redo log buffer. The parameter LOG_SMALL_ENTRY_MAX_SIZE sets a threshold for whether the redo allocation latch will be acquired for the duration of the redo log buffer write. If the size of the redo is smaller (in bytes) than LOG_SMALL_ENTRY_MAX_SIZE, the redo allocation latch will be used. If the redo is larger, a redo copy latch will be used. So if you see latch contention in the form of sleeps or spins on the redo allocation latch, consider reducing LOG_SMALL_ENTRY_MAX_SIZE.

NOTE There is a school of opinion for setting LOG_SMALL_ENTRY_MAX_SIZE to 0 and always using the redo copy latches. We contend that things Oracle are rarely so black and white. Always test a setting like this, and always be willing to accept that something else will work better.

Other Shared Pool Latching Problems

Latching issues in the shared pool are usually caused by insufficient memory allocation. As far as database parameters go, there isn't a lot to tune with respect to the shared pool beyond memory. Of course, maintain your typical vigilance over I/O distribution and bad SQL.

Tuning Buffer Block Waits

Data block waits listed in the V$WAITSTAT view can indicate an insufficient number of free lists available on the table or index where the wait is occurring. You may need to increase it. In Oracle8i you can dynamically increase or decrease the number of free lists in an object by using the ALTER TABLE statement with the FREELISTS keyword in the STORAGE clause.

NOTE By the way, don't expect to see waits in V$WAITSTAT for the FREELIST class. This statistic applies only to free list groups. Free list groups are used in Oracle Parallel Server (OPS) configurations, so it's unlikely that you'll use them if you are not using OPS.

Another concern is the setting of the object's INITRANS parameter. The INITRANS parameter defaults to 1, but if there is substantial DML activity on the table, you may need to increase the setting. This parameter, as well, can be adjusted dynamically. Note that by increasing either free lists or INITRANS for an object, you are reducing the total space available in a block for actually storing row data. Keep this in mind.

It can be hard to identify exactly what object is causing the buffer block wait problems. Perhaps the easiest way is to try to capture the waits as they occur, using the V$SESSION_WAIT view. Remember that this view is transitory, and you might need to create a monitoring script to try and catch some object usage trends. Another way to monitor object usage is to enable table monitoring and watch the activity recorded in the SYS.DBA_TAB_MODIFICATIONS view. You can create a job to copy those stats to a permanent table before you update the statistics. See Chapter 16 for more on table monitoring.

WARNING Carefully measure the performance impact of monitoring. It generally is insignificant, but with a system that is already "performance challenged," you may further affect overall performance by enabling monitoring. Nevertheless, the potential gains from knowing which tables are getting the most activity may well override performance concerns. Remember that short-term pain for long-term gain is not a bad thing. You can pay me now, or you can pay me later.

It's the same old saw: The easiest way to reduce buffer block waits is to tune your I/O and then tune your SQL. Statements and databases that run efficiently will reduce the likelihood of buffer block waits.

By the way—others suggest that reducing the block size of your database is another solution. This approach might or might not reduce waiting; in any case, it's not a good idea. The overwhelming advantages of larger block sizes cannot be ignored.

Last Word: Stay on Top of I/O Throughput!

We discussed proper placement of database datafiles in Chapter 4. If you're running multiple databases, I/O distribution becomes critical. In addition, file placement, partitioning, tablespaces, and physical distribution all affect I/O throughput to an even greater degree. Thus the concepts discussed in Chapter 4 have direct application in tuning methodologies. We'll close this chapter with seven tenets for maximizing I/O throughput:

1. Separate data tablespaces from index tablespaces.
2. Separate large, frequently used tables, into their own tablespaces. If you partition tables, separate each partition into its own tablespace.
3. Determine which tables will frequently be joined together and attempt to distribute them onto separate disks. If you can also manage to put them on separate controllers as well, so much the better.
4. Put temporary tablespaces on their own disks, particularly if intense disk sorting is occurring.
5. Beware of the system tablespace. Often times DBAs think it is not heavily used. You might be surprised how frequently it is read from and written to. Look at V$FILESTAT and see for yourself.
6. Separate redo logs onto different disks and controllers. This is for both performance reasons and recoverability reasons.
7. Separate your archived redo logs onto different disks. The archiving process can have a significant impact on the performance of your system if you do not distribute the load out correctly.

TIP One last bit of advice. On occasion, it's the actual setups of the disk and file systems that are hindering performance. Make sure you ask your system administrator for help if you are having serious performance problems. He or she might have additional monitoring tools on hand that can help you solve your problem. A lazy DBA takes advantage of all resources at his or her disposal, always.

CHAPTER 18

Oracle8i Parallel Processing

FEATURING:

Parallelizing Oracle operations	*844*
Using parallel DML and DDL	*845*
Executing parallel queries	*849*
Performing parallel recovery operations	*854*
Tuning and monitoring parallel processing operations	*855*

Parallel processing is the process of using a multiprocessor computer to divide a large task into smaller operations to be executed in parallel. In Oracle, a single database operation can be divided into subtasks, which are performed by several different processors working in parallel. The result is faster, more efficient database operations.

In this chapter, we discuss several options for effectively implementing parallel processing. The chapter begins with some basics of parallelizing operations, and then discusses how to use parallel DML and DDL, execute parallel queries, and perform parallel recovery operations. Finally, you will learn about the parallel processing parameters and how to monitor and tune parallel processing operations.

Parallelizing Oracle Operations

In Oracle8i, parallel processing is easy to configure, and it provides speed and optimization benefits for many operations, including the following:

- Batch bulk changes
- Temporary rollup tables for data warehousing
- Data transfer between partitioned and nonpartitioned tables
- Queries
- Recovery operations

Prior to Oracle8i, you needed to configure your database instance for DML operations. Oracle8i automatically assigns these values. Setting the init.ora parameter PARALLEL_AUTOMATIC_TUNING to TRUE will establish all of the necessary parameters to default values that will work fine in most cases. (Oracle recommends that PARALLEL_AUTOMATIC_TUNING be set to TRUE whenever parallel execution is implemented.)

NOTE Setting the PARALLEL_AUTOMATIC_TUNING parameter to TRUE automatically sets other parallel processing parameters. If necessary, you can adjust individual parallel processing parameters in the init.ora file to tune your parallelized operations. See the "Tuning and Monitoring Parallel Operations" section later in this chapter for details.

When you use parallel processing, the database evaluates the number of CPUs on the server and the number of disks on which the table's data is stored in order to determine the default *degree of parallelism (DOP)*. The default degree of parallelism is determined by two initialization parameters. First, Oracle estimates the number of blocks in the table being accessed (based on statistics in the data dictionary) and divides that number by the value of the initialization parameter PARALLEL_DEFAULT_SCANSIZE. Next, you can limit the number of query servers to use by default by setting the initialization parameter PARALLEL_DEFAULT_MAX_SCANS. The smaller of these two values is the default degree of parallelism. For example, if you have a table with 70,000 blocks and the parameter PARALLEL_DEFAULT_SCANSIZE is set to 1000, the default degree of parallelism is 70.

Rather than accepting the default degree of parallelism, you can tell Oracle what the degree of parallelism should be. You can assign a degree of parallelism when you create a table with the CREATE TABLE command or modify a table with the ALTER TABLE command. Also, you can override the default degree of parallelism by using the PARALLEL hint (as explained in the "Using Query Hints to Force Parallelism" section later in this chapter). To determine the degree of parallelism, Oracle will first look at the system parameters, then the table settings, and then the hints in the SQL statements.

NOTE When you are joining two or more tables and the tables have different degrees of parallelism associated with them, the highest value represents *the maximum degree of parallelism.*

Using Parallel DML and DDL

You can use parallel DML to speed up the execution of INSERT, DELETE, and UPDATE operations. Also, any DDL operations that both create and select can be placed in parallel. The PARALLEL option can be used for creating indexes, sorts, tables—any DDL operation, including SQL*Loader.

Enabling and Disabling Parallel DML

When you consider what is involved in performing standard DML statements for INSERT, UPDATE, and DELETE operations on large tables, you will be able to see the advantage of parallel processing. To use parallel DML, you first need to enable it. Use the following statement to enable parallel DML:

```
ALTER SESSION ENABLE PARALLEL DML;
```

When you're finished with the task you want to perform in parallel, you can disable parallel DML, as follows:

```
ALTER SESSION DISABLE PARALLEL DML;
```

Alternatively, simply exiting the session disables parallel DML.

You can also use the ALTER SYSTEM command to enable and disable the PARALLEL option.

Creating a Table with Parallel DML

Let's work through an example to demonstrate parallel DML in action. In this example, you will use parallel DML to create a table that combines information from two other existing tables. The example involves data from a product-buying club of some sort (such as a music CD club or a book club). The two tables that already exist are PRODUCT and CUSTOMER.

The PRODUCT table contains information about the products that a customer has ordered. It has the following columns:

CUST_NO

PROD_NO

PROD_NAME

PROD_STAT

PROD_LEFT

PROD_EXPIRE_DATE

PROD_OFFERS

The CUSTOMER table contains information about each customer, including the customer's name, address, and other information. It has the following columns:

CUST_NO

CUST_NAME

CUST_ADD

CUST_CITY

CUST_STATE

CUST_ZIP

CUST_INFO

Using parallel DML, you will create a third table named PROD_CUST_LIST. This table will contain combined information from the PRODUCT and CUSTOMER tables, based on specific criteria. It will have the following columns:

CUST_NO

PROD_NAME

PROD_NO

CUST_NAME

CUST_ADD

CUST_CITY

CUST_STATE

CUST_ZIP

PROD_LEFT

PROD_OFFERS

The CUSTOMER table has a one-to-many relationship with the PRODUCT table. Using parallel DML is a fast way to create the PROD_CUST_LIST table, since this method uses the power of multiple CPUs.

For the PROD_CUST_LIST table, you will identify all customers who have five products left prior to their club contract's expiration (PROD_LEFT = 5). You might use this information to send a discounted renewal option to these customers. You also will include customers whose contract has expired and who have been sent three or fewer renewal offers (PROD_OFFERS <= 3). You may want to offer these customers a special incentive to get them back. Listing 18.1 shows the code to create the table.

Listing 18.1: Creating a Table with Parallel DML

```
SQL> ALTER SESSION ENABLE PARALLEL DML;

SQL> INSERT
INTO prod_cust_list (SELECT
b.cust_no
, a.prod_name
, a.prod_no
, a.prod_left
, a.prod_offers
, b.cust_name
, b.cust_add
, b.cust_city
```

```
, b.cust_state
, b.cust_zip
FROM
product a, customer b
WHERE a.cust_no = b.cust_no
AND a.prod_left = 5
AND a.prod_expire_date <= SYSDATE
AND a.prod_offers <= 3);

COMMIT;

ALTER SESSION DISABLE PARALLEL DML;
```

The first ALTER SESSION command enables parallel processing. The INSERT statement that follows processes the operation in parallel. The final ALTER SESSION statement disables the PARALLEL option.

What you accomplished here with the INSERT statement can be done with the DELETE statement and UPDATE statement as well. You can see how this feature could be useful for creating and updating data warehousing applications, as well as for reporting from them.

Using Parallel DDL

Parallel DDL (PDDL) is a misnomer; rather than literally creating an object in parallel, PDDL *loads* the data in parallel. PDDL applies to situations in which you build the object in the same statement in which you define it. The example in Listing 18.1 created a third table with the SELECT INTO clause. This is parallel DDL, because the code creates the table and populates it with data at the same time. Similarly, the SELECT command and associated INSERT command can be split into parallel processes. Thus, any of your DDL operations that both create and select can be placed in parallel.

Here is an example of using parallel DDL to create an index:

```
SQL> CREATE INDEX product_cust_no_n1
    ON product
    (cust_no)
    PARALLEL;
```

In this example, index creation results in a full table scan, but it is accomplished in parallel. The SELECT portion is run using PARALLEL.

Parallel Loading with SQL*Loader

If you have a lot of data to load via SQL*Loader (discussed in depth in Chapter 22), using the PARALLEL option can reduce the load time. However, if you think about what SQL*Loader is accomplishing in a direct-path load operation, you will know that parallel loading is a bit more complex. In a direct-path load, SQL*Loader skips the portion of trying to look for space in existing blocks. It goes to the table's high-water mark and starts inserting rows in the new blocks, while periodically reestablishing the new high-water mark.

Multiple processes will need to know what each of the other processes is accomplishing. Since only one process can access the table header block at a time, setting PARALLEL=TRUE for multiple direct loads changes what the loading processes do. In this case, each process creates its own temporary tablespace in the tablespace that is being loaded. The indexes are not maintained. Once each process has completed the load it is assigned, each temporary segment is merged into the table by adding the extents to the header block of the table.

Because the parallel load is accomplished in this fashion, each process needs to have its own input file. This requires some planning on your part, rather than leaving the task up to the Parallel Manager. You must drop all indexes and re-create them when the load is complete.

Executing Parallel Queries

The ideal environment for implementing a parallel query (PQ) is one in which tables and indexes are partitioned, so that the query can access multiple partitions. Using partitioning in conjunction with parallelism is the best way to speed up the execution of your SQL code. Parallel queries on partitioned tables execute quickly through the use of *partition pruning*—a very large table is separated into many different sections, and then the parallel operations access only the parts needed, rather than the whole table. (See Chapter 24 for details on Oracle partitioning.)

Parallel query operation (PQO) employs a producer-consumer input/output approach. A SQL statement is handled through a *client process,* the *Query Coordinator* (QC), and *parallel execution* (PX) processes. The client process sends the SQL statement to the QC. The QC takes the original SQL, breaks it apart, and sends it to the various CPUs. The *PX slave* receives the SQL from the QC and then gathers the data from the desired tables. The producer part of the PX slave accesses the database (produces data). The consumer part of the PX slave accepts (consumes) data from the producer. The PX slave returns the results to the QC, where the results are combined into one return statement and returned to the client process.

The total number of PX slaves on the instance is controlled by the PARALLEL_MAX_SERVERS parameter in `init.ora`. PX slaves are borrowed from a pool of slaves in the instance as needed. Communication between slaves is handled by exchanging messages through a message queue in the SGA. For example, if the PARALLEL_MAX_SERVERS parameter is set to 8, the number of PX slaves borrowed from a pool of slaves is a maximum of eight. The PARALLEL_MAX_SERVERS parameter might also be set to a lower value, depending on how the memory pool is set up and how many other processes are presently running with the PARALLEL option on. You can adjust the size of the message buffer and the PARALLEL_MAX_SERVER parameter, as described in the "Tuning and Monitoring Parallel Operations" section later in this chapter.

Using One PX Slave

The following is an example of a parallel query executed using one PX slave, using the CUSTOMER table from the example presented in the "Creating a Table with Parallel DML" section earlier in this chapter.

```
SQL> SELECT
       COUNT(1)
     FROM product;
```

Figure 18.1 shows the process flow when the parallel query is invoked. First, the server process that communicates with the client process becomes the QC. The QC is responsible for handling communications with the client and managing an additional set of PX slave processes to accomplish most of the work in the database. The QC enlists multiple PX slave processes, splits the workload between those slave processes, and passes the results back to the client. The example shown in Figure 18.1 depicts three PX slave processes, which are considered to be one PX slave.

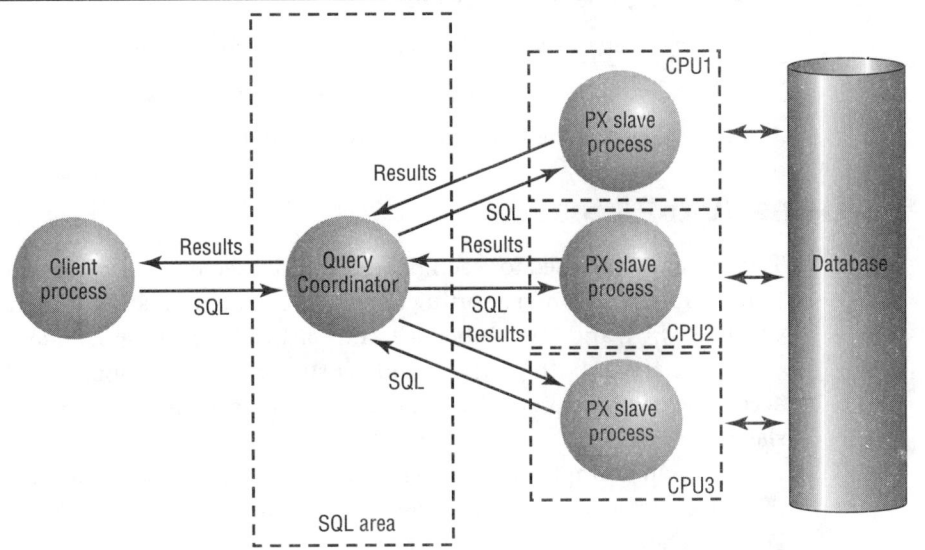

FIGURE 18.1

Parallel query execution with one PX slave

Here's how the query is handled behind the scenes:

1. The client process sends the SQL statement to the Oracle server process.
2. The server process, which is controlled by PARALLEL_MAX_SERVERS, does the following:
    - Develops the best parallel access path to retrieve the data
    - From the original SQL, creates multiple queries that access specific table partitions and/or table ROWID ranges
    - Becomes QC to manage PX slave processes
    - Recruits PX slave processes to execute the rewritten queries
    - Assigns partitions and ROWID ranges to process for the PX slave processes
3. The PX slave processes do the following:
    - Accept queries from the QC
    - Process assigned partition and ROWID ranges assigned by the QC
    - Communicate results to other PX slave processes via messages through message queues

4. The QC does the following:
   - Receives the result sets from the PX slave processes
   - Performs final aggregation if necessary
   - Returns the final result set to the client process

Using Two PX Slaves

Two PX slaves are used for each parallel query execution path for a merge or a hash join operation, or when a sorting or an aggregation operation (functions such as AVG, COUNT, MAX, and MIN) is being accomplished in the original query. In this case, each slave acts as both producer and consumer in the relationship. The slaves that access the database produce data, which is then consumed by the second set of PX slaves.

Here is an example of a parallel query executed using two PX slaves, using the PRODUCT table from the example presented in the "Creating a Table with Parallel DML" section earlier in this chapter:

```
SQL> SELECT
    prod_name
    , COUNT(1)
    FROM product
GROUP BY prod_name;
```

In a sorting operation (GROUP BY), the first set of PX slave processes will select rows from the database and apply limiting conditions. The result will be sent to the second set of PX slave processes for sorting. The second set of PX slave processes has the task of sorting rows within a particular range. Each of the PX (producer) slave processes that retrieved data directly sends its results to the designated slave process, according to the sort key.

Figure 18.2 shows the process flow when two PX slaves are used. This figure depicts two columns of PX slave processes with communication between each column, representing two slave processes. The row of PX slave processes next to the database is considered the producer, because these slave processes get the data, and the second row of PX slave processes is considered the consumer, because these processes receive the data from the first set of PX slave processes to send back to the QC.

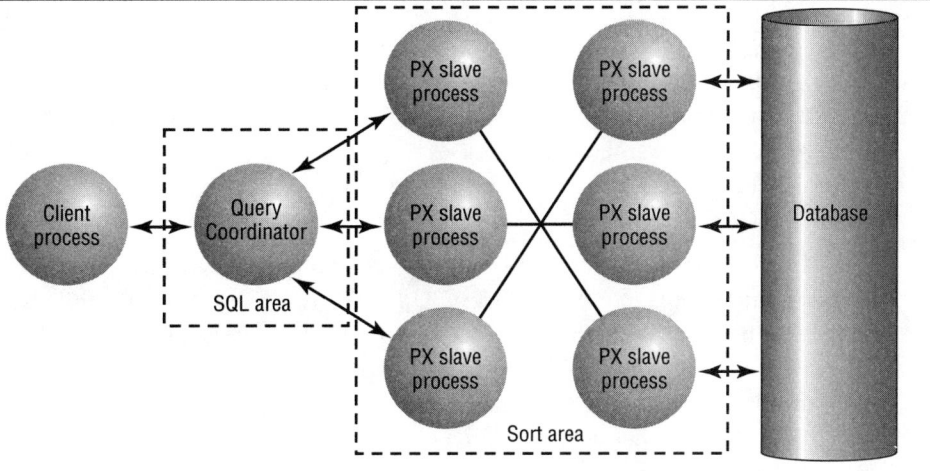

FIGURE 18.2
Parallel query execution with two PX slaves

Using Query Hints to Force Parallelism

Using hints to override the degree of parallelism established on a table is an easy way to manage the work to be performed. For example, suppose you have a table that has the PARALLEL option turned on and set to 2. Now you need to get the SUM(AMOUNT) for each quarter from this table, so you want to increase the degree of parallelism to get the results faster. For example, if you raise the degree of parallelism to 6, you divide the work six ways and speed up the operations.

 NOTE As noted earlier in the chapter, the order of operation is system parameter first; then table settings, which can override system parameters; then hints, which override table settings.

You can enable parallelism with the PARALLEL hint and disable it with the NOPARALLEL hint. The PARALLEL hint has three parameters:

- The table name
- The degree of parallelism
- The instance setting

Since there are no keywords in the hint, you must be careful with the syntax. In the following example, a hint is used to tell the Optimizer to use a degree of parallelism of 3 when querying the CUSTOMER table.

```
SELECT /*+ PARALLEL(customer,3) */
FROM customer;
```

You can also use hints to specify the number of instances that should be involved in performing the query. Simply include a value for the instances after the degree of parallelism parameter, as in this example:

```
SELECT /*+ PARALLEL(customer,5,3) */
FROM customer;
```

This example sets a degree of parallelism of 5 and sets instances to 3, to use three instances for resolving the query. This effectively sets 15-way parallelism.

When you want to disable parallelism for the query, use the NOPARALLEL hint. The following disables the PARALLEL option used in the preceding example, without modifying the `init.ora` parameters:

```
SELECT /*+ NOPARALLEL(customer) */
FROM customer;
```

Performing Parallel Recovery Operations

During an Oracle database recovery operation, the recovery server process has a lot to do. It reads a recovery record from the log file; reads the block from the datafile, if necessary, and places it into the buffer cache; and then applies the recovery record. It repeats this process until all of the recovery records have been applied. This means that the recovery server process is busy performing a great deal of reading, writing, and blocking on input/output during database recovery. Given that database recovery is often a time-pressured operation, the ability to speed it up by parallelization is clearly welcome.

NOTE Prior to Oracle 7.1, the only form of parallel recovery was to start up multiple user sessions to recover separate datafiles at the same time. Each session read through the redo logs independently and applied changes for its specified datafile. This method depended on the ability of the I/O subsystem to parallelize the separate operations. If the operating system couldn't parallelize, you would see little improvement in performance.

Oracle 7.1 and later offer true parallel recovery capabilities. With this feature, the recovery server process acts as a coordinator for several slave processes. The recovery server process reads a recovery record from the redo log file and assigns the recovery record to a parallel slave process, repeating these steps until all recovery records have been applied. The slave process performs the other steps: It receives each recovery record from the recovery server process, reads a block into buffer cache if necessary, and applies the recovery record to the data block. The slave process continues until it is told that the recovery is complete.

You can invoke parallel recovery in either of two ways:

- Set RECOVERY_PARALLELISM in the `init.ora` file.
- Supply a PARALLEL clause with the RECOVER command in Server Manager. (See Chapter 10 for more information about the RECOVER command.)

You must have set PARALLEL_MAX_SERVERS to above 0 before you can enable parallel recovery, because it uses the parallel servers as the recovery slaves. The RECOVERY_PARALLELISM parameter specifies the number of processes that will participate in parallel recovery during recovery. The RECOVERY_PARALLELISM setting cannot be greater than the PARALLEL_MAX_SERVERS setting. Oracle will not exceed the value of PARALLEL_MAX_SERVERS for recovery, even if the DBA requests a higher degree of parallelism. The PARALLEL_MAX_SERVERS parameter is discussed in more detail in the next section.

Contrary to Oracle's claim that there is little benefit to using parallel recovery with a setting of less than 8, personal experience reveals that the best performance is achieved with RECOVERY_PARALLELISM set to two times the CPU count. Systems with faster disk channels may benefit from a higher setting, perhaps three times the CPU count. We recommend tuning toward disk channel saturation.

NOTE If your system is using asynchronous I/O, there will be little benefit to using parallel recovery.

Tuning and Monitoring Parallel Operations

Oracle8i uses many initialization parameters to control how various parallel-processing operations will operate. As explained earlier in the chapter, when you set the `init.ora` parameter PARALLEL_AUTOMATIC_TUNING to TRUE, Oracle automatically sets other parallel processing parameters. If necessary, you can adjust the other parameters individually to tune parallel operations on your system. Table 18.1 lists the `init.ora` parameters for parallel server processes, along with a brief description, the default value, and the valid values for each parameter.

TABLE 18.1: *INIT.ORA* PARAMETERS FOR PARALLEL SERVER PROCESSES

Parameter	Default Value	Description
FAST_START_PARALLEL_ROLLBACK	FALSE (no parallel recovery)	Specifies the number of processes spawned to perform parallel recovery. For parallel recovery, you can set this to LOW (number of recovery servers may not exceed 2 × CPU count) or HIGH (number of recovery servers may not exceed 4 × CPU count).
LARGE_POOL_SIZE	0	Controls whether large objects are stored in the large pool section of the shared pool. The minimum value is 600KB.
PARALLEL	FALSE	Controls whether direct loads are performed using parallel processing.
PARALLEL_ADAPTIVE_MULTI_USER	FALSE	Varies the degree of parallelism based on the total perceived load on the system.
PARALLEL_AUTOMATIC_TUNING	FALSE	Automatically sets other parallel parameters.
PARALLEL_BROADCAST_ENABLED	FALSE	Optimizes parallelized joins involving very large tables joined to small tables.
PARALLEL_EXECUTION_MESSAGE_SIZE	Depends on operating system; about 2KB	Controls the amount of shared pool space used by parallel query operations.
PARALLEL_INSTANCE_GROUP	NULL	Defines the instance group (by name) used for query server processes.
PARALLEL_MAX_SERVERS	0	Sets the maximum number of parallel processes that can be created for the instance. The maximum setting is 3599.
PARALLEL_MIN_PERCENT	0	Sets the minimum percentage of requested parallel processes that must be available in order for the operation to execute in parallel. The maximum setting is 100.
PARALLEL_MIN_SERVERS	0	Sets the minimum number of parallel processes created at instance startup to be used by parallel operations in the database. Valid values are 0 to the value of PARALLEL_MAX_SERVERS.
PARALLEL_SERVER	FALSE	Enables Oracle Parallel Server (OPS).

Continued

TABLE 18.1: *INIT.ORA* PARAMETERS FOR PARALLEL SERVER PROCESSES (CONTINUED)		
Parameter	Default Value	Description
PARALLEL_SERVER_INSTANCES	1	Specifies the number of instances configured.
PARALLEL_THREADS_PER_CPU	Depends on operating system	Computes the degree of parallelism for parallel operations where the degree of parallelism is not set.
PARALLEL_THREADS_PER_CPU	Depends on operating system	Specifies the number of parallel query operation threads executed per CPU.
PARALLEL_TRANSACTION_RECOVERY	FALSE	Specifies whether recovery is in parallel mode.
PROCESSES	Depends on CPU count and MAX_PARALLEL_SERVERS	Sets the number of operating system user processes that can simultaneously connect to Oracle. The minimum value is 6.
RECOVERY_PARALLELISM	0	Defines the number of processes that will participate in parallel recovery during instance or media recovery. This cannot be set to more than the PARALLEL_MAX_SERVERS setting.
SESSIONS	((1.1*PROCESSES)+5)	Sets the number of user and system sessions. Valid values are 1 to 2^{31}.
TRANSACTIONS	(1.1*SESSIONS)	Sets the number of concurrent active transactions. Valid values are 4 to 2^{32}.

Oracle recommends that PARALLEL_AUTOMATIC_TUNING be set to TRUE whenever parallel execution is implemented. This setting will automatically set the PARALLEL_ADAPTIVE_MULTI_USER, PROCESSES, SESSIONS, PARALLEL_MAX_SERVERS, PARALLEL_THREADS_PER_CPU, and PARALLEL_EXECUTION_MESSAGE_SIZE parameters.

The following parameters can be adjusted with the ALTER SYSTEM command:

- FAST_START_PARALLEL_ROLLBACK
- PARALLEL_ADAPTIVE_MULTI_USER
- PARALLEL_INSTANCE_GROUP
- PARALLEL_THREADS_PER_CPU

Here is an example of changing the PARALLEL_THREADS_PER_CPU setting:
`ALTER SYSTEM SET parallel_threads_per_cpu = 8;`

This will set the system parameter PARALLEL_THREADS_PER_CPU to 8. You can alter each of the other parameters in the same way.

The following sections discuss several parameters that can affect parallel execution performance dramatically, views for monitoring parallel query processing, and parallel query tuning.

Setting the Message Buffer Size

Oracle uses message buffers for interoperational parallel processes. One buffer is required for each producer-consumer connection (described in the "Executing Parallel Queries" section earlier in this chapter). Generally, increasing the size of the message buffer increases throughput between the producer and consumer PX slaves, which in turn reduces execution time. The number of connections for a particular query is, at the most, the square of the maximum degree of parallelism of the query, because each producer has a connection to each consumer. For example, if the maximum degree of parallelism of the query is 2, there could be as many as 4 connections. If the maximum degree of parallelism is 8, there will be 64 connections. Based on this relationship, one can deduce that memory requirements for message buffers increase greatly as the value of the degree of parallelism increases.

The system-wide amount of memory required for the message buffers also depends on the number of concurrent queries executing and the size of the message buffer. The following formula is used for calculating the buffer space in Oracle 8i:

buffer space = (3 * PARALLEL_EXECUTION_MESSAGE_SIZE) * (CPU_COUNT + 2) * PARALLEL_MAX_SERVERS

The `init.ora` parameter PARALLEL_EXECUTION_MESSAGE_SIZE sets the message buffer size. The default value for the PARALLEL_EXECUTION_MESSAGE_SIZE parameter is 2KB. If your system has enough memory, increasing this value to between 4KB and 8KB will likely increase performance between the consumer and producer PX slaves, if the message buffers are indeed a bottleneck. (If your process is I/O bound, this is a good indication that the message buffers are a bottleneck.) Since the PARALLEL_EXECUTION_MESSAGE_SIZE value directly increases and decreases the need for shared pool space, and the shared pool is part of the SGA, increasing the size of this parameter will require you to increase the size of the SGA as well. If there is not enough space, parallel queries will fail with an ORA-4031 memory allocation failure message.

Setting the Message Buffer Location

Another important decision is where the message buffers will reside—in which SGA pool. If PARALLEL_AUTOMATIC_TUNING is set to FALSE, the buffers will be in the shared pool. If this parameter is set to TRUE, the buffers will be in the large pool. Since the shared pool often has resource contention, it is recommended that you set the PARALLEL_AUTOMATIC_TUNING value to TRUE, so that the message buffers will be placed in the large pool.

To properly configure the size of the large pool, tune the other parameters that affect parallel execution (see Table 18.1) and bring up the instance with PARALLEL_AUTOMATIC_TUNING set to TRUE. Make sure that all parameters affected by this parameter being set to TRUE are configured to meet your needs. The only way you will know if the parameters are configured properly is to start processing.

You can retrieve the total size of the message pool from V$SGASTAT with this query:

```
SQL> SELECT
pool, SUM(bytes)
FROM v$sgastat
WHERE name = 'PX msg pool';
```

TIP We've found that when we set PARALLEL_AUTOMATIC_TUNING to TRUE, the settings rarely need to be modified. At most, we've needed to place a hint in the SQL to increase the degree of parallelism for only a few processes. In one case, for example, a process that was I/O bound was running on a computer that had four CPUs, which were not even being used. We modified the SQL code to increase the degree of parallelism and use all the CPUs. The process ran in less than half the time it had taken earlier in the week.

Setting the Minimum and Maximum Parallel Servers

When you execute your SQL in a parallel operation, Oracle will increase the number of query servers as demand requires, up to the maximum number of parallel execution servers for an instance, specified by the PARALLEL_MAX_SERVERS parameter. Oracle recommends that you use the same value across all instances in the parallel server environment.

The PARALLEL_MAX_SERVERS parameter is used to size the large pool, which is part of the SGA. If you didn't allocate enough memory to the SGA, Oracle will use only what is available. To avoid problems, make sure that PARALLEL_MAX_SERVERS is set properly. You want to ensure that there is adequate memory for times of peak database utilization. If PARALLEL_MAX_SERVERS is set too high, memory shortages may occur during high memory allocation, resulting in degraded performance. When PARALLEL_MAX_SERVERS is set too low, some of your queries may not have enough available memory resources to perform in parallel.

PARALLEL_MIN_SERVERS is the opposite of PARALLEL_MAX_SERVERS. Oracle will decrease the number of query servers as demand requires, down to the amount set by the PARALLEL_MIN_SERVERS parameter. This parameter specifies the minimum number of parallel execution servers for an instance. If there is not enough memory in the SGA to handle this minimum, the SQL will not be executed in parallel.

The good news is that setting PARALLEL_AUTOMATIC_TUNING to TRUE will automatically set these two parameters for you. In my experience, the automatic settings work well. As you run through your day-to-day operations, you should be able to tell if these two parameters need adjustment. Keep in mind that if you adjust either of these parameters, you will be affecting the SGA and how it is allocated.

Viewing Parallel Query Information

Several dynamic performance views (V$ views) can help you evaluate the runtime performance of parallel queries. Armed with the knowledge you gain from these monitoring tools, you should be able to identify parallel performance problem areas. Table 18.2 lists the V$ tables of interest for monitoring parallel processing

TABLE 18.2: ORACLE V$ VIEWS FOR PARALLEL PERFORMANCE MONITORING

View Name	Description
V$PQ_SYSSTAT	Shows system-level statistics for parallel queries
V$PQ_SESSTAT	Shows session-level statistics for parallel queries
V$PQ_SLAVE	Displays statistics for each active parallel query in the instance
V$PQ_TQSTAT	Displays statistics for all parallel queries and query operations

Tuning Parallel Query Processes

Although many parallel queries perform well, you may encounter some problem areas. When this happens, you must be ready to tune the processes. You will need to enhance or rewrite the SQL involved in the parallel operations. To accomplish this, you need to understand how Oracle implements parallelism and the various parameters that affect the parallel configuration and performance. With this foundation, you can learn how to decode parallel execution plans and to identify areas for improvement.

For example, Listing 18.2 shows an execution plan that reveals SQL that could be improved.

Listing 18.2: A Sample Execution Plan

```
EXPLAIN PLAN
SET STATEMENT_ID = 'markb' FOR
SELECT
   a.task_number
   , b.expenditure_number
   , sum(b.amount)
FROM
   tasks a
   , expenditures b
WHERE
   a.task_id = b.task_id
   AND to_char(b.creation_date,'dd-mon-yyyy')
       BETWEEN '01-JAN-2000' AND '31-DEC-2000'
GROUP BY
   a.task_number
   , b.expenditure_number;

SELECT STATEMENT COST = 19326822
    2.1 SORT GROUP
       3.1 SORT GROUP BY
          4.1 HASH JOIN
             5.1 TABLE ACCESS FULL 'EXPENDITURES'
             5.2 PARTITION RANGE ITERATOR
                6.1 TABLE ACCESS FULL   'TASKS'
```

You can see that we are doing a full table scan on both tables. This would not be necessary if we were using an index on the driving table. All we would need to do is get rid of the `to_char` on `b.creation_date`, and then the index would take effect, letting the parallel query access the data in parallel without a full table scan. This would allow us to access both the data and the associated index in parallel, speeding up the execution of the SQL.

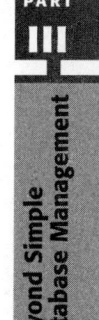

CHAPTER 19

Oracle8i Data Warehousing Features

FEATURING:

Data marts and data warehouses	**864**
Query rewrite	**866**
Materialized views	**872**
Dimensions	**891**
Other data warehousing features	**902**

Oracle8i contains many features designed to improve the ability of the Oracle8i database to support data warehousing features. In this chapter we'll discuss several elements in Oracle8i that are designed to make data warehousing easier. First we'll examine the data warehousing concept overall, and make sure you understand some relevant terms. The principal portion of the chapter is devoted to explaining the components of summary management provided in Oracle8i. These include query rewriting, materialized views, and dimensions. Following that we will look at some of the other Oracle8i features and SQL tools for application in data warehousing environments. Some of these are covered more thoroughly elsewhere in this book.

Understanding Data Warehousing

The average size of the Oracle database has grown rapidly over the years. Early databases stored information for this department or that department. One system might store sales data, another HR information, and another might store accounts receivable and payable. This compartmentalization complicated things for enterprise management. First they had to go among multiple sources of information, and then they had to correlate that information in numerous reports, aggregating it by hand or in separate spreadsheets.

Data marts evolved first. The various organization elements had a need for historical data and for this information to be summarized and aggregated for analysis purposes. But the data marts were still generally separated departmentally, and it remained a difficult task to correlate information between departments.

Enter the *data warehouse*—designed to take data from various systems throughout the enterprise and manipulate it as required, joining departmental data elements, creating aggregates, summaries, and doing any required "cleansing" tasks that might be required. The manipulated data is then made available for further analysis. That is one of the primary purposes of a data warehouse: analysis of historical data (as opposed to OLTP, which works with current data). Generally the data in a data warehouse comes from multiple sources.

This chapter isn't about creating a data warehouse; that would take a whole book in and of itself. It *is* about helping you understand some basic tenets of the data warehousing approach to databases.

The Fact/Dimension Schema

Data warehouses are often built using what is called a *star schema* and are rarely seen in third normal form. The star schemas consist of two types of tables: dimension tables and fact tables. The *dimension tables,* often referred to as *lookup* or *reference tables,* support the data to be loaded into the fact tables. That is, they contain the information that describes what will be stored in the fact tables. The denormalized, star schema format improves performance by eliminating joins of multiple tables.

Fact tables contain the detail records, or measures, of the data warehouse. Each row in the fact table is some information that is related to one or more dimension tables. Thus each row contains some measurable information (such as the gross pay for a department), as well as the related dimensions (such as the department ID and the pay period).

Typically, the fact/dimension schema design is called a star schema because the fact table sits at the center and all of its related dimension tables radiate around it. An example might be an HR database. In this design, you might have these dimension tables: employee table, benefits provider table, perhaps a table of pay periods, and a department table. In the fact table for this schema would be the employee number that relates to the employee table, and the pay periods that relate to the pay period table. Also in the fact table you might store the department information for an employee, the net pay amount, and perhaps information about payments to various benefit providers. Typically, fact/dimension schemas have many fact tables. Often the fact tables will use the same dimension tables; this is known as a *snowflake schema*. Oracle's optimizer has built-in features that take advantage of both star and snowflake schemas.

The fact table can also be an aggregate of the detail records rather than a collection. For example, it might consist of aggregate data for each department's net pay and benefits contribution. Perhaps the company is self-insured for medical costs; the fact table would display each department's contributions to the self-insured health fund and each department's overall expenses paid for health care. Problems with aggregate tables are many. They often required substantial programming to populate and maintain. If the underlying detail-level data changes, any related aggregate information must be recalculated—a potentially expensive process. You'll see in later sections that Oracle provides features to simplify your work with these summary tables.

NOTE Because things such as product codes change over time, the data warehouse must accommodate these changes. For example, if we want a report on all white socks of size 11 sold over the last four years, what happens if the product code for those socks changed two years ago? How do we get all the relevant data? Many such questions must be considered when creating a data warehouse. And the same questions must be answered continually as the warehouse grows and encompasses more of the enterprise.

The Components of Summary Management

Summary management is the process of managing aggregate data based on underlying detail data. In addition, summary management allows the user to get to the data as easily as possible. This chapter discusses the three principal components of summary management in Oracle8i: query rewrite, materialized views, and dimensions.

Query Rewrite

The ability to rewrite SQL queries is known as *query rewrite,* and it is the first element of summary management. Query rewrite allows the optimizer to take a SQL query against a detail table (or a join of several detail tables) and rewrite it so that it uses one or more existing *materialized views (Mviews)* instead. (Materialized views are the second element of summary management and are covered later.) Query rewrite, disabled by default, must be enabled if you want the optimizer to use it. It also must be enabled if you are to use function-based indexes, another new feature in Oracle8i (see Chapter 6).

The beauty of query rewrite is that it is seamless to the user, who can write a query against four base tables and end up with a query that actually executes against a single materialized view. This represents significant performance advantages for queries, and it all happens under the covers.

This section explains query rewrite and its relationship to the operations of the Oracle optimizer, and shows you how to enable and use query rewrite in database processing. You'll also see how to establish the desired integrity level for the optimizer when considering query rewrite.

Using Query Rewrite

Rules abound when you want to use query rewrite. (Frankly, there are so many rules that we sometimes wonder if query rewrite is worth all the trouble!) We'll get to those rules shortly—but first, here are the three kinds of Oracle SQL statements that can use the query rewrite features of Oracle8i:

- SELECT
- CREATE TABLE...AS SELECT
- INSERT INTO...SELECT

In addition to these, query rewrite is also supported in

- Subqueries as a part of UNION, UNION ALL, INTERSECT, and MINUS queries
- Subqueries in INSERT, DELETE, and UPDATE statements
- Inline views

Query rewrite is only supported when using the cost-based optimizer (CBO). Thus it is very important that all tables involved in the query, as well as any possible rewrite candidates (that is, materialized views), are analyzed. The CBO code will take the existing query and calculate the cost of executing the query without rewrite. The optimizer then chooses the possible query rewrite paths (for example, using a materialized view instead). It uses an integrative approach to this determination, adding and eliminating materialized views that it might use. Depending on the costs of the access paths, the CBO will choose either to use the original schema objects in the query, or to rewrite the query and take advantage of existing materialized views.

Rules for Query Rewrite

Now let's look at all those rules. Oracle will choose to rewrite a query only when the following very specific conditions are met:

- You must have enabled query rewrite for the session or it must be enabled globally.
- If an Mview contains one or more remote tables, only local tables of the query can be considered for rewrite.
- Neither the Mview nor the base tables of the Mview can be owned by SYS.
- If the query to be rewritten is for a materialized view, the materialized view must have been enabled for query rewrite.
- If the query to be rewritten is for a materialized view, the parameter settings to indicate the required rewrite integrity level should be set such that a rewrite to

use a materialized view will be possible. For example, if a materialized view is not fresh and query rewrite integrity is set to ENFORCED, the materialized view will not be used.

- If the query to be rewritten is for a materialized view, some part of the row source returned by the query must be returned from a precomputed result stored in the materialized view.

- In some cases, you must define a dimension in order for the optimizer to correctly rewrite the query.

- The query defining the Mview cannot contain nonrepeatable expressions such as the ROWID or SYSDATE. A query built on such an Mview will not be eligible for rewrite.

- The Mview cannot contain columns of RAW, LONG RAW, or Object REFs.

- The Mview cannot contain block set functions such as the INTERSECT, UNION, MINUS, and UNION ALL operators (but the query to be rewritten can include these set functions).

- The columns of the Mview, if built with the PREBUILT clause, must match the precision of the SELECT statement associated with the Mview. If this is not the case, use of the WITH REDUCED PRECISION clause in the CREATE MATERIALIZED VIEW command will allow for query rewrite.

- The Mview cannot contain a HAVING or CONNECT BY clause.

- The Mview cannot contain an OR clause in the WHERE clause.

Note that most of these rules revolve around materialized views rather than function-based indexes. For the most part, query rewrite is associated with materialized views rather than function based indexes.

How Does It Work?

Let's take a look at what the optimizer does when performing query rewrite for materialized views. Generally it follows one of two methods (in this order) to determine if rewrite is possible: First, it does SQL text matching; then, failing that, it uses what is called the general query rewrite method.

SQL Text-Matching vs. General Query Rewrite

In the *SQL text-matching* method, the optimizer performs a comparison of the SQL statement syntax to see if the text matches the SQL syntax of an existing materialized view. The match may be a full or partial match. If the SQL text-matching test fails,

Oracle then looks at the various join conditions using what is called the *general query rewrite method*. This method performs four different checks to determine if a given query can be rewritten. Should any of these checks succeed, the query can be rewritten. The following four elements are checked to determine query rewrite eligibility:

- Join compatibility
- Data sufficiency
- Grouping compatibility
- Aggregate compatibility

When performing the *join compatibility check*, Oracle compares the join condition in the original SQL statement against the joins in the materialized views. This is to ensure that the join criteria between the query and the materialized views are compatible.

In the *data sufficiency check*, the optimizer checks the columns of the materialized view to see if they can be used to satisfy the query. The use of *constraints* (primary key and foreign key) and *dimensions* can be very helpful for this stage. Primary keys and dimensions (particularly the DETERMINES clause of a given dimension) give Oracle a better picture of columns and their relationships as it proceeds through the data sufficiency check.

The next check is performed on the *grouping compatibility*. This check only occurs if a GROUP BY is contained in both the materialized view and the query rewrite candidate. The grouping defined in the query is compared with the grouping in the materialized view. A match occurs if the grouping contained in the materialized view is at the same or a broader level than the grouping in the SQL statement. For example, if the grouping in the materialized view is based on a quarterly grouping, and your SQL query is grouping by year, the query would be rewriteable. If, however, the materialized view grouping is quarterly and the SQL statement's is weekly, the check fails and a rewrite using the materialized view is not possible.

The *aggregate compatibility check* is performed last. This only occurs when the materialized view and the SQL statement both contain aggregate functions such as SUM( ) or AVG( ). For example, say the query calls for an average of a column of rows be determined. If the materialized view has a column that contains the COUNT( ) and SUM( ) of the same rows, the average could be calculated by using the formula SUM( ) / COUNT( ).

Failing all of these checks, the optimizer will not be able to rewrite the SQL statement.

Requirements for Constraints and Dimensions

Constraints and dimensions not only can assist the optimizer in attempting to do query rewrites, but are in fact required at times. They need not be present for matching

SQL text tests. But if the general query rewrite checks are to succeed, constraints and dimensions may be required. To make sure you have maximum availability to use query rewrite, make sure your constraints and dimensions are appropriately established. Table 19.1 lists the relevant requirements for the general query rewrite checks.

TABLE 19.1: REQUIREMENTS FOR CONSTRAINTS AND DIMENSIONS WITH GENERAL QUERY

General Query Rewrite Check	Dimension Required?	Constraint (PK or FK) Required?
Matching SQL text	N	N
Join compatibility	N	Y
Data sufficiency	Y (or constraint)	Y (or dimension)
Grouping compatibility	Y	Y
Aggregate compatibility	N	N

Enabling Query Rewrite

To enable query rewrite, you must set the `init.ora` parameter QUERY_REWRITE_ENABLED to TRUE. If it's disabled, this parameter can be adjusted dynamically with the database up, using the ALTER SYSTEM or ALTER SESSION command. For example, you would issue the command

    ALTER SESSION SET QUERY_REWRITE_ENABLED=TRUE;

to enable query rewrite in your session. The command

    ALTER SESSION SET QUERY_REWRITE_ENABLED=TRUE;

would turn it on for the entire system.

NOTE When creating materialized views, you must explicitly enable query rewrite with each individual view.

Even if you have query rewrite enabled, you may find that query rewrites are not occurring. This happens because several other `init.ora` parameters and object settings can affect the use of query rewrite, as described in Table 19.2.

TABLE 19.2: *INIT.ORA* PARAMETERS AFFECTING QUERY REWRITE

Init.ora Parameter	Default Setting	Valid Settings	Parameter's Role
QUERY_REWRITE_ENABLED	FALSE	TRUE FALSE	Controls the optimizer's ability to rewrite a query.
OPTIMIZER_MODE	CHOOSE	RULE CHOOSE FIRST_ROWS ALL_ROWS	Using RULE causes the optimizer to use rule-based optimization rather than CBO, so query rewrite is not supported.
COMPATIBLE	Varies	Varies	If set to less than 8.1.0, causes query rewrite to be disabled.
QUERY_REWRITE_INTEGRITY	ENFORCED	STALE_TOLERATED TRUSTED ENFORCED	Related to materialized views. Determines the currency requirement of the data in the materialized view. See "Setting the Rewrite Integrity Level" in this chapter.

Another way of enabling query rewrite is to use SQL hints to suggest to the optimizer that query rewriting is to be attempted; you do this with the REWRITE hint. You can also use SQL to force the optimizer *not* to rewrite the query, by using the NOREWRITE hint.

We will discuss the security aspects of query rewrite in the section on materialized views.

Setting the Rewrite Integrity Level

Oracle also controls the level of query rewrite that is allowed, via the setting of the QUERY_REWRITE_INTEGRITY parameter. This parameter defaults to a value of ENFORCED, which is the most restrictive setting. Other options include TRUSTED and STALE_TOLERATED.

ENFORCED   With the QUERY_REWRITE_INTEGRITY parameter set to ENFORCED, Oracle will only use those materialized views known to have up-to-date data in their base tables. So you can always be sure that your SQL queries will be rewritten only if the Mview is absolutely current. In addition, queries will not be rewritten unless constraints are defined on the tables in the Mview, and they must be validated.

TRUSTED   Probably the most common setting for this parameter. When QUERY_REWRITE_INTEGRITY is set to TRUSTED, the relationships between the base tables of the materialized view are trusted, and Oracle considers the base table data and the materialized view to be correct. This allows you to use the ENABLE NOVALIDATE clause when enabling a constraint. Also, Oracle will consider that all information in a RELY constraint and any dimension to be correct. Even with TRUSTED set, Oracle nevertheless will not use a "stale" Mview.

STALE_TOLERATED   When QUERY_REWRITE_INTEGRITY is set to STALE_TOLERATED, the optimizer will consider all valid materialized views for query rewrite, even if the data contained in those views is stale. This is the most permissive mode in which to run query rewrite; be cautious with its use because incorrect results can be generated.

Materialized Views

As stated earlier, data warehouses often need to aggregate data, typically to provide fast access to common queries. Answers to questions such as "How much chocolate did we sell during the 4th Quarter?" may well be answered much more quickly by querying tables with precalculated aggregated data. Otherwise, without indexes to provide the data through indexed lookups, we might have to scan through a table full of several years' sales records and calculate all the chocolate sales for just the 4th Quarter. Instead, we can create a materialized view containing the calculated aggregates we are likely to query—say, summarized sales for all product types by quarter. Rather than 500 or so sales records in the main detail table for the 4th Quarter, we have one aggregate record for all 4th Quarter chocolate sales. When we want to know the chocolate sales in any quarter, we need read only one record. Speeding up queries in this fashion is the purpose of a *materialized view*.

A materialized view (Mview) is based on a SQL statement much as is a regular view in Oracle. Generally, materialized views are used to compute aggregates from either a single table or a multitable join. One primary difference between a regular and a materialized view is that the materialized view actually stores the result set from the SQL statement in the CREATE MATERIALIZED VIEW statement, and thus requires storage for those rows. Rather than having to calculate the required subtotals, aggregates, or other amounts every time, the materialized view can store those values as row data. The process of returning the related calculations is substantially simplified and requires far fewer I/Os.

When using materialized views, you can subdivide the measures (contained in columns) in a fact table. There are three types of measures:

- A *simple measure* is just a noncalculated value within the column.
- In a *computed measure,* the column value represents the result of an expression of one or more simple measures. An example might be SUM(*pay*) / COUNT(*), to generate the average pay for all employees for a given period.
- A *multitable measure* is the result of an expression that involves measures from multiple tables, for example, the sum of the number of employees in the EMP table, and the total bonus money paid to these employees in the bonus table for a given period.

Another significant difference between a normal view and an Mview is that the Mview can be updated to properly reflect the data contained in the base tables of the view. Thus, as detail records in the base tables change, the Mview changes as well. In some cases this alteration may be reflected after any change is committed; in other cases, the change may be reflected only after an update routine is executed against the Mview. See "Materialized View Refresh Methods" later in the chapter for more information on refresh methods.

As discussed, Oracle can benefit from the rewriting of a SQL statement to take advantage of an existing materialized view. The developer need not know of the view's existence in order to benefit from its presence. Query rewrite on a Mview depends on the proper setup of the query rewrite facility and whether the rules for query rewrite are followed.

Creating a Materialized View

This section explains materialized view creation and the related security requirements that must be satisfied in order to create these objects. We'll also show you some examples of using the CREATE MATERIALIZED VIEW command.

NOTE As discussed in Chapter 25, materialized views are also used for distributed replication of database data (formally known as *snapshots*). In previous versions of Oracle, snapshots were used for simple replication. In Oracle8i, the terms *snapshot* and *materialized view* are used synonymously a great deal of the time. Both elements contain the results of a query on one or more tables. In fact, when you create a snapshot, upon completion, Oracle reports "Materialized View Created." In Oracle8i, CREATE MATERIALIZED VIEW is a synonym for CREATE SNAPSHOT.

Options for Creating Mviews

An Mview is created with the SQL command CREATE MATERIALIZED VIEW. See Appendix E for the complete syntax.

A number of options are available when creating a materialized view.

- You can create the materialized view as an index-organized table.
- You can partition a materialized view.
- You can create a materialized view using the NOLOGGING command to reduce redo generation.
- Oracle's parallel features (Chapter 18) fully support queries using materialized views such as parallelized SELECT statements.
- As with other objects in Oracle, you should carefully consider the settings of the STORAGE clause (INITIAL, NEXT, etc.) as well as the physical attributes clause (PCTFREE, PCTUSED, etc.) and the tablespace assignment.

There may well be cases where you will want the view created, but you do not yet wish to populate it. This functionality is provided through the use of the BUILD DEFERRED clause. The opposite clause, BUILD IMMEDIATE, is the default. By default, Oracle will not rewrite SQL queries to use a given materialized view. Thus, if you wish for your Mview to be a candidate for query rewrite, include the ENABLE QUERY REWRITE clause in the CREATE MATERIALZED VIEW command.

TIP When first creating the Mview, use the ORDER BY clause to order the rows by primary key. Even though the ORDER BY clause won't be used in subsequent refreshes, having the table data in loaded order can substantially help performance when the related primary key index is being used. Note that query rewrite is not affected by use of the ORDER BY clause.

When you create a materialized view, one associated index is also created to help manage the view. The USING INDEX clause is used to set the STORAGE parameters of that index. If this clause isn't present, the default values for the user's default tablespace are substituted.

NOTE Although the CACHE clause is available for use when creating an Mview (as for creating most objects that store data), you should use the keep buffer pool instead.

Privileges Required for Working with Mviews

To create materialized views in the current schema, the user must have

- The CREATE MATERIALIZED VIEW grant.
- Either the CREATE TABLE or CREATE ANY TABLE grant.
- At least SELECT privileges for each base table of the view, or SELECT ANY TABLE privileges.

To create materialized views in another schema, the user must have

- The CREATE ANY MATERIALIZED VIEW grant for that schema.
- At least SELECT privileges for each base table of the view, or SELECT ANY TABLE privileges.

Also, the schema in which the view is being created must have

- The CREATE TABLE privilege.
- Access to all of the base tables in the view, or SELECT ANY TABLE privileges.

Keep in mind that the internal workings of the creation and maintenance of an Mview may require creation of an index and a view, and the privileges required for those operations. (See Chapter 25's section on Mview privileges.)

A final twist: If you want to create the Mview enabled for query rewrite, the owner of the base tables of the view must have the QUERY REWRITE or GLOBAL QUERY REWRITE privileges. In addition, if the owner of the Mview is not the owner of the base tables, the owner of the Mview must have the GLOBAL QUERY REWRITE privilege.

Mview Examples

Listings 19.1, 19.2, and 19.3 are several different examples of the use of the CREATE MATERIALIZED VIEW command, including the creation of a partitioned Mview.

Listing 19.1: An Mview with a Join and Aggregate

```
CREATE MATERIALIZED VIEW
mv_emp_dept
BUILD IMMEDIATE
REFRESH FAST ON DEMAND
ENABLE QUERY REWRITE
AS
SELECT b.dname, COUNT(a.deptno)
FROM emp a, dept b
WHERE a.deptno=b.deptno
Group BY b.dname;
```

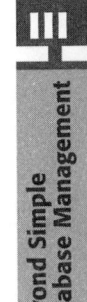

Materialized view created.

```
SQL> SELECT * FROM mv_emp_dept;

DNAME           COUNT(A.DEPTNO)
--------------  ---------------
ACCOUNTING                    3
RESEARCH                      5
SALES                         6
```

Listing 19.2: A Single-Table Aggregate Mview

```
-- Create the log first
SQL> CREATE MATERIALIZED VIEW LOG ON scott.emp
WITH ROWID (hiredate)
INCLUDING NEW VALUES;

-- Create the Mview single table aggregate
SQL> CREATE MATERIALIZED VIEW
mv_emp_date_agg
BUILD IMMEDIATE
REFRESH FAST ON COMMIT
ENABLE QUERY REWRITE
AS
SELECT TO_CHAR(hiredate,'yyyy')
"Hire Year", COUNT(*)
"Number Hired" FROM EMP
GROUP BY
TO_CHAR(hiredate,'yyyy');

Materialized view created.

-- query the Mview
SQL> SELECT * FROM
mv_emp_date_agg;

Hire Number Hired
---- ------------
1980            1
1981           10
```

```
1982           2
1983           1
```

Listing 19.3: A Partitioned Mview

```
DROP MATERIALIZED VIEW mv_emp_date_agg;
CREATE MATERIALIZED VIEW
mv_emp_date_agg
PARTITION BY RANGE (hireyear)
(
    PARTITION p1 VALUES LESS THAN ('1999')
    tablespace pre_1999_data,
    PARTITION p2 VALUES LESS THAN ('2000')
    TABLESPACE data_1999,
    PARTITION p3 VALUES LESS THAN ('2001')
    TABLESPACE data_2000,
    PARTITION p4 VALUES LESS THAN ('2002')
    TABLESPACE data_2001
)
BUILD IMMEDIATE
REFRESH COMPLETE ON DEMAND
ENABLE QUERY REWRITE
AS
SELECT TO_CHAR(hiredate,'yyyy') Hireyear,
COUNT(*) "Number Hired"
FROM emp
GROUP BY  TO_CHAR(hiredate,'yyyy');
```

Altering or Dropping an Mview

Of course, we need to be able to alter the various characteristics of a materialized view. With the ALTER MATERIALIZED VIEW command, we can change the storage and physical attributes of an Mview, the refresh method, or the view's eligibility for query rewrite. Check Appendix E for the syntax of this command.

To change a materialized view, you must either own the view, or you must have the ALTER ANY MATERIALIZED VIEW privilege.

It may well happen that an Mview becomes invalid because dependency objects have been changed. Use the ALTER MATERIALIZED VIEW <view_name> ENABLE QUERY REWRITE command to revalidate a materialized view.

Here are some examples of altering Mviews:

```
ALTER MATERIALIZED VIEW mv_emp_date_agg
PCTFREE 10
PCTUSED 60
STORAGE (NEXT 100k);

ALTER MATERIALIZED VIEW mv_emp_date_agg
ADD PARTITION p5 VALUES LESS THAN ('2003')
TABLESPACE data_2002;

ALTER MATERIALIZED VIEW mv_emp_date_agg
DISABLE QUERY REWRITE;
```

When you want to get rid of an Mview that you've created, it's as simple as using the DROP MATERIALIZED VIEW command. Appendix E has the syntax for this command, and you've already seen it used here in this chapter.

```
DROP MATERIALIZED VIEW mv_emp_date_agg;
```

As you might expect, if you want to drop an Mview in a schema other than your own, you need the DROP ANY MATERIALIZED VIEW privilege.

"But I Already Have Aggregate Tables!"

So, you were ahead of the curve, and you already have a warehouse full of tables that act like materialized views. Oracle rewards you by allowing you to create an Mview on an existing table. To do this, you use the ON PREBUILT TABLE clause of the CREATE MATERIALIZED VIEW command.

There are a few rules to follow for using existing aggregate tables:

- The number of columns and column names in the table must match those in the query used in the CREATE MATERIALIZED VIEW command.
- The table must be in the same schema as the materialized view being created.
- The table must have the same name as the materialized view being created.

Note: Keep in mind that the Mview you create with the ON PREBUILT TABLE clause will replace the table of the same name. Thus, that table will be converted into an Mview.

Continued

CONTINUED

Here's an example of use of the ON PREBUILT TABLE clause:

```
-- Create the table that we will convert to a MV
CREATE TABLE emp_agg as
SELECT TO_CHAR(hiredate,'yyyy') Hireyear,
COUNT(*) "Number Hired"
FROM EMP
GROUP BY  TO_CHAR(hiredate,'yyyy');
Table created.

-- Now, convert this into a MV using the ON PREBUILT TABLE clause.
-- Note the name of the Mview is the same as the prebuilt table name.
CREATE MATERIALIZED VIEW
emp_agg
ON PREBUILT TABLE
REFRESH COMPLETE ON DEMAND
ENABLE QUERY REWRITE
AS
SELECT TO_CHAR(hiredate,'yyyy') Hireyear,
COUNT(*) "Number Hired"
FROM EMP
GROUP BY  TO_CHAR(hiredate,'yyyy');
```

Data Dictionary Views for Mviews

Several data dictionary views are provided for use with Mviews. They're listed in Table 19.3.

TABLE 19.3: MVIEW DATA DICTIONARY VIEWS

View Name	Description
DBA_MVIEWS	General information on materialized views in the database.

Continued

TABLE 19.3: MVIEW DATA DICTIONARY VIEWS (CONTINUED)	
View Name	Description
ALL_REFRESH_DEPENDENCIES	The last refresh information for objects on which Mviews are dependent.
DBA_MVIEW_ANALYSIS	Detailed information on Mviews, such as last refresh time and SCN.
DBA_MVIEW_DETAIL_RELATIONS	Mviews and their dependent base tables.
DBA_MVIEW_JOINS	Information on join conditions within Mviews.
DBA_MVIEW_KEYS	Various information on Mview relationships. For use with DBA_MVIEW_DETAIL_RELATIONS to get more details on Mview relationships.

Refreshing Mviews

When you create a materialized view, you want to make sure that Oracle keeps it updated to reflect the current data in the underlying tables. There are different ways to do this, depending on the type of materialized view you are using. The refresh mode available for a given Mview depends on whether it has joins and aggregates, joins and no aggregates, or is an aggregate Mview without any joins.

There are two *refresh options*:

- REFRESH ON COMMIT causes the Mview to be refreshed upon the COMMIT of any transaction that is changing the underlying base tables of the view.
- REFRESH ON DEMAND delays the refresh of the materialized view until a warehouse refresh job is executed. We will discuss warehouse refresh later in this chapter.

You also need to select the *refresh method* to be used by Oracle when actually refreshing the view. There are five refresh method choices, each with its own use restrictions: FAST, COMPLETE, FORCE, NEVER, and ALWAYS.

Let's take a closer look at the refresh options and refresh methods.

Mview Refresh Options

As mentioned, two refresh options are made available when you create a materialized view. You can also alter an Mview to change its refresh option.

Refresh on Commit

The REFRESH ON COMMIT option of the CREATE MATERIALIZED VIEW command is allowed in only two cases. The first is when the Mview is based on a single table (and is likely aggregating one or more columns of that table). The second case is when the Mview is created by joining two or more tables together, but the view contains no aggregates. Other restrictions also apply. Generally when you are doing a refresh on commit, you'll want to be able to use the fast refresh method, and restrictions are associated with that as well.

Refresh on Demand

The REFRESH ON DEMAND option of the CREATE MATERIALIZED VIEW command is the default refresh option for any Mview created.

Mview Refresh Methods

The various refresh methods can be a bit confusing—in particular fast refresh and complete refresh. Here we'll examine their functionality and the rules associated with them.

Fast Refresh

A *fast refresh*, also known as an *incremental refresh*, causes only the changed rows in the Mviews to be changed. Only rows that contain aggregates based on the changed rows of the base view will be changed in the Mview. Fast refresh is probably the best option, but there are a number of restrictions on it.

If you wish to do a fast refresh of your Mview upon commitment of changes to the base table, an associated Mview log must be created on the base table. To do this, use the CREATE MATERIALIZED VIEW LOG command, and in the WITH clause define which columns you want to track in the log. In order to fast refresh the Mview, you must include the columns involved in the primary key of the base table. (More information on Mview logs can be found later in this chapter.)

Here are the general rules for employing fast refresh:

- The tables in the FROM clause cannot be views.
- Mviews cannot contain nonrepeating expressions such as SYSDATE or ROWNUM, or nonrepeating PL/SQL functions.
- LONG RAW and LONG data types are not supported for fast refresh.
- You cannot use the HAVING and CONNECT BY clauses.
- The WHERE clause can only contain inner and outer equijoins. All joins must be connected with ANDs.
- Fast refresh does not support subqueries, inline views, or use of the UNION, UNION ALL, INTERSECT, or MINUS operations.

The restrictions on use of fast refresh depend on the type of Mview. They are as follows:

View with joins and aggregates The SELECT list must include all the columns of the GROUP BY clause.

- An aggregate function is not required, but if one is used it can only include the following: SUM, COUNT(*column*), COUNT(DISTINCT *column*), COUNT(*), AVG, VARIANCE, STDDEV, MIN, and MAX.
- There may be other restrictions. You may well be able to use the fast refresh method, but still have to refresh on demand.

NOTE You cannot perform fast refreshes for updates to base tables of Mviews that contain joins and aggregates. Fast refreshes are only possible for operations that add data to the Mview using direct load operations (for example, direct load path SQL*Loader imports or INSERTS using the APPEND hint).

Single-table aggregate Mview Fast refresh (and even refresh on commit) is allowed with this type of view. Restrictions include the following:

- The SELECT list must contain all GROUP BY columns.
- You can use expressions in the SELECT and GROUP BY columns, but the expressions must be the same in both columns.
- In a single-table Mview to be fast refreshed, the WHERE clause is not supported.
- A COUNT(*) must be included in the Mview SELECT list.
- The MIN and MAX functions are not supported.
- An Mview log must exist and must contain all columns to be referenced in the Mview. You must include the INCLUDING NEW VALUES clause of the Mview log.
- If the AVG or SUM function is used, you must also use the COUNT function and include the same expression in the COUNT function as the AVG or SUM function. For example if you include a SUM(pay), you'll also need to include a COUNT(pay) in the query of the Mview.

Mviews containing only joins   Mviews with joins only cannot contain any GROUP BY clauses.

- If the WHERE clause contains outer joins, unique constraints must exist on the join columns of the inner join table.
- The ROWIDs of all the tables in the FROM list must appear in the SELECT list within the query defining the Mview.
- You must have an Mview log on each base table of the Mview, and the logs must contain the ROWIDs of the base tables.

Complete Refresh
If you choose complete refresh, your Mview will be completely rebuilt rather than just updated with the incremental changes to the base tables. Often, this is the only refresh method available for use. Its benefits include the fact that you don't need to create a snapshot (Mview) log from the base tables of the Mview. The drawback, however, is that the underlying table of the Mview is truncated before the refresh, and so there are no rows in the view until the refresh completes.

Force Refresh
Using the Force method tells Oracle that a fast refresh is the preferred method of updating the view, but to do a complete refresh if a fast refresh is not possible.

Always and Never
Always causes an unconditional refresh of the materialized view, and Never suppresses the refresh altogether.

The Data Warehouse Refresh Facility (DBMS_MVIEW)
If your Mviews cannot be set to REFRESH ON COMMIT (which means they are set to REFRESH ON DEMAND), then you need another method of updating the Mviews that you have in your system. This is the purpose of the Warehouse Refresh facility of Oracle8i, which is present in the form of the DBMS_MVIEW package.

The DBMS_MVIEW package contains a number of different procedures, but for the purposes of refreshing Mviews we are interested in the following:

- DBMS_MVIEW.REFRESH, which refreshes a specific Mview
- DBMS_MVIEW.REFRESH_ALL_MVIEWS, which refreshes all Mviews
- DBMS_MVIEW.REFRESH_DEPENDENT, which refreshes all Mviews that are dependent on one or more base tables

NOTE The DBMS_MVIEW package is also used to manage remote Mview updates. See Chapter 25 for more information on simple replication with Mviews.

Setting Up DBMS_MVIEW

The primary consideration for setting up the Warehouse Refresh facility is properly setting up the Oracle Job Scheduler. Table 19.4 lists the parameters that you need to configure and their purpose. Once you have set these parameters, you are ready to refresh the Mviews.

TABLE 19.4: JOB SCHEDULER PARAMETERS PERTINENT TO DBMS_MVIEW

Parameter Name	Default Value	Description
JOB_QUEUE_PROCESSES	0	Determines the number of job queue processes that Oracle will start when the database starts. Each queue is capable of running one job at a time. Thus, if multiple queues are started, you can run refreshes in parallel.
JOB_QUEUE_INTERVAL	60	Determines the amount of time (in seconds) that will elapse before a job queue process looks for another job to execute.
UTL_FILE_DIR	None	Defines external directories that can be written to by the UTL_FILE procedure.

NOTE JOB_QUEUE_PROCESSES is dynamically modifiable using the ALTER SYSTEM command. Changing the other parameters requires bouncing the database.

Using DBMS_MVIEW.REFRESH

The REFRESH procedure of the DBMS_MVIEW command is an overloaded procedure. This is to allow the DBA to pass in either a single table or a comma-delimited list of tables for refresh. This procedure has the following definitions:

```
Argument Name                   Type                    In/Out  Default?
------------------------------  ----------------------  ------  --------
```

MATERIALIZED VIEWS

```
LIST                            VARCHAR2                 IN
METHOD                          VARCHAR2                 IN      DEFAULT
ROLLBACK_SEG                    VARCHAR2                 IN      DEFAULT
PUSH_DEFERRED_RPC               BOOLEAN                  IN      DEFAULT
REFRESH_AFTER_ERRORS            BOOLEAN                  IN      DEFAULT
PURGE_OPTION                    BINARY_INTEGER           IN      DEFAULT
PARALLELISM                     BINARY_INTEGER           IN      DEFAULT
HEAP_SIZE                       BINARY_INTEGER           IN      DEFAULT
ATOMIC_REFRESH                  BOOLEAN                  IN      DEFAULT

Argument Name                   Type                     In/Out  Default?
------------------------------  -----------------------  ------  --------
TAB                             TABLE OF VARCHAR2(227)   IN/OUT
METHOD                          VARCHAR2                 IN      DEFAULT
ROLLBACK_SEG                    VARCHAR2                 IN      DEFAULT
PUSH_DEFERRED_RPC               BOOLEAN                  IN      DEFAULT
REFRESH_AFTER_ERRORS            BOOLEAN                  IN      DEFAULT
PURGE_OPTION                    BINARY_INTEGER           IN      DEFAULT
PARALLELISM                     BINARY_INTEGER           IN      DEFAULT
HEAP_SIZE                       BINARY_INTEGER           IN      DEFAULT
ATOMIC_REFRESH                  BOOLEAN                  IN      DEFAULT
```

Note that most of these parameters have default values, so in many cases you'll only need to provide the table (or list of tables) to update and then the update method you wish to use. Table 19.5 describes the parameters for the REFRESH procedure.

 TIP Often the DBA will create a job (using the DBMS_JOBS package) in the Job Scheduler to automate the execution of DBMS_MVIEW.REFRESH. See Chapter 20 for more information on DBMS_JOBS.

TABLE 19.5: DBMS_MVIEW.REFRESH PARAMETERS

Refresh Parameter	Purpose
LIST	A comma-delimited list of Mviews to refresh.
TAB	A single Mview to refresh.

Continued

TABLE 19.5: DBMS_MVIEW.REFRESH PARAMETERS (CONTINUED)	
Refresh Parameter	**Purpose**
METHOD	The refresh method to use: A=Always, F=Fast, ?=Force, and C=Complete.
ROLLBACK_SEG	The name of a specific rollback segment to use when performing the refresh.
PUSH_DEFERRED_RPC	Set to TRUE always; used for updateable snapshots and has no effect with warehouse-based Mviews.
REFRESH_AFTER_ERRORS	Indicates whether the job should continue refreshing other Mviews if an error is encountered with any previous Mview refresh. Set to TRUE to continue the job.
PURGE_OPTION	Set to FALSE always.
PARALLELISM	Set to 0 always.
HEAP_SIZE	Set to 0 always.
ATOMIC_REFRESH	If TRUE, all refreshes are in one transaction. If False, all refreshes are in their own transaction.

Listing 19.4 is an example of running DBMS_MVIEW.REFRESH.

Listing 19.4: Using DBMS_MVIEW.REFRESH

```
-- Query the existing view. Note that we have 14 records.
SQL> SELECT empno, ename FROM EMP;
     EMPNO ENAME
---------- ----------
      7369 SMITH
      7499 ALLEN
      7521 WARD
      7566 JONES
      7654 MARTIN
      7698 BLAKE
      7782 CLARK
      7788 SCOTT
      7839 KING
      7844 TURNER
      7876 ADAMS
      7900 JAMES
      7902 FORD
```

```
         7934 MILLER
14 rows selected.

-- Query the associated Mview
SQL> SELECT * FROM  emp_agg;

HIRE Number Hired
---- ------------
1980           1
1981          10
1982           2
1983           1

-- Add a new record.
SQL> INSERT INTO emp VALUES
  (8000,'FREEMAN','KING',NULL, SYSDATE, 4000,2000,10);
1 row created.
SQL> commit;

-- Note, the Mview is not updated.
SQL> SELECT * FROM  emp_agg;

HIRE Number Hired
---- ------------
1980           1
1981          10
1982           2
1983           1

-- Use the warehouse refresh facility to update the Mview.
SQL> BEGIN
  2      DBMS_MVIEW.REFRESH('EMP_AGG','A');
  3  END;
  4  /
PL/SQL procedure successfully completed.

-- Now, look at the Mview, it's updated!
SQL> SELECT * FROM  emp_agg;
```

```
HIRE   Number Hired
----   ------------
1980              1
1981             10
1982              2
1983              1
2001              1
```

Using DBMS_MVIEW.REFRESH_ALL_MVIEWS

Of course, you're likely to need a procedure that just refreshes all Mviews that are in need of refreshing. The REFRESH_ALL_MVIEWS procedure fits the bill. This procedure will refresh all stale snapshots (ones that have pending updates from the base tables).

```
Argument Name                  Type                    In/Out   Default?
------------------------------ ----------------------- ------   --------
NUMBER_OF_FAILURES             BINARY_INTEGER          OUT
METHOD                         VARCHAR2                IN       DEFAULT
ROLLBACK_SEG                   VARCHAR2                IN       DEFAULT
REFRESH_AFTER_ERRORS           BOOLEAN                 IN       DEFAULT
ATOMIC_REFRESH                 BOOLEAN                 IN       DEFAULT
```

The parameters of the REFRESH_ALL_MVIEWS procedure are consistent with the parameters shown in Table 19.5 for the REFRESH procedure. Also, note that most of these parameters do have default values, so the only parameter you need to send to the procedure is the first one (which is an OUT type, so be careful there!)

Listing 19.5 is an example of the use of DBMS_MVIEW.REFRESH_ALL_MVIEWS.

Listing 19.5: Using DBMS_MVIEW.REFRESH_ALL_MVIEWS

```
DECLARE
     Failures BINARY_INTEGER;
BEGIN
     DBMS_MVIEW.REFRESH_ALL_MVIEWS(failures);
     DBMS_OUTPUT.PUT_LINE('Procedure had '||failures||' failures.');
END;
/
Procedure had 0 failures.
PL/SQL procedure successfully completed.
```

Using DBMS_MVIEW.REFRESH_DEPENDENT

Often, you'll know about changes to a given base table that may potentially affect many Mviews. This can occur, for example, after a load process has added data to the table. The REFRESH_DEPENDENT procedure of DBMS_MVIEW allows you to refresh all Mviews that are based on one or more updated dependent tables. This procedure refreshes all Mviews that have not already been refreshed. Like the DBMS_MVIEW.REFRESH procedure, REFRESH_DEPENDENT is overloaded. This allows you to pass in one or several tables to the procedure for refresh.

```
Argument Name                  Type                    In/Out Default?
------------------------------ ----------------------- ------ --------
NUMBER_OF_FAILURES             BINARY_INTEGER          OUT
LIST                           VARCHAR2                IN
METHOD                         VARCHAR2                IN     DEFAULT
ROLLBACK_SEG                   VARCHAR2                IN     DEFAULT
REFRESH_AFTER_ERRORS           BOOLEAN                 IN     DEFAULT
ATOMIC_REFRESH                 BOOLEAN                 IN     DEFAULT


Argument Name                  Type                    In/Out Default?
------------------------------ ----------------------- ------ --------
NUMBER_OF_FAILURES             BINARY_INTEGER          OUT
TAB                            TABLE OF VARCHAR2(227)  IN
METHOD                         VARCHAR2                IN     DEFAULT
ROLLBACK_SEG                   VARCHAR2                IN     DEFAULT
REFRESH_AFTER_ERRORS           BOOLEAN                 IN     DEFAULT
ATOMIC_REFRESH                 BOOLEAN                 IN     DEFAULT
```

Listing 19.6 is an example of the REFRESH_DEPENDENT procedure.

Listing 19.6: Using DBMS_MVIEW.REFRESH_DEPENDENT

```
DECLARE
    Failures BINARY_INTEGER;
BEGIN
    DBMS_MVIEW.REFRESH_DEPENDENT(failures, 'EMP,DEPT');
    DBMS_OUTPUT.PUT_LINE('Procedure had '||failures||' failures.');
END;
/
PL/SQL procedure successfully completed.
```

Mview Logs

Fast (incremental) refreshes depend heavily upon the presence of an Mview log. If you want to be able to fast refresh an Mview, you must create an *Mview log* on each base table that is a part of that materialized view. These Mview logs (also called *snapshot logs*) record each change that occurs to the base table. They are read during the Mview refresh process so that the view can be properly updated without having to scan all the tables on which the view is based.

Creating Mview Logs

To create an Mview log, use the CREATE MATERIALIZED VIEW LOG command. As with any other schema object that will store information, you can define the storage characteristics of the Mview log with the STORAGE clause. You can also define the tablespace that will store the Mview log, as well as the logging characteristics.

When you create an Mview log, you use the WITH clause to define how the Mview stores the changes to its base table. Options available for designating storage of the change information include ROWID, Primary Key (the default) or both the ROWID and primary key. In addition, you can specify a list of columns to be recorded in the Mview. All columns referenced in the Mview definition query must be referenced in the Mview log.

The INCLUDING NEW VALUES clause, which is required for a fast refresh, is an optional part of the Mview log. This clause causes both the old and new values of the changed rows to be stored in the Mview log. The default, EXCLUDING NEW VALUES will cause the new values not to be stored.

To create an Mview log in a schema that is not your own, you must have the following privileges:

- CREATE ANY TABLE
- CREATE ANY TRIGGER
- SELECT (on the underlying master table)
- COMMENT ANY TABLE

Following is an example of the SQL used to create an Mview log:

```
CREATE MATERIALIZED VIEW LOG ON building_income
TABLESPACE users
NOLOGGING
WITH PRIMARY KEY, ROWID
INCLUDING NEW VALUES;
```

Altering and Dropping Mview Logs

Often you will need to modify the STORAGE clause, modify the partitioning strategy in some way, or change the default degree of parallelism. Perhaps, through the use of the ADD clause, you want to alter the Mview log so that it starts storing the primary key. Maybe you need to modify the list of columns to be stored in the Mview Log. This is all facilitated through the use of the SQL command ALTER MATERIALIZED VIEW LOG.

NOTE The ADD clause of ALTER MATERIALIZED VIEW LOG only adds items to be recorded in the Mview log, such as the ROWID or an additional list of columns. If anything is to be removed from the Mview, the view itself must be dropped and re-created.

The same grants are required for modifying an Mview log as are required to create it. Here's an example of this command; see Appendix E for complete syntax:

```
ALTER MATERIALIZED VIEW LOG ON EMP
ADD ROWID;
```

Sometimes you just need to drop the Mview log because it's not being used anymore. Sometimes you need to drop it because you want to change the nature of what is being stored in the log. In either case, use the DROP MATERIALZED VIEW LOG command to remove the log.

If the Mview log is not in your schema, you must have the DROP ANY TABLE privilege.

Here's an example of this simple command; see Appendix E for syntax.

```
DROP MATERIALIZED VIEW LOG ON EMP;
```

Data Dictionary Views of Mview Logs

To query information on Mview logs from the data dictionary, Oracle has the *_SNAPSHOT_LOGS (DBA, ALL, and USER). These views provide information such as the Mview log owner, the view name, the SQL text that makes up the view, and a great deal of additional information.

The DBA_SNAPSHOT_LOG_FILTER_COLS view provides a list of the columns on which the snapshot logs are built.

 NOTE There is no synonym created for the DBA_SNAPSHOT_LOG_FILTER_COLS view. If you need to reference it from a schema other than SYS, you must prefix the view with the SYS schema.

Dimensions

The purpose of a dimension in Oracle is clearly reflected in its name: A *dimension* is used to define the hierarchical nature of data. In other words, a dimension defines a parent-child relationship between the columns in your tables. This information is used by the optimizer to enable certain query rewrite operations (see Table 19.1). Although dimensions are an optional feature of materialized views in Oracle8i, you must use them if you want these query rewrite operations to function.

An example of a dimension would be a time relationship among various data elements. An employee's pay, for instance, might be divided into several linear elements: Lifetime Pay, Yearly Pay, Quarterly Pay, Monthly Pay, Weekly Pay, and the Hourly Pay Rate. Within a data warehouse, you might have a table called PAY_TABLE, and within that table you'd have the employee's ID and net or gross pay (among other things). You could then create an Mview that contains columns based on these linear elements (LIFETIME_PAY, YEARLY_PAY, QUARTERLY_PAY, and so on). This Mview, once created, would speed up management queries on pay information, and providing an easy way to drill up or down through the various pay levels.

With the table and the Mview created, you would then create a dimension to define the time relationships for the Oracle optimizer. Then, when you query the base table using an aggregate function, such as summing the pay by quarter, the dimension helps the optimizer to determine whether the Mview can be used instead of the base table. This informed decision is made possible because the dimension defines the relationships between hourly, weekly, and yearly pay.

Creating a Dimension

So, this new dimension stuff sounds great, you say, and you want to try it. You probably won't be surprised to find that the command for creating a dimension is the CREATE DIMENSION command. Also not surprisingly, you need the CREATE DIMENSION privilege to create a dimension in your own schema, and the CREATE ANY DIMENSION privilege to create one in any other schema. You must also have at least SELECT privileges on the objects referenced in the dimension. And, of course, the objects must already exist.

Defining the Dimension

When you issue the CREATE DIMENSION command (see Appendix E for the complete syntax), you will proceed to define three different elements for the dimension:

- The LEVEL clause
- The HIERARCHY clause
- The ATTRIBUTE clause

LEVEL   In the LEVEL clause, you define the columns of the table(s) in the dimension. If the dimension consists of a single table it is called a *normalized dimension*; if it consists of two or more tables, it is called a *denormalized dimension*. Each level can be named and can consist of up to 32 columns from one table only. To allow incorporation of multiple tables in the dimension, you can define multiple LEVELs. Within the LEVEL clause, you will assign each column to a given identifier name that will be referenced when defining the dimension's HIERARCHY. Also, a given column can only exist in a single dimension.

NOTE   There are some restrictions when you assign multiple tables to a dimension. First, you must have foreign key relationships established between the tables of the dimensional HIERARCHY. All columns defined in the dimension should be defined as NOT NULL. The NOT NULL requirement is required but not enforced.

HIERARCHY   In the HIERARCHY clause, you define the relationship of the LEVELs, creating the actual hierarchy. You start by listing the most atomic level as defined in the LEVEL clause (such as Hourly Pay) and move to the most encompassing level of the hierarchy (such as Lifetime Pay). Thus, each subsequent level of the hierarchy is a child of the preceding level of the hierarchy. Another example of a hierarchy would be a City, State, and Country relationship. You would start creating the HIERARCHY with the City, and work your way up to Country.

Within the HIERARCHY clause is a JOIN clause that defines the join relationship of the various columns in the dimension.

NOTE   As in the LEVEL clause, NULLs in the table columns are not recommended for the HIERARCHY clause. They can cause incorrect results to be returned (no error will be generated, however). Each child key in the HIERARCHY must join with a parent-level column.

ATTRIBUTE   The ATTRIBUTE clause is next. Some dimensions include some one-to-one relationships between an attribute and other dimensional attributes; for example, in a hierarchy of Cubicle, Office, Floor, and Building. In the Cubicle level, there is also a one-to-one relationship between the Office and the Employee who occupies the Cubicle. In the Office (which in our example can take up part of a Floor), there is a relationship between the Office and the Person who signed

the lease on that Office. In the Building, there is a Manager, so we have a one-to-one relationship there as well. Each of these relationships could be defined for a given dimension in the ATTRIBUTE clause. Finally, you can include multiple hierarchies and attributes in a single dimension.

In sum, here are the fundamental rules for creating and defining a dimension:

- A parent dimension can have one or more children.
- A child dimension can have only one parent.
- The relationship between a dimensional HIERARCHY level and any dependent ATTRIBUTEs must be one-to-one only.
- Columns of each HIERARCHICY level must be NOT NULL.
- A column of a HIERARCHY cannot be associated with more than one dimension.
- You cannot create cyclical hierarchical relationships.

A Dimension Example

Listing 19.7 provides an extended example of the creation of a dimension. In this example, we will create a materialized view that has multiple base tables. This Mview will also be created using inline views. As a result, this is the most complicated Mview created in this chapter.

After creating the Mview, we create a dimension on the columns of the Mview. This dimension has two hierarchies:

- A HIERARCHY for the rollup of the rents paid to the Management Company of several buildings. What are the LEVELs? The rents are paid at the Office level. The business rules say that a given Office can exist on only one Floor and that you may have multiple Offices on each Floor. Thus, we have a one-to-many relationship between Floors and Offices. Again, each Floor is assigned to a given Building and a given Floor may exist in only one Building (but the same Floor ID may be used in multiple Buildings). The rollup is then from Office to Floor to Building, and that hierarchy is defined in the first LEVEL.
- The second HIERARCHY is from the Floor Agent who is responsible for collecting the rents on a given Floor, to the Building Manager who is responsible for managing the Building.

Finally, the dimension relates the ATTRIBUTEs of the Floor number to the Floor Agent, and the Building number to the Building Manager.

After creating the dimension, we query the base table of the Mview and find that indeed, our query has been rewritten.

Listing 19.7: Creating a Dimension

```
-- Note: The account in which you will be running this code
-- must have been granted GLOBAL QUERY REWRITE privileges directly,
-- not through a role. If your account does not have this privilege,
-- remove the ENABLE QUERY REWRITE line from the CREATE
-- MATERIALIZED VIEW command, and it will work.
DROP MATERIALIZED VIEW mv_building_income;
DROP TABLE building_income;
DROP TABLE floor_agent;
DROP TABLE building_manager;
DROP DIMENSION building_dim;

CREATE TABLE building_income
(
    today_date              DATE,
    office_number           NUMBER,
    floor_number            NUMBER,
    building_number         NUMBER,
    rent_paid               NUMBER,
    floor_agent             NUMBER,
    building_manager        NUMBER,
CONSTRAINT pk_building_income PRIMARY KEY
(today_date, office_number, floor_number, building_number)
USING INDEX TABLESPACE index_tbs
STORAGE (INITIAL 10K NEXT 10K) );

CREATE TABLE floor_agent
( floor_agent               NUMBER,
  agent_name                varchar2(40) );

CREATE TABLE building_manager
( building_manager          NUMBER,
  manager_name              varchar2(40) );

-- Need to create an mview log

INSERT INTO floor_agent VALUES
(1, 'Franks, Peter');
INSERT INTO floor_agent VALUES
```

```sql
(2, 'Blowfeld, Sirge');
INSERT INTO building_manager VALUES
(1, 'Coleman, Kathy');
INSERT INTO building_manager VALUES
(2, 'Sheraton, John');
INSERT INTO building_income VALUES
( SYSDATE, 1, 1, 1, 1000, 1, 1);
INSERT INTO building_income VALUES
( SYSDATE, 2, 2, 1, 2000, 2, 1);
INSERT INTO building_income VALUES
( SYSDATE, 3, 2, 1, 335, 1, 1);
INSERT INTO building_income VALUES
( SYSDATE, 1, 1, 2, 1000, 1, 2);
INSERT INTO building_income VALUES
( SYSDATE, 1, 2, 2, 1000, 2, 2);
commit;

ANALYZE TABLE building_income COMPUTE STATISTICS;

-- This is a complex Mview, so it cannot refresh fast.
CREATE MATERIALIZED VIEW
mv_building_income
BUILD IMMEDIATE
REFRESH COMPLETE ON DEMAND
ENABLE QUERY REWRITE
AS
SELECT TRUNC(a.today_date) todays_date,
a.building_number,
a.floor_number,
SUM(a.floor_total) todays_floor,
SUM(b.building_total) todays_building
FROM
(SELECT TRUNC(today_date)  as today_date,
building_number, floor_number, SUM(rent_paid) as floor_total
from building_income
GROUP BY today_date, building_number, floor_number) a,
(SELECT TRUNC(today_date)  as today_date, building_number,
SUM(rent_paid) as building_total
FROM building_income
```

```sql
              GROUP BY today_date, building_number) b
WHERE   a.today_date=b.today_date
AND a.building_number=b.building_number
GROUP BY trunc(a.today_date), a.building_number, a.floor_number;

CREATE DIMENSION building_dim
LEVEL office is building_income.office_number
LEVEL floor is building_income.floor_number
LEVEL building is building_income.building_number
LEVEL floor_agent is building_income.floor_agent
LEVEL building_manager is building_income.building_manager
HIERARCHY floor_rollup
(
office   CHILD OF
floor    CHILD OF
building
)
HIERARCHY management_rollup
(
floor_agent CHILD OF
building_manager
)
ATTRIBUTE floor DETERMINES building_income.floor_agent
ATTRIBUTE building DETERMINES building_income.building_manager;

ANALYZE TABLE mv_building_income COMPUTE STATISTICS;

exec DBMS_OLAP.VALIDATE_DIMENSION('BUILDING_DIM','SCOTT',TRUE,TRUE);

PL/SQL procedure successfully completed.

SELECT * FROM   mview$_exceptions;
no rows selected

-- Now, let's look at the results of the Mview and test to see if query
-- rewrite is working!
-- We have query_rewrite turned off by default on this system, so we
-- will enable it.
ALTER SESSION SET query_rewrite_enabled=TRUE;
```

```
SET AUTOTRACE ON

-- Now, run the query against the base table and see what happens!
SELECT TRUNC(a.today_date) todays_date,
a.building_number,
a.floor_number,
SUM(a.floor_total) todays_floor,
SUM(b.building_total) todays_building
FROM
(SELECT TRUNC(today_date)   as today_date,
building_number, floor_number, SUM(rent_paid) as floor_total
FROM building_income
GROUP BY today_date, building_number, floor_number) a,
(SELECT TRUNC(today_date)   as today_date, building_number,
SUM(rent_paid) as building_total
FROM building_income
GROUP BY today_date, building_number) b
WHERE  a.today_date=b.today_date
AND a.building_number=b.building_number
GROUP BY trunc(a.today_date), a.building_number, a.floor_number;
```

TODAYS_DA	BUILDING_NUMBER	FLOOR_NUMBER	TODAYS_FLOOR	TODAYS_BUILDING
19-MAY-01	1	1	1000	3335
19-MAY-01	1	2	2335	3335
19-MAY-01	2	1	4000	4000

```
Execution Plan
----------------------------------------------------------
     0      SELECT STATEMENT Optimizer=CHOOSE (Cost=1 Card=3 Bytes=51)
     1    0   TABLE ACCESS (FULL) OF 'MV_BUILDING_INCOME' (Cost=1 Card=3
               Bytes=51)
-- Note that query rewrite occurred. We queried the building_income
-- table in our query above but the rewrite facility changed it to
-- use our materialized view!
```

About those inline queries—they will make the query rewrite very difficult at times. This is because you are not likely to write queries that will successfully pass the query rewrite rules. For example, take the following query:

```
SELECT /*+ REWRITE */
TRUNC(today_date), building_number, floor_number, SUM(rent_paid)
FROM building_income
GROUP BY trunc(today_date), building_number, floor_number;
```

You might think that this query would be rewritten to take advantage of the Mview called MV_BUILDING_INCOME created in Listing 19.7. However, Oracle can't find any match that will allow it to rewrite this query, and so it uses the BUILDING_INCOME table instead. The moral of this story is that you should always be careful about assuming that a particular query will get rewritten; it may very well not be.

Altering and Dropping Dimensions

The ALTER DIMENSION command allows you to manage your dimensions. This command allows you to:

- Add or drop hierarchy, levels and attributes to the dimension.
- Recompile the dimension

Here's an example:

```
ALTER DIMENSION building_dim COMPILE;
ALTER DIMENSION building_dim ADD ATTRIBUTE building
   DETERMINES state_table.state;
```

Following is an example of the DROP DIMENSION command, which is used to drop a dimension from the database:

```
DROP DIMENSION building_dim;
```

Displaying Dimensions

This section shows you how to put your dimensions to work. First we'll look at the relevant data dictionary views, and then we'll examine a special Oracle-supplied package called DEMO_DIM that can simplify the task of documenting dimensions.

Data Dictionary Views for Dimensions

Table 19.6 lists views for dimension management.

TABLE 19.6: DIMENSION DATA DICTIONARY VIEWS

View name*	Dimension Information
DBA_DIMENSIONS	General information.
DBA_DIM_LEVELS	Defined dimension levels.
DBA_DIM_LEVEL_KEY	Columns defined at the dimension level.
DBA_DIM_HIERARCHIES	Hierarchies defined within a dimension.
DBA_DIM_CHILD_OF	Hierarchical relationships between defined levels in a dimension.
DBA_DIM_JOIN_KEY	Joins between dimension tables (since a dimension can contain more than one table).
DBA_DIM_ATTRIBUTES	Attributes defined in a dimension.

* In addition to these DBA_ views, the same elements are available in USER_ and ALL_ views.

The DEMO_DIM Package

If you query some of the views listed in Table 19.6, you'll find that they complicate somewhat your dimension management tasks. Oracle's DEMO_DIM package makes things a bit easier.

DEMO_DIM must be installed; it's located in the $ORACLE_HOME/rdbms/demo directory in the form of a script called smdim.sql. When you run this script, it loads two procedures (PRINT_DIM and PRINT_ALLDIMS) that can then be run to document the dimensions. After installing the script, you have to grant execute privilege on DEMO_DIM to either PUBLIC or the individual users who will be running the package.

NOTE The procedures in the DEMO_DIM package use the DBMS_OUTPUT package, so before running DEMO_DIM you must issue the command set serveroutput on.

PRINT_DIM

The PRINT_DIM procedure allows you to print out the contents of a given dimension. You pass one parameter to PRINT_DIM, which is the name of the dimension that you want reported. Note that you cannot pass a schema name to the procedure, so you must be in the schema that owns the dimension. Following is an example of running PRINT_DIM.

```
SQL> exec demo_dim.print_dim('BUILDING_DIM');
DIMENSION SCOTT.BUILDING_DIM
LEVEL BUILDING IS SCOTT.BUILDING_INCOME.BUILDING_NUMBER
LEVEL BUILDING_MANAGER IS SCOTT.BUILDING_INCOME.BUILDING_MANAGER
LEVEL FLOOR IS SCOTT.BUILDING_INCOME.FLOOR_NUMBER
LEVEL FLOOR_AGENT IS SCOTT.BUILDING_INCOME.FLOOR_AGENT
LEVEL OFFICE IS SCOTT.BUILDING_INCOME.OFFICE_NUMBER
HIERARCHY FLOOR_ROLLUP (
OFFICE
CHILD OF FLOOR
CHILD OF BUILDING
)
HIERARCHY MANAGEMENT_ROLLUP (
FLOOR_AGENT
CHILD OF BUILDING_MANAGER
)
ATTRIBUTE FLOOR DETERMINES SCOTT.BUILDING_INCOME.FLOOR_AGENT
ATTRIBUTE BUILDING DETERMINES SCOTT.BUILDING_INCOME.BUILDING_MANAGER
```

PRINT_ALLDIMS

The PRINT_ALLDIMS procedure prints out all dimensions in all schemas. It takes no parameters. Following is an example:

```
SQL> exec demo_dim.print_alldims
DIMENSION SCOTT.BUILDING_DIM
LEVEL BUILDING IS SCOTT.BUILDING_INCOME.BUILDING_NUMBER
LEVEL BUILDING_MANAGER IS SCOTT.BUILDING_INCOME.BUILDING_MANAGER
LEVEL FLOOR IS SCOTT.BUILDING_INCOME.FLOOR_NUMBER
LEVEL FLOOR_AGENT IS SCOTT.BUILDING_INCOME.FLOOR_AGENT
LEVEL OFFICE IS SCOTT.BUILDING_INCOME.OFFICE_NUMBER
HIERARCHY FLOOR_ROLLUP (
OFFICE
CHILD OF FLOOR
CHILD OF BUILDING
)
HIERARCHY MANAGEMENT_ROLLUP (
FLOOR_AGENT
CHILD OF BUILDING_MANAGER
)
ATTRIBUTE FLOOR DETERMINES SCOTT.BUILDING_INCOME.FLOOR_AGENT
```

```
ATTRIBUTE BUILDING DETERMINES SCOTT.BUILDING_INCOME.BUILDING_MANAGER

PL/SQL procedure successfully completed.
```

Other Data Warehousing Features

Before we wrap up this chapter, we want to point out some of the other data warehousing features available in Oracle8i.

Features Covered Elsewhere

These features have their own chapters in this book:

Oracle8i constraint features for data warehouses   For certain types of query rewrites to be possible, constraints among related tables must be in place and must be enabled. Refer to Chapters 1 and 6 for more information on creating, altering, and dropping constraints.

Transportable tablespaces   Chapter 12 discusses transportable tablespaces, which are used in some data warehouses to transport source data sets. For example, other data marts or OLTP systems may be transported for the data warehouse to cleanse and load into its various tables.

Parallel query execution   A badly tuned parallel query can just ruin your day. With the large data sets present in data warehouses, parallel processing can make a substantial difference in the time taken for a query to run. Chapter 18 explains parallel processing and contains instructions for properly configuring Oracle's parallel query operations.

SQL Features for Data Warehouse Queries

Oracle added some nice SQL features in Oracle8i for data warehouse queries: the ROLLUP, CUBE, and GROUPING keywords, and what are called top-N (and bottom-N) queries.

ROLLUP

The new ROLLUP operator is useful for creating cross-tab reports where you have many different levels of subtotaling and then finally a grant total. The ROLLUP operator is implemented as a part of the GROUP BY clause of a SELECT statement. The

ROLLUP operator can be used with a materialized view. The Mview will continue to be fully refreshable and query rewrite will be possible.

Let's look again at our BUILDING_INCOME table (created in Listing 19.7) for an example. Suppose we want to print a subtotal of rents received for each Floor, and for each Building by day. To produce this output, we can use the ROLLUP operator, as shown in the following query:

```
SQL> SELECT TRUNC(today_date), building_number, floor_number,
  2  SUM(rent_paid) from building_income
  3  GROUP BY rollup(trunc(today_date), building_number, floor_number);
```

TRUNC(TOD	BUILDING_NUMBER	FLOOR_NUMBER	SUM(RENT_PAID)
19-MAY-01	1	1	1000
19-MAY-01	1	2	2335
19-MAY-01	1		3335
19-MAY-01	2	1	2000
19-MAY-01	2		2000
19-MAY-01			5335
21-MAY-01	1	3	300
21-MAY-01	1		300
21-MAY-01			300
			5635

What did we get in this output?

1. On the first two lines, we see that on May 19, Building 1 got payments for Floors 1 and 2.
2. On the third line, we get a rollup for that day's payments for Building 1.
3. On the next line, Building 2 got one payment, and the rollup for that payment is on the following line.
4. Note that on the next line both the building number and the floor number columns are NULL. This indicates that this row is a rollup for the entire day, which ends up at $5,335.
5. Next we see the income for May 21 and then two more rollup lines.
6. Finally, the last line gives a grand total for all the income generated.

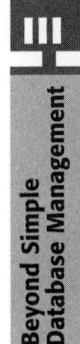

CUBE

The CUBE operator allows you to perform various types of rollups within the same SQL statement. For example, we can roll up the rent receipts of all of the Agents, and at the same time be rolling up the total rent received for a given Building. Like the ROLLUP operator, CUBE is used as a part of the GROUP BY expression and can be used in Mviews with no restrictions.

Following is an example of a query using the CUBE operator:

```
  1  SELECT TRUNC(today_date), building_number, floor_agent, SUM(rent_paid)
  2  from building_income
  3* GROUP BY cube(trunc(today_date), building_number, floor_agent);
SQL> /
```

TRUNC(TOD	BUILDING_NUMBER	FLOOR_AGENT	SUM(RENT_PAID)
19-MAY-01	1	1	1335
19-MAY-01	1	2	2000
19-MAY-01	1		3335
19-MAY-01	2	1	1000
19-MAY-01	2	2	1000
19-MAY-01	2		2000
19-MAY-01		1	2335
19-MAY-01		2	3000
19-MAY-01			5335
21-MAY-01	1	1	300
21-MAY-01	1		300

TRUNC(TOD	BUILDING_NUMBER	FLOOR_AGENT	SUM(RENT_PAID)
21-MAY-01		1	300
21-MAY-01			300
	1	1	1635
	1	2	2000
	1		3635
	2	1	1000
	2	2	1000
	2		2000
		1	2635
		2	3000
			5635

Information produced in this case includes total rent received by Building, total rent received by Floor Agent for each Building, total rent received by Floor Agents for all Buildings as well as total rent received for all Buildings.

GROUPING

Sometimes the NULL columns that occur when using the CUBE and ROLLUP operators can cause headaches for developers. They need an easy way to determine what kind of total is being reported for the column, and that it is in fact a total. The GROUPING function allows you to define additional columns to be returned in the query that will tell you these facts. What you end up with is essentially a bitmap at the end of your row set, which your application can then use in deciding how to handle the data. The GROUPING operator can be used with the CUBE and ROLLUP operators.

Here is an example of using the GROUPING function along with the ROLLUP operator. Notice that the D, B, and F columns now provide a bitmap indicating what type of total is provided in the column.

```
SQL> SELECT TRUNC(today_date), building_number, floor_number,
  2  SUM(rent_paid),
  3  GROUPING (trunc(today_date)) as D,
  4  GROUPING (building_number) as B,
  5  GROUPING (floor_number) as F
  6  from building_income
  7  GROUP BY rollup(trunc(today_date), building_number, floor_number);
```

TRUNC(TOD	BUILDING_NUMBER	FLOOR_NUMBER	SUM(RENT_PAID)	D	B	F
19-MAY-01	1	1	1000	0	0	0
19-MAY-01	1	2	2335	0	0	0
19-MAY-01	1		3335	0	0	1
19-MAY-01	2	1	2000	0	0	0
19-MAY-01	2		2000	0	0	1
19-MAY-01			5335	0	1	1
21-MAY-01	1	3	300	0	0	0
21-MAY-01	1		300	0	0	1
21-MAY-01			300	0	1	1
			5635	1	1	1

Top-N Queries

Oracle users have been frustrated for some time by the inability to easily determine the bottom-N or top-N rows in a given query. Two issues are involved in this problem.

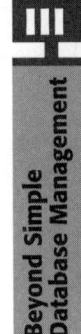

First, the ROWNUM clause of a SQL statement is always executed before any ORDER BY operation. Second, although inline views are allowed, until Oracle8i they did not support the ORDER BY operation.

Now in Oracle8i, the ORDER BY clause is supported in inline views. Top-N queries are now quite easy to do (as are bottom-N queries). Simply create the inline view with an ORDER BY clause (ordering in ascending or descending order as required), and then use the ROWNUM clause to limit the result set.

The following code provides examples of both a top-N and bottom-N query:

```
-- This gives us the bottom 5 floor rent payments
SQL> SELECT * FROM
  2  (SELECT floor_number, rent_paid FROM building_income
  3  ORDER BY rent_paid)
  4  WHERE ROWNUM <= 5;

FLOOR_NUMBER   RENT_PAID
------------   ---------
           3         300
           2         335
           1        1000
           1        1000
           1        1000

-- This gives us the top 5 floor rent payments
SQL> SELECT * FROM
  2  (SELECT floor_number, rent_paid FROM building_income
  3  ORDER BY rent_paid desc)
  4  WHERE ROWNUM <= 5
  5  ;

FLOOR_NUMBER   RENT_PAID
------------   ---------
           2        2000
           1        1000
           1        1000
           1        1000
           2         335
```

Oracle continues to add more and more functionality to its support of VLDBs. Many of these data warehousing features can significantly improve the performance of queries against these databases.

CHAPTER 20

Oracle8i Supplied Packages

FEATURING:

Using the Oracle8i supplied packages	908
Scheduling jobs with the Job Scheduler	914
Communicating through pipes	921

Oracle supplies packages that add powerful and flexible weapons to the DBA's arsenal of database tools. These packages are provided for two main reasons. One purpose is to supply the DBA with enhanced database management and reporting functions. The other purpose is to provide the developer with enhanced development tools to allow for better and more efficient use of database resources.

We have provided examples of the use of various packages throughout this book. For example, in Chapter 12, we covered how to use the DBMS_TTS package to check transportable tablespaces. Chapter 14 covered the LogMiner feature, which is available through the DBMS_LOGMNR package. In Chapter 15, you saw examples of how to use the DBMS_SYSTEM package to set events.

In this chapter, we provide an overview of using the Oracle8i supplied packages, and then focus on two packages that provide very useful functions: the DBMS_JOB package, which works with the Oracle8i Job Scheduler, and the DBMS_PIPE package, which allows sessions to communicate with each other.

Using the Oracle8i Supplied Packages

The Oracle8i packages have many purposes, including the following:

- Analyzing the Oracle8i database
- Checking for software corrupted data blocks
- Converting ROWIDs
- Providing job queuing facilities for the database, allowing for quasi-parallel PL/SQL threading
- Allowing the DBA to generate database statistics
- Updating snapshots and materialized views
- Providing various forms of I/O for PL/SQL
- Managing the shared pool
- Generating dynamic SQL

Table 20.1 lists the most commonly used packages. Also, we have provided Appendix D on the CD as a quick reference to the Oracle supplied packages.

TABLE 20.1: COMMONLY USED ORACLE SUPPLIED PACKAGES

Package Name	Purpose
DBMS_ALERT	Provides support for the asynchronous notification of database events
DBMS_APPLICATION_INFO	Allows registration of an application name with the database for auditing, certain types of debugging, and performance tracking purposes
DBMS_AQ	Lets you add a message or remove a message from a message queue
DBMS_AQADM	Contains administrative functions for advanced queuing
DBMS_DDL	Allows you to compile and analyze Oracle database objects
DBMS_DEBUG	Supports PL/SQL code debugging
DBMS_DESCRIBE	Describes a stored procedure and its arguments
DBMS_IOT	Supports ANALYZE and constraint exception operations on index-organized tables
DBMS_JOB	Allows you to manage the Oracle Job Scheduling facility
DBMS_LOB	Provides various routines that can be used to manage and manipulate Oracle internal and external LOBs
DBMS_LOCK	Allows you to request various levels of locks using Oracle's Lock Management services
DBMS_LOGMNR	Allows you to use Oracle's LogMiner facility to mine redo logs
DBMS_LOGMNR_D	Creates an object dictionary that allows LogMiner to cross reference transactions in redo logs with the names of the objects in the database
DBMS_MVIEW	A synonym for DBMS_SNAPSHOT
DBMS_OBFUSCATION_TOOLKIT	Allows you to apply encryption to a given column value
DBMS_OFFLINE_OG	Allows for offline instantiation of a master table in a multiple-master replication group
DBMS_OFFLINE_SNAPSHOT	Allows for offline instantiation of snapshots
DBMS_OLAP	Provides additional functionality and management of summaries, dimensions, and query rewrites
DBMS_OUTPUT	Provides the ability to move output to a buffer for display and to retrieve that information by PL/SQL programs
DBMS_PCLXUTIL	Provides for intra-partition parallelism when creating partition-wise local indexes

Continued

TABLE 20.1: COMMONLY USED ORACLE SUPPLIED PACKAGES (CONTINUED)

Package Name	Purpose
DBMS_PIPE	Allows different Oracle sessions to communicate through a pipe
DBMS_PROFILER	Provides an interface into PL/SQL that allows for debugging and performance profiling
DBMS_RANDOM	Provides seed-based random number generation
DBMS_REFRESH	Allows for the creation of snapshot groups that can be refreshed together, so they are transactionally consistent to a given point in time (requires the Distributed option)
DBMS_REPAIR	Provides certain data corruption detection and repair procedures
DBMS_REPCAT	Provides routines to administer and update the Oracle replication catalog and environment (requires the Replication option)
DBMS_REPCAT_ADMIN	Allows for the creation of users for the symmetric replication facility (requires the Replication option)
DBMS_REPCAT_INSTANTIATE	Allows for instantiation of deployment templates (requires the Replication option)
DBMS_REPCAT_RGT	Lets you control the maintenance and definition of refresh group templates (requires the Replication option)
DBMS_REPUTIL	Provide routines to generate shadow tables, triggers, and packages for table replication
DBMS_RESOURCE_MANAGER	Allows you to maintain plans, consumer groups, and plan directives
DBMS_RESOURCE_MANAGER_PRIVS	Allows you to maintain the various privileges associated with resource consumer groups
DBMS_RLS	Provides support for Oracle's virtual private database functionality, which supplies database-controlled, row-level security
DBMS_ROWID	Provides procedures to analyze and dissect Oracle8i ROWIDs
DBMS_SESSION	Provides access to various statements available when running the SQL ALTER SESSION statement
DBMS_SHARED_POOL	Lets you control the behavior of objects in the shared pool, such as pinning objects to prevent their removal
DBMS_SNAPSHOT	Lets you refresh individual snapshots and purge snapshot logs (requires the Distributed option); a synonym for DBMS_MVIEW
DBMS_SPACE	Provides various segment space information
DBMS_SPACE_ADMIN	Provides locally managed tablespace segment space administration functionality, much of which is not available through standard SQL

Continued

TABLE 20.1: COMMONLY USED ORACLE SUPPLIED PACKAGES (CONTINUED)

Package Name	Purpose
DBMS_SQL	Allows for the dynamic operation of dynamic SQL, such as the execution of DDL within PL/SQL routines
DBMS_STATS	Allows for the gathering of statistics of objects within the database
DBMS_TRACE	Allows for starting and stopping PL/SQL tracing
DBMS_TRANSACTION	Allows you to control transactions from a stored procedure
DBMS_TTS	Verifies the transportable tablespace set and determines if it is self-contained
DBMS_UTILITY	Provides various utility routines used by the DBA, such as analysis routines
OUTLN_PKG	Allows you to manage stored outlines in Oracle
UTL_COLL	Allows PL/SQL programs to use collection locators to query and update the database
UTL_FILE	Allows PL/SQL programs to read and write operating system text files in real time
UTL_HTTP	Enables various HTTP callouts from PL/SQL and SQL, so that you can write code that accesses data on the Internet, through, for example, a URL
UTL_INADDR	Provides a procedure that supports Internet addressing
UTL_RAW	Provides various SQL functions that allow you to manipulate RAW datatypes, including APPEND, CONCAT, SUBSTR, and casting functions
UTL_REF	Enables PL/SQL to access an object by providing a reference to the object
UTL_SMTP	Provides functionality to send e-mail
UTL_TCP	Supports PL/SQL functionality for simple TCP/IP-based communications

Running the Supplied Packages

Running the Oracle8i supplied packages the first time (or even subsequent times!) can be a frustrating exercise. You may find that they do not exist in the database you created, and you will need to install them. Also, sometimes, you need to use named notation for parameters to call the packages correctly.

Installing Supplied Packages

Most of the packages that you will use in Oracle are installed when you run either the `catalog.sql` or `catproc.sql` SQL script, both of which must be executed after database creation. Some of the supplied packages, however, must be installed using special scripts. The following are some of the most commonly used packages that need to be installed before you can use them:

- DBMS_SHARED_POOL, which is installed by running the `dbmspool.sql`
- DBMS_IOT, which is installed by running the `dbmsiotc.sql` script
- DBMS_RANDOM, which is installed by running the `dbmsrand.sql` script.

If the package you want to use doesn't exist on your system, search the $ORACLE_HOME/rdbms/admin directory files to see if one of these scripts creates that package. When you load these packages into the database, make sure that you do so when connected as SYSDBA or SYS, as shown in this example:

```
SQL> @d:\oracle\ora816\rdbms\admin\dbmsrand.sql
Package created.
Package body created.
Synonym dropped.
Synonym created.
Grant succeeded.
Grant succeeded.
```

Calling the Parameters of a Stored Package

Some packages require the use of named notation in order to use all of the parameters that you want. *Named notation* simply means that you will name the parameter for the package and the value for that parameter, rather than just listing the value. This is often required when procedures have several optional parameters, and you may not need, or want, to provide values for those parameters. Named notation uses the exact name of the parameter, then the characters => to indicate named notation, followed by the parameter value itself. See Chapter 14 for examples of using named notation with the DBMS_LOGMNR.START_LOGMNR package. There are other examples of using named notation throughout this book.

Getting Information about Supplied Packages

So, with all these wonderful supplied packages, you might be wondering how you can find out what parameters to send which procedure. If you have a stored package that you think you should run, but you can't remember the name of the function or procedure within that stored procedure, all you need do is issue the DESC command from SQL*Plus. For example, to see the description of the DBMS_LOGMNR package, issue the following command:

```
SQL> DESC dbms_logmnr
```

If you are logged in as an owner that has the rights to use that package, you will be shown each procedure or function in the package, along with the different parameters for each procedure.

If you cannot remember the name of a particular package, you can query the DBA_OBJECTS view, using the OWNER and OBJECT_NAME columns. This may show you the stored package you are looking for (all of the Oracle supplied packages are owned by SYS, by the way). You can further qualify the query to show only packages by using the OBJECT_TYPE column. Here is an example of a query that uses all three columns and its results.

```
-- Get the package names.
SQL>  SELECT owner, object_name, object_type
  2    FROM dba_objects
  3   WHERE object_name like 'DBMS_LOG%'
  4     AND object_type='PACKAGE'
  5   ORDER BY 2;


OWNER       OBJECT_NAME            OBJECT_TYPE
---------   --------------------   ------------
SYS         DBMS_LOGMNR            PACKAGE
SYS         DBMS_LOGMNR_D          PACKAGE
```

Also check the DBA_OBJECTS view (and the documentation, of course!) when installing a new version of Oracle to see if any new and interesting packages have been added.

TIP If you have any questions or problems regarding the supplied packages, check the release-specific documentation. Also, if you have access to Oracle's MetaLink support forum (for Oracle-supported customers, accessed through http://www.support.oracle.com/metalink) or Oracle's free Technet forum (accessed through http://technet.oracle.com), you can find some additional documentation on certain procedures. Also, you can surf over to RevealNet Pipelines (http://www.revealnet.com/Pipelines/piplines.htm), where I frequently act as a sysop, and ask questions about stored procedures or do a quick search on your topic.

Scheduling Jobs with the Job Scheduler

Oracle's Job Scheduling facility is a fairly robust system that allows you to schedule various Oracle PL/SQL jobs. Jobs in the Job Scheduler can be set up to run just once, or they can be scheduled as reoccurring jobs. This allows the Job Scheduler to be used to "multithread" PL/SQL jobs. Built correctly, multiple PL/SQL jobs can run in parallel, reducing overall run times. I have literally seen such parallel threading of jobs decrease overall run times by 50 to 60 percent, so it's well worth the effort to learn how to use the Job Scheduler.

The DBMS_JOB supplied package is used to interface with the Oracle Job Scheduler. You use this package to create jobs to be executed, to break jobs (for example, if you don't want them to run for a period of time), to remove jobs, or to alter jobs in the job queue.

Enabling the Job Scheduler

Before you can use the Job Scheduler, it must be enabled by setting the initialization parameter JOB_QUEUE_PROCESSES to a value other than the default value of 0. This parameter enables the Job Scheduling facility, and it can be dynamically changed with the ALTER SYSTEM command, as shown here:

```
ALTER SYSTEM SET job_queue_processes=4;
```

You can check the value of the JOB_QUEUE_PROCESSES parameter by querying the V$PARAMETER view, like this:

```
SELECT name, value
FROM v$parameter
WHERE name LIKE 'job_queue_processes';
```

NAME	VALUE
job_queue_processes	4

On Unix systems (and on other systems where multiple processes are running Oracle), setting the JOB_QUEUE_PROCESSES parameter to a value greater than 1 will cause the Job Scheduler processes to be started when the database starts. Systems that use multithreaded processes, like Windows NT, will have new threads started. Once enabled, the Oracle Job Scheduling facility is controlled through the use of the DBMS_JOB package.

The other parameter that impacts the Job Scheduler is JOB_QUEUE_INTERVAL, which defines how often the job queue processes will wake up and search for a new job to be executed. The JOB_QUEUE_INTERVAL parameter is measured in seconds and defaults to 60 seconds.

Adding a Job to the Job Scheduler

To add a job to the Job Scheduler, use the DBMS_JOB.SUBMIT procedure to submit the job for execution. As each job is submitted to the Job Scheduler, it is assigned a job number. This job number is returned to the user through the DBMS_JOB.SUBMIT procedure, or you can query the DBA_JOBS view to determine the job number of the assigned job. You can choose to run the job just once, by not assigning it a rerun interval, or you may choose to run the job repeatedly at a specified frequency, by assigning it a rerun interval. The *interval* of the job executions simply means how long will it be between the execution of a given job. Listing 20.1 shows an example of adding a job to the Job Scheduler.

Listing 20.1: Adding a Job to the Job Scheduler

```
VAR job_num NUMBER;
BEGIN
        DBMS_JOB.SUBMIT(job=>:job_num,
        what=>'INSERT INTO time_table VALUES (SYSDATE);',
        next_date=>SYSDATE,
        interval=>'SYSDATE + 1/24');
COMMIT;
END;
/
```

This example creates a job that will insert the system date and time into a table called TIME_TABLE. The first parameter, JOB, will hold the job number that Oracle automatically assigns to this newly created job. The next parameter, WHAT, defines the job that is to be executed. In this case, we are simply using a SQL statement as the job to be executed. Notice the presence of the trailing semicolon, indicating that all SQL rules are to be followed. Next, the NEXT_DATE parameter indicates the first time the job should be executed. We used SYSDATE to indicate that the job should be executed immediately upon the submission of the job to the Job Scheduler. Finally, the INTERVAL variable indicates that this job should run once an hour. (Setting the job interval is discussed in more detail in the "Running a Job at Intervals" section, coming up shortly.)

Also, notice the COMMIT command. When you are creating a job, the use of the COMMIT command is required to ensure that the first execution of a job occurs. If

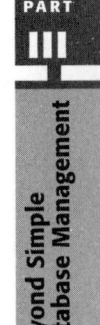

you do not issue a COMMIT command, then the next COMMIT in the session creating a job will cause the job to run, or the job will run when the session is completed.

You can also have a function, a procedure, a package, or even an external routine run by the Job Scheduler. Listing 20.2 shows an example of adding a job that runs a procedure.

Listing 20.2: Adding a Job that Executes a Procedure

```
-- Create a procedure called run_job.
CREATE OR REPLACE PROCEDURE run_job AS
BEGIN
     INSERT INTO time_table VALUES (SYSDATE);
END run_job;
/

-- Now, submit the job.
BEGIN
     DBMS_JOB.SUBMIT(job=>:job_num,
     what=>'run_job;',
     next_date=>SYSDATE,
             interval=>'SYSDATE + 1/24');
     COMMIT;
     END;
/
```

NOTE A procedure executed as a job can take parameters and be passed those parameters by the Job Scheduler, just as any procedure can.

Jobs in the Job Scheduler can have one of two job statuses: broken or not broken. When a job is *broken*, the job will not execute until the broken status has been changed. Typically, jobs will be broken because they fail 16 times. Also, the DBA may choose to break the job using the DBMS_JOB.BROKEN procedure. The DBMS_JOB.BROKEN procedure allows you to mark a job in the Job Scheduler with a broken status or to remove the broken status from a job. A DBA may choose to break a job to prevent it from running because some form of maintenance is being executed, or perhaps because some part of the job itself it being replaced. To determine if a job has been broken, you can check the DBA_JOBS data dictionary view, as shown in the next section.

Running a Job Once

If you make the job interval NULL, the job will run only once (if it is successful). If successful, the job will be removed from the Job Scheduler. If the job is not successful, the Job Scheduler will retry the job for the number of retries allowed, and then break the job. Once the problem has been fixed, you can restart the job, and if it runs successfully, it will be removed from the Job Scheduler.

To run a job, use the DBMS_JOB.RUN command. Here is an example of finding a specific job number, which is required to execute the job, and then running an existing job.

```
-- Query the dba_jobs view to determine the job number we wish to run.
SELECT job, what, broken, failures
FROM dba_jobs;

       JOB WHAT                                            B   FAILURES
---------- ---------------------------------------------- - ----------
         1 INSERT INTO time_table VALUES (SYSDATE);       N          0
         2 INSERT INTO time_two VALUES (SYSDATE);         Y         17
         3 INSERT INTO time_two VALUES (SYSDATE);         N         13
         4 INSERT INTO time_three VALUES (SYSDATE);       N          0
         6 run_job;                                       N          0

-- We want to run the job that does the insert into the
-- TIME_TABLE table. This is job number 1. Use the dbms_job.run
-- command to run this job.
EXEC dbms_job.run(1);
```

In this example, you see that there are four jobs currently available to run. The job number is shown in the JOB column. The WHAT column shows the statement(s) that will be executed. We decided to run job 1, which we did by using the DBMS_JOB.RUN command.

Running a Job at Intervals

You can have a job run repeatedly by assigning an interval to the job when you add it to the Job Scheduler. The parameter that you use to define the interval is a VARCHAR2 type rather than a DATE type. This is because you may need to use some rather odd-looking values for the interval parameter.

The interval parameter is expressed in days, so a 1 for this parameter represents one day, a 2 is two days, and so on. But what if you want a job to run with a greater

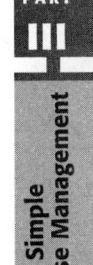

frequency than a day? Oracle allows you to do this by providing a way to define a part of a day.

To specify part of a day, you need to divide the day into units. Thus, a day is 24 hours, 1440 minutes, or 86,400 seconds. Once you determine the unit of time that you need to divide the day into, you determine what period of that increment you want to represent. For example, if you want to represent an hour, that is 1/24 day. If you want to represent a half hour, that is 1/48 day (because there are 48 half hours in the day). Perhaps you want your job to run every 5 minutes. In this case, you should use the value 5/1440. The 1440 represents the number of minutes in the day, and the 5 indicates that every 5 units of that 1440 increment (or every 5 minutes), the job will execute. In the examples in Listings 20.1 and 20.2, the jobs are set up to run every hour. Listing 20.3 shows an example of creating a job that will run every minute.

Listing 20.3: Running a Job at 1-Minute Intervals

```
BEGIN
    DBMS_JOB.SUBMIT(job=>:job_num,
    what=>'run_job;',
    next_date=>SYSDATE,
        interval=>'SYSDATE + 1/1440');
    COMMIT;
    END;
/
```

Modifying Jobs

With the DBMS_JOB.CHANGE procedure, you can change a variety of job information, including what should be executed when the job is run, the interval of time between each job execution, and the next time that the job should be executed. For example, suppose that you want to modify job 6, which currently runs every hour, so that it runs every minute. Listing 20.4 shows how to use the DBMS_JOB.CHANGE procedure to change the interval.

Listing 20.4: Changing a Job Interval

```
BEGIN
    DBMS_JOB.CHANGE(job=>6,what=>NULL, next_date=>NULL,
    interval=>'SYSDATE + 1/1440');
    COMMIT;
END;
/
```

Notice the NULL values passed to the WHAT and NEXT_DATE parameters in this example. Because there are no default values for these parameters, they must be given some value when running the procedure. Since NULL values are passed to these parameters, no changes will be made to their settings.

As another example, suppose that you want to have the next job execution occur in three days. Listing 20.5 shows how you could accomplish this modification.

Listing 20.5: Changing a Job's Time of Execution

```
BEGIN
    DBMS_JOB.CHANGE(job=>6,what=>NULL, next_date=>SYSDATE + 3,
    interval=>NULL);
    COMMIT;
END;
/
```

Suspending or Removing a Job

If you wish to suspend the execution of a job, use the DBMS_JOB.BROKEN procedure. You can also use this procedure to restart the execution of a job. Here is an example of breaking a job:

```
EXEC dbms_job.broken(6,TRUE);
```

In this case, job 6 will be broken after this statement is executed. The first parameter is obviously the job number. The second parameter is a Boolean value (TRUE/FALSE) that indicates if the job is broken (TRUE) or not (FALSE).

If you wish to unbreak a job, issue the following command:

```
EXEC dbms_job.broken(6,FALSE);
```

If you need to completely remove a job from the Job Scheduling facility, use the DBMS_JOB.REMOVE procedure, as in this example:

```
EXEC dbms_job.remove(2);
```

This example removes job 2, which is a broken job. (You can see this in the query of the DBA_JOBS view shown earlier, in the "Running a Job Once" section.)

Monitoring the Job Scheduler

The DBA_JOBS (and the USER_ and ALL_ varieties as well) data dictionary view provides a great deal of information about the various jobs in the job queue. The information includes when the job last ran, when it is scheduled to run again, what the job is, how many errors have occurred when the job has tried to run previously, and how often the job actually runs. Table 20.2 describes the most commonly used columns of the DBA_JOBS data dictionary view.

TABLE 20.2: COMMONLY USED COLUMNS IN THE DBA_JOBS VIEW

Column	Description
JOB	The job number assigned to the job
WHAT	The actual job (PL/SQL routine) that will be executed
LOG_USER	The user who submitted the job to the job queue
PRIV_USER	The user whose privileges are ascribed to the job
SCHEMA_USER	The default user who is used to parse the job (this is the schema that should contain the job)
LAST_DATE	The last date that the job was successfully run
THIS_DATE	If the job is executing, this column will be populated; if the job is not executing, this column will be NULL (can be used to determine how long a job has been running)
NEXT_DATE	The next execution date for the job
TOTAL_TIME	The overall time that the system has spent on the job
BROKEN	Indicates if the job is broken (which means it will not be scheduled for execution)
FAILURES	Indicates how many times this job has failed since its last success (16 successive failures will cause the job to become broken)

Here is an example of querying the DBA_JOBS view and its results:

```
SELECT job, what, TO_CHAR(last_date,'mm/dd/yyyy hh24:mi:ss') last_date,
TO_CHAR(next_date, 'mm/dd/yyyy hh24:mi:ss') next_date, failures, broken
FROM dba_jobs;

JOB WHAT                          LAST_DATE            NEXT_DATE            FAILURES B
--- ------------------------      -------------------  -------------------  -------- -
  1 begin my_procedure; end;      06/16/2001 13:31:53  06/16/2001 13:36:53         0 N
```

The results show a procedure called MY_PROCEDURE that is scheduled to run. It last ran on June 16 at 1:31 P.M., and it's ready to go again at 1:36 P.M. on the same day. No failures appear to have occurred with the execution of this job, and it's not broken.

Communicating through Pipes

The DBMS_PIPE package allows two or more sessions of an Oracle instance to communicate with each other. When the pipe is established, an area in the SGA is allocated for that pipe. Other sessions can attach to that area of shared memory, and then pass messages back and forth. Because all messaging is done through the SGA, be aware that all messages sent through pipes will be lost once the instance is shut down.

NOTE Oracle's Advanced Queuing feature provides for persistency of messages. See Oracle's documentation for information about Advanced Queuing.

The DBMS_PIPE package is very handy when you wish to perform real-time communications between Oracle sessions. For example, you might want to monitor the operation of multiple threads. You could establish a pipe between the running processes and an application that you have written to monitor those processes. You can also use a pipe for debugging triggers and stored PL/SQL code.

There are two different kinds of pipes in Oracle: public pipes and private pipes. Let's look at each of these types in a bit more detail.

Using Public Pipes

Public pipes are asynchronous in nature, and any user who has access to the pipe can read or write to that pipe through the DBMS_PIPE package (as long as they have EXECUTE privileges to the package). Once a user reads from the pipe, the message is removed from the pipe. Therefore, there is a risk that the user you intended the message for in the public pipe will never receive that message.

Public pipes can be either created implicitly or explicitly. An implicit public pipe is created automatically the first time it is referenced, and no specific creation procedure is required. An explicit public pipe is created by calling the CREATE_PIPE function and setting the private pipe type flag to N. You must de-allocate an explicitly created pipe with the REMOVE_PIPE function.

Using Private Pipes

Access to private pipes is much more restricted than access to implicit public pipes. Any session that wishes to connect to the private pipe created by your session must be logged in using the same user ID as the session that created the pipe: SYSDBA or

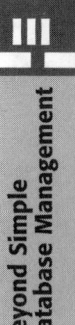

INTERNAL. Also, you can access the pipe through stored procedures that are running under the same user domain authorization as the creator of the pipe.

A private pipe is created by using the CREATE_PIPE function. The pipe is defined as a private pipe if the private pipe type flag is set to Y and there are no implicit private pipes. The name of the private pipe to be created cannot be the same as the name of any other existing private or public pipe. Like public pipes, private pipes are deallocated by using the REMOVE_PIPE function.

Sending and Receiving Messages

You send and retrieve messages through the public and private pipes in the same fashion. To make pipes work, you first need a sending side and a receiving side session on the same database. The sending side will establish the pipe, using either a private or public pipe (the public pipe can be an implicit pipe or an explicitly named pipe).

Sending a Message through a Pipe

If you wish to use an explicitly named pipe, use the DBMS_PIPE.CREATE_PIPE function. After creating the pipe (or not, if you are using a public implicit pipe), the next step is to pack the message with the DBMS_PIPE.PACK_MESSAGE procedure. If you are using an implicit pipe, it will be created when you pack it. Finally, once the message has been packaged, you will send the message through the pipe with the DBMS_PIPE.SEND_MESSAGE function. Listing 20.6 provides an example of sending a message through a pipe.

NOTE Listing 20.6 and Listing 20.7 (presented in the next section) are designed to run together. Listing 20.6 provides one side of the pipe (the sending side), and Listing 20.7 provides the other side of the pipe (the receiving side). To see the results of these examples, you would run Listing 20.7 first to set up the receiving side, and then run Listing 20.6 to send the message. Make sure to issue the SET SERVEROUTPUT ON command, as shown in these examples, or you will not see the output.

Listing 20.6: Setting Up the Sending Side of a Pipe
```
SET SERVEROUTPUT ON
DECLARE
V_pipe_name        VARCHAR2(30):='mypipe';
V_pipe_message     VARCHAR2(8192);
V_return           NUMBER;
BEGIN
```

```
        Dbms_output.put_line('Sending the message through the pipe!');
        -- Call dbms_pipe.create pipe to create an explicit pipe.
        -- This will be a public pipe by default.
        v_return:=Dbms_pipe.create_pipe(pipename=>v_pipe_name,
        private=>FALSE);
        IF v_return=0
        THEN
             Dbms_output.put_line('Pipe Open.');
        ELSE
             Dbms_output.put_line('error opening pipe.');
        END IF;

        -- Now, let's create a message to send through the pipe.
        V_pipe_message:='Do, or do not, there is no try.';
        Dbms_pipe.pack_message(v_pipe_message);

        -- Now, send the message through the pipe.
        -- Wait only 60 seconds.
        V_return:=Dbms_pipe.send_message(v_pipe_name, 60);
        IF v_return=0
        THEN
             Dbms_output.put_line('Message Sent.');
        ELSE
             Dbms_output.put_line('error sending message.');
        END IF;

        -- Our work is done.
        V_return:=Dbms_pipe.remove_pipe(v_pipe_name);
        IF v_return=0
        THEN
             Dbms_output.put_line('Pipe Closed.');
        ELSE
             Dbms_output.put_line('error closing pipe.');
        END IF;
END;
/
```
Here is the output from the sending session:
Sending the message through the pipe!
Pipe Open.

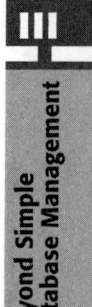

```
Message Sent.
Pipe Closed.

PL/SQL procedure successfully completed.
```

Receiving a Message through a Pipe

On the receiving side, things work pretty much in the reverse. First, you can explicitly open the pipe with the CREATE PIPE command, or you can choose to use an implicit pipe if you are going to be reading a public pipe. Then you use the DBMS_PIPE stored function RECEIVE_MESSAGE to receive a message from the pipe. After receiving the message, you can use the DBMS_PIPE.UNPACK_MESSAGE to unpack the message from the pipe. When you're finished with the pipes, use the DBMS_PIPE.REMOVE_ PIPE procedure to remove them. Listing 20.7 provides an example of receiving a message from a pipe.

Listing 20.7: Setting Up the Receiving Side of a Pipe

```
SET SERVEROUTPUT ON
DECLARE
V_pipe_name        VARCHAR2(30):='mypipe';
V_pipe_message     VARCHAR2(8192);
V_return           NUMBER;
BEGIN
    Dbms_output.put_line('Receiving the message through the pipe!');
    -- Call dbms_pipe.create pipe to create an explicit pipe.
    -- This will be a public pipe by default.
    v_return:=Dbms_pipe.create_pipe(pipename=>v_pipe_name,
    private=>FALSE);
    IF v_return=0
    THEN
        Dbms_output.put_line('Pipe Open.');
    ELSE
        Dbms_output.put_line('error opening pipe.');
    END IF;

    -- Now, send the message through the pipe.
    -- Wait only 60 seconds.
    V_return:=Dbms_pipe.receive_message(v_pipe_name, 60);
    IF v_return=0
    THEN
```

```
            Dbms_output.put_line('received the message through the pipe!');
        ELSE
            Dbms_output.put_line('error receiving the message through the
            pipe!');
        END IF;

        -- Now, unpack the message.
        Dbms_pipe.unpack_message(v_pipe_message);

        -- What was the message?
        Dbms_output.put_line('The message was: '||v_pipe_message);

        -- Our work is done.
        V_return:=Dbms_pipe.remove_pipe(v_pipe_name);
    IF v_return=0
        THEN
            Dbms_output.put_line('Pipe Removed.');
        ELSE
            Dbms_output.put_line('error removing pipe.');
        END IF;
END;
/
```

Here is the output from the receiving session:

```
Receiving the message through the pipe!
Pipe Open.
received the message through the pipe!
The message was: Do, or do not, there is no try.
Pipe Removed.

PL/SQL procedure successfully completed.
```

We have covered just a few of the many Oracle stored procedures that can simplify the Oracle DBA's life. Packages such as DBMS_DDL, DBMS_LOB, DBMS_OUTPUT, and DBMS_UTILITY can be very helpful to the DBA. As described earlier in this chapter, you can use the DESC command from SQL*Plus to see the procedures and functions in any of the Oracle-supplied packages.

CHAPTER 21

Oracle8i Database Security

FEATURING:

Managing Oracle user accounts	928
Enforcing row-level security	950
Enforcing column-level security	968

A primary responsibility of DBAs is to ensure that the data under their watchful eyes is protected from both accidental loss and deliberate acts of sabotage. One of the main ways to control access to a database is through user accounts. For more advanced database security, you can control access to portions of data in a table. One way to enforce row-level security is provided through Oracle8i's virtual private database feature (also known as *fine-grained access control*). You can also encrypt data within the database itself. Other Oracle security solutions include securing the network and the system the database is on itself (using the Oracle Security Server).

This chapter covers some of the techniques that you can use to secure your database. We describe managing user accounts and authentication, including setting up profiles and roles. Then we cover Oracle's features for providing row-level and column-level security.

Managing Oracle User Accounts

In Oracle, you can set up various forms of authentication for your users. After you have defined users, you can assign profiles to them, grant and revoke privileges, and create roles for ease of management.

One step you can take to provide some extra protection for your database is to set up password file authentication. Let's see how that is done, and then move onto the procedures for setting up and managing user accounts, profiles, and roles.

NOTE There is a subtle, but distinct, difference between the terms *schema* and *user* in Oracle. A *user* in Oracle is the person who signs into the database. Passwords and security grants to objects are associated with users. A schema is what owns the objects that are created by a given user. A schema can own objects created by the user that owns the schema, or the schema may own objects that are created by a different database user.

Setting Up Password File Authentication

By default, access to Oracle administration privileges is validated at the operating system level. The method of validation varies by operating system. For example, on Unix systems, this validation is based on the username and if the user is a member of a specific Unix group, typically called DBA. Thus, if your account is a member of the DBA group in Unix, you will be able to administer the database (through Server Manager or SQL*Plus, for example).

It should be obvious that this form of validation is a potential security hole. To plug it, you can change the default behavior and instead authenticate access to highly privileged database accounts regardless of the operating system user account that is being used. This is facilitated through the use of a password file. The password file is designed to provide an additional level of security for privileged Oracle accounts.

While using the password file is optional in many cases, you must set up password file authentication if you wish to use certain Oracle utilities (such as RMAN in Oracle 8.1.7) to manage the database. Also, some Oracle Enterprise Manager functions require password file authentication to be in place.

To use password file authentication for privileged database user accounts, you must first create the password file. Then you need to set up the database so that it knows it should use that password file.

Creating the Password File

To create the password file in Oracle8i, use the ORAPWD program (this program's name may be different on different platforms, but it is the same on Unix and NT systems in Oracle8i). The ORAPWD program takes three parameters; two are required and the third is optional. To see these parameters, just run ORAPWD by itself:

```
D:\ORACLE\ORA816\BIN>orapwd
Usage: orapwd file=<fname> password=<password> entries=<users>
  where
  file - name of password file (mand),
  password - password for SYS and INTERNAL (mand),
  entries - maximum number of distinct DBA and OPERs (opt),
  There are no spaces around the equal-to (=) character.
```

As you can see, the first parameter is the name of the password file. The password file takes a standard naming convention: <*sid*>pwd.ora, where <*sid*> is the name of the database. Thus, for my database named ROBERT, my password file is called robertpwd.ora. The default location for the password file varies by operating system. On NT systems, the password file is located in $ORACLE_HOME\database. On Unix systems, it's in $ORACLE_HOME\dbs.

NOTE On many systems, the location of the password file (and even its name) can be changed by altering your system environment. Check your operating system documentation for more information about defining alternate paths for your password file.

The next parameter of the ORAPWD command is the name of the password for the SYS and INTERNAL account. This is the password you will use when logging in to the database using SYS or CONNECT INTERNAL (or / AS SYSDBA).

The final, optional, parameter of the ORAPWD command is the number of entries for additional privileged users who will be granted SYSDBA or SYSOPER privileges. If you use the default value, Oracle will store enough entries to fill one database block. The default generally is around four entries for a 512KB operating system block size. The actual number of entries will likely be greater than that number, since Oracle will fill the entire operating system block. Using the ENTRIES parameter, you can define a larger number of privileged users.

Here is an example of creating a password file:

```
D:\ORACLE\ORA816\BIN>orapwd file=testpwd.ora password=robert entries=10
D:\ORACLE\ORA816\BIN>dir testpwd.ora
 Volume in drive D has no label.
 Volume Serial Number is 3C0E-D639
 Directory of D:\ORACLE\ORA816\BIN

05/27/01  10:09p                 2,560 testpwd.ora
               1 File(s)         2,560 bytes
                            40,697,856 bytes free
```

If the existing database password file is lost or becomes corrupted, you can easily re-create it using ORAPWD. Also, if you change the password of an account listed in the password file (which will be any account with SYSDBA or SYSOPER privileges), the password file will be updated as well.

Setting Up the Database to Use the Password File

After you've created the password file, the only other setup required to use password file authentication is to change a single database parameter. This is the REMOTE_LOGIN_PASSWORDFILE parameter, which is set to None by default (indicating that privileged database access is authenticated by the operating system). To enable password file authentication, change this parameter to either of the following settings:

- If you set REMOTE_LOGIN_PASSWORDFILE to Exclusive, the password file is not shared. In this mode, the password file is used by only one database, and it may contain passwords for users other than SYS and INTERNAL.

- If you set this parameter to Shared, the password file is shared by many databases. The main restriction is that this password file can contain only the passwords for SYS and INTERNAL logons, so this setting is less useful than Exclusive.

Once you've altered the parameter, you will need to take down the database and bring it back up again before the change will take effect. Once you've completed this final step, the database and highly privileged accounts will be database authenticated instead of operating system authenticated.

Creating User Accounts

When you create a user account in Oracle, using the CREATE USER command, you also define the way that the user's access to the database is authenticated. When the user is authenticated, the user account name is verified, the password (if one is used) is validated, and the username's security privileges are checked. If all of these validations succeed, the user is signed in.

> **NOTE** The Oracle Advanced Security Option (or whatever name is the flavor of the month) provides for network authentication, using various external authentication protocols, as well as global user authentication. *Global users* are users defined within a centralized enterprise directory, and access to databases is controlled via that directory using SSL. Also, multitier authentication and authorization can occur when users connect to the database through a proxy server. OCI provides calls that support this type of authentication.

Creating Database-Authenticated Users

For increased security, you can have the database validate and authenticate the user signing in. An example of creating this type of user account is shown in Listing 21.1.

Listing 21.1: Creating a Database-Authenticated User Account

```
CREATE USER chris IDENTIFIED BY carter
DEFAULT TABLESPACE users
TEMPORARY TABLESPACE temp
QUOTA ON users UNLIMITED;
```

Let's take a closer look at the settings for a user account:

Username Listing 21.1 creates a user named Chris. Usernames are not case sensitive. There are a few restrictions on usernames. First, a username cannot be longer than 30 bytes. A username can contain only alphanumeric characters from your character set and the following special characters: _, $, and #. Also, a username cannot be a reserved word (such as CREATE). Finally, as you might suspect, you cannot duplicate usernames in the same database.

Password   The IDENTIFIED BY clause indicates the password you are assigning to the user. A password is mandatory for a database-authenticated user. In Listing 21.1, the password for the Chris account is Carter. Passwords are not case sensitive.

Default tablespace   The DEFAULT TABLESPACE clause assigns the user's default tablespace. In Listing 21.1, Chris is assigned a default tablespace of USERS. This means that any objects that Chris creates will be created in the USERS tablespace by default. If you don't define a default tablespace, Oracle will assign the default tablespace as the SYSTEM tablespace. So, be sure to assign a default tablespace other than SYSTEM!

Temporary tablespace   The TEMPORARY TABLESPACE clause indicates the user's temporary tablespace, which is TEMP in Listing 21.1. This means that all temporary segments (created during sorting or when using global temporary tables for user Chris) will be created in the TEMP tablespace. As with the default tablespace, the default for the temporary tablespace setting is the SYSTEM tablespace, so you will want to make sure that you define another temporary tablespace when creating a user.

WARNING   You never want to allow any user account to have the SYSTEM tablespace as its default tablespace or temporary tablespace. After you create a database, you should even change the default and temporary tablespace for the SYSTEM account! (Generally, we do not change the SYS default tablespace account assignment.)

Quota   In the final line in Listing 21.1, you see that the user is assigned an UNLIMITED quota on the USERS tablespace. The QUOTA ON clause allows you to control how much space the user can use in a given tablespace. By default, all tablespaces (except those defined as a temporary tablespace) are assigned a quota of 0. Thus, if you want a user to be able to use a tablespace, you must allocate a quota to the tablespace for that user (unless you grant the user a role with unlimited tablespace usage).

Creating Operating System–Authenticated Users

You might create an operating system–authenticated user account for databases where security is not an issue, so letting the operating system authenticate the user is sufficient to allow database access. In these cases, the user account on the operating system and the database user account will be the same name.

By default, Oracle disables operating system authentication. You can enable use of operating system authentication by setting the database parameter REMOTE_OS_AUTHENT to TRUE (it defaults to FALSE) in the database's `init.ora` file.

Often, administrators will define a prefix for operating system-authenticated account names to indicate that the accounts are externally identified accounts. In Oracle8i, you can define this prefix name through the OS_AUTHENT_PREFIX parameter (which typically defaults to ops$) in the `init.ora` file.

WARNING Using any prefix other than a blank one can be a potential security threat. If hackers who know your naming schema for remotely authenticated users are able to gain access to your system, all they need to do is find out which users have the prefix, and they will know they can easily circumvent database security. We strongly recommend against using operating system authentication in your database.

Creating an operating system–authenticated user is much like creating a database-authenticated user. The only difference is that you replace the IDENTIFIED BY <*password*> clause with the IDENTIFIED EXTERNALLY clause. Listing 21.2 provides an example of creating a user who is authenticated via the operating system.

Listing 21.2: Creating an Operating System-Authenticated User Account

```
CREATE USER user$chris IDENTIFIED EXTERNALLY
DEFAULT TABLESPACE users
TEMPORARY TABLESPACE temp
QUOTA ON users UNLIMITED;
```

In this example, the username is given the user$ prefix (so the OS_AUTHENT_PREFIX parameter must also be set to user$). The default tablespace, temporary tablespace, and quota settings are the same as those in Listing 21.1, described in the previous section.

Privileged Users

Privileged users are those users who can perform special database activities, such as starting up and shutting down the database. In Oracle 8i, the SYSDBA and SYSOPER privileges supersede the INTERNAL user and its privileges (and, in fact, INTERNAL will be done away with in Oracle 9i). By default, SYS is not a privileged user, unless you are signing in as SYS using SYSDBA.

The SYSDBA privilege is assigned to a user account and gives that account the same privileges that the INTERNAL account has. The SYSDBA privilege encompasses all system privileges, including ADMIN OPTION, which allows granting system privileges to other users. The SYSDBA basically allows any database administration activity to take place, so take care when you grant this privilege.

The SYSOPER privilege is assigned to a user account that will perform specific types of database operational activities. SYSOPER can issue the following commands: STARTUP, SHUTDOWN, ALTER DATABASE OPEN/MOUNT, ALTER DATABASE BACKUP, ALTER TABLESPACE BEGIN/END BACKUP, ARCHIVE LOG, and RECOVER. Also, the SYSOPER has the RESTRICTED SESSION privilege.

NOTE If you are using operating system authentication for users, you will not need to grant SYSDBA or SYSOPER privileges to any account. This discussion applies only to database authentication of privileged user accounts.

Logging On as a Privileged User

When logging on, users with the SYSDBA or SYSOPER privilege must indicate that they wish to log on with that privilege. To do so, they include the string AS SYSDBA (or AS SYSOPER) in their logon string. For example, with my username Robert, I would connect using the following connect string:

```
CONNECT robert as sysdba
```

In some cases, such as at the SQL*Plus command line or when using the EXP and IMP utilities, you will need to include the ID and privilege in double quotation marks, as in this example:

```
D:\ORACLE\admin\recover>sqlplus "robert as sysdba"
SQL*Plus: Release 8.1.6.0.0 - Production on Sun May 27 22:34:45 2001
(c) Copyright 1999 Oracle Corporation.  All rights reserved.
Enter password:
Connected to:
Oracle8i Enterprise Edition Release 8.1.6.0.0 - Production
With the Partitioning option
JServer Release 8.1.6.0.0 - Production
SQL> QUIT
```

If you don't include the double quotation marks (single quotes do not work either!), you'll get an error, like this:

```
D:\ORACLE\admin\recover>sqlplus robert/robert as sysdba
Usage: SQLPLUS [ [<option>] [<logon>] [<start>] ]
where <option> ::= - | -? | [ [-M <o>] [-R <n>] [-S] ]
```

MANAGING ORACLE USER ACCOUNTS

```
<logon>   ::= <username>[/<password>][@<connect_string>] | / | /NOLOG
<start>   ::= @<filename>[.<ext>] [<parameter> ...]
  "-"  displays the usage syntax
  "-?" displays the SQL*Plus version banner
  "-M <o>" uses HTML markup options <o>
  "-R <n>" uses restricted mode <n>
  "-S" uses silent mode
```

If you attempt to sign into an account as SYSDBA or SYSOPER, Oracle will not generate an error as long as you use the correct password. However, if you try to execute a privileged action (such as shutting down the database), Oracle will generate an error indicating that you have insufficient privileges.

Viewing Privileged Users

If you are using database authentication, you can determine who is assigned the status of a privileged user using the V$PWFILE_USERS view. Here is a description of the view and an example of a query to list privileged users:

```
SQL> DESC v$pwfile_users;
 Name                                      Null?    Type
 ----------------------------------------- -------- ------------
 USERNAME                                           VARCHAR2(30)
 SYSDBA                                             VARCHAR2(5)
 SYSOPER                                            VARCHAR2(5)

SQL> SELECT * FROM v$pwfile_users;
USERNAME                       SYSDB SYSOP
------------------------------ ----- -----
INTERNAL                       TRUE  TRUE
SYS                            TRUE  TRUE
ROBERT                         TRUE  FALSE
DODO                           FALSE TRUE
```

 NOTE Not all database users will appear on this report. You will see only those users with privileged status (assigned to SYSDBA or SYSOPER).

In this example, you see that INTERNAL and SYS are both assigned SYSDBA and SYSOPER privileges. The ROBERT account is assigned SYSDBA privileges, but not SYSOPER, and the DODO account is assigned SYSOPER but not SYSDBA privileges.

Notice that the SYSTEM account does not appear in this listing. This is because it is not, by default, set up to be a privileged account.

If you are using operating system authentication, you will need to determine who is assigned to the specific group for privileged users, such as the DBA group in Unix. Then use your operating system's procedures to view the group's members.

Maintaining User Accounts

You may need to alter a user account to change the user's password, profile, or perhaps lock a bad guy out of the system. This is facilitated through the ALTER USER password command. The ALTER USER command allows you to make the following changes:

- Change a user password.
- Change a user's profile.
- Change a user's default or temporary tablespace settings.
- Alter a user's tablespace quota.
- Alter a user's default role.
- Expire the user's password, or lock out the account completely.

Here are a few examples of using the ALTER USER command:
```
ALTER USER todd DEFAULT TABLESPACE ted_data
QUOTA unlimited on ted_data;

ALTER USER badboy PASSWORD EXPIRE;

ALTER USER eddie PROFILE normal_user;
```

The DROP USER command is used to remove user accounts from the database:
```
DROP USER michael;
```

The DROP USER command will drop a user without any dependent objects. If there are dependent objects owned by that user, you will need to use the CASCADE clause, which will cause those objects to be dropped along with the user.
```
DROP USER michelle CASCADE;
```

 WARNING Take care when using the CASCADE command to drop user accounts. You don't want to cause other users' objects to become invalid!

Of course, once you have created users, you need a way to figure out how they are configured. The main data dictionary view that you can refer to for user information is the DBA_USERS view (as well as its ALL_ and USER_ versions). In addition, views like V$SESSION and V$PROCESS can give you real-time information on what users are doing.

Setting Up User Profiles

User profiles allow DBAs to control users by establishing certain rules that user accounts will follow. You can specify allowable resource usage, such as the total number of sessions that a user can have open, as well as password controls, such as when passwords expire.

 NOTE Strong passwords and forcing passwords to change often are key security issues. You should enforce a clear password policy.

Creating Profiles

To create a profile, use the CREATE PROFILE command. Once the profile is created, you can assign it to users. Listing 21.3 provides an example creating a profile.

Listing 21.3: Creating a Profile

```
CREATE PROFILE standard_user LIMIT
SESSIONS_PER_USER 3
CONNECT_TIME 30
IDLE_TIME 5
LOGICAL_READS_PER_SESSION 2000000
LOGICAL_READS_PER_CALL 2000
FAILED_LOGIN_ATTEMPTS 3
PASSWORD_LIFE_TIME 45
PASSWORD_GRACE_TIME 5
PASSWORD_REUSE_TIME 365
PASSWORD_REUSE_MAX UNLIMITED
PASSWORD_LOCK_TIME 1/24;
```

This example begins with the CREATE PROFILE command, followed by the name of this profile, STANDARD_USER. The keyword LIMIT puts the parameters included in the profile into effect. Most parameters can be set to UNLIMITED to indicate that they are to be ignored for that particular profile.

User Profile Resource Settings

To use resource limits in a profile, the RESOURCE_LIMIT parameter in the database parameter file must be set to TRUE (it defaults to FALSE). This parameter can be set dynamically with the ALTER SYSTEM command.

The profile in Listing 21.3 sets five resource limits for the users assigned to this profile:

- The total number of concurrent sessions (SESSIONS_PER_USER) is set to 3.
- The maximum connect time for a user session (CONNECT_TIME) is set to 30 minutes.
- The maximum idle time for any user session (IDLE_TIME) is set to 5 minutes.
- The total number of logical reads per session (LOGICAL_READS_PER_SESSION) is set to 2,000,000.
- The total number of logical reads per each call in each session (LOGICAL_READS_PER_CALL) is set to 2000.

You can also set CPU limits, a composite limit, and a shared pool allocation amount (for MTS). Table 21.1 lists the resource settings available for user profiles.

TABLE 21.1: RESOURCE LIMITS FOR USER PROFILES

Parameter	Description
SESSIONS_PER_USER	Limits the user to a maximum number of concurrent sessions.
CPU_PER_SESSION	Limits the amount of CPU per session, in 1/100 second units.
CPU_PER_CALL	Limits the amount of CPU per call for a given session, in 1/100 second units.
CONNECT_TIME	Limits the total time allowed for a single session, in minutes.
IDLE_TIME	Limits the total time that a given session can be idle, in minutes.
LOGICAL_READS_PER_SESSION	Sets the maximum number of data blocks that can be read per session. This includes blocks read from memory or disk.
LOGICAL_READS_PER_CALL	Sets the maximum number of data blocks that can be read per call. This includes blocks read from memory or disk.

Continued

TABLE 21.1: RESOURCE LIMITS FOR USER PROFILES (CONTINUED)

Parameter	Description
COMPOSITE_LIMIT	Allows you to define a composite limit, based on the weighted costs of the CPU_PER_SESSION, CONNECT_TIME, LOGICAL_READS_PER_SESSION, and PRIVATE_SGA statistics. You can alter the weight given to any of these parameters by using the ALTER RESOURCE COST command.
PRIVATE_SGA	If using MTS, controls how much of the shared pool can be allocated to the PGA of a given session. This value can be expressed in bytes (b) or kilobytes (k).

User Profile Password Settings

Following the resource settings in Listing 21.3 are the password limits for this user profile:

- The total number of logon attempts that fail because the user entered the wrong password (FAILED_LOGIN_ATTEMPTS) is set to 3.

- Users must change their passwords (PASSWORD_LIFE_TIME) every 45 days.

- Users have a grace period (PASSWORD_GRACE_TIME) of 5 days after a password has expired to change the password.

- The amount of time allowed between reuse of the same password (PASSWORD_REUSE_TIME) is 365 days.

- The number of times that a password must be changed before an old password can be reused (PASSWORD_REUSE_MAX) is set to UNLIMITED. This is required since the PASSWORD_REUSE_TIME parameter is set in this profile.

- A user account will be locked out after the maximum failed logon attempts limit is reached (PASSWORD_LOCK_TIME) for one hour (1/24 day).

You might have noticed the odd-looking value for the PASSWORD_LOCK_TIME parameter. This parameter is expressed in days, so a 1 for this parameter would be one day. However, you probably don't want to lock out an account for a whole day due to failed logon attempts. To define a part of a day, you divide a day into units. Thus, a day is 24 hours, 1440 minutes, or 86,400 seconds. For example, to represent one hour, use 1/24. For a half hour, use 1/48 (there are 48 half hours in the day). To unlock an account after 2 minutes, use the value 2/1440.

Another option for setting password limits is to use the PASSWORD_VERIFY_FUNCTION parameter to create a password validation function. Using this function, you can verify any changes to account passwords to ensure that they meet specific criteria that you define for those passwords. This allows DBAs to enforce password policies such as strong passwords or a requirement for certain characters to be contained within the password. The password verify function must be owned by SYS and takes three parameters, as shown here:

```
SYS.YOUR_PASSWORD_FUNCTION_NAME_HERE
(   user_id         IN      VARCHAR2(30),
    new_password    IN      VARCHAR2(30),
    old_password    IN      VARCHAR2(30)
) RETURN BOOLEAN;
```

Notice that you name the password verify function. This means that your database may contain more than one function, and different profiles may use different functions. The function should return a BOOLEAN value (TRUE or FALSE) indicating if the password passes the test. This function will be executed each time the password is changed (for example through the ALTER USER IDENTIFIED BY command) and the password is verified.

NOTE Password controls are all well and good, but one of the problems is that there often is not a way for the users to actually change their passwords. Many users do not have direct access to the database through a facility such as SQL*Plus, so they cannot issue an ALTER USER command (which will be used to alter the user password). Also, users coming in through applications will not realize that their passwords are about to expire. These issues will need to be dealt with programmatically.

Table 21.2 summarizes the password settings available for user profiles.

TABLE 21.2: PASSWORD CONTROLS FOR USER PROFILES

Parameter	Description
FAILED_LOGIN_ATTEMPTS	Specifies the total number of failed logon attempts that may occur before the account is automatically locked out. The account will be unlocked after PASSWORD_LOCK_TIME expires.

Continued

TABLE 21.2: PASSWORD CONTROLS FOR USER PROFILES (CONTINUED)	
Parameter	Description
PASSWORD_LIFE_TIME	Indicates the maximum time allowed between password changes, expressed in days. Once this number of days has been exceeded, the account will be locked out, unless the PASSWORD_GRACE_TIME parameter is set. The DBA (or security administrator) will need to reset the account if this occurs.
PASSWORD_REUSE_TIME	Indicates the maximum number of days that must pass before a password can be reused. This must be set to UNLIMITED if PASSWORD_REUSE_MAX is set.
PASSWORD_REUSE_MAX	Indicates the number of times that a password must be changed before an old password can be reused. This must be set to UNLIMITED if PASSWORD_REUSE_TIME is set.
PASSWORD_LOCK_TIME	Indicates how long a password will be locked if the account is locked out automatically due to a violation of the restriction set by FAILED_LOGIN_ATTEMPTS.
PASSWORD_GRACE_TIME	Sets the amount of time, in days, that an account will be able to be logged in to after a password has expired. After this time, the account will be locked out.
PASSWORD_VERIFY_FUNCTION	Specifies the use of a user-defined function that allows you to define rules for the use of passwords. With this function, you can enforce the use of strong passwords, for example.

Using Profiles

Once you have created a profile, you can assign that profile to users via the CREATE USER or ALTER USER commands. For example, if you wished to create a user account called Michael and assign the STANDARD_USER profile (created earlier in Listing 21.3), the CREATE USER statement would look something like this:

```
CREATE USER michael IDENTIFIED BY sinclair
PROFILE standard_user
DEFAULT TABLESPACE users
TEMPORARY TABLESPACE temp;
```

If the Michael user account already exists, you would use the ALTER USER command to modify his account, like this:

```
ALTER USER michael
PROFILE standard_user;
```

Maintaining Profiles

The ALTER PROFILE command allows you to add, remove, or change resource and password parameters in existing profiles. Listing 21.4 provides an example of the use of the ALTER PROFILE command.

Listing 21.4: Changing a Profile

```
ALTER PROFILE standard_user LIMIT
SESSIONS_PER_USER 5
CONNECT_TIME UNLIMITED
IDLE_TIME 10
FAILED_LOGIN_ATTEMPTS 5
PASSWORD_LOCK_TIME 1/48;
```

This example alters the STANDARD_USER profile, created in Listing 21.3. Here, we are changing the total number of concurrent sessions that an account can have open at one time to five using the SESSION_PER_USER parameter. Then we allowed all user sessions to be connected for an unlimited amount of time with the CONNECT_TIME parameter. Also, we changed the amount of time that a session can sit idle to 10 minutes using the IDLE_TIME parameter. We also changed two password parameters. The first change allows five logon attempts to fail before we lock out the account. The second change locks out the account for 30 minutes (the original setting was an hour).

To drop a profile, use the DROP PROFILE command:

```
DROP PROFILE slow_queries;
```

If users are assigned to the profile, you will need to use the CASCADE option. This will cause all existing users to be removed from the profile that is being dropped. They will, by default, then be assigned to the DEFAULT profile.

As you might guess, the DBA_PROFILES, USER_PROFILES, and ALL_PROFILES views provide information about profiles currently set up in your database. Each profile and its settings are listed in the view. If you wish to determine which profile a user is assigned to, check the DBA_USERS view (or its corresponding USER_ or ALL_ view). This view includes a PROFILES column, which lists the profile to which the user is assigned.

Defining Grants

Once you have created users, you probably want them to be able to do something. In order for a user account to be able to do anything in Oracle, it must have been given the ability to do that. *Grants* are the facility through which access to database objects, or the ability to perform some action on the database (such as create a tablespace) is regulated. If the user doesn't have the grant, the user cannot perform the action. Therefore, grants are a part of the foundation of Oracle's security. You can grant privileges to specific users, roles (discussed in the next section), or to PUBLIC. Granting privileges to PUBLIC basically gives every account the privilege.

Grants come in two flavors:

- *System-level grants* are given to allow the user to execute specific SQL commands (such as the SQL command CREATE TABLE or CREATE INDEX).
- *Object-level grants* give the user the ability to perform some action on an existing object (such as select from or insert into a given table).

 TIP A quick reference to system and object grants can be found in Appendix G on the CD.

Issuing and Revoking System-Level Grants

System-level grants allow you to do anything from altering clusters to updating tables. There are a number of privileges that can be granted (or revoked) to a specific user. To issue a grant, use the GRANT command, as in these examples:

```
GRANT CREATE TABLE TO ted;
GRANT CREATE SESSION TO fred;
```

If you wish to allow the user the ability to grant the same privileges to others, use the WITH ADMIN OPTION when granting that user privileges:

```
GRANT CREATE ANY TABLE TO ted WITH ADMIN OPTION;
```

This will allow that user to grant the same privilege to other users. (Generally, we hesitate to use this option because it's a potential security hole.) If the WITH ADMIN OPTION is not used, the user receiving the grant cannot give that grant to others.

System-level grants can be used as soon as they are issued, so you don't need to log on or log out to use them. You can also use the GRANT ALL command (or GRANT ALL PRIVILEGES command) to grant all privileges to a given account.

If you need to revoke a specific privilege, use the REVOKE privilege, as in this example:

```
REVOKE CREATE ANY TABLE FROM lon;
```

Note that if you revoke a system privilege from one user, and that user assigned that privilege to other users, the other users will still continue to have that privilege. Thus, if you fired Nat, and he had earlier given Sid the CREATE SESSION grant, Sid will still have the CREATE SESSION privilege after you revoke it from Nat's account.

Issuing and Revoking Object-Level Grants

Object-level grants allow you to perform some DML action (such as INSERT rows into a table) on a specific object. For example, if Rich created a table in the schema called PROD, and he wanted Tim to be able to access it, Rich would need to give Tim access to that object. Rich would do this through the use of the GRANT command.

If you wish to grant someone access to an object for DML operations and you wish them to be able to grant that same access to others as well, you use the WITH GRANT OPTION keyword (similar to the WITH ADMIN OPTION keyword that you use for system grants). You can also use the ALL keyword to grant all privileges on an object to a user. Here is an example:

```
GRANT ALL ON my_table TO freddie WITH GRANT OPTION;
```

The GRANT command also allows you to control the ability to INSERT or UPDATE a specific column in a table, as well as using a specific column in a foreign key reference. You simply list the column after you indicate the type of grant you are giving. Here are some more examples of using the object-level GRANT command:

```
GRANT SELECT on user_information TO george;
GRANT UPDATE(user_name) on user_information TO my_user;
```

As with system-level grants, the effects of granting (or revoking) object privileges are immediate, so you don't need to log out and back in to use them.

TIP Create owning schemas to own the schema objects you are going to create. Grant other user accounts access to these objects, but do not allow users to access the schema owning account.

A major difference between system and object grants is what happens when you revoke a grant from a user. Let's say that you granted Ted access to a table called TEST_RESULTS using the WITH GRANT OPTION. If Ted grants access to that table to Sid and Danny, when you revoke Ted's access to that object, the revoke will cascade down to Sid and Danny. Suddenly, Sid and Danny will find themselves unable to access the object (unless they have grants to that same object through some other means, such as a role or a grant from another user). So, be careful how you administer your grants. (I tend to avoid using the WITH GRANT option.) Here are some examples of revoking object privileges:

```
REVOKE ALL ON my_table FROM freddie;
REVOKE ALL ON my_table FROM freddie CASCADE CONSTRAINTS;
```

Viewing Grant Information

These are several data dictionary views that are useful for managing both system-level and object-level grants. These views are listed in Table 21.3.

TABLE 21.3: VIEWS FOR GRANTS

View (DBA, USER, and ALL)	Description
_SYS_PRIVS	Lists all system privileges that a user has. Also indicates if the user can grant those same privileges.
_TAB_PRIVS	Lists all table privileges that a user has. Also indicates if the user can grant those same privileges.
_COL_PRIVS	Lists all column privileges granted on the system.
_COL_PRIVS_MADE	Lists all column privileges granted by the user.
_COL_PRIVS_RECD	Lists all column privileges granted to the user.

Setting Up Roles

If you had a system with thousands of users, you can imagine that it might become a bit tedious to grant individual users each system and object grant that they needed. Additionally, the maintenance might become very burdensome, as you would need to update the grants for each user each time you added or removed an object from the database. Roles were designed to deal with just this problem.

A *role* is somewhat like a user in that privileges (system or object) are granted to the role. The difference is that you cannot log on using a role name. Once the privileges are granted to the role using the GRANT command, the role (which perhaps is like one big privilege) is granted to any number of users who require those privileges. You can see how roles make administration of the database much easier. If you add an object, you simply add the new grants to that object to a single role, rather than individual users. The users receive the grants to that object through the role.

Predefined Roles

Once an Oracle database is created, three predefined roles are created: CONNECT, RESOURCE, and DBA. Depending on the products installed, additional roles may be created as well; in a normal database, you will find more than 10 default roles installed. Generally, it is a better idea to use your own roles for administrative purposes, rather than use the ones that Oracle provides. This is because the CONNECT, RESOURCE, and DBA roles contain many privileges that you may not want to give users, and may, in fact, represent security risks.

Oracle also provides some administrative roles—such as EXP_FULL_DATABASE, IMP_FULL_DATABASE, and RECOVERY_CATALOG_OWNER—that are associated with specific Oracle utilities such as Export, Import, and RMAN. You should use these roles as recommended in the documentation for these products. You can, of course, re-create those roles and the privileges they are granted if you desire, but in the case of these products, you don't want to neglect a privilege that the utility might require. If you want to take a look at the different privileges that are granted to the various default roles that Oracle creates, see the "Viewing Role Information" section, coming up shortly.

A Caveat about Roles and PL/SQL

If you are going to access a database object in your PL/SQL (for example, issue SELECT statements against it), you must be aware of the interaction of roles, users, and PL/SQL. By default, a PL/SQL object is compiled (and executed) using the rights of the creator of the PL/SQL routine. In this case, privileges to all objects that the object will need should be granted directly to that user, rather than through a role. This is because the validation routine that Oracle goes through to ensure the user has the correct rights to that object occurs at compile time.

Since roles can be enabled or disabled at any time, there is no way to guarantee that the role will be enabled when you execute the procedure. Thus, when using DEFINER rights, stored procedures will fail to compile if any object access is facilitated through roles. The bottom line is that if you create a PL/SQL routine using the default AUTHID DEFINER clause, you must have directly granted the required access to the objects to the schema that is creating the object for that object to compile.

Continued

> **CONTINUED**
>
> If, on the other hand, you use the AUTHID CURRENT_USER clause of the CREATE PROCEDURE, CREATE FUNCTION, CREATE PACKAGE, or CREATE TYPE command, the privileges of the user running the program will be those that are used, and validation occurs at runtime. This removes the problems with using roles and PL/SQL routines. See Appendix F on the CD for more details on the distinctions between AUTHID CURRENT_USER and AUTHID DEFINER.

Creating Roles

Four methods of authentication are provided for roles: no authentication, operating system authentication (not supported with MTS), database authentication, and central naming authentication. Implementation of operating system authentication of roles varies by operating system, so see your operating system's documentation for more information about implementing this method.

You create roles by using the CREATE ROLE command, followed by the role name. (A role name cannot be the same name as a username.) If you wish to make the role password-protected, use the IDENTIFIED BY clause, followed by the password for the role. You can also specify that a role should be authenticated by an external method, such as by the operating system logon. To indicate that the role is authenticated through a central naming mechanism, such as Oracle Internet Directory, use the GLOBALLY clause.

Here are a couple of examples of creating roles in Oracle8i:

```
CREATE ROLE read_all_data;
CREATE ROLE secret_role IDENTIFIED BY secret_role;
```

The first role, READ_ALL_DATA, is not password-protected. The second role, SECRET_ROLE, is password-protected. The only time that the role password will be required is when a user tries to enable the role with the SET ROLE statement.

When you create a user, you cannot define a default role. However, you can use the ALTER USER to define default roles for that user. Thus, you can cause specific roles to not be enabled by default when a user logs in to the database initially. This might be handy for users who have DBA privileges, but you want to make them cautiously use those privileges, and perhaps even secure those privileges a bit more by requiring that a separate password be entered when enabling the role.

WARNING A nasty little snag is the MAX_ENABLED_ROLES parameter in `init.ora`. This parameter places a ceiling on the total number of roles that can be assigned in a database. The default is 20. Typically, a good-sized Oracle8i database will have more than 20 roles assigned, so you will need to increase this parameter. This problem occurs more often when doing upgrades from Oracle7 because of the additional default roles in Oracle8i.

As you probably expected, you can remove roles with the DROP ROLE command:
```
DROP ROLE bad_role;
```

Granting Roles

Once you create a role, you will then grant either system or object privileges to that role, just as you would to a user. Next, you can grant the roles to users using the GRANT command, like this:
```
GRANT SELECT ON my_table TO read_all_data;
```
Here is the order of grant/role operations:

1. Create the role.
2. Assign privileges to the role using the GRANT command.
3. Grant the role to database users using the GRANT command.

If you are assigning system privileges to a role, you can use the WITH ADMIN OPTION to allow users assigned the role to grant the system privileges to other users. If you grant the role using the WITH ADMIN OPTION, you are giving the grantee of the role the following privileges:

- The grantee can grant the role to another user.
- The grantee can revoke the role from another user.
- The grantee can change the password of the role or its authorization method.
- The grantee can drop the role.

You cannot use the WITH GRANT OPTION when granting object privileges to a role.

There are some restrictions to granting roles. First, the UNLIMITED TABLESPACE system privilege cannot be granted to a role. Also the INDEX and REFERENCES privileges cannot be granted to a role, nor can a role be granted to itself. Also, circular references to roles are not allowed (for example, granting role DATA_OWNER to role DATA_ALL, and then granting the DATA_ALL role back to DATA_OWNER).

Enabling Roles

By default, all roles are enabled for a user when the user logs in. However, you can change your enabled roles by using the SET ROLE command, as follows:

```
SET ROLE read_all_data;
```

If the IDENTIFIED BY clause was used in the role's definition, the user will need to provide the password to this role when using the SET ROLE command. This is accomplished through the IDENTIFIED BY clause of the SET ROLE command:

```
SET ROLE secret_role IDENTIFIED BY secret_role;
```

Viewing Role Information

Several data dictionary views provide information about roles. These views are listed in Table 21.4. You will probably want to use these views in combination with the views that show information about grants to get a complete picture of the nature of various roles in the database.

TABLE 21.4: VIEWS FOR ROLES

View	Description
DBA_ROLES	Lists all roles in the database and if they require authentication to use.
DBA_ROLE_PRIVS	Lists the grantee of all roles. (The *grantee* is the user or role granted the role.) The view also indicates if the ADMIN option was granted and if the role is part of the user's default list of roles.
SESSION_ROLES	Lists the currently enabled roles for a session.
ROLE_ROLE_PRIVS	Lists information on roles assigned to other roles. It is valid for only the roles that the current user has access to (including nondefault roles).
ROLE_SYS_PRIVS	Lists all system privileges for roles that the user has access to.
ROLE_TAB_PRIVS	Lists all table privileges (INSERT, UPDATE, etc.) granted to roles that the current user has access to.

Enforcing Row-Level Security

We have discussed how to control entire sets of data within tables, granting access to some users and not to others. However, you may want users to have access to some rows in a table, but not be able to access other rows. This is known as *row-level security*.

Oracle8i has a new feature called *virtual private database (VPD)* or *fine-grained access control (FGAC)* that can be used to control access to table data. Prior to the introduction of the FGAC feature, the DBA's ability to provide row-level security on tables was fairly limited. Generally, the only method available was the use of views and, occasionally, triggers. Using views for access control is not as flexible as Oracle8i's new FGAC, but this method has the benefit of being fairly easy to set up.

Another common method used to secure data in a database is to "lock down" all of the data, and make it accessible only through calls to stored procedures. This approach has the benefit of tightly controlling access to the data in the database, but this is a major shortcoming as well. Restricting access to data via stored procedures tends to put a cramp in ad hoc users' styles. You might set up stored procedures to control DML activity and grant SELECT privileges only to ad hoc users, but then you are losing some control over your ability to restrict read access to data. If you want to use stored procedures, consider combining them with views or FGAC to achieve a fairly well-secured database.

Using Views for Row-Level Security

Views may be a viable option if you have a few security requirements that are easy to implement and the views have a minimal impact on the database. As your security requirements get more complex, the views that you need to create to go with them also become more complex and, generally, less efficient. The other problem with using views to secure databases is that some views cannot be updated. Thus, as your security requirements increase, you may find that you suddenly are unable to update the table you are securing with a view. This adds to the complexity of the structure, as you then need to add additional views, procedures, and the like.

Listing 21.5 provides an example of a view used to secure a table.

Listing 21.5: Securing a Table's Data with a View

```
-- Create the table.
CREATE TABLE user_information
(  user_name      VARCHAR2(30),
   information    VARCHAR2(2000) );
```

```
-- Create the view.
CREATE OR REPLACE VIEW secured_information AS
SELECT information
FROM user_information
WHERE user_name=USER
WITH CHECK OPTION;
```

In this example, the USER keyword indicates that the view should just show information on the current user. You would probably create a BEFORE INSERT trigger on the table to make sure that the username was loaded into the USER_NAME column when you inserted data into the table (that way, you could insert through the view itself).

Using FGAC

Roles and grants are somewhat of an all-or-nothing proposition. Either you can access an object or you cannot access it. What if you want to be able to control a user's access to the data within a table? For example, let's say that you are writing a package for a government agency, and different personnel are cleared for different security levels. The data they are going to access is of the same nature, so it logically belongs in the same table. But how do you ensure that a user with the lowest clearance level cannot see records classified at higher clearance levels? Prior to Oracle8i, the solution might have been to use views, or perhaps to just split up the data into different tables, granting the different users access as required. These solutions are administratively complicated and provide less-than-ideal performance. From a design standpoint, they just seem screwy, don't they?

Sometimes, security is moved to the application level, but how safe do you think that makes your secrets? A well-placed hacker with a copy of SQL*Plus could just find his way into your database and hack to his heart's content, with nothing but a password between him and your data.

Enter FGAC. This feature of Oracle8i Enterprise Edition allows you to design your database tables such that access to the data within these tables is controlled directly at the database level.

NOTE FGAC is available only with the Enterprise Edition of Oracle8i. If you are not running Oracle8i Enterprise Edition, you will not be able to use the features of this powerful security option.

FGAC Features

FGAC provides what is known as *enhanced security*. No matter how users sign in—from an application or from some ad hoc tool (like SQL*Plus or Microsoft Access)—they will be able to see only the information that they are allowed to see. FGAC is not the final solution to protecting your database, but it does go a long way toward securing your data.

FGAC has several benefits:

- It transparently enforces *security policies*. Security policies are rules established to determine who has access to what data.

- FGAC allows you to modify security policies transparently, without the user noticing (unless the security policy change affects them in some way, of course).

- FGAC is a scalable option. FGAC is based on the use of SQL, thus the SQL statements that are generated are stored in the shared pool and are available for reuse as long as reusability rules are followed.

- FGAC is flexible and allows complex security policies to be enforced. Multiple criteria can be enforced, and final access decisions don't need to be made until runtime, making FGAC even more flexible.

Your Mission, If You Choose to Accept It ... Securing a Table

You are sitting in a dark office. You can barely make out the faces of the two men and one woman sitting at the table, but they know what you can do. After all, you are an Oracle DBA, and you are carrying around that Sybex book *Mastering Oracle8i*, so you must be a sharp cookie! These dark figures work for the CSS (Center for Secret Stuff), and they need you to secure their database data. They have a data model with a table called SECRET_STUFF (we don't like this name a whole lot, so we will change it shortly), which contains—you guessed it—all of their secret information. The problem is that they want all of their agents to have access to this data (and they would like the public to be able to access some of it), but they want to be able to restrict access to the data in the table based on the agent's security clearance.

The table is fairly simple. It has three columns:

- SECRET_ID, which is just a monotonically increasing number

- SECRET_DATE, which is when this data was collected

- SECRET_INFORMATION, which contains the secret information that they need you to help secure

Your mission is to secure the information based on a security clearance level. They have four clearance levels: Public, Secret, Top Secret, and If You Know You Die.

You have decided to take on this challenge. In doing so, you will follow five basic steps:

1. Clearly define the security policy.
2. Modify the table as required to support the security policy and implementation of FGAC.
3. For each user who signs into the database, define their security level upon logon for later use. You will create a package to define the security level. This package is called the *application context-setting package*.
4. Use an event trigger at logon to execute this context-setting package.
5. Create a second package that will handle the actual security enforcement. This package will append a WHERE clause statement onto the SQL being passed to the table to control access to the table.
6. Register the security-checking package created in step 5 with the database so that it is executed every time.

In the next few pages, we will look at each of these steps in detail. In the end, you will have created the security-checking package needed by your client. You will then collect your pay and watch your back as you exit the building.

Defining the Security Policy and Modifying the Table

As noted earlier, the client has established four levels of security clearance. You are going to assign numbers to these levels, as follows:

Public	0
Secret	10
Top Secret	20
If You Know You Die	100

You are also going to create a table that lists each user and assigns a security level to that user (you would probably want to secure that table as well, but we only have so many pages in this book!).

 NOTE In the real world, we would define other policies related to security. This would include such things as who is authorized to give access to the data, and through what means this access will be granted. This is not a book on security administration, so we won't spend a great deal of time on those issues.

Having defined the security policy, you need to create the SQL statements to create the initial schemas you will use, as shown in Listing 21.6.

Listing 21.6: Setting Up the Security Policy

```
-- Create the schemas and basic stuff.
CONNECT SYSTEM
DROP USER spy_owner CASCADE;
DROP USER boss_spy;
DROP USER public_access;
DROP USER secret_spy;
DROP USER top_secret_spy;
DROP USER license_to_kill;

-- Now, create the object-owning schema, spy_owner.
CREATE USER spy_owner IDENTIFIED BY spy_owner
DEFAULT TABLESPACE spy_data
TEMPORARY TABLESPACE temp
QUOTA UNLIMITED ON spy_data;

-- Now, create the users who will want to access the data.
CREATE USER boss_spy IDENTIFIED BY boss_spy
DEFAULT TABLESPACE spy_data
TEMPORARY TABLESPACE temp;

CREATE USER public_access IDENTIFIED BY public_access
DEFAULT TABLESPACE spy_data
TEMPORARY TABLESPACE temp;

CREATE USER secret_spy IDENTIFIED BY secret_spy
DEFAULT TABLESPACE spy_data
TEMPORARY TABLESPACE temp;

CREATE USER top_secret_spy IDENTIFIED BY top_secret_spy
DEFAULT TABLESPACE spy_data
TEMPORARY TABLESPACE temp;

CREATE USER license_to_kill IDENTIFIED BY license_to_kill
DEFAULT TABLESPACE spy_data
TEMPORARY TABLESPACE temp;
```

```sql
-- Now issue the grants needed.
-- spy_owner needs more grants than the other users.
GRANT CONNECT TO spy_owner;
GRANT CREATE PUBLIC SYNONYM TO spy_owner;
GRANT DROP PUBLIC SYNONYM TO spy_owner;
GRANT CREATE PROCEDURE TO spy_owner;
GRANT CREATE ROLE TO spy_owner;

GRANT CREATE SESSION TO spy_owner;
GRANT CREATE SESSION TO boss_spy;
GRANT CREATE SESSION TO public_access;
GRANT CREATE SESSION TO secret_spy;
GRANT CREATE SESSION TO top_secret_spy;
GRANT CREATE SESSION TO license_to_kill;

-- Connect as spy_owner to create the objects.
CONNECT spy_owner/spy_owner

-- Now, create the tables we will need.
CREATE TABLE tbl_security_codes
( security_id     NUMBER PRIMARY KEY,
  security_code   VARCHAR2(30) )
TABLESPACE spy_data
STORAGE (INITIAL 100k NEXT 100k);

CREATE TABLE tbl_user_id
( user_id         NUMBER PRIMARY KEY,
  user_name       VARCHAR2(30),
  security_level NUMBER )
TABLESPACE spy_data
STORAGE (INITIAL 100k NEXT 100k);

CREATE TABLE tbl_secured_information
( min_security_id      NUMBER,
  secret_information   VARCHAR2(2000) )
TABLESPACE spy_data
STORAGE (INITIAL 100k NEXT 100k);

-- Create public synonyms to these objects.
```

```sql
DROP PUBLIC SYNONYM tbl_secured_information;
DROP PUBLIC SYNONYM tbl_user_id;
DROP PUBLIC SYNONYM tbl_security_codes;
CREATE PUBLIC SYNONYM tbl_secured_information FOR tbl_secured_information;
CREATE PUBLIC SYNONYM tbl_user_id FOR tbl_user_id;
CREATE PUBLIC SYNONYM tbl_security_codes FOR tbl_security_codes;

-- Create a role to give access to these objects to the spies.
CREATE ROLE spy_access identified BY spy_access;

-- Grant privileges to the role to access tables.
GRANT SELECT ON tbl_security_codes TO spy_access;
GRANT SELECT ON tbl_user_id TO spy_access;
GRANT SELECT ON tbl_secured_information TO spy_access;

-- Grant the role to the users.
GRANT spy_access TO boss_spy;
GRANT spy_access TO public_access;
GRANT spy_access TO secret_spy;
GRANT spy_access TO top_secret_spy;
GRANT spy_access TO license_to_kill;

-- Now, populate the security code table.
INSERT INTO tbl_security_codes VALUES (0, 'PUBLIC');
INSERT INTO tbl_security_codes VALUES (10, 'SECRET');
INSERT INTO tbl_security_codes VALUES (20, 'TOP SECRET');
INSERT INTO tbl_security_codes VALUES (100, 'IF YOU KNOW YOU DIE');

-- Populate the users table (10000 indicates spy management,
-- access to everything!).
INSERT INTO tbl_user_id VALUES (1,'BOSS_SPY',10000);
INSERT INTO tbl_user_id VALUES (2,'PUBLIC_ACCESS',0);
INSERT INTO tbl_user_id VALUES (3,'SECRET_SPY',10);
INSERT INTO tbl_user_id VALUES (4,'TOP_SECRET_SPY',20);
INSERT INTO tbl_user_id VALUES (5,'LICENSE_TO_KILL',100);

-- Populate some secret data!!
INSERT INTO tbl_secured_information VALUES
(0, 'This is boring public information');
```

```
INSERT INTO tbl_secured_information VALUES (10, 'Men are NOT from Mars!!');
INSERT INTO tbl_secured_information VALUES
(20, 'But the Aliens are from Mars!!');
INSERT INTO tbl_secured_information VALUES
(100, 'And they are here to take over the world.');
COMMIT;
```

Listing 21.6 creates a table that stores all the secret code levels and associates a number with those levels. For example, level 0 is public information, and level 20 is top secret. It also defines five employees (using their secret code names so as to not give away their true spy identities). For example, the chief of the spies is called boss spy. The public access account is for a public-access kiosk that the bureau is setting up in the lobby. Then there is secret spy, who really isn't that much of an agent (in fact, we think he may work for Microsoft). Because your client is not too sure of him, his access is not as great as that of the next user, top secret spy. Finally, you have top dog spy, code-named license to kill (he's the guy sitting deep in the shadows, smoking his third pack of Camels).

Each of these spies is assigned a classification level. For example, secret spy is a class 10, so he can see any documents with security codes 10 or 0; top secret can see codes 20, 10, and 0, and so on. Notice that boss spy is level 10,000, so she can see everything (and we hope she is trustworthy!).

But there's a problem: Right now, all of the users can see any of the classified data. This security breach is apparent from the following query:

```
CONNECT public_access/public_access
SELECT * FROM tbl_secured_information;
SQL> SELECT * FROM tbl_secured_information;

MIN_SECURITY_ID SECRET_INFORMATION
--------------- ----------------------------------------
              0 This is boring public information
             10 Men are NOT from Mars!!
             20 But the Aliens are from Mars!!
            100 And they are here to take over the world.
```

To correct this problem, you will set up an FGAC security policy on the TBL_SECURED_INFORMATION table. You will start in the next section, by creating an application context package.

Creating an Application Context Package

You will create an application context package that establishes a private user context area upon user logon. (I'm not sure why they decided to call this the application

context package; user sign-on context package seems like a more appropriate name.) The *context area* is an area of private memory that is unique to every session connected to the database. You will create placeholders in this memory area to store some values that are set at logon. Later in the process, you will read the context memory area and retrieve these stored memory areas for use. This is an optional step. You could define the context area every time the user accesses the object, but this approach is faster, because you do these checks only once.

You place values into the context area by creating a package or function that is called each time users log on to the database. For this project, you will store the user's assigned security level into a context variable whenever the user logs in. This way, you can quickly retrieve this security value from the context area when you need it. This saves multiple trips to the security table to look up the security ID each time you need that value.

Before you can use a context namespace, you must first create the context namespace, which needs to be done only once for each specific context area. The context namespace is created using the CREATE CONTEXT command (or you can use CREATE OR REPLACE CONTEXT, if you prefer). When you create the context namespace, you define the package that will be used to set the values to be stored in the context namespace. Typically, when you create the context, the associated package will not have been created yet, and that's okay. You will create that package next.

NOTE Creating the context namespace is similar to programming with a pointer. You first create the pointer, and then you allocate memory to it. The same is true with a context. You first create the context, and then the context setting package "allocates" what is to be stored to the context. (Okay, so all comparisons have limitations!)

After you have created the context area, you will use the DBMS_SESSION.SET_CONTEXT package to store a value in a context area. This package allows you to create what amounts to variables and assign values to these variables. These variables and their assigned values are then poked into memory for quick retrieval later. The DBMS_SESSION.SET_CONTEXT procedure takes three parameters. Here is the procedure definition:

```
PROCEDURE DBMS_SESSION.SET_CONTEXT
( NAMESPACE      VARCHAR2,
  ATTRIBUTE      VARCHAR2,
  VALUE          VARCHAR2);
```

When you call the SET_CONTEXT procedure from your context setting package or function, you simply pass it the name of the context you want to use, the name of the context variable you wish to create, and the value you wish to store associated with that variable.

When you create the application context package, this package will take one parameter, which is the username of the user who is signing onto the database. You use the username to cross-reference with the TBL_USER_ID table columns USER_NAME and SECURITY_LEVEL to determine what the proper security level setting for the user should be. You then set a context variable called security_level to the correct security level for the user. You will use a database logon trigger to call the package.

Listing 21.7 shows the creation of a context and then the creation of the context-checking package.

Listing 21.7: Creating the Context and Context-Checking Package

```
-- Grant the required privilege to create the context.
CONNECT system/robert
GRANT CREATE ANY CONTEXT TO spy_owner;
GRANT DROP ANY CONTEXT TO spy_owner;
GRANT CREATE ANY TRIGGER TO spy_owner;
GRANT ADMINISTER DATABASE TRIGGER TO spy_owner;

-- Now, connect and create the context. We will reference the
-- currently nonexisting package pkg_spy_owner_context_01 as the
-- context-checking package. We will write this package next.
CONNECT spy_owner/spy_owner

-- Drop any preexisting context.
DROP CONTEXT spy_owner.cont_spy_owner_01;

-- Create the context. Note that we could have used CREATE OR
-- REPLACE instead.
CREATE CONTEXT cont_spy_owner_01
USING spy_owner.pkg_spy_owner_context_01;

-- Now, create the pkg_spy_owner_context_01 package header.
CREATE OR REPLACE package spy_owner.pkg_spy_owner_context_01
AUTHID DEFINER AS
PROCEDURE proc_get_spy_context(p_usern IN VARCHAR2);
END;
```

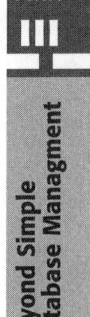

```
/

-- Now, create the package body.
CREATE OR REPLACE PACKAGE BODY pkg_spy_owner_context_01
AS
PROCEDURE proc_get_spy_context(p_usern IN VARCHAR2)
IS
V_Spy_clearance    NUMBER;
BEGIN

    -- Now, take the p_usern, look it up in our
    -- tbl_userid table and get the correct clearance
    -- for this spy.
    SELECT security_level
    INTO v_spy_clearance
    FROM spy_owner.tbl_user_id
    WHERE user_name=p_usern;

  -- These next two lines will store the username and the
  -- user clearance level in the context for later use.
SYS.DBMS_SESSION.SET_CONTEXT('cont_spy_owner_01','v_spy_clearance',
  v_spy_clearance);
SYS.DBMS_SESSION.SET_CONTEXT('cont_spy_owner_01','spy_id',p_usern);
END proc_get_spy_context;
END pkg_spy_owner_context_01;
/
```

NOTE Notice the use of the DROP CONTEXT command in the example. This command will drop any existing context. To create a context, you must have the CREATE ANY CONTEXT privilege. To drop a context requires the DROP ANY CONTEXT privilege.

Keep in mind that setting the context, as done in Listing 21.7, and the actual implementation of FGAC are two different things. You are only setting the context area with the username and the clearance code because it will make the performance of your security policy (which truly implements FGAC) better.

Executing the Context Package at User Logon

Once the context-checking package is in place, you need to create a database logon event trigger to call the application context package. It is the job of this trigger to fire when the user logs in to the database. The user's context area will be created, and then the application context package will be executed, determining the security level of the user.

To create this logon trigger, you use the built-in SQL function SYS_CONTEXT. This function returns the value of a specific context variable to the calling program or SQL statement. Oracle provides a built-in context namespace for each user session called USERENV. You will use this built-in context namespace to get the username of the user who is logging in to the database. You will then pass that username to the application context-checking package. You will use the values stored in the context areas shortly. Listing 21.8 shows the logon trigger.

Listing 21.8: Setting the Application Context with a Logon Trigger

```
CONNECT spy_owner/spy_owner

-- The logon trigger
CREATE OR REPLACE TRIGGER tr_db_logon_01
AFTER LOGON ON DATABASE
DECLARE
     spy_id     VARCHAR2(30);
BEGIN
     spy_id:=sys_context('USERENV','SESSION_USER');
     pkg_spy_owner_context_01.proc_get_spy_context(spy_id);
EXCEPTION
     WHEN others THEN
NULL;
END;
/
```

Creating the Security Enforcement Package

The next step is to create the security enforcement package. The security enforcement package will be executed when a user attempts to access the table that the security enforcement package will be assigned to in the next step. To enforce the row-level security, the security enforcement package adds a *dynamic predicate* to the SQL statement that is being executed. The dynamic predicate becomes an additional restriction to be appended to the SQL statement to be executed (basically, extending the WHERE clause to include restrictions for the implementation of row security).

You can actually take advantage of FGAC by just writing this policy package and taking the next step, which is to register the package with the database. You don't need to use contexts to use FGAC.

In this example, you will append a predicate that basically says something to this effect:

WHERE users_security_level>=tbl_secured_information.min_security_id

Thus, if the user's security level is greater than the minimum required security level in the TBL_SECURED_INFORMATION table, the user will be able to perform a given operation on that table (such as UPDATE or SELECT). The security enforcement package (called PKG_TBL_SECURED_INFO_01 in this example) will construct this predicate and return it as a VARCHAR2 datatype to the database, where it will be applied to the SQL statement. Listing 21.9 provides an example of the creation of the security enforcement package.

NOTE The additional predicate does not appear in data dictionary views of the SQL statement, such as V$SQL.

Listing 21.9: Creating the Security Enforcement Package

```
CONNECT spy_owner/spy_owner
CREATE OR REPLACE PACKAGE pkg_spy_auth
AUTHID DEFINER AS
FUNCTION fu_spy_check(p_schema VARCHAR2, p_name VARCHAR2)
RETURN VARCHAR2;
END;
/

CREATE OR REPLACE PACKAGE body pkg_spy_auth
AS
FUNCTION fu_spy_check(p_schema VARCHAR2, p_name VARCHAR2)
RETURN VARCHAR2 AS
V_predicate VARCHAR2(2000);
V_clearance NUMBER;
BEGIN
    V_clearance:=sys_context('cont_spy_owner_01','v_spy_clearance');
    IF v_clearance IS NOT NULL
    THEN
```

```
                V_predicate:= ' min_security_id <= '||v_clearance;
        ELSE
                V_predicate:= ' 1 = 2';
        END IF;
RETURN v_predicate;
END fu_spy_check;
END pkg_spy_auth;
/
```

This package retrieves from the cont_spy_owner_01 context the clearance level of the person logged in to the database. It then checks to see if v_clearance is NULL, which will be the case if the user signs in as someone who is not in the security clearance table (TBL_USER_ID). If the user's security clearance is set to NULL, the package creates a predicate that makes the SQL statement return no rows. Since the clause 1 = 2 is always going to evaluate as FALSE, this guarantees that you prevent access to the table to unauthorized users. Always include this clause to make sure your data is secured.

If the clearance is not NULL, the package creates a predicate that indicates that the column MIN_SECURITY_ID should be less than or equal to the clearance level assigned. Once this procedure is associated with the TBL_SECURED_INFORMATION table, all queries will have this predicate attached to the end of them, thus enforcing the security.

NOTE Some functions, such as DBMS_OUTPUT, will not execute in FGAC security enforcement packages. The package will compile but no output will be forthcoming. Also, autonomous transactions will cause a row-level security package to fail when executed. This is likely seen as a circumvention of security by Oracle. The UTL_FILE package, strangely enough, appears to work fine.

Registering the Security Enforcement Package

Now that you have written the security enforcement package, the final step is to enforce the rules represented by this package and relate that package to a table. The security enforcement package is related to the table through the use of the DBMS_RLS package.

NOTE Oracle does not allow any security policies to apply to the SYS schema.

The DBMS_RLS package is used to register your security enforcement package with the table that you wish that package to administer, as well as to manage the security enforcement packages. This package includes the DBMS_RLS.ADD_POLICY, DBMS_RLS.DROP_POLICY, DBMS_RLS.ENABLE_POLICY, and DBMS_RLS.REFRESH_POLICY procedures. In this example, you use the DBMS_RLS.ADD_POLICY procedure to register the security enforcement package. Let's take a quick look at that procedure:

```
PROCEDURE dbms_rls.add_policy
Argument Name       Type            In/Out  Default?
------------------  --------------  ------  --------
OBJECT_SCHEMA       VARCHAR2        IN      DEFAULT
OBJECT_NAME         VARCHAR2        IN
POLICY_NAME         VARCHAR2        IN
FUNCTION_SCHEM      VARCHAR2        IN      DEFAULT
POLICY_FUNCTION     VARCHAR2        IN
STATEMENT_TYPES     VARCHAR2        IN      DEFAULT
UPDATE_CHECK        BOOLEAN         IN      DEFAULT
ENABLE              BOOLEAN         IN      DEFAULT
```

Listing 21.10 shows how to use this procedure to register the security enforcement package created with the database so it will execute on any DML statement that is executed on the table TBL_SECURED_INFORMATION.

Listing 21.10: Adding the Policy with the DBMS_RLS.ADD_POLICY Procedure

```
CONNECT SYS/yourpassword
BEGIN
Dbms_rls.add_policy('SPY_OWNER','TBL_SECURED_INFORMATION',
'SPY_OWNER','SPY_OWNER', 'PKG_SPY_AUTH.FU_SPY_CHECK',
'SELECT, INSERT, UPDATE, DELETE',
TRUE, TRUE);
END;
/
```

As you can see, the DBMS_RLS.ADD_POLICY procedure takes several parameters. Table 21.5 describes each parameter.

TABLE 21.5: PARAMETERS FOR THE DBMS_RLS.ADD_POLICY PROCEDURE

Argument	Default Value	Description
Object_schema	NULL	The schema that contains the table or view that you wish to register the policy for. If NULL, the current user schema will be used.
Object_name	None	The name of the table or view that the policy is being added to.
Policy_name	None	The name of the policy being assigned to the table or view. This name must be unique for each object.
Function_schema	NULL	The name of the schema that owns the policy function that is to be used. If NULL, the current user that you are logged in as will be used.
Policy_function	None	The name of the function/package that is used to create the dynamic predicate (this is the security enforcement package).
Statement_types	All	The statement types that the policy should apply to (SELECT, INSERT, UPDATE, DELETE).
Update_check	FALSE	Causes the value to be checked again after an UPDATE or INSERT statement completes.
Enable	TRUE	Enables the policy. The policy can be selectively enabled or disabled with the DBMS_RLS.ENABLE procedure.

NOTE When you begin planning your security with FGAC, you may end up crafting multiple policies for the same table. Oracle supports this type of approach, allowing you to register multiple policies for the same table.

The other procedures in the DBMS_RLS package allow you to manage your policies. You can drop policies with the DROP_POLICY procedure, enable or disable policies with the ENABLE_POLICY procedure, and use the REFRESH_POLICY procedure to cause all SQL statements associated with the policy to be re-parsed.

Testing the Security Enforcement Package

So, you've written code, set up logon triggers, created the security enforcement package, and added it as a security policy. You're ready to go! Listing 21.11 provides the test. In this test, you log on to the database as each user and try to SELECT from the table. Let's see what happens.

Listing 21.11: Looking for a Security Breach

```
SQL> CONNECT spy_owner/spy_owner
Connected.
SQL> SELECT * FROM tbl_secured_information;
MIN_SECURITY_ID SECRET_INFORMATION
--------------- -------------------------------
              0 This is boring public information
             10 Men are NOT from Mars!!
             20 But the Aliens are from Mars!!
            100 And they are here to take over the world.

SQL> CONNECT public_access/public_access
Connected.
SQL> /
no rows selected

SQL> CONNECT secret_spy/secret_spy
Connected.
SQL> /

MIN_SECURITY_ID SECRET_INFORMATION
--------------- ---------------------------------
              0 This is boring public information
             10 Men are NOT from Mars!!

SQL> CONNECT top_secret_spy/top_secret_spy
Connected.
SQL> /

MIN_SECURITY_ID SECRET_INFORMATION
--------------- -------------------------------
              0 This is boring public information
             10 Men are NOT from Mars!!
             20 But the Aliens are from Mars!!

SQL> CONNECT license_to_kill/license_to_kill
```

```
Connected.
SQL> /

MIN_SECURITY_ID SECRET_INFORMATION
--------------- ------------------------------
              0 This is boring public information
             10 Men are NOT from Mars!!
             20 But the Aliens are from Mars!!
            100 And they are here to take over the world.
```

The Good, the Bad, and the Ugly about FGAC

As is typical of any new feature, there are some good things and some bad things about using FGAC. The fact that FGAC works in the background, so that it is invisible to the user, is one of the advantages of using FGAC. And, of course, there is the benefit of making your database more secure.

The main negative aspect to FGAC is the complexity involved in implementing the feature. However, once you have done it a couple of times, it becomes easier.

Another issue with FGAC is the fact that it has the potential to negatively impact performance. Since the predicate to be added changes the SQL statement, you can end up with an execution plan that is different from what you expected. Since you have almost no way of knowing what predicate is being attached to the SQL statement, it makes tuning that SQL statement much more difficult. The complete SQL statement, with the predicate, doesn't show up in the V$SQL view, and the predicate doesn't appear if you enable Autotrace. If you look in a trace file, you will not see a predicate associated with your session.

Predicates can impact performance. Depending on the predicate to be added, you could end up with more table joins than you expected, quickly turning a simple two table join into a three- or four-table join (or more). As a developer, DBA, or database architect, you need to consider the impacts of predicates and make sure that indexes are created to assist the database in properly handling the addition of the predicates.

There is one way to determine what predicate is being added when you are running SQL statements: Add event 10730. Setting this event will provide you with a trace file that contains the complete SQL statement you issued. This SQL statement will also include the dynamic FGAC predicate attached. If you are using Oracle version 8.1.5, your output will look somewhat different in that only the predicate will appear. In Oracle version 8.1.6 and later, you will find that the entire SQL statement appears, as shown here:

```
ALTER SESSION SET EVENTS= '10730 trace name context forever, level 10';
```

```
*** 2001-06-03 09:51:16.034
*** SESSION ID:(8.3) 2001-06-03 09:51:16.014
-----------------------------------------------------------------
Logon user     : SPY_OWNER
Table or View  : SPY_OWNER.TBL_SECURED_INFORMATION
Policy name    : SPY_OWNER
Policy function: SPY_OWNER.PKG_SPY_AUTH.FU_SPY_CHECK
RLS view :
SELECT  "MIN_SECURITY_ID","SECRET_INFORMATION" FROM "SPY_OWNER".
"TBL_SECURED_INFORMATION" "TBL_SECURED_INFORMATION"
WHERE ( min_security_id <= 10000)
```

Enforcing Column-Level Security

Do you need to secure your data even more? You may want to go an additional step and encrypt the data within the columns of the tables in your Oracle database. This functionality is facilitated through triggers and the DBMS_OBFUSCATION_TOOLKIT package.

Oracle8i does not install the OBFUSCATION toolkit by default. You will need to run the catobtk.sql script, stored in the $ORACLE_HOME/rdbms/admin directory. You should run this script only when connected as INTERNAL or as SYS; otherwise, the toolkit will not work properly.

After you run the script, you will find that your database has a new package called DBMS_OBFUSCATION_TOOLKIT. This package contains two overloaded procedures (thus, it's just like having four scripts). Here is a description of the four scripts:

```
SQL> DESC dbms_obfuscation_toolkit
PROCEDURE DESDECRYPT
 Argument Name              Type            In/Out Default?
 --------------------       --------------- ------ --------
 INPUT                      RAW             IN
 KEY                        RAW             IN
 DECRYPTED_DATA             RAW             OUT

PROCEDURE DESDECRYPT
 Argument Name              Type            In/Out  Default?
 --------------------       --------------- ------- --------
 INPUT_STRING               VARCHAR2        IN
```

```
                         KEY_STRING                VARCHAR2         IN
                         DECRYPTED_STRING          VARCHAR2         OUT

             PROCEDURE DESENCRYPT
              Argument Name               Type              In/Out Default?
              ------------------------    --------------    ------ --------
              INPUT                       RAW               IN
              KEY                         RAW               IN
              ENCRYPTED_DATA              RAW               OUT

             PROCEDURE DESENCRYPT
              Argument Name               Type              In/Out Default?
              ------------------------    --------------    ------ --------
              INPUT_STRING                VARCHAR2          IN
              KEY_STRING                  VARCHAR2          IN
              ENCRYPTED_STRING            VARCHAR2          OUT
```

Notice that the two main themes of the procedures are to encrypt data and decrypt data. There is one set of procedures for string data and another set for RAW datatypes. The parameter names are different for each procedure. When using an OBFUSCATION toolkit procedure, you must use named notation to refer to the correct parameter name; otherwise, Oracle may generate an error because it will not be sure which script to use.

Encrypting Data

To encrypt data, use the DESENCRYPT procedure. It's fairly straightforward, as shown in Listing 21.12. This listing creates a table called USER_INFORMATION. We want to encrypt the data going into one of the columns of this table, the INFORMATION column. We do this by creating a trigger that fires each time a row is inserted into the table.

Listing 21:12: Encrypting Data Using the DESENCRYPT Procedure

```
SQL> DESC user_information
 Name                                       Null?    Type
 ------------------------------------------ -------- -----------------
 USER_NAME                                           VARCHAR2(30)
 INFORMATION                                         VARCHAR2(2000)

CREATE OR REPLACE TRIGGER tr_user_information_01
BEFORE INSERT ON user_information
```

```
FOR EACH ROW
DECLARE
v_stuff    varchar2(2048);
v_temp     varchar2(2048);
-- Must be at least 8 bytes!
v_keystring varchar2(8):='locked00';
BEGIN

    -- This string must be a multiple of 8 bytes.
    v_temp:=rpad(:new.information, (length(:new.information) +
    (8 - mod(length(:new.information),8) ) ) );

    dbms_obfuscation_toolkit.desencrypt
    (
        input_string => v_temp,
        key_string=>v_keystring,
        encrypted_string=>v_stuff
    );
    :new.information:=v_stuff;
END;
/
```

Notice that we needed to pad the input string to be a length that is a multiple of eight. This is a requirement of the package for string manipulation. Also notice that we furnished the key string (locked00). You must use the same string to later decrypt the data. The key string needs to be no less than 8 bytes (or characters in the case of single-byte character sets) because of a bug in Oracle.

After loading this trigger, any time a user inserts data into the table, it will be protected. SELECT statements on the table will reveal only gibberish in the secured columns (unless they are decrypted), as in this example:

```
SQL> INSERT INTO user_information VALUES ('SYS','TEST');
1 row created.
SQL> SELECT * FROM user_information;

USER_NAME                    INFORMATION
------------------------     ------------
SYS                          ‡L↕♥M
```

You will see an example of decrypting the data in the next section. The same basic process applies to RAW data encryption.

Decrypting Data

One of the problems with decrypting data is that it cannot be done simply in a SQL statement. Because of the way the procedure is written, the return value for the unencrypted string comes to us by way of an IN/OUT variable that must be defined. Thus, PL/SQL is about the only way to get at what you need. Listing 21.13 provides an example of retrieving encrypted data from the database and displaying its contents.

Listing 21.13: Retrieving Encrypted Data

```
SET SERVEROUTPUT ON
DECLARE
v_key      VARCHAR2(8):='locked00';
v_outpu    VARCHAR2(2048);
v_stuff    VARCHAR2(2048);

BEGIN

FOR v_cursor_one in (select * from user_information WHERE user_name='&1')
LOOP
     dbms_obfuscation_toolkit.DESDecrypt
     (
          input_string=>v_cursor_one.information,
          key_string=>v_key,
          decrypted_string=>v_stuff
     );
     dbms_output.put_line('User name '||v_cursor_one.user_name);
     dbms_output.put_line('Information '||v_stuff);
END LOOP;
END;
/
Enter value for 1: SYS
old    8: for v_cursor_one in
(select * from user_information where user_name='&1')
new    8: for v_cursor_one in
(select * from user_information where user_name='SYS')
User name SYS
Information TEST
PL/SQL procedure successfully completed.
```

As you can see, we retrieved the row from the table that we created earlier. Then we decrypted the data before we displayed it.

CHAPTER 22

SQL*Loader

FEATURING:

Introduction to SQL*Loader	974
The input files	979
The "output": discards and rejects	991
SQL*Loader log files	994
Loading objects, collections, LOBs, and partitioned objects	996
Running SQL*Loader	1001

In SQL*Loader, Oracle has provided a tool that enables us to take data from an external source and load it into Oracle. This is generally accomplished with flat files that are in both a comma-delimited as well as fixed-length format. Over the years, our personal experience with SQL*Loader has been good, and we've found it an efficient tool for converting databases from many different sources into Oracle.

This chapter explains the elements and operations of SQL*Loader. You'll examine the parts of the important control file and all of its options that are available, and see examples of creating a control file. We'll discuss the input datafile, the output files (BADFILE and DISCARDFILE), and the log file. You'll read about the various methods of loading data, and how to execute SQL*Loader from the command line or using a script.

NOTE The case studies in the Oracle documentation are good examples that will help you understand how to use SQL*Loader.

Introduction to SQL*Loader

SQL*Loader will bring data in from a source external to Oracle and place that data into Oracle tables. There are two sources of input: the control file and the actual input datafile. The datafile, of course, contains the data you wish to load into Oracle. The control file describes the data to be loaded, its location, how it is to be loaded the data, and more.

There's a log file, as well, that tracks information about the load from beginning to end.

Discarded and rejected rows are placed in two separate files for your convenience. Discarded rows are the items that did not match the selection criteria of the control file, and rejected rows are items containing incorrect data and have been rejected by either Oracle processing or by the SQL*Loader utility.

Figure 22.1 represents the relationship between SQL*Loader and the input and output files.

FIGURE 22.1

*Basic components of a SQL*Loader session*

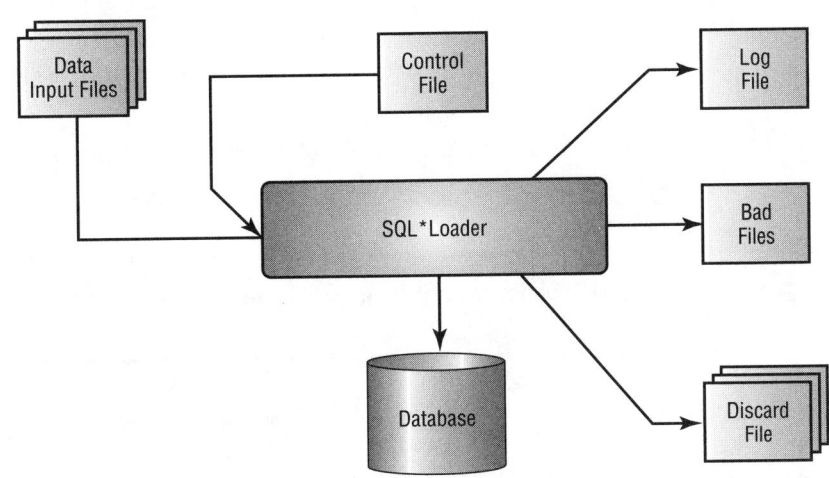

SQL*Loader's Capabilities

You gain many advantages and capabilities when you use SQL*Loader, including the following:

- It is a prebuilt Oracle utility, supported by Oracle.
- Choice of three different record formats for the input datafiles.
- You can filter out unwanted data.
- You can load data from one input source into multiple Oracle tables.
- You can validate and transform data as it is being loaded.
- Data is loaded speedily and accurately into your tables.
- Ability to reuse the control file for multiple runs.

All of these features and more are discussed in this chapter. We'll cover the logical areas of input (control file and data files), the "output" (bad file, discard file, and log file), and the types of data loads possible (direct, conventional, and parallel).

Conventional and Direct Path Loads

With SQL*Loader you have two methods of loading data: the conventional path load and the direct path load. You specify the load path when creating the control file, in the OPTIONS section of the control file. If you specify the DIRECT parameter, then direct path load will be utilized; otherwise, the conventional path load is used by default.

- Conventional path load uses the standard SQL INSERT statement to load the data.
- Both the direct path and parallel direct path methods load data directly into a database.

NOTE SQL*Loader will not create tables, so the tables to be loaded must exist prior to invoking SQL*Loader.

Depending on how your control file is set up you will need to have INSERT privileges on the table that is being loaded and if you are using the REPLACE or TRUNCATE option you will also require DELETE privileges on the table as well.

Although direct path load can load data into the Oracle table faster, the direct path method has more restrictions. Conventional path is what is used most often.

For more information about all three load methods, consult Oracle's documentation on SQL*Loader.

Conventional Path Load

Conventional path load is the default load type and will be used if you do not specify a load method. You can use any of the record formats with this method (Variable Record Format, Fixed Record Format, and Stream Record Format). Oracle parses each row in accordance with the control file's INTO TABLE clause specifications. Each row is then loaded into a series of bind arrays that match the columns specified in the control file. When the bind array is full, an array INSERT is executed, and the process continues until all data has been processed.

NOTE If any errors occur on a LOB field, the column is left empty for the row being inserted.

Since SQL*Loader competes with all other processes for buffer space and resources, the same conventional path load may run for five minutes one time and half an hour the next. In addition to competing for the buffer space, SQL*Loader incurs extra overhead for creating the SQL INSERT statements that are actually sent to Oracle for inserting rows into the table.

When to Use a Conventional Path Load

There are many reasons to use conventional path load and circumstances under which it will most benefit database processing.

- When speed is not important; that is, it doesn't matter how long the SQL*Loader session takes.
- When space is an issue (conventional path load will insert data under the high-water mark).
- When direct path load cannot be utilized.
- When the table into which you are loading has a column type of LOB.
- When the table into which you are loading has a column type of VARRAY.
- When table constraints are present.

Direct Path Load

Direct path load handles the input data differently than does conventional path load. Instead of filling a bind array buffer, direct path load parses the input data in accordance with the control file's layout and field specifications. Oracle then converts the data for each and every field into a matching column array structure. Next, the column array structures are created to form an Oracle data block and build index keys. These database blocks are then written directly to the database. Multiple buffers are used for these formatted blocks.

Writing the data blocks directly to the database bypasses most of the overhead associated with conventional path load. Bypassing the multiple inserts constraint checking that is associated with the conventional path load makes direct path load faster. However, after direct patch load you will have to rebuild the indexes and reestablish the primary and foreign key constraints to make the tables useful again.

To run SQL*Loader with direct path loading, just set DIRECT=TRUE on the command line or in the OPTIONS clause of the control file. Also, the `catldr.sql` script must already have been run. This script is generally run when the database is created as part of the procedure CATPROC.SQL.

Restrictions on Direct Path Load

The direct path load has several restrictions, including the following. (For a complete list, consult the Oracle documentation.)

- SQL strings are not allowed in the control file.
- The table into which you are loading data cannot contain LOB or VARRAY column types.

- The table into which you are loading data cannot contain object columns, nested table columns, or clustered tables.
- Table constraints cannot be enabled.
- Triggers are not fired.

Parallel Direct Path Load

The main difference between direct path load and *parallel direct path load* is that the load is performed in parallel (see Chapter 18 for a full explanation of parallel processing). All the restrictions on using direct path load also apply for parallel direct path load. In addition, there are a few other limitations:

- Local and global indexes are not maintained during parallel direct path load. That means all indexes on the table being loaded will need to be re-created.
- All triggers on the table being loaded must be disabled.
- All referential integrity and check constraints must be disabled on the table being loaded.
- Only the APPEND loading method is allowed.

Reserved Words

Like SQL, SQL*Loader uses reserved words (keywords) when identifying its instructions. If you have a table, column, or any other object named with a SQL*Loader reserved word, you must place quotation marks around that object name. Table 22.1 is an alphabetical list of these reserved words.

TABLE 22.1: SQL*LOADER RESERVED WORDS

AND	DOUBLE	NULLCOLS	SORTDEVT
APPEND	ENCLOSED	NULLIF	SORTED
BADDN	EOF	OBJECT	SORTNUM
BADFILE	EXCEPTIONS	OID	SQL/DS
BEGINDATA	EXTERNAL	OPTIONALLY	STORAGE
BFILE	FIELDS	OPTIONS	STREAM
BLANKS	FILLER	PART	SUBPARTITION
BLOCKSIZE	FIXED	PARTITION	SYSDATE
BY	FLOAT	PIECED	TABLE

Continued

TABLE 22.1: SQL*LOADER RESERVED WORDS (CONTINUED)			
BYTEINT	FORMAT	POSITION	TERMINATED
CHAR	GENERATED	PRESERVE	THIS
CHARACTERSET	GRAPHIC	RAW	TRAILING
COLUMN	INDDN	READBUFFERS	TRUNCATE
CONCATENATE	INDEXES	READSIZE	UNLOAD
CONSTANT	INFILE	RECLEN	UNRECOVERABLE
CONTINUE_LOAD	INSERT	RECNUM	USING
CONTINUEIF	INTEGER	RECORD	VARCHAR
COUNT	INTO	RECOVERABLE	VARCHARC
DATA	LAST	REENABLE	VARGRAPHIC
DATE	LOAD	REF	VARIABLE
DECIMAL	LOBFILE	REPLACE	VARRAW
DEFAULTIF	LOG	RESUME	VARRAWC
DELETE	LONG	SDF	VARRAY
DISABLED_CONSTRAINTS	MAX	SEQUENCE	WHEN
DISCARDDN	MLSLABEL	SID	WHITESPACE
DISCARDFILE	NESTED	SINGLEROW	WORKDDN
DISCARDMAX	NEXT	SKIP	YES
DISCARDS	NO	SMALLINT	ZONED

The Input Files

SQL*Loader has two files that are considered to be input files: the control file, which tells the utility how to handle the load, and the data files (flat files) that store the data. (You can also place the data itself in the control file, using the keyword BEGINDATA.)

The Control File

The control file (we call it the "traffic cop") is a text file that describes to SQL*Loader what is to be accomplished. It contains instructions on where the datafile is located, whether the table being loaded is to be appended to or completely replaced, how to parse the input file, and much more.

The control file's three sections comprise sessionwide information, the name and format of the tables to be loaded, and the optional BEGINDATA clause indicating where the input data is located. Following is a diagram showing the syntax for the control file clauses, and Listing 22.1 is a simple example of a control file.

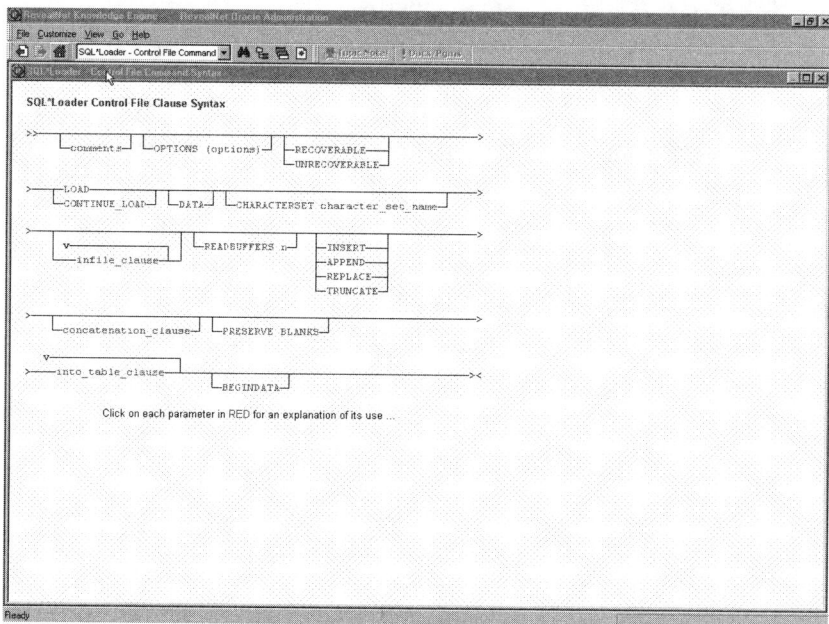

Listing 22.1: Sample Control File

```
-- First section: sessionwide information
OPTIONS (errors=10000
        ,bindsize=100000000
        ,parallel=true)
LOAD DATA
INFILE '/m1_load2/m1_load.dat'  -- Identifies the input data
TRUNCATE                         -- The loading mode
- Second section: INTO TABLE blocks
INTO TABLE pa_serv_type_translations  -- The table to load data into
FIELDS TERMINATED BY ',' optionally ENCLOSED BY '"'
   (M1_PROGRAM_TYPE      char,
    M1_PROJECT_TYPE      char,
    M1_PRODUCT           char,
    PA_CLASS_CODE        char,
```

```
        PA_SERVICE_TYPE_CODE    char,
        PA_FLWTHRU_PROJTASK     char,
        PA_TEMPLATE_SEG1        char,
        PA_BUDGET_PROJTASK      char)
-- Third section
BEGINDATA
-- data for load belongs here
```

Sessionwide Information

The control file's sessionwide or "global" information can be placed in the control file or in a script file. When it's in a script file, you can easily modify the script and change the characteristics of the load without tampering with the control file itself. In addition, you can easily use the script to run the load multiple times without modification. Listing 22.2 is an example of a script file to hold the sessionwide information.

Listing 22.2: A Script with the Control File's Sessionwide Information

```
sqlload $USER_PASS
    \control=1461c1.ctl
     log=servtype.log
     data=servtype.csv
    \bad=servtype.bad
     discard=servtyp.dis
    parallel=true
    \errors=10000 rows=1000 bindsize=100000000
```

 TIP Oracle has supplied a collection of case studies in the SQL*Loader documentation that may be of use to you in constructing your control files.

OPTIONS Clause

The OPTIONS section contains the SQLLOAD command-line options. You can specify these options within the control file, in a batch or script file, or when you run the SQLLOAD command itself. If the put the options in a separate batch or script file, the SQL*Loader session will be run from there as well.

Since the default settings will be invoked for your run, you only need to identify the options that you want to modify. Table 22.2 describes the command options allowed and lists their default settings.

TABLE 22.2: SQLLOAD COMMAND OPTIONS

Command Option	Default Value	Description
BINDSIZE	64KB	The bind buffer array size.
DIRECT	False	Tells Oracle to use direct path load.
ERRORS	50	Number of errors allowed before processing is aborted.
LOAD	All	Number of rows to load.
PARALLEL	False	Tells Oracle to use parallel loading.
ROWS	64	Number of rows to be loaded prior to issuing a COMMIT.
SILENT	Null	If you specify a SILENT option, you tell Oracle not to broadcast the specified message type (Header, Feedback, Error, Discards, or All). The default of NULL states that all will be broadcasted.
SKIP	0	Number of rows to skip in the input datafile prior to beginning the load.

LOAD Statement

This statement specifies whether SQL*Loader will start with a clean load or continue with a load that was previously aborted (CONTINUE_LOAD). Most often you'll start with a clean load (LOAD DATA).

When CONTINUE_LOAD is utilized, you'll need to use the SKIP command in the INFILE specification to skip past the rows that have already been loaded.

```
-- Sample control file for start of clean load
LOAD DATA

-- Sample control file that will restart after skiping 10 rows
   of the input datafile (flat file)
LOAD CONTINUE_LOAD
SKIP 10
```

INFILE Clause

This clause specifies the name of the input file that holds the data. (See the later section "Input Datafiles.") Optionally, you can specify the * parameter, which tells Oracle that the input data is contained in the control file immediately following the keyword BEGINDATA.

After you have identified the input file, you can optionally identify the BADFILE and DISCARDFILE output files. (See the later section "Discards and Rejects.")

- The BADFILE is the file where you want to place the rows that have errors. You can specify a path as well as a file. If you do specify a path, quotes must be placed around the full path name. If no bad file is named, one will be created for you; it will have the control file's name with an extension of .bad.

- The DISCARDFILE is the file where you will place discarded rows. You can specify a path as well as a file. If you do specify a path, quotes must be placed around the full path name. If no discard file is named, any row that is discarded will be lost.

You can specify a READBUFFERS clause when using direct path load, to load an entire large file. (See the later section on load types.) This clause can be useful when loading record types that exceed 255 characters, such as the LONG record type. The default for READBUFFERS is 4. If you receive an ORA-02374 error during a direct path load, increase this value; otherwise, it's best left at the default.

Listing 22.3 demonstrate each of these control file elements.

Listing 22.3: Control File Statements

```
-- Statement to say the the data is in the control file
INFILE *

-- Statement to have one input file and the directory path
INFILE '/m1_load2/m1_load.dat'

-- Statement to have one input file default directory
INFILE m1_load.dat

-- Statement to identify the output files
INFILE '/m1_load2/m1_load.dat'
BADFILE servtype.bad
DISCARD servtype.dis

-- Statement to identify multiple load files
INFILE *
INFILE '/m1_load2/m1_load.dat'
BADFILE servtype.bad
DISCARD servtype.dis
-- Notice we specified both a datafile and the '*' that says the data is
```

```
-- in the control file. This is permitted, or you can specify multiple
-- load files. Only the m1_load.dat is identified to have a badfile and a
-- discard file. Since I didn't specify a discard file for the INFILE *,
-- a discard file will not be produced and only the bad data from
-- m1_load.dat will be placed in the servtype.bad. The bad data from
-- INFILE * will be placed in the control file name.dat.

-- Statement to identify the readbuffers
INFILE '/m1_load2/m1_load.dat'
BADFILE servtype.bad
DISCARD servtype.dis
READBUFFERS 7
```

Loading Mode

The next clause dictates how the rows will be loaded into the Oracle table. You can specify the mode here in the global section or with the INTO TABLE clause.

- INSERT states that you are going to load data into an empty table. If Oracle finds any rows in the table, SQL*Loader will abort.

- APPEND states that you will be adding data to the table. The table does not have to be empty.

- REPLACE will delete all data in the table with the DELETE command prior to beginning the load process.

TRUNCATE will empty the table with the TRUNCATE command.

```
-- Specifies a load using the truncate method
INFILE '/m1_load2/m1_load.dat'
BADFILE servtype.bad
DISCARD servtype.dis
TRUNCATE
```

You can also specify one of these commands with the INTO TABLE clause of a multitable load. The INTO TABLE clause will take precedence if utilized there.

Concatenation

The *concatenation clause* is used to create one logical row from many physical rows. This lets you bring in one datafile that has logical rows and build one row for insertion into Oracle. There are two options to this clause. CONCATENATE is utilized to join two or more rows into one logical row for processing, and CONTINUEIF is used to join two or more rows together based on a certain conditional clause.

Listing 22.4 contains examples of both concatenation options.

Listing 22.4: Concatenation Options

```
-- We specify concatenate 4. This will take 4 lines and concatenate
-- into 1 line. We will end up with two lines
-- 100 Test Project 0001 Build Task
-- 200 Test Project 2 0002 Labor Task
INFILE '/m1_load2/m1_load.dat'
BADFILE servtype.bad
DISCARD servtype.dis
TRUNCATE
CONCATENATE 4

-- Sample data file for concatenate
-- This datafile is made up of a project number, project name,
-- task number, task name
100
Test Project
0001
Build Task
200
Test Project 2
0002
Labor Task
-- For the CONTINUEIF clause, we will need some logic.
-- We specified CONCATENATE 4. This will take 4 lines and concatenate
-- into 1 line. We will end up with two lines:
-- 100 Test Project This is a project that we will Place all the notes
-- in.  We have Had several project managers and we are presently
-- Behind schedule
-- 200 Test Project We are presently on schedule and Will remain that
-- way unless some Unforeseen delay happens
INFILE '/m1_load2/m1_load.dat'
BADFILE servtype.bad
DISCARD servtype.dis
TRUNCATE
CONTINUEIF LAST = '~'
-- Sample data file for continueif
-- This datafile is made up of a project number, project name, and
-- project notes.
-- Input file begins with this next line:
```

```
100~
Test Project~
This is a project that we will
Place all the notes in.  We have
Had several project managers and we are presently
Behind schedule~
200~
Test Project 2~
We are presently on schedule and
Will remain that way unless some
Unforeseen delay happens~
-- input file ends with previous line
```

INTO TABLE Section

This clause tells Oracle what table we are loading data into. It also specifies the format of the data in the input file, which is loaded as specified in the loading mode clause (INSERT, APPEND, REPLACE, or TRUNCATE). INTO TABLE is possibly the most complex clause of SQL*Loader's control file.

NOTE For an in-depth breakdown of this control file section, you can go to Chapters 3 through 6 of the Oracle documentation on SQL*Loader.

If you specify INTO TABLE with one of the options INSERT, APPEND, REPLACE, or TRUNCATE, as described earlier, that option will take precedence over the INSERT, APPEND, REPLACE, or TRUNCATE identified in the sessionwide section of the control file.

```
- Second section one table to load
INTO TABLE pa_serv_type_translations
INSERT  -- could be append, replace or truncate
```

Following are the clauses that you can use with INTO TABLE.

SORTED INDEXES   The SORTED INDEXES clause is only utilized with the direct path load. It tells SQL*Loader that the input data is presorted using the key of the listed indexes. This allows SQL*Loader to optimize its performance by eliminating the sort phase when using direct path load.

```
LOAD DATA
    INFILE '/m1_load2/m1_load.dat'
    INSERT
```

```
INTO TABLE pa_serv_type_translations
  SORTED INDEXES (pa_svctyp)
(PA_SERVICE_TYPE_CODE  char,
 PA_FLWTHRU_PROJTASK   char,
 PA_TEMPLATE_SEG1      char,
 PA_BUDGET_PROJTASK    char)
```

You can also specify a multiple-column index. If you do, you should keep the input data ordered so the first index column matches the first column in the index, the second column matches the second column in the index, and so on. In short, if we were to use a multicolumn index on the preceding example, the first column of the index would be PA_SERVICE_TYPE_CODE, and the second column of the index would be PA_FLWTRHU_PROJTASK.

SINGLEROW   The SINGLEROW option instructs Oracle to put the data into the table one row at a time. This option can only be used with the APPEND loading mode. Use it when temporary storage is small or when the number of rows to be loaded is small compared to the size of the table.

OPTIONS   This clause is only valid for parallel loads. The OPTIONS clause is used with the FILE= option to specify separate files for each table being loaded. This clause has no relationship to the OPTIONS clause in the sessionwide area of the control file.

REENABLE   The REENABLE clause is used to turn constraints (unique and foreign key) back on automatically after the table has been loaded. The second part of REENABLE is the EXCEPTIONS table section. It identifies the table into which will be loaded the ROWIDs of rows that failed the constraint clause. In short, you can see what rows are preventing the constraints from being reenabled. When no EXCEPTIONS clause is present, the reenable process will stop when the first bad row is reached.

WHEN   The WHEN clause specifies conditional loading.

- A field condition clause can be added to compare a named field to a literal.
- We use delimiter specification to tell SQL*Loader how the data is to be parsed. The TERMINATED BY clause indicates the field separator, and the ENCLOSED clause tells SQL*Loader that we have enclosed or optionally enclosed fields within the datafile with a specified character. This allows us to load a string of data that has a comma in it even though we may have designated the comma as the field terminator.

- The TRAILING NULLCOLS clause tells SQL*Loader that any relatively positioned columns that are not present in the physical record should be loaded as NULL values.

FIELDS The FIELDS clause tells SQL*Loader what the field terminator is (TERMINATED BY) and whether the fields are enclosed by a character (OPTIONALLY ENCLOSED BY).

COLUMN_NAME Each COLUMN_NAME clause defines the load of a specific value into that column. You can use the following keywords to characterize the columns to be generated:

- RECNUM inserts a record number as the record is loaded.
- SYSDATE loads the current system date in the rows as they are loaded.
- CONSTANT loads a specific value.
- SEQUENCE loads a sequence number in the row.
- COLUMN_SPEC tells what the specifications are for each column in the load file.

BEGINDATA Section

In this section we can optionally place the data that will be loaded with SQL*Loader. You will identify data here when INFILE * is specified. Listing 22.5 is an example.

Listing 22.5: Control File with a BEGINDATA Section

```
OPTIONS (errors=10000
        ,bindsize=100000000
        ,parallel=true)
LOAD DATA
INFILE *
TRUNCATE

INTO TABLE pa_serv_type_translations
FIELDS TERMINATED BY ',' optionally ENCLOSED BY '"'
  (PA_SERVICE_TYPE_CODE   char,
   PA_SERVICE_TYPE_DESC   char)

BEGINDATA
1,svc_type1,
2,svc_type2,
3,svc_type3,
4,svc_type4,
```

The Input Datafiles (Flat Files)

SQL*Loader considers the control file an input file. The second input file is the actual data to be loaded. SQL*Loader can read data from more than one file at a time. These input files are identified in the INFILE clause within the control file.

There are three record formats available: variable (delimited), fixed, and stream. You can have a logical record extension with any of these record types.

Variable Record Format

When you use *variable record format,* you must identify the length of each line at the beginning of each and every line, so that SQL*Loader will know where the record begins and ends. Errors are harder to detect visually when variable format is used, because each line can be of a different length.

In Listing 22.6, SQL*Loader is instructed to look for a datafile called var_example.dat and that the format is variable. The first three positions of this file tell the length of each line in the file. You can also see that each row contains two fields by looking at the column list.

Listing 22.6: Variable Record Format for Input Datafile

```
LOAD DATA
INFILE 'var_example.dat' 'var 3'
INTO TABLE mdb_examp
FIELDS TERMINATED BY ',' OPTIONALLY ENCLOSED BY '"'
(col1 varchar(6),
  col2 varchar(15))

var_example.dat:   -- This is the datafile to load
013Oracle,Hello,
0098i,World,
016is up,I am here,
017to,I am not here,
019"8.1.7",I am there,
```

The resulting datafile has five rows, each consisting of two fields. The row lengths are 13, 9, 16, 17, and 19. You can determine this visually by looking at the first three bytes of every row. The data will be loaded into five different rows in the table MDB_EXAMP. Notice that the comma character is included in the character count of each record.

NOTE If the record length is not specified, it defaults to 5.

Fixed Record Format

In *fixed record format*, all the records (rows) in the datafile are of the same length. This option offers the best loader performance and is easy to specify in the control file. The INFILE line contains the filename and the number of positions each row will take, as it does for the variable record format. Listing 22.7 is an example of a control file and datafile with the fixed record format.

Listing 22.7: Fixed Record Format for Input Datafile
```
LOAD DATA
INFILE 'fix_example.dat' "fix 48"
INTO TABLE mdb_examp
FIELDS TERMINATED BY ',' OPTIONALLY ENCLOSED BY '"'
(col1 varchar2(9),
  col2 varchar2(15),
  col3 varchar2(12),
  col4 varchar2(9))

fix_example.dat:   -- This is the datafile to load
Mark      ,Blomberg       ,Programmer  ,06/30/77,
Robert    ,Freeman        ,DBA         ,04/01/85,
David     ,Rosson         ,Analyst     ,07/20/75,
```

In this example, all rows in the datafile have a length of 48 bytes. It will be quite easy to identify visually any rows that are shorter or longer than this, by using an editor with the wrap option turned off—just open the file and scan down the right side of the file. Any row that does not match the 48-byte length will be either shorter or longer. You can then fix the rows in question or extract the desired data again.

Stream Record Format (SRF)

Like fixed record format, *stream record format* (SRF) is very flexible. One drawback to SRF, however, is that Oracle needs to compute the record size by parsing the datafile (looking for the specified delimiter). This process can be time consuming.

 NOTE INFILE * uses SRF format.

Listing 22.8 is an example of a control file that specifies a datafile for stream record format. The terminator string is the tilde (~).

Listing 22.8: Stream Record Format for Input Datafile

```
LOAD DATA
INFILE 'srf_example.dat' "str '~'"
INTO TABLE mdb_examp
FIELDS TERMINATED BY ',' OPTIONALLY ENCLOSED BY '"'
(col1 varchar2(9),
 col2 varchar2(15),
 col3 varchar2(12),
 col4 varchar2(9))

srf_example.dat:   -- This is the datafile to load
Mark,Blomberg,Programmer,06/30/77,~
Robert,Freeman,DBA,04/01/85,~
David,Rosson,Analyst,07/20/75,~
```

Logical Records

All three record types can have logical extension records. This allows us to state that more then one row will make up a logical record for loading into the Oracle table. This is accomplished with the CONCATENATE or CONTINUEIF clause, as explained in the "Concatenation" section.

The "Output": Discards and Rejects

The bad file is where all the bad rows are placed that can't be loaded. When identifying the bad file you will give it any file name allowed by your operating system. A full path and file name will be required if you don't want the file to be placed in the current working directory. This is the file where bad records that can't be loaded are placed.

The discard file is the location where Oracle will store all the rows that do not meet the selection criteria. Here as with the bad file, any name allowed by your operating system is acceptable. You will need to identify the full pathname for any location other then the working directory.

When SQL*Loader reads the input file and begins evaluating rows for loading or exclusion, the excluded files are sent to two locations: the bad file and the discard file. As illustrated in Figure 22.2, the first point of possible rejection is when the fields get validated. The second point is when SQL*Loader validates the data against the WHEN clause.

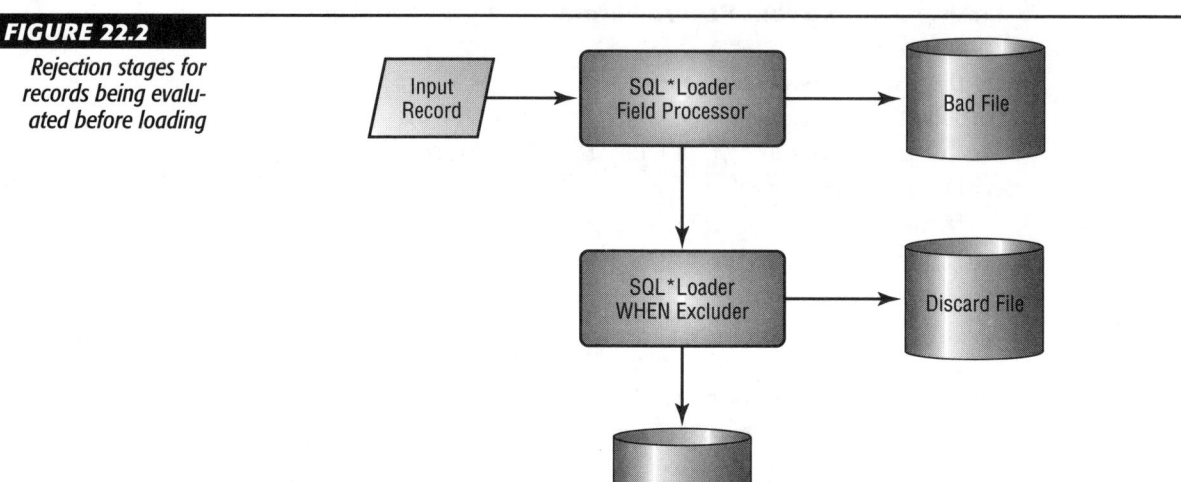

FIGURE 22.2
Rejection stages for records being evaluated before loading

Bad File

The bad file is a listing of the actual data from the datafile that is rejected either by SQL*Loader processing or by Oracle processing. Some of the possible reasons for these rejects are shown in the following listing from an actual performed load.

```
415DB01,MD40015,NETEQ,37100,210,600,"Dearborn Hub","01/01/2000 00:00:00",
    " ",OTHER_PLNT_PGMS,"Hub/Headend - Metro"
415WL01,MD40015,NETEQ,37100,210,600,"West Headend","01/01/2000 00:00:00",
    " ",OTHER_PLNT_PGMS,"Hub/Headend - Metro"
436AC00,MD40036,NMSS,37200,210,600,"City Telemetry","01/19/2000 00:00:00",
    " ",OTHER_PLNT_PGMS,"Metro Detroit Telemetry"
436AT00,MD40036,NMSS,37200,210,600,"ATwp Telemetry","01/19/2000 00:00:00",
    " ",OTHER_PLNT_PGMS,"Metro Detroit Telemetry"
```

SQL*Loader Rejects   Rows are rejected by SQL*Loader when something is wrong with the input format. For example, the datafile may have a field identified to be a length of 15 whereas the table's is 10; or a delimiter may be missing on one of the columns.

Oracle Rejects Once the row has been accepted by SQL*Loader, the Oracle processing software attempts to load it into the table. A number of errors can occur here, including ORA-00001 (unique constraint), ORA-01722 (invalid number), and many more. In Appendix F on the CD, the "Exception Handling" section has a table that lists some of the error possibilities that cause row rejection.

Discard File

As SQL*Loader executes each of the rows in the input datafile, they may not be eligible for loading based on the WHEN clause. You can tell SQL*Loader to create a discard file by including DISCARD *filename* in the OPTIONS clause of the control file. Oracle will create the discard file only if the DISCARD clause is used *and* a WHEN condition is designated in the INTO TABLE section of the control file. Listing 22.9's example of such a WHEN clause places the rows that we do not want loaded into the discard file. We only want to load rows where the project type is something other than FLOWTHR.

Listing 22.9: Sample Control File with WHEN Clause

```
OPTIONS (errors=10000
        ,bindsize=100000000
        ,parallel=true)
LOAD DATA
INFILE '/m1_load2/m1_load.dat'   -- Identifies the input data
TRUNCATE                         -- The loading mode

INTO TABLE pa_serv_type_translations  -- The table to load data into
WHEN m1_project_type != 'FLOWTHR'
FIELDS TERMINATED BY ',' optionally ENCLOSED BY '"'
   (M1_PROGRAM_TYPE        char,
    M1_PROJECT_TYPE        char,
    M1_PRODUCT             char,
    PA_CLASS_CODE          char,
    PA_SERVICE_TYPE_CODE   char,
    PA_FLWTHRU_PROJTASK    char,
    PA_TEMPLATE_SEG1       char,
    PA_BUDGET_PROJTASK     char)

BEGINDATA
-- data for load belongs here
```

You can let the discard file build until the load is complete, or you can set a maximum number of rows allowed in the file. When that maximum is reached, the load process will be stopped and logged as having reached the maximum number of discards allowed.

 NOTE Discarded records are different from rejected records in that they don't necessarily contain bad data. They are discarded because they contain rows that do not match the record selection criteria defined in the control file (in the WHEN clauses).

If appropriate, you can edit the rows in the discard file so they will pass the WHEN clause requirement and then attempt to load them again. This is done by copying the data from the discard file and overwriting the existing data in the INFILE, or changing the name of the INFILE to the name of the discard file you have fixed.

SQL*Loader Log Files

From the time you begin execution of SQL*Loader until it completes its processing, a log file is kept. This file contains information about all aspects of the load. Following are some key items of interest from a log file (these items are in boldface in Listing 22.10).

- Location of the control file, input datafile, bad file, and discard file
- Number of rows to load and how many were loaded
- Number of errors allowed and actual errors encountered
- Makeup of the control file
- When the load started and ended

For more thorough coverage of the elements of SQL*Loader's log files, consult the SQL*Loader documentation.

Listing 22.10: Example of SQL*Loader Log File

```
Control File:    /pac146/ctl/1463c.ctl
Datafile:        /pac146/data/mlprj_midmo.txt
  Bad File:      /pac146/data/mlprj_midmo.bad
  Discard File:  /pac146/data/mlprj_midmo.dis
 (Allow all discards)
```

Number to load: ALL
Number to skip: 0
Errors allowed: 10000
Bind array: 1000 rows, maximum of 100000000 bytes
Continuation: none specified
Path used: Conventional

Table "PA"."PA_PROJECT_CONVERSIONS", loaded from every logical record.
Insert option in effect for this table: APPEND

```
   Column Name                       Position   Len  Term Encl Datatype
------------------------------       ---------- ---- ---- ---- ---------
M1_PROJECT_ID                        FIRST       *    ,   O(") CHARACTER
M1_PROG_NUM                          NEXT        *    ,   O(") CHARACTER
M1_PROJ_TYPE                         NEXT        *    ,   O(") CHARACTER
M1_BUSINESS_UNIT                     NEXT        *    ,   O(") CHARACTER
M1_MARKET                            NEXT        *    ,   O(") CHARACTER
M1_PRODUCT                           NEXT        *    ,   O(") CHARACTER
M1_PROG_DESC                         NEXT        *    ,   O(") CHARACTER
M1_OPEN_DATE                         NEXT        *    ,   O(") CHARACTER
M1_PROJ_MGR                          NEXT        *    ,   O(") CHARACTER
M1_PROG_TYPE                         NEXT        *    ,   O(") CHARACTER
M1_PROJ_DESC                         NEXT        *    ,   O(") CHARACTER
```

Record 175: Rejected - Error on table "PA"."PA_PROJECT_CONVERSIONS".
ORA-00001: unique constraint (PA.PA_PROJECT_CONV_PK) violated

Record 182: Rejected - Error on table "PA"."PA_PROJECT_CONVERSIONS".
ORA-00001: unique constraint (PA.PA_PROJECT_CONV_PK) violated

Record 192: Rejected - Error on table "PA"."PA_PROJECT_CONVERSIONS".
ORA-00001: unique constraint (PA.PA_PROJECT_CONV_PK) violated

Record 194: Rejected - Error on table "PA"."PA_PROJECT_CONVERSIONS".
ORA-00001: unique constraint (PA.PA_PROJECT_CONV_PK) violated

Record 196: Rejected - Error on table "PA"."PA_PROJECT_CONVERSIONS".
ORA-00001: unique constraint (PA.PA_PROJECT_CONV_PK) violated

```
Record 198: Rejected - Error on table "PA"."PA_PROJECT_CONVERSIONS".
ORA-00001: unique constraint (PA.PA_PROJECT_CONV_PK) violated

Table "PA"."PA_PROJECT_CONVERSIONS":
  251 Rows successfully loaded.
  28 Rows not loaded due to data errors.
  0 Rows not loaded because all WHEN clauses were failed.
  0 Rows not loaded because all fields were null.

Space allocated for bind array:                   2860000 bytes(1000 rows)
Space allocated for memory besides bind array:    2947302 bytes

Total logical records skipped:       0
Total logical records read:          279
Total logical records rejected:      28
Total logical records discarded:     0

Run began on Tue Oct  3 14:47:39 2000
Run ended on Tue Oct  3 14:47:40 2000

Elapsed time was:     00:00:01.41
CPU time was:         00:00:00.18
```

Loading Objects, Collections, and LOBs

Objects, collections, and LOBs are not regular column types, and this section discusses how the loading of these objects is supported in SQL*Loader processing. (We assume you are already familiar with Oracle's support of these objects.)

Objects

SQL*Loader supports the loading of column objects and row objects.

Column Objects

The objects stored in the column of a table are referred to as *column objects*. Theoretically, column objects are stored wholly in a single column position within a row. Column objects do not have identifiers and therefore cannot be referenced by an outside source.

Loading a column object with SQL*Loader is as easy as loading any other object type. Listing 22.11 is an example.

Listing 22.11: Loading a Column Object

```
LOAD DATA
INFILE 'var_example_co.dat' "var 6"
INTO TABLE projects
FIELDS TERMINATED BY ',' OPTIONALLY ENCLOSED BY '"'
  (proj_no
   proj_name,
   proj_mgr        COLUMN OBJECT
      (prj_mgr_name      CHAR(30),
       prj_mgr_age       INTEGER EXTERNAL(5),
       prj_mgr_id        INTEGER EXTERNAL(5)) )

var_example_co.dat
000028002,Installs,Mark B.,43,75,
000037010,Head End,"Robert Freeman",36,25,
```

Notice that the column specifications are given just as they are with any other control file, except that the column object is surrounded by parentheses. The datafile will follow the layout of the INFILE clause in the control file. The example (var_example_co.dat) has two rows in the file. The first six positions of the datafile tell the control file how long the line is. The rest of the line consists of the proj_no, proj_name, proj_mgr, which is a column object containing the prj_mgr_name, prj_mgr_age, and prj_mgr_id. This example uses the variable record format.

Row Objects

Unlike column objects, *row objects* are stored in tables that are known as object tables. These object tables have columns that are compatible to the attributes of the object. Row objects have an extra system-created column, SYS_NC_OID$. This column stores identifiers for each object in the table, called OIDs. Columns in all other tables can thus reference the column of the row object by using the OIDs attached to the row object. Listing 22.12 is an example control file and datafile for loading a row object.

Listing 22.12: Loading a Row Object

```
LOAD DATA
INFILE 'ro_example.dat'
DISCARDFILE 'co_example.dsc'
BADFILE 'ro_example.bad'
REPLACE
```

```
    INTO TABLE employee
    FIELDS TERMINATED BY ',' OPTIONALLY ENCLOSED BY '"'
       (name     CHAR(30)              NULLIF name=BLANKS,
        age      INTEGER EXTERNAL(3)   NULLIF age=BLANKS,
        emp_id   INTEGER EXTERNAL(5))

    ro_example.dat
    Robert Freeman, 36, 75,
    Mark Blomberg, 43, 25,
```

Collections

Nested tables and VARRAYs are *collection types,* which are defined as a set of elements treated as a single element. These two collection types are supported with SQL*Loader.

Nested Tables   A nested table is actually a table within a table. This means you can have a table's column be defined as a nested table, and that column can store multiple values. One great advantage here is that nested tables do not have a limited number of entries per row.

VARRAYs   VARRAYs are similar to nested tables in that they can store multiple values in a single row. Simply put, a VARRAY is a varying array. When working with this type of collection, you must specify the number of elements that the array will have.

In SQL*Loader, loading nested tables and VARRAYs works a little differently. Listing 22.13 shows a control file to demonstrate this using a department table and projects table.

Listing 22.13: Loading a Collection

```
LOAD DATA
INFILE 'ct_example.dat' "str '|\n' "
INTO TABLE department
FIELDS TERMINATED BY ',' OPTIONALLY ENCLOSED BY `"'
TRAILING NULLCOLS
(dept_no     CHAR(3),
 dept_name   CHAR(20) NULLIF dname=BLANKS ,
 emp_cnt     FILLER INTEGER EXTERNAL(5),
 employees   VARRAY COUNT(emp_cnt)
   (name)    FILLER CHAR(10),
```

```
    employees COLUMN OBJECT
       (emp_name)    CHAR(30),
        emp_age      INTEGER EXTERNAL(3),
        emp_id       CHAR(7) NULLIF emps.emps.emp_id=BLANKS)),
    projects  NESTED TABLE SDF(CONSTANT 'pr.txt' "fix 71")
       (project_id     char(5)   INTEGER EXTERNAL(5),
        project_name   char(30)  CHAR
                         NULLIF projects.project_name=BLANKS,
        proj_desc      LOBFILE( proj_desc.txt) CHAR(2000)
                  TERMINATED BY "<>\n"))
```

In this example we have a VARRAY of employees and a nested table of projects. If the filler column EMP_CNT is 0, then the array is initialized to EMPTY; and if the COUNT is greater then 0, then the VARRAY is created with the number of elements equal to EMP_CNT. As for the nested table of projects, we just load the data into the nested table, since it has no limitations on rows as does the VARRAY.

LOBs

Following are the four types of LOBs (Large Objects) supported by SQL*Loader processing:

- BLOB is a Binary Large Object that can store up to 4GB of data. This type actually stores its data in the table.

- CLOB is a Character Large Object that can store up to 4GB of data. This type actually stores its data in the table.

- NCLOB is a national character set of CLOB. This type actually stores its data in the table.

- BFILE means Binary Large Object. This type is only a pointer to an external file supported and maintained by the operating system. Unlike the other three LOB types, the BFILE has no size limit imposed by Oracle but is limited by the operating system.

Listing 22.14 has two examples of loading LOBs in SQL*Loader. In the first, the LOBs are loaded from a delimited field; the second example loads LOBs from LOB files.

NOTE During the load process, SQL*Loader reads the LOB file in 64KB chunks and stores the data like any other record type. In order for Oracle to load physical records larger than 64KB, you must use the READSIZE command-line parameter to specify a larger record size.

Listing 22.14: Loading LOBs

```
LOAD DATA
INFILE 'lob_example.dat' "str '|'"
INTO TABLE candidate
FIELDS TERMINATED BY ','
   (name         CHAR(25),
     "RESUME"    CHAR(507) ENCLOSED BY '<beg_lob>' AND '<end_lob>')
```

lob_example.dat
```
Mark Blomberg,<startlob>        Mark D. Blomberg
                                1234 East Park Vista
                                mblomberg@here.com
            Resume info here   <endlob>
|Robert Freeman,<startlob>       Robert G. Freeman
                                1234 West Bay Drive
                                rfreeman@east.com
            Resume info here   <endlob>
LOAD DATA
INFILE 'lob2_example.dat'
   INTO TABLE candidate
   FIELDS TERMINATED BY ','
   (name        CHAR(20),
    ext_fname   FILLER CHAR(40),
     "RESUME"   LOBFILE(ext_fname) TERMINATED BY EOF)

Mark Blomberg,mdb_resume.txt,
Robert Freeman,'/candidate/rgf_resume.txt',
```

Mdb_rsume.txt
```
                                Mark D. Blomberg
                                1234 East Park Vista
                                mblomberg@here.com
            Resume info here
```

Rgf_resume.txt
```
                                Robert G. Freeman
                                1234 West Bay Drive
                                rfreeman@east.com
            Resume info here
```

In the first example, the control file specifies that the separator between records is the | character, and that the LOB has the identifying markers of <beg_lob> and <end_lob>. This object could be used to store a person's name and resume, facilitating quick online access of a person's employment qualifications. You could add other columns to the table to hold other relevant information.

Loading Partitioned Objects

As fully discussed in Chapter 24, in Oracle a partitioned table is one that is separated (grouped) into logical sets. SQL*Loader supports loading of partitioned tables with all load types (conventional path, direct path, and parallel direct path). SQL*Loader has made this transparent and you will not need to do any extra control file setup or data processing to handle this type of table. All the topics covered in this chapter apply to partitioned tables, as well.

Loading of the following partitioned objects is supported in Oracle 8i SQL*Loader:

- A single partition of a partitioned table
- Multiple partitions of a partitioned table
- All partitions of a partitioned table
- Nonpartitioned table

Running SQL*Loader

You can run SQL*Loader from the command line, from a script, or using a parameter file. In this section, all examples demonstrate execution of SQL*Loader in a Unix environment.

SQL*Loader from the Command Line

Command-line execution of SQL*Loader is easy. From the system prompt, you enter **sqlldr** with the required series of keywords and values. (Refer to your Oracle documentation for the specific command to execute on your operating system.) If you issue **sqlldr** with no keywords, SQL*Loader displays all the available keywords and default values. Listing 22.15 shows the keywords and default values that are the same across all operating systems.

Listing 22.15: SQL*Loader Command Options (All Platforms)

```
Sqlldr
        userid -- Oracle username/password
       control -- Control file name
           log -- Log file name
           bad -- Bad file name
          data -- Data file name
       discard -- Discard file name
    discardmax -- Number of discards to allow
                  (Default all)
          skip -- Number of logical records to skip
                  (Default 0)
          load -- Number of logical records to load
                  (Default all)
        errors -- Number of errors to allow
                  (Default 50)
          rows -- Number of rows in conventional path bind array
                  or between direct path data saves
                  (Default: Conventional Path 64, Direct path all)
      bindsize -- Size of conventional path bind array in bytes
                  (System-dependent default)
        silent -- Suppress messages during run
                  (header, feedback, errors, discards, partitions, all)
        direct -- Use direct path
                  (Default FALSE)
       parfile -- Parameter file: name of file that contains
                  parameter specifications
      parallel -- Perform parallel load
                  (Default FALSE)
      readsize -- Size (in bytes) of the read buffer
          file -- File to allocate extents from
```

Here is an example of starting SQL*Loader from the command line:

```
sqlldr userid=mark/mark_sql control=1461c1.ctl log=servtype.log
   data=servtype.csv bad=servtype.bad discard=servtyp.dis
   parallel=true errors=10000 rows=1000 bindsize=100000000
```

Using a Parameter File

Parameter file execution of SQL*Loader is easy as well. You create a file that will hold the parameters and their values. Then you can specify that file when issuing the SQLLDR command.

```
SQLLDR PARFILE=par_file_examp.par

--Par_file_examp.par
userid=mark/mark_sql
control=1461c1.ctl
log=servtype.log
data=servtype.csv
bad=servtype.bad
discard=servtyp.dis
parallel=true
errors=10000
rows=1000
bindsize=100000000
```

 NOTE Depending on your operating system, you may not be allowed to have spaces between the equals sign and the parameter value.

SQL*Loader Script File Execution

Executing SQL*Loader from a script file is similar to using the command line and the parameter file. Within the script, you call SQL*Loader (**sqlload**), and then you designate a combination of command-line parameters as well as the parameter file.

```
./load_sql.sh

-- contents of load_sql.sh
sqlldr mark/mark_sql
   \control=1461c1.ctl
     log=servtype.log
     data=servtype.csv
   \bad=servtype.bad
     discard=servtyp.dis
```

```
          parallel=true
          \errors=10000  rows=1000  bindsize=100000000
```

SQL*Loader DDL Syntax

First, here is the overall syntax for SQL*Loader:

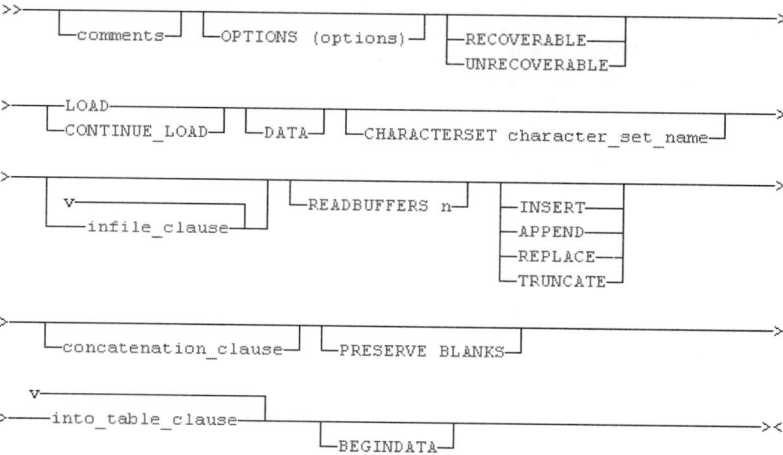

The infile_clause is used to identify the files that actually hold the data to be loaded into the Oracle table. This clause also identifies the files for bad records and discarded rows.

infile_clause Syntax

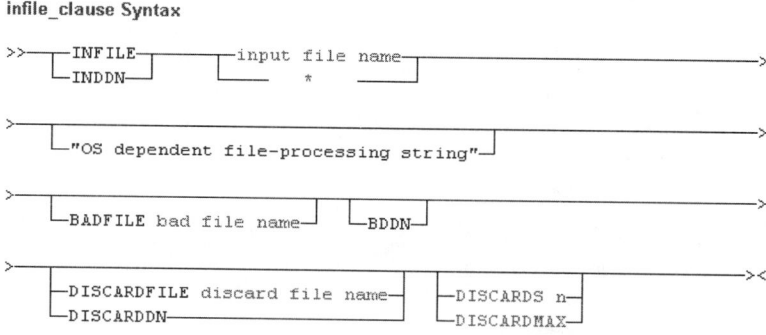

The concatenation clause creates one logical row from one or more physical records from the input data. The two options for this clause are CONCATENATE and CONTINUEIF.

concatenation_clause Syntax:

```
>>--+--CONCATENATE--+--n------+-------------------------------><
    |               +--(n)----+
    |
    +--CONTINUEIF--+-------+--+--pos_spec--operator--+--'char_string'--+--+--+
                  +--THIS-+  |                       +--X'hex_byte'----+  |
                  +--NEXT-+  |                                            |
                             +--LAST--operator--+--'char_string'----------+
                                                +--X'hex_byte'-----------+
```

Each and every table to be loaded is specified with a separate into_table_clause, shown in the next two diagrams.

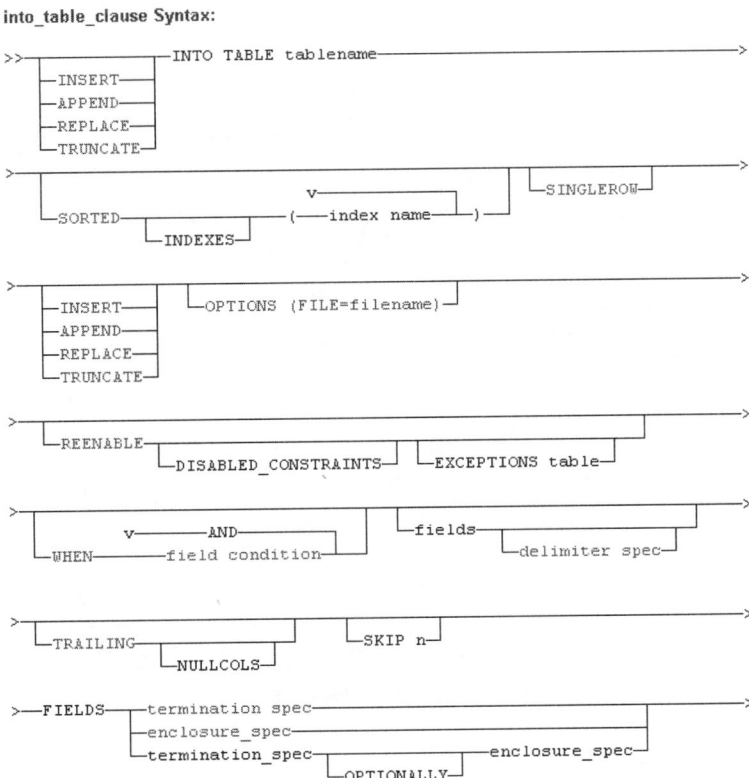

into_table_clause Syntax:

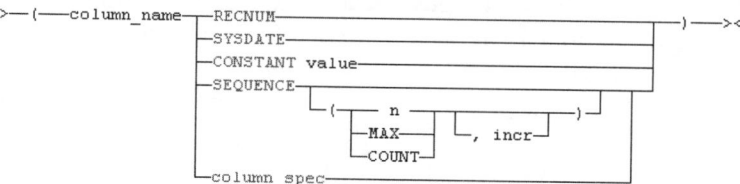

The field_condition_clause, generally part of the column_specification, compares the named field to a given value. Optionally, a null can be inserted into the column, utilizing the NULLIF or DEFAULTIF clause of column_specification. The delimiter specification designates how the data is to be parsed in the input file, including termination characters and enclosure identifiers. The column_specification tells SQL*Loader how each field in the input record is to be interpreted.

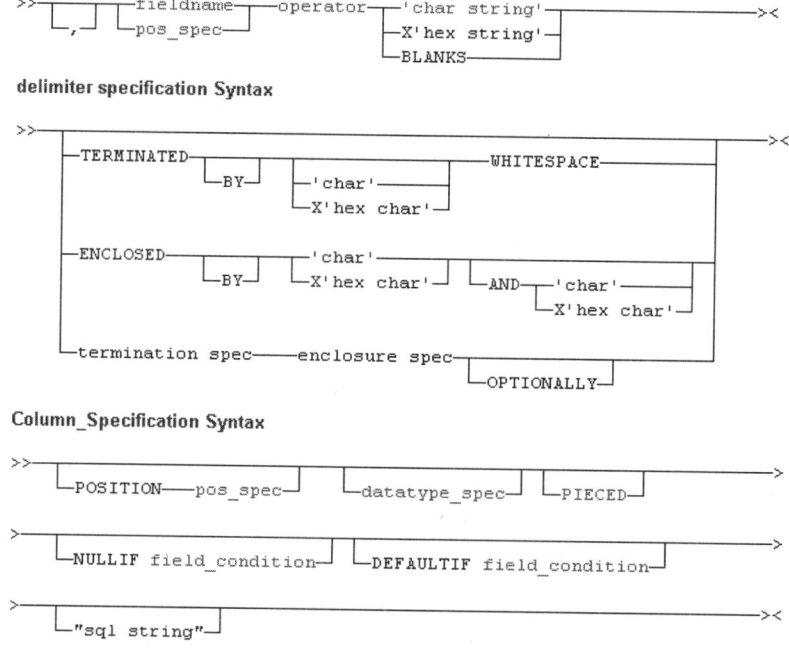

The data_type_specification is used by the column_specification for mapping the external representations of data in the input file into the internal representations within the database table.

data_type_specifications Syntax

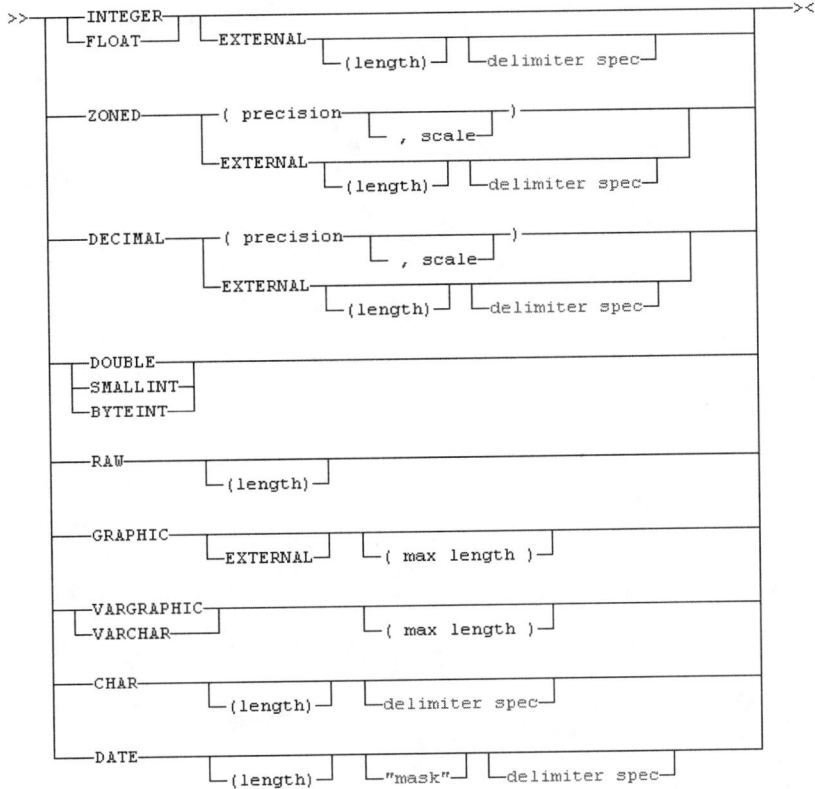

PART IV

Oracle8i Distributed Database

LEARN TO:

- *Administer database links*
- *Manage partitions*
- *Create and maintain database objects in multiple locations*
- *Use Java with Oracle8i*

CHAPTER 23

Oracle Database Links

Database link architecture	*1012*
Administering database links	*1018*
Using database links	*1022*

A *database link* is exactly what its name implies: a connection between two database servers allowing clients to access both servers as one logical unit. This is the central concept in *distributed database systems*. This chapter covers the basic concepts of database links: how they work, how to manage and name them, and how to use them.

Database Link Architecture

What is a database link and why would you use it? Simply put, a database link is a pointer from one physical database to another physical database. The two databases can be on the same or separate physical computers. The database link is *only* a one-way communication from the originating database to the destination database.

Keep in mind that the link is merely a pointer defined in the data dictionary table, and that is what makes the connection between the databases. This means a client connected to local database EAST_PROD can use a link stored in database EAST_PROD to access information in a remote database MID_PROD, but users connected to database MID_PROD cannot use the same link to access data in database EAST_PROD. When MID_PROD local users want to access data on EAST_PROD, they must define a link that is stored in the data dictionary of database EAST_PROD.

The database links provide a means for users to manipulate objects within the remote database. Users can issue DML statements such as SELECT, INSERT, UPDATE, and DELETE. The remote server executes all operations on objects in the remote database, and only the results of those operations are passed back to the server that issued the call through the link. Thus, database links make distributed database processing a reality in the Oracle world.

In order for a connection through a database link to occur, each database in the distributed system must have a unique *global database name* in the network domain. This global database name uniquely identifies a database server in a distributed system. You'll find complete coverage of the global name concept in Chapter 9.

In Figure 23.1, a user can access four different distributed databases from a single central corporate database. The user will be able to access the tables that are on the PROD (Production) database on any of the four divisions (NW_DIV, NE_DIV, SW_DIV, and SE_DIV), depending on how links are established.

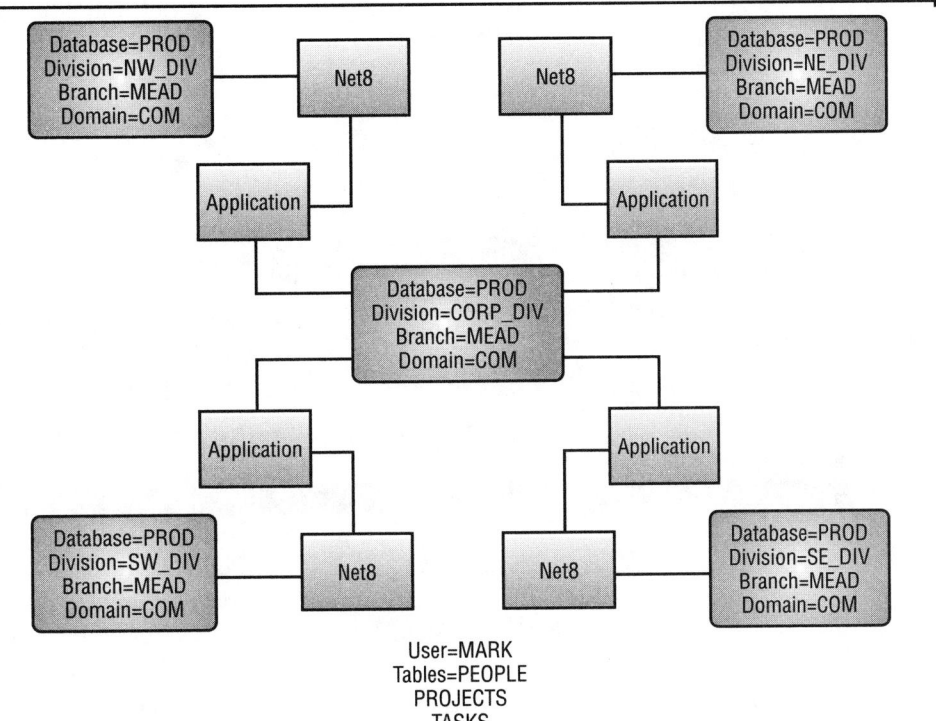

FIGURE 23.1

An arrangement of database links

Advantages Offered by Database Links

One advantage of a database link is that it enables connection to a remote database server and allows limited access (or unlimited, depending on how you configure the remote server account) to outside users. You don't have to keep the same set of data on two different databases to support an enterprise with multiple locations. Database links allow query access of data on the remote system. Thus MARK, a local user on the corporate production database (PROD in the example in Figure 23.1), can link to and access the data at remote database PROD.NE_DIV without having to be a user on that database.

Let's consider a project-related example of linked databases, using Figure 23.1 as a guide. Say we have projects established in local databases around the nation, each tracking all information for its particular region. We have databases named NW_DIV, SW_DIV, NE_DIV, and SE_DIV. You're working at corporate headquarters (the database named CORP_DIV) and you have the responsibility of checking the status of all the national projects. Instead of having to keep a set of data from each region, you can establish a link to each of the _DIV locations. By accessing their data, you can run reports and queries on the most current version of each region's data. This is known as *distributed processing*.

Database Link Types

When you want to create a database link, you need to decide what type of link you wish to create. The three types of database links are private, public, and global. Table 23.1 gives a brief description of each type, and you'll learn more about them as you work through this chapter. The table also summarizes the pros and cons of each link type. You'll want to consider these against the requirements of your own distributed environment.

TABLE 23.1: TYPES OF DATABASE LINKS

Link Type	Owner	Allowed Access	Advantage	Disadvantage
Private	User who created the link	Only the user who created the link	Most secure link	Only the user who created the link can access it.
Public	PUBLIC user	All users and PL/SQL programs	Many users can access the link	Many users can access the link, so not as secure. Like all public entities, it is accessible to a large audience, which can mean heavy network traffic.
Global	PUBLIC user	All users and PL/SQL programs	Many users can access the link. Management is global and thus easier to do	Disadvantages are the same as for a public link.

NOTE If your database is running multithreaded server (MTS), your public, private, and global database links can all be established as *shared links*. The primary purpose of a shared database link is to take advantage of MTS's ability to handle multiple database connections through one server process. This reduces the overall load on the database server.

Connection Methods

Having decided what link type you wish to create, you then choose a type of *connection method* to be used when you create the link. The connection method of a link determines how Oracle accesses the remote host through the database link. The connection method also determines what objects your link has access to. In addition, your each connection option has particular influence on the security of the remote database to which you connect.

- In a *connected user link,* the originating user connects as him/herself. The user on the originating database must have an account on the destination database with the same username as that on the originating database.

- A *fixed user link* makes the connection as the user identified in the link. That is, if MARK (a user at the originating site) connects with a fixed link to the Projects database with the username/password combination of DEN_REM/GUEST, then MARK will have all the rights and privileges granted to DEN_REM.

- The *current user link* is an aspect of the Oracle Advanced Security Option and should be employed with caution. In a current user link, the user always connects as a global user and can thus access the remote database without the user's global password being stored in the link definition. For example, ROBERT can access a procedure that MARK wrote, accessing MARK's account and MARK's schema on the Projects database.

WARNING The most secure of these connection methods is the connected user link, which grants limited access on remote databases to local users. Of course, the most secure method is, by virtue of its secure nature, more difficult to use. We find that fixed user links are employed most often in the real world. Beware of fixed user links, however, because the user account name and password are stored *unencrypted* in the SYS.LINK$ data dictionary view. Although this view is only accessible to DBA-level accounts, this still represents a major security hole.

Connected User Links

The following statement creates a public link to the NW_DIV database. In this arrangement, when user APP_OWN accesses the public link to NW_DIV in a query, the connected user will be APP_OWN.

```
CREATE PUBLIC DATABASE LINK NW_DIV USING 'NW_DIV' ;
```

As you can see, the CREATE statement for a connected user link does not have a CONNECT string. The CONNECT string is used to establish connection to the remote database as a specified user. One advantage of using this link is that the user connects to the remote database as himself/herself, keeping the same username on both the source and destination databases. Better yet, no password is used and therefore cannot be intercepted. This is a relatively secure method for establishing the connection.

For a *connected user link*, the user must have privileges on the remote database. This can be considered both an advantage and disadvantage. On the positive side, the requirement means the user cannot accomplish anything without the privileges. On the negative side, the DBA has to establish and maintain those privileges.

One more item concerning the connected user link: Oracle does allow a connected user to be authenticated by the host system or through other authentication services. If you intend to use connected user links for connecting to a remote database, you'll have to set the REMOTE_OS_AUTHENT initialization parameter to TRUE (the default). To see the value of this parameter, use the following SQL:

```
SELECT name, value, isdefault, ismodified, description
FROM v$parameter
WHERE name = 'remote_os_authent' ;
```

Fixed User Links

With a *fixed user link*, the user connects to the remote database with a username and password. For instance, MARK (the DBA) creates a public database link in ROBERT's schema and specifies a fixed user of RODNEY/CONSULTANT. Now any user on the source system can connect to the remote system using the proper username/password; however, they will be connecting as RODNEY/CONSULTANT. This allows the connection to be enabled and disabled quickly and easily, leaving the remote link up only as long as necessary.

Here's an example of the fixed user link:

```
CREATE DATABASE LINK my_link
    CONNECT TO robert IDENTIFIED BY enterprise
    USING 'proj_us';
```

In this example, our database link is named MY_LINK. We will connect to a Net8 service called PROJ_US. We will connect as the ROBERT user, with ENTERPRISE as the password.

One big drawback to the fixed user connection is that usernames and passwords are stored in the LINK$ table and are unencrypted. As stated earlier, this opens a gap in the security arrangements. Any user with SELECT ANY TABLE access can easily gain access if the O7_DICTIONARY_ACCESSIBILITY parameter is set to TRUE (which is the default). You can look at this parameter with the following SQL:

```
SELECT name, value, isdefault, ismodified, description
FROM v$parameter
WHERE name = 'O7_DICTIONARY_ACCESSIBILITY' ;
```

NOTE We strongly suggest that O7_DICTIONARY_ACCESSIBILITY be set to FALSE in your Oracle8i database to avoid this security nightmare.

Current User Links

A *current user link* always connects as a global user. A global user must be authenticated through an X.509 certificate and a private key, and the user must be established on both the remote database and the source database.

Following is an example of a current user link:

```
CREATE PUBLIC DATABASE LINK my_link
CONNECT TO CURRENT_USER USING 'proj_us' ;
```

In the previous example we are creating a database link called MY_LINK. Since we use the CURRENT_USER keyword, this is a current user link and will attach to the remote database (PROJ_US) as the currently logged-in user.

Following are the drawbacks of current user links:

- The current user is the same as the connected user when access is not established from a stored function, procedure, or other object—that is, when the link is used directly (SQL statement). If MARK accesses the link with a SQL statement, then MARK could actually look like ROBERT if the current user is established as ROBERT.

- The current user is the user who owns the object when the link is established through a function, procedure, or other object. For example, if MARK accesses the link through the function GET_PAYROLL_INFO, which was created by ROBERT, then the CURRENT_USER is ROBERT.

- You cannot use a current user link through an object's owner when connected as an enterprise user, if that object's owner exists in a shared global schema. For example, if ROBERT is the owner of object GET_HELP and exists in the shared global schema, when MARK executes GET_HELP he cannot gain access as the CURRENT_USER ROBERT.

Schema Object Names on a Distributed System

Oracle uses the following syntax to name objects and keep them unique across a distributed system:

schema.schema_object@global_database_name

where the variables have the following definitions:

- schema is a collection of tables, views, and grants making up a logical grouping. Each user owns a single schema.
- schema_object is the table, view, index, or other object within the schema.
- global_database_name is the unique name of the remote database. Remember that this name *must* match the DB_NAME and DB_DOMAIN concatenated together, unless GLOBAL_NAMES is set to FALSE.

Take a look at this example of a link and the SQL to access data on that database:
PROJ.NE_DIV.MEAD.COM

```
SELECT Proj_num, Amount
FROM robert.proj@PROD.NE_DIV.MEAD.COM
WHERE amount <= 200000 ;
```

This will get the project number and amount from the PROJ table in the ROBERT schema, where the amount is less than or equal to 200000. Note that if GLOBAL_NAMES were set to FALSE, then the following statement could be used. We can substitute the global name with any name we want, as shown here:

```
SELECT Proj_num, Amount
FROM robert.proj@ENTERPRISE
WHERE amount <= 200000 ;
```

Administering Database Links

As with anything else Oracle, you have some administrative tasks to perform on your links. In this section we'll look at some fundamentals on how to create and drop database links, understanding schema object name resolution, and a couple of relevant data dictionary views.

NOTE For more on database link administration, see Chapter 2 of the Oracle documentation for Oracle8i Distributed Database Systems.

Creating Database Links

To create a database link, use the CREATE DATABASE LINK statement. For creating a public database link, use the optional syntax CREATE PUBLIC DATABASE LINK. Once the link is created, you can use the link in your SQL code to access objects in the remote database. Table 23.2 lists the SQL statements necessary to establish various connections and links to a remote database.

TABLE 23.2: LINK COMMANDS

Type of Link	Type of Connection	SQL Command to Create the Link
Private	Connected user	CREATE DATABASE LINK Prod USING 'proj_us' ;
Private	Fixed user	CREATE DATABASE LINK Prod CONNECT TO robert IDENTIFIED BY enterprise USING 'proj_us' ;
Private	Current user	CREATE DATABASE LINK cur_test CONNECT TO CURRENT_USER USING 'prod_us' ;
Public	Connected user	CREATE PUBLIC DATABASE LINK nw_div USING 'nw_div' ;
Public	Fixed user	CREATE PUBLIC DATABASE LINK proj CONNECT TO robert IDENTIFIED BY enterprise USING 'prod_us';

NOTE Keep in mind that you will need to establish Net8 connectivity to the remote database before you can create a database link to it. The process of configuring databases for Net8 is discussed in detail in Chapter 9.

Dropping Database Links

To drop a database link use the DROP DATABASE LINK command:

```
DROP DATABASE LINK <link name>;
```

 NOTE There is no ALTER DATABASE LINK command in Oracle8i.

Schema Object Name Resolution

What's in a name? A lot. When deciding which object you want to use, be aware that Oracle uses a hierarchical object access methodology. Within the Oracle database each and every schema in a database is unique by virtue of the schema name and other rules (such as the rule that a given table within a schema must have a unique name). In the end, all objects in that schema are unique. (See the earlier section, "Schema Object Names on a Distributed System.")

Things can get muddy, however, when you introduce the distributed environment, or synonyms, or both. All of a sudden you may well have a given object present in your schema called PROJECTS, and at the same time you might have a PROJECTS synonym that points to a PROJECTS object in a distributed database. It's easy to see that you must exercise care when designing the database and creating objects in a schema—a caution you've heard and read before, no doubt. You need to make sure that the object is not going to inadvertently cause problems for some other object that might be accessed by the user.

Within disparate distributed systems, object names are guaranteed to be unique across the distributed environment because Oracle uses a hierarchical naming schema. We don't need to be particularly concerned if an object in one production database has the same name as an object in another database. We can have identical names for all our objects in these production databases. For a given databases schema, each link name must be unique, and this makes each of those objects uniquely accessible. Because of this, Oracle will actually be able to determine that we are accessing different tables and return the correct results to us. The only aside to this is that some caution must be taken when you have a public database link and a private database link with the same name.

Oracle may need a little help with pulling out the correct column. We can assist by aliasing the column and the object being queried, as in the following example:

```
SELECT a.Proj_num, a.amount, b.project_manager, b.status
FROM projects@PROJ_MASTER a,
```

```
projects@PROJECT_MGR_MASTER b
WHERE a.proj_id=b.proj_id;
```

In this SELECT statement, we have a join that is accessing two different remote databases. It appears we are going after two tables with the same name, PROJECTS. Of course, one of these PROJECTS tables is in the database pointed to by the PROJ_MASTER database link. The other is in the database pointed to by the PROJECT_MGR_ MASTER database link. We assume that these two links point to two disparate remote databases. As you can see, the STATUS column is common within both of the objects we are querying. Note how we need to alias the columns to get the query to operate correctly.

Using Synonyms

In addition to using the full name of a link, Oracle allows us to create *synonyms* to specific objects using the database links that we establish. Synonyms serve several purposes. First, they serve to hide the actual destination of the database link and the object being accessed, from the user. Synonyms also serve to make coding easier, by allowing you to assign a name to the given link that describes the link, and the object being accessed through that link. Here is an example of the creation of a public synonym for an object that is accessed through a database link.

```
CREATE PUBLIC SYNONYM PROD_NEDIV for ROBERT.PROD@NE_DIV;
```

Data Dictionary Objects Relevant to Database Links

Of course, you may need to look up the database links in your database. What remote databases are they pointing to? You will also want to document the database links in your database so that you can re-create them if the need arises. The DBA_DB_LINKS and SYS.LINK$ views are the primary data dictionary objects for acquiring database link information.

The DBA_DB_LINKS View   The DBA_DB_LINKS view (and its related ALL_DB_LINKS and USER_DB_LINKS views) provides information on each database link. Included in the view is the name of the database link, the host, and the connecting account name used by the link uses to connect to the remote database. Also included is the creation date of the database link. You can use this view to find the name of the appropriate database link that you need to use in your queries.

The LINK$ Data Dictionary Table   The LINK$ data dictionary table, owned by the SYS schema, is a base data dictionary table that contains various information on every database link. Only the SYS user has access to this base table, and no grants are given to it, either directly to other user accounts or indirectly through any role. Be cautious when you're considering giving access to this base table, since it contains in cleartext the password of the username that the link connects to on the remote database.

Using Database Links

After creating the link as described earlier, we can start with a simple SQL statement that accesses the PROJECTS table to get all the active projects in the NE_DIV.

```
SELECT  proj_num, status
FROM    Projects@ne_div
WHERE   Status = 'ACTIVE' ;
```

Notice that when accessing the table PROJECTS, we added the location where PROJECTS resides. This is necessary because we are accessing a table on the NE_DIV database, which is not our home database.

Understanding object naming is very important for accessing just the right database and table you want. You will need to design your object-naming convention prior to creating links for a distributed system. See Chapters 3 and 9 for further information on naming.

 TIP The Oracle documentation contains a wealth of information on Oracle distributed databases, as does Technet (technet.oracle.com).

CHAPTER 24

Database Partitioning

FEATURING:

Partitioning in Oracle8i	1024
Partitioning basics	1025
Partitioning indexes	1036
The importance of partition pruning	1039
Partition-wise joins	1040
Partition management	1043

This chapter offers examples of all types of partitioning for both tables and indexes, with some administrative considerations to keep in mind. (Partitioning of materialized views works the same as for tables and indexes.) The features described in this chapter are available with Oracle8i Enterprise Edition's partitioning option.

NOTE Partitioning is like any other part of a successful Oracle implementation: Always design and test your solutions carefully.

Partitioning in Oracle8i

Two new partitioning methods were introduced in Oracle8i: hash partitioning and composite partitioning. When combined with the existing range partitioning capability, we now have a choice of partitioning methods and can pick the best solution for a particular situation. Like range partitioning, the two new methods work with standard DML statements run against the partitioned tables.

In addition to the new partitioning methods, several enhancements to partitioning technology were introduced in Oracle8i.

Partition Merging You can take two separate and distinct partitions of the same table and bring them back into one partition. This is accomplished with the ALTER TABLE...MERGE PARTITIONS command. The partitions to be merged must be utilizing range partitioning.

Updateable Partition Keys Another new feature is the ENABLE ROW MOVEMENT option for the CREATE TABLE and ALTER TABLE commands. It allows movement of data from one partition to another. The moved data is no longer associated with the old partition. In essence, you modify the keys associated to the two partitions.

Enhanced Partition Elimination This feature lets you skip past data in partitions that is not relevant to SQL queries. For instance, if you have a table that is partitioned into 12 separate partitions (by month) and a SQL query against data from March (the third partition), you can skip over the other 11 partitions and improve the performance of your SQL. This is accomplished transparently by Oracle via partition pruning, discussed later in this chapter.

Partition-Wise Joins   When tables are joined in parallel processing (see Chapter 18), earlier versions of Oracle split the joined table into many pieces, depending on the degree of parallelism, and then gathered and recombined the pieces based on the join column. In Oracle8i, the recombining step can be skipped if the data is partitioned on the join key. This can reduce consumption of memory and temporary storage space, and potentially decrease the time taken for queries to return their results. Oracle handles this transparently, provided your table/tables are partitioned and parallel processing is activated.

Support for LOBs   Oracle8i supports partitioning of tables with LOB columns.

Support for Index-Organized Tables   In Oracle8i you can partition index-organized tables. This is of most use to OLTPs, historical (data warehousing) databases, and VLDBs.

NOTE   Another new partitioning method (list partitioning) is available in Oracle9i.

Partitioning Basics

Partitioning is the process of taking a very large database element and turning it into smaller, more manageable objects. Partitioning makes it easier to gather data from the smaller parts rather than accessing the whole table. It is only available for databases using cost-based optimization.

There are three methods of partitioning:

- In *range partitioning,* the object is split based on a range of values.
- In *hash partitioning,* the object is split based on a hash function.
- In *composite partitioning,* the data is split first with the range method and then further subpartitioned with the hash partitioning method.

You can partition tables, indexes, materialized views, and materialized views indexes, as long as they are not part of a cluster and do not contain a LONG or LONG RAW datatype.

NOTE   You cannot do partitioning of clustered tables or indexes on clustered tables.

Among the many advantages to partitioning, discussed at length in Chapter 11 of the *Oracle8i Concepts* documentation, is that splitting a VLDB into many parts improves performance. I/O performance can be significantly increased by splitting separate partitions across physical devices (load balancing). The transparency of Oracle's operations is a big benefit to the programmer and DBA alike. As previously mentioned, it's not necessary to write code in order to gain benefits from partition elimination or partition-wise joins. What this means is that you can take an existing table and partition it using any of the three methods—without having to change the code that accesses these tables.

 TIP Listings 24.1 through 24.3 demonstrate how to create a partitioned table using each of the partitioning methods. Check the Oracle documentation for more examples.

Partition Naming

Naming of partitions follows the same convention as naming of all objects in Oracle. Just keep in mind that the name of the partition or subpartition must be unique.

For composite partitioning, the names of partitions and subpartitions are in the same namespace. That is, a partition and a subpartition belonging to the same parent table or index cannot have the same name.

You can rename a partition or subpartition; however, you cannot create any synonyms on a partition or subpartition name.

Range Partitioning

Put simply, range partitioning is the process of breaking an object into smaller parts based on the values in a column. This is accomplished with the PARTITION BY clause. You have the ability to take an existing object and partition it or create it as a partitioned object. The following diagrams show the DDL syntax for range partitioning.

PARTITIONING BASICS

```
>—PARTITION BY RANGE (column_list) (—partition_definition—)——>
```

partition_definition Command Syntax

```
>—PARTITION————————VALUES LESS THAN (value_list)——————>
           └─partition─┘

>——┬─segment_attribute_clause─┬──┬─OVERFLOW─────────────────────────┬──>
   ├─COMPRESS─────────────────┤  └────────segment_attributes_clause─┘
   └─NOCOMPRESS───────────────┘

>——┬─LOB_storage_clause────┬──┬─partition_level_subpartitioning─┬──>
   └─varray_storage_clause─┘
```

segment_attribute_clause Command Syntax

```
>——┬─physical_attributes_clause─┬──>
   ├─TABLESPACE tablespace──────┤
   ├─LOGGING────────────────────┤
   └─NOLOGGING──────────────────┘
```

LOB_storage_clause Command Syntax

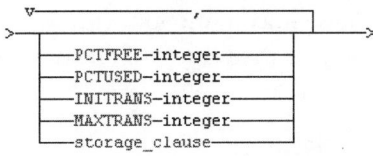

varray_storage_clause Command Syntax

```
>—VARRAY varray item STORE AS LOB——┬─LOB_segname (LOB_parameters)─┬──>
                                   ├─LOB_segname─────────────────┤
                                   └─(LOB_parameters)────────────┘
```

physical_attributes_clause Command Syntax

```
>——┬─PCTFREE—integer──┬──>
   ├─PCTUSED—integer──┤
   ├─INITRANS—integer─┤
   ├─MAXTRANS—integer─┤
   └─storage_clause───┘
```

storage clause Command Syntax

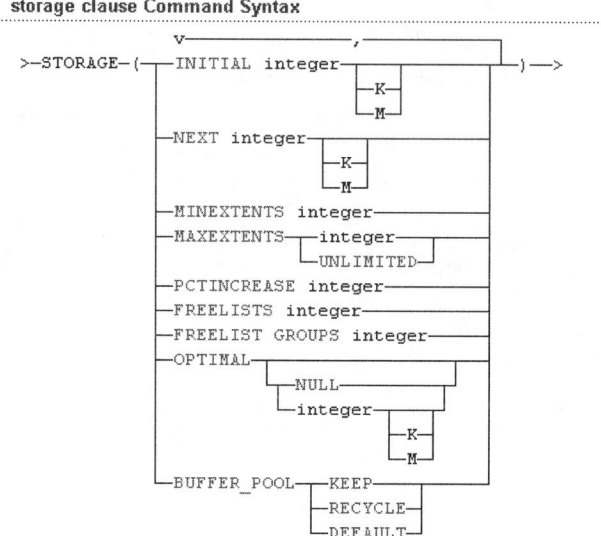

LOB_parameters Command Syntax

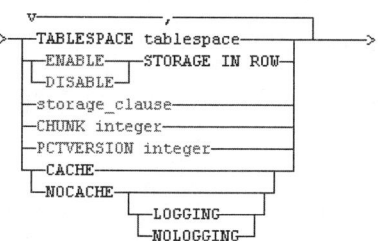

Listing 24.1 demonstrates partitioning of the PROJECTS table into 12 pieces, one partition for each month depending on the project's start date. Notice that we specify the PARTITION BY RANGE clause in conjunction with the column on which we want to partition (column_list) as well as the values that belong in each partition (value_list).

Listing 24.1: Range Partitioning

```
CREATE TABLE projects
(project_number    number         not null
, project_name     varchar2(20)   not null
, start_date       date           not null
, end_date         date           not null
```

```
, amount          number(12,2)    not null
, month_num       number(2)       not null)
PCTFREE 5
PCTUSED 30
STORAGE (INITIAL 100M
     NEXT 100M
     PCTINCREASE 0)
PARTITION BY RANGE (MONTH_NUM)
(PARTITION MONTH01 VALUES LESS THAN (2)
   PCTFREE 5
   PCTUSED 30
   TABLESPACE DATA01
      STORAGE (INITIAL 100M
            NEXT 100M)
 PARTITION MONTH02 VALUES LESS THAN (3)
   PCTFREE 5
   PCTUSED 30
      TABLESPACE DATA02
      STORAGE (INITIAL 100M
            NEXT 100M)
 PARTITION MONTH03 VALUES LESS THAN (4)
   PCTFREE 5
   PCTUSED 30
   TABLESPACE DATA03
      STORAGE (INITIAL 100M
            NEXT 100M)
 PARTITION MONTH04 VALUES LESS THAN (5)
   PCTFREE 5
   PCTUSED 30
   TABLESPACE DATA04
      STORAGE (INITIAL 100M
            NEXT 100M)
 PARTITION MONTH05 VALUES LESS THAN (6)
   PCTFREE 5
   PCTUSED 30
   TABLESPACE DATA05
      STORAGE (INITIAL 100M
            NEXT 100M)
 PARTITION MONTH06 VALUES LESS THAN (7)
```

```
            PCTFREE 5
            PCTUSED 30
            TABLESPACE DATA06
                STORAGE (INITIAL 100M
                        NEXT 100M)
    PARTITION MONTH07 VALUES LESS THAN (8)
            PCTFREE 5
            PCTUSED 30
            TABLESPACE DATA07
                STORAGE (INITIAL 100M
                        NEXT 100M)
    PARTITION MONTH08 VALUES LESS THAN (9)
            PCTFREE 5
            PCTUSED 30
            TABLESPACE DATA08
                STORAGE (INITIAL 100M
                        NEXT 100M)
    PARTITION MONTH09 VALUES LESS THAN (10)
            PCTFREE 5
            PCTUSED 30
            TABLESPACE DATA09
                STORAGE (INITIAL 100M
                        NEXT 100M)
    PARTITION MONTH10 VALUES LESS THAN (11)
            PCTFREE 5
            PCTUSED 30
            TABLESPACE DATA10
                STORAGE (INITIAL 100M
                        NEXT 100M)
    PARTITION MONTH11 VALUES LESS THAN (12)
            PCTFREE 5
            PCTUSED 30
            TABLESPACE DATA11
                STORAGE (INITIAL 100M
                        NEXT 100M)
    PARTITION MONTH12 VALUES LESS THAN (MAXVALUE)
            PCTFREE 5
            PCTUSED 30
            TABLESPACE DATA12
```

```
              STORAGE (INITIAL 100M
                      NEXT 100M));
```

With the PROJECTS table partitioned as above, you can access parts (partitions) of the table instead of the whole table. Should this partitioning turn out to be inefficient based on the way the data is being accessed, you can put a section of partitions back together with the ALTER TABLE MERGE PARTITIONS command. You'll thus be able to adjust to your changing data requirements. Should you need to partition a table after it has been created, you'd use the ALTER TABLE command. In its PARTITION BY clause, you'd be able to partition the existing table.

Hash Partitioning

Hash partitioning, new with Oracle8i, distributes rows evenly into many partitions based on a hashing function. One advantage to this method is that partitions will be evenly sized. This facilitates separation of the partitions across disks, to assist with load balancing and minimize risk of data loss (whole table) should you lose an I/O device. In short, hash partitioning lends itself to situations where the data does not lend itself to range partitioning.

Following is the DDL syntax diagram for hash partitioning.

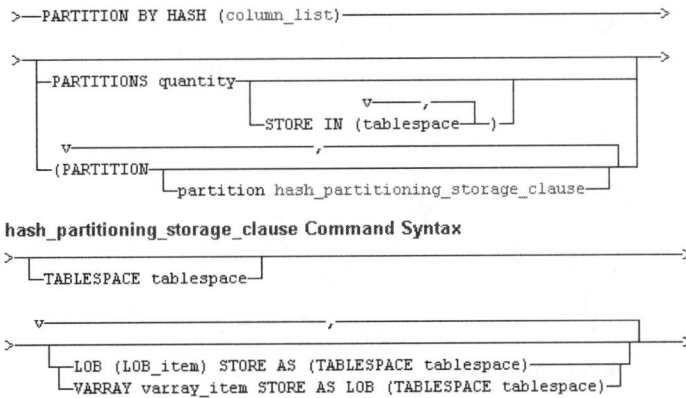

hash_partitioning_storage_clause Command Syntax

NOTE It's an accepted fact that SQL performance improves with load balancing. Keep in mind that load balancing will be more difficult under hash partitioning, because the partitioning is done by Oracle and not controlled by the DBA.

Following are conditions under which to consider using hash partitioning:

- When you cannot determine the amount of data that will reside in each of the partitions.
- When partition pruning is important, as discussed later in this chapter. Pruning lets you select data only from certain partitions to meet the needs of your SQL query, rather than accessing the whole table. This will increase your I/O performance.
- When use of partition-wise joins is important, as discussed later in the chapter. With this construct we can take a large join operation and break it into smaller joins that will be performed either sequentially or in parallel.

In hash partitioning, the goal is to distribute the data evenly. Thus it is best to use a power of 2 (making sure the number of partitions is evenly divisible by 2) in this method—it gives you the best opportunity for an even spread of the data. In Listing 24.2, we have six partitions and thus partitioning with the power of 2.

Listing 24.2: Hash Partitioning

```
CREATE TABLE projects
(project_number   number         not null
, project_name    varchar2(20)   not null
, start_date      date           not null
, end_date        date           not null
, amount          number(12,2)   not null
, month_num       number(2)      not null)
PCTFREE 5
PCTUSED 30
STORAGE (INITIAL 100M
   NEXT 100M
   PCTINCREASE 0)
PARTITION BY HASH (start_date)
   (PARTITION MONTH01 TABLESPACE DATA01
   , PARTITION MONTH02 TABLESPACE DATA02
   , PARTITION MONTH03 TABLESPACE DATA03
   , PARTITION MONTH04 TABLESPACE DATA04
   , PARTITION MONTH05 TABLESPACE DATA05
   , PARTITION MONTH06 TABLESPACE DATA06)
ENABLE ROW MOVEMENT ;
```

Notice that we've used start_date this time as the PARTITION BY HASH value, instead of month_num. The month_num value used with the range partitioning method allows us to control the breakpoint in the data. In the case of hash partitioning, where we are working toward even distribution among partitions, we choose the start_date. We have elected to spread the partitions across several tablespaces to help with load balancing. Also notice that the data is divided across six different partitions, giving a power of 2 distribution.

Another point to note is that the last line of code in this example is ENABLE ROW MOVEMENT. Using this option allows rows in one partition to move to another partition if they're needed. (You must include this statement to enable row movement; the option is disabled by default.)

Composite Partitioning

Composite partitioning is a combination of the hash and range methods. You get the benefits of the hash method's automatic distribution of data, as well as the range method's easy availability (knowing what partitions are holding what data) and partition management. You can break up the data as desired in the partition, and then further subpartition the data to achieve an even distribution—composite partitioning is a great tool for load balancing.

Some other benefits of composite partitioning are

- Naming and storing the subpartitions how and where we want.
- Creating range-partitioned global indexes.
- Naming the index subpartitions as desired, and storing them where we want.
- Building local indexes on composite partitioned tables. These indexes will be stored in the same tablespace as the table subpartition.

Following is the DDL syntax for composite partitioning.

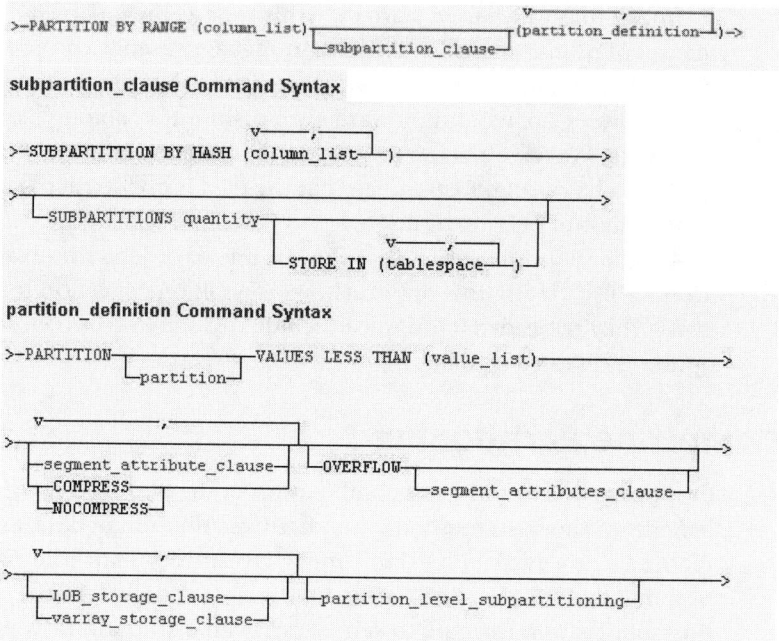

Listing 24.3 is an example utilizing composite partitioning. We are range-partitioning by order_date and then further hash-partitioning by product_id. This partitioning arrangement will give us a pretty good spread across our database.

Listing 24.3: Composite Partitioning

```
CREATE TABLE sales_orders
(order_id        number          not null
, order_number   number          not null
, order_date     date            not null
, cancel_date    date            not null
, quantity       number(12)      not null
, amount         number(12,2)    not null
, product_id     number(2)       not null)
PCTFREE 5
PCTUSED 30
STORAGE (INITIAL 100M
   NEXT 100M
   PCTINCREASE 0)
PARTITION BY RANGE(order_date)
   SUBPARTITION BY HASH(product_id) SUBPARTITIONS 4
```

```
            STORE IN (DATA06, DATA07, DATA08, DATA09)
                (PARTITION DATA06 VALUES LESS THAN('01-APR-2000'),
                 PARTITION DATA07 VALUES LESS THAN('01-JUL-2000'),
                 PARTITION DATA08 VALUES LESS THAN('01-OCT-2000'),
                 PARTITION DATA09 VALUES LESS THAN('01-DEC-2000'));
```

Partitioning on LOB Columns

Oracle8i allows use of LOB columns as the partitioning column. (An object cannot, however, have a partition key that contains a LOB datatype.)

Bear in mind that the LOB is stored as an object on the disk and not in the table itself. We can designate where we want storage location for the LOB object, and that technique is highly recommended. In designating the storage location of the LOB, you can further enhance the I/O performance through load balancing. The basic rules for LOB partitioning are as follows:

- If you specify the tablespace (recommended) where the LOB is to be stored, that value is used.
- If you let the default tablespace be assigned, that value is used (for example, when you let the index be located with the table).
- If neither of these is utilized, the LOB is stored with the table partition that it belongs to.

Following is an example of assigning the tablespace for where the data will be going (we prefer this arrangement). In assigning the tablespace, you maintain a better understanding of the partitioning setup and will be able to do load balancing more efficiently.

```
CREATE TABLE projects_p
    (project_number    number
    ,project_blob      blob
    ,project_clob      clob
    ,project_nclob     nclob)
PARTITION BY RANGE (project_number)
(PARTITION project_number VALUES LESS THAN (200000)
    TABLESPACE blob_p1
 PARTITION project_number VALUES LESS THAN (400000)
    TABLESPACE clob
 PARTITION project_number VALUES LESS THAN (800000)
    TABLESPACE nclob);
```

In this example we have elected to identify the tablespace where the LOBs are to be located. LOBS in this database are now separated (load balanced) into different partitions.

Partitioning Indexes

Partitioning your indexes is as important as partitioning your tables. If you partition your tables but not your indexes, you achieve performance improvement in your tables—but their indexes still require nonpartitioned access. So you won't realize the full benefit of partitioning. This section discusses range, hash, and composite partitioning, as well as partitioning global indexes.

A local index partition is guaranteed to match the partition of the table that the index belongs to. This is accomplished by automatically creating and dropping the necessary index partitions based on the partitioning of the table. You cannot add, drop, or split an index partition for a local index.

Range Partitioning of an Index

Following are discussions of two different methods for partitioning indexes using the range method.

```
CREATE INDEX pt_projects
   ON projects (month_num)
   LOCAL;
```

This first example creates the index `pt_projects`, where the partitioning will be the same as the table `projects`. Since we don't specify the PARTITION clause, we'll end up with 12 partitions for the index. Since we don't specify a location for the index, it will be placed in the same tablespace as the table partitions.

The next example is a better choice for partitioning our index. Here, we specify the breakout of the partitions and define the location for storing them.

```
CREATE INDEX pt_projects
ON projects(month_num)
    LOCAL(
        PARTITION imonth1          TABLESPACE idx1,
        PARTITION imonth2          TABLESPACE idx2,
        PARTITION imonth3          TABLESPACE idx3,
        PARTITION imonth4          TABLESPACE idx4,
        PARTITION imonth5          TABLESPACE idx5,
        PARTITION imonth6          TABLESPACE idx6,
```

```
        PARTITION imonth7      TABLESPACE idx7,
        PARTITION imonth8      TABLESPACE idx8,
        PARTITION imonth9      TABLESPACE idx9,
        PARTITION imonth10     TABLESPACE idx10,
        PARTITION imonth11     TABLESPACE idx11,
        PARTITION imonth12     TABLESPACE idx12);
```

Hash Partitioning of an Index

Following is an example of creating an index using the hash partitioning method. Just as we do for table partitioning, we simply cite the number of partitions we want. Oracle creates the index and distributes the data in accordance with the hash algorithm.

```
CREATE INDEX pt_projects
ON projects(month_num)
  LOCAL
    STORE IN (idx1, idx2, idx3, idx4, idx5, idx6);
```

This example creates an index on the table `projects`. The STORE IN clause indicates that the index method is hash and will distribute the data in the index partitions evenly between the six indicated locations (`idx1...idx6`).

Composite Partitioning of an Index

Composite partitioning of an index is just like composite partitioning for a table. Listing 24.4 is an example, using the SALES table.

Listing 24.4: Composite Partitioning of an Index

```
CREATE INDEX sales_idx
ON sales_orders(order_date)
    STORAGE (INITIAL 1M, MAXEXTENTS UNLIMITED)
    LOCAL
    STORE IN (idx1, idx2, idx3, idx4)
    (PARTITION q1_2000
    , PARTITION q2_2000
    , PARTITION q3_2000
    , PARTITION q4_2000
        (SUBPARTITION q4_2000_s1 TABLESPACE is1,
         SUBPARTITION q4_2000_s2 TABLESPACE is2,
         SUBPARTITION q4_2000_s3 TABLESPACE is3,
         SUBPARTITION q4_2000_s4 TABLESPACE is4);
```

This example creates a composite partitioned index. The STORE IN clause specifies four different tablespaces where we can store the indexes (`idx1`, `idx2`, `idx3`, and `idx4`). We decided to override the fourth partition and create subpartitions, storing the results in the tablespaces `is1`, `is2`, `is3`, and `is4`. The end result will be that partitions q1_2000, q2_2000, and q3_2000 will be stored in one of the four tablespaces `idx1`, `idx2`, `idx3`, or `idx4`; and p4_2000 will be stored in tablespaces `is1`, `is2`, `is3`, and `is4`.

Global Indexes

Global indexes contain keys that refer to more than one partition. They are created using the GLOBAL attribute of the CREATE INDEX command rather than the LOCAL attribute. (All the preceding examples of partitioned indexes are local indexes.)

We prefer not to useglobal indexes because they require frequent table maintenance; in addition, they can never be considered equipartitioned even if structurally they appear to be. One advantage of global indexes is that they don't have to have the same partitioning as the master table.

Listing 24.5 demonstrates creating a global index with partitioning.

Listing 24.5: Creating a Partitioned Global Index

```
CREATE INDEX pt_gl_projects
ON projects (month_num)
GLOBAL
   PARTITION BY RANGE (month_num)
      (PARTITION i_gl_projects1  VALUES LESS THAN (2)
         TABLESPACE proj_index1,
       PARTITION i_gl_projects2  VALUES LESS THAN (3)
         TABLESPACE proj_index2,
       PARTITION i_gl_projects3  VALUES LESS THAN (4)
         TABLESPACE proj_index3,
       PARTITION i_gl_projects4  VALUES LESS THAN (5)
         TABLESPACE proj_index4,
       PARTITION i_gl_projects5  VALUES LESS THAN (6)
         TABLESPACE proj_index5,
       PARTITION i_gl_projects6  VALUES LESS THAN (7)
         TABLESPACE proj_index6,
       PARTITION i_gl_projects7  VALUES LESS THAN (8)
         TABLESPACE proj_index7,
       PARTITION i_gl_projects8  VALUES LESS THAN (9)
         TABLESPACE proj_index8,
       PARTITION i_gl_projects9  VALUES LESS THAN (10)
```

```
        TABLESPACE proj_index9,
    PARTITION i_gl_projects10   VALUES LESS THAN (11)
        TABLESPACE proj_index10,
    PARTITION i_gl_projects11   VALUES LESS THAN (12)
        TABLESPACE proj_index11,
    PARTITION i_gl_projects12   VALUES LESS THAN (maxvalue)
        TABLESPACE proj_index12));
```

The Importance of Partition Pruning

Oracle's ability to recognize partitions and subpartitions gives you an important inroad to increased productivity for your queries. Through partition *pruning,* you capitalize even more on this advantage. By utilizing the important partitions and eliminating or "pruning" the unnecessary partitions, you will get better returns from your SQL statements.

Oracle can prune away partitions that do not meet the selection criteria of the SQL statement being executed. For instance, if you write a query to access only the first three months (partitions) of the PROJECTS table, there is no need to retrieve data from the remaining nine partitions. Oracle's pruning technique dramatically reduces data read-through, resulting in substantial improvements in query performance.

When the Oracle optimizer resolves that all the data requirements are satisfied by the rows in the selected partition, it removes the remaining partitions from the WHERE clause prior to executing the query.

NOTE The optimizer will not prune partitions when the SQL code applies a function (other than the TO_DATE() function) to the partitioning column.

Oracle can also prune partitioned indexes, even when the table's partitions are required to successfully execute the SQL statement. For instance, suppose we are after items in three of four partitions and we have partitioned the indexes on different columns. We may be able to improve the performance of operations on large tables by reducing (pruning) the amount of data that the SQL statement needs to access or modify.

Pruning also increases the availability of unneeded partitions for other database operations, such as

- Loading data into unused partitions

- Purging data from unused partitions
- Backup and restoration of unused partitions
- Reorganization
- Index building

Partition-Wise Joins

A *partition-wise join* is a large join operation divided into smaller parts and executed in parallel. The results of the smaller joins are then brought back together as if the separation had never taken place. This utilizes Oracle's capabilities of both parallel processing and partitioning.

For a partition-wise join to occur, the following conditions must exist:

- Both tables in the join statement must be equipartitioned.
- Either the tables or the indexes in the join operation must use the same partitioning method.
- Both tables or indexes must have the same partitioning columns.
- Both tables or indexes must have the same number of partitions.
- In range partitioning, the same partition bounds are required.
- In composite partitioning, only one of the tables need be equipartitioned.

Example of a Partition-Wise Join

Figure 24.1 represents four equipartitioned objects (tables and indexes) in a project/task relationship. The PROJECTS and TASKS tables are divided into two partitions each, by project number. The indexes have the same partitioning bounds. Specifically:

- PROJECTS is a table with two partitions, range-partitioned on column PROJECT_NO. The first partition contains project numbers up to 200000. The second partition contains project numbers up to 400000.
- PROJECTS_N1 is an index on column PROJECT_NO of the PROJECTS table. Both the table and index are range-partitioned on column PROJECT_NO into two partitions, which have the same partition bounds as the PROJECTS table's partitions. These are the elements that begin to develop the requirements listed just above.

- TASKS is a table with two partitions, range-partitioned on column PROJECT_NO (this is the same as the PROJECTS table). PROJECT_NO is a foreign key that references PROJECT_NO in PROJECTS.
- TASKS_N1 is an index on columns (PROJECT_NO, TASK_NO) in TASKS. Again, we are range-partitioned on PROJECT_NO into two partitions, which have the same partition bounds as the partitions of PROJECTS.

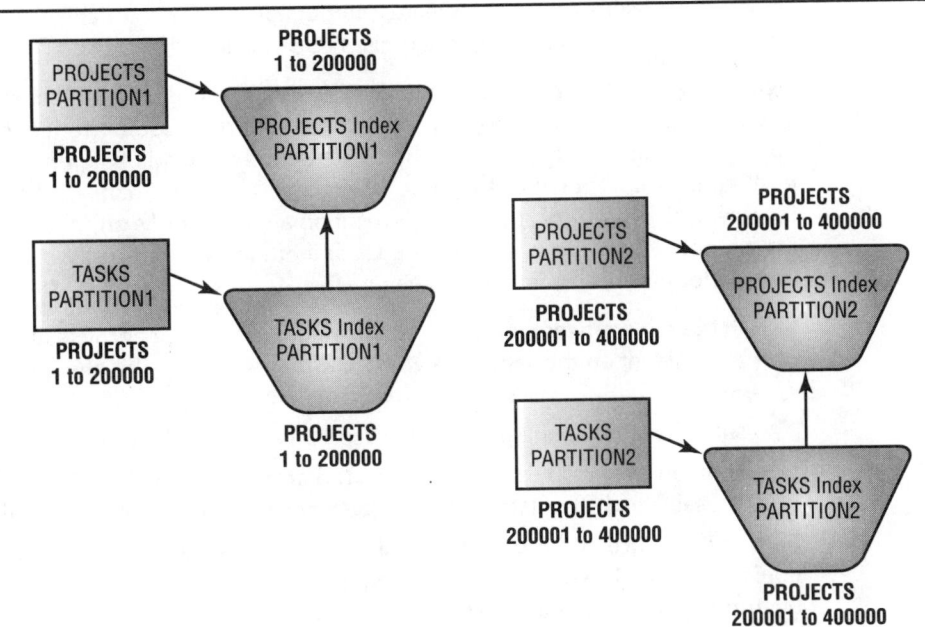

FIGURE 24.1
Equipartitioned tables and indexes

If a performance gain can be achieved with partition-wise joining, Oracle will use it. In some cases pruning can be achieved with a partition-wise join resulting in a bigger performance gain. This is all handled by Oracle and is transparent to the user and developer.

Performance versus Availability

Both partitioning and disk striping are techniques utilized to reduce contention for disk access. In database design, you may have occasion to consider using either or both. If you're after performance gains, you'll want to stripe your partition across as many I/O devices as possible to get the greatest throughput. If data availability is the goal, you should place the partition on as few disks as possible.

Figure 24.2 is a common representation of two methods of partitioning and striping. These are extreme examples but do demonstrate database performance using both approaches utilized together. The top figure shows what will happen when you stripe each partition to its own disks (more availability; less performance). The bottom figure represents the results of striping each partition across all disks on your system; depending on how your system is configured, this bottom arrangement would give you the best performance. Notice the following:

- In the top arrangement, you see lessened performance because all your partitions are resident on the same disks. All I/O is happening on the one device.
- If just one of the disks becomes unavailable (bottom example), all the partitions suffer because all the partitions are spread across all the disks.
- From an availability standpoint, the top arrangement is better. If a disk becomes unusable, only the data on that disk is unusable and not all the partitions.

Both performance and processing availability are at issue when you design your partitioning solution. The reliability of your equipment is part of the equation, as well. It has been our experience that most enterprises have better results making do with slower data retrieval than coping with no data being retrieved at all.

FIGURE 24.2
Two arrangements of partitioning plus disk striping

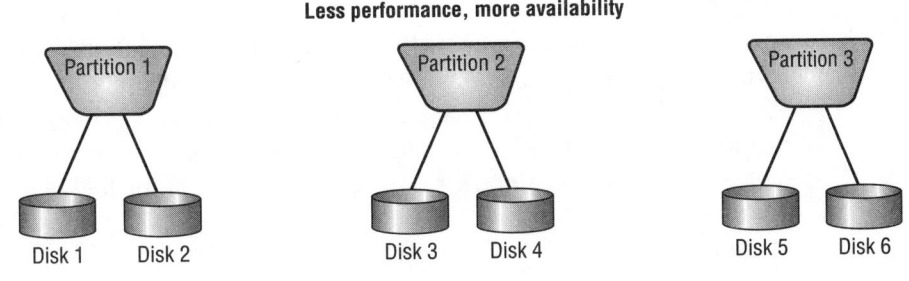
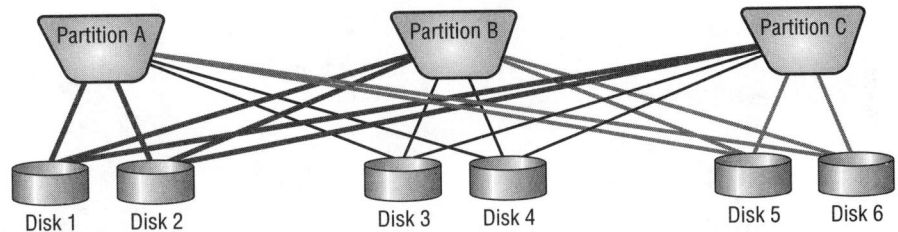

Partition Management

This section discusses merging, splitting, exchanging, and dropping partitions. It lists partition-related attributes and offers several helpful data dictionary views.

Merging

The MERGE PARTITIONS option lets you take a table that is partitioned into, say, five parts and bring that back to four parts. Partitions to be merged must be adjacent. Here's an example of the merge command.

```
ALTER TABLE projects
MERGE PARTITIONS projects_q1, projects_q2
INTO projects_a2000 ;
```

Here we're merging projects_q1 (first quarter data) and projects_q2 (second quarter data) into a new partition called projects_a2000 (annual data for 2000). This might be useful when trying to redistribute data from monthly to quarterly and from quarterly to annual.

Splitting

Splitting a partition does exactly that—you split an object that is partitioned into parts and make more partitions. For example, say your PROJECTS table is partitioned into four parts, one for each quarter. Your user community is requesting lots of reports and writing SQL that needs the data separated by month. You can repartition the table to accommodate this, by splitting a partition with the following command:

```
ALTER TABLE projects
SPLIT PARTITION projects_expense
AT project_number (200000)
INTO PARTITION projects_flow less then (200000)
    PARTITION projects_const (maxvalue);
```

This breaks the partition called `projects_expense` into two partitions called `projects_flow` and `projects_const`. This will not touch any other partitions assigned to the PROJECTS table.

Exchanging

Partition exchanging is a new feature as of Oracle8i. You have the ability to move data into a partitioned table from any nonpartitioned table. This will be accomplished one partition at a time. Here's an example:

```
ALTER TABLE projects_p8
EXCHANGE projects_w1 WITH projects
INCLUDING INDEXES
WITH VALIDATION
EXCEPTIONS INTO mdb_exceptions ;
```

This code will move data from the PROJECTS table into a partitioned table `projects_p8`; in addition; you'll move the data from the partitioned table `projects_p8` to the Projects table. The command EXCHANGE means literally to exchange data from one partition to another.

Dropping Partitions

Before you drop a partition, be sure you want to do it. When you drop a partition, you drop that partition and all the data stored in it—there's no exception.

 WARNING Even if you're certain you want to take this step, back up the affected data or move it into a place from which it can be restored.

Either of the following commands will drop a partition:
```
ALTER TABLE projects
DROP PARTITON projects_p8 ;
```

The second example will drop the partition `projects_p8` from the `projects` table. The partition and all the data stored there will be gone.

One last thing: you can't use the DROP PARTITION command if the object only contains one partition.

Attributes and Partitioning

We all know and understand attributes. Partitions have the same column and constraint definitions. However, the storage specifications may differ from partition to partition, as will other physical attributes such as PCTFREE, PCTUSED, INITRANS, and MAXTRANS. (Subpartitions do not follow this convention. All subpartitions must have the same physical attributes as the partition to which they belong.)

The Appendix F syntax diagrams for CREATE/ALTER TABLE and CREATE/ALTER INDEX include many attributes concerning partitioning, about 15 of them. Table 24.1 is a complete list of these options.

TABLE 24.1: OPTIONS FOR CONTROLLING ATTRIBUTES IN PARTITIONING

Command	Description
ADD_HASH_PARTITION_CLAUSE	Adds a new hash partition to the "high" end of a partitioned table.
ADD_RANGE_PARTITION_CLAUSE	Adds a new range partition to the "high" end of a partitioned table.
COALESCE_PARTITION_CLAUSE	Distributes partition contents into one or more remaining partitions (determined by the hash function), and then drops the selected partition. Only applies to hash-partitioned tables.
DROP_PARTITION_CLAUSE	Removes the partition and its stored data from a partitioned table. Applies only to range- or composite-partitioned tables.
EXCHANGE_PARTITION/ SUBPARTITION_CLAUSE	Converts a partition or subpartition into a nonpartitioned table, and a nonpartitioned table into a partition or subpartition.

Continued

TABLE 24.1: OPTIONS FOR CONTROLLING ATTRIBUTES IN PARTITIONING (CONTINUED)

MERGE_PARTITION_CLAUSE	Merges the contents of two adjacent table partitions into one new partition, and then drops the two original partitions.
MODIFY_DEFAULT_ATTRIBUTES_CLAUSE	Specifies new default values for the attributes of the table.
MODIFY_PARTITION_CLAUSE	Modifies physical attributes of the partition.
MODIFY_SUBPARTITION_CLAUSE	Lets you allocate or deallocate storage for an individual subpartition.
MOVE_PARTITION_CLAUSE	Moves the table partition to another segment.
MOVE_SUBPARTITION_CLAUSE	Moves the table subpartition to another segment.
RENAME_PARTITION/ SUBPARTITION_CLAUSE	Renames a table partition or subpartition CURRENT_NAME to NEW_NAME.
ROW_MOVEMENT_CLAUSE	Determines whether a row can be moved to a different partition or subpartition because of a change to one or more of its key values.
SPLIT_PARTITION_CLAUSE	Creates two new partitions, each with a new segment and new physical attributes, and new initial extents.
TRUNCATE_PARTITION/ SUBPARTITION_CLAUSE	Removes all rows from a partition or, if the table is composite-partitioned, all rows from the partition's subpartitions.

TIP We highly recommend that you try and test as many of these attribute options as your system will allow. They are critical in design and implementation when partitioning your objects.

Data Dictionary Views Useful in Partitioning

Partitioning is only available for databases using cost-based optimization. Table 24.2 lists data dictionary views at your disposal for viewing partitioning statistics for any given object. Notice that all are available for ALL_, DBA_, and USER_ areas. The USER_ views display only items that the user owns, and ALL_ is the broadest view of results from all the tables and indexes that have partition related information. You'll find many uses for this information.

TABLE 24.2: DATA DICTIONARY VIEWS USEFUL IN PARTITIONING

Objects	Description
TAB_PARTITIONS*	Tables and their partitioning information
TAB_SUBPARTITIONS*	Tables and their subpartitioning information
IND_PARTITIONS*	Partitioned indexes, with related information
IND_SUBPARTITIONS*	Subpartitions, with related information
PART_COL_STATISTICS*	Column statistics associated with the partitions
SUBPART_COL_STATISTICS*	Column statistics associated with the subpartitions

* All these data dictionary items are available in ALL_, DBA_, and USER_ views.

Here's a query using the USER_TAB_PARTITIONS view. Output will list the partition name, number of rows in the partition, number of blocks occupied by the partition, and the average row length in the partition. The resulting data will vary depending on your setup.

```
SELECT partition_name
, num_rows
, blocks
, avg_row_len
FROM user_tab_partitions ;
```

CHAPTER 25

Simple and Advanced Replication

FEATURING:

- **Simple replication with materialized views** — 1050
- **Refresh groups** — 1055
- **Advanced replication** — 1059

Replication is exactly what it sounds like: creating and maintaining database objects in multiple locations. Simply stated, replication is a process by which you copy and maintain database objects in more then one database. Using materialized views, you can create an environment in which data can be duplicated from one database to another, for a simple form of replication. Advanced replication is more complex, but Oracle 8i provides several tools to help you develop and maintain an advanced replication environment.

This chapter discusses methods for both simple and advanced replication. First, we describe how to use materialized views for simple replication. Then we cover how to create and manage refresh groups, which can be used with simple and advanced replication schemes. Finally, we detail advanced replication, including some step-by-step instructions.

Simple Replication with Materialized Views

Oracle8i materialized views (Mviews) store data based on a query. In short, an Mview is a table that stores a predefined set of data. When you create an Mview, you specify the SQL used to populate it.

In Chapter 19, you learned about Mviews as a data warehousing feature. That chapter covered the basics of creating, refreshing, and managing Mviews and Mview logs. Mviews can also serve as a tool for performing simple replication. Here, we will look at this application of Mviews.

NOTE In previous versions of Oracle, snapshots were used for simple replication. In Oracle8i, the terms *snapshot* and *materialized view* are used synonymously. They both contain the results of a query on one or more tables. In fact, when you create a snapshot, upon completion, Oracle reports "Materialized View Created." In Oracle8i, CREATE MATERIALIZED VIEW is a synonym for CREATE SNAPSHOT.

An important aspect of using Mviews for replication is that you can keep your Mviews up to date with the appropriate refresh option. Oracle refreshes Mviews in the manner that you specify when you create the views. You can even group refresh operations to coordinate the refresh schedules of related tables (master tables). This will assist in keeping your Mviews accurate and timely with other views of the related sources. Using refresh groups is discussed in the "Refresh Groups" section later in this chapter.

For example, suppose that you want to replicate project and task information for reporting, but you do not want all of the data in the associated tables. You could create one or more Mviews with the desired data in them, specifying the refresh option and mode. That's all there is to simple replication with Mviews.

Listing 25.1 shows an example of creating an Mview for simple replication. This Mview contains ten columns: five from a table containing projects information and five from a table containing tasks information. It uses the PARALLEL option to parallelize the view creation operation.

 TIP To make the best use of an Mview, make sure that the SQL that creates the view is optimized and the frequency for refresh is in accordance with the way the view is used. Also, if possible, take advantage of partitioning and parallel processing.

Listing 25.1: Creating a Materialized View for Simple Replication

```
CREATE MATERIALIZED VIEW proj_task_mv
  PCTFREE 0 TABLESPACE mviews
  STORAGE (INITIAL 16k NEXT 16k PCTINCREASE 0)
  PARALLEL
  BUILD DEFERRED
  REFRESH COMPLETE
  ENABLE QUERY REWRITE
  AS
  SELECT
   p.proj_num
   , p.proj_name
   , p.proj_start
   , p.proj_end
   , p.proj_status
   , t.task_num
   , t.task_name
   , t.task_start
   , t.task_end
   , t.task_status
  FROM
   pa_projects p
   , pa_tasks   t
  WHERE p.project_id = t.project_id;
```

Notice the BUILD and REFRESH options. These were discussed in Chapter 19, but let's review them here in relation to replication.

 NOTE The ENABLE QUERY REWRITE option specifies that the Mview is eligible to be used for query rewrite. See Chapter 19 for a detailed discussion of the query rewrite feature.

Choosing an Mview Build Option

Oracle supplies two methods for building a materialized view:

BUILD DEFERRED This option, used in Listing 25.1, creates the structure for the view, but the view will be populated at a later time manually by, using DBMS_MVIEW.REFRESH. You might use this option if the build process will take hours to complete or could hamper daily processing in another way. This view will have an UNUSABLE value associated with it, so it cannot be used for query rewrite until it is populated.

BUILD IMMEDIATE This option builds and populates the view when the command is issued. You might use this option if you need to have immediate access to the data in the view or if you know that the build process will not interfere with daily processing.

Choosing an Mview Refresh Option

As explained in Chapter 19, Oracle provides three options for refreshing your Mview (FAST, COMPLETE, or FORCE), along with two options for the method to use for refreshing (ON COMMIT or ON DEMAND). Table 25.1 summarizes how the REFRESH options and modes work together.

TABLE 25.1: MATERIALIZED VIEW REFRESH METHODS

Option	Mode	Description
FAST	ON COMMIT	Uses the Mview log (described in Chapter 19) and will update the view when a COMMIT is performed on the master table
FAST	ON DEMAND	Occurs only if you add data using a direct-path method (SQL*Loader in direct-path mode)

Continued

SIMPLE REPLICATION WITH MATERIALIZED VIEWS

TABLE 25.1: MATERIALIZED VIEW REFRESH METHODS (CONTINUED)

Option	Mode	Description
COMPLETE	ON COMMIT	Completely rebuilds the Mview every time a COMMIT occurs on the master table (not recommended)
COMPLETE	ON DEMAND	Creates a new view or completely refreshes the data.
FORCE	ON COMMIT	Uses FAST refresh if possible; otherwise, uses COMPLETE refresh (not recommended)
FORCE	ON DEMAND	Uses FAST refresh if possible; otherwise, uses COMPLETE

Let's look at some examples of using the various options and modes.

 NOTE When you specify the ON DEMAND mode, you must use one of the procedures in the DBMS_MVIEW package to refresh your views. See Chapter 19 for details.

Creating an Mview with the FAST/ON COMMIT Refresh Option

The FAST/ON COMMIT combination will keep the Mview up-to-date with what the original data represents. Listing 25.2 shows an example of creating this type of view.

Listing 25.2: Using REFRESH FAST ON COMMIT

```
CREATE MATERIALIZED VIEW proj_task_mv
  BUILD IMMEDIATE
  REFRESH FAST ON COMMIT
  AS
  SELECT
  p.proj_num
  , p.proj_name
  , p.proj_start
  , p.proj_end
  , p.proj_status
  , t.task_num
  , t.task_name
  , t.task_start
  , t.task_end
  , t.task_status
```

```
FROM
  pa_projects p
  , pa_tasks   t
WHERE p.project_id = t.project_id ;
```

TIP If you want to be able to update an Mview, include the FOR UPDATE keywords. When FOR UPDATE is specified in the definition of an Mview, Oracle allows a subquery, primary key, or ROWID in the Mview to be updated. When used in conjunction with advanced replication, discussed later in this chapter, these updates will be propagated to the master table of the Mview.

In this example, the view will be built immediately (because of the BUILD IMMEDIATE option). An Mview log will be created when the Mview is created, allowing the fast refresh to work. The Mview log will be updated immediately following a COMMIT on the master table (in this case, either PA_PROJECTS or PA_TASKS). The ON COMMIT option will refresh the Mview when a row in one of the tables that make up the view has a COMMIT submitted against it.

NOTE When you use the ON COMMIT option, check the alert log and trace file to make sure that no errors were encountered. Should any errors occur during the refresh operation, you will need to fix the error and manually refresh the Mview using the DBMS_MVIEW package.

Creating an Mview with the FORCE/ON COMMIT Refresh Option

The FORCE/ON COMMIT combination will also update the Mview when a COMMIT is completed on the master table. The Mview will be evaluated by Oracle each and every time a COMMIT is completed on the master table. If Oracle decides that a fast refresh can be completed, then that operation will take place. However, if Oracle decides that the fast refresh cannot be completed successfully, a complete refresh is performed. Considering that a complete refresh could take some time and impact the day-to-day operations, you probably don't want this to happen, so you will want to avoid using the FORCE/ON COMMIT combination. Instead, use the COMPLETE option or even the FORCE/ON DEMAND option. That way, you will be able to plan for a complete refresh and make sure that it occurs after standard operating hours, when the users have gone home.

Creating an Mview with the FAST/ON DEMAND Refresh Option

When you use the FAST/ON DEMAND combination, your Mview will be refreshed only if you are adding data using a direct-path method (a SQL*Loader direct-path load). Listing 25.3 shows an example of using this refresh method.

Listing 25.3: Using REFRESH FAST ON DEMAND

```
CREATE MATERIALIZED VIEW proj_task_mv
  BUILD IMMEDIATE
  REFRESH FAST ON DEMAND
  AS
  SELECT
   p.proj_num
  , p.proj_name
  , p.proj_start
  , p.proj_end
  , p.proj_status
  , t.task_num
  , t.task_name
  , t.task_start
  , t.task_end
  , t.task_status
  FROM
   pa_projects p
  , pa_tasks   t
  WHERE p.project_id = t.project_id ;
```

In this example, if you are loading data into the PA_PROJECTS or PA_TASKS table using SQL*Loader with the direct-path load option, your Mview will also be updated.

Refresh Groups

Refresh groups are used to manage the refresh schedule for the objects in the refresh group. By placing Mviews in refresh groups, you can coordinate the refresh schedules of related tables (master tables) that make up the Mviews. Refresh groups are a handy tool for both simple replication and advanced replication (discussed later in this chapter).

NOTE Remember that the terms *materialized view (Mview)* and *snapshot* are synonyms in Oracle8i. In this chapter, we use the term Mview. In the Oracle documentation, you may see both terms, used interchangeably.

Each refresh group can contain from 1 to 400 Mviews. An Mview can belong to only one group at a time.

For managing refresh groups, Oracle supplies the DBMS_REFRESH package. The procedures in this package are listed in Table 25.2.

TABLE 25.2: DBMS_REFRESH PROCEDURES

Procedure	Description
ADD	Adds a snapshot or an Mview to an existing refresh group
CHANGE	Changes the interval at which the refresh will occur for the group
DESTROY	Deletes the refresh group
MAKE	Creates a refresh group
REFRESH	Manually refreshes the objects in the refresh group
SUBTRACT	Deletes an object from a refresh group

Let's look at how these procedures are used to create and modify refresh groups.

Creating a Refresh Group

Creating a refresh group is easy. First, and most important, you must decide which views will belong to which refresh groups and what the refresh schedule will be for each group. Then you can use the DBMS_REFRESH package's MAKE procedure to create the group. Listing 25.4 shows an example of how to create a refresh group.

Listing 25.4: Creating a Refresh Group

```
DBMS_REFRESH.MAKE (
    name                IN VARCHAR2,
    {list
     | tab              IN DBMS_UTILITY.UNCL_ARRAY,}
    next_date           IN DATE,
    interval            IN VARCHAR2,
    implicit_destroy    IN BOOLEAN DEFAULT FALSE,
```

```
    lax                    IN BOOLEAN DEFAULT FALSE,
    job                    IN BINARY INTEGER DEFAULT 0,
    rollback_seg           IN VARCHAR2 DEFAULT NULL,
    push_deferred_rpc      IN BOOLEAN DEFAULT TRUE,
    refresh_after_errors   IN BOOLEAN DEFAULT FALSE,
    purge_option           IN BINARY_INTEGER := 1,
    parallelism            IN BINARY_INTEGER := 0,
    heap_size              IN BINARY_INTEGER : 0);

EXECUTE dbms_refresh.make(
    'projects',  -- name
    'inst.projects, op_stat',
    SYSDATE,
    'next_date(SYSDATE + 1)',
    TRUE,
    FALSE);
```

This example creates a refresh group called projects. In this group are the Mviews INST.PROJECTS and OP_STAT (for installed projects and operating status). The next date will be SYSDATE, and the interval will be SYSDATE +1, or every day.

NOTE The MAKE procedure is overloaded, and the LIST and TAB parameters are mutually exclusive. In other words, if you specify the LIST parameter, you cannot specify the TAB parameter.

Notice that Listing 25.4 specifies only the name of the refresh group, the Mviews that are part of the group, and the refresh schedule. The refresh group will use the defaults for all of the other parameters.

Adding Members to a Refresh Group

You can add an Mview to an existing group by using the DBMS_REFRESH package's ADD option. Listing 25.5 shows an example of adding a member to a refresh group.

Listing 25.5: Adding an Mview to a Refresh Group

```
DBMS_REFRESH.ADD (
    name   IN VARCHAR2,
    {list  IN VARCHAR2,
```

```
     |tab  IN DBMS_UTILITY.UNCL_ARRAY, }
     lax   IN BOOLEAN DEFAULT FALSE);

EXECUTE dbms_refresh.add(
    'projects',
    'clo_proj',
    FALSE);
```

This example will add a new Mview to the projects group (created in Listing 25.4). The new Mview is named CLO_PROJ (for closed projects).

Removing Members from a Refresh Group

Use the SUBTRACT procedure of the DBMS_REFRESH package to remove Mviews from a refresh group. Listing 25.6 shows an example that removes the Mview added in Listing 25.5.

Listing 25.6: Removing an Mview from a Refresh Group

```
DBMS_REFRESH.SUBTRACT (
    name    IN VARCHAR2,
    {list   IN VARCHAR2,
    |tab    IN DBMS_UTILITY.UNCL_ARRAY,}
    lax     IN BOOLEAN DEFAULT FALSE );

EXECUTE dbms_refresh.subtract(
    'projects',
    'clo_proj',
    FALSE);
```

Changing a Refresh Group's Schedule

To modify a refresh group's schedule, use the CHANGE procedure of the DBMS_REFRESH package. Suppose that, after setting up the refresh group to be refreshed daily, you later find that you only need to refresh the views in this group weekly. Listing 25.7 shows how to modify the refresh schedule to reflect that change.

Listing 25.7: Changing a Refresh Group's Schedule

```
DBMS_REFRESH.CHANGE (
    name              IN VARCHAR2,
    next_date         IN DATE DEFAULT NULL,
    interval          IN VARCHAR2 DEFAULT NULL,
```

```
    implicit_destroy       IN BOOLEAN DEFAULT NULL,
    rollback_segment       IN VARCHAR2 DEFAULT NULL,
    push_deferred_rpc      IN BOOLEAN DEFAULT NULL,
    refresh_after_errors   IN BOOLEAN DEFAULT NULL,
    purge_option           IN BINARY_INTEGER := 1,
    parallelism            IN BINARY_INTEGER := 0,
    heap_size              IN BINARY_INTEGER : 0);

EXECUTE dbms_refresh.change(
    'projects',
    NULL,
    'next_date(SYSDATE + 1, ''MONDAY'')';
```

This example changes the schedule so that views in this refresh group will be refreshed every Monday.

Deleting a Refresh Group

To delete a refresh group, use the DESTROY procedure of the DBMS_REFRESH package, as in the following example:

```
DBMS_REFRESH.DESTROY ( name   IN VARCHAR2 )

EXECUTE dbms_refresh.destroy(projects);
```

Another way to delete a group is through the IMPLICIT_DESTROY parameter available with the MAKE and CHANGE procedures. This will delete the group and then re-create it with the new parameters.

Advanced Replication

Advanced replication can support bi-directional transaction capture and replication, and it provides comprehensive replication conflict detection and resolution. Oracle has made several improvements in advanced replication with the release of 8i, including the following:

- Oracle has internalized several of the PL/SQL replication packages. More of the replication code is now placed in the database engine.
- Oracle now allows larger refresh groups. As stated in the previous section, up to 400 Mviews are allowed in one refresh group.

- For multiple-site replication, you now have the ability to create snapshot templates. The DBA can create a snapshot (centrally) and distribute it to many different sites.

 TIP To learn more about snapshot templates, see the "Snapshot Concepts and Architecture" section in the Oracle documentation.

- To assist with advanced replication setup, Oracle supplies a Replication Manager deployment wizard that will help with the selection of objects, parameters, and authorizations.
- Offline instantiation is now possible. The DBA can package the templates and associated data onto removable media (such as tape or a CD-R) and ship this item to the remote site. The remote site can perform a fast refresh after the offline instantiation is completed.

Over the past few years, advanced replication has gained the reputation of being difficult, both to set up and administer. Here, we'll provide a step-by-step approach to advanced replication design and setup. The goal is to demonstrate how, with a bit of effort, you can reap the benefits of using Oracle's advanced replication tools. But first, we need to go over the requirements and components of advanced replication.

Advanced Replication Requirements

Advanced replication uses two sites: the master definition site and the master site. The *master definition site* is the database that has all the objects that you wish to replicate. All SUSPEND and RESUME commands are to be entered from this site, and they will be automatically propagated to the master site (or sites). The *master site* is the database that will hold the replicated objects. One master definition site can be replicated to multiple master sites.

The following requirements are necessary for implementing advanced replication:

- Install the Distributed and Replication option.
- Run `catrep.sql` (in $ORACLE_HOME/rdbms/admin/) as INTERNAL.
- Establish the same passwords for REPSYS and REPADMIN on the master and master definition sites.
- Set up mandatory parameters in the `init.ora` file, as listed in Table 25.3.

TABLE 25.3: *INIT.ORA* PARAMETERS ASSOCIATED WITH ADVANCED REPLICATION

Parameter	Mandatory Value	Description
SHARED_POOL_SIZE	25M	A major piece of the SGA where Oracle caches PL/SQL programs.
GLOBAL_NAMES	TRUE	Determines whether or not a database link is required to have the same name as the database to which it connects.
JOB_QUEUE_PROCESSES	2	Sets the number of SNP*n* background processes per instance, where *n* is 0 to 9 followed by A to Z.
OPEN_LINKS	6	The maximum number of concurrent open connections to remote databases per user process in one session. If set to 0, no distributed transactions are allowed.
JOB_QUEUE_INTERVAL	Less than interval for DBA_JOBS submitted	Sets the interval between wake-ups for the SNP*n* background processes of the instance.
JOB_QUEUE_KEEP_CONNECTIONS	FALSE	Determines whether or not to keep network connections between the execution of jobs.

Here are examples of the settings listed in Table 25.2 in an init.ora file:

```
shared_pool_size: 25M
global_names = true
job_queue_processes = 2
open_links = 6
job_queue_interval = 2
job_queue_keep_connections = false
```

The value for the OPEN_LINKS parameter should equal or exceed the number of databases referred to in a single SQL statement that references multiple databases, so that all the databases can be open to execute the statement. You should increase this value if many different databases are accessed over time. For example, if OPEN_LINKS is set to 2, and queries alternately access databases A, B, and C, performance would slow down while one connection was broken and another connection was made. In this case, you should increase the OPEN_LINKS value to 3 or more to avoid the wait.

Remote Procedure Calls for Replication

There are three Oracle packages that are critical for the replication environment to work properly: DBMS_DEFER_SYS, DBMS_DEFER, and DBMS_DEFER_QUERY. These packages are necessary for handling deferred transactions and remote procedure calls (RPCs), as described in the following sections.

The DBMS_DEFER_SYS Package

Administrative tasks like scheduling, executing, and deleting queued transactions are performed when one of the DBMS_DEFER_SYS package procedures is invoked. Table 25.4 lists the procedures that are available with this package. The views referred to in Table 25.4 are described in the "Viewing Replication Information" section, coming up shortly.

TABLE 25.4: DBMS_DEFER_SYS PROCEDURES

Procedure	Description
ADD_DEFAULT_DEST	Adds a destination database to the DEFDEFAULTDEST view
COPY	Creates a copy of a deferred transaction with a new destination
DELETE_DEF_DESTINATION	Removes a destination database from the DEFSCHEDULE view
DELETE_DEFAULT_DEST	Removes a destination database from the DEFDEFAULT-DEST view
DELETE_ERROR	Deletes a transaction from the DEFERROR view
DELETE_TRAN	Deletes deferred transactions
DISABLED	Determines if propagation of the deferred transaction queue from the current site to a given site is enabled
EXCLUDE_PUSH	Acquires an exclusive lock that prevents deferred transaction PUSH
EXECUTE_ERROR	Forces execution of a transaction that originally failed, leaving a record in DEFERROR
EXECUTE_ERROR_AS_USER	Reexecutes a deferred transaction that did not complete successfully
PURGE	Purges pushed transactions from the deferred transaction queue at your current master or snapshot site
PUSH	Forces a deferred call queue at your current master or snapshot site to be pushed to another master site

Continued

TABLE 25.4: DBMS_DEFER_SYS PROCEDURES (CONTINUED)

Procedure	Description
REGISTER_PROPAGATOR	Registers the given user as the propagator for the local database
SCHEDULE_PURGE	Schedules a job to purge pushed transactions from the deferred transaction queue at your current master or snapshot site
SCHEDULE_PUSH	Schedules a job to push the deferred transaction queue to a remote master destination
SET_DISABLED	Disables or enables propagation of the deferred transaction queue from the current site to a given destination site
UNREGISTER_PROPAGATOR	Unregisters a user as the propagator from the local database
UNSCHEDULE_PURGE	Stops automatic purges of pushed transactions from the deferred transaction queue at a snapshot or master site
UNSCHEDULE_PUSH	Stops automatic pushes of the deferred transaction queue from a snapshot or master site to another master site

The DBMS_DEFER Package

The DBMS_DEFER package builds deferred RPCs. Table 25.5 lists the procedures available with this package.

TABLE 25.5: DBMS_DEFER PROCEDURES

Procedure	Description
CALL	Builds a deferred call to a remote procedure
COMMIT_WORK	Performs a transaction commit after checking for well-formed deferred RPCs
DATATYPE_ARG	Provides the data that is to be passed to a deferred RPC
TRANSACTION	Allows you to specify destination sites for the ensuing call(s) to the DBMS_DEFER.CALL procedure

The DBMS_DEFER_QUERY Package

The DBMS_DEFER_QUERY package provides access to parameters passed to deferred calls. Table 25.6 lists the procedures available with this package.

TABLE 25.6: DBMS_DEFER_QUERY PROCEDURES

Procedure	Description
GET_ARG_FORM	Determines the form of an argument in a deferred RPC
GET_ARG_TYPE	Determines the type of an argument in a deferred RPC
GET_CALL_ARGS	Gets the arguments for the given RPC
GET_DATAYTPE_ARG	Determines the value of an argument in a deferred RPC

Replication Views

Oracle has supplied a wide variety of views to assist with day-to-day operations. Table 25.7 lists the data dictionary views that assist with the management of replication.

TABLE 25.7: VIEWS FOR REPLICATION

View	Description
DEFCALL	Contains information about all deferred RPCs. Queries the SYSTEM.DEF$_CALL table.
DEFCALLDEST	Contains the destination database(s) for each deferred RPC in DEFCALL. Queries SYSTEM.DEF$_CALL, SYSTEM.DEF$_DESTINATION, SYSTEM.DEF$_CALLDEST, SYSTEM.DEF$_ERROR, and SYSTEM.REPCAT$_REPPROP.
DEFDEFAULTDEST	Contains the default destinations for deferred RPCs. Queries SYSTEM.DEF$DEFAULTDEST.
DEFERROR	Contains error information for deferred calls that could not be applied at their destination. Queries SYSTEM.DEF$_ERROR.
DEFERRORCOUNT	Contains the count of errors for each destination. Queries SYSTEM.DEF$_ERROR.
DEFSCHEDULE	Contains information about the scheduling of deferred jobs. Queries SYSTEM.DEF$_DESTINATION and SYS.JOB$.

Continued

TABLE 25.7: VIEWS FOR REPLICATION (CONTINUED)	
View	Description
DEFTRAN	Contains information about all deferred calls. Queries SYSTEM.DEF$_CALL and SYS.USER$.
DEFTRANDEST	Contains the destination database(s) for each deferred transaction. Queries SYSTEM.DEF$_CALL, SYSTEM.DEF$_DESTINATION, SYSTEM.DEF$_ERROR, SYSTEM.DEF$_CALLDEST, and SYSTEM.REPCAT$_REPPROP.

Setting Up Advanced Replication

Now that we've covered the requirements, RPCs, and views for replication, we're ready to tackle the actual setup for advanced replication. Here, I will present a method that has been developed and used by several DBAs (including myself) at several sites. You can use these steps as a guide, modifying them to suit your own requirements for your replicated environment. I recommend the following steps for planning and implementing replication:

1. Create two users: REPADMIN AND REPSYS.
2. Create the replication administration users at the master site.
3. At the master site, create the objects to be replicated.
4. At the master definition site, create a replication schema.
5. At the master definition site, create the required replication group.
6. Add the objects to the group.
7. Generate replication support for the object.
8. Add one or more master sites to the group.

Let's look at each of these steps in detail.

Creating the REPADMIN AND REPSYS Users

The REPADMIN user performs administrative tasks related to advanced replication. The REPSYS user performs operations on SYS's behalf, as required by the advanced replication packages. SYSTEM will hold the replication tables.

As noted earlier in this chapter, the master definition site is the database that contains the objects that you will be replicating. At the master definition site, set up the database links and grant the users the appropriate privileges. Listing 25.8 shows how this step is accomplished. In this and the following listings, the items that you will need to replace for your own environment are in boldface.

Listing 25.8: Creating the REPADMIN AND REPSYS Users

```
-- Run this first on the master_definition_site database as SYS.
-- This sets up the advanced replication users. You will need to
-- replace the global name with the global name that you will use.
-- You will also need to input several items for your situation.
-- You will need to set the sizes of the tablespaces you establish.
SET ECHO ON
SPOOL create_ad_mds_rep.out
CONNECT sys/&sys_password
ALTER DATABASE RENAME global_name TO GLOBAL_NAME;

CREATE USER repsys IDENTIFIED BY &repsys_password
DEFAULT TABLESPACE  def_tablespace
TEMPORARY TABLESPACE temp_tablespace
QUOTA UNLIMITED ON def_tablespace;

CREATE PUBLIC DATABASE LINK REP.WORLD USING 'REP.WORLD';
DROP DATABASE LINK REP.WORLD;

CREATE DATABASE LINK REP.WORLD
CONNECT TO repsys IDENTIFIED BY &repsys_passwd;

CREATE USER repadmin IDENTIFIED BY &repadmin_passwd
DEFAULT TABLESPACE def_tablespace
TEMPORARY TABLESPACE temp_tablespace
QUOTA UNLIMITED ON def_tablespace;

GRANT dba TO repadmin;
GRANT EXECUTE ON dbms_defer
    TO repadmin WITH GRANT OPTION;
GRANT EXECUTE ON dbms_defer_query
    TO repadmin;
EXECUTE dbms_repcat_admin.grant_admin_any_repgroup('repadmin');
EXECUTE dbms_repcat_auth.grant_surrogate_repcat('repsys');
CONNECT repadmin/&repadmin_passwd
```

```
DROP DATABASE LINK REP.world;

CREATE DATABASE LINK REP.WORLD
    CONNECT TO repadmin
IDENTIFIED BY &repadmin_passwd;
GRANT EXECUTE ON sys.dbms_defer TO USER;

CONNECT USER/USER_PASSWORD
DROP DATABASE LINK REP.world;

CREATE DATABASE LINK REP.WORLD
    CONNECT TO USER
IDENTIFIED BY &USER_PASSWORD;
SPOOL off;
```

Provided that you have designed your setup appropriately (which database you are going to replicate and where you are going to replicate it to), you now have established a script that can be used again and again. Remember to replace the boldfaced code with your own identifiers.

Creating the Replication Administration Users at the Master Site

The master site will contain the replicated objects. Your next step is to create the replication administration users at the master site, with the appropriate database links and database privileges. Listing 25.9 shows how to accomplish this step.

Listing 25.9: Creating the Users at the Master Site

```
-- Run this next set of commands on the master site, signed in as SYS.
SET ECHO ON
SPOOL create_ad_ms_rep.out
CONNECT sys/&sys_passwd
ALTER DATABASE RENAME global_name TO REP.WORLD;

CREATE USER repsys IDENTIFIED BY &repsys_passwd
DEFAULT TABLESPACE   DEF_TABLESPACE
TEMPORARY TABLESPACE TEMP_TABLESPACE
QUOTA UNLIMITED ON DEF_TABLESPACE;

GRANT connect
     ,resource
```

```
TO repsys;
DROP PUBLIC DATABASE LINK NEW_EMP.WORLD;

CREATE PUBLIC DATABASE LINK NEW_EMP.WORLD USING 'NEW_EMP';
DROP DATABASE LINK NEW_EMP.WORLD;

CREATE DATABASE LINK NEW_EMP.WORLD CONNECT TO repsys
IDENTIFIED BY &repsys_passwd;

CREATE USER repadmin IDENTIFIED BY &repadmin_passwd
DEFAULT TABLESPACE def_tablespace
TEMPORARY TABLESPACE temp_tablespace
QUOTA UNLIMITED ON def_tablespace
/

GRANT dba TO repadmin;
GRANT EXECUTE ON dbms_defer TO repadmin with grant option;
GRANT EXECUTE ON dbms_defer_query TO repadmin;
EXECUTE dbms_repcat_admin.grant_admin_any_repgroup('repadmin');
EXECUTE dbms_repcat_auth.grant_surrogate_repcat('repsys');
CONNECT repadmin/&repadmin_passwd
DROP DATABASE LINK NEW_EMP.WORLD;

CREATE DATABASE LINK NEW_EMP.WORLD CONNECT TO repadmin
IDENTIFIED BY &repadmin_passwd;

GRANT EXECUTE ON sys.dbms_defer TO USER;
CONNECT USER/&USER_PASSWORD
DROP DATABASE LINK NEW_EMP.WORLD;

CREATE DATABASE LINK NEMP.WORLD connect to USER
identified by &USER_passwd;
SPOOL off;
SET ECHO off
```

You will now execute the next steps signed in as REPADMIN.

Creating the Objects to Be Replicated at the Master Site

At the master site, pre-create the objects that you want to replicate. I have tested this several times and found that if the table is changing on a regular basis (such as in an

OLTP environment), it is better to create the structures. Then you can allow the Replication Manager to copy the rows while creating the replication objects.

Creating a Replication Schema at the Master Definition Site

To create the replication schema at the master definition site, use the DBMS_REPCAT.CREATE_MASTER_SCHEMA command. Here is an example:

```
EXEC dbms_repcat.create_master_schema('USER');
```

Creating the Replication Group at the Master Definition Site

To create the replication group at the master definition site, use the DBMS_REPCAT.CREATE_MASTER_REPGROUP command. This command has the following syntax:

```
DBMS_REPCAT.CREATE_MASTER_REPGROUP (
    gname              IN VARCHAR2,
    group_comment      IN VARCHAR2 : = ' ' ,
    master_comment     IN VARCHAR2 : = ' ' )
```

Here is an example of its use:

```
EXEC dbms_repcat.create_master_repgroup('REP_GROUP');
```

Adding Objects to the Replication Group

After you have a replication group, you can add objects to it. Use the DBMS_REPCAT.CREATE_MASTER_REPOBJECT command, which has the following syntax:

```
DBMS_REPCAT.CREATE_MASTER_REPOBJECT (
    sname                IN VARCHAR2,
    oname                IN VARCHAR2,
    type                 IN VARCHAR2,
    use_existing_object  IN BOOLEAN : = TRUE
    ddl_text             IN VARCHAR2 : =
    comment              IN VARCHAR2
    retry                IN BOOLEAN : = FALSE
    copy_rows            IN BOOLEAN : = TRUE,
    gname                IN VARCHAR2 : = ' ' )
```

Here is an example of its use:

```
EXEC dbms_repcat.create_master_repobject(
    SNAME=>'USER'
    ,ONAME=>'PROJECTS'
    ,TYPE=>'TABLE'
    ,USE_EXISTING_OBJECT=>TRUE
    ,COPY_ROWS=>TRUE
    ,GNAME=>'OBJ_GROUP');
```

Generating Replication Support for the Object

You will need some advanced replication triggers and packages to support replication. To generate them, use the DBMS_REPCAT.GENERATE_REPLICATION_SUPPORT command, which has the following syntax:

```
DBMS_REPCAT.GENERATE_REPLICATION_SUPPORT (
    gname              IN VARCHAR2,
    oname              IN VARCHAR2,
    type               IN VARCHAR2,
    package_prefix     IN VARCHAR2 : = NULL,
    procedure_prefix   IN VARCHAR2 : = NULL,
    distributed        IN BOOLEAN  : = TRUE,
    gen_rep2_trigger   IN BOOLEAN  : = FALSE,
    gen_obj_owner      IN VARCHAR2 : = ' ' )
```

Here is an example of its use:

```
EXEC dbms_repcat.generate_replication_support('OBJ_LOCATED',
  'OBJ_NAME','OBJ_TYPE');
```

Adding Master Sites to the Group

You can add one or more master sites to the group, using the DBMS_REPCAT.ADD_MASTER_DATABASE command. This command has the following syntax:

```
DBMS_REPCAT.ADD_MASTER_DATABASE (
    gname                IN VARCHAR2,
    master               IN VARCHAR2,
    use_existing_objects IN BOOLEAN  : = TRUE,
    copy_rows            IN BOOLEAN  : = TRUE,
    comment              IN VARCHAR2 : = ' ',
    propagation_mode     IN VARCHAR2 : = 'ASYNCHRONOUS'
    fname                IN VARCHAR2 : NULL);
```

Here is an example:

```
EXEC dbms_repcat.add_master_database(
    SNAME  => 'USER'
    ,oname => 'PROJECTS'
    ,type=>'TABLE'
    ,USE_EXISTING_OBJECT=>true
    ,copy_rows => true
    ,gname => 'PROJECTS_RUN');
```

You will now be able to check what is going on with the replication, as described in the next section.

Checking for Replication Errors

We have gone through the steps to establish a replicated environment. You will now need to check for errors. This is something that should be done on a regular basis.

 TIP For my own work, I set up reoccurring jobs that perform replication checking for me and log the results to my e-mail.

You can use the DBA_REPCATLOG view to check for errors in administrative tasks, such as adding groups, This view will also show any administrative tasks that are still pending. Here is an example of a query to select columns with ERROR status in DBA_REPCATLOG:

```
SELECT oname,
       request,
       message
  FROM dba_repcatlog
 WHERE status = 'ERROR'
```

You will now need to decide what to do with the errors—fix them or continue on with the errors.

You can also check DEFERROR for any jobs that have been submitted. If you find errors, you can fix them with DBMS_DEFER_SYS.EXECUTE_ERROR, or you can delete the errors with DBMS_DEFER_SYS.DELETE_ERROR.

Detecting Replication Conflicts

Replication conflicts are something that can and will probably happen. An example of this is when you are replicating a reporting site from a production site and you are updating the same table on the reporting site. You could easily have two different updates going on at the same time to the same table. You will need to address the conflict, since the system data will not move until the conflict is resolved somehow, generally manually.

Whenever possible, you should design a replication system that avoids conflicts. In your design, take into account all sources of data and when data can be replicated. However, many applications require that some percentage of data be updatable at multiple sites.

Types of Conflicts

Advanced replication includes facilities for detecting and resolving three types of conflicts: update, uniqueness, and delete. These are described in the following sections.

Update Conflicts

An update conflict is exactly what it sounds like: A conflict will happen when the replication of data from one site is updating a row and another site is attempting to update the same row. You will not be able to avoid this type of conflict. The best you can do is to code an exception routine and manage it on a case-by-case basis.

NOTE Remember that with Oracle, the update doesn't need to happen at exactly the same time to cause a conflict; it can occur at nearly the same time. What "nearly" means is an Oracle decision, and you cannot influence it by coding. In short, it is when Oracle decides that a deadlock has occurred.

Uniqueness Conflicts

A uniqueness conflict will occur when the replication of a row attempts to violate any unique key on the destination table. For example, suppose that one site is updating a row in the PROJECTS table (PROJECT_NAME) and another site is updating a different row in the same table. However, a unique constraint exists on the column PROJECT_NAME, and the two updates are trying to update the table with the same name. The standard Oracle error for a unique key violation will occur. This can also happen when only one site is attempting to change the PROJECT_NAME to one that is already in existence. You can code for this, log the error, and notify the user that the PROJECT_NAME is already in use. The user can then change the name to another value and let the replication take place.

TIP To avoid uniqueness conflicts, you can use a composite key for unique keys and primary keys. This is a method that I highly recommend and it will avoid all unique conflicts. Unfortunately, this becomes a bit more difficult when the primary key is a sequence counter. You will need to make sure that all sites use the same sequence generator, check the counters at the other sites, or have a range of numbers that are blocked for each site.

Delete Conflicts

A delete conflict occurs when one site and another site are attempting to delete the same row, or one site is updating the row and the other site is attempting to delete the row. To avoid a delete conflict, you will need to create a technique that will mark a row for deletion and then delete the rows at a later time. This means that the DELETE statement cannot occur in your replicated code.

Viewing Conflicts

Oracle's REPCAT views show all of the conflicts that have occurred and what method is being used to resolve them. Each of the views comes in USER, ALL, and DBA versions. Table 25.6 lists the REPCAT views.

TABLE 25.6: REPCAT VIEWS

View (DBA, USER, and ALL)	Description
_REPCOLUMN_GROUP	Lists all of the column groups defined for the database
_REPCONFLICT	Lists the types of conflicts that you have a specified resolution for
_REPGROUPED_COLUMN	Lists all of the columns in each column group in the database
_REPPARAMETER_COLUMN	Identifies columns that are used by the conflict resolution methods to resolve a conflict
_REPPRIORITY	Lists priority levels for each priority or site priority group
_REPPRIORITY_GROUP	Lists all of the priority groups and site priority groups defined for the database
_REPRESOLUTION	Provides more specific information about the conflict resolution method used to resolve conflicts on each object
_REPRESOLUTION_METHOD	Shows all available conflict resolution methods

Resuming Master Activity

If you ever need to resume the activity for a replication job, the following command will accomplish this.

```
DBMS_REPCAT.RESUME_MASTER_ACTIVITY (
    gname       IN VARCHAR2,
    override    IN BOOLEAN : = FALSE)
```

```
EXEC dbms_repcat.resume_master_activity('PROJECTS_RUN');
```

You will now have a replication job that runs until you shut it down or other fatal errors occur that cause it to stop operations.

CHAPTER 26

High Availability

FEATURING:

Using a standby database	**1076**
Using Oracle Parallel Server	**1093**
Using Fail Safe	**1105**

Because uptime relates directly to revenue generation, and downtime means losing work hours as well as potential customers, the impact of either on the bottom line is evident. The actual cost of downtime can range anywhere from a couple of hundred dollars to a couple of thousand dollars per second, depending on the nature of business and the time of the day. As more companies scale up their business processes for the global market, demand for 24/7 access to applications is not uncommon. In response to such demand, companies spend a considerable amount of time and money to design and implement a high-availability (HA) solution.

Technically speaking, HA is defined as 99.9 percent uptime—no more than 8 hours and 45 minutes of downtime in a year. There is also a trend toward achieving 99.999 percent uptime, also known as *five nines,* equaling no more than 5 minutes and 15 seconds of downtime in a year. The five nines standard is achievable, but it requires significant planning and investment. Oracle8i supplies five tools to help you get there: replication, Net8, the standby database, Oracle Parallel Server (OPS), and Oracle Fail Safe. This chapter covers the use of the standby database, OPS, and Oracle Fail Safe. Replication is discussed in Chapter 25, and Net8 is covered in Chapter 9.

Using a Standby Database

Oracle introduced the standby database with release 7.3 in response to a growing need for increased redundancy and efficient recoverability. Enhancements introduced in Oracle8i make the standby database simpler to maintain, with greater flexibility and usability.

A *standby database* is a near synchronous copy or copies of a production, or primary, database. It is maintained in a state of recovery and kept current through the application of archived redo logs sourced from the primary database. Figure 26.1 shows the standby database architecture.

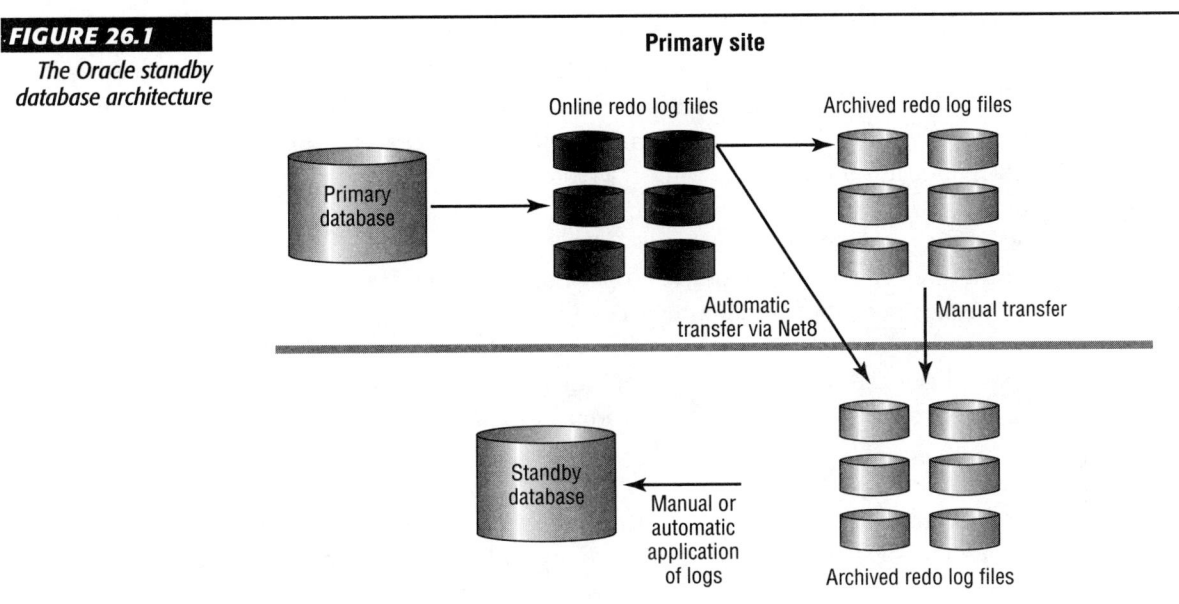

FIGURE 26.1
The Oracle standby database architecture

Should the primary database become unusable, the standby database can be activated as a failover solution to reduce recovery time and minimize data loss, even as a disaster recovery solution if the standby host is maintained in a geographically remote location.

To activate a standby database, the standby database must be mounted but not open. Activation terminates recovery, and the database can be opened for normal processing as the primary database. A standby database can also be opened in read-only mode, which is useful for separating report processing from the primary host.

Standby Database Modes

A standby database can be run in managed recovery, manual recovery, or read-only mode. You can run the standby database in only a single mode at any given time, although you can switch between each mode as necessary. For example, you might run your standby database in managed recovery mode during the day, open it in read-only mode at night for batch-report processing, and switch back to managed recovery mode in the morning.

Managed Recovery Mode

When the standby database is in *managed recovery mode*, archived redo logs are propagated by the primary database to the standby host over Net8 and then applied to the standby database. This process is managed entirely by Oracle. For each archive (ARCH) process on the primary host, a remote file server process is spawned on the standby host, which reads the stream from the primary database, writes the archive logs, and updates the standby control file. The standby database reads the standby control file and applies the newly propagated redo log archive.

The primary database is limited to five archive destinations, one of which must be local. Consequently, the primary database is limited to a maximum of four remote hosts. This means that a maximum of four standby databases can be maintained in managed recovery mode for any one primary database.

Manual Recovery Mode

Unlike with managed recovery mode, *manual recovery mode* does not place a limit on the number of standby databases. You could configure four standby databases in managed recovery mode, and then configure any number of standby databases in manual recovery mode, limited only by the standby database environment (such as CPU, memory, and storage availability).

With manual recovery, archived redo logs must be manually propagated and applied to the standby database to keep it current with the primary database. Manual recovery mode is useful in environments where a Net8 connection cannot be maintained between the primary and standby hosts, or if managed recovery fails due to an interruption to the Net8 connection.

Read-Only Mode

In *read-only mode*, recovery is terminated and the database is opened for read-only processing. While in read-only mode, redo log archives are still received and the standby control file is updated, but the recovery does not continue until the database is placed back into managed recovery mode.

Creating the Standby Database

Before you prepare the standby database, you must identify where the standby database will reside and determine whether to use managed recovery or manual recovery. You also need to decide whether the standby database will have the same directory structure as the primary database. Although maintenance of the standby database is easier if the directory structure matches that of the primary database, it is possible to use a different structure.

It is also possible to build the standby database on the same host as the primary database. In that case, the directory structure of the standby database will be different from that of the primary database, and you will need to set certain configuration parameters to allow for the differences.

If the purpose of the standby database is for a failover or disaster recovery plan, you will want to store the standby database on a separate physical host, preferably at a remote site. If the purpose of the standby database is for supplemental reporting, you may decide to store the standby database on a separate host locally, or even put the standby database on the same host as the primary database.

In most situations, managed recovery is preferred to ensure near synchronization with the primary database. However, you may decide to go with manual recovery because of your system's environment (for example, perhaps the system is used for other databases) or because the data is stable enough that concurrent synchronization is not required.

Once you have decided where to host the standby database and whether to use managed recovery or manual recovery, you are ready to create the standby database. Here are the steps for creating a standby database:

1. Back up the primary database.
2. Create the standby control file.
3. Copy the database files to the standby host.
4. Configure Net8.
5. Configure the primary instance.
6. Configure the standby instance.
7. Mount the standby database.
8. Rename files on the standby site.
9. Enable parameters for the primary instance.
10. Enable recovery.

These steps are discussed in detail in the following sections.

Backing Up the Primary Database

When you back up your primary database, make sure that the primary database is in ARCHIVELOG mode. You will need the archived redo logs to keep the standby database current with the primary database. Either query the V$DATABASE view or issue the ARCHIVE LOG LIST statement, as follows:

```
SQL> CONNECT INTERNAL
SQL> ARCHIVE LOG LIST
```

```
Database log mode              Archive Mode
Automatic archival             Enabled
Archive destination            /u02/PRMRY/arch
Oldest online log sequence     174
Next log sequence to archive   175
Current log sequence           179
```

You can use a recent backup or make a new backup of your primary database's datafiles. You will create the standby datafiles from this backup. You may create the standby database datafiles from either an online or offline backup. (See Chapters 10 and 13 for more on datafile backups.)

Creating the Standby Control File

All databases need control files, of course, and standby databases are no exception. With a standby database, you use a standby control file. You create the standby control file after you have created the backup of the datafiles. To create the standby control file, connect to the primary database and issue the ALTER DATABASE CREATE STANDBY CONTROLFILE statement. Make sure that the path and filename of the standby control file are different from the control file of the primary database:

```
ALTER DATABASE CREATE STANDBY CONTROLFILE AS '/tmp/stdby.ctl';
```

Copying the Database Files to the Standby Host

After you have created both a backup of the primary database and a standby control file, transfer the backup datafiles and the standby control file to the standby host. If you are creating the standby database on the same host as the primary database, be careful not to overwrite the primary database files.

Configuring Net8

To implement managed recovery, you will need to configure Net8 so that archived redo logs generated by the primary database will be copied to the standby host and applied to the standby database. If your plan is to use manual recovery, you will not need to configure Net8. Instead, you must use methods provided by your operating system to copy archived redo logs to the standby host and manually apply the archived redo logs to the standby database.

To configure Net8, you will need to set up the tnsnames.ora file on the primary host and the listener.ora file on the standby host. The tnsnames.ora file will reference the service name of the standby instance, and the listener.ora file will configure the listener to receive connection requests from the primary database. The settings in the tnsnames.ora file must correlate with the settings in the listener.ora file.

Listing 26.1 is an example of a tnsnames.ora entry configured to reference the service name of the standby database.

Listing 26.1: Referencing the Standby Database in the tnsnames.ora File

```
stdby=
  (description=
    (address=
      (protocol=tcp)
      (port=1512)
      (host=sbhost)
    )
    (connect_data=(sid=stdby)
    )
  )
```

Listing 26.2 shows an example of a listener.ora entry configured for the standby instance.

Listing 26.2: Configuring the Standby Instance in the listener.ora File

```
listener=
  (address_list=
    (address=
      (protocol=tcp)
      (port=1512)
      (host=sbhost)
    )
  )
sid_list_listener=
  (sid_list=
    (sid_desc=
      (sid_name=stdby)
      (ORACLE_HOME=/u01/app/oracle/product/8.1.7)
    )
  )
```

Once you have configured the listener.ora file, you will need to start the listener or reload the listener, if it is already running. If the listener is not running, start it with this command:

```
$ lsnrctl start
```

If the listener is already running, you can enable the new configuration without stopping the listener by using the reload option:

```
$ lsnrctl reload
```

Configuring the Primary Instance

To implement managed recovery, you will need to configure the primary instance to archive redo logs to the standby host. If you plan to use manual recovery, you do not need to make any configuration changes to the primary instance.

To configure the primary instance to archive redo logs to the standby host, you will need to set up the `init.ora` file for the primary instance with information about where to archive these logs. You do not need to shut down the primary instance to enable these parameters. Instead, you can manually enable them using the ALTER SYSTEM command, as described in the "Enabling Parameters for the Primary Instance" section later in this chapter.

The archive destination is specified by using the LOG_ARCHIVE_DEST_n parameter, where n is an integer from 1 to 5. Up to five destinations may be defined, but one destination must be a local device. When setting these parameters, the keyword LOCATION specifies a valid path for the local archive destination, and the keyword SERVICE specifies a service name referenced in the `tnsnames.ora` file. The SERVICE keyword must be specified for all standby archive destinations, whether local or remote. Here is an example of using the LOG_ARCHIVE_DEST_n parameters in the `init.ora` file of the primary instance:

```
log_archive_dest_1 = 'location=/u02/arch/PRMRY'
log_archive_dest_2 = 'service=stdby'
```

There are several options that you can set with the LOG_ARCHIVE_DEST_n parameter, as described in the following sections.

Setting a Mandatory or Optional Destination

You can specify whether a destination is mandatory or optional by using the MANDATORY or OPTIONAL keyword, respectively. Oracle recommends that you specify the local archived redo log destination as MANDATORY. The following is an example of using the MANDATORY and OPTIONAL keywords:

```
log_archive_dest_1 = 'location=/u02/arch/PRMRY MANDATORY'
log_archive_dest_2 = 'service=stdby OPTIONAL'
```

Specifying Access after a Failed Write

By default, Oracle will not attempt to access a destination following an error. You can specify that Oracle should attempt to access an archived redo log destination again after a failed write using the REOPEN keyword. The REOPEN keyword specifies the number of seconds Oracle will wait before the archiver process should attempt to access a failed destination again. The default value of the REOPEN keyword when specified without qualification is 300 seconds. (If you do not specify the REOPEN keyword, the default value is 0.) You can override the default by using REOPEN=n, where

n is the number of seconds to wait. The following is an example of using the REOPEN keyword:

```
log_archive_dest_2 = 'service=stdby OPTIONAL REOPEN=60'
```

Setting the Minimum Successful Write Destinations

The LOG_ARCHIVE_MIN_SUCCEED_DEST parameter specifies the minimum number of destinations where the archiver process must successfully write archived redo logs before the source redo log is available for new writes. When archived redo logs are written, the count of successful writes to all MANDATORY destinations and OPTIONAL nonstandby destinations is measured to satisfy the setting of the LOG_ARCHIVE_MIN_SUCCEED_DEST parameter. The default setting for LOG_ARCHIVE_MIN_SUCCEED_DEST is 1, and valid values are 1 through 5.

Enabling or Deferring a Destination

It is possible to define archived redo log destinations without enabling those destinations. Whether or not an archived redo log destination is enabled is specified using the LOG_ARCHIVE_DEST_STATE_n parameter, where n is an integer from 1 to 5, corresponding to the respective LOG_ARCHIVE_DEST_n parameter. Valid values are ENABLE or DEFER. ENABLE, the default setting, tells Oracle to archive to the defined destination. The DEFER setting allows you to define the destination without actually archiving to that destination. The deferred destination can later be enabled dynamically using the ALTER SESSION or ALTER SYSTEM command. The following example illustrates how to define an archived redo log destination without enabling it:

```
log_archive_dest_state_2 = DEFER
log_archive_dest_2 = 'service=stdby'
```

Configuring the Standby Instance

You can create the initialization parameter file for the standby instance by copying the initialization parameter file from the primary instance. With a few exceptions, the initialization parameters for the primary instance and the standby instance should have the same settings.

Setting Standby Initialization Parameters

The following parameters are particularly important when you are configuring the standby instance:

- The COMPATIBLE parameter settings should be identical for the primary and standby instances.
- The DB_NAME parameter settings should also be identical in both files.
- The CONTROL_FILES parameter for the standby instance should be set to the fully qualified name of the standby control file.

- The LOG_ARCHIVE_DEST_n (described earlier in the "Configuring the Primary Instance" section) specifies the location of the archived redo logs for manual recovery. This parameter should be set whether you are configuring managed or manual recovery.

- The optional parameter LOG_ARCHIVE_TRACE causes an audit trail of archived redo logs received from the primary database to be written to a trace file.

- In a managed recovery environment, the STANDBY_ARCHIVE_DEST parameter sets the location to write the archived redo logs received from the primary database. Set LOG_ARCHIVE_DEST_n and STANDBY_ARCHIVE_DEST to identical values for easier maintenance.

Setting Parameters for a Standby on the Same Host as the Primary

When the primary and standby databases reside on the same host, several other standby initialization parameters are important. These include the DB_FILE_NAME_CONVERT, LOG_FILE_NAME_CONVERT, and LOCK_NAME_SPACE parameters.

The DB_FILE_NAME_CONVERT and LOG_FILE_NAME_CONVERT parameters in the standby initialization parameter file enable automatic name conversion of datafiles and archived redo logs, respectively. Ideally, the directory structures in the primary and standby databases should be identical. However, if they are not (because the primary and standby databases reside on the same host or for some other reason), you will need to update the standby control file with the new filenames.

The DB_FILE_NAME_CONVERT and LOG_FILE_NAME_CONVERT parameters each specify two strings. The first string is that portion of the path structure of the primary database to be converted. The second string is the new path structure to replace the structure specified by the first string. Here's an example of the DB_FILE_NAME_CONVERT parameter set in the standby database initialization parameter file:

```
db_file_name_convert = /u01/oradata/PRMRY, /u01/oradata/STDBY
```

The LOCK_NAME_SPACE parameter also must be set for the standby instance when the primary and standby databases reside on the same host, as follows:

```
lock_name_space = stdby
```

If this parameter is not set for the two instances, you will receive an ORA-1102 error.

Mounting the Standby Database

When you are ready to start the standby database, follow these steps:

1. Connect to Oracle from SQL*Plus:
   ```
   $ sqlplus /NOLOG
   SQL> CONNECT INTERNAL
   ```

2. Start the instance without mounting the database:
   SQL> STARTUP NOMOUNT

3. Mount the database as a standby database:
   SQL> ALTER DATABASE MOUNT STANDBY DATABASE;

Renaming Files on the Standby Site

If you are unable to correctly rename all of the datafiles and redo log files for the standby database using conversion parameters, you will need to manually rename these files before starting recovery. For example, suppose that the DB_FILE_NAME_CONVERT parameter was set to convert the path /u01/oradata/PRMRY to /u01/oradata/STDBY. However, a datafile was erroneously created following the path /u01/app/oracle/admin/PRMRY, and you are unable to take the downtime to correct this error. You can still move this datafile on the standby site to the correct path, but you will need to manually rename this datafile in the standby control file.

To manually rename a datafile, with the standby database mounted, use the ALTER DATABASE RENAME FILE command, as follows:

```
SQL> ALTER DATABASE RENAME FILE
  2>   '/u01/app/oracle/admin/PRMRY/temp01.dbf' to
  3>   '/u01/oradata/STDBY/temp01.dbf';
```

Enabling Parameters for the Primary Instance

If you are implementing managed recovery, you have configured the initialization parameter file of the primary instance to archive redo logs to the standby site (as described in the "Configuring the Primary Instance" section earlier in this chapter). However, if you have not shut down and restarted the instance, these new settings have not taken effect. You can enable these new parameter settings dynamically without shutting down the instance by using the ALTER SYSTEM command.

For example, suppose that you set the LOG_ARCHIVE_DEST_2 parameter as follows:

```
log_archive_dest_2 = "service=stdby"
```

You can now enable this parameter with the following command:

```
SQL> ALTER SYSTEM SET log_archive_dest_2 = "service=stdby";
```

Enabling Recovery

Your next step is to start the recovery process of the standby database. How you start the recovery depends on the type of recovery you have chosen for your environment.

Enabling Manual Recovery

If you chose to use the manual recovery process, you can initiate recovery by issuing the following command:

```
SQL> RECOVER STANDBY DATABASE;
```

This command tells Oracle to use the location specified in the initialization file.

Alternatively, you can start manual recovery with this command:

```
SQL> RECOVER FROM '/u02/arch/STDBY' STANDBY DATABASE;
```

As you can see, this command gives the location of the archived log files to be used for the current recovery session.

You can also use the above commands with the UNTIL CANCEL option:

```
SQL> RECOVER STANDBY DATABSE UNTIL CANCEL;
```

```
SQL> RECOVER FROM '/u02/arch/STDBY' STANDBY DATABASE UNTIL CANCEL;
```

When using this command, Oracle will prompt you for each archived redo log file that it wants to apply and wait for you to acknowledge the prompt before continuing.

Enabling Managed Recovery

If you are using the managed recovery option, you will first need to check to see if a *gap sequence* exists. Since Oracle rolls the standby database forward by sequentially applying the archived redo log files, it cannot enter into a managed recovery session if there is a missing log. A gap sequence exists when the primary database generated a log sequence that was not archived to the standby site. A gap sequence may occur for a number of reasons, such as the following:

- The standby database was created from an old backup or from an inconsistent (online) backup.
- You shut down the standby database(s) before shutting down the primary database.
- There was a network failure.

If a gap sequence exists, you will need to manually apply the missing archived redo log files to bring the standby database in synch with the primary site.

You can query the standby database to see if a gap sequence exists using SQL*Plus, as follows:

```
SELECT high.thread#, "LowGap#", "HighGap#"
FROM
     (
     SELECT thread#, MIN(sequence#)-1 "HighGap#"
     FROM
```

```sql
    (
        SELECT a.thread#, a.sequence#
        FROM
        (
            SELECT *
            FROM v$archived_log
        ) a,
        (
            SELECT thread#, MAX(next_change#)gap1
            FROM v$log_history
            GROUP BY thread#
        ) b
        WHERE a.thread# = b.thread#
        AND a.next_change# > gap1
    )
    GROUP BY thread#
) high,
(
    SELECT thread#, MIN(sequence#) "LowGap#"
    FROM
    (
        SELECT thread#, sequence#
        FROM v$log_history, v$datafile
        WHERE checkpoint_change# <= next_change#
        AND checkpoint_change# >= first_change#
    )
    GROUP BY thread#
) low
 WHERE low.thread# = high.thread#;
```

This query will generate an output similar to the following:

```
THREAD#    LowSeq#    HighSeq#
--------   --------   ---------
     1        171        174
```

This shows that a gap sequence exists for thread #1 and that logs 171 through 174 should be manually applied to the standby database. If the HIGHSEQ# and LOWSEQ# columns both show the same number, a gap sequence does not exist for that particular thread.

If there is a gap sequence, query the V$ARCHIVED_LOG view in the primary database to obtain the names of the log files that need to be manually applied, as follows:

```
SQL> SELECT name
  2> FROM v$archived_log
  3> WHERE sequence# >= 171
  4> AND sequence# <= 174;

NAME
----------------------------------------
/u02/arch/primary/arch_PRMRY_1_171.log
/u02/arch/primary/arch_PRMRY_1_172.log
/u02/arch/primary/arch_PRMRY_1_173.log
/u02/arch/primary/arch_PRMRY_1_174.log
```

You will then need to copy these archived log files from the primary database's archiving destination to the standby database's receiving destination. After the files have been copied, issue either the RECOVER STANDBY DATABASE UNTIL CANCEL or RECOVER AUTOMATIC STANDBY DATABASE command to apply the necessary log files.

Once the gap sequence has been resolved, you can initiate a managed recovery session for your standby database, as follows:

```
SQL> RECOVER MANAGED STANDBY DATABASE;
```

When you use this statement, Oracle will wait indefinitely for the new archived log files to be received and automatically apply them to your standby database.

If you want to specify a waiting period, use the TIMEOUT option and specify the length of time to wait, in minutes:

```
SQL> RECOVER MANAGED STANDBY DATABASE TIMEOUT 10;
```

In this example, Oracle will wait for 10 minutes for new archived log files to arrive before it will time out and cancel the managed recovery session.

Testing the Standby Database

You are now ready to test the failover functionality of your newly created standby database. However, if you simply activated the standby database, you would need to open the database using the RESETLOGS command. Of course, once the standby database has been opened with RESETLOGS, the only way to resume in standby mode is to re-create the standby database. The solution to this problem is to test your standby database failover functionality by first using cancel-based recovery, and then starting the standby database in read-only mode.

For a managed recovery process, cancel the recovery session and shut down the standby instance by issuing this command:

SQL> RECOVER MANAGED STANDBY DATABASE CANCEL

For manual recovery, use the following commands:

SQL> RECOVER CANCEL
SQL> SHUTDOWN IMMEDIATE

Next, start the standby database and put it in MOUNT mode:

SQL> STARTUP NOMOUNT
SQL> ALTER DATABASE MOUNT STANDBY DATABASE;

Then, in MOUNT mode, open the database in read-only mode:

SQL> ALTER DATABASE OPEN READ ONLY;

Once the standby database has been opened in read-only mode, you can query the standby database to verify that the transactions executed on the primary site are propagated to the standby site.

Maintaining a Standby Database

The previous sections walked you through a step-by-step process of creating a standby database. So now that you have a fully operational standby database, what's next?

Like everything else, your standby database will require some administration and maintenance. Generally, the only maintenance that is required for a standby database is to keep it in synch with the primary database. Some problems you may run into while managing standby databases include the need to resolve redo log sequence number gaps as they occur. Other tasks include making sure that the physical structure of the standby database matches that of the primary database and manually propagating any data that was applied to the primary site via the DIRECT or UNRECOVERABLE mode. Let's take a closer look at these situations.

 TIP The standby database can also be backed up, but not while the database is in recovery mode. Either shut down the standby database or open it in read-only mode. Make the backups. Then resume recovery.

Resolving Gap Sequences

Common causes for gap sequences (after the standby database is operational) are network failures and shutting down the standby database while the primary database is still open. You will need to be aware of these situations and regularly monitor the standby database to ensure that a gap sequence does not occur. If you do find a gap sequence, you will need to manually resolve it, as explained in the "Enabling Managed Recovery" section earlier in this chapter.

Matching Changes in the Physical Structure

Standby database recovery is possible only as long as the physical structure matches that of the primary database. Certain physical structure changes are transmitted automatically to the standby database via redo application. Such changes include renaming a primary database's datafile, changing the mode of a tablespace from offline to online or vice versa, changing the status of a tablespace from read-only to read/write or vice versa, and dropping a tablespace.

Other structural changes require a certain degree of manual maintenance on the standby database. Such changes include re-creating the control file and adding a tablespace/datafile to the primary database.

Re-creating the Standby Control File

Creating new members or groups on the primary database does not affect the standby database. Similarly, enabling or disabling threads does not affect the standby database either. However, it is recommended that if you enable or disable threads, or add or drop groups or members on the primary database, you re-create the standby control file. This keeps the redo log file configuration on the primary and the standby databases in synch.

WARNING If for some reason, the unarchived log files need to be cleared on the primary instance, you will invalidate the entire standby database. Your only option at that time will be to re-create the standby database.

Changing certain initialization parameters requires re-creating the control file. If you re-create the primary database's control file, you will invalidate the standby database's control file. Therefore, you will need to re-create the standby database's control file. Follow these steps to re-create a standby control file (note that these steps assume that the primary database's control files have been re-created):

1. Cancel the recovery session and shut down the standby instance.

    - For managed recovery, issue:
      SQL> RECOVER MANAGED STANDBY DATABASE CANCEL

    - For manual recovery, use:
      SQL> RECOVER CANCEL
      SQL> SHUTDOWN IMMEDIATE

2. Log in to the primary instance and use the following statement to create a standby control file:
   ```
   SQL> ALTER DATABASE CREATE STANDBY CONTROLFILE AS '/tmp/stdby.ctl';
   ```
3. Archive the online redo log file on the primary database:
   ```
   SQL> ALTER SYSTEM ARCHIVE LOG CURRENT;
   ```
4. Copy the newly created standby control file from the primary host to the standby host and start the standby instance in recovery mode:
   ```
   SQL> STARTUP NOMOUNT
   SQL> ALTER DATABASE MOUNT STANDBY DATABASE;
   SQL> RECOVER STANDBY DATABASE
   ```

NOTE If you restored a control file from backup on the primary database or opened the primary database with the RESETLOGS command, you will need to re-create the standby database.

Adding Tablespaces/Datafiles

Whenever a new datafile is added to the primary site, the same file needs to be added to the standby site (or sites) as well. Suppose that you add a new datafile to the primary site like this:

```
SQL> ALTER TABLESPACE TEMP ADD DATAFILE '/u01/oradata/PRMRY/temp02.dbf'
     SIZE 200M;
```

Redo generated from this statement will add the name of the new datafile to the standby control file. However, in order for the standby database to continue recovery, you must copy the file to its corresponding location. You can also cancel the recovery session on the standby site and create the datafile.

To switch log files on the primary site to initiate archival of the redo logs to the standby site, issue the following statement:

```
SQL>  ALTER SYSTEM SWITCH LOGFILE;
```

Next, ensure that the standby database is running in recovery mode. Initiate manual recovery, if necessary:

```
SQL> CONNECT INTERNAL
SQL> STARTUP NOMOUNT
SQL> ALTER DATABASE MOUNT STANDBY DATABASE;
SQL> RECOVER MANAGED STANDBY DATABASE;
```

For manual recovery of the standby database, substitute the last statement with this one:

```sql
SQL> RECOVER STANDBY DATABASE UNTIL CANCEL;
```

Once all the archived redo log files have been applied to the standby database, use CANCEL or RECOVER MANAGED STANDBY DATABASE CANCEL statements (or press Ctrl+C) to cancel the recovery session.

Now that you have added related information about the new datafile to the standby control file, you need to create the relevant file(s) on the standby site. To create the datafile, use the ALTER DATABASE CREATE DATAFILE command:

```sql
SQL> ALTER DATABASE CREATE DATAFILE '/u01/oradata/STDBY/temp02.dbf'
     AS '/u01/oradata/STDBY/temp02.dbf';
```

You can now resume normal activity on both the primary database (for example, transaction processing) and the standby database (such as managed recovery mode).

Making Manual Changes

Since direct-path loads and changes made using the NOLOGGING / UNRECOVERABLE option do not generate redo, changes made to the primary database cannot be automatically transmitted to the standby database. The recovery process on the standby database will still read all of the archived log files in a sequential manner and continue the recovery process. However, an error message will be generated in the standby database's alert log file, stating that the block was changed using the NOLOGGING option and therefore cannot be recovered.

Your only options to synchronize the primary and the standby databases in such cases are as follows:

- Re-create the standby database.
- Back up the affected tablespaces from the primary database, transfer them to the standby database, and resume recovery.
- Cancel recovery on the standby database, take the affected datafiles offline, and then drop them when the standby database is activated. This option may not be feasible because it will result in data loss.

Opening a Standby Database in Read-Only Mode

You can open a standby database in read-only mode once the recovery session has been canceled. Tablespaces in a read-only standby database need to be created as temporary and locally managed, and they should contain only temporary files. Also, all the required user permissions and privileges must be set to access these tablespaces. Since this cannot be done at the standby site, all these privileges must be given at the primary site. This allows for queries that generate on-disk sorting operations without generating any redo entries or affecting the data dictionary.

To open a standby database in read-only mode, first start the standby database in MOUNT mode:

```
SQL> STARTUP NOMOUNT
SQL> ALTER DATABASE MOUNT STANDBY DATABASE;
```

In MOUNT mode, you can open the database in read-only mode with the following command:

```
SQL> ALTER DATABASE OPEN READ ONLY;
```

Data Guard to the Rescue

Oracle introduced Data Guard with Oracle8i as an option to administer and maintain your standby databases on Unix platforms. Built to protect against data corruptions and disasters, Data Guard can be configured to automate failovers. Another feature of Data Guard is that it can allow for a time delay. This means that it waits a specified amount of time before applying the archived redo log files to the standby database. In Oracle8i, Data Guard also can be used in conjunction with a remote mirroring technology to support a zero data loss environment.

Data Guard will be fully released with Oracle9i. It is supposed to have a GUI that will plug into Oracle Enterprise Manager (OEM), providing for ease of management. Also, the zero data loss option will be built in with the Oracle9i version of Data Guard—the LGWR process on the primary database will write to its online redo log files and to the archived log files on a remote site simultaneously.

Using Oracle Parallel Server

Oracle Parallel Server (OPS) is a combination of hardware and software configuration that allows you to use the power of multiple servers as one server. OPS is commonly installed in a clustered environment. Several *nodes* (servers) combine to form a *cluster*. The idea behind the OPS architecture is to allow transactions to be divided and executed simultaneously on several nodes. These nodes access a single database that usually resides on a centralized storage array.

OPS can be used for various database configurations. Data warehousing and decision support systems can readily use the robustness of the OPS architecture to split and run multiple batch jobs concurrently. OPS can also be configured in various OLTP and hybrid configurations, primarily for the purposes of load balancing and availability.

To a front-end application, an OPS configuration is transparent. This means that functionally, running on an OPS does not appear any different to the application than running on a single-instance database. However, since the application can be distributed and the database accordingly partitioned, there is a large performance gain in an OPS environment.

NOTE In earlier versions of OPS (versions 8.0.x and earlier), significant performance gains were experienced in cases where the data-to-node affinity was greater. In environments where the applications were not OPS-aware (properly distributed), a database running an OPS configuration would actually perform slower than a single-instance database. This was because of processes called *pinging* and *false pinging*. These topics, along with enhancements in Oracle8i that avoid database pings, are discussed later in this chapter, in the "Oracle 8i OPS Enhancements" section.

The OPS Architecture

OPS allows for multiple instances (running on the same or different nodes) to mount and access the same database. OPS allows read-consistent data to be read from multiple instances. This is handled using Parallel Cache Management (PCM) locks. Each PCM lock occupies approximately 100 bytes of memory and is responsible for inter-instance data block access.

As you might expect, there is a lot that goes on behind the scenes to allow multiple instances to access a single database. A fairly complex hardware configuration and software solution are combined to allow for such an architecture. Figure 26.2 illustrates the OPS architecture, and the following sections describe its components in more detail.

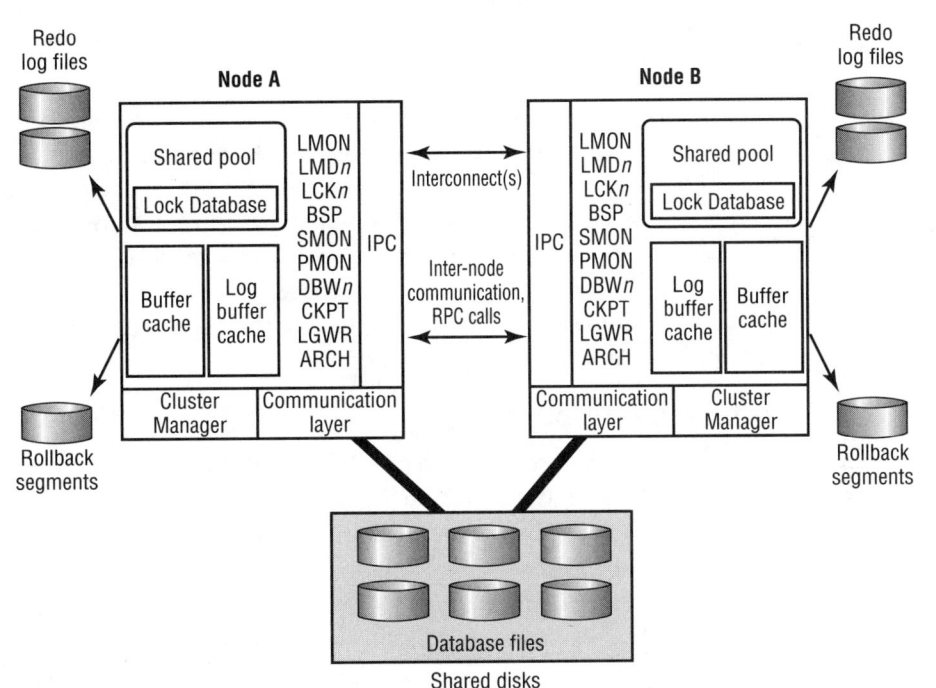

FIGURE 26.2
The Oracle Parallel Server architecture

Hardware Cluster Configurations

A clustered environment is built by linking two or more *nodes* via a high-speed *interconnect*. A node is essentially a server that joins with other servers to form a cluster. A node, like any other server, is made up of a CPU, memory, and storage. Interconnects are high-speed communication links between nodes. They form a private network for all inter-node and inter-instance communications. An interconnect can be an Ethernet or a fiber connection between two nodes.

There are practically an infinite number of configurations for a node, and therefore cluster configurations vary significantly from vendor to vendor, as well as from environment to environment.

CPU and Memory Configurations

CPUs and memory configurations can be divided into two main categories:

- In uniform memory access (UMA), the CPUs in a cluster access shared memory at the same speed. This is also referred to as *symmetrical multiprocessing* (SMP).

- In nonuniform memory access (NUMA), the CPUs access all parts of the memory, but their speed varies.

Storage-Access Configurations

Like memory access, disk access can also be uniform and nonuniform. In a uniform disk access configuration, nodes access a shared centralized storage array via SCSI or fiber connections. In a nonuniform disk access configuration, each node has a certain number of storage devices locally attached to it. Disk access for that node is much faster because it is local; for other nodes, the disk access becomes remote and is handled via special software over the interconnects.

The most common hardware configuration for an OPS environment is multiple SMP nodes connected to a shared disk farm.

Software Components

Several software components collectively support the OPS environment. These include the Cluster Manager, the Distributed Lock Manager (DLM or iDLM), the Block Server Process (BSP), and the Inter-Process Communication (IPC) component, which serve the following functions:

- The Cluster Manager is a vendor-provided software component that resides on each node locally and manages the node's membership in a cluster. The Cluster Manager provides failure-detection services (stopping services and isolating a node from the cluster if a failure is detected), monitors each node for any hardware and software changes, and scans all the nodes for any new instances that start.

- The DLM provides transparency to data access from different instances, as well as fault tolerance and deadlock detection. The DLM in Oracle8i consists of the Lock Database function and four background processes (LMON, LMD*n*, LCK*n*, and BSP), which work as follows:

  - The Lock Database contains resources for all inter-instance activities, such as locks and PCM and non-PCM enqueues.

  - The LMON background process monitors the entire cluster and manages locks and enqueue resources. In cases of failures, the LMON triggers DLM to rebuild the Lock Database, and the SMON initiates instance recovery. LMON also monitors incoming status messages from other instances.

  - The LMD background process manages and processes all incoming PCM enqueue requests.

- The LCK background process manages and processes all incoming non-PCM enqueue requests.
- The BSP produces and transmits consistent images of data blocks to the requesting instances over the interconnect. This process is new in Oracle8i and is an integral part of the Cache Fusion technology.
- The IPC component provides the protocol and interfaces that Oracle uses to transmit and receive messages among its instances. The IPC is based on an asynchronous, queued messaging model.

Oracle8i OPS Enhancements

As mentioned earlier, OPS uses PCM locks to allow read-consistent data to be read from multiple instances. In earlier Oracle versions, PCM locks were statically specified in the init.ora file by the GC_FILES_TO_LOCKS initialization parameter. Any adjustments to this parameter required the database to be taken down and brought back up again ("bounced"). Since this parameter specifies locks per datafile, it should be set to the same value in all of the different init.ora files. (See Table 26.1, later in this chapter, for more details on instance-specific initialization parameters.) The result was that there would be a set number of instances using a specified number of PCM locks to cover each and every database block.

For example, suppose that you had a 80GB database with an 8KB block size, and you allowed a 1:20 ratio for the PCM locks. This would mean that for a total of 10,485,760 database blocks, there were 524,288 PCM locks. Setting these locks would require an additional 50MB of memory per instance. What would happen when a request was made to modify one of the database blocks?

Let's say that a server process on Instance A on Node 1 needed to read a block from a specified file. Because the PCM lock ratio was set to 1:20, it would mean that the server process would not only read that particular block, but would also read the next 19 blocks covered by that PCM lock. In this process, a lock would be placed on the affected data block, indicating that it was being modified by Instance A.

Now, let's say that Instance B on Node 2 made a read-only request for the same block. In this scenario, Instance B would need to wait for Instance A to either write the block back to the datafile or provide it with a read-consistent image. In either case, Instance A would need to flush some data back to the datafile in order for Instance B to be able to read. This is known as a database *ping*.

What would happen if Instance B made a read-only request for any of the other 19 blocks covered by that particular PCM lock? Again, Instance A would need to flush the unmodified blocks back to the datafile in order for Instance B to be able to read it. This process is known as *false pinging*.

As new instances were added, the chances of pinging as well as false pinging would increase. This could result in serious performance problems. Therefore, in environments where applications were not OPS-aware (properly distributed), earlier versions of OPS could cause headaches.

With Oracle 8.0.*x*, Oracle introduced a new mechanism for dynamically setting PCM locks called *DBA locking,* or *shared* or *dynamic locking.* A DBA now could dynamically assign a PCM lock per database block for a specific period of time. This provided relief from false pinging, but with the added management costs of assigning and releasing the PCM locks.

Now in Oracle8i, Oracle has introduced a new concept called *Cache Fusion.* Cache Fusion allows for an instance to transmit a read-consistent image of a data block to a requesting instance directly over the high-speed interconnect, thus significantly reducing database pings. Cache Fusion technology in Oracle8i works well for scenarios where an instance requests a particular block that is being modified by another instance (a "write-read" scenario). However, it does not prevent a ping in cases where an instance requests to modify a block that is being read by another instance (a "read-write" scenario) or where an instance requests to modify a data block that is currently being modified by another instance (a "write-write" scenario).

OPS Limitations

OPS is a robust, highly scalable, and highly available configuration. However, it may not be ideal for every environment. There are certain factors that need to be considered before implementing OPS. One of the biggest drawbacks of OPS is that the applications need to be built with OPS in mind. This means that OPS may not be a viable solution for certain third-party, out-of-the-box solutions.

OPS requires all of the database files to be created as raw devices. When creating a database on raw devices, you need to spend a lot more time planning the file sizes as well as their locations. Certain Cluster Managers also need to be shut down whenever adding new raw devices. This means that you need to either create all of the files for the entire lifetime of the database prior to its creation or allow for some amount of downtime. In addition to this, backup and recovery processes also require additional overhead.

Creating the OPS Database

Creating an OPS environment includes installing and configuring several hardware and software components. The following sections provide details on creating an OPS database, preparing multiple initialization files, and then starting instances and mounting the database in parallel mode.

NOTE We assume that you have already configured the required underlying software and hardware components. Follow the manufacturers' recommendations to configure your hardware and OPS environment infrastructure.

Preparing for Installation

The preparatory steps include installing and configuring the following components on each participating node in the cluster:

Operating system-specific software Load the specific operating system on each participating node in the cluster. Also ensure that all vendor-recommended patches have been installed. It is always good practice to check the hardware compatibility list for every software component to be installed. Any conflicts should be resolved prior to proceeding.

Operating system-dependent layer Install software components such as the Cluster Manager, the IPC component, and shared disk subsystem management software. Since each of these components is a vendor-supplied component (from a vendor other than Oracle), follow the manufacturer's installation and configuration procedures. It is always good practice to run any vendor-recommended diagnostics after installation of these components.

Raw devices One of the limitations of implementing OPS is that all the datafiles, control files, and redo log files must be created as raw devices. Also, some operating systems mandate that the Cluster Manager be stopped when adding new raw devices. This means that you need to create all the raw devices for the entire lifetime of the database prior to creating the database, or you must allow for a certain amount of downtime later.

NOTE You must create at least the initial raw devices prior to creating the database. Also, if you intend to use the Oracle Universal Installer and the Database Configuration Assistant, you need to create an ASCII file with all the raw device filenames. The DBCA_RAW_CONFIG environment variable must be set to point to this file.

Oracle software The Oracle Universal Installer (OUI) is OPS-aware. When you use it to install the Oracle software, it will present you with the choice of selecting nodes. But before you invoke the OUI, there is a certain amount of preconfiguration that is required. Basically, OUI requires that the Oracle user should be able to do remote login (rlogin) to all the nodes. The .rhosts or the hosts.equiv file on Unix systems should be set accordingly. You will need to create the OSOPER and OSDBA groups as well.

Creating the Database Manually

Creating an OPS database is much like creating a single-instance database, although there are a few differences, as you will learn in this section. You can use the Database Configuration Assistant to create the OPS database, or you can manually create it. The following are the basic steps to manually create the OPS database:

1. Create instance-specific initialization files.
2. Create the database.
3. Create additional rollback segments.
4. Start the database in parallel mode.
5. Configure Net8 on each node.

The following sections describe these steps in more detail.

Creating the Initialization Files

You will need an initialization file for every instance that you start. You can use the $ORACLE_HOME/opsm/admin/init.ora (on Unix) file as a starting point. This file contains some of the OPS-specific initialization parameters. Copy and rename this file accordingly. Table 26.1 describes the instance-specific initialization parameters, and Table 26.2 describes the database-specific initialization parameters.

TABLE 26.1: INSTANCE-SPECIFIC INITIALIZATION PARAMETERS

Parameter	Description
IFILE	Identifies the path and name of the include file. In an OPS environment, some initialization parameters are identical for all the instances, so this parameter can be used to specify a common file that contains all database-specific initialization parameters.
INSTANCE_NAME	Identifies the name of the instance. Each instance in an OPS configuration must have a unique name.
INSTANCE_NUMBER	Maps the instance to a free list group of a database object with the free list group of the storage parameter. This value must be set the same as the value of the thread parameter for that instance.

Continued

TABLE 26.1: INSTANCE-SPECIFIC INITIALIZATION PARAMETERS (CONTINUED)

Parameter	Description
THREAD	Specifies the number of the redo thread to be used by the instance. Each instance in an OPS configuration must have its own redo thread to write to. Also, the instance will not mount the database if its redo thread has been disabled.
ROLLBACK_SEGMENTS	Sets rollback segments to be used by an instance. At least two rollback segments per instance are required. When creating the database, you need to create enough rollback segments for every instance. Note that except for the system rollback segment, public rollback segments cannot be shared among instances.
PARALLEL_SERVER	Allows instances to mount the database in shared mode. This should be set to TRUE for all instances.
GC_FILES_TO_LOCKS	Statically allocates and distributes PCM locks per datafile. Because the PCM locks control inter-instance access to blocks within a datafile, the values for GC_FILES_TO_LOCKS must be set identically in all instances.

TABLE 26.2: DATABASE-SPECIFIC INITIALIZATION PARAMETERS

Parameter	Description
DB_NAME	Specifies the name of the database.
DB_DOMAIN	Specifies the database domain. It is always good practice to set the database domain identical to the network domain.
CONTROL_FILES	Specifies the names of the raw devices to be used as control files.
BACKGROUND_DUMP_DEST	Specifies the location where the background processes write their trace files.
USER_DUMP_DEST	Specifies the location when user processes need to write a trace file.
SERVICE_NAMES	Specifies the database service names. By default, the service name is set to the global name of the database. It is possible to have multiple service names in an OPS configuration. To implement this, set the service_names initialization parameter in the instance-specific init.ora file.

The trick to creating an instance-specific init.ora file is that most of the instance-specific parameters will have different values, whereas all the database-related parameters will be set the same throughout instances.

Using the CREATE DATABASE Command to Create the Database

Certain CREATE DATABASE options play an important role in how your OPS environment will be configured:

MAXDATAFILES A database that is going to be accessed by multiple instances generally tends to have a larger number of datafiles than a single-instance database. This is because every instance requires its own redo thread as well as rollback segments. Since any changes to the MAXDATAFILE parameter require re-creating the control file, it is a good idea to initially set this to a large value.

MAXINSTANCES This parameter places the high limit on the number of instances that can access the database concurrently. It is always recommended that you set the MAXINSTANCES value to more than the maximum number of instances than you ever plan to run concurrently.

MAXLOGHISTORY This parameter sets the high limit on the number of archived redo log files that can be stored in the control file. This number should be set much higher than the default value (which varies by operating system). This value directly impacts the ability to automatically recover an OPS node.

MAXLOGFILES This parameter sets the high limit on the number of log groups that can be created for the database. Since each instance that you start requires its own redo thread, it is wise to set MAXLOGFILES to a high value.

Listing 26.3 shows a sample script that creates a database called TEST to be opened by multiple instances.

Listing 26.3: Creating an OPS Database

```
CREATE DATABASE "TEST"
MAXDATAFILES 1024
MAXINSTANCES 10
MAXLOGFILES 15
MAXLOGMEMBERS 5
MAXLOGHISTORY 1000
CHARACTER SET UTF8
CONTROLFILE REUSE
LOGFILE
    GROUP 1 ('/dev/vx/rdsk1/TEST/redo01_log01.dbf',
```

```
                    '/dev/vx/rdsk2/TEST/redo01_log02.dbf',
                    '/dev/vx/rdsk3/TEST/redo01_log03.dbf') SIZE 10M REUSE,
       GROUP 2 ('/dev/vx/rdsk1/TEST/redo02_log01.dbf',
                    '/dev/vx/rdsk2/TEST/redo02_log02.dbf',
                    '/dev/vx/rdsk3/TEST/redo02_log03.dbf') SIZE 10M REUSE,
DATAFILE
      '/dev/vx/rdsk/oradata/TEST/system01.dbf' size 400M REUSE;
```

The script in Listing 26.3 is no different from a regular CREATE DATABASE script, other than the fact that it creates two redo log groups. Also, notice the high values of the MAXDATAFILES, MAXINSTANCES, MAXLOGFILES, and MAXLOGHISTORY parameters.

Once you have created the database and all of the required tablespaces, run the $ORACLE_HOME/rdbms/admin/catalog.sql and $ORACLE_HOME/rdbms/admin/catproc.sql scripts. Also run the $ORACLE_HOME/rdbms/admin/catparr.sql script.

Creating Additional Rollback Segments

You will need to create additional private or public rollback segments for each of your instances. Use the CREATE ROLLBACK SEGMENT or the CREATE PUBLIC ROLLBACK SEGMENT statement to create additional rollback segments.

Private rollback segments are set in the instance-specific initialization files and can be used only by that specific instance. They are brought online when the instance is started. On the other hand, public rollback segments can be created by any instance and used by any other instance. Once an instance acquires a public rollback segment, it continues to use it until the instance is shut down. After the instance releases the public rollback segment, it can be acquired and used by any other instance.

Starting the Database in Parallel Mode

To start the database in parallel mode, use either of the following commands:

```
SQL> STARTUP SHARED
SQL> STARTUP PARALLEL
```

You can also set the RETRY option, specifying the number of retries, as follows:

```
SQL STARTUP OPEN TEST RETRY 10
```

With the RETRY option set, Oracle will continue to mount the database every 5 seconds until either the database is opened or the retry limit has been reached. In this example, Oracle will try at least ten times to mount and open the TEST database.

Configuring Net8

When you use OPS, you can automatically fail over applications to other open instances. Listing 26.4 illustrates how to configure the tnsnames.ora file so that the same alias will allow you to connect to the database via an alternate instance, in the event that the primary instance is down.

Listing 26.4: Configuring Automatic Failover

```
test = (description=
            (address_list=
                (address=
                    (protocol=tcp)(host=node1)(port=1521))
                (address=
                    (protocol=tcp)(host=node2)(port=1521))
            )
            (connect_data=(sid=test))
        )
```

Starting with Oracle8i, Oracle introduced the Transparent Application Failover (TAF) component. You can use the TAF component to reconnect an established connection through a chosen backup instance in cases of failure. Listing 26.5 shows how to use the TAF component.

Listing 26.5: Configuring the TAF Component

```
test = (description=
            (failover_mode=on)
                (address=
                    (protocol=tcp)(host=node1)(port=1521)
                )
                (address=
                    (protocol=tcp)(host=node2)(port=1521)
                )
                (connect_data=
                    (service_name=test)
                )
        )
```

Additionally, you can also use the LOAD_BALANCE option to perform a random selection of the address. If the chosen address does not respond, Oracle automatically transfers the connection request to the next available address. Listing 26.6 shows how to use the LOAD_BALANCE option for this function.

Listing 26.6: Configuring Load Balancing

```
test = (description=
            (load_balance=on)
```

```
            (address=
                (protocol=tcp)(host=node1)(port=1521)
            )
            (address=
                (protocol=tcp)(host=node2)(port=1521)
            )
        (connect_data=
            (service_name=test)
        )
    )
```

Using Oracle Fail Safe

Oracle Fail Safe is an add-on option for Oracle databases and is used to deploy highly available solutions on Windows NT and Windows 2000 clusters. It consists of the Fail Safe Server and the Fail Safe Manager. The server component works in conjunction with the Microsoft Cluster Server (MSCS) software and other resource libraries to provide fast, automated failovers.

The Fail Safe Manager is a GUI component used for configuration, maintenance, and load balancing within the cluster. A command-line utility, FSCMD, is also available for performing configuration and maintenance tasks via scripts.

NOTE Check the Hardware Compatibility List (HCL) for Microsoft Cluster Server before beginning the installation and configuration of the Windows cluster. Fail Safe 3.1 also supports the Windows 2000 Datacenter configurations.

Cluster configuration in a Fail Safe environment is similar to cluster configuration in an OPS environment. The Fail Safe Server software, along with the Oracle database software, is installed on each node in the cluster. The datafiles reside on the shared disk subsystem. The shared disk subsystem is attached to each node via a SCSI or fiber connection.

Even though the cluster configuration of Fail Safe is similar to that of OPS, the logical configuration can vary. Two configurations are common:

Active/passive In an active/passive configuration, the primary node picks up the entire workload, while the secondary node waits in a standby mode. As soon as a failure is detected, applications fail over to the secondary node, which then becomes the primary node. Failovers in this configuration are much faster than other high-availability solutions. Figure 26.3 illustrates this configuration.

FIGURE 26.3
An active/passive Fail Safe configuration

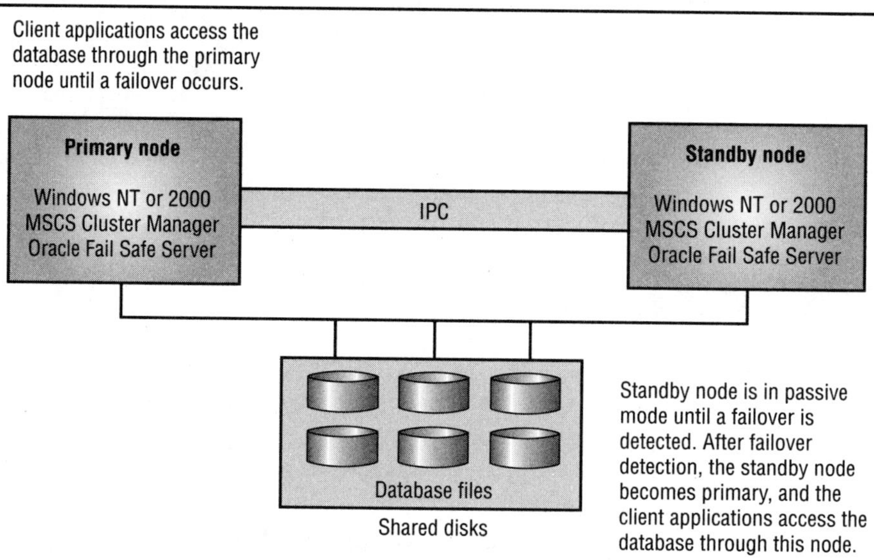

Client applications access the database through the primary node until a failover occurs.

Primary node
Windows NT or 2000
MSCS Cluster Manager
Oracle Fail Safe Server

IPC

Standby node
Windows NT or 2000
MSCS Cluster Manager
Oracle Fail Safe Server

Database files
Shared disks

Standby node is in passive mode until a failover is detected. After failover detection, the standby node becomes primary, and the client applications access the database through this node.

Active/active In an active/active configuration, applications access both the primary and the secondary nodes for different tasks. Of course, there is the tradeoff of resource availability and usability versus performance and load balancing. Also, since both nodes are active, failovers are not as responsive as they are in active/passive mode. Typically, most of the workload is still picked up by the primary node, and only critical pieces of applications are allowed to fail over to the secondary node. A good example of the active/active configuration is where the primary node is the primary database server and the secondary node also serves as a web server. Figure 26.4 illustrates this configuration.

FIGURE 26.4

An active/active Fail Safe configuration

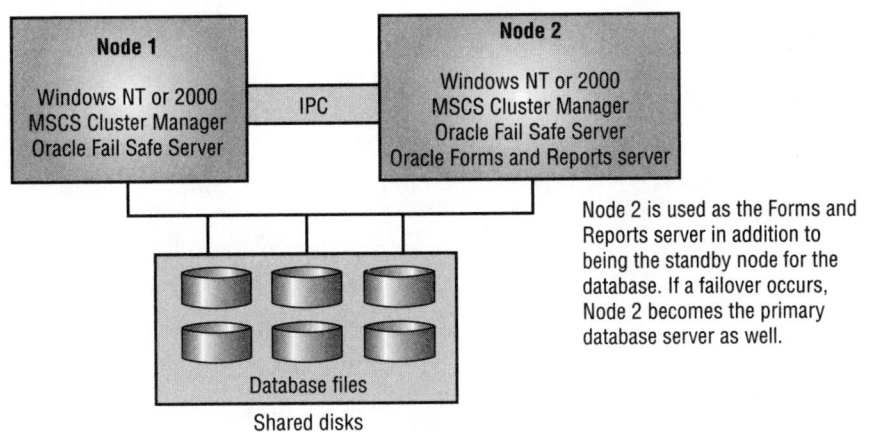

You can implement Fail Safe in various Windows-based multitier environments. Parallel Fail Safe is now also available for some HP-UX and Solaris environments. Newer releases of Oracle Fail Safe have built-in functionality for seamless failovers of Oracle Applications 11i, Oracle Forms and Reports, and Oracle9i Internet Application Servers (including Oracle portals). Third-party application vendors such as SAP, Baan, J. D. Edwards, and PeopleSoft are also validating their software solutions with Oracle Fail Safe.

CHAPTER 27

Oracle8i and the Internet

Using Java in Oracle8i	*1111*
Java configuration	*1115*
Java installation	*1118*
Creating Java stored procedures	*1120*
Java utilities	*1121*
Java security	*1123*
Oracle Internet File System (iFS)	*1124*
XML SQL Utility (XSU)	*1124*

For good or bad…no, let's be honest—for good *and* bad, the Internet has changed how we live and do business. From ordering pizza to trading stocks, banking, auctioning off old treasures, tracking shipments—and countless other possibilities and realities—we live in a wired economy. Since the proliferation of the Internet economy, we've watched business move faster, fortunes rise and fall, and technology change at an alarming rate. For good and bad, the Internet has affected every aspect of our lives…and it's here to stay.

If you have any doubts about the influence of the Internet, just look at what major companies such as Oracle, Microsoft, and Sun Microsystems are doing. They are practically betting the future of their companies on the innovations they have brought to this virtual e-volution. Sun Microsystems pioneered Java. Microsoft has built its consumer operating system around the online user. And Oracle has built a complete suite of products around Internet development, deployment, and database management.

Behind every e-commerce website is data—data about products, data about purchases, data about consumers, the list goes on. You need a database to manage all this data, and Oracle has extended its database platform to support the technological demands of a Web-enabled market.

In some sense, the title of this chapter should really be "Oracle8i and Java," since Java is the foundation for the new Internet-focused features in Oracle8i. Here we'll introduce you to Java as it is implemented in Oracle8i, especially the Java Virtual Machine (JVM). This chapter prepares you, as an Internet DBA, to support a Java-enabled database. We'll look at a number of Java/database-related topics, starting with integration of Java support and the JVM in Oracle8i. We'll explain the Java pool and go over creation of Java stored procedures. You'll get a look at the LOADJAVA utility, as well as some other Internet-related features in Oracle8i specifically. Security issues related to Java are mentioned, as well.

Other Critical Knowledge for Internet DBAs

As an Internet DBA, you may need to become acquainted with the following Oracle8i products and features. These subjects are too complex to be fully covered in a general Oracle database administration book. The Oracle documentation has plenty of information on these elements, however, as do Technet.oracle.com and www.oracle.com.

- Application Server
- HTTP Server
- Oracle Internet Directory
- Internet File System (iFS)
- XML

Using Java in Oracle8i

The integration of Java support in Oracle8i is the foundation for Internet development in the Oracle database. Oracle8i includes extensive support for Java within the database and for use of Oracle8i databases with Java.

Basic Methods

There are three basic ways to use Java in Oracle8i:

- Java Database Connectivity (JDBC) provides a driver-based interface that allows access to the Oracle8i database from Java applications.
- SQLJ is a Java precompiler that turns embedded SQL statements into Java. SQLJ operates similarly to other Oracle precompilers, such as Pro*C or Pro*COBOL. You might think of SQLJ as "Pro*Java."
- The JDeveloper tool integrates JDBC and SQLJ into a complete development environment.

Integration of Java into Oracle8i is a two-way street. Java can call SQL and PL/SQL, and PL/SQL and SQL can call Java. Java programs call their SQL and PL/SQL counterparts using the JDBC driver, which is embedded into the Java Virtual Machine architecture residing in the Oracle8i database. In the other direction, Oracle8i offers two features. In Oracle8i, Java namespaces map to database schemas. This facilitates dependency maintenance to allow storage of Java in the database. Oracle8i also provides extended DDL, such as CREATE PROCEDURE AS JAVA, for embedding Java code easily into Oracle8i.

Using the JDBC Driver

There are three versions of the JDBC driver at work in Oracle8i, all of which use the same syntax, APIs, and Oracle extensions. This allows portability of Java code between robust clients, Web-based Java applets, and Java stored procedures.

- The JDBC OCI driver is most similar to traditional ODBC drivers because it uses the Oracle Call Interface and Net8, thus requiring the Oracle8i Client to be installed on the machine running the Java program.
- JDBC Thin is used for executing Java programs inside web browsers. This driver communicates through Java sockets, not OCI or Net8. Thus, machines using JDBC Thin do not need the Oracle8i Client installed on them, which makes these applications highly scalable.
- The JDBC KPRB driver is used in Java programs that are stored directly within Oracle8i.

In addition to supporting all JDBC 1.22 functionality standards, and everything in JDBC 2.0 except XA support on the client side, Oracle8i extends the JDBC functionality by supporting Oracle-specific extensions for ROWID, REFCURSOR, object types, REFs, and LOBs. You can also use row prefetching and array operations, all Oracle character sets, and PL/SQL or Java stored procedures.

Using SQLJ

If you have done any development in any programming language using the Oracle-supported precompilers, such as Pro*C or Pro*COBOL, you already know how SQLJ functions in the overall compilation of source code into an executable program. To review, you start with Java code containing embedded SQL statements. You then apply the SQLJ processor to your source code to convert the embedded SQL calls into Java. The result is a file containing source code that is all Java and that contains JDBC calls. From there, you apply the Java compiler to your source code to convert it into a Java class. The result is an executable Java program.

Embedding SQL statements within SQLJ is considerably simpler than writing equivalent JDBC calls within Java programs, because you don't have to set up character strings, explicitly bind your own variables, and issue PARSE and EXECUTE statements yourself. The only issue to consider when using SQLJ is deciding which JDBC driver is appropriate for the application you are developing. You will use JDBC OCI for robust clients and server-to-server connections, JDBC Thin drivers for Java applets in web browsers, and JDBC KPRB for Java stored procedures.

JDeveloper

This suite of Java enterprise development tools allows you to build server-side application components for use in network-based applications. JDBC and SQLJ are both components of JDeveloper, which also includes wizards for rapid application development. JDeveloper uses its own Java compiler and debugger, along with interfaces that allow you to see database objects in Oracle8i, such as tables and PL/SQL procedures. This suite of tools integrates with Oracle Application Server as well, to allow methods for deploying distributed CORBA-based applications and for generating dynamic HTML for Internet applications.

The Java Virtual Machine (JVM)

If Java is the foundation for Internet development in the Oracle8i database, then the Java Virtual Machine is the cornerstone of that foundation. The JVM is a scalable, general-purpose Java execution environment that is compliant with the Sun Java Java Development Kit (JDK) specification and has been optimized to leverage the Oracle architecture. Oracle8i incorporates the JVM architecture directly into the database, allowing you to use Java programs in cooperation with Oracle8i.

NOTE The one constant in life is change, and thus you should be aware of the following Oracle JDK version compliance: Oracle 8.1.5 is compliant with JDK 1.1; Oracle 8.1.6 is compliant with JDK 1.2.

Java is complementary to PL/SQL and fulfills other application needs. SQL and PL/SQL can be called from Java programs through an embedded JDBC driver in the database. In turn, Java procedures can be called from SQL and PL/SQL once they have been published as a PL/SQL program. Java has been introduced to complement PL/SQL, not replace it. You need not rewrite PL/SQL programs to Java. Because PL/SQL and Java interoperate cleanly in Oracle8i, the best answer may in fact be to utilize a combination of both languages.

The JVM runs in the same address space in memory as Oracle8i and is integrated with Oracle8i in several other ways, as well. For example, the Oracle8i JDBC driver is embedded into the JVM to allow for faster processing of SQL and PL/SQL by avoiding the Net8 connectivity layer. The mechanisms for calling C procedures from PL/SQL using EXTPROC have been extended to allow PL/SQL to call Java procedures. Net8 has been enhanced to permit you to publish Java programs, which then allow you to call Java functions from SQL using Net8. Additional features allow you to connect to Oracle8i without using Net8 at all—using an embedded, Java-based object request broker that is compliant with CORBA 2.0 standards—and to permit access to Java programs in the Oracle8i database.

The following items are the Java components responsible for executing Java programs:

Bytecode Compiler   Converts a Java-language program into a Java class. Java classes are binary programs, which can be executed on the host machine.

Native Compilation   Used for optimizing Java byte code programs so that they will run faster.

Java Runtime Interpreter   Used for executing a Java class.

The following items are Java components used for managing Java programs within the JVM and in the Oracle8i database:

Java Class Loader   Permits the movement of Java classes into and out of the Oracle8i database.

Library Manager and Standard Libraries   Support functionality required for basic use of Java and for use of Java within Oracle8i.

Finally, here are the Java components used for the development of Java code and memory-management functionality:

SQLJ Translator   Enables the use of embedded SQL in Java programs by pre-compiling SQL into Java language constructs.

Object Memory Management   Allocates and frees memory in blocks called object memories.

Memory Manager and Garbage Collector   Handles Object Memory Management and other JVM memory-related functions.

JServer Accelerator

The JServer Accelerator (NCOMP) utility is new with Oracle 8.1.7. It is designed to increase the speed of Java code execution by creating platform-specific shared libraries that can be deployed to the server.

In 8.1.5 and 8.1.6, the core classes that are shipped with JVM are already in NCOMP format, but there is not a utility that would do it for user classes. All user classes are translated into byte code, and a byte code interpreter, stored internally in the database, interprets each class at runtime. This is a slow method and the JServer Accelerator allows for the Java classes to already be in a natively compiled C language format.

This NCOMP format has shown to be from two to five times faster at runtime than non-NCOMP formats. The individual results still depend on the application. SQL-intensive applications may only see a small a performance gain, but other applications may see a substantial increase.

> ### Java vs. PL/SQL
>
> Which is faster—Java or PL/SQL? In general, PL/SQL is best for data-intensive programs and Java is best for compute-intensive coding.
>
> PL/SQL is better and more efficient than Java for managing SQL datatypes. In a scenario with many database read/writes and very little computation, code written in PL/SQL always runs significantly (about ten times) faster than similar code written in Java.
>
> Java is more suited for the writing of programs that implement intensive logic and use object-oriented coding. In a scenario with much computation and few database read/writes, code written in Java always runs significantly (up to five times) faster than similar code written in PL/SQL.

Java Configuration

Before installing Java in your Oracle8i database, you should become familiar with the new `init.ora` configuration parameters that support Java, as well as the SHARED_POOL_SIZE parameter. All these parameters must be considered in your Oracle configuration. The settings required for running `initjvm.sql` are all listed here for your reference.

JAVA_SOFT_SESSIONSPACE_LIMIT   Identifies a soft limit on memory used by Java in a session. Each user can specify a soft memory limit for their session. When a session is started, the memory limit set by this parameter is allocated for the session. When the session exceeds this soft limit, a trace is generated under USER_DUMP_DEST and a warning is written to the alert log. The default value is 1MB.

JAVA_MAX_SESSIONSPACE_SIZE Used to limit the memory usage for the Java objects during the user's session. When the session exceeds this value, an out-of-memory error is generated and the executing Java procedure is terminated by Oracle. To avoid problems during normal operations, the default value for this parameter is 4GB.

SHARED_POOL_SIZE Defines the size of your shared pool in bytes. Shared pool memory is used during the Java class loading and resolving process. During this process, the loader uses approximately 8KB for each class. The initialization process loads about 8000 classes. Hence, you need to set SHARED_POOL_SIZE to at least 65MB.

JAVA_POOL_SIZE Based on the amount of JAVA_POOL_SIZE, the JServer's memory manager stores all the Java states (except `load` and `resolve` as described under SHARED_POOL_SIZE) during runtime execution. This portion of memory also stores the shared in-memory representation for the Java objects and the Java objects information that is migrated to the session at the end-of-call. Different behavior can be observed if you are running in MTS mode. As a general guideline, the JAVA_POOL_SIZE should be set to 50MB or higher for large applications. The default of 20MB should be adequate for typical Java stored procedure usage.

To determine how much Java pool memory is being used, query V$SGASTAT:

```
SELECT *
FROM V$SGASTAT
WHERE pool = 'java pool';
```

Add free memory to memory in use, to determine the size of the Java pool.

Overall system requirements The following are the recommended system requirements. The requirements for your system may be greater, and you will have to monitor and tune accordingly.

- SHARED_POOL_SIZE should be 65MB or higher.
- JAVA_POOL_SIZE should be 50 MB or higher.
- You should have 50MB free in the SYSTEM tablespace.
- You should have 250MB of rollback segment space.

MTS vs. Dedicated Server

DBAs need to be mindful of Oracle configuration in terms of Java support. Within the Oracle instance there are two defined memory spaces: the Shared Global Area (SGA) and the Program Global Area (PGA). Essentially, the SGA is defined at a fixed size by parameters in the `init.ora` file, but the PGA is variable and will grow or shrink as the need arises.

The Java pool is included within the SGA, in addition to memory constructs such as the shared pool, db buffer cache, and redo buffer cache. If the server is running in MTS mode, then the SGA also contains a variable memory space known as the User Global Area (UGA). The shared pool and Java pool are fixed-size memory constructs allocated at instance startup. In the `init.ora` file, the shared pool is sized in bytes with the SHARED_POOL_SIZE parameter, and the Java pool is sized in bytes by the JAVA_POOL_SIZE parameter.

The PGA contains a variable memory space called the Call Global Area (CGA). If the server is running in dedicated mode, then the PGA also hosts the UGA.

In a dedicated server, the Java pool includes the shared part of each Java class which are about 4–8KB per class. However, the per-session variables for each Java class are stored in the UGA, which is within the variable sized PGA. For this reason, the size of the Java pool can be relatively smaller.

Using MTS, the Java pool includes the shared part of each Java class, just as in a dedicated server model. Yet, because of the construct of MTS, some of the UGA information is stored in memory allocated from the Java pool, which is a fixed size. Each UGA will grow and shrink as needed, but the total memory allocated for all UGA constructs must be able to fit within the fixed-size Java pool. Thus, when using MTS, the Java pool in this configuration will be sized relatively larger.

Java Scripts

As with other things Oracle, the Java options in Oracle have some associated SQL scripts that you'll use from time to time. The following scripts are located in $ORACLE_HOME/javavm/install:

initjvm.sql This script is the heart of the JVM installation process. It loads the initial set of Java classes necessary to support Java, initializes the SQL tables for the CORBA namespace, and publishes some top-level entry points through call specifications.

rmjvm.sql The `rmjvm.sql` script removes any trace of Java usage; this includes core classes, user created classes, and all the Java objects from the data dictionary. It should only be run if you wish to remove all Java objects from a database. Once this script is run, all of your Java objects will be gone, unless you have a backup.

jvmu815.sql This script should be run when upgrading a database from 8.1.5 to 8.1.6 when Java was used in the 8.1.5 database. It preserves user classes while replacing system classes, whereas if you ran `rmjvm.sql` followed by `initjvm.sql`, it would remove user classes and replace system classes.

Java Installation

Before using the JVM, you must install the JVM classes in the Oracle8i database. This step is performed using the `initjvm.sql` located in `$ORACLE_HOME/javavm/install`. Executing this script as user SYS loads your initial set of Java classes and creates a set of roles called JAVAUSERPRIV and JAVASYSPRIV for authorizing users to run Java. This script also creates a package called DBMS_JAVA. Before running this script, ensure that your database has at least one rollback segment that can grow as large as 100MB to accommodate all the rollback generated by Oracle8i.

The Java Virtual Machine can be installed using one of the following two methods:

- An Oracle8i typical or minimal install installs JVM automatically.
- An Oracle8i custom install installs JVM, when the JVM option is selected.

The Java Virtual Machine can be activated in a new or existing database by the following means:

- Create a database with the database assistant and choose to activate Java. (This will cause `initjvm.sql` to be run automatically, thus taking longer to create the database.)
- Manually run the `initjvm.sql` script as internal or SYS. (The script can take over an hour to run.)

The `initjvm.sql` script does the following to install the JVM:

- Creates and loads the Java classes into the SYS schema using the CREATE or REPLACE JAVA SYSTEM command.
- Creates public synonyms for the loaded classes to be accessible to all users.
- Creates roles that can be used with Java.
- Defines database startup and shutdown triggers.
- Configures the JVM for CORBA and EJBs.
- Creates the DBMS_JAVA package by calling the `initdbj.sql` script.
- Installs SQLJ by calling the `initsqlj.sql` script.

Verifying Java Installation

You can verify successful installation by querying the data dictionary. The following query checks that the number of Java objects created is greater than zero:

```
SELECT count(*)
FROM dba_objects
WHERE object_type LIKE '%JAVA%';
```

If the above query returns a number less than 4000, the installation was not successful.

And this query checks for any invalid Java classes using a Java stored procedure:

```
SELECT dbms_java.longname(name)
FROM sys.obj$
WHERE type# = 29 and status != 1;
```

If the above query fails or returns any rows, then something is wrong with the JVM installation.

NOTE The banner in SVRMGRL/SQLPLUS shows that Java Options have been installed.

Common Errors While Installing or Using JVM

The following are common errors you may run into while installing or using JVM:

ORA-3113: End-of-file on communication channel running *initjvm.sql*
An ORA-3113 can occur when there is a lack of resources. Verify the following:

- SHARED_POOL_SIZE is at least 65 MB
- JAVA_POOL_SIZE is at least 50 MB
- 50MB free space in the SYSTEM tablespace
- 250MB of rollback segment space

ORA-4030: Out of process memory when trying to allocate %s bytes (%s,%s) running *initjvm.sql*
This problem can be solved by setting all ULIMIT parameters to UNLIMITED, though the command for doing so will vary from platform to platform. Refer to your platform-specific documentation.

ORA-4031: Unable to allocate X bytes of shared memory This problem may be due to the setting for SHARED_POOL_SIZE, JAVA_POOL_SIZE, or both.

Creating Java Stored Procedures

Now that you have installed and configured Java in your Oracle8i database, it is time to create your first Java stored procedure. Java programs or classes can be stored in the Oracle database, as an alternative or complement to PL/SQL programs. Java can be used for all types of database triggers, for stored procedures and functions, and in member methods for object types in the Oracle8i OBJECTS option. After completing the following steps for developing Java stored procedure in your Oracle8i database, you can call Java stored procedures from within SQL statements or from PL/SQL blocks.

To create a Java stored procedure, complete the following steps:

1. **Write the Java program**.

   For our example, the following code is saved to the file `hello.java`.
   ```
   public class Hello {
   static public String Message(String name) {
   return "Hello, " + name;
    }
   }
   ```

2. **Load the program into the database**.

   Use the LOADJAVA utility from the O/S prompt to load the Java program into the database:
   ```
   $ loadjava -u system/manager -v -r Hello.java
   ```

   You may also load the Java program manually from SQL*Plus:
   ```
   SQL> create or replace java source named "Hello" as
     2  public class Hello {
     3    static public String Message(String name) {
     4      return "Hello, " + name;
     5    }
     6  }
     7 /
   ```

3. **Publish the Java program to SQL (PL/SQL Wrapper)**.

   To call a Java procedure from SQL or PL/SQL, you must publish the procedure to SQL. This is also referred to as creating a PL/SQL Wrapper. Once the procedure is published, or wrapped, it can be called from any PL/SQL routine or SQL statement.

Continuing with our example:
```
SQL> create or replace procedure sayhello (name VARCHAR2)
  2  as language java
  3  name 'Hello.Message (java.lang.String)';
```

4. **Call the Java program from SQL or PL/SQL.**
```
SQL> select sayhello('world!') from dual;
SAYHELLO('world!')
------------------
Hello, world!
```

Java Utilities

The following sections present the LOADJAVA and DROPJAVA utilities. These utilities are used to load and drop Java classes in the database. You can find more information on these utilities in the *Oracle8i Java Tools Reference* in the Oracle8i documentation.

Using the LOADJAVA Utility

The LOADJAVA Utility assists in the loading of Java classes/source into the database. The utility is invoked from the Operating System prompt and behaves much like the Export/Import Utility.

When the utility is invoked, it connects to the database and attempts to load the Java files into the schema of the connecting user, or into the schema of the user who is specified in the -SCHEMA parameter.

Based on this, the schema that the objects are loaded into must meet the following three criteria:

- The user must exist.
- The user must have sufficient quota in the default tablespace.
- There must be enough free space in the tablespace.

Common options for the LOADJAVA utility include the following:

USER   You're logging into the database as this user.

SCHEMA   This is the schema you want the objects loaded into (if it is different from the user parameter). If this option is not specified, the objects are loaded into the LOGON schema.

VERBOSE   This enables the VERBOSE mode, in which progress messages are displayed (recommended).

RESOLVE   After all the objects are loaded and compiled, this option resolves all external references in those classes. If RESOLVE isn't specified, files are loaded but not compiled or resolved until runtime.

OCI8   This directs LOADJAVA to communicate with the database using the OCI JDBC driver (default driver).

THIN   This directs LOADJAVA to communicate with the database using the thin JDBC driver.

When the LOADJAVA utility is used, six objects are created in the users' schema, if they do not already exist. These objects assist in the loading of the Java objects into the database.

JAVA$CLASS$MD5$TABLE   This is a hash table that tracks the loading of Java objects into a schema. If you use the LOADJAVA utility to load the objects, you must use the DROPJAVA utility to drop the objects otherwise this table is not updated. Two indexes are also created for this table.

CREATE$JAVA$LOB$TABLE   This table contains the name of the Java object, the date it was loaded, and has a BLOB column to store the Java object. One index is also created for this table.

LOADLOBS   This package is used to load the Java object into the BLOB column in the CREATE$JAVA$LOB$TABLE.

Using the DROPJAVA Utility

The DROPJAVA Utility converts the filenames into the names of schema objects, drops the objects, and then deletes their corresponding row in the JAVA$CLASS$MD5$TABLE. The following options are included with the DROPJAVA utility:

OCI8   This directs DROPJAVA to communicate with the database using the OCI JDBC driver (default driver).

SCHEMA   This is the schema from which you wish to drop objects.

THIN   This directs DROPJAVA to communicate with the database using the thin JDBC driver.

VERBOSE   This enables the VERBOSE mode, in which progress messages are displayed (recommended).

Java Security

In Oracle 8.1.5, security is provided only through the use of database roles. In Oracle 8.1.6, JServer security is based on Java 2 security, which allows developers to assign privileges on a class-by-class basis. The Java-related roles in 8.1.5 still exist in 8.1.6 for backward compatibility; however, Oracle recommends that you specify each permission explicitly, rather than use the roles.

In 8.1.5 the initjvm.sql script creates two roles named JAVAUSERPRIV and JAVASYSPRIV. The privileges for each role are described here.

JAVAUSERPRIV privileges:

- Open a TCP/IP socket
- Read or write from a file using UTL_FILE_DIR

JAVASYSPRIV privileges:

- Includes all the privileges associated with JAVAUSERPRIV
- Create a subprocess
- Listen on a specific network port
- Set the socket factory
- Set the stream handler
- Read or write from any file

In Java 2 security, you create security policies or permissions for each specific class. Within Oracle8i, you specify the policy through the DBMS_JAVA package, and the security policy is stored within the *policy table*. This is a new table within the database that exclusively manages Java 2 security permissions. You can grant or revoke permissions dynamically by using PL/SQL through DBMS_JAVA procedures, or by using Java through the class ORACLE.AURORA.RDBMS.SECURITY.POLICYTABLEMANAGER.

The following two views have been added in Oracle 8.1.6 to view the policy table. Both views contain information about granted and restricted permissions.

DBA_JAVA_POLICY Allows you to see all rows within the policy table.

USER_JAVA_POLICY Only allows you to see permissions relevant to the current user.

NOTE Refer to the *Java Developer's Guide* for more information on Java security.

Additional Internet Features

Before we end our discussion, it's worth mentioning few words about Oracle iFS and XML.

Oracle Internet File System (iFS)

To extend use of Oracle8i as a file system, iFS is an application written in Java that permits users to access database data as though it were stored in files on a disk. Oracle's *Internet File System,* or *iFS,* is an extension to the Oracle8i database. Oracle iFS provides a union of the relational database and the traditional file system; it provides the reliability, availability, and scalability of Oracle8i with the look and feel of a standard file system.

From the user's perspective, iFS appears to be standard file system on the network, whether the user accesses the contents through Windows Explorer, a web browser, an FTP client, or some other file system browser. Relational data or hybrid documents of relational and nonrelational data can appear as files. Oracle iFS also supports text searches and queries of those files and data stored in iFS.

For the developer, iFS is the single data store for a variety of applications. For the administrator, iFS provides a single point of administration for both file systems and messaging. Oracle iFS is bundled with the database CD pack and is available for free to anyone with an Oracle database license.

XML SQL Utility (XSU)

The XML SQL Utility (XSU) can generate XML from the results of SQL and JDBC queries. The XML output can be produced as text or as trees of objects conforming to the DOM standard. The XSU can also produce the associated DOM, DTD, or RESULTSET object of a query. The XSU can be used to insert, update, and delete XML data in database tables and preserve the structure of XML documents when they are saved to the database.

INDEX

Note to the reader: Throughout this index **boldfaced** page numbers indicate primary discussions of a topic. *Italicized* page numbers indicate illustrations.

Symbols

!= operator, and accidentally forcing table scans, 775
* (asterisk), in SELECT statement for all columns, 33
@ sign, for object reference by database link, 295–296
_allow_read_only_corruption parameter, 490
_allow_resetlogs_corruption parameter, 490
_corrupted_rollback_segments parameter, 489
_LATCH_WAIT_POSTING parameter, 798
_LOG_SIMULTANEOUS_COPIES parameter, 800
_offline_rollback_segments parameter, 489
_SPIN_COUNT parameter, 797

A

access control. *See* fine-grained access control (FGAC)
access paths, **741–744**
 in execution plan, 735
account, vs. schema, 142
ACID, 6–7
active instance, 14
ADD procedure (DBMS_REFRESH), 1056
ADD_DEFAULT_DEST procedure (DBMS_DEFER_SYS), 1062
ADD_HASH_PARTITION_CLAUSE command, 1045
ADD_RANGE_PARTITION_CLAUSE command, 1045
administrative region in Oracle Names, 411
administrative roles, 946
ADMIN_TABLES function (DBMS_REPAIR), 332
Advanced Networking Option (ANO), 420
Advanced Security Option (ASO), **420–421**
aggregate compatibility check, 869
aggregate tables, 865
aggregation, 38–39
 materialized views with, and fast refresh, 882
AIX
 post-wait driver, 89
 Universal Installer for, 51
alert log, **330**
ALL_ views, 144, **158–159**
ALLOCATE CHANNEL command (RMAN), 543, 549, **551–552**
ALLOCATE CHANNEL FOR MAINTENANCE command, 543, 552
_allow_read_only_corruption parameter, 490
_allow_resetlogs_corruption parameter, 490
ALL_REFRESH_DEPENDENCIES view, 880

ALL_ROWS hint, 763
ALTER CLUSTER command, **275**
ALTER commands, 216
ALTER DATABASE ADD LOGFILE command, 322
ALTER DATABASE BACKUP CONTROLFILE TO TRACE command, 318
ALTER DATABASE CLEAR LOGFILE command, 476
ALTER DATABASE command (RMAN), 548
ALTER DATABASE CONVERT command, 83–84
ALTER DATABASE DROP LOGFILE command, 322
    for redo log, 109–110
ALTER DIMENSION command, 899
ALTER INDEX statement, **256–258**
    COALESCE, 258
    DISABLE and ENABLE, 257
    REBUILD, 257
ALTER MATERIALIZED VIEW command, 877–878
ALTER MATERIALIZED VIEW LOG command, 890–891
ALTER OUTLINE statement, 785–786
ALTER PROFILE command, 942
ALTER ROLLBACK SEGMENT command, 279–280
ALTER SEQUENCE command, 298–299
ALTER SESSION command, 120
ALTER SESSION SET EVENTS command, 632–633
ALTER SESSION SET SQL_TRACE command, 721
ALTER SYSTEM BACKUP CONTROL FILE TO command, 480
ALTER SYSTEM command, 120
    for ARCHIVELOG mode parameter changes, 430–431
    to change JOB_QUEUE_PROCESSES parameter, 914
    for RESOURCE_LIMIT parameter changes, 938
ALTER SYSTEM SET EVENTS command, 632–633
ALTER TABLE command, **240–241**
    DEALLOCATE UNUSED clause, 241
    END BACKUP, 446
    for IOTs, 266–268
    MERGE PARTITIONS, 1024, 1031, 1043
    MOVE , and LOBs, 309
    for nested tables, 363–364
    for object table, **355**
    for VARRAY, 360
ALTER TABLESPACE command, 225, **228–229**
    BEGIN BACKUP, 445
    OFFLINE, 460
    for READ ONLY, 524
    to set read/write mode, 527
ALTER USER command, 936, 942
ANALYZE command
    to create histogram, 718
    for database objects, **323–329**
    DBMS_STATS package vs., **778–780**
    DELETE STATISTICS clause, **328**
    for list of chained rows, 714–715
ANALYZE VALIDATE command, **328–329**
AND_EQUAL hint, 765
ANO (Advanced Networking Option), 420
anonymous blocks in PL/SQL, 39, **40–41**
anti-joins, 36
APPC (Advanced Program-to-Program Communication) architecture, 391
APPEND hint, 768
application context package, 957–960

application context-setting package, 953
ARCH process, 191, 430
 directories for, 433
 trace file creation, 330
archive log backups, lists, 609–610
archived redo logs, 91, 203
 ARCHIVELOG mode and, 429
 backup, **442–443**, 450
 minimum destinations for successful writes, 1083
 naming standards, 117
 recovery, **455–456**, **585–586**
ARCHIVELOG mode, 136
 backups with Recovery Manager, **566–572**
 cold backups in, **441–442**
 hot backups in, **443–450**
  completion, 446–449
  current log sequence number, 445
  datafile backup, 446
  example, 447–449
  identifying database files and tablespaces, 444–445
  redo log switch, 446
  steps, 444
  tablespaces in hot backup mode, 445–446
 for moving datafiles, 321
 parameters, 128
 recoveries, **450–480**
  complete recovery, **454–466**
  incomplete recovery, **466–480**
  preparing for, **450–452**
  RECOVER command, **452–454**
Asian languages, 208
ASO (Advanced Security Option), **420–421**
asterisk (*), in SELECT statement for all columns, 33
atomicity of relational database, 6
attributes, 337, 338
 partitions and, **1045–1046**
 of types, 340
  viewing information, 345
 types as, **342–343**
AUDIT_FILE_DEST parameter, 125
auditing, and migration, 82
AUTOEXTEND clause, of CREATE TABLESPACE command, 227–228
automatic failover, 1104
availability, performance vs., **1042**, *1043*
Available Product Components window in UI, 56–58, *57*
Available Products window in UI, 54–55, *55*
AVG() function, 38

B

background process, 188
 monitoring, 190
BACKGROUND_DUMP_DEST parameter, 125, 1101
backup, 1079–1080. *See also* recovery; Recovery Manager (RMAN)
 ARCHIVELOG mode, **429–435**
  completing process, **433–434**
  init.ora file modification, **430–433**
  online redo log groups, **434–435**
 ARCHIVELOG mode backups, **441–450**
  archived redo logs, **442–443**
  cold backups, **441–442**
  hot backups, **443–450**
 ARCHIVELOG mode recoveries, **450–480**
  complete recovery, **454–466**
  incomplete recovery, **466–480**
  RECOVER command, **452–454**

control file backups, **480–485**
    files to consider, 485
    forcing open database, **489–490**
    before migration, **81**
    NOARCHIVELOG mode, **435–441**
        cold backup recovery, **439–441**
        cold backups, **436–438**
    offsite, 428
    physical vs. logical, 424
    planning, **424–428**
        backup strategy, 424–425
        for disaster, **425–428**
    RESETLOGS and recovery, **486–489**
        why and when to use, 486–487
BACKUP command (RMAN), 550
backup control file, 437
backup images, 92
backup pieces in Recovery Manager, **544**
backup sets in Recovery Manager, 543–544
backup specification list, 554–556
bad file, 983
    output from SQL*Loader, 991, **992–993**
base cardinality, 708
base incremental backup, 563
base tables
    in data dictionary, 143
    updates, 285–286
baseline for tuning, 630, 689
    importance, **751**
BATCH COMMAND mode, for namesctl utility, 416
BEGINDATA section, in SQL*Loader control file, 988
benchmarks, 689
    for latch contention, 834
Bequeath protocol, 391

BFILE datatype, 30
    SQL*Loader support, 999
binary data, LONG RAW datatype for, 209
bind variables, **703–704**, **793–794**
bitmap indexes, **249–250**
    creating, 254
BLOB datatype, 30, 211
    SQL*Loader support, 999
Block Server Process (BSP), 191, 1097
blocking lock
    alarm generation for, 828
    catblock.sql script for views to resolve, **828–831**
    V$LOCK view to find, 809–810
blocks, 19, **176–177**, *177*
    compression by Recovery Manager, 539
    determining size, **113–115**
    images in redo logs, 443
bottom-N queries, 906
bounded range scans, **251**, 743
branch, in execution plan tree, 738
broken job, 916
browned-out indexes, monitoring, **670–672**
BSP (Block Server Process), 191, 1097
B*Tree indexes, **248–249**, *249*
    creating, 252
buffer block waits, tuning, **840–841**
buffer busy waits
    list of files with, 153
    statistics, 817
buffer cache, sizing, **121–122**
buffer waits, **819**
BUFFER_POOL parameter, 224
BUFFER_POOL_KEEP parameter, 122
BUFFER_POOL_RECYCLE parameter, 122
bugs, one-off patches to fix, 64–65

byte strings, LONG RAW datatype for, 209
Bytecode Compiler (Java), 1114

C

cache buffers LRU chain, 800
cache for name resolution, 414–415
Cache Fusion, 1098
CACHE hint, 769
CACHE option
    for CREATE SEQUENCE command, 298
    for heap table creation, 232
    for table creation including LOBs, 309–310
Call Global Area (CGA), 187, 1117
CALL procedure (DBMS_DEFER), 1063
cancel-based recovery, 475
cardinality, use by estimator, 708
Cartesian joins, 36, 747
CASCADE CONSTRAINTS clause, of DROP
    TABLE command, 241–242
CASCADE operation, and foreign key
    constraints, 20–21
CATALOG command (RMAN), 548
catalog.sql script, 134, 143
catblock.sql script, 134, **828–831**
catobtk.sql script, 968
catperf.sql script, 134, 648
catproc.sql script, 134, 143
catrep.sql script, 134
CD-ROM, running Universal Installer from, 52
CGA (Call Global Area), 187, 1117
chained rows, 217
    finding tables with, 713
    fixing tables with, **714–717**
    and performance, 712–713
change-based recovery, **472–475**, **584**

CHANGE command (RMAN), 548
CHANGE procedure (DBMS_REFRESH), 1056,
    1058–1059
change vectors, 203–204
channels
    allocating in Recovery Manager, **551–552**
    releasing in Recovery Manager, 553
CHAR datatype, 30, **207–208**
character datatypes, **207–209**
    CHAR datatype, **207–208**
    NLS types, **208–209**
    VARCHAR2 datatype, **208**
CHARTOROWID function, 214
check constraints, 21, **303**
CHECK_OBJECT function (DBMS_REPAIR), 332
Checkpoint (CKPT), 190–191
checkpoints, **192–195**
    checkpoint processing, **193–194**
    incremental checkpoints, **194–195**
Chen, Peter, 6
child latches, 799
child step, in execution plan, 736
CHOOSE hint, 763
CHUNK clause, for table creation including
    LOBs, 309
circular reuse records, 202
CKPT (Checkpoint), 190–191
class, 337
client for Net8
    configuration, **401–406**
    discovery of Names servers, 412–413
    MTS management on, **410–411**
client process in parallel queries, 849
client/server connections, in Net8, **390–391**
client-side daemon process, for name resolution,
    413–414

CLOBs, 211
    SQL*Loader support, 999
clone database, for point-in-time recovery, 534
clone parameter file, for point-in-time recovery, 534
closed backup. *See* cold backups
CLUSTER hint, 763
cluster index, creating, 273
cluster key, 270
Cluster Manager, 1096
clusters, **269–276**
    altering, **275**
    creating, **271–275**
    dropping, **275**
    hash, **270–271**
    indexed, **270**
    validation, 329
    viewing information, **276**
clusters of nodes (servers), 1093
CMADMIN (OCM Administrative Process), 420
CMGW (OCM Gateway Process), 420
coalesce function, 258
    to manage index browning, 258–259
COALESCE_PARTITION_CLAUSE command, 1045
Codd, E.F., 6
cold backups, 429, 435
    in ARCHIVELOG mode, **441–442**
    in NOARCHIVELOG mode, **436–438**
        recovery, **439–441**
    in Recovery Manager, **564**
        in NOARCHIVELOG mode, **564–566**
collection objects, 337, **357–365**
    information about, **364–365**
    nested tables, **361–364**
        altering and dropping, **363–364**
        creating, 361–362

    selecting from, **377–379**
    SQL*Loader support, 998–999
    VARRAYS, **357–360**
        altering and dropping, 360
        creating, **358–360**
column-level security, **968–971**
column objects, 346, 347
    SQL*Loader support, 996–997
columns in database, 6
command line
    for namesctl utility, 416
    for SQL*Loader, 1001–1003
    for Universal Installer, 52–53
comments
    for hints in SQL statements, 762
    in init.ora file, 16
    in Oracle SQL, 31
COMMIT command, 192, 204
    and locks, 802
commits, fetches across, 200
COMMIT_WORK procedure (DBMS_DEFER), 1063
COMPATIBLE parameter, 774
    for standby instance, 1083
complete recovery, **454–466**
complete refresh, for materialized views, 883
Component Locations window in UI, 58–59, *59*
composite partitioning, 1025, **1033–1035**
    for indexes, **1037–1038**
compression
    of extents, by Oracle Export utility, **501**
    of index-organized tables (IOTs), **266**
    of indexes, **253**
    by Recovery Manager, 539
computed measure in materialized view, 873

concatenation
  clause in SQL*Loader control file, 984–986
  in execution plan, 745
conditional loading, by SQL*Loader, 987–988
Configuration Assistant, **406–407**
configuration files, 18
CONNECT BY operation, in execution plan, 744
CONNECT command (RMAN), 548
CONNECT INTERNAL command, 22
CONNECT role, 946
CONNECT SYS AS SYSDBA command, 23
connect time failover, for Net8 client, 403
connected user link, 1015, **1016**
connect_timeout parameter, in listener.ora file, 399
consistency in relational database, 6
  in Oracle, **19**
constraints, **20–21**, 234, **300–307**
  enabling, **304–305**
    with deferred checking, 304
    with RELY setting, 305
    without validation, 304–305
  naming, **303**
  requirements, 869–870
  types, **300–303**
  viewing information, **305–307**
constructor methods, **366**
context area, 958
control files, 18, **202**
  adding, **322**
  backup types and, 564
  backups, **480–485**, 528
  documentation for, **163–164**
  dumping header, 637
  locating for backup, 436–437
  location, 126

naming standards, 117
planning for, 111
recovery, **594–595**
  without recovery catalog, **587–589**
  for standby database, 1080
  re-creating, 1090–1091
control files for SQL*Loader, 974, **979–988**
  BEGINDATA section, 988
  sessionwide information, **981–986**
    concatenation clause, 984–986
    INFILE clause, 982–984
    LOAD statement, 982
    loading mode, 984
    OPTIONS clause, 981–982
  INTO TABLE section, **986–988**
    COLUMN_NAME, 988
    FIELDS clause, 988
    OPTIONS clause, 987
    REENABLE, 987
    SINGLEROW option, 987
    SORTED INDEXES clause, 986–987
    WHEN clause, 987–988
Control Panel, Services window, 69
CONTROL_FILE_RECORD_KEEP_TIME parameter, 202
CONTROL_FILES parameter, 126, 1101
  for standby instance, 1083
conventional path load, 975, **976–977**
coordinator, for disaster recovery, 427
COPY command (RMAN), 550, 573–574
COPY procedure (DBMS_DEFER_SYS), 1062
copying datafiles
  to standby host, 1080
  for transportable tablespace, 525–526
CORE_DUMP_DEST parameter, 125
_corrupted_rollback_segments parameter, 489

cost-based mode optimization, for SQL statements, **707–708**, **761–770**
COUNT() function, 38
COUNT, in execution plan, 746
COUNT method for VARRAY, 375
CREATE CATALOG command (RMAN), 548
CREATE CLUSTER command, 270
    HASHKEYS keyword, 273–274
    for indexed cluster, 271–273
    SIZE keyword, 274
CREATE CONTEXT command, 958
CREATE CONTROL FILE command, NOMOUNT mode for, 313
CREATE DATABASE command, **129**, 133–134, 142
    for Oracle Parallel Server database, 1102–1103
    and redo logs, 109
    and SYSTEM tablespace, 224
CREATE DATABASE LINK command, 295, 1019
Create Database screen, 61
CREATE DIMENSION command, **892–899**
    ATTRIBUTE clause, 893–894
    HIERARCHY clause, 893, 894
    LEVEL clause, 893
    privileges, 892
create directory, 94
CREATE FUNCTION command, 42–43
CREATE INDEX command, **251–256**
    ON CLUSTER keyword, 273
    COMPRESS parameter, 253
    PARTITION clause, 1036
    REVERSE keyword, 252
CREATE MATERIALIZED VIEW command, **873–878**
    BUILD IMMEDIATE vs. BUILD DEFERRED, 874
    ON PREBUILT TABLE clause, 878–879
    refresh options, 880–881
CREATE MATERIALIZED VIEW LOG command, 890
CREATE OR REPLACE FUNCTION command, 42
CREATE OR REPLACE PROCEDURE command, 41
CREATE OR REPLACE TYPE BODY command, 367–368
CREATE OR REPLACE VIEW command, 283, 384
CREATE PROCEDURE command, 41
CREATE PROFILE command, 937
CREATE PUBLIC DATABASE LINK command, 295
CREATE PUBLIC SYNONYM command, 293
CREATE ROLE command, 947
CREATE ROLLBACK SEGMENT command, 279
CREATE SCRIPT command (RMAN), 548, 596–597
CREATE SEQUENCE command, 297–298
CREATE SYNONYM command, 293
CREATE TABLE AS SELECT command, 237–238, 716
CREATE TABLE command, 231–234
    GLOBAL TEMPORARY keyword, 239
    INCLUDING clause, 265
    with LOBs, 307–310
    for object table, 351
    OID clause, 352
    OIDINDEX clause, 354
    ORGANIZATION INDEX clause, 263–264
    OVERFLOW clause, 265
    PCTTHRESHOLD clause, 265
    PCTUSED parameter, 265
    with primary key and index location, 235–236

with two-column primary key and foreign key constraint, 236–237
CREATE TABLESPACE command, 137, **226–228**
   AUTOEXTEND clause, 227–228
CREATE TYPE command, 338, **340–341**, 348
   and method definition, 366
   for VARRAY, 358–360
CREATE USER command, **931–933**, 941
CREATE VIEW command, 283–284, 380–382
CREATE_PIPE function, in DBMS_PIPE package, 922
CROSSCHECK command (RMAN), 548, 600–602
.ctl file extension, 117
CUBE operator, **904–905**
cumulative backup, 563
cumulative patches, 64
current user link, 1015, **1017–1018**
CURRVAL pseudocolumn, 299–300
cursors
   information about, 640
   in SQL statement processing, **700–701**
CURSOR_SHARING parameter, **772–773**
CURSOR_SPACE_FOR_TIME parameter, **773**
custom install, 56
CYCLE option, for CREATE SEQUENCE command, 298

D

danger threshold, 827
data dictionary
   accessing views, **147–148**
      from PL/SQL, **148–150**
   architecture, **142–148**
      creation scripts, **143–144**
      dynamic performance views, **145–146**
      protection, **146–148**
      views, **144**
   LINK$, 297
   to manage extent allocation, 178
   and migration, 82
   objects relevant to database links, **1021–1022**
   queries on views to document database, **160–172**
      control files, 163–164
      current index key structures, 169–170
      current parameters, 164–166
      database tablespaces and datafiles, 160–162
      dependencies, 171–172
      list of current grants, 169
      list of current roles, 168
      list of foreign key relationships, 170–171
      online redo logs, 162–163
      users' setups in database, 167–168
   recover catalog views, **598–600**
   script to build views, 134
   space allocation, **129–131**
   to store views, 283
   tables to manage types, **344–346**
   using, **151–160**
      ALL_ views, **158–159**
      DBA_ views, **156–157**
      USER_ views, **157–158**
      V$ dynamic performance views, **159–160**
      X$ tables, **151–155**
data dictionary cache, 184
   hit ratio calculation, **653**
   monitoring, **653–654**
data dictionary views. *See also* DBA_ views
   for dimensions, 899–900

for materialized views, **879–880**
of Mview logs, 891
for partitions, **1046–1047**
related to histograms, 718
of stored outlines, 786
data distribution, histograms to analyze, **717–718**
Data Guard, 1093
data locks, 803
data marts, 864
data partitions. *See* partitions
data redundancy, normalization and, 7
data-retention standards, 98
data segment, 179, 180
data striping, 101, 659
    horizontal vs. vertical, 102–103, *103*
    and partitioning, 1042, *1043*
data sufficiency check by optimizer, 869
data tablespaces, 226. *See also* tablespaces
data warehouses, **864–866**. *See also* summary management
    and block size, 113, 114
    fact/dimension schema, **865–866**
    refresh facility, **883–889**
    SQL features for queries, **902–906**
        CUBE operator, **904–905**
        GROUPING function, **905**
        ROLLUP operator, **902–903**
        top-N queries, **905–906**
    transportable tablespaces and, **530–531**
database administration subdirectory, 94
database administrators, what they are, **4–5**
database buffer cache, **182–183**
    latches, 800
    monitoring, **646–652**
    tracking usage, 152–153

database buffer cache hit ratio, 646
    calculating, 647
    tuning, 649–650
database checkpoint, 193
database components, 91–92
Database Configuration Assistant (DCA), **135–136**
    and scripts, 144
database consistency, **19**
database control files, 92
    in Recovery Manager, 541
    view to display information, 640
database control structures, **192–205**
    checkpoints, **192–195**
        checkpoint processing, **193–194**
        incremental checkpoints, **194–195**
    control files, **202**
    database datafiles, **201–202**
    redo logs, **202–205**
        switches, **204–205**
    rollback segments and undo, **197–200**
    SCN (System Change Number), **195–197**
        database consistency checks, 196–197
        database recovery services, 197
        read-consistent images, 196
    transaction commits and rollbacks, **192**
database creation, **128–138**
    data dictionary space allocations, **129–131**
    with Database Configuration Assistant (DCA), **135–136**
    determining block size, **113–115**
    final steps, **136–138**
        Oracle network configuration, 137
        password changes, 137
        rollback segment configuration, 136
        tablespace creation, 137–138

manually, **133–134**
naming standards, **115–117**
parameter file (init.ora) creation, **117–128**
physical requirements, **97–112**
    disk configuration, **101–107**
    disk space requirements, **97–100**
    memory requirements, **111–112**
    sizing database files, **108–111**
preparing for, **96–97**, **128–131**
summary of steps, **138–139**
database datafiles, **201–202**
database files
    identifying for hot backup, 444–445
    management, **320–323**
database links, **1012–1018**, *1013*
    administration, **1018–1022**
        creation, **1019–1020**
    advantages of, **1013–1014**
    connection methods, **1015–1018**
    data dictionary objects relevant to, **1021–1022**
    setup, **294–297**
    types, **1014–1015**
    using, **1022**
Database Migration Assistant (DMA), 60, **84**
database objects
    ANALYZE command, **323–329**
        for statistics, **324–328**
    supporting tables and indexes, **292–312**
        constraints, **300–307**
        database links setup, **294–297**
        LOBs, **307–312**
        sequences, **297–300**
        synonyms, **292–294**
database parameter file. *See* init.ora file
database user authentication, **931–932**

Database Writer (DBW*n*), 189
databases
    backups, 1079–1080. *See also* backup
        resynchronization before, **594**
    changing name, **318–319**
    complete recovery, **462–465**
    diagnosing problems, **329–333**
        with DBMS_REPAIR, **332–333**
        with DBV (DBVerify), **331–332**
        with trace files and alert log, **329–331**
    forcing open, **489–490**
    for Import utility, 505
    instances vs., **14–17**, *15*
    monitoring
        for availability, 691–694
        items to monitor, 690
    monitoring threats, **664–673**
        browned-out indexes, **670–672**
        inefficient block usage in object, **669–670**
        resource usage, **672–673**
        segment fragmentation, **667–668**
        tablespace free space fragmentation, **666–667**
        user setup, **665**
    Recovery Manager connection to, **547**
    registration with recovery catalog, **593–594**
    RESETLOGS to create another version, 486–489
    resetting, **595–596**
    shutdown process, **315–317**
    startup, **312–315**
        MOUNT mode, **314**
        NOMOUNT mode, **313–314**
        OPEN mode, **314–315**
        restricted mode, **315**
datafile checkpoint, 193

datafiles, 18
    adding to standby database, 1091–1092
    backups, **569–570**
    copies, **573–574**
        for transportable tablespace, 525–526
    headers, **201**
    locating for backup, 436–437
    management, **321–322**
    naming standards, 117
    recovery, 456–460
        to another location, **590**
        with Recovery Manager, 581
    for SQL*Loader, **989–991**
    views for information about, 640
DATATYPE_ARG procedure (DBMS_DEFER), 1063
DATE datatype, 30
db file scattered read waits, **819–820**
db file sequential read waits, **820–821**
DBA CONNECT method, 22
DBA locking, 1098
DBA role, 946
DBA_ views, 144, **156–157**
    DBA_CLUSTERS view, 276
    DBA_COLL_TYPES view, 364–365
    DBA_CONS_COLUMNS view, 305
    DBA_CONSTRAINTS view, 305
    DBA_DB_LINKS view, 296–297, 1021
    DBA_DEPENDENCIES view, 343–344
    DBA_EXTENTS view, **245–246**
    DBA_IND_COLUMNS view, 261–262
    DBA_INDEXES view, **259–261**
        IOTs in, 268
    DBA_JAVA_POLICY, 1123
    DBA_JOBS view, 919–920
    DBA_LOCKS view, 830–831
    DBA_METHOD_PARAMS view, 372
    DBA_METHOD_RESULTS view, 372
    DBA_MVIEW_ANALYSIS view, 880
    DBA_MVIEW_DETAIL_RELATIONS view, 880
    DBA_MVIEW_JOINS view, 880
    DBA_MVIEW_KEYS view, 880
    DBA_MVIEWS view, 879
    DBA_NESTED TABLES view, 365
    DBA_OBJECTS view, 346
    DBA_OBJECT_TABLES view, **356**
    DBA_REFS view, 357
    DBA_REPCATLOG view, 1071
    DBA_ROLLBACK_SEGS view, 280–281
    DBA_SEGMENTS view, **246–247**
    DBA_SYNONYMS view, 294
    DBA_TAB_COLUMNS view, **244–245**
    DBA_TABLES view, 235, **242–244**
        to determine high-water mark, 777
        IOTs in, 268
    DBA_TYPE_ATTRS view, 345–346
    DBA_TYPE_METHODS view, 372
    DBA_TYPES view, 345
    DBA_USERS, 942
    DBA_VIEWS view, 288–289
    DBA_WAITERS view, 831
    for dimensions, 900
    for LOBs, 312
    for materialized views, **879–880**
    of Mview logs, 891
    for partitions, **1046–1047**
    related to histograms, 718
    for statistics, 326
    of stored outlines, 786
DB_BLOCK_BUFFERS parameter, 121–122, 183, 649
DB_BLOCK_LRU_LATCHES parameter, 122

DB_BLOCK_SIZE parameter, 183
DB_DOMAIN parameter, 1101
.dbf file extension, 117
DB_FILE_MULTIBLOCK_READ_COUNT
    parameter, 182
    and block size, 114
DB_FILE_NAME_CONVERT parameter, 1084
DB_FILES parameter, 126
DBID, 542
DBMS_ALERT package, 909
DBMS_APPLICATION_INFO package, 909
DBMS_AQ package, 909
DBMS_AQADM package, 909
DBMS_DDL package, 909
DBMS_DDL.ANALYZE_OBJECT procedure, 719
DBMS_DEFER package, 1063
DBMS_DEFER_QUERY package, 1064
DBMS_DEFER_SYS package, **1062–1063**
DBMS_DESCRIBE package, 909
DBMS_IOT package, 909
DBMS_JOB package, 909
    BROKEN procedure, 919
    CHANGE command, 918
    REMOVE procedure, 919
    RUN command, 917
    SUBMIT procedure, 915
DBMS_LOCK package, 909
DBMS_LOGMNR package, 909
    START_LOGMNR procedure, 620–623
DBMS_LOGMNR_D package, 909
    BUILD procedure, 616
DBMS_MVIEW package, **883–889**, 909
    job scheduler parameters, 884
    REFRESH procedure, 884–888
        example, 886–888
        parameters, 885–886

REFRESH_ALL_MVIEWS procedure, 888
REFRESH_DEPENDENT procedure, 888–889
DBMS_OBFUSCATION_TOOLKIT package, 909, 968–969
    decrypting data, **971**
    DESENCRYPT procedure, **969–970**
DBMS_OFFLINE_OG package, 909
DBMS_OFFLINE_SNAPSHOT package, 909
DBMS_OLAP package, 909
DBMS_OUTPUT package, 909
DBMS_PCLXUTIL package, 909
DBMS_PIPE package, 910, **921–925**
    CREATE_PIPE function, 922
    PACK_MESSAGE function, 922
    RECEIVE_MESSAGE function, 924
    REMOVE_PIPE function, 924
    SEND_MESSAGE function, 922
    UNPACK_MESSAGE function, 924
dbmspool.sql script, 134
DBMS_PROFILER package, 910
DBMS_RANDOM package, 910
DBMS_REFRESH package, 910, 1056
DBMS_REPAIR package, **332–333**, 910
DBMS_REPCAT package, 910
DBMS_REPCAT_ADMIN package, 910
DBMS_REPCAT_INSTANTIATE package, 910
DBMS_REPCAT_RGT package, 910
DBMS_REPUTIL package, 910
DBMS_RESOURCE_MANAGER package, 910
DBMS_RESOURCE_MANAGER_PRIVS package, 910
DBMS_RLS package, 910, 963–964
    ADD_POLICY procedure, 964–965
DBMS_ROWID package, 910
DBMS_SESSION package, 910
    SET_CONTEXT procedure, 958–959

DBMS_SHAPSHOT package, 910
DBMS_SHARED_POOL package, 910
DBMS_SPACE package, 910
DBMS_SPACE_ADMIN package, 910
DBMS_SQL package, 911
DBMS_STATS package, **778–783**, 911
    vs. ANALYZE command, **778–780**
    common procedures, 779
    example of use, 780–781
    maintaining current statistics, 782–783
DBMS_SYSTEM.SET_EV procedure, 637–638
DBMS_TRACE package, 911
DBMS_TRANSACTION package, 911
DBMS_TTS package, 911
DBMS_UTILITY package, 911
    ANALYZE_DATABASE procedure, 719
    ANALYZE_PART_OBJECT procedure, 720
    ANALYZE_SCHEMA procedure, 719
DB_NAME parameter, 1101
    for standby instance, 1083
DBSM_DEBUG package, 909
DBV (DBVerify), **331–332**
DBWn (Database Writer), 189
DCA (Database Configuration Assistant), **135–136**
    and scripts, 144
DDL (Data Definition Language), 31
    parallel processing, **848**
    production with INDEXFILE, **516–517**
    SQL*Loader syntax, **1004–1007**
DDL locks, 803
deadlock, preventing, 799
DEC data type, 206
DECIMAL data type, 206
DECLARE section in anonymous block, 41
declustering tables, 377

dedicated server processes, 189
default buffer cache, 646
    calculating hit ratio, 647
default buffer pool, 183
default degree of parallelism, 845
DEFAULT TABLESPACE, 146–147
default tablespace, for user accounts, 932
DEFCALL view, 1064
DEFCALLDEST view, 1064
DEFDEFAULTDEST view, 1064
DEFERRABLE clause of ALTER TABLE ADD CONSTRAINT command, 304
DEFERROR view, 1064
DEFERRORCOUNT view, 1064
definer's rights, 149
defragmentation with Export and Import utilities, **502**
DEFSCHEDULE view, 1064
DEFTRAN view, 1065
DEFTRANDEST view, 1065
degree of parallelism, 845
    hints to override, **853–854**
delayed block cleanout, 199
delete conflicts in replication, 1072
DELETE EXPIRED BACKUPSET command (RMAN), 549
DELETE EXPIRED command (RMAN), 549
DELETE method, for VARRAY, 375
DELETE SCRIPT command (RMAN), 549
DELETE statement, 31
    recovery after, **465–466**
DELETE STATISTICS clause for ANALYZE command, **328**
DELETE_DEFAULT_DEST procedure (DBMS_DEFER_SYS), 1062

DELETE_DEF_DESTINATION procedure (DBMS_DEFER_SYS), 1062
DELETE_ERROR procedure (DBMS_DEFER_SYS), 1062
DELETE_TRAN procedure (DBMS_DEFER_SYS), 1062
DEMO_DIM package, **900**
denormalized dimension, 893
denormalized state, data storage in, 7
dependencies
    for objects, documentation, 171–172
    of Oracle products, 55
    of types, **343–344**
depreciated parameters, 81
DESENCRYPT procedure, **969–970**
DESTROY procedure (DBMS_REFRESH), 1056, 1059
dictionary cache miss ratios, calculating, **654**
dictionary data locks, 803
dictionary file, creating for LogMiner, 616–617
differential backup, 563
dimension tables in data warehouse, 865
dimensions, **891–902**
    altering and dropping, 899
    defining, 892–894
    displaying, 899–902
    example, 894–899
    requirements, 869–870
direct loads, 183
direct-mode export, **501–502**
direct path load, 975, **977–978**
directories. *See also* Oracle Flexible Architecture (OFA)
    for ARCH process, 433
    OFA rules for, 90–91
directory service. *See also* Oracle Names

DISABLE STORAGE IN ROW clause, for table creation including LOBs, 308–309
DISABLED procedure (DBMS_DEFER_SYS), 1062
disaster recovery planning, **425–428**
    documentation, 427–428
    testing plan, 428
    timelines, 427
discard file, output from SQL*Loader, 991, **993–994**
discarded rows from SQL*Loader, 974
DISCARDFILE, 983
discovery of Names servers, 412–413
disk mirroring, 102
disk space requirements, **97–100**
    avoiding single point of failure, **107**
    calculating, 98–100
    for COMPUTE STATISTICS, 324
    for install, 62, 63
dispatcher processes, view to monitor, 640
DISPLAY parameter, 51
distinct cardinality, 708
distributed computing environment, 390
Distributed Database Recovery process, 191
Distributed Lock Manager (DLM), 1096
distributed processing, 1014
DISTRIBUTED_TRANSACTIONS process, 191
DLM (Distributed Lock Manager), 1096
DMA (Database Migration Assistant), 60, **84**
DML (Data Manipulation Language), 31
    parallel processing, **845–846**
DML locks, 803
D*nnn* processes, 191
documentation
    for database, **88–89**, **160–172**
        control files, 163–164
        current index key structures, 169–170

current parameters, 164–166
database tablespaces and datafiles,
   160–162
dependencies, 171–172
list of current grants, 169
list of current roles, 168
list of foreign key relationships, 170–171
online redo logs, 162–163
users' setups in database, 167–168
   of events, 632
   for migration, 80
dot notation to access object in another user's
   schema, 292
DOUBLE PRECISION data type, 206
driving table
   in execution plan tree, 738–739
   for rule-based SQL optimization, 705–706,
      758–760
DRIVING_SITE hint, 767
DROP commands, 217
   DROP CATALOG command (RMAN), 549
   DROP CLUSTER command, **275**
   DROP CONTEXT command, 960
   DROP DATABASE LINK command, 296, 1020
   DROP INDEX command, 259
   DROP MATERIALIZED VIEW command, 878
   DROP PARTITION command, **1044–1045**
   DROP PUBLIC SYNONYM command, 294
   DROP ROLLBACK SEGMENT command, 280
   DROP SEQUENCE command, 299
   DROP SYNONYM command, 294
   DROP TABLE command, 241–242
      for IOTs, 268
      for object table, **356**
   DROP TABLESPACE command, **229**
   DROP TYPE command, 342
      for VARRAY, 360

DROP USER command, 936
DROP VIEW command, 284
DROP_PARTITION_CLAUSE command, 1045
DROPJAVA utility, **1122**
dump directories for database, 94
dump files
   from Oracle Export utility, 492
      multiple, 503
   sizing, 127
DUMP_ORPHAN_KEYS function
   (DBMS_REPAIR), 332
duplexing backups, **575**
DUPLICATE command (RMAN), 550
durability in relational database, 7
dynamic locking, 1098
dynamic performance views, **145–146**
dynamic predicate, 961–962

E

e-mail notification of monitoring, from
   database, 694–695
EBU, 538
editable buffer in SQL*Plus, 27
effective cardinality, 708
EIS (Executive Information Systems), and block
   size, 113, 114
Ellison, Larry, 12
encapsulation, 337
enhanced security, 952
enqueue, 796, 821. *See also* locks
Entity Relationship model, 6
environment settings, **21–22**
   for migration, 75, 81–82
      in Unix, 78
   when starting Universal Installer, 51–52

equijoin, 35
error messages
    files not copied during install, 63
    from installing or using Java Virtual Machine, **1119–1120**
    ORA-1550, Snapshot Too Old message, **198–200**
    ORA-06532 errors, 617–618
    out of extents, 83
estimator for SQL statement costs, 708–709
event codes, **633**
events, **632–638**. See also wait management
    enabling, **632–635**
    monitoring, **826–827**
    for monitoring database, **635–638**
    trace parameters, **634**
    trace types, **634**
EXCHANGE_PARTITION/SUBPARTITION_CLAUSE command, 1045
exchanging partitions, **1044**
EXCLUDE_PUSH procedure (DBMS_DEFER_SYS), 1062
exclusive DDL lock, 803
exclusive lock mode, 807
EXECUTE SCRIPT command (RMAN), 550, 597
EXECUTE_ERROR procedure (DBMS_DEFER_SYS), 1062
EXECUTE_ERROR_AS_USER procedure (DBMS_DEFER_SYS), 1062
execution plans
    data access methods, **741–744**
        full table scans, 742
        index accesses, 743–744
        sample table lookups, 743
        table ROWID lookups and index scans, 742–743
    generating, **720–734**
        with EXPLAIN PLAN, 733
        ratios in TKPROF output, 728–729
        TKPROF to reformat trace file, 722–731
        tracing other users' sessions, 733–734
        tracing sessions and TKPROF, 720–722
        using SQL*Plus Autotrace, 731–733
    non-data operations, **744–748**
        hash joins, 747
        merge joins, 747
        nested loops, 747
    reading and interpreting, **734–740**
        following execution order, 738–740
        order of operations, 735–738
    stability, **783–786**
    trace file of steps in decision, 748
Executive Information Systems (EIS), and block size, 113, 114
EXISTS method for VARRAY, 375
EXIT command (namesctl), 417
exp directory, 94
EXPLAIN PLAN command, 733
exporting. See also Oracle Export utility
    tablespaces for point-in-time recovery, 535
EXTEND method for VARRAY, 375
extended ROWIDs, 230–231
extents, 19, **178–179**
    compression by Oracle Export utility, **501**
    objects of multiple, 667
external data. See also SQL*Loader
external LOBs, BFILES as, **310**
external naming, 394

F

fact tables in data warehouse, 865

Fail Safe Manager, 1105
Fail Safe Server, 1105
failed write, access after, 1082–1083
FAILED_LOGIN_ATTEMPTS, 939, 940
failover
    connect time, 403
    preconnect, 405–406
    transparent application (TAF), **403–406**
false pinging, 1094, 1097
fast refresh for materialized views, 881–883
fast start recovery, 315
FAST_START_IO_TARGET parameter, 194
FET$ data dictionary table, 178
fetch phase in SQL statement processing, 704
fetches across commits, 200
FGAC (fine-grained access control). *See* fine-grained access control (FGAC)
File Locations window in UI, 53–54, *54*
files in Oracle, **18**
    path setup in init.ora file, **124–125**
FILESIZE parameter
    for export files, 503
    when importing, 515
FILESPERSET parameter, for BACKUP command, 571
FILTER, in execution plan, 746
fine-grained access control (FGAC), 928, 950, **951–968**
    application context package, 957–960
    context package execution at user logon, 961
    features, **952**
    good and bad about, 967–968
    security enforcement package, 961–963
        registration, 963–965
        testing, 965–967
    security policy definition, 953–957

FIRST method, for VARRAY, 375
first normal form, 8
FIRST_ROWS hint, 763
FIX_CORRUPT_BLOCKS function (DBMS_REPAIR), 332
fixed block header, 177
fixed record format for SQL*Loader datafile, **990**
fixed user link, 1015, **1016–1017**
FLOAT data type, 206
FLUSH command (namesctl), 417
FLUSH_NAME command (namesctl), 417
FOR UPDATE clause in execution plan, 746
    problems from, 776–777
force refresh for materialized views, 883
forcing open database, **489–490**
foreign key constraints, 12, **20–21**, **302–303**
    CREATE TABLE command with, 236–237
foreign key relationships, 9–10, 11
    list of, 170–171
    locks and, 811–812
free buffer wait, 821–822
free lists, 181
FREELIST GROUPS parameter, **223**
FREELISTS parameter, **223**
FROM clause, in SQL query, 33
FSCMD command-line utility, 1105
FTP, to obtain patches, 65
full backup, 564
    with Recovery Manager, **467–469**
full database recovery, with Recovery Manager, 580
FULL hint, 763
full table scans, **742**
    vs. index use, 755–756
    and performance, 650
    reducing impact, 777–778

fully versioned path, 93–94
function-based indexes, **251**, **255–256**, **774–775**
functions, **42–43**
fuzziness, 201

G

gap sequences
    in managed recovery of standby database, 1086–1087
    resolving, 1089–1090
GC_FILES_TO_LOCKS parameter, 1097, 1101
GET_ARG_FORM procedure (DBMS_DEFER_QUERY), 1064
GET_ARG_TYPE procedure (DBMS_DEFER_QUERY), 1064
GET_CALL_ARGS procedure (DBMS_DEFER_QUERY), 1064
GET_DATATYPE_ARG procedure (DBMS_DEFER_QUERY), 1064
global database link, 1014
global database name, 16, 392, 1012
global indexes, **1038–1039**
GLOBAL TEMPORARY table, 351
global users, 931
    current user link connection as, 1017
GLOBAL_NAMES parameter, 1061
GRANT command, 216
grants, documentation, 169
GROUP BY cardinality, 708
GROUP BY clause, for aggregation, 38–39
grouping compatibility, 869
GROUPING function, **905**
groups, for online redo logs, **434–435**
GV$ views, 145

H

hard drives. *See also* RAID (Redundant Array of Inexpensive Disks)
hard parse, 701–702
    monitoring and managing excessive, **770–773**
hardware requirements
    for database creation, **97–112**
        disk configuration, **101–107**
        disk space requirements, **97–100**
        memory requirements, **111–112**
        sizing database files, **108–111**
    disk space for install, 62, 63
    of Universal Installer, 47
hash clusters, **270–271**
    creating, 271, **273–275**
HASH hint, 764
hash joins, 747
    in execution plan, 745, **747**
hash partitioning, 1025, **1031–1033**
    for indexes, **1037**
hash table, 274
HASH_AJ hint, 767
HASH_AREA_SIZE parameter, 710, 747–748
HASHKEYS keyword, 273
HASH_SJ hint, 767
headers
    for block, 176
    in datafiles, **201**
heap tables, **229–247**
    altering, **240–241**
    creating, **231–240**
        from existing table definition, 237–238
        with LOBs, 307–310
        options when, 232–233

with primary key and index location, 235–236
with two-column primary key and foreign key constraint, 236–237
de-allocating unused space, **241**
dropping, **241–242**
fundamentals, **229–231**
PCTFREE parameter and, 218
validation, 328
viewing information, **242–247**
  DBA_EXTENTS view, **245–246**
  DBA_SEGMENTS view, **246–247**
  DBA_TAB_COLUMNS view, **244–245**
  DBA_TABLES view, **242–244**
HELP command (namesctl), 417
help for Recovery Manager, 545–546
hidden parameters, 154–155
high-availability solutions. *See also* Oracle Parallel Server (OPS)
  Oracle Fail Safe, **1105–1107**, *1107*
  standby database, **1076–1093**
    architecture, *1077*
    creating, **1078–1089**
    modes, **1077–1078**
high-water mark, 241
  and performance, 777
hints
  for cost-based SQL statements, **761–770**
    access method, 763–766
    join operation, 766–767
    join order, 766
    miscellaneous, 769–770
    optimization approach, 763
    parallel execution, 768–769
  to override degree of parallelism, **853–854**

histograms
  in Oracle optimizer, **717–718**
  in SQL statement tuning, 754
historical data. *See* data warehouses
hit ratio calculation
  for data dictionary cache, **653**
  for library cache, **655**
HKEY_LOCAL_MACHINE folder, 70
horizontal data striping, vs. vertical, 102–103, *103*
Host naming, 393
hot backups, 429
  in ARCHIVELOG mode, **443–450**
    completion, 446–449
    current log sequence number, 445
    datafile backup, 446
    example, 447–449
    identifying database files and tablespaces, 444–445
    redo log switch, 446
    steps, 444
    tablespaces in hot backup mode, 445–446
  in Recovery Manager, **564**
hot blocks, 182
  determining, 153

I

I/O
  contention monitoring, **658–664**
    rollback segment usage, **662–664**
    session file I/O, **660–662**
    system file I/O, **658–660**
  distribution, **835–836**
  and index use, 755
  reduction in SQL statement tuning, 752

resources
    disk configuration, 105–106
    OFA rules for, 91
  throughput maximization, **841**
IFILE parameter, 127, 1100
iFS (Internet file system), 1124
image copies in Recovery Manager, 545, 573
IMP command. *See* Oracle Import utility
importing tablespaces
    for point-in-time recovery, 535
    for transportable tablespace, 526–527
incarnation
    information about, 611–612
    RESETLOGS to create, 486–489, 596
INCREMENT BY keyword, for CREATE SEQUENCE command, 297, 298
incremental backups, in Recovery Manager, **563**, **570–572**
incremental checkpoints, **194–195**
incremental refresh, for materialized views, 881
index browning, **258–259**
INDEX clause, for table creation including LOBs, 308
INDEX hint, 764
INDEX JOIN, in execution plan, 745
index-organized tables (IOTs), **262–269**
    altering, 266–268
    compressing, **266**
    creating, **263–265**
    logical ROWIDs, **263**
    viewing, **268–269**
index-range-scan lookup, 742–743
index segment, 179, 180
index tablespaces, 226
    placement on disks, 104–105
INDEX_ASC hint, 764

INDEX_COMBINE hint, 764
INDEX_DESC hint, 765
indexed clusters, **270**
    adding tables to, 272–273
    CREATE CLUSTER command for, 271–273
indexes, **247–262**
    accesses, 743–744
    altering, **256–258**
        enabling and disabling, 257
        rebuilding, 257–258
    bitmap indexes, **249–250**
        creating, 254
    bounded and unbounded range scans, **251**
    B*Tree indexes, **248–249**, *249*
        creating, 252
    column considerations, **250**
    compressing, **253**
    creating, **251–256**
        NOLOGGING option, 254
        with parallel processing, **254–255**
    documentation of current structures, 169–170
    dropping, 259
    function-based, **251**, **255–256**
    global, **1038–1039**
    monitoring browned-out, **670–672**
    partitions for, **1036–1039**
    scans and ROWID lookup, **742–743**
    in SQL statement tuning, **753–758**
        disabling, **755–758**
        rule-based, **760–761**
    statistics on, 324–328
    unique, **252–253**
    validation, 328
    viewing information, **259–262**
        DBA_IND_COLUMNS view, 261–262

DBA_INDEXES view, **259–261**
INDEXES_STATS view, 262
INDEXES_STATS view, 262
INDEX_FFS hint, 765
INDEXFILE, DDL production with, **516–517**
INDEX_JOIN hint, 764
inefficient block usage in object, monitoring, **669–670**
INITIAL parameter, **220–221**
initialization files, for Oracle Parallel Server, 1100–1102
initjvm.sql script, 134, 1117, 1118
   roles, 1123
init.ora file, **16–17**
   _INIT_SQL_FILE, 130
   advanced replication parameters, 1061
   ALL_ROWS, 711
   ALWAYS_ANTI_JOIN, 710
   ARCHIVELOG mode parameters, **430–433**
   backup, 485
   BITMAP_MERGE_AREA_SIZE, 710
   BUFFER_POOL_KEEP, 122
   BUFFER_POOL_RECYCLE, 122
   CONTROL_FILES parameter, 126
   creating, **117–128**
   CURSOR_SPACE_FOR_TIME parameter, **773**
   DB_BLOCK_BUFFERS parameter, 121–122, 183, 649
   DB_FILE_MULTIBLOCK_READ_COUNT parameter, 710
   DB_FILES parameter, 126
   example, 119
   file path setup, **124–125**
   FIRST_ROWS, 711
   GC_FILES_TO_LOCKS parameter, 1097
   GLOBAL_NAMES parameter, 1061
   HASH_AREA_SIZE, 710, 747–748
   HASH_JOIN_ENABLED, 710
   HASH_MULTIBLOCK_IO_COUNT, 710
   JAVA_MAX_SESSIONSPACE_SIZE, 1116
   JAVA_POOL_SIZE, 124
   JAVA_POOL_SIZE parameter, 1116
   JAVA_SOFT_SESSIONSPACE_LIMIT, 1115
   JOB_QUEUE_INTERVAL parameter, 914–915, 1061
   JOB_QUEUE_KEEP_CONNECTIONS parameter, 1061
   JOB_QUEUE_PROCESSES parameter, 914, 1061
   LARGE_POOL_SIZE, 124
   location, **118–119**
   LOG_BUFFER, 124
   MAX_DUMP_FILE_SIZE parameter, 721
   MAX_ENABLED_ROLES parameter, 948
   in migration process, 79
   MTS_CIRCUITS parameter, 409
   MTS_DISPATCHERS parameter, 408–409
   MTS_MAX_DISPATCHERS parameter, 409
   MTS_MAX_SERVERS parameter, 409
   MTS_SERVER parameter, 409
   MTS_SESSIONS parameter, 409
   OPEN_LINKS parameter, 1061
   OPTIMIZER_FEATURES_ENABLED, 710
   OPTIMIZER_INDEX_CACHING, 711
   OPTIMIZER_INDEXER_COST_ADJUST, 710
   OPTIMIZER_MAX_PERMUTATIONS, 711
   OPTIMIZER_PERCENT_PARALLEL, 711
   other issues, **126–128**
   parallel processing parameters, 856–857
   PARALLEL_AUTOMATIC_TUNING, 844, 855, 857
   PARALLEL_EXECUTION_MESSAGE_SIZE, 858

PARALLEL_MAX_SERVERS, 126, 850
parameters impacting optimizer, 710–712
query rewrite parameters, 871
QUERY REWRITE_ENABLED parameter, 870
SERVICE_NAMES parameter, 393
setting parameters, **120**
SHARED_POOL_SIZE parameter, **123**, 184, 771–772, 1116
    for replication, 1061
SORT_AREA_SIZE parameter, 711
SQL_TRACE parameter, 721
in startup, 313
System Global Area (SGA), configuration, **120–124**
TIMED_STATISTICS parameter, 721
and tracing, 721
USER_DUMP_DEST parameter, 125, 127, 330, 637, 721
INITRANS parameter, 177, **219–220**
inline storage, 211
inline views, **287–288**
inner join, 35
input files for SQL*Loader, **979–991**
    control files, **979–988**
    datafiles, **989–991**
INSERT statement, 31
    to query object types, **372–374**
Install process window, *62*, 62–63
Installation Types window in UI, 55–56
installing Java, **1118–1120**
    verifying, **1119**
installing Oracle
    Configuration Tools window, *64*
    postinstallation steps, 63
    preinstall steps, **48–50**
        general for all platforms, 48–49
        in Unix, 49–50
        in Windows NT, 50
    Universal Installer, **47–48**
        Available Product Components, 56–58, *57*
        Available Products, 54–55, *55*
        Component Locations, 58–59, *59*
        Create Database screen, 61
        File Locations, 53–54, *54*
        Install process window, *62*, 62–63
        Installation Types, 55–56
        migrating existing databases, 60
        Oracle Protocol Support, 59, *60*
        products not installed by default, 57–58
        starting, **51–53**
        Summary screen, 61, *61*
installing Oracle Statspack, **677–680**
installing Oracle8i supplied packages, **912**
instance recovery, 314–315
INSTANCE_NAME parameter, 1100
INSTANCE_NUMBER parameter, 1100
instances, 337
    creating for object in PL/SQL, 350
    vs. databases, **14–17**, *15*
    information about, 640
    of member methods, SELF parameter, 366
    service names definition, 392
INT data type, 207
INTEGER data type, 207
integrity rules, 7
    foreign key relationships, 11–12
Inter-Process Communication (IPC), 1097
interconnect, for hardware clusters, 1095
internal locks, 803
    types, 805
INTERNAL user, 933

Internet. *See also* Java
    critical components for, 1111
    impact, 1110
Internet file system (iFS), 1124
INTERPRETER mode for namesctl utility, 416
INTERSECTION, in execution plan, 745
interval of job executions, 915
invalid hints, 762
IOTs. *See* index-organized tables (IOTs)
IPC (Inter-Process Communication), 391, 1097
isolation in relational database, 6
Ixora, 86

J

Java, **1111–1115**
    basic methods, **1111–1113**
    configuration, **115–118**
        MTS vs. dedicated server, **1116–1117**
    installation, **1118–1120**
        verifying, **1119**
    Java Virtual Machine (JVM), **1113–1114**
        common errors when installing or using, **1119–1120**
    JServer Accelerator, **1114–1115**
    vs. PL/SQL, 115
    scripts, **1117–1118**
    security, **1123**
    stored procedures creation, **1120–1121**
    utilities, **1121–1122**
Java-based installer, 47
Java Class Loader, 1114
Java Database Connectivity (JDBC), 1111, **1112**
Java pool, 187
Java Runtime Environment (JRE), 47
Java Runtime Interpreter, 1114

Java stored procedures, 42
JAVA_MAX_SESSIONSPACE_SIZE parameter, 1116
JAVA_POOL_SIZE parameter, 124, 1116, 1117
JAVA_SOFT_SESSIONSPACE_LIMIT parameter, 1115
JAVASYSPRIV role, 1118
    privileges, 1123
JAVAUSERPRIV role, 1118
    privileges, 1123
JDBC (Java Database Connectivity), 1111, **1112**
JDeveloper tool, 1111, **1113**
job commands in Recovery Manager, 548
job queue processes, 191
Job Scheduler, **914–920**
    adding job, **915–918**
        running job at intervals, 917–918
        running job once, 917
    enabling, **914–915**
    modifying jobs, **918–919**
    monitoring, **919–920**
    parameters for DBMS_MVIEW package, 884
    suspending or removing job, **919**
JOB_QUEUE_INTERVAL parameter, 914–915, 1061
JOB_QUEUE_KEEP_CONNECTIONS parameter, 1061
JOB_QUEUE_PROCESSES parameter, 914, 1061
join cardinality, 708
join compatibility check, by optimizer, 869
joined object views, **383**
joins, **11–12**, *12*, **34–36**
    anti-joins, 36
    Cartesian joins, 36
    effects of NULL columns, **36–38**
    equijoin, 35

guidelines for using, 748
inner join, 35
materialized views with, and fast refresh, 882
outer joins, 35–36
partition-wise, 1025, **1040–1041**
self joins, 36
theta joins, 35
JRE (Java Runtime Environment), 47
JServer Accelerator, **1114–1115**
JVM (Java Virtual Machine), **1113–1114**
jvmu815.sql script, 1117–1118

K

keep buffer pool, 183
key preserved columns, 285

L

large pool, 187
LARGE_POOL_SIZE parameter, 124
LAST method, for VARRAY, 375
latch activity wait, 822
latch free wait, 822
latches
    contention, **797–799**
        general tuning, **837–841**
        latch wait posting, 798
        monitoring for, **832–835**
        no-wait mode latches, 799
        parent/child latches, 799
        willing-to-wait latch, 797–798
    information about, **800–801**
    for monitoring, **799–800**
    statistics on, 640
    what it is, **796–801**

_LATCH_WAIT_POSTING parameter, 798
LCK*n* process, 191
LDAP (Lightweight Directory Access Protocol), 393
LD_LIBRARY_PATH parameter, 21
LEADING hint, 767
leftmost column, 250
LGWR (Log Writer), 189–190
library cache, 184
    latches, 800
        monitoring, **654–658**
    view to display objects in, 640
library cache hit ratio, **655**
library cache lock and pin waits, 822
library cache pin hit ratio, **656–657**
library cache reload ratio, 771
    calculating, **655–656**
Library manager and Standard libraries (Java), 1114
license, 49
LIKE operator, and accidentally forcing table scans, 776
LIMIT method, for VARRAY, 375
LINK$ data dictionary table, 297, 1021–1022
LIST command (RMAN), 549
LIST COPY command (RMAN), 574
LISTENER, 191
    configuration in Net8, **395–401**
listener.ora configuration file, 394
    sample, 396–400
        control parameters, 399–400
        listener address section, 397–398
        static service section, 398
    and standby database, 1080–1081
lists from Recovery Manager, **607–612**
    archive log backups, 609–610

incarnation information, 611–612
parameters, 607–608
recoverable backups, 610–611
LMD (Lock Manager Daemon), 191
LMON process, 191
load balancing
client, **402–403**
hash partitioning and, 1031
LOADJAVA utility, 1120, **1121–1122**
LOB (latest large object) datatype, 30, **209–213**, **307–312**
accessing through SQL, **310–312**
BFILES, **310**
BLOB datatype, 211
CLOBs, 211
monitoring allocations, 153–154
NCLOB datatype, 211
partitioning on columns, **1035–1036**
and read consistency, 212
restrictions, 213
SQL*Loader support, 999–1001
storage, 211–212
VARRAY data as, 360
viewing information, 312
local indexes, 1038
local naming, 393
Lock Manager Daemon (LMD), 191
LOCK TABLE command, 200
LOCK_NAME_SPACE parameter, 1084
locks, **802–812**
conversions, 807–808
escalation, 807
example of monitoring, with V$LOCK, **808–811**
and foreign key problems, 811–812
monitoring, **827–831**
optimistic or pessimistic strategy, 812
and SELECT FOR UPDATE, 812
types and modes, **803–808**
exclusive or shared mode, 806–807
type codes, 803–805
log buffer space waits, 822–823
.log file extension, 117
log file parallel write waits, 823
log file sequential read waits, 823
log file single write waits, 823
log file switch waits, 824
log file sync waits, 824
log files
for materialized views, **889–891**
of Oracle installation, 63
from SQL*Loader, **994–996**
log on
executing context package at, 961
as privileged user, **934–935**
log sequence number-based recovery, **583–584**
Log Writer (LGWR), 189–190
LOG_ARCHIVE parameters, 128
LOG_ARCHIVE_DEST parameter, 125
LOG_ARCHIVE_DEST_N parameter, 125
LOG_ARCHIVE_DEST_STATE_*n* parameter, 1083, 1084
LOG_ARCHIVE_DUPLEX_DEST parameter, 125
LOG_ARCHIVE_MIN_SUCCEED_DEST parameter, 1083
LOG_ARCHIVE_TRACE parameter, 330, 1084
LOG_BUFFER parameter, 124
LOG_CHECKPOINT_INTERVAL parameter, 194
LOG_CHECKPOINTS_TO_ALERT parameter, 195
LOG_CHECKPOINT_TIMEOUT parameter, 195
log_directory parameter, in listener.ora file, 399

log_file parameter, in listener.ora file, 399
LOG_FILE_NAME_CONVERT parameter, 1084
LOGGING option
    for heap table creation, 233
    for table creation including LOBs, 309
    for tablespaces, 226
logging parameter, in listener.ora file, 399
logical backup, 424, 492. *See also* Oracle Export utility
    EXP to create, 72
logical I/O, reduction in SQL statement tuning, 752
logical Oracle, **18–19**
logical reads, vs. physical reads, 646
logical records, for SQL*Loader datafile, 991
logical ROWIDs, in IOTs, **263**
logical volume manager, 835
LogMiner
    CREATE TABLE AS SELECT command with, 238
    features, **614**
    limitations, **615**
    retrieving results, **624–626**
    selecting redo logs for, **618–620**
        viewing list, **620**
    setup, **615–617**
        dictionary file creation, 616–617
        UTL_FILE_DIR parameter, 615
    using, **620–624**
    viewing results, **623–624**
_LOG_SIMULTANEOUS_COPIES parameter, 800
LOG_SMALL_ENTRY_MAX_SIZE parameter, 839
LOG_STATS command (namesctl), 417
LONG datatype, 30, 209
LONGRAW datatype, 30, 209
lookup tables, in data warehouse, 865

LRU (least recently used) blocks in SGA, 181, *182*
LRU algorithm, 152
LRU latches, 122
lsnrctl utility, 400–401
LU6.2 (Logical Unit Type 6.2) protocol, 391

M

MAKE procedure (DBMS_REFRESH), 1056
managed recovery mode for standby database, **1078**
manual recovery mode for standby database, **1078**
many-to-many join, 11, *12*
map and order methods, **370–371**
master definition site for advanced replication, 1060
    changing replication group, 1069
    changing replication schema, 1069
master site for advanced replication, 1060
    objects to be replicated at, **1068–1069**
    replication administration users at, **1067–1068**
materialized views, 708, **872–891**
    creating, **873–878**, 1052
    data dictionary views, **879–880**
    DBMS_MVIEW to refresh, **883–889**
    examples, **875–877**
        with join and aggregate, 875–876
        partitioned, 877
        single-table aggregate, 876–877
    logs, **889–891**
    privileges for working with, **875**
    refresh groups for, **1055–1059**
    replication with, **1050–1055**

MAXDATAFILES parameter, 129
MAX_DUMP_FILE_SIZE parameter, 127, 721
MAX_ENABLED_ROLES parameter, 126
MAXEXTENTS parameter, **222–223**
   and de-allocation of table space, 241
   and object monitoring, 698
maximum degree of parallelism, 845
maximum parallel servers, setting, 859–860
MAXTRANS parameter, 177, **219–220**
MAXVALUE option, for CREATE SEQUENCE command, 298
Mean Time Between Failure (MTBF), 101
Mean Time to Recover (MTTR), 101
measures in materialized views, 873
media management layer in Recovery Manager, 542
media recovery, 315
member methods, **366–369**
memory allocation
   for database buffer cache, 184
   information about, 641
memory, in clustered environment, 1095–1096
Memory Manager and Garbage Collector (Java), 1114
memory requirements, for database creation, **111–112**
memory structures. *See* Oracle memory structures
MERGE hint, 769
MERGE JOIN, in execution plan, 744, **747**
merge joins, 747
MERGE_AJ hint, 767
MERGE_PARTITION_CLAUSE command, 1046
message buffer location, setting, 859
message buffer size, setting, 858

metadata
   data dictionary based tables for storing, 143
   exporting for transportable tablespace, 524–525
methods, 337, 338, **365–372**
   constructor methods, **366**
   information about, **372**
   map and order methods, **370–371**
   member methods, **366–369**
midpoint insertion, 182
midpoint of SGA, 181, *182*
MIG (Migration utility), 74
   checklist for using, **75–80**
MIGPREP, **74–75**
MIGRATE schema, 74
migrated rows
   fixing tables with, **714–717**
   and performance, 712
migrating existing databases, 60
migrating to Oracle8i, **70–75**
   advice, **80–84**
      ALTER DATABASE CONVERT problems, 83–84
      on auditing, 82
      on backup, 81
      on database parameters, 81–82
      on migration utility notes, 82–83
      on system items, 82
   checklist, **75–80**
   with Data Migration Assistant, **84**
   existing 7.1+ database, **73–75**
   pre-7.1 database, **71–73**
      with export and import utilities, 72
      migrating to 7 then to Oracle8i, 73
      with SQL*Plus COPY command, 72–73
   vs. upgrade, **71**

MINEXTENTS parameter, **222–223**
mini-checkpoint, 194
minimal install, 56
minimum parallel servers, setting, 859–860
MINUS, in execution plan, 745
MINVALUE option, for CREATE SEQUENCE command, 298
miss ratios for dictionary cache, calculating, **654**
MODIFY_DEFAULT_ATTRIBUTES_CLAUSE command, 1046
MODIFY_PARTITION_CLAUSE command, 1046
MODIFY_SUBPARTITION_CLAUSE command, 1046
monitoring
    database threats, **664–673**
        browned-out indexes, **670–672**
        inefficient block usage in object, **669–670**
        resource usage, **672–673**
        segment fragmentation, **667–668**
        tablespace free space fragmentation, **666–667**
        user setup, **665**
    events for, **632–638**
    I/O contention, **658–664**
        rollback segment usage, **662–664**
        session file I/O, **660–662**
        system file I/O, **658–660**
    latch contention, **832–835**
    latches for, **799–800**
    locks, **827–831**
    methodology, **688–698**
        application tools, **689–690**
        baselines, benchmarks and trends, **689**
        database to send e-mail notification, **694–695**
        items to monitor, **690–694**
        scripts, **826–834**
    SGA (System Global Area), **645–658**
        data dictionary cache, **653–654**
        database buffer cache, **646–652**
        library cache, **654–658**
    vs. tuning database, 630
MONITORING option, for heap table creation, 233
monitoring tools, **673–680**
    gathering system statistics, **674–676**
    Oracle Statspack, **676–688**
mounting standby database, **1084–1085**
MOVE_PARTITION_CLAUSE command, 1046
MOVE_SUBPARTITION_CLAUSE command, 1046
moving
    datafiles, **321–322**
    index-organized tables (IOTs), 267
    online redo logs, **322–323**
    tablespaces, 528
MRU (most recently used) blocks in SGA, 181, *182*
MTBF (Mean Time Between Failure), 101
MTS (multithreaded server model), **407–411**
    configuration, **408–409**
    managing on client, **410–411**
    viewing information, **410**
MTS_CIRCUITS parameter, 409
MTS_DISPATCHERS parameter, 408–409
MTS_MAX_DISPATCHERS parameter, 409
MTS_MAX_SERVERS parameter, 409
MTS_SERVER parameter, 409
MTS_SESSIONS parameter, 409
MTTR (Mean Time to Recover), 101
multiplexing, 544
MULTIPLIER parameter, 83

multitable measure in materialized view, 873
Mviews. *See* materialized views

N

named notation, 622
    for package parameters, 912
Named pipes protocol, 391
names
    of databases, changing, **318–319**
    for files on standby site, 1085
    in Net8, methods for resolving, **393–394**
    for partitions, 1026
    for roles, 947
    for schema objects on distributed system, 1018
        resolution, **1020–1021**
namesctl utility, **416–419**
    common commands, 417–419
    passwords for, 416–417
names.ora configuration file, 395, 415–416
naming standards, **115–117**. *See also* Oracle Flexible Architecture (OFA)
    for constraints, **303**
    for database, 116
    for database objects, 116–117
    for objects, 341
National Language Support (NLS) character types, 207, **208–209**
Native Compilation (Java), 1114
NCHAR datatype, 30
NCLOB datatype, 30, 211
    SQL*Loader support, 999
NCOMP format, 1114–1115
nested cursor, 379
NESTED LOOP, in execution plan, 745, **747**

nested tables, **361–364**
    altering and dropping, **363–364**
    creating, 361–362
    INSERT statement to query, 374
    SQL*Loader support, 998–999
    UPDATE statement for, 376
Net8
    Advanced Security Option, **420–421**
    basics, **390–394**
        client/server connections, **390–391**
        naming methods, **393–394**
        protocols supported, **391**
        service names, **392–393**
    configuration, **394–407**
        of client, **401–406**
        with Configuration Assistant, **406–407**
        file backup, 485
        of listener, **395–401**
        for Oracle Parallel Server, 1103–1105
        for standby database, 1080–1081
    MTS (multithreaded server model), **407–411**
        configuration, **408–409**
        managing on client, **410–411**
        viewing information, **410**
    Oracle Connection Manager, **419–420**
    Oracle Names, **411–419**
        how it works, **411–415**
        names servers configuration, **415–416**
        names servers management, **416–419**
network
    configuration, 137
    TNSPING to test setup, **29**
NEXT method, for VARRAY, 375
NEXT parameter, **221**
NEXTVAL pseudocolumn, 299–300

NLS (National Language Support) character types, 207, **208–209**
no-wait mode latches, 799
NOAPPEND hint, 768
NOARCHIVELOG mode
    cold backup recovery, **439–441**
    cold backups in, 435, **436–438**
        with Recovery Manager, **564–566**
    determining, 429
    recovery in, **575–579**
NOCACHE hint, 769
NOCACHE option
    for heap table creation, 232
    for table creation including LOBs, 310
NOCYCLE option, for CREATE SEQUENCE command, 298
nodes, in execution plan tree, 738
nodes (servers), in clustered environment, 1095
NO_EXPAND hint, 765
NO_INDEX hint, 765
NOLOGGING option
    for heap table creation, 233
    for table creation including LOBs, 309
NOLOGGING option for tablespaces, 226
NOMAXVALUE option, for CREATE SEQUENCE command, 298
NO_MERGE hint, 769
NOMINVALUE option, for CREATE SEQUENCE command, 298
NOMONITORING option, for heap table creation, 233
non-equijoin, 35
noncontiguous extents, 667–668
nonuniform memory access, 1096
NOPARALLEL hint, 768
NOPARALLEL_INDEX hint, 769
NOREVERSE keyword, 257
NOREWRITE hint, 766
normal database operations, and disk space requirements, 98
normal hash cluster, 270
normalization, **7–11**
    first normal form, 8
    second normal form, 8–9
    third normal form, 7, 9–11
normalized dimension, 893
NOT NULL constraints, 300
    and accidentally forcing table scans, 775
NOT NULL keyword, 234
NO_UNNEST hint, 770
NULL job interval, 917
NULL lock holders, 806
NULL values, **21**
    and accidentally forcing table scans, 775
    effects on joins, **36–38**
    and foreign key constraints, 20
    preventing, 300
NUMBER datatype, 30, **205–207**
    precision and scale, 205–206
    subtypes, 206–207
numbering of Oracle software, 71
NUMERIC data type, 206
NVARCHAR2 datatype, 30

O

object-level grants, **944–945**
object management
    configuring physical attributes, **217–219**
        INITRANS parameter, **219–220**
        MAXTRANS parameter, **219–220**
        PCTFREE parameter, **218–219**, *219*
        PCTUSED parameter, **218–219**, *219*

overview, **216–224**
storage parameters, **220–224**
    BUFFER_POOL parameter, 224
    FREELIST GROUPS parameter, **223**
    FREELISTS parameter, **223**
    INITIAL parameter, **220–221**
    MAXEXTENTS parameter, **222–223**
    MINEXTENTS parameter, **222–223**
    NEXT parameter, **221**
    OPTIMAL parameter, **223–224**
    PCTINCREASE parameter, **221–222**
Object Memory Management (Java), 1114
object-oriented database, 336
    Oracle as, 13
object tables, 337, 338, **351–357**
    altering, **355**
    creating, **351–355**
    dropping, **356**
    information about, **356–357**
    relational views on, **386–387**
    views with relational tables and, 385–386
objects in Oracle, **336–338**. *See also* database objects; heap tables; indexes; user-defined object types
    column objects, 346
    dependencies for, documentation, 171–172
    invalidated, 172
    listing access to, 158–159
    monitoring those near maximum extents, 698
    names on distributed system, 1018
        resolution, **1020–1021**
    queries, **372–379**
        with INSERT statement, **372–374**
        with SELECT statement, **376–379**
        with UPDATE statement, **374–376**
    row objects, 346
    vs. segments, 179
    SQL*Loader support, **996–998**
    validating structure, **328–329**
    views, **380–387**
OCM Administrative Process (CMADMIN), 420
OCM Gateway Process (CMGW), 420
OFA (Oracle Flexible Architecture), 16. *See* Oracle Flexible Architecture (OFA)
OFFLINE PENDING state, for rollback segment, 280
offline tablespaces, 460
_offline_rollback_segments parameter, 489
OID clause, of CREATE TABLE command, 352
OID (object ID), 346–347
    as primary key, 352, 360
OIDINDEX clause, of CREATE TABLE command, 354
Oklahoma City bombing, 426
OLTP (online transaction processing system), 7
    block size for, 113, 114
ON COMMIT keyword, 239
ON DELETE CASCADE option, for foreign keys, 302
ON DELETE SET NULL option, for foreign keys, 303
one-off patches, 64–65
one-to-many join, 11, *12*
one-to-one join, 11, *12*
online redo logs, 91
    after SHUTDOWN ABORT, 317
    as critical point of failure, 107
    documentation for, **162–163**
    groups, **434–435**
    locating for backup, 437
    mirroring and distribution, *108*

moving, **322–323**
re-creating, 109–110
recovery from loss of, **475–480**
sizing, **108–110**
suggested sizes, 109
online transaction processing system (OLTP), 7
  block size for, 113, 114
op code, 204
open backup. *See* hot backups
open cursors, maximum number, 126
OPEN_CURSORS parameter, 701
OPEN_LINKS parameter, 1061
operating system user authentication, **932–933**
operations, 7
OPS (Oracle Parallel Server), 14
OPTIMAL parameter, **223–224**
  and migration, 82
  for rollback segment, 199
optimistic locking strategy, 812
ORA-1550, Snapshot Too Old message, **198–200**
ORA-06532 errors, 617–618
Oracle
  file placement, **104–106**
    avoiding single point of failure, **107**
  patches, **64–65**
  removing software, **66–70**
Oracle Base directory, 93
Oracle Connection Manager, **419–420**
Oracle control file, as critical point of failure, 107
Oracle Directory Naming, 393
Oracle executables, 92
Oracle Export utility, **492–504**
  command-line mode, **496–498**
    common parameters, 494–495
  compression of extents, **501**

direct-mode export, **501–502**
files, 92
interactive mode, **496**
for migration, 72
parameter-file-driven, **498–499**
support for multiple export files, **503–504**
table-level export, **500–501**
user-level export, **499–500**
uses for, 492
what can be exported, **493–494**
Oracle Fail Safe, **1105–1107**, *1107*
Oracle Flexible Architecture (OFA), 16, **89–96**
  benefits, **89–90**
  structure, **90–95**
    basic rules, 90–91
    database administration subdirectory, 94
    database components, 91–92
    Oracle Base and Oracle Home, 92–94
    Oradata directories, 95
    roadmap, 95–96
Oracle Home Name, 54
Oracle Home Path, 54
Oracle Import utility, **504–517**
  common parameters, 506–508
  DDL production with INDEXFILE, **516–517**
  full import mode, 505, **509–511**
  for migration, 72
  to move transportable tablespace, 526
  row array type commits, 514
  support for multiple export files, **515–516**
  table-level import mode, 505, **513–514**
  user-level import mode, 505, **511–513**
  what can be imported, **504–505**
Oracle Internet file system (iFS), 1124
Oracle memory structures, **112**, **181–188**
  Java pool, 187

large pool, 187
PGA (Process Global Area), **187**
request and response queues, 188
SGA (System Global Area), **181–187**
    database buffer cache, **182–183**
    redo log buffer, **184–185**
    shared pool, **184**
    size, **185–186**
sort areas, 187–188
Oracle Metalink, 86
Oracle Names, 393, **411–419**
    administrative region in, 411
    how it works, **411–415**
        client discovery of Names servers, 412–413
        name resolution optimization, 413–415
        service registration, 412
    names servers configuration, **415–416**
    names servers management, **416–419**
Oracle optimizer, **705–720**
    analysis with Oracle supplied packages, **719–720**
    cost-based mode optimization, **707–708**
    histograms, **717–718**
    migrated and chained rows, **712–717**
    rule-based optimization, **705–706**
    set up, **709–712**
    SQL text-matching by, 868–869
Oracle Parallel Server (OPS), 14, **1093–1105**
    architecture, **1094–1097**, *1095*
        hardware cluster configurations, 1095–1096
        software components, 1096–1097
    creating database, **1098–1105**
        installation preparation, 1099–1100
        manual creation, 1100–1105

    limitations, **1098**
    Oracle8i enhancements, **1097–1098**
Oracle PL/SQL, **39–43**
    basic structure, **39–40**
    program units, **40–43**
        anonymous blocks, **40–41**
        functions, **42–43**
        packages, 43
        procedures, **41–42**
        triggers, 43
Oracle processes, **188–191**
    optional processes, **191**
    required processes, **189–191**
        CKPT (Checkpoint), 190–191
        DBW*n* (Database Writer), 189
        LGWR (Log Writer), 189–190
        PMON (Process Monitor), 190
        SMON (System Monitor), 190
    server processes, **188–189**
Oracle Protocol Support window in UI, 59, *60*
Oracle services
    creating in Windows NT, **132**
    removing, 69–70
    stopping, 68–69
Oracle Software Source Path, 54
Oracle SQL, **29–38**. *See also* SQL
Oracle Statspack, **676–688**
    automating statistics collection, **683–684**
    custom report generation, **687–688**
    installing in database, **677–680**
    taking database snapshots, **681–683**
    viewing report, **684–687**
Oracle storage architecture, **176–181**, *179*
    blocks, **176–177**, *177*
    extents, **178–179**
    segments, **179–181**

Oracle8i. *See also* installing Oracle
    fundamental principles, **19–21**
        constraints, **20–21**
        database consistency, **19**
        environment settings, **21–22**
        NULL values, **21**
        transactions, **19–20**
    internals, **13–19**
        instances vs. databases, **14–17**, *15*
        physilogical Oracle, **17–19**
    introduction, **5–13**
        history, **12–13**
        relational theory, **6–12**
    platforms, 46
    SQL interface tools, **22–29**. *See also* SQL*Plus
        Server Manager, **22–23**
        TNSPING, **29**
ORACLE_BASE parameter, 22, 51, 93
ORACLE_HOME parameter, 22, 49, 52, 58–59, 93
ORACLE_SID parameter, 22, 52
    for database connection, 547
ORACLE_TRACE_COLLECTION_PATH parameter, 125
ORACLE_TRACE_FACILITY_PATH parameter, 125
Oradata directories, **95**
ORADIM command, **132**
ORAPWD program, 929–930
order methods, **370–371**
order of precedence, object references in schemas, 293–294
ORDERED hint, 766
ORDERED_PREDICATES hint, 770
OS_AUTHENT_PREFIX parameter, 933
out of extents error message, 83
out-of-line storage, 212
outer joins, 35–36
OUTLN_PKG package, 786, 911
output from SQL*Loader, **991–994**, *992*
    bad file, 991, **992–993**
    discard file, 991, **993–994**
overflow segment, 264

P

packages, 43
    Oracle8i supplied, **908–913**
        calling parameters, **912**
        information about, **912–913**
        installing, **912**
        running, 911–912
        support for, 913
PACK_MESSAGE function, in DBMS_PIPE package, 922
paging memory, and performance, 649
parallel channels, determining number, 543
parallel direct path load, **978**
parallel execution process, 849
PARALLEL hint, 768
parallel loading, with SQL*Loader, **849**
parallel mode, starting database in, 1103
parallel processing, **844–845**
    DDL (Data Definition Language), **848**
    DML (Data Manipulation Language), **845–846**
        to create tables, **846–848**
    index creation with, **254–255**
    in recovery operations, **854–855**
    tuning and monitoring, **855–861**
        init.ora parameters, 856–857
        message buffer location, 859

message buffer size, 858
minimum and maximum parallel servers, 859–860
parallel queries, **849–854**
information about, 641
PX slaves in, **849–852**, *851*, *853*
tuning processes, 860–861
viewing information, 860
PARALLEL_AUTOMATIC_TUNING parameter, 844, 855, 857
PARALLEL_DEFAULT_MAX_SCANS parameter, 845
PARALLEL_EXECUTION_MESSAGE_SIZE parameter, 858
PARALLEL_INDEX hint, 768
PARALLEL_MAX_SERVERS parameter, 126, 850, 855, 859–860
PARALLEL_MIN_SERVERS parameter, 860
PARALLEL_SERVER parameter, 1101
PARALLEL_THREADS_PER_CPU parameter, 857
parameter files, 18. *See also* init.ora file
and migration, 81–82
modifying, 120
for SQL*Loader execution, 1003
parameters
documentation for current use, **164–166**
hidden, 154–155, 838
in init.ora file, 16
parent/child latches, 799
parent/child relationship, foreign key constraints for, **20–21**
parent step, in execution plan, 736
parsing
CURSOR_SHARING parameter and, 772–773
CURSOR_SPACE_FOR_TIME parameter and, **773**

hard parse, 701–702
monitoring and managing excessive, **770–773**
phase in SQL statement processing, **701–703**
soft parse, 701
partition-wise joins, 1025, **1040–1041**
partitioned tables, transporting, **529–530**
partitions, **1024–1025**
attributes and, **1045–1046**
basics, **1025–1036**
composite partitioning, **1033–1035**
hash partitioning, **1031–1033**
on LOB columns, **1035–1036**
names, 1026
range partitioning, **1026–1031**
data dictionary views for, **1046–1047**
enhanced elimination, 1024
importing, 511
for indexes, **1036–1039**
composite partitioning, **1037–1038**
hash partitioning, **1037**
range partitioning, **1036–1037**
management, **1043–1047**
dropping, **1044–1045**
exchanging, **1044**
merging, 1024, **1043**
splitting, **1044**
pruning, 849, **1039–1040**
password file authentication, **928–931**
creating password file, **929–930**
database setup to use password file, **930–931**
PASSWORD_GRACE_TIME, 939, 941
PASSWORD_LIFE_TIME, 939, 941
PASSWORD_LOCK_TIME, 939, 941
PASSWORD_REUSE_MAX, 939, 941
PASSWORD_REUSE_TIME, 939, 941

passwords
   changing after database creation, 137
   for namesctl utility, 416–417
   for roles, 947
   user profile settings, 939–941
passwords parameter, in listener.ora file, 399
PASSWORD_VERIFY_FUNCTION parameter, 940, 941
patches, **64–65**, **86**
   need for, 49
path, fully versioned, 93–94
PATH parameter, 22, 52
PCTFREE parameter, 177, **218–219**, *219*, 669
PCTINCREASE parameter, **221–222**
PCTUSED parameter, 177, **218–219**, *219*, 669
PCTVERSION keyword, for table creation including LOBs, 309
performance. *See also* V$ dynamic performance views
   vs. availability, **1042**, *1043*
   cluster size and hashkeys impact, 274
   extents and, 223
   FGAC and, 967
   Java vs. PL/SQL, 115
   locks and, 803
   monitoring tools, **673–680**
      gathering system statistics, **674–676**
      Oracle Statspack, **676–688**
   normalization and, 7
   paging memory and, 649
   partitions and, 1026
   shared pool size and, 184
   tuning problem databases, **630–631**
   view creation and, 284
   views as problems, 287
permanent tablespace, 226

pessimistic locking strategy, 812
pfile directory, 94
PGA (Process Global Area), **187**
physical attributes of objects
   INITRANS parameter, **219–220**
   MAXTRANS parameter, **219–220**
   PCTFREE parameter, **218–219**, *219*
   PCTUSED parameter, **218–219**, *219*
physical backup, 424
physical I/O, reduction in SQL statement tuning, 752
physical Oracle, **18**
physical reads, logical reads vs., 646
physical requirements. *See* hardware requirements
physilogical Oracle, **17–19**
pin hit ratio for library cache, calculating, **656–657**
PING command (namesctl), 418
pinging, 1094, 1097
pinning objects, 154
pipes, **921–925**
   private pipes, 921–922
   public pipes, 921
   receiving messages, 924–925
   sending messages, **922–924**
PL/SQL, Java vs., 115
PL/SQL (Procedural Structured Query Language). *See also* Oracle PL/SQL
   accessing data dictionary views from, **148–150**
   to create method instance, 368
   report on objects in database, **166–167**
   and roles, **946–947**
   user-defined object types in, **350**
PL/SQL wrapper, creating, 1120–1121

plan generator, for SQL statement costs, 709
planning backup, **424–428**
    backup strategy, 424–425
    for disaster, **425–428**
PLAN_TABLE, for Autotrace, 731–732
PMON (Process Monitor), 190
point-in-time recovery, transportable tablespaces for, **532–535**
policy table, for Java security, 1123
polymorphism, 337
precision of NUMBER data type, 204–205
preconnect failover, 405–406
predefined roles, **946**
predicates in WHERE clause, 33
primary database, for point-in-time recovery, 532
primary instance, configuration for standby database, 1082–1083
primary key constraints, **20**, **301**
    adding to table, 240
    CREATE TABLE command with, 235–237
    privileges to create index, 232
PRINT SCRIPT command (RMAN), 598
PRINT_ALLDIMS procedure, **901–902**
PRINT_DIM procedure, **900–901**
PRIOR method, for VARRAY, 375
private database link, 1014
private process memory, 187
private SQL area, 700. *See also* cursors
private synonym, 293
privileged users, **933–936**
    log on, **934–935**
    viewing, **935–936**
privileges, 216
    CREATE PUBLIC SYNONYM, 293
    to create tables, 232

Procedural Structured Query Language (PL/SQL). *See also* Oracle PL/SQL
procedures, **41–42**
process free lists, 181
Process Global Area (PGA), **187**
process memory, private, 187
Process Monitor (PMON), 190
process trace files, 329–330
processes. *See* Oracle processes
    maximum number, 126
profile scripts, 26
protocols, Net8 support for, **391**
proxy copy, 542
public database link, 1014
public synonym, 293
PURGE procedure (DBMS_DEFER_SYS), 1062
PUSH procedure (DBMS_DEFER_SYS), 1062
PUSH_SUBQ hint, 770
PX slaves in parallel queries, **849–852**, *851*, *853*

Q

Q*nnn* processes, 191
queries. *See* SQL
QUERY command (namesctl), 418
Query Coordinator, 849
query rewrite, **866–872**
    constraints and dimensions requirements, 869–870
    enabling, 870–871
    how it works, 868–870
    rewrite integrity level, 871–872
    rules, 867–868
QUERY REWRITE privilege, for function-based index creation, 255
query transformer, 707–708

QUERY_REWRITE_ENABLED parameter, 774
QUERY_REWRITE_INTEGRITY parameter, 774, 871–872
queues, request and response, 188
QUIT command (namesctl), 418
QUOTA, 232
quota for user accounts, 932

R

RAID (Redundant Array of Inexpensive Disks), 101–104
range partitioning, 1025, **1026–1031**
    for indexes, **1036–1037**
RAW datatype, 209
RBA (redo byte address), 203
read consistency, 198
    LOB datatype and, 212
read-only mode, for standby database, **1078**, 1092–1093
read-only tablespaces, 81, 524
    setting, 529
    sharing, **528**
read/write mode, placing tablespaces in, 527
READ_EV procedure, 633
REAL data type, 207
REBUILD_FREELISTS function (DBMS_REPAIR), 333
RECEIVE_MESSAGE function, in DBMS_PIPE package, 924
RECO process, 191
RECOVER command, **452–454**
    parameters, 453
RECOVER command (RMAN), 550, **558–559**
RECOVER DATABASE command, 451

RECOVER DATABASE UNTIL CHANGE command, 472
RECOVER DATABASE UNTIL TIME command, 468
RECOVER DATAFILE command, 456
recoverable backups, lists, 610–611
recovery
    in ARCHIVELOG mode, **450–480**
        complete recovery, **454–466**
        incomplete recovery, **466–480**
        preparing for, **450–452**
        RECOVER command, **452–454**
    backup control file for, **480–483**
    cancel-based, 475
    change-based, **472–475**
    datafiles, 456–460
    log sequence number-based, **583–584**
    from loss of online redo logs, **475–480**
    NOARCHIVELOG mode, cold backup recovery, **439–441**
    parallel processing in, **854–855**
    point-in-time, transportable tablespaces for, **532–535**
    RESETLOGS and, **486–489**
        why and when to use, 486–487
    of standby database, **1085–1088**
    SYSTEM tablespace, **465**
    tablespaces, **460–462**
        with rollback segments, **465–466**
    time-based, **467–472, 582–583**
recovery catalog, **590–603**
    control file recovery without, **587–589**
    creating, **591–594**
        database creation, 591
        schema creation, 592–593
    database registration with, **593–594**

purging records, 602–603
recovery from complete database loss
  without, **584–585**
Recovery Manager (RMAN), 538
  architecture, **540–545**
    database control files, 541
    image copies, 545
    media management layer, 542
    RMAN backup pieces, 544
    RMAN backup sets, 543–544
    RMAN channels, 542–543
    RMAN recovery catalog, 543
    snapshot control file, 545
    target database, 541–542
  backup reports, **604–607**
    DEVICE TYPE option, 607
    NEED BACKUP option, 604–605
    OBSOLETE option, 606
    report object definition, 606
    SCHEMA option and AT clause, 606–607
    UNRECOVERABLE option, 605–606
  commands, **548–559**
    backup commands, **550–556**
    command-line parameters, 546–547
    recovery commands, **556–559**
  features, **538–540**
  limitations, **540**
  lists, **607–612**
    archive log backups, 609–610
    incarnation information, 611–612
    parameters, 607–608
    recoverable backups, 610–611
  performing backups, **562–575**
    archived redo logs, 573
    in ARCHIVELOG mode, **566–572**
    datafile copies, 573–574
    duplexing backups, **575**
    types, **562–564**
  recovery catalog, **590–603**
    control file recovery, **594–595**
    creating, **591–594**
    database synchronization, **594**
    maintaining, **598–603**
    resetting database, **595–596**
    storing RMAN scripts, **596–598**
  recovery operations, **575–590**
    archived redo logs, **585–586**
    ARCHIVELOG mode complete recovery, **579–581**
    ARCHIVELOG mode incomplete recovery, **582–584**
    for complete database loss without recovery catalog, **584–585**
    control file recovery without recovery catalog, **587–589**
    datafile to another location, **590**
    NOARCHIVELOG mode backup recovery, **575–579**
  reviewing output, **559–562**
  running, **545–562**
    connecting to databases, **547**
RECOVERY_PARALLELISM parameter, 855
recursive relationship, creating parent and child tables with, 348–349
recursive SQL, 701
recycle buffer pool, 183
redo, **203–204**
redo allocation latch, tuning problems, 839
redo buffer latches, 800
redo byte address (RBA), 203
redo copy latch, tuning problems, 838–839
redo log buffer, **184–185**

redo logs, 18, 91, **202–205**. *See also* LogMiner
   archived, 91, 203
   as bottleneck, 823
   as critical point of failure, 107
   Database Configuration Assistant (DCA) and, 135
   information about switches, 640
   mirroring and distribution, *108*
   naming standards, 117
   re-creating, 109–110
   selecting for mining, **618–620**
   sizing, **108–110**
   sizing buffer, 124
   suggested sizes, 109
   switches, **204–205**
   viewing list, **620**
redo records, 204
   LGWR process to move from buffer to log, 189
Redundant Array of Inexpensive Disks (RAID), 101–104
reference tables, in data warehouse, 865
referential integrity constraints, and transportable tablespace, 522–523
refresh groups, **1055–1059**
   adding members, **1057–1058**
   changing schedule, **1058–1059**
   creating, **1056–1057**
   deleting, **1059**
   removing members, **1058**
refresh options for materialized views and replication, **1050–1055**
   FAST/ON COMMIT option, 1053–1054
   FAST/ON DEMAND option, 1055
   FORCE/ON COMMIT option, 1054
refresh options, for materialized views, 880–881

REFRESH procedure (DBMS_REFRESH), 1056
REFs, 347, 349
   ALTER TABLE command for scoping, 355
   view describing those present in attributes, 357
   when creating object table, 354
REGISTER command (namesctl), 418
REGISTER DATABASE command (RMAN), 549
REGISTER_PROPAGATOR procedure (DBMS_DEFER_SYS), 1063
registration
   of security enforcement package, 963–965
   of service names, 395–396
Registry
   backup, 69
   removing services from, 70
rejected rows, from SQL*Loader, 974
relational database, Oracle as, 13
Relational Software, Inc., 12
relational tables, 229. *See also* heap tables
   creating object views on, **383–386**
   user-defined object types in, **350**
   views with object tables and, 385–386
relational theory, **6–12**, 336
   joins, **11–12**
   normalization, **7–11**
relational views, on object tables, **386–387**
RELEASE CHANNEL command (RMAN), 550, 553
RELOAD command (namesctl), 418
reload ratio for library cache, calculating, **655–656**
RELY setting for constraints, 305
REMOTE, in execution plan, 746
remote procedure calls, for replication, **1062–1064**

REMOTE_LOGIN_PASSWORDFILE parameter, 930
REMOVE_PIPE function, in DBMS_PIPE package, 924
removing Oracle software, **66–70**
RENAME_PARTITION/SUBPARTITION_CLAUSE command, 1046
REOPEN keyword, 1082–1083
REPADMIN user, **1065–1067**
REPEAT command (namesctl), 418
REPLACE SCRIPT command (RMAN), 549, 597–598
replication, 1050
   advanced, **1059–1073**
      requirements, **1060–1061**
     checking for errors, **1071**
     detecting conflicts, **1071–1073**
       delete conflicts, 1072
       uniqueness conflicts, 1072
       update conflicts, 1072
   with materialized views, **1050–1055**
   refresh groups for, **1055–1059**
   remote procedure calls for, **1062–1064**
   resuming master activity, **1073**
   setting up advanced, **1065–1070**
     adding master sites to group, 1070
     adding objects to replication group, 1069
     generating support for object, 1070
     REPADMIN and REPSYS users creation, **1065–1067**
     replication administration users at master site, **1067–1068**
     replication group at master definition site, 1069
     replication schema at master definition site, 1069
   views, **1064–1065**

REPORT command (RMAN), 549
reports from Recovery Manager, **604–607**
   DEVICE TYPE option, 607
   NEED BACKUP option, 604–605
   OBSOLETE option, 606
   report object definition, 606
   SCHEMA option and AT clause, 606–607
   UNRECOVERABLE option, 605–606
reports, repository for, 788
REPSYS user, **1065–1067**
request and response queues, 188
required processes, **189–191**
   CKPT (Checkpoint), 190–191
   DBWn (Database Writer), 189
   LGWR (Log Writer), 189–190
   PMON (Process Monitor), 190
   SMON (System Monitor), 190
reserved words in SQL*Loader, 978–979
RESET DATABASE command (RMAN), 549, 595–596
RESETLOGS command, 466, 476–477, 1088
   recovery and, **486–489**
     why and when to use, 486–487
RESET_STATS command (namesctl), 418
RESOURCE role, 946
resource usage, monitoring, **672–673**
RESOURCE_LIMIT parameter, 938
response time, improving, **750–752**
RESTART command (namesctl), 418
RESTORE command (RMAN), 550, **557–558**
   UNTIL clause, 559
restricted ROWIDs, 231
RESYNC CATALOG command (REMAN), 594
RevealNet, 86
   Knowledge Base for Oracle Administration, 167

reverse-key indexes
    creating, 252
    to manage index browning, 258
REVERSE keyword, 257
reverse transversal algorithm, for parsing execution plan, 735
REWRITE hint, 765
rewrite integrity level, setting, **871–872**
RMAN. *See* Recovery Manager (RMAN)
RMAN backup pieces in Recovery Manager, 544
RMAN backup sets in Recovery Manager, 543–544
RMAN channels in Recovery Manager, 542–543
RMAN recovery catalog in Recovery Manager, 543
rmjvm.sql script, 1117
roles, **945–949**
    authentication methods for, 947
    creating, **947–948**
    documentation, 168
    enabling, 949
    granting, **948**
    for Java, 1118
    maximum number, 126
    and PL/SQL, **946–947**
    predefined, **946**
    viewing information, 949
ROLLBACK command, 192
rollback segment tablespaces, 226
    configuration, 136
    disk space requirements, 100
rollback segments, 179, 180
    altering, **279–280**
    creating, **279**
    dropping, 280
    importing and, 514
    information about, 641
    for instances, 1103
    monitoring usage, **662–664**
    OPTIMAL parameter, **223–224**
    planning, **277–279**
    tablespace recovery with, **465–466**
    and undo, **197–200**
    viewing information, **280–282**
rollbacks, and locks, 802
ROLLBACK_SEGMENTS parameter, 118, 127, 1101
rolling back transactions, in startup, 315
ROLLUP operator, **902–903**
root node, **248–249**
row array type commits, 514
row cache objects latch, 800
row directory in block header, 177
row exclusive lock mode, 806
row-level security, **950–968**
    with FGAC, **951–968**
        application context package, 957–960
        context package execution at user logon, 961
        features, **952**
        good and bad about, 967–968
        security enforcement package, 961–963
        security enforcement package registration, 963–965
        security enforcement package testing, 965–967
        security policy definition, 953–957
row lock, 803
row migration
    fixing tables with, **714–717**
    and performance, 712
row objects, 346
    SQL*Loader support, 997–998

row share lock mode, 806
row source, in execution plan, 735
ROWID datatype, 30, 213–214, 229–231, 346
    extended ROWIDs, 230–231
    logical in IOTs, **263**
    lookups and index scans, **742–743**
    restricted ROWIDs, 231
ROWID hint, 763
ROWIDTOCHAR function, 214
ROW_MOVEMENT_CLAUSE command, 1046
rows in database, 6
rule-based optimization for SQL statements, **705–706**
    allowances for, **711–712**
    driving table, **758–760**
RULE hint, 763
RUN command (RMAN), 550–551

S

sample table lookups, 743
save_config_on_stop parameter, in listener.ora file, 399
scalar datatypes, 30, **205–214**, 337
    character datatypes, **207–209**
        CHAR datatype, **207–208**
        NLS types, **208–209**
        VARCHAR2 datatype, **208**
    LOBs, **209–213**
        BLOB datatype, 211
        CLOBs, 211
        NCLOB datatype, 211
        and read consistency, 212
        restrictions, 213
        storage, 211–212
    LONG datatype, 209
    LONG RAW datatype, 209
    NUMBER datatype, **205–207**
        precision and scale, 205–206
        subtypes, 206–207
    RAW datatype, 209
    ROWID datatype, 213–214
    UROWID datatype, 213–214
scale of NUMBER data type, 204–205
SCHEDULE_PURGE procedure (DBMS_DEFER_SYS), 1063
SCHEDULE_PUSH procedure (DBMS_DEFER_SYS), 1063
scheduling. *See* Job Scheduler
schema
    account vs., 142
    importing to copy objects between, 512
    object names on distributed system, 1018
        resolution, **1020–1021**
    objects in shared SQL statements, 702–703
    for recovery catalog, 592–593
    vs. users, 928
SCN (System Change Number), **195–197**
    database consistency checks, 196–197
    database recovery services, 197
    read-consistent images, 196
scoping the REF, 354
scripts. *See also* sql.bsq script
    archived redo log recovery, 586
    catblock.sql, **828–831**
    catobtk.sql, 968
    for cold backup, **565–566**
    for cumulative incremental backup, 572–573
    database loss recovery, 585
    for dictionary creation, **143–144**
    for differential incremental backup, 571–572
    for full database backup, **467–469**

monitoring, **826–834**
for NOARCHIVE mode recovery preparation, 576
for Oracle Statspack install, 677
profile, 26
spauto.sql, 684
spreport.sql, **684–687**
SQL control file recovery, 588–589
sql.bsq, 129–130
    common changes to tables in, 130–131
    execution, 142
for SQL*Loader execution, **1003–1004**
storing RMAN, **596–598**
for system statistics gathering, **674–676**
utlxplan.sql, 733
utlxpls.sql, 733
second normal form, 8–9
Secure Sockets Layer (SSL), 391
security, 137, **950–968**. *See also* user accounts
    Advanced Security Option (ASO), **420–421**
    column-level, **968–971**
    database links and, 297
    in Java, **1123**
    row-level, **950–968**
    row-level, with FGAC, **951–968**
        application context package, 957–960
        context package execution at user logon, 961
        features, **952**
        good and bad about, 967–968
        security enforcement package, 961–963
        security enforcement package registration, 963–965
        security enforcement package testing, 965–967
        security policy definition, 953–957
    views for, **950–951**

segment fragmentation, monitoring, **667–668**
segments, 18, **179–181**
    objects vs., 179
SELECT statement, 31, 33
    to query object types, **376–379**
    FOR UPDATE clause, and locks, 812
    VALUE function, 379
SELECT_CATALOG_ROLE role, 157
selectivity, use by estimator, 708
self joins, 36
SELF parameter
    for map and order methods, 370
    of member method instances, 366
SEND_MESSAGE function, in DBMS_PIPE package, 922
SEQUENCE, in execution plan, 746
Sequenced Packet Exchange (SPX), 391
sequences, **297–300**
    in determining archive log file recovery, 455
sequential reads, and block size, 113
server processes, **188–189**
    in SGA, 181
server sessions, in Recovery Manager, 539
service names
    of databases, 15–16
    in Net8, **392–393**
    registration, 395–396
        in Oracle Names, 412
SERVICE_NAMES parameter, 1101
session file I/O, monitoring, **660–662**
session parameters, documentation, 164
sessions
    tracing, 720–722
    wait statistics, 813
SET command (RMAN), 549
SET DEFAULT_DOMAIN command (namesctl), 418

SET DUPLEX command, 575
SET FORWARDING_AVAILABLE command (namesctl), 418
SET LOG_STATS_INTERVAL command (namesctl), 418
SET NAMESCTL_TRACE_LEVEL command (namesctl), 418
SET PASSWORD command (namesctl), 418
set processing, **32**
SET REQUESTS_ENABLED command (namesctl), 418
SET RESET_STATS_INTERVAL command (namesctl), 418
SET ROLE statement, 947, 949
SET SERVER command (namesctl), 418
SET TRACE_LEVEL command (namesctl), 418
SET UNTIL statement, 582
SET_DISABLED procedure (DBMS_DEFER_SYS), 1063
SET_EV procedure, 633
SETSIZE parameter, for BACKUP command, 571
SET_SQL_TRACE_IN_SESSION procedure, 734
SGA (System Global Area), 14, **181–187**
    configuration, **120–124**
    database buffer cache, **182–183**
    and Java, 1116–1117
    monitoring, **645–658**
        data dictionary cache, **653–654**
        database buffer cache, **646–652**
        library cache, **654–658**
    redo log buffer, **184–185**
    shared pool, **184**
    size, **185–186**, 200
share DDL lock, 803
share row exclusive lock mode, 807
share table lock mode, 807

shared database link, 1015
shared locking, 1098
shared memory, 796
shared pool, **184**
    latches, 800
    monitoring reserved area, **657–658**
    sizing, **123**
    tuning, 836–837
shared server processes, 188–189
shared SQL area, 701
    rules for comparing statements in, 702–703
SHARED_POOL_RESERVED_MIN_ALLOC parameter, 837
SHARED_POOL_RESERVED_SIZE parameter, 837
SHARED_POOL_SIZE parameter, **123**, 184, 771–772, 1116
    for replication, 1061
sharing read-only tablespaces, **528**
SHOW CACHE_CHECKPOINT_INTERVAL command (namesctl), 418
SHOW DEFAULT_DOMAIN command (namesctl), 418
SHOW FORWARDING_AVAILABLE command (namesctl), 418
SHOW LOG_FILE_NAME command (namesctl), 418
SHOW LOG_STATS_INTERVAL command (namesctl), 419
SHOW NAMESCTL_TRACE_LEVEL command (namesctl), 419
SHOW REQUESTS_ENABLED command (namesctl), 419
SHOW RESET_STATS_INTERVAL command (namesctl), 419
SHOW SERVER command (namesctl), 419
SHOW STATUS command (namesctl), 419

SHOW SYSTEM_QUERIES command (namesctl), 419
SHOW TRACE_FILE_NAME command (namesctl), 419
SHOW TRACE_LEVEL command (namesctl), 419
SHOW VERSION command (namesctl), 419
SHUTDOWN ABORT command, 197, 316
   risks, 480
   vs. SHUTDOWN IMMEDIATE command, **317–318**
SHUTDOWN command, for cold backup, 437
SHUTDOWN command (namesctl), 419
SHUTDOWN command (RMAN), 549
SHUTDOWN IMMEDIATE command, 316
   for cold backup, 437
   SHUTDOWN ABORT command vs., **317–318**
shutdown process, and checkpoint, 197
SHUTDOWN TRANSACTIONAL command, **316–317**
SID (site identifier), 15
SID (System identifier), 116
   finding user assigned to, 810
simple measure in materialized view, 873
single-row hash cluster, 271
site identifier (SID), 15
site profile script, 26
sizing
   database files, 99, **108–111**
   datafiles, 321
SKIP_CORRUPTED_BLOCKS function (DBMS_REPAIR), 333
sleep operation, by waiting processes, 797
SMALLINT data type, 207
SMON (System Monitor), 190
snapshot, 198, 873. *See also* materialized views
   from Oracle Statspack, **681–683**

snapshot control file in Recovery Manager, 545
Sneed, Bob, 112
S*nnn* processes, 191
snowflake schema, 865
SNP*n* process, 191
soft parse, 701
sort areas, 187–188
SORT, in execution plan, 746
SORT_AREA_SIZE parameter, 127
SORTED INDEXES clause, in SQL*Loader control file, 986–987
sorting, memory allocation for, 732
spauto.sql script, 684
spcreate.sql script, 677
speed
   of disk access, 104
   of Oracle installation, 63
spin operation, by waiting processes, 797
_SPIN_COUNT parameter, 797
SPLIT_PARTITION_CLAUSE command, 1046
splitting partitions, **1044**
spreport.sql script, **684–687**
SPX (Sequenced Packet Exchange), 391
SQL. *See* Oracle SQL
   data dictionary role in recursive operations, 151
   datatypes, **30**
   DML and DDL languages, **31**
   operations, **34–39**. *See also* joins
      aggregation, 38–39
      correlated subqueries, 34
      subqueries, 34
   queries, **33–34**
   queries on data dictionary views to document database, **160–172**
      control files, 163–164
      current index key structures, 169–170

current parameters, 164–166
database tablespaces and datafiles, 160–162
dependencies, 171–172
list of current grants, 169
list of current roles, 168
list of foreign key relationships, 170–171
online redo logs, 162–163
users' setups in database, 167–168
set processing, **32**
SQL statement tuning, **749–778**
   of cost-based statements, **761–770**
   full table scans, impact, **777–778**
   hard parse, monitoring excessive, **770–773**
   high-water mark, 777
   indexes, **753–758**
     disabling, **755–758**
     function-based, **774–775**
   proactive component, **787–794**
     bind variables, **793–794**
   quantifying goals, **749–750**
   of rule-based statements, **758–761**
     driving table selection, 758–760
     indexes, 760–761
   table scans, accidental force, 775–776
   throughput and response time improvement, **750–752**
     baselines, 751
     I/O reductions, 752
   FOR UPDATE clause, 776
SQL statements
   CREATE DATABASE command, **129**, 133–134
   data warehouse query features, **902–906**. *See also* execution plans
     CUBE operator, **904–905**
     GROUPING function, **905**
     ROLLUP operator, **902–903**
     top-N queries, **905–906**
   end, 31
   inline views as part of, **287–288**
   INSERT statement, to query object types, **372–374**
   listing text for view, 640
   monitoring and notification, **794**
   Oracle optimizer, **705–720**
     analysis with Oracle supplied packages, **719–720**
     cost-based mode optimization, **707–708**
     histograms, **717–718**
     migrated and chained rows, **712–717**
     rule-based optimization, **705–706**
     set up, **709–712**
   processing, **700–704**
     bind variables, **703–704**
     cursors, **700–701**
     execution, fetch and close, **704**
     parse phase, **701–703**
   SQL*Plus command vs., 27
   unchangeable, 786–787
SQL text-matching by optimizer, 868–869
sql.bsq script, 129–130
   common changes to tables in, 130–131
   execution, 142
SQLJ, 1111, **1112–1113**
SQLJ Translator, 1114
SQLLOAD command, 981
SQL*Loader
   bad file, 991–994
   basic components, *975*
   collection loading, **998–999**
   discard file, 991–994
   input files, **979–991**

control files, **979–988**
datafiles, **989–991**
introduction, **974–979**
   capabilities, 975
   conventional and direct path loads, **975–978**
   reserved words, **978–979**
LOB loading, **999–1001**
log files, **994–996**
object loading, **996–998**
   column objects, 996–997
   row objects, 997–998
parallel loading with, **849**
partitioned object loading, **1001**
running, **1001–1007**
   from command line, **1001–1003**
   DDL syntax, **1004–1007**
   script file execution, **1003–1004**
sqlnet.ora configuration file, 395
   NAMES.PREFERRED_SERVER parameter, 412, 413
SQL*Plus, **24–28**
   to access LOBs, **310–312**
   commands
      parameters, 25
      vs. SQL statements, 27
   COPY command for migrating database, **72–73**
   starting, **24–26**
      profile scripts, 26
   using, **27–28**
   window, 24
SQL*Plus Autotrace, **731–733**
   output from, 732–733
SQL_TRACE parameter, 721
SSL (Secure Sockets Layer), 391

stage directory, for patches, 65
staging redo logs, **618–619**
standards. *See* Oracle Flexible Architecture (OFA)
standby database, **1076–1093**
   creation
      copying files to standby host, 1080
      enabling recovery, 1085–1088
      mounting standby instance, 1084–1085
      Net8 configuration, 1080–1081
      parameters for primary instance, 1085
      primary database backup, 1079–1080
      primary instance configuration, 1082–1083
      renaming files on standby site, 1085
      standby control file, 1080
      standby instance configuration, 1083–1084
      testing, 1088–1089
   maintenance, **1089–1093**
      manual changes, 1092
      matching changes in physical structure, 1090–1092
      resolving gap sequences, 1089–1090
      opening in read-only mode, 1092–1093
STANDBY_ARCHIVE_DEST parameter, 125, 1084
STAR hint, 766
star schemas, 865
START command (namesctl), 419
START WITH keyword, for CREATE SEQUENCE command, 297, 298
STAR_TRANSFORMATION hint, 770
STARTUP command, **312–315**
   MOUNT mode, **314**
   NOMOUNT mode, **313–314**
   OPEN mode, **314–315**
   restricted mode, **315**

STARTUP command (namesctl), 419
STARTUP command (RMAN), 549
STARTUP NOMOUNT command, 133
startup_wait_time parameter, in listener.ora file, 399
static member methods, 367
    creating, **368–369**
statistics, 779
    ANALYZE command for, **324–328**
        COMPUTE STATISTICS clause, **324**
        DELETE STATISTICS clause, **328**
        ESTIMATE STATISTICS clause, **325**
        viewing information, 326–327
    DBMS_STATS package, **778–783**
        vs. ANALYZE command, **778–780**
        common procedures, 779
        example of use, 780–781
        maintaining current statistics, 782–783
    views to provide, 640–642
Statspack, **676–688**
STOP command (namesctl), 419
stopping Oracle services, 68–69
storage. *See* Oracle storage architecture
STORAGE clause, for table creation including LOBs, 308–309
storage parameters
    BUFFER_POOL parameter, 224
    FREELIST GROUPS parameter, **223**
    FREELISTS parameter, **223**
    INITIAL parameter, **220–221**
    MAXEXTENTS parameter, **222–223**
    MINEXTENTS parameter, **222–223**
    NEXT parameter, **221**
    OPTIMAL parameter, **223–224**
    PCTINCREASE parameter, **221–222**

stored outlines
    creating, **784–785**
    data dictionary views, 786
    using and modifying, **785–786**
stored procedures, 39
    creating in Java, **1120–1121**
stream record format, for SQL*Loader datafile, **990–991**
striping. *See* data striping
structures, 7
SUBTRACT procedure (DBMS_REFRESH), 1056, 1058
SUM() function, 38
summary management, 866
    dimensions, **891–902**
        altering and dropping, 899
        defining, 892–894
        displaying, 899–902
        example, 894–899
    materialized views, **872–891**
        creating, **873–878**
        data dictionary views, **879–880**
        logs, **889–891**
        refreshing, **880–889**
    query rewrite, **866–872**
        constraints and dimensions requirements, 869–870
        enabling, 870–871
        how it works, 868–870
        rewrite integrity level, 871–872
        rules, 867–868
Summary screen, 61, *61*
Sun environment, Oracle best practices in, 112
suspending job, 919
svrmgr1 command, 22
SWITCH command (RMAN), 550, 590

symmetrical multiprocessing, 1095
synonyms, **292–294**
    for database links, 1021
SYS account
    creating, 142
    ownership of data dictionary, 146
SYSDBA privileges, 933–934
SYS.FET$, 143
SYS.FILE$, 143
SYS.LINK$ data dictionary view, user account name and password storage in, 1015
SYSOPER privileges, 933–934
system file I/O, monitoring, **658–660**
System Global Area (SGA), **181–187**
    configuration, **120–124**
    database buffer cache, **182–183**
    and Java, 1116–1117
    redo log buffer, **184–185**
    shared pool, **184**
    size, **185–186**
System identifier (SID), 116
system-level grants, **943–944**
system-level parameters, documentation, 164
system memory, 112
System Monitor (SMON), 190
SYSTEM rollback segment, 82
system statistics, gathering, **674–676**
SYSTEM tablespace, **224**
    defining datafile for, 129
    objects created in, 146
    recovery, **465**
    sizing, 111
SYS.UET$, 143

T

table directory in block header, 177
table-level export, **500–501**
table-level import mode, 505, **513–514**
table lock, 803
table scans, accidentally forced, **775–776**
tables. *See* index-organized tables (IOTs). *See also* heap tables; object tables
    adding to indexed cluster, 272–273
    full scans, and performance, 650
    parallel processing to create, **846–848**
    statistics on, 324–328
    transporting partitioned, **529–530**
tablespace datafiles, 92
tablespaces, 18. *See also* transportable tablespaces
    adding to standby database, 1091–1092
    altering, **228–229**
    backups
        in hot backup mode, 443
        identifying for hot backup, 444–445
        with Recovery Manager, **569**
    creating, 137–138, **226–228**
    Database Configuration Assistant (DCA) and, 135
    dropping, **229**
    free space fragmentation, monitoring, **666–667**
    management, **224–229**
    monitoring space, 696
        contiguous space, 696–697
        free space, 697–698
    OFA rules for, 91
    placement on disks, 105
    query for report, 160–162

recovery, **460–462**
    with Recovery Manager, 580–581
    with rollback segments, **465–466**
sharing read-only, **528**
storage parameters
    BUFFER_POOL parameter, 224
    FREELIST GROUPS parameter, **223**
    FREELISTS parameter, **223**
    INITIAL parameter, **220–221**
    MAXEXTENTS parameter, **222–223**
    MINEXTENTS parameter, **222–223**
    NEXT parameter, **221**
    OPTIMAL parameter, **223–224**
    PCTINCREASE parameter, **221–222**
types
    data tablespaces, 226
    index tablespaces, 226
    rollback segment tablespaces, 226
    SYSTEM tablespace, **224**
    temporary tablespaces, **225**
for user accounts, 146
TAF (transparent application failover), **403–406**
    configuration, 1104
target database in Recovery Manager, 541–542
TCP/IP (Transmission Control Protocol/Internet Protocol), Net8 support, 391
TCP/IP with SSL, Net8 support, 391
tempfiles, 225
temporary files, 18
    for Oracle install on NT, 50
temporary segments, 179, 180, 217
temporary tables, creating, **239–240**
temporary tablespaces, **225**
    creating, 137, 226
    disk space requirements, 100
    placement on disks, 104
    for user accounts, 146–147, 932

test database, to calculate disk space requirements, 98–99
testing enabled events, 632
theta joins, 35
third normal form, 7, 9–11
thread checkpoint, 194
THREAD parameter, 1101
thresholds for monitoring, 827
throughput
    improving, **750–752**
    maximizing, **841**
time-based recovery, **467–472, 582–583**
time to live (TTL), for client name cache, 414
TIMED_QUERY command (namesctl), 419
TIMED_STATISTICS parameter, 127, 643–645, 721
    setting, **725**
timelines for disaster recovery, 427
TKPROF
    command-line parameters, 723–724
    examples of running, 730
    to format trace file, 720–722
    output generated, 725–727
    ratios in output, 728–729
    to reformat trace file, **722–731**
    syntax, 723
tnsnames.ora configuration file, 395, 401–402
    and standby database, 1080–1081
top-N queries, **905–906**
touch counter for SGA blocks, 182, 651–652
touch-point algorithm, 152
trace files, **329–331**, 480
    for recovery, **483–485**
    TKPROF to reformat, **722–731**
trace_directory parameter in listener.ora file, 399
trace_file parameter in listener.ora file, 399

trace_filelen parameter in listener.ora file, 399
trace_fileno parameter in listener.ora file, 399
trace_level parameter in listener.ora file, 399
trace_timestamp parameter in listener.ora file, 400
tracing sessions, 720–722
transaction commits and rollbacks, **192**
transaction free lists, 181
TRANSACTION procedure (DBMS_DEFER), 1063
transaction slots, 199
transactions, **19–20**
    characteristics, 6–7
transient objects, 338
transparent application failover (TAF), **403–406**
    configuration, 1104
transportable tablespaces, **520–522**
    creating set, **522–526**
        checking for self-containment, 523–524
        copying datafiles, 525–526
        exporting metadata, 524–525
        making tablespaces read-only, 524
    and data warehouse, **530–531**
    management, **531**
    plugging in set, **526–528**
        importing tablespace, 526–527
        making data accessible, 527
        moving tablespaces, 528
    requirements, **520–521**
    using for point-in-time recovery, **532–535**
    what can be transported, **521–522**
trends, 689
triggers, 43
TRIM method, for VARRAY, 375
troubleshooting. *See also* recovery
    database problems, **329–333**
        with DBMS_REPAIR, **332–333**
        with DBV (DBVerify), **331–332**
        with trace files and alert log, **329–331**
TRUNCATE command
    recovery after, **466–480**
    and SHUTDOWN ABORT, 317
TRUNCATE_PARTITION/SUBPARTITION_CLAUSE command, 1046
TTL (time to live), for client name cache, 414
tuning. *See also* latches; locks; SQL statement tuning
    buffer block waits, **840–841**
    general advice, **834–837**
        I/O distribution checkup, **835–836**
        shared pool, 836–837
    parallel processing, **855–861**
    redo allocation latch problems, 839
    redo copy latch problems, 838–839
    wait management, **813–826**
tuning problem databases, **630–631**
TWO_TASK parameter, 22
types (user-defined datatypes), 338. *See also* user-defined object types
typical install, 55

U

UET$ data dictionary table, 178
UGA (User Global Area), 187, 1117
UI. *See* Universal Installer
unbounded range scans, **251**, 743
undo, rollback segments and, **197–200**
undocumented parameters, 154–155
uniform memory access, 1095
uninstalling Oracle software, **66–70**
UNION-ALL, in execution plan, 745
UNION, in execution plan, 745

unique constraints, **301–302**
unique indexes, **252–253**
unique key constraints, **20**
uniqueness conflicts in replication, 1072
Universal Installer, **47–48**
   Available Product Components, 56–58, *57*
   Available Products, 54–55, *55*
   Component Locations, 58–59, *59*
   Create Database screen, 61
   File Locations, 53–54, *54*
   Install process window, *62*, 62–63
   Installation Types, 55–56
   Inventory window, *67*, 67
   migrating existing databases, 60
   Oracle Protocol Support, 59, *60*
   products not installed by default, 57–58
   to remove Oracle software, **66–70**
     starting, 66
     from Windows NT, 68–70
   starting, **51–53**
   Summary screen, 61, *61*
Unix
   preinstall steps for Oracle, 49–50
   starting Universal Installer, 51–53
     environment settings, 51–52
   user session as process, 188
UNNEST hint, 770
unnesting subqueries, 708
unnesting syntax in SELECT statement, 377–378
UNPACK_MESSAGE function, in DBMS_PIPE package, 924
UNREGISTER command (namesctl), 419
UNREGISTER_PROPAGATOR procedure (DBMS_DEFER_SYS), 1063
UNSCHEDULE_PURGE procedure (DBMS_DEFER_SYS), 1063

UNSCHEDULE_PUSH procedure (DBMS_DEFER_SYS), 1063
UNTIL command (RMAN), 549
update conflicts in replication, 1072
UPDATE statement, 31
   to query object types, **374–376**
updating to Oracle8i, **70–75**
   vs. migration, **71**
   withing major versions, **84–86**
     vs. patches, 86
UPGRADE CATALOG command (RMAN), 549
UROWID datatype, 30, 213–214
USE_CONCAT hint, 765
USE_HASH hint, 767
USE_MERGE hint, 767
USE_NL hint, 766
use_plug_and_play parameter, in listener.ora file, 400
user accounts, **928–949**
   creating, **931–933**
     database authentication, **931–932**
     operating system authentication, **932–933**
   default and temporary tablespace for, 146
   grants, defining, **943–945**
   maintaining, **936–937**
   password file authentication, **928–931**
     creating password file, **929–930**
     database setup to use password file, **930–931**
   privileged users, **933–936**
     log on, **934–935**
     viewing, **935–936**
   roles, **945–949**
     creating, **947–948**
     enabling, 949

granting, **948**
and PL/SQL, **946–947**
predefined, **946**
viewing information, 949
user profiles, **937–942**
  maintaining, **942**
  password settings, **939–941**
  resource settings, **938–939**
  using, **941–942**
user-defined object types, 338, *339*, **339–350**
  creating, **340–341**
  data dictionary tables to manage, **344–346**
  determining dependencies, **343–344**
  forward declaring, **347–349**
  methods, **365–372**
    constructor methods, **366**
    information about, **372**
    map and order methods, **370–371**
    member methods, **366–369**
  modifying and dropping, **341–342**
  in PL/SQL, **350**
  in relational tables, **350**
  using as attributes, **342–343**
user files, 92
User Global Area (UGA), 187, 1117
user-level export, **499–500**
user-level import mode, 505, **511–513**
user lock, 803
user processes, in SGA, 181
user profile script, 26
user session
  information about, 641
  tracing, 637, 733–734
user setup, monitoring, **665**
user trace files, 330
USER_ views, 144, **157–158**

USER_DUMP_DEST parameter, 125, 127, 330, 637, 721, 1101
USERENV namespace, 961
usernames, 931
users
  documentation of setup, 167–168
  finding for SID (System Identifier), 810
  schema vs., 928
USERS tablespace, 137
utlbstat.sql script, **674–676**
  report sections, 675
UTL_COLL package, 911
utlestat.sql script, **674–676**
UTL_FILE package, 911
UTL_FILE_DIR parameter, 125, 615
UTL_HTTP package, 911
UTL_INADDR package, 911
UTL_RAW package, 911
UTL_REF package, 911
UTL_SMTP package, 911
UTL_STMP package, 694–695
UTL_TCP package, 911
utlxplan.sql script, 733
utlxpls.sql script, 733

V

V$ dynamic performance views, 143, **159–160**, **638–645**
  additional information from, **643–645**
  for backup and recovery, 451–452
  creation, **638–639**
  for MTS information, **410**
  for parallel queries, 860
  for performance monitoring, **639–642**

V$CONTROLFILE_RECORD_SECTION view,
   for control files documentation, 163
V$FILESTAT view, 658
V$FIXED_TABLE view, 151
V$FIXED_VIEW_DEFINITION view, 145, 639
V$LATCH view, 799, 800–801, 832
V$LATCH_CHILDREN view, 801
V$LATCH_PARENT view, 801
V$LOCK view, **803**, 827–829
V$LOGMNR_CONTENTS view, 623–624
V$LOGMNR_LOGS view, 618
V$PARAMETER data dictionary view, 120
   for control files documentation, 163
V$PWFILE_USERS view, 935
V$RESOURCE_LIMIT, 672–673
V$ROLLNAME view, 281–282
V$ROLLSTAT view, 281–282
V$SESSION view, 810
V$SESSION_LONGOPS view, 794
V$SESSION_WAIT view, **824–826**
V$SGASTAT dynamic performance view, for
   SGA size, 185–186
V$SQL view, **788–793**
   report on high disk I/O, 791–792
   report on high sort count, 790–791
   report on ratio of buffer gets to rows
      processed, 792–793
V$SQLAREA view, 790
V$SYSSTAT view, 647
   for wait statistics, 813
      V$SESSION_EVENT, **815–816**, 818
      V$SYSTEM_EVENT, **814–815**, 818
      V$WAITSTAT, **817–818**
validation
   enabling constraints without, 304–305
   of object structure, **328–329**

VARCHAR2 datatype, 30, **208**
variable record format, for SQL*Loader datafile,
   989
variable transaction header, 177
VARRAYS, **357–360**
   altering and dropping, 360
   creating, **358–360**
   INSERT statement to query, **372–373**
   vs. nested tables, 361
   SQL*Loader support, 998–999
   UPDATE statement for, **374–376**
vendors, emergency contacts during disaster,
   427–428
vertical data striping, vs. horizontal, 102–103,
   103
VIEW, in execution plan, 746
view merging, 707
views, **282–289**. *See also* DBA_ views
   for constraints, **305–307**
   creating, **283–284**
   for data dictionary, **144**
      accessing, **147–148**
   for database links, **296–297**
   for datafiles, 321–322
   dynamic performance, **145–146**
   for grant information, 945
   for index information, **259–262**
      DBA_IND_COLUMNS view, 261–262
      DBA_INDEXES view, **259–261**
      INDEXES_STATS view, 262
   inline, **287–288**
   on object tables, **386–387**
   for objects, creating, **380–387**
   for recovery catalog, **598–600**
   with relational and object tables, 385–386
   for replication, **1064–1065**

for replication conflicts, 1073
for role information, 949
for row-level security, **950–951**
for synonyms, 294
using, **284–287**
viewing information, **288–289**
virtual file systems, logical volume manager in, 835
virtual private database, 950

W

wait management, **813–826**
   common events, **818–824**
      buffer waits, **819**
      db file scattered read, **819–820**
      db file sequential read, **820–821**
      enqueue, 821
      free buffer wait, 821–822
      latch activity wait, 822
      latch free wait, 822
      library cache lock and pin, 822
      log buffer space, 822–823
      log file parallel write, 823
      log file sequential read, 823
      log file single write, 823
      log file switch, 824
      log file sync, 824
      write complete, 824
   views
      V$SESSION_EVENT, **815–816**, 818
      V$SYSTEM_EVENT, **814–815**, 818
      V$WAITSTAT, **817–818**
warning threshold, 827
   for database monitoring, 690–694

WHERE clause
   and indexes, 753
   in SQL query, 33–34
whole backup, 564
wildcard searches, indexes for, 776
willing-to-wait latch, 797–798
Windows NT
   ORADIM command, **132**
   preinstall steps for Oracle, 50
   removing Oracle software, **68–70**
   starting Universal Installer, 51, 66
write complete waits, 824

X

X$ tables, 143, **151–155**
   X$BH table, **152–153**
   X$KCBFWAIT table, 153
   X$KCBWBPD table, 648
   X$KCBWS table, 648
   X$KSMLRU table, 153–154
   X$KSPPI table, 154–155
   X$SKPPCV table, 154–155
X$BH view, 650–651
XML SQL utility (XSU), 1124
XSU (XML SQL utility), 1124

TELL US WHAT YOU THINK!

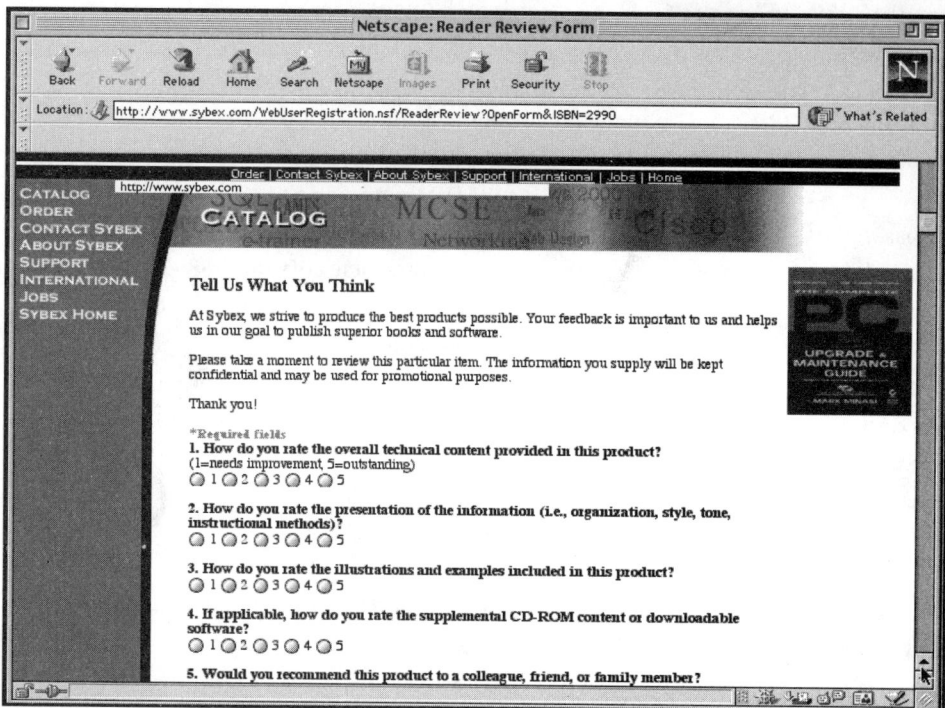

Your feedback is critical to our efforts to provide you with the best books and software on the market. Tell us what you think about the products you've purchased. It's simple:

1. Visit the Sybex website
2. Go to the product page
3. Click on **Submit a Review**
4. Fill out the questionnaire and comments
5. Click **Submit**

With your feedback, we can continue to publish the highest quality computer books and software products that today's busy IT professionals deserve.

www.sybex.com

SYBEX Inc. • 1151 Marina Village Parkway, Alameda, CA 94501 • 510-523-8233